LAND OWNERSHIP AND USE

LAND OWNERSHIP AND USE

Third Edition

CURTIS J. BERGER
Lawrence A. Wien Professor of Law
Columbia University

Little, Brown and Company
Boston   Toronto

Library of Congress Catalog Card No. 81-86687
ISBN 0-316-09154-5

Third Printing

HAL

*Published simultaneously in Canada
by Little, Brown & Company (Canada) Limited*

Printed in the United States of America

To Viv

SUMMARY OF CONTENTS

CONTENTS

PREFACE
TO THE THIRD EDITION

Another seven years have passed, and once again I must pen a preface. Because this edition already contains two prefaces, which together express my view about the coverage and stress of a first-year property course, this preface should be read in conjunction with its predecessors.

Those who are acquainted with the earlier editions of Land Ownership and Use will see that I have succumbed, finally, to the entreaties of those teachers who believe (as I do) that personal property offers a wonderful first exposure to legal thought and analysis. Chapter 2, Of Property in Things, is brand new and, I confess, borrowed heavily and with gratitude from Professor Bernard Keenan of the Suffolk University Law School. Personal property does not appear in the first and second editions because, in the ideal curriculum, Property would not be taught until the second semester. By then, most law students have acquired analytical competence that makes much of personal property, however skillfully taught, pedagogically redundant. But since Property still remains a year-long enterprise at most law schools, instructors whose students begin Property in their first weeks may wish to start with Chapter 2.

In one respect, this edition has a slightly changed organization. I have brought together all the landlord and tenant materials (except those dealing with the running of covenants) at Chapters 4-6. Many book users have urged this concentration, and I am satisfied it makes sense. Moreover, the concentration appears relatively early in the course and, coming in the wake of freehold estates, gives students a more contemporaneous, as well as directly personal, vision of the property system.

Finally, in this edition I have expanded the materials on marital property, rent control, and condo conversions, have responded further to the growing constitutionalization of our once intensely private realm, have reflected the ongoing work on the Restatement (Second) of Property, and have added another dash or two of economics to the brew.

New York City
July 1982

PREFACE
TO THE SECOND EDITION

The last step in preparing the second edition has been to reread the preface to the first edition to see what I could still embrace. Happily, nearly everything. I am less emphatic about delaying the student's exposure to real estate transactions and have included introductory conveyancing materials. These should ready students for the more intricate tax and financing issues of upper-class electives. And I have omitted the urban renewal and public housing materials, which time and changing governmental philosophy have dated. Otherwise, instructors who are acquainted with the first edition will find much that is familiar here.

For teachers of property, the years since 1968 have brought a rich harvest of key statutes and decisions: the Civil Rights Act of 1968, *Javins,* the National Environmental Policy Act of 1969, *Ramapo, Mount Laurel,* the Uniform Residential Landlord and Tenant Act, *Roth,* and *Shack;* to name a few. I have tried to capture the detail and the mood of these eventful years. I have also tried for greater teachability—expanding the textual treatment where this could facilitate instruction, and making the organization more explicit where this could enlarge the student's grasp. And, finally, I have tried to indicate the continuing challenge of this demanding and endlessly provocative subject.

New York City
June 1975

PREFACE
TO THE FIRST EDITION

This book represents one teacher's conclusions about the assembly of materials for a first-year property course. As such, the book reflects certain basic convictions about coverage; intracurricular relationships; the use of classroom time; the skills a lawyer should acquire; the role of courts, legislatures, and other decision-makers; and, not least, the interests and ambitions of the young people we teach. In general, the convictions are the following:

First: Conveyancing does not belong in the first-year curriculum. Real estate transactions—as they are practiced today—are pregnant with considerations of income taxation, financing, and contracts. Except possibly for contracts, a beginning law student lacks the necessary background in these areas, and if we ignore them we waste everyone's time. An additional justification for deferring transactions until an advanced course is that they should be taught partly by the problem method and through exercises in drafting or negotiation—approaches to instruction that are better left to the second or third year.

Second: It seems irrelevant to concentrate on future interests in a course that emphasizes land in present-day America. Except for the defeasible estates, which remain a common device for enforcing private and public conditions on the use or alienation of land, future interests now serve their major role as tools of estate planning. Most students eventually take a course in wealth transmission; there they can study future interests in a far more meaningful context.

Third: Resource allocation, and the means to achieve it, deserve equal billing with the more conventional chapters on estates in land. I regard the land-planning materials in the last third of the book as so basic that I seriously considered putting them first, both to make clear this high regard and to offset our tendencies to hurry through or cut final chapters. But every text has its own sequential logic, and it seemed vital that students first absorb some of the language of property. I hope, however, that the instructor who uses this book will not misallocate his or her own resources of time, so that the students must await a third-year seminar to become thoroughly acquainted with the land-planning materials, or worse yet, become lawyers knowing nothing about zoning, eminent domain, urban renewal, etc.

Fourth: Property is no longer a common-law (or even a private-law) discipline, a realization that has been slow to arrive. State and local legislatures—and, of course, the federal government—are recasting the institution of property with breathtaking speed; to what end is what this course examines. Thus, the book begins with major excerpts from the Civil Rights Bill of 1966, and throughout, where it has seemed fit, statutory material appears. As a teacher, I demand that students become as adept in their handling of statutes as they are professional in their dealings with cases.

Some of my older colleagues, still deadened by their own sterile, anachronistic encounter with property as students, wonder that I find the subject so relevant and stimulating. Yet, this is where in the law school curriculum we first consider man's struggle to control his environment, to find beauty, comfort, and order in his daily life, and to achieve a sense of consequence in his relations with government and fellow man. What is more timely, vital, or exciting?

ACKNOWLEDGMENTS

The author wishes to acknowledge the permissions kindly granted to reproduce the materials listed below.

American Law Institute, Restatement (Second) of Property (Tentative Drafts 1973-1979). Copyright © 1979 by the American Law Institute. Reprinted with permission.

Abrams, C., Man's Struggle for Shelter in an Urbanizing World 12-14, 21-22 (1964). Reprinted with permission of The Massachusetts Institute of Technology and the President and Fellows of Harvard College. Footnotes omitted.

Axelrod, A., Berger, C., & Johnstone, Q., Land Transfer and Finance 66-67, 103, 156-158, 159, 505, 506, 531-534, 537-538, 666-667, 674-675 (2d ed. 1978). Copyright © 1978 by Axelrod, Berger, and Johnstone. Reprinted with permission.

Berger, Book Review (Mandelker, Green Belts and Urban Growth), 61 Mich. L. Rev. 628, 630-631, 632-633 (1963). Reprinted with permission.

Berger, Condominium: Shelter on a Statutory Foundation, 63 Colum. L. Rev. 987 (1963). Reprinted with permission.

Berger, Hard Leases Make Bad Law, 74 Colum. L. Rev. 791, 814-815 (1974). Reprinted with permission.

Brown, R., Personal Property 76-78 (Raushenbush 3d ed. 1975). Reprinted with permission.

Calabresi & Melamed, Property Rules, Liability Rules, and Inalienability, 85 Harv. L. Rev. 1089-1093, 1115-1124 (1972). Copyright © 1972 by the Harvard Law Review Association. Reprinted with permission.

Chafee, The Music Goes Round and Round: Equitable Servitudes and Chattels, 69 Harv. L. Rev. 1250, 1258 (1956). Reprinted with permission.

Chicago Title & Trust Co., Contract of Sale (rev. 1968). Reprinted with permission.

Comment, The Public Use Limitation on Eminent Domain: An Advance Requiem, 58 Yale L.J. 599, 614 (1949). Reprinted with permission of the Yale Law Journal Co. and Fred B. Rothman & Co.

Costonis, J., Space Adrift 3, 4 (1974). Reprinted with permission of the University of Illinois Press.

Delafons, J., Land-Use Controls in the United States 62-63 (1962). Reprinted with permission.

Directive Committee on Regional Planning, The Case for Regional Planning 77-79 (1947). Reprinted with permission of the Yale University Press.

Duhl, The Parameters of Urban Planning, in Planning for Diversity and Choice 34 (Anderson ed. 1968). Reprinted with permission of The MIT Press, Cambridge, Mass.

Dukeminier, Zoning for Aesthetic Objectives: A Reappraisal, 20 L. & Contemp. Probs. 218, 231 (1955). Copyright © 1955 by Duke University. Reprinted with permission.

Dukeminier & Stapleton, The Zoning Board of Adjustment: A Case Study in Misrule, 50 Ky. L.J. 273, 321, 322, 332-339 (1962). Reprinted with permission.

Editorial, More on the Zone Defense Against Smut, The New York Times, February 15, 1977, p. 30. Reprinted with permission.

Editor's Comments, Golden v. Town of Ramapo: Establishing a New Dimension in American Planning Law, 4 Urban Law. ix, xii-xiii (1972). Reprinted with permission.

Ennis, Landmark Mansion on 79th St. to Be Razed, The New York Times, September 17, 1964, p. 1. Reprinted with permission.

Fagin, Regulating the Timing of Urban Development, 20 L. & Contemp. Probs. 298, 300-302 (1955). Copyright © 1955 by Duke University. Reprinted with permission.

Fine, The Condominium Conversion Problem: Causes and Solution, 1980 Duke L.J. 306. Copyright © 1980 by Duke Law Journal. Reprinted with permission.

Freedman, Letter to the Editor, The New York Times, February 15, 1977, p. 30. Reprinted with permission.

Goodman, ed., Principles and Practice of Urban Planning 537 (1968). Reprinted with permission.

Gribetz & Grad, Housing Code Enforcement: Sanctions and Remedies, 66 Colum. L. Rev. 1254, 1259-1260 (1960). Reprinted with permission.

Haar et al., Computer Power and Legal Reasoning: A Case Study of Judicial Decision Prediction in Zoning Amendment Cases, 1977 Am. B. Found. Research J. 651, 657, 747-750. Reprinted with permission.

Hammond, Limitations upon Possibilities of Reverter and Rights of Entry: Current Trends in State Legislation 1953-1954, 589, 590-592 (1955). Reprinted with permission of University of Michigan Law School.

Hines, Real Property Joint Tenancies: Law, Fact, and Fancy, 51 Iowa L. Rev. 582, 586, 607, 608, 617 (1966). Reprinted with permission.

Hohfeld, Some Fundamental Legal Conceptions as Applied in Judicial Reasoning, 23 Yale L.J. 16, 28-33, 44-49, 52-53, 55, 58-59 (1913). Reprinted with permission of the Yale Law Journal Co. and Fred B. Rothman & Co.

Housing Codes and Their Enforcement 195-196 (October 1966). Reprinted with permission of the Legislative Drafting Research Fund of Columbia University.

Huber, Creditors' Rights in Tenancies by the Entireties, 1 B.C. Ind. & Comm. L. Rev. 197, 205-207 (1960). Copyright © 1960 by Boston College Law School. Reprinted with permission.

Institute of Real Estate Management. Income/Expense Analysis (1979). Reprinted with permission.

International City Management Assn., Principles and Practice of Urban Planning (Washington, D.C. 1968). Reprinted with permission.

McMichael, S., & O'Keefe, P., Leases 118-119, 124 (5th ed. 1959). Reprinted with permission.

Mitchell, Laura Remson, When Housing Is Tight, Are Rent Controls Necessary? Calif. J. 53, 54-55 (1978). Reprinted with permission of the author and publisher.

Munchow, H., The Use of Deed Restrictions in Subdivision Development (Institute for Research in Land Economics and Public Utilities 1928). Reprinted with permission.

Norwick, Letter to the Editor, The New York Times, February 15, 1977, p. 30. Reprinted with permission.

Nuccio, Abandoned Property, The New York Times, March 30, 1964, p. 44. Reprinted with permission.

Ozbekian, "Can" Implies "Ought," in Planning for Diversity and Choice 208 (Anderson ed. 1968). Reprinted with permission of The MIT Press, Cambridge, Mass.

Outdoor Recreation Resources Review Commission, Outdoor Recreation for America 151 (1962). Reprinted with permission.

Phillips, C., From the Crash to the Blitz, 1929-1939, 2-3 (1969). Copyright © 1969 by The New York Times Company. Reprinted with permission of the Macmillan Publishing Co., Inc.

Posner, R., Economic Analysis of Law 10-15 (2d ed. 1973). Reprinted with permission.

Powell, R., Law of Real Property (Rohan ed. 1973). Copyright © 1973 by Matthew Bender & Co., Inc. Reprinted with permission.

Prather, Foreclosure of the Security Interest, 1957 Ill. L.F. 420, 427-430. Copyright © 1957 by the Board of Trustees of the University of Illinois. Reprinted with permission.

Reeves, Handbook of Interest, Annuity and Related Fiscal Tables (1966). Reprinted with permission.

Reich, The New Property, 73 Yale L.J. 733, 734-737, 738-740, 741, 745, 756, 778-779 (1964). Reprinted with permission of the Yale Law Journal Co. and Fred B. Rothman & Co.

Reno, The Enforcement of Equitable Servitudes in Land, 28 Va. L. Rev. 951, 972-977 (1942). Reprinted with permission of the Virginia Law Review and Fred B. Rothman & Co.

Reps, Pomeroy Memorial Lecture: Requiem for Zoning, 56 Planning, Selected Papers of the ASPO National Planning Conference 1964. Reprinted with permission.

Rye Tax Protester Returns to Jail, The New York Times, January 16, 1964, p. 46. Copyright © 1964 by The New York Times Co. Reprinted with permission.

Smith, An Inverse Condemnation Puzzle: The *Agins* Case Lands in Limbo, Natl. L.J., August 4, 1980, p. 52, 54. Reprinted with permission.

Sternlieb, G., & Burchell, R., Residential Abandonment xxii-xxvi (1973). Reprinted with permission.

Sternlieb, G., & Hughes, J., The Future of Rental Housing 3-5, 8-11, 12-13, 83-91 (1981). Reprinted with permission.

Stoebuck, A General Theory of Eminent Domain, 47 Wash. L. Rev. 553, 597 (1972). Reprinted with permission of the Washington Law Review Association.

Tell, Detroit's Fray: Progress v. Poverty, Natl. L.J., June 1, 1981, p. 1. Reprinted with permission.

Urban Land Institute, The Homes Association Handbook 21 (TB 50 rev. ed. (1966). Reprinted with permission of ULI—The Urban Land Institute, 1200 18th Street, N.W., Washington, D.C., 20036.

Williams, Planning Law and Democratic Living, 20 L. & Contemp. Probs. 317-318 (1955). Copyright © by Duke University School of Law. Reprinted with permission.

Zillman & Deeny, Legal Aspects of Solar Energy Development, 25 Ariz. St. L.J. 25, 28-29, 33-35 (1976). Copyright © 1976 by Arizona State Law Journal. Reprinted with permission.

LAND OWNERSHIP AND USE

PART I

THE INSTITUTION OF PROPERTY

Chapter 1

What Is Property?

§1.1 Law and Property; Property and Law

BENTHAM, THEORY OF LEGISLATION: PRINCIPLES OF THE CIVIL CODE

111-113 (Hildreth ed. 1931)

The better to understand the advantages of law, let us endeavour to form a clear idea of *property*. We shall see that there is no such thing as natural property, and that it is entirely the work of law.

Property is nothing but a basis of expectation; the expectation of deriving certain advantages from a thing, which we are said to possess, in consequence of the relation in which we stand towards it.

There is no image, no painting, no visible trait, which can express the relation that constitutes property. It is not material, it is metaphysical; it is a mere conception of the mind.

To have a thing in our hands; to keep it; to make it; to sell it; to work it up into something else; to use it;—none of these physical circumstances, nor all united, convey the idea of property. A piece of stuff which is actually in the Indies may belong to me, while the dress I wear may not. The aliment which is incorporated into my very body may belong to another, to whom I am bound to account for it.

The idea of property consists in an established expectation; in the persuasion of being able to draw such or such an advantage from the thing possessed, according to the nature of the case. Now this expectation, this persuasion, can only be the work of law. I cannot count upon the enjoyment of that which guarantees it to me. It is law alone which permits me to forget my natural weakness. It is only through the protection of law, that I am able to enclose a field, and to give myself up to its cultivation, with the sure though distant hope of harvest.

But it may be asked, what is it that serves as a basis to law, upon which to begin operations, when it adopts objects which under the name of property, it promises to protect? Have not men, in the primitive state, a *natural* expecta-

3

tion of enjoying certain things,—an expectation drawn from sources anterior to law?

Yes. There have been from the beginning, and there always will be, circumstances, in which a man may secure himself by his own means, in the enjoyment of certain things. But the catalogue of these cases is very limited. The savage who has killed a deer, may hope to keep it for himself, so long as his cave is undiscovered; so long as he watches to defend it, and is stronger than his rivals; but that is all. How miserable and precarious is such a possession! If we suppose the least agreement among savages to respect the acquisitions of each other, we see the introduction of a principle to which no name can be given, but that of law. A feeble and monetary expectation may result from time to time from circumstances purely physical; but a strong and permanent expectation can result, only from law. That which in the natural state was an almost invisible thread, in the social state, becomes a cable.

Property and law are born together, and die together. Before laws were made there was no property; take away laws, and property ceases.

COMMUNITY REDEVELOPMENT AGENCY v. ABRAMS
15 Cal. 3d 813, 543 P.2d 905, 126 Cal. Rptr. 423 (1975)

SULLIVAN, J. In this action in eminent domain both parties have appealed from a judgment which, inter alia, awarded compensation to the condemnee, a pharmacist, for the value of certain "ethical drugs" located on the condemned real property but refused to award any compensation for loss of business goodwill resulting from the taking. In dealing with the questions thus presented we are required to address a broad question of constitutional law which, to borrow the image used by one learned commentator in a similar context, has proved remarkably "resistant to analytical efforts." (See Sax, Takings, Private Property and Public Rights (1971) 81 Yale L.J. 149, 149.) Simply stated, the question is this: When and to what extent do the state and federal Constitutions require that the "just compensation" to be paid upon the taking or damaging of private property for public use[2] include payment over and above the fair market value of the property taken on account of business losses sustained by the condemnee as a result of the taking?

Sixty years ago we answered this question in decisive fashion, and thereby stated the rule which presently applies in this state and, generally speaking, in all other jurisdictions of this nation. ". . . [t]he real contention of

2. The Fifth Amendment to the United States Constitution, made applicable to the states by the Fourteenth Amendment, (Chicago, Burlington, etc. R'd v. Chicago (1897) 166 U.S. 226, 233-241, 17 S. Ct. 581, 41 L. Ed. 979), provides in relevant part: ". . . nor shall private property be taken for public use, without just compensation."

Article I, section 19 (replacing former art. I, §14) of the California Constitution provides in relevant part: "Private property may be taken or damaged for public use only when just compensation, ascertained by a jury unless waived, has first been paid to, or into court for, the owner."

appellant . . . [is] that business is property, and when the taking by the state or its agencies interferes with, impairs, damages, or destroys a business, compensation may be recovered therefor. We are not to be understood as saying that this should not be the law when we do say that it is not our law. It is quite within the power of the legislature to declare that a damage to that form of property known as business or the goodwill of a business shall be compensated for, but unless the constitution or the legislature has so declared, it is the universal rule of construction that an injury or an inconvenience to a business is *damnum absque injuria*, and does not form an element of the compensating damages to be awarded." (Oakland v. Pacific Coast Lumber etc. Co. (1915) 171 Cal. 392, 398, 153 P. 705, 707.)

It now appears that while this matter was pending on appeal the Legislature acted in this respect. New section 1263.510 of the Code of Civil Procedure—signed into law by the Governor on October 1, 1975, as a part of a comprehensive revision of the eminent domain law of this state—will operate to render goodwill compensable to a certain extent in cases arising on or after January 1, 1976 (see new §1230.065). This legislation, however, as all parties hereto readily concede, can have no application to the present proceeding, which was commenced in 1971—nor shall what we have to say below be construed to reflect any views on the part of this court relative to the validity or interpretation of the legislation itself. In the posture of the instant case, the question remains one of constitutional dimension: Must the settled rules of constitutional interpretation in this area now give way, in light of the changing conditions of urban society, to rules of similar constitutional stature providing for compensation for lost business goodwill and other incidental damages consequent upon exercise of the power of eminent domain?

I

The facts of the case before us are these: In the course of implementing its Watts Redevelopment Project, the Community Redevelopment Agency of Los Angeles (Agency) brought this action in eminent domain to acquire real property owned by defendant Arthur J. Abrams. For 27 years preceding the trial Abrams, a pharmacist, had operated his pharmacy on the subject property. His parcel lay within an area of approximately 20 square blocks condemned for the project, and the total condemnation not only took the pharmacy property but eliminated the neighborhood from which Abrams' clientele came.

In his answer to the complaint he claimed as elements of the just compensation required by constitutional provisions (see fn. 2, *ante*) not only the value of the real property but also (1) the value of his inventory of so-called "ethical drugs"—or drugs which may be sold only on prescription—which were in opened containers, and (2) the value of his business goodwill. In support of the latter element Abrams alleged that by reason of his age (64) and a rheumatoid arthritis condition from which he suffered he was incapable of relocating his business in a new area and thereby retaining or maintaining his business goodwill, and that as a result of this circumstance and the further fact that under state law his inventory of "ethical drugs," insofar as it was in containers already opened, could not be sold to another pharmacist without a certification of purity—the cost of which would exceed the value of the subject drugs—his inventory of "ethical drugs" in opened containers would be rendered valueless by the taking of his real property.

The trial court found on the basis of substantial evidence that by reason of his age and physical condition Abrams was incapable of relocating his business in a new area; that the business goodwill of Abrams' pharmacy had been taken, damaged, and destroyed by the taking of his real property; and that the market for Abrams' stock of "ethical drugs" had been likewise destroyed. As here relevant it concluded as a matter of law that Abrams was entitled to compensation pursuant to article I, section 14, of the state Constitution for his stock of "ethical drugs" in open containers, but that he was not entitled to be compensated for business goodwill. On the basis of these findings and conclusions the trial court awarded Abrams $10,000, the stipulated value of the drugs in open containers, in addition to the value which the jury placed on the real property and fixtures; no award was made for loss of business goodwill. These appeals followed.

II

Defendant Abrams' arguments on the subject of compensation for business goodwill proceed on two distinct levels. The first is a general attack on the rule of noncompensability, based upon its asserted irrational and arbitrary character. The second is more specific, based upon the particular facts of this case: It urges that whatever be the general rule as to the compensability of business goodwill, compensation should be made when the condemnee is incapable of relocating his business and thus transferring *any part* of his goodwill. We first address ourselves to the more general challenge.

It is urged that the rule of noncompensability for business goodwill is irrational because goodwill is itself "property" in this state and as such should be subject to compensation like any other "property." It is pointed out that goodwill is declared by statute to be property;[4] that it is treated as such in matters of private law in the areas of tort, contract, business affairs, marital dissolution, and probate; and that it is taxable as such. [Citations omitted.] The only area in which business goodwill is denied the status of property,

4. Section 654 of the Civil Code provides: "The ownership of a thing is the right of one or more persons to possess and use it to the exclusion of others. In this Code, the thing of which there may be ownership is called property."

Section 655 of the Civil Code provides: "There may be ownership of all inanimate things which are capable of appropriation or of manual delivery; of all domestic animals; of all obligations; of such products of labor or skill as the composition of an author, *the good will of a business,* trade marks and signs, and of rights created or granted by statute." [Italics added.]

Section 14102 of the Business and Professions Code provides: "*The good will of a business is property* and is transferable." [Italics added.]

defendant asserts, is when the government "takes and destroys" it for public use. The result, it is urged, is not only a violation of constitutional "just compensation" clauses (see fn. 2, *ante*) but a denial of equal protection of the laws.

The foregoing contentions betray a fundamental misunderstanding. The courts of this state have never taken the position that business goodwill is not property—indeed, such a position would be wholly inconsistent with statutory provisions to the contrary (see fn. 4, *ante*). What the courts have established is that "that form of property known as business or the goodwill of a business" (Oakland v. Pacific Coast Lumber etc. Co., *supra*, 171 Cal. 392, 398, 153 P. 705) is not the form of property to which constitutional provisions requiring just compensation refer. As the leading commentator has stated the essentially universal rule, "An established business, or what is called 'good will,' has never been held to be by itself property *in the constitutional sense.* [1]"

". . . While it may be an added element of value to a particular piece of land taken, a business is less tangible in nature and more uncertain in its vicissitudes than the rights which the constitution undertakes to protect absolutely. Although in some cases the destruction of an established business works a much greater hardship than many injuries for which the constitution makes compensation necessary, diminution of its value is considered a vaguer injury than the type of taking or appropriation with which the constitution deals. A business might be destroyed by the construction of a more popular street into which travel was diverted or by a change in the location of a railroad station, a subway entrance, or even a transfer point for street cars (as well as by competition), but there would be as little claim in the one case as in the other."

"The case is no different when the business is destroyed by taking the land on which it was conducted." (4 Nichols, Eminent Domain, (3d ed. 1974) §13.3, pp. 13-148.2-13-149.3; fns. 2 and 3 omitted; italics added.)[5]

It is clear from the foregoing that defendant's linguistic arguments based upon the status of goodwill as property simply ignore established precedents and, in so doing, beg the real question we face today. The fact that business goodwill is legislatively declared to be property and is treated as such in various legal contexts, does not render per se *irrational* a rule which refuses to treat it as such in a constitutional sense for purposes of awarding compensation in eminent domain. The inquiry must go much deeper—into an examination of the reasons for this distinction. Only when that examination has been made can it be determined whether the considerations of constitutional policy underlying it are presently valid. . . .

[T]he rule denying compensation for business goodwill . . . is uniformly applied in all cases to which it is applicable—i.e., in all cases wherein the condemnor takes the fee upon which a business is conducted and does not *by the nature of its action* wholly preclude the condemnee from transferring its

1. "Good will is generally held property in matters of private law. . . ."
5. Compare 1 Orgel, Valuation Under Eminent Domain, *supra*, section 1, page 5: "It goes without saying that the courts have never construed the 'just compensation' clause of a federal or state constitution as requiring payment for all injuries imposed upon persons or property by acts of government. Any such requirement would make government itself impossible."

going-concern or goodwill value to another location. . . . [T]his rule is based on the conviction that it is "fair on the whole" to treat all such condemnees alike, refusing to create distinctions on the basis of "the remote possibility that the owner will be unable to find a wholly suitable location for the transfer of going-concern value." (Kimball Laundry Co. v. United States, 338 U.S. 1, 15 (1949), 69 S. Ct. at p. 1442.) We are thus brought to the question which lies at the core of our inquiry: Does the erosion by modern conditions of the assumptions underlying this rule require its abrogation as a matter of constitutional law and its replacement with a constitutionally grounded and judicially administered rule of compensation more responsive to present-day realities? It is to this question that we now turn our attention.

III

We judicially notice the following as facts "of generalized knowledge that are so universally known that they cannot reasonably be the subject of dispute" (Evid. Code, §451, subd. (f)): The conditions of modern American life, including the increased concentration of people in urban centers and the need for increased governmental activity in the areas of transportation and urban redevelopment, have resulted in the disruption and displacement of increased numbers of people and businesses by government projects. Moreover, the peculiar nature of urban redevelopment programs, which act upon large areas of contiguous property, often involves the uprooting of entire neighborhoods and the consequent dispersal of their business and residential occupants to other areas. (See generally An Act to Provide Compensation For Loss of Goodwill Resulting From Eminent Domain Proceedings, *supra*, 3 Harv. J. Legis. 445, 447-448 (memo.); Note, Eminent Domain Valuation in an Age of Redevelopment: Incidental Losses, *supra* 67 Yale L.J. 61.)

While the effects of this process are severe in both a personal and social sense for the residential occupants of areas subjected to redevelopment, its effects upon business occupants may be even more serious. One such effect relates to the business goodwill which such a businessman has built up in the location of which he is deprived by condemnation. In some cases, as for example in the case of a mail order business whose clientele is not rooted in the area affected by redevelopment, business goodwill may be transferred with relative ease to a new location outside the redevelopment area. At the other end of the spectrum, however, are businesses which depend on a clientele within the redevelopment area. In many such cases business goodwill is based almost wholly upon the businessman's personal acquaintance with his customers and his knowledge of their particular needs. Such goodwill is by its nature not freely transferable within the context of wholesale condemnation pursuant to urban redevelopment, for the inevitable effect of such condemnation is to disperse the businessman's clientele throughout the urban area, with the result that any new location chosen by him will be unable to continue to profitably serve a significant portion of them.

It is clear that to apply the rule of noncompensability for loss of business goodwill to cases in which the assumption underlying it—i.e., that such goodwill is not "taken" or "damaged" but remains subject to transfer to a new location—does not hold true is in effect to require the affected parties to bear a disproportionate share of the true cost of the public undertaking. It is the increased incidence of this occurrence, brought about by the modern urban conditions adverted to above, which has been the basis of scholarly comment critical of the rule. . . . The question before us is whether these considerations require that we hold *as a matter of constitutional law* that business goodwill is now to be considered a compensable element of damage in eminent domain.

As we have repeatedly emphasized, it is the underscored language which is the kernel of the controversy before us. To recognize that there are substantial numbers of cases in which the assumption underlying the rule of noncompensability for business goodwill is not borne out by the particular facts is not necessarily to conclude that alteration of the *constitutional* rule is required. It is at this point that a consideration of institutional functions and capacities must come into play.

It is strenuously urged that because ultimate responsibility for determining the amount of compensation to be paid for property taken under constitutional "just compensation" clauses lies with the courts [citations omitted], it is the courts who must fashion rules insuring that losses of business goodwill occasioned through condemnation be compensated.

This argument, at least insofar as it implies that the sole institution which may provide standards of compensation is the courts, proceeds upon an invalid premise, to wit, that the "just compensation" prescribed by constitutional provisions contemplates total indemnification for damage sustained through condemnation. However, as we have pointed out above (see text accompanying fn. 5, *ante*), the law simply does not equate "just compensation" with total indemnification.[9] We have not far to look in California jurisprudence for cases other than those involving business goodwill in which *demonstrable loss* resulting from condemnation has been held not to constitute an element of *constitutionally required* "just compensation." For example, in County of Los Angeles v. Ortiz, 6 Cal. 3d 141, 98 Cal. Rptr. 454, 490 P.2d 1142, we held that a condemnee's litigation expenses, although clearly resulting in a loss to the condemnee which he would not have sustained absent condemnation, did not, under a virtually unbroken line of authority, form an element of damage required to be paid by the Constitution. Such costs, we concluded, were "of policy as distinguished from constitutional dimension" and the allowance of

---

9. We are of course aware of language in some cases which indicates that "The owner is to be put in as good a position pecuniarily as he would have occupied if his property had not been taken from him." (People ex rel. Dept. Pub. Wks. v. Lynbar, Inc. (1967) 253 Cal. App. 2d 870, 880, 62 Cal. Rptr. 320, 327, see also United States v. Miller (1942) 317 U.S. 369, 373, 63 S. Ct. 276, 87 L. Ed. 336.) This language which we have previously characterized as "panoramic" (County of Los Angeles v. Ortiz, 6 Cal. 3d 141, 147, 98 Cal. Rptr. 454, 490 P.2d 1142), makes up in idealism what it lacks in universal application.

their recovery rested with the Legislature rather than the courts. (6 Cal. 3d at pp. 148-149, 98 Cal. Rptr. at p. 459, 490 P.2d at p. 1147.)[10] Similarly, in Town of Los Gatos v. Sund (1965) 234 Cal. App. 2d 24, 44 Cal. Rptr. 181, it was held that expenses of moving personal property involved in the business conducted on the condemned property, although clearly incurred by the condemnee as a result of the condemnation, were not compensable under constitutional "just compensation" provisions, and that any appeal for their allowance must be made to the Legislature.[11] What these cases show is simply that compensation provided for the taking of real property through eminent domain may be "just" within the meaning of the constitutional provisions without providing complete reimbursement to the owner for all losses suffered by him as a result of condemnation, and that in at least some cases in which the constitutional measure of compensation falls demonstrably short of that required to make the condemnee "whole," his recourse must be to the Legislature.

The central issue, then, is whether compensation for loss of business goodwill should be included within the constitutional minimum required by "just compensation" clauses or whether it should continue to be excluded from that measure and remain subject to legislative competence for the redress of demonstrable losses. We have concluded that valid reasons of policy, based primarily upon considerations of institutional competence, counsel in favor of judicial deference to the legislative branch in fashioning standards and procedures responsive to present realities in this area.

Loss of business goodwill due to condemnation of business premises is just one of a number of areas in which demonstrable loss and inconvenience are suffered by those who are uprooted from their homes and businesses by the modern phenomenon of urban redevelopment programs. The damage sustained ranges from the relatively imponderable (for example, educational damage caused young persons by midstream changes in schools) to the relatively tangible (for example, expenses incurred by a family or a business in moving personal property from condemned realty to a new location). In the specific area with which we are here concerned—to wit, loss of business goodwill—there are similar problems. Thus, even assuming as defendant insists that the goodwill possessed by a business at one location is capable of accurate translation into a dollar amount, to what extent must the assumption of transferability (upon which, as we have seen, the rule of noncompensability rests)

10. Partial legislative response in this area has come in the form of new section 1249.3 of the Code of Civil Procedure (enacted in 1974), which requires the parties to make final settlement offers prior to trial and awards the defendant his litigation expenses when it appears after trial that the plaintiff's offer was unreasonably low. Litigation expenses, including reasonable attorney's fees, appraisal fees, and fees for the services of other experts, are also awarded by statute when the eminent domain proceeding is ultimately abandoned (Code Civ. Proc., §1255a) or the defendant secures a judgment that the condemnor may not acquire the real property (Code Civ. Proc., §1246.4). Further provisions in this area are included in the 1975 act (new Code Civ. Proc., §1268.610).

11. Legislative response in this area appeared in 1971 amendments to the state Relocation Assistance Act, specifically with the addition of subdivision (a)(2) to section 7262 of the Government Code.

break down in the particular case to justify compensation, and what amount
of compensation is appropriate when the breakdown of the assumption is less
than total?

The courts, although rarely making explicit reference to the overall
problem, have, by their case by case rulings in accordance with established
principles such as that we consider today, demonstrated a fundamental awareness of the real dimensions of the underlying problem. In the words of one
perceptive commentator, "the courts recognize that they cannot, through the
enunciation of doctrine which decides cases, adequately stake out the limits of
fair treatment; that if the quest for fairness is left to a series of occasional
encounters between courts and public administrators it can but partially be
fulfilled; and that the political branches, accordingly, labor under their own
obligations to avoid unfairness regardless of what the courts may require."
(Michelman, Property, Utility, and Fairness: Comments on The Ethical
Foundations of "Just Compensation" Law, 80 Harv. L. Rev. 1165, 1252.)[12]

It is manifest that state and federal legislative bodies have begun to
demonstrate their awareness of such obligations. The federal Uniform Relocation Assistance and Real Property Acquisition Policies Act (42 U.S.C. §4601
et seq.) and the interlocking California Relocation Assistance Act (Gov. Code,
§7260 et seq.) have made substantial strides in the direction of providing—in

12. The cited article by Professor Michelman, which must be acknowledged a landmark in
the field of compensation analysis, goes far to explicate the nature of the broad problem of
compensation for public takings and the role of courts, legislatures, and other public bodies in
providing solutions for that problem. Professor Michelman's thesis is stated in brief in the following paragraph from his article:

A serious objection to the habit of leaving fairness discipline to the courts is that we may
thereby miss opportunities to make good use of settlement methods too artificial or innovative for judicial adoption. A court, it seems, must choose between denying all compensation
and awarding "just" compensation; the loss is either a "taking" of "property" or it is not.
If "just" compensation is essentially incalculable, or if the cost of computing it is very high,
the court may be led to classify a situation as non-compensable. If choice must be relegated
to this framework, we shall not be able to exploit the substitutability of settlement costs and
demoralization costs.* It may be that even though that stettlement which would reduce
demoralization costs to zero would be prohibitively costly, there exists some relatively
cheap form of settlement which would reduce demoralization costs so effectively that, by
using it, we can reduce the total of settlement plus demoralization cost below what they
would be in the absence of any settlement. Such a settlement technique, if one exists, is very
likely to require legislative adoption.

(Michelman, *supra*, 80 Harv. L. Rev. at pp. 1253-1254; fns. omitted.)

* "Demoralization costs" are defined as the total of (1) the dollar value necessary to
offset disutilities which accrue to losers and their sympathizers specifically from the realization that no compensation is offered, and (2) the present capitalized dollar value of lost
future production (reflecting either impaired incentives or social unrest) caused by demoralization of uncompensated losers, their sympathizers, and other observers disturbed by the
thought that they themselves may be subjected to similar treatment on some other occasion. "Settlement costs" are measured by the dollar value of the time, effort, and resources
which would be required in order to reach compensation settlements adequate to avoid
demoralization costs. Included are the costs of settling not only the particular compensation claims presented, but also those of all persons so affected by the measure in question
or similar measures as to have claims not obviously distinguishable by the available settlement apparatus.

(Michelman, *supra*, 80 Harv. L. Rev. at p. 1214; fns. omitted.)

the words of the declaration of policy of the federal act—"fair and equitable treatment of persons displaced as a result of [public] programs in order that such persons shall not suffer disproportionate injuries as a result of programs designed for the benefit of the public as a whole." (42 U.S.C. §4621.) Thus, provision is now made for the payment of moving and related expenses (42 U.S.C. §4622; Gov. Code, §7262), acquisition of replacement housing (42 U.S.C. §§4623, 4624, 4626; Gov. Code, §§7263, 7263.5, 7264, 7264.5), and advisory services (42 U.S.C. §4625; Gov. Code §7261). As to the matter of business relocation, the acts provide for in lieu payment (based upon average net earnings) of up to $10,000 in cases wherein the business cannot be relocated without substantial loss of patronage and is not a part of an enterprise having another establishment or establishments in the same or similar business which are not being acquired. (42 U.S.C. §4622(c); Gov. Code, §7262, subd. (c).) (See generally 6A Nichols, Eminent Domain, *supra,* ch. 34; Comment: Relocation Assistance in California: Legislative Response to the Federal Program (1972) 3 Pacific L.J. 114.)

The foregoing acts do not address themselves directly to the matter here before us, i.e., loss of business goodwill. However it is clear that the provision for in lieu payments adverted to above represent an attempt to provide some compensation (up to the maximum of $10,000) for business losses occasioned through condemnation.[15] More importantly, the recent action of the Legislature in enacting new section 1263.510 of the Code of Civil Procedure—which section will in future cases provide compensation for loss of goodwill in coordination with applicable provisions of the Relocation Assistance Act[16]—manifests an explicit legislative recognition of the problem and a willingness to address itself to it.[17]

---

15. This, like the other provisions of the respective relocation acts, is clearly an effort by the legislative arm of government to introduce what Professor Michelman would term a "relatively cheap form of settlement [designed to] reduce demoralization costs so effectively that, by using it, we can reduce the total of settlement plus demoralization costs below what they would be in the absence of any settlement." (See fn. 12, *ante.*)

16. New section 1263.510, effective January 1, 1976, provides:

(a)   The owner of a business conducted on the property taken, or on the remainder if such property is part of a larger parcel, shall be compensated for loss of goodwill if the owner proves all of the following:

(1)   The loss is caused by the taking of the property or the injury to the remainder.

(2)   The loss cannot reasonably be prevented by a relocation of the business or by taking steps and adopting procedures that a reasonably prudent person would take and adopt in preserving the goodwill.

(3)   Compensation for the loss will not be included in payments under Section 7262 of the Government Code.

(4)   Compensation for the loss will not be duplicated in the compensation otherwise awarded to the owner.

(b)   Within the meaning of this article, "goodwill" consists of the benefits that accrue to a business as a result of its location, reputation for dependability, skill or quality, and any other circumstances resulting in probable retention of old or acquisition of new patronage.

17. Although, as we have observed at the outset of this opinion, the provisions of new section 1263.510 are not applicable to this proceeding, we believe it appropriate to make reference to them as a manifestation of continued legislative concern in this area.

In view of all of the foregoing we have concluded that sound reasons of constitutional and judicial policy counsel against a present reinterpretation of constitutional "just compensation" clauses to require compensation for business goodwill affected or damaged by exercise of the power of eminent domain. The present discrete limits upon constitutionally compelled compensation, while seeming arbitrary and irrational from the point of view of total indemnification for losses sustained through condemnation, suffer from neither of those vices when viewed in the proper context of institutional functions and capabilities. The courts, in essentially limiting the scope of constitutionally compelled compensation to the fair market value of real property taken or damaged by public projects, have in essence recognized their limitations in providing overall fair treatment for persons who suffer injuries as a result of public projects. The legislative branch of government, recognizing its peculiar competence in this area, has undertaken responsive steps and evidences a willingness to continue to deal with the difficult and involved questions of social policy which underlie the task. In these circumstances wisdom lies in the direction of judicial deference to the legislative branch. We therefore reaffirm the longstanding and uniform rule of constitutional interpretation which holds that the provisions of the state and federal Constitutions providing for the payment of just compensation upon the taking or damaging of private property for public use (see fn. 2, *ante*) do not require that compensation be paid for the loss of business goodwill sustained due to the exercise of the power of eminent domain, and that recourse for recoupment of injury of this kind must lie with the legislative branch. We further hold that this rule is based upon sound considerations of governmental policy and does not operate to deny affected parties the equal protection of the laws. . . . [The Court, extending the above analysis, concludes that the pharmacist was not constitutionally entitled to recover the value of the ethical drugs inventory. Can you supply the reasoning?—ED.]

To recapitulate, we hold (1) that under the law applicable to the case at bench, and in particular under pertinent *constitutional* provisions, defendant condemnee was not entitled to recover compensation either for loss of business goodwill or for the loss of value of his inventory of "ethical drugs," resulting from condemnation of the real property owned by him; (2) that accordingly the trial court did not err in concluding that he was not entitled to be compensated for loss of business goodwill; but (3) that the court did err in awarding him compensation for his inventory of ethical drugs. The judgment must therefore be reversed, but we find nothing in the record impelling us to order a new trial. The case was fully tried and we apprehend no necessity to take further evidence. On remand the court should make findings of fact and conclusions of law in conformity with the views herein expressed and entered judgment accordingly.

The judgment is reversed and the cause is remanded to the trial court to proceed with the disposition thereof under the directions and in conformity with the views herein expressed. Defendant shall recover his costs on plaintiff's appeal; plaintiff shall recover its costs on defendant's appeal.

WRIGHT, C.J., and McCOMB, TOBRINER, MOSK, CLARK and RICHARD-
SON, JJ., concur.

NOTES AND QUESTIONS

1. Reread the excerpt from Jeremy Bentham. With respect to the value
of business goodwill, did the pharmacist lose because he had no property or
did he have no property because he lost?

2. Suppose that, two months prior to the condemnation, a gas main
explosion destroyed the pharmacist's building. If negligence of a privately
owned utility had caused the explosion, would the pharmacist's right to compensation in tort cover any part of his business goodwill? Would your analysis
be unchanged if the city had negligently caused the explosion? Does the nature of property partly depend on who seeks what from whom?

3. Consider the court's discussion of the responsibility (as between
court and legislature) for defining the nature of property. Are you persuaded
that, with respect to the compensability of goodwill in eminent domain, courts
should follow the legislature's lead? Why so? Why not? Is the original rule of
noncompensability judge-made or statutory?

4. You need not fully understand, this early in the course, the economic
theory that underlies goodwill (or business advantage). More extended treatment appears at §18.2b, *infra*.

5. A most significant contribution to an *analytical* basis for understanding property was made by Wesley Hohfeld. Excerpts from his much-cited
article appear below. After reading the excerpts, consider how "Hohfeldian"
terms might be used to describe the various property interests present in the
Abrams case.

§1.2   Property as a Hohfeldian Relationship

HOHFELD, SOME FUNDAMENTAL LEGAL CONCEPTIONS AS APPLIED IN JUDICIAL REASONING
23 Yale L.J. 16 (1913)

FUNDAMENTAL JURAL RELATIONS CONTRASTED WITH ONE ANOTHER

One of the greatest hindrances to the clear understanding, the incisive
statement, and the true solution of legal problems frequently arises from the
express or tacit assumption that all legal relations may be reduced to "rights"
and "duties," and that these latter categories are therefore adequate for the
purpose of analyzing even the most complex legal interests, such as trusts,

options, escrows, "future" interests, corporate interests, etc. Even if the difficulty related merely to inadequacy and ambiguity of terminology, its seriousness would nevertheless be worthy of definite recognition and persistent effort toward improvement; for in any closely reasoned problem, whether legal or non-legal, chameleon-hued words are a peril both to clear thought and to lucid expression. As a matter of fact, however, the above mentioned inadequacy and ambiguity of terms unfortunately reflect, all too often, corresponding paucity and confusion as regards actual legal conceptions. That this is so may appear in some measure from the discussion to follow.

The strictly fundamental legal relations are, after all, sui generis; and thus it is that attempts at formal definition are always unsatisfactory, if not altogether useless. Accordingly, the most promising line of procedure seems to consist in exhibiting all of the various relations in a scheme of "opposites" and "correlatives," and then proceeding to exemplify their individual scope and application in concrete cases. An effort will be made to pursue this method:

Jural Opposites	right	privilege	power	immunity
	no-right	duty	disability	liability

Jural Correlatives	right	privilege	power	immunity
	duty	no-right	liability	disability

Rights and Duties. As already intimated, the term "rights" tends to be used indiscriminately to cover what in a given case may be a privilege, a power, or an immunity, rather than a right in the strictest sense; and this looseness of usage is occasionally recognized by the authorities. As said by Mr. Justice Strong in People v. Dikeman [7 How. Pr. 124, 130 (1852)]: "The word 'right' is defined by lexicographers to denote, among other things, *property, interest, power, prerogative, immunity, privilege* (Walker's Dict. word 'Right'). In law it is most frequently applied to property in its restricted sense, but it is often used to designate *power, prerogative,* and *privilege.* . . ."

Recognizing, as we must, the very broad and indiscriminate use of the term, "right," what clue do we find, in ordinary legal discourse, toward limiting the word in question to a definite and appropriate meaning. That clue lies in the correlative "duty," for it is certain that even those who use the word and the conception "right" in the broadest possible way are accustomed to thinking of "duty" as the invariable correlative. As said in Lake Shore & M.S.R. Co. v. Kurtz [10 Ind. App. 60, 37 N.E. 303, 304 (1894)]:

"A duty or a legal obligation is that which one ought or ought not to do. 'Duty' and 'right' are correlative terms. When a right is invaded, a duty is violated."

In other words, if X has a right against Y that he shall stay off the former's land, the correlative (and equivalent) is that Y is under a duty toward X to stay off the place. If, as seems desirable, we should seek a synonym for the term "right" in this limited and proper meaning, perhaps the word "claim" would prove the best. The latter has the advantage of being a mono-syllable. . . .

Privileges and "No-Rights." As indicated in the above scheme of jural rela-tions, a privilege is the opposite of duty, and the correlative of a "no-right." In the example last put, whereas X has a *right* or *claim* that Y, the other man, should stay off the land, he himself has the *privilege* of entering on the land; or, in equivalent words, X does not have a duty to stay off. The privilege of entering is the negation of a duty to stay off. As indicated by this case, some caution is necessary at this point; for, always, when it is said that a given privilege is the mere negation of a *duty,* what is meant, of course, is a duty having a content or tenor precisely *opposite* to that of the privilege in question. Thus, if, for some special reason, X has contracted with Y to go on the former's own land, it is obvious that X has, as regards Y, both the privilege of entering and the *duty of entering.* The privilege is perfectly consistent with this sort of duty,—for the latter is of the *same* content or tenor as the privilege;—but it still holds good that, as regards Y, X's privilege of entering is the precise negation of a duty *to stay off.* Similarly, if A has not contracted with B to perform certain work for the latter, A's privilege of *not* doing so is the very negation of a duty of *doing* so. Here again the duty contrasted is of a content or tenor exactly opposite to that of the privilege.

Passing now to the question of "correlatives," it will be remembered, of course, that a duty is the invariable correlative of that legal relation which is most properly called a right or claim. That being so, if further evidence be needed as to the fundamental and important difference between a right (or claim) and a privilege, surely it is found in the fact that the correlative of the latter relation is a "no-right," there being no single term available to express the latter conception. Thus, the correlative of X's right that Y shall not enter on the land is Y's duty not to enter; but the correlative of X's privilege of entering himself is manifestly Y's "no-right" that X shall not enter. . . .

Powers and Liabilities. As indicated in the preliminary scheme of jural relations, a legal power (as distinguished, of course, from a mental or physical power) is the opposite of legal disability, and the correlative of legal liability. But what is the intrinsic nature of a legal power as such? Is it possible to analyze the conception represented by this constantly employed and very important term of legal discourse? Too close an analysis might seem meta-physical rather than useful; so that what is here presented is intended only as an approximate explanation, sufficient for all practical purposes.

A change in a given legal relation may result (1) from some superadded fact or group of facts not under the volitional control of a human being (or human beings); or (2) from some superadded fact or group of facts which are under the volitional control of one or more human beings. As regards the second class of cases, the person (or persons) whose volitional control is para-mount may be said to have the (legal) power to effect the particular change of legal relations that is involved in the problem.

This second class of cases—powers in the technical sense—must now be further considered. The nearest synonym for any ordinary case seems to be (legal) "ability,"—the latter being obviously the opposite of "inability," or "disability." The term "right," so frequently and loosely used in the present connection, is an unfortunate term for the purpose,—a not unusual result being confusion of thought as well as ambiguity of expression. The term "capacity" is equally unfortunate; for, as we have already seen, when used with discrimination, this word denotes a particular group of operative facts, and not a legal relation of any kind.

Many examples of legal powers may readily be given. Thus, X, the owner of ordinary personal property "in a tangible object" has the power to extinguish his own legal interest (rights, powers, immunities, etc.) through that totality of operative facts known as abandonment; and—simultaneously and correlatively—to create in other persons privileges and powers relating to the abandoned object,—e.g., the power to acquire title to the latter by appropriating it. *Similarly*, X has the power to transfer his interest to Y,—that is, to extinguish his own interest and concomitantly create in Y a new and corresponding interest. So also X has the power to create contractual obligations of various kinds. Agency cases are likewise instructive. By the use of some *metaphorical* expression such as the Latin, qui facit per alium, facit per se, the true nature of agency relations is only too frequently obscured. The creation of an agency relation involves, inter alia, the grant of legal powers to the so-called agent, and the creation of correlative liabilities in the principal. That is to say, one party, P, has the power to create agency powers in another party, A,—for example, the power to convey P's property, the power to impose (so-called) contractual obligations on P, the power to discharge a debt owing to P, the power to "receive" title to property so that it shall vest in P, and so forth. . . .

As regards all the "legal powers" thus far considered, possibly some caution is necessary. If, for example, we consider the ordinary property owner's power of alienation, it is necessary to distinguish carefully between the *legal* power, the *physical* power to do things necessary for the "exercise" of the legal power, and, finally, the *privilege* of doing these things—that is, if such privilege does really exist. It may or may not. Thus, if X, a landowner, has contracted with Y that the former will not alienate to Z, the acts of X necessary to exercise the power of alienating to Z are privileged as between X and every party other than Y; but, obviously, as between X and Y, the former has no privilege of doing the necessary acts; or conversely, he is under a duty to Y not to do what is necessary to exercise the power.

In view of what has already been said, very little may suffice concerning a *liability* as such. The latter, as we have seen, is the correlative of power, and the opposite of immunity (or exemption). While no doubt the term "liability" is often loosely used as a synonym for "duty," or "obligation," it is believed, from an extensive survey of judicial precedents, that the connotation already adopted as most appropriate to the word in question is fully justified. A few cases tending to indicate this will now be noticed. In McNeer v. McNeer [142 Ill. 388, 397 (1892)], Mr. Justice Magruder balanced the conceptions of power and liability as follows:

"So long as she lived, however, his interest in her land lacked those *elements of property*, such as *power of disposition* and *liability to sale on execution* which had formerly given it the character of a vested estate."

In Booth v. Commonwealth [16 Gratt. 519, 525 (Va. 1861)], the court had to construe a Virginia statute providing "that all free white male persons who are twenty-one years of age and not over sixty, shall be *liable* to serve as jurors, except as hereinafter provided." It is plain that this enactment imposed only a *liability* and not a *duty*. It is a liability to have a duty created. The latter would arise only when, in exercise of their powers, the parties litigant and the court officers had done what was necessary to impose a specific duty to perform the functions of a juror. . . .

Immunities and Disabilities. As already brought out, immunity is the correlative of disability ("no-power"), and the opposite, or negation, of liability. Perhaps it will also be plain, from the preliminary outline and from the discussion down to this point, that a power bears the same general contrast to an immunity that a right does to a privilege. A right is one's affirmative claim against another, and a privilege is one's freedom from the right or claim of another. Similarly, a power is one's affirmative "control" over a given legal relation as against another; whereas an immunity is one's freedom from the legal power or "control" of another as regards some legal relation.

A few examples may serve to make this clear. X, a landowner, has, as we have seen, power to alienate to Y or to any other ordinary party. On the other hand, X has also various immunities as against Y, and all other ordinary parties. For Y is under a disability (i.e., has no power) so far as shifting the legal interest either to himself or to a third party is concerned; and what is true of Y applies similarly to every one else who has not by virtue of special operative facts acquired a power to alienate X's property. If, indeed, a sheriff has been duly empowered by a writ of execution to sell X's interest, that is a very different matter: correlative to such sheriff's power would be the *liability* of X,—the very opposite of immunity (or exemption). It is elementary, too, that as against the sheriff, X might be immune or exempt in relation to certain parcels of property, and be liable as to others. Similarly, if an agent has been duly appointed by X to sell a given piece of property, then, as to the latter, X has, in relation to such agent, a liability rather than an immunity. . . .

In the latter part of the preceding discussion, eight conceptions of the law have been analyzed and compared in some detail, the purpose having been to exhibit not only their intrinsic meaning and scope, but also their relations to one another and the methods by which they are applied, in judicial reasoning, to the solution of concrete problems of litigation. Before concluding this branch of the discussion a general suggestion may be ventured as to the great practical importance of a clear appreciation of the distinctions and discriminations set forth. If a homely metaphor be permitted, these eight conceptions,—right and duties, privileges and no-rights, powers and liabilities, immunities and disabilities,—seem to be what may be called "the lowest common denominators of the law." Ten fractions (1/3, 2/5, etc.) may, *superficially*, seem so different from one another as to defy comparison. If, however, they are expressed in terms of their lowest common denominators (5/15, 6/15, etc.), comparison becomes easy, and fundamental similarity may be discovered. The same thing is of course true as regards the lowest generic conceptions to which any and all "legal quantities" may be reduced.

Reverting, for example, to the subject powers, it might be difficult at first glance to discover any essential and fundamental similarity between conditional sales of personality, escrow transactions, option agreements, agency relations, powers of appointment, etc. But if all these relations are reduced to their lowest generic terms, the conceptions of legal power and legal liability are seen to be dominantly, though not exclusively, applicable throughout the series. By such a process it becomes possible not only to discover essential similarities and illuminating analogies in the midst of what appears superficially to be infinite and hopeless variety, but also to discern common principles of justice and policy underlying the various jural problems involved. An indirect, yet very practical, consequence is that it frequently becomes feasible, by virtue of such analysis, to use as persuasive authorities judicial precedents that might otherwise seem altogether irrelevant. If this point be valid with respect to powers, it would seem to be equally so as regards all of the other basic conceptions of the law. In short, the deeper the analysis, the greater becomes one's perception of fundamental unity and harmony in the law.

NOTES AND QUESTIONS

1. The Restatement of Property (1936) relied heavily on Hohfeld for several of its basic terms. The similarity between the passages above and the Restatement paragraphs below is apparent.

> §1. *Right.* A right, as the word is used in this Restatement, is a legally enforceable claim of one person against another, that the other shall do a given act or shall not do a given act.
>
> *Comment: a. Correlative duty.* The relation indicated by the word "right" may also be stated from the point of view of the person against whom that right exists. This person has a duty, that is, is under a legally enforceable obligation to do or not to do an act. The word "duty" is used in this Restatement with this meaning.
>
> *Illustration:* 1. A is the owner of Blackacre. B is any other person. A normally has a right that B shall not walk across Blackacre. . . .
>
> §2. *Privilege.* A privilege, as the word is used in this Restatement, is a legal freedom on the part of one person as against another to do a given act or a legal freedom not to do a given act.
>
> *Comment: a. Correlative absence of right.* The relation indicated by the word "privilege" may also be stated from the point of view of the person against whom

the privilege exists. From the point of view of this other person it may be said that there is no right on his part that the first person should not engage in the particular course of action or of nonaction in question.

Illustration: 1. A is the lessee of a farm. The lease contains a covenant with the landlord B that A will cultivate field one, and that he will not cultivate field two, and has no covenant as to field three. As between A and B, A has both the duty and privilege of cultivating field one; he has both the duty and the privilege of not cultivating field two; except so far as he is affected by the law of waste, he has the privilege of cultivating and the privilege of not cultivating field three.

§3. *Power.* A power, as the word is used in this Restatement, is an ability on the part of a person to produce a change in a given legal relation by doing or not doing a given act.

Comment: a. Correlative liability. The relation indicated by the word "power" may also be stated from the point of view of the person whose legal relation is thus liable to be changed. This subjection of the second person to having his legal relation affected by the conduct of the person having the power is a "liability" and the word is used in this Restatement with this meaning.

Illustrations: 1. A, the owner of Blackacre, gives B a power of attorney to transfer Blackacre to a purchaser. B has a power. A is under a liability. . . . 3. B has the recorded title to Blackacre. He transfers the land to A. A does not record his deed. B makes a formally sufficient conveyance of the same land to C who buys in ignorance of the conveyance to A, and who pays full value for the land and records his deed. B in so conveying to C exercised a power to destroy A's interest and A was under a corresponding liability with regard to B. B has no privilege to do so and in doing so violates A's rights. . . .

§4. *Immunity.* An immunity, as the word is used in this Restatement, is a freedom on the part of one person against having a given legal relation altered by a given act or omission to act on the part of another person.

Comment: a. Correlative disability. The relation indicated by the word "immunity" may also be stated from the point of view of the person with respect to whom the immunity exists, that is, who has no ability so to alter the given legal relation. This second person has, in this particular, a disability with regard to the first person and the word "disability" is used in this Restatement with this meaning. . . .

Illustration: 1. A owns Blackacre in fee simple absolute. B is a judgment creditor of A. B has a power with regard to Blackacre and A has a liability. A discharges in full B's judgment debt. So far as B's powers as a judgment creditor are concerned, A now has an immunity and B has a disability with regard to Blackacre.

2. Over the years, Hohfeld has had both his staunch defenders and vigorous assailants. Good examples of the latter include Husik, Hohfeld's Jurisprudence, 72 U. Pa. L. Rev. 263 (1924); Radin, A Restatement of Hohfeld, 51 Harv. L. Rev. 1141 (1938); Stone, An Analysis of Hohfeld, 48 Minn. L. Rev. 313 (1963). The attack is met in Corbin, Jural Relations and Their Classification, 30 Yale L.J. 226 (1921); Hoebel, Fundamental Legal Concepts as Applied in the Study of Primitive Law, 51 Yale L.J. 951 (1942).

3. Unfortunately, neither Hohfeld nor the Restatement could have

been much help to either the lawyers trying or the justices deciding the *Abrams* case. If you doubt this, try to build an argument that supports the claimant and uses only Restatement phrases. Have you done more than to describe the legal consequences you would like established by a favorable court decision? Has your argument any persuasive power? Any predictive power?

§1.3   Property and Social Change: The Right to Exclude

BLACKSTONE, COMMENTARIES
575-576 (Ehrlich ed. 1959)

Trespass quare clausum fregit—But in the limited and confined sense, in which we are at present to consider it, it signifies no more than an entry on another man's ground without a lawful authority, and doing some damage, however inconsiderable, to his real property. For the right of meum and tuum (mine and thine) or property, in lands being once established, it follows, as a necessary consequence, that this right must be exclusive; that is, that the owner may retain to himself the sole use and occupation of his soil: every entry, therefore, thereon without the owner's leave, and especially if contrary to his express order, is a trespass or transgression.

The law of England has treated every entry upon another's lands (unless by the owner's leave, or in some very particular cases), as an injury or wrong, for satisfaction of which an action of trespass will lie; but determines the quantum of that satisfaction, by considering how far the offense was willful or inadvertent, and by estimating the value of the actual damages sustained.

STATE v. SHACK
58 N.J. 297, 277 A.2d 369 (1971)

The opinion of the Court was delivered by WEINTRAUB, C.J. Defendants entered upon private property to aid migrant farmworkers employed and housed there. Having refused to depart upon the demand of the owner, defendants were charged with violating N.J.S.A. 2A:170-31 which provides that "[a]ny person who trespasses on any lands . . . after being forbidden so to trespass by the owner . . . is a disorderly person and shall be punished by a fine of not more than $50." Defendants were convicted in the Municipal Court of Deerfield Township and again on appeal in the County Court of Cumberland County on a trial de novo. R. 3:23-8(a). We certified their further appeal before argument in the Appellate Division.

Before us, no one seeks to sustain these convictions. The complaints were prosecuted in the Municipal Court and in the County Court by counsel engaged by the complaining landowner, Tedesco. However Tedesco did not respond to this appeal, and the county prosecutor, while defending abstractly the constitutionality of the trespass statute, expressly disclaimed any position as to whether the statute reached the activity of these defendants.

Complainant, Tedesco, a farmer, employs migrant workers for his seasonal needs. As part of their compensation, these workers are housed at a camp on his property.

Defendant Tejeras is a field worker for the Farm Workers Divison of the Southwest Citizens Organization for Poverty Elimination, known by the acronym SCOPE, a nonprofit corporation funded by the Office of Economic Opportunity pursuant to an act of Congress, 42 U.S.C.A. §§2861-2864. The role of SCOPE includes providing for the "health services of the migrant farm worker."

Defendant Shack is a staff attorney with the Farm Workers Division of Camden Regional Legal Services, Inc., known as "CRLS," also a nonprofit corporation funded by the Office of Economic Opportunity pursuant to an act of Congress, 42 U.S.C.A. §2809(a)(3). The mission of CRLS includes legal advice and representation for these workers.

Differences had developed between Tedesco and these defendants prior to the events which led to the trespass charges now before us. Hence when defendant Tejeras wanted to go upon Tedesco's farm to find a migrant worker who needed medical aid for the removal of 28 sutures, he called upon defendant Shack for his help with respect to the legalities involved. Shack, too, had a mission to perform on Tedesco's farm; he wanted to discuss a legal problem with another migrant worker there employed and housed. Defendants arranged to go to the farm together. Shack carried literature to inform the migrant farmworkers of the assistance available to them under federal statutes, but no mention seems to have been made of that literature when Shack was later confronted by Tedesco.

Defendants entered upon Tedesco's property and as they neared the camp site where the farmworkers were housed, they were confronted by Tedesco who inquired of their purpose. Tejeras and Shack stated their missions. In response, Tedesco offered to find the injured worker, and as to the worker who needed legal advice, Tedesco also offered to locate the man but insisted that the consultation would have to take place in Tedesco's office and in his presence. Defendants declined, saying that they had the right to see the men in the privacy of their living quarters and without Tedesco's supervision. Tedesco thereupon summoned a State Trooper who, however, refused to remove defendants except upon Tedesco's written complaint. Tedesco then executed the formal complaints charging violations of the trespass statute.

I

The constitutionality of the trespass statute, as applied here, is challenged on several scores.

It is urged that the First Amendment rights of the defendants and of the migrant farmworkers were thereby offended. Reliance is placed on Marsh v. Alabama, 326 U.S. 501 (1946), where it was held that free speech was assured by the First Amendment in a company-owned town which was open to the public generally and was indistinguishable from any other town except for the fact that the title to property was vested in a private corporation. Hence a Jehovah's Witness who distributed literature on a sidewalk within the town could not be held as a trespasser. Later, on the strength of that case, it was held that there was a First Amendment right to picket peacefully in a privately owned shopping center which was found to be the functional equivalent of the business district of the company-owned town in *Marsh*. Amalgamated Food Employees Union Local 590 v. Logan Valley Plaza, Inc., 391 U.S. 308 (1968). See, to the same effect, the earlier case of Schwartz-Torrance Investment Corp. v. Bakery and Confectionery Workers' Union, 61 Cal. 2d 766, 40 Cal. Rptr. 233, 394 P.2d 921 (Sup. Ct. 1964), cert. denied, 380 U.S. 906 (1964). Those cases rest upon the fact that the property was in fact opened to the general public. There may be some migrant camps with the attributes of the company town in *Marsh* and of course they would come within its holding. But there is nothing of that character in the case before us, and hence there would have to be an extension of *Marsh* to embrace the immediate situation.

Defendants also maintain that the application of the trespass statute to them is barred by the Supremacy Clause of the United States Constitution, Art. VI, cl. 2, and this on the premise that the application of the trespass statute would defeat the purpose of the federal statutes, under which SCOPE and CRLS are funded, to reach and aid the migrant farmworker. The brief of the United States, amicus curiae, supports that approach. Here defendants rely upon cases construing the National Labor Relations Act, 29 U.S.C.A. §151 et seq., and holding that an employer may in some circumstances be guilty of an unfair labor practice in violation of that statute if the employer denies union organizers an opportunity to communicate with his employees at some suitable place upon the employer's premises. See NLRB v. Babcock and Wilcox Co., 351 U.S. 105 (1956), and annotation, 100 L. Ed. 984 (1956). The brief of New Jersey Office of Legal Services, amicus curiae, asserts the workers' Sixth Amendment right to counsel in criminal matters is involved and suggests also that a right to counsel in civil matters is a "penumbra" right emanating from the whole Bill of Rights under the thinking of Griswold v. Connecticut, 381 U.S. 479 (1965), or is a privilege of national citizenship protected by the privileges and immunities clause of the Fourteenth Amendment, or is a right "retained by the people" under the Ninth Amendment, citing a dictum in United Public Workers v. Mitchell, 330 U.S. 75, 94 (1947).

These constitutional claims are not established by any definitive holding. We think it unnecessary to explore their validity. The reason is that we are satisfied that under our State law the ownership of real property does not include the right to bar access to governmental services available to migrant

workers and hence there was no trespass within the meaning of the penal
statute. The policy considerations which underlie that conclusion may be
much the same as those which would be weighed with respect to one or more
of the constitutional challenges, but a decision in nonconstitutional terms is
more satisfactory, because the interests of migrant workers are more expansively served in that way than they would be if they had no more freedom than
these constitutional concepts could be found to mandate if indeed they apply
at all.

II

Property rights serve human values. They are recognized to that end
and are limited by it. Title to real property cannot include dominion over the
destiny of persons the owner permits to come upon the premises. Their well-
being must remain the paramount concern of a system of law. Indeed the
needs of the occupants may be so imperative and their strength so weak, that
the law will deny the occupants the power to contract away what is deemed
essential to their health, welfare, or dignity.

Here we are concerned with a highly disadvantaged segment of our
society. We are told that every year farmworkers and their families numbering
more than one million leave their home areas to fill the seasonal demand for
farm labor in the United States. The Migratory Farm Labor Problem in the
United States (1969 Report of Subcommittee on Migratory Labor of the
United States Senate Committee on Labor and Public Welfare), p. 1. The
migrant farmworkers come to New Jersey in substantial numbers. The report
just cited places at 55,700 the number of man-months of such employment in
our State in 1968 (p. 7). The numbers of workers so employed here in that
year are estimated at 1,300 in April; 6,500 in May; 9,800 in June; 10,600 in
July; 12,000 in August; 9,600 in September; and 5,500 in October (p. 9).

The migrant farmworkers are a community within but apart from the
local scene. They are rootless and isolated. Although the need for their labors
is evident, they are unorganized and without economic or political power. It is
their plight alone that summoned government to their aid. In response, Congress provided under Title III-B of the Economic Opportunity Act of 1964 (42
U.S.C.A. §2701 et seq.) for "assistance for migrant and other seasonally employed farmworkers and their families." Section 2861 states "the purpose of
this part is to assist migrant and seasonal farmworkers and their families to
improve their living conditions and develop skills necessary for a productive
and self-sufficient life in an increasingly complex and technological society."
Section 2862(b)(1) provides for funding of programs "to meet the immediate
needs of migrant and seasonal farmworkers and their families, such as day care
for children, education, health services, improved housing and sanitation (including the provision and maintenance of emergency and temporary housing
and sanitation facilities), legal advice and representation, and consumer training and counseling." As we have said, SCOPE is engaged in a program funded

under this section, and CRLS also pursues the objectives of this section although, we gather, it is funded under §2809(a)(3), which is not limited in its concern to the migrant and other seasonally employed farmworkers and seeks "to further the cause of justice among persons living in poverty by mobilizing the assistance of lawyers and legal institutions and by providing legal advice, legal representation, counseling, education, and other appropriate services."

These ends would not be gained if the intended beneficiaries could be insulated from efforts to reach them. It is in this framework that we must decide whether the camp operator's rights in his lands may stand between the migrant workers and those who would aid them. The key to that aid is communication. Since the migrant workers are outside the mainstream of the communities in which they are housed and are unaware of their rights and opportunities and of the services available to them, they can be reached only by positive efforts tailored to that end. The Report of the Governor's Task Force on Migrant Farm Labor (1968) noted that "One of the major problems related to seasonal farm labor is the lack of adequate direct information with regard to the availability of public services," and that "there is a dire need to provide the workers with basic educational and informational material in a language and style that can be readily understood by the migrant" (pp. 101-102). The report stressed the problem of access and deplored the notion that property rights may stand as a barrier, saying "In our judgment, 'no trespass' signs represent the last dying remnants of paternalistic behavior" (p. 63).

A man's right in his real property of course is not absolute. It was a maxim of the common law that one should so use his property as not to injure the rights of others. Broom, Legal Maxims (10 ed. Kersley 1939), p. 238; 39 Words and Phrases, "Sic Utere Tuo et Alienum Non Laedas," p. 335. Although hardly a precise solvent of actual controversies, the maxim does express the inevitable proposition that rights are relative and there must be an accommodation when they meet. Hence it has long been true that necessity, private or public, may justify entry upon the lands of another. For a catalogue of such situations, see Prosser, Torts (3d ed. 1964), §24, pp. 127-129; 6A American Law of Property (A. J. Casner ed. 1954) §28.10, p. 31; 52 Am. Jur., "Trespass," §§40-41, pp. 867-869. See also Restatement, Second, Torts (1965) §§197-211; Krauth v. Geller, 31 N.J. 270, 272-273 (1960).

The subject is not static. As pointed out in 5 Powell, Real Property (Rohan 1970) §745, pp. 493-494, while society will protect the owner in his permissible interests in land, yet

> such an owner must expect to find the absoluteness of his property rights curtailed by the organs of society, for the promotion of the best interests of others for whom these organs also operate as protective agencies. The necessity for such curtailments is greater in a modern industrialized and urbanized society than it was in the relatively simple American society of fifty, 100, or 200 years ago. The current balance between individualism and dominance of the social interest depends not only upon political and social ideologies, but also upon the physical and social facts of the time and place under discussion.

Professor Powell added in §746, pp. 494-496:

> As one looks back along the historic road traversed by the law of land in
> England and in America, one sees a change from the viewpoint that he who
> owns may do as he pleases with what he owns, to a position which hesitatingly
> embodies an ingredient of stewardship; which grudgingly, but steadily, broadens
> the recognized scope of social interests in the utilization of things. . . .
> To one seeing history through the glasses of religion, these changes may
> seem to evidence increasing embodiments of the golden rule. To one thinking in
> terms of political and economic ideologies, they are likely to be labeled evidences
> of "social enlightment," or of "creeping socialism" or even of "communistic
> infiltration," according to the individual's assumed definitions and retained or
> acquired prejudices. With slight attention to words or labels, time marches on
> toward new adjustments between individualism and the social interests.

This process involves not only the accommodation between the right of
the owner and the interests of the general public in his use of his property, but
involves also an accommodation between the right of the owner and the right
of individuals who are parties with him in consensual transactions relating to
the use of the property. Accordingly substantial alterations have been made as
between a landlord and his tenant. See Reste Realty Corp. v. Cooper, 53 N.J.
444, 451-453 (1969); Marini v. Ireland, 56 N.J. 130, 141-143 (1970).

The argument in this case understandably included the question
whether the migrant worker should be deemed to be a tenant and thus entitled
to the tenant's right to receive visitors, Williams v. Lubbering, 73 N.J.L. 317,
319-320 (Sup. Ct. 1906), or whether his residence on the employer's property
should be deemed to be merely incidental and in aid of his employment, and
hence to involve no possessory interest in the realty. See Scottish Rite Co. v.
Salkowitz, 119 N.J.L. 558 (E. & A. 1938); New Jersey Midland Ry. Co. v.
Van Syckle, 37 N.J.L. 496, 506 (E. & A. 1874); Gray v. Reynolds, 67 N.J.L.
169 (Sup. Ct. 1901); McQuade v. Emmons, 38 N.J.L. 397 (Sup. Ct. 1876);
Morris Canal & Banking Co. v. Mitchell, 31 N.J.L. 99 (Sup. Ct. 1864); Schu-
man v. Zurawell, 24 N.J. Misc. 180 (Cir. Ct. 1946). These cases did not reach
employment situations at all comparable with the one before us. Nor did they
involve the question whether an employee who is not a tenant may have
visitors notwithstanding the employer's prohibition. Rather they were concerned with whether notice must be given to end the employee's right to
remain upon the premises, with whether the employer may remove the discharged employee without court order, and with the availability of a particular judicial remedy to achieve his removal by process. We of course are not
concerned here with the right of a migrant worker to remain on the employer's
property after the employment is ended.

We see no profit in trying to decide upon a conventional category and
then forcing the present subject into it. That approach would be artificial and
distorting. The quest is for a fair adjustment of the competing needs of the
parties, in the light of the realities of the relationship between the migrant
worker and the operator of the housing facility.

Thus approaching the case, we find it unthinkable that the farmer-employer can assert a right to isolate the migrant worker in any respect significant for the worker's well-being. The farmer, of course, is entitled to pursue his farming activities without interference, and this defendants readily concede. But we see no legitimate need for a right in the farmer to deny the worker the opportunity for aid available from federal, State, or local services, or from recognized charitable groups seeking to assist him. Hence representatives of these agencies and organizations may enter upon the premises to seek out the worker at his living quarters. So, too, the migrant must be allowed to receive visitors there of his own choice, so long as there is no behavior hurtful to others, and members of the press may not be denied reasonable access to workers who do not object to seeing them.

It is not our purpose to open the employer's premises to the general public if in fact the employer himself has not done so. We do not say, for example, that solicitors or peddlers of all kinds may enter on their own; we may assume for the present that the employer may regulate their entry or bar them, at least if the employer's purpose is not to gain a commercial advantage for himself or if the regulation does not deprive the migrant worker of practical access to things he needs.

And we are mindful of the employer's interest in his own and in his employees' security. Hence he may reasonably require a visitor to identify himself, and also to state his general purpose if the migrant worker has not already informed him that the visitor is expected. But the employer may not deny the worker his privacy or interfere with his opportunity to live with dignity and to enjoy associations customary among our citizens. These rights are too fundamental to be denied on the basis of an interest in real property and too fragile to be left to the unequal bargaining strength of the parties. See Henningsen v. Bloomfield Motors, Inc., 32 N.J. 358, 403-404 (1960); Ellsworth Dobbs, Inc. v. Johnson, 50 N.J. 528, 555 (1967).

It follows that defendants here invaded no possessory right of the farmer-employer. Their conduct was therefore beyond the reach of the trespass statute. The judgments are accordingly reversed and the matters remanded to the County Court with directions to enter judgments of acquittal.

For reversal and remandment—CHIEF JUSTICE WEINTRAUB and JUSTICES JACOBS, FRANCIS, PROCTOR, HALL and SCHETTINO—6.

For affirmance—None.

NOTES AND QUESTIONS

1. The excerpt from Blackstone (page 21), which was written in the mid-1700s, treats as an injury or wrong, for which trespass will lie, "every entry upon another's land (unless by the owner's leave, or in some very particular cases)." What "particular cases" might Blackstone have been writing about? Apart from holdings like State v. Shack, would the list of "particular cases" be any longer today?

2. "Property rights serve human values" (State v. Shack, page 21, *supra*). Would you agree that a landowner's right to exclude, protected by criminal trespass statutes and civil trespass remedies, serves "human values"? If so, which human values?

3. Professor Richard Posner has written extensively about law and economics. Consider carefully the following excerpt from his writings, in defense of exclusivity. Is his argument necessary to your understanding of the right to exclude? Is it sufficient? Posner, R., Economic Analysis of Law 10-15 (1973)*:

The Economic Theory of Property Rights

Imagine a society in which all property rights have been abolished. A farmer plants corn, fertilizes it, and erects scarecrows, but when the corn is ripe his neighbor reaps and sells it. [1] The farmer has no legal remedy against his neighbor's conduct since he owns neither the land that he sowed nor the crop. After a few such incidents the cultivation of land will be abandoned and the society will shift to methods of subsistence (such as hunting) that involve less preparatory investment. [2]

This example suggests that the legal protection of property rights has an important economic function: to create incentives to use resources efficiently. Although the value of the crop in our example, as measured by consumer willingness to pay, may have greatly exceeded the cost in labor, materials, and forgone alternative uses of the land, without property rights there is no incentive to incur these costs because there is no reasonably assured reward for incurring them. The proper incentives are created by the parceling out among the members of society of mutually exclusive rights to the use of particular resources. If every piece of land is owned by someone, in the sense that there is always an individual who can exclude all others from access to any given area, then individuals will endeavor by cultivation or other improvements to maximize the value of land.

The creation of exclusive rights is a necessary rather than sufficient condition for the efficient use of resources. The rights must be transferable. Suppose the farmer in our example owns the land that he sows but is a bad farmer; his land would be more productive in someone else's hands. The maximization of value requires a mechanism by which the farmer can be induced to transfer rights in the property to someone who can work it more productively. A transferable property right is such a mechanism.

An example will illustrate. Farmer A owns a piece of land that he anticipates will yield him $100 a year, in excess of labor and other costs, indefinitely. The value of the right to a stream of future earnings can be expressed as a present sum. Just as the price of a share of common stock expresses the present value of the anticipated earnings to which the shareholder will be entitled, so the

* Copyright 1972, 1973 by Richard A. Posner. Reprinted by permission of the author and Little, Brown and Company.
1. The example is somewhat artificial: presumably the "buyer" could simply grab the corn and would be under no obligation to pay for it.
2. Some interesting anthropological evidence relevant to this point may be found in Harold Demsetz, Toward a Theory of Property Rights, 57 Am. Econ. Rev. Papers & Proceedings 347 (1967).

present value of a parcel of land that yields an annual net income of $100 can be calculated and is the minimum price that A will accept in exchange for his property right. Farmer B believes that he can use A's land more productively than A. Stated another way, B thinks he could net more than $100 a year from working A's land. The present value of B's higher expected earnings stream will, of course, exceed the present value calculated by A. Assume the present value calculated by A is $1000 and by B $1500. Then sale of the property right by A to B will yield benefits to both parties if the price is anywhere between $1000 and $1500. At a price of $1250, for example, A receives $250 more than the land is worth to him and B pays $250 less than the land is worth to *him*. Thus, there are strong incentives for the parties voluntarily to exchange A's land for B's money, and if B is as he believes a better farmer than A, the transfer will result in an increase in the productivity of the land. Through a succession of such transfers, resources are shifted to their highest valued, most productive uses and efficiency in the use of economic resources is maximized.

The foregoing discussion suggests three criteria of an efficient system of property rights. The first is *universality*. Ideally, all resources should be owned, or ownable, by someone, except resources so plentiful that everybody can consume as much of them as he wants without reducing consumption by anyone else (sunlight is a good, but not perfect, example—why?). No issue of efficient use arises in such a case.

The second criterion—but one that requires, as we shall see, careful qualification—is *exclusivity*. We have assumed so far that either the farmer can exclude no one or he can exclude everyone, but of course there are intermediate stages: the farmer may be entitled to exclude private individuals from reaping his crop, but not the government in time of war. It might appear that the more exclusive the property right, the greater the incentive to invest the right amount of resources in the development of the property. Suppose our farmer estimates that he can raise a hog with a market value of $100 at a cost of only $50 in labor and materials. Suppose further that there is no alternative combination of resources and land use that would yield a greater excess of value over cost: in the next best use his net income from the land would be only $20. He will raise the hog. But now suppose his property right is less than exclusive in two respects. First, he has no right to prevent an adjacent railroad from accidentally emitting engine sparks that may set fire to the hog's pen, killing it prematurely. Second, he has no right to prevent the local government from rezoning his land from agricultural to residential use and compelling him to sell the hog at disadvantageous terms before it is grown. In light of these contingencies he must reevaluate the yield of his land: he might discount the $100 to reflect the probability that the yield may be much less, perhaps zero. Suppose, after discounting, the expected revenue from raising the hog (market value times the probability that it will reach the market) is only $60. He will not raise the hog. He will shift to the next best use of the land, which we said was less valuable. [3]

The analysis, however, is incomplete. While the farmer will be induced, as a consequence of no longer enjoying an exclusive property right, to shift to an alternative land use that *seems* less efficient, overall efficiency may be increased. The removal of the hog may result in an increase in the value of surrounding

3. The profit from raising the hog is now $10, since his costs are $50. The next best use, we said, yields a profit of $20.

residential land greater than the reduction in the value of the farmer's parcel. The cost of preventing the emission of engine sparks may be larger than the reduction in the value of the farmer's land when he switches from hog raising to, say, growing radishes. To this, the very alert reader may be tempted to reply that if the increase in value to others from a different use of the farmer's land exceeds the decrease to him, they can buy his right: the railroad can purchase an easement to emit sparks; the surrounding homeowners can purchase a covenant from the farmer not to raise hogs. Often, however, the costs of effecting a transfer of rights—transaction costs—are prohibitive; but more on this shortly.

The third criterion of an efficient system of property rights is *transferability*. If a property right cannot be transferred, there is no way of shifting a resource from a less productive to a more productive use through voluntary exchange. The costs of transfer may be high to begin with; a legal prohibition against transferring may, depending on the penalties for violation, make the costs utterly prohibitive. We shall see that when the costs of transferring property rights are high, the attempt to achieve our second criterion, exclusivity, may actually reduce the efficiency of the property rights system.

4. When the New Jersey court decided State v. Shack in 1971, the First Amendment claim, which the court decided finally not to accept because nonconstitutional grounds would serve the migrant workers "more expansively" (page 24 *supra*), could still be seriously advanced because of the two Supreme Court decisions cited in the opinion, Marsh v. Alabama, 326 U.S. 501 (1946) and Amalgamated Food Employees Local 590 v. Logan Valley Plaza, Inc., 391 U.S. 308 (1968). In the *Marsh* case (still good law), the corporate owner of Chickasaw, Alabama—a company town—sought to ban religious pamphleteering on the town's sidewalks. Because Chickasaw had, except for its ownership, "all the characteristics of any other American town," 326 U.S. 501, 502, it was subject to the Fourteenth Amendment and could not deny its residents the constitutional guarantees of free speech and religion. The *Marsh* case was later followed in the *Logan Valley Plaza* case. There the owner of a shopping center sought to prevent a union engaged in organizational activity from handbilling and picketing within the parking area. The Supreme Court upset a state court injunction barring the activity, by analogizing the shopping center to a community business block. Writing in dissent, Justice Black (the author of Marsh v. Alabama) argued:

> The question is, under what circumstances can private property be treated as though it were public? The answer that *Marsh* gives is when that property has taken on all the attributes of a town, i.e., "residential buildings, streets, a system of sewers, a sewage disposal plant and a 'business block' on which business places are situated." 326 U.S., at 502. I can find nothing in *Marsh* which indicates that if one of these features is present, e.g., a business district, this is sufficient for the Court to confiscate a part of an owner's private property and give its use to people who want to picket on it. [391 U.S. at 332]

Beginning in 1972, influenced by the Black dissent, the Court delivered *Logan Valley Plaza* to the precedential scrap heap. In Lloyd Corp., Ltd. v.

Tanner, 407 U.S. 551 (1972), the Court held that First Amendment protection did not extend to persons engaged in antiwar protest in the interior mall area of a shopping center whose owner insisted that the protesters leave. Justice Powell, writing for the Court, stressed that the handbilling was unrelated to any activity within the center and that the protesters had adequate alternative means of carrying their message.

Two later decisions, Hudgens v. NLRB, 424 U.S. 507 (1976) and Pruneyard Shopping Center v. Robins, 447 U.S. 74 (1980) cast away the remaining shreds of the shopping center-company town equivalence.

During the interval between *Logan Valley Plaza* and *Lloyd Corp.*, a United States district court relying upon the earlier case barred the owner of a migrant farm—on First Amendment grounds—from denying reasonable access to agency representatives who were seeking to assist migrant workers. Folgueras v. Hassle, 331 F. Supp. 615 (W.D. Mich. 1971). Cf. also People v. Rewald, 65 Misc. 2d 453, 318 N.Y.S.2d 40 (County Ct. 1971). *Lloyd Corp.* and its progeny notwithstanding, might the supremacy clause still provide a *constitutional* basis for refusing farm owners the power to exclude representatives of federally funded agencies seeking to assist migrant workers? Might it also be shown—to return to Marsh v. Alabama—that a migrant farm has more "company town" attributes than a suburban shopping center? Cf. Illinois Migrant Council v. Campbell Soup Co., 574 F.2d 374 (7th Cir. 1978) (denied plaintiff right of access to privately owned migrant farm).

5. In Pruneyard Shopping Center v. Robins, *supra*, the Supreme Court upheld a California state court decision barring the shopping center from denying reasonable access to individuals seeking signatures from center patrons to a pro-Zionist petition. The California court based its decision on the state's constitutional counterpart to the First Amendment. Quoting an earlier opinion, the court described the state constitutional guarantee as "[a] protective provision more definitive and inclusive than the First Amendment." 23 Cal. 3d 899, 908 (1979). Justice Rehnquist, writing for the Supreme Court on the appeal, agreed that the *Lloyd* and *Hudgens* cases would still allow reasonable entry onto a shopping center in the interests of a state constitutional free-speech guarantee. The shopping center owner in *Pruneyard* argued vainly that its own property and first amendment rights had been violated. How would that argument be stated?

Drawing from the analogy of State v. Shack, might the California court have decided *Pruneyard* on nonconstitutional grounds?

The courts of Washington (divided 5 to 4) and Connecticut have also found state constitutional support for a shopping center entry over the owner's objection. In Alderwood Associates v. Washington Environmental Council, 635 P.2d 108 (Wash. 1981), the court allowed individuals to solicit signatures within the shopping mall for a ballot initiative. Cologne v. Westfarm Associates, 50 U.S.L.W. 2434 (Conn. Super. Ct.) also involved efforts to gather signatures for a political petition.

6. The Supreme Court of New Jersey has again refused to extend its criminal trespass statute in behalf of a private landowner seeking to regulate

entry. State v. Schmid, 84 N.J. 835, 423 A.2d 615 (1980). The landowner was Princeton University. The "trespasser," a nonstudent and member of the United States Labor Party, was arrested while distributing political literature on the university campus. Princeton required off-campus persons to obtain a distribution permit, which Schmid had neither procured nor sought.

Although the New Jersey court refused to find a First Amendment violation (Princeton University was neither a "company town" nor a state instrumentality), the court found that the New Jersey Constitution offered Schmid "an alternative and independent source of individual rights." In weighing defendant's right of political free speech against the University's desire to control outside access to its campus, the court decided that the regulatory scheme, which failed to contain any reasonable standards for granting or denying access, violated defendant's state constitutional rights.

The United States Supreme Court granted a hearing on the issue, "Does a private university have the right to determine without state interference what expressive activities by strangers it will permit on its campus and under what circumstances?" 101 S. Ct. 2312 (1981). After oral argument, the Court dismissed the appeal upon learning that Princeton had rescinded its permit requirement. 50 U.S.L.W. 4159 (1982).

7. In a case of apparent first impression in New York, plaintiffs sued television newsmen in civil trespass for entering their home in the company of a Humane Society investigator. The investigator held a warrant authorizing him to search plaintiffs' home for improperly cared-for animals and the defendant newsmen had come along to film the search. The court rejected the newsmen's defense that the First Amendment created a right of entry. Anderson v. WROC-TV, 109 Misc. 2d 904,—N.Y.S.2d—(Sup. Ct. 1981). Is State v. Shack distinguishable?

8. Suppose that the owner of a migrant camp himself lives in a quiet suburban community. Organizers for a farm workers' union picket on the sidewalk in front of the camp owner's home. They carry signs that read: "X treats his workers like animals." The picketers are arrested under a local ordinance making it unlawful "to picket before or about the residence of any individual." Is the ordinance valid? Cf. Garcia v. Gray, 507 F.2d 539 (10th Cir. 1974).

§1.4   Property and Social Change: The Privilege of Sale

STATEMENT OF CONGRESSMAN FLYNT
112 Cong. Rec. 17,333 (Aug. 3, 1966)

Mr. Flynt (D. Ga.). Mr. Chairman, title IV of H.R. 14765 should be stricken from the pending bill. It has no place in the laws of a democratic, representative government.

This proposal strikes at the very heart of a free enterprise system in which the fee simple ownership of real property is a vital part.

The right of private ownership of property in fee simple has been a privilege and right of the American people. Until this legislation was proposed, we had believed that as long as a property owner paid the taxes on his property, and as long as he did not use it for illegal or immoral purposes, that he could do what he pleased with it, occupy it or leave it unoccupied, and rent it or sell it as he saw fit and to whom he saw fit.

If a member of any group, a majority or a minority group, wants to buy or rent a particular piece of property, he has always had that right, provided the owner would be equally willing to sell it or rent it to him. A contract for the purchase and sale of real property has historically required a meeting of the minds between a willing buyer and a willing seller. The only exceptions to this rule have been when the right of eminent domain has been exercised and when property has been sold under court order.

If the language of title IV of H.R. 14765 is enacted into law, it could set off a chain reaction which could eventually result in legislation, Executive orders, or judicial decrees that a property owner could be required to sell or rent property even though he might prefer to retain it and even to occupy it personally.

The right of private ownership of property is an integral part of a free enterprise system. If the Congress of the United States undertakes to destroy the basic rights and concepts of private ownership of property, then it will, at the same time, begin to wipe out the free enterprise system in this country and on this planet.

Human rights cannot exist without property rights, and a healthy respect for both. Any attempt to destroy or weaken the right of private ownership of property is an attempt to destroy a system of private capital, and to substitute a totalitarian form of government in its place, whether it is called socialism, state socialism, or communism.

The statement above appears in the House Debates on Title IV of the proposed Civil Rights Act of 1966, which would have created a federal fair housing law. Two years later, Congress finally passed a similar statute.

TITLE VIII, CIVIL RIGHTS ACT OF 1968
42 U.S.C. §§3601-3619 (1970)

§3601.　Declaration of Policy

It is the policy of the United States to provide, within constitutional limitations, for fair housing throughout the United States.

§3602. DEFINITIONS

As used in this subchapter—

(a) "Secretary" means the Secretary of Housing and Urban Development.

(b) "Dwelling" means any building, structure, or portion thereof which is occupied as, or designed or intended for occupancy as, a residence by one or more families, and any vacant land which is offered for sale or lease for the construction or location thereon of any such building, structure, or portion thereof.

(c) "Family" includes a single individual.

(d) "Person" includes one or more individuals, corporations, partnerships, associations, labor organizations, legal representatives, mutual companies, joint-stock companies, trusts, unincorporated organizations, trustees, trustees in cases under Title II, receivers, and fiduciaries.

(e) "To rent" includes to lease, to sublease, to let and otherwise to grant for a consideration the right to occupy premises not owned by the occupant.

(f) "Discriminatory housing practice" means an act that is unlawful under section 3604, 3605, or 3606 of this title.

(g) "State" means any of the several States, the District of Columbia, the Commonwealth of Puerto Rico, or any of the territories and possessions of the United States.

§3603. EFFECTIVE DATES OF CERTAIN PROHIBITIONS

. . . (b) Exemptions. Nothing in section 3604 of this title (other than subsection (c)) shall apply to—

(1) any single-family house sold or rented by an owner: *Provided,* That such private individual owner does not own more than three such single-family houses at any one time: *Provided further,* That in the case of the sale of any such single-family house by a private individual owner not residing in such house at the time of such sale or who was not the most recent resident of such house prior to such sale, the exemption granted by this subsection shall apply only with respect to one such sale within any twenty-four month period: *Provided further,* That such bona fide private individual owner does not own any interest in, nor is there owned or reserved on his behalf, under any express or voluntary agreement, title to or any right to all or a portion of the proceeds from the sale or rental of, more than three such single-family houses at any one time: *Provided further,* That after December 31, 1969, the sale or rental of any such single-family house shall be excepted from the application of this title only if such house is sold or rented (A) without the use in any manner of the sales or rental facilities or the sales or rental services of any real estate broker, agent, or salesman, or of such facilities or services of any person in the business of selling or renting dwellings, or of any employee or agent of any such broker,

agent, salesman, or person and (B) without the publication, posting or mailing, after notice, of any advertisement or written notice in violation of section 3604(c) of this title; but nothing in this proviso shall prohibit the use of attorneys, escrow agents, abstractors, title companies, and other such professional assistance as necessary to perfect or transfer the title, or

(2)   rooms or units in dwellings containing living quarters occupied or intended to be occupied by no more than four families living independently of each other, if the owner actually maintains and occupies one of such living quarters as his residence.

(c)   For the purposes of subsection (b), a person shall be deemed to be in the business of selling or renting dwellings if—

(1)   he has, within the preceding twelve months, participated as principal in three or more transactions involving the sale or rental of any dwelling or any interest therein, or

(2)   he has, within the preceding twelve months, participated as agent, other than in the sale of his own personal residence in providing sales or rental facilities or sales or rental services in two or more transactions involving the sale or rental of any dwelling or any interest therein, or

(3)   he is the owner of any dwelling designed or intended for occupancy by, or occupied by, five or more families.

§3604.   Discrimination in the Sale or Rental of Housing

As made applicable by section 3603 and except as exempted by sections 3603(b) and 3607, it shall be unlawful—

(a)   To refuse to sell or rent after the making of a bona fide offer, or to refuse to negotiate for the sale or rental of, or otherwise make unavailable or deny, a dwelling to any person because of race, color, religion, sex,[1] or national origin.

(b)   To discriminate against any person in the terms, conditions, or privileges of sale or rental of a dwelling, or in the provision of services or facilities in connection therewith, because of race, color, religion, sex, or national origin.

(c)   To make, print, or publish, or cause to be made, printed, or published any notice, statement, or advertisement, with respect to the sale or rental of a dwelling that indicates any preference, limitation, or discrimination based on race, color, religion, sex, or national origin, or an intention to make any such preference, limitation, or discrimination.

(d)   To represent to any person because of race, color, religion, sex, or national origin that any dwelling is not available for inspection, sale, or rental when such dwelling is in fact so available.

(e)   For profit, to induce or attempt to induce any person to sell or rent any dwelling by representations regarding the entry or prospective entry into

---

1. Congress, in 1974, added "sex" to the objects of unlawful discrimination. Pub. L. 93-383.—Ed.

the neighborhood of a person or persons of a particular race, color, religion, sex, or national origin.

§3605. DISCRIMINATION IN THE FINANCING OF HOUSING

After December 31, 1968, it shall be unlawful for any bank, building and loan association, insurance company or other corporation, association, firm or enterprise whose business consists in whole or in part in the making of commercial real estate loans, to deny a loan or other financial assistance to a person applying there for the purpose of purchasing, constructing, improving, repairing, or maintaining a dwelling, or to discriminate against him in the fixing of the amount, interest rate, duration, or other terms or conditions of such loan or other financial assistance, because of the race, color, religion, sex, or national origin of such person or of any person associated with him in connection with such loan or other financial assistance or the purposes of such loan or other financial assistance, or of the present or prospective owners, lessees, tenants, or occupants of the dwelling or dwellings in relation to which such loan or other financial assistance is to be made or given: *Provided,* That nothing contained in this section shall impair the scope or effectiveness of the exception contained in section 3603(b).

§3606. DISCRIMINATION IN THE PROVISION OF BROKERAGE SERVICES

After December 31, 1968, it shall be unlawful to deny any person access to or membership or participation in any multiple-listing service, real estate brokers' organization or other service, organization, or facility relating to the business of selling or renting dwellings, or to discriminate against him in the terms or conditions of such access, membership, or participation, on account of race, color, religion, sex, or national origin.

§3607. EXEMPTION

Nothing in this title shall prohibit a religious organization, association, or society, or any nonprofit institution or organization operated, supervised or controlled by or in conjunction with a religious organization, association, or society, from limiting the sale, rental or occupancy of dwellings which it owns or operates for other than a commercial purpose to persons of the same religion, or from giving preference to such persons, unless membership in such religion is restricted on account of race, color, or national origin. Nor shall anything in this title prohibit a private club not in fact open to the public, which as an incident to its primary purpose or purposes provides lodgings which it owns or operates for other than a commercial purpose, from limiting the rental or occupancy of such lodgings to its members or from giving preference to its members. . . .

The remaining provisions of Title VIII, 42 U.S.C. §§3608-3617 (1970), contain the enforcement procedures. Section 3608 lodges administration in the Secretary of HUD (Housing and Urban Development). Aggrieved persons may file a complaint with HUD. The Secretary has 30 days to try conciliation. If that fails, the complainant may then file a civil action in federal court. (But until the trial takes place, conciliation efforts may continue.) Where applicable state or local fair housing laws exist, however, and these laws give substantially similar rights and remedies, the Secretary must refer the administrative complaint to the nonfederal agency (§3610). In the civil action, the federal court may grant injunctions, actual damages, not more than $1000 punitive damages, court costs, and reasonable attorney fees to the prevailing plaintiff (§3612). Section 3613 authorizes the U.S. Attorney General to initiate civil suits to press issues of "general public importance" or to challenge patterns or practices of resistance by any person to the rights granted by Title VIII.

Congress, more than one century before the passage of Title VIII, enacted the Civil Rights Act of 1866. Section 1 of the Act, now 42 U.S.C.A. §1982, provides:

> *Be it enacted by the Senate and House of Representatives of the United States of America in Congress assembled,* That all persons born in the United States and not subject to any foreign power, . . . are hereby declared to be citizens of the United States; and such citizens, of every race and color, without regard to any previous condition of slavery or involuntary servitude . . . shall have the same right, in every State and Territory in the United States, to make and enforce contracts, to sue, be parties, and give evidence, to inherit, purchase, lease, sell, hold, and convey real and personal property, and to full and equal benefit of all laws and proceedings for the security of person and property, as is enjoyed by white citizens, and shall be subject to like punishment, pains, and penalties, and to none other, any law, statute, ordinance, regulation, or custom, to the contrary notwithstanding.

In 1968, shortly after Title VIII became law, the Supreme Court considered the scope of §1982 in Jones v. Alfred H. Mayer Co., 392 U.S. 409 (1968). Defendant builder had refused to sell plaintiffs a newly constructed subdivision home for the sole reason, according to the complaint, that one of the plaintiffs was a Negro. Plaintiffs sought injunctive and other relief under section 1982. In a landmark judgment, the Court held that the section bars *all* racial discrimination, private as well as public, in the sale or rental of property, and that the statute, so construed, was a valid exercise of the congres-sional power to enforce the Thirteenth Amendment.

Justice Stewart, writing for the Court, contrasted the two "fair housing" statutes:

> At the outset, it is important to make clear precisely what this case does *not* involve. Whatever else it may be, 42 U.S.C.A. §1982 is not a comprehensive open housing law. In sharp contrast to the Fair Housing Title (Title VIII) of the Civil Rights Act of 1968, Pub. L. 90-284, 82 Stat. 73, the statute in this case deals only with racial discrimination and does not address itself to discrimination on grounds of religion or national origin. It does not deal specifically with dis-crimination in the provision of services or facilities in connection with the sale or rental of a dwelling. It does not prohibit advertising or other representations that indicate discriminatory preferences. It does not refer explicitly to discrimination in financing arrangements or in the provisions of brokerage services. It does not empower a federal administrative agency to assist aggrieved parties. It makes no provision for intervention by the Attorney General. And, although it can be enforced by injunction it contains no provision expressly authorizing a federal court to order the payment of damages. [392 U.S. at 413-414.]

Real estate professionals, bent on bias, yield to no one in their ingenuity. These schemes are among those that courts have struck down under Title VIII:

(a) Using a credit check as a ruse, rental agents routinely denied apart-ments to black applicants. United States v. Reddock, 467 F.2d 897 (5th Cir. 1972).

(b) Subdivider refused to sell lots to black buyers unless they dealt with an "approved" builder. Williams v. Matthews Co., 499 F.2d 819 (8th Cir. 1974).

(c) Landlord refused to rent apartments to single women without cars, contending that women faced too great a risk of assault walking to and from apartments. United States v. Reece, 457 F. Supp. 43 (D. Mont. 1978). The same landlord would not consider alimony and child support payments in determining whether divorced women met income requirements.

(d) Real estate salesman told black couple that they would not be happy living in the house or in the part of subdivision in which they were interested and suggested to the couple that they contact a bro-kerage firm owned by blacks and specializing in the sale of homes to black purchasers. Bradley v. John M. Brabham Agency, Inc., 463 F. Supp. 27 (D.S.C. 1978).

(e) Building and loan association "red-lined" neighborhoods in which minority group families were concentrated and refused to make loans in those areas. Laufman v. Oakley Bldg. & Loan Co., 408 F. Supp. 489 (D. Ohio 1976).

A recurring issue when plaintiffs claim a practice or pattern of discrimination is whether Title VIII or §1982 requires proof of discriminatory motive or intent. In the case which follows, plaintiffs could show only that the landlord's rental practices had a disproportionate impact upon black and Hispanic tenant applicants.

BOYD v. THE LEFRAK ORGANIZATION
509 F.2d 1110 (2d Cir. 1975)

HAYS, CIRCUIT JUDGE. Plaintiffs commenced this action seeking injunctive and declaratory relief on the ground that the use by The Lefrak Organization ("Lefrak") and Life Realty, Inc. ("rental office") of certain financial criteria to determine eligibility for tenancy in their apartments violated the Civil Rights Act of 1968, 42 U.S.C. §3601 et seq. (1970) ("Fair Housing Act") and the Civil Rights Act of 1866, 42 U.S.C. §1982 (1970) ("Civil Rights Act"). The named plaintiffs, black recipients of public assistance in New York City, whose applications to rent apartments were rejected by defendants, sue on behalf of "all public assistance recipients within the New York Metropolitan Area who have sought or may seek to rent accommodations in the residential buildings owned or operated by the Lefrak interests." Defendants are operators of 119 buildings within the City of New York, containing 15,484 apartments, with rental ranges running from $140 to $400 per month. The financial standard challenged herein is the requirement, applied by defendants in the rental of all their apartments, that an applicant, or applicant and spouse, have a weekly net income[1] equal to at least 90% of the monthly rental of the apartment applied for ("the 90% rule") or, alternatively, obtain a co-signer of the lease whose weekly net income is equal to 110% of a month's rent ("co-signer requirement").[2] The rental office and Lefrak appeal from a judgment entered in the United States District Court for the Eastern District of New York, after a trial before the Honorable Tom C. Clark, Associate Justice of the United States Supreme Court, retired (sitting by designation), without a jury. The court below declared the financial criteria used by the rental office and Lefrak to be in violation of the Fair Housing Act and the Civil Rights Act of 1866, and enjoined defendants from applying the 90% rule and co-signer requirement to plaintiffs and members of the class they represent. We reverse. . . .

The Fair Housing Act prohibits discrimination in housing because of "race, color, religion, or national origin." 42 U.S.C. §3604 (1970). Plaintiffs argue that defendants by utilizing the 90% rule have violated this prohibition.

---

1. To arrive at net income all taxes, fixed obligations and debts are deducted from gross income.
2. The income of the co-signer's spouse is not taken into account, and in determining net income, the co-signer's own rent is treated as a fixed obligation and deducted.

They reason that the 90% rule excludes all public assistance recipients except for the very small number who can obtain an acceptable co-signer, that a large majority of public assistance recipients in New York City are black or Puerto Rican, and that therefore the use of the 90% rule is racially discriminatory. The premise of plaintiffs' argument is that "[w]elfare recipiency . . . must be seen as the 'functional equivalent' of race." Appellee's brief at 36. Such an equivalency between race and income has been rejected by the Supreme Court in James v. Valtierra, 402 U.S. 137, 91 S. Ct. 1331, 28 L. Ed. 2d 678 (1971). Plaintiffs in that case, relying on a line of reasoning similar to that advanced by plaintiffs here, challenged an article of the California state constitution which provided that no low-rent housing projects should be developed, constructed or acquired by a state public body until the project was approved by the majority of those voting at a community election. Despite implicit recognition of the correlation between racial minority and low income, the Court refused to equate the two factors. The Court, in upholding the validity of the provision, said: "The Article requires referendum approval for any low-rent public housing project, not only for projects which will be occupied by a racial minority." Id. at 141, 91 S. Ct. at 1333.

As in *Valtierra,* supra, the rule under consideration here cannot be said to rest on distinctions based on race. See 402 U.S. at 141, 91 S. Ct. 1331. While blacks and Puerto Ricans do not have the same access to Lefrak apartments as do whites, the reason for this inequality is not racial discrimination but rather the disparity in economic level among these groups. . . . A businessman's differential treatment of different economic groups is not necessarily racial discrimination and is not made so because minorities are statistically overrepresented in the poorer economic groups. The fact that differentiation in eligibility rates for defendants' apartments is correlated with race proves merely that minorities tend to be poorer than is the general population. In order to utilize this correlation to establish a violation of the Fair Housing Act on the part of a private landlord, plaintiffs would have to show that there existed some demonstrable prejudicial treatment of minorities over and above that which is the inevitable result of disparity in income. Cf. James v. Valtierra, *supra.* Just as this court will not impose even on the government an affirmative duty to construct low-income housing when the decision not to build is not racially motivated, Citizens Committee for Faraday Wood v. Lindsay, 507 F.2d 1065, 1071 (2d Cir. 1974); Acevedo v. Nassau County, 500 F.2d 1078, 1080-1081 (2d Cir. 1974), so we will not impose an affirmative duty on the private landlord to accept low income tenants absent evidence that his motivation is racial rather than economic in origin.

The conclusion that defendants' seemingly neutral rule is in fact aimed at excluding a racial minority finds no support in the record. The percentage of blacks in appellants' apartments (about 19.8%) closely approximates the percentage of blacks in the population of New York City (21%). There is no claim that black public assistance recipients are treated differently from white public assistance recipients. Nor is there any evidence that public assistance recipients have been excluded from Lefrak apartments for any reason other than inability to meet the financial standard. On the other hand, the evidence indicates that when the financial standard could be met as, for example, by obtaining an acceptable co-signer, public assistance recipients, including those belonging to minority ethnic groups, were rented apartments on the same terms as were any other qualifying applicants. To use ethnic distribution of tenants excluded from appellants' apartments as a basis for inferring discriminatory practices in this situation is like imputing discriminatory motives to producers of high priced goods because such goods more often find their way into the hands of wealthier white consumers than into the hands of the poor. As this court has said in the context of the equal protection clause, "[t]he mere fact that a requirement, otherwise proper, may have a greater impact on the poor, does not render it invalid. . . ." English v. Town of Huntington, 448 F.2d 319, 324 (2d Cir. 1971).

A landlord in the private sector [6] is entitled to choose whom he will accept as tenants as long as he does not discriminate on one of the statutorily condemned bases. Certainly he may seek assurance that prospective tenants will be able to meet their rental responsibilities. "[T]here is no requirement that welfare recipients, or any other individuals, may secure apartments . . . without regard to their ability to pay." Male v. Crossroads Associates, 469 F.2d 616, 622 (2d Cir. 1972).

Plaintiffs claim that the 90% rule, and indeed any economic standard computed on a percentage-of-income basis, is an inappropriate measure of a public assistance recipient's rent-paying ability because, unlike the working person the amount which a recipient receives for his non-shelter needs remains the same regardless of the amount of his shelter allowance [7] and because increased shelter allowances can be obtained by recipients if approved by the New York City Department of Social Services. While it may be true that a public assistance recipient's ability to pay rent is related to the Department of Social Services' willingness to approve shelter allowances, the private landlord in choosing his tenants is free to use any grounds he likes so long as no discriminatory purpose is shown. See Madison v. Jeffers, 494 F.2d 114, 116-117 (4th Cir. 174); Pughsley v. 3750 Lake Shore Drive Cooperative Building, 463 F.2d 1055, 1056 (7th Cir. 1972). His choice is not limited by any obligation to accommodate a special class of low income applicants.

Plaintiffs' reliance on Griggs v. Duke Power Co., 401 U.S. 424, 91 S. Ct. 849, 28 L. Ed. 2d 158 (1971) and other cases interpreting the Fair Employment Act, 42 U.S.C. §2000e et seq. (1970) is misplaced. The "business neces-

---

6. There is concededly no state action in this case.

7. Public assistance recipients receive a grant issued semi-monthly to meet shelter and other needs. New York Social Services Law §131-a (McKinney's Consol. Laws, c. 55, 1974). The amount they receive for food, clothing, and other non-shelter needs is fixed by statute and is based on a statewide "standard of need". Id. Shelter needs (rent) of the recipient household are met on an "as paid" basis, i.e., whatever the household actually pays for shelter, and there are no upper limits on this portion of their grant. A recipient obtains a shelter allowance by first locating an apartment to rent, and then requesting approval of the rental from the New York City Department of Social Services; however, approval is not given until a landlord has agreed to rent a particular apartment to the recipient.

sity" test developed in that context, whereby employers must demonstrate the business necessity of employment tests which have an unequal impact on minority job applicants, has never been applied in any Fair Housing Act case, either public or private, and we find it to be inapposite here. Cf. Jefferson v. Hackney, 406 U.S. 535, 549 n. 19, 92 S. Ct. 1724, 32 L. Ed. 2d 285 (1972). . . .

Similarly because there has been no finding of racially-motivated discrimination, appellants have not violated the Civil Rights Act of 1866, 42 U.S.C. §1982 (1970). See Jones v. Alfred H. Mayer Co., 392 U.S. 409, 421, 88 S. Ct. 2186, 20 L. Ed. 2d 1189 (1968); Madison v. Jeffers, 494 F.2d 114, 116-117 (4th Cir. 1974); Pughsley v. 3750 Lake Shore Drive Cooperative Building, 463 F.2d 1055, 1056 (7th Cir. 1972).

Accordingly, the judgment of the district court is reversed.

MANSFIELD, CIRCUIT JUDGE (dissenting). With due respect, the majority opinion seems to me to be grounded upon the erroneous concept that, in order to establish a violation of the Fair Housing Act, 42 U.S.C. §3601 et seq., direct evidence of a racially discriminatory motive or purpose on the part of the alleged violator must be adduced. In my view such proof is not required.

This case should be governed by the principle, firmly established by the Supreme Court in its interpretation and enforcement of analogous civil rights legislation, to the effect that, where a facially neutral practice has a serious and substantial *de facto* discriminatory impact, it prima facie violates a statutory prohibition against racial discrimination unless the alleged violator can show that the practice is necessary for non-racial reasons. Griggs v. Duke Power Co., 401 U.S. 424, 91 S. Ct. 849, 28 L. Ed. 2d 158 (1971). In *Griggs* the question was whether an employer's use of employee-testing procedures which had the effect of excluding a disproportionate number of Negroes from employment violated the Civil Rights Act of 1964, 42 U.S.C. §2000e et seq. (Title VII) in the absence of proof of a discriminatory intent on the part of the employer. In holding that the proof was sufficient to establish such a violation, Chief Justice Burger, speaking for a unanimous court, stated: "The Act proscribes not only overt discrimination but also practices that are fair in form, but discriminatory in operation. The touchstone is business necessity. If an employment practice which operates to exclude Negroes cannot be shown to be related to job performance, the practice is prohibited. . . .

Congress, in passing the Fair Housing Act, sought to eliminate artificial and arbitrary barriers to housing that operate to discriminate against persons because of their race, just as it had through Title VII acted to remove similar racially discriminatory barriers to employment. It must be recognized that if these laws were to depend for their effectiveness upon proof of the landlord's subjective intent, which is rarely obtainable, they would largely be rendered useless. Racial discrimination cannot, of course, be condoned because it is accomplished through a sophisticated or indirect method, cf. Lane v. Wilson, 307 U.S. 268, 275, 59 S. Ct. 872, 83 L. Ed. 1281 (1939). Nor should it be excused on the theory that it is the product of thoughtlessness rather than willfulness. In either event, the harmful effect is the same. Enforcement of the anti-discrimination provisions of the Fair Housing Act must therefore be judged by objective standards, in line with the principle that the Act be given a "generous construction," Trafficante v. Metropolitan Life Insurance Co., 409 U.S. 205, 212, 93 S. Ct. 364, 34 L. Ed. 2d 415 (1972). In recognition of the old adage that actions speak louder than words, to make out a prima facie violation of the Act it should be sufficient to show that the challenged practice excludes a disproportionately high percentage of minority persons as compared with non-minority. The burden of going forward with a non-racial justification should then shift to the person using the practice.

Plaintiffs in this case have not suggested that "welfare recipients, or any other individuals, may secure apartments . . . without regard to their ability to pay," Male v. Crossroads Associates, 469 F.2d 616, 622 (2d Cir. 1972). Nor does anyone question the importance to a landlord of a prospective tenant's payment of rent, upon which the landlord depends for the successful operation of his real estate enterprise. Toward that end the landlord, of course, may adopt reasonably appropriate economic standards or tests designed to assure the tenant's future ability to pay rent on an on-going basis. See, e.g., United States v. Grooms, 348 F. Supp. 1130, 1134 (M.D. Fla. 1972). But where the formula has the effect of excluding a disproportionately high percentage of a minority group, the landlord should in fairness be prepared to demonstrate the business necessity of his facially neutral rule. "It is no answer that defendants would have exploited whites as well as blacks," Clark v. Universal Builders, 501 F.2d 324, 331 (7th Cir. 1974).

The Supreme Court's decision in James v. Valtierra, 402 U.S. 137, 91 S. Ct. 1331, 28 L. Ed. 2d 678 (1971), so heavily relied upon by the majority, is inapposite. That case did not deal with the interpretation of a federal civil rights statute, which is the issue before us, but with the constitutionality of a state law under attack as violative of the Equal Protection Clause, an entirely different issue requiring application of totally different principles.[1] In deciding that a state's constitutional provisions for community referenda with respect to proposed housing projects did not violate the Equal Protection Clause, the Court was not concerned with statutory interpretation but with the constitutionality of a presumptively valid statute. It concluded that the community's interest in determining the level of local governmental expenditure justified the state constitutional amendment under attack, even though some persons might be disadvantaged by the mandatory referendum procedure. Here we are dealing with the entirely different question of determining the scope and meaning of a statute which expressly prohibits discrimination in housing because of "race, color, religion, or national origin." In my view, in order to give effect to Congress' objective, this legislation must be interpreted as prohibiting conduct which, according to objective standards, has the effect of discriminat-

---

1. Citizens Committee for Faraday Wood v. Lindsay, 507 F.2d 1065 (2d Cir. 1974), and Acevedo v. Nassau County, 500 F.2d 1078, 1080 (2d Cir. 1974), also relied on by the majority, likewise deal with constitutional claims, not enforcement of a civil rights law. . . .

ing because of race, unless a non-racial justification is shown. See United States v. Grooms, 348 F. Supp. 1130 (M.D. Fla. 1972). Otherwise the law would become for the most part a dead letter, in view of the difficulty of proving discriminatory intent upon the part of the person alleged to have violated it.

Applying these principles here, plaintiffs made out a clear prima facie showing that the 90% Rule has had a disproportionately high racial impact. The evidence is undisputed that the effect of the 90% Rule is to exclude from appellant's apartments all but a handful of welfare recipients who apply. Indeed there was direct evidence that the rental agent for Lefrak apartments, Anthony Cuccia, told plaintiff Boyd, "We don't rent to welfare recipients." Jerry Richter, Vice-President of Lefrak, further advised plaintiff's attorney that Lefrak had a policy of not renting to public assistance recipients.

To exclude public assistance recipients in New York City is the equivalent of excluding minority persons. According to the 1970 census 77% of all welfare recipients in New York City were minority persons, the great majority of whom were Black and Puerto Rican. Since that time the figure has increased. A 1971 study, for instance, reveals that 90.1% of those receiving assistance under the program for Aid to Dependent Children are minority persons. A review of all categories of public assistance, see Goodwin v. Wyman, 330 F. Supp. 1038 (S.D.N.Y. 1971), aff'd per curiam, 406 U.S. 964, 92 S. Ct. 2420, 32 L. Ed. 2d 664 (1972), indicates that minorities predominate substantially.

Although minority persons would, under the 90% Rule, continue to be eligible to rent appellants' apartments, they constitute but a small number of those, minority and non-minority, who are eligible. There was expert testimony to the effect that 92.5% of Black and Puerto Rican households would be excluded. Such testimony indicated that under the 90% Rule eligibility of white households in New York City would be four times as great as that of Black households and ten times as great as that of Puerto Rican households.[3] Furthermore, accepting the fact that appellants have rented apartments to a substantial number of wealthier minority persons, not on welfare, who can satisfy the 90% Rule,[4] the percentage of minority households in appellants' apartments would be much higher under a less stringent rule. To compound the disproportionately high racial impact of the 90% Rule, the evidence before the trial judge further disclosed that of the public assistance recipients who applied to appellants for apartments the percentage of non-minority appellants who were accepted was approximately twice the percentage of Black

3. These statistics as well as the impact of the 90% Rule must also be considered in light of an earlier history of alleged racial discrimination that led to the institution by the government in August 1960 of its suit against appellants under the Fair Housing Act, alleging a pattern and practice of discrimination, which was settled by entry of a consent decree in January 1971.
4. The majority's statement that 19.8% of appellants' apartments are rented to Blacks is open to question. It assumes that once an apartment was rented to a Black family the occupancy did not thereafter change to a white family. The figure was also based only on appellants' Brooklyn buildings.

applicants accepted. The 90% Rule, therefore, operates as "built-in head-winds" for minority groups.

Faced with the discriminatory consequences of their conduct appellants failed to offer any satisfactory non-racial explanation, such as business necessity. There was no showing, for instance, that experience in the rental of apartments of the type here under consideration had demonstrated that the 90% Rule was reasonably necessary to insure tenants' payment of rent and that there had been losses, substantial defaults, or failure to collect back rental payments under less stringent rules. Nor was there proof that welfare recipients as tenants have a greater incidence of rent failures or defaults than other tenants. Plaintiffs, in contrast, offered persuasive evidence that the 90% Rule was not adopted as a "business necessity" measure. Fifty-six percent of all New York City households renting apartments in the Lefrak rental range here under consideration do not meet the 90% Rule, i.e., the household's weekly net income is not equal to at least 90% of the monthly rental of its apartment. Indeed, in New York City 47.4% of the white renters and 57.6% of the Black and Puerto Rican renters exceed that ratio. The trial judge further found that 53.1% of the white households renting apartments in the Lefrak rental range, 70.4% of the Black households, and 74.8% of the Puerto Rican households, do not satisfy the 90% Rule. Still there is no showing that landlords renting to these tenants have suffered losses or been faced with bankruptcy. Furthermore, the 90% Rule fails to take into consideration the fact that the amount allocated by the Department of Social Services ("DSS") to a welfare recipient for payment of his rent is not fixed at a specific figure but is equal to the recipient's actual rent when approved by DSS, and, in the event he defaults in the payment of his rent, the rent is thereafter paid by a "two party" DSS check (i.e., payable jointly to the recipient and landlord), which does not affect the level and amount of subsistence separately paid to the recipient. Indeed DSS may even pay the rent directly to the landlord, N.Y. Social Services Law §131-a(7). The welfare recipient's ability to pay, therefore, is not properly measurable by his or her aggregate income. Furthermore, the recipient's income includes non-cash benefits (e.g., food stamps, Medicaid)[5] not available to the non-welfare tenant. Id., §131-a. The ability of welfare recipients to pay Lefrak rents is also attested to by the existence, unknown to Lefrak, of some 461 welfare-recipient households in its apartments in 1972 and the fact that, out of 15,484 Lefrak apartments, only 108 dispossess notices were issued in 1972 and 43 in 1973.

Thus, according to the trial judge's findings of fact, which are fully supported and are not asserted by the majority to be clearly erroneous, the 90% Rule has a disproportionately high racially discriminatory impact and appellants have failed to show that the Rule is based on business necessity or other nonracial grounds. Application of the principles prescribed by the Su-

5. See N.Y. Social Services Law §363 et seq.; Title 18 N.Y.C.R.R. Part 435.

preme Court in *Griggs* therefore mandates affirmance of the district court's decision.

NOTES AND QUESTIONS

1. You should reread §1982 and the excerpts from Title VIII. Contrast the scope of §1982 with that of Title VIII. What forms of housing discrimination are reached by both? By neither? By Title VIII alone? By §1982 alone? If X, a black or Hispanic client, consults you after being thwarted by a home-builder whom X charges with racial discrimination, what do you consider in weighing whether to proceed either under §1982 or Title VIII? Are the two procedures mutually exclusive?

Should you also investigate your state and local fair housing procedures? What should you know about them?

2. Title VIII expressly provides for an award of actual or compensatory damages. In the usual case, where the defendant has illegally refused to sell a house or rent an apartment, how would the court measure the plaintiff's economic injury? Courts have also treated humiliation, emotional distress, and mental anguish as compensable items. Seaton v. Sky Realty Co., Inc., 491 F.2d 634 (7th Cir. 1974); Bishop v. Pecsok, 431 F. Supp. 34 (D.C. Ohio 1976).

3. Although few persons had believed prior to the decision in Jones v. Alfred H. Mayer Co. that §1982 could reach purely private discrimination, §1982 has become a sometimes useful legal companion to Title VIII. Although §1982 contains no damage provision, federal courts, by analogy to the "state action" civil rights measure, 42 U.S.C.A. §1983, have allowed successful §1982 plaintiffs to recover both compensatory and punitive damages. Moreover, §1982 defendants have failed to place the $1,000 Title VIII cap upon punitive damages awards. See generally Friedman, Damages in Housing Bias Litigation, 21 N.Y.L. Forum 551 (1976); Parker v. Shonfeld, 409 F. Supp. 876 (D.C. Cal. 1976) ($10,000 exemplary damages award under §1982 "neither unreasonable nor excessive"). The National Law Journal, August 10, 1981, reported one award of $288,691, which included $200,000 in punitive damages. Id. at 3, col. 1.

4. Compare Boyd v. The Lefrak Organization with Metropolitan Housing Development Corp. v. Village of Arlington Heights, 558 F.2d 1283 (7th Cir. 1977), *cert. denied,* 434 U.S. 1025 (1978). Plaintiffs sued to compel the village defendant to rezone the plaintiffs' property to permit the construction of 190 federally subsidized housing units for lower income families. The Village Board of Trustees had earlier refused to rezone, basing its refusal upon a desire to protect property values and to preserve the zoning plan integrity. When Arlington Heights made that decision, only 27 (!) of the Village's 64,000 residents, compared to 18 percent of the residents in the entire Chicago metropolitan area, were black. If the project were built, as many as 40 percent of the area families eligible for the subsidized units would have been black.

Plaintiffs, who included the prospective nonprofit developer and a black worker (who was employed locally and eligible for a unit in the project) based their suit upon the Equal Protection Clause and the two federal "fair housing" statutes. The trial court dismissed the suit after finding that the Village's refusal to rezone was motivated by factors unrelated to racial discrimination. 373 F. Supp. 208 (N.D. Ill. 1974). The court of appeals reversed, however, on the ground that the zoning decision had a discriminatory impact; in that context, the Village's refusal could not be upheld absent a compelling interest in support of the decision. Since the Village had failed to supply a compelling justification, its action violated the Equal Protection Clause. 517 F.2d 409 (7th Cir. 1974).

The Supreme Court reversed, holding that a showing of discriminatory intent would be required to establish an Equal Protection violation. The Court then remanded the case for a determination of whether the Village's conduct, in the absence of discriminatory intent, violated Title VIII. 429 U.S. 252 (1977).

Upon remand, the Seventh Circuit decided that a Title VIII violation could take place, *under some circumstances,* by a showing of discriminatory effect without a showing of discriminatory intent. The court refused, however, to rule that every action that produces discriminatory effects causes Title VIII illegality.

In applying this malleable rule to the case at bar, the Seventh Circuit examined four "critical" factors:

(a) how strong the plaintiff's showing of discriminatory effect is;
(b) whether there is some evidence of discriminatory intent, though less than needed to show a constitutional violation;
(c) what the defendant's interest is in taking the action complained of;
(d) the nature of the relief plaintiff seeks: in this case, plaintiff was seeking to build interracial housing itself rather than trying to compel defendant to do so. In discussing this factor, the court wrote that "to require a defendant to appropriate money, utilize his land for a particular purpose, or take other affirmative steps toward integrated housing is a massive judicial intrusion on private authority." [558 F.2d 1283, 1293]

This examination led the Seventh Circuit to return the suit to the district court to determine whether any parcel existed in Arlington Heights that was both already properly zoned and suitable for subsidized low-cost housing. The Village would have the burden of identifying such a site and, should the Village falter, plaintiffs would be entitled to the relief sought.

The plaintiffs and defendant then compromised their dispute. A suitable parcel was located, lying just beyond the Village boundaries. The Village agreed to annex the parcel and to permit the development to proceed on that site. The plaintiffs in turn agreed to undertake the project and (to the extent federal law permitted) to give residents of Arlington Heights (99.6 percent white) priority in occupying the units. Over the objections of nearby landowners, the district court approved the settlement. 469 F. Supp. 836 (N.D. Ill. 1979), *aff'd,* 616 F.2d 1006 (7th Cir. 1980).

As the tenants' attorney in Boyd v. The Lefrak Organization, how would you reason from the *Arlington Heights* decision, assuming it were already the law? As the landlord's attorney?

5. Re-examine Title VIII. What is the statutory language applying to local governmental acts, including zoning decisions, which would bar a racially discriminatory impact upon housing availability?

One of the First Title VIII suits against a municipality involved the city of Black Jack, Missouri. St. Louis County adopted a master plan in 1965 for a 1,700-acre unincorporated area. In 1969, a nonprofit sponsor acquired an 11.9-acre parcel (zoned for apartments) within this area on which to build a subsidized housing project for low- and moderate-income ghetto residents. Area residents protested and in 1970 incorporated the entire 1,700 acres as the City of Black Jack. The city at once adopted its own zoning ordinance barring any new multiple-family dwellings including the project that had triggered the controversy. Black Jack was then virtually all white.

Pursuant to his powers under §3613, the U.S. Attorney General sued to invalidate the ordinance, alleging that it precluded the building of integrated townhouse apartments and, accordingly, had a racially discriminatory effect. The trial court denied relief. 372 F. Supp. 319 (E.D. Mo. 1974). The appellate court reversed and directed a permanent injunction against enforcement of the ordinance. United States v. City of Black Jack, Missouri, 508 F.2d 1179 (8th Cir. 1974), *cert. denied,* 422 U.S. 1042 (1975).

In finding a racially discriminatory effect, the court stressed that the ordinance would prevent 85 percent of the blacks living in the St. Louis metropolitan area from obtaining housing in Black Jack. The court also referred to the overall pattern of housing segregation within the St. Louis area as having the "racial shape of a donut, with the negroes in the hole and with mostly whites occupying the ring." 508 F.2d 1179.

The project sponsors, the Inter-Religious Center for Urban Affairs (ICUA), and eight prospective project residents had brought a companion case, also seeking to invalidate the ordinance. After the 1974 Eighth Circuit decision, the sponsor agreed to accept from Black Jack a $450,000 payment (original cost: $238,000) for the building site, which scuttled the project.[2] The consent decree, which approved this settlement, gave leave to the individual plaintiffs to seek further *equitable* relief, and they moved for a decree directing the city "to undertake measures whereby it can reasonably be expected that, within a reasonable time, [multiracial, moderate-income housing units roughly comparable to those originally planned] will be available in the City of Black Jack." The district court denied plaintiffs any form of relief. 454 F.

2. Between 1970 and 1976, construction costs escalated from $1,381,000 to more than three million dollars. This also weakened the sponsor's resolve to continue the project.

Supp. 1223 (E.D. Mo. 1978). Once again, the appeals court reversed and remanded for further proceedings, 605 F.2d 1033 (8th Cir. 1979).

> The class has shown it suffers a significant deprivation because of the absence of low-cost housing in Black Jack, which is the effect of defendants' discriminatory conduct. Thus the need for further relief has been established. [605 F.2d 1033, 1039]

Plaintiffs suggested several methods by which the city might accomplish the stated goals without expending its own funds. Ibid.

6.   Possibly the most dramatic instance in which the attorney general has invoked Title VIII is the suit against Parma, Ohio. The defendant, Cleveland's largest suburb, had a 1970 population exceeding 100,000 people, of whom only fifty were black. Despite the city's explanation for its segregated condition—economic factors and associational preference, the district court found a series of actions, motivated by racially discriminatory intent, to be violative of Title VIII. These actions included:

(a) rejection of a fair housing resolution;
(b) refusal to sign a cooperation agreement with the county housing authority to build public housing;
(c) denial of a building permit for a specific low- and moderate-income project;
(d) passage of a thirty-five-foot height-restriction ordinance;
(e) passage of an ordinance requiring voter approval for low-income housing;
(f) refusal to submit an adequate housing assistance plan in a community block development grant application.

United States v. City of Parma, 494 F. Supp. 1049, (N.D. Ohio 1980).

The Sixth Circuit affirmed the lower court ruling as to discrimination, 661 F.2d 562 (6th Cir. 1981). Moreover, it upheld that part of the remedial plan that included:

(a) establishment of a mandatory fair-housing educational program for all city officials and employees;
(b) enactment of a resolution welcoming all persons, regardless of race, to reside in Parma;
(c) undertaking a comprehensive campaign of newspaper advertising to promote Parma as an equal housing-opportunity community;
(d) action to allow the construction of public housing and the certification of low-income families for §8 subsidies;
(e) a permanent injunction barring the city and its officers from engaging in socially discriminatory conduct.

Any comment?

7. The Equal Protection Clause of the Fourteenth Amendment, on which basis plaintiffs in the *Arlington Heights* case argued unsuccessfully, has had one notable application in dealing with *private* housing discrimination. The landmark decision Shelley v. Kraemer, 334 U.S. 1 (1947), barred state courts from injunctively enforcing privately created racially restrictive covenants, and several years later Barrows v. Jackson, 346 U.S. 249 (1953), denied courts the alternative power to award damages for a covenant violation. While refusing to outlaw such convenants if parties voluntarily obeyed them, the Court held that judicial enforcement would be an exercise of state power in support of racial discrimination and thus prohibited by the Equal Protection Clause. This "state action" theory has been much criticized even by scholars sympathetic with the two decisions. See, e.g., Henkin, Shelley v. Kraemer: Notes for a Revised Opinion, 110 U. Pa. L. Rev. 473 (1962).

The passage of Title VIII and the expanded scope of §1982 have made racially restrictive covenants malum per se.

8. Notwithstanding the two federal statutes and a spate of state and local fair housing laws, racially segregated housing remains firmly embedded throughout the country. A 1978 study by the Urban Institute concluded:

> The persistence of housing segregation contrasts with the increase in integration that has occurred in other facets of life. . . . [I]n the midst of these changes, segregation in private housing stands out as a seemingly unyielding obstacle . . . [I]t . . . underlies a host of economic and social problems . . . : white flight to the suburbs, the fiscal decline of many central cities, and problems with quality public education. [A. Schnare, The Persistence of Racial Segregation in Housing VII (The Urban Institute, 1978)]

That same year, the New York-based Regional Plan Association sought to measure the magnitude of racial segregation in the New York region. Relying upon 1970 census data (admittedly somewhat dated but not necessarily unrepresentative of 1978 conditions), the Association found that less than 10 percent of all census tracts within the region were racially "balanced," that is, held about the average regional proportion of black families (9 to 17 black families per 100 total families). Blacks were substantially underrepresented in more than 70 percent of all census tracts and substantially overrepresented in about 20 percent. Nearly two-thirds of the region's black families were confined to about 1.35 percent of the region's residential land. Regional Plan Association, Housing Segregation in the Tri-State Region (1978), updated and condensed in Regional Plan News (July, 1979), p. 2.

In analyzing these data, the study authors estimated that only 6 percent of the racial imbalance could be explained by income differences between black families and white families, and that other factors—voluntary and involuntary—were to blame. Involuntary factors included direct discrimination *and* lack of information about housing opportunities. Id. at 2.

The study also borrowed from a 1977 audit of real estate market practices undertaken by the National Commission against Discrimination in Housing (NCDH). This audit revealed widespread, but less overt, discrimination tactics. In the New York area, for example, the NCDH audit conducted 140 paired tests (black and white "checkers"). For example, prospective white home buyers tended to be offered many more listings than were their black counterparts. Blacks were more frequently asked to provide financial information, but were invited to complete applications only one-third as frequently as whites. Id. at 3.

In evaluating the effectiveness of government intervention, the NCDH study states:

> The complaints filed depend on how well-known and accessible the agency is to its constituents (either directly, or through private fair housing organizations), and how effective the complaint process is perceived to be. The attitude of "not dealing with the system," the notion that recourse is futile, is widespread among minorities. The average processing time per complaint by HUD has been substantially reduced, from 10.9 months in 1974 to 3.3 months in 1977, with a concomitant increase in successful resolutions and number of complaints processed. The elapsed time, however, is often still too long for effective action. The process is cumbersome, lacks enforcement teeth, and seldom includes follow-up. . . .

> Individuals or groups can institute private legal action both under the Civil Rights Act of 1968 and the Civil Rights Act of 1866. The number of such suits is limited because few victims of discrimination are willing to wait as long as two to three years for redress, to risk the time and the psychological strain, or are able to afford the upfront fees charged by lawyers, even on a contingency basis. [Id. at 4, 5]

9. Typically, law students are expected to concentrate on the law, that is, the statutes and cases that define legal rights and duties and the remedies to enforce those relationships. Occasionally, law students are reminded that the "customary law," that is, the de facto rights and duties that individuals actually enjoy and suffer, may deviate considerably from the formal legal doctrine. The sources at note 7, plus your own experience, establish such deviation in the case of housing opportunity.

But carry your thoughts one level deeper. Why, in your opinion, does housing discrimination remain so epidemic?

10. Discrimination against families with children in rental housing is said to have reached crisis proportions in some areas. For example, in the San Francisco peninsula area, one survey reported that 70 to 80 percent of apartment units were not open to children. Several large California cities and at least six states have passed laws preventing child discrimination. Nat'l Comm. Against Discrimination in Housing, Trends in Housing (Oct. 1981), at 10.

What are the arguments for and against child discrimination laws? What should such laws provide or not provide?

§1.5   The New Wealth

REICH, THE NEW PROPERTY
73 Yale L.J. 733 (1964)

The institution called property guards the troubled boundary between individual man and the state. It is not the only guardian; many other institutions, laws, and practices serve as well. But in a society that chiefly values material well-being, the power to control a particular portion of that well-being is the very foundation of individuality.

One of the most important developments in the United States during the past decade has been the emergence of government as a major source of wealth. Government is a gigantic syphon. It draws in revenue and power, and pours forth wealth: money, benefits, services, contracts, franchises, and licenses. Government has always had this function. But while in early times it was minor, today's distribution of largess is on a vast, imperial scale.

The valuables dispensed by government take many forms, but they all share one characteristic. They are steadily taking the place of traditional forms of wealth—forms which are held as private property. Social insurance substitutes for savings; a government contract replaces a businessman's customers and goodwill. The wealth of more and more Americans depends upon a relationship to government. Increasingly, Americans live on government largess—allocated by government on its own terms, and held by recipients subject to conditions which express "the public interest."

The growth of government largess, accompanied by a distinctive system of law, is having profound consequences. It affects the underpinnings of individualism and independence. It influences the workings of the Bill of Rights. It has an impact on the power of private interests, in their relation to each other and to government. It is helping to create a new society. . . .

I.   The Largess of Government

A.   THE FORMS OF GOVERNMENT-CREATED WEALTH

The valuables which derive from relationships to government are of many kinds. Somre primarily concern individuals; other flow to businesses and organizations. Some are obvious forms of wealth, such as direct payments of money, while others, like licenses and franchises, are indirectly valuable.

Income and benefits. For a large number of people, government is a direct source of income although they hold no public job. Their eligibility arises from legal status. Examples are Social Security benefits, unemployment compensation, aid to dependent children, veterans benefits, and the whole scheme of state and local welfare. These represent a principal source of income to a substantial segment of the community. Total federal, state and local social welfare expenditures in 1961 were almost fifty-eight billion dollars.

Jobs. More than nine million persons receive income from public funds because they are directly employed by federal, state, or local government. The size of the publicly employed working force has increased steadily since the founding of the United States, and seems likely to keep on increasing. If the three to four million persons employed in defense industries, which exist mainly on government funds, are added to the nine million directly employed, it may be estimated that fifteen to twenty per cent of the labor force receives its primary income from government.

Occupational licenses. Licenses are required before one may engage in many kinds of work, from practicing medicine to guiding hunters through the woods. Even occupations which require little education or training, like that of longshoremen, often are subject to strict licensing. Such licenses, which are dispensed by government, make it possible for their holders to receive what is ordinarily their chief source of income.

Franchises. A franchise, which may be held by an individual or by a company, is a partial monopoly created and handed out by government. Its value depends largely upon governmental power; by limiting the number of franchises, government can make them extremely remunerative. A New York City taxi medallion, which costs very little when originally obtained from the city, can be sold for over twenty thousand dollars. The reason for this high price is that the city has not issued new transferable medallions despite the rise in population and traffic. A television channel, handed out free, can often be sold for many millions. Government distributes wealth when it dispenses route permits to truckers, charters to bus lines, routes to air carriers, certificates to oil and gas pipelines, licenses to liquor stores, allotments to growers of cotton or wheat, and concessions in national parks.

Contracts. Many individuals and many more businesses enjoy public generosity in the form of government contracts. Fifty billion dollars annually flows from the federal government in the form of defense spending. These contracts often resemble subsidies; it is virtually impossible to lose money on them. Businesses sometimes make the government their principal source of income, and many "free enterprises" are set up primarily to do business with the government.

Subsidies. Analogous to welfare payments for individuals who cannot manage independently in the economy are subsidies to business. Agriculture is subsidized to help it survive against better organized (and less competitive) sectors of the economy, and the shipping industry is given a dole because of its inability to compete with foreign lines. Local airlines are also on the dole. So are other major industries, notably housing. Still others, such as the railroads, are eagerly seeking help. Government also supports many nonbusiness activities, in such areas as scientific research, health, and education. Total federal subsidies for 1964 were expected to be just under eight and a half billion dollars.

Use of public resources. A very large part of the American economy is publicly owned. Government owns or controls hundreds of millions of acres of public lands valuable for mining, grazing, lumbering, and recreation; sources of energy such as the hydroelectric power of all major rivers, the tidelands reservoirs of oil, and the infant giant of nuclear power; routes of travel and commerce such as the airways, highways, and rivers; the radio-television spectrum which is the avenue for all broadcasting; hoards of surplus crops and materials, public buildings and facilities; and much more. These resources are available for utilization by private businesses and individuals; such use is often equivalent to a subsidy. The radio-television industry uses the scarce channels of the air, free of charge; electric companies use publicly-owned water power; stockmen graze sheep and cattle on public lands at nominal cost; ships and airplanes arrive and depart from publicly-owned docks and airports; the atomic energy industry uses government materials, facilities, and know-how, and all are entitled to make a profit.

Services. Like resources, government services are a source of wealth. Some of these are plainly of commercial value; postal service for periodicals, newspapers, advertisers, and mail-order houses, insurance for home builders and savings banks; technical information for agriculture. Other services dispensed by government include sewage, sanitation, police and fire protection, and public transportation. The Communications Satellite represents an unusual type of subsidy through service: the turning over of government research and know-how to a quasi-private organization. The most important public service of all, education, is one of the greatest sources of value to the individual. . . .

C.   LARGESS AND THE CHANGING FORMS OF WEALTH

The significance of government largess is increased by certain underlying changes in the forms of private wealth in the United States. Changes in the forms of wealth are not remarkable in themselves; the forms are constantly changing and differ in every culture. But today more and more of our wealth takes the form of rights or status rather than of tangible goods. An individual's profession or occupation is a prime example. To many others, a job with a particular employer is the principal form of wealth. A profession or a job is frequently far more valuable than a house or bank account, for a new house can be bought, and a new bank account created, once a profession or job is secure. For the jobless, their status as governmentally assisted or insured persons may be the main source of subsistence.

The automobile dealer's chief wealth is his franchise from the manufacturer which gives him exclusive sales rights within a certain territory, for it is his guarantee of income. His building, his stock of cars, his organization, and his goodwill may all be less valuable than his franchise. Franchises represent the principal asset of many businesses: the gasoline station, chain restaurant, motel or drug store, and many other retail suppliers. To the large manufacturer, contracts, business arrangements, and organization may be the most valuable assets. The steel company's relationships with coal and iron producers and automobile manufacturers and construction companies may be worth more than all its plant and equipment.

The kinds of wealth dispensed by government consist almost entirely of those forms which are in the ascendancy today. To the individual, these new forms, such as a profession, job, or right to receive income, are the basis of his various statuses in society, and may therefore be the most meaningful and distinctive wealth he possesses.

II. THE EMERGING SYSTEM OF LAW

Wealth or value is created by culture and by society; it is culture that makes a diamond valuable and a pebble worthless. Property, on the other hand, is the creation of law. A man who has property has certain legal rights with respect to an item of wealth; property represents a relationship between wealth and its "owner." Government largess is plainly "wealth," but it is not necessarily "property."

Government largess has given rise to a distinctive system of law. This system can be viewed from at least three perspectives; the rights of holders of largess, the powers of government over largess, and the procedure by which holders' rights and governmental power are adjusted. At this point, analysis will not be aided by attempting to apply or to reject the label "property." What is important is to survey—without the use of labels—the unique legal system that is emerging.

A. INDIVIDUAL RIGHTS IN LARGESS

As government largess has grown in importance, quite naturally there has been pressure for the protection of individual interests in it. The holder of a broadcast license or a motor carrier permit or a grazing permit for the public lands tends to consider this wealth his "own," and to seek legal protection against interference with his enjoyment. The development of individual interests has been substantial, but it has not come easily.

From the beginning, individual rights in largess have been greatly affected by several traditional legal concepts, each of which has had lasting significance:

Right vs. privilege. The early law is marked by courts' attempts to distinguish which forms of largess were "rights" and which were "privileges." Legal protection of the former was by far the greater. If the holder of a license had a "right," he might be entitled to a hearing before the license could be revoked; a "mere privilege" might be revoked without notice or hearing.

[Query: Is Professor Reich using the right-privilege dichotomy as did Hohfeld, §1.2 *supra*?]

The gratuity principle. Government largess has often been considered a "gratuity" furnished by the state. Hence it is said that the state can withhold, grant, or revoke the largess at its pleasure. Under this theory, government is considered to be in somewhat the same position as a private giver.

The whole and the parts. Related to the gratuity theory is the idea that, since government may completely withhold a benefit, it may grant it subject to any terms or conditions whatever. This theory is essentially an exercise in logic: the whole power must include all of its parts.

Internal management. Particularly in relation to its own contracts, government has been permitted extensive power on the theory that it should have control over its own housekeeping or internal management functions. Under this theory, government is treated like a private business. In its dealings with outsiders it is permitted much of the freedom to grant contracts and licenses that a private business would have. . . .

These sentiments are often voiced in the law of government largess, but individual interests have grown up nevertheless. The most common forms of protection are procedural, coupled with an insistence that government action be based on standards that are not "arbitrary" or unauthorized. Development has varied mainly according to the particular type of wealth involved. The courts have most readily granted protection to those types which are intimately bound up with the individual's freedom to earn a living. They have been reluctant to grant individual rights in those types of largess which seem to be exercises of the managerial functions of government, such as subsidies and government contracts. . . .

In all of the cases concerning individual rights in largess the exact nature of the government action which precipitates the controversy makes a great difference. A controversy over government largess may arise from such diverse situations as denial of the right to apply, denial of an application, attaching of conditons to a grant, modification of a grant already made, suspension or revocation of a grant, or some other sanction. In general, courts tend to afford the greatest measure of protection in revocation or suspension cases. The theory seems to be that here some sort of rights have "vested" which may not be taken away without proper procedure. On the other hand, an applicant for largess is thought to have less at stake, and is therefore entitled to less protection. The mere fact that a particular form of largess is protected in one context does not mean that it will be protected in all others.

While individual interests in largess have developed along the lines of procedural protection and restraint upon arbitrary official action, substantive rights to possess and use largess have remained very limited. In the first place, largess does not "vest" in a recipient; it almost always remains revocable. . . .

When the public interest demands that the government take over "property," the Constitution requires that just compensation be paid to the owner. But when largess is revoked in the public interest, the holder ordinarily receives no compensation. For example, if a television station's license were revoked, not for bad behavior on the part of the operator, but in order to provide a channel in another locality, or to provide an outlet for educational television, the holder would not be compensated for its loss. This principle applies to largess of all types.

In addition to being revocable without compensation, most forms of largess are subject to considerable limitations on their use. Social Security cannot be sold or transferred. A television license can be transferred only with FCC permission. The possessor of a grazing permit has no right to change, improve, or destroy the landscape. And use of most largess is limited to specified purposes. Some welfare grants, for example, must be applied to support dependent children. On the other hand, holders of government wealth usually do have a power to exclude others, and to realize income.

The most significant limitation on use is more subtle. To some extent, at least, the holder of government largess is expected to act as the agent of "the public interest" rather than solely in the service of his own self-interest. The theory of broadcast licensing is that the channels belong to the public and should be used for the public's benefit, but that a variety of private operators are likely to perform this function more successfully than government; the holder of a radio or television license is therefore expected to broadcast in "the public interest." The opportunity for private profit is intended to serve as a lure to make private operators serve the public. . . .

III. THE PUBLIC INTEREST STATE

What are the consequences of the rise of government largess and its attendant legal system? What is the impact on the recipient, on constitutional guaranties of liberty, on the structure of power in the nation? It is important to try to picture the society that is emerging, and to seek its underlying philosophy. The dominant theme, as we have seen, is "the public interest," and out of it there grows the "public interest state.". . .

V. TOWARD INDIVIDUAL STAKES IN THE COMMONWEALTH

Ahead there stretches—to the farthest horizon—the joyless landscape of the public interest state. The life it promises will be comfortable and comforting. It will be well planned—with suitable areas for work and play. But there will be no precincts sacred to the spirit of individual man.

There can be no retreat from the public interest state. It is the inevitable outgrowth of an interdependent world. An effort to return to an earlier economic order would merely transfer power to giant private governments which would rule not in the public interest, but in their own interest. If individualism and pluralism are to be preserved, this must be done not by marching backwards, but by building these values into today's society. If public and private are now blurred, it will be necessary to draw a new zone of privacy. If private property can no longer perform its protective functions, it will be necessary to establish institutions to carry on the work that private property once did but can no longer do.

In these efforts government largess must play a major role. As we move toward a welfare state, largess will be an ever more important form of wealth. And largess is a vital link in the relationship between the government and private sides of society. It is necessary, then, that largess begin to do the work of property.

The chief obstacle to the creation of private rights in largess has been the fact that it is originally public property, comes from the state, and may be withheld completely. But this need not be an obstacle. Traditional property also comes from the state, and in much the same way. Land, for example, traces back to grants from the sovereign. In the United States, some was the gift of the King of England, some that of the King of Spain. The sovereign extinguished Indian title by conquest, became the new owner, and then granted title to a private individual or group. Some land was the gift of the sovereign under laws such as the Homestead and Preemption Acts. Many other natural resources—water, minerals and timber—passed into private ownership under similar grants. In America, land and resources all were originally government largess. In a less obvious sense, personal property also stems from government. Personal property is created by law; it owes its origin and continuance to laws supported by the people as a whole. These laws "give" the property to one who performs certain actions. Even the man who catches a wild animal "owns" the animal only as a gift from the sovereign, having fulfilled the terms of an offer to transfer ownership.

Like largess, real and personal property were also originally dispensed on conditions, and were subject to forfeiture if the conditions failed. The conditions in the sovereign grants, such as colonization, were generally made explicit, and so was the forfeiture resulting from failure to fulfill them. In the case of the Preemption and Homestead Acts, there were also specific conditions. Even now land is subject to forfeiture for neglect; if it is unused it may be deemed abandoned to the state or forfeited to an adverse possessor. In a very similar way, personal property may be forfeited by abandonment or loss. Hence, all property might be described as government largess, given on condition and subject to loss.

If all property is government largess, why is it not regulated to the same degree as present-day largess? Regulation of property has been limited, not because society had no interest in property, but because it was in the interest of society that property be free. Once property is seen not as a natural right but as a construction designed to serve certain functions, then its origin ceases to be decisive in determining how much regulation should be imposed. The conditions that can be attached to receipt, ownership, and use depend not on where property came from, but on what job it should be expected to perform. Thus in the case of government largess, nothing turns on the fact that it originated in government. The real issue is how it functions and how it should function. . . .

D. FROM LARGESS TO RIGHT

The proposals discussed above, however salutary, are by themselves far from adequate to assure the status of individual man with respect to largess. The problems go deeper. First, the growth of government power based on the dispensing of wealth must be kept within bounds. Second, there must be a zone of privacy for each individual beyond which neither government nor private power can push—a hiding place from the all-pervasive system of regulation and control. Finally, it must be recognized that we are becoming a society based upon relationship and status—status deriving primarily from source of livlihood. Status is so closely linked to personality that destruction of one may well destroy the other. Status must therefore be surrounded with the kind of safeguards once reserved for personality.

Eventually those forms of largess which are closely linked to status must be deemed to be held as of right. Like property, such largess could be governed by a system of regulation plus civil or criminal sanctions rather than a system based upon denial, suspension and revocation. As things now stand, violations lead to forfeitures—outright confiscation of wealth and status. But there is surely no need for these drastic results. Confiscation, if used at all, should be the ultimate, not the most common and convenient penalty. The presumption should be that the professional man will keep his license, and the welfare recipient his pension. These interests should be "vested." If revocation is necessary, not by reason of the fault of the individual holder, but by reason of overriding demands of public policy, perhaps payment of just compensation would be appropriate. The individual should not bear the entire loss for a remedy primarily intended to benefit the community.

The concept of right is most urgently needed with respect to benefits like unemployment compensation, public assistance, and old age insurance. These benefits are based upon a recognition that misfortune and deprivation are often caused by forces far beyond the control of the individual, such as technological change, variations in demand for goods, depressions, or wars. The aim of these benefits is to preserve the self-sufficiency of the individual, to rehabilitate him where necessary, and to allow him to be a valuable member of a family and a community; in theory they represent part of the individual's rightful share in the commonwealth. Only by making such benefits into rights can the welfare state achieve its goal of providing a secure minimum basis for individual well-being and dignity in a society where each man cannot be wholly the master of his own destiny.

CONCLUSION

The highly organized, scientifically planned society of the future, governed for the good of its inhabitants, promises the best life that men have ever known. In place of the misery and injustice of the past there can be prosperity, leisure, knowledge, and rich opportunity open to all. In the rush of accomplishment, however, not all values receive equal attention; some are temporarily forgotten while others are pushed ahead. We have made provision for nearly everything, but we have made no adequate provision for individual man.

This article is an attempt to offer perspective of the transformation of society as it bears on the economic basis of individualism. The effort has been to show relationships; to bring together drivers' licenses, unemployment insurance, membership in the bar, permits for using school auditoriums, and second class mail privileges, in order to see what we are becoming.

Government largess is only one small corner of a far vaster problem. There are many other new forms of wealth: franchises in private businesses, equities in corporations, the right to receive privately furnished utilities and services, status in private organizations. These too may need added safeguards in the future. Similarly, there are many sources of expanded governmental power aside from largess. By themselves, proposals concerning government largess would be far from accomplishing any fundamental reforms. But, somehow, we must begin.

At the very least, it is time to reconsider the theories under which new forms of wealth are regulated, and by which governmental power over them is measured. It is time to recognize that "the public interest" is all too often a reassuring platitude that covers up sharp clashes of conflicting values, and hides fundamental choices. It is time to see that the "privilege" or "gratuity" concept, as applied to wealth dispensed by government, is not much different from the absolute right of ownership that private capital once invoked to justify arbitrary power over employees and the public.

Above all, the time has come for us to remember what the framers of the Constitutions knew so well—that "a power over a man's subsistence amounts to a power over his will." We cannot safely entrust our livelihoods and our rights to the discretion of authorities, examiners, boards of control, character committees, regents, or license commissioners. We cannot permit any official or agency to pretend to sole knowledge of the public good. We cannot put the independence of any man—least of all our Barskys and our Anastaplos—wholly in the power of other men.

If the individual is to survive in a collective society, he must have protection against its ruthless pressures. There must be sanctuaries or enclaves where no majority can reach. To shelter the solitary human spirit does not merely make possible the fulfillment of individuals; it also gives society the power to change, to grow, and to regenerate, and hence to endure. These were the objects which property sought to achieve, and can no longer achieve. The challenge of the future will be to construct, for the society that is coming, institutions and laws to carry on this work. Just as the Homestead Act was a deliberate effort to foster individual values at an earlier time, so we must try to build an economic basis for liberty today—a Homestead Act for rootless twentieth century man. We must create a new property.

Professor Reich's article "The New Property" and its sequel, "Individual

Rights and Social Welfare: The Emerging Legal Issues," 74 Yale L.J. 1254 (1965), anticipated and helped nurture two important streams of Supreme Court decisions during the early Burger Court years. One group of cases dealt with the protection of privately created wealth against summary loss resulting from state-sanctioned procedures. Here we find Sniadach v. Family Finance Corp., 395 U.S. 337 (1969) (debtor entitled to due process hearing before wages can be garnished) and Fuentes v. Shevin, 407 U.S. 67 (1972) (buyer entitled to due process hearing before credit-seller can reposses goods after default). The second group of cases, which Professor Reich influenced more directly, involved the loss of governmentally created benefits (Query: "entitlements"?). In each instance, the court required that a fact-finding hearing precede a benefit termination: Goldberg v. Kelly, 397 U.S. 254 (1970) (termination of welfare benefits); Bell v. Burson, 402 U.S. 535 (1971) (revocation of driver's license); Morissey v. Brewer, 408 U.S. 471 (1972) (revocation of parole).

Perry v. Sindermann, 408 U.S. 593 (1972) and Board of Regents v. Roth, 408 U.S. 564 (1972), which both involve government employment, are related to the second genre of cases. The plaintiff in Perry v. Sindermann had been a teacher in the Texas state college system for ten years, under a series of short-term contracts. His final contract was not renewed after a newspaper advertisement highly critical of the state regents appeared over his name. The regents charged him with insurbordination but gave him no opportunity for a hearing to challenge the basis of the nonrenewal.

The Supreme Court affirmed the decision of the court of appeals, which had directed the trial court to offer plaintiff a hearing on two contested issues of fact: First, whether the defendant's decision not to renew the contract was based on protected free speech; if so, nonrenewal would violate the First and Fourteenth Amendments whether plaintiff held tenure or not. Second, whether (under Texas custom) the plaintiff had an "expectancy" of re-employment despite his lack of formal tenure; if so, procedural due process entitled plaintiff to a statement of reasons and a hearing before college officials upon their decision not to retain him.

> We have made clear in *Roth* . . . that "property" interests subject to procedural due process protection are not limited by a few rigid, technical forms. Rather, "property" denotes a broad range of interests that are secured by "existing rules or understandings". . . . A person's interest in a benefit is a "property" interest for due process purposes if there are such rules or mutually explicit understandings that support his claim of entitlement to the benefit and that he may invoke at a hearing. [408 U.S. 593, 601 (1972)]

The plaintiff in Board of Regents v. Roth taught political science in the Wisconsin state university system. After one year, his initial contract was not renewed. Tenure, which Wisconsin Law granted only after four years of year-to-year employment, would have entitled plaintiff to remain at the job "during efficiency and good behavior." Under the same law, nontenured teachers—such as plaintiff—were not entitled to an explanation for contract nonrenewals, nor was any review or appeal procedure provided.

Plaintiff attacked the regents' decision not to rehire him, claiming a violation of his right to free speech[3] and to a hearing on the reasons for nonretention. The Court, despite expansive language about the forms of property that are entitled to due process protection, held that a state college could refuse to renew the contract of a *nontenured* professor and not state a reason or afford an evidentiary hearing as to cause, except where the employee could make a prima facie showing that either his "liberty" or free speech rights had been impaired.

> In these circumstances, the respondent surely had an abstract concern in being rehired, but he did not have a *property* interest sufficient to require the University authorities to give him a hearing when they declined to renew his contract of employment.

> There might be cases in which a state refused to reemploy a [nontenured] person under such circumstances that interests in liberty would be implicated. But this is not such a case.

> The state, in declining to rehire the respondent did not make any charge against him that might seriously damage his standing and associations in his community. It did not base the nonrenewal of his contract on a charge, for example, that he had been guilty of dishonesty, or immorality. Had it done so, this would be a different case. For "where a person's good name, reputation, honor, or integrity is at stake because of what the government is doing to him, notice and an opportunity to be heard are essential" (citing Wisconsin v. Constantineau, 400 U.S. 433, 437). . . . In the present case, however, there is no suggestion whatever that the respondent's "good name, reputation, honor, or integrity" is at stake. [408 U.S. 564, 573]

In Arnett v. Kennedy, 416 U.S. 134 (1974), the Supreme Court tried to apply *Roth* and *Sindermann* to the discharge of a tenured federal employee. The case badly divided the justices. The Lloyd-La Follette Act protects civil service employees against removal except "for such cause as will promote the efficiency of the service." The same act sets forth procedures for determining "such cause." These do not require a pretermination hearing, but do allow the discharged employee a trial-type hearing at the appeal stage. Discharged under this procedure, plaintiff claimed a denial of due process because the law failed to accord him a trial-type hearing prior to removal. The Supreme Court validated the statute.

Writing for a three-man (!) plurality, Justice Rehnquist argued that the worker's substantive property right was linked inexorably to the statutory procedure that protected the right, and that here the right was "not a guarantee against removal without cause in the abstract, but such a guarantee as enforced by the procedures which Congress has designated for the determina-

---

3. [Plaintiff's free speech claim was not before the Supreme Court because the trial court had stayed proceedings on that issue.]

tion of cause." Chief Justice Burger and Justice Stewart joined in the opinion. Justices Powell and Blackmun concurred in the result, to form the five-man majority, but rejected the substance = remedy linkage as "incompatible with the principles laid down in *Roth* and *Sindermann*."

> Indeed, it would lead directly to the conclusion that whatever the nature of an individual's statutorily created property interest, deprivation of that interest could be accomplished without notice or a hearing at any time. This view misconceives the origin of the right to procedural due process. That right is conferred not by legislative grace but by constitutional guarantee. While the legislature may elect not to confer a property interest in federal employment, it may not constitutionally authorize the deprivation of such an interest, once conferred, without appropriate procedural safeguards. [416 U.S. 134, 1 (1974)]

The two justices then analyzed the policy in favor of a pretermination hearing (a vindicated employee would not suffer a "temporary" interruption of income) and against such a hearing (discipline and morale problems would result from prolonged retention of an unsatisfactory employee; additional administrative costs would be incurred), and decided that on balance a prior evidentiary hearing would not be required because the present law reasonably accommodated the competing interests.

Justices Marshall, Douglas, and Brennan struck the opposite balance; they believed that the Constitution required that an impartial decision-maker hold a prior evidentiary hearing. To support this conclusion, they noted that almost one-fourth of all appeals from agency dismissals resulted in a finding that the termination was illegal, but that the appeal process might take more than a year and routinely took at least two months.

Justice White also believed that due process protected the employee before his discharge and that the statutory arrangement giving the employee a right to make a *written* presentation satisfied the minimum requirements, but that the failure to provide an "impartial decision-maker" tainted the process.

Plaintiff further claimed that his discharge, because he was in effect accused of dishonesty, implicated his liberty interest and that for this reason as well, due process required a predismissal hearing. Even the three pluralists conceded that plaintiff was constitutionally entitled to "an opportunity to clear his name" but ruled that the post-dismissal appeal would satisfy due process. Justices Powell and Blackmun joined in that ruling. The four dissenting justices would have ordered a predismissal hearing on the liberty issue.

BISHOP v. WOOD

426 U.S. 341, 96 S. Ct. 2074, 48 L. Ed. 2d 684 (1976)

MR. JUSTICE STEVENS delivered the opinion of the court.

Acting on the recommendation of the Chief of Police, the City Manager of Marion, N.C., terminated petitioner's employment as a policeman without affording him a hearing to determine the sufficiency of the cause for his discharge. Petitioner brought suit contending that since a city ordinance classified him as a "permanent employee," he had a constitutional right to a pretermination hearing. During pretrial discovery petitioner was advised that his dismissal was based on a failure to follow certain orders, poor attendance at police training classes, causing low morale, and conduct unsuited to an officer. Petitioner and several other police officers filed affidavits essentially denying the truth of these charges. The District Court granted defendants' motion for summary judgment.[2] The Court of Appeals affirmed,[3] and we granted certiorari. [Citation omitted.]

The questions for us to decide are (1) whether petitioner's employment status was a property interest protected by the Due Process Clause of the Fourteenth Amendment, and (2) assuming that the explanation for his discharge was false, whether that false explanation deprived him of an interest in liberty protected by that Clause.

I

Petitioner was employed by the city of Marion as a probationary policeman on June 9, 1969. After six months he became a permanent employee. He was dismissed on March 31, 1972. He claims that he had either an express or an implied right to continued employment.

A city ordinance provides that a permanent employee may be discharged if he fails to perform work up to the standard of his classification, or if he is negligent, inefficient, or unfit to perform his duties.[5] Petitioner first contends that even though the ordinance does not expressly so provide, it should be read to prohibit discharge for any other reason, and therefore to confer tenure on all permanent employees. In addition, he contends that his period of service, together with his "permanent" classification, gave him a sufficient expectancy of continued employment to constitute a protected property interest.

A property interest in employment can, of course, be created by ordinance, or by an implied contract.[6] In either case, however, the sufficiency of

2. 377 F. Supp. 501 (W.D.N.C. 1973).

3. A three-judge panel of the Court of Appeals affirmed, with one judge dissenting, 498 F. 2d 1341 (1974); then, after granting rehearing en banc, the court affirmed without opinion by an equally divided court.

5. Article II, §6, of the Personnel Ordinance of the city of Marion, reads as follows:

Dismissal. A permanent employee whose work is not satisfactory over a period of time shall be notified in what way his work is deficient and what he must do if his work is to be satisfactory. If a permanent employee fails to perform work up to the standard of the classification held, or continues to be negligent, inefficient, or unfit to perform his duties, he may be dismissed by the City Manager. Any discharged employee shall be given written notice of his discharge setting forth the effective date and reasons for his discharge if he shall request such a notice.

6. In Perry v. Sindermann, 408 U.S. 593, 601, 33 L. Ed. 2d 570, 92 S. Ct. 2694, the Court said that a "person's interest in a benefit is a 'property' interest for due process purposes if there are . . . rules or mutually explicit understandings that support his claim of entitlement to the benefit and that he may invoke at a hearing."

the claim of entitlement must be decided by reference to state law.[7] The North Carolina Supreme Court has held that an enforceable expectation of continued public employment in that State can exist only if the employer, by statute or contract, has actually granted some form of guarantee. Still v. Lance, 279 N.C. 254, 182 S.E. 2d 403 (1971). Whether such a guarantee has been given can be determined only by an examination of the particular statute or ordinance in question.

On its face the ordinance on which petitioner relies may fairly be read as conferring such a guarantee. However, such a reading is not the only possible interpretation; the ordinance may also be construed as granting no right to continued employment but merely conditioning an employee's removal on compliance with certain specified procedures.[8] We do not have any authoritative interpretation of this ordinance by a North Carolina state court. We do, however, have the opinion of the United States District Judge who, of course, sits in North Carolina and practiced law there for many years. Based on his understanding of state law, he concluded that petitioner "held his position at the will and pleasure of the city." This construction of North Carolina law was upheld by the Court of Appeals for the Fourth Circuit, albeit by an equally divided court. In comparable circumstances, this Court has accepted the interpretation of state law in which the District Court and the Court of Appeals have concurred even if an examination of the state-law issue without such guidance might have justified a different conclusion.

In this case, as the District Court construed the ordinance, the City Manager's determination of the adequacy of the grounds for discharge is not subject to judicial review; the employee is merely given certain procedural rights which the District Court found not to have been violated in this case. The District Court's reading of the ordinance is tenable; it derives some support from a decision of the North Carolina Supreme Court, Still v. Lance, *supra;* and it was accepted by the Court of Appeals for the Fourth Circuit. These reasons are sufficient to foreclose our independent examination of the state-law issue.

Under that view of the law, petitioner's discharge did not deprive him of a property interest protected by the Fourteenth Amendment.

---

7. "Property interests, of course, are not created by the Constitution. Rather, they are created and their dimensions are defined by existing rules or understandings that stem from an independent source such a state law—rules or understandings that secure certain benefits and that support claims of entitlement to those benefits." Board of Regents v. Roth, 408 U.S. 564, 577, 33 L. Ed. 2d 548, 92 S. Ct. 2701.

8. This is not the construction which six Members of this Court placed on the federal regulations involved in Arnett v. Kennedy, 416 U.S. 134, 40 L. Ed. 2d 15, 94 S. Ct. 1633. In that case the Court concluded that because the employee could only be discharged for cause, he had a property interest which was entitled to constitutional protection. In this case, a holding that as a matter of state law the employee "held his position at the will and pleasure of the city" necessarily establishes that he had *no* property interest. The Court's evaluation of the federal regulations involved in *Arnett* sheds no light on the problem presented by this case.

II

Petitioner's claim that he has been deprived of liberty has two components. He contends that the reasons given for his discharge are so serious as to constitute a stigma that may severely damage his reputation in the community; in addition, he claims that those reasons were false.

In our appraisal of petitioner's claim we must accept his version of the facts since the District Court granted summary judgment against him. His evidence established that he was a competent police officer; that he was respected by his peers; that he made more arrests than any other officer on the force; that although he had been criticized for engaging in high-speed pursuits, he had promptly heeded such criticism; and that he had a reasonable explanation for his imperfect attendance at police training sessions. We must therefore assume that his discharge was a mistake and based on incorrect information.

In Board of Regents v. Roth, 408 U.S. 564, 33 L. Ed. 2d 548, 92 S. Ct. 2701, we recognized that the nonretention of an untenured college teacher might make him somewhat less attractive to other employers, but nevertheless concluded that it would stretch the concept too far "to suggest that a person is deprived of 'liberty' when he simply is not rehired in one job but remains as free as before to seek another." Id., at 575, 33 L. Ed. 2d 548, 92 S. Ct. 2701. This same conclusion applies to the discharge of a public employee whose position is terminable at the will of the employer when there is no public disclosure of the reasons for the discharge.

In this case the asserted reasons for the City Manager's decision were communicated orally to the petitioner in private and also were stated in writing in answer to interrogatories after this litigation commenced. Since the former communication was not made public, it cannot properly form the basis for a claim that petitioner's interest in his "good name, reputation, honor, or integrity" was thereby impaired. And since the latter communication was made in the course of a judicial proceeding which did not commence until after petitioner had suffered the injury for which he seeks redress, it surely cannot provide retroactive support for his claim. A contrary evaluation of either explanation would penalize forthright and truthful communication between employer and employee in the former instance, and between litigants in the latter.

Petitioner argues, however, that the reasons given for his discharge were false. Even so, the reasons stated to him in private had no different impact on his reputation than if they had been true. And the answers to his interrogatories, whether true or false, did not cause the discharge. The truth or falsity of the City Manager's statement determines whether or not his decision to discharge the petitioner was correct or prudent, but neither enhances nor diminishes the petitioner's claim that his constitutionally protected interest in liberty has been impaired. A contrary evaluation of his contention would enable every discharged employee to assert a constitutional claim merely by alleging that his former supervisor made a mistake.

The federal court is not the appropriate forum in which to review the multitude of personnel decisions that are made daily by public agencies.[14] We must accept the harsh fact that numerous individual mistakes are inevitable in the day-to-day administration of our affairs. The United States Constitution cannot feasibly be construed to require federal judicial review for every such error. In the absence of any claim that the public employer was motivated by a desire to curtail or to penalize the exercise of an employee's constitutionally protected rights, we must presume that official action was regular and, if erroneous, can best be corrected in other ways. The Due Process Clause of the Fourteenth Amendment is not a guarantee against incorrect or ill-advised personnel decisions.

The judgment is affirmed.

MR. JUSTICE BRENNAN, with whom MR. JUSTICE MARSHALL concurs, dissenting.

Petitioner was discharged as a policeman on the grounds of insubordination, "causing low morale," and "conduct unsuited to an officer." *Ante,* at 343, 48 L. Ed. 2d 689. It is difficult to imagine a greater "badge of infamy" that could be imposed on one following petitioner's calling; in a profession in which prospective employees are invariably investigated, petitioner's job prospects will be severely constricted by the governmental action in this case. Although our case law would appear to require that petitioner thus be accorded an opportunity "to clear his name" of this calumny, see, e.g., Board of Regents v. Roth, 408 U.S. 564, 573, and n.12, 33 L. Ed. 2d 548, 92 S. Ct. 2701 (1972); Arnett v. Kennedy, 416 U.S. 134, 157, 40 L. Ed. 2d 15, 94 S. Ct. 1633 (1974) (opinion of Rehnquist, J.), the Court condones this governmental action and holds that petitioner was deprived of no liberty interest thereby. . . .

The Court purports to limit its holding to situations in which there is "no public disclosure of the reasons for the discharge," *ante,* at 348, 48 L. Ed. 2d 692, but in this case the stigmatizing reasons have been disclosed, and there is no reason to believe that respondents will not convey these actual reasons to petitioner's prospective employers.[2] The Court responds by asserting that since the stigma was imposed "after petitioner had suffered the injury for which he seeks redress, it surely cannot provide retroactive support for his claim." Ibid. But the "claim" does not arise until the State has officially branded petitioner in some way, and the purpose of the due process hearing is to accord him an

14. The cumulative impression created by the three dissenting opinions is that this holding represents a significant retreat from settled practice in the federal courts. The fact of the matter, however, is that the instances in which the federal judiciary has required a state agency to reinstate a discharged employee for failure to provide a pretermination hearing are extremely rare. The reason is clear. For unless we were to adopt Mr. Justice Brennan's remarkably innovative suggestion that we develop a federal common law of property rights, or his equally far-reaching view that almost every discharge implicates a constitutionally protected liberty interest, the ultimate control of state personnel relationships is, and will remain, with the States; they may grant or withold tenure at their unfettered discretion. In this case, whether we accept or reject the construction of the ordinance adopted by the two lower courts, the power to change or clarify that ordinance will remain in the hands of the City Council of the city of Marion.

2. It is only common sense, to be sure, that prospective employers will inquire as to petitioner's employment during the 33 months in which he was in respondents' service.

opportunity to clear his name; merely because the derogatory information is filed in respondents' records and no "publication" occurs until shortly after his discharge from employment does not subvert the fact that a postdeprivation hearing to accord petitioner an opportunity to clear his name has been contemplated by our cases.[3] . . .

These observations do not, of course, suggest that a "federal court is . . . the appropriate forum in which to review the multitude of personnel decisions that are made daily by public agencies." *Ante,* at 349, 48 L. Ed. 2d 693. However, the federal courts are the appropriate forum for ensuring that the constitutional mandates of due process are followed by those agencies of government making personnel decisions that pervasively influence the lives of those affected thereby; the fundamental premise of the Due Process Clause is that those procedural safeguards will help the government avoid the "harsh fact" of "incorrect or ill-advised personnel decisions." *Ante,* at 350, 48 L. Ed. 2d 693. Petitioner seeks no more than that, and I believe that his "property" interest in continued employment and his "liberty" interest in his good name and reputation dictate that he be accorded procedural safeguards before those interests are deprived by arbitrary or capricious government action.

MR. JUSTICE WHITE, with whom MR. JUSTICE BRENNAN, MR. JUSTICE MARSHALL, and MR. JUSTICE BLACKMUN join, dissenting. . . . In the concluding paragraph of its discussion of petitioner's property interest, the majority holds that since neither the ordinance nor state law provides for a hearing, or any kind of review of the City Manager's dismissal decision, petitioner had no enforceable property interest in his job. The majority concludes: "In this case, as the District Court construed the ordinance, the City Manager's *determination of the adequacy of the grounds for discharge* is not subject to judicial review; the employee is merely given certain procedural rights which the District court found not to have been violated in this case. The District Court's reading of the ordinance is tenable. . . ." *Ante,* at 347. (Emphasis added.)

The majority thus implicity concedes that the ordinance supplies the "grounds" for discharge and that the City Manager must determine them to be "adequate" before he may fire an employee. The majority's holding that petitioner had no property interest in his job in spite of the unequivocal language in the city ordinance that he may be dismissed only for certain kinds of cause rests, then, on the fact that state law provides no *procedures* for assuring that the City Manager dismiss him only for cause. The right to his job appar-

---

3. The Court asserts that to provide petitioner with a post-deprivation hearing when the stigmatizing reasons become known during litigation "would penalize forthright and truthful communication . . . between litigants." *Ante,* at 349, 48 L. Ed. 2d 692. Of course, there are various sanctions under our judicial system to ensure that testimony is "forthright and truthful" without necessitating denial of petitioner's due process rights. And I suppose the Court would declare that according a discharged employee a post-deprivation hearing as soon as it is clear his former employer is stigmatizing his name when it communicates with prospective employers would similarly discourage "forthright and truthful" communication between employers in that situation. However, the purpose of the due process hearing is to provide petitioner a mechanism for clearing his name of a cloud that is not in fact "truthful."

ently given by the first two sentences of the ordinance is thus redefined, according to the majority, by the procedures provided for in the third sentence and as redefined is infringed only if the procedures are not followed.

This is precisely the reasoning which was embraced by only three and expressly rejected by six Members of this court in Arnett v. Kennedy, *supra*. . . .

MR. JUSTICE BLACKMUN, with whom MR. JUSTICE BRENNAN joins, dissenting.

I join Mr. Justice White's dissent for I agree that the Court appears to be adopting a legal principle which specifically was rejected by a majority of the Justices of this Court in Arnett v. Kennedy, 416 U.S. 134, 40 L. Ed. 2d 15, 94 S. Ct. 1633 (1974).

I also feel, however, that Still v. Lance, 279 N.C. 254, 182 S.E.2d 403 (1971), the only North Carolina case cited by the Court and by the District Court, is by no means the authoritative holding on state law that the Court, *ante*, at 345 and n.9, 48 L. Ed. 2d 690, seems to think it is. In *Still* the Supreme Court of North Carolina considered a statute that contained no "for cause" standard for failure to renew a teacher's contract at the *end* of a school year. In holding that this provision did not create a continued expectation of employment, the North Carolina court noted that it "does not limit the right of the employer board to terminate the employment of a teacher at the end of a school year to a specified cause or circumstance." 279 N.C., at 260, 182 S.E.2d, at 407. This provision, the court observed, stood in sharp contrast with another provision of the statute relating to termination of employment *during* the school year and providing that when "it shall have been determined that the services of an employee are not *acceptable* for the remainder of the current school year" (emphasis added), ibid., notice and hearing were required.

The Marion ordinance in the present case contains a "for cause" standard for dismissal and, it seems to me, is like that portion of the statute construed in *Still* pertaining to termination of employment during the year. As such, it plainly does not subject an employee to termination at the will and pleasure of the municipality, but, instead, creates a proper expectation of continued employment so long as he performs his work satisfactorily. At this point, the Federal Constitution steps in and requires that appropriate procedures be followed before the employee may be deprived of his property interest.

NOTES AND QUESTIONS

1. As to the plaintiff in Bishop v. Wood, was he denied a hearing because he had no property or did he have no property (protected by due process) because he was denied a hearing?

2. Compare Bishop v. Wood with Goss v. Lopez, 419 U.S. 565 (1975). Nine public high school students filed a §1983 action against the Columbus Board of Education alleging that their suspension without hearing of any kind

violated procedural due process. None of the suspensions exceeded ten days. The Supreme Court (5 to 4) held that the suspension implicated both the students' property interest in educational benefits temporarily denied and their liberty interest in reputation, and that those interests were substantial enough to bar summary suspension. Having determined that due process applied, the Court then had to decide what process was due. In the case of relatively brief suspensions (ten days or less), students would be entitled to a presuspension oral or written notice of the charges against them, an explanation of the evidence to support the charge, and an opportunity to present their side of the story. The Court indicated that more formal procedures might be required in the case of longer suspensions or expulsion.

Can you reconcile the *Goss* (1975) and *Bishop* (1976) decisions? During the interval between the two cases, Justice Stevens succeeded Justice Douglas, which shifted the balance of power in this area; internally, Justices Stewart and Blackmun traded positions. Apart from the Court's changed composition, however, might one find other ways to explain the result differences?

3. Compare Goss v. Lopez with Ingraham v. Wright, 430 U.S. 651 (1977). By a narrow majority, the Supreme Court held that the paddling of students as a means of maintaining school discipline did not require that students be given prior notice and an opportunity to be heard. Although the justices acknowledged that the paddling implicated the students' liberty interest (to say nothing of various portions of their anatomy), due process would be satisfied by the available civil and criminal sanctions under Florida state law against teachers who abused their disciplinary power. As Justice White noted in dissent, students paddled erroneously because of a teacher's good-faith mistake would not be protected adequately by a tort action or criminal complaint.

4. Start with a clean slate. On the assumption that the courts would find a protected property or liberty interest in each of the following situations, what process, in your opinion, should be due:

(a) a first-year student at a state university law school facing dismissal after flunking property and contracts;

(b) a first-year student at a state university law school facing dismissal after a proctor reports that the student looked at some class notes during a closed-book examination;

(c) A fourth-year student at a state university medical school facing dismissal after her supervising physician reports that the student lacks a satisfactory manner with patients and is inattentive to personal appearance (see Horowitz v. Board of Curators, 538 F.2d 1317 (8th Cir. 1976));

(d) an apartment tenant facing a cut-off of electrical service from a municipal utility because of nonpayment (see Craft v. Memphis Light, Gas and Water Division, 534 F.2d 684 (6th Cir. 1976));

(e) a tenant in a city-owned low-rent housing project facing eviction as an "undesirable" (see Escalera v. Housing Authority, §3.6 *infra*)?

PART II

FORMATION OF INTERESTS
IN THINGS

Chapter 2

Personal Property Issues

§2.1   Wild Animals

PIERSON v. POST
3 Cai. R. 175 (N.Y. 1805)

Tompkins, J. delivered the opinion of the court. This cause comes before us on a return to a certiorari directed to one of the justices of Queens county.

The question submitted by the counsel in this cause for our determination is, whether Lodowick Post, by the pursuit with his hounds in the manner alleged in his declaration, acquired such a right to, or property in, the fox as will sustain an action against Pierson for killing and taking him away?

The cause was argued with much ability by the counsel on both sides, and presents for our decision a novel and nice question. It is admitted that a fox is an animal *ferae naturae,* and that property in such animals is acquired by occupancy only. These admissions narrow the discussion to the simple question of what acts amount to occupancy, applied to acquiring right to wild animals.

If we have recourse to the ancient writers upon general principles of law, the judgment below is obviously erroneous. Justinians Institutes, lib. 2, tit. 1, s. 13, and Fleta, lib. 3, c. 2, p. 175, adopt the principle, that pursuit alone vests no property or right in the huntsman; and that even pursuit, accompanied with wounding, is equally ineffectual for that purpose, unless the animal be actually taken. The same principle is recognised by Bracton, lib. 2, c. 1, p. 8.

Puffendorf, lib. 4, c. 6, s. 2, and 10, defines occupancy of beasts *ferae naturae,* to be the actual corporal possession of them, and Bynkershock is cited as coinciding in this definition. It is indeed with hesitation that Puffendorf affirms that a wild beast mortally wounded, or greatly maimed, cannot be fairly intercepted by another, whilst the pursuit of the person inflicting the wound continues. The foregoing authorities are decisive to show that mere pursuit gave Post no legal right to the fox, but that he became the property of Pierson, who intercepted and killed him.

It therefore only remains to inquire whether there are any contrary principles, or authorities, to be found in other books, which ought to induce a different decision. Most of the cases which have occurred in England, relating to property in wild animals, have either been discussed and decided upon the principles of their positive statute regulations, or have arisen between the huntsman and the owner of the land upon which beasts *ferae naturae* have been apprehended; the former claiming them by title of occupancy, and the latter ratione soli. Little satisfactory aid can, therefore, be derived from the English reporters.

Barbeyrac, in his notes on Puffendorf, does not accede to the definition of occupancy by the latter, but on the contrary, affirms, that actual bodily seizure is not, in all cases, necessary to constitute possession of wild animals. He does not, however, describe the acts which, according to his ideas, will amount to an appropriation of such animals to private use, so as to exclude the claims of all other persons, by title of occupancy, to the same animals; and he is far from averring that pursuit alone is sufficient for that purpose. To a certain extent, and as far as Barbeyrac appears to me to go, his objections to Puffendorf's definition of occupancy are reasonable and correct. That is to say, that actual bodily seizure is not indispensable to acquire right to, or possession of, wild beasts; but that, on the contrary, the mortal wounding of such beasts, by one not abandoning his pursuit, may, with the utmost propriety, be deemed possession of him; since, thereby, the pursuer manifests an unequivocal intention of appropriating the animal to his individual use, has deprived him of his natural liberty, and brought him within his certain control. So also, encompassing and securing such animals with nets and toils, or otherwise intercepting them in such a manner as to deprive them of their natural liberty, and render escape impossible, may justly be deemed to give possession of them to those persons who, by their industry and labor, have used such means of apprehending them.

The case now under consideration is one of mere pursuit, and presents no circumstances or acts which can bring it within the definition of occupancy by Puffendorf, or Grotius, or the ideas of Barbeyrac upon that subject.

The case cited from 11 Mod. 74—130, I think clearly distinguishable from the present; inasmuch as there the action was for maliciously hindering and disturbing the plaintiff in the exercise and enjoyment of a private franchise; and in the report of the same case, (3 Salk. 9,) Holt, Ch. J., states, that the ducks were in the plaintiff's decoy pond, and so in his possession, from which it is obvious the court laid much stress in their opinion upon the plaintiff's possession of the ducks, ratione soli.

We are the more readily inclined to confine possession or occupancy of beasts *ferae naturae,* within the limits prescribed by the learned authors above cited, for the sake of certainty, and preserving peace and order in society. If the first seeing, starting, or pursuing such animals, without having so wounded, circumvented or ensnared them, so as to deprive them of their natural liberty, and subject them to the control of their pursuer, should afford the basis of actions against others for intercepting and killing them, it would prove a fertile source of quarrels and litigation.

However uncourteous or unkind the conduct of Pierson towards Post, in this instance, may have been, yet his act was productive of no injury or damage for which a legal remedy can be applied. We are of opinion the judgment below was erroneous, and ought to be reversed.

LIVINGSTON, J. Whether a person who, with his own hounds, starts and hunts a fox on waste and uninhabited ground, and is on the point of seizing his prey, acquires such an interest in the animal, as to have a right of action against another, who in view of the huntsman and his dogs in full pursuit, and with knowledge of the chase, shall kill and carry him away?

This is a knotty point, and should have been submitted to the arbitration of sportsmen, without poring over Justinian, Fleta, Bracton, Puffendorf, Locke, Barbeyrac, or Blackstone, all of whom have been cited; they would have had no difficulty in coming to a prompt and correct conclusion. In a court thus constituted, the skin and carcass of poor reynard would have been properly disposed of, and a precedent set, interfering with no usage or custom which the experience of ages has sanctioned, and which must be so well known to every votary of Diana. But the parties have referred the question to our judgment, and we must dispose of it as well as we can, from the partial lights we possess, leaving to a higher tribunal, the correction of any mistake which we may be so unfortunate as to make. By the pleadings it is admitted that a fox is a "wild and noxious beast." Both parties have regarded him, as the law of nations does a pirate, "hostem humani generis," and although "de mortuis nil nisi bonum," be a maxim of our profession, the memory of the deceased has not been spared. His depredations on farmers and on barn yards, have not been forgotten; and to put him to death wherever found, is allowed to be meritorious, and of public benefit. Hence it follows, that our decision should have in view the greatest possible encouragement to the destruction of an animal, so cunning and ruthless in his career. But who would keep a pack of hounds; or what gentleman, at the sound of the horn, and at peep of day, would mount his steed, and for hours together, "sub jove frigido," or a vertical sun, pursue the windings of this wily quadruped, if, just as night came on, and his stratagems and strength were nearly exhausted, a saucy intruder, who had not shared in the honors or labors of the chase, were permitted to come in at the death, and bear away in triumph the object of pursuit? Whatever Justinian may have thought of the matter, it must be recollected that his code was compiled many hundred years ago, and it would be very hard indeed, at the distance of so many centuries, not to have a right to establish a rule for ourselves. In his day, we read of no order of men who made it a business, in the language of the declaration in this cause, "with hounds and dogs to find, start, pursue, hunt, and chase," these animals, and that, too, without any other motive than the preservation of Roman poultry; if this diversion had been then in fashion, the lawyers who composed his institutes, would have taken care not to pass it by, without suitable encouragement. If any thing, therefore, in the digests or pandects shall appear to militate against the defendant in error, who, on this occasion, was the fox hunter, we have only to say tempora mutantur; and if men themselves change with the times, why should not laws also undergo an alteration?

It may be expected, however, by the learned counsel, that more particular notice be taken of their authorities. I have examined them all, and feel great difficulty in determining, whether to acquire dominion over a thing, before in common, it be sufficient that we barely see it, or know where it is, or wish for it, or make a declaration of our will respecting it; or whether, in the case of wild beasts, setting a trap, or lying in wait, or starting, or pursuing, be enough; or if an actual wounding, or killing, or bodily tact and occupation be necessary. Writers on general law, who have favored us with their speculations on these points, differ on them all; but, great as is the diversity of sentiment among them, some conclusion must be adopted on the question immediately before us.

Now, as we are without any municipal regulations of our own, and the pursuit here, for aught that appears on the case, being with dogs and hounds of imperial stature, we are at liberty to adopt one of the provisions just cited, which comports also with the learned conclusion of Barbeyrac, that property in animals *ferae naturae* may be acquired without bodily touch or manucaption, provided the pursuer be within reach, or have a reasonable prospect (which certainly existed here) of taking, what he has thus discovered an intention of converting to his own use.

When we reflect also that the interest of our husbandmen, the most useful of men in any community, will be advanced by the destruction of a beast so pernicious and incorrigible, we cannot greatly err, in saying, that a pursuit like the present, through waste and unoccupied lands, and which must inevitably and speedily have terminated in corporal possession, or bodily seisin, confers such a right to the object of it, as to make any one a wrongdoer, who shall interfere and shoulder the spoil. The justice's judgment ought therefore, in my opinion, be affirmed.

Judgment of reversal.

NOTES AND QUESTIONS

1. Compare Pierson v. Post with Ghen v. Rich, 8 F. 159 (D. Mass. 1881). Plaintiff, a professional whaler, had mortally wounded a fin-back whale with a gun-fired bomb lance made expressly for that purpose. Killed in the easterly part of Massachusetts Bay, the whale sank to the bottom, but a few days later rose to the surface and eventually floated to shore. There, a stranger found the beached carcass and sold it to the defendant, who stripped off the blubber and tried out, i.e., purified, the oil. When plaintiff learned of this, he sued defendant and recovered a judgment for the market value of the oil less the cost of preparing it for market.

The usage on Cape Cod, for many years, has been that the person who kills a whale in the manner and under the circumstances described, owns it, and this right has never been disputed until this case. . . . [The usage] requires in the first taker the only act of appropriation that is possible in the nature of the case. Unless it is sustained, this branch of industry must necessarily cease, for no person would engage in it if the fruits of his labor could be appropriated by any chance finder. . . . That the rule works well in practice is shown by the extent of the industry which has grown up under it, and the general acquiescence of a whole community interested to dispute it. It is by no means clear that without regard to usage the common-law would not reach the same result. [8 Fed. at 160, 162]

The defendant in Ghen v. Rich did not know that plaintiff had killed the whale but knew, or could readily have learned, that a professional whaler, using a bomb lance, had caused the mortal injury. How important is that?

2. Compare Pierson v. Post with Keeble v. Hickeringill, 103 Eng. Rep. 1127, the early 18th century English case that Judge Tompkins distinguishes in his opinion. Plaintiff's land contained a pond on which the plaintiff set decoys in order to attract wildfowl, which he shot and marketed. Defendant, in order to disrupt plaintiff's business, discharged guns that frightened the wild-fowl away. Plaintiff obtained a money judgment for his damages.

[T]his action is brought for disturbing the wild ducks coming to [plaintiff's] decoy and so is in the nature of disturbing him from exercising his trade. Where a violent or malicious act is done to a man's occupation, profession, or way of getting livelihood, there an action lies in all cases. But if a man doth him damage by using the same employment; as if Mr. Hickeringill had set up another decoy on his own ground near the plaintiff's, and that had spoiled the custom of the plaintiff, no action would lie, because he had as much liberty to make and use a decoy as the plaintiff. . . . [Id. at 1128]

3. The lands in Pierson v. Post were "wild and uninhabited." Suppose that the plaintiff Post had owned these lands, however. Would (should) this have changed the result? Compare State v. Repp, 104 Iowa 305, 73 N.W. 829 (1898) (title in landowner) with McKee v. Gratz, 260 U.S. 127 (1922) (general custom to hunt or fish on wild, unenclosed lands: jury may imply a license to do so).

CONTI v. ASPCA
77 Misc. 2d 61, 353 N.Y.S.2d 288 (Civ. Ct. 1974)

RODELL, J. Chester is a parrot. He is fourteen inches tall, with a green coat, yellow head and an orange streak on his wings. Red splashes cover his left shoulder. Chester is a show parrot, used by the defendant ASPCA in various educational exhibitions presented to groups of children.

On June 28, 1973, during an exhibition in Kings Point, New York, Chester flew the coop and found refuge in the tallest tree he could find. For seven hours the defendant sought to retrieve Chester. Ladders proved to be too short. Offers of food were steadfastly ignored. With the approach of darkness, search efforts were discontinued. A return to the area on the next morning revealed that Chester was gone.

On July 5th, 1973 the plaintiff, who resides in Belle Harbor, Queens County, had occasion to see a green-hued parrot with a yellow head and red splashes seated in his backyard. His offer of food was eagerly accepted by the bird. This was repeated on three occasions each day for a period of two weeks. This display of human kindness was rewarded by the parrot's finally entering the plaintiff's home, where he was placed in a cage.

The next day, the plaintiff phoned the defendant ASPCA and requested advice as to the care of a parrot he had found. Thereupon the defendant sent two representatives to the plaintiff's home. Upon examination, they claimed that it was the missing parrot, Chester, and removed it from the plaintiff's home.

Upon refusal of the defendant ASPCA to return the bird, the plaintiff now brings this action in replevin.

The issues presented to the Court are twofold: One, is the parrot in question truly Chester, the missing bird? Two, if it is in fact Chester, who is entitled to its ownership?

The plaintiff presented witnesses who testified that a parrot similar to the one in question was seen in the neighborhood prior to July 5, 1973. He further contended that a parrot could not fly the distance between Kings Point and Belle Harbor in so short a period of time, and therefore the bird in question was not in fact Chester.

The representatives of the defendant ASPCA were categorical in their testimony that the parrot was indeed Chester, that he was unique because of his size, color and habits. They claimed that Chester said "hello" and could dangle by his legs. During the entire trial the Court had the parrot under close scrutiny, but at no time did it exhibit any of these characteristics. The Court called upon the parrot to indicate by name or other mannerism an affinity to either of the claimed owners. Alas, the parrot stood mute.

Upon all the credible evidence the Court does find as a fact that the parrot in question is indeed Chester and is the same parrot which escaped from the possession of the ASPCA on June 28, 1973.

The Court must now deal with the plaintiff's position, that the ownership of the defendant was a qualified one and upon the parrot's escape, ownership passed to the first individual who captured it and placed it under his control.

The law is well settled that the true owner of lost property is entitled to the return thereof as against any person finding same. (In re Wright's Estate, 15 Misc. 2d 225, 177 N.Y.S.2d 410) (36A C.J.S. Finding Lost Goods §3).

This general rule is not applicable when the property lost is an animal. In such cases the Court must inquire as to whether the animal was domesticated or ferae naturae (wild).

Where an animal is wild, its owner can only acquire a qualified right of property which is wholly lost when it escapes from its captor with no intention of returning.

Thus in Mullett v. Bradley, 24 Misc. 695, 53 N.Y.S. 781, an untrained and undomesticated sea lion escaped after being shipped from the West to the East Coast. The sea lion escaped and was again captured in a fish pond off the New Jersey Coast. The original owner sued the finder for its return. The court held that the sea lion was a wild animal (ferae naturae), and when it returned to its wild state, the original owner's property rights were extinguished.

In Amory v. Flyn, 10 Johns. (N.Y.) 102, plaintiff sought to recover geese of the wild variety which had strayed from the owner. In granting judgment to the plaintiff, the court pointed out that the geese had been tamed by the plaintiff and therefore were unable to regain their natural liberty.

This important distinction was also demonstrated in Manning v. Mitcherson, 69 Ga. 447, 450-451, 52 A.L.R. 1063, where the plaintiff sought the return of a pet canary. In holding for the plaintiff the court stated "To say that if one has a canary bird, mocking bird, parrot, or any other bird so kept, and it should accidentally escape from its cage to the street, or to a neighboring house, that the first person who caught it would be its owner is wholly at variance with all our views of right and justice."

The Court finds that Chester was a domesticated animal, subject to training and discipline. Thus the rule of ferae naturae does not prevail and the defendant as true owner is entitled to regain possession.

The Court wishes to commend the plaintiff for his acts of kindness and compassion to the parrot during the period that it was lost and was gratified to receive the defendant's aassurance that the first parrot available would be offered to the plaintiff for adoption.

Judgment for defendant dismissing the complaint without costs.

NOTE

During a storm, a Himalayan tiger escapes from a zoo and is captured several days later. To whom does the tiger belong: the zoo or the party capturing the escaped beast? Should the outcome depend only upon whether the animal is "domesticated, subject to training and discipline," to borrow a phrase from the parrot opinion? Compare Reese v. Hughes, 144 Miss. 304, 109 So. 731 (1926) (original owner loses title if fugitive animal has no tendency to return) with Stephens & Co. v. Albers, 81 Colo. 488, 256 P. 15 (1927) (original owner retains title if escaped animal is far from its native habitat and reasonably identifiable).

COMMONWEALTH v. AGWAY, INC.

210 Pa. Super. Ct. 150, 232 A.2d 69 (1967)

Jacobs, J. The Commonwealth of Pennsylvania brought this suit in trespass to recover damages for the value of fish killed as a result of pollution of the South Branch of French Creek and French Creek near Union City. The complaint alleged that the discharge of certain chemicals into the creek caused the death of some 12,000 fish and 60,000 minnows, all such fish being in a state of freedom in the inland waters of the Commonwealth.

The court below dismissed the complaint on the grounds that the Commonwealth did not have a property interest in such ferae naturae that would support a suit in trespass for damages, and that the exclusive remedy for the Commonwealth was the penal provisions of The Fish Law of 1959, Act of December 15, 1959, P.L. 1779, as amended, 30 P.S. §1 et seq.[1]

The controlling question in this case is whether the Commonwealth has a property interest in fish in a state of freedom, the invasion of which will support an action in trespass for monetary damages. We agree with the court below that the Commonwealth has no such property interest and affirm the dismissal of the complaint.

Fish running wild in the streams of a state or nation are ferae naturae. 2 Blackstone, Commentaries 403. They are not the subject of property until they are reduced to possession, Wallis v. Mease, 3 Binney 546 (1811) and, if alive, property in them exists only so long as possession continues. See, e.g., Mullet v. Bradley, 24 Misc. 695, 53 N.Y.S. 781 (1898); Reese v. Hughes, 144 Miss. 304, 109 So. 731 (1926); James v. Wood, 82 Me. 173, 19 A. 160, 8 A.L.R. 448 (1889); Young v. Hichens, 1 Dav. & Mer. 592, 6 Q.B. 606 (1844). The Commonwealth does not allege a property interest by way of possession of the fish. Instead, it admits the fish were in a state of freedom in Pennsylvania waters, but asserts that it has a property interest either as sovereign or proprietor in all wild game and fish in the Commonwealth sufficient to allow its recovery of damages.

Neither this court nor the court below nor the Commonwealth has discovered any case which has held that a state has such a property interest in wild game and fish that it could be the subject of a tortious invasion. To support its position the Commonwealth relies on cases involving the validity of

---

1. That act provides, inter alia:

§200. No person shall put or place in any waters within or on the boundaries of this Commonwealth any electricity, explosives or any poisonous substances whatsoever for the purpose of catching, injuring or killing fish. . . .

§202. Any person violating the preceding provisions of this article shall, on conviction as provided in chapter 14 of this act, be sentenced to pay a fine of not less than one hundred dollars ($100.00) nor more than one thousand dollars ($1,000.00).

§310. It is the intent of this act to prescribe an exclusive system for the angling, catching and taking of fish, and for their propagation, management and protection in waters within, bounding on, or adjacent to, this Commonwealth. . . .

regulatory measures enacted by states to preserve and protect wild game, and argues that since such cases refer to wild game as the property of the state, it follows that the state also "owns" wild game for purposes of a suit in trespass.

Game and fish in a wild state often have been described as the property of the state, but an examination of the cases demonstrates that the interest of the state is that of a sovereign, not an owner. Thus in Commonwealth v. Papsone, 44 Pa. Super. 128, *aff'd*, Patsone v. Commonwealth, 231 Pa. 46, 79 A. 928, 232 U.S. 138, 34 S. Ct. 281, 58 L. Ed. 539 (1910), although this court referred to wild animals as the property of the sovereign, the case itself involved only the validity of hunting regulations and the holding was based solely on the sovereign power of the state to regulate and prohibit hunting and did not depend on any state property rights in the wild game.

In McCready v. Virginia, 94 U.S. 391, 24 L. Ed. 248 (1877), all that was decided was that the state could reserve to its own residents the exclusive right to grow oysters on the bed of a tidal river. While the case refers to the state as owning the tide waters and the fish in them it recognizes the limited meaning of such ownership by saying "so far as they are capable of ownership." Likewise in Geer v. State of Connecticut, 161 U.S. 519, 16 S. Ct. 600, 40 L. Ed. 793 (1895), in holding that Connecticut could prohibit the transportation of any killed game beyond the state the court based its decision on the power of the state to regulate the acquisition of title by an individual. Both cases demonstrate the exercise of the sovereign power and not the assertion of proprietary rights of the state.

In two instances the United States Supreme Court has referred to state ownership of wild game with some skepticism. In State of Missouri v. Holland, 252 U.S. 416, 434, 40 S. Ct. 382, 64 L. Ed. 641, 648 (1920), Justice Holmes said of the proposition that states own wild game: "To put the claim of the State upon title is to lean upon a slender reed. Wild birds are not in the possession of anyone; and possession is the beginning of ownership." In Toomer v. Witsell, 334 U.S. 385, 68 S. Ct. 1156, 92 L. Ed. 1460 (1946), the Supreme Court found a violation of the Privileges and Immunities Clause in a South Carolina statute which imposed a fishing license fee on nonresidents 100 times greater than the fee imposed on residents. The court said there: "The whole ownership theory, in fact, is now generally regarded as but a fiction expressive in legal shorthand of the importance to its people that a state have power to preserve and regulate the exploitation of an important resource." 334 U.S. 402, 68 S. Ct. 1165, 92 L. Ed. 1474. The confusion as to whether a state owns fish in the sense of owning other state property was traced by the court to Roman times: "The fiction apparently gained currency partly as a result of the confusion between the Roman term *imperium* or governmental power to regulate, and *dominium* or ownership. Power over fish and game was, in origin, *imperium*." Ibid. at footnote 37, 68 S. Ct. 1156.

Regardless of the terminology historically applied, we deal here with a power of the state to preserve and control a natural resource for the enjoyment of all citizens. The Commonwealth has the power for the common good to determine when, by whom and under what conditions fish running wild may be captured and thus owned and the power to control the resale and transportation of such fish thereby qualifying the ownership of the captor. It has this power as a result of its sovereignty over the land and the people. But it is not the owner of the fish as it is of its lands and buildings so as to support a civil action for damages resulting from the destruction of those fish which have not been reduced to possession.

Affirmed.

WRIGHT, J., files a concurring opinion.

WRIGHT, J. (concurring). I am not prepared to agree with the majority that the Commonwealth lacks sufficient property interest in fish upon which to predicate a trespass action for their negligent destruction. Fish constitute an important natural resource providing both food and recreation for our citizens. The Pennsylvania Fish Commission operates a number of hatcheries and regularly stocks the waters of the Commonwealth, including the stream here involved. I am concurring in the result on the ground, primarily relied upon by the court below, that The Fish Law of 1959 contains an express statement by the legislature that it is intended "to prescribe an exclusive system for . . . their propagation, management and protection."

NOTE

The *Agway* opinion cites Geer v. Connecticut, 161 U.S. 519 (1896) which the Supreme Court has since overruled. Hughes v. Oklahoma, 441 U.S. 322, 325 (1979).

Hughes operated a commercial minnow business near Wichita Falls, Texas. An Oklahoma game ranger arrested Hughes for transporting into Texas a load of natural minnows which he had purchased from an Oklahoma dealer. Oklahoma law barred the extraterritorial shipment of natural minnows seined within the state. Convicted under the state law, Hughes appealed to the Supreme Court. The Court agreed with Hughes that the statute offended the Commerce Clause and, in reaching that conclusion, overruled Geer v. Connecticut.

The earlier case had allowed Connecticut to forbid the transportation beyond the state of game birds lawfully killed within the state. That decision rested on the holding that no interstate commerce was involved since the state had the power "as representative for its citizens who 'owned' in common all wild animals within the State, to control not only the *taking* of game but the *ownership* of game that had been lawfully reduced to possession. By virtue of this power, Connecticut could qualify the ownership of wild game taken within the State by, for example, prohibiting its removal from the State." 441 U.S. 327.

Justice Brennan, writing for the Court in Hughes v. Oklahoma, recalled that the two dissenters in the *Geer* case had rejected as "artificial" and "formalistic" the dichotomy between "ownership" and "commerce" in wild game and would have affirmed the State's power to protect wild game only "so far as such protection . . . does not contravene the power of Congress in the regulation of interstate commerce." After eighty-three years, during which *Geer* suffered steady erosion, the dissenters finally had their way.

But the *Hughes* decision spawned its own dissent written by Justice Rehnquist for himself and Chief Justice Burger:

> Admittedly, a state does not "own" the wild creatures within its borders in any conventional sense of the word. . . . But the concept expressed by the "ownership" doctrine is not obsolete. . . . This Court long has recognized that the ownership language of *Geer* and similar cases is simply a shorthand way of describing a State's substantial interest in preserving and regulating the exploitation of the fish and game and other natural resources within its boundaries for the benefit of its citizens. . . . [T]he range of regulations that a State may adopt under these circumstances is extremely broad, particularly where, as here, the burden on interstate commerce is, at most, minimal. [441 U.S. 322, at 341-344]

§2.2   Lost and Found Goods

ARMORY v. DELAMIRIE
93 Eng. Rep. 664 (K.B. 1722)

The plaintiff being a chimney sweeper's boy found a jewel and carried it to the defendant's shop (who was a goldsmith) to know what it was, and delivered it into the hands of the apprentice, who under pretence of weighing it, took out the stones, and calling to the master to let him know it came to three halfpence, the master offered the boy the money, who refused to take it, and insisted to have the thing again: whereupon the apprentice delivered him back the socket without the stones. And now in trover against the master these points were ruled:

1.   That the finder of a jewel, though he does not by such finding acquire an absolute property or ownership, yet he has such a property as will enable him to keep it against all but the rightful owner, and consequently may maintain trover.

2.   That the action well lay against the master, who gives a credit to his apprentice, and is answerable for his neglect.

3.   As to the value of the jewel several of the trade were examined to prove what a jewel of the finest water that would fit the socket would be worth; and the Chief Justice directed the jury, that unless the defendant did produce the jewel, and shew it not to be of the finest water, they should presume the strongest against him, and make the value of the best jewels the measure of their damages: which they accordingly did.

NOTE

By contrast, compare South Staffordshire Water Co. v. Sharman, 2 Q.B. 44 (1896). P hired D, a workman, to clean out a pool on P's land. D found two gold rings in the mud at the bottom of the pool. The owner of the rings could not be found. Held: P entitled to recover rings: "where a person has possession of house or land, with a manifest intention to exercise control over it and the things which may be upon or in it, then, if something is found on that land, whether by an employee of the owner or by a stranger, the presumption is that the possession of that thing is in the owner of the locus in quo."

HURLEY v. CITY OF NIAGARA FALLS
30 A.D.2d 89, 289 N.Y.S.2d 889 (4th Dept. 1968)

Bastow, J. This appeal presents the issue of the respective rights to "lost property" as between the finder thereof and the owners of a private residence in the light of Article 7-B of Personal Property Law added thereto by Chapter 860 of the Laws of 1958.

The defendants, Moraca, since the early 1950s have owned a residence in the city of Niagara Falls. In 1962 they contracted with plaintiff to build a recreation room in the basement. While attempting to remove a pipe plaintiff found $4,990 in currency hidden behind a wooden block on the floor of a cabinet-type sink. There were several bundles of bills each bound by a so-called bank wrapper. The packages appeared to have been water soaked from time to time. The bills had consecutive serial numbers. The Moracas knew nothing about the money and after prior litigation, Moraca v. Hurley, 22 A.D.2d 473, 256 N.Y.S.2d 722, it was turned over to the local Police Department.

At common law the principle was early (1722) established that the finder acquires a right in a found chattel good against the whole world except the true owner (Armory v. Delamirie, 1 Strange 505, 93 E.R. 664). Among the many subtleties that developed in this area of the law one was presented by the conflicting claims of the finder and the owner of the premises where the finding occurred. In answering this question the decisions through the years developed two further refinements. First, whether the finding occurred in a place open to the public or in a private place (Cf. Cohen v. Manufacturers Safe Deposit Co., 297 N.Y. 266, 270, 78 N.E.2d 604). Second, whether the chattels had been lost or mislaid. "A loss is always involuntary; there can be no intent to part with the ownership of lost property. Mislaid property is property which the owner voluntarily and intentionally laid down in a place where he can again resort to it, and then forgets where he put it. Property is not 'lost' unless the owner parts with it involuntarily and unintentionally, and does not at any time thereafter know where to find it." (1 Am. Jur. 2d, Abandoned, Lost and Unclaimed Property, §2; Foulke v. N.Y. Consolidated R.R. Co., 228 N.Y. 269, 273, 274, 127 N.E. 237, 9 A.L.R. 1384).

The general common law rule is that the finder of mislaid property on premises of another acquires no special property in it and that the right of possession as against all except the true owners is in the owner or occupant of the premises where the property is discovered. The rule is based on the legal fiction that mislaid property is presumed to have been left in the custody of the owner or occupier of the premises upon which it is found. (1 Am. Jur. 2d, Abandoned, Lost and Unclaimed Property, §23; 1 N.Y. Jur. Abandoned and Escheated Property, §37; Dolitsky v. Dollar Savings Bank, 203 Misc. 262, 265, 118 N.Y.S.2d 65).

A further exception, however, to the common law doctrine of mislaid property (and one here pertinent) is the rule that treasure trove which by modern definition includes paper money and not only buried treasure but money hidden in places above the ground (23 Tulane L.R. 409 and cases therein cited), belongs to the finder and not to the owner of the locus (1 Am. Jur. 2d, Abandoned, Lost and Unclaimed Property, §21).

Article 7-B was added to the Personal Property Law as the result of recommendations, studies and hearings of the Law Revision Commission in successive years (Report of N.Y. Law Rev. Comm., p. 367 et seq.; N.Y. Legis. Doc., 1957, No. 65(L); Report of N.Y. Law Rev. Comm., p. 19 et seq., N.Y. Legis. Doc., 1958, No. 65(A)). The earlier document (pp. 393-428; 481-483) contains exhaustive studies of the law of lost property made at the direction of the Commission. It is made clear that the recommendations were designed to abolish the distinction between lost and mislaid property (N.Y. Legis. Doc., 1957, No. 65(L), note (5), p. 375).

This is made explicit in section 251 of the article where (subd. 3) "lost property" is defined as including lost or mislaid property and further provides that "Abandoned property, waifs and treasure trove . . ." and other property which is found, shall be presumed to be lost property. This section (subd. 5) further defines a "finder" as the person who first takes possession of lost property. "Property" is defined (subd. 1), with irrelevant exceptions, as "money, goods, chattels and tangible personal property."

The general scheme of the enactment (§252) requires the finder of property of $10 or more in value to deposit it with the proper police authorities upon whom are imposed certain obligations (§253). Upon expiration of the time required for retention by the police,[1] if the property has not been returned to the owner or has not been the object of any other written claim, it shall be turned over to the finder in whom title then vests (§§254, 257).

This right of the finder is subject, however, to certain exceptions (§256), here immaterial,[2] except subdivision two which provides that an employer shall have the rights of a finder where the property is found by an employee under a duty to deliver it to his employer. Upon the trial a feeble effort was

---

1. The retention period ranges from 6 months for property valued at $500 or less up to 3 years for property valued at $3,000 or more.—ED.

2. One exception involves a finder whose presence on the premises is a crime. But even he gets to keep the property if the owner of the premises fails to make a claim within the prescribed period.—ED.

made to establish that plaintiff was an employee of defendants, Moraca. The trial court found that he was an independent contractor and the proof sustains that finding.

We reject the contention of respondents that the absence from the statute of an express provision giving a finder of property on private premises a right paramount to the owner thereof makes applicable the former common law rule. That rule, as stated, was based on the reasoning that such property was in the constructive possession of the owner and could not be "lost" in the sense of the law of lost property—it was merely "mislaid." (36A C.J.S. Finding Lost Goods §1).

The statute (§251, subd. 3), as we have seen, abolished the distinction between "lost" and "mislaid" property. There is no indication that the Legislature intended the former "public place—private place" distinction to survive. This view is fortified by other provisions of the enactment (§256, subds. 3 and 4) which establish differing procedures where property is found in certain public places (safe deposit premises, banks and transportation facilities).

We conclude that plaintiff, as the person who first took possession of the money, was the finder thereof. The statutory period for the retention by the police having expired it should be delivered to him at which time title thereto shall vest in him.

The judgment should be reversed and such relief granted to plaintiff.

Judgment unanimously reversed on the law and facts, with costs, and judgment granted for plaintiff.

GOLDMAN, DEL VECCHIO, WITMER and HENRY, JJ., concur.

HURLEY v. CITY OF NIAGARA FALLS

25 N.Y.2d 687, 254 N.E.2d 917, 306 N.Y.S.2d 689 (1969)

Order affirmed, without costs, in the opinion at the Appellate Division.

BURKE, BREITEL, JASEN and GIBSON, JJ., concur.

SCILEPPI, J., dissents and votes to reverse in the following opinion in which FULD, C.J., and BERGAN, J., concur.

SCILEPPI, J. (dissenting). Article 7-B (§252, subd. 1) of the Personal Property Law, Consol. Laws, c. 41, provides in relevant part that "any person who finds lost property of the value of ten dollars or more or comes into possession of property of the value of ten dollars or more with knowledge that it is lost property . . . shall, within ten days after the finding or acquisition of possession thereof, either return it to the owner or report such finding or acquisition of possession and deposit such property in a police station or police headquarters of the city where the finding occurred".

In the latter part of 1962 the appellants, Mr. and Mrs. Moraca, engaged Edward Hurley, the respondent herein, to remodel the basement of their home located in the City of Niagara Falls. While attempting to remove a pipe under a sink, Hurley found $4,990 in currency hidden behind a block on the floor of the cabinet enclosing the sink. The Moracas told Hurley that the money was not theirs and they had no idea how it had gotten there. Hurley then suggested and the Moracas agreed that for the purposes of safekeeping, Hurley should place the money in the safe at the Niagara Falls Air Force Base where Hurley was a full-time civilian employee. Hurley, however, did not take the money to the Base but rather took it home with him and sometime thereafter, apparently long after the 10-day statutory period had elapsed, unsuccessfully attempted to spend some of the money in a department store.

On cross-examination Hurley testified:

Q. Did somebody representing the store call the Police Department?
A. Yes, sir.
Q. What did you tell the police officer in reference to this money?
A. I didn't tell him anything, sir. I asked him if I could contact my attorney.
Q. Did the police officer ask you where you got the money or found the money?
A. Yes, he asked me where I got the money from.
Q. What did you tell the police officer?
A. I told him at the time that I might have got it in change.
The Court: May have got it in change?
The Witness: In change, cashing a check.
By Mr. Gellman:
Q. You did not tell the police officer the truth, is that correct?
A. I did not tell the police officer the truth, yes, sir.

Sometime thereafter, apparently in 1964, the appellants instituted an action against Hurley for conversion. It was not until after the Appellate Division unanimously affirmed the dismissal of the action as being premature (Moraca v. Hurley, 22 A.D.2d 473, 256 N.Y.S.2d 722) that the money in question was finally turned over to the proper authorities—more than two years after Hurley had found it.

The respondent argues that the mere failure to comply with the statute in no way affects the statutorily vested rights of the finder to the property. We do not agree; for even assuming, arguendo, that Hurley's rights under the statute are superior to those of the Moracas, it is our opinion that Hurley's failure to comply with the statutory provisions precludes him from asserting any rights under the statute which he so flagrantly disregarded.

While it is true that the statute does not expressly provide for defeating the rights of the finder by his failure to comply (although it does impose possible criminal punishment for willful noncompliance [§252, subd. 3]), it is inconceivable that the Legislature, in enacting article 7-B, ever intended such a strict application of the statute so as to bring about the offensive result reached by the majority. In a real sense the majority is permitting a person who intentionally violates the criminal law to profit by his own wrong. This is manifestly repugnant to basic concepts of justice and common sense.

Surely the far better rule to follow and the one which would best bring about the policy of the statute to increase the likelihood of restoring the property to its true owner is to view the finder's statutory rights in the property from the movement of acquisition as being vested subject to being divested by his failure to, at the very least, substantially comply with the statute.

Of course, it is fundamental that one cannot establish title in himself merely by showing someone else to have no rights in the property. It is, therefore, evident that, based on the above discussion merely defeating Hurley's rights to the property, we could not, without more, hold that the Moracas have title to the property in question.

It is our opinion, however, that even if we assume that compliance with the statute is not a prerequisite to obtaining rights thereunder, the Moracas' rights are superior to Hurley's under the statute.

Section 256 of article 7-B provides for certain exceptions to the general rule giving the first one to take physical possession of the property superior rights. Subdivision 2 of section 256 provides: "2. If the finder is an officer or employee of the state or of a public corporation and takes possession of the property in the course of his official duty, the state or public corporation shall be deemed to be the finder for the purposes of section two hundred fifty-four and section two hundred fifty-seven of this chapter. *If, in any other case, the finder is an employee under a duty to deliver the lost property to his employer, the employer shall have the rights of the finder as provided in section two hundred fifty-four if, before the property is delivered to the finder by the police, he shall file with the police having custody of the property a written notice asserting such rights.*" (Emphasis added.)

While it is true that the trial court determined that Hurley was an independent contractor, we need not give the term "employee" as used in the statute such a restrictive reading so as to limit it to only those employees whose liability would be imputed to their employers. Rather the term should be construed broadly to encompass all persons engaged to perform tasks; and if in the course of performing those tasks, property is found on the premises of the employer, the "employee" is under a duty to deliver it to his employer.

If we were to reach a contrary conclusion it would necessarily follow, e.g., that if A buys a used desk and hires B, a carpenter, to repair it, B would acquire superior rights, under the statute, to any valuables he might find in a compartment of the desk which had been placed there by a prior owner. Certainly such an unjust result should be avoided by placing the interpretation on the statute as we have evidenced above.

Accordingly, the order of the Appellate Division should be reversed and the judgment of Supreme Court, Niagara County, reinstated.

Order affirmed, etc.

FAVORITE v. MILLER

176 Conn. 310, 407 A.2d 974 (1978)

BOGDANSKI, J. On July 9, 1776, a band of patriots, hearing news of the Declaration of Independence, toppled the equestrian statue of King George

III, which was located in Bowling Green Park in lower Manhattan, New York. The statue, of gilded lead, was then hacked apart and the pieces ferried over Long Island Sound and loaded onto wagons at Norwalk, Connecticut, to be hauled some fifty miles northward to Oliver Wolcott's bullet-molding foundry in Litchfield, there to be cast into bullets. On the journey to Litchfield, the wagoners halted at Wilton, Connecticut, and while the patriots were imbibing, the loyalists managed to steal back pieces of the statue. The wagonload of the pieces lifted by the Tories was scattered about in the area of the Davis Swamp in Wilton and fragments of the statue have continued to turn up in that area since that time.

Although the above events have been dramatized in the intervening years, the unquestioned historical facts are: (1) the destruction of the statue; (2) cartage of the pieces to the Wolcott Foundry; (3) the pause at Wilton where part of the load was scattered over the Wilton area by loyalists; and (4) repeated discoveries of fragments over the last century.

In 1972, the defendant, Louis Miller, determined that a part of the statute might be located within property owned by the plaintiffs. On October 16 he entered the area of the Davis Swamp owned by the plaintiffs although he knew it to be private property. With the aid of a metal detector, he discovered a statuary fragment fifteen inches square and weighing twenty pounds which was embedded ten inches below the soil. He dug up this fragment and removed it from the plaintiffs' property. The plaintiffs did not learn that a piece of the statue of King George III had been found on their property until they read about it in the newspaper, long after it had been removed.

In due course, the piece of the statue made its way back to New York City, where the defendant agreed to sell it to the Museum of the City of New York for $5500. The museum continues to hold it pending resolution of this controversy.

In March of 1973, the plaintiffs instituted this action to have the fragment returned to them and the case was submitted to the court on a stipulation of facts. The trial court found the issues for the plaintiffs, from which judgment the defendant appealed to this court. The sole issue presented on appeal is whether the claim of the defendant, as finder, is superior to that of the plaintiffs, as owners of the land upon which the historic fragment was discovered.

Traditionally, when questions have arisen concerning the rights of the finder as against the person upon whose land the property was found, the resolution has turned upon the characterization given the property. Typically, if the property was found to be "lost" or "abandoned," the finder would prevail, whereas if the property was characterized as "mislaid," the owner or occupier of the land would prevail.

Lost property has traditionally been defined as involving an involuntary parting, i.e., where there is no intent on the part of the loser to part with the ownership of the property. Foster v. Fidelity Safe Deposit Co., 264 Mo. 89, 174 S.W. 376 (1915); Kuykendall v. Fisher, 61 W. Va. 87, 56 S.E. 48 (1906); 1 Am. Jur. 2d 4, Abandoned, Lost, and Unclaimed Property, §2; annot., 170

A.L.R. 706. Abandonment, in turn, has been defined as the voluntary relinquishment of ownership of property without reference to any particular person
or purpose; Ellis v. Brown, 177 F.2d 677 (6th Cir. 1949); Jackson v. Steinberg,
186 Or. 129, 200 P.2d 376 (1948), *rehearing denied,* 186 Or. 129, 205 P.2d 562
(1949); annot., 170 A.L.R. 708; i.e., a "throwing away" of the property concerned; Foulke v. New York Consolidated R. Co., 228 N.Y. 269, 273, 127 N.E.
237 (1920); while mislaid property is defined as that which is intentionally
placed by the owner where he can obtain custody of it, but afterwards forgotten. Foster v. Fidelity Safe Deposit Co., *supra;* Loucks v. Gallogly, 1 Misc. 22,
23 N.Y.S. 126 (1892); annot., 9 A.L.R. 1388, 1390.

It should be noted that the classification of property as "lost," "abandoned," or "mislaid" requires that a court determine the intent or mental state
of the unknown party who at some time in the past parted with the ownership
or control of the property.

The trial court in this case applied the traditional approach and ruled in
favor of the landowners on the ground that the piece of the statue found by
Miller was "mislaid." The factual basis for that conclusion is set out in the
finding, where the court found that "the loyalists did not wish to have the
pieces [in their possession] during the turmoil surrounding the Revolutionary
War and hid them in a place where they could resort to them [after the war],
but forgot where they put them."

The defendant contends that the finding was made without evidence and
that the court's conclusion "is legally impossible now after 200 years with no
living claimants to the fragment and the secret of its burial having died with
them." While we cannot agree that the court's conclusion was legally impossible, we do agree that any conclusion as to the mental state of persons engaged
in events which occurred over two hundred years ago would be of a conjectural nature and as such does not furnish an adequate basis for determining
rights of twentieth century claimants.

The defendant argues further that his rights in the statue are superior to
those of anyone except the true owner (i.e., the British government). He
presses this claim on the ground that the law has traditionally favored the
finder as against all but the true owner, and that because his efforts brought
the statue to light, he should be allowed to reap the benefits of his discovery. In
his brief, he asserts: "As with archeologists forever probing and unearthing the
past, to guide man for the betterment of those to follow, explorers like Miller
deserve encouragement, and reward, in their selfless pursuit of the hidden, the
unknown."

There are, however, some difficulties with the defendant's position. The
first concerns the defendant's characterization of himself as a selfless seeker
after knowledge. The facts in the record do not support such a conclusion. The
defendant admitted that he was in the business of selling metal detectors and
that he has used his success in finding the statue as advertising to boost his
sales of such metal detectors, and that the advertising has been financially
rewarding. Further, there is the fact that he signed a contract with the City

Museum of New York for the sale of the statuary piece and that he stands to profit thereby.

Moreover, even if we assume his motive to be that of historical research alone, that fact will not justify his entering upon the property of another without permission. It is unquestioned that in today's world even archeologists must obtain permission from owners of property and the government of the country involved before they can conduct their explorations. Similarly, mountaineers must apply for permits, sometimes years in advance of their proposed expeditions. On a more familiar level, backpackers and hikers must often obtain permits before being allowed access to certain of our national parks and forests, even though that land is public and not private. Similarly, hunters and fishermen wishing to enter upon private property must first obtain the permission of the owner before they embark upon their respective pursuits.

Although few cases are to be found in this area of the law, one line of cases which have dealt with this issue has held that except where the trespass is trivial or merely technical, the fact that the finder is trespassing is sufficient to deprive him of his normal preference over the owner of the place where the property was found. Barker v. Bates, 30 Mass. (13 Pick.) 255, 23 Am. Dec. 678 (1832); Brown, Personal Property (2d Ed.) §12, p. 24, n.10; Hibbert v. McKiernan, 2 K.B. 142 (1948). The basis for the rule is that a wrongdoer should not be allowed to profit by his wrongdoing. Note, 21 Minn. L. Rev. 191 (1937); Morton, "Public Policy and the Finders Cases," 1 Wyo. L.J. 101, 105 (1947). Another line of cases holds that property, other than treasure trove,[2] which is found embedded in the earth is the property of the owner of the locus in quo. . . . The presumption in such cases is that possession of the article found is in the owner of the land and that the finder acquires no rights to the article found.

The defendant, by his own admission, knew that he was trespassing when he entered upon the property of the plaintiffs. He admitted that he was told by Gertrude Merwyn, the librarian of the Wilton Historical Society, *before* he went into the Davis Swamp area, that the land was privately owned and that Mrs. Merwyn recommended that he call the owners, whom she named, and obtain permission before he began his explorations. He also admitted that when he later told Mrs. Merwyn about his discovery, she again suggested that he contact the owners of the property, but that he failed to do so.

In the stipulation of facts submitted to the court, the defendant admitted entering the Davis Swamp property "with the belief that part of the 'King George Statue' . . . might be located within said property and with the inten-

---

2. Treasure trove has traditionally been strictly and narrowly defined as "any gold or silver in coin, plate, or bullion found concealed in the earth or in a house or other private place." 1 Am. Jur. 2d 6, Abandoned, Lost, and Unclaimed Property, §4. This strict definition is well established in American law. Ferguson v. Ray, 44 Or. 557, 77 P. 600 (1904); Danielson v. Roberts, 44 Or. 108, 74 P. 913 (1904) (gold coin); Zech v. Accola, 253 Wis. 80, 33 N.W.2d 232 (1948) (paper certificates); 1 Am. Jur. 2d 6, op. cit., §4; annot., 170 A.L.R. 707. Since the fragment of the statue recovered by the defendant was of gilded lead, he makes no claim that the fragment constituted treasure trove.

tion of removing [the] same if located." The defendant has also admitted that the piece of the statue which he found was embedded in the ground ten inches below the surface and that it was necessary for him to excavate in order to take possession of his find.

In light of those undisputed facts the defendant's trespass was neither technical nor trivial. We conclude that the fact that the property found was embedded in the earth and the fact that the defendant was a trespasser are sufficient to defeat any claim to the property which the defendant might otherwise have had as a finder.

Where the trial court reaches a correct decision but on mistaken grounds, this court has repeatedly sustained the trial court's action if proper grounds exist to support it. Morris v. Costa, 174 Conn. 592, 392 A.2d 468; DiMaggio v. Cannon, 165 Conn. 19, 24, 327 A.2d 561. The present case falls within the ambit of that principle of law and we affirm the decision of the court below

There is no error.

In this opinion the other Judges concurred.

UNITED STATES v. MORRISON
492 F.2d 1219 (Ct. Cl. 1974)

HARKINS, J: On July 31, 1968, plaintiff was a Sergeant E-5 in command of a squad of the 3d Platoon, B Company, 1st Battalion, 50th Infantry, on a search-and-destroy patrol in the Central Highlands of South Vietnam. During the course of this patrol, plaintiff's squad searched a cave and discovered, among other items, $150,000 in United States currency and 550,000 South Vietnamese piasters.

Plaintiff is not a "finder" of the $150,000. When plaintiff discovered the money and took it into possession, he did so as an agent of the United States; the $150,000 was "captured" public property taken from the enemy or "abandoned" property within the meaning of Article 103 of the Uniform Code of Military Justice. Accordingly, plaintiff's petition must be dismissed.

Sight of the American money generated considerable excitement in plaintiff's squad and order was restored only with difficulty. Some of the bills were grabbed and passed around, and it was proposed that the money be divided among the squad members for personal use. Plaintiff suggested to his platoon leader that the money should be split up among the squad members. After a warning by the platoon leader that the squad would get into trouble if they tried to divide the money, the excitement was calmed. The money was redeposited in the can, and possession of the can and the money was relinquished to the platoon leader. In due course, the papers and money were turned over to the company commander, reported by radio to brigade headquarters, and extracted by helicopter to brigade headquarters where a count was made. The can contained $150,000 in United States currency, all in $50 bills. Approximately 30 of the 3,000 bills were marked with oriental characters that subsequently were determined to be Chinese. No translation of the Chinese characters is available. . . .

Plaintiff asserts that the $150,000 in United States currency constitutes "treasure trove" and from his capacity as a "finder" claims the right to its possession against all the world other than the true owner. The law of "finders" does not apply to this money. Plaintiff's rights are determined by statute and duly authorized administrative regulation. It is not necessary to resort to the ancient arcane principles that were developed in the Common Law of England prior to the American Revolution to determine the rights of a squad leader in the United States military forces to 3,000 United States $50 bills that were located in a cave in the Central Highlands of South Vietnam in the course of a search-and-destroy patrol.

On July 31, 1968, plaintiff was subject to Article 103 of the Uniform Code of Military Justice. This article deals with captured or abandoned property, and is derived from the constitutional power of Congress to "make Rules concerning Captures on Land and Water." Article 103 requires military personnel on duty in a combat zone, on penalty of court-martial, to (a) secure all public property that is taken from the enemy and (b) turn over to the proper authority all captured or abandoned property in their possession, custody, or control. In addition, article 103 prohibits military personnel from buying, selling, trading, or dealing in captured or abandoned property on his own account or from engaging in looting or pillaging. Article 103 reflects the policy that a soldier may not make a profit out of the disorders of war. The article recognize the difficulties involved in policing an army when abandoned property situations and looting situations are involved. . . .

A directive of the United States Military Assistance Command implements the provisions of article 103 for captured or seized currencies taken in field operations in Vietnam. This directive applies to all United States forces conducting operations within the Republic of Vietnam and was in force at the time plaintiff's squad located and searched the cave on July 31, 1968. MACV Dir. 37-20 applies to any currency, either public currency or private currency, including United States dollars, Military Payment Certificates (MPC), and GVN or NVN piasters, that United States forces personnel may capture or seize in the possession of a detainee or as part of a cache.

All public currency so taken is stated to be the "property of the United States Government." Public currency is defined as all currency which is the "property of the enemy force, state, government, or political subdivision thereof."

Private currency is property that can be identified by the individual who can establish ownership. Private currency is any currency seized or captured by United States forces personnel and "identifiable as the personal property of an individual."

The source of, or the true owner of, the money located in the cave is unknown. The record does not establish the identity of the parties that deposited the money in the ammunition cans or placed the cans in the cave. No individual has identified or established a claim to the money as personal property. In the circumstances of this case, the $150,000 must be treated as public property unless or until the true owner identifies it and establishes a superior personal property right. Until proven otherwise, the currency found in the cave should be considered to be public currency and, as such, the property of the United States Government.

When in the cave, and when he saw and took possession of the money, plaintiff was in a combat situation in an area not under effective control of either the South Vietnam forces or of the United States forces. If the currency was property of the enemy, it was taken in combat and is captured public property. As a general rule, all property located in enemy territory, regardless of its ownership, in time of war is regarded as enemy property subject to the laws of war.

Hypothetically, the currency located in the cave could be considered to be private currency placed in the cave by unknown South Vietnamese or other civilian parties, or even by South Vietnamese or American military personnel. In such event, the $150,000 private currency would be contraband under local law and would be abandoned property as that term is used in article 103. In article 103, the word "abandoned" covers not only property abandoned by the enemy, but also by civilian populations "in flight from the perils of the combat zone." The term "abandoned" in article 103 is broader than the common law concept of "abandoned" property in that it includes property that was left behind or cast aside in situations where the right to possession was not voluntarily surrendered. In the circumstances of this case, the nature of the war in Vietnam would have caused any private owner of the money to abandon it to escape the "perils of the combat zone." No South Vietnamese or American, civilian or military, who had cached profits from black market operations would assert title to the money in the cave in the circumstances, particularly when its discovery occurred on a search-and-destroy patrol by heavily armed combat troops. In such event, the $150,000 would be private property cast aside and abandoned with no intent of asserting ownership or possessory rights.

Plaintiff's claim is disposed of by the nature of plaintiff's mission at the time the discovery was made. Seizure of the currency was plaintiff's military responsibility, and possession of the currency was taken as an agent of the United States. Plaintiff can assert no right to possession. This case is not concerned with, and no decision is made as to, what the result would be if plaintiff were not on a combat mission and acting well within the scope of his assigned official duties. Nor is this case concerned with a "finding" made by a member of an army of occupation or by military personnel in pursuit of wholly personal activities that lay outside the scope of assigned official responsibilities.

Upon the findings of fact and the foregoing opinion, which are adopted by the court and made a part of the judgment herein, the court concludes as a matter of law that plaintiff is not entitled to recover, and the petition is dismissed.

§2.3   Bailments

PRESTON v. PRATHER
137 U.S. 604 (1890)

The plaintiffs below, the defendants in error here, were citizens of Missouri, and for many years have been copartners, doing business at Maryville, in that State, under the name of the Nodaway Valley Bank of Maryville. The defendants below were citizens of different States, one of them of Michigan and the others of Illinois, and for a similar period have been engaged in business as bankers at Chicago, in the latter State. In 1873 the plaintiffs opened an account with the defendants, which continued until the spring of 1883. The average amount of deposits by them with the defendants each year during this period was between two and four hundred thousand dollars. Interest was allowed at the rate of two and one-half per cent on the deposits above three thousand dollars, but nothing on deposits under that sum.

On the 7th of July, 1880, the plaintiffs purchased of the defendants four per cent bonds of the United States to the nominal amount of twelve thousand dollars.

The letter directing the purchase concluded with a request that the defendants send to the plaintiffs a description and the numbers of the bonds, and hold the same as a special deposit. In the subsequent account of the purchase rendered by the defendants the plaintiffs were informed that the bonds were held on special deposit subject to their order. The numbers of the bonds appear upon the bond register kept by the defendants, and the bonds remained in their custody until some time between November, 1881, and November, 1882, when they were stolen and disposed of by their assistant cashier, one Ker, who absconded from the State on the 16th of January, 1883. The present action was brought to recover their value.

[It appeared that about a year before he absconded, information was given to the bank that some one in its employ was speculating on the Board of Trade in Chicago, and an inquiry revealed the fact that Ker was that person. Although he was supposed to be dependent entirely on his salary, and although he had free access to the vaults where the securities of the bank, including these bonds, were deposited, he was continued in the service of the bank until the theft took place.

At trial a jury was waived by stipulation. The court found special findings of fact, which were not excepted to, and gave judgment for the plaintiffs. 29 Fed. Rep. 498. The defendants sued out this writ of error.] . . .

Mr. Justice FIELD, after stating the case, delivered the opinion of the court.

By the defendants it was contended below in substance, and the contention is renewed here, that the bonds being placed with them on special deposit for safe-keeping, without any reward, promised or implied, they were gratuitous bailees, and were not chargeable for the loss of the bonds, unless the same resulted from their gross negligence, and they deny that any such negligence is imputable to them.

On the other hand, the plaintiffs contended below, and repeat their contention here, that, assuming that the defendants were in fact simply gratuitous bailees when the bonds were deposited with them, they still neglected to keep them with the care which such bailees are bound to give for the protection of property placed in their custody; and further, that subsequently the character of the bailment was changed to one for the mutual benefit of the parties.

Undoubtedly, if the bonds were received by the defendants for safe-keeping, without compensation to them in any form, but exclusively for the benefit of the plaintiffs, the only obligation resting upon them was to exercise over the bonds such reasonable care as men of common prudence would usually bestow for the protection of their own property of a similar character. No one taking upon himself a duty for another without consideration is bound, either in law or morals, to do more than a man of that character would do generally for himself under like conditions. The exercise of reasonable care is in all such cases the dictate of good faith. An utter disregard of the property of the bailor would be an act of bad faith to him. But what will constitute such reasonable care will vary with the nature, value and situation of the property, the general protection afforded by the police of the community against violence and crime, and the bearing of surrounding circumstances upon its security. The care usually and generally deemed necessary in the community for the security of similar property, under like conditions, would be required of the bailee in such cases, but nothing more. The general doctrine, as stated by text writers and in judicial decisions, is that gratuitous bailees of another's property are not responsible for its loss unless guilty of gross negligence in its keeping. But gross negligence in such cases is nothing more than a failure to bestow the care which the property in its situation demands; the omission of the reasonable care required is the negligence which creates the liability; and whether this existed is a question of fact for the jury to determine, or by the court where a jury is waived.

. . . As stated above, the reasonable care which persons should take of property entrusted to them for safe-keeping without reward will necessarily vary with its nature, value and situation, and the bearing of surrounding circumstances upon its security. The business of the bailee will necessarily have some effect upon the nature of the care required of him, as, for example, in the case of bankers and banking institutions, having special arrangements, by vaults and other guards, to protect property in their custody. Persons therefore depositing valuable articles with them, expect that such measures will be taken as will ordinarily secure the property from burglars outside and from thieves within, and that whenever ground for suspicion arises an examination will be made by them to see that it has not been abstracted or tampered with; and also that they will employ fit men, both in ability and integrity, for the discharge of their duties, and remove those employed whenever found wanting in either of these particulars. An omission of such measures would in most cases be deemed culpable negligence, so gross as to amount to a breach of good faith, and constitute a fraud upon the depositor.

It was this view of the duty of the defendants in this case, who were engaged in business as bankers, and the evidence of their neglect, upon being notified of the speculations in stocks of their assistant cashier who stole the bonds, to make the necessary examination respecting the securities deposited with them, or to remove the speculating cashier, which led the court to its conclusion that they were guilty of gross negligence. It was shown that about a year before the assistant cashier absconded the defendant Kean, who was the chief officer of the banking institution, was informed that there was some one in the bank speculating on the Board of Trade at Chicago. Thereupon Kean made a quiet investigation, and the facts discovered by him pointed to Ker, whom he accused of speculating. Ker replied that he had made a few transactions, but was doing nothing then and did not propose to do anything more, and that he was then about a thousand dollars ahead, all told. It was not known that Ker had any other property besides his salary. His position as assistant cashier gave him access to the funds as well as the securities of the bank, and he was afterwards kept in his position without any effort being made on the part of the defendants to verify the truth of his statement, or whether he had attempted to appropriate to his own use the property of others. . . .

. . . The court below, in giving its decision, Prather v. Kean, 29 Fed. Rep. 498, after observing that the defendants knew that Ker had been engaged in business which was hazardous and that his means were scant, and after commenting upon the demoralizing effect of speculating in stocks and grain, as seen in the numerous peculations, embezzlements, forgeries and thefts plainly traceable to that cause, and the free access by Ker to valuable securities, which were transferable by delivery, easily abstracted and converted, and yet his being allowed to retain his position without any effort to see that he had not converted to his own use the property of others, or that his statements were correct, held that it was gross negligence in the defendants not to discharge him or place him in some position of less responsibility. In this conclusion we fully concur.

The second position of the plaintiffs is also well taken, that, assuming the defendants were gratuitous bailees at the time the bonds were placed with them, the character of the bailment was subsequently changed to one for the mutual benefit of the parties. It appears from the findings that the plaintiffs, subsequently to their deposit, had repeatedly asked for a discount of their notes by the defendants, offering the latter the bonds deposited with them as collateral, and that such discounts were made. When the notes thus secured were paid, and the defendants called upon the plaintiffs to know what they should do with the bonds, they were informed that they were to hold them ιᴗr the plaintiffs' use as previously. The plaintiffs had already written to the defendants that they desired to keep the bonds for an emergency, and also that they wished at times to overdraw their account, and that they would consider the bonds as security for such overdrafts. From these facts the court was of opinion that the bonds were held by the defendants as collateral to meet any sums which the plaintiffs might overdraw; and the accounts show that they did subsequently overdraw in numerous instances.

The deposit, by its change from a gratuitous bailment to a security for loans, became a bailment for the mutual benefit of both parties, that is to say, both were interested in the transactions. For the bailor it obtained the loans, and to that extent was to his advantage; and to the bailee it secured the payment of the loans, and that was to his advantage also. The bailee was therefore required, for the protection of the bonds, to give such care as a prudent owner would extend to his own property of a similar kind, being in that respect under an obligation of a more stringent character than that of a gratuitous bailee, but differing from him in that he thereby became liable for the loss of the property if caused by his neglect, though not amounting to gross negligence.

It follows, therefore, that whether we regard the defendants as gratuitous bailees in the first instance, or as afterwards becoming bailees for the mutual benefit of both parties, they were liable for the loss of the bonds deposited with them. And the measure of the recovery was the value of the bonds at the time they were stolen.

Judgment affirmed.

NOTES AND QUESTIONS

1. The opinion in Preston v. Prather distinguishes between two of the several classes of bailment: gratuitous bailments, and bailments for the mutual benefit of the parties. The line that divides them is sometimes murky; so, too, is the attendant standard of care that devolves upon the bailee.

As to whether the bailment is gratuitous or for mutual benefit, consider, for example, the case of Peet v. The Roth Hotel Company, 191 Minn. 151, 253 N.W. 546 (1934). There the plaintiff, not a hotel guest, left her engagement ring in an envelope with the hotel cashier with instructions that it would be called for by one of the hotel's regular patrons. Somehow, the envelope disappeared before delivery, and plaintiff sued the hotel for the value of the ring. On these facts, the court charged that a bailment had been formed for the reciprocal benefit of the parties and that, if negligent, defendant would be liable. On appeal, the charge and plaintiff's verdict were upheld.

As to the appropriate standard of care, is there really any difference between that required of a gratuitous bailee (for example, the neighbor who agrees to watch your dog when you're away shopping) and the "mutually benefited" bailee (for example, the neighbor who agrees to watch your dog in your absence as part of a reciprocal promise to take care of her dog when she is away)?

2. At the far end of the spectrum from a gratuitous bailment is one for the benefit of the bailee. Can you give two or three examples? What standard of care would you impose upon the bailee?

KNOWLES v. GILCHRIST CO.
362 Mass. 642, 289 N.E.2d 881 (1972)

TAURO, C.J. The plaintiff (bailor) in an action of tort and contract in the Municipal Court against the defendant Gilchrist Company (bailee) seeks to recover damages for loss of certain articles of furniture in the bailee's possession pursuant to an agreement by the bailee to reupholster and return furniture to the bailor. There was a finding for the bailor in the amount of $800. The bailee claimed a report to the Appellate Division on the basis of the judge's refusal to allow the following requests for rulings. (1) On all the evidence a finding for the bailee is required. (2) On all the law, a finding for the bailee is required. (3) The evidence is insufficient to warrant a finding for the bailor as to the extent of her damage. The Appellate Division vacated the Municipal Court's finding for the bailor and ordered judgment for the bailee. The bailor appeals.

The Appellate Division rested its decision on the basis of our cases which have held that the bailor has the burden of proving by a fair preponderance of the evidence that the bailee broke the bailment contract by its negligence in caring for the goods. The Appellate Division decided that denial of the bailee's requests for rulings was error because the bailor introduced no evidence that the loss was caused by the bailee's negligence.

We think the Appellate Division's decision requires a reexamination of the Massachusetts common law rule which places on the bailor the burden of proving that the bailee negligently broke its bailment contract. Well established case authority in Massachusetts and in most other States has followed this rule despite the obvious problems in situations where, because the property was in the bailee's exclusive possession, the bailor has no knowledge of or access to the facts concerning its loss.

Originally, Massachusetts case law made a distinction between tort and contract actions in deciding where the burden of proof would be fixed. In Cass v. Boston & Lowell R. R., 14 Allen 448 (1867), the plaintiff bailor brought a contract action against a warehouseman to recover for the bailee's failure to return the goods entrusted to it. This court held that when the bailor alleged and proved that the bailee had received the bailor's property and failed to deliver it upon timely demand, the bailee had the burden of proving that the goods had been lost without any fault on its part. The pleadings were held to be decisive on the issue of burden of proof. This court noted that "The instructions of the court [as to the burden of proof] of course must correspond to the form of the action. The rule which has been often stated, that a decision should not be made to turn upon the state of the pleadings, . . . has no application to the case" (p. 451). Since the bailor had sued in *contract*, he had not alleged that the bailee was negligent. The *Cass* opinion placed the burden of proving the absence of negligence on the party who alleged it in its pleadings, namely, the bailee. This line of reasoning led the court to conclude that the burden of proof lies on the *bailor* in tort actions because the bailor must allege negligence in his pleadings. The court concluded, "[W]hen a plaintiff founds his action upon negligence, or a culpable omission of duty, the burden is upon him to establish it by proof" (pp. 451-452). However, since the plaintiff in the *Cass* case had sued in contract, the defendant bailee had to "show an excuse for the non-performance of . . . [its] promise; and the burden of proof was upon . . . [it] to establish . . . [its] excuse." The *Cass* case, *supra*, at 452.

Chief Justice Bigelow in his dissenting opinion in the *Cass* case also relied on a pleading rationale to allocate the burden of proof. His position was that ultimately the plaintiff bailor had to show a want of due care on the bailee's part to prove that the bailee breached his contract. Since the bailee "did not agree to keep or deliver the property absolutely and unconditionally, if nothing else is shown but a failure to deliver it, without any facts from which negligence can be inferred, the plaintiff stops short in establishing any ground for recovery." The *Cass* case, *supra,* 14 Allen at 456. Although he attacked the majority's ruling which resolved the issue by looking to the *format* of the pleadings, Chief Justice Bigelow adopted a parallel premise that the burden of proving all the essential elements of any cause of action lies on the party that *pleads* that cause of action. In his view, since the bailor must ultimately claim negligence when the bailee alleges impossibility as a defense to nondelivery, the burden of proving the bailee's negligence must lie on the bailor.

Just twenty years later, this court adopted Chief Justice Bigelow's dissent as the law and in effect overruled the *Cass* case in the *Willett* case. In the *Willett* case, this court reversed on the basis of a trial court's instruction which placed the burden of proof in a breach of contract suit on the bailee to show that the damage to the bailed property occurred without his fault. The court noted (142 Mass. p. 357, 7 N.E. p. 777) that "The fundamental rule as to the burden of proof is, that, whenever the existence of any fact is necessary in order that a party may make out his case, or establish a defense, the burden is on such party to show the existence of such fact." Thus, the *Willett* case established the rule, which is followed by most other jurisdictions, that the bailor has the burden of proving the bailee's negligence, regardless of whether the bailor's action sounds in tort or contract.

One serious problem created by fixing the burden of proof on the bailor is well illustrated by this court's decision in Little v. Lynn & Marblehead Real Estate Co., 301 Mass. 156, 16 N.E.2d 688. In a case with very similar facts to those in the instant case, the bailor sued the bailee after a fire in the bailee's premises destroyed the bailor's property. The bailee introduced evidence which established only that the fire prevented the return of the bailed property to the bailor. This court noted, "The fact that the fire originated in the defendant's premises is not evidence that it was started by the defendant; nor is it evidence that the fire was caused by any negligence on its part. . . . [Citations omitted.] The defendant is liable if its negligence caused the fire, 'but until its cause is known or fairly found from the evidence [the fire] cannot be said to be due to [the defendant's] negligence.' Stewart v. DeNoon, 220 Penn. St. 154, 161, 69 A. 587, 589." The *Little* case, *supra*, at 159, 16 N.E.2d at 690. Under this rule, since the bailor has the burden of proving the bailee's negligence, the bailee can simply plead impossibility as a defense, introduce evidence of a fire and rest as the bailee did in the instant case, even though the bailee may be the only party with access to the facts surrounding the loss.

In response to the obvious inequities and difficulties created by fixing the burden of proof on the bailor, recent decisions by State and Federal courts have held that the bailor can establish an inference or presumption of negligence merely by showing a bailment and failure to deliver by the bailee. Once the bailor makes this showing, the burden of *production* shifts to the bailee to go forward with evidence to rebut this presumption. See Buntin v. Fletchas, 257 F.2d 512 (5th Cir.); Moss v. Bailey Sales & Serv. Inc., 385 Pa. 547, 123 A.2d 425; Trammell v. Whitlock, 150 Tex. 500, 242 S.W.2d 157. The United States Supreme Court adopted this procedure for proof of negligence in Commercial Molasses Corp. v. New York Tank Barge Corp., 314 U.S. 104, 62 S. Ct. 156, 86 L. Ed. 89. The court noted (pp. 110-111, 62 S. Ct. p. 160) that, in exclusive bailment cases, "the burden of proving the breach of duty or obligation rests upon him who must assert it as the ground of the recovery which he seeks. . . . Since the bailee in general is in a better position than the bailor to know the cause of the loss and to show that it was one [not] involving the bailee's liability, the law lays on him the duty to come forward with the information available to him. . . . It does not cause the burden of proof to shift, and if the bailee does go forward with evidence enough to raise doubts as to the validity of the inference [of negligence on the bailee's part], which the trier of fact is unable to resolve, the bailor does not sustain the burden of persuasion which upon the whole evidence remains upon him, where it rested at the start."

This court followed the Supreme Court's lead in Bean v. Security Fur Storage Warehouse, Inc., 344 Mass. 674, 184 N.E. 2d 64. Noting the unfairness of a rule which allowed the bailee to remain silent despite the fact that the bailed property was lost or damaged while in its exclusive control, we held, "While the burden of proving negligence would continue to rest upon the plaintiff, the receipt of the coat by the defendant and its disappearance while in the possession of the defendant, which offers no explanation of the disappearance, would permit a finding that the defendant was negligent. . . . [T]his means that the burden of going forward with the evidence falls upon the defendant." The *Bean* case, *supra*, at 676, 184 N.E.2d at 66.

Although this court has never specifically addressed the precise question whether the bailee has to offer more evidence than the mere existence of a fire of unknown origin or other exculpatory cause to satisfy his burden of production, our holding in the *Little* case, *supra,* suggests that the burden of production imposed on the bailee is a minimal one which is satisfied by evidence of an exculpatory cause for the loss of the bailed property. Thus, it appears that our cases have adopted the rule followed by a majority of the States that the bailee may satisfy his burden of production and rebut the presumption of negligence arising from his failure to return goods entrusted to him by proof of loss arising from a fire or other extraordinary event. "When he [the bailee] shows the property was damaged or destroyed by fire, the burden is upon the bailor to establish by a preponderance of the evidence that the loss by fire was a proximate result of bailee's negligence." McElroy v. General Texas Asphalt Co., 427 S.W.2d 719, 720 (Tex. Civ. App.).

The irrational result of this holding is that evidence of a fire is sufficient evidence of due care on the bailee's part to overcome the bailor's inference of negligence. Moreover, it leaves the bailor in the same position of having to produce evidence of the bailee's negligence although it may have no access to such information. The imposition of such a minimal burden of production on the bailee defeats the rule's basic purpose because the bailee can simply note that a theft or a fire of unknown origin made delivery of the bailed goods impossible and rest his case.

Realizing the obvious defects of such a rule, many State courts have recently imposed a more stringent burden of production on the bailee. The Alaska Supreme Court's decision in Harris v. Deveau, 385 P.2d 283, reflects this modern trend in bailment cases. That court held (p. 286), "Regardless of the type of bailment and the degree of care required of the bailee, the trend of modern authorities is in support of the rule that in order to throw the duty of proceeding with actual proof of negligence upon a bailor who has made out a prima facie case by showing that the chattel involved was damaged or destroyed while in the possession of the bailee, the bailee must not only prove that the damage or loss occurred by reason of theft, fire or other cause beyond his control, but produce further evidence in explanation of the actual damage or loss which would indicate exercise of care on his part in the protection of the property. It is reasoned, and we think rightly so, that the bailee being in possession of the chattel is in a better position to explain the origin of the fire or the circumstances of the theft or other cause which would determine whether the loss or damage was due to negligence. He should disclose, to the extent that he is able, the manner in which the damage or loss occurred, the facts and circumstances attending such damage or loss and the precautions taken to prevent it." See also Clemenson v. Whitney, 238 Ill. App. 308, 313-314; Sherber v. Kinney Sys. Inc., (N.Y.) 42 Misc. 2d 530, 533, 248 N.Y.S.2d 437.

However, we feel that defining the bailee's burden of production in this manner resolves only in part the problem created by fixing the ultimate risk of nonpersuasion (or burden of proof by a fair preponderance of the evidence) on the bailor. A stringent burden of production on the bailee mitigates but does not cure the evil of imposing the burden of proof (or persuasion) on the party who has little or no access to the facts surrounding the loss or damage of the bailed property. The *Harris* holding, *supra,* does force the bailee to give some affirmative evidence of his due care in handling the bailed property. But once the bailee has done so, the presumption of negligence established by the bailor's case disappears and the burden of production shifts back to the bailor to refute the bailee's evidence of due care. See the *Commerical Molasses Corp.* case, *supra,* 314 U.S. at 111, 62 S. Ct. 146. Thus, the bailor is still placed in the inequitable position of bearing the burden of proof even though he may not have access to the information needed to rebut the bailee's affirmative evidence of due care. This essential unfairness is even more pronounced in cases, like the instant one, where the bailor is a consumer. The consumer's unfamiliarity with the bailee's trade practices and commercial customs *aggravates* the difficult task that all bailors face in trying to rebut the inference of due care which the bailee has created by selecting the most favorable facts from all the information exclusively available to him.

Therefore, we decline to follow prior cases such as the *Willett* case, *supra,* 142 Mass. 356, 7 N.E. 776, which allocate the burden of proof in bailment cases principally on the basis of the pleadings. We have long abandoned the notion of strict adherence to pleadings when to do so would give preference to form over substance. Instead, we must determine upon sound policy grounds how to fairly allocate the burden of proof. McCormick and Wigmore mention, among others, one policy factor which aids courts in determining where the burden of proof should rest.

"A doctrine often repeated by the courts is that where the facts with regard to an issue lie peculiarly in the knowledge of a party, that party has the burden of proving the issue." McCormick, Evidence (2d ed.) §337, p. 787. Since negligence is the determinative issue in the ordinary bailment case, the burden of proof should rest on the party who is in the best position to determine what actually happened to the goods and what safeguards existed both before and after the precipitating event that destroyed or damaged the bailed property. Clearly, the bailee has greater access to the information needed to show negligence or due care.

We are confirmed in our conclusion by the fact that in a closely similar situation the Legislature long ago placed the burden of proof on the bailee. Where a warehouse receipt is issued, the Uniform Warehouse Receipts Act places the burden upon the warehouseman to establish the existence of a lawful excuse for refusal or failure to deliver the goods on a proper demand, and the Uniform Commercial Code carries forward the same rule. G.L. c. 105, §§15, 27, inserted by St. 1907, c. 582, §§9, 22. G.L. c. 106, §7-403(1)(b), inserted by St. 1957, c. 765, §1.

Therefore, we hold that once the bailor proves delivery of the property to the bailee in good condition and the failure to redeliver upon timely demand, the burden of proof is irrevocably fixed upon the bailee to prove by a fair preponderance of the evidence that he has exercised due care to prevent the property's loss or destruction. Our holding extends to all bailment for hire cases, whether brought in tort or contract, in which the bailee has exclusive control over the property at the time it was destroyed or damaged. Excluded from this category would be cases where the bailee has contractually obligated himself irrespective of due care.

The order of the Appellate Division is reversed. The case is remanded to the Municipal Court for a new trial.

So ordered.

BRAUCHER, J. (dissenting in part). I concur fully in the court's ruling that the burden of proof should be on the defendant in this case to prove that it exercised due care. But I think the finding of the trial judge was warranted under the rule of Bean v. Security Fur Storage Warehouse, Inc., 344 Mass. 674, 676, 184 N.E.2d 64, "That the burden of going forward with the evidence falls upon the defendant." The report shows only that the furniture was delivered to the defendant at its warehouse on one day, and that there was a fire at the warehouse the next day. Such a showing does not carry the defendant's burden, and "an issue of fact" was "presented." Ibid. I therefore dissent from the decision so far as it orders a new trial.

NOTES AND QUESTIONS

1. The opinion places upon the bailee for hire the burden of presenting exculpatory evidence where he has exclusive control over the property at the time it was damaged or destroyed. Should that burden extend to every manner of bailee?

2. An attended public garage is a common specimen of bailee for hire. X leaves her car and keys with the attendant but when she returns two hours later, the car is missing. Later the auto is found undamaged some blocks away, but $10,000 of jewelry has disappeared from the glove compartment. X sues the garage for her loss. What is the defendant's liability? Does the bailment extend to the jewelry? Cf. Schulte v. North Terminal Garage Co., 291 Mass. 251, 197 N.E. 16 (1935). Is the standard of care for the car different from that for the jewelry?

KERGALD v. ARMSTRONG TRANSFER EXPRESS CO.
330 Mass. 254, 113 N.E.2d 53 (1953)

LUMMUS, J.

This is an action of contract, begun by writ dated August 26, 1949, in which the plaintiff sues for the loss of her trunk and its contents. The defendant is an intrastate common carrier. There was evidence that the plaintiff arrived with her trunk at the South Station in Boston late in an evening in May, 1949, and went to the defendant's office there. She was not asked the value of her trunk, but was given a small pasteboard check by the defendant which was not read to her and which she did not read, but put in her purse. The trunk was to be delivered at her home in Boston. The defendant failed to deliver her trunk, and admitted that it had been lost. The small check had on one side the order number and the words "Read contract on reverse side," and on the other the words, "The holder of this check agrees that the value of the baggage checked does not exceed $100 unless a greater value has been declared at time of checking and additional payment made therefore."

The defendant excepted to the denial of its motion for a directed verdict for the plaintiff in the sum of $100. The defendant excepted to the refusal of several requested instructions to the effect that the plaintiff was bound by the limitation printed upon the check, whether she read it or not. The judge instructed the jury, over the exception of the defendant, that the plaintiff is bound by that limitation if she had knowledge of it when she took the check, and otherwise is not. The jury returned a verdict for the plaintiff for $1,700, and the defendant brought the case here.

Where what is given to a plaintiff purports on its face to set forth the terms of a contract, the plaintiff, whether he reads it or not, by accepting it assents to its terms, and is bound by any limitation of liability therein contained, in the absence of fraud. . . . [Citations omitted.]

On the other hand, where as in this case what is received is apparently a means of identification of the property bailed, rather than a complete contract, the bailor is not bound by a limitation upon the liability of the bailee unless it is actually known to the bailor.

The cases in this Commonwealth so clearly show the law applicable to the facts of this case that we need not discuss decisions elsewhere. But we may say that our conclusions are supported by well reasoned cases in New York as well as other jurisdictions.

In our opinion no error is disclosed by the record.

Exceptions overruled.

NOTES AND QUESTIONS

1. "The bailor is not bound by a limitation upon the liability of the bailee unless it is actually known to the bailor." (Where the bailor receives a claim or identification check.) What steps should the bailee take to inform bailor of the liability limits? Would a conspicuously posted notice be enough, or must the bailee also prove that his customer saw the notice and knew its character and purpose? Cf. Palazzo v. Katz Parking Systems, Inc., 64 Misc. 2d 720, 315 N.Y.S.2d 384 (N.Y. Civ. Ct. 1970).

2. Should the bailee's attempt to limit or disclaim liability be nullified, even where adequate notice exists, on public policy grounds? What do you

think of the following Massachusetts statute, which the legislature passed in 1972?

> In any action of contract or tort in which the defendant is the Owner or Operator of a privately or publicly owned or operated garage, lot or other facility used for parking or storage for a fee, it shall not constitute a defense that said owner or operator by means of language appearing on any sign, ticket, or receipt sought to disclaim, limit or exclude his legal liability. Such a disclaimer or limitation is void as against public policy. [Mass. Gen. Law C. 231 §85 M]

3. Consider I.C.C. Metals, Inc. v. Municipal Warehouse Co., 50 N.Y.2d 657, 409 N.E.2d 849 (1980). In 1974 plaintiff delivered three lots of an industrial metal called indium, valued at $100,000, to defendant's commercial warehouse. Plaintiff was aware of the $50 limitation on liability but chose not to pay a premium for increased limits. In 1976 plaintiff called for the indium, but it could not be found. Defendant had no explanation other than its speculation that theft had occurred. Plaintiff sued in conversion. Defendant sought to impose the $50 liability ceiling. The court of appeals affirmed a summary judgment awarding plaintiff the full value of the indium:

> A warehouse which fails to redeliver goods to the person entitled to their return upon a proper demand, may be liable for either negligence or conversion, depending upon the circumstances. . . . It has long been the law in this State that a warehouse, like a common carrier, may limit its liability for loss of or damage to stored goods even if the injury or loss is the result of the warehouse's negligence, so long as it provides the bailor with an opportunity to increase that potential liability by payment of a higher storage fee. . . . If the warehouse converts the goods, however, strong policy considerations bar enforcement of any such limitation upon its liability. Uniform Comm. Code §7-204(2). . . .
>
> The rule requiring a warehouse to come forward with an explanation for its failure to return bailed goods or be cast in damages in negligence is based upon practical necessity. . . . There exists no sound reason to apply a different rule to [a conversion action] where, as here, the bailee comes forward with insufficient proof of its explanation for the loss of the bailed goods. . . . The rule requiring a warehouse to explain the loss of or damage to the goods lest it be held liable would be severely undermined could a warehouse avoid the bulk of potential liability in such a case by means of a contractual provision.

In dissent, Judge Jasen wrote:

> Here, plaintiff has presented no proof whatsoever of an intentional wrongdoing by defendant. . . . As a matter of public policy, I believe the burden of proving a wrongful act such as conversion should remain upon the party claiming it, rather than the one accused of the wrongdoing. . . . If the bailor is seeking to circumvent the contractual limitation on damages, agreed upon by the parties as a condition of the bailment, the bailor should be put to the task of demonstrating

that the bailee converted the goods to its own use or the use of another. To hold otherwise is to permit the bailor to have its cake and eat it too. This is so because the bailor, as in this case, need not declare the full value of the goods and, as a result, is required to pay only a *de minimus* bailment fee, rather than a fee based on actual value; yet, upon loss of the goods, it may seek compensation for their full value even though it was never disclosed to the bailee.

If the bailed chattel does disappear mysteriously, how does the bailee ever exonerate itself from a claim of conversion?

4. Suppose the bailor pays the higher storage rate based upon the declared value of the goods. If the goods then are damaged or disappear, must the bailor still allege (and prove) the bailee's negligence or intentional wrongdoing? Or does the higher storage rate imply that the bailee has guaranteed the goods' return?

McGLYNN v. NEWARK PARKING AUTHORITY
86 N.J. 551, 432 A.2d 99 (1981)

POLLOCK, J. The primary issue in this case is whether the operator of an enclosed park and lock garage is liable for theft of property from and damage to a car parked in the garage.

Plaintiffs, McGlynn and Backer, parked their cars in the Military Park Garage operated by the defendant, Parking Authority. While the cars were parked, vandals damaged the cars and stole property from them. Both McGlynn and Backer recovered judgments in the Essex County District Court, and the Authority appealed. We granted direct certification of both appeals. 84 N.J. 412-413, 420 A.2d 329 (1980). We affirm both judgments.

I

Military Park Garage is a cavernous underground parking facility in the center of Newark. The garage has three levels of underground parking with several entrances for cars and additional entrances and exits for pedestrians. On entering, a driver receives a printed ticket from a machine. Drivers park in any availabe space, lock their automobiles and retain the keys. To exit, a driver must stop the car at a toll booth, present the ticket and pay the parking fee.

The facts in both cases are similar. Both McGlynn and Backer drove their cars to the garage and received tickets from the dispensing machine. Neither McGlynn nor Backer read the tickets or knew what was printed on them. On the morning of December 7, 1977, McGlynn parked his Mercedes-Benz convertible on the second underground level, locked it and took his keys. Upon returning in the afternoon, he discovered that someone had slashed the convertible top and had stolen his portable cassette recorder together with forty cassettes. The recorder had been located in the cradle between the two front seats, and the cassettes had been stored in a plastic container located on the floor behind the front seat. In the evening of October 30, 1977, Backer parked his 1972 Datsun 240Z on the first underground level. When he returned the next morning, four hubcaps were missing and the antenna was broken. Both McGlynn and Backer reported the incidents to employees of the Authority. McGlynn was not charged for parking in the garage. Backer completed a claim form and returned it to the Authority. Both McGlynn and Backer asserted that the Authority had breached a bailment contract with them and that its negligence had caused their damage.

During his trial, McGlynn testified that he had never seen a security guard in the garage, but that he had parked in the garage because he thought it would be safe. In both cases, the only witness for the Authority was the supervisor of the garage. In *McGlynn*, the supervisor testified that the security procedures in effect on the day of the incident included the patrolling of three levels and stairways by garage attendants and city police, as well as the deployment of at least two attendants on each level of the garage. He conceded that there had been prior incidents of theft and vandalism. In *Backer*, the supervisor had not been in the garage while Backer's car was parked. Nonetheless, he testified that during the period when Backer's car was parked there would have been one or two attendants on duty and Newark Police would have been patrolling the garage.

In both cases, the Authority attempted to introduce into evidence the limitation of liability clause allegedly found on the tickets. The trial judge would not allow the tickets to be introduced because the Authority had not pleaded limitation of liability as an affirmative defense.

In *McGlynn*, the trial judge found that a bailment existed and instructed the jury that upon proof of damage, a presumption of negligence arose. The jury returned a verdict of $1,050.

In *Backer*, the same judge, sitting without a jury, found again that a bailment existed and that a presumption of negligence arose upon proof of damage. The court determined that the presumption established a prima facie case that was not rebutted by the Authority. Accordingly, the court awarded Backer damages of $150.

II

Traditionally, courts have analyzed parking lot or garage cases in terms of whether a bailment, license or lease relationship existed between the customer and the operator of the parking lot. Annot., "Liability for loss of or damage to automobile left in parking lot or garage," 7 A.L.R.3d 927 (1966). Depending on the characterization selected, a different standard of care was imposed upon the parking lot operator. Id. If the relationship was characterized as a bailment, proof of damage to the bailed goods created a presumption of negligence and established a prima facie case. See, e.g., Bachman Chocolate

Mfg. Co. v. Lehigh Warehouse & Transp. Co., 1 N.J. 239, 242, 62 A.2d 806 (1949) (proof of damage to cocoa beans stored in warehouse established prima facie case against bailee). The bailee could rebut this presumption by coming forward with evidence showing that the loss was not caused by his negligence or that he exercised due care. Id. If, however, the relationship was character- ized as a license to park or a lease of space, the customer did not receive the benefit of the presumption. Consequently, the customer had the duty to prove affirmatively the negligence of the operator. McFarland v. C.A.R. Corp., 58 N.J. Super. 449, 452, 156 A.2d 488 (App. Div. 1959).

In addition, under the traditional approach, even if the relationship between the garage operator and the parker were found to be a bailment, the contents of the vehicle would not necessarily be included within the bailment. To be included within the bailment, the contents had to be plainly visible or of a kind normally kept in a car. See Cerreta v. Kinney Corp., 50 N.J. Super. 514, 517-518, 142 A.2d 917 (App. Div. 1958); Annot., "Liability of owner or operator of parking lot or garage for loss of or damage to contents of parked motor vehicle," 78 A.L.R.3d 1057, 1069-1073 (1977).

This Court, however, has never decided whether a bailment relationship exists between the operator of an enclosed park and lock garage and its cus- tomers. In related situations, lower courts have focused on the criteria of pos- session and control in determining whether the relationship was one of license, lease or bailment. See, e.g., HyGrade Oil Co. v. New Jersey Bank, 138 N.J. Super. 112, 116, 350 A.2d 279 (App. Div. 1975), certif. den. 70 N.J. 518, 361 A.2d 532 (1976) (judgment for bank customer reversed and case remanded to determine if there was delivery of money to night depository of bank because "it is essential to the creation of a bailment that the property be turned over to the possession and control of the bailee"); Marsh v. Amer. Locker Co., 7 N.J. Super. 81 at 84-86, 72 A.2d 343 (App. Div. 1950), aff'd o.b., 6 N.J. 81, 77 A.2d 315 (1950) (insufficient delivery and control to create bailment where package containing jewelry was deposited in locker at railroad station). . . .

In parking lot and garage cases, the relevant indicia of possession and control include whether the lot is enclosed, whether a claim ticket is issued, whether the claim ticket identifies the car or merely indicates time and date of entry, whether the parking is by an attendant or the automobile operator and whether the operator retains the keys.

Rather than consider possession and control in the context of a bailment, we believe it is more useful and straightforward to consider them in defining the duty of care a garage operator owes to its customers. Fairness and reason suggest that we abandon the quest for the elements of bailment and seek an adjustment of the rights and duties of the parties in light of the realities of their relationship. See State v. Shack, 58 N.J. 297, 307, 277 A.2d 369 (1971); R. Brown, supra, §10.1 at 210. Thus, the indicia of possesion and control must be analyzed, along with all other relevant circumstances, to determine the duty the operator owes to its customers. Our approach is consistent with those courts in other states that have discarded bailment, license and lease as ancient labels ill-suited for the analysis of problems like those posed by the present cases. . . .

Whether the garage operator is under a duty to take reasonable steps to prevent harm to the vehicles parked in the garage and to their contents depends, in large part, upon whether the risk of harm is reasonably forseeable. See Hill v. Yaskin, 75 N.J. 139, 143, 380 A.2d 1107 (1977); W. Prosser, Law of Torts §43 at 250 (4 ed. 1971). In a related area, we have imposed liability on landlords for failing to take reasonable measures to protect their tenants from the foreseeable criminal conduct of others. See Trentacost v. Brussel, 82 N.J. 214, 223, 412 A.2d 436 (1980) ("[f]oreseeability of harm . . . is the crucial factor in determining 'whether a *duty* exists to take measures to guard against [criminal activity]' "); Restatement (Second) of Torts, *supra*, §§302B, 448. Imposing a duty of reasonable care on the operator of an enclosed garage to protect cars and items reasonably expected to be within those cars is consistent with *Trentacost*. In the present cases, the Authority knew of prior incidents of vandalism; the Authority also controlled access to the parked cars. The prior incidents of vandalism indicated the foreseeability of the risk that criminal acts of others would cause harm to the automobiles and their contents. This foreseeable risk of harm extended not only to the parked cars, but to all items that the garage operator would reasonably expect to find within the cars.

Ultimately, however, the imposition of a duty depends upon policy considerations such as the effect of the imposition of the risks and burdens of an activity. 2 F. Harper and F. James, The Law of Torts §18.6 at 1052 (1956). In comparison with a parker, the garage owner is better situated to protect a parked car and to distribute the costs of protection through parking fees. Furthermore, at an enclosed garage, car owners expect to receive back their cars in the same condition in which they left them. The imposition of a duty to protect parked vehicles and their contents is consistent with this expectation. Thus, we hold that the operator of an enclosed garage is under a duty to exercise reasonable care to protect the parked cars and those items one would expect reasonably to find within them. In a modern society, where car radios and cassette players are common, it is reasonable to expect that a car will contain a small cassette player and cassettes. Thus, in this case the duty of the Authority extended to the cassettes and cassette player in the McGlynn vehicle as well as to the hubcaps and outside antenna of the Backer vehicle.

Sufficient performance of the duty to exercise reasonable care will vary in other kinds of parking lots and garages. The care due to one who parks and locks his own car differs from the care due to another who entrusts his car and keys to an attendant ("valet parking"). Due care may vary also if the parking facility is an unfenced lot, rather than an enclosed garage. In the final analysis, the exercise of reasonable care will depend on the totality of the circumstances pertaining to a specific parking facility. Thus, whether an operator has discharged its duty of reasonable care must be determined on a case-by-case basis after an evaluation of all of the relevant circumstances. . . .

The judgments of the Essex County District Court are affirmed.

§2.4   Adverse Possession of Chattels

O'KEEFFE v. SNYDER
83 N.J. 478, 416 A.2d 862 (1980)

POLLOCK, J. This is an appeal from an order of the Appellate Division granting summary judgment to plaintiff, Georgia O'Keeffe, against defendant, Barry Snyder, d/b/a Princeton Gallery of Fine Art, for replevin of three small pictures painted by O'Keeffe. O'Keeffe v. Snyder, 170 N.J. Super. 75, 405 A.2d 840 (1979). In her complaint, filed in March, 1976, O'Keeffe alleged she was the owner of the paintings and that they were stolen from a New York art gallery in 1946. Snyder asserted he was a purchaser for value of the paintings, he had title by adverse possession, and O'Keeffe's action was barred by the expiration of the six-year period of limitations provided by N.J.S.A. 2A:14-1 pertaining to an action in replevin. Snyder impleaded third party defendant, Ulrich A. Frank, from whom Snyder purchased the paintings in 1975 for $35,000.

The trial court granted summary judgment for Snyder on the ground that O'Keeffe's action was barred because it was not commenced within six years of the alleged theft. The Appellate Division reversed and entered judgment for O'Keeffe. *O'Keeffe, supra,* 170 N.J. Super. at 92, 405 A.2d 840. A majority of that court concluded that the paintings were stolen, the defenses of expiration of the statute of limitations and title by adverse possession were identical, and Snyder had not proved the elements of adverse possession. Consequently, the majority ruled that O'Keeffe could still enforce her right to possession of the paintings.

The dissenting judge stated that the appropriate measurement of the period of limitation was not by analogy to adverse possession, but by application of the "discovery rule" pertaining to some statutes of limitation. He concluded that the six-year period of limitations commenced when O'Keeffe knew or should have known who unlawfully possessed the paintings, and that the matter should be remanded to determine if and when that event had occurred. Id. at 96-97, 405 A.2d 840.

We granted certification to consider not only the issues raised in the dissenting opinion, but all other issues. 81 N.J. 406, 408 A.2d 800 (1979). We reverse and remand the matter for a plenary hearing in accordance with this opinion.

I

The record, limited to pleadings, affidavits, answers to interrogatories, and depositions, is fraught with factual conflict. Apart from the creation of the paintings by O'Keeffe and their discovery in Snyder's gallery in 1976, the parties agree on little else.

O'Keeffe contended the paintings were stolen in 1946 from a gallery, An

American Place. The gallery was operated by her late husband, the famous photographer Alfred Stieglitz.

An American Place was a cooperative undertaking of O'Keeffe and some other American artists identified by her as Marin, Hardin, Dove, Andema, and Stevens. In 1946, Stieglitz arranged an exhibit which included an O'Keeffe painting, identified as *Cliffs*. According to O'Keeffe, one day in March, 1946, she and Stieglitz discovered *Cliffs* was missing from the wall of the exhibit. O'Keeffe estimates the value of the painting at the time of the alleged theft to have been about $150.

About two weeks later, O'Keeffe noticed that two other paintings, *Seaweed* and *Fragments,* were missing from a storage room at An American Place. She did not tell anyone, even Stieglitz, about the missing paintings, since she did not want to upset him.

Before the date when O'Keeffe discovered the disappearance of *Seaweed,* she had already sold it (apparently for a string of amber beads) to a Mrs. Weiner, now deceased. Following the grant of the motion for summary judgment by the trial court in favor of Snyder, O'Keeffe submitted a release from the legatees of Mrs. Weiner purportedly assigning to O'Keeffe their interest in the sale.

O'Keeffe testified on depositions that at about the same time as the disappearance of her paintings, 12 or 13 miniature paintings by Marin also were stolen from An American Place. According to O'Keeffe, a man named Estrick took the Marin paintings and "maybe a few other things." Estrick distributed the Marin paintings to members of the theater world who, when confronted by Stieglitz, returned them. However, neither Stieglitz nor O'Keeffe confronted Estrick with the loss of any of the O'Keeffe paintings.

There was no evidence of a break and entry at An American Place on the dates when O'Keeffe discovered the disappearance of her paintings. Neither Stieglitz nor O'Keeffe reported them missing to the New York Police Department or any other law enforcement agency. Apparently the paintings were uninsured, and O'Keeffe did not seek reimbursement from an insurance company. Similarly, neither O'Keeffe nor Stieglitz advertised the loss of the paintings in Art News or any other publication. Nonetheless, they discussed it with associates in the art world and later O'Keeffe mentioned the loss to the director of the Art Institute of Chicago, but she did not ask him to do anything because "it wouldn't have been my way." O'Keeffe does not contend that Frank or Snyder had actual knowledge of the alleged theft.

Stieglitz died in the summer of 1946, and O'Keeffe explains she did not pursue her efforts to locate the paintings because she was settling his estate. In 1947, she retained the services of Doris Bry to help settle the estate. Bry urged O'Keeffe to report the loss of the paintings, but O'Keeffe declined because "they never got anything back by reporting it." Finally, in 1972, O'Keeffe authorized Bry to report the theft to the Art Dealers Association of America, Inc., which maintains for its members a registry of stolen paintings. The record does not indicate whether such a registry existed at the time the paintings disappeared.

In September, 1975, O'Keeffe learned that the paintings were in the Andrew Crispo Gallery in New York on consignment from Bernard Danenberg Galleries. On February 11, 1976, O'Keeffe discovered that Ulrich A. Frank had sold the paintings to Barry Snyder, d/b/a Princeton Gallery of Fine Art. She demanded their return and, following Snyder's refusal, instituted this action for replevin.

Frank traces his possession of the paintings to his father, Dr. Frank, who died in 1968. He claims there is a family relationship by marriage between his family and the Stieglitz family, a contention that O'Keeffe disputes. Frank does not know how his father acquired the paintings, but he recalls seeing them in his father's apartment in New Hampshire as early as 1941-1943, a period that precedes the alleged theft. Consequently, Frank's factual contentions are inconsistent with O'Keeffe's allegation of theft. Until 1965, Dr. Frank occasionally lent the paintings to Ulrich Frank. In 1965, Dr. and Mrs. Frank formally gave the paintings to Ulrich Frank, who kept them in his residences in Yardley, Pennsylvania and Princeton, New Jersey. In 1968, he exhibited anonymously *Cliffs* and *Fragments* in a one day art show in the Jewish Community Center in Trenton. All of these events precede O'Keeffe's listing of the paintings as stolen with the Art Dealers Association of America, Inc. in 1972.

Frank claims continuous possession of the paintings through his father for over thirty years and admits selling the paintings to Snyder. Snyder and Frank do not trace their provenance, or history of possession of the paintings, back to O'Keeffe.

As indicated, Snyder moved for summary judgment on the theory that O'Keeffe's action was barred by the statute of limitations and title had vested in Frank by adverse possession. For purposes of his motion, Snyder conceded that the paintings had been stolen. On her cross motion, O'Keeffe urged that the paintings were stolen, the statute of limitations had not run, and title to the paintings remained in her.

II

The Appellate Division accepted O'Keeffe's contention that the paintings had been stolen. However, in his deposition, Ulrich Frank traces possession of the paintings to his father in the early 1940's, a date that precedes the alleged theft by several years. The factual dispute about the loss of the paintings by O'Keeffe and their acquisition by Frank, as well as the other subsequently described factual issues, warrant a remand for a plenary hearing. See Judson v. Peoples Bank & Trust Co. of Westfield, 17 N.J. 67, 110 A.2d 24 (1954).

In reversing the cross motions for summary judgment, the Appellate Division erred in accepting one of two conflicting versions of material fact: the theft of the paintings in March, 1946 as asserted by O'Keeffe as against the possession of the paintings by the Frank family since the early 1940's. Instead of recognizing the existence of this controversy, the Appellate Division misconstrued Snyder's concession that the paintings had been stolen. That concession was made to enable the trial court to determine Snyder's motion for summary judgment that title had passed by adverse possession. The concession was not available to resolve O'Keeffe's cross motion for summary judgment. Hence, there is an issue of material fact, whether the paintings were stolen, that compels remand for trial.

Without purporting to limit the scope of the trial, other factual issues include whether (1) O'Keeffe acquired title to *Seaweed* by obtaining releases from the legatees of Mrs. Weiner; (2) the paintings were not stolen but sold, lent, consigned, or given by Stieglitz to Dr. Frank or someone else without O'Keeffe's knowledge before he died; and (3) there was any business or family relationship between Stieglitz and Dr. Frank so that the original possession of the paintings by the Frank family may have been under claim of right.

III

On the limited record before us, we cannot determine now who has title to the paintings. That determination will depend on the evidence adduced at trial. Nonetheless, we believe it may aid the trial court and the parties to resolve questions of law that may become relevant at trial.

Our decision begins with the principle that, generally speaking, if the paintings were stolen, the thief acquired no title and could not transfer good title to others regardless of their good faith and ignorance of the theft. Proof of theft would advance O'Keeffe's right to possession of the paintings absent other considerations such as expiration of the statute of limitations.

Another issue that may become relevant at trial is whether Frank or his father acquired a "voidable title" to the paintings under N.J.S.A. 12A:2-403(1). That section, part of the Uniform Commerial Code (U.C.C.), does not change the basic principle that a mere possessor cannot transfer good title. 2 Anderson, Uniform Commercial Code (2d ed. 1971) §2-403:6 at 41 (Anderson). Nonetheless, the U.C.C. permits a person with voidable title to transfer good title to a good faith purchaser for value in certain circumstances. N.J.S.A. 12A:2-403(1). If the facts developed at trial merit application of that section, then Frank may have transferred good title to Snyder, thereby providing a defense to O'Keeffe's action. No party on this appeal has urged factual or legal contentions concerning the applicability of the U.C.C. Consequently, a more complete discussion of the U.C.C. would be premature, particularly in light of our decision to remand the matter for trial.

On this appeal, the critical legal question is when O'Keeffe's cause of action accrued. The fulcrum on which the outcome turns is the statute of limitations in N.J.S.A. 2A:14-1, which provides that an action for replevin of goods or chattels must be commenced within six years after the accrual of the cause of action.

The trial court found that O'Keeffe's cause of action accrued on the date of the alleged theft, March, 1946, and concluded that her action was barred. The Appellate Division found that an action might have accrued more than six years before the date of suit if possession by the defendant or his predecessors satisfied the elements of adverse possession. As indicated, the Appellate Division concluded that Snyder had not established those elements and that the O'Keeffe action was not barred by the statute of limitations. . . .

IV

On the assumption that New Jersey law will apply, we shall consider significant questions raised about the interpretation of N.J.S.A. 2A:14-1. The purpose of a statute of limitations is to "stimulate to activity and punish negligence" and "promote repose by giving security and stability to human affairs". . . .

To avoid harsh results from the mechanical application of the statute, the courts have developed a concept known as the discovery rule. . . . The discovery rule provides that, in an appropriate case, a cause of action will not accrue until the injured party discovers, or by exercise of reasonable diligence and intelligence should have discovered, facts which form the basis of a cause of action. . . .

[W]e conclude that the discovery rule applies to an action for replevin of a painting under N.J.S.A. 2A:14-1. O'Keeffe's cause of action accrued when she first knew, or reasonably should have known through the exercise of due diligence, of the cause of action, including the identity of the possessor of the paintings. See N. Ward, Adverse Possession of Loaned or Stolen Objects—Is Possession Still 9/10ths of the Law?, published in Legal Problems of Museum Administration (ALI-ABA 1980) at 89-90.

In determining whether O'Keeffe is entitled to the benefit of the discovery rule, the trial court should consider, among others, the following issues: (1) whether O'Keeffe used due diligence to recover the paintings at the time of the alleged theft and thereafter; (2) whether at the time of the alleged theft there was an effective method, other than talking to her colleagues, for O'Keeffe to alert the art world; and (3) whether registering paintings with the Art Dealers Association of America, Inc. or any other organization would put a reasonably prudent purchaser of art on constructive notice that someone other than the possessor was the true owner.

V

The acquisition of title to real and personal property by adverse possession is based on the expiration of a statute of limitations. R. Brown, The Law of Personal Property (3d ed. 1975), §4.1 at 33 (Brown). Adverse possession does not create title by prescription apart from the statute of limitations. Walsh, Title by Adverse Possession, 17 N.Y.U.L.Q. Rev. 44, 82 (1939) (Walsh); see Developments in the Law—Statutes of Limitations, 63 Harv. L. Rev. 1177 (1950) (Developments).

To establish title by adverse possession to chattels, the rule of law has been that the possession must be hostile, actual, visible, exclusive, and continuous. Redmond v. New Jersey Historical Society, 132 N.J. Eq. 464, 474, 28 A.2d 189 (E. & A. 1942); 54 C.J.S. Limitations of Actions §119 at 23. *Redmond* involved a portrait of Captain James Lawrence by Gilbert Stuart, which was bequeathed by its owner to her son with a provision that if he should die leaving no descendants, it should go the the New Jersey Historical Society. The owner died in 1887, when her son was 14, and her executors delivered the painting to the Historical Society. The painting remained in the possession of the Historical Society for over 50 years, until 1938, when the son died and his children, the legatees under his will, demanded its return. The Historical Society refused, and the legatees instituted a replevin action.

The Historical Society argued that the applicable statute of limitations, the predecessor of N.J.S.A. 2A:14-1, had run and that plaintiffs' action was barred. The Court of Errors and Appeals held that the doctrine of adverse possession applied to chattels as well as to real property, *Redmond, supra,* 132 N.J. Eq. at 473, 28 A.2d 189, and that the statute of limitations would not begin to run against the true owner until possession became adverse. Id. at 475, 28 A.2d 189. The Court found that the Historical Society had done nothing inconsistent with the theory that the painting was a "voluntary bailment or gratuitous loan" and had "utterly failed to prove that its possession of the portrait was 'adversary', 'hostile'." Id. at 474-475, 28 A.2d at 195. The Court found further that the Historical Society had not asserted ownership until 1938, when it refused to deliver the painting to plaintiff, and that the statute did not begin to run until that date. Consequently, the Court ordered the painting to be returned to plaintiffs.

The only other New Jersey case applying adverse possession to chattels is Joseph v. Lesnevich, 56 N.J. Super. 340, 153 A.2d 349 (App. Div. 1949). In *Lesnevich,* several negotiable bearer bonds were stolen from plaintiff in 1951. In October, 1951, Lesnevich received an envelope containing the bonds. On October 21, 1951, Lesnevich and his business partner pledged the bonds with a credit company. They failed to pay the loan secured by the bonds and requested the credit company to sell the bonds to pay the loan. On August 1, 1952, the president of the credit company purchased the bonds and sold them to his son. In 1958, within one day of the expiration of six years from the date of the purchase, the owner of the bonds sued the credit company and its president, among others, for conversion of the bonds. The Appellate Division found that the credit company and its president held the bonds "as openly and notoriously as the nature of the property would permit". *Lesnevich, supra,* 56

N.J. Super. at 355, 153 A.2d at 357. The pledge of the bonds with the credit company was considered to be open possession.

As *Lesnevich* demonstrates, there is an inherent problem with many kinds of personal property that will raise questions whether their possession has been open, visible, and notorious. In *Lesnevich,* the court strained to conclude that in holding bonds as collateral, a credit company satisfied the requirement of open, visible, and notorious possession.

Other problems with the requirement of visible, open, and notorious possession readily come to mind. For example, if jewelry is stolen from a municipality in one county in New Jersey, it is unlikely that the owner would learn that someone is openly wearing that jewelry in another county or even in the same municipality. Open and visible possession of personal property, such as jewelry, may not be sufficient to put the original owner on actual or constructive notice of the identity of the possessor.

The problem is even more acute with works of art. Like many kinds of personal property, works of art are readily moved and easily concealed. O'Keeffe argues that nothing short of public display should be sufficient to alert the true owner and start the statute running. Although there is merit in that contention from the perspective of the original owner, the effect is to impose a heavy burden on the purchasers of paintings who wish to enjoy the paintings in the privacy of their homes.

In the present case, the trial court and Appellate Division concluded that the paintings, which allegedly had been kept in the private residences of the Frank family, had not been held visibly, openly, and notoriously. Notwithstanding that conclusion, the trial court ruled that the statute of limitations began to run at the time of the theft and had expired before the commencement of suit. The Appellate Division determined it was bound by the rules in *Redmond* and reversed the trial court on the theory that the defenses of adverse possession and expiration of the statute of limitations were identical. Nonetheless, for different reasons, the majority and dissenting judges in the Appellate Division acknowledged deficiencies in identifying the statute of limitations with adverse possession. The majority stated that, as a practical matter, requiring compliance with adverse possession would preclude barring stale claims and acquiring title to personal property. *O'Keeffe, supra,* 170 N.J. Super. at 86, 405 A.2d 840. The dissenting judge feared that identifying the statutes of limitations with adverse possession would lead to a "handbook for larceny". Id. at 96, 405 A.2d 840. The divergent conclusions of the lower courts suggest that the doctrine of adverse possession no longer provides a fair and reasonable means of resolving this kind of dispute. . . .

We are persuaded that the introduction of equitable considerations through the discovery rule provides a more satisfactory response than the doctrine of adverse possession. The discovery rule shifts the emphasis from the conduct of the possessor to the conduct of the owner. The focus of the inquiry will no longer be whether the possessor has met the tests of adverse possession, but whether the owner has acted with due diligence in pursuing his or her personal property.

For example, under the discovery rule, if an artist diligently seeks the recovery of a lost or stolen painting, but cannot find it or discover the identity of the possessor, the statute of limitations will not begin to run. The rule permits an artist who uses reasonable efforts to report, investigate, and recover a painting to preserve the rights of title and possession. . . .

A purchaser from a private party would be well-advised to inquire whether a work of art has been reported as lost or stolen. However, a bona fide purchaser who purchases in the ordinary course of business a painting entrusted to an art dealer should be able to acquire good title against the true owner. Under the U.C.C. entrusting possession of goods to a merchant who deals in that kind of goods gives the merchant the power to transfer all the rights of the entruster to a buyer in the ordinary course of business. N.J.S.A. 12A:2-403(2). In a transaction under that statute, a merchant may vest good title in the buyer as against the original owner. See *Anderson, supra,* §2-403:17 et seq. The interplay between the statute of limitations as modified by the discovery rule and the U.C.C. should encourage good faith purchases from legitimate art dealers and discourage trafficking in stolen art without frustrating an artist's ability to recover stolen art works.

The discovery rule will fulfill the purposes of a statute of limitations and accord greater protection to the innocnet owner of personal property whose goods are lost or stolen. Accordingly, we overrule Redmond v. New Jersey Historical Society, *supra,* and Joseph v. Lesnevich, *supra,* to the extent that they hold that the doctrine of adverse possession applies to chattels.

By diligently pursuing their goods, owners may prevent the statute of limitations from running. The meaning of due diligence will vary with the facts of each case, including the nature and value of the personal property. For example, with respect to jewelry of moderate value, it may be sufficient if the owner reports the theft to the police. With respect to art work of greater value, it may be reasonable to expect an owner to do more. In practice, our ruling should contribute to more careful practices concerning the purchase of art.

The considerations are different with real estate, and there is no reason to disturb the application of the doctrine of adverse possession to real estate. Real estate is fixed and cannot be moved or concealed. The owner of real property knows or should know where his property is located and reasonably can be expected to be aware of open, notorious, visible, hostile, continuous acts of possession on it.

Our ruling not only changes the requirements for acquiring title to personal property after an alleged unlawful taking, but also shifts the burden of proof at trial. Under the doctrine of adverse possession, the burden is on the possessor to prove the elements of adverse possession. Wilomay Holding Co. v. Peninsula Land Co., 36 N.J. Super 440, 443, 116 A.2d 484 (App. Div. 1955), *certif. den.* 19 N.J. 618, 118 A.2d 128 (1955). Under the discovery rule, the burden is on the owner as the one seeking the benefit of the rule to establish facts that would justify deferring the beginning of the period of limitations.

VI

Read literally, the effect of the expiration of the statute of limitations under N.J.S.A. 2A:14-1 is to bar an action such as replevin. The statute does not speak of divesting the original owner of title. By its terms the statute cuts off the remedy, but not the right of title. Nonetheless, the effect of the expiration of the statute of limitations, albeit on the theory of adverse possession, has been not only to bar an action for possession, but also to vest title in the possessor. There is no reason to change that result although the discovery rule has replaced adverse possession. History, reason, and common sense support the conclusion that the expiration of the statute of limitations bars the remedy to recover possession and also vests title in the possessor.

Professor Brown explains the historical reason for construing the statute of limitations as barring the right of title as well as an action for possession: "The metamorphosis of statutes simply limiting the time in which an action may be commenced into instrumentalities for the transfer of title may be explained perhaps by the historical doctrine of disseisin which, though more customarily applied to land, was probably originally controlling as to chattels also. By this doctrine the wrongful possessor as long as his possession continued, was treated as the owner and the dispossessed occupant considered merely to have a personal right to recapture his property if he could." [Brown, *supra*, §4.1 at 34.] See 3 Am. Jur. 2d, Adverse Possession, §202 at 290-292; 3 American Law of Property, §15.16 at 834.

Before the expiration of the statute, the possessor has both the chattel and the right to keep it except as against the true owner. The only imperfection in the possessor's right to retain the chattel is the original owner's right to repossess it. Once that imperfection is removed, the possessor should have good title for all purposes. Ames, The Disseisin of Chattels, 3 Harv. L. Rev. 313, 321 (1890) (Ames). As Dean Ames wrote: "An immortal right to bring an eternally prohibited action is a metaphysical subtlety that the present writer cannot pretend to understand." Id. at 319.

Recognizing a metaphysical notion of title in the owner would be of little benefit to him or her and would create potential problems for the possessor and third parties. The expiration of the six-year period of N.J.S.A. 2A:14-1 should vest title as effectively under the discovery rule as under the doctrine of adverse possession.

Our construction of N.J.S.A. 2A:14-1 is consistent with the construction of N.J.S.A. 2A:14-6, one of the statutes pertaining to title by adverse possession of real estate. That statute recites that one with right or title of entry into real estate shall make such entry within 20 years after the accrual of the right or be barred. It does not expressly state that the expiration of 20 years vests title in the possessor. Two other statutes pertaining to the adverse possession of real estate, N.J.S.A. 2A:14-30 and 31, expressly state that adverse possession for the statutory period shall vest title in the possessor. Notwithstanding the difference in wording between N.J.S.A. 2A:14-6 and N.J.S.A. 2A:14-30 and 31, the former statute has always been construed as vesting title in the adverse possessor at the end of the statutory period. See, e.g., Braue v. Fleck, 23 N.J. 1, 16, 127 A.2d 1 (1956).

To summarize, the operative fact that divests the original owner of title to either personal or real property is the expiration of the period of limitations. In the past, adverse possession has described the nature of the conduct that will vest title of a chattel at the end of the statutory period. Our adoption of the discovery rule does not change the conclusion that at the end of the statutory period title will vest in the possessor.

We reverse the judgment of the Appellate Division in favor of O'Keeffe and remand the matter for trial in accordance with this opinion.

HANDLER, J., dissenting. The Court today rules that if a work of art has been stolen from an artist, the artist's right to recover his or her work from a subsequent possessor would be barred by the statute of limitations if the action were not brought within six years after the original theft. This can happen even though the artist may have been totally innocent and wholly ignorant of the identity of the thief or of any intervening receivers or possessors of the stolen art. The Court would grudgingly grant some measure of relief from this horrendous result and allow the artist to bring suit provided he or she can sustain the burden of proving "due diligence" in earlier attempting to retrieve the stolen artwork. No similar duty of diligence or vigilance, however, is placed upon the subsequent receiver or possessor, who, innocently or not, has actually trafficked in the stolen art. Despite ritualistic disavowals, the Court's holding does little to discourage art thievery. Rather, by making it relatively more easy for the receiver or possessor of an artwork with a "checkered background" to gain security and title than for the artist or true owner to reacquire it, it seems as though the Court surely will stimulate and legitimatize art thievery.

I believe that there is a much sounder approach in this sort of case than one that requires the parties to become enmeshed in duplicate or cumulative hearings that focus on the essentially collateral issues of the statute of limitations and its possible tolling by an extended application of the discovery doctrine. The better approach, I would suggest, is one that enables the parties to get to the merits of the controversy. It would recognize an artist's or owner's right to assert a claim against a newly-revealed receiver or possessor of stolen art as well as the correlative right of such a possessor to assert all equitable and legal defenses. This would enable the parties to concentrate directly upon entitlement to the artwork rather than entitlement to bring a lawsuit. By dealing with the merits of the claims instead of the right to sue, such an approach would be more conducive to reconciling the demands for individual justice with societal needs to discourage art thievery. In addition, such a rule would comport more closely with traditional common law values emphasizing the paramountcy of the rights of a true owner of chattels as against others whose possession is derived from theft. Simultaneously, it would acknowledge that the claims of the true owner as against subsequent converters may in appropriate circumstances be counterbalanced by equitable considerations. I therefore dissent.

It is the general rule that "a bona fide purchaser of personal property taken tortiously or wrongfully, as by trespass or theft, does not acquire a title good against the true owner." Kutner Buick, Inc. v. Strelecki, 111 N.J. Super. 89, 97, 267 A.2d 549, 554 (Ch. Div. 1970) (purchaser of stolen motor vehicle).

It follows from this well-established principle that, generally, as between the true owner who has lost personal property through theft and a subsequent good faith purchaser for value, the former is entitled to the goods over the latter. Title remains in the true owner rather than flowing to the bona fide purchaser when " 'the wrongdoer sells the chattel to [such] innocent purchaser . . . because the wrongdoer had [title] to give.' " Kutner Buick, Inc. v. Strelecki, *supra,* 111 N.J. Super. at 97, 267 A.2d at 553 (quoting from National Retailers Mut. Ins. Co. v. Gambino, 1 N.J. Super. 627, 629, 64 A.2d 927 (Law Div. 1948)).

These basic tenets are fully applicable to creative works of art and govern ownership claims in the case of the theft or wrongful appropriation of artistic creations such as those involved in this case. E.g., Porter v. Wertz, 68 A.D.2d 141, 149, 416 N.Y.S.2d 254, 259 (App. Div. 1979) (true owners of a painting by Maurice Utrillo, entitled *Chateau de Lion-sur-Mer,* could recover either the painting or damages as against defendant gallery which purchased the painting from an individual who had acquired it wrongfully from another person who was not authorized by the owner to sell it); cf. Lieber v. Mohawk Arms, Inc., *supra,* 64 Misc. 2d at 208, 314 N.Y.S.2d at 512 (owner of personal effects of Adolf Hitler entitled to recover these unique items stolen from him by transferor of defendant bona fide purchaser).

Consequently, if we were to view this record as presenting only the undisputed fact that the paintings were stolen and could thus not be validly transferred thereafter to Snyder as bona fide purchaser, plaintiff O'Keeffe would clearly be entitled to prevail. And, in that posture, I would subscribe to the result urged in the dissenting opinion of Justice Sullivan, *ante* at 877-878, namely, a reversal and entry of judgment in favor of plaintiff. Under all of the circumstances, however, I do not believe that such a disposition woud be appropriate and would instead counsel a remand, albeit with a focus and under guidelines very different from those expressed in the majority opinion.[2]

---

2. I am constrained to agree with the Court that the cross-motions for summary judgment have not satisfactorily eliminated all disputes as to material facts. It seems manifest that the parties brought their respective motions in order to obtain dispositive rulings as to the defenses of the statute of limitations and the doctrine of adverse possession. If defendants were entitled to prevail under either of these defenses, this would have terminated the litigation (the result actually reached by the trial court). Since, in my view, these defenses are not available, rulings in favor of

III

"As a general rule, a defendant in a replevin action may interpose any defense which questions the plaintiff's title or right to possession, or upholds his own taking or unlawful detention." 66 Am. Jur. 2d, Replevin, §47 at 864 (1973) (footnotes omitted). See 20 N.J. Practice, *supra,* §1739 at 509-510. While the fundamental principle is that a wrongdoer cannot, as against the true owner, convey good title even to a bona fide purchaser, that precept is not absolute. Some exceptions to this common law rule are derived from judicial rulings, others, from statutes. Dobbs, *supra,* §4.7 at 282, 286; N.J.S.A. 12A:2-403(2) (U.C.C. §2-403(2)) (U.C.C. codifies the common law notion of voidable or equitable title where goods have been "entrusted" by the owner "to a merchant who deals in goods of that kind").

Aside from specialized defenses peculiar to sales transactions, there are also general equitable defenses—such as laches, unclean hands, estoppel or mistake—cognizable in equity actions or in other actions in which such defenses may be raised. Dobbs, *supra,* §2.4 at 45 et seq. Notwithstanding in this case a failure to denominate each and every equitable defense which might be available to him, defendant Snyder has adequately invoked the defenses which would be germane in addressing plaintiff's claim for the return of the paintings. He has asserted his own ownership of the paintings, implying thereby that, under all of the circumstances surrounding the original disappearance of the paintings, their subsequent possession by others, and his eventual purchase for value, his own entitlement to possession of them exceeds that of O'Keeffe. He has also alleged laches as against plaintiff, undoubtedly intending to establish that she delayed unduly in bringing an action to recover her paintings against those whom she knew or ought to have known were in possession thereof and that, as a result, he ultimately stands to suffer a loss.

Equitable considerations have special pertinency in the instant proceedings. They appropriately require the fullest exposure of all facets of the controversy: the uniqueness of the chattels—paintings created by a renowned artist whose artworks have in general grown greatly in value; the theft or mysterious disappearance of these paintings several decades ago; the subsequent possession and enjoyment of the paintings by the Frank family; Frank's subsequent attempts to sell the paintings, and their eventual acquisition by Snyder; the experience and status of Snyder in the art world, and whether he sufficiently investigated the provenance of the O'Keeffe paintings and acted with commensurate due care and reasonable prudence when he purchased them. The difficulties caused by the lengthy interim between the original disappearance of the paintings and their ultimate surfacing in Snyder's gallery also has a

---

plaintiff would have the effect only of a partial summary judgment under R. 4:46-2 because other issues remain unresolved in the case. Such a result would require a remand to decide such remaining issues. See Rotwein v. General Accident Group, 103 N.J. Super. 406, 424-425, 247 A.2d 370 (Law Div. 1968).

definite bearing upon the equities in this case. These considerations, I believe, should be given direct application as constituent elements of the primary claims and the affirmative defenses of the parties rather than be given at most, as required by the majority opinion, oblique application as an aspect of the discovery rule relevant only as to whether O'Keeffe is entitled to assert a claim for the stolen paintings.

IV

I am mindful that the majority is concerned with the importance of the policy of repose and the discouragement of stale claims. At times, however, these policies must yield to other equally important policies. Compare, for example, Velmohos v. Maren Engineering Corp., 83 N.J. 282, 293, 416 A.2d 372 (1980), with Galligan v. Westfield Centre Service, Inc., 82 N.J. 188, 192-193, 412 A.2d 122 (1980). The majority has in this case gone well beyond a simple and understandable desire for quietude in litigation. It has actually placed the entire burden of proof as to the absence of comparative fault upon the original owner-artist, albeit in the sheep's clothing of the discovery rule. *Ante* at 869-870, 873-874. I see no justification for removing that burden from the defendant, who may assert equities in his favor to establish his entitlement to the artwork. Ward, *supra* at 96. I respectfully repeat that the Court's anxiety in this regard can be fully and properly accommodated in this case without first fictionalizing the tortious character of Snyder's conversion and then applying as the only pertinent statute of limitations that which was triggered as of the date of the original theft, subject to an artificial and novel extension of the discovery rule, all of which does not really allow the parties to get to the heart of the matter.

All of the factors which trouble the majority, I suggest, can and should be addressed in the context of a remand directing the trial court to consider the defendant's affirmative defenses, to recognize that defendant bears the burden of proof with respect to those defenses, and, ultimately, to weigh the respective interests of the parties by balancing the equities in order to determine who should bear the loss of the paintings.

For these reasons, I dissent.

NOTES AND QUESTIONS

1. Can you summarize the disagreement between Justice Pollock and Justice Handler? If you were Georgia O'Keeffe's attorney, which of the two theories propounded would better serve your client? Why?

2. To establish title to chattels by adverse possession, the rule of law has been that the possession must be hostile, actual, visible, exclusive, and continuous. A majority of the appellate division concluded that defendant had

not proved the elements of adverse possession, which defense the court viewed as identical to an expired statute of limitations. Which was the missing element?

3.   X owns a rare book, which he mislays on a park bench. Y finds the book, takes it home, and places it in his library. Ten years later X learns that Y has the book. May X recover the book? (The replevin limitations period is six years.)

4.   X owns a rare book, which he mislays on a park bench. Y finds the book and sells it to the Bibliophile Shop, which resells it to Z. Ten years later X learns that Z has the book. May X recover the book? (The replevin limitations period is six years.)

5.   Compare Lieber v. Mohawk Arms, Inc., 64 Misc. 2d 206, 314 N.Y.S.2d 510 (Sup. Ct. 1970). Plaintiff, then in the U.S. Army, was among the first soldiers to occupy Munich, Germany. There he entered Adolf Hitler's apartment and removed the Fuehrer's uniform jacket and cap. In 1968 these items were stolen by plaintiff's chauffeur and sold to a New York dealer in historical Americana. The dealer sold it to the defendant who purchased in good faith. Through collectors' circles the plaintiff soon discovered the whereabouts of his stolen property, demanded its return, and sued when the defendant refused. Held: judgment for the plaintiff. The defendant, despite its good faith, had no title since its possession was derived from a thief. Nor could the defendant plead that a third party, the Bavarian Government, had right of possession superior to the plaintiff.

§2.5   Gifts of Chattels

R. BROWN, PERSONAL PROPERTY
Raushenbush ed. 1975, at 76-78

§7.1.   DEFINITION, CLASSES, AND GENERAL REQUIREMENTS OF GIFTS

A gift may be defined as a voluntary transfer of his property by one to another without any consideration or compensation therefor. There may, of course, be gifts of real as well as of personal property, but the law concerning transfers of real and personal property has developed along entirely different lines.

A gift is distinguished from other voluntary transfers primarily by its gratuitous character. If there be valid legal consideration for the transfer, then the transaction is of the nature of a contract or a sale and is governed by the particular rules applicable thereto. A gift is also a present transfer of an interest in the property. If the gift is to take effect only at some time in the future, it is in substance a mere promise to give, and unenforceable in law for lack of a valid consideration. Gifts of the character now under consideration are also distinct from testamentary dispositions of property. Gifts by the last will and testament of a deceased person do not take effect upon the execution of the instrument, but only upon death. Although as will be seen there is a certain close relationship between so-called gifts causa mortis and gifts by the last will and testament of the donor, the latter type of dispositions is controlled by express statutes relating to the making of wills. . . . [T]here are two general classes of gifts, gifts inter vivos, and gifts causa mortis. The former are the ordinary present unconditional gifts between living persons; the latter are those made in contemplation of immediate approaching death. The requirements for the making of a valid gift of either type are substantially the same although some courts, because of the greater opportunity for fraudulent claims in gifts causa mortis due to the ensuing death of the donor, are apt to be more strict in the case of gifts of that type, than in the case of gifts inter vivos. The chief distinction between the two classes of gifts is in their effect when made. The gift inter vivos is immediate and irrevocable when once made. The widespread lay impression that to "take back" a completed gift is legally permissible (though perhaps ethically improper), is simply incorrect. In the case of the gift causa mortis on the other hand, the gift, until the death of the donor is revocable by him, and is indeed ipso facto revoked by his escape from the contemplated death, the expectation of which prompted the gift in question.

For the making of a valid gift, either inter vivos or causa mortis there are three general requisites. The first of these is that there must be either a deed by the donor transferring the property in question, or in the more common case of the parol gift, a delivery of the subject matter by the donor to the donee, or some other act or course of conduct on the part of the donor, which is accepted by the courts as equivalent thereto. The second requirement is that the donor must possess the intent to give. And the third is that the donee must accept. The burden of proof is on the donee to show that these requirements have been met.

SCHERER v. HYLAND

75 N.J. 127, 380 A.2d 698 (1977)

PER CURIAM. Defendant, the Administrator ad litem of the Estate of Catherine Wagner, appeals from an Appellate Division decision, one judge dissenting, affirming a summary judgment by the trial court holding that Ms. Wagner had made a valid gift causa mortis of a check to plaintiff. We affirm.

The facts are not in dispute. Catherine Wagner and the plaintiff, Robert Scherer, lived together for approximately fifteen years prior to Ms. Wagner's death in January 1974. In 1970, the decedent and plaintiff were involved in an automobile accident in which decedent suffered facial wounds and a broken hip. Because of the hip injury, decedent's physical mobility was substantially impaired. She was forced to give up her job and to restrict her activities.

After the accident, plaintiff cared for her and assumed the sole financial responsibility for maintaining their household. During the weeks preceding her death, Ms. Wagner was acutely depressed. On one occasion, she attempted suicide by slashing her wrists. On January 23, 1974, she committed suicide by jumping from the roof of the apartment building in which they lived.

On the morning of the day of her death, Ms. Wagner received a check for $17,400 drawn by a Pennsylvania attorney who had represented her in a claim arising out of the automobile accident. The check represented settlement of the claim. Plaintiff telephoned Ms. Wagner at around 11:30 A.M. that day and was told that the check had arrived. Plaintiff noticed nothing unusual in Ms. Wagner's voice. At about 3:20 P.M., decedent left the apartment building and jumped to her death. The police, as part of their investigation of the suicide, asked the building superintendent to admit them to the apartment. On the kitchen table they found the check, endorsed in blank, and two notes handwritten by the decedent. In one, she described her depression over her physical condition, expressed her love for Scherer, and asked him to forgive her "for taking the easy way out." In the other, she indicated that she "bequeathed" to plaintiff all of her possessions, including "the check for $17,400.00 . . . ." The police took possession of the check, which was eventually placed in an interest-bearing account pending disposition of this action.

Under our wills statute it is clear that Ms. Wagner's note bequeathing all her possessions to Mr. Scherer cannot take effect as a testamentary disposition. N.J.S.A. 3A:3-2. A *donatio causa mortis* has been traditionally defined as a gift of personal property made by a party in expectation of death, then imminent, subject to the condition that the donor die as anticipated. Establishment of the gift has uniformly called for proof of delivery.

The primary issue here is whether Ms. Wagner's acts of endorsing the settlement check, placing it on the kitchen table in the apartment she shared with Scherer, next to a writing clearly evidencing her intent to transfer the check to Scherer, and abandoning the apartment with a clear expectation of imminent death constituted delivery sufficient to sustain a gift causa mortis of the check. Defendant, relying on the principles established in Foster v. Reiss, 18 N.J. 41, 112 A.2d 553 (1955), argues that there was no delivery because the donor did not unequivocally relinquish control of the check before her death. Central to this argument is the contention that suicide, the perceived peril, was one which decedent herself created and one which was completely within her control. According to this contention, the donor at any time before she jumped from the apartment roof could have changed her mind, re-entered the apartment, and reclaimed the check. Defendant therefore reasons that decedent did not make an effective transfer of the check during her lifetime, as is required for a valid gift causa mortis.

The majority and dissenting opinions in Foster v. Reiss contain thorough analyses of the evolution of the delivery requirement of the gift causa mortis. See also Mechem, "The Requirement of Delivery in Gifts of Chattels and of Choses in Action Evidenced by Commercial Instruments," 21 Ill. L. Rev. 341,

457, 568 (1926); Burton, "The Requirement of Delivery as Applied to Gifts of Choses in Action," 39 Yale L.J. 837 (1930). For commentary on Foster v. Reiss, see Bordwell, "Testate and Intestate Succession," 10 Rutgers L. Rev. 293, 297 (1955); Note, 10 Rutgers L. Rev. 457 (1955); Note, 54 Mich. L. Rev. 572 (1956). We see no need to retrace that history here.

There is general agreement that the major purpose of the delivery requirement is evidentiary. Proof of delivery reduces the possibility that the evidence of intent has been fabricated or that a mere donative impulse, not consummated by action, has been mistaken for a completed gift. Since "these gifts come into question only after death has closed the lips of the donor," the delivery requirement provides a substantial safeguard against fraud and perjury. See Keepers v. Fidelity Title and Deposit Co., 56 N.J.L. 302, 308, 28 A. 585 (E. & A. 1893). In *Foster,* the majority concluded that these policies could best be fulfilled by a strict rule requiring actual manual tradition of the subject-matter of the gift except in a very narrow class of cases where "there can be no actual delivery" or where "the situation is incompatible with the performance of such ceremony." 18 N.J. at 50, 112 A.2d at 559. Justice Jacobs, in his dissenting opinion (joined by Justices Brennan and Wachenfeld) questioned the reasonableness of requiring direct physical delivery in cases where donative intent is "freely and clearly expressed in a written instrument." Id. at 56, 112 A.2d at 562. He observed that a more flexible approach to the delivery requirement had been taken by other jurisdictions and quoted approvingly from Devol v. Dye, 123 Ind. 321, 24 N.E. 246, 7 L.R.A. 439 (Sup. Ct. 1890). That case stated:

> [G]ifts causa mortis . . . are not to be held contrary to public policy, nor do they rest under the disfavor of the law, when the facts are clearly and satisfactorily shown which make it appear that they were freely and intelligently made. Ellis v. Secor, 31 Mich. 185. While every case must be brought within the general rule upon the points essential to such a gift, yet, as the circumstances under which donations mortis causa are made must of necessity be infinite in variety, each case must be determined upon its own peculiar facts and circumstances. Dickeschild v. Bank, 28 W. Va. 341; Kiff v. Weaver, 94 N.C. 274. The rule requiring delivery, either actual or symbolical, must be maintained, but its application is to be militated and applied according to the relative importance of the subject of the gift and the condition of the donor. The intention of a donor in peril of death, when clearly ascertained and fairly consummated within the meaning of well-established rules, is not to be thwarted by a narrow and illiberal construction of what may have been intended for and deemed by him a sufficient delivery. . . .

The balancing approach suggested in Devol v. Dye has been articulated in the following manner:

> Where there has been unequivocal proof of a deliberate and well-considered donative intent on the part of the donor, many courts have been inclined to

overlook the technical requirements and to hold that by a "constructive" or "symbolic" delivery is sufficient to vest title in the donee. However, where this is allowed the evidence must clearly show an intention to part presently with some substantial attribute of ownership. [Gordon v. Barr, 13 Cal. 2d 596, 601, 91 P.2d 101, 104 (Sup. Ct. Cal. 1939)]

In essence, this approach takes into account the purposes served by the requirement of delivery in determining whether that requirement has been met. It would find a constructive delivery adequate to support the gift when the evidence of donative intent is concrete and undisputed, when there is every indication that the donor intended to make a present transfer of the subject matter of the gift, and when the steps taken by the donor to effect such a transfer must have been deemed by the donor as sufficient to pass the donor's interest to the donee. We are persuaded that this approach, which does not minimize the need for evidentiary safeguards to prevent frauds upon the estates of the deceased, reflects the realities which attend transfers of this kind.

In this case, the evidence of decedent's intent to transfer the check to Robert Scherer is concrete, unequivocal, and undisputed. The circumstances definitely rule out any possibility of fraud. The sole question, then, is whether the steps taken by the decedent, independent of her writing of the suicide notes, were sufficient to support a finding that she effected a lifetime transfer of the check to Scherer. We think that they were. First, the act of endorsing a check represents, in common experience and understanding, the only act needed (short of actual delivery) to render a check negotiable. The significance of such an act is universally understood. Accordingly, we have no trouble in viewing Ms. Wagner's endorsement of the settlement check as a substantial step taken by her for the purpose of effecting a transfer to Scherer of her right to the check proceeds. Second, we note that the only person other than the decedent who had routine access to the apartment was Robert Scherer. Indeed, the apartment was leased in his name. It is clear that Ms. Wagner before leaving the apartment placed the check in a place where Scherer could not fail to see it and fully expected that he would take actual possession of the check when he entered. And, although Ms. Wagner's subsequent suicide does not itself constitute a component of the delivery of this gift, it does provide persuasive evidence that when Ms. Wagner locked the door of the apartment she did so with no expectation of returning. When we consider her state of mind as it must have been upon leaving the apartment, her surrender of possession at that moment was complete. We find, therefore, that when she left the apartment she completed a constructive delivery of the check to Robert Scherer. In light of her resolve to take her own life and of her obvious desire not to be deterred from that purpose, Ms. Wagner's failure manually to transfer the check to Scherer is understandable. She clearly did all that she could do or thought necessary to do to surrender the check. Her donative intent has been conclusively demonstrated by independent evidence.

The law should effectuate that intent rather than indulge in nice distinctions which would thwart her purpose. Upon these facts, we find that the constructive delivery she made was adequate to support a gift causa mortis.

Defendant's assertion that suicide is not the sort of peril that will sustain a gift causa mortis finds some support in precedents from other jurisdictions. E.g., Ray v. Leader Federal Sav. & Loan Ass'n, 40 Tenn. App. 625, 292 S.W.2d 458 (Ct. App. 1953). See generally Annot., "Nature and validity of gift made in contemplation of suicide," 60 A.L.R.2d 575 (1958). We are, however, not bound by those authorities nor do we find them persuasive. While it is true that a gift causa mortis is made by the donor with a view to impending death, death is no less impending because of a resolve to commit suicide. Nor does that fixed purpose constitute any lesser or less imminent peril than does a ravaging disease. Indeed, given the despair sufficient to end it all, the peril attendant upon contemplated suicide may reasonably be viewed as even more imminent than that accompanying many illnesses which prove ultimately to be fatal. Cf. Berl v. Rosenberg, 169 Cal. App. 2d 125, 336 P.2d 975, 978 (Dist. Ct. App. 1959) (public policy against suicide does not invalidate otherwise valid gift causa mortis). And, the notion that one in a state of mental depression serious enough to lead to suicide is somehow "freer" to renounce the depression and thus the danger than one suffering from a physical illness, although it has a certain augustinian appeal, has long since been replaced by more enlightened views of human psychology. In re Van Wormer's Estate, 255 Mich. 399, 238 N.W. 210 (Sup. Ct. 1931) (melancholia ending in suicide sufficient to sustain a gift causa mortis). We also observe that an argument that the donor of a causa mortis gift might have changed his or her mind loses much of its force when one recalls that a causa mortis gift, by definition, can be revoked at any time before the donor dies and is automatically revoked if the donor recovers.

Finally, defendant asserts that this gift must fail because there was no acceptance prior to the donor's death. Although the issue of acceptance is rarely litigated, the authority that does exist indicates that, given a valid delivery, acceptance will be implied if the gift is unconditional and beneficial to the donee. See, e.g., Sparks v. Hurley, 208 Pa. 166, 57 A. 364, 366 (Sup. Ct. 1904); Graham v. Johnston, 243 Iowa 112, 49 N.W.2d 540, 543 (Sup. Ct. 1951). The presumption of acceptance may apply even if the donee does not learn of the gift until after the donor's death. Taylor v. Sanford, 108 Tex. 340, 344, 193 S.W. 661, 662 (Sup. Ct. 1912) (assent to gift of deed mailed in contemplation of death but received after grantor's death should be presumed unless a dissent or disclaimer appears). A donee cannot be expected to accept or reject a gift until he learns of it and unless a gift is rejected when the donee is informed of it the presumption of acceptance is not defeated. See id. at 344, 193 S.W. at 662. Here the gift was clearly beneficial to Scherer, and he has always expressed his acceptance.

Judgment affirmed.

NOTES AND QUESTIONS

1. Foster v. Reiss, 18 N.J. 41, 112 A.2d 553 (1955), the case on which defendant relied in vain, offers a poignant counterpart to Scherer v. Hyland. There, decedent had entered a hospital to undergo major surgery. Shortly before leaving her hospital room, she wrote the following note in Hungarian to her husband:

> My Dearest Papa:
>
> In the kitchen, in the bottom of the cabinet, where the blue frying pan is, under the wine bottle, there is one hundred dollars. Along side the bed in my bedroom, in the rear drawer of the small table in the corner of the drawer, where my stockings are, you will find about seventy-five dollars. In my purse there is six dollars, where the coats are. Where the coats are, in a round tin box, on the floor, where the shoes are, there is two hundred dollars. This is Dianna's. Please put it in the bank for her. This is for her schooling.
>
> The Building Loan book is yours, and the Bank book, and also the money that is here. In the red book is my son's and sister's and my brothers address. In the letter box is also my bank book.
>
> Give Margaret my sewing machine and anything else she may want; she deserves it as she was good to me.
>
> God be with you. God shall watch your steps. Please look out for yourself that you do not go on a bad road. I cannot stay with you. My will is in the office of the former Lawyer Anekstein, and his successor has it. There you will find out everything.
>
> Your Kissing, loving wife,
Ethel Reiss   1951-5-4.

The decedent placed the note inside the drawer of her bedside table, asked an old friend to tell her husband about it, and underwent surgery from which she died apparently without regaining consciousness.

Because decedent's will left the bulk of her estate to her children, the executors sued the husband to recover the passbooks. A badly divided Supreme Court reversed a lower court judgment for the husband, holding that insufficient delivery had occurred to establish a gift causa mortis.

The court in its opinion stated that gifts causa mortis are not favored in the law. Why might this be? Note, however, that not all courts would agree. Cf. Devol v. Dye, 123 Ind. 321, 24 N.E. 246 (1890) (cited in Scherer v. Hyland).

Which outcome do you prefer: Foster v. Reiss or Scherer v. Hyland? Why?

2. Consider whether a completed gift has occurred in the following situations:

(a) Father on his deathbed gives his daughter the keys to the family car and says: "I want the car to be yours." Father dies shortly after.

(b) Father on his daughter's birthday gives her the keys to the family car and says: "This is your birthday present. Drive the car in good health!" Father dies suddenly the next day.

(c) Father on his deathbed gives his son the keys to the family car and says: "I want your sister Sally to have the car." Father dies shortly after.

3. Compare the following situations:

(a) Father says to his son: "I am leaving you the Picasso in the living room when I die."

(b) Father says to his son: "The Picasso in the living room is yours. Be sure that you take it when I die."

BLANCHETTE v. BLANCHETTE
362 Mass. 518, 287 N.E.2d 459 (1972)

BRAUCHER, J.

This is a petition brought in connection with the divorce of the parties by the petitioner Marie to determine her interest in certain property including 168 shares (the stock) of the American Telephone & Telegraph Company (the company). The petition was referred to a master who heard the parties, filed a report, and made general findings, among others, that the respondent Robert was the sole owner of the stock and that there was no gift or attempted gift of the stock to Marie.

Marie objected to that part of the report which related to the stock. After a hearing, the judge issued a decree overruling Marie's exceptions, confirming the report, declaring the stock to be the sole property of Robert and ordering Marie to execute any documents necessary to give effect to the ownership of the stock, as determined by the decree, upon the records of the company. Marie appeals from the decree, contending that the subsidiary facts reported by the master do not support his general findings with respect to the ownership of the stock.

The master's report having been confirmed, his findings establish the facts in the case. Foot v. Bauman, 333 Mass. 214, 219. Flynn v. Seekonk, 352 Mass. 71, 72. We summarize them. The parties were married on November 17, 1945. While married they both worked, with a few interruptions, at steady jobs. In 1955 Robert was working for the company, and under a company plan began to buy shares of stock in the company at eighty-five per cent of market value through a weekly deduction from his pay.

Robert wanted to avoid the expense of probate and legal proceedings if he should die. When he expressed this desire in connection with the stock purchase plan to the people where he worked, he was told that the only way to achieve it was to have the stock issued to himself and Marie as joint tenants. The stock could have been issued to the parties as tenants in common, but Robert purposely avoided that option.

When he started to acquire the stock, he told Marie he put them in both their names as joint tenants "in case something happened" to him and that they would then be hers "without probate or lawyer." The certificates were issued at his request to "Robert L. Blanchette & Mrs. Marie A. Blanchette, Joint Tenants." He executed assignments to himself and Marie "as Joint Tenants with rights of survivorship and not as Tenants in Common," and she also signed some of the documents in this form. The last certificate was issued on June 30, 1964.

Marie took no part in the purchase of the stock and did not know when the stock certificates were issued or how many shares were acquired. Her impression was that they would be hers only after Robert's death and she did not think she had the right to sell any interest in them or to do anything with them without his signature. She signed dividend checks; on many occasions Robert signed her name to the checks. Robert never told her that she owned half of the stock. The certificates were kept in a wardrobe in their bedroom when they were separated on February 7, 1965, and at that time Marie did demand one of two bankbooks usually kept in the same place, but she did not ask for any of the stock. She was content with the bankbook. There is no finding that she made any claim to the stock before the parties' divorce on May 14, 1969.

The master's general findings included the following: Robert "never at any time indicated by conduct or words that he intended to transfer any present interest in these stocks to his wife." The words "Joint Tenants" were used "only because this form of issuance was the only one authorized by Robert's employer which approximated his desire to make his wife 'his beneficiary' if he died. Robert did not in any way attempt to make a gift of these stocks to his wife and no gift of these stocks was in fact made."

The master's findings must stand unless they are inconsistent, contradictory or plainly wrong. We have applied to share certificates in joint names the same principles we have applied to joint bank accounts. [Citations omitted.] In disputes arising while both parties to a joint bank account are still alive we have frequently upheld allegations or findings that there was no donative intent. [Citations omitted.] A finding as to the respective interests of the parties in joint deposits during their lives is a pure question of fact. [Citations omitted.]

Share certificates are less likely than bank accounts to be put in joint names merely for convenience, and in two cases we have disapproved findings that share certificates were placed in joint names without donative intent. MacLennan v. MacLennan, 316 Mass. 593, 597. Zambunos v. Zambunos, 324 Mass. 220, 223. Compare McPherson v. McPherson, 337 Mass. 611, 614 (real estate); Goldman v. Finkel, 341 Mass. 492, 494 (real estate). In both of those cases, as in this one, the intention was clear that the husband was to have sole control during his life and that whatever should remain at his death, if the wife survived, should ripen into full ownership by her. The finding that no present gift was intended would logically have the effect of frustrating the intention of the parties by rendering their arrangement testamentary and void. We avoided that result by substituting a finding of an intention to make a present gift of a joint interest, with the effect intended by the parties. In effect, there was a present gift of a future interest, subject to a reserved life estate in the husband and to his power to revoke his wife's interest. The result was based on our duty to draw proper inferences from the subsidiary findings unaffected by the conclusions of the trier of fact. We have the same duty in reviewing the subsidiary findings and conclusions of a master. Robinson v. Pero, 272 Mass. 482, 484, and cases cited. International Tel. & Tel. Corp. v. Hartford Acc. & Indem. Co., 357 Mass. 282, 287, and cases cited.

We think, however, that it is not necessary to modify the decree here, as was done in the *MacLennan* and *Zambunos* cases, to declare that the certificates are held in joint account, subject to the right of control reserved by the respondent. By contesting this suit the respondent has fully manifested his intention to exercise his right of control, and he has been prevented from doing so by the pendency of the suit. The decree does substantial justice, and a modification would be purely formal except so far as it might permit intervening events to affect unjustly the rights of the parties. Compare White v. White, 346 Mass. 76, 79-80. To the extent that the *MacLennan* and *Zambunos* cases would require modification, therefore, we overrule those cases. The decree is to be affirmed without modification.

To avoid misunderstanding, we emphasize that nothing we say here is intended to impair the right of the survivor to joint bank accounts or to share certificates in joint names, where the donor has died without manifesting an intention to defeat the gift. If the owner of funds, with the assent of another, deposits the funds in an account in both their names, payable to either or the survivor, the deposit if so intended may take effect as a novation, creating contract rights against the bank in both parties in accordance with the deposit agreement. The statute of wills is not involved. As between the bank and the named depositors, the deposit agreement is binding. G.L. c. 167, §14. Sawyer v. National Shawmut Bank, 306 Mass. 313, 316.

The effect of such a deposit is a present and complete gift of the contract right intended, and it is not fatal that the original owner of the funds retains possession of the bankbook and a right to withdraw funds from the account and thus to defeat the gift. In numerous cases where the original owner had died, we have upheld the right of the survivor to the balance in the account. We have not regarded the form of the account as conclusive between the parties, but have allowed the representative of the estate of the decedent to show by attendant facts and circumstances that the decedent did not intend to make a present completed gift of a joint interest in the account. Thus we have upheld findings of undue influence. . . .

In cases of conflicting evidence we have required that the question of donative intent be submitted to the trier of fact. The burden of proof is on the person seeking to show that the transaction is not to be taken at face value.

Where as in the present case the intention has been clear that the donee's interest was to ripen into full ownership on the donor's death, we have overturned findings that there was no donative intent.

We recognize that under the cases cited the arrangement of the parties provides a substitute for a will. But we see no harm in that. "If an owner of property can find a means of disposing of it inter vivos that will render a will unnecessary for the accomplishment of his practical purposes, he has a right to employ it. The fact that the motive of a transfer is to obtain the practical advantages of a will without making one is immaterial." National Shawmut Bank v. Joy, 315 Mass. 457, 471-472, and cases cited. . . .

Our law in this situation is in harmony with that in many other States. "The formal requisites of wills serve two main purposes: to insure that dispositions are carefully and seriously made, and to provide reliable evidence of the dispositions. Those purposes are adequately served by the institutional setting and the signed writing normally involved in taking out insurance, opening a bank account, buying United States Savings Bonds, or entering a government pension system." 1951 Rep. N.Y. Law Rev. Commn. 587, 597. In a very large number of cases joint bank accounts have been given effect as a "poor man's will." . . .

Decree affirmed.

DE CICCO v. BARKER
339 Mass. 457, 159 N.E.2d 534 (1959)

WILLIAMS, J. In this suit in equity the plaintiff seeks to obtain from the defendant the return of six engagement rings given by him to her in contemplation of marriage. The defendant demurred to the plaintiff's bill on the ground that the suit was prohibited by G.L. c. 207, §47A. The demurrer was overruled by interlocutory decree and the defendant appealed. She then answered and made counterclaim for the return by the plaintiff of two rings given to him by her. The case was referred to a master who reported the following facts. The parties met in December, 1952. The plaintiff was then married. In February, 1954, his wife became "very" ill and was hospitalized. He discussed with the defendant the possibility of marriage if his wife died. In March they picked out a six carat diamond ring which the plaintiff purchased and gave to the defendant. He also gave her at some time three other rings. His wife died on April 6. About May 3 the defendant gave the plaintiff a "man's diamond ring . . . in contemplation of marriage, and as an engagement ring." The plaintiff negotiated for the purchase of a house which the defendant had selected and they installed there a quantity of her furniture and numerous articles purchased by him as gifts for her. At some time between the wife's death and the following November the parties had agreed to marry. In January, 1955, the defendant broke the engagement without "adequate cause" or "fault" on the part of the plaintiff. The master found that the six carat diamond ring was given by the plaintiff to the defendant as an "engagement ring . . . upon the implied condition that the parties would be married when and if his wife died" and that the other rings given by him were "absolute gifts." The master's report was confirmed and a final decree entered dismissing both the plaintiff's bill and the defendant's counterclaim. The plaintiff appealed.

It is generally held that an engagement ring is in the nature of a pledge, given on the implied condition that the marriage shall take place. If the contract to marry is terminated without fault on the part of the donor he may recover the ring. Gikas v. Nicholis, 96 N.H. 177, 71 A.2d 785, 24 A.L.R.2d 576; Priebe v. Sinclair, 90 Cal. App. 2d 79, 202 P.2d 577. See 24 A.L.R.2d 579. General Laws c. 207, §47A, on which the defendant relies, was inserted by St. 1938, c. 350, §1. It provides that "Breach of contract to marry shall not constitute an injury or wrong recognized by law, and no action, suit or proceeding shall be maintained therefor." Its title, "An Act abolishing causes of action for breach of contract to marry, with a view to preserving the marriage institution and protecting the public morals," is indicative of its purpose. See 33 Mich. L. Rev. 979. We held in Thibault v. Lalumiere, 318 Mass. 72, 60 N.E.2d 349, 158 A.L.R. 613, that after breach of such a contract a woman could not maintain an action in tort to recover damages for embraces and caresses to which she had submitted during the engagement. The present suit is different in character. It is a proceeding not to recover damages either directly or indirectly for breach of the contract to marry but to obtain on established equitable principles restitution of property held on a condition which the defendant was unwilling to fulfil. It seeks to prevent unjust enrichment. Authority for the maintenance of such a suit is found in the Restatement: Restitution, §58, and in the judicial decisions in other States having statutes similar to §47A. Gikas v. Nicholis, 96 N.H. 177, 71 A.2d 785, 24 A.L.R.2d 576; Pavlicic v. Vogtsberger, 390 Pa. 502, 136 A.2d 127. See 29 Cornell L.Q. 401. We think it is not the kind of suit which the Legislature intended to abolish and that the plaintiff is entitled to recover his engagement ring.

It was said in the Thibault opinion that §47A "abolished any right of action, whatever its form, that was based" [318 Mass. 72, 60 N.E.2d 351] upon breach of promise. Further consideration leads us to think that the statement was too inclusive and that a proceeding may be maintained which although occasioned by breach of contract to marry, and in a sense based upon the breach, is not as was the action in the Thibault case brought to recover for the breach itself.

The interlocutory decree overruling the defendant's demurrer is affirmed. The final decree is reversed in so far as it provides for the dismissal of the plaintiff's bill and is affirmed as to the dismissal of the defendant's counterclaim. A new final decree is to be entered providing that the defendant deliver to the plaintiff the six carat diamond engagement ring.

So ordered.

LOWE v. QUINN
27 N.Y.2d 397, 267 N.E.2d 251 (1971)

FULD, C.J. The plaintiff, a married man, sues for the return of a diamond "engagement" ring which he gave the defendant in October of 1968 upon her promise to wed him when and if he became free; he had been living apart from his wife for several years and they contemplated a divorce. About a month after receiving the ring, the defendant told the plaintiff that she had "second thoughts" about the matter and had decided against getting married. When he requested the return of the ring, she suggested that he "talk to [her] lawyer". Convinced of the futility of further discussion, he brought this action to recover the ring or, in the alternative, the sum of $60,000, its asserted value.

Following a motion by the defendant for summary judgment dismissing the complaint and a cross motion by the plaintiff to amend his complaint "to include causes of action for fraud, unjust enrichment and monies had and received," the court at Special Term denied the defendant's application and granted the plaintiff's. The Appellate Division reversed and granted the defendant's motion, directing summary judgment against the plaintiff.

An engagement ring "is in the nature of a pledge for the contract of marriage" (Beck v. Cohen, 237 App. Div. 729, 730, 262 N.Y.S. 716, 718) and, under the common law, it was settled—at least in a case where no impediment existed to a marriage—that, if the recipient broke the "engagement," she was required, upon demand, to return the ring on the theory that it constituted a conditional gift. (See, e.g., Wilson v. Riggs, 267 N.Y. 570, 196 N.E. 584, *aff'g* 243 App. Div. 33, 276 N.Y.S. 232; Beck v. Cohen, 237 App. Div. 729, 262 N.Y.S. 716, *supra;* Goldstein v. Rosenthal, 56 Misc. 2d 311, 288 N.Y.S.2d 503; Jacobs v. Davis [1917], 2 K.B. 532; see, also, Note, 24 A.L.R.2d 579.) However, a different result is compelled where, as here, one of the parties is married. An agreement to marry under such circumstances is void as against public policy (see, e.g., Haviland v. Halstead, 34 N.Y. 643; Williams v. Igel, 62 Misc. 354, 116 N.Y.S. 778; Davis v. Pryor, 8 Cir., 112 F. 274), and it is not saved or rendered valid by the fact that the married individual contemplated divorce and that the agreement was conditioned on procurement of the divorce. (See, e.g., Smith v. McPherson, 176 Cal. 144, 167 P. 875; Leupert v. Shields, 14 Col. App. 404, 60 P. 193; Noice v. Brown, 38 N.J.L. 228; see, also, 49 Harv. L. Rev. 648.) Based on such reasoning, the few courts which have had occasion to consider the question have held that a plaintiff may not recover the engagement ring or any other property he may have given the woman. (See Malasarte v. Keye, 13 Alaska 407, 412; Morgan v. Wright, 219 Ga. 385, 133 S.E.2d 341; Armitage v. Hogan, 25 Wash. 2d 672, 171 P.2d

830.) Thus, in Armitage v. Hogan, 25 Wash. 2d 672, 171 P.2d 830, *supra,*
which is quite similar to the present case, the high court of the State of Washington declared (pp. 683, 685, 171 P.2d): ". . . if it be admitted for the sake of
argument that [defendant] respondent did agree to marry [plaintiff] appellant, and that the ring was purchased . . . in consideration of such promise,
such agreement would be illegal and void, as appellant was, at that time, and
in fact has at all times since been, a married man. . . . [p. 683, 171 P.2d 837]

"Regardless of the fact that appellant states this action is based on fraud
and deceit, we are of the opinion that, under the facts in the case, appellant's
claimed cause of action is based upon an illegal and immoral transaction, and
that this court should not lend its aid in furthering such transaction. [p. 685,
171 P.2d 838]".

There are cases, it is true, which refuse to apply the doctrine of "unclean
hands"—invoked by the courts in the cited decisions—when the conduct relied
upon is not "directly related to the subject matter in litigation" but it is
difficult to see how the delivery of the ring or the action to procure its return
may be deemed unrelated to the contract to marry. There can be no possible
doubt that the gift of the engagement ring was part and parcel of, directly
related to, the agreement to wed.

Nor does section 80-b of the Civil Rights Law create a cause of action.
That provision, enacted in 1965, recites in part that "Nothing in this article
contained shall be construed to bar a right of action for the recovery of a
chattel . . . when the sole consideration for the transfer of the chattel . . . was
a contemplated marriage which has not occurred". That section must, however, be read in connection with section 80-a which effected the abolition of
actions for breach of promise to marry. Section 80-b was added to overcome
decisions such as Josephson v. Dry Dock Sav. Inst., 292 N.Y. 666, 56 N.E.2d
96, in order to make it clear that a man not under any impediment to marry
was entitled to the return of articles which he gave the woman, even though
breach of promise suits had been abolished as against public policy. (See, e.g.,
Goldstein v. Rosenthal, 56 Misc. 2d 311, 314, 288 N.Y.S.2d 503, *supra.*) This
statute, however, does not alter the settled principle denying a right of recovery where either of the parties to the proposed marriage is already married.

The order appealed from should be affirmed, with costs.

SCILEPPI, J. (dissenting).

PART III

FORMATION OF INTERESTS
IN LAND

Chapter 3

Estates in Land: The Freehold Estates

§3.1 The Estate-in-Land Concept

"Estates" in land are a form of legal shorthand: they represent various bundles of property interests—i.e., rights, privileges, powers, etc., that one can enjoy with respect to land. They also reflect a view of property that emerged from England's post-Conquest feudal order. The word "estate" once denoted "status"; in thirteenth-century England, a man's social status depended on the extent of his land holdings and, equally relevant, on the tenure by which he held. Quite simply, a "free" man held a "freehold" estate; a villein or serf held a "nonfreehold" estate. Practical differences, relating chiefly to access to the courts, accompanied this distinction. In time, the feudal system vanished and new means appeared for acquiring status. Still, we have kept the term "estate" as a genus for classifying property in land. Moreover, we have also preserved, largely out of habit, the dichotomy between "freehold" and "nonfreehold" estates.

The *right to possession* is a focal point for estate analysis, although it is only one of the many property interests we will consider. In the attention given the right to possession, the stress has been temporal, one devoted to *when* the right begins, and to its *duration*. (Later, we will consider possession from another vantage: *who* is entitled to possession?) By analyzing possession along a plane of time, we can divide estates into "present" interests, entitling someone to possession now, and "future" interests, entitling someone to possession when (and if) the present interest ends. For example, if you occupy your apartment on a two-year lease, yours is a present interest, and your landlord's is a future interest.

Present and future interests come in several species, and we will mention most of them in this text. It is quite a trick to keep them sorted out, and Table 1 is intended to improve your chances of doing so. The terms will mean little to you just now, but they will be old acquaintances someday. Incidentally, correct usage is essential; otherwise, classification will not serve even its minimum role of giving lawyers a common tongue. Therefore, do not say "remainder" when you mean "reversion."

Note that the table has three divisions. First, it separates the "freehold" from the "nonfreehold" interests. Second, it separates the "present" from the "future" interests. Finally, it distinguishes the future interests that a grantor reserves for himself from the future interests that a grantor creates in third

TABLE 1

Present Interest	Future Interest	
	in grantor	*in third person*
FREEHOLD INTERESTS		
Fee simple absolute	None	None
Fee tail	Reversion	Vested remainder Contingent remainder* Executory interest*
Defeasible estates		
(a) Fee simple determinable (also called base fee, qualified fee, or fee on [special] limitation)	Possibility of reverter	Executory interest*
(b) Fee simple subject to a condition subsequent (also called fee on condition)	Power of termination (right of entry, right of reacquisition)	Executory interest*
Life estate	Reversion	Vested remainder‡ Contingent remainder* Executory interest*
NONFREEHOLD INTERESTS		
Term of years (estate for years)	Reversion	Vested remainder†
Tenancy at will (estate at will)		Executory interest†
Periodic tenancy		(Fee subject to term)†

* The contingent remainder and the executory interest both can follow the fee tail or the life estate. Although these two future interests stem from different sources, the unlikenesses between them are largely gone. Where dissimilarity remains, you will probably hear about it in a trusts and estates course. For now, simply be aware that both interests exist. Cf. O. Moynihan, Introduction to Real Property 205–207 (1962); Dukeminier, Contingent Remainders and Executory Interests: A Requiem for the Distinction, 43 Minn. L. Rev. 13 (1958).

Under common-law terminology, only an executory interest can follow a *defeasible* estate where the future interest is created *in third persons*. Under some statutes, however, remainder has displaced executory interest, as the proper usage, in all situations. See, e.g., N.Y. Est., Powers and Trusts L. 6-4.3 (McKinney 1967).

† These occur infrequently.

‡ Vested remainders come in three styles: indefeasibly vested; vested subject to open; vested subject to complete defeasance. See, e.g., N.Y. Est., Powers and Trusts L. §§6-4.7–6-4.9 (McKinney 1967); §3.4, *infra*.

persons. You will discover why it sometimes matters when we examine defeasible estates; see pages 161-170.

§3.2   The "Fee Simple Absolute" (A "to B and His Heirs")

The crown jewel in the estate packet is the fee simple absolute, rapturously described by one writer as "the totality of rights that a man may have with respect to that piece of land." Bigelow, Cases on Rights in Land 20 (3d ed. 1945). But as we shall see, there is little that is absolute in the fee simple absolute; moreover, the totality of property interests enjoyed by one owner in fee simple absolute may vary greatly from that of her neighbor who also owns in fee simple absolute. To give one example: A owns Lot 1 encumbered by a $50,000 first mortgage and a 20-year lease; B owns Lot 2 free and clear—no mortgage, no lease; yet both A and B may own their respective pieces of land in fee simple absolute.

One right is common to all estates in fee simple absolute—the right of inheritance which an heir enjoys if her ancestor dies intestate while owning the land. For example: were A, owning Lot 1 in fee simple absolute, to die intestate survived by D, her sole heir, D would then own the lot in fee simple absolute. And if D were then to die intestate, still owning Lot 1 in fee simple absolute, succession would continue to her heirs. And so on, through the generations.[1] But even this right of intestate succession may be subject to state and federal taxes.

It is sometimes said that the holder of a fee simple absolute also has the power to transfer her entire estate (or some lesser part), in her lifetime or at her death (by will), but these are powers also enjoyed by landowners having some less exalted estates. Furthermore, the power to transfer is often qualified by doctrines regarding competency, by privately created restraints on alienation, and by common-law or statutory schemes designed to enhance the financial security of surviving husbands and wives. Indeed, the only unique quality of a fee simple absolute is its "general inheritance." And in an era when valuable land seldom passes by intestate succession, "general inheritance" is not all that much.

Although the descendability of land is a venerable part of the common-law tradition, it was not always so, and herein hangs a tale that would sometimes concern an unwary draftsman or an adroit lawyer. In the first decades of the feudal system, the relationship of lord and tenant was so charged with personal undertaking that the typical grant ended with the tenant's life; the land would then revert to the lord who was free to make whatever new arrangements he wished. Perhaps the lord *would* grant the parcel to the dece-

---

1. What becomes of land if an owner dies intestate without surviving heirs? Cf. 6 Powell, Real Property 619-629 (Rohan ed. 1973); Conn. Gen. Stat. Ann. §45-296 (Supp. 1973) (escheat).

dent's male heir—on his agreement to perform the services charged to his ancestor; but the lord might grant to others if the heir seemed unwilling or unable to shoulder his father's role.

In time, tenants were given advance assurance that at their death succession would be permitted; in short, grants "to B (the tenant) and his heirs" replaced grants "to B." And since primogeniture was much in vogue, the choice of the phrase "and his heirs" was significant: it denoted that succession was contemplated indefinitely, not only for the first generation. This estate in land became known as "fee simple absolute," and, after primogeniture disappeared, it took on the quality of general inheritance—that is, any class of heirs was entitled to succession.

As sometimes happens, legal arteries harden. The phrase "and his heirs," which denoted the "fee simple absolute," became the exclusive formula for creating this estate. We have this on the hallowed authority of Littleton:

> Tenant in fee simple is he which hath lands or tenements to hold to him and his heirs forever. . . . If a man would purchase lands . . . in fee simple, it behoveth him to have these words in his purchase, "To have and to hold to him and to his heirs": for these words, his heirs, make the estate of inheritance. For if a man purchase lands by these words, To have and to hold to him forever, or by these words, To have and to hold to him and his assigns forever; in these two cases he hath but an estate for term of life, for that there lack these words, his heirs, which words only make an estate of inheritance in all feoffments and grants. (Tenures, B. 1, c. 1 (1481))

Thus, even a conveyance "to B in fee simple absolute," however evident the grantor's intent, would have transferred no more than a deed inscribed "to B for life."

Formalism did not die with the fifteenth century. Blind adherence to form over substance, the necessity of invoking the "traditionally honored collocations of letters," as one writer called this mumbo jumbo, marked the law long after Littleton's remains were buried. For example, as recently as 1957, a Connecticut court ruled that a 12-year-old deed running "to B and assigns forever" failed to convey a fee simple absolute, although nothing in the deed suggested a contrary intent. [2]

Most states, however, have now rejected this barren formalism. Usually they have done so by statute, of which the following is typical:

> The use of terms of inheritance or succession are not necessary to create a fee simple estate, and every grant, conveyance, or mortgage of lands . . . shall convey or mortgage the entire interest which the grantor could lawfully grant, convey, or mortgage, unless it clearly appears by the deed, mortgage, or instrument that the grantor intended to convey or mortgage a less estate. [Ohio Rev. Code §5301.02 (1965)]

2. Cole v. Steinlauf, 144 Conn. 629, 136 A.2d 744 (1957). Four years later, the same court sharply questioned the earlier result. Dennen v. Searle, 149 Conn. 126, 137-138, 176 A.2d 561, 568 (1961).

A survey made in 1973 listed 39 states and the District of Columbia as having a comprehensive statute, and 9 other states as having enacted a partial remedy. (In Hawaii, the courts acted on their own initiative.) 2 Powell, Real Property 33-41 (Rohan ed. 1977). In the land of its birth, the need for the phrase "and his heirs" ended with the English law of Property Act of 1925, §60.

NOTES AND QUESTIONS

1. By passing a law that upsets a long-settled view of property, the legislature poses another issue which we will meet often: does the statute apply to transactions completed before the law's effective date; if so, does such retroaction deprive persons of vested property rights or interfere unduly with the obligation of contracts? For example: a prestatutory deed runs from A "to B and his assigns forever." While A seems to have intended a fee simple absolute, his improper usage has given B a life estate only, which would leave in A the reversion following B's death. The state then enacts a law that would retroactively deprive A of his reversion. Is this a deprivation without due process? Is it relevant that the reversion was accidental—the result of a draftsman's carelessness or neglect, and that the thrust of the statute is intent-promoting (whereas the thrust of the common law was intent-defeating)? In the absence of a statute which applies to B's deed, how might B rectify the apparent mistake?

Most statutes either do not mention the past (see, e.g., the Ohio statute *supra*) or are explicitly prospective, but an occasional statute covers deeds already in existence. One example is the English Law of Property Act of 1925, §60, which has made it sufficient, for deeds executed after December 31, 1881, to use the words "in fee simple" without reference to "heirs."

2. A title examiner should be thoroughly familiar both with current property doctrine and its evolutionary course. He must analyze each deed or other document in the chain of title by reference to doctrine existing when the instrument became effective (for an inter vivos transfer, the date of execution; for a will, the date of the testator's death), unless, of course, later reforms apply to earlier instruments. So pervasive has been the influence of statutory change that the skilled "title man" must have a healthy respect for the historical process.

3. From earliest times a fee simple absolute could be devised by will without use of the phrase "and his heirs." This difference arose because testamentary land transfers were first recognized by Chancery, which had little patience with the rigidity of fifteenth-century common-law conveyancing. Any clear expression of the testator's intent to devise a fee simple absolute was sufficient. 2 Powell, Real Property 30-33 (Rohan ed. 1977).

4. Although it is no longer necessary in most states, draftsmen still invoke the litany "and his heirs" to create a fee simple absolute. Why so?

How does the phrase "to A and his heirs" differ from "to A and his assigns"?

Corporations may have successors, but they never have heirs. How might a draftsman transfer land in fee simple absolute to a corporate grantee? Cf. Modern Legal Forms §3201 (Belshiem ed. 1966).

5. Where it is unclear whether the grantor intended to create a fee simple absolute or some "lesser" interest, what should be the presumption? Would you endorse the Restatement view? "In determining whether a 'conveyance expresses an intent to create an estate other than a fee simple absolute,' every reasonable doubt as to the existence of such an intent is resolved against the finding of such an intent." Restatement of Property §39, Comment b.

6. Two phrases are much bruited by appellate judges: "words of purchase" and "words of limitation." To understand them, one should begin with the concept of "purchase" as it is used in classifying estates. (In another context, that of recording act protection, purchase has a different, more familiar meaning.) Purchase is *any transfer* of a property interest that is accomplished by a conveyance or a will. (Thus, transfer by intestate succession is not a purchase.) If A deeds Lot 1 to B, a purchase occurs (and B is a purchaser), whether A sells the land or gives it away. "Words of purchase" are those words in a conveyance or a will that express the transfer, e.g., "A grants to B."

"Words of limitation" express the extent or limit of the purchaser's estate. An example should make this clear. Suppose that "A grants Lot 1 to B for the life of B." "For the life of B" is the phrase that qualifies B's interest by limiting him to a life estate. As such, we speak of this phrase as "words of limitation."

7. Why, in a conveyance "to B and his heirs," do the heirs receive only a contingent interest—the right to succession if B dies intestate while owning the land? On their face, "to B and his heirs" seem like words of purchase that would endow B's heirs as fully as "to B and his son John" would endow son John. Three reasons for this surprising result follow, all steeped in early common law.

The first is metaphysical: to speak of property in persons yet unidentified or yet unborn was alien to the feudal mind for whom land ownership could not be imagined except in relation to someone *in being* who was entitled to present or future possession of the res. The second is twelfth-century avarice: as we shall see, an important source of feudal revenue, the incidents of primer seisin and relief (the ancient counterparts of estate taxes), depended on the fiction that B's heirs did not really acquire property by a conveyance to his ancestor. Finally, perhaps in response to this fiction, the common-law courts permitted B, by an inter vivos transfer, to deprive his heir of succession; only if B did not convey during his lifetime would the heir enjoy his "birthright." D'Arundel's Case, Bracton's Notebook, pl. 1054 (1225).

§3.3   The "Fee Simple Conditional" and the "Fee Tail" (A "to B and the Heirs of His Body")

a.   Fee Simple Conditional

The commercial land transaction rarely occurred in Bracton's England. Land meant wealth and status, and one simply did not retail this symbol and source of power. But the family head, while wanting to maintain his estate intact, also had to consider the sometimes urgent financial needs of his children and children-in-law, needs best satisfied by donations of land, either as part of a marriage settlement or as an estate-planning scheme to treat younger sons more fairly than did primogeniture. Landowners also had to worry about the risk of forfeiture—for disloyalty or crime; often it was prudent to place title in those family members whose activities were less likely to bring official disgrace. But a device was needed to prevent the transferee from frittering away or forfeiting the dynastic base. In making his gift to B, A wanted assurance that the land would in time descend to B's heir.

After D'Arundel's Case (1225), use of the fee simple absolute was not the answer; B could sever the line of descent by making a transfer during his lifetime. Draftsmen thought, however, that the phrase "to B and the heirs of his body" would prevent this. The change was ever so slight. Only three little words were added to the symbolic notation for fee simple absolute, yet the grantor's intention was unmistakable: he wanted a different reading of B's powers and liabilities. And, in an era that exalted form, it would have been unthinkable for the courts to treat "heirs of his body" language as having no significance.

Powerful, however, was the demand for freer alienability, and the courts, even then, were rather disposed to support this demand. They quickly found a formula. On a conveyance "to B and the heirs of his body," B was permitted to alienate a fee simple absolute as soon as he produced an heir of the designated class. All that was needed was a live birth (the heir might die minutes later), and B was free, at any time before his death, to defeat the donor's desire. Only if B did not convey, and did not lose the land involuntarily, would descent, as provided for in the grant, then take place. Moreover, the descendants might similarly convey, once they had demonstrated their power of procreation. Because B had a fee simple "conditional upon the birth of the heirs of his body," his estate became known as a fee simple conditional.

b.   De Donis and the Advent of Fee Tail

This judicial gloss did not contribute to the happiness of major landowners who, as early as 1258, petitioned the King for some redress. It arrived finally, in 1285, when De Donis Conditionalibus, 13 Edw. 1, c. 1 (Statute of Westminster), became law. With a directness that is refreshing, De Donis made perfectly clear that a donee could not substitute his preferences for those of the giver:

> Wherefore our lord the king, perceiving how necessary and expedient it should be to provide remedy in the aforesaid cases, hath ordained, that the will of the giver according to the form in the deed of gift manifestly expressed shall be from henceforth observed, so that they to whom the land was given under such condition shall have no power to aliene the land so given, but that it shall remain unto the issue of them to whom it was given after their death, or shall revert unto the giver or his heirs if issue fail either by reason that there is no issue at all, or if any issue be, it fail by death, the heir of such issue failing.

The estate was no longer called "fee simple conditional"; henceforth, "fee tail" would designate the phrase "to B and the heirs of his body." "Fee tail" derived from "tailler," an early French infinitive, meaning "to carve"; one could say that the grantor carved out an estate (fee) to fit his liking.

Let us pause a moment to check your understanding of the property interests created by fee tail. Assume a conveyance by A "to B and the heirs of his body." B is the "tenant in tail." He has a present estate, for life; his transferee would get no more; neither would a creditor or the King (in case of forfeiture). At B's death, the land descends to the members of the designated class, B's lineal heirs, if they exist. Moreover, B's lineal heirs also enjoy only a life estate; at their death, the process of descent continues. If B dies without the enumerated heirs, or if the line of descent fails in any later generation, the entailed estate reverts to the grantor, or if he is already dead, to his heirs. A's future interest, his prospect of recovering the land if B's issue fails, is called a "reversion." Had A created this prospect in third persons, for example, A "to B and the heirs of his body, then to C and his heirs," C's future interest would be called a "remainder." Query: would any property then be left in A and his heirs?

If he wished, a grantor could carve out fee tail estates with an even greater deftness of hand. For example, A might transfer land "to B and the heirs (male) (female) of his body," or "to B and the heirs of his body by his wife C." Why might a grantor choose a more circumscribed line of descent?

c. The Courts Assault Fee Tail

For nearly two centuries much of the privately owned land in England was entailed, defying a mounting clamor that land be more productive and more freely alienable. Entail was attacked on other counts, too: it was said that fee tail encouraged disrespect for regal and parental authority, and disregard for one's debts:

> Children grew disobedient when they knew they could not be set aside: farmers were ousted of their leases made by tenants in tail; for, if such leases had

been valid, then under colour of long leases the issue might have been virtually disinherited: creditors were defrauded of their debts; for, if tenant in tail could have charged his estate with their payment, he might also have defeated his issue, by mortgaging it for as much as it was worth: . . . and treasons were encouraged; as estates tail were not liable to forfeiture, longer than for the tenant's life. So that they were justly branded, as the source of new contentions and mischiefs unknown to the common law; and almost universally considered as the common grievance of the realm. But as the nobility were always fond of this statute, because it preserved their family estates from forfeitures, there was little hope of procuring repeal by the legislature. [2 Blackstone, Commentaries *116]

No system can survive insistent demands for its reform. If the lords in Parliament would not act, some other artifice would be found. The means chosen illustrate both the unending resourcefulness of the practicing lawyer and the common law's receptivity to purely formal legal triumphs. Two techniques, the common recovery and the fine, were developed for barring the entail; i.e., cutting off the tenant's heirs. Of the two, the common recovery was the more ingenious, and for many years was also the more effective, since it cut off not only the tenant's heirs, but also the reversioner or remainderman (the fine did not reach these latter interests until the sixteenth century).

The invention of common recovery culminated a steady assault on De Donis. First, tenants in tail had been allowed to satisfy De Donis by substituting lands of equal value for the entailed estate. Next, the courts had accepted, in place of the entailed lands, a judgment of equivalent value, regardless of its collectibility. Then, with these doctrines firmly entrenched, the lawyers needed only to stage a collusive lawsuit—the common recovery—in order to manufacture the worthless judgment that could substitute for the entailed lands. Let us watch the lawyers cast the suit.

B is the tenant in tail who is bent on barring the entail. He must find an "adverse" party (call him C) willing to cooperate in the proceedings (C was often the person to whom B wished to sell a fee simple absolute). B must also locate an assetless someone who would agree, for a small fee, to let a judgment be taken against him. In time, the court crier (call him X) was quite likely to fill this role. With the cast chosen and rehearsed, a conspiratorial drama in five acts was then played out:

Act One: C sues B in an action for the recovery of the entailed lands, C falsely alleging that he has title.

Act Two: B "vouches in" X for breach of warranty, B falsely alleging that he had acquired the lands from X, with warranties of title. [3]

Act Three: X appears, admits both the conveyance and the warranties of title, asks for an adjournment, and then defaults.

3. One of the common-law warranties, quiet enjoyment, would result in a judgment for damages against the grantor if the grantee's possession were disturbed by someone having paramount title.

Act Four: The court gives judgment to C that he recover the lands in fee simple absolute. B complies with the judgment.

Act Five: The court gives judgment to B in his claim against X. This judgment, known as the common recovery, replaces the entailed estate.

Although its beginnings were some time earlier, common recovery received official notice and approval in 1472 with the decision in Taltarum's Case, Y.B. 12 Edw. 4, Mich. term, pl. 25. Thereafter, De Donis was a dead letter; the tenant in tail could repudiate the donor's intention whenever he wished. So widespread were the disentailing practices that they are mentioned by Hamlet in his musings on the skull of a lawyer;[4] and a lawyer who dared criticize the common recovery was sharply reproved by the Chief Justice of the Common Pleas who referred to the device as a "legal pillar" and "founded upon great reason and authority." Mary Portington's Case, 10 Co. Rep. 35b at 40a, 77 Eng. Rep. 976, 984 (1614). So profitable were the disentailing schemes for solicitors, courts, and governmental offices that the *statutory* repeal of De Donis was not achieved until 1834, when fines and recoveries were abolished, and a simple conveyance by deed served to bar the entail.

d. Fee Tail in the United States

Fee tail was never popular in the United States, partly because manorial holdings were uncommon beyond some areas in the South and along the Hudson River, and partly because the fee tail was already an ineffective dynastic device when American colonization began. Still, fee tail language occasionally appears, usually in wills—more often through inadvertence than design—and most American jurisdictions have enacted statutes to arrest its force. One example of the problem that arises when fee tail language appears today is illustrated in the following case.

MORRIS v. ULBRIGHT
558 S.W.2d 660 (Mo. Sup. Ct. 1977)

DONNELLY, J. This is an action to quiet title to land.

On March 8, 1947, Lina A. Ulbright and Frank O. Ulbright, her husband, executed a deed which conveyed the property in question to Logan Mitchell Ulbright "and his bodily heirs." The natural son, and only child, of Logan Mitchell Ulbright was Logan M. Ulbright, Jr. On October 4, 1950, Marion V. Morris and Ruby N. Morris adopted Logan M. Ulbright, Jr. and his name was changed to Logan Marion Morris.

---

4. ". . . This fellow might be in his time a great buyer of land, with his statutes, his recognizances, his fines, his double vouchers, his recoveries. Is this the fine of his fines, and the recovery of his recoveries, to have his fine pate full of fine dirt? . . ." Act 5, scene 1.

Lina A. Ulbright and Frank O. Ulbright are deceased.

On February 9, 1964, the heirs of Lina A. Ulbright conveyed to T.B. Alspaugh and Sara Jane Alspaugh.

On February 12, 1972, Logan Mitchell Ulbright died.

On January 24, 1973, the Alspaughs conveyed to Dorothy A. Ulbright and Ralph C. Ulbright.

Logan Marion Morris is plaintiff and claims title under the deed executed March 8, 1947. Dorothy A. Ulbright and Ralph C. Ulbright are defendants and claim title under the deed executed January 24, 1973.

The trial court entered summary judgment in favor of defendants. Plaintiff appealed to the Kansas City District of the Court of Appeals where the judgment of the trial court was reversed. The case was then transferred to this Court, by order of this Court, and will be decided here "the same as on original appeal." Mo. Const. Art. V, §10.

The parties agree that the deed of March 8, 1947, created an estate tail; that under the deed and Section 442.470, RSMo 1969, the first taker (Logan Mitchell Ulbright) took a life estate; and that the heir of the body (Logan M. Ulbright, Jr.—Logan Marion Morris) took a contingent remainder in the fee. Davidson v. Davidson, 350 Mo. 639, 167 S.W.2d 641 (1943). It is not seriously disputed that had Logan M. Ulbright, Jr., not been adopted on October 4, 1950, he would have taken in fee simple absolute upon the death of Logan Mitchell Ulbright on February 12, 1972. Defendants contend, however, that because of the provisions of Section 453.090, RSMo 1969, the adoption of plaintiff on October 4, 1950, "acted to remove the Plaintiff from the bloodstream of his natural father Logan Mitchell Ulbright and with no exception ceased and determined all rights and duties between Plaintiff and his natural father."

Section 453.090, RSMo 1969, provides that when a child is adopted in accordance with the provisions of Chapter 453, "all legal relationships and all rights and duties between such child and his natural parents . . . shall cease and determine."

The essential question in this case then becomes: Does plaintiff's interest, if any, in the land derive from Lina A. Ulbright and Frank O. Ulbright (grantors in the deed of March 8, 1947) or is plaintiff's interest, if any, one of inheritance from his natural father Logan Mitchell Ulbright (life tenant under the deed of March 8, 1947)? If the latter, plaintiff's interest was cut off by the adoption. If the former, it was not.

In 1 H. Tiffany, The Law of Real Property §48 at 70 (3rd ed. 1939), we find the following: "On the death of a tenant in tail, the land passes to the next heir of the body of the original donee; but such heir, though he takes because he is the heir of the body, takes not by descent, but as a substituted purchaser from the original donor, per formam doni, as it is expressed. . . ."

This proposition finds express support in Pollock v. Speidel, 17 Ohio St. 439, 49 Am. Dec. 467 (1867) and implied support in Davidson v. Davidson, supra, and Byrd v. Allen, 351 Mo. 99, 171 S.W.2d 691 (1942). See also 31 C.J.S. Estates §21, at 47 (1964).

In addition, Section 442.490, RSMo 1969, provides that when a remainder shall be limited to the heirs of the body of a person to whom a life estate is given, the remaindermen who qualify as heirs of the body "shall be entitled to take as *purchasers* in fee simple, by virtue of the remainder so limited in them." (Emphasis ours).

Accordingly, we are of the opinion that plaintiff derived his title as purchaser under the deed from Lina A. Ulbright and Frank O. Ulbright and not by inheritance from his natural father. Grimes v. Rush, 355 Mo. 573, 197 S.W.2d 310 (1946). We hold that his interest in the land was not extinguished by the adoption and provisions of §453.090, *supra,* because his interest in the land does not derive from his natural father.

The judgment is reversed and the cause remanded. . . .

FINCH, J., dissenting.

I respectfully dissent. The principal opinion concludes that the essential question for determination is whether plaintiff takes his interest, if any, as purchaser from Lina A. Ulbright and Frank O. Ulbright, grantors in the deed of March 8, 1947, or whether he takes by inheritance from his natural father who was the life tenant under said deed. It correctly concludes that one who qualifies as an heir of the body takes his interest by purchase and not by inheritance, but, in my view, this conclusion is not determinative of the issues before us.

The principal opinion simply assumes that under §442.490 plaintiff qualified as an heir of the body. Such an assumption, in my view, is contrary to the plain language of §442.490, which provides: "Where a remainder shall be limited to the heirs, or heirs of the body, of a person to whom a life estate in the same premises shall be given, *the persons who, on the termination of the life estate, shall be the heir or heirs of the body of such tenant for life* shall be entitled to take as purchasers in fee simple, by virtue of the remainder so limited in them." [Emphasis supplied]

The statute does not purport to *identify* who shall take the property as a purchaser. On the contrary, the statute expressly conditions the vesting of the estate by purchase to those who may be identified as the heir or heirs of the body of the life tenant. . . .

In determining the identity of those qualifying as a "bodily heir," it must be noted that the word "heir" is one of technical legal significance. It is defined in Black's Law Dictionary (4th ed. 1951) as: "the person *appointed by law* to succeed to the estate in case of intestacy." An "heir of the body" is a subclass of "heir"—i.e., "an heir begotten or borne [*sic*] by the person referred to. . . ." In Missouri, the phrase has been held to mean "an heir begotten of the body; a lineal descendant." Clarkson v. Hatton, 143 Mo. 47, 56, 44 S.W. 761, 762 (1898). The Restatement of Property §306 (1936) provides:

> When a limitation is in favor of the "heirs of the body" of a designated person, or is in other words of similar import, then, unless a contrary intent of the conveyor is found from additional language or circumstances, the persons so

described are the lineal descendants of the designated ancestor who *under the applicable local law* would succeed to the property if such ancestor died owning the property and intestate. . . . [Emphasis supplied]

It has long been recognized in this state that the law of inheritance is a creature of statute. In re Cupples Estate, 272 Mo. 465, 473, 199 S.W. 556, 558 (1917). Furthermore, "the right of the Legislature to prescribe the right of descent and inheritance cannot be doubted. It is not a natural right." *Cupples, supra* at 471, 199 S.W. at 557. Thus it is readily apparent from the foregoing that the relationship of one person as an "heir of the body" of another is a legal relationship which is established by statute rather than a natural relationship which exists as of right independent of a statutory grant.

It is axiomatic that a man does not have heirs until he dies. How then does anyone receive a contingent remainder in fee by purchase before the life tenant's death? Logically, because the nature of the contingency is that those who will take the property are unascertainable until the death of the life tenant, nobody can be said to own a remainder interest at all until such death, at which point the estate vests in possession or falls in for want of takers. However, it may be said that those who are *presumptive* heirs of the body at any given moment do have at least an expectancy interest. That is, once a child is born to the life tenant it is clear that at any given moment the life tenant could die and the remainder in fee would immediately vest in both interest and possession in the surviving child by virtue of the fact that the child would then be identified as an heir of the body under the existing intestacy statute, from which such identity derives. This expectancy of the presumptive heir is recognized in Missouri to be of sufficient weight to constitute a contingent remainder which may be "conveyed" by quitclaim deed. §442.020; Grimes v. Rush, 355 Mo. 573, 197 S.W.2d 310 (Mo. 1946). Of course, any interest claimed under such a deed would be subject to the same contingency of the grantor being properly identified as an heir of the body under the intestacy statute upon the death of the life tenant. . . .

Since 1917, some 30 years prior to the execution of this deed, the statutes of this state have provided that, upon adoption, all legal relationships and rights between the natural parent and adopted child shall "cease and determine." The relationship of a child to a parent as "heir" is determined upon death and is clearly a legal relationship because it arises solely by statute. The status of one as "presumptive heir" is likewise a legal relationship. Such relationships are clearly terminated as between the natural parent and adopted child at the time of the decree of adoption. Thus, absent some other language in the instrument indicating a contrary intention, an adopted child is neither the "heir" nor "heir of the body" of the natural parent. . . .

Such a result is not disconsonant with the underlying policy of the entail statute. Though some states have abolished the fee tail estate entirely by vesting the fee in the first grantee, Missouri's statutory provision allows the grantor to keep the land in the family for at least one generation as a balance between the interest of the grantor to keep the land in the family permanently and the interest of the state in free alienability. If any intent on the part of the grantors here may be discerned, their selection of the fee tail form of transfer evidences an intent to keep the land in the family. The construction of the adoption statutes . . . and urged herein furthers that policy and likely intent. I would therefore affirm the judgment.

NOTES AND QUESTIONS

1. The plaintiffs in Morris v. Ulbright brought an action to quiet title, a common procedural mode for resolving land ownership disputes. They claimed to have acquired whatever interest Lina A. Ulbright and Frank O. Ulbright had retained after the 1947 conveyance. What was that interest called?

2. Statutes abolishing the common-law fee tail estate have taken three distinct forms. Examples of each follow.

> (a) *Estate for life plus remainder.* "In cases where, by the common or stat-ute law of England, any person might become seized in fee tail of any lands . . . such person . . . shall become seized thereof for his natural life only; and the remainder shall pass in fee simple absolute to the person to whom the estate tail would, on the death of the first grantee, devisee or donee in tail, first pass according to the course of the common law, by virtue of such devise, gift, grant or convey-ance." Rev. Stat. Mo. §442.470 (1969), Morris v. Ulbright, *supra.*
>
> (b) *Estates in fee tail preserved for one generation.* "No person seized in fee simple shall have a right to devise any estate in fee tail for a longer time than to the children of the first devisee; . . ." R.I. Gen. Laws §33-6-10 (1969).
>
> (c) *Estate in fee simple.* Estates tail have been abolished, and every estate which would be a fee tail . . . shall be a fee simple; and if no valid future estate is limited thereon, a fee simple absolute. Where a future estate in fee is limited on any estate which would be a fee tail . . . such future estate is valid and vests in possession on the death of the first taker, without issue living at the time of his death." N.Y. Est., Powers & Trusts Law §6-12 (1967).

See 2 Powell, Real Property ¶198 (Rohan ed. 1977).

3. Assume that A has made the following devises. After the death of B, who would have title under each of the above statues?

> (a) To B and the heirs of his body. B dies childless, leaving X as his sole heir.
>
> (b) To B and the heirs of his body. B dies leaving one child, S.

(c) To B and the heirs of his body, remainder to C and his heirs. B die childless, leaving X as his sole heir.

(d) To B and the heirs of his body, remainder to C and his heirs. B dies, leaving one child, S.

4. Today, only four states—Delaware, Maine, Massachusetts, and Rhode Island (for estates created by deed)—recognize the fee tail, and in each, disentailing is readily achieved by deed. Moreover, a levying creditor or a foreclosing mortgagee may also convert a fee tail into a fee simple interest.

§3.4   Defeasible Estates

Consider the following:

In 1895, A transferred his family homestead to the local chapter of the Grand Order of Little Frogs (GOLF), "so long as it uses the property for its fraternal purposes." Ever since, GOLF has maintained a chapter house on the site, but it members now wish to sell the property, which has become highly valuable commercial acreage, and reinvest the sales proceeds on less expensive land and more sumptuous quarters elsewhere.

Is there any reason why GOLF cannot make this switch?

To give a complete answer you must make the following analysis:

(a) What property (or contract) interests were created by the 1895 conveyance?

(b) Who has standing to challenge GOLF's proposed action? [5]

(c) Are there defenses to the challenge? Any partial list of defenses might include:

(1) *The Rule Against Perpetuities:* Has the conveyance created any *contingent* future interests? Are they subject to the Rule Against Perpetuities? If so, do they violate the Rule Against Perpetuities? Cf. First Universalist Society of North Adams v. Boland, page 164, *infra.*

(2) *Restraint on alienation:* Has the conveyance created an invalid restraint on alienation? Cf. Mountain Brow Lodge v. Toscano, page 170, *infra.*

(3) *Procedural defenses:* Has there been waiver, estoppel, laches, or a running of the statute of limitations? Cf. pages 183-185, *infra.*

(4) Is there any *statute* specifically regulating the 1895 conveyances? Cf. Cline v. Johnson County Board of Education, page 178, *infra.*

(d) What are the social policies for and against letting this challenge stand?

5. GOLF might seek, instead, a declaratory judgment permitting it to sell the property free of any cloud on title. In that event, whom must GOLF join as parties defendant?

a. Nature of the Interests Created

HAGAMAN v. BOARD OF EDUCATION OF WOODBRIDGE TWP.

117 N.J. Super. 446, 285 A.2d 63 (App. Div. 1971)

LANE, J. The complaint seeks possession of real property conveyed by plaintiff's parents to defendant on October 20, 1925. Both parties moved for summary judgment. The trial court, 112 N.J. Super. 221, 270 A.2d 736, granted defendant's motion. The judgment that was entered "ORDERED that Summary Judgment be and is hereby granted to the defendant, Board of Education of the Township of Woodbridge, dismissing plaintiff's complaint." Plaintiff appeals.

The deed to defendant contained a provision:

> It is the understanding of the parties to this conveyance that the here-inabove described land is conveyed solely for the purpose of being used for the erection and maintenance of a public school or schools and that the Board of Education of Woodbridge Township, N.J., will erect a school thereon on or before the school year of 1926 and use such building for school purposes.

From the affidavits and admissions in the pleadings it was uncontroverted that defendant erected a school building on the property and used the property for school purposes until approximately 1968. In that year the school building was closed. The students who formerly would have attended the school began to attend two new schools within the area. At the time of the trial the property in question was used as a recreational park or playground. It was equipped with swings, a sliding board, monkey bars and basketball courts. During the summer it was supervised by a full-time playground supervisor. Organized and supervised play activities were carried on. On March 2, 1971 after the judgment was rendered the school building was destroyed by fire.

Plaintiff argues that the deed expresses a clear and unequivocal intention to convey a fee simple determinable or a fee simple subject to a condition subsequent and that he is entitled to possession because the property is no longer being used for the maintenance of a public school.

In determining the meaning of a deed, prime consideration is the intent of the parties. . . .

An estate in fee simple determinable is an estate in fee simple which automatically determines upon the occurrence of a given event. The grantor retains a possibility of reverter upon the occurrence of the stated event. . . . Generally, the intent to create such an estate is indicated by the use of words denoting duration of time such as "while," "during," "so long as." . . . "The absence of some one of these phraseologies makes it likely that a court will find a covenant, a trust, or some other type of interest less drastic in its sanctions." 2 Powell, Real Property §187 at 45-47. . . . However, ". . . particular forms of expression standing alone and without resort to the purpose of the instrument in question are not determinative. . . ." Oldfield v. Stoeco Homes, Inc., 26 N.J. 246, 256, 139 A.2d 291, 296. Words of limitation merely stating the purpose for which the land is conveyed usually do not indicate an intent to create an estate in fee simple determinable although other language in the instrument, the amount of the consideration and the circumstances surrounding the conveyance may indicate such an intent. Restatement, Property §44, comment m, at 129-130; 2 Powell, Real Property §187 at 48-49. When a conveyance contains only a clause of condition or of covenant, such clause does not usually indicate an intent to create a fee simple determinable. Restatement, Property §44, comment n, at 130.

An estate in fee simple subject to a condition subsequent is an estate in fee simple which upon the occurrence of a given event gives to the grantor or his successor in interest the right to reenter and terminate the estate. Upon the occurrence of the given event, the forfeiture of the estate is not automatic. . . . The intent to create such an estate may be indicated by the use of such words as "on condition that," "provided that." . . . However, such language is not necessarily determinative. . . . Generally, an intent to create a fee simple subject to a condition subsequent is established when the conveyance contains one of the above phrases and a provision that if the given event occurs the grantor may enter and terminate or has a right to re-enter. Restatement, Property §45, comment j, at 139; 2 Powell, Real Property §188 at 58-58.1. "Conditions subsequent must be so created as to leave no doubt regarding the grantor's intention." 4 Thompson, Real Property §1875 at 578. A mere statement of the use to which the conveyed land is to be devoted is not sufficient to create an estate in fee simple subject to a condition subsequent. . . . Absent clear intention to create a fee simple subject to a condition subsequent, a conveyance with words of condition may be found to create a covenant, a trust, or a mere precatory expression. . . .

Language in an instrument which is alleged to create a fee simple determinable or a fee simple subject to a condition subsequent is strictly construed. "A recognized rule of construction indicates that an instrument, when a choice exists, is to be construed against rather than in favor of a forfeiture." Lehigh Valley R.R. Co. v. Chapman, 35 N.J. 177, 188, 171 A.2d 653, 660. . . .

If a choice is between an estate in fee simple determinable and an estate on condition subsequent, the latter is preferred. . . . Where it is doubtful whether a clause in a deed is a covenant or a condition, the former is preferred. . . . When a condition in a deed is relied upon to defeat an estate, it should be strictly construed and its violation must be clearly established. . . .

In the present case there are no words indicating an intent to create a fee simple determinable or a fee simple subject to a condition subsequent. There are no words creating either a right of re-entry or a possibility of a reversion [*sic*].

Plaintiff does not have a right to possession to the property under the deed. This holding by the trial court was correct. . . .

The judgment is affirmed.[6]

NOTES AND QUESTIONS

1. Rewrite the clause in the school deed, *supra,* to illustrate a *fee simple determinable* with the grantor reserving the future interest for himself. What is the future interest called? Cf. Restatement of Property §44; Powell, Real Property 187 (Powell & Rohan abr. ed. 1968); Table 1, *supra.*

2. Rewrite the clause in the school deed, *supra,* to illustrate a *fee simple subject to a condition subsequent* with the grantor reserving the future interest for himself. What is the future interest called? Cf. Restatement of Property §45; Powell, Real Property 188 (Powell & Rohan abr. ed. 1968); Table 1, *supra.*

3. If the school deed had created a fee simple determinable, would the outcome in this case have been different? What if the deed had created a fee simple subject to a condition subsequent?

4. Draftsmen do not always draft, and judges do not always respond, with the same attention to or respect for the careful distinctions that are suggested above. The examples can be multiplied, but here are several:

(a) The city of Long Beach quitclaimed some tidelands to the state of California. In the deed were these words: "This conveyance is made upon the express condition that the property conveyed hereby shall be used for a park . . . and should said property . . . be used for any other purpose, then, in that event, the property hereby conveyed shall immediately revert unto the grantor herein, its successors or assigns." A California court ruled that a fee simple subject to a condition subsequent had been created, and that the grantor had retained a "power of reentry" [*sic*]. People v. City of Long Beach, 200 Cal. App. 2d 609, 19 Cal. Rptr. 585 (1962).

(b) An 1868 deed to school trustees provided: "[This conveyance] is made and accepted subject to the following conditions and reservations, viz.: . . . and whenever the property hereby conveyed shall cease to be used for school and meeting purposes . . . then and in that case the same shall revert to and become the property of the first part[y]." A New York court decided that

6. Compare with Matter of Rieger, 60 A.D.2d 299, 400 N.Y.S.2d 881 (3d Dept. 1977). Testator's will devised real property to the Girl Scouts and Boy Scouts organizations "to be retained and used by the Girl and Boy Scouts . . . for the purposes of their organizations." The court held that, in the absence of any of the phrases required to limit an estate, the testator had failed to reserve any rights in himself, his heirs, or his origins. The court further held, in the wake of a finding that the land was unsuited to the charitable beneficiaries' needs, that the directions in the will would permit a sale of the property and the reinvestment of the proceeds so as to promote scouting activities.—ED.

this language manifested the grantor's intent to create a fee simple subject to a condition subsequent. Fausett v. Guisewhite, 16 A.D.2d 82, 225 N.Y.S.2d 616 (1962). Cf. also United Methodist Church v. Kunz, 78 Misc. 2d 565, 357 N.Y.S.2d 637 (Sup. Ct. 1974).

(c) A railway acquired a 66-foot strip of land by a deed which read: "Said second party hereby agrees to and with said first party that in case said Railway shall at any time be abandoned then the lands heretofore described shall revert to the grantors." In reversing the trial judge, a New York appellate court decided unanimously that this deed had conveyed a fee upon special limitation, and that the grantors had retained a possibility of reverter. Nichols v. Haehn, 8 A.D.2d 409, 187 N.Y.S.2d 773 (1959).

Is there any neutral principle to explain these cases?

5. Rewrite the clause in the school deed, *supra,* to illustrate (i) a fee simple determinable and (ii) a fee simple subject to a condition subsequent with the grantor creating the future interest in X, a third party. What is the future interest called? Cf. Restatement of Property, §§46, 47; Powell, Real Property 189 (Powell & Rohan abr. ed. 1968); Table 1, *supra.*

As will shortly appear, pages 161-170, *infra,* these estates create serious technical problems for the draftsman.

6. What social policy, if any, would seem to underlie the constructional preference for a fee simple subject to a condition over a fee simple determinable? Should it make any difference whether the grantee paid for the property or received it as a charitable gift?

7. Rewrite the clause in the school deed, *supra,* to illustrate a covenant rather than a condition or limitation. If the school deed had created a covenant, would the outcome in this case have been different? Consider the remedies for breach of covenant. Consider also the possible defenses to a breach of covenant suit. Compare these with the remedies and the defenses that are available in a suit to enforce a condition or a limitation.

8. What social policy, if any, would seem to underlie the constructional preference for a covenant over a defeasible estate? Should it make any difference whether the grantee paid for the property or received it as a charitable gift?

9. White Land Co. v. Christenson, 14 S.W.2d 369 (Tex. Civ. App. 1928), once was called "the high water mark of constructional aversion" to the defeasible estate. Goldstein, Rights of Entry and Possibilities of Reverter as Devices to Restrict the Use of Land, 54 Harv. L. Rev. 248, 261 (1940). In the White Land case, the court treated as a covenant the following deed language: "If said [grantee] . . . shall build a residence on said lots the residence so built . . . shall not cost less than $5,000. . . . In case the said grantee . . . shall ever violate any one of said conditions contained herein and made a part of the covenants of this deed, the said land and all improvements therein shall immediately revert to and become the property of the grantor. . . ."

Clark v. City of Grand Rapids, 334 Mich. 646, 55 N.W.2d 137 (1952), offers a somewhat less startling display of constructional preference.

b. Standing to Enforce Forfeiture—The Alienability and Descendability of the Future Interest

The plaintiff in Hagaman v. Board of Education, *supra,* had acquired his interest from his parents, the school board's grantors. If the court had labeled the conveyance a fee simple determinable, would it matter whether plaintiff's interest came to him via deed, will, or intestate succession? Consider the same question if the conveyance had been called a fee simple subject to a condition subsequent.

For its part, the Restatement of Property treats the possibility of reverter as alienable (§159), devisable (§165), and descendable (§164). Although the power of termination is also regarded as devisable (§165) and descendable (§164), it is said not to be generally capable of inter vivos transfer (§160) unless it supplements a reversionary interest; e.g., the landlord's interest in the fee (§161-c). (Two other exceptions to the rule also appear). The Restatement once asserted (by a split decision of 41 to 35) the surprising principle that a power of termination is destroyed by an attempt to make a "forbidden" transfer, §160, Comment c. The destructibility rule had its American origins in Rice v. Boston & Worcester R.R., 94 Mass. (12 Allen) 141 (1866), and may have worked its way into the case law of six states (Colorado, Maine, Massachusetts, Michigan, New York, and Oregon). It has since lost both its Restatement support, see American Law Institute, Restatement of the Law 416 (1948 Supp.), and some of its limited following elsewhere, see 2 A Powell, Real Property ¶282 (Rohan ed. 1977)

The nonalienability rule still survives in many jurisdictions, although England ended it more than a century ago. 7 Wm. 4 & 1 Vict., c. 26, §3 (1837) (applies to wills only), 7 & 8 Vict., 76, §5 (1844). An American trend to make powers of termination more freely alienable is now definitely underway. See, e.g., N.Y. Est., Powers & Trusts Law §6-5.1 (1979); 2 A Powell, *supra,* at 494-497. Is there any policy justification for barring the inter vivos transfer of powers of termination? Is there any policy justification for treating the possibility of reverter as being more alienable than the power of termination? On this latter issue, two law teachers have written:

> It is, therefore, believed that the whole dichotomy, between determinable fees with possibilities of reverter and fees subject to condition subsequent with rights of entry, is just another example of needless double-talk, of obscure historical origins and unfortunate contemporary policy consequences, which might well disappear from the books. When the consequences a donor seeks are within the policy of the community, no informed draftsman will trust his donor's intent to so frail a carrier as the difference between "so long as" and "but if"; when the consequences a donor seeks are forbidden by community policy, no element of rationality suggests that he should be permitted to exceed the community's bounds by one verbal form and not by another. [McDougal and Haber, Property, Wealth, Land 286 (1948)]

See also, Dunham, Possibility of Reverter and Powers of Termination—Fraternal or Identical Twins? 20 U. Chi. L. Rev. 215 (1952).

Illinois and Oregon take the exceptional view that neither interest is alienable or devisable. Ill. Rev. Stat. c. 30, §37b (Smith-Hurd 1969); City of Klamath Falls v. Bell, 7 Or. App. 330, 338; 490 P.2d 515, 519 (1971).

Consider the following situation: fifty years ago, X transferred one acre from a ten-acre parcel to a school district "so long as the premises are used for educational purposes." Thereafter X sold the remaining acreage to Acme Builders, who now operate garden apartments on the site. The X-Acme Builders deed did not refer to the earlier transfer. X died intestate leaving two heirs, D and S. The school district seeks a declaratory judgment vesting itself with fee simple absolute title. Whom must the plaintiff join as parties defendant? Why?

c. Defenses to a Suit to Enforce Forfeiture—The Rule Against Perpetuities

We have already seen, in the sections on fee simple conditional and fee tail, the running struggle between the landed rich who sought to tie up their holdings dynastically and various others (including ungrateful descendants) who wanted free alienability. Action invited reaction, with the battle's edge leaning towards the freehanders. By the seventeenth century, the law had ruined the fee tail as a dynastic instrument, but a new device for tying up land unto the generations—the so-called executory interest—had gained widespread usage. Finally, in the celebrated Duke of Norfolk's Case, 3 Ch. Cas. 1, 22 Eng. Rep. 931 (1681), the even more celebrated Lord Chancellor Nottingham coined a rule against "perpetuities" that could invalidate some, but not all, executory interests and—as the rule evolved—other contingent future interests. See Gulliver, Future Interests 371-388 (1959), for a factual synopsis and edited opinion of the Duke of Norfolk's Case.

The Rule Against Perpetuities has few rivals for the torment it can cause law students and the havoc it can occasionally wreak on badly drafted wills and other property transfers. Any attempt to master the rule would take several weeks of effort, and since you are certain to meet the rule again if you study trusts and estates, you might defer your mastery until then. For present purposes, you will be well served to recognize a simple statement of the rule, to work out several untricky examples, to understand the rule's social policy, and to see the rule applied to the future interests that follow a defeasible estate.

The common-law statement of the Rule Against Perpetuities. For a contingent future interest to be valid, the interest must vest, if it vests at all, within twenty-one years after some life in being when the interest is created.

While simply stated, the Rule is sometimes treacherous to apply. Before you try a few examples, here are some "clarifying" guidelines.

(a) For purposes of the Rule Against Perpetuities, a future interest is contingent when (1) a condition (e.g., survivorship) must be satisfied before the interest holder will be sure to take, or (2) the identity of the prospective interest holder is not yet determined (e.g., the heirs of a living person).

(b) We refer to the "life in being" as the "measuring life." The measuring life is someone who is alive on the effective date of the instrument creating the contingent future interest. For inter vivos transfers (usually gifts), the effective date is when the deed or trust instrument is delivered; for wills, the effective date is when the testator dies.

(c) Thus, the perpetuities period (life in being plus twenty-one years) begins to run, in the case of a deed or trust instrument, on the delivery date, and in the case of a will, on the testator's death.

(d) We apply the common-law rule *prospectively.* We ask whether the contingent future interest is certain to vest, if it vests at all, within the perpetuities period. An alternative way to put the question, and one that I believe simplifies analysis, is to ask: when will we be sure to learn whether the contingency is satisfied? If that "determination date" falls within the perpetuities period, the future interest is valid; otherwise it is void ab initio. Because we look ahead when we ask the question, it makes no difference whether, as events later unfold, the future interest vests or fails within a life in being plus twenty-one years. Because we deal theoretically with the contingency, we sometimes call the common-law rule the "what might happen" rule.

(e) Accordingly, the rule is intent-defeating, and courts often have stretched the rule to thwart rather than to abet the grantor's or testator's objectives. For some lurid examples, as well as the classical treatments of the subject, see two articles by Barton Leach: Perpetuities in a Nutshell, 51 Harv. L. Rev. 638 (1938), and Perpetuities: The Nutshell Revisited, 78 Harv. L. Rev. 973 (1965).

(f) One of the most puzzling aspects of the rule is the choice of measuring lives. Remember that the purpose of a measuring life is to identify some living person about whom we can say that within twenty-one years after that person's death we will be sure to learn whether or not the contingency is satisfied. If no such person exists the interest is void.

Very often, an appropriate measuring life will be someone named in the instrument (example 2, *infra*). Sometimes, we must infer a measuring life (example 6, *infra*). But unless there is someone alive when the instrument becomes effective whose death certainly will not occur more than twenty-one years before the "determination" date, the interest must fail.

Now test your understanding of the rule by working through the following examples. In each case you should ask a threshold question: whether there is a *contingent* future interest. If so, then you should ask whether the interest must vest, if it vests at all, within the perpetuities period—i.e., within twenty-one years after some life in being at the creation of the interest. Once subject to the rule, a future interest must either satisfy the rule or be invalid.

(1)   A to "B for life, remainder to C and his heirs."

Suggested analysis: In this example, the future interest, which is held by C, is noncontingent (see point (a), *supra*). Accordingly, C's interest is not subject to the rule and we can avoid further analysis. C holds a valid future interest.

(2)   A to "B for life, remainder to C and his heirs if C survives B" (B and C are living persons).

Suggested analysis: In this example, C holds a contingent remainder because of its condition of survivorship.[7] This contingent future interest *is* subject to the rule. We must therefore consider whether C's interest satisfies the rule.

I suggest that you proceed by asking when we will be sure to learn whether the contingency is satisfied, that is, whether C's contingent interest will become vested.

If you answered: When B dies, you have answered correctly. At B's death, C either will have survived (in which event, C's interest vests), or will not have survived (in which event, C's interest can never vest).

To go on: does this "determination" date occur during the perpetuities period, that is, during a life in being (measuring life) plus twenty-one years? Once again, you should have answered yes, since B can serve as our measuring life.[8] We will certainly know before the end of the perpetuities period (B's life plus twenty-one years) whether C's interest will vest, if it vests at all. Because we can say yes absolutely as to the "determination" date, C's interest satisfies the rule *even though C's interest may never become vested.*

(3)   A makes a gift to "the first child of B (who is alive and childless at the date of the gift) to attain the age of twenty-five years."

Suggested analysis: In this example, the future interest, which is held by "B's first child to attain . . . twenty-five," is contingent, since we cannot now identify the interest holder. Accordingly, the interest is subject to the Rule. Does it satisfy the Rule? No, it does not. Why not?

Once again, we ask the "determination" question: when will we be sure to learn who, if anyone, satisfies the contingency? Will we be sure to learn during the perpetuities period (some life in being plus twenty-one years)? Not during B's life, since B can give birth to a child C who might reach twenty-five *more* than *twenty-one* years after B's death. Nor can we name any other *living* person about whom we can surely say that within twenty-one years after that person dies we can identify "B's first child to attain . . . twenty-five." Thus, this contingent future interest violates the Rule Against Perpetuities and is *void ab initio.*

Now more nearly on your own, try a few other simple examples.

---

7. If B were already dead (a situation arising, for example, if B were alive when A signed the will but not sometime later) C, if living, would have a vested interest, not subject to the Rule.
   8. So, too, can C.

(4) A to "B for life, remainder to the heirs of C (a living person)."

(5) A to "B for life, remainder to C and his heirs if C survives B, otherwise to D and his heirs." (C and D are living persons.)

(6) A leaves everything by will to "my first grandchild to attain the age of twenty-one years." (At A's death, A has one daughter, D, who is childless.)

(7) A makes an inter vivos gift to "the first child of B to attain the age of twenty-five years." (B is alive and has one child, C, who is twenty-four years old.)

Application of the rule to future interests created by a defeasible estate: The First Universalist case, *infra,* deals with executory interests, possibilities of reverter, and powers of termination—all three of the future interests that can exist when one creates a defeasible estate. Notice some sloppy language in the opinion. For good or bad, the distinctions that this court makes as to the rule's application still govern the present law.

FIRST UNIVERSALIST SOCIETY OF NORTH ADAMS v. BOLAND

155 Mass. 171, 29 N.E. 524 (1892)

BILL IN EQUITY, filed in the Superior Court, for the specific performance of an agreement by the plaintiff to sell and by the defendant to purchase land. The case was submitted to the Superior Court, and, after judgment for the plaintiff, to this court, on appeal, on an agreed statement of facts; and was as follows.

On April 9, 1842, Joseph D. Clark and twenty-five or thirty other persons formed the plaintiff society, with a constitution which adopted as the basis of its religious faith the profession of belief accepted by the General Convention of the Universalists at its session at Winchester, New Hampshire, in 1803, and provided for three trustees to be the executive power of the society and to see that all votes of the society were carried out. On April 3, 1854, Clark for the expressed consideration of nine hundred dollars conveyed the land in question by a deed containing the usual covenants to the plaintiff society,

> to have and to hold to the said First Universalist Society and their assigns, so long as said real estate shall by said society or its assigns be devoted to the uses, interests, and support of those doctrines of the Christian religion embraced in the Confession of Faith adopted by the General Convention of Universalists held at Winchester, New Hampshire, in the year eighteen hundred and three. And when said real estate shall by said society or its assigns be diverted from the uses, interests, and support aforesaid to any other interests, uses, or purposes than as aforesaid, then the title of said society or its assigns in the same shall forever cease, and be forever vested in the following named persons, and such persons shall be the legal representatives of any of such persons at the time the same so

vests as aforesaid in the following undivided parts and proportions, to wit: to Stephen M. Whipple 140/1000, Alanson Cady 140/1000, John F. Arnold 114/1000, Joseph D. Clark 70/1000. [Here followed the names of 37 others after each of which was placed a fraction in thousandths.] To have and to hold the above granted premises, with the privileges and appurtenances thereto belonging, to the said grantees, their heirs and assigns, to them and their use and behoof forever, as aforesaid. . . .

Upon the land so conveyed to the plaintiff a church was erected, which from the time of its erection to the present time has been occupied and used for religious worship by the plaintiff society, without any change in the profession of faith mentioned in the deed of April 3, 1854, or in its constitution. The agreement in question was made by the parties on April 20, 1891, but the defendant, upon the tender of a deed to him from the plaintiff, refused to carry it out, on the ground, among others, that the plaintiff society never was seised in fee simple, but at most obtained only a qualified or conditional fee, and could not convey a good and clear title. . . .

ALLEN, J. The limitation over, which is contained in the deed of Clark to the plaintiff in 1854, is void for remoteness. Wells v. Heath, 10 Gray, 17, 25, 26. Brattle Square Church v. Grant, 3 Gray, 142, 152. The fact that the grantor designated himself as one of the persons amongst many others to take under this limitation, does not have the effect to make the limitation valid. He was to take with the rest, and stand upon the same footing with them.

Where there is an invalid limitation over, the general rule is that the preceding estate is to stand, unaffected by the void limitation. The estate becomes vested in the first taker, according to the terms in which it was granted or devised. . . . There may be instances in which a void limitation might be referred to for the purpose of giving a construction to the language used in making the prior gift, provided any aid could be gained thereby. In the present case, we do not see that any such aid can be gained. The estate given to the first taker does not depend at all upon the validity or invalidity of the limitation over, and the construction of the language used is not aided by a reference thereto.

The grant to the plaintiff was to have and to hold, etc., "so long as said real estate shall by said society or its assigns be devoted to the uses, interests, and support of those doctrines of the Christian religion," as specified. "And when said real estate shall by said society or its assigns be diverted from the uses, interests, and support aforesaid to any other interests, uses, or purposes than as aforesaid, then the title of said society or its assigns in the same shall forever cease, and be forever vested in the following named persons," etc. These words do not grant an absolute fee, nor an estate on condition, but an estate which is to continue till the happening of a certain event, and then to cease. That event may happen at any time, or it may never happen. Because the estate may last forever, it is a fee. Because it may end on the happening of the event, it is what is usually called a determinable or qualified fee. The grant was not upon a condition subsequent, and no re-entry would be necessary; but by the terms of the grant the estate was to continue so long as the real estate should be devoted to the specified uses, and when it should no longer be so devoted, then the estate would cease and determine by its own limitation. Numerous illustrations of words proper to create such qualified or determinable fees are to be found in the books, one of which, as old as Walsingham's case, 2 Plowd. 557, is "as long as the church of St. Paul shall stand." . . .

Since the estate of the plaintiff may determine, and since there is no valid limitation over, it follows that there is a possibility of reverter in the original grantor, Clark. This is similar to, though not quite identical with, the possibility of reverter which remains in the grantor of land upon a condition subsequent. The exact nature and incidents of this right need not now be discussed, but it represents whatever is not conveyed by the deed, and it is the possibility that the land may revert to the grantor or his heirs when the granted estate determines. . . .

Clark's possibility of reverter is not invalid for remoteness. It has been expressly held by this court, that such possibility of reverter upon breach of a condition subsequent is not within the rule against perpetuities. Tobey v. Moore, 130 Mass. 448. French v. Old South Society, 106 Mass. 479.[9] If there is any distinction in this respect between such possibility of reverter and that which arises upon the determination of a qualified fee, it would seem to be in favor of the latter. But they should be governed by the same rule. If one is not held void for remoteness, the other should not be. The very many cases cited in Gray, Rule against Perpetuities, §§305-312, show conclusively that the general understanding of courts and of the profession in America has been that the rule as to remoteness does not apply; though the learned author thinks this view erroneous in principle. . . .

Bill dismissed.

NOTES AND QUESTIONS

1. In present-day terms, what social values are promoted by a rule that would invalidate contingent future interests that might not vest within a prescribed period? If there are such values, is it sound to submit executory interests to the rule while excluding possibilities of reverter and powers of termination? Again, if there are such values, should the prescribed period be fixed—e.g., the contingency must occur within thirty years (Mass. Gen. Laws Ann. Ch. 184A, §3 (1977)), instead of depending upon the uncertain duration

---

9. Careful reading of the two "precedents" upon which the opinion relies reveals that neither held directly that the power of termination was immune from the rule. Ironically, a contemporary decision in England, birthplace of the rule, held exactly to the contrary. Re Trustees of Hollis Hospital and Hague's Contract [1899] 2 Ch. 540—Ed.

of lives in being? Cf. Hiddleston v. Nebraska Jewish Education Socy., 186 Neb. 786, 186 N.W.2d 904 (1971) (concurring opinion).

2. In the immediate case, did the court's decision abet or thwart Clark's objectives in granting the land to the church on a defeasible estate, and an executory interest in himself and third parties? Which among the following were the winners and the losers: the congregation, Clark's heirs, the town of North Adams, and the charitable impulse? Should we give any attention to the fact that Clark received $900 for the land and did not give it away free?

3. You represent a landowner who wishes to transfer land to a church "so long as the premises are used for church purposes" but wants "X (a third person) and his heirs" to hold the future interest. How might you accomplish that objective without violating the Rule Against Perpetuities?

4. As we shall see, some states have statutorily extended the Rule Against Perpetuities to include possibilities of reverter or powers of termination, or have otherwise limited their permissible duration. See pages 177-183, *infra.* In England, the common-law rule applied to the power of termination, a result confirmed by Law of Property Act 1925, section 4(3). Some years later, Parliament extended the rule to the possibility of reverter (The Perpetuities and Accumulations Act 1964, §12), ending some confusion over whether the common law rule already applied. R.H. Maudsley, The Modern Law of Perpetuities 70-71 (1979).

In this country, the American Law Institute has again declared that the possibility of reverter and the power of termination remain exempt from the rule, absent statutory change. Restatement (Second) of Property (Tent. Draft No. 2, 68-69, 1979).

Note, however, that statutes that apply the rule to the possibility of reverter and power of termination carry an exception in the case of a landlord holding those interests. Reconsider in this light your answer to question 3, *supra.*

5. A latter-day sequel to the *First Universalist* case is found in Brown v. Independent Baptist Church of Woburn, 325 Mass. 645, 91 N.E.2d 922 (1950). The decedent, Sarah Converse, left a will in 1849 devising land to the "independent Baptist Church of Woburn . . . so long as they shall continue a Church." Thereafter the land was to go to named legatees. In addition, the will contained a residuary clause naming the same persons as residuary legatees. In 1939 the church closed its doors, having fallen, it seems, upon the seven lean years. In the equity suit to try title to the land, the parties agreed that the church held a determinable fee, and that the executory devise (an executory interest created by will) failed to satisfy the Rule Against Perpetuities. Relying upon the *First Universalist* case, the court held that a possibility of reverter remained in Sarah Converse, and, in the absence of a specific devise under her will, passed under the residuary clause—to the same persons who could not take under the void executory devise. A lone justice ruled that this interest, too, should be subject to the rule, but his brethren disagreed because

of the "fundamental difference in character" between the attempted executory devise and the residuary gift to the same persons.

6.   Still another illustration of the absurdity resulting from the American rule appears in City of Klamath Falls v. Bell, 7 Or. App. 330, 490 P.2d 515 (1971). A corporation in 1925 had donated land to the city so long as it used the site as a library; the deed also contained an executory interest. Library use continued until 1969, when the site (and building thereon) became vacant. The city then sought a declaratory judgment vesting title in itself. It named as defendants the executory interest holders and the individual shareholders of the corporate donor (now dissolved). These were the same persons.

The court held that the gift over (executory interest) was void under the Rule Against Perpetuities. The court then held that defendants, *qua* sole shareholders of the corporate donor, were entitled to and had received all of the remaining assets of the corporation, including the possibility of reverter that rose from the ashes of the void executory interest.

7.   No case can match the absurdity of Jee v. Audley, 29 Eng. Rep. 1186 (Ch. 1787). There a gift failed that was made to the daughters of an elderly couple (both were past 70); the court reasoned that daughters not yet born might bless the couple. This decision gave rise to the "fertile octogenarian" rule.

But the present almost matches the past. Consider, for example, United Virginia Bank/Citizens & Marine v. Union Oil Co. of California, 214 Va. 48, 197 S.E.2d 174 (1973). In 1966, a landowner gave an option for the purchase of a one-acre lot to be valid for 120 days to begin "at the time the City of Newport News . . . acquires [a specified right of way]." In an action by the landowner's executor to invalidate the option, the court held—after first declaring options subject to the rule—that a violation had occurred and that the option was unenforceable. At the time of the decision, only seven years after the option was issued, it seemed likely that the specified acquisition would happen soon. But the court's logic would have invalidated the option even if the 120-day trigger had been certain to occur shortly.

The Rule Against Perpetuities is continually undergoing statutory adjustment, often the result of forward-looking reform. See, e.g., N.Y. Est., Powers & Trusts Law §§9-1.1 to 9-1.8 (McKinney Supp. 1980-1981). Perhaps the most far-reaching reform is the so-called wait-and-see rule which the American Law Institute approved for inclusion in Restatement (Second) of Property §1.4 (Donative Transfers, Tent. Draft No. 2, 1979). That section provides: ". . . a donative transfer of an interest in property fails, if the interest *does not vest*, if it ever vests, within the period of the rule against perpetuities." (italics added)

In his rationale for adoption of "wait-and-see" (admittedly having limited statutory acceptance), the Reporter wrote:

> Most non-vested interests that conceivably might vest too remotely, so far as the rule against perpetuities is concerned, will not in fact vest too remotely, if

given an opportunity to vest. Every non-vested interest that conceivably might vest too remotely could be made valid by simply providing that such non-vested interest will take effect if, and only if, it vests within 21 years after the death of the survivor of named lives in being on the date the period of the rule against perpetuities begins to run. [10] In all jurisdictions, such non-vested interest would be valid and it would be necessary to wait and see whether the interest in fact vests in time. In other words, the what-might-happen approach is nothing more than a trap that is easily avoided by appropriate drafting. The adoption of the wait-and-see approach in this Restatement is largely motivated by the equality of treatment that is produced by placing the validity of all non-vested interests on the same plane, whether the interest is created by a skilled draftsman or one not so skilled. [Id. at 17]

Wait-and-see entered English law in The Perpetuities and Accumulations Act 1964. Writing about the English statute, one of its leading exponents commented:

> Two factors of special importance rise out of this principle; though they have commonly been overlooked. First: when Waiting and Seeing, which are the "lives" which are to be used for the purpose of measuring the period of life in being plus 21 years? The situation now is very different from what it was under the common law rule. Under that rule, the lives in being "picked" themselves. . . . Since, to be valid, it was necessary to show that the interest must vest, if it vest at all, during the period of a life or lives in being plus 21 years, the life in being was the person within 21 years of whose death the interest must vest, if it vest at all. The measuring lives at common law were those who validated a valid gift. If the limitation was void; if, in other words, it was not possible to say that it must vest, if at all, during 21 years of the death of some person living, the question of who were the lives in being did not arise. There were none.

> Thus, when enacting a system of Wait and See, it is essential to say who are the measuring lives for the purpose of Waiting and Seeing. That is the first point. The second point is that, when a system of Wait and See is enacted, the common law rule should be abolished. This point is even more obvious than the first. The common law rule said that a disposition was valid if it *must* vest, if it vest at all, within the period. Wait and See says that a disposition is valid if it *does in fact* vest within the period. As a matter of simple logic, an interest which *must* vest, if it vest at all within the perpetuity period, *will* vest, if it vest at all, within the period. Thus, Wait and See "contains" the common law rule, and there is no need for the latter. [R. H. Maudsley, The Modern Law of Perpetuities, 4-6 (1979)]

The Restatement (Second) contains an elaborate compilation of measuring lives. Id. at §1.3.

10. In this connection, consider the possible longevity of a contingent future interest that is directed to take effect, if at all, "21 years after the death of the survivor of the now-living descendants of the late Senator Robert F. Kennedy." Suppose that the instrument creating this interest became effective in 1970, when the youngest of Senator Kennedy's eleven surviving children was only two years old.—ED.

Finally, if the "not so skilled" draftsman stumbles into the perpetuities trap and wait-and-see fails to rescue him, the Restatement (Second) offers yet another saving device:

> If under a donative transfer an interest in property fails because it does not vest or cannot vest within the period of the rule against perpetuities, the transferred property shall be disposed of in the manner which most closely effectuates the transferor's manifested plan of distribution, which is within the limits of the Rule Against Perpetuities. [Id. at §1.5]

Reconsider the *First Universalist* case in the light of Restatement (Second), §§1.3-1.5. The executory interest would remain valid for twenty-one years after the death of all defined measuring lives, including (among others) the transferor, Clark, and each of the forty-one named beneficiaries. If, when this period ended, the church still held the property, the executory interest would not have been saved, even by wait-and-see. But §1.5 would then give the court a chance to determine how "most closely [to effectuate] the transferor's manifested plan of distribution." In your opinion, what would more nearly conform to Clark's presumed intention: vesting a fee simple absolute in the church; creating a possibility of reverter in Clark's heirs? Might a court decide differently if the executory interest failed, let us say, after sixty years under wait-and-see than if the executory interest were void ab initio under the common law rule?

d. Defenses to a Suit to Enforce Forfeiture—Restraint on Alienation

MOUNTAIN BROW LODGE NO. 82 v. TOSCANO
257 Cal. App. 2d 22, 64 Cal. Rptr. 816 (1968)

GARGANO, J. This action was instituted by appellant, a non-profit corporation, to quiet its title to a parcel of real property which it acquired on April 6, 1950, by gift deed from James V. Toscano and Maria Toscano, both deceased. Respondents are the trustees and administrators of the estates of the deceased grantors and appellant sought to quiet its title as to their interest in the land arising from certain conditions contained in the gift deed.

The matter was submitted to the court on stipulated facts and the court rendered judgment in favor of respondents. However, it is not clear from the court's findings of fact and conclusions of law whether it determined that the conditions were not void and hence refused to quiet appellant's title for this reason, or whether it decided that appellant had not broken the conditions and then erroneously concluded that "neither party has a right to an anticipatory decree" until a violation occurs. Thus, to avoid prolonged litigation the parties have stipulated that when the trial court rendered judgment refusing to quiet appellant's title it simply decided that the conditions are not void and that its decision on this limited issue is the only question presented in this appeal. We shall limit our discussion accordingly.

The controversy between the parties centers on the language contained in the habendum clause of the deed of conveyance which reads as follows:

> Said property is restricted for the use and benefit of the second party, only; and in the event the same fails to be used by the second party or in the event of sale or transfer by the second party of all or any part of said lot, the same is to revert to the first parties herein, their successors, heirs or assigns.

Respondents maintain that the language creates a fee simple subject to a condition subsequent and is valid and enforceable. On the other hand, appellant contends that the restrictive language amounts to an absolute restraint on its power of alienation and is void. It apparently asserts that, since the purpose for which the land must be used is not precisely defined, it may be used by appellant for any purpose and hence the restriction is not on the land use but on who uses it. Thus, appellant concludes that it is clear that the reversionary clause was intended by grantors to take effect only if appellant sells or transfers the land.

Admittedly, the condition of the habendum clause which prohibits appellant from selling or transferring the land under penalty of forfeiture is an absolute restraint against alienation and is void. The common law rule prohibiting restraint against alienation is embodied in Civil Code section 711 which provides: "Conditions restraining alienation, when repugnant to the interest created, are void." However, this condition and the condition relating to the use of the land are in the disjunctive and are clearly severable. In other words, under the plain language of the deed the grantors, their successors or assigns may exercise their power of termination "if the land is not used by the second party" or "in the event of sale or transfer by second party." Thus, the invalid restraint against alienation does not necessarily affect or nullify the condition on land use (Los Angeles Investment Company v. Gary, 181 Cal. 680, 186 P. 596, 9 A.L.R. 115).

The remaining question, therefore, is whether the use condition created a defeasible fee as respondents maintain or whether it is also a restraint against alienation and nothing more as appellant alleges. Significantly, appellant is a non-profit corporation organized for lodge, fraternal and similar purposes. Moreover, decedent, James V. Toscano, was an active member of the lodge at the time of his death. In addition, the term "use" as applied to real property can be construed to mean a "right which a person has to use or enjoy the property of another according to his necessities" (Mulford v. LeFranc (1864), 26 Cal. 88, 102). Under these circumstances it is reasonably clear that when the grantors stated that the land was conveyed in consideration of "love and affection" and added that it "is restricted for the *use* and benefit of the second party" they simply meant to say that the land was conveyed upon condition that it would be used for lodge, fraternal and other purposes for which the non-profit corporation was formed. Thus, we conclude that the portion of the habendum clause relating to the land use, when construed as a whole and in light of the surrounding circumstances, created a fee subject to a condition subsequent with title to revert to the grantors, their successors or assigns if the land ceases to be used for lodge, fraternal and similar purposes for which the appellant is formed. [2] No formal language is necessary to create a fee simple subject to a condition subsequent as long as the intent of the grantor is clear. It is the rule that the object in construing a deed is to ascertain the intention of the grantor from words which have been employed and from surrounding circumstances.

It is of course arguable, as appellant suggests, that the condition in appellant's deed is not a restriction on land use but on who uses it. Be this as it may, the distinction between a covenant which restrains the alienation of a fee simple absolute and a condition which restricts land use and creates a defeasible estate was long recognized at common law and is recognized in this state. [3] Thus, conditions restricting land use have been upheld by the California courts on numerous occasions even though they hamper, and often completely impede, alienation. A few examples follow: Mitchell v. Cheney Slough Irrigation Co., 57 Cal. App. 2d 138, 134 P.2d 34 (irrigation ditch); Aller v. Berkeley Hall School Foundation, 40 Cal. App. 2d 31, 103 P.2d 1052 (exclusively private dwellings); Rosecrans v. Pacific Electric Railway Co., 21 Cal. 2d 602, 134 P.2d 245 (to maintain a train schedule); Schultz v. Beers, 111 Cal. App. 2d 820, 245 P.2d 334 (road purposes); Firth v. Marovich, 160 Cal. 257, 116 P. 729 (residence only).

Moreover, if appellant's suggestion is carried to its logical conclusion it would mean that real property could not be conveyed to a city to be used only for its own city purposes, or to a school district to be used only for its own school purposes, or to a church to be used only for its own church purposes. Such restrictions would also be restrictions upon who uses the land. And yet we do not understand this to be the rule of this state. For example, in Los Angeles Investment Company v. Gary, *supra,* 181 Cal. 680, 186 P. 596, land had been conveyed upon condition that it was not to be sold, leased, rented or occupied by persons other than those of Caucasian race. The court held that the condition against alienation of the land was void, but upheld the condition

---

2. It is arguable that the gift deed created a fee simple determinable. However, in doubtful cases the preferred construction is in favor of an estate subject to a condition subsequent (2 Witkin, Summary Calif. Law., Real Prop. §97, pp. 949-50).

3. The distinction between defeasible estates and future interests that also curtail alienation was recognized at common law. In fact, the creation of future interests, through trusts and similar devises, whose vesting could be indefinitely postponed, resulted in the development of the rule against perpetuities. Significantly, the rule against perpetuities has no application to defeasible estates because reversions, possibilities of reverter and powers of termination are inherently vested in nature (Strong v. Shatto, 45 Cal. App. 29, 187 P. 159; Caffroy v. Fremlin, 198 Cal. App. 2d 176, 17 Cal. Rptr. 668).

restricting the land use. Although a use restriction compelling racial discrimination is no longer consonant with constitutional principles under more recent decisions, the sharp distinction that the court drew between a restriction on land use and a restriction on alienation is still valid. For further example, in the leading and often cited case of Johnston v. City of Los Angeles, 176 Cal. 479, 168 P. 1047, the land was conveyed to the City of Los Angeles on the express condition that the city would use it for the erection and maintenance of a dam, the land to revert if the city ceased to use it for such purposes. The Supreme Court held that the condition created a defeasible estate, apparently even though it was by necessity a restriction on who could use the land. . . .

For the reasons herein stated, the first paragraph of the judgment below is amended and revised to read:

> 1. That at the time of the commencement of this action title to the parcel of real property situated in the City of Los Banos, County of Merced, State of California, being described as:
> Lot 20 Block 72 according to the Map of the Town of Los Banos was vested in the MOUNTAIN BROW LODGE NO. 82, INDEPENDENT ORDER OF ODD FELLOWS, subject to the condition that said property is restricted for the use and benefit of the second party only; and in the event the same fails to be used by the second party the same is to revert to the first parties herein, their successors, heirs or assigns.

As so modified the judgment is affirmed. Respondents to recover their costs on appeal.

The petition for rehearing is denied.

CONLEY, J., concurs.

STONE, J. I dissent. I believe the entire habendum clause which purports to restrict the fee simple conveyed is invalid as a restraint upon alienation within the ambit of Civil Code section 711. It reads: "Said property is restricted for the use and benefit of the second party, only; and in the event the same fails to be used by the second party or in the event of sale or transfer by the second party of all or any part of said lot the same is to revert to the first parties herein, their successors, heirs or assigns."

If the words "sale or transfer," which the majority find to be a restraint upon alienation, are expunged, still the property cannot be sold or transferred by the grantee because the property may be used by only the I.O.O.F. Lodge No. 82, upon pain of reverter. This use restriction prevents the grantee from conveying the property just as effectively as the condition against "sale or transfer . . . of all or any part of said lot." (Los Angeles Investment Co. v. Gary, 181 Cal. 680, 682, 186 P. 596; Property Restatement, §404 et seq.; 2 Witkin, Summary of Cal. Law, Real Property, p. 1004; Simes, Perpetuities in California since 1951; 18 Hastings L.J., p. 248.)

Certainly, if we are to have realism in the law, the effect of language must be judged according to what it does. When two different terms generate the same ultimate legal result, they should be treated alike in relation to that result.

Section 711 of the Civil Code expresses an ancient policy of English common law.* The wisdom of this proscription as applied to situations of this kind is manifest when we note that a number of fraternal, political and similar organizations of a century ago have disappeared, and others have ceased to function in individual communities. Should an organization holding property under a deed similar to the one before us be disbanded one hundred years or so after the conveyance is made, the result may well be a title fragmented into the interests of heirs of the grantors numbering in the hundreds and scattered to the four corners of the earth.

The majority opinion cites a number of cases holding use restrictions in deeds to be valid, but these restrictions impose limitations upon the manner in which the property may be used. The majority equates these cases with the restriction in the instant case to use *by* only Lodge No. 82. It seems to me that a restriction upon the use that may be made of land must be distinguished from a restriction upon *who* may use it. In the first place, a restriction upon the kind of use does not restrain alienation because the property may be conveyed to *anyone,* subject to the restriction. Moreover, as Professor Simes points out in his article, "Restricting Land Use in California by Rights of Entry and Possibility of Reverter," 13 Hastings Law Journal No. 3, page 293, where changed circumstances are shown a court of equity will free land from a property use restriction.

There is a judicially-created exception to public policy against restraint of alienation embodied in Civil Code section 711 which is broadly defined as "restraint on alienation when reasonable as to purpose." (Coast Bank v. Min-

---

* The conceptual argument is that the law defines the exact nature of every estate in land, that each has certain incidents which are provided by law, and that one of the principal incidents of a fee is alienability. Manning, The Development of Restraints on Alienation Since Gray, 48 Harv. L. Rev. 373 (1935).

The first of the two reasons most often given for holding restraints void is that a restraint is repugnant to the nature of the fee. Murray v. Green, 64 Cal. 363, 28 P. 118 (1883); Eastman Marble Co. v. Vermont Marble Co., 236 Mass. 138, 128 N.E. 177 (1920); Andrews v. Hall, 156 Neb. 817, 58 N.W.2d 201 [42 A.L.R.2d 1239] (1963); 5 Tiffany, Real Property §1343 (3d ed. 1939); Manning, *supra,* at 401. However, Lord Coke believed that restraints were void, not only because they were repugnant to the fee, but because "it is absurd and repugnant to reason" that a tenant in fee simple should be restrained "of all his power to alien." Co. Litt. 223a.

The second and more practically oriented reason for holding restraints void is that a restraint, by taking land out of the flow of commerce, is detrimental to the economy. Gray, Restraints on Alienation §21 (2d ed. 1895); 6 Powell, Real Property 1 (1958); 5 Tiffany, op. cit. *supra,* §1343. Other reasons have been accepted on occasion by courts: to encourage improvement of property; hampering effective use of property if the buyer could put it to better use than the seller; removal from trade of increasing amounts of capital; not allowing an individual to appear more prosperous than he is, i.e., a borrower may appear to own property outright, thus able to sell it in payment of a debt, where in reality the property is restrained; balance of dead hand control, i.e., recognizing the right of the individual to control property after death, by the proposition that life is for the living and should be controlled by the living and not by the extended hand of the dead. Bernhard, The Minority Doctrine Concerning Direct Restraints on Alienation, 57 Mich. L. Rev. 1173, 1177 (1959). (12 U.C.L.A. Law Rev. No. 3, fn. p. 956.)

derhout, . . . 61 Cal. 2d 311, 38 Cal. Rptr. 505, 392 P.2d 265.) In discussing this subject, a comment in 12 U.C.L.A. Law Review No. 3, says, in part, at pages 955-958:

> The alienability of realty has long been a jealously guarded incident of a fee simple estate. All jurisdictions invalidate absolute restraints on alienation, and *an overwhelming majority void restraints partial as to persons and temporary as to time.* California has codified the common law rule of restraints on alienation in Civil Code section 711. This provision not only voids restraints created by the grantor of an estate in a deed or conveyance but has been judicially interpreted to void restraints created by covenants executed separately from a deed. In mitigation of the harshness stemming from the rule invalidating restraints, both case law and statutory exceptions have been promulgated in most jurisdictions. In California, a restraint on the transfer of shares in a corporation has been upheld, as have the restraints created by the spendthrift trust, a lease for a term of years, and a restraint on the alienability of a life estate. The decision in *Minderhout* distinguished California as the first state not to invalidate a restraint on alienation when reasonable as to purpose. (Emphasis added.)

As I view the restraint in the instant case, it accomplishes no reasonable purpose within the rationale of Coast Bank v. Minderhout, *supra,* that would justify the indefinite suspension of alienation. . . .

NOTES AND QUESTIONS

1. The rule against direct restraints on alienation is much older than the Rule Against Perpetuities. Littleton wrote around 1475 that if a feoffment in fee simple (but not fee tail) were made on condition that the feoffee not alienate to anyone, the condition would be void as "against reason"; not so, however, a condition against alienating to a specified person. Littleton, Tenures §§360-362. Lord Coke in his commentaries on Littleton placed the earliest prohibition against such a restraint in the statute Quia Emptores (1290). Coke on Littleton ff. 206b, 233a.

2. Restraints on alienation fall into three classes: disabling restraints, forfeiture restraints, and promissory restraints. Examples of each follow.

(a) A to B in fee simple absolute. B may not transfer without A's consent. (disabling restraint)
(b) A to B, provided, however, that A shall have the power to terminate if B should transfer without A's consent. (forfeiture restraint)
(c) A to B in fee simple absolute. B covenants not to transfer without A's consent. (promissory restraint)

Looking at these several restraints abstractly, can you think of any reason for one to be more (or less) valid than another?

3. "When two different terms generate the same ultimate legal result, they should be treated alike in relation to that result." (Dissenting opinion in Mountain Brow Lodge No. 82 v. Toscano, *supra*.)

What do you think of the majority opinion distinction between a valid restraint on use (even when limited to one party) and an invalid restraint on alienation? Does the revised habendum clause of the deed give the lodge any additional rights, powers, etc. in the site?

4. Why should (or shouldn't) a donor be able to attach strings to a gift of land, whether as to mode of use, identity of the user, or identity of the owner?

Looking at each of the following gift conveyances, try to measure (from shortest to longest) the length of the donor's strings.

(a) D to the city of Los Angeles so long as the premises are used as a park.
(b) D to the city of Los Angeles so long as it uses the premises as a park.
(c) D to the city of Los Angeles so long as it continues to own the premises.

5. Do you believe that the court would have found repugnant either of the following gifts?

(a) D to the lodge for its use. If the lodge should sell or transfer the land, D shall be paid the value of the land measured as of the date of gift.
(b) D to the lodge for its use. If the lodge should ever wish to sell or transfer the land, D shall first be given the opportunity to reacquire the land for the sum of the value of the land measured as of the date of gift, plus the current value of any lodge-built improvements.

6. All the judges agreed that the prohibition against sale or transfer violated Civil Code §711: "Conditions restraining alienation, *when repugnant to the interest created,* are void." Stop and think about this, however. Is the prohibition invalid because it is "repugnant," or is the prohibition repugnant because it is invalid? Do you see the circularity that the judges seem to be blind to? Haven't they all assumed a legal conclusion without giving any reasons?

In this connection, does it (should it) make any difference whether the restraint appears in a fee simple absolute or in a defeasible estate? Is it at all persuasive that the fee simple absolute has potentially infinite duration, which implies broad, limitless powers of alienation, whereas a defeasible estate by its very nature can be cut short if the holder takes some disfavored action, and that alienation may well be the proscribed action? Or are we simply distinguishing between a disabling restraint and a forfeiture restraint (note 2, *supra*)?

And looking ahead to landlord-tenant estates, what do you think of a lease that bars the tenant, upon pain of forfeiture, from assigning his interest without landlord's consent? See §5.13, *infra*.

7. The dissenting justice writes of restraints on alienation that are "reasonable as to purpose" and indicates that such restraints are valid, a judicially created exception, he states, to the public policy against restraints on alienation. Should not the exception overtake the principle, so as to test all restraints on alienation, direct and indirect, against a "rule of reason"? If this were so, what factors would you stress in weighing the reasonableness of a restraint: its duration? whether the transfer was for value? the continuing relationship, if any, between grantor and grantee? the purpose for which the restraint is sought? any others? Compare Restatement (Second) of Property §4.2(3) (Tent. Draft No. 3, 1980). And should restraints on use be similarly tested?

8. A due-on clause commonly appears in real estate mortgages to provide, at the lender's election, for immediate full payment of the unpaid mortgage balance if the borrower transfers the mortgaged property without the lender's consent. Why might lenders install such clauses in a mortgage and seek to enforce them? Does such a proviso restrain alienation? If so, is the restraint unreasonable? Compare Wellenkamp v. Bank of America, 21 Cal. 3d 943, 582 P.2d 970, 148 Cal. Rptr. 379 (1978) (due-on clause unenforceable absent impairment of security or risk of default) with Malouff v. Midland Federal Savings & Loan Ass'n, 181 Colo. 294, 509 P.2d 1240 (1973) (due-on clause generally enforceable). Cf. also First Federal Savings & Loan Ass'n v. Peterson, 516 F. Supp. 732 (N.D. Fla. 1981) (Federal Home Loan Bank Board regulation allowing member associations to use due-on clauses overrides contrary state law).

e. Defenses to a Suit to Enforce Forfeiture—Legislation Limiting Possibilities of Reverter and Powers of Termination

HAMMOND, LIMITATIONS UPON POSSIBILITIES OF REVERTER AND RIGHTS OF ENTRY: CURRENT TRENDS IN STATE LEGISLATION 1953-1954

589, 590-592 (1955)

In examining statutes which affect possibilities of reverter and rights of entry, two basic policies of the law must be kept in mind because the use of a possibility of reverter or a right of entry in a conveyance of land may bring these policies into conflict. Any legislation in this field should seek to resolve this conflict.

The first of the two policies concerned is that land should be freely alienable; that is, land should be transferable by its owner with a minimum of difficulty of any kind. This policy is believed to promote the fullest and best economic use of land in the interests of society. There are two important elements in the free alienability of land. First, to be freely alienable, or marketable, land must have a title that is free of defects and restrictions. Defects in title make purchase hazardous, and restrictions diminish the potential useful-ness of the land. Second, the state of title must be easily discoverable so that prospective purchasers may know whether the title is marketable. Such legis-lation as recording acts and marketable title acts are attempts to make the title to real property readily discoverable and also, in some instances, attempts to provide a basis for curing defects in title, thereby effectuating the policy of free alienability of land.

The second important policy here involved is that owners should be free to dispose of their land, imposing such limitations, conditions, and restrictions as they choose. This policy is in accord with democratic political ideas and free enterprise economic philosophy. It recognizes the right of the individual to acquire property, to own property, and to dispose of property with a minimum of interference. . . .

The conflict between the policies of free alienability and of the right to dispose of land as one chooses comes about as a result of the fact that there is no limitation upon the length of time that possibilities of reverter and rights of entry remain enforceable interests. Each interest remains a part of the title to the land until the interest is in some way eliminated. Thus, each interest may operate to cause a forfeiture or reverter at a remote future time. Whenever such an interest appears in a title to land, account must be taken of it by a title examiner in approving his client's prospective purchase of the land. Because of the ever present possibility that the land will revert or be forfeited, many prospective purchasers hesitate to buy. Thus, the title is rendered partially unmarketable. In addition, if considerable time has elapsed since the creation of the interest, it may be difficult to secure a discharge of the interest. This may be because the owner cannot be found, because he demands unreasonable compensation for giving a discharge, or because there are numerous owners of the interest who either cannot all be found or who cannot all be persuaded to give discharges of their interests. Also, it may be difficult or impossible to determine whether circumstances may have occurred which render the interest unenforceable. The result is that it is often difficult to discover the true state of title where a possibility of reverter or right of entry appears in the title. This, combined with the restrictive effect of the limitation or condition itself, tends to hamper the free alienability of land.

CLINE v. JOHNSON COUNTY BOARD OF EDUCATION
548 S.W.2d 507 (Ky. 1977)

PALMORE, J. The issue in this case is whether KRS 381.221(1) is consti-tutional. Enacted in 1960, it provided that every possibility of reverter and right of entry [upon breach of a condition subsequent] created prior to July 1, 1960, would cease to be valid or enforceable 30 years after its creation unless before July 1, 1965, a declaration of intent to preserve it were recorded. We are of the opinion that the judgment of the trial court holding it valid was correct.

There is no factual dispute, nor any necessity for summarizing the manner in which the issue was joined by the pleadings and presented for judgment.

By a deed executed in 1910 Walker Wells and others, some of whom were ancestors of the appellants, conveyed a half-acre parcel of land in Johnson County to the board of education for the sum of $45.00. The habendum clause provided that the property was to be held by the grantee and its successors "so long as used for school purposes and when no longer used for school purposes to revert to parties of the first part . . . said parties of the first part [sic] reserve right to remove school house and furnishings from said premises when they may desire as it is understood that the land only reverts back to while the house and furnishings remain the property of the County Board of Education or school district."

Appellants contend that although the reversionary interest retained by their ancestors was not preserved by the recording of a notice as required by KRS 381.221(1), because the property is no longer being used for school purposes the fee reverts to them regardless of the statute. Their position is that a possibility of reverter is a vested property right and that its abolition impairs a contract right in violation of Sec. 19 of the Kentucky Constitution. In the main, the Kentucky cases cited in support of that position hold that a possibility of reverter is an alienable interest in property. That much may be conceded, but it does not necessarily follow perforce that the statute is invalid.

In terms of legal technicality, we recognize that a possibility of reverter is not the same thing as a mere expectancy, which might be described as a hope coupled with some degree of probability. From a practical standpoint, however, there are more similarities than differences. As suggested by its very name, the prospects of a reverter are no less fleeting and amorphous than are those of an expectancy, and no more valuable. The differences are more historic than they are real. That they may, historically, be considered as "vested" no more shields them against the police power of the state than are the vested-in-possession rights of landowners protected from devaluation by zoning laws. A regulation, for example, that eliminates the prospect of converting a piece of real estate to commercial usage is most likely to effect more loss in terms of actual value than is a law that merely requires the owner of a possibility of reverter to renew it of record within a reasonable time as a condition precedent to enforcing it in the future.

In Atkinson v. Kish, Ky., 420 S.W.2d 104, 109 (1967), footnote 5, it was said that because "a reversionary right of entry, like a possibility of reverter, *amounts* to no more than an expectancy" (emphasis added), it does not come within the constitutional protection of "vested rights." Dictum though it may have been, we reach the same ultimate conclusion here.

In Biltmore Village v. Royal, Fla., 71 So. 2d 727, 41 A.L.R.2d 1380 (1954), the Florida Supreme Court held invalid a statute cancelling reverter provisions in plats or deeds after 21 years unless enforced within one year from the effective date of the act. In so doing, it recognized that the one-year saving provision was of no avail to those whose rights of enforcement had not accrued. Our statute, on the contrary, provided a period of five years in which the owner of the right was not required to enforce it, but only to record notice of his intent to preserve it.

Although a possibility of reverter was not an alienable estate under Illinois law, as it is under our law, in Trustees of Schools of Township No. 1 v. Batdorf, 6 Ill. 2d 486, 130 N.E.2d 111 (1955), the Supreme Court of that state held valid a statute terminating all such interests that had not fallen in within 50 years after their creation. In reaching that result it commented as follows:

> The statute reflects the General Assembly's appraisal of the actual economic significance of these interests, weighed against the inconvenience and expense caused by their continued existence for unlimited periods of time without regard to altered circumstances . . . Our problem . . . [is] reasonableness of the method chosen by the General Assembly. We are unable to say that that method offends the constitutional provisions relied upon.

In Board of Education of Central Sch. Dist. No. 1 v. Miles, 15 N.Y.2d 364, 259 N.Y.S.2d 129, 207 N.E.2d 181 (1965), the New York Supreme Court took the view that a statute eliminating this kind of property interest unless preserved by a recorded notice does not come within the scope of the police power. We think that it does, and, in the words of the Illinois opinion, that the General Assembly could properly determine that the economic significance of these interests is so outweighed by the inconvenience and expense caused by their continued existence for unlimited periods of time that the only constitutional problem is the reasonableness of the method chosen to deal with them. We are of the opinion that the method chosen in the form of KRS 381.221(1), allowing five years in which to file a preservation notice, was entirely reasonable.

The judgment is affirmed.

All concur.

CALDWELL v. BROWN

553 S.W.2d 692 (Ky. 1977)

PER CURIAM. On November 5, 1869, J. D. Cundiff conveyed to the Louisville & Nashville Railroad one acre adjoining its right-of-way on the condition that the lot was to be used for depot purposes. The deed provided: "Said parcel of ground to revert to said party of the first part should the party of the second part at any time abandon or fail to use it for the purposes herein set forth."

The railroad company ceased to use the lot for depot purposes, dismantled the buildings it had placed on the lot, and made no further use of the property. On January 6, 1969, it conveyed the lot to Arthur and Delvia Caldwell by quit-claim deed.

On July 14, 1969, Mae H. Brown and Cora Weindel as heirs of J. D. Cundiff filed this action to quiet their title to the lot, claiming that title had reverted to them upon the abandonment of the lot by the railroad and, consequently, the quit-claim deed to Caldwell was void. The judgment of the trial court held the reservation in the 1869 deed to be a possibility of reverter, and the title to the lot had automatically vested in Brown and Weindel upon its abandonment by the railroad. Finally, the court held that Caldwell acquired no interest by the quit-claim deed as the railroad had no title to convey. The trial court also held that KRS 381.221 did not apply.

Caldwell asserts upon appeal that KRS 381.221 did apply and that the failure of Brown and Weindel to timely file a notice of intent extinguished their rights under the possibility of reverter. KRS 381.221 is a part of the Kentucky Perpetuities Act of 1960 and provides that every possibility of reverter and every right of entry created prior to July 1, 1960, cease to be enforceable thirty years after its creation unless a declaration of intention to preserve it was recorded before July 1, 1965.

It is admitted that Brown and Weindel did not file the required declaration of intention to preserve. KRS 381.221 was enacted by the 1960 General Assembly and became effective June 16, 1960. On July 16, 1973, Cora Weindel testified as follows:

Q. Do you know approximately when the L & N ceased using that as a depot?

A. Oh, it's been about twenty-five or thirty years ago.

This is the only evidence in the record concerning the time of abandonment by the railroad. A rather elementary mathematical calculation makes it clear that the railroad ceased using the lot as a depot as early as 1943 and, in no event, later than 1948. Caldwell correctly stated that under the common law the language in the 1869 deed created a possibility of reverter which carried with it an automatic termination on cessation of the use. This being true, the possibility of reverter did not exist on June 16, 1960, as the reversion had already occurred. KRS 381.220 could not have controlled this issue.

The judgment is affirmed.

All concur.

NOTES AND QUESTIONS

1. Statutes limiting the duration of a possibility of reverter or power of termination (other than those applying the Rule Against Perpetuities to those interests) usually take one of two forms: the absolute cut-off of the future

interest after a specified interval and the conditional cut-off, which happens unless the interest holder records notice of his intention to preserve it.

Illinois's Reverter Act of 1947, Ill. Rev. Stat. ch. 30, §37e (1969, Supp. 1978), represents the first genre. After forty years, the interests cease. The state court validated the statute even as to interests already in being. Trustees of Schools of Twp. No. 1 v. Batdorf, 6 Ill. 2d 486, 130 N.E.2d 111 (1955). Compare Biltmore Village v. Royal, 71 So. 2d 727 (Fla. 1954) (twenty-one year cut-off invalid as to existing interests).

The Kentucky statute, discussed in the *Cline* and *Caldwell* cases, illustrates the second genre. The *Cline* opinion refers to the New York statute, N.Y. Real Prop. L. §345 (McKinney 1976), that also required interest holders, as to interests created more than thirty years earlier, to record a "declaration of intention to preserve"; the statute gave them three years to comply. The court of appeals held the statute invalid as to outstanding interests but enforceable as to interests created after the statute's adoption. Board of Education v. Miles, 15 N.Y.2d 364, 207 N.E.2d 181 (1965).

The New York statute also provides for renewals (at ten-year intervals) of the declaration of intention to preserve.

2. In his opinion in the *Miles* case, *supra*, Judge Van Voorhis wrote that one of the New York statute's defects was its requirement that persons record their declaration of intention (and the ten-year renewals thereof) before the future interest "matured," that is, before anyone could identify the parties in interest if the reverter were to take effect. Might not that be equally true as to possibilities of reverter created after §345 became law? What is the legal basis for distinguishing between the two situations?

The New York statute became effective in 1962. Assume a 1962 conveyance from A to a school district so long as the premises are used for school purposes. A dies intestate in 1980 leaving two heirs, X and Y, who are both alive in 1992. Who should file the 1992 declaration of intention if the grantee has continued to use the premises for school purposes? Suppose a 1932 conveyance from A to the school district, A's 1950 death intestate, and the same heirs, X and Y, alive in 1962. Is there any practical reason why the 1932 and 1962 conveyances should not be subject to the same recordation duty?

If you were A's lawyer in 1982, as he was about to transfer land to a school district on a defeasible estate, what steps would you recommend to your client to better the chances of compliance with §345 thirty years later? Note that the declaration cannot be filed until twenty-seven years have passed.

3. At least two other statutory modes exist to weaken the persistent grip of a long-standing possibility of reverter or power of termination.

(a) Conditions that "are nominal" and of no "substantial" benefit "to the party in whose favor they run are void and unenforceable." Mich. Comp. Laws Ann. §554.46 (1967); Wis. Stat. Ann. §700.15 (Supp. 1973); Ariz. Rev. Stat. §33-436 (1956). For a review of cases construing these terms, see Hammond, *supra*, at 606-609; see also N.Y. Real Prop. Actions Law §1951 (1963), which deals with *restrictions* that are of no "substantial" benefit, and Mohawk Containers, Inc. v. Hancock, §11.6, *infra*, for a judicial response.

(b) After a fixed period, any possibility of reverter or power of termination shall be enforceable only by equitable remedies as though it were a covenant or restriction. Fla. Stat. Ann. §689.18 (1969) (twenty-one years).

4. Review the *Hammond* excerpts, *supra,* and the various statutory devices we have mentioned. How well do these devices respond to each of the following goals?

(a) removing title defects
(b) promoting economic efficiency
(c) respecting donative desire

5. Later on, you will meet more statutes curbing burdens on land use, this time aimed at covenants and equitable servitudes. Some of the devices and many of the legal or practical problems that you have just discussed will be reprised in a somewhat different context, §11.6, *infra.*

f. Defenses to a Suit to Enforce Forfeiture—Waiver, Estoppel, the Statute of Limitations, and Other Procedural Ploys

Even if the defeasible estate does not flout the Rule Against Perpetuities, restrain alienation unreasonably, or fail to satisfy some other statutory or social policy, the holder of the future interest may still face a procedural defense that will thwart his efforts to regain possession of the property.

One such barrier is the statute of limitations for an action to recover real property. We will be more directly concerned with each state's variant of this statute when we later examine adverse possession, but for now you should be aware that the holder of the future interest may not wait forever to enforce his rights after the limiting event has occurred or the condition is breached.

In this context, note the following distinction between a fee simple determinable and a fee simple subject to a condition subsequent, which appears in the Restatement of Property:

> §44. Fee Simple Determinable—Form of Limitation. An estate in fee simple determinable . . . provides that the estate shall *automatically* expire upon the occurrence of a stated event. (Emphasis added.)

> §45. Fee Simple Subject to a Condition Subsequent—Form of Limitation. An estate in fee simple subject to a condition subsequent . . . provides that upon the occurrence of a stated event the conveyor or his successor in interest *shall have the power* to terminate the estate so created. (Emphasis added.)

This contrast between the "automatic" forfeiture and the power (election) to terminate may have theoretical importance in the following hypothetical.

In 1960, A transfers real estate to B "so long as it is used for lodge purposes." B holds a determinable fee, A holds a possibility of reverter. In 1969, B violates the limitation, but A takes no action. The statute of limitations for the recovery of possession of real property is ten years. In 1980, A brings an action against B to recover the property. The statute of limitations might well bar the action, since the right to possession vests automatically in A when the violation occurs.

Suppose, instead, that the 1960 transfer had created a fee simple subject to a condition subsequent in B; A would retain a power of termination. In 1969, B breaches the condition, and again A takes no action until 1980, when A notifies B of his election to terminate. In theory, the ten-year statute of limitations for the recovery of possession should begin to run only in 1980; until A makes his election, declaring B in breach, A is not entitled to possession and has no cause of action to recover possession. In practice, however, this distinction seems largely to have been ignored. Cf. Annot., 19 A.L.R.2d 720, 732 (1951).

Besides the bar of the statute of limitations, the future interest holder may also face defenses of waiver or estoppel. Professors Leach and Logan, in Future Interests and Estate Planning 64-67 (1961), have collected a number of factual situations that have triggered these defenses. For example, A conveys land to B conditioned on the premises not being used for the sale of liquor. B proves that other lots in the same subdivision were subject to the same condition, that the condition was violated repeatedly, and that no enforcement occurred. B now argues that A's failure to enforce the condition elsewhere constitutes a waiver not only for those lots but also for B's own lot. Would you agree? Cf. Brown v. Wrightman, 5 Cal. App. 391, 90 P. 467 (1907).

One such waiver dispute evoked the following discussion, which, even for a legal area where lawyers and judges sling terms around with furious, misguided abandon, boggles credulity.

> Fees upon condition subsequent, or conditional fees as they are called, are an ancient form of estate. . . . They place no restraint upon alienation but merely limit the estate conveyed. The taker never has a fee absolute. His estate is defeasible upon condition broken and re-entry into possession by the grantor within fifteen years of the breach causing reverter. . . . Omission to re-enter for fifteen years or waiver of an absolute right of re-entry terminates all possibility of reverter, for the estate does not revest automatically, as does a qualified or determinable fee, when the limitation upon which it depends fails. Before breach the grantor has a possibility of reverter, a kind of inchoate right of re-entry. Even this may be formally released or waived. [Resnick v. Croton Park Colony, 3 Misc. 2d 109, 114, 151 N.Y.S.2d 328, 334-335 (Sup. Ct. 1955)]

The party seeking forfeiture must also worry about the rule of strict construction that will treat any ambiguity in the conveyance to the prejudice of the claimant. Leslie Enterprises, Inc. v. Metropolitan Dade County, 293 So. 2d 73 (Fla. Dist. Ct. App. 1974), involved a 1964 grant of a defeasible estate from plaintiff to defendant: "In the event the above described property should be abandoned or should not be used for a public park or recreational purposes, then, and in that event, by operation of law, the title to said property shall revert to the Grantor. . . ." Id. at 74.

In the ensuing six years, the grantee did nothing with the land except to plant five trees. Yet grantor's suit to enforce the forfeiture failed because the reverter clause did not impose a time limit for the county's action. "It is well settled that such restrictions are not favored in law if they have the effect of destroying an estate, that they will be construed strictly and will be most strongly construed against the grantor. . . . Such forfeiture provisions are particularly undesirable when they operate against the public." Id. at 75.

§3.5   Life Estates (A "to B for Life")[11]

As you have seen, the earliest conveyances of land in the common-law system created a life estate—one ending with the death of the transferee. As commercial transactions in land increased and as new estate forms emerged, the life estate lost some of its preeminence, but, even today, it serves a major role in estate planning—i.e., the donative transmission of wealth from one generation to the next. Thus, a husband or wife may want at death to create a life estate in the surviving spouse with a remainder over to third parties. Although the testator in this case could devise the real estate directly to the survivor for his or her life, this would seldom prove wise. The recipient would be locked into the property in the sense that he or she could not sell a fee simple absolute, or enter into a long-term lease, or obtain a mortgage. To allow flexibility, most donors would now use a trust, giving the trustee "legal" title to the trust assets, in fee simple absolute, and creating an *equitable* life estate in the beneficiary. Having the power of sale, lease, or mortgage, the trustees can then make decisions vis-à-vis the property that will best serve the interests of the beneficiary and the aims of the trustor.

In the formation stage, two issues may arise: (1) Was a life estate intended? See Morgan v. Green, page 187 *infra*. (2) If so, what is the measuring life? To tackle the second issue first: suppose a transfer from A "to B for life," when does B's life estate end? At A's death? At B's death? Absent any other clue to the grantor's intent, custom regards the measuring life as B's. What becomes of the land at B's death? What is this future interest called? Cf. Table 1, page 142 *supra*. Is it subject to the Rule Against Perpetuities?

Problem: what are the measuring lives in the following examples?

11. When created by deed, trust indenture, or will, the life estate is described as "conventional." In §§8.2 and 8.3, *infra*, you will meet life estates that the law imposes upon land.

(1) A "to B and C for life."
(2) A "to B and C for their joint lives."
(3) A "for life to B and C and the survivor of them."
(4) A "to B for the life of the survivor of all persons listed in the 1982-
     1983 Manhattan telephone directory." (Cf. Restatement of Property
     §107; N.Y. Est., Powers & Trusts Law §9-1.1(b) (1970).)

Note also that one can create a defeasible life estate. A common instance
is H "to W for life, but if W should remarry, then to S." What is S's interest
called?

a. Life Estate pur Autre Vie

Suppose that a life tenant, B, before his death conveys his entire interest
to C. What estate does C get? Since B can not convey an estate greater than
his own, C's interest ends at B's death. Until then, C does enjoy a life estate,
but the measuring life is one other than his own, thus, a life estate pur autre vie
(the Gallic influence). It is as if the grantor, A, had created an estate "to C, for
the life of B."

The life estate pur autre vie must be further analyzed when the life
tenant dies before the end of the measuring life. In the example A "to C, for
the life of B," what becomes of the land at C's death, if B is still alive? The
grantor might have anticipated this event by designating a successor on C's
predecease; also, if the grantor had not acted, C might himself have named a
taker, either by inter vivos transfer, or by will. The designee would be known
as the "special occupant."

But, suppose both have failed to name a special occupant. A is not
entitled to regain the land quite yet, for he has deferred his right to possession
until the death of B. Nor would the early common law let the land descend to
C's heirs, for it regarded the life estate as noninheritable. To close this hiatus,
the law simply allowed the first occupant—called a "general occupant"—to
enjoy the remaining term. This crude device lasted until 1677 when it was
abolished by statute (29 Ca. 2, c. 3, §12). Today, if a special occupant is not
named, the remaining life term passes by intestacy to the tenant's heirs.

Remainders. As you now know, the future interest that follows the end of
the life estate often is created in third persons. A simple illustration would be:
A devises Blackacre "to B for life, *remainder* to C and her heirs." At B's death,
the land passes to the named third person.

As you also know, remainders may be either contingent or vested. We
looked at contingent remainders in our treatment of the Rule Against Perpetuities. A simple illustration would be: A devises Blackacre "to B for life,
remainder to C and her heirs, if C survives B." Because of the condition of
survivorship, C holds a contingent remainder. Suppose now that C fails to
survive B: What happens to Blackacre at B's death? If you intuit that the land

reverts to A,[12] your hunch is sound. When creating a contingent remainder, the creator either expressly or implicitly must consider that the contingency will not be satisfied (if, for example, C predeceases B), or that, after the life estate ends, time may elapse before the contingency disappears. (For example, a remainder in the heirs of C vests only at C's death; if C outlives the life tenant, the property must revert to the creator during the interval between the death of B and the death of C.)

There are three kinds of vested remainder: indefeasibly vested, vested subject to open, and vested subject to complete defeasance. Illustrations of each follow.

(a) A devises Blackacre "to B for life, remainder to C and her heirs" (indefeasibly vested).
(b) A devises Blackacre "to B for life, remainder to each of B's children who reach the age of twenty-one years" (at A's death, B has two children, ages twenty-two and nineteen) (vested subject to open).[13]
(c) A devises Blackacre "to B for life, remainder to C and her heirs, but if C fails to survive B, then to D and his heirs" (at A's death, B and C are both alive) (vested subject to complete defeasance).[14]

Remainders (and their near relative, executory interests) will cause you endless worry in another course, and we have greatly abbreviated their explanation. Fair-sized differences in legal results attend the decision that a remainder is "vested," rather than "contingent," and you will be expected to understand what those differences are and how lawyers and courts go about arguing or deciding which remainder they have. For the present, it is enough to be acquainted with the terms.

Occasionally the lawyer's attention will be drawn to the issue of the grantor's intention: what did the grantor have in mind when he created the estate? When the issue concerns a possible life estate, the controversial language is likely to appear in a will, which means that the testator is dead and quite unable to explain his (or his lawyer's) choice of words. The following case presents a typical dispute.

MORGAN v. GREEN
263 Ark. 125, 562 S.W.2d 612 (1978)

HICKMAN, J. This appeal questions whether a clause in a will granted a mere life estate, or gave the life tenant an absolute power of alienation. The

---

12. Since A has already died, what becomes of Blackacre?—ED.
13. Although the twenty-two-year-old child holds a vested remainder, it is subject to diminution ("subject to open") as other siblings reach the age of twenty-one. We call this remainder a "class gift." Although "vested," it is subject to the Rule Against Perpetuities—an exception, alas, to the principle stated earlier that the rule does not cover vested future interests.
14. In this illustration, D holds an executory interest. C's interest is not subject to the Rule Against Perpetuities; D's interest, however (as does every executory interest), comes under the rule.

chancellor, after careful consideration, decided on summary judgment the will of Eva Morgan did not grant her son, Jeff Morgan, the power to sell sixty acres—it only gave Morgan a life estate. We disagree with the chancellor and reverse his decision.

The relevant portions of Morgan's will provided:

> Section III: I give, devise and bequeath to my beloved son, Jeff Morgan, *a life interest in the real estate described herein with the right to mortgage, sell or in any manner to alienate the said property during his lifetime with remainder over.* . . .

> Section IV: At the death of Jeff Morgan, *the remainder over is vested in the following persons* or their heirs and assigns as tenants in common. . . . (Emphasis added.)

Eva Morgan died in 1959 and her son took possession of sixty acres of land devised to him. In 1963, Jeff Morgan sold the land by warranty deed. He died in 1973, and appellee, Reba Green, who stood to have an interest in the sixty acres if it had remained unsold, filed suit to set aside the deed.

The case was decided on summary judgment for Green. The present owner brings this appeal.

It is our duty in interpreting documents to apply our best judgment consistent with certain rules of construction. We seek to find the intent of the testator. This intention is gathered from a consideration of the entire instrument. Jackson v. Robinson, 195 Ark. 431, 112 S.W.2d 417 (1938); Lawrence v. Lawrence, 225 Ark. 500, 283 S.W.2d 697 (1955). Words and sentences used in a will are to be construed in their ordinary sense so as to arrive at the real intention of the testator. Morris v. Dosch, 194 Ark. 153, 106 S.W.2d 159 (1937). We do not consider, as a controlling factor, whether a power of sale is in the same clause as the grant of a life estate or in a separate clause. Union & Mercantile Trust Co. v. Hudson, 143 Ark. 519, 220 S.W. 820 (1920). Applying these rules of construction to Morgan's will we merely have to examine her words. Her son Jeff was granted a life estate "with the right to mortgage, *sell, or in any manner to alienate the said property* during his lifetime. . . ." This simply means that he was given the right to sell the real estate—not just his interest in the property. We pointed out in a similar case that such words would be meaningless if they did not grant the life tenant the power to sell the property. He already has the right to sell his interest. Pearrow v. Vaden, 201 Ark. 1146, 148 S.W.2d 320 (1941).

We do not find the words "remainder over" in the will granted to Green a vested remainder interest in the property. The words simply provided for the disposition of the property if Morgan did not dispose of it during his lifetime.

It is not necessary for us to reach the other argument raised by the appellants since the decree is reversed and remanded with directions to enter a decree for the appellants.

Reversed.

FOGLEMAN and HOWARD, JJ., dissent.

FOGLEMAN, J., dissenting. I dissent because I agree with the chancellor's careful analysis of our decisions on the question involved. I also agree with the careful, thorough analysis of our cases by the Hon. John E. Miller, the distinguished Judge (now Senior Judge) of the Western District of Arkansas, in Bone v. United States, 238 F. Supp. 97 (1965). The majority's categorical statement, that the phrase quoted simply means that the life tenant was given the right to sell, not his life estate, but the real estate, is simplistic and not supported by our decisions. . . .

One troublesome aspect of the division of property interests into present and future estates is the potential conflict between those in possession who seek to maximize present enjoyment of the asset and those awaiting possession who want the asset to reach them undiminished in value. This conflict can arise in several ways:

(a) Is the life tenant committing *waste?* For example, the asset consists of a timber stand. May the life tenant chop down the trees? Or take another example: the asset consists of an apartment house. Must the life tenant keep the building rented, even at a loss, to prevent vacancy blight? We will examine the waste problem in §12.1, *infra.*

(b) The municipality levies a special tax assessment for permanent improvements to the real estate. Who bears the cost: the life tenant or the remainderman? Cf. Annot., 10 A.L.R.3d 1309 (1966); compare Gaugh v. Gatewood, 380 S.W.2d 84 (Ky. 1964) (apportionment), with Hamilton v. Kinnebrew, 161 Ga. 495, 131 S.E. 470 (1926) (life tenant), and with Morrow v. Person, 195 Tenn. 370, 259 S.W.2d 665 (1953) (remainderman). How would you devise a formula for apportionment?

(c) The life tenant would like to sell the asset and reinvest the proceeds in something more immediately productive. Are there circumstances when equity can (should) direct such a sale and reinvestment? Consider the following case.

BAKER v. WEEDON
262 So. 2d 641 (Miss. 1972)

PATTERSON, J. This is an appeal from a decree of the Chancery Court of Alcorn County. It directs a sale of land affected by a life estate and future interests with provision for the investment of the proceeds. The interest therefrom is to be paid to the life tenant for her maintenance. We reverse and remand.

John Harrison Weedon was born in High Point, North Carolina. He lived throughout the South and was married twice prior to establishing his final residence in Alcorn County. His first marriage to Lula Edwards resulted in two siblings, Mrs. Florence Weedon Baker and Mrs. Delette Weedon Jones.

Mrs. Baker was the mother of three children, Henry Baker, Sarah Baker Lyman and Louise Virginia Baker Heck, the appellants herein. Mrs. Delette Weedon Jones adopted a daughter, Dorothy Jean Jones, who has not been heard from for a number of years and whose whereabouts are presently unknown.

John Weedon was next married to Ella Howell and to this union there was born one child, Rachel. Both Ella and Rachel are now deceased.

Subsequent to these marriages John Weedon bought Oakland Farm in 1905 and engaged himself in its operation. In 1915 John, who was then 55 years of age, married Anna Plaxco, 17 years of age. This marriage, though resulting in no children, was a compatible relationship. John and Anna worked side by side in farming this 152.95-acre tract of land in Alcorn County. There can be no doubt that Anna's contribution to the development and existence of Oakland Farm was significant. The record discloses that during the monetarily difficult years following World War I she hoed, picked cotton and milked an average of fifteen cows per day to protect the farm from financial ruin.

While the relationship of John and Anna was close and amiable, that between John and his daughters of his first marriage was distant and strained. He had no contact with Florence, who was reared by Mr. Weedon's sister in North Carolina, during the seventeen years preceding his death. An even more unfortunate relationship existed between John and his second daughter, Delette Weedon Jones. She is portrayed by the record as being a nomadic person who only contacted her father for money, threatening on several occasions to bring suit against him.

With an obvious intent to exclude his daughters and provide for his wife Anna, John executed his last will and testament in 1925. It provided in part:

> Second; I give and bequeath to my beloved wife, Anna Plaxco Weedon all of my property both real, personal and mixed during her natural life and upon her death to her children, if she has any, and in the event she dies without issue then at the death of my wife Anna Plaxco Weedon I give, bequeath and devise all of my property to my grandchildren, each grandchild sharing equally with the other.

> Third; In this will I have not provided for my daughters, Mrs. Florence Baker and Mrs. Delette Weedon Jones, the reason is, I have given them their share of my property and they have not looked after and cared for me in the latter part of my life.

Subsequent to John Weedon's death in 1932 and the probate of his will, Anna continued to live on Oakland Farm. In 1933 Anna, who had been urged by John to remarry in the event of his death, wed J. E. Myers. This union lasted some twenty years and produced no offspring which might terminate the contingent remainder vested in Weedon's grandchildren by the will.

There was no contact between Anna and John Weedon's children or grandchildren from 1932 until 1964. Anna ceased to operate the farm in 1955 due to her age and it has been rented since that time. Anna's only income is $1000 annually from the farm rental, $300 per year from sign rental and $50 per month by way of social security payments. Without contradiction Anna's income is presently insufficient and places a severe burden upon her ability to live comfortably in view of her age and the infirmities therefrom.

In 1964 the growth of the city of Corinth was approaching Oakland Farm. A right-of-way through the property was sought by the Mississippi State Highway Department for the construction of U.S. Highway 45 bypass. The highway department located Florence Baker's three children, the contingent remaindermen by the will of John Weedon, to negotiate with them for the purchase of the right-of-way. Dorothy Jean Jones, the adopted daughter of Delette Weedon Jones, was not located and due to the long passage of years, is presumbly dead. A decree pro confesso was entered against her.

Until the notice afforded by the highway department the grandchildren were unaware of their possible inheritance. Henry Baker, a native of New Jersey, journeyed to Mississippi to supervise their interests. He appears, as was true of the other grandchildren, to have been totally sympathetic to the conditions surrounding Anna's existence as a life tenant. A settlement of $20,000 was completed for the right-of-way bypass of which Anna received $7500 with which to construct a new home. It is significant that all legal and administrative fees were deducted from the shares of the three grandchildren and not taxed to the life tenant. A contract was executed in 1970 for the sale of soil from the property for $2500. Anna received $1000 of this sum which went toward completion of payments for the home.

There was substantial evidence introduced to indicate the value of the property is appreciating significantly with the nearing completion of U.S. Highway 45 bypass plus the growth of the city of Corinth. While the commercial value of the property is appreciating, it is notable that the rental value for agricultural purposes is not. It is apparent that the land can bring no more for agricultural rental purposes than the $1000 per year now received.

The value of the property for commercial purposes at the time of trial was $168,500. Its estimated value within the ensuing four years is placed at $336,000, reflecting the great influence of the interstate construction upon the land. Mr. Baker, for himself and other remaindermen, appears to have made numerous honest and sincere efforts to sell the property at a favorable price. However, his endeavors have been hindered by the slowness of the construction of the bypass.

Anna, the life tenant and appellee here, is 73 years of age and although now living in a new home, has brought this suit due to her economic distress. She prays that the property, less the house site, be sold by a commissioner and that the proceeds be invested to provide her with an adequate income resulting from interest on the trust investment. She prays also that the sale and investment management be under the direction of the chancery court.

The chancellor granted the relief prayed by Anna under the theory of economic waste. His opinion reflects:

> . . . [T]he change of the economy in this area, the change in farming conditions, the equipment required for farming, and the age of this complainant leaves the real estate where it is to all intents and purposes unproductive when viewed in light of its capacity and that a continuing use under the present conditions would result in economic waste.

The contingent remaindermen by the will, appellants here, were granted an interlocutory appeal to settle the issue of the propriety of the chancellor's decree in divesting the contingency title of the remaindermen by ordering a sale of the property.

The weight of authority reflects a tendency to afford a court of equity the power to order the sale of land in which there are future interests. Simes, Law of Future Interest, section 53 (2d ed. 1966), states:

> By the weight of authority, it is held that a court of equity has the power to order a judicial sale of land affected with a future interest and an investment of the proceeds, where this is necessary for the preservation of all interests in the land. When the power is exercised, the proceeds of the sale are held in a judicially created trust. The beneficiaries of the trust are the persons who held interests in the land, and the beneficial interests are of the same character as the legal interests which they formally held in the land.

See also Simes and Smith, The Law of Future Interest, §1941 (2d ed. 1956).

This Court has long recognized that chancery courts do have jurisdiction to order the sale of land for the prevention of waste. Kelly v. Neville, 136 Miss. 429, 101 So. 565 (1924). In Riley v. Norfleet, 167 Miss. 420, 436-437, 148 So. 777, 781 (1933), Justice Cook, speaking for the Court and citing *Kelly, supra,* stated:

> . . . The power of a court of equity on a plenary bill, with adversary interest properly represented, to sell contingent remainders in land, under some circumstances, though the contingent remaindermen are not then ascertained or in being, as, for instance, to preserve the estate from complete or partial destruction, is well established.

While Mississippi and most jurisdictions recognize the inherent power of a court of equity to direct a judicial sale of land which is subject to a future interest, nevertheless the scope of this power has not been clearly defined. It is difficult to determine the facts and circumstances which will merit such a sale.

It is apparent that there must be "necessity" before the chancery court can order a judicial sale. It is also beyond cavil that the power should be exercised with caution and only when the need is evident. Lambdin v. Lambdin, 209 Miss. 672, 48 So. 2d 341 (1950). These cases, *Kelly, Riley* and *Lambdin, supra,* are all illustrative of situations where the freehold estate was deteriorating and the income therefrom was insufficient to pay taxes and maintain the property. In each of these this Court approved a judicial sale to preserve and maintain the estate. The appellants argue, therefore, that since Oakland Farm is not deteriorating and since there is sufficient income from rental to pay taxes, a judicial sale by direction of the court was not proper.

The unusual circumstances of this case persuade us to the contrary. We are of the opinion that deterioration and waste of the property is not the exclusive and ultimate test to be used in determining whether a sale of land affected by future interest is proper, but also that consideration should be given to the question of whether a sale is necessary for the best interest of all the parties, that is, the life tenant and the contingent remaindermen. This "necessary for the best interest of all parties" rule is gleaned from Rogers, Removal of Future Interest Encumbrances—Sale of the Fee Simple Estate, 17 Vanderbilt L. Rev. 1437 (1964); Simes, Law of Future Interest, *supra;* Simes and Smith, The Law of Future Interest, §1941 (1956); and appears to have the necessary flexibility to meet the requirements of unusual and unique situations which demand in justice an equitable solution.

Our decision to reverse the chancellor and remand the case for his further consideration is couched in our belief that the best interest of all the parties would not be served by a judicial sale of the entirety of the property at this time. While true that such a sale would provide immediate relief to the life tenant who is worthy of this aid in equity, admitted by the remaindermen, it would nevertheless under the circumstances before us cause great financial loss to the remaindermen.

We therefore reverse and remand this cause to the chancery court, which shall have continuing jurisdiction thereof, for determination upon motion of the life tenant, if she so desires, for relief by way of sale of a part of the burdened land sufficient to provide for her reasonable needs from interest derived from the investment of the proceeds. The sale, however, is to be made only in the event the parties cannot unite to hypothecate the land for sufficient funds for the life tenant's reasonable needs. By affording the options above we do not mean to suggest that other remedies suitable to the parties which will provide economic relief to the aging life tenant are not open to them if approved by the chancellor. It is our opinion, shared by the chancellor and acknowledged by the appellants, that the facts suggest an equitable remedy. However, it is our further opinion that this equity does not warrant the remedy of sale of all of the property since this would unjustly impinge upon the vested rights of the remaindermen.

Reversed and remanded.

b. Valuation of Life Estates

We must sometimes value a life estate. In Baker v. Weedon, *supra,* if the property had been sold, some arrangement respecting the proceeds would clearly have been needed to reflect the divided interests. A similar situation arises if land subject to a life tenancy is condemned. One solution, mentioned in Baker v. Weedon, is to place the award in a court-supervised account; the life tenant would then receive the income until his death, when the remainder-man would get the corpus. Although this procedure is sometimes used, courts shy away from unnecessary administration. The alternative solution, immediate valuation of the life estate, is usually preferred, and for some purposes, such as estate tax computation, immediate valuation is required.

Valuation of life estates is relatively simple, although it is based on two artificial conventions: that the duration of the life estate is measured by the tenant's projected life expectancy; that the earning power of the asset will equal a specified annual rate.

As to the life estate's duration, statutes usually prescribe which mortality table one should use in projecting a life expectancy. In New York the direction appears at §403, Real Property Actions and Proceedings Law (McKinney 1979), and specifies the Commissioners' Standard Ordinary Human Mortality and Expectancy Table compiled by the National Association of Insurance Commissioners in 1958. The importance of redating the statute to conform to ever-growing human life expectancies was overlooked for almost 100 years by the New York legislature, which until 1966 had designated the American Experience Table compiled in 1868. You can see at once why remaindermen might yearn for the good old days.

Age of Life Tenant	Expectancy (1958)	Expectancy (1868)
1	68.30	47.45
21	49.46	41.
61	16.12	14.10

As to the asset's earning power, this too is statutorily defined. The New York rate is 4 percent: Real Prop. Acts. Law §402 (1979); the federal rate for estate tax computation has been 6 percent since 1971:[15] Int. Rev. Reg. §20.2031-10(e). If the statutory rate is low (high) relative to current market conditions, who benefits: the life tenant? the remainderman? Does it depend on why the computation is made?

Let us try an example to see how the system works. Suppose that the value of Lot 1, located in New York, is $100,000; that B, age 30, has a life estate; that C and his heirs have the remainder. Consulting the prescribed table (partly reproduced, Table 2, infra) we find that B enjoys (rounded off) a 41-year expectancy. Assuming a 4 percent rate, we must then calculate the sum of money which, if invested at this rate (compounded annually), will yield $4000 yearly (4% × $100,000) for 41 years and exhaust itself with the final payment—in short, an annuity. We consult a second table (partly reproduced, Table 3, infra), giving the present value of the right to receive $1.00 yearly for stated durations (N years), and we find this right valued at $19.99 where the

15. The rate had previously been 3.5 percent.

TABLE [2]
Human Expectancy*

Age	Years of Expectancy	Age	Years of Expectancy
25	45.82	40	32.18
26	44.90	41	31.29
27	43.99	42	30.41
28	43.08	43	29.54
29	42.16	44	28.67
30	41.25	45	27.81
31	40.34	46	26.95
32	39.43	47	26.11
33	38.51	48	25.27
34	37.60	49	24.45
35	36.69		
36	35.78		
37	34.88		
38	33.97		
39	33.07		

* National Association of Insurance Commissioners, C.S.O. approved, 1958.
Source: Reeves, Handbook of Interest, Annuity and Related Fiscal Tables (1966).

annuity lasts 41 years. Since B is to receive $4000 yearly, the present value of his life estate is $79,960 (4000 × $19.99). Since the total value of Lot 1 is $100,000, C's remainder interest is worth only $20,040 ($100,000 − $79,960).

Lest you say, "Isn't this awful!" remember our assumptions. At the end of 41 years, C should have intact $100,000. This he will achieve if the $20,040 is invested for the entire term so as to yield 4 percent interest compounded annually. To confirm this, we consult yet another table (partly reproduced, Table 4, *infra*) giving the accumulated value of $1.00 at the end of N years, if invested at specified rates. At 4 percent compound interest, $1.00 would increase to $4.9993 after 41 years. C's starting $20,040 would become $100,000 ($20,040 × $4.993).

Problems: Calculate the present value of B's life estate and C's remainder interest, making the following assumptions (round off life expectancies to whole years):

(1) value of parcel $250,000, B's age 25, interest rate 5%.
(2) value of parcel $175,000, B's age 28, interest rate 6%.
(3) value of parcel $ 50,000, B's age 35, interest rate 7%.

Answers: (1) $223,500, $26,500
               (2) $160,650, $14,350
               (3) $ 45,920, $ 4,080

Query: At any given age, the life expectancies of a white male, white

TABLE [3]
Present Value of $1 Per Annum Receivable at Future Dates (N)
Discount Rate

N	4%	5%	6%	7%
31	17.588	15.592	13.929	12.531
32	17.873	15.802	14.084	12.646
33	18.147	16.002	14.230	12.753
34	18.411	16.192	14.368	12.854
35	18.664	16.374	14.498	12.947
36	18.908	16.546	14.620	13.035
37	19.142	16.711	14.736	13.117
38	19.367	16.867	14.846	13.193
39	19.584	17.017	14.949	13.264
40	19.792	17.159	15.046	13.331
41	19.993	17.294	15.138	13.394
42	20.185	17.423	15.224	13.452
43	20.370	17.545	15.306	13.506
44	20.548	17.662	15.383	13.557
45	20.720	17.774	15.455	13.605
46	20.884	17.880	15.524	13.650
47	21.042	17.981	15.589	13.691
48	21.195	18.077	15.650	13.730
49	21.341	18.168	15.707	13.766
50	21.482	18.255	15.761	13.800

Source: Reeves, Handbook of Interest, Annuity and Related Fiscal Tables (1966).

female, nonwhite male, and nonwhite female vary widely. Should the designated mortality tables embody these differences?[16]

New York's Real Prop. Acts. Law §404 (1979) provides: "In all valuations made under this article, no significance shall be given to the ancestry, health or habits of the person whose life is involved. Each valuation shall be based exclusively on the actuarial data." (Section 401 specifies when the article shall be used.)

In the absence of a statutory mandate, courts prefer to consider such relevant matters as general health and habits. Thus, a New York court has held that "in view of the decedent's terminal illness immediately prior to his death, his life expectancy at that moment was practically nil and that the use

16. In a related context New York partly recognizes this difference. Insurance Law §205(3)(a)(i) prescribes the mortality table for use in fixing premiums and present values for ordinary life policies. It is this table that Real Prop. Acts. Law §403 specifies for use in valuing life estates. But the insurance law permits insurers to use an age for insured females up to three years younger than the insured's actual age.

Federal estate tax tables differentiate between male and female expectancies. Int. Rev. Reg. §20.2031-10(e).

TABLE [4]

Accumulation of $1 at Compound Interest in N Years

Interest Rate

N	4%	5%	6%	7%
31	3.373	4.538	6.088	8.145
32	3.508	4.764	6.453	8.715
33	3.648	5.003	6.840	9.325
34	3.794	5.253	7.251	9.978
35	3.946	5.516	7.686	10.676
36	4.103	5.791	8.147	11.423
37	4.268	6.081	8.636	12.223
38	4.438	6.385	9.154	13.079
39	4.616	6.704	9.703	13.994
40	4.801	7.039	10.285	14.974
41	4.993	7.391	10.902	16.022
42	5.192	7.761	11.557	17.144
43	5.400	8.149	12.250	18.344
44	5.616	8.557	12.985	19.628
45	5.841	8.985	13.764	21.002
46	6.074	9.434	14.590	22.472
47	6.317	9.905	15.465	24.045
48	6.570	10.401	16.393	25.728
49	6.833	10.921	17.377	27.529
50	7.106	11.467	18.420	29.457

Source: Reeves, Handbook of Interest, Annuity and Related Fiscal Tables (1966).

of mortality tables to value his reversionary interest must give way to realism."
Matter of Cushing, 49 Misc. 2d 454, 267 N.Y.S.2d 747 (Surr. Ct. 1966) (N.Y.
estate tax proceeding). Accord: Hall v. United States, 353 F.2d 500 (7th Cir.
1965) (federal estate tax proceeding); Mercantile-Safe Deposit and Trust Co.
v. United States, 368 F. Supp. 743 (D. Md. 1974) (idem); Rev. Rul. 66-307,
1966-2 Cum. Bull. 429.

§3.6   The Condominium

BERGER, CONDOMINIUM: SHELTER ON A STATUTORY FOUNDATION

63 Colum. L. Rev. 987 (1963)

Mrs. Sullivan: "I am glad to hear about this [condominium] type of ownership. It is the first time I heard of it."

Mr. Addonizio: "This is a new concept, as far as I am concerned, but it is very interesting."

Senator Sparkman: "I must say I am intrigued by it. . . ."

Seldom have hard-nosed lawmakers greeted innovation more cordially than they have greeted the condominium. For whatever reason—whether the persuasiveness of its Puerto Rican proponents, the allure of a concept whose origins are said to predate Caesar, the inattention of its natural enemies, or simply its inherent merit—Congress was quick to bring condominium apartments within the Federal Housing Administration's (FHA) mortgage insurance powers by adding Section 234 to the National Housing Act. There has followed an astonishing burst of activity among legal writers, writers, bar committees, state assemblies, and members of the real estate profession. Today, familiarity with condominium is widespread; yet only three years ago Congress's housing experts were hearing of it for the first time.

What is this condominium that has aroused such sudden interest? According to its Latin meaning, condominium is co-ownership; however, co-ownership is not today its primary feature. The most common modern instance of condominium is a multi-unit dwelling each of whose residents enjoys exclusive ownership of his individual apartment. With "title" to an apartment goes a cotenant's undivided interest in the common facilities—the land, the hallways, the heating plant, etc. Remarkably flexible, condominium is susceptible of an endless variety of legal formulations and can be adapted to a multiplicity of land uses or project designs. But in all of its forms its principal goal remains constant: to enable occupants of a multi-unit project to achieve more concomitants of ownership than are now available either to renters or to cooperators. The realization of this goal depends mainly on whether the individual units will gain independent dignity as mortgage security and as a basis for property taxation. . . .

A still greater disadvantage [of the cooperative] is that, for purposes of mortgage financing and property taxation, the co-operator's stock-lease "estate" lacks sufficient personality to support an individual obligation. As a result the entire cooperative structure is burdened by a blanket mortgage and a single tax assessment. By saddling the venture with overall liens, the stock-cooperative imposes upon the tenants the duty of meeting collectively the tax and debt service obligations as they fall due; frequently the two items exceed two-thirds of the monthly assessment. Stipulate a vigorous economy, modest inflation, housing undersupply, healthy reserves, a competitive location, and no problems of disrepair or obsolescence, and the concern over this financial interdependence is academic. If a tenant defaults, the cooperative may quickly terminate his status and find a replacement able to discharge the delinquent's pro rata obligation. There is no assurance, however, of the performance of satisfactory conditions. Unsatisfactory conditions, moreover, breed further delinquency by stepping up the need for new cooperators at a time when their supply is shrinking. Since the blanket tax and financing burden remains fairly constant, any additional charges upon the surviving cooperators may affect adversely both their ability to pay and their desire to remain current. The calamitous experience of stock-cooperatives during the early 1930's reveals the risks inherent in the snowballing of individual defaults. Higher standards for the selection of tenants, larger down payment requirements, and the immediate funding of reserves would be forms of prophylaxis, but they would also discourage the wider use of cooperatives among lower- and middle-income families.

Even if the risk of financial interdependence has been overdrawn, the blanket mortgage scheme imposes serious disadvantages upon the cooperator. He lacks the flexibility with regard to debt reduction, refinancing, or resale that the home owner enjoys. He cannot shift his assets or take advantage of earnings peaks or asset increments to reduce or eliminate the mortgage affecting his unit. Refinancing, which is often needed to effect modernization, modify debt service charges, "borrow against one's equity," or facilitate resale, is not possible unless the cooperator can persuade his fellow stockholders to refinance the blanket debt. This disadvantage is especially significant at the time of resale if the unit has an enhanced equity value and if the venture permits the cooperator to realize the gain, for the seller is more likely to deal with a buyer who must borrow in order to arrange the purchase. If the seller himself takes back the financing, he must defer the conversion into cash of his equity value. The new stockholder-tenant, who carries the heavier costs of a secondary loan whatever its source, may pose an added hazard for his fellow interdependent cooperators.

By enabling the unit owner to undertake an individual financing program, the condominium offers a major and perhaps critical advantage over the present-day cooperative. Yet the condominium relinquishes none of the ownership benefits afforded by stock-cooperatives—voice in its management, permanence of tenure, avoidance of profit to the landlord, and tax savings. . . .

II. The Need for a Statutory Foundation

In considering whether condominium is a feasible form of ownership under the common law or whether it requires special statutory provision, as it has in Latin America and Europe, one might note that England and Scotland have assimilated flat-ownership without benefit of statute, and, in the United States, there are instances of condominium that predate legislative recognition. In 1947, twelve ex-servicemen who wanted to buy jointly a building on Manhattan's East 84th Street containing a dozen units were unable to get a Veterans' Administration guarantee on a blanket mortgage. Therefore they created an entity resembling a condominium whereby each received a deed describing his respective apartment space and an undivided interest in the common premises. For each unit they were able to obtain a separate loan and persuade the VA to guarantee the mortgage. Quite recently interest in condominium has sparked more than fifty ventures, principally in Florida, Utah, and the

San Francisco Bay area, where investors relied, temporarily at least, upon the compatibility of existing state law. Probably the area with the most extensive experience in common-law condominium is southern California. There, separate ownership and financing, but not taxation, of apartment units, have become commonplace under a plan bearing the jaunty label—"Own-Your-Own Apartments." During the four-year period ending in 1961, the Real Estate Commissioner gave preliminary approval for nearly two hundred own-your-own projects in the Los Angeles area.

Condominium, it appears, can exist under the common law, but whether it will flourish without statutory provision is doubtful. Although the Manhattan venture has enjoyed fifteen successful years, it has not seeded similar projects in New York, and the California own-your-own plan has failed to attract the major institutional leaders. Moreover, the recent growth of condominiums in Florida, California, and Utah was probably based in part on a belief that in each state statutory provision was imminent. Furthermore, the real estate community's pressure for enabling statutes undoubtedly reflects a feeling that legislation is badly needed.

What kind of legislation does condominium in its embryonic state require? There is immediate need for an official imprimatur—an enabling statute that blesses the condominium concept and erases any doubts that our legal system can tolerate ownership estates in airspace lots. This alone should stimulate the interest and elicit the confidence of lenders, consumers, and suppliers. The statute would ensure that unit ownership is recognized as an interest in real property—a status denied by some courts to the stock-lease arrangement for a cooperative—and that unit mortgages, whether insured or conventional, qualify for institutional investment.

But the major burdens of such a statute are threefold: (1) to provide a procedure for the establishment and dissolution of a condominium and to secure a uniform pattern of legal documentation; (2) to accommodate existing legislation dealing with taxation, recording procedures, liens, land-use control, and security regulatory techniques to the special needs of the condominium; and (3) to anticipate possible judicial antagonism involving such matters as bars on partition and covenants real. . . .

III.   Creation of the Condominium

To inform interested parties of the nature of the enterprise and its internal organization two important documents must be executed and recorded—the declaration and the operating by-laws.

The declaration serves roughly the same function for the condominium as the subdivision map and restrictive covenants serve in a tract development. It includes a legal description of the underlying land, a description in layman's terms of the building, apartment units, and common facilities, and a statement in fractions of each owner's share of rights and duties with respect to the common premises. This fraction fixes permanently the unit owner's pro rata burden of the common expenses and his share in any profit or distribution of capital. It is also the measure of his voice in the management. Because taxing officials will need a formula for apportioning a project's total value among the separate units, the fraction may be used to compute each apartment's assessment. And finally, the fraction may provide a basis for limiting the unit owner's individual liability for liens and for the claims of the project's creditors.

Beyond these essential features, the content of the declarations may vary in accordance with the requirements of individual statutes. Nevertheless, most declarations will contain provisions regarding the establishment of an entity to manage the condominium's day-to-day affairs, measures to be taken against delinquent owners—such as the power to lien an individual unit, designation of persons upon whom process may be served, arrangements for blanket casualty and liability insurance, and procedures to be followed in the event of project destruction or obsolescence. The statutes may mandate some of these provisions, for example, the designation of persons to receive process; they will legitimate others, such as the power to impose assessment liens.

The declaration will also include various restraints upon the unit owner's freedom to alienate. Two involve the physical and legal integrity of the project: a restraint against partition of the common areas while the structure remains intact and subject to the condominium regime, and a bar against transfers that would divide ownership of a unit from ownership of the corresponding share of the common areas. Frequently the declaration will also restrict the unit owner's freedom to choose a vendee or tenant. . . .

Finally, the declaration will normally include the condominium plans and either a subdivision map or a statement of metes and bounds describing each of the units. These descriptions . . . are later incorporated in the deed of conveyance that the condominium member receives when he acquires his interest.

For the internal administration of a condominium, by-laws are needed to regulate matters such as building maintenance, budgeting, assessment and collection, capital improvements, and occupant control. . . .

Heretofore the most common form of condominium management has been the unincorporated "Association of Owners." Unit ownership automatically bestows the status of association membership, which carries the privileges of voting for a board of directors and taking part in the association's business meetings. In turn, the board elects the association officers and, together with these and perhaps a manager, it directs the condominium's daily operations. . . .

———————————————

Rohan and Reskin, Condominium Law and Practice, app. A (1974), contains an extensive bibliography. We will return to the condominium shortly, after we have introduced the stock cooperative, §4.6, *infra*.

Chapter 4

Estates in Land: The Nonfreehold Estates

§4.1 The Landlord and Tenant Estates

Largely because of its function, the lease was not at once admitted into the family of estates. The lease had dubious origins: moneylenders used it to evade the Church's bar on usury. Upon receipt of the loan, the borrower would lease his lands to the lender, who would remain in possession for the lease term. In fixing the term, the parties would make it of sufficient duration to allow the lender to recoup, from the land's harvest, his original outlay together with the unlawful interest. [1] Because of his disreputable status, the lessee was originally denied the legal protection that the courts accorded "free" men—the essence of whose holdings was "the permanent and normal economic basis of the family." [2] Thus, a life tenant might seek a writ of right (recovery) if his possession were unlawfully disrupted, but not so the lessee. As against strangers, the lessee had no protection; his only recourse was a suit against the lessor for breach of covenant (for quiet enjoyment). Other, more trifling difficulties beset the leasehold interest. [3]

The early leases served one other important function. They were a form of agrarian contract wherein landowners arranged to have their lands farmed by the nonlandowning poor. Whereas husbandry leases grew steadily in importance, security leases were gradually replaced by other devices. By the early thirteenth century, as the lease gained respectability, the courts' preju-

---

1. The ways of man are such that even today hard-pressed borrowers and overreaching lenders use a similar device to avoid the appearance of usury. The borrower "sells" his land to the lender, who, upon getting the deed, delivers an option. This enables the seller to repurchase the land at the option price, set, as you would suppose, to equal the original sales price (the loan principal) plus the interest amount. By using this sham, the parties do not put in writing the interest rate. Also, if the borrower seeks later to invoke the usury statute, he must prove that the sale-and-option was a disguised usurious transaction. Sometimes, but not always, the borrower prevails. Compare Freedman v. Hendershott, 77 Idaho 213, 290 P.2d 738 (1955), and State v. Bosworth, 124 Vt. 3, 197 A.2d 477 (1963), with Sledge Lumber Corp. v. Southern Builders Equipment Co., 257 N.C. 435, 126 S.E.2d 97 (1962).
   2. T. Plucknett, A Concise History of the Common Law 573 (5th ed. 1956).
   3. Id. at 571.

dice against it began to weaken. But the courts, instead of letting the old remedies reach new parties, patched together a succession of new remedies, available only to lessees. Of these, the writ of "trespass de ejectione firmae" (ejectment) was most sweeping in the relief given, for it entitled the lessee to recover his lands from any person who had wrongfully supplanted him. Indeed, ejectment worked so efficiently compared with its freehold counterpart that the courts eventually sanctioned its use for all estates in land. [4] But, to this day, we still speak of leasehold estates as "nonfreehold"—a gentle, quite harmless reminder that many of our property institutions are rooted deep in English soil.

For purposes of further classification, leasehold estates are arranged into several categories. These are: (a) term of years, (b) tenancy at will, (c) "occupancy" at sufferance, (d) periodic tenancy, (e) statutory tenancy, and (f) proprietary (cooperative) lease.

§4.2 The Common-Law Landlord and Tenant Estates

a. Term of Years (Estate for Years)

The Restatement (Second) of Property §1.4 defines this estate as having a "fixed or computable period of time." The term is fixed when both a beginning and termination date are specified. The term is computable when a specified formula will produce the two necessary dates. Regardless of the length of the term, usage refers to the tenancy as "term of years." Thus, estates for one week, six months, or 999 years [5] all bear a generic likeness. Unless the parties validly agree otherwise, the term begins immediately after midnight on the starting date and ends just before midnight on the termination date.

A lease term may sometimes begin upon the happening of an event; e.g., L "to T, for twenty years, the term to begin when the improvements are erected and a certificate of occupancy is obtained." In that situation, the landlord-tenant relationship must await the stated occurrences. Also, because T holds a *contingent* future interest (the stipulated events are not certain to occur), the Rule against Perpetuities will apply.

Although the term of years must have a fixed (or computable) duration, the term may be defeasible; e.g., L "to T for fifty years, unless T shall die sooner," or, more commonplace, L "to T for two years, but if T does not pay the rent, etc., L may terminate the lease." Whether the defeasible event results in an automatic termination of the tenancy or an option to terminate is a

---

4. Most important of all, ejectment also became a *landlord's* remedy.

5. A few states have placed statutory limits on a leasehold term. See, e.g., Calif. Civ. Code §717 (West Supp. 1981) (agricultural leases—51 years); Alabama Code tit. 47 §18 (1958) (all leases—99 years).

matter for the parties' agreement; sometimes murkiness clouds that agreement.[6]

Ordinarily the estate for years ends automatically at the expiration of the fixed term. But sometimes the lease will provide that tenant must give advance notice (thirty, sixty, ninety, etc. days) of his intention to remove, and that the failure to give such requisite notice can—at landlord's election—extend the original term, sometimes for an entire second term. Since tenant's forgetfulness, rather than his desire to remain, often leads to the failure to give notice, some states now require that landlord remind tenant of the notice provision if landlord plans to enforce it. See, e.g., N.Y. Gen. Oblig. Law §5-905 (McKinney 1964) (landlord must notify tenant in writing at least fifteen days and not more than thirty days before tenant's notice is due).

The corollary to this situation is when the lease contains a tenant's option to renew, but requires tenant to give landlord advance notice of his election. Tenant's failure to serve timely notice can cost him his renewal privilege. In the absence of statutes requiring landlord to remind tenant of the notice date, the neglectful tenant must rely, not always with success, upon the courts for relief from forfeiture.

Whether an estate for years *has* been created may be more than an academic quibble. Requirements as to writing, recordation, and notice of termination, as well as the lease's actual duration, may rest on the label.

b.   Tenancy at Will (Estate at Will)

The Restatement (Second) of Property §1.6 defines a tenancy at will as one "created to endure only so long *as both* the landlord and the tenant desire." Such an estate, at common law, ended on the very day that a terminating notice from one of the parties was received by the other. You might ask when such an estate would arise in the normal dealings between landlord and tenant. After all, it would seem unusual for parties to enter into an arrangement that either party could end abruptly. For the landlord it might mean a sudden loss of income; for the tenant, an unplanned-for loss of shelter or investment in crops, good will, or fixtures.

As a rule, the tenancy at will is not the product of agreement, but instead is read into an arrangement *after the fact*—by a court to which the parties have carried a dispute. A few examples should suffice to suggest areas of possible controversy:

(1)   While negotiating a lease (or a renewal of his term), T takes possession (or remains in possession) of the premises. The negotiations fail. Held: T is a tenant at will. Carteri v. Roberts, 140 Cal. 164, 73 P. 819 (1903).

6. Compare Brause v. 2968 Third Avenue Inc., 41 Misc. 2d 348, 244 N.Y.S.2d 587 (Civ. Ct. 1963) with Remedco Corp. v. Bryn Mawr Hotel, 45 Misc. 2d 586, 257 N.Y.S.2d 525 (Civ. Ct. 1965).

(2)   Because of a dangerous illness, T is unable to vacate the premises until fifteen days after the expiration of the term. Held: T is a tenant at will. Herter v. Mullen, 159 N.Y. 28, 53 N.E. 700 (1899). But see Mason v. Wierengo, 113 Mich. 151, 71 N.W. 489 (1897).

(3)   T takes possession under a letting for an undefined period and there is no reservation of a periodic rent. Held: T is a tenant at will. Carruth v. Carruth, 77 Ga. App. 131, 48 S.E.2d 387 (1948).

(4)   T takes possession under an oral lease in a jurisdiction requiring *all* leases to be written. T is a tenant at will. See, e.g., Mass Ann. Laws c. 183, §3 (1955).

Since a tenancy at will involves mutuality, what if the parties agree that either L or T, but not both, may terminate at will? Ignoring some contrary case law,[7] as well as the original Restatement,[8] the editors of the Restatement (Second) refused to convert such arrangements into a tenancy at will except where, under all the circumstances, an arrangement became unconscionable; in that instance, either party might terminate at will. Id. at §1.6, Comment g. Otherwise, a lease from L "to T for two years, unless L notifies T that the lease is terminated" would be seen as a determinable term of years.

The Restatement also asserts that the death of either party ends a tenancy at will, as does a transfer of either party's interest in the tenancy. Id. at §1.6, Comments c, d. Logically, why this result?

Statutes in many states have modified the common-law tenancy at will by requiring one or both parties to give notice of termination. Thus, in New York the landlord must give thirty days' notice (N.Y. Real Prop. Law §228) (McKinney 1968); in Georgia, the tenant must give thirty days' notice and the landlord sixty days' notice for an implied tenancy at will, but no notice, as at common law, for an express tenancy at will (Ga. Code Ann. §61-105 (1966)). What are the various policy reasons for requiring notice, for treating the tenant more protectively than the landlord, or for distinguishing express from implied tenancies at will?

c.   Occupancy at Sufferance

Often confused with the tenancy at will is the estate, or more properly, the occupancy at sufferance. Quite simply, an occupant at sufferance is someone once having a valid tenancy[9] (or other possessory interest)[10] who has since lost the legal right to remain. A tenant will most often become an occu-

---

7. See, e.g., Foley v. Gamester, 271 Mass. 55, 57, 170 N.E. 799, 800 (1930).

8. Restatement of Property §21 drew a distinction between a lease terminable at the landlord's will and one terminable at the tenant's will. In the former case, the election to terminate was extended to the tenant, thereby creating a tenancy at will. In the latter case, the Restatement did not impose mutuality upon the parties, but regarded the landlord bound until the tenant terminated.

9. Ergo, a squatter is not an occupant at sufferance.

10. The occupant is sometimes a vendor who refuses to vacate after title passes, or a vendee in possession who refuses to vacate after the deal collapses.

pant at sufferance when he is ordered, after failing to pay the rent, to vacate the premises. At common law, the occupant at sufferance was subject to removal without further notice (causing the confusion with tenancy at will), and was not liable for rent during the sufferance period (distinguishing the tenancy at will).

Most states now give the landlord a statutory money claim against the occupant at sufferance, usually for the reasonable rental value; see, e.g., Colo. Rev. Stat. §§58-1-4 and 58-1-10 (1963). See also Restatement (Second) of Property §14.5. But a few states measure this claim by the previous rent, see, e.g., Rogers v. Kolp, 272 S.W.2d 793 (Tex. Civ. App. 1954), or by double the previous rent, see, e.g., Ga. Code Ann. §61-305 (1966). The landlord may also have a claim for special damages reasonably foreseeable by the former tenant. Restatement (Second) of Property §14.6. During the holdover period, however, the Restatement (Second) would require the landlord to perform his regular leasehold duties. Id. at §14.7.

d. Periodic Tenancy

Suppose that a tenant rents an apartment at a *fixed* monthly rental. Landlord and tenant agree that either party may end the arrangement by giving the other party thirty days' notice.

This arrangement, widely used by urban dwellers, would probably be construed as a periodic tenancy—one in which the estate continues automatically for successive periods unless either party acts, *through the giving of notice,* to terminate the estate. The periodic tenancy originated in the sixteenth century, as courts sought to ameliorate the hardship that the tenancy at will often occasioned. When a tenancy at will carried with it a periodic rent, courts began to read into the tenancy a requirement of notice should either landlord or tenant wish the estate to end. The length of required notice would vary with the period covered by a rent payment: six months' notice for a yearly rental; [11] one month's notice for a monthly rental; one week's notice for a weekly rental. [12] Moreover, the date stated in the notice for ending the tenancy had to coincide with the end of a period; otherwise the notice was defective. Thus, a landlord's notice dated October 15 terminating a month-to-month tenancy as of November 15 would be ineffectual if the tenant's rental term ran from the first to the 30th of each month. In addition, unless the landlord served a new notice, on or before November 1, terminating the tenancy as of November 30, the tenant would be privileged to remain after December 1. As pointed out, the duty of giving notice was reciprocal. Therefore, unless the tenant was also careful to have his notices conform to the common law requirement, he, too,

11. 28 Mott St. Co. v. Summit Import Corp., 64 Misc. 2d 860, 316 N.Y.S.2d 259 (Civ. Ct. 1970), illustrates how the 6 months' notice requirement can plague a landlord.

12. The rule for determining the time in which an act must be done is to exclude the first day and include the last. Thus, a 30-day notice, to be effective on October 31, must be served by October 1. Cf. Seminole Housing Corp. v. M & M Garages, Inc., 78 Misc. 2d 755, 359 N.Y.S.2d 711 (Civ. Ct. 1974).

might have leasehold duties for longer than he wanted. Statutes in some jurisdictions have now modified the notice requirements. See, e.g., Cal. Civ. Code
§1946 (1954) (month-to-month tenancy terminable by thirty days' notice
given *at any time*); N.Y. Real Prop. L. §232a (in New York City, only the
landlord is required to give thirty days' notice to end month-to-month tenancy).

§4.3　Must the Lease Be in Writing?

The English Statute of Frauds, 29 Car. 2, c. 3 (1677), required a writing for
any lease longer than three years. American statutes have followed the English
pattern, although many have reduced the permitted maximum for oral leases
to one year; see, e.g., N.Y. Gen. Oblig. Law §5-703 (1964). A few statutes
have barred oral leases altogether; see, e.g., Mass. Ann. Laws c. 259, §1
(1956); Snider v. Deban, 249 Mass. 59, 144 N.E. 69 (1924). Should an oral
term of years ever be permitted?

Suppose that on January 1 the parties agree to a lease for a one-year
term to begin on February 1. Many statutes providing for written leases of *more*
than one year also require a writing when a contract is "not to be performed
within the space of one year from the making thereof." Is an agreement to
lease a contract? If so, does the January 1 agreement come within this provision? Compare Ward v. Hasbrouck, 169 N.Y. 407, 62 N.E. 434 (1902) (a lease
for one year to take effect in the future need not be in writing), with Cromme-
lin v. Thiess, 31 Ala. 412 (1858) (contra). Restatement (Second) of Property
adopts the New York rule. Id. at §2.1, Comment f.

When a writing is required, it must identify the parties, identify the
premises, specify the duration of the lease, and state the rent to be paid. The
writing must also be signed by the party to be charged, or by his lawful agent.
Id. at §2.2. Some states go even further, however, and require in every instance that both parties sign the writing before either one may enforce its
provisions against the other. See, e.g., Penn. Stat. Ann. tit. 68, §250.202
(1965).

Suppose that T takes possession under a two-year oral letting in a state
requiring a writing for leases longer than one year. What is the nature of T's
tenancy? See Restatement (Second) of Property §2.3.

§4.4　The Status of the Holdover Tenant

Problem: T's two-year lease expires on August 31. The rent is $3600 yearly,
payable $300 monthly in advance. T for personal reasons fails to vacate the
apartment until September 10. L sues T for September rent ($300), which T

refuses to pay. T tenders ten days' rent ($100), which L refuses to accept. As of September 1, what is T's holdover status? As of October 1? November 1? Discuss the possibilities in the light of the foregoing text and the materials which follow.

DONNELLY ADVERTISING CORP. v. FLACCOMIO
216 Md. 113, 140 A.2d 165 (Ct. App. 1958)

HORNEY, J. This is an appeal by the Donnelly Advertising Corporation of Maryland (the tenant), from a judgment for $350 obtained by Annie Flaccomio (the landlord), in the Superior Court of Baltimore City (Mason, J., sitting without a jury). The judgment represents two months' rent which the trial court held was due under an "implied" lease which arose as a result of the tenant holding over after the expiration of a written lease which expired on March 20, 1956.

On November 16, 1955, the tenant acquired all of the property of the Morton Company, Inc. (the previous tenant), including the lease from the landlord to the previous tenant. The term of the original lease, which began on August 1, 1947, and ended on March 20, 1953, had been extended by written agreements for three successive terms of one year each, the last extension ending, as stated, on March 20, 1956. Each of the written agreements provided that the extended term would be on "the same terms and conditions of the original lease." The tenant was obliged to pay rent of $175 per month, plus ground rent of $60 per annum, water rent, and various taxes. . . .

Since a decision of this case depends primarily on the interpretation of a series of letters between the parties, it is necessary to discuss and analyze such letters with particularity. . . . On February 29, 1956, the tenant wrote to the landlord confirming a verbal offer made by it on February 23, 1956, to pay a rental reduced from $2,100 a year to $1,000 a year, but for a five-year term instead of a one-year term. On March 12, 1956, the attorney for the landlord replied to this offer: " . . . [the landlord] is not willing to rent her property for less than the amount it has been bringing for the past several years, as she said she could have put stores here but for this lease."

By March 20, 1956, the expiration date of the lease, nothing further had been done. Until this date, the tenant had offered to lease at a lower rental, but the landlord had flatly refused to accept the offer. On March 23, 1956, the third day after it had begun to hold over, the tenant wrote the following letter to the landlord:

> Due to the fact that the present lease has expired, and as you are aware, we are attempting to renegotiate a new lease with you.
> We will continue on the same rental basis from month to month until such time as we can come to some agreement as to the future.
> We reserve the right to vacate the property upon (30) days' written notice at any time should we fail to be able to make satisfactory arrangements.
> Check for one month is enclosed.

On March 30, 1956, the tenant received the following letter from the landlord's attorney:

> Your lease has expired and I have authorized . . . [the landlord] to deposit the one check which pays for the current month, but . . . [the landlord] desires me to inform you that she is not willing for you to continue on a month to month basis, but she will rent year to year.
>
> Please arrange to sign a lease for a year or remove your property from the premises and restore the premises to its former condition prior to the lease.

Nothing further was heard from the tenant until April 16, 1956, when the landlord received a check for the rent from April 20, 1956 to May 20, 1956. In the letter accompanying the check the tenant stated that it would not continue to lease the property beyond May 20, 1956. Therein the tenant also stated that there had not been a renewal of the "previous agreement." On the same day, April 16, 1956, the landlord's attorney wrote to the tenant enclosing the bill for the ground rent which the tenant was obliged to pay under the original lease. The attorney added:

> I have heretofore notified you that [the landlord] is not willing to rent this property from month to month but must be from year to year so that if you are not out of there immediately and have not moved your equipment we shall consider that you are taking it for another year under the same terms or I shall have to issue ejectment proceedings, whichever we find most advantageous to us.
>
> You must understand that . . . [the landlord] does not wish to lose any of her rights in the property by letting you stay there without a lease and it is my duty to protect her in this respect.

On April 20, 1956, the tenant replied to the attorney, stating that it would send $30 in payment of six months' ground rent to the owner of the reversion. On April 25, 1956, the attorney wrote to the tenant that: "Inasmuch as you have gone over two months since the termination of the lease, I believe that under the law you have automatically renewed the lease for another term of year to year." The tenant countered on April 27, 1956, by stating that it would vacate on May 20, 1956, but once again, on May 2, 1956, the attorney for the landlord insisted that the lease had been "automatically renewed . . . for a period of a year on the same terms."

This suit was brought to recover the rent claimed to be due for the months beginning May 21, 1956, and June 21, 1956, respectively, on the theory that the tenant was holding over under an implied lease for one year beginning March 21, 1956, and ending March 20, 1957, since it remained on the premises after March 20, 1956, until May 15, 1956. . . . [T]he trial court accepted the landlord's implied lease theory and awarded her a judgment for two months' rent and costs.

Estates from year to year are a class of estates at will, from which they originated. Such estates may endure for one or more years, and are now terminable in Baltimore City at the end of thirty days' notice expiring at that period of the year at which the tenancy commenced, or that period fixed by the parties for the tenancy to end. The tenancy is created by express agreement or by implication. A peculiar form of this tenancy occurs where a tenant for years holds over after the expiration of the term, and the landlord accepts rent accruing after such expiration. The *provisions and covenants* of the original lease, so far as they are consistent with a yearly holding, *continue,* and the parties are mutually bound by them. . . .

However, the general rule is that a tenant who has remained after the expiration of the term is not a tenant holding over, and thus liable for a full year's rent, if . . . the tenant has definitely established one of two circumstances: either (i) that the landlord *consented* to the tenant remaining in the premises on a month-to-month basis, or some other specified time, for a temporary period, or (ii) that the parties were *actually engaged in negotiations* as to a renewal of the lease when the previous term ended. We think it is clear that the tenant failed to prove either of the determining factors.

We are unable to hold, under any reasonable construction of the acts of the parties, including particularly the correspondence between them, that the landlord gave the tenant either express or implied consent to remain on the premises after the date of the expiration of the lease.

The tenant insists that the existence of "negotiations" led it to believe that it could hold over for that purpose. The weakness of this theory, which makes it untenable, is that it would permit a tenant, who blithely writes a letter to the landlord offering a lower rental for a renewal lease, to remain on the premises after the expiration date with impunity. Under such circumstances, even if the landlord rejected the offer, the tenant could successfully defend by asserting that it was not a tenant holding over, but was simply engaging in negotiations. In the case at bar, even if actual negotiations had been in progress before the expiration of the lease, such negotiations were obviously unsuccessful and were abandoned. Certainly the existence of abandoned negotiations would not justify a tenant remaining on the premises, and it would be unreasonable to permit the tenant to dictate to the landlord the terms under which would continue to remain after it had held over for several days, and then claim that such tactics constituted negotiations still in progress. That is precisely what the tenant did in its letter of March 23, 1956.

Finally, we cannot hold that the trial court was clearly wrong in finding that the landlord had not committed herself to a month-to-month lease by reason of the letter of March 29, 1956, and the acceptance of a month's rent. We think there is no persuasive evidence that a *new* lease from month to month was substituted for the implied lease which arose as a result of the tenant holding over after the expiration of the *old* lease which expired on March 20, 1956. In all of the correspondence there is not the slightest indication that the landlord would consent to anything but a renewal of the old written lease from year to year or the execution of a new written lease embodying precisely the same terms and conditions as were in the old lease, and there is nothing in the record to refute this. The fact that the landlord wanted and kept insisting upon either a renewal of the old or the execution of a new written lease would not be fatal to her right to claim under the implied lease.

By operation of law, the tenant holding over becomes a trespasser, in the sense of being wrongfully in possession, or a tenant from year to year at the election of the landlord, regardless of the wishes of the tenant . . . The fact that the tenant sent a check for one month's rent after the crucial date, proposing that it be accepted as a tenant from month-to-month does not alter the situation. The landlord never agreed to the proposal, so there was no substitution of a new lease for the implied lease which arose by operation of law, nor was there any alteration in the terms and conditions of the then existing implied lease. While it is true that the landlord, in accepting the check, did not at that time expressly elect to treat the tenant as a tenant holding over, it is clear that she definitely declined the tenant's proposal. For this reason we think the acceptance of the check, which was in the exact amount the landlord was entitled to receive for a month's rent under the old lease and from a *tenant holding over* under the implied lease for another year, did not bar her recovery of subsequent installments. . . . We think the landlord was not barred from subsequently making the election to hold the tenant under the implied lease after her previous demand and ultimatum had been declined and ignored, and the tenant continued to remain in the premises. Moreover, we think it is a persuasive indication that the tenant must have had some doubt that it was not a tenant from month to month in that it paid one-half of the yearly ground rent when it became due.

Even if it is assumed that the acceptance by the landlord of a month's rent constituted tacit consent that the tenant could remain on the premises pending negotiations for a new written lease or a further extension of the old one, it is clear that such negotiations finally ceased on April 16, 1956, yet the tenant continued to remain on the premises until it saw fit to vacate. . . .

The judgment of the lower court should be affirmed.

BRUNE, C.J., and PRESCOTT, J., dissent.

PRESCOTT, J. (dissenting). I do not wish any one to think that I disagree with the principles of law as they are so clearly enunciated by Judge Horney in his brilliant majority opinion. It is the treatment of the facts and their effect that prevent my concurrence. These facts, as related in the majority opinion, seem clearly to demonstrate that the parties had begun, and were conducting, negotiations having as their object a renewal of the lease—both sides, legitimately, attempting to obtain advantageous terms. The appellant and its predecessors had leased the property since 1947; the original lease had been extended *three* successive terms by written agreements; the tenant wrote the appellee's attorney as early as December 8, 1955, concerning the lease; and verbal and written negotiations before March 20, 1956, the expiration date of the lease, followed. *Three days* after the expiration date, the tenant wrote to the landlord the first letter quoted in the majority opinion. In it, the tenant specifically stated the parties were negotiating for a new lease and offered to continue on the previous rental basis from month to month until such time as the negotiations were successful or broke down. A check for one month's rent was enclosed. Within a week, the landlord's attorney replied. The letter did not deny that negotiations were being conducted by the parties; nor did it make any claim that the tenant was holding over under a lease imposed by law for a year. On the contrary, it explicitly stated the check was *accepted* for the current month's rent and then went on to say, the landlord "desires me to inform you that she is not willing for you to *continue on a month to month basis,* but she will rent year to year." It is extremely difficult to comprehend how the tenant could "continue" on a month to month basis, if it never occupied that status, as the majority opinion holds. It was not until April 16, 1956, that any claim was made that the tenant was holding over under a new lease imposed by law. The tenant took the position, which seems proper especially when its letter so stated, that, upon the acceptance of its check for one month's rent, it became a tenant from month to month, and, in order to terminate this tenancy, it must give the landlord thirty days' notice, which it did. This made the expiration date May 20, 1956. The rent was paid in full until that time, and the tenant properly vacated the premises by that date. The above facts seem to make it clear the tenant was not only remaining in possession of the property with the tacit, but the express, consent of the landlord. She was anxious, as she had done before, to obtain a written lease for a year upon favorable terms. The dilapidated condition of the property rendered it particularly desirable for her to lease to some one in such a business as that conducted by the appellant. For these reasons, I think the appellant should have prevailed.

BRUNE, C.J., has authorized me to say he concurs in this opinion.

NOTES AND QUESTIONS

1. Restatement (Second), Property, §14.4 adopts the following rule on holdover tenancies:

> Except to the extent the parties to a lease validly agree otherwise, the landlord, if there is no incoming tenant, or the incoming tenant if there is one, may elect, solely on the basis of the tenant's improper holding over after the termination of his lease, unilaterally to hold the tenant to another term, unless equitable considerations justify giving the tenant an extension of time to vacate the leased property and the tenant vacates the leased property before the end of the extended period.

The length of the holdover term relates to the rental period of the original lease. If rent was computed on a monthly basis, a month-to-month periodic holdover tenancy results. If rent was computed on an annual basis (even though payable monthly), the holdover tenancy is year-to-year. Id., Comment f. In a few jurisdictions, a holdover term of years—i.e., one month, one year—replaces the periodic holdover tenancy.

2. The common-law (Restatement) rule finds its justification in the following excerpt:

> The rule [that a periodic tenancy may result] imposes a penalty upon the individual tenant wrongfully holding over, but ultimately operates for the benefit of tenants as a class by its tendency to secure the agreed surrender of terms to incoming tenants who have severally yielded possession of other premises in anticipation of promptly entering into the possession of the new. This makes for confidence in leasehold transactions. Again, the terms of the leases of property which is rented for business, commercial, residential, and agricultural uses tend to begin and end at a customary date or during a particular season of the year, as determined by the nature of the use of the specific property, and as the value of any piece of property is largely dependent upon its actual or potential continuing yield in periodic rent, the social and economic importance of the landlord being able certainly to deliver, and the prospective tenant so to obtain possession on the stipulated day, is obvious. [A.H. Fetting Mfg. Jewelry Co. v. Waltz, 160 Md. 50, 54, 152 A. 434, 436 (1930)]

3. Some states, via statute, would treat the holdover tenant less harshly. For example, N.Y. Real Prop. Law §232-c (McKinney 1968) provides:

> Where a tenant whose term is longer than one month holds over after the expiration of such term, such holding over shall not give to the landlord the option to hold the tenant for a new term solely by virtue of the tenant's holding over. In the case of such a holding over by the tenant, the landlord may proceed, in any manner permitted by law, to remove the tenant, or, if the landlord shall accept rent for any period subsequent to the expiration of such term, then, unless an agreement either express or implied is made providing otherwise, the tenancy created by the acceptance of such rent shall be a tenancy from month to month commencing on the first day after the expiration of such term.

In proposing the change, the Law Revision Commission sought to relieve tenants of "a penalty . . . disproportionate to the fault of the tenant and the damage the landlord may suffer." Law Revision Commission, 1959 Leg. Doc. 65(D); 1959 Report, Recommendations and Studies 139, quoted in Ungar v. Schwartz, 30 Misc. 2d 152, 156, 213 N.Y.S.2d 993, 998 (Nassau Co. Dist. Ct. 1961).

On balance, which do you prefer, the Restatement or the New York rule? In considering that question, imagine why a tenant might fail to vacate when his or her term expired.

4. Even the Restatement softens the tenant's plight if "equitable circumstances justify." Two illustrations appear: all moving companies strike and the tenant has no available alternative; tenant suffers a heart attack the night before the lease expires *and* the doctor advises that he should not be moved (italics added). Can you think of other "equitable circumstances"?

5. In the *Donnelly Advertising Co.* case, suppose that, after sending the March 23 letter, tenant had changed its mind about wanting to leave on thirty days' notice. If tenant had written on April 16 that it now wished to remain for the balance of the year, could landlord then change her mind and treat tenant as an occupant at sufferance? Cf. Crechale & Polles, Inc. v. Smith, 295 So. 2d 275, 277 (Miss. 1974) (landlord's election when once exercised is binding upon the landlord as well as the tenant).

6. T is a month-to-month tenant at a monthly rental of $100. T receives a thirty-day notice that his rental is being raised to $150 at the beginning of the next term. Without replying, T remains in possession. L refuses to accept T's $100 rental tender and sues for $150. Result? Cf. Reimer v. Kaslov, 61 Misc. 2d 960, 307 N.Y.S.2d 760 (Civ. Ct. 1970).

7. T's lease expires August 31. L rents the premises to X for a term beginning September 1. T holds over, preventing timely possession by X. What are X's rights against T? Against L? Cf. §5.6 *infra.*

§4.5   Statutory Rent Control

A severe housing shortage is sometimes the signal for government restraint—via rent control—on the acquisitiveness of landlords. An early instance concerned the Jewish ghettos of Rome; filled to overflowing, their rents far exceeded levels elsewhere in the city. In response, Pope Clement VIII issued the bull Viam Veritatis (1604) barring ghetto landlords from raising rents or evicting tenants. Rent control also appeared in France, Spain, and Portugal well before the present century.

It was the impetus of the two world wars, however, that brought rent control to the United States and greatly extended its influence throughout Europe. From 1919 to 1921 Congress imposed rent ceilings on housing within the District of Columbia; and at least three states—New York, Massachusetts, and New Jersey—attempted it briefly. The advent of World War II brought pervasive federal control; through the Office of Price Administration, virtually all urban rental housing was regulated.

Federal rent controls ended in 1947, and thereafter most states allowed free market forces to determine rent levels. New York State asserted control until 1962, but after 1962 only New York City and Boston among major cities continued to fix rents.

President Nixon's New Economic Policy, announced in August 1971, returned virtually *all* rentals to federal control, except where local regulation persisted. Guidelines promulgated in December 1971 called for the fixing of a basic rental for every controlled unit, and for automatic annual increments (2.5 per cent) to cover hikes in operating costs. Landlords could, in addition, recoup outlays for capital expenditures and higher real estate taxes. But as suddenly as they had begun, federal controls over rentals (and other prices) ended in January 1973.

Inflation did not abate with demise of the NEP, nor had Americans seen the last of rent control. State and local regulations began to mushroom everywhere. By mid-1976, the Wall Street Journal reported controls not only in New York City and Boston, but also in 105 other cities in New York State, 100 municipalities in New Jersey, Cambridge and two other cities in Massachusetts, a half-dozen communities in Connecticut, Baltimore and three counties in Maryland, the District of Columbia, Miami Beach, and several Alaskan cities. By 1980, controls had spread to California, covering 50 percent of the state's ten million tenants. And, the Wall Street Journal reported (Feb. 1, 1980), groups in thirty states were seeking to bring controls to their cities.

Rent control laws usually levy severe penalties upon the landlord who exceeds the ceiling or who does not furnish a tenant the services to which he is entitled. But in time of housing shortage, most tenants need the further protection of a secure tenure—an assured right to remain where they are if they are not in default. To create this security, rent control has devised the so-called *statutory* tenancy. It is a subspecies of periodic (month-to-month) tenancy, one that only the tenant can terminate while the control continues, unless the tenant defaults or the landlord can satisfy one of a few statutory exceptions (for example, lessor's "immediate and compelling necessity" to recover the premises for his personal use and occupancy). Even though the tenancy may have begun with a term of years, when the initial term ends, the tenant need not vacate. Instead, the parties may either enter into a new written lease or convert to a statutory tenancy. A tenant who wishes to terminate a statutory tenancy must give the notice required of a month-to-month tenant.

Wartime rent controls easily passed constitutional muster, notably in Block v. Hirsch, 256 U.S. 135 (1921). But the persistence of rent regulation, no longer related to wartime emergency, has forced courts to re-examine the regulatory rationale, as well as to review the formulae for setting and the procedures for adjusting rentals.

ORANGE TAXPAYERS COUNCIL, INC. v. CITY OF ORANGE
83 N.J. 246, 416 A.2d 353 (1980)

PASHMAN, J. This is the third of three related cases challenging municipal power to prevent the deterioration of rented residential housing. [1] Here we consider the validity of a rent control ordinance which prohibits increases in rent without a certification that a dwelling is in "substantial compliance" with municipal housing regulations.

1. The other cases, also decided today, are Dome Realty Inc. v. City of Paterson, 83 N.J. 212, 416 A.2d 334 (1980), and State v. C.I.B. International, 83 N.J. 262, 416 A.2d 362 (1980).

On November 15, 1976, the City of Orange enacted Ordinance MCD 27-76 "to regulate, control and stabilize rents and to create a Rent Control Board within the City of Orange. . . ." The enactment codified and replaced the various ordinances regarding rent control which had been passed since 1972. It applied to all rented housing besides hotels, motels, one- and two-family dwellings and three-family, owner-occupied dwellings. The ordinance prohibited increases in rentals except under three sets of circumstances. When a lease expired or a periodic lease terminated, a landlord could charge an increase in rent proportionate to the increase in the Consumer Price Index [2] over the period of the former lease. Such periodic increases were originally limited to an annual rate of 4%. [3] A landlord could also petition for an increase to avoid economic hardship if he could not meet his "usual[,] customary and normal" operating expenses, including mortgage payments and maintenance costs. Finally, the ordinance permitted a landlord to seek additional rent for "major capital improvements or service [improvements]." An increase by reason of hardship or capital improvements was limited to 15% of a tenant's rent.

While no further official authorization was needed for periodic increases, each proposed increase in rentals due to hardship or capital improvements required the approval of the city's Rent Leveling Board. The board consisted of five members and two alternates appointed by the City Council for three-year terms. The ordinance granted the board authority to promulgate rules and regulations to implement the ordinance. Such regulations would "have the force of law." An aggrieved landlord or tenant could appeal decisions of the Rent Leveling Board to the City Council within 20 days of the date of determination.

The ordinance contains several provisions designed to insure a multiple dwelling's compliance with municipal standards for safety and habitability. When seeking a periodic increase in rents, a landlord must give formal notice to his tenants of the calculations involved in the increase, "and a certification that said dwelling and housing space is in *substantial compliance* with the applicable Property Maintenance Codes." Petitions for increases due to hardship or capital improvements required "a certification from the Property Maintenance Department of the City of Orange that the building and grounds are in Substantial Compliance with the Property Maintenance Code." The ordinance provided that the landlord must apply for official certification no more than one month prior to filing his petition with the Rent Leveling Board.

The ordinance defined "substantial compliance" as follows:

> "Substantial Compliance" means that the housing space and dwelling are free from all heat, hot water, elevator and all health, safety and fire hazards as well

2. Specifically, the ordinance employed the Consumer Price Index of all items for the New York City metropolitan area, as compiled by the Bureau of Labor Statistics, United States Department of Labor.

3. Amendments to the rent control ordinance raised that ceiling to 7% on September 7, 1979, and lowered it to 5% on November 9, 1979.

as 90% qualitatively free of all other violations of the Orange Property Maintenance Code and the Property Maintenance Code of the State of New Jersey
where applicable.

As written, the definition appeared to mandate compliance with both the
State and municipal housing codes. After the Appellate Division's decision in
this case, however, the Rent Leveling Board issued regulations requiring substantial compliance with only the municipal housing code for the issuance of
certificates.

Orange Taxpayers Council, Inc., a coalition of owners of rental properties in Orange, and several individual landlords instituted this challenge to the
rent control ordinance on March 10, 1977. Filing a verified complaint in lieu
of prerogative writs, R. 4:69, plaintiffs named as defendants the City of Orange, its Rent Leveling Board, each of the board's members and its secretary,
the Orange Tenants Association, an unincorporated association of tenants residing in Orange, and Barbara Davis, the association's president. Plaintiffs
alleged numerous grounds for the invalidation of Orange's rent control
scheme. Among them were challenges to the requirements that a landlord
provide or obtain a certification of "substantial compliance" as a condition for
any increase in rents.

The parties filed cross motions for summary judgment on the legality of
the certification scheme. In a letter opinion the trial court held it invalid.
According to the court, the requirement that an apartment be in "substantial
compliance" with housing regulations was unrelated to the purposes of rent
control. It found that the ordinance imposed penalties on landlords for violations of State as well as municipal housing regulations. Relying upon the
Appellate Division decision in Modular Concepts, Inc. v. South Brunswick
Tp., 146 N.J. Super. 138, 369 A.2d 32 (App. Div. 1977), certif. den., 74 N.J.
262, 377 A.2d 667 (1977), the court held that the City of Orange did not
possess authority to establish penalties for the violation of State regulations.
Even as a measure designed to enforce only local housing standards, the court
ruled that the ordinance exceeded the limits of delegated municipal authority.
By prohibiting increases in rent for dwellings that were not in "substantial
compliance," the ordinance prescribed penalties for violations in excess of the
$500 limit provided in N.J.S.A. 40:49-5. The court also noted that by requir-
ing "substantial compliance" before permitting higher rents, the ordinance
prevented landlords from seeking an increase to finance repairs for existing
violations. Accordingly, the trial court granted judgment for plaintiffs.

Defendants sought and were granted leave to appeal this decision to the
Appellate Division. Finding no facial defect in the certification requirement,
the Appellate Division reversed the trial court. Orange Taxpayers Council,
Inc. v. City of Orange, 169 N.J. Super. 288, 404 A.2d 1186 (App. Div. 1979).
It held that Orange's scheme to insure the safety and habitability of rent-
regulated dwellings was a reasonable exercise of municipal authority. Addressing the contention that compliance with housing regulations was not reason-

ably related to the purposes of rent control, the court observed, "Rent control would be self-defeating were landlords permitted to reduce maintenance expenditures and allow buildings to deteriorate because their profits have been regulated downward." Id. at 303, 404 A.2d at 1193.

We granted plaintiffs' petition for certification, but limited our review to whether a municipality could require the production of a certificate of "substantial compliance" as a prerequisite to an increase in controlled rents. 81 N.J. 399, 408 A.2d 793 (1979). As to that issue we now affirm.

The power of a municipality to control rents within its borders, in the absence of specific legislative authorization by the State, was recognized in the landmark case of Inganamort v. Borough of Fort Lee, 62 N.J. 521, 303 A.2d 298 (1973). Writing for the Court, Chief Justice Weintraub observed, "The police power is vested in local government to the very end that the right of property may be restrained when it ought to be because of sufficient local need." Id. at 538, 303 A.2d at 307. The Court in *Inganamort* found that a shortage of rental housing and the consequent risk that landlords would exploit tenants presented a proper occasion for local government "to devise measures tailored to the local scene[,] . . . to meet varying conditions or to achieve the ultimate goal more effectively." Id. at 528, 303 A.2d at 302. The "reservoir of police power" conferred by N.J.S.A. 40:48-2 was held to contain a delegation of legislative authority sufficient to support rent control by municipalities. See 62 N.J. at 536, 303 A.2d 298.

While *Inganamort* acknowledged the existence of municipal police power to regulate rents, the scope of that power remained largely unexplored until 1975. At that time, in a series of three decisions, Hutton Park Gardens v. West Orange Town Council, 68 N.J. 543, 350 A.2d 1 (1975); Brunetti v. Borough of New Milford, 68 N.J. 576, 350 A.2d 19 (1975); Troy Hills Village v. Parsippany-Troy Hills Tp., 68 N.J. 604, 350 A.2d 34 (1975), the Court addressed various questions concerning the manner in which a municipality may exercise its police power to control rents. The fundamental principle enunciated in these decisions was that municipal rent control ordinances "are subject to the same narrow scope of review under principles of substantive due process as are other [forms of legislative price regulations]." *Hutton Park Gardens,* 68 N.J. at 563-564, 350 A.2d at 12.

> [W]here, in the opinion of the legislature, regulation of prices serves the public interest, a state is entirely free to impose such regulation, provided only that it does not employ means which are arbitrary, discriminatory or demonstrably irrelevant to a legitimate purpose. [Id. at 558, 350 A.2d at 8]

Application of this principle led to a three-part analysis for assessing local rent control provisions. The first part is "whether the legislative body could rationally have concluded that the unrestrained operation of the competitive market was not in the public interest." Id. at 564, 350 A.2d at 12. [Citations omitted.]

The second inquiry is whether the regulatory scheme when examined in its entirety permits a "just and reasonable return" to the owners of rental properties. [Citations omitted.]

Finally, the means adopted to accomplish regulation in the public interest must be rationally related to the purposes of the rent control ordinance. [Citations omitted.]

When a plaintiff attacks a legislative enactment as simply arbitrary and unreasonable—a violation of his substantive due process rights—his claim is that he has been deprived of property for reasons unrelated to the welfare of the community. Judicial deference to the judgment of elected lawmakers requires that municipal rent control ordinances, like other legislative enactments, carry a presumption of validity. Although the presumption is not irrebuttable, it places a heavy burden upon the proponent of invalidity. See *Hutton Park Gardens,* 68 N.J. at 564-565, 350 A.2d 1. To succeed in his challenge, he must

> show that the legislative body could not have had any set of facts within its contemplation which would have permitted it to rationally conclude that the competitive rental housing market was not operating in the public interest. [Citations omitted.]

When confiscation is the issue, and the attack is upon the terms of the enactment itself and not the consequence of its application, the plaintiff's task is equally onerous. Only if a rent leveling ordinance is "so restrictive as to facially preclude any possibility of a just and reasonable return" may a court declare it invalid without considering the actual effects of the ordinance upon landlords. *Hutton Park Gardens,* 68 N.J. at 571, 350 A.2d 1; see *Brunetti,* 68 N.J. at 592, 350 A.2d 19.

When these principles are applied to the case before us, it becomes clear that we must reject plaintiffs' claims. As their principal argument, plaintiffs challenge as arbitrary and unreasonable the requirement that an apartment be in "substantial compliance" with local housing regulations before a landlord can charge higher rents. Thus, they contend that the enforcement of minimum standards of safety and habitability is completely unrelated to the goals of rent control. This proposition cannot be accepted.

We have ourselves described as "possible rationales for adopting [a rent control] ordinance . . . a housing shortage, widespread imposition of exorbitant rents, monopoly control of the rental housing market or *prevalence of substandard housing.*" *Brunetti,* 68 N.J. at 594, 350 A.2d at 28 (emphasis added). See *Hutton Park Gardens,* 68 N.J. at 564, 394 A.2d 65. Both "the problems of substandard dwellings and exorbitant rentals . . . stem from the critical condition of the housing market." Inganamort v. Borough of Fort Lee, 120 N.J. Super. 286, 310, 293 A.2d 720, 733 (Law Div. 1972), *aff'd,* 62 N.J. 521, 303 A.2d 298 (1973). No one would applaud the wisdom of lawmakers who by controlling the price of rental housing but not its quality, insured that their constituents could live in affordable dwellings that are unsafe, unsanitary and harmful to health. A municipality's authority to act "for the preservation of the public health, safety and welfare" of its residents, N.J.S.A. 40:48-2, permits it to go beyond mere regulation of price. There is no doubt that a municipality can employ its delegated police power to regulate the forces of the marketplace to help its residents obtain decent housing within their means.

This was precisely the goal of the City of Orange when it imposed a requirement of "substantial compliance" in its rent control ordinance. The preamble to the ordinance under scrutiny expressed official concern about both "increases in rents and subsequent deterioration of [residential] dwelling units." The same concerns were expressed in the city's original rent control ordinance in 1972. It appears that by enacting the "substantial compliance" requirement, the city could have acted—and indeed, did act—upon a rational perception of the "health, safety and welfare" of its citizens. We therefore find that the requirement is not an arbitrary and unreasonable feature of Orange's rent control ordinance.

The only feature of the ordinance which on its face gives rise to a claim of confiscation is the requirement that a dwelling be in "substantial compliance" with housing regulations before the Rent Leveling Board grants an increase in rents for economic hardship or capital improvements. As the trial court noted, "[t]he landlord seeking an increase to cure violations by a capital improvement or hardship increase cannot even file the petition because such a landlord could not get the certificate." The effect of this requirement, however, is not the preclusion of "any possibility of a just and reasonable return," *Hutton Park Gardens,* 68 N.J. at 571, 350 A.2d at 16. The purpose of requiring substantial compliance before granting an increase is to insure that tenants will not finance indirectly, by way of rent increases, those repairs which housing regulations and the landlord's implied warranty of habitability, see Trentacost v. Brussel, 82 N.J. 214, 412 A.2d 436 (1980), already obligate him to undertake. In the past we have recognized a tenant's right to receive reductions or rebates of rent when premises violate minimum standards of safety and health. See Berzito v. Gambino, 63 N.J. 460, 308 A.2d 17 (1973); see also N.J.S.A. 2A:42-85 et seq. Since the notion of a "just and reasonable return" embraces a landlord's responsibilities to his tenants as well as his right to receive sufficient income, we perceive no inherent defect in an ordinance that prevents increases in rent for defective premises.

For the foregoing reasons, the judgment of the Appellate Division is affirmed.

NOTES AND QUESTIONS

1. Both those who advocate and oppose rent control have, in their argument, been long on rhetoric and short on empirical back-up. Those who regard such controls as anathema have claimed that:

(a) holding the return on investment below market levels lowers the value of property investment, thereby reducing assessed valuations and shifting local tax burdens onto commercial, industrial, and non-rental residential properties.

(b) rent control, and even the threat of rent control, dries up new construction.

(c) artificially low rents aggravate housing decay by weakening reinvestment and ordinary maintainance.

(d) rent control tends to benefit more affluent tenants rather than the poor.

(e) rent control tends to favor established residents over transients or newcomers, and in some communities whites over minorities.

(f) rent control procedures especially burden small-scale owners unable to hire lawyers or accountants to help penetrate the bureaucratic maze.

Proponents, who reject much of the above, would argue:

(a) where shortages of rental housing exist, uncontrolled rents rise faster than the overall increase in consumer prices.

(b) the poor and persons on fixed incomes (especially the elderly) can least afford rising, uncontrolled rentals.

(c) even where rent controls exist, landlords far too often are able to secure unwarranted increases.

2. Mitchell, When Housing Is Tight, Are Rent Controls Necessary? 9 Calif. J. 53, 54-55 (1978):

A Tale of Two Studies

Is rent control a blessing or a disaster? One of the most frustrating things for anyone trying to answer that question objectively is the absence of any research that is accepted by both sides as authoritative and unbiased. Rent control studies generally seem to support the point of view of those who financed or requested them. At best, the conclusions of such studies appear suspect.

Taken together, however, two of the most recent studies—both of rent control in New Jersey—may provide a glimmer of truth. In 1976, John Gilderbloom, a graduate student in urban affairs at the University of California at Santa Barbara, was asked by the California Department of Housing and Community Development to examine the effects of rent control. Gilderbloom was then working as a department intern. His initial report, prepared under extreme time pressure, was based on data gathered by others concerning rent control in several states.

He was later given the go-ahead to expand the study. He prepared a supplementary report based on additional data he gathered himself in New Jersey. More recently, he has processed his data through a computer, using special techniques to isolate the rent control factor from others affecting the rental housing market. He compared a group of 26 cities that had had what he calls "moderate" rent controls for three to four years with a group of 37 uncontrolled cities. He found no evidence of negative effects from moderate, short-run controls. (Although prepared under state auspices, Gilderbloom's study has not been issued as an official state report.)

Gruen, Gruen & Associates were hired by the anti-rent control California Housing Council in response to Gilderbloom's studies. The Gruen report warned of developing problems in New Jersey's rent-controlled cities.

Understandably, rent control advocates like to point to Gilderbloom's work, while opponents are able to counter with the Gruen report. Surprisingly, however, the Gruens and Gilderbloom seem to agree on the basic facts concerning the effects of rent control:

Both accept the conclusions of traditional literature on rent control. While highly restrictive controls, like a rent freeze, keep rent levels lower than they otherwise would be under the existing market conditions, they also tend, over time, to result in decreased maintenance, a declining level of new rental housing construction, increased abandonment and falling rental property values. This last tends to shift the local tax burden to owners of other types of property, including homeowners. Thus, long-term application of highly restrictive controls helps to perpetuate or even worsen the tight housing market that led to the establishment of such controls in the first place.

"Moderate" (Gilderbloom's term) or "investment-neutral" (the Gruens' term) controls only limit windfall profits taken by landlords who have been reaping unearned benefits from a tight housing market. Such controls are not designed to grant across-the-board rent relief. Typically, they permit modest general rent increases plus additional hikes in the face of certain increased costs. They often exempt new construction entirely. Over the short run, at least, such controls exhibit no evidence of the negative effects that characterize highly restrictive, long-term controls.

There is a wide range between a rent freeze and an investment-neutral type of rent control. It seems reasonable to conclude that the more restrictive the control, the lower general rent levels are held and the worse the negative impacts on the quantity and quality of rental housing are likely to be. Similarly, the less restrictive the control, the less the effect on both general rent levels and the quantity and quality of rental housing.

The difference between the Gruens and Gilderbloom lies in their prediction of whether moderate controls will tend to become more restrictive over time. The Gruens say, yes. Gilderbloom says, maybe.

Just as some rent control critics have asserted that many modern rent controls are still too new for negative effects to have surfaced, Gilderbloom says it is too early to verify or dismiss any trend toward greater restrictiveness. Although he agrees that some cities have toughened their controls, he says that others have loosened or eliminated them.

The Gruens acknowledge that some cities, like Miami Beach, Florida, have ended their temporary controls. But they think the more likely path is for moderate controls to become tougher. They believe that rent control advocates want to limit rents, not just windfall profits. Since moderate controls permit rents to rise, they believe pressure will grow to tighten the controls instead of removing them, especially when landlords' costs are rising rapidly and pushing up rent levels.

Both positions regarding future changes in moderate rent control laws are based on general observation rather than on any systematic analysis of hard data. Those interested in rent control and its potential effects will have to decide for themselves which point of view to accept.

3. The regulatory scheme, to be constitutionally acceptable, must "when examined in its entirety permit a 'just and reasonable return' to the owners of rental properties." Orange Taxpayers Council, Inc. v. City of Orange, page 216, *supra*.

Suppose that you are counsel to a legislative committee which is about to consider a rent control bill. What evidence should committee members entertain on the issue of "just and reasonable return"?

4. As we have stated, rent regulations generally involve a statutorily protected tenure: the landlady may not remove a tenant, once occupancy begins, except in the case of tenant default or for one of the several reasons contained in the statute—e.g., the landlady wishes to occupy the premises herself. At least one state, New Jersey, has extended statutory tenure to nearly all residential tenants, whether or not their municipality may also have enacted a rent control ordinance.

2A:18-61.1   Removal of Residential Tenants; Grounds

No lessee or tenant or the assigns, under-tenants or legal representatives of such lessee or tenant may be removed by the county district court or the Superior Court from any house, building, mobile home or land in a mobile home park or tenement leased for residential purposes, other than owner-occupied premises with not more than two rental units or a hotel, motel or other guest house or part thereof rented to a transient guest or seasonal tenant, except upon establishment of one of the following grounds as good cause:

a. The person fails to pay rent due and owing under the lease whether the same be oral or written;

b. The person has continued to be, after written notice to cease, so disorderly as to destroy the peace and quiet of the occupants or other tenants living in said house or neighborhood;

c. The person has willfully or by reason of gross negligence caused or allowed destruction, damage or injury to the premises;

d. The person has continued, after written notice to cease, to substantially violate or breach any of the landlord's rules and regulations governing said premises, provided such rules and regulations are reasonable and have been accepted in writing by the tenant or made a part of the lease at the beginning of the lease term;

e. The person has continued, after written notice to cease, to substantially violate or breach any of the covenants or agreements contained in the lease for the premises where a right of re-entry is reserved to the landlord in the lease for a violation of such covenant or agreement, provided that such covenant or agreement is reasonable and was contained in the lease at the beginning of the lease term;

f.   The person has failed to pay rent after a valid notice to quit and notice of increase of said rent, provided the increase in rent is not unconscionable and complies with any and all other laws or municipal ordinances governing rent increases.

g.   The landlord or owner (1) seeks to permanently board up or demolish the premises because he has been cited by local or State housing inspectors for substantial violations affecting the health and safety of tenants and it is economically unfeasible for the owner to eliminate the violations; (2) seeks to comply with local or State housing inspectors who have cited him for substantial violations affecting the health and safety of tenants and it is unfeasible to so comply without removing the tenant;

h.   The owner seeks to retire permanently the residential building or the mobile home park from residential use or use as a mobile home park, provided this paragraph shall not apply to circumstances covered under paragraph g. of this section.

i.   The landlord or owner proposes, at the termination of a lease, reasonable changes of substance in the terms and conditions of the lease, including specifically any change in the term thereof, which the tenant, after written notice, refuses to accept.

j.   The person, after written notice to cease, has habitually and without legal justification failed to pay rent which is due and owing.

k.   The landlord or owner of the building is converting from the rental market to a condominium or a cooperative. Where the tenant is being removed pursuant to this subsection, no warrant for possession shall be issued until this act has been complied with. . . .

m.   The landlord or owner conditioned the tenancy upon and in consideration for the tenant's employment by the landlord or owner as superintendent, janitor or in some other capacity and such employment is being terminated.

If a New Jersey-like proposal were before you, as a legislator, what would be your response? Why?

5.   A student comment discusses the current rent-control situation in New Jersey and analyzes three formulas for establishing rate of return: return on fair market value; return on investment; and a (ratio of) net operating income (that is, rental less all costs except for depreciation, mortgage payments, and interest) to annual rental income. Comment, Rethinking Rent Control: An Analysis of "Fair Return," 12 Rutgers L.J. 617 (1981).

The author criticizes the first mode (despite its widespread use) because value reflects projected revenue, which presumably would either reflect rental controls (ergo, circularity) or the scarce conditions leading to controls (ergo, inflated values). Id. at 640-641. The return-on-investment formula, the author notes, might prejudice the owner who acquired the property donatively or when dollars were worth more than they are today, although he offers suggestions to deal with those situations. Id. at 644-646. The author describes the third approach as "the most easily administered basis for determining rate of return" and concludes that a rent-control ordinance would not be confiscatory if net operating income exceeded a given percentage of annual rental income. Id. at 647. New York City's Maximum Base Rent formula uses 42.4 percent. Id. at 650.

§4.6　The Stock Cooperative (the Proprietary Lease)

Origins and growth of the stock cooperative. The cooperative apartment (co-op) occupies a tiny and somewhat uneasy toehold in the housing market. It is found chiefly in a few urban centers, and it remains heavily dependent upon either income tax advantage (for luxury units) or government subsidy (for middle-income units).

The co-op appeals to those persons who wish to combine apartment occupancy and the advantages of home ownership. The Internal Revenue Code offers a major monetary advantage to the homeowning taxpayer: he may take itemized deductions for property tax payments and financing charges; yet he is not required, as reformers have urged, to impute as income the rental value of his dwelling. The homeowner, furthermore, has an equity he may devise, alienate, or borrow against, and the value of his equity is likely to increase over the years in our land-scarce and inflationary economy. (To be sure, he also shoulders the risk of a short-term decline.) Residential leaseholds, on the other hand, seldom generate increments of value for the lessee. And finally, in our status-ridden society, home ownership for many consumers connotes social arrival and, as such, is a significant factor in their selection of housing.

We cannot date or place the co-op's invention, but an 1886 lawsuit involving a co-op, Barrington Apartment Assn. v. Watson, 45 Sup. Ct. (38 Hun.) 545 (1886), suggests Manhattan, in the decades after the Civil War, as a possibility. In the years preceding the Great Depression, the luxury co-op began to abound in Chicago and New York—two cities where the well-to-do practiced the apartment habit, and, in 1927, the first middle-income co-op, Amalgamated Houses, rose in the Bronx. The depression struck all forms of real estate hard; because of their financial interdependence (page 197, *infra*), co-ops were especially prone. Some have estimated that fewer than one of ten co-ops survived ruin, and even the highly subsidized Amalgamated Houses barely made it. When World War II began, the co-op movement was in near collapse.

In the postwar era, the co-op has regained and surpassed its former status. Several facts explain this recovery. Congress, in 1942, passed the forerunner of Int. Rev. Code §216, creating tax parity (regarding deductions for interest and property taxes) between homeowner and co-op owner. The war-occasioned rise in tax rates gave the upper-income apartment dweller further incentive to reduce his tax burden by switching from a rental to a co-op unit. The tenant's desire, in this rare instance, paralleled his landlord's, for the latter, faced with the wearying prospect of rent control, often wanted to sell out; his easiest (and most profitable) chance of doing so lay in conversion to co-op and the giving of first option to his present tenants—a procedure rent control allowed, at least in New York. Congress, in 1950, once again spurred co-op activity when it added §213 to the National Housing Act, authorizing the FHA to insure the co-op mortgage. And middle-income co-ops received a major stimulus from the New York legislature in 1956, when it enacted the Mitchell-Lama Law (Private Housing Finance Law §§10–37) with its twin inducements of long-term, low-interest loans and property tax abatement.

Legal arrangement. Title to the land and building is held by a single entity—usually a corporation, although a trust is sometimes used. Only those who are to become apartment "owners," the co-op owners, may obtain a corporate (trust) interest; each co-op owner acquires shares based on the value of his apartment. The right to occupy the apartment is embodied in a "proprietary" lease between the corporation (trust), as landlord, and the co-op owner as tenant. Under the lease provisions, the co-op owner pays a periodic rental or assessment; this charge covers the co-op owner's pro rata share of the project's expenses, including debt service, maintenance, taxes, insurance, capital improvements, and reserves. Ordinarily the lease is for an initial term of three to five years, but is automatically renewable for like terms at the tenant's election.

Management of the co-operative is performed by a board of directors, who are elected by the project members in accordance with the governing bylaws. The directors fix the amount of the periodic assessment, and enforce the lease against delinquent stockholder-tenants. Default may result in a member's eviction and in the forced sale of his stock and lease.

For a fuller discussion of the stock cooperative, see Hennessey, Co-operative Apartments and Town Houses, 1956 U. Ill. L.F. 22; Isaacs, "To Buy or Not to Buy: That is the Question" . . . What is a Cooperative Apartment? 13 Record of N.Y.C.B.A. 203 (1958); Notes, 61 Harv. L. Rev. 1407 (1948); 111 U. Pa. L. Rev. 638 (1963); 68 Yale L.J. 542 (1959); Rohan and Reskin, Cooperative Housing Law and Practice (1967) (bibliography included).

PROBLEM

To test your understanding of the difference between the stock cooperative and the condominium, assume a developer X who plans to build two structures, a 100-unit stock-cooperative and an identical 100-unit condominium. The units within each building are themselves identical. Every unit has a market value of $100,000. Assume further that 80 percent financing will be available. This means that lenders will provide mortgages equal to 80 percent of a unit's (or, in the case of the cooperative, the structure's) value. What legal shape will the two projects take? How will the financing be arranged?

Now assume that the projects are completed and that Y and Z have agreed to purchase one of the stock-cooperative and condominium units, respectively. Each has $20,000 in cash and is otherwise a qualified buyer. What documents will Y receive at the closing (time of transfer)? What documents must Y subscribe? Similarly, as to Z.

FINE, THE CONDOMINIUM CONVERSION PROBLEM: CAUSES AND SOLUTIONS
1980 Duke L.J. 306

In many major urban and suburban areas, condominiums and co-operatives are becoming a significant element of the housing market. A primary feature of the condominium boom, accounting for the largest share of new condominium units on the market, is the conversion of rental apartments to condominiums. One survey estimates that conversions have doubled from approximately 50,000 units in 1977 to 100,000 units in 1978. Approximately seventy-five percent of these conversions took place in seven major markets: New York, Chicago, Houston, Seattle, Denver, Los Angeles, and Washington, D.C. When the data are compiled, it is likely that 130,000 units have been converted in 1979.

The surge in condominium conversions is attributable to a number of factors. Demand for condominiums is strong, particularly for converted units, which are generally priced lower than newly constructed units. At the same time, conversion provides an opportunity for landlords with ever decreasing profits to sell their properties for substantial gains.

Condominium conversion has many benefits. Conversion meets the strong demand for condominium ownership and offers one of the best long-range solutions for urban decay. There are, however, many negative effects associated with the process. Conversion displaces existing tenants who do not want or cannot afford to buy units in the converted building. Each conversion also reduces available rental housing, making it difficult for displaced tenants to find suitable alternative housing. The burden of the conversion boom clearly falls most heavily on the poor and the elderly, groups that can least afford to purchase the converted units.

GRACE v. TOWN OF BROOKLINE
399 N.E.2d 1038 (1979)

LIACOS, J. A condominium developer, a condominium owner and a potential condominium purchaser challenge, as unauthorized by statute and prohibited by the Massachusetts and the United States Constitutions, two amendments to art. XXXVIII of the bylaws of the town of Brookline. The disputed amendments protect tenants by regulating the procedure for their eviction from apartments converted into condominium units. We uphold their validity.

The plaintiffs filed a complaint in the county court for declaratory and injunctive relief on November 3, 1978. On November 10, 1978, a single justice of this court denied the plaintiffs' request for a preliminary injunction, an allowed a motion by the Attorney General of the Commonwealth to intervene as a party-defendant. The parties subsequently submitted a stipulation of facts, and on March 6, 1979, a single justice reserved and reported the case for decision by a full bench.

The pertinent facts stipulated are as follows. From 1970 until December 31, 1975, the town of Brookline generally regulated and controlled rents and evictions under the general rent control enabling provisions of St. 1970, c. 842. On December 16, 1975, a Brookline special town meeting rescinded its approval of c. 842. In its place, under the authority specifically granted to Brookline by St. 1970, c. 843, the town meeting adopted art. XXXVIII of the Brookline by-laws (referred to hereafter as the "by-law"). Brookline has regulated rents and evictions pursuant to c. 843 and the by-law since January 1, 1976.

Section 9(a) of the by-law enumerates the bases on which the rent control board may issue certificates of eviction with regard to rent-controlled housing units. Prior to July 25, 1978, §9(a) provided two grounds for eviction of tenants residing in rent controlled apartments which were slated for, or had already undergone, conversion to condominiums. Section 9(a)(8) allowed a landlord to obtain a certificate of eviction if he sought to occupy a unit for himself or a member of his immediate family; section 9(a)(10) authorized a landlord to bring an action to recover possession of a unit "for any other just cause." The first of these provisions permitted a purchaser of a newly converted condominium unit who sought occupancy to apply for a certificate of eviction. The second allowed a developer to seek certificates of eviction for an entire building intended for conversion to condominium units. The rent control board of Brookline routinely granted developers such certificates upon compliance with particular guidelines it had promulgated.

On July 25, 1978, a special town meeting of Brookline voted to amend §9(a)(8) and (10) of the by-law. The effect of the amendment to §9(a)(10) was to render certificates of eviction unavailable to condominium developers. At the same time, the amendment to §9(a)(8) preserves, for the condominium purchaser who seeks to occupy the unit, the opportunity to evict a tenant who refuses to vacate voluntarily. However, if the tenant was in possession of the unit when the new landlord acquired ownership, that tenant is protected by a mandatory six-month stay of issuance of a certificate of eviction. The amendment to §9(a)(8) also provides for an additional six-month delay if the board determines that a hardship exists. After approval by the Attorney General, pursuant to G.L. c. 40, §32, both amendments took effect on September 27, 1978.

The plaintiff Grace is a developer of a condominium project in Brookline. On January 13, 1978, he purchased several buildings in order to convert the thirty-five apartments therein for sale as condominiums. After entering into purchase and sale agreements with prospective purchasers who were not tenants and who intended to occupy the units, Grace applied to the board for certificates of eviction. In each case decided before July 25, 1978, on finding compliance with the guidelines, the board granted Grace a certificate of eviction.

Prior to enactment of the by-law amendments, the plaintiff Lonabocker contracted to buy one of the units owned by Grace. She obtained a commitment for mortgage financing and sold her residence, expecting to occupy the condominium. After July 25, 1978, Lonabocker and Grace were disqualified from applying for a certificate of eviction. Because she was unable to obtain occupancy of the unit, Lonabocker's mortgage financing was cancelled. She has not purchased the unit.

The plaintiff Ehrenworth purchased a unit from Grace on October 20, 1978, in order to occupy it as his residence. At the time of the purchase, the unit was occupied by a tenant. Ehrenworth filed an application for a certificate of eviction which was approved by the board on December 19, 1978. As of March 2, 1979, the date of the parties' stipulation, the board had not issued a certificate of eviction, by virtue of the operation of §9(a)(8), as amended. Since purchasing the unit from Grace, and until at least March 2, 1979, Ehrenworth received rent from the tenant occupying the unit. The rental receipts, however, were insufficient to offset the monthly carrying charges incurred by Ehrenworth on the unit. Grace agreed to bear the difference between the rents collected and the costs incurred for a period of one year from the passage of title.

On November 14, 1978, a Brookline special town meeting voted to amend the by-law further by imposing a general six-month moratorium on the issuance of any certificate of eviction against a tenant who was in possession of an apartment when it was purchased as a condominium unit. The moratorium, which was approved by the Attorney General on December 28, 1978, bore an expiration date of June 15, 1979.

The plaintiffs raise two constitutional arguments in contesting the validity of the amendments. They claim that on their face the amendments effect a taking without just compensation and deprive them of the equal protection of the laws. As with the statutory arguments, plaintiffs must satisfy a heavy burden if they are to prevail on these claims. See Turnpike Realty Co. v. Dedham, 362 Mass. 221, 233, 284 N.E.2d 891 (1972), *cert. denied*, 409 U.S. 1108 (1973). We conclude that they have not met their burden.

1. The plaintiffs' "taking" argument rests on an apparent distinction between the regulation of use and the transfer of rights. They suggest that the amendments are illegal because, rather than regulate what uses are or are not permitted, the amendments determine who, as between a tenant in possession

and an owner, shall enjoy a permitted use. In effect, the plaintiffs contend, the amendments transfer the right to possess from the owner to the tenant and compel the condominium owner to become a landlord.

The United States Supreme Court consistently has upheld rent control statutes as proper exercises of the police power in times of public emergency. See Bowles v. Willingham, 321 U.S. 503, 517, 64 S. Ct. 641, 88 L. Ed. 892 (1944); Edgar A. Levy Leasing Co. v. Siegel, 258 U.S. 242, 42 S. Ct. 289, 66 L. Ed. 595 (1922); Marcus Brown Holding Co. v. Feldman, 256 U.S. 170, 41 S. Ct. 465, 65 L. Ed. 877 (1921); Block v. Hirsh, 256 U.S. 135, 41 S. Ct. 458, 65 L. Ed. 865 (1921). This court also has upheld such acts, including the enabling legislation for the local provisions challenged today. [Citations omitted].

The import of these cases is that a shortage of housing threatens the public interest (Block v. Hirsh, *supra*, 256 U.S. at 156, 41 S. Ct. 458), and that legislation which preserves the rental market for low, moderate, and fixed income persons promotes health, safety, and welfare generally. In short, a housing crisis justifies the exercise of the police power.

A particular provision, nevertheless, may go too far. "For just as there comes a point at which the police power ceases and leaves only that of eminent domain, it may be conceded that regulations of the present sort pressed to a certain height might amount to a taking without due process of law." Id. See generally Pennsylvania Coal Co. v. Mahon, 260 U.S. 393, 43 S. Ct. 158, 67 L. Ed. 322 (1922). The character of governmental action is one of several factors relevant to a determination of whether a taking has occurred. See Penn Cent. Transp. Co. v. New York City, 438 U.S. 104, 124, 98 S. Ct. 2646, 57 L. Ed.2d 631 (1978). In a strict sense, the amendments do effect a transfer of rights incident to ownership: the tenant in possession at the time of conversion is permitted to remain in possession even though the owner seeks recovery for his own personal use. In our view, however, this redistribution of rights is not unlike the redistribution of rights effected by rent and eviction control generally.

During a housing shortage, the Legislature has wide latitude to control rents and evictions. See, e.g., Mayo v. Boston Rent Control Adm'r, *supra* (landlord may not evict in order to perform renovation that would increase rents). How wide that latitude is, we need not determine now since the amendments go no further than the provisions upheld in the cases cited. The by-law amendments in issue do not attempt to create rental housing from owner-occupied units, nor do they bring under control units not previously subject to the by-law. They merely limit the property owners' right to remove units from the rental market, by delaying recovery for personal occupancy. But cf. Rivera v. R. Cobian Chinea & Co., 181 F.2d 974, 978 (1st Cir. 1950). The period of delay required by these amendments does not render the provisions confiscatory.

In reaching this conclusion we are especially mindful that the property held by the plaintiffs is not rendered worthless by the amendments. Compare Pennsylvania Coal Co. v. Mahon, *supra*, with Goldblatt v. Hempstead, 369

U.S. 590, 594, 82 S. Ct. 987, 8 L. Ed. 2d 130 (1962), and Turnpike Realty Co. v. Dedham, *supra*, 362 Mass at 236-237, 284 N.E.2d 891. Inasmuch as the amendments permit the condominium purchaser to take possession eventually, a unit purchased for conversion has value as a condominium even while it remains tenant-occupied. Cf. Golden v. Planning Bd. of Ramapo, 30 N.Y.2d 359, 380-381, 334 N.Y.S.2d 138, 285 N.E.2d 291, *appeal dismissed*, 409 U.S. 1003, 93 S. Ct. 436, 34 L. Ed. 2d 294 (1972). Moreover, until the tenant vacates, the condominium purchaser is entitled to receive rent. By statute, rent for a controlled unit must yield a "fair net operating income." St. 1971, c. 673, §1. In order to obtain this yield, the owner may seek such individual adjustment as may be necessary. Id. Significantly, both plaintiffs Grace and Ehrenworth obtained adjustments for the units they owned to the levels of rent sought.

   2. In their equal protection argument, the plaintiffs appear to challenge the amendments as both under-inclusive and over-inclusive: under-inclusive because they do not apply to all purchasers or owners of residential rental property; over-inclusive because they apply to fair-minded condominium purchasers as well as to those who would harass and pressure tenants to vacate.

   Underlying both equal protection contentions is the assumption that Brookline has drawn a distinction based solely on the form of ownership. The plaintiffs assert that in a number of cases from other jurisdictions, purportedly cited with approval in Goldman v. Dennis,—Mass.—,—, 375 N.E.2d 1212 courts have held that "[p]lanning controls . . . cannot be employed by a municipality to exclude condominiums or discriminate against the condominium form of ownership, for it is use rather than form of ownership that is the proper concern and focus of zoning and planning regulation." Maplewood Village Tenants Ass'n v. Maplewood Village, 116 N.J. Super. 372, 377, 282 A.2d 428, 431 (Ch. Div 1971). See Miami Beach v. Arlen King Cole Condominium Ass'n, 302 So. 2d 777 (Fla. App. 1974).

   Contrary to the plaintiffs' interpretation of *Goldman*, that case neither approves nor disapproves of the reasoning of cases like *Maplewood Village Tenants Ass'n*. Those cases were cited simply as inapposite to the matter then before us. Likewise, they do not control the issue before us. None involved condominium conversion in the context of rent and eviction control. Nor did those cases rest their decisions on the constitutional guaranty of equal protection of the laws. Instead, each held that under the applicable zoning enabling acts, regulation based on the form of ownership was unauthorized. We perceive no reason why Brookline may not draw up regulations based on the form of ownership so long as such a classification is rationally related to the purposes of rent and eviction control.

   We have no difficulty in concluding that the challenged classification rationally furthers the purposes of rent and eviction control. The record suggests that conversion of controlled units into condominiums has been occurring with accelerating frequency. Consequently, Brookline reasonably could have concluded that condominium conversion posed a singular threat to the purpose of rent control. There is no denial of equal protection because Brookline chose to focus its response on that threat. [Citations omitted.] The town also might have concluded reasonably that, due to the potential for harassment of tenants by condominium purchasers anxious to obtain possession, "a particular limitation . . . would protect against its occurrence, and that the expense and other difficulties of individual determinations justified the inherent imprecision of [the] prophylactic rule." Weinberger v. Salfi, 422 U.S. 749, 777, 95 S. Ct. 2457, 2473, 45 L. Ed. 2d 522 (1975). Consequently, there is no denial of equal protection because the amendments apply whether or not the purchaser is guilty of harassment.

CONCLUSION

For the reasons stated, we conclude that the amendments to art. XXXVIII of the Brookline by-laws, adopted on July 25, 1978, are valid. The promulgation of these by-law amendments by the town meeting was within the authority granted to the town of Brookline by St. 1970, c. 843. The by-law amendments are not in conflict with G.L. c. 183A or G.L. c. 239, nor do they violate the rights of the plaintiffs under Federal or State constitutional provisions. This case is remanded to the single justice for the entry of a judgment declaring the rights of the parties in accordance with this opinion.

So ordered.

The Brookline ordinance is one of several legislative methods intended to strengthen the hand or the finances of rental tenants whose landlords seek conversion into a cooperative or condominium. Other techniques include:

(a) outright prohibition against conversion, sometimes for specified intervals—e.g., 30 to 120 days, sometimes indefinitely—e.g., until the vacancy rate in rental apartments within the community rises above 5 percent.

(b) building conversion not to become effective unless a specified percentage of present rental tenants agree to purchase units within the building, see e.g., N.Y. Gen. Bus. Law §352-eeee (McKinney Supp. 1981) (35 percent).

(c) transfer tax levy upon the sale of converted units from the developer to the original purchasers, with the revenue earmarked for rental subsidies for displaced tenants.

The Uniform Condominium Act §4-110, which to date has had few adoptions, would give present tenants a ninety-day right to purchase their unit, and, for nonpurchasing tenants, a three-year protection against eviction measured from the date the conversion plan is first presented. In addition, the Code would bar local legislation, limiting restrictions to the state level.

Given the competing interests of the demand for homeownership, the stability of urban neighborhoods, the continuing importance of rental apartments as a shelter mode, the desire of rental tenants—especially the poor and elderly—not to be forced from their "homes", and the economic well-being of apartment owners, how best can these interests be reconciled legislatively?

Two years after the *Brookline* decision, the Massachusetts court upheld an even more drastic ordinance emanating from the city of Cambridge. This law barred the removal of any nonpurchasing tenant from a converted rental project unless the city rent-control board issued a permit, which generally it could refuse. In upholding the law against the claim that persons purchasing such units would suffer an unconstitutional taking of property, the court reasoned that plaintiffs could not establish a taking "simply by showing that they have been denied the ability to exploit a property interest that they heretofore had believed was available." Flynn v. City of Cambridge,—Mass.—, 418 N.E.2d 335 (1981).

Chapter 5

Landlord and Tenant: Tenant Rights and Remedies

We have already noted that the early lease defined a relation between the landed gentry and feudal England's land-working poor. Much of the present (or very recent) law of landlord and tenant traces its genes to these primitive origins, reproduced through centuries of rural society. This sense of history brings little comfort—certainly not to the elderly New York widow unable to make her landlord fix a leaky toilet because Yorkshire farmers were required (and able) to make their own repairs.

But things are stirring. The law of landlord and tenant has seen more change since 1960 than took place in the preceding six hundred years—and that is only prologue to the sweeping changes that lie just ahead. Thus, your task will be twofold in studying these materials. You will want to see where the law is rooted. But you will also want to ponder where it should head. You will find, I think, that the questions are not so hard, and that the answers are not so easy.

Law students (like everyone else) tend to judge issues against their own experience—for most of you, this means many years as tenants. Without implying any bias for your antagonist, I urge that you remember—as you explore the issues ahead—that most landlords are businessmen (or think they are), and that their legitimate concern for the economic vitality of property must be factored into any solutions you propose.

§5.1 "Model" Apartment Lease

A stranger from Mars, on hearing that leases often use thousands of words, might expect the lease to set forth fully the tenant's rights, as well as his duties. This would be true if the tenant were a major supermarket chain leasing 20,000 square feet in a shopping center. Not true, however, for residential

tenants the country over who—if they read their leases—would find a monotony of "shall-nots" and penalties, and little cognizance of rights and remedies.
Read through the lease form below,[1] a so-called model apartment lease, endorsed by the Association of the Bar of the City of New York. How many
rights does the model give tenants? How many remedies? Compare for landlords.

MODEL APARTMENT LEASE

*Standard Form of Apartment Lease Approved by the Association of the Bar of the City of
New York*

LEASE, made as of the _____ day of _____, 19_____, between

_____,

Parties;
Addresses

having an address at_____, _____ (the
"Landlord") and _____,
having an address at _____,
_____ (the "Tenant").

Apartment

WITNESSETH: The Landlord leases to the Tenant Apartment
_____ (the "Apartment") on the_____ floor of the building (the
"Building") having the street address_____,

Use
Term of
Lease
Rent

for use by the Tenant solely as a private residence. The term of this
lease shall commence on _____, 19_____, and shall end on _____,
19_____, or earlier if this lease is terminated in accordance with the
provisions of Article 9. The annual rent shall be $_____, payable in
equal monthly installments of $_____ each, in advance, on the first
day of each calendar month during the term, except that, unless this
lease is a renewal, the first monthly installment shall be paid on the
signing of this lease. All other sums required to be paid by the Tenant
under this lease shall be deemed additional rent.

The parties further agree as follows:

Payment
of Rent

1. The Tenant (a) will pay the rent to the Landlord, without
deduction, at the Landlord's address set forth above or at such other
address as the Landlord may designate by notice given to the Tenant,
and (b) will not withhold rent for any reason.

Landlord Not
Responsible
for Failure to
Deliver
Possession of

2. The Tenant waives the provisions of Section 223–a of the
New York Real Property Law (which would otherwise permit the Tenant to cancel this lease and hold the Landlord responsible for damages)
in the event that the Landlord is unable or fails to deliver possession of
the Apartment to the Tenant on the commencement of the term of this

1. It might be fun here to examine your own lease carefully. You probably haven't done so
before.

Apartment on Time; Rent Abatement

lease, but the Tenant shall not be required to pay rent until the Apartment is no longer leased to, or occupied by, anyone else. The term of this lease shall end on the date set forth above regardless of the date on which possession of the Apartment is delivered to the Tenant or the date on which the Tenant first occupies the Apartment.

Tenant to Take Care of Apartment; Repairs by Tenant

Tenant to Comply with Laws, etc.

Tenant to Indemnify Landlord Against Liability

3. The Tenant will take good care of the Apartment and all of its equipment, and will not permit same to be damaged or destroyed. The Tenant will make all repairs to the Apartment and its equipment required by reason of the misuse or negligence of the Tenant or any other person occupying or using the Apartment (other than the Landlord or its agents or employees); will abide by and comply with all laws, regulations, rules and orders of the federal, state and municipal governments, and of any of their departments, and the regulations of the New York Board of Fire Underwriters, applicable to the Tenant's use of the Apartment or any alterations to, or installations in, the Apartment made by the Tenant, whether or not approved by the Landlord, and shall indemnify the Landlord against any liability incurred by the Landlord because of injury to person or property resulting from any act of omission of Tenant or any occupant of, or person allowed by the Tenant to enter or use the Apartment.

4. Without the Landlord's prior written consent, the Tenant will not:

No Apartment Alterations, Wallpapering, Painting, etc. by Tenant

Tenant Not To Deface Apartment or Install Locks or Appliances

(a) make any alterations, additions or improvements (collectively "alterations") in or on the Apartment, including, but not limited to panelling, painting, wallpapering, flooring, window installations, "built-in" decorations, partitions and railings, or drill into, or in any way deface or permit the defacing of any part of the Apartment, or install any locks or chain-guards or alter or change any lock cylinders or otherwise prevent authorized entry to the Apartment;

(b) install any dishwashing, clothes washing or drying machines or heating, ventilating, humidifying or air-conditioning units, or place any water filled furniture in the Apartment;

No Pets

(c) keep any animal [2] in the Apartment;

Other Limitations on Tenant's Use of Apartment

(d) do or permit anything to be done in the Apartment which will increase the rate of fire insurance on the Building;

(e) install any shades, blinds, screens, window guards or treatments;

---

2. Humor sometimes slips into a standard lease. Apply the principle of ejusdem generis to this passage from a San Diego form: "Tenant agrees that neither he nor his guests shall keep or bring into said premises . . . any animal, bird, fowl, pet, water bed, piano or other musical instrument." Berger, Hard Leases Make Bad Law, 74 Colum. L. Rev. 791, 833 (1974).—Ed.

(f) attach any awning or other projections to the outside walls of the Building or place any signs in any windows; or

(g) permit the accumulation of refuse in the Apartment or allow cooking or other objectionable odors to escape therefrom.

Removal of Tenant's Property and Alterations (at Landlord's Option) and Repair of Damage to Apartment by Tenant at Tenant's Expense

At or before the end of the term of this Lease, the Tenant shall remove all of the Tenant's furniture and other property from the Building and the Apartment and shall repair all injury done to the Apartment and the Building by the moving in, installation or removal of the Tenant's furniture and other property. If the Tenant fails to remove such property or to make or complete such repairs, such property may be removed and repairs may be made by the Landlord, at the expense of the Tenant, and an amount equal to the expense incurred by the Landlord shall be paid by the Tenant, on demand, whether or not the term of this lease has ended. All alterations to the Apartment made by either party shall become the property of the Landlord, and shall remain and be surrendered with the Apartment at the end of the term of this lease unless the Landlord elects, by notice given to the Tenant not less than thirty (30) days prior to the end of the term, to have alterations made by the Tenant removed, in which event the Tenant shall promptly remove such alterations. If the Tenant fails to remove such alterations by the end of the term of this lease, the Landlord may remove same at the expense of the Tenant, and the expense incurred by the Landlord shall be paid by the Tenant, on demand. At the end

Surrender of Apartment and Abandoned Property

of the Term of this lease, the Tenant will surrender and deliver to the Landlord possession of the Apartment in as good condition as it was at the beginning of the term, subject to reasonable wear and tear, except for damage by fire or other casualty or cause for which the Tenant is not responsible under any of the provisions of this lease. If any of the Tenant's property remains in the Building or the Apartment after the Tenant has moved from the Apartment, such property shall be deemed abandoned by the Tenant and, at the election of the Landlord, either shall be kept as the Landlord's property or be removed by the Landlord as set forth above.

Landlord's Rules

5. The Tenant will observe and comply with such reasonable rules as the Landlord may prescribe (on notice to the Tenant) for the safety, care and cleanliness of the Building, and the comfort, quiet and convenience of other occupants of the Building.

Services Furnished by Landlord; Electricity

6. Unless this is a sublease, the Landlord shall furnish:

(a) elevator service (if there are one or more elevators in the Building);

(b) hot and cold water, in reasonable quantities;

(c) heat as required by law;

(d) air-conditioning (if the Building has central air-conditioning equipment or there are individual units owned by the Landlord) during the summer except that it shall be the Tenant's responsibility to clean and change filters in any such individual units; and

(e) electricity for lights, small appliances and air-conditioning equipment or individual units in the Apartment which are owned by the Landlord, unless the Apartment is separately metered, in which event the Tenant shall purchase electricity directly from the utility company serving the Building.

Landlord Not Liable for Interruption or Curtailment of Services

Interruption or curtailment of any or all such services, if caused by strikes, mechanical difficulties or any other cause reasonably beyond the Landlord's control, shall not entitle the Tenant to make any claim against the Landlord or to withhold or reduce any installment of rent.

Damage by Fire

7. If the Building, the Apartment or means of access thereto is damaged or destroyed by fire or other casualty and the Landlord shall decide not to repair, restore or rebuild it, this lease shall terminate and the rent shall be apportioned as of the date on which the damage shall have occurred. If this lease is not so terminated, the Landlord shall repair the damage to the Apartment and means of access thereto as soon as practicable, and if the damage has made the Apartment untenantable, in whole or in part, there shall be an apportionment of the rent until the damage has been repaired (unless such damage was caused by the Tenant). The Landlord and the Tenant agree that the foregoing provisions of this Article are an express agreement made in lieu of the provisions of Section 227 of the New York Real Property Law which provide that a tenant may terminate a lease if an apartment is rendered untenantable. Neither the Landlord's decision not to repair, restore or rebuild, nor its obligation to repair damage shall be deemed to release the Tenant from any liability to the Landlord arising out of the Tenant's acts or omissions and any resulting damage from fire or other casualty. The Tenant shall look first to any insurance which it carries before making any claim against the Landlord for recovery for loss or damage resulting from fire or other casualty not caused by the Tenant's acts or omissions, shall name the Landlord as an additional insured under any casualty policy held by the Tenant, and to the extent that such insurance is in force and collectible and to the extent permitted by law, the Tenant releases, and waives all right of recovery against the Landlord for any such law. The Tenant under-

Tenant to Rely First on Insurance and To Make No Claims Against Landlord For Insured Loss; Tenant to Name Landlord as Additional Insured on Tenant's Policies

stands that the Landlord will not carry insurance on the Tenant's alterations, furniture, furnishings, equipment, appliances, decorations and personal effects, and agrees that the Landlord will not be obligated to repair any damage to, or to replace, the same.

Eminent Domain

8. If the Building or the Apartment (or any part thereof or means of access thereto) is taken or condemned by virtue of eminent domain, the Landlord, on notice to the Tenant, may terminate this lease as of the date when the same shall be so taken or condemned, and the rent shall be apportioned as of said date. No part of any award for the Building shall belong to the Tenant, and the Tenant shall not be entitled to any payment for its leasehold estate in the Apartment.

Tenant's Refusal or Failure to Perform

Termination of Lease; Tenant to Remain Liable

9. (a) If the Tenant refuses or fails to perform any of the Tenant's agreements or obligations under this lease, including the Tenant's obligation to pay rent and additional rent the Landlord may give notice of such fact to the Tenant, and if such refusal or failure has not been cured within ten (10) days after the giving of such notice, then the Landlord may give the Tenant notice that the Landlord has elected to terminate this lease as of a date fixed by the Landlord (which shall not be less than five (5) days after the date of such notice), and on the date specified in the Landlord's notice the term of this lease shall end, and the Tenant shall then surrender and deliver possession of the Apartment to the Landlord, but the Tenant shall remain liable to the Landlord by reason of the Tenant's refusal or failure mentioned above.

Landlord's Resumption of Possession

Tenant to Pay Damages; Landlord has No Obligation to Relet

(b) If (i) the Tenant refuses or fails to pay rent or additional rent when due, or (ii) this lease has been terminated by the Landlord pursuant to subparagraph (a) of this Article 9, then and in either of such events the Landlord may at any time thereafter re-enter and take possession of the Apartment by any lawful means, and remove the Tenant and other occupants and their effects, by dispossess proceedings, or otherwise, without being liable to prosecution or damages. In any such case, the Landlord, at the Landlord's option may relet the Apartment, and receive the rent from the next tenant, applying the same first to the payment of any expenses that the Landlord incurred in connection with said taking of possession and reletting, including without limitation reasonable legal fees and disbursements, brokerage fees, advertising costs, the cost of cleaning, repairing and decorating the Apartment and its equipment and appliances, and then to the payment of rent and the cost of performance of the other agreements and obligations of the Tenant as provided in this lease; and whether or not the Landlord has relet the Apartment (it being agreed that the Landlord shall have no obligation to relet the Apartment), the Tenant shall pay to the Landlord on the first day of each calendar month, the rent and other sums for which the Tenant is responsible, less the proceeds of the reletting remaining after deduction of the amount of all of the aforementioned expenses, if any, as ascertained from time to time.

**No
Assignment
or Subletting
By Tenant**

10. Except as otherwise provided in Sections 226-b and 236 of the New York Real Property Law (which permit subleases or the termination of leases in certain circumstances), the Tenant shall neither assign this lease nor sublease the Apartment or any part thereof without the Landlord's prior consent. If this lease is assigned by the Tenant,

**Landlord
May Accept
Rent from
Others**

or if the Apartment is subleased or occupied by anyone other than the Tenant, the Landlord may collect rent from the assignee, subtenant or occupant, and apply the net amount collected to the rent and additional rent payable under the terms of this lease, and no such collection shall be deemed a waiver of these restrictions against assignment and subleasing, or the acceptance of such assignee, subtenant or occupant as the tenant under this lease, or a release of the Tenant from further performance of the covenants contained in this lease.

**Subordination
to Mortgages
and Ground
and
Underlying
Leases**

11. This lease shall be subject and subordinate to the lien of all mortgages on the Building and to all ground or underlying leases which now or hereafter may be a lien on or affect the Building, so that a foreclosure of any such mortgage or termination of any such lease shall result in a termination of this lease unless the mortgagor or landlord of any such lease shall otherwise elect, in which event the Tenant, upon request, shall enter into a new lease (for the balance of the term of this Lease taken as if this Lease had not termiated) with such mortgagor or landlord on terms substantially identical to the terms and provisions of this lease.

**Waiver of
Trial by Jury**

12. It is mutually agreed by and between the Landlord and the Tenant that each party waives trial by jury in any action, proceeding or counterclaim which may be brought by the other party on any matters arising out of or in any way connected with this lease (except for personal injury or property damage), the relationship of the Landlord and the Tenant, the Tenant's use or occupancy of the Apartment, or any emergency or other statutory remedy. It is further agreed that if the Landlord commences any summary proceeding, the Tenant will not interpose any counterclaim of whatever nature or description in any such proceeding except as permitted by statute.

**Limitation on
Landlord's
Liability**

13. The Landlord shall not be liable for damage or injury to person or property occurring within the Building or the Apartment, unless caused by or resulting from the negligence of the Landlord or any of the Landlord's agents, servants or employees.

**Inspection of
Apartment;
Entry for
Repairs, etc.**

14. Prospective purchasers of the Building and, during the last six (6) months of the term of this lease, prospective tenants of the Apartment shall be permitted to enter the Apartment at any time between 9 A.M. and 8 P.M. to view the Apartment; and the Landlord and its agents and employees shall be permitted at any time to examine the Apartment at any reasonable hour, and workmen may enter at any time when authorized by the Landlord, to make or facilitate re-

pairs, improvements or decorations in any part of the Building. If the Tenant shall not be personally present to permit any such entry, the Landlord may enter by a master key, or if the Tenant has prevented entry, forcibly, without being liable in damages.

Notices and Consents

15. Any notice by either party to the other, or consent by the Landlord, must be in writing and shall be deemed to be duly given only if personally delivered to the Tenant or mailed by registered or certified mail (return receipt requested) in a postpaid envelope, addressed (a) if to the Tenant, at the Building, and (b) if to the Landlord, at its address, set forth above (or such other address as the Landlord may specify by notice given to the Tenant) or, if none is set forth above, then at the Building.

No Representations or Agreements by Landlord

16. The Tenant has inspected the Building and the Apartment and is thoroughly acquainted with their condition, and agrees to accept them "as is" except that, on or about the date on which the term of this lease commences, the Landlord agrees to do the following work:

The Tenant acknowledges that the taking of possession of the Apartment by the Tenant shall be conclusive evidence that the Apartment and the Building were in good and satisfactory condition at the time such possession was so taken, except as to latent defects. The Landlord agrees that the Apartment and all areas used in conjunction therewith in common with other tenants will be fit for human habitation and for the uses set forth in this lease and that, except to the extent such condition has been caused by the Tenant or any occupant of, or person permitted by the Tenant to use, the Apartment, the Tenant shall not be subjected to any conditions which would be dangerous, hazardous or detrimental to the Tenant's life, health or safety. The Landlord has not made any other representations or agreements, except as contained in this lease.

Quiet Enjoyment

17. The Tenant, on paying the rent and performing its obligations under this lease, shall and may peaceably and quietly have, hold and enjoy the Apartment for the term of this Lease, subject to mortgages and ground and underlying leases to which this lease is subject and subordinate.

Successors and Assigns

Landlord Released on Assignment

18. The provisions of this lease shall bind and enure to the benefit of the Landlord and the Tenant, and their respective successors, legal representatives and assigns. From and after each conveyance and transfer of Landlord's interest in the Building and the land on which the Building stands, the Landlord shall be released from and the Land-

lord's grantee shall become liable for, all unfulfilled obligations of the Landlord under this lease.

Security Deposit

19. The Tenant has delivered to the Landlord the sum of $_____ as security for the faithful performance and observance by the Tenant of its agreements and obligations under this lease. Such security (a) has been deposited in _____, a banking institution located at _____, _____, _____, and delivery of this lease to the Tenant constitutes written notice thereof, or (b) will be deposited in a banking institution and the Tenant will be notified of the name and address of such institution. If there are six (6) or more family dwelling units in the Building, then the account into which such security has been or will be deposited is or will be an interest bearing security account, and unless applied to unpaid rent or additional rent the Landlord will deliver or cause to be delivered to the Tenant, such interest as is allowed on said account at the end of the term, less the one percent (1%) per annum administration expense allowed by law. It is agreed that if the Tenant fails to perform any of the Tenant's agreements or obligations under this lease, including, but not limited to, the Tenant's agreement to pay rent and additional rent, the Landlord may apply or retain the whole or any part of the security so deposited, and any interest accrued thereon, to the extent required for the payment of any rent and additional rent or any other sum which the Tenant is required to pay or for any sum which the Landlord may expend or may be required to expend by reason of the Tenant's failure to perform any of the Tenant's agreements and obligations under this lease, including, but not limited to, any damages or deficiency in the reletting of the Apartment, whether such damages or deficiency accrue before or after summary dispossess proceedings or other re-entry by the Landlord. In the event that the Tenant shall fully and faithfully comply with all of the Tenant's agreements and obligations under this lease, the security and any interest collected and due shall be returned to the Tenant after the end of the term of this lease and the surrender and delivery of possession of the Apartment to the Landlord as required by this lease.

IN WITNESS WHEREOF, the parties hereto have signed this instrument, the day and year above written.

_____
Landlord

_____
Tenant

NOTES AND QUESTIONS

1. The Bar Association form lease is a 1978 revision of an earlier model to reflect various substantive changes (viz. paragraphs 10, 16, and 19) in the law. The lease was also designed to satisfy "The Plain Language Law," which the New York Legislature adopted in 1977. Gen. Oblig. L. §5-701(b) requires that every written lease for residential purposes must be "written in non-technical language and in a clear and coherent manner using words with common and every day meanings." The penalty for noncompliance consists of the tenant's actual damages (quere?) plus fifty dollars. How well do you believe the Bar Association succeeded in using plain language? Compare, for example, paragraph 12 of the Model Lease with the following paragraph in a widely used New York City printed form:

> *Jury trial and counterclaims:* Landlord and Tenant agree not to use their right to a Trial by Jury in any action or proceeding brought by either, against the other, for any matter concerning this Lease or the Apartment. This does not include actions for personal injury or property damage and warranty of habitability actions. Tenant gives up any right to bring a counterclaim or set-off in any action by Landlord against Tenant on any matter directly or indirectly related to this lease. [Blumbert T327—Apartment Lease February, 1981]

2. Writers have occasionally urged that state legislatures promulgate statutory form residential leases that would fully detail the rights and duties, as well as the remedies, of both landlord and tenant. See, e.g., Berger, Hard Leases Make Bad Law, 74 Colum. L. Rev. 791, 819-821 (1974); Bentley, An Alternative Residential Lease, 74 Colum. L. Rev. 836, 879-880 (1974); Kirby, Contract Law and the Form Lease: Can Contract Law Provide the Answer?, 71 Nw. U.L. Rev. 204, 235-237 (1976). Such mandated forms regularly appear in the insurance field. What are the arguments for and against requiring residential landlords and tenants to use state-approved form leases?

3. Recall your own experience as a tenant. Were you tendered a form lease? Did you read it before signing? Did you understand its terms? Did it seem to present fairly the rights and duties of both landlord and tenant?

§5.2   Tenant's Right to Share His or Her Apartment

Leases often limit the occupancy of a residential unit to the tenant and members of the tenant's "immediate family." Consider whether the landlord may enforce this provision against a tenant who shares his or her apartment with a live-in friend, whether of the same or different gender.

HUDSON VIEW PROPERTIES v. WEISS

106 Misc. 2d 251, 431 N.Y.S.2d 632 (Civ. Ct. 1980)

WILK, J. Landlord brings this holdover proceeding to evict tenant on the ground that she is violating a substantial obligation of her tenancy by living with a man to whom she is unrelated by blood or marriage.

Tenant moves to dismiss landlord's petition for failure to state a cause of action. . . .

The facts are, for the most part, uncontested. For purposes of this motion, where they are disputed, I accept the facts as submitted by landlord. Tenant has been living in the same apartment building for 46 years. In January, 1967, tenant, her former husband and their children moved into the rent controlled apartment that she presently occupies under the terms of a lease signed by her former husband. The lease provides, in part, that "the demised premises and any part thereof shall be occupied only by tenant and members of the immediate family of tenant".

Tenant's former husband moved out of the apartment in August, 1976. In December, 1979, a man with whom tenant "has a close and loving relationship" began sharing the apartment with tenant. He treats the apartment as his primary residence.

Consistent with the mandate of Fraydun Enterprises v. Ettinger[1] (91 Misc. 2d 119), landlord has given tenant an opportunity to cure the violation of the lease by ejecting her companion or by bringing him within the ambit of her immediate family (presumably through marriage or adoption).

Tenant contends that the lease provision which prohibits her current living arrangement is void because it violates section 296 (subd. 5, par. [a]) of the Human Rights Law (Executive Law) and section B1-7.0 (subd. 5, par. [a]) of the Law on Human Rights of the City of New York (Administrative Code of City of New York, §B1-7.0, subd. 5, par. [a]).

Section 296 of the Human Rights Law prohibits discrimination in several areas.

Section 296 (subd. 5, par. [a]) provides that:

[i]t shall be an unlawful discriminatory practice for the owner, lessee, sub-lessee, assignee, or managing agent of, or other person having the right to sell, rent or lease a housing accommodation, constructed or to be constructed, or any agent or employee thereof:
(1) To refuse to sell, rent, lease or otherwise to deny to or withhold from any person or group of persons such a housing accommodation because of the race, creed, color, national origin, sex, or disability or marital status of such person or persons. . . .

---

1. While the court held a similar lease clause enforceable, it was not asked to and did not pass upon the effect of the Human Rights Laws.

The Law on Human Rights of the City of New York contains language virtually identical to that of section 296 (subd. 5, par. [a]).

The initial question is whether these facts fall within the "marital status" prohibition of the statute, which was amended in 1975 to include such classification. Although the phrase "marital status" is not further defined by the Legislature, section 300 of the Human Rights Law requires that this statute be liberally construed (300 Gramatan Ave. Assoc. v. State Div. of Human Rights, 45 N.Y.2d 176, 183; City of Schenectady v. State Div. of Human Rights, 37 N.Y.2d 421).

The State Division of Human Rights, the body responsible for enforcement of this law, has consistently taken the position that a refusal to sell or rent to unmarried and unrelated couples constitutes unlawful discrimination on the basis of marital status (Matter of Kramarsky v. Price, Supreme Ct., Schuyler County, April 5, 1978, Index No. 78-29 [other citations omitted]. A reasonable and rational construction of a statute by the agency responsible for its administration should be upheld (Matter of Howard v. Wyman, 28 N.Y.2d 434, 438). . . .

The legislative addition of "marital status" to the Human Rights Laws reflects the profound changes we have experienced in contemporary mores and the now common-place practice of unmarried couples establishing households. Although there is little legislative history to guide us, the language of the statute is manifestly clear. This law prohibits landlords from differentiating between those who are married and those who are not married, all other facts being equal. This is precisely what landlord seeks to do. Tenant may continue to reside in her apartment with her companion if they marry. To require that she leave because their relationship lacks the imprimatur of State or benefit of clergy is to terminate her tenancy because of her marital status. . . .

Landlord's reliance on the contract clause of the United States Constitution is misplaced. In the first instance, it is not clear that the contract clause applies to the facts of this case. However, it is beyond dispute that the contract clause does not subordinate all societal relations to the protection of private contracts. Individual contractual obligations may fall to the State's responsibility to promote "the general good of the public" (Allied Structural Steel Co. v. Spannaus, 438 U.S. 234, 241).

Landlord's remaining constitutional argument is equally unavailing. The due process clauses of the Federal and State Constitutions speak of "life" and "liberty" before "property" and, even when considered in conjunction with the contract clause, do not create a constitutional preference for the protection of property rights. Legislation which is reasonably designed to promote the general welfare of society is not ipso facto unconstitutional because it also affects private property rights (Modjeska Sign Studios v. Berle, 43 N.Y.2d 468, 474).

The addition of "marital status" to section 296 (subd. 5, par. [a]) of the Human Rights Law is well within the purview of the legitimate exercise of government to erect barriers against discrimination based on status. A prohibition against discrimination based on marital status is consistent with both evolving notions of morality and the realities of contemporary urban society, where couples openly live in heterosexual and homosexual units without sanction of State or clergy.

That portion of the lease attempting to sanction discrimination based upon marital status is unenforceable. . . . Tenant's motion is granted and the petition is dismissed.

HUDSON VIEW PROPERTIES v. WEISS
109 Misc. 2d 589, 442 N.Y.S.2d 367 (App. T. 1981)

PER CURIAM. Order entered July 28, 1980 is reversed, with $10 costs; the tenant's motion to dismiss the petition (CPLR 3211, subd. [a], par. 7) is denied. . . .

. . . We are cognizant that section 300 of the Executive Law provides that "[t]he provisions of this article [including of course §296, subd. 5, par. (a)] shall be construed liberally for the accomplishment of the purposes thereof" and that section B1-11.0 of the Administrative Code similarly so provides (see, also, City of Schenectady v. State Div. of Human Rights, 37 N.Y.2d 421, 428). There is nonetheless little in this sparse record to suggest that the landlord, in seeking to enforce the restrictive covenant in the lease limiting occupancy to the tenant and members of tenant's immediate family, had any interest in the marital status of the tenant Weiss or the occupant Wertheimer, other than that Wertheimer was not a member of Weiss' immediate family. An interest in ascertaining whether an occupant qualifies for occupancy of a demised premises, under a lease provision authorizing occupancy by tenant and members of tenant's immediate family (i.e., whether the occupant is a spouse, son, parent or other relation within the scope of "immediate family") does not ipso facto connote discrimination on the basis of "marital status"; thus we are not persuaded by this sparse record that there has been a showing of discrimination by the landlord against the tenant upon the basis of her "marital status". While clearly no cause of action lies under a restrictive covenant in a lease limiting occupancy to the tenant and members of tenant's immediate family, where the tenant has married a newly arrived occupant, it does not follow that a landlord is automatically precluded by section 296 (subd. 5, par. [a]) of the Executive Law from enforcing such a restrictive covenant where the tenant and the new occupant are, for whatever reason, unmarried. In summary, landlord's cause of action predicated upon the covenant in the specified lease restricting occupancy of the subject premises to the tenant and members of tenant's immediate family does not appear to us to constitute discrimination per se on the basis of tenant's "marital status". In concluding that tenant failed to demonstrate that she is entitled to a dismissal of landlord's petition pursuant to CPLR 3211 (subd. [a], par. 7), we do not, however, foreclose the tenant from offering proof at the time of trial that she is entitled to prevail in this proceeding because the landlord in maintaining this proceeding is indeed unlawfully discriminating against her on the basis of her "marital status" (Executive Law, §296, subd. 5, par. [a]). Contrary to the argument made by the landlord, the proscriptions set forth in section 296 (subd. 5, par. [a]) of the Executive Law do not only apply to circumstances existing at the inception of a landlord-tenant relationship. A landlord's conduct during the course of a tenancy may be shown to violate the provisions of section 296 (subd. 5, par. [a]).

ASCH, J. (dissenting). In my opinion, this court should affirm Judge Wilk's dismissal and hold that, under the peculiar facts of this case, to oust Ms. Weiss would be violative of section 296 of article 15 of the Executive Law (Human Rights Law). . . .

. . . [I]t should be noted that the grounds for the dissent are fairly narrow. Concededly, the occupants of the apartment "maintain a close and loving relationship". Yet, it is indisputable that the landlord required a formal marriage as the essential condition for continuing the tenancy. The marriage certificate does not always supply a litmus test for love. Further, under the Human Rights Law, it cannot serve as the key which opens the door to the tenancy of an apartment.

The landlord still has ample discretion to select and reject tenants provided that he does not use categories interdicted under the law, such as, marital status, in screening their suitability.

I would affirm the lower court's dismissal of the petition.

Concur: TIERNEY, J.P., and RICCOBONO, J.; ASCH, J., dissents in a separate memorandum opinion.

HUDSON VIEW PROPERTIES v. WEISS
— A.D.2d — , — N.Y.S.2d — (App. Div. 1982) (N.Y.L.J., Feb. 17, 1982)

Order, Appellate Term, Supreme Court, First Department, entered on July 17, 1981, unanimously reversed, on the law, without costs and without disbursements, for the reasons stated by Asch, J., dissenting at Appellate Term and Wilk, J., at Civil Court and the motion to dismiss the petition of petitioner-respondent granted (Ross, J., concurs in the result only). Order filed.

SANDLER, ROSS, CARRO, and SILVERMAN, JJ.

NOTES AND QUESTIONS

1. Might (should) the *Weiss* case have been similarly decided if New York did not statutorily bar discrimination because of a tenant's "marital status"?

2.   The Census Bureau reported, as of March 1980, the presence of 1.56 million households composed of two unrelated adults of opposite sex. Ten years earlier the number was 523,000. N.Y. Daily News, October 19, 1981, at 45, col. 1. Are such statistics at all relevant in a landlord's suit to enforce the "immediate family" clause in its lease?

3.   Invoking the "immediate family" clause in its lease, landlord sued to recover possession of an apartment whose tenant acknowledged that she had developed a "warm and loving relationship" with her female apartment-mate. Refusing to extend Hudson View Properties v. Weiss, the court granted land-lord a final judgment. To hold otherwise in the case of "homosexuals living together . . . the court would lend itself to the ultimate destruction of the family unit, the foundation of society." Avest Seventh Corp. v. Ringelheim, 109 Misc. 2d 284, 286,—N.Y.S.2d—(Civ. Ct. 1981).

4.   Suppose that a tenant takes in a roommate simply to share expenses, or (e.g., in the case of an elderly or infirm tenant) to gain companionship. In those circumstances should a court enforce the "immediate family" clause?

5.   Suppose that a landlord substitutes for the "immediate family" clause a provision limiting full-time occupancy to one person, the tenant named in the lease. Would *Hudson View Properties* be decided differently?

6.   A related issue involves the refusal of landlords to rent apartments to couples of child-bearing age or to households having minor children. Leases sometimes even call for termination if the tenants bear or adopt a minor child. The California Supreme Court has recently placed a lid on such restrictions. Marina Point, Ltd. v. Wolfson, 180 Cal. Rptr. 496 (1982).

§5.3   The Doctrine of Unconscionability

New York Real Property Law §235-c provides:

> 1.   If the court as a matter of law finds a lease or any clause of the lease to have been unconscionable at the time it was made the court may refuse to enforce the lease, or it may enforce the remainder of the lease without the uncon-scionable clause, or it may so limit the application of any unconscionable clause as to avoid any unconscionable result.
>
> 2.   When it is claimed or appears to the court that a lease or any clause thereof may be unconscionable the parties shall be afforded a reasonable oppor-tunity to present evidence as to its setting, purpose and effect to aid the court in making the determination.

New York is now one of several states that has brought the doctrine of unconscionability into the law of landlord and tenant. Consider the doctrine's application in the following case. Have lap dogs joined widows and orphans as a sympathetic object?

HOLLYWOOD LEASING CORP. v. ROSENBLUM

100 Misc. 2d 120, 418 N.Y.S.2d 887 (Civ. Ct. 1979)

SHILLING, J. In this holdover summary proceeding, landlord petitioner maintains that tenant respondents, by keeping a dog in their residential apartment, are committing a substantial breach of their lease which contains a provision prohibiting the harboring of animals on the premises without written consent of the landlord. The lease in question, a standard residential form lease, also contains a clause prohibiting waiver by the landlord of any provision therein, as well as a clause providing that no oral representations have been made by landlord or its agents, other than those contained within the four corners of the form lease itself. Landlord relies on the afore-mentioned provisions in instituting summary proceedings to evict tenants from their apartment.

Tenants, for their answer, maintain as an affirmative defense to this proceeding, that the lease provision in question is unconscionable in that at the time the lease was executed they had had extensive discussions with landlord's agents about their desire to obtain a dog to provide companionship for their small child who had recently lost a sibling through death; that the lease was signed at tenant's kitchen table with the puppy in tenant's lap and the landlord's agent patting the dog on its head; that the agent stated at that time that tenants should disregard the no-pet provision of the lease and represented orally that landlord consented to the presence of the dog, having all apparent authority to do so. Although common instincts might dictate that such a clause be crossed out of the lease, the testimony adduced at trial is unrefuted that tenants are laymen, that they relied on agent's representations at the time of execution of the lease, and that other tenants in the same building keep animals in their apartments regardless of standard form leases containing similar no-pet provisions. It is also a fact that at no time has landlord alleged that tenant's particular dog has created a nuisance or danger on the premises.

Therefore, as a matter of law, this court finds that, pursuant to section 235-c of the Real Property Law, the lease provision in question is unconscionable under the circumstances existing at the time of execution of the lease, and that said clause will not be enforced against tenants in order to avoid an unconscionable result. Petition dismissed with prejudice.

Generally, the law regarding the harboring of animals in violation of a written lease provision is not settled; indeed, the courts are not in accord as to whether the mere fact that a tenant is keeping a dog on the premises is a violation of such magnitude as to constitute a breach of a substantial obligation of the terms of the tenancy (thus warranting eviction) in the absence of proof that the animal is an actual danger or nuisance to other residents or in the absence of a specific clause in the lease deeming such violation a substantial breach. " 'Substantial' is a word of general reference which takes on color and precision from its total context. Having little if any meaning when considered in abstract or in vacuum, it must be defined with reference to the particular legal and factual state in which it occurs." (New York Life Ins. Co. v. Dick, 71 Misc. 2d 52, 61; Rasch, New York Landlord and Tenant, Summary Proceedings [2d ed.] §1063, and cases cited therein.)

There is no doubt, however, that in and of itself, a clause prohibiting the harboring of animals in residential premises is reasonable and enforceable. (Riverbay Corp. v. Klinghoffer, 34 A.D.2d 630; Pollack v. Green Constr. Corp., 40 A.D.2d 996, *aff'd* 32 N.Y.2d 720.) The court does not contest this holding, but finds that, under the specific factual circumstances of the instant case, the enforcement of such a lease provision would produce an unconscionable result.

The doctrine of unconscionability is relatively new to the law of landlord-tenant. Effective 1976, section 235-c of the Real Property Law, like the statutory warranty of habitability, attempts to place the tenant in legal parity with the landlord by recognizing that a residential lease is more akin to the purchase of shelter and services rather than the conveyance of a feudal estate, and that the law of sales, derived from contract principles, provides an analogy better suited than the outmoded law of property to determine the respective obligations of landlord and tenant. (Park West Mgt. Corp. v. Mitchell, 47 N.Y.2d 316, citing Green v. Superior Ct., 10 Cal. 3d 616, 626–627.)

Section 235-c of the Real Property Law is derived from section 2-302 of the Uniform Commercial Code (L. 1962, ch. 553, eff. Sept. 27, 1964). The Uniform Commercial Code codified the doctrine, essentially equitable in nature, which was used by the common-law courts to invalidate contracts under certain conditions. An unconscionable contract was one "such as no man in his senses and not under delusion would make on the one hand, and as no honest and fair man would accept on the other." (Earl of Chesterfield v. Janssen, 2 Ves. Sen. 125, 155; 28 Eng. Rep. 82, 100 [1750]; cf. Hume v. United States, 132 U.S. 406.) A contractual clause would not be enforced where it was "so monstrous and extravagant that it would be a reproach to the administration of justice to countenance or uphold it." (Greer v. Tweed, 13 Abb. Prac. [N.S.] 427, 429.)

As codified under the Uniform Commercial Code, the term "unconscionability" is not defined, nor are the factors or elements thereof enumerated. The official comment under section 2-302 explains that "[t]he basic test is whether, in the light of the general commercial background and the commercial needs of the particular trade or case, the clauses involved are so one-sided as to be unconscionable under the circumstances existing at the time of the making of the contract. . . . The principle is one of the prevention of oppression and unfair surprise". Commentators have elaborated on this broad explication to distinguish procedural unconscionability, wherein evidence of the contract-formation process must be scrutinized, and substantive unconscionability, wherein substantive elements of unconscionability must be identified in the content of the contract per se, either as an overall "elaborate lopsidedness" of the contract in its entirety, or as an example of "one-clause naughtiness". (Leff, Unconscionability and the Code—The Emperor's New Clause, 115 U. of Pa. L. Rev. 485, 512, 513; Murray, Unconscionability: Unconscionability, 31 U. of Pitt. L. Rev. 1.) Case law in this area has stressed various elements for determining the existence of unconscionability in a particular factual situation. High pressure sales tactics, failure to disclose terms of the contract, misrepresentation and fraud on the part of the seller (i.e., the party offering the contract, often on a take-it-or-leave-it basis; here, the landlord), refusal to bargain on certain crucial terms, clauses hidden in fine print and unequal bargaining power aggravated by the fact that the consumer, in many cases, cannot speak English, have been recognized as procedurally unconscionable. (Nu Dimension Figure Salons v. Becerra, 73 Misc. 2d 140; Brooklyn Union Gas Co. v. Jimeniz, 82 Misc. 2d 948.) Inflated prices, including grossly inadequate consideration given by the seller, unfair disclaimers of warranty and termination clauses have been deemed substantively unconscionable. (Industralease Automated & Scientific Equip. Corp. v. R.M.E. Enterprises, 58 A.D.2d 482.) These examples are, by no means, exhaustive. The concept of unconscionability must necessarily be applied flexibly depending on all the facts and circumstances of a given case. The weight given to each factor is as variable as the facts of each case. (Matter of Friedman, 64 A.D.2d 70.)

A consideration of case law and economic reason has led courts to extend the principles of section 2-302 of the Uniform Commercial Code to landlord-tenant situations. With the transformation of the housing market by rapid urbanization and population growth, and the growing trend toward characterizing a lease as a contract, the medieval concept of "Caveat lessee" is being eliminated. "[L]essees . . . are usually occasional customers, not acquainted with the carefully drafted legal terms set forth in such printed form leases. The landlord and his agents, assisted by expert legal counsel, carefully draft the lease in language designed solely for the landlord's protection. When the landlord presents the lease to the lessee for acceptance and execution he is usually fully cognizant of the fact that the other party has not read or bargained for many of the incidental terms of the contract. The terms of the printed contract are usually nonnegotiable. In most cases the tenant is not represented by counsel. The landlord's position is superior. He not only possesses superior knowledge, but offers a scarce commodity. . . . The landlord is a merchant in a sellers' market place. . . . If one is a merchant, he has a special skill or particular knowledge; and for this reason he is held by the court to a completely different set of rules which are generally more strict than the rules that apply to nonmerchants. . . . A merchant is to be held to a higher standard of conduct by the court. . . . The lessee that has no choice but to sign an unconscionable lease agreement or not take the premises must be protected against the bad bargain he enters into. The lease in such cases is the equivalent of a consumer contract. The concept of laissez-faire, that is if the purchaser does not agree to lease of the seller he can go elsewhere, has no place in our enlightened society where lessor and lessee do not deal on equal terms and where lessee for all practical purposes does not have the option of shopping around for available renting accommodations of his choice." (Seabrook v. Commuter Housing Co., 72 Misc. 2d 6, 7-8.)

The dominant belief of the laissez-faire system of late 18th and 19th century America was that parties were free to contract as they chose without interference by the courts, regardless of resulting harsh or oppressive terms. This almost sacred adherence to the concept of freedom of contract found its justification in the basic principle of contract law that one is bound by the writing one signs. Only recently has it been recognized that there can be no genuine assent where bargaining power is unequal and where often the only choice presented is "take-it-or-leave-it." Today, the use of the form contract has become a necessary and economically advantageous component of the mass transaction. The code does not alter axiomatic contract principles but rather strengthens and transforms the outmoded concept of unrestrained freedom of contract to that of freedom of intended bargain. The doctrine of unconscionability deals with the pathology of nonbargaining. "There is no freedom of contract in the equal treatment of unequals." (Murray, p. 28.) Underlying all contracts in such a system are the code's basic obligations of good faith and fair dealing. (Uniform Commercial Code, §§1-203, 2-103.)

In the instant case, the landlord has clearly violated such obligations. Despite oral representations and assurances to the tenants at the time of execution of the lease that they may have a pet, landlord now chooses to invoke a written clause prohibiting animals without landlord's written consent. Under circumstances such as these, the lease cannot be regarded as a sacrosanct document and landlord cannot be permitted to resort to the drastic remedy of eviction. Of crucial consideration is the fact that there have been no allegations that tenants' particular dog is a nuisance or danger to others. There is no indication as to why landlord has waited several years to invoke this form clause and this court will not allow it to do so simply because it is there. As a matter of law, pursuant to section 235-c of the Real Property Law, the court finds the clause unconscionable and unenforceable. Petition dismissed with prejudice.

NOTES AND QUESTIONS

1. What was unconscionable: the clause prohibiting pets, the clause prohibiting pets as applied to the tenants' dog in this case, the clause barring oral changes in the lease, the landlord's behavior, or none of the above? Might tenant have prevailed without reference to the doctrine of unconscionability?

2. The court stressed that tenants were laymen and also quoted from an earlier opinion describing most tenants as "occasional consumers, not acquainted with the carefully drafted legal terms set forth in such printed form leases." Should the case have been decided differently if tenants had been first-year law students? experienced attorneys? real estate brokers? Compare Hal-

prin v. 2 Fifth Avenue Co., 101 Misc. 2d 943, 948, 422 N.Y.S.2d 275, 279 (Sup. Ct. 1979) (although tenants were "sophisticated, intelligent and highly educated persons, including, inter alia, lawyers, corporate executives . . . and a college professor," this does not preclude a finding of unconscionability) with Graziano v. Tortora Agency, 78 Misc. 2d 1094, 1096, 359 N.Y.S.2d 489,— (Civ. Ct. 1974) (where tenant is "knowledgeable, sophisticated real estate broker, the court cannot take seriously this kind of litigant complaining of an unfair advantage taken against it in a real estate transaction.") The *Halprin* decision was later reversed; the appellate division did not think the disputed clause all that offensive. 75 A.D.2d 565 (1980). The court's memorandum decision fails to consider, however, whether the tenants' sophistication would have prevented a successful unconscionability claim.

   3.   The Uniform Residential Landlord and Tenant Act (URLTA) borrowed §1.303, *infra,* its unconscionability provision, almost verbatim from the Uniform Commercial Code. Eleven of the states (Arizona, Florida, Hawaii, Iowa, Kansas, Kentucky, Montana, Nebraska, New Mexico, Oregon, and Tennessee) that have enacted URLTA have retained substantially all of §1.303. Note also the similarity of the New York statute, p. 249 *supra,* with §1.303. Does either the statutory language or comment help a lawyer decide when a lease, or part thereof, *is* unconscionable?

Section 1.303   Unconscionability

> (a) If the court, as a matter of law, finds
>> (1) a rental agreement or any provision thereof was unconscionable when made, the court may refuse to enforce the agreement, enforce the remainder of the agreement without the unconscionable provision, or limit the application of any unconscionable provision to avoid an unconscionable result; or
>> (2) a settlement in which a party waives or agrees to forego a claim or right under this Act or under a rental agreement was unconscionable when made, the court may refuse to enforce the settlement, enforce the remainder of the settlement without the unconscionable provision, or limit the application of any unconscionable provision to avoid an unconscionable result.
> (b) If unconscionability is put into issue by a party or by the court upon its own motion the parties shall be afforded a reasonable opportunity to present evidence as to the setting, purpose, and effect of the rental agreement or settlement to aid the court in making the determination.

Comment

   This Section, adapted from the Uniform Commercial Code and the Consumer Credit Code, is intended to make it possible for the courts to police explicitly against rental agreements, clauses, settlements, or waivers of claim or right which they find to be unconscionable. This Section is intended to allow the courts to pass directly on the issue of unconscionability and to make a conclusion of law as to unconscionability. The basic test is whether, in light of the background and setting of the market, the conditions of the particular parties to the rental agreement, settlement or waiver of right or claim are so one-sided as to be unconscionable under the circumstances existing at the time of the making of the agreement or settlement. Thus, the particular facts involved in each case are of utmost importance since unconscionability may exist in some situations but not in others. Either landlords or tenants may, in appropriate circumstances, avail themselves of this Section.

4.   Weaver v. American Oil Co., 257 Ind. 458, 276 N.E.2d 144 (1971), is the leading pre-URLTA leasehold unconscionability decision. The lessee, a filling station operator, had signed a printed form contract which contained a "hold harmless" clause requiring him, inter alia, to indemnify the oil company lessor for any negligence of the *oil company* occurring on the leased premises. An oil company employee negligently sprayed gasoline upon the lessee's assistant, and suit was brought to determine the lessee's liability to the oil company under this clause. In refusing to enforce the "hold harmless" clause, the court drew upon the analogy with §2-302 of the Uniform Commercial Code:

> Caveat lessee is no more the current law than caveat emptor. Only in this way can justice be served and the true meaning of freedom of contract preserved. The analogy is rational. We have previously pointed out a similar situation in the Uniform Commercial Code, which prohibits unconscionable contract clauses in sales agreements.
>
> When a party can show that the contract, which is sought to be enforced, was in fact an unconscionable one, due to a prodigious amount of bargaining power on behalf of the stronger party, which is used to the stronger party's advantage and is unknown to the lesser party, causing a great hardship and risk on the lesser party, the contract provision, or the contract as a whole, if the provision is not separable, should not be enforceable on the grounds that the provision is contrary to public policy. The party seeking to enforce such a contract has the burden of showing that the provisions were explained to the other party and *came to his knowledge* and there was in fact *a real and voluntary meeting of the minds and not merely an objective meeting*. . . .
>
> We do not mean to say or infer that parties may not make contracts exculpating one of his negligence and providing for indemnification, but it must be done *knowingly* and *willingly* as in insurance contracts made for that very purpose. [Court's emphasis] [257 Ind. 458, 464, 465, 276 N.E.2d 144, 148]

The court had earlier stressed that the lessee was a high-school dropout who had signed the lease without legal counsel.

The *Weaver* opinion evoked an angry dissent:

> Chief Justice Arterburn, speaking for a majority of this court, has concluded that the defendant was in an inferior position with respect to the lease and

treats the lease as we might treat an *adhesion* contract. I find justification for neither. An adhesion contract is one that has been drafted unilaterally by the dominant party and then presented on a "take it or leave it" basis to the weaker party, who has no real opportunity to bargain about its terms. (Restatement 2d, Conflicts of Law §332a, Comment *e*) (17 C.J.S. Contracts §10, p. 581.) Here we have a printed form contract prepared by American. There was great disparity between the economic positions of American and Defendant; and Defendant was a man of limited educational and business background. However, there is nothing from which we can find or infer that the printed lease provisions were not subject to negotiation or that, with respect to this particular lease, Defendant was not in a bargaining position equal to that of American. The fact that Defendant did not avail himself of the opportunity to read the agreement but elected to accept it as presented does not warrant the inference that his only options were to "take it or leave it." That the "hold harmless" clause was or might have been in small print, as suggested by the majority, can hardly have significance in light of the claim and finding that the defendant did not read any portion of the document. . . .

[I]t is clear that the uniform commercial code sections on sales cited by the majority can have no application; and Chief Justice Arterburn was careful to point out that it was referred to only to illustrate the acceptance of legal philosophies permitting and fostering fair dealings and substantive justice rather than blind and often unjust adherence to hard and fast rules. But we have neither the duty nor the right to abandon established principles whenever, in our judgment, it is necessary to avert a hardship. And should the Legislature see fit to vest us with either or both, I question that we have the requisite wisdom. It is for this reason, I believe, that our mandate is not simply to administer justice but to do so *under the law*. I hold no special interest in preserving the policy of enforcing indemnity and exculpatory contracts. It may well be that they should be greatly curtailed. But the majority opinion does not so hold. Defendant's dilemma does not spring from an unconscionable advantage taken of him either by deceit of American or by virtue of a superior bargaining position. It clearly stems from either an unwillingness or indifference upon his part to utilize the resources available to him or from a willingness to assume the risks in exchange for the rewards that he hoped to gain. Presumably he has had the benefits contracted for, and the majority decision is a grant of retrospective unilateral contractual immunity to the careless and speculative and places a premium upon ignorance. I fear that it will stand as an invitation to any litigant, who finding himself burdened by his own contract, will say that he did not understand its provisions and ask us for relief that we have neither the duty, right nor wisdom to grant. . . .
[Id. at 474, 476, 276 N.E.2d 144, 153-155]

In your opinion, who has the better of the argument?

Contrast *Weaver* with Levine v. Shell Oil Co., 28 N.Y.2d 205, 269 N.E.2d 799 (1971) ("hold harmless" clause enforceable; "no showing that the agreement . . . either a contract of adhesion or . . . unconscionable").

See also O'Callaghan v. Waller & Beckwith Realty Co., 15 Ill. 2d 436, 155 N.E.2d 545 (1958) (court enforces "exculpatory" clause despite tenant's claim of unconscionability).

5. Consider whether you believe that, as a matter of law, a court should deem unconscionable any of the following clauses appearing in a residential lease:

(a) Tenant agrees to a jury trial waiver. See In re Estate of Greenberg, 102 Misc. 2d 308, 425 N.Y.S.2d 909 (N.Y. App. Div. 1979); Koslowski v. Palmieri, 94 Misc. 2d 555, 404 N.Y.S.2d 799 (Civ. Ct. 1978), reversed on other grounds, 98 Misc. 2d 885, 414 N.Y.S.2d 599 (App. T. 1979) (such clause not unconscionable).

(b) Tenant agrees to forfeit one month's rent, although landlord suffers no damage, for premature termination of lease. See Zemp v. Rowland, 31 Or. App. 1005, 572 P.2d 637 (1977) (such clause not unconscionable, but one judge dissents).

6. Can a lease provision that restates the common law be unconscionable? Can a lease by its omission be unconscionable—for example, where a lease systematically fails to apprise tenant of his common-law or statutory rights and remedies? Cf. Berger, Hard Leases Make Bad Law, 74 Colum. L. Rev. 791, 821-833 (1974).

7. The Commonwealth of Pennsylvania sued to enjoin twenty-five large landlords from using standard form agreements, which the complaint described as "unconscionable contracts of adhesion." In dismissing the complaint, the trial court wrote:

> If there ever was a description of a sociologically desirable legislative program for the entire commonwealth through the improper use of "judicial intervention", the aforesaid statement from the commonwealth's brief sets it forth. Unless and until the General Assembly of Pennsylvania or some higher court directs this court, in effect, to establish social legislation (no matter how desirable it may be), this court will condemn and refuse such "judicial intervention". Courts in this country are about the business of determining people's rights, based upon presented facts and applicable law. If the particular provisions of leases used in this commonwealth (only generally referred to and certainly not set forth with any specificity by the commonwealth in its complaint) are as onerous as alleged, then the proper method to test the legality of such leases is to bring a specific action, with respect to specific harm done to some specific citizen, against specific defendants on specific leases. If the commonwealth desires a broad approach, the matter should be laid before the General Assembly. . . .
>
> In reality, the commonwealth is requesting this court to determine for an entire industry that provisions of agreements which are onerous to the attorney general, but which have not yet been declared illegal or unconstitutional per se, be declared illegal, null and void. The commonwealth's approach in this case would be analogous to the Department of Environmental Resources bringing a lawsuit against 25 owners of buildings with smokestacks and four builders of smokestacks, seeking to enjoin them from emitting particulate matter from

smokestacks in excess of that department's regulation, with the intent of enjoining all such smokestacks in the commonwealth. . . .

There can be no question that under the law of this commonwealth contracts of adhesion are violative of public policy and should be given no legal effect. It is also quite clear, however, that the phrase "contracts of adhesion" cannot be attached a priori to every form lease, but rather contracts of adhesion can only be determined based upon appropriate facts concerning specific parties under specific circumstances. As our supreme court has noted, contracts containing clauses which could be declared to constitute contracts of adhesion will not be so declared under lease contracts between corporations with equal bargaining power. Cf. Employers Liability Assurance Corp. Ltd. v. Greenville Business Men's Assoc., 224 A.2d 620 (1966).

The commonwealth argues that the form leases generally described are contracts of adhesion because "poor" persons who are prospective tenants must accept the terms of the landlord's form lease or obtain no housing whatsoever. While this court abhors the use of form leases which are overly protective and unfairly drawn to the benefit of the landlord, before such lease may be determined to be a contract of adhesion and therefore of no legal effect, specific facts pertaining to specific instances and specific tenants and landlords must be alleged and proven. [Pennsylvania v. Monumental Properties, Inc., Pa. Cmwl. Ct., Nov. 7, 1973]

On appeal to the Pennsylvania Supreme Court, the commonwealth won on the narrow issue that the state's consumer protection law covered unfair or deceptive practices in connection with the leasing of housing. The court remanded the suit for trial on the issues of unfairness and deception. Pa. Sup. Ct., Dec. 5, 1974.

8. Compare the doctrine of unconscionability with the doctrine of fair dealing, §5.12, *infra*.

BERGER, HARD LEASES MAKE BAD LAW
74 Colum. L. Rev. 791, 814-815 (1974)

While this may be so, a larger issue remains that the present system fails to moot. It is the issue of "contract integrity"—the integrity of the paper that seals the bargain. Here I use "integrity" in a dual sense. I refer both to the honesty or fairness of the contract and to its even-handed completeness.

In the context of the lease, let me illustrate what I mean. A and B make a lease. What they negotiate, however, is far less detailed than the instrument they sign. The negotiated oral transaction seldom goes beyond the monthly rental and the duration of the lease. These terms often are flexible, and the final bargain responds to the urgency with which each party needs to obtain or get rid of the space. Thus, even during an apartment shortage, some owners may readily make a rent concession if their buildings are renting poorly. Conversely, some tenants will pay dearly for apartments they badly want even during a market glut. Thus, as to the *negotiated* bargain, chronic disparity between landlord and tenant would be hard to prove.

If the negotiated bargain were the entire transaction, the written lease would be one paragraph long. But, of course, the landlord-tenant relation is far more complex, and the non-bargained part of the transaction occupies most of the written form. This is where the principle of contract integrity enters. It would require:

1. That the lease fairly describe all the unspoken expectations of the parties. For example, if the tenant expects to receive and the landlord expects to furnish heat, hot and cold running water, trash removal, a minimum level of security, or janitorial service, these rights and duties should be set forth.

2. That the lease fairly describe all basic statutory and common-law rights of the parties. For example, where statute requires landlord to hold the tenant's security deposit in an interest-bearing account, interest payable annually to the tenant, the lease should say so.

3. That the lease describe the tenant's remedies with the same completeness and detail that it describes the landlord's remedies. Thus, tenants would read in their lease of rent-withholding, repair-and-offset, or rescission, where these remedies were available.

4. That the lease distinguish *fairly* between major ("substantial") and minor ("insubstantial") duties, and indicate what penalties follow the breach of each.

5. That the lease not contain any surprises. A tenant who expected to get delivery of the apartment on April 1 should not discover, if the previous tenant unlawfully holds over, that the landlord may recover rent even though the apartment is not ready. If the landlord wants to bargain for such a surprising right, he must *ask* for it during the oral negotiations.

6. That the lease be written for a layman's understanding.

Contract integrity and contract unconscionability occupy the opposing ends of a spectrum. Between them lie many shades of tolerated agreement. Since unconscionability is a doctrine of last resort, virtually any contract that does not shock the conscience is presumptively valid. But I suggest that the legal system should espouse a higher norm, one that contract integrity can help fulfill. Each party who signs an agreement should sense its truth and essential fairness and should believe that the paper fully states his rights and remedies, that it captures both parties' understanding, that it conceals no hookers, and that it is understandable. Uninformed or misinformed parties to a contract are easily terrorized or disarmed into foregoing their rights and remedies, and contract integrity would help prevent that. I also believe, and have tried to show, that hard leases often make bad law, and while no reform can root out the defects of intellect or of fairness among our judges, contract integrity would allow courts to apply their powers of reason and their spirit of impartiality to a dispute far more readily than does today's standard form lease.

§5.4   Which Law Applies: Contract or Conveyance?

As we saw in Chapter 4, tenancies are one form of common-law estate in land. The legal device for the creation of such estates, to wit, the lease, has traditionally been viewed as a conveyance of an interest in land, just as the deed is a conveyance that transfers, inter vivos, a fee simple absolute. Because it was seen as a conveyance, and not as a contract, the lease—and, derivatively, the rights of landlord and tenant—continued mostly to be shaped by tenets of property law long after contract law had formulated principles that, if applied to the dispute at hand, might have changed the outcome. Although, as you are about to witness, contract rules have begun to permeate strongly the law of landlord and tenant, old notions fade slowly. The following decision illustrates the uneasy dichotomy between the lease *qua* conveyance and the lease *qua* contract.

219 BROADWAY CORP. v. ALEXANDER'S, INC.
46 N.Y.2d 506, 389 N.E.2d 467, 415 N.Y.S. 2d 985 (1979)

JASEN, J. The specific issue raised on this appeal is whether a complaint which alleges a breach of a written lease, yet explicitly concedes that such lease was never delivered, states a cause of action.

Plaintiff, 219 Broadway Corp., alleges that its representatives and those of defendant, Alexander's, Inc., conducted extensive negotiations between August, 1974 and June, 1975 with the expectation that mutually acceptable terms could be reached concerning the leasing of certain premises by defendant, as lessor, to plaintiff, as lessee. Plaintiff planned to utilize this property, located on Broadway between 219th Street and 220th Street in New York City, as a parking lot.

As a result of the negotiations, an agreement was reached as to the terms of the lease and an instrument was drafted which provided for plaintiff to lease the subject premises from defendant for a 10-year term at an annual rental rate of $6,000 for the initial five years and $6,600 for the remaining five years. The lease and an accompanying memorandum for recording were duly signed by the plaintiff on June 25, 1975, and thereafter forwarded to the attorneys for the defendant. Plaintiff alleges, upon information and belief, that "subsequent thereto, the defendant executed the said lease and memorandum thereof but refused and still refuses to deliver the said lease to the plaintiff."

In August, 1975, the attorneys for the defendant informed the plaintiff's attorneys that the defendant had leased the premises to a third party. Plaintiff, learning of this turn of events, commenced this action by service of a summons and complaint in which it seeks specific performance of the lease, or, in the alternative, money damages resulting from its breach. Defendant moved to dismiss the complaint on the ground that it failed to state a cause of action. (CPLR 3211, subd. [a], par. 7.) Special Term denied defendant's motion, reasoning that "the signatures of [the] lessor and lessee are sufficient to validate a lease." The Appellate Division unanimously reversed, holding, inter alia, that absent delivery, a lease is ineffective. An appeal to this court ensued from the order of the Appellate Division. There should be an affirmance.

Initially, we note the procedural posture in which this case comes before us. The sole question presented for our review is whether the plaintiff's complaint states a cause of action. As such, we accept, as we must, each and every allegation forwarded by the plaintiff without expressing any opinion as to the plaintiff's ability ultimately to establish the truth of these averments before the trier of the facts. (See, e.g., Becker v. Schwartz, 46 N.Y.2d 401, 408; Cohn v. Lionel Corp., 21 N.Y.2d 559, 562; Kober v. Kober, 16 N.Y.2d 191, 193.) If we find that the plaintiff is entitled to a recovery upon any reasonable view of the stated facts, our judicial inquiry is complete and we must declare the plaintiff's complaint to be legally sufficient. (See, e.g., Dulberg v. Mock, 1 N.Y.2d 54, 56; Condon v. Associated Hosp. Serv. of N.Y., 287 N.Y. 411, 414.)

In addressing the issue presented, we take cognizance of the hybrid nature of a lease. Only recently we have noted that "a lease, especially a modern lease, is generally more than a simple conveyance of an interest in land for a fixed period of time. Typically it is also a contract which requires the parties, particularly the tenant, to fulfill certain obligations while the lease is in effect." (Geraci v. Jenrette, 41 N.Y.2d 660, 665.) Thus, it can be said, and we would be remiss not to recognize, that a lease achieves two ends, to wit: the conveyance of an estate in real property from lessor to lessee and the delineation of the parties' rights and obligations pursuant thereto.

Plaintiff, seizing upon this judicial acknowledgment of the dual function of a lease, would argue that the validity of the instrument, as a conveyance of an estate in land, should be governed by what are said to be contract principles. Since it is alleged in plaintiff's complaint that the lease and the accompanying memorandum for recording were duly "executed" by both the plaintiff and the defendant, plaintiff contends that it has adequately demonstrated, at the pleading stage, its right to demand specific performance, or, in the alternative, to recover money damages. Specifically, plaintiff cites compliance with section 5-703 of the General Obligations Law to bolster its position.* Inasmuch as that provision imposes no requirement that a lease be delivered to

---

* Section 5-703 of the General Obligations Law provides:

　　1.　An estate or interest in real property, other than a lease for a term not exceeding one year, or any trust or power, over or concerning real property, or in any manner relating thereto, cannot be created, granted, assigned, surrendered or declared, unless by act or operation of law, or by a deed or conveyance in writing, subscribed by the person creating, granting, assigning, surrendering or declaring the same, or by his lawful agent, thereunto authorized by writing. But this subdivision does not affect the power of a testator in the disposition of his real property by will; nor prevent any trust from arising or being extinguished by implication or operation of law, nor any declaration of trust from being proved by a writing subscribed by the person declaring the same.

　　2.　A contract for the leasing for a longer period than one year, or for the sale, of any real property, or an interest therein, is void unless the contract or some note or memorandum thereof, expressing the consideration, is in writing, subscribed by the party to be charged, or by his lawful agent thereunto authorized by writing.

take effect, plaintiff asserts that the lease, and all rights and obligations of the parties thereunder, became fully binding once the instrument was duly signed by the defendant. With this contention, we cannot agree.

By its very terms, section 5-703 of the General Obligations Law speaks only to the requirement that conveyances and contracts concerning real property be memorialized in writing. Nowhere does the statute provide, or its language even remotely suggest, that its provisions were intended to supplant the traditional prerequisites for the conveyance of an interest in real property. In the absence of such legislative directive, the issue posed on this appeal, namely whether a lease must be delivered to take effect, must be resolved by application of time-weathered principles of real property law. (Cf. Kahn v. Kahn, 43 N.Y.2d 203, 209.)

Plaintiff's reliance upon our holding in Geraci v. Jenrette (41 N.Y.2d 660, *supra*) to support its contention that a lease can be enforced against the party sought to be charged once facts sufficient to demonstrate compliance with section 5-703 of the General Obligations Law are alleged is misplaced. Our holding in *Geraci* was limited to a determination of whether a lease is, or is not, a contract within the Statute of Frauds (General Obligations Law, §5-703, subd. 2). In view of our disposition that it was, it became unnecessary to consider the further issue of whether parties who have signed a lease could be bound by its terms, absent a showing of delivery.

While, as previously noted, a lease is often chameleonic in both character and function, its fundamental purpose remains to serve as a vehicle for the conveyance of an interest in real property. Until this end is achieved, any rights or obligations of the parties which may be embodied in the lease remain dormant. Thus, the threshold inquiry in this case becomes whether, under the facts alleged, the lease served to convey an estate in real property from the defendant to the plaintiff.

A lease, as in the case of conveyances of an interest in land generally, requires the fulfillment by the parties of certain prerequisites to take effect. It is the well-established rule in this State that delivery is one such requirement, the absence of which, without more, renders the lease ineffective. [Citations omitted.]

The requirement that a lease be delivered to be effective as a conveyance of an interest in land is not peculiar to this State alone, but is ingrained in the common-law principles of real property in many States. [Citations omitted.]

---

3. A contract to devise real property or establish a trust of real property, or any interest therein or right with reference thereto, is void unless the contract or some note or memorandum thereof is in writing and subscribed by the party to be charged therewith, or by his lawfully authorized agent.

4. Nothing contained in this section abridges the powers of courts of equity to compel the specific performance of agreements in cases of part performance.

In Geraci v. Jenrette (41 N.Y.2d 660, *supra*), this court held that a lease is a contract within the meaning of subdivision 2 of this section, and is therefore void unless signed by the person against whom enforcement is sought.

The underlying justification for viewing delivery as fundamental to the conveyance of an interest in land is not grounded in the blind application of what some may consider archaic principles of property law. On the contrary, delivery serves a very practical end. It is a common practice in the contemporary business world for parties to draft and sign instruments of conveyance prior to the time at which they intend their contemplated transaction to become irrevocable. By requiring delivery, the law facilitates the true expectations of the parties by ensuring that the interest in the property is not conveyed until that moment when the parties so intend.

Inasmuch as delivery is required for a lease to take effect and being concerned, as we are, with the legal sufficiency of the plaintiff's complaint, we proceed to an examination of plaintiff's allegations bearing upon the issue of delivery. Plaintiff's sole allegation in this regard is that a written lease and memorandum for recording were duly "executed" by it and, after being forwarded, were subsequently "executed" by the defendant. Plaintiff concedes that the defendant never returned the written lease. In light of these bare assertions, we now hold that the plaintiff has failed to state a cause of action for which recovery can be sought. Since plaintiff did not allege a delivery of the lease—indeed, it alleged nondelivery—it may not now be heard to seek enforcement of a written lease which, as a matter of law, never became effective.

In determining whether pleaded allegations are sufficient to allege a delivery, we recognize that the concept of delivery is not given to precise definition or controlled by fixed formalities. It can be said, however, with as much certainty as this sometimes elusive concept permits, that a delivery of a lease so as to give it effect requires acts or words or both acts and words which clearly manifest that it is the intent of the parties that an interest in the land is, in fact, being conveyed to the lessee. (See, generally, 1 Rasch, New York Landlord and Tenant [2d ed.], §18; 3 Thompson, Real Property [1959 ed.], §1059; cf. Ten Eyck v. Whitbeck, 156 N.Y. 341, 352; Bianco v. Furia, 41 Misc. 2d 292; 15 N.Y. Jur., Deeds, §47.)

The due signature of the lease instrument is but one step in the process of conveying an interest in land. Delivery requires something more. There must be evidence of an unequivocal intent that the interest intended to be conveyed is, in fact, being conveyed. The mere signing of the instrument by parties not in the presence of each other, without more, does not evince such intent. (See Whitford v. Laidler, 94 N.Y. 145, 151-152, *supra;* P & R Realty Corp. v. Hagel, 191 Misc. 732, 734, *supra;* cf. Marden v. Dorthy, 160 N.Y. 39, 49.)

In reaching the conclusion that we do, we observe, as did the Appellate Division, that the "complaint does not allege breach by [defendant] of an executory contract to enter into a lease for the parking lot." (61 A.D.2d 917.) Accordingly, we do not reach the question whether, had there been such an allegation, the complaint should have been dismissed. Nor do we reach or consider the broad question whether, and in what circumstances, signature alone will suffice to create an enforceable contract.

In sum, we hold that a plaintiff must plead allegations sufficient to allege a delivery to state a cause of action for a breach of a written lease. On the record before us, plaintiff has failed to do so.

Accordingly, the order of the Appellate Division should be affirmed, with costs.

NOTES AND QUESTIONS

1. You are the landlord's attorney. Your client, having lost in the case above, asks whether it might have prevailed on an "executory" contract theory. What is your honest answer?

2. Compare Mallory Associates v. Barving Realty Co., 300 N.Y. 297, 90 N.E.2d 468 (1949). Plaintiff tenant leased defendant's hotel, located in Norfolk, Virginia, for a fifteen-year term. The lease, signed in New York, required tenant to make a $65,000 security deposit. When landlord commingled the deposit with its own funds, rather than keeping it in a separate trust fund as required by New York law, tenant sued in conversion. Landlord argued that the law of Virginia, which allowed commingling, applied because a lease relates to an interest in real property and under governing conflict of laws doctrine, the law of the situs prevails. The New York Court of Appeals, however, held for the tenant:

> [T]he personal covenants between the contracting parties, though contained in a contract affecting realty are governed by the lex loci contractus; and as the contract of lease was made in New York, and the deposit was delivered to the leasor in New York, and the rent was payable in New York, the law of New York governs *as to the purely personal covenants.* (Italics added.) [300 N.Y. 301, 90 N.E.2d 471 (1949)]

Be careful to note, however, that "as to the purely personal covenants," the New York (and other) courts remain schizoid as to whether to apply property or (where it differs) contract principle.

3. "Contract or Conveyance" is a recurring theme. You will hear it when exploring these leasehold issues:

(a) Is a writing necessary? See §4.3, *supra.*
(b) Where the premises are destroyed by fire, is tenant excused from further performance? See Note 5, page 298, *infra.* If the premises are taken in eminent domain?
(c) Where landlord substantially breaches a material covenant, may tenant rescind? See University Club v. Deakin, and Dyett v. Pendleton, pages 265 and 282, *infra.*
(d) Where tenant abandons the premises, must landlord mitigate the damages? See Sommer v. Kridel, §6.7, *infra.*

(e) Where tenant states that he will not pay future rent installments, may landlord claim an anticipatory breach? See Sagamore Corp. v. Willcutt, §6.7, *infra*.

4. Useful discussion appears in 1 American Law of Property 202-207 (Casner ed. 1952); Comment, The California Lease—Contract or Conveyance? 4 Stan. L. Rev. 244 (1952); Friedman, The Nature of a Lease in New York, 33 Cornell L.Q. 165 (1947).

§5.5　Tenant's Exclusive Right to Sell

Retail tenants often obtain an exclusive right to sell, usually stated as a landlord's promise not to lease another store in the same center to a merchant carrying a similar line of goods. The following materials, which deal with the tenant's remedies when competition occurs, raise two sets of recurring issues whenever landlord breaches a duty:

(a) The interdependence of a landlord's covenant and the tenant's covenant to pay rent that, in contract terms, may be restated as the materiality of a landlord's covenant. Where interdependence or materiality exists, tenant may rescind after landlord's breach. Where interdependence or materiality does not exist, landlord's breach will not excuse tenant from paying rent. In that case, tenant must respond by seeking damages or an injunction or both.

(b) How does tenant measure his damages?

UNIVERSITY CLUB v. DEAKIN
265 Ill. 257, 106 N.E. 790 (1914)

Mr. Justice Cook delivered the opinion of the court. Defendant in error, the University Club of Chicago, brought suit in the municipal court of Chicago against Earl H. Deakin, the plaintiff in error, to recover rent alleged to be due under a lease. A trial was had before the court without a jury and resulted in a judgment for $2007.66. Deakin prosecuted an appeal to the Appellate Court for the First District, where the judgment of the municipal court was affirmed. A writ of certiorari having been granted by this court, the record has been brought here for review.

On March 31, 1909, defendant in error leased to plaintiff in error, for a term of one year, a store room in its building at the corner of Michigan avenue and Monroe street, in the city of Chicago, at a rental of $5000 for the year. The lease provided that plaintiff in error should use the room for a jewelry and art shop and for no other purpose. It also contained the following clause, numbered 12: "Lessor hereby agrees during the term of this lease not to rent any other store in said University Club building to any tenant making a specialty of the sale of Japanese or Chinese goods or pearls." Shortly after this lease was made defendant in error leased to one Sandberg, for one year, a room in the University Club building, two doors from the corner, at a rental of $2500. The following provision was inserted in the Sandberg lease: "It is further distinctly understood and agreed by and between the parties hereto that at no time during the term of this lease will the lessee herein use the demised premises for a collateral loan or pawnshop or make a specialty therein of the sale of pearls." On May 1, 1909, being the first day of the term of the lease, plaintiff in error took possession of the premises and thereafter paid the rent, in monthly installments, for May and June. During the latter part of June plaintiff in error, through his attorney, sought to obtain from defendant in error a cancellation of his lease on the ground that by leasing a room in the University Club building to Sandberg and permitting him to display and sell pearls therein defendant in error had violated the provision of plaintiff in error's lease above quoted, and that for such violation plaintiff in error was entitled to terminate the lease. Defendant in error refused to cancel the lease, and on June 30 plaintiff in error vacated the premises, surrendered the keys and refused to pay any further installments of rent. This suit was brought to enforce payment of subsequent installments of rent accruing under the lease for the time the premises remained unoccupied after June 30.

The evidence offered by plaintiff in error tended to show that Sandberg had made a specialty of the sale of pearls in connection with the conduct of his general jewelry business ever since he took possession of the room leased to him, and that plaintiff in error vacated the premises and surrendered possession because of the failure of defendant in error to enforce the twelfth clause of his lease. The evidence offered by defendant in error tended to prove that Sandberg had not made a specialty of the sale of pearls, and that when plaintiff in error first made known his desire to assign or cancel his lease he gave as his only reason that his health was failing and that he had been advised by his physician to leave the city of Chicago.

Propositions were submitted to the court by both parties to be held as the law of the case. The court held, at the request of plaintiff in error, that the lease sued upon was a bi-lateral contract, and upon a breach of an essential covenant thereof by the lessor the lessee had a right to refuse further to be bound by its terms and to surrender possession of the premises, and that a breach of the twelfth clause of the lease would be a good defense to an action for rent if the tenant surrendered possession of the premises within a reasonable time after discovery of the breach. The court refused to hold as law propositions submitted by defendant in error stating the converse of the propositions so held at the request of plaintiff in error. The court properly held that the lease in question was a bi-lateral contract. It was executed by both parties and contained covenants to be performed by each of them. The propositions so held with reference to the effect of a breach of the twelfth clause of the lease correctly stated the law. By holding these propositions the court properly construed the twelfth clause as a vital provision of the lease and held that a breach of that provision by the lessor would entitle the lessee to rescind. Where there is a failure to comply with a particular provision of a contract and there is no agreement that the breach of that term shall operate as a discharge, it is always a question for the courts to determine whether or not the default is in a matter which is vital to the contract. . . . While there was no provision in this contract that plaintiff in error should have the option to terminate it if the terms of the twelfth clause were not observed, it is apparent that it was the intention of the parties to constitute this one of the vital provisions of the lease. It was concerning a matter in reference to which the parties had a perfect right to contract, and it will be presumed that plaintiff in error would not have entered into the contract if this clause had not been made a part of it. It is such an essential provision of the contract that a breach of it would warrant plaintiff in error in rescinding the contract and surrendering possession of the premises. . . .

The following proposition was submitted by defendant in error and held by the court as the law of the case: "That plaintiff performed all the obligations imposed upon it by its covenant that it would not rent any other store in its building to a tenant making a specialty of the sale of pearls, by incorporating in its lease to the second tenant that said second tenant should not make a specialty of the sale of pearls in the demised premises."

From a consideration of all the propositions of law held and refused, it appears that the judgment of the trial court was reached from the application of the proposition just quoted to the facts in the case. The court erred in holding this proposition as the law. By covenanting with plaintiff in error not to rent any other store in this building, during the term of plaintiff in error's lease, to any tenant making a specialty of the sale of pearls, defendant in error assumed an obligation which could not be discharged by simply inserting in the contract with the second tenant a covenant that such tenant should not make a specialty of the sale of pearls. It was incumbent upon it to do more than to insert this provision in the second lease. By the terms of its contract with plaintiff in error it agreed that no other portion of its premises should be leased to any one engaged in the prohibited line of business, and if it failed to prevent any subsequent tenant from engaging in the business of making a specialty of the sale of pearls, it did so at the risk of plaintiff in error terminating his lease and surrendering possession of the premises.

This precise question has never been passed upon by this court, so far as we are able to ascertain. Defendant in error cites and relies upon Lucente v. Davis, 101 Md. 526, which supports its theory. We cannot yield our assent to the doctrine there announced. Defendant in error cannot escape its obligation by the mere insertion of a clause in the lease with the second tenant prohibiting him from engaging in the line of business named. Plaintiff in error contracted for the exclusive right to engage in this particular business in that building. There was no privity between him and Sandberg, and he was powerless to enforce the provisions of the contract between defendant in error and

Sandberg.[3] It is idle to say that an action for damages for a breach of contract would afford him ample remedy. He contracted with defendant in error for the sole right to engage in this specialty in its building, and if defendant in error saw fit to ignore that provision of the contract and suffer a breach of the same, plaintiff in error had the right to terminate his lease, surrender possession of the premises and refuse to further perform on his part the provisions of the contract.

For the errors indicated the judgment of the Appellate Court and the judgment of the municipal court are reversed and the cause is remanded to the municipal court for a new trial.

Reversed and remanded.

NOTES AND QUESTIONS

1.   If landlord had won a decree enjoining Sandberg from any further sale of pearls and Sandberg had violated the injunction, would injured tenant still be able to rescind? See Bookman v. Cavalier Court, Inc., 198 Va. 183, 93 S.E.2d 318 (1956).

2.   Courts have regularly treated the landlord's covenant to bar competition as a vital part of the lease enabling tenant to rescind once he establishes breach. Cf. also Kulawitz v. Pacific Woodenware & Paper Co., 25 Cal. 2d 664, 155 P.2d 24 (1944). Courts have similarly regarded the covenant for quiet enjoyment. See §5.7, *infra*.

By contrast, consider the recent case of Schulman v. Vera, 108 Cal. App. 3d 552, 166 Cal. Rptr. 620 (1980). The *commercial* tenant had rented space on a ten-year lease. Included in the lease were a tenant's covenant to pay rent and a landlord's covenant to repair any damage to the roof or exterior walls of the building. When tenant failed to pay rent, landlord sued for possession; tenant pleaded as an affirmative defense the landlord's breach of the covenant to repair the roof. Landlord's motion to strike the affirmative defense was granted and the appellate court upheld the ruling:

> A covenant to repair on the part of the lessor and a covenant to pay rent on the part of the lessee are usually considered as independant covenants, and unless the covenant to repair is expressly or impliedly made a condition precedent to the covenant to pay rent, the breach of the former does not justify the refusal on the part of the lessee to perform the latter. [108 Cal. App. 3d 558-559, 166 Cal. Rptr. 623. Accord: Stewart v. Childs, Co., 86 N.J.L. 648, 92 A. 392 (1914)]

---

3. Privity in property law is a several-headed concept. Privity here would have permitted Deakin to sue Sandberg on the latter's promise not to sell pearls. Since Sandberg's promise ran to the landlord, Deakin would have enjoyed the requisite privity only if he had acquired some interest from the landlord *after* Sandberg made his promise. Cf. Restatement of Property §547, page 602, *infra*. Consider, however, whether Deakin could have asserted rights as the third-party beneficiary of Sandberg's promise. See also Freedman v. Seidler, page 270, *infra*.—Ed.

Although language in the *Schulman* opinion, 108 Cal. App. 3d 562, 166 Cal. Rptr. 626, intimates that the court might have decided differently if the landlord had been suing for the rent and not possession, the landlord's right to possession depended upon an antecedent right to collect his rent in full despite his breach of the repair covenant.

Can you formulate any criteria for helping one to decide whether a landlord's covenant is vital? What about tenant's covenants? Suppose, in Schulman v. Vera, the premises were a dwelling unit that the landlord had failed to repair. Cf. Green v. Superior Court, page 301, *infra.* Suppose that the tenant promises to take good care of the premises and fails to do so. Cf. Model Apartment Lease ¶3, §5.1, *supra.*

3.   If landlord breaches a vital covenant, may tenant ever remain on the premises and pay no rent at all? Cf. Smith v. McEnany, page 279, *infra.*

4.   If the tenant is entitled to terminate the lease because of the land-lord's default, absent a valid agreement as to the measure of damages, damages may include one or more of the following items, wherever appropriate, so long as no double recovery is involved:

(a) the fair market value (premium value) of the lease as of the termination date

(b) the loss sustained by the tenant due to reasonable (and foreseeable) expenditures made by the tenant before the landlord's default

(c) reasonable relocation costs

(d) (in the case of business premises) loss of anticipated business profits proven to a reasonable degree of certainty

(e) interest on the amount recovered at the legal rate for the period appropriate under the circumstances

Restatement (Second) of Property §10.2 (1977)

The fair market value of the lease, (a) *supra,* is the present value of the difference between a higher fair rental value of the unit and the agreed-upon or bargained-for rental (reserved rental) over the unexpired term of the lease. The following discussion, appearing in McMichael and O'Keefe, Leases 118-119, 124 (5th ed. 1959), elaborates the above rule:

". . . *In property where there is no capital investment made by the lessee, the leasehold has value only if the rent reserved in the lease is less than the true economic rental value.* [4] *The measure of leasehold value is the present-day discounted worth of the sum of the annual differentials for the remaining lease term.*

"The discount theory is based on the economic fact that present money, because of its earning potential, commands a premium over future money. $3312.12 invested today at 8 percent interest will pay an annuity of $1000 for four years at the end of which period the capital sum will have been ex-

---

4. This differential usually comes from a change in market conditions during the term of the lease.—ED.

hausted. The difference between the $4000 in total annual payments and the $3312.12 is the discount. Obviously, the discount will vary as the assumed interest rate varies. . . .

"Anyone buying an annuity will discount it for interest as of the date of purchase. The lessee who holds a lease at less than the fair rental value has in effect an annuity (the differential between the fair rental value and the rent reserved in the lease) which stems from his leasehold interest. There is, of course, an assumption that this differential will be maintained during the remainder of the lease term.

"Translating the leasehold interest into value is the same as discounting the 'annuities' for the balance of the lease. Take as an example the property with an assumed worth of $100,000 and a rental value of $8000 per annum net (8 percent of fee value). Let it be further assumed that the property is leased for a term of years, with 15 years remaining, at $6000 per annum.

"The differential between the rental value and the lease rental is $2000 per annum. This represents the lessee's 'annuity' for 15 years. Discounted at 8 percent interest, the leasehold would be valued at $17,000.

"In this same case, if the fee or lessor's interest were appraised, it would suffer a diminution in value because the lease is unfavorable from the lessor's or fee owner's point of view. The same mathematics would apply and a proper valuation of the fee interest would be $100,000 minus $17,000 or $83,000.

"Similarly (although the value of the fee is not our primary concern), a lease to a *responsible* tenant at a rental in excess of true rental value might give property a value above the free and clear market value.

"If we take the case above of the property valued at $100,000 with a fair rental value of $8000 and assume it to be rented for $10,000 per annum, it would give the lessor or fee owner an 'annuity' of $2000 over and above the fair rental value predicated, of course, on the tenant's responsibility and ability to pay. In this case, the fee might be valued at $100,000 plus $17,000 or $117,000. The leasehold interest would be valueless. . . ."

Suppose that tenant chooses not to rescind, yet wants to prevent future violations and to recover for past violations. What is the measure of his rights? Ponder this as you read Freedman v. Seidler.

FREEDMAN v. SEIDLER
233 Md. 39, 194 A.2d 778 (1963)

HORNEY, J. In this equity action for injunctive relief and a money judgment for damages allegedly sustained as the result of the breach by one tenant of the restrictive covenant in the lease between himself and the landlords prohibiting competition with another tenant of the same landlords, the questions on appeal relate to the dismissal of the final injunctive order, the award of damages and the allowance of counsel fees.

Since 1950 Minnie Seidler (often herein referred to as the injured tenant) had operated a women's specialty shop at 3514 Eastern Avenue in Baltimore City for the sale of millinery, handbags, gloves, hosiery, costume jewelry, belts and accessories. In April 1958 she entered into a renewal of her lease for another term of five years. In the lease, the landlords covenanted "not to lease any other property owned by Landlords and fronting on Eastern Avenue . . . to any other person, firm or corporation which would conduct therein a business in direct competition with the business of the Tenant."

In September 1960, Israel Freedman (often herein referred to as the offending tenant), who specialized in the sale of men's, women's and children's shoes, entered into a lease with the same landlords for the rental of 3516 Eastern Avenue. Prior thereto he had attempted to purchase the right to sell handbags and hosiery in the shoe shop he intended to operate next door to the specialty shop, but the negotiations were unsuccessful. Accordingly, the lease for the shoe shop provided that the premises were to be used for the retail sale of shoes "and other kindred articles" and the tenant was specifically excluded from offering for sale any "millinery, handbags, hosiery and gloves and costume jewelry." When, however, the offending tenant opened his store on September 22, 1960, he placed signs in the window advertising: "Free . . . Nylon hose with purchase of . . . shoes $3.99 and up" and "Free gift of handbag with purchase of shoes of $5.99 and up." He also placed handbags in the window in connection with the display of shoes. According to the offending tenant, the signs were taken out of the window when the distribution of hosiery and handbags ceased on October 25, 1960, but some handbags were displayed for a "little while longer." According to the injured tenant, however, the signs remained in the window until the latter part of November 1960 and the handbags were displayed for an additional month.

The original action was brought by Minnie Seidler, the injured tenant, against Nathan Katz and others, the landlords. Besides requesting an order to require the landlords to prohibit Israel Freedman, the offending tenant, from conducting his business "in competition with and to the detriment" of her business by taking action against him, the injured tenant claimed damages for the violation of the covenant in her lease. The landlords impleaded the offending tenant as a third party and the injured tenant elected to so amend the action as to join the offending tenant as a defendant. Therein, the injured tenant in addition to seeking permanent injunctive relief against the offending tenant, also sought damages for the violation of the restrictive covenant in the lease between the landlords and the offending tenant.

At the trial, the offending tenant testified that he was not offering hosiery and handbags for sale, but rather was giving them away as part of a promotional program to aid his sales of shoes. In support of her claim for damages, the injured tenant testified that as a result of the "give away" of the hosiery and handbags, "[w]e had a drastic reduction in our business" and that the "business fell off terribly." She stated that the decline started "as soon as those bags were given away and we have suffered since." A sales clerk, who had been employed by the injured tenant from April 1951 to August 1962, testified to the effect that after the promotional program began there was a decline in business and that many of the regular customers stopped buying at the specialty shop. Neither the owner of the specialty shop nor the sales clerk testified as to the percentage the business fell off nor as to the loss in profits sustained during the promotional program and subsequent periods. The only other witness who testified as to damages was an accountant employed by the injured tenant to prepare a financial report showing his computation of her loss of profits during the period from September 22, 1960, to March 31, 1963, to be used in the trial of this case. In substance, the testimony of the accountant was contained in the financial report. Based upon a comparison of sales and profits for the years 1959-1960-1961, he testified that in 1960, until the beginning of the offending tenant's promotional scheme, gross sales averaged 10.87% ahead of 1959. By computing this percentage increase in sales with the sales made from September 22, 1960, until the business was discontinued on July 31, 1962, the report showed that the losses in net profits for the period from September 22, 1960, through July 31, 1962, were as follows: $1673.41 from September 22 to December 31, 1960; $3655.20 from January 1 to December 31, 1961; and $2364.23 from January 1 to July 31, 1962. No evidence was produced to show the difference in value between the lease of the injured tenant with the covenant unbroken and the same lease with the covenant broken.

At the conclusion of the trial, the lower court continued injunctive relief by permanently enjoining Israel Freedman, the shoe shop owner, from conducting his business in competition with the business of Minnie Seidler, the specialty shop owner; awarded her a money judgment against Israel Freedman for $7328.61 with costs, representing damages of $5328.61 and counsel fees of $2000; and dismissed the bill of complaint against Nathan Katz and the other landlords. Israel Freedman appealed, claiming (i) that the injunctive provisions of the decree should be reversed; (ii) that the damages awarded were speculative and conjectural and without rational foundation. . . .

Insofar as Minnie Seidler is concerned, the decretal order directing the issuance of a permanent injunction against Israel Freedman should be dismissed as moot. It seems clear, since the operation of the specialty shop had been discontinued more than six months before the date of the final decree, that the change in circumstances which occurred after the issuance of the preliminary injunction, rendered the continuation of injunctive relief unnecessary. . . .

We do not agree that the damages awarded by the lower court were speculative and conjectural or without rational foundation, but we think they were excessive and for that reason the judgment for money damages should be modified.

It is well settled in this State that a covenant in a lease to the effect that the tenant shall have the *exclusive* right of conducting a specified business on the leased premises may be injunctively enforced against both the landlord . . .

and a subsequent tenant of another part of the landlord's premises, who, at the time he entered into the lease, had notice of the right granted to the original tenant.[5] . . . Since the record is clear that the offending tenant was aware of the exclusive right of the injured tenant to sell handbags, hosiery and other specialties at 3514 Eastern Avenue before he leased 3516 Eastern Avenue, we think his "giving away" of handbags and hosiery (the values of which were included in the selling price of the shoes) was tantamout to selling them, and that the injured tenant was therefore entitled to seek injunctive relief against the landlords and the offending tenant to prevent the further breach of the covenant in her lease guaranteeing no competition. . . .

. . . The only defense to the adjunctive relief sought was that the damages were too speculative and conjectural and could not be determined with reasonable certainty. Consequently, we shall concern ourselves only with the nature and extent of the damages sustained by the injured tenant as a result of the competitive activities of the offending tenant.

The general rule is that an injured tenant may sue a landlord who has breached a covenant pledging no competition in an action at law for damages. See Parker v. Levin, 285 Mass. 125, 188 N.E. 502, 90 A.L.R. 1446 (1934), a landmark case in this area. Although a covenantee may be entitled to at least nominal damages for any breach of such a covenant, the courts in this country are not in agreement as to the proper measure to be used in ascertaining *damages* substantial damages sustained by the breach. But two measures seem to be utilized more often than the rest. Some courts consider the difference in what the value of the leasehold would be with the covenant against competition unbroken and the same leasehold with the covenant broken, and allow evidence of loss of profits as tending to show the value of the difference. Parker v. Levin, *supra*. Other courts allow the injured tenant to recover the lost profits caused by the prohibited competition (without considering any other element) if he can prove the amount thereof by competent evidence satisfactory to the court. See, for example, Krikorian v. Dailey, 171 Va. 16, 197 S.E. 442 (1938). See also the law note, entitled Lessors' Covenants Restricting Competition: Drafting Problems, in 63 Harv. L.R. 1400. Other cases in this field are collected in 90 A.L.R. 1449.

Since it appears that loss of profits is the governing factor in both the above measures, we see no reason why loss of profits, when a reasonable method of computing such losses has been utilized, cannot be used as a measure for assessing damages caused by a breach of a covenant guaranteeing no competition. Nor is there any reason why such measure should not be applied

5. Compare with University Club v. Deakin, page 265, *supra*, where the court states as obiter dicta that T(1) cannot sue T(2) in the absence of privity. Here the court allows suit where T(2) has notice of the rights of T(1). Note here that T(1) is suing on the L-T(1) covenant, not on the T(2)-L covenant. At common law, the claim of T(1) against T(2) on the L-T(1) covenant has to overcome even more difficult hurdles than did a suit based on the T(2)-L covenant. These hurdles have largely disappeared, and the Maryland court adopts an especially relaxed view. For more elaborate discussion of the enforceability of covenants against nonsignatories, see §§10.4-10.6, *infra*.—ED.

to the case at bar. We think the financial report prepared by the accountant—and there was no evidence to the contrary—was a reasonable basis for computing the loss of profits through December 31, 1961. However, we are of the opinion that the damages recoverable by the injured tenant should have been limited to the period during which the breach of covenant actually took place, that is, from September 22, 1960, through December 31, 1960. The financial report of the accountant shows that the loss of profits during this period was $1673.41. Accordingly we shall reduce the amount of damages awarded by the lower court from $5328.61 to $1673.41. . . .

The provisions of the decree granting a permanent injunction and allowing a counsel fee are reversed; the award of damages is modified by reducing the judgment to $1673.41, and the award, as modified, is affirmed; the appellant to pay the costs.

NOTES AND QUESTIONS

1.   Where tenant does not rescind the lease after landlord's breach, through choice if the covenant is material, Freedman v. Seidler, *supra,* or because rescission is not permitted, if the covenant is either nonmaterial or "independent," tenant is entitled to recover damages to reflect any diminution in the value of the premises. The court in Freedman v. Seidler measured tenant's damages as the difference in the leasehold's value with the noncompetiton covenant unbroken and with the same covenant broken, and allowed tenant to introduce evidence of lost profits as indicating that difference in value. That may well be the prevailing view. The Restatement (Second) of Property §11.1 (1977) defines an alternative measure:

> If the tenant is entitled to an abatement of the rent, the rent is abated to the amount of that proportion of the rent which the fair rental value after the event giving the right to abate bears to the fair rental value before the event.

Compare the tenant's recovery under the *Freedman* and Restatement methods (assuming that tenant has paid the reserved rental in advance) where the unexpired term is one year, the fair rental value of the premises before the event (covenant unbroken) is $15,000 yearly, the fair rental value of the premises after the event (covenant broken) is $10,000 yearly, and the reserved rental is $13,000 yearly. Suppose that the reserved rental were $15,000 yearly? $6,000 yearly? Which one of the two formulae do you prefer? Why?

2.   The Restatement (Second) of Property §7.2 (1977), although it agrees that the landlord's failure to bar competition under a leasehold covenant places the landlord in default, notes also that some noncompetition promises are invalid as illegal restraints on trade. Id. at Comment a. Under what circumstances might such promises be illegal?

§5.6 Tenant's Right to Possession When Term Begins

On August 1, L rents T an apartment for two years to start September 1. X, the present occupant, holds a lease expiring August 31. That day L phones T to say that X cannot leave until October 1 (when X's new house will be finished). In the meantime, T's present apartment has been rerented as of September 10. What are T's rights and remedies vis-à-vis L?

DIEFFENBACH v. McINTYRE
208 Okla. 163, 254 P.2d 346 (1952)

BINGAMAN, J. This action was brought by plaintiff Mildred E. McIntyre against the defendant Nevin J. Dieffenbach, seeking to recover rental paid, damages for repairs made upon a building leased by her from the defendant, and anticipated profits lost by her because of her removal from the building. The trial court submitted the cause to the jury as to the rental paid and cost of repairs, but refused to permit the introduction of evidence as to loss of anticipated profits. Defendant appeals from the judgment against him rendered on a verdict by the jury in favor of plaintiff, and plaintiff cross-appeals from the refusal of the court to permit her to introduce evidence as to loss of anticipated profits.

Undisputed facts are that plaintiff, prior to the time she leased the building from defendant, was operating a beauty parlor in one of the downtown buildings in Tulsa; that she was required to vacate the rooms used by her in said building on or before May 1, 1946, and that during the month of April she sought to find another place in which to conduct her beauty parlor. She got in touch with defendant, who was attorney in fact for his mother-in-law, who owned a building farther removed from the business section of Tulsa, and sought to lease a portion thereof from him for a term of years. The transaction finally resulted in her leasing the entire building, which consisted of four units of several rooms each, two upstairs and two downstairs. She installed her beauty parlor in one of the downstairs units, but upon failure to obtain the possession of the entire building removed therefrom to other quarters on or about the 1st of August, 1946.

Plaintiff testified that at or prior to the time she signed the lease on the building, which lease ran for a term of three years at a rental of $500 per month, she was assured by defendant that he had raised the rent on the other three units in the building from $50 to $150 per month and had given thirty day notices requiring them to remove,[6] and that they could not possibly remain there and pay the rental which he had fixed as the new rate on the

---

6. What is the legal effect of a notice requiring a month-to-month tenant either to move out in thirty days or stay and pay a higher rental? Cf. page 215, Note 6.—ED.

property. Thereafter, she testified, he informed her that he could not give her possession until the 1st of June, and she made arrangements to stay in her old quarters for another month. On the 1st of June, when she was ready to move in, two of the units in the building were still occupied, and she hesitated to move in, but upon assurance from defendant to her attorney that he would obtain possession of the two occupied units on or before June 7th, she moved into the unit which she proposed to use as a beauty parlor. When the lease was signed she paid defendant one month's rent of $500, and she expended additional sums in fixing up the unit occupied by her. She testified that defendant failed to oust the tenants from the two units occupied by them, although one of them subsequently left, and that the occupant of the other unit offered her the regular $50 per month rental, but she refused to accept the same, telling them that arrangements for payments should be made with defendant. This unit was still occupied when she left the building and the tenants testified that they thereafter paid defendant the regular rental of $50 per month and were still occupying the unit and paying such rental at the time of the trial. . . .

Defendant in his brief asserts that the major and paramount question for decision is whether as a matter of law the defendant, when he executed the lease of April 30th, transferred to the plaintiff the legal right to possession, and was under no further obligation, or whether he was obligated to go further and place the plaintiff in actual possession of the property on June 1st. In arguing this question he asserts that the lease transferred the legal right to possession to the plaintiff, which was all he was required to do; that the occupants holding over after the term of their rental periods had expired by reason of his notices to them were trespassers, or tenants at sufferance of plaintiff, and that he was not required to place the plaintiff in possession as against them. . . .

Defendant calls attention to the fact that the so-called American rule as to the placing of a lessee in possession required only that he be placed in legal possession, while the other or English rule holds that there is an implied covenant to place the lessee in actual possession, see, Hannan v. Dusch, 154 Va. 356, 153 S.E. 824, 70 A.L.R. 141, and asserts that the American rule is generally prevalent in the United States. This state, among numerous others, has followed the other or so-called English rule, and holds that the lessor is required to place the lessee in actual possession of the property. King v. Coombs, 36 Okl. 396, 122 P. 181; Flannagan v. Dickerson, 103 Okl. 206, 229 P. 552. In these cases we recognized and adhered to the rule holding that the lease contained an implied obligation to place the lessee in actual possession. In Hannan v. Dusch, *supra*, the court cited and discussed numerous cases which adhered to either one rule or the other, and in the note to that case a number of these cases are analyzed. The states listed in the opinion, 154 Va. 356, 153 S.E. 824, 70 A.L.R. on page 142, show that a large majority of the states follow the so-called English rule adopted and followed by this court in the cases above cited, and in Stewart v. Murphy, 95 Kan. 421, 148 P. 609, it is stated that by the great weight of authority the covenant to put the lessee in possession at the beginning of the term is implied, citing numerous cases.

It follows that in the instant case the lessee was entitled to be put in possession of the entire building by the lessor on or before June 1, 1946, and the failure of the defendant to so place her in possession, or at least to place her in possession June 7, at which time he assured her attorney she would receive possession of the entire building, was a breach of the lease.

Defendant contends that the breach was only a partial breach since it did not interfere with the operation of the beauty parlor by plaintiff, but we think it was a complete breach, since it forced the plaintiff either to bring ouster proceedings against the tenants holding over, or to continue to pay $500 a month rent for a portion of the premises only. . . . [7]

It follows that judgment for plaintiff as rendered by the lower court must be and hereby is affirmed. . . .

NOTES AND QUESTIONS

1. A 1977 state-by-state survey listed 15 states that espouse the English rule (implied covenant to deliver physical possession), 9 states that espouse the "modified English" rule of URLTA, *infra,* note 2, 11 states that assert the American rule (implied covenant to deliver "legal" possession only), 1 state that uses a "modified American" rule, and 14 states plus the District of Columbia that have not yet had to choose among the several possibilities— Weissenberger, The Landlord's Duty to Deliver Possession: The Overlooked Reform, 46 U. Cin. L. Rev. 937, 966-968 (1977).

When the tenant fails to gain possession because the premises are occupied by the landlord, by a third person with the "consent" of the landlord, or by a third person having paramount title, the landlord is in breach under both the English *and* American rules. Cf. quiet enjoyment, §5.7, *infra.* But when the premises are occupied by a third person without right to be there, for example a holdover tenant, the American rule would require the incoming tenant to pay the agreed-upon rental and to wage his cause against the wrongful occupant.

The legal basis for the American rule, which is essentially satisfied if the landlord enjoys good title and has not already rented the premises to someone else, is discussed in Weissenberger, *supra,* pages 946-950. The rule seems to have stemmed from "a misplaced reliance on the covenant of quiet enjoyment," id. at 947, and the view that the incoming tenant, having the legal right to possession, is the only party with standing to evict the wrongful occupant, id. at 948.

The arguments supporting the English rule are well summarized by Weissenberger, id. at 951-952. How might the arguments run?

2. The Uniform Residential Landlord and Tenant Act contains the following language on the delivery of possession:

---

7. Why not prorate plaintiff's duty to pay rent among the three units until the fourth unit becomes available?—ED.

§2.103. At the commencement of the term a landlord shall deliver possession of the premises to the tenant in compliance with the rental agreement . . .
[T]he landlord may bring an action for possession against any person wrongfully
in possession. . . .

§4.102. (a) If the landlord fails to deliver possession of the dwelling unit to
the tenant as provided in Section 2.103, rent abates until possession is delivered
and the tenant may (1) terminate the rental agreement upon at least [5] days'
written notice to the landlord and upon termination the landlord shall return all
prepaid rent and security; or (2) demand performance of the rental agreement
by the landlord and, if the tenant elects, maintain an action for possession of the
dwelling unit against the landlord or any person wrongfully in possession and
recover the actual damages sustained by him. . . .

Weissenberger, *supra,* describes this provision as "modified English." Do
the modifications weaken or strengthen the tenant's hand? Id. at 956-960.

3.   In New York, where the American rule received some of its strongest
support, the legislature had other thoughts in 1962 when it enacted N.Y. Real
Prop. Law §223-a:

In the absence of an express provision to the contrary, there shall be
implied in every lease of real property a condition that the lessor will deliver
possession at the beginning of the term. In the event of breach of such implied
condition the lessee shall have the right to rescind the lease and to recover the
consideration paid. Such right shall not be deemed inconsistent with any right of
action he may have to recover damages.

Note, however, paragraph 2 of the Model Apartment Lease, *supra,* page
236. Does this paragraph, which is quite standard throughout the state, vitiate
not only much of Real Prop. Law §223-a but also much of the American rule
as well? Is such a provision unconscionable? Cf. Seabrook v. Commuter Housing Co., 72 Misc. 2d 6, 338 N.Y.S.2d 67 (Civ. Ct. 1972), *aff'd on other grounds,*
79 Misc. 2d 168, 363 N.Y.S.2d 566 (App. T. 1973).

4.   Restatement (Second) of Property §6.2 (1977) contains an elaborate
statement of the tenant's rights and remedies when a third person is wrongfully
in possession as the lease term begins. But the statement may be rendered
virtually meaningless by the qualifying phrase "except to the extent the parties to the lease validly agree otherwise."

5.   Problem: The reserved rent is $1,000 monthly. The premises are
worth $1200 monthly. T finds that the premises are occupied by holdover H.
If H remains wrongfully in possession for two months, but T does not rescind
the lease, what are T's rights and duties vis-à-vis H and landlord L under the
English and American rules? Suppose the premises are worth $800 monthly?

6.   Under the English rule:

(a) Trespasser takes possession on the second day of the term, but before the tenant has moved in. Is the landlord in breach? *No*

(b) May tenant recover from the landlord the added cost of taking a hotel room until the apartment is ready? The cost of taxis to his new apartment to check for mail? The cost of boarding his cat? Cf. Shreiber v. Kleban, 63 Misc. 2d 628, 312 N.Y.S.2d 1007 (Civ. Ct. 1970).

(c) Will even a brief delay in occupancy permit tenant to rescind?

§5.7   Tenant's Right to Quiet Enjoyment

The common law reads into every lease, except when some express term of the lease contradicts it,[8] a landlord's covenant that tenant shall quietly enjoy the premises. To prove a breach of the covenant for quiet enjoyment, the tenant must establish (a) an interference with his use of the demised premises; and (b) the fact that this interference has been caused by the landlord, or by someone having title paramount to that of the landlord, or by someone who derived authority for his acts from the landlord. 2 Powell, Real Property ¶225[3] (Rohan ed. 1973).

Breach would follow routinely if landlord had previously rented the same premises to another tenant (compare with wrongful holdover, §4.4, *supra*), if landlord's default on a mortgage caused tenant to lose his premises,[9] or if landlord without cause were to lock tenant out of his apartment.[10] Were any of these events to occur, tenant could rescind the lease and sue to recover his losses, which would include the premium value of the lease's unexpired term[11] and consequential damages. But *total, actual eviction*, by the landlord, by parties having paramount title, or by parties deriving their authority from landlord, is only one trigger for a claimed breach of quiet enjoyment. The materials that follow show other possibilities.

a.   Partial, Actual Eviction

SMITH v. McENANY
170 Mass. 26, 48 N.E. 781 (1897)

HOLMES, J. This is an action upon a lease for rent, and for breach of a covenant to repair. There is also a count on an account annexed, for use and occupation, etc., but nothing turns on it. The defense is an eviction. The land

---

8. Leases often express quiet enjoyment in some form. See, e.g., Model Apartment Lease ¶17, page 242, *supra*.

9. Or forced him to enter into a new lease with a new landlord (i.e., to attorn) as the price for remaining.

10. Lockout may sometimes be all right. See Note 1, page 368, *infra*.

11. To measure this value, see discussion at page 269, *supra*.

is a lot in the city of Boston, the part concerned being covered by a shed which was used by the defendant to store wagons. The eviction relied on was the building of a permanent brick wall for a building on adjoining land belonging to the plaintiff's husband, which encroached nine inches by the plaintiff's admission, or as his witness testified from measurements, thirteen and a half inches, or, as the defendant said, two feet, for thirty-four feet along the back of the shed. The wall was built with the plaintiff's assent, and with knowledge that it encroached on the demised premises. The judge ruled that the defendant had a right to treat this as an eviction determining the lease. The plaintiff asked to have the ruling so qualified as to make the question depend upon whether the wall made the premises "uninhabitable for the purpose for which they were hired, materially changing the character and beneficial enjoyment thereof." This was refused, and the plaintiff excepted. The bill of exceptions is unnecessarily complicated by the insertion of evidence of waiver and other matters; but the only question before us is the one stated, and we have stated all the facts which are necessary for its decision.

The refusal was right. It is settled in this State, in accordance with the law of England, that a wrongful eviction of the tenant by the landlord from a part of the premises suspends the rent under the lease. The main reason which is given for the decisions is, that the enjoyment of the whole consideration is the foundation of the debt and the condition of the covenant and that the obligation to pay cannot be apportioned. . . . It also is said that the landlord shall not apportion his own wrong, following an expression in some of the older English books. . . . But this does not so much explain the rule as suggest the limitation that there may be an apportionment when the eviction is by title paramount, or when the lessor's entry is rightful. . . . It leaves open the question why the landlord may not show that his wrong extended only to a part of the premises. No doubt the question equally may be asked why the lease is construed to exclude apportionment, and it may be that this is partly due to the traditional doctrine that the rent issues out of the land, and that the whole rent is charged on every part of the land. . . . The land is hired as one whole. If by his own fault the landlord withdraws a part of it, he cannot recover either on the lease or outside of it for the occupation of the residue. . . .

It follows from the nature of the reason for the decisions which we have stated, that when the tenant proves a wrongful deforcement by the landlord from an appreciable part of the premises, no inquiry is open as to the greater or less importance of the parcel from which the tenant is deforced. Outside the rule de minimis, the degree of interference with the use and enjoyment of the premises is important only in the case of acts not physically excluding the tenant, but alleged to have an equally serious practical effect,[12] just as the intent is important only in the case of acts not necessarily amounting to an entry and deforcement of the tenant. Skally v. Shute, 132 Mass. 367. The inquiry is for the purpose of settling whether the landlord's acts had the al-

[handwritten margin note: This is where Holmes construes the lease →]

---

12. See constructive eviction, page 282, *infra*—ED.

leged effect; that is, whether the tenant is evicted from any portion of the land. If that is admitted, the rent is suspended, because, by the terms of the instrument as construed, the tenant has made it an absolute condition that he should have the whole of the demised premises, at least as against willful interference on the landlord's part. . . .

We must repeat that we do not understand any question except the one which we have dealt with to be before us. An eviction like the present does not necessarily end the lease; Leishman v. White, 1 Allen, 489, 490; or other obligations of the tenant under it, such as the covenant to repair. . . .

Exceptions overruled.

NOTES AND QUESTIONS

1.   A leading New York case on partial, actual eviction is Fifth Avenue Building Co. v. Kernochan, 221 N.Y. 370, 117 N.E. 579 (1917). The landlord sued for rent. The leased premises included a vault beneath the sidewalk maintained under a license from the city of New York. The city revoked the license, thus excluding the tenant from part of his space. In denying the landlord full recovery, Judge Cardozo wrote for the court:

> Eviction as a defense to a claim for rent does not depend upon a covenant for quiet enjoyment, either express or implied. It suspends the obligation of payment either in whole or in part, because it involves a failure of the consideration for which rent is paid [authorities cited]. We are dealing now with an eviction which is actual and not constructive. If such an eviction, though partial only, is the act of the landlord, it suspends the entire rent because the landlord is not permitted to apportion his own wrong. If the eviction is the act of a stranger by force of paramount title, the rent will be apportioned, and a recovery permitted for the value of the land retained. . . . A covenant for quiet enjoyment either express or implied, is essential where eviction by title paramount is the subject of a claim for damages. It is not essential where the tenant asserts a failure, either complete or partial, of the consideration for the rent. . . .

Do you understand the subtle distinction between failure of consideration (as a defense to a claim for rent) and breach of a covenant for quiet enjoyment (as the subject of a claim for damages)? In the *Kernochan* case, how would a court measure the landlord's recovery?

2.   Consider the holding in Randall-Smith, Inc. v. 43rd St. Estates Corp., 17 N.Y.2d 99, 215 N.E.2d 494, 268 N.Y.S.2d 306 (1966). There the landlord forcibly ejected a tenant from 10 percent of the rented offices. In the tenant's suit for treble damages (cf. §6.1, *infra*) the court declared that, for a partial eviction, the actual damages were the difference between the actual rental value and the agreed-upon but unpaid rent. No note was taken of the fact that the partial eviction was the act of the landlord. Is the holding consistent with Smith v. McEnany?

3.   In a case involving a luxury apartment, a lower New York court suspended a tenant's entire rent when the eleven-room apartment agreed upon in the lease was found to have only ten rooms. Fifth Avenue Estates, Inc. v. Scull, 42 Misc. 2d 1052, 249 N.Y.S.2d 774 (1964) (App. T. 1964). Is the "no apportionment of wrong" rule sensible regardless of the magnitude (or minuteness) of the wrong? Compare with the requirement for constructive eviction, *infra*, that tenant show a substantial interference with his quiet enjoyment. What is the significance of Justice Holmes's statement in Smith v. McEnany that "an eviction like the present does not necessarily end the lease"? Is the test for rescission different from the test for suspension?

4.   Landlord refuses to air-condition offices after 6 P.M. and on weekends, making the offices unusable during the summer. Partial actual eviction? See Barash v. Pennsylvania Terminal Rental Estate Corp., 26 N.Y.2d 77, 256 N.E.2d 707, 308 N.Y.S.2d 649 (1970), page 290, *infra*.

b.   Constructive Eviction

DYETT v. PENDLETON
8 Cow. 727 (N.Y. 1826)

[The facts appear in the concurring opinion of Sen. Crary.]

. . . The facts offered to be proved on the trial are, substantially, that in February, 1820, from time to time, and at sundry times, the plaintiff introduced into the house, (two rooms upon the second floor and two rooms upon the third floor whereof had been leased to the defendant,) divers lewd women or prostitutes, and kept and detained them in the said house all night, for the purpose of prostitution; that the said lewd women or prostitutes would frequently enter the said house in the day time, and after staying all night, would leave the same by daylight in the morning; that the plaintiff sometimes introduced other men into the said premises, who, together with him, kept company with the said lewd women or prostitutes during the night; that on such occasions, the plaintiff and the said lewd women or prostitutes, being in company in certain parts of the said house, not included in the lease to the defendant, but adjacent thereto, and in the occupation or use of the plaintiff, were accustomed to make a great deal of indecent noise and disturbance, the said women or prostitutes often screaming extravagantly, and so as to be heard throughout the house, and by the near neighbors, and frequently using obscene and vulgar language so loud as to be understood at a considerable distance; that such noise and riotous proceedings, being from time to time continued all night, greatly disturbed the rest of persons sleeping in other parts of the said house, and particularly in those parts thereof demised to the defendant; that the practices aforesaid were matters of conversation and reproach in the neighborhood, and were of a nature to draw, and did draw, odium and infamy upon the said house, as being a place of ill fame, so that it was no longer respectable for moral and decent persons to dwell or enter therein; that all the said immoral, indecent and unlawful practices and proceedings were by the procurement or with the permission and concurrence of the plaintiff; that the defendant, being a person of good and respectable character, was compelled, by the repetition of the said indecent practices and proceedings, to leave the said premises, and did, for that cause, leave the same on or about the beginning of March, 1820, after which he did not return thereto, &c.

This evidence, being objected to by the plaintiff's counsel, was rejected by the court, and is now to be considered as true. . . .

[The main opinion follows.]

SPENCER, SENATOR. It seems to be conceded that the only plea which could be interposed by the defendant below, to let in the defence which he offered, if any would answer that purpose, was, that the plaintiff had entered in and upon the demised premises, and ejected and put out the defendant. Such a plea was filed; and it is contended on the one side, that it must be literally proved, and an actual entry and expulsion established: while on the other side it is insisted, that a constructive entry and expulsion is sufficient, and that the facts which tended to prove it, should have been left to the jury. . . .

. . . The agreement set forth in the plea, contains a covenant that the defendant shall have "peaceable, quiet and indisputable possession" of the premises. This is in its nature, a condition precedent to the payment of rent,[13] and whether the possession was peaceable and quiet, was clearly a question of fact for the jury. Such conduct of the lessor as was offered to be proved in this case, went directly to that point; and without saying at present, whether it was or was not sufficient to establish a legal disturbance, it is enough that it tended to that end, and should have been received, subject to such advice as the judge might give to the jury.

The opinion of the supreme court proceeds upon the ground that there must be an actual physical eviction, to bar the plaintiffs; and in most of the cases cited, such eviction was proved; and all of them show that such is the form of the plea. But the forms of pleading given, and the cases cited, do not establish the principle on which the recovery of rent is refused, but merely furnish illustrations of that principle, and exemplifications of its application. The principle itself is deeper and more extensive than the cases. It is thus stated by Baron Gilbert, in his essay on rents, p. 145:

> A rent is something given by way of retribution to the lessor, for the land demised by him to the tenant, and consequently the lessor's title to the rent is founded upon this: that the land demised, is enjoyed by the tenant during the term included in the contract; for the tenant can make no return for a thing he has not. If therefore the tenant be deprived of the thing letten, the obligation to

13. Can it also be said that the payment of rent is condition precedent to quiet enjoyment? Cf. Model Apartment Lease ¶17, page 242, *supra.* Cf. also Herstein v. Columbia Pictures Corp., 4 N.Y.2d 117, 149 N.E.2d 328 (1958).—ED.

pay the rent ceases, because such obligation has its force only from the consideration, which was the enjoyment of the thing demised.

And from this principle, the inference is drawn, that the lessor is not entitled to recover rent in the following cases: 1st. If the lands demised be recovered by a third person, by a superior title, the tenant is discharged from the payment of rent after eviction by such recovery. 2d. If a part only of the lands be recovered by a third person, such eviction is a discharge only of so much of the rent as is in proportion to the value of the land evicted. 3d. If the lessor expel the tenant from the premises, the rent ceases. 4th. If the lessor expel the tenant from a part only of the premises, the tenant is discharged from the payment of the whole rent; and the reason for the rule why there shall be no apportionment of the rent in this case as well as in that of an eviction by a stranger, is, that it is the wrongful act of the lessor himself, "that no man may be encouraged to injure or disturb his tenant in his possession, whom, by the policy of the feudal law, he ought to protect and defend."

This distinction, which is as perfectly well settled as any to be found in our books, establishes the great principle that a tenant shall not be required to pay rent, even for the part of the premises which he retains, if he has been evicted from the other part by the landlord. As to the part retained, this is deemed such a disturbance, such an injury to its beneficial enjoyment, such a diminution of the consideration upon which the contract is founded, that the law refuses its aid to coerce the payment of any rent. Here, then, is a case, where actual entry and physical eviction are not necessary to exonerate the tenant from the payment of rent; and if the principle be correct as applied to a part of the premises, why should not the same principle equally apply to the whole property demised, where there has been an obstruction to its beneficial enjoyment, and a diminution of the consideration of the contract, by the acts of the landlord, although those acts do not amount to a physical eviction? If physical eviction be not necessary in the one case, to discharge the rent of the part retained, why should it be essential in the other, to discharge the rent of the whole? If I have not deceived myself, the distinction referred to settles and recognizes the principle for which the plaintiff in error contends, that there may be a constructive eviction produced by the acts of the landlord. . . .

. . . Believing that [the tenant's testimony] tended to establish a constructive eviction and expulsion against the consent of the tenant; that it tended to prove a disturbance of his quiet possession, and a failure of the consideration on which only the tenant was obliged to pay rent, I am of opinion that it ought to have been received; and that therefore the judgment of the supreme court should be reversed, with directions to issue a venire denovo. . . .

[Then there is SENATOR CRARY's peroration:]

The whole science of law consists in the application of a few simple principles to the "affairs and bosoms of men." In Collins v. Blantern, (2 Wils. R. 350,) it is said by lord chief justice Wilmot, that "all writers upon our law agree in this: no polluted hand shall touch the pure fountains of justice." I should lay hold upon this principle, if there was no other, for the purpose of chastising vice and impudence, on the one hand, and protecting virtue and innocence, on the other. When the defendant is told that every right, when withheld, shall have its remedy, and every injury its proper redress, and that personal security, which includes reputation, is one of his absolute rights, and then told he must live in a brothel, against his will, or, at least, pay rent for it, he cannot but see the disparity between the text and the comment, and if the one is right, the other must be wrong.

If the evidence offered does not technically prove an eviction, yet, as there is no other plea under which the defence can be made, for the sake of giving effect to it, I should resort not to the statute law, nor to the common law, but to the great principles of morality, on which both are founded; and if, in the long tract of ages which are past, I could find no case parallel with the present, I should decide against the plaintiff, satisfied that if the same case had ever existed, the principal actor in it had not aspired to immortality by publishing his own infamy.

[And finally there is the dissent:]

COLDEN, SENATOR. . . . It is conceded, on all hands, that to excuse the non-performance of a covenant to pay rent, an entry of the lessor and an eviction of the lessee must be pleaded. But the plaintiff in error contends that the evidence he offered, should have been received as proof of an entry and eviction. This doctrine appears to be entirely new, and no case was cited to shew that it was not so. Indeed, the counsel of the plaintiff in error seemed to appeal to the moral, rather than to the municipal law. And if we were to decide this case according to the dictates of morality, we might be disposed to pronounce a judgment in his favor. It is true that the moral law and the law of the land should not be at variance; but if they be so, it is not for us, in our judicial capacity, to reconcile them. We are, in rendering our judgments, not to determine as we may think the law of our country should be, but as we find it established; and the question now presented for our decision is, whether a lessee, finding himself temporarily disturbed in the enjoyment of the demised premises by the misconduct or immoral practices of the lessor, may abandon the tenement for the whole term, and be exonerated from the payment of rent. If this question were to be answered in the affirmative, it would, in my opinion, introduce a new and very extensive chapter in the law of landlord and tenant; for if the encouragement or practice of lewdness, on premises under the same roof with the tenements leased, would warrant an abdication by the tenant, and release him from his covenant to pay rent, there is no reason why, if the landlord should by any other means render the occupation of the premises inconvenient or uncomfortable, the same consequences should not ensue. It would be so if the landlord were to maintain a house of ill fame adjoining or opposite to, or in the same street with the demised premises; if he were to set up a noisy or noxious manufactory near the tenements he had let; or if the landlord should happen to have the plague of a scolding wife under the same roof with his tenant, the tenant might feel himself authorized to leave the premises, and claim an exoneration from the payment of rent.

A decision that matters of this nature may be put in issue in an action of covenant for the non-payment of rent, would be to afford grounds for litigation on which there would be perpetual contentions. If the lessor illegally interferes with his lessee's enjoyment of the demised premises, otherwise than by an entry and eviction, the tenant has his remedy by civil suit or public prosecution . . . But merely because the tenant is interrupted or incommoded in the enjoyment of the demised premises, I am convinced the law does not allow him to redress himself by abandoning the tenement and withholding the rent. . . .

[But a majority were for reversal. For reversal, 16. For affirmance, 6.]

NOTES AND QUESTIONS

1. Tenant must show a substantial impairment of his quiet enjoyment. Since the tenant must also abandon the premises to plead constructive eviction, the defense cannot be tested until tenant has moved elsewhere. What exposure does tenant face if a court rules, after the fact, that the impairment was insubstantial? Does substantial mean "material"?

2. Why must abandonment precede the plea of constructive eviction? Abandonment must also be prompt. What if tenant cannot find another apartment? Or can only find an apartment at an appreciably higher rent? Who pays the tenant's moving expenses?

3. Suppose the tenant in Dyett v. Pendleton had decided not to move. Could he have sued the landlord in damages? What were the tenant's damages?

4. Could the tenant have sued to enjoin landlord from continuing his activities?

c. Partial, Constructive Eviction

EAST HAVEN ASSOCIATES v. GURIAN
64 Misc. 2d 276, 313 N.Y.S.2d 927 (Civ. Ct. 1970)

SANDLER, J. The most important of the several interesting issues presented by the proof in this case is whether or not the doctrine of constructive eviction is available to a residential tenant when a landlord is responsible for conditions that render part of the premises uninhabitable, and the tenant abandons that part but continues to reside in the rest of the premises. Put in another way, the question is whether New York law should recognize the doctrine of partial constructive eviction as a counterpart to partial actual eviction precisely as it has recognized for over a century constructive eviction as a counterpart to actual eviction. (See Dyett v. Pendleton, 8 Cow. 727.)

After a careful review of the authorities, I have concluded that the concept of partial constructive eviction is sound in principle, is supported by compelling considerations of social policy and fairness, and is in no way precluded by controlling precedent.

On May 26, 1963, the defendant entered into a lease with the then owner of 301 East 69 Street, with respect to apartment 18E under which the defendant agreed to pay rent for the apartment from December 1, 1963 to November 30, 1966 in the amount of $425 per month. The apartment in question had a terrace.

In April, 1966, the plaintiff acquired the building. At the end of July, 1966, the defendant and his family vacated the apartment and refused to pay rent for the months of August, September, October and November, 1966, the remaining period of the lease. Accordingly, plaintiff sued for the total of the four months rent, for the reasonable value of legal services, and for specific items of damages allegedly caused by the defendants. As to the last, I find the proof wholly deficient and these claims are accordingly dismissed.

The defense to the suit for rent rests upon the claim that the defendant was constructively evicted from the apartment as a result of the misconduct and neglect of the landlord, which allegedly rendered the terrace uninhabitable.

In addition, the defendant sues for damages to his furniture caused by the landlord's neglect, but this claim clearly must fail since the proof established that the damage complained of occurred before the plaintiff acquired the building. Finally, the defendant seeks return of his security in the amount of $425.

The central factual issue turns on the condition of the terrace and the factors causing that condition.

I find that from early 1965 the central air conditioner emitted quite steadily a green fluid and a stream of water overflow that fell in significant quantities on the terrace. I further find that the incinerator spewed forth particles of ash that were deposited in substantial part upon the terrace. The result was to render the terrace effectively unusable for its intended purposes, and the defendant and his family promptly abandoned the terrace, although it had been a prime factor in inducing them to enter the lease.

Nevertheless, I am unable to conclude that the departure of the defendant and his family from the apartment at the end of July, 1966 constituted their constructive eviction from the entire premises. The evidence clearly discloses that the terrace had become unusable no later than the early spring of 1965, and quite possibly earlier. The law is clear that the abandonment must occur with reasonable promptness after the conditions justifying it have developed. (See 1 Rasch, Landlord and Tenant, §877, and cases cited.)

Unquestionably, this rule should be given a flexible interpretation in light of the practical difficulties these days in finding satisfactory apartments.

Moreover, tenants have a right to rely on assurances that the landlord will correct the objectionable conditions.

Although the question is troublesome, I have concluded that a delay of at least 17 months in moving, without any significant proof of an early sustained effort to find other apartments, cannot be reconciled with the current requirements of law.

Turning to the issue of partial eviction, the proof quite plainly established that the terrace had been promptly abandoned once the condition complained of had developed. I am satisfied that conforming the pleadings to the proof to permit consideration of the issue of partial eviction would serve the interests of justice. (CPLR 3025, subd. [c.].)

Although the matter is not clear, I am inclined to believe that the proof before me spelled out an actual partial eviction. It seems to me that the tangible and concrete physical character of the substances falling on the terrace provides a substantial basis for such a finding.

However, I do not rest my decision on that ground in veiw of the decision of the New York Court of Appeals in Barash v. Pennsylvania Term. Real Estate Corp. (26 N.Y.2d 77). Although the facts of the *Barash* case do not preclude such a finding, the wording of the opinion plainly suggests a disposition to define actual eviction rather narrowly. I therefore turn to consider the status of partial constructive eviction under New York law.

In his authoritative treatise, Rasch flatly asserted that constructive eviction requires "surrender of the entire possession by the tenant." (See 1 Rasch, Landlord and Tenant, §876.)

None of the cases he cites, however, supports that sweeping assertion. These cases, with many others, repeat the general formula that constructive eviction requires abandonment of the premises. None of the cases I have examined squarely address[es] the question here presented of the legal effect of abandonment of only that part of the premises rendered uninhabitable.

The doctrine of constructive eviction was developed by analogy to actual eviction on the basis of a vary simple and obvious proposition. If a tenant is effectively forced out of leased premises as a result of misconduct by a landlord that substantially impairs enjoyment of the leased premises, the same legal consequences should follow as though the tenant were physically evicted.

In the eloquent landmark decision that firmly established constructive eviction in New York law, Dyett v. Pendleton (8 Cow. 727, *supra*) the following was said at page 734:

> Suppose the landlord had established a hospital for the small pox, the plague, or the yellow fever, in the remaining part of this house; suppose he had made a deposit of gunpowder, under the tenant, or had introduced some offensive and pestilential materials of the most dangerous nature; can there by any hesitation in saying that if, by such means, he had driven the tenant from his habitation, he should not recover for the use of that house, of which, by his own wrong, he had

deprived his tenant? It would need nothing but common sense and common justice to decide it.

Why should a different test be applied where the tenant, through comparable means, is effectively deprived of the use of part of his residence and abandons that part? Ought not the same consequences to follow as would follow an "actual partial eviction"?

I am unable to see any basis in "common sense and common justice" for treating the two situations differently.

Support for this view appears in the careful phrasing of the first decision to establish the requirement of abandonment in constructive eviction cases (Edgerton v. Page, 20 N.Y. 281, 284, 285). The Court of Appeals squarely rested the requirement on the unfairness of suspending rent while the tenant continued to occupy the "entire premises." "I cannot see upon what principle the landlord should be absolutely barred from a recovery of rent, when his wrongful acts stop short of depriving the tenant of the possession of *any portion* of the premises. . . . The true rule, from all the authorities is, that while the tenant remains in possession of the *entire premises* demised, his obligation to pay rent continues."

While some later opinions have been less carefully worded, I know of none that requires a different result.

While the view here expressed seems to me inherent in "common sense and common justice" that gave rise originally to the doctrine of constructive eviction, the result is independently compelled by considerations of fairness and justice in the light of present realities.

It cannot be seriously disputed that a major shortage in residential housing has prevailed in our metropolitan area for several decades. The clear effect has been to undermine so drastically the bargaining power of tenants in relation to landlords that grave questions as to the fairness and relevance of some traditional concepts of landlord-tenant law are presented.

The very idea of requiring families to abandon their homes before they can defend against actions for rent is a baffling one in an era in which decent housing is so hard to get, particularly for those who are poor and without resources. It makes no sense at all to say that if part of an apartment has been rendered uninhabitable, a family must move from the entire dwelling before it can seek justice and fair dealing.

Accordingly, I hold that when the defendant and his family ceased to use the terrace, a partial constructive eviction occurred with the same legal consequences as attends a partial "actual" eviction.

These consequences were comprehensively defined in Peerless Candy Co. v. Halbreich (125 Misc. 889). It is clear that from the time of the partial eviction, the defendant had the right to stop paying rent. Accordingly, I find against the plaintiff on its action for rent and legal expenses, and for the defendant on his action to recover the security deposit of $425.

Judgment should be entered for the defendant for $425 with interest from August 1, 1966.

NOTES AND QUESTIONS

1. The facts in Barash v. Pennsylvania Terminal Rental Real Estate Corp., 26 N.Y.2d 77, 256 N.E.2d 707, 308 N.Y.S.2d 649 (1970), were these: Tenant charged landlord with wrongful failure to air-condition his offices evenings and weekends, causing the offices to become "hot, stuffy, and unusable and uninhabitable" at those times. Claiming a partial actual eviction, tenant sought an order relieving him from payment of rent. Two lower courts refused to dismiss the tenant's complaint, but the court of appeals reversed.

> The tenant, who has not abandoned the premises, asserts that there has been an actual eviction, though partial only, thus permitting him to retain possession of the premises without liability for rent. To support this contention it is claimed that failure to supply fresh air constitutes actual eviction, if only, albeit, during the hours after 6:00 P.M. and on weekends. . . .
>
> All that tenant suffered was a substantial diminution in the extent to which he could beneficially enjoy the premises. Although possibly more pronounced, tenant's situation is analogous to cases where there is a persistent offensive odor, harmful to health, arising from a noxious gas, an open sewer . . . , or defective plumbing. . . . In all such cases there has been held to be only a constructive eviction. . . . Given these well-established rules, proper characterization of the instant failure to ventilate follows easily. . . . The tenant has neither been expelled nor excluded from the premises, nor has the landlord seized a portion of the premises for his own use or that of another. He has, by his alleged wrongful failure to provide proper ventilation, substantially reduced the beneficial use of the premises. . . . Since the eviction, if any, is constructive and not actual, the tenant's failure to abandon the premises makes the first cause of action insufficient in law. . . .

2. "The fallacy . . . is quite evident and manifest. Applying 'common sense and common justice,' a tenant deprived of the beneficial use and enjoyment of a portion of the demised premises cannot be placed in a better bargaining advantage than a tenant who is deprived of the beneficial use and enjoyment of the entire demised premises. For, if a tenant must abandon the demised premises to claim the benefit of a total constructive eviction, then, certainly, a tenant deprived of the beneficial use and enjoyment of a portion of the premises must either vacate the said premises or pay rent if he elects to remain in possession." Leonforte, J., in dismissing defense of partial constructive eviction where tenant unable to use the terrace of his fourth-floor apartment, but remained in possession. Zweighaft v. Remington, 66 Misc. 2d 261, 263, 320 N.Y.S.2d 151, 153 (Civ. Ct. 1971). Who has the better of the argument, Justice Sandler or his brother Leonforte?

d. The Disorderly Neighbor

COLONIAL COURT APARTMENTS, INC. v. KERN
282 Minn. 533, 163 N.W.2d 770 (1968)

PER CURIAM. This is an appeal from an order of the municipal court denying plaintiff's alternative motion for judgment notwithstanding the findings or for a new trial in an action for rent. The trial court found for defendant, holding that there had been a constructive eviction. Plaintiff contends that the findings are not supported by the record.

From the record it appears that plaintiff, Colonial Court Apartments, Inc., rented an apartment to defendant, Irene Kern, for a 1-year term to begin January 1, 1966. The apartment immediately above was occupied by a young couple. When Mrs. Kern leased from plaintiff, she expressed her desire for a quiet apartment and was assured that the building was well insulated and not noisy. It is agreed that the building was well constructed and well maintained. However, almost from the start of her occupancy, Mrs. Kern complained that some young neighbors interfered with her enjoyment of the apartment, alleging that they gave noisy parties twice a week, ran water early in the morning, operated a dishwasher at late hours, subjected her to insulting and abusive language, and disturbed her sleep to the point where she had to go elsewhere for rest. After she had lodged several complaints, the landlord terminated the young couple's lease, effective February 28, 1966. However, due to the pregnancy of the wife, it was agreed that they could remain in the apartment until the baby was born on condition that there would be no further disturbances and with the understanding that they would vacate as soon as possible thereafter. This agreement was explained to defendant. There were no further disturbances until shortly after the baby was born, at which time the objectionable conduct was resumed. On May 12, 1966, the landlord received a letter from the young couple expressing their intention to vacate by June 1, 1966. In response, the landlord wrote informing them that they were responsible for rent to June 30, 1966, because they had not given the full 30-day statutory notice, and went on to explain that "your notice and the first possibility to vacate, according to law, will be June 30." They were advised that if the landlord could rerent the apartment sooner he would do so. On Memorial Day of 1966, in response to Mrs. Kern's complaint about another loud party the night before, the landlord told her that the neighbors would be out by June 1. On June 16, the young couple still being in possession, defendant vacated the apartment, feeling that she could no longer endure the continued disturbances and annoyances. The trial court found:

> That the noise emanating from the Lindgren apartment so disturbed and interfered with Defendant's rest, that she found it necessary to drive to her parent's home in Eau Claire, Wisconsin, on the average of twice a month, on week ends, to get a good night's sleep on the Friday nights of said week ends.

That Plaintiff took no further action with respect to removing the source of Defendant's disturbance by requiring performance by Lindgrens of their agreement to vacate as soon as possible following the said birth of their child until, on May 12, 1966, Plaintiff was advised by the said Lindgrens that they intended to vacate their apartment effective June 1, 1966. Whereupon, on May 16, 1966, Plaintiff, through its authorized agent, notified the said Lindgrens that their notice of intention to vacate was insufficient and that their first possibility of vacating according to law would be June 30, 1966.

A constructive eviction is said to occur when the beneficial enjoyment of an apartment by the lessee is so interfered with by the landlord as to justify an abandonment. It does not suppose an actual ouster or dispossession by the landlord. Santrizos v. Public Drug Co., 143 Minn. 222, 173 N.W. 563. Ordinarily, the rule is that the acts of one tenant do not constitute a constructive eviction of another tenant of the same landlord unless they materially disturb the latter tenant in the use, occupancy, and enjoyment of the demised premises or the natural consequence thereof is to injure the other tenant. 52 C.J.S., Landlord and Tenant, §448b. City Power Co. v. Fergus Falls Water Co., 55 Minn. 172, 56 N.W. 685.

The facts relating to the objectionable conditions of the premises are materially less serious than those referred to in other Minnesota decisions, where the enjoyment of the demised premises was made impossible or diminished to a material degree by circumstances involving defective and unhygienic conditions. [Citations omitted.]

In fairness it should be said that the trial court could well have found that the landlord took such reasonable measures as were warranted under the circumstances to correct the conditions of which defendant complained. He might also have found that the landlord's letter to the tenants that their "first possibility to vacate, according to law, will be June 30," referred to liability for rent rather than a requirement to remain in possession. Nevertheless, we are not warranted in making an exception to our well-established rule that in reviewing the record the testimony must be considered in the light most favorable to the prevailing party, and if support for the findings may be found in the evidence as a whole, such findings will not be disturbed. The findings of fact by the trial court and the jury stand on equal footing and are entitled to the same weight and will not be reversed on appeal unless they are manifestly and palpably contrary to the evidence. 1B Dunnell, Dig. (3 ed.) §415b. In Santrizos v. Public Drug Co., 143 Minn. 222, 223, 173 N.W. 563, 564, we said: "The definition of what constitutes constructive eviction does not get us far. Usually the question whether there is a constructive eviction is one of fact with each case largely dependent upon its particular circumstances." Although the evidence bearing on the issue of constructive eviction leaves something to be desired, we are constrained, nevertheless, to hold that there is sufficient evidence in the record to substantiate the trial court's determination.

Affirmed.

NOTES AND QUESTIONS

1. Compare Stewart v. Lawson, 199 Mich. 497, 165 N.W. 716 (1917), where tenant unsuccessfully claimed a constructive eviction because of the "intolerably offensive" conduct and language of other tenants in the building:

> "From the doctrine that the landlord is not responsible for the acts of strangers, it would follow that an act done by one tenant in a tenement house without the authority, consent, or connivance of the landlord cannot be treated as an eviction by other tenants." It is clear under this rule that no eviction took place which would bar a recovery of the rent, there being no evidence that the tenants causing the disturbance had any title interest in the premises or that [landlord] in any way encouraged it. The most that can be said is that [landlord] suffered it to continue. This would not be sufficient to bind her, unless she gave some active support or encouragement to their wrongful acts. [199 Mich. at 499, 165 N.W. at 717]

Stewart v. Lawson, when it was decided, seems to have stated correctly the prevailing view. Even though landlord might have sued to enjoin a tenant's offensive conduct or, alternatively, brought eviction proceedings, the landlord's failure to act was not seen as an implied authority for the tenant to create the disturbance. By contrast, however, courts would hold landlords responsible, so as to permit a complaining tenant to terminate his lease, where the disturbances emanated from the hallways and elevators—a "common nuisance which the landlord had the complete power to abate." Phyfe v. Dale, 72 Misc. 383, 130 N.Y.S. 231 (App. T. 1911).

Are there any arguments to support the Stewart v. Lawson rule? the Phyfe v. Dale exception?

2. Restatement (Second) of Property §6.1, Comment d, imputes to the landlord the conduct of third parties if it takes place on property in which the landlord has an interest, provided that landlord can legally control the conduct.

3. Might the complaining tenant also assert that landlord, by failing to quell the disturbance, has breached the implied convenant of habitability, §5.8, *infra?* See Millbridge Apartments v. Linden, 151 N.J Super. 168, 376 A.2d 611 (D. Ct. 1977).

4. On the complaint of the tenants in the apartment below, a landlord sought to evict a "noisy" young couple and their two children, ages four and two. In dismissing the summary dispossess proceeding, the trial judge wrote:

> From the court's opportunity to observe them, both the respondents and the tenants below seem to be people who under other circumstances would be congenial and happy neighbors. It is unfortunate that they have had to come to court to face each other in an eyeball to eyeball confrontation.
>
> The respondents are a young couple with two small children, ages four and two. It was admitted by them that the children do run and play in their

apartment, but they say they keep shoes off their feet when at home. The father says that he does walk back and forth at various times when at home, particularly to the refrigerator during the TV commercials and, also, to other areas of the apartment as necessity requires, but denies that he does this excessively or in a loud or heavy manner. They maintain that whatever noises emanate from their apartment are the normal noises of everyday living.

The tenants below, the Levins, are a middle-aged couple who go to business each day. They are like many others of our fellow citizens, who daily go forth to brave the vicissitudes of the mainstream of city life. At the end of the toilsome day, like tired fish, they are only too happy to seek out these quiet backwaters of the metropolis to recuperate for the next day's bout with the task of earning a living. They have raised their own child and are past the time when the patter of little feet overhead is a welcome sound. They say they love their new apartment and that it is just what they have been looking for and would hate to have to give it up because of the noise from above. Mrs. Levin is associated with the publisher of a teen-age magazine and realizes that she is in a bind between her desire for present comfort and the possible loss of two future subscribers. She consequently hastens to add that she loves children and has no objection to the Sokolows because of them—that it is solely the noise of which she complains. So we have the issue.

The landlord's brief states that in its view, the conduct that is even more objectionable than the noise, is the "unco-operative attitude of the Tenants." This observation is probably prompted by testimony to the effect that Mr. Sokolow, one of the upstairs tenants, is reported to have said "This is my home, and no one can tell me what to do in my own home." This is a prevalent notion that stems from the ancient axiom that a man's home is his castle.

The difficulty of the situation here is that Mr. Sokolow's castle is directly above the castle of Mr. Levin. That a man's home is his castle is an old Anglo-legal maxim hoary with time and the sanction of frequent repetition. It expressed an age when castles were remote, separated by broad moors, and when an intruder had to force moat and wall to make his presence felt within. The tranquillity of the King's peace, the seclusion of a clandestine romance and the opportunity, like Hamlet, to deliver a soliloquy from the ramparts without fear of neighborly repercussions, were real. Times however change, and all change is not necessarily progress, as some sage has perceptively reminded us. For in an era of modernity and concentrated urban living, when high-rise apartment houses have piled castle upon castle for some 20 or more stories in the air, it is extremely difficult to equate these modern counterparts with their drawbridged and turreted ancestors. The builders of today's cubicular confusion have tried to compensate for the functional construction by providing lobbies in Brooklyn Renaissance that rival in décor the throne room at Knossos. They have also provided built-in airconditioning, closed circuit television, playrooms and laundromats. There are tropical balconies to cool the fevered brow in the short, hot northern Summer, which, the other nine months, serve as convenient places to store the floor mop and scrub pail. On the debit side they also contain miles of utility and sanitary piping which convey sound throughout the building with all the gusto of the mammoth organ in the Mormon Tabernacle at Salt Lake City. Also, the prefabricated or frugally plastered walls have their molecules so critically near the separation level that they oppose almost no barrier at all to alien sounds from neighboring apartments. This often forces one into an embarrassingly auditory intimacy with the surrounding tenants. Such are the hazards of modern apartment house living. One of my brother Justices, the Honorable Harold J. Crawford, has opined that in this day in our large cities it is fruitless to expect the solitude of the sylvan glen. (Matter of Twin Elm Management Corp. v. Banks, 181 Misc. 96.) In this we concur. Particularly so, when we consider that all of us are daily assaulted by the "roaring traffic's boom," the early-morning carillon of the garbage cans and the determined whine of homing supersonic jets. Further, children and noise have been inseparable from a time whence the mind of man runneth not to the contrary. This court, therefore, is not disposed to attempt anything so schizophrenic at this late date.

Weighing the equities in this difficult controversy, the court finds that the Sokolows were there first, with a record as good tenants. The Levins underneath seem to be good tenants also. This was attested to by the superintendent who was called upon to testify. He made the understatement of the year when he said: "I kept out of the middle of this fight. It's near Christmas and this is no time for me to fight with tenants"—a piece of homely pragmatism which would have gladdened the heart of William James.

In his own crude way the superintendent may have suggested the solution to this proceeding. This is a time for peace on earth to men of good will. As the court noted above, they are all nice people and a little mutual forbearance and understanding of each other's problems should resolve the issues to everyone's satisfaction.

The evidence on the main question shows that in October the respondents Sokolow were already in a fixed relationship to the landlord. The Levins, on the other hand, were not—their position was a mobile one. They had the opportunity to ascertain what was above them in the event they decided to move in below. They elected to move in and afterwards attempted to correct the condition complained of. Since upon the evidence the overhead noise has been shown to be neither excessive nor deliberate, the court is not constrained to flex its muscles and evict the respondents. Upon the entire case the respondents are entitled to a final order dismissing the petition. [Louisiana Leasing Co. v. Sokolow, 48 Misc. 2d 1014, 266 N.Y.S.2d 447 (N.Y. City Civ. Ct. 1966)]

5.   Does the tenant whose enjoyment is disturbed have legal recourse against the disturbing tenant? Suppose that the disturbance is a leasehold violation (e.g., "no pets may be kept"), but falls short of a common-law nuisance?

§5.8   Tenant's Right to "Habitable" Premises

GADE v. NATIONAL CREAMERY CO.

324 Mass. 515, 87 N.E.2d 180 (1949)

WILLIAMS, J. These are three actions of contract or tort for property damage arising from the collapse on May 8, 1945, of the first floor of the building numbered 5 and 6 Fulton Place, Boston. This floor was equipped as a refrigerator room, thirty-seven feet by twenty feet in area and nine feet in height, and was supplied with the necessary brine from pipes of the Quincy Market Cold Storage and Warehouse Company. The floor of the room was of wood planking supported by timbers thirteen inches by twelve inches, placed ten inches apart. Although the building was about one hundred fifty years old, it did not appear how long the first floor had been fitted up for refrigeration. The property had been purchased by the defendants Harry Weiner and his wife Alice H. Weiner in 1942, and the first floor was rented by them to the National Creamery Company, a corporation, as tenant in will, in 1944, to be used for the storage of pickled herring in barrels. Four hundreds fifteen barrels, each weighing from three hundred thirty to three hundred forty pounds, were therein put in storage by the creamery company. The barrels were piled on end in two tiers with some twenty-five barrels rolled sidewise on top. Esther L. Gade purchased the premises from the Weiners about April 16, 1945, and the rent, which had been paid in advance for the month of April by the creamery company, was adjusted with Gade by the Weiners. The creamery company was notified of the change in ownership. On May 8, 1945, the floor of this refrigerator room collapsed and many of the three hundred sixty-five barrels which at that time remained in storage fell into the cellar. There was evidence that the floor timbers had become rotted where they joined the walls in the rear of the building. Damage resulted both to the building and to a substantial number of the barrels of herring. . . .

The second action is by National Creamery Company against Esther L. Gade for breach of an implied warranty of structural fitness. A second count for negligence in the plaintiff's declaration has been waived. The plaintiff excepted to the direction of a verdict for the defendant. In the ordinary lease of real estate there is no implied warranty that the premises are fit for occupancy or for the particular use contemplated by the lessee. The lessee takes the premises as he finds them. . . . The plaintiff, however, contends that the present case comes within the exception to the general rule stated in Ingalls v. Hobbs, 156 Mass. 348, 31 N.E. 286, where, in reference to the lease of a completely furnished dwelling house for a single season at a summer watering place, it was held that there was an implied agreement that the house was fit for habitation, without greater preparation than one hiring it for a short time might reasonably be expected to make in appropriating it to the use for which it was designed. The principle of Ingalls v. Hobbs, although extended to include in the implied agreement the structural condition of the house, Ackarey v. Carbonaro, 320 Mass. 537, 70 N.E.2d 418, has been recognized as a departure from the general rule, Hacker v. Nitschke, 310 Mass. 754, 39 N.E.2d 644, 139 A.L.R. 257, and in its application has been limited to factual conditions similar to those on which the decision was based. . . . The renting of a refrigeration room for commercial purposes and for an indefinite time, although the room was needed by the tenant for immediate occupancy, is not within the Ingalls v. Hobbs exception. There was no error in directing a verdict for the defendant.

The third action is by National Creamery Company against Harry Weiner and Alice H. Weiner also for breach of implied warranty of structural fitness. In this case also a second count for negligence has been waived. The plaintiff's exceptions are to the direction of a verdict for the defendant Alice H. Weiner at the conclusion of the evidence and the entry of a verdict for the defendant Harry Weiner under leave reserved after a verdict for the plaintiff. For the reasons stated in our discussion of the second action, the judge was right in directing and entering verdicts for the two defendants.

Exceptions overruled.

[In the first action, Esther Gade sued the creamery company both in waste and negligence. The court affirmed the judgment below in favor of the plaintiff landlady. There was evidence that the tenant had delayed defrosting the refrigerator pipes, causing an ice accumulation of approximately 5,000 pounds.]

NOTES AND QUESTIONS

1. The author of a well-known treatise wrote in 1906:

The rule that there is no implied warranty of fitness applies in a case where the subject-matter of the lease is a dwelling house. The lessor does not undertake that it is fitted for the use for which it is let, or for any purpose, or that it will remain in a tenantable condition. This involves both the right of the landlord to collect rent and his freedom from liability for injuries caused by defects in the premises. If there has been no misrepresentation or fraud, the landlord is entitled to his rent although the premises turn out to be useless. Moreover, the landlord is not liable for damage caused by defects in the premises unless he is guilty of laying a trap or of maintaining a nuisance. . . . When a tenant inspects premises, he takes the risk of their condition, and he cannot complain because the landlord did not disclose defects in respect to which he had full opportunity of informing himself. If the tenant desires to hold his landlord responsible for the security of the leased building, he should have a covenant to that effect incorporated in the lease. So, where there are no express covenants in a lease, and the landlord is neither dishonest nor negligent, it has been declared to be settled law that the rule of caveat emptor applies as to the condition of the leased premises. The tenant assumes the risk, and no liability attaches to the landlord. . . . [Jones, Landlord & Tenant §576 (1906)]

Despite courts' reluctance to intrude upon "settled law," they were finding an exception for furnished premises on short-term leases. Ingalls v. Hobbs, 156 Mass. 348, 31 N.E. 286 (1892), is the leading case:

But there are good reasons why a different rule should apply to one who hires a furnished room or a furnished house for a few days or a few weeks or months. Its fitness for immediate use of a particular kind, as indicated by its appointments, is a far more important element entering into the contract than where there is a mere lease of real estate. One who lets for a short term a house provided with all furnishings and appointments for immediate residence may be supposed to contract with reference to a well understood purpose of the hirer to use it as a habitation. An important part of what the hirer pays for is the opportunity to enjoy it without delay, and without the expense of preparing it for use. It is very difficult, and often impossible, for one to determine on inspection whether the house and its appointments are fit for the use for which they are immediately wanted, and the doctrine of caveat emptor, which is ordinarily applicable to the lessee of real estate, would often work injustice if applied to cases of this kind. It would be unreasonable to hold, under such circumstances, that the landlord does not impliedly agree that what he is letting is a house suitable for occupation in its condition at the time.

Accord: Young v. Povich, 121 Me. 141, 116 A. 26 (1922), discussed in 22 Colum. L. Rev. 595 (1922). One cannot help speculating over the underlying factors for the short-term, furnished premises exception. At least five possibilities emerge:

(a) That the courts were discontented with the caveat tenant rule and were seeking to narrow its ambit. But see the *Gade* case, *supra*.

(b) That a short-term hirer of furnished premises has different expectations regarding the use of his unit than either a long-term hirer of furnished premises or any hirer of unfurnished premises, and that these expectations are more deserving of legal protection. This is what the *Ingalls* courts seems to be saying.

(c) That a short-term tenant should not be expected to make either the cash or sweat outlay for repairs that will benefit him only briefly.

(d) That a short-term hirer of furnished premises has less opportunity to make a prior inspection. For example, the summer cottage by the shore, which is usually furnished, often is rented sight unseen.

(e) That a short-term tenant of furnished premises is easy prey to unconscionable landlords. In an urban center, what categories of persons take short-term leases of furnished units?

By the way, when does a lease graduate from short- to long-term?

3.   Another exception has sometimes been drawn for premises within a building not yet finished when the lease was made. See, e.g., J. D. Young Corp. v. McClintic, 26 S.W.2d 460 (Tex. Civ. App. 1930). But in Oliver v. Hartzell, 170 Ark. 512, 280 S.W. 979 (1926), the rule of caveat tenant applied where the building was far enough completed to permit the tenant to judge its suitability before making the lease.

4.   If premises are leased for a single use barred by zoning, can the tenant argue that the landlord gave his assurance of fitness for the specified use? See Hyland v. Parkside Investment Co., 10 N.J. Misc. 1148, 162 A. 521 (Sup. Ct. 1932).

5.   *Damage or destruction during the leasehold term.* At common law, destruction of leased buildings did not end the tenant's duty to pay rent. This was explained on the theory that the lessee had received an estate in *land;* fire,

flood, or acts of war might ravish the structures, but the land itself would remain relatively intact. In a rural economy, when farm buildings were easily replaced and were seldom the central factor in a lease, this seemingly harsh rule may have worked little mischief. Unless he had negligently caused building damage, the tenant was under no duty to restore, and one might even suppose that he took greater pains to avoid destruction than he otherwise would. See Note, 24 Geo. L.J. 197 (1935). Moreover, where it mattered, the parties might embody a different set of rights and duties in their lease.

As the lease moved into the city, where apartment tenancies became widespread, both courts and legislatures rewrote the existing rule. In a New York case, the court of appeals discharged an upper-story tenant from further rent after the building burned; its theory: the tenant had no interest in the land, only in the attached building. Graves v. Beidan, 26 N.Y. 498 (1863). Shortly before the *Graves* decision (but after the destructive fire which caused that litigation), the New York legislature passed a law permitting a lessee to surrender the premises whenever they were destroyed or so injured as to be "untenantable, and unfit for occupancy." Exceptions were drawn for tenant's fault or for an express written agreement to the contrary. N.Y. Real Prop. Law §227 (1962). Substantially similar statutes have since been enacted in many states. See 2 Powell, Real Property ¶233 [3] (Rohan ed. 1973).

Few clauses in a commercial lease are harder to draw than the fire (or other casualty) provision. Complete destruction poses relatively few problems; it is easily defined, and, moreover, it seldom occurs. Partial destruction, however, is not easily specified and the statute offers little help. The terms "untenantable" and "unfit for occupancy" would seem to invite litigation.

Re-examine the fire clause (¶7) in the Model Apartment Lease, page 239, *supra.*

NOTE: THE ADVENT OF HOUSING CODES

1. "The beginning of modern code enforcement in America may be placed at the turn of the century, with the enactment in 1901 of the Tenement House Act for New York City. Thus, housing codes and code enforcement for the benefit of the inhabitants are of very recent origin, when compared, for instance, with the common law antiquities of the law of landlord and tenant. Prior to our century, to be sure, there had been building codes and other laws relating to dwellings, but their major concern had been the protection of the city from conflagration and building collapse. Regulations to protect the tenants themselves were scant, and were generally limited to provisions aimed at preventing nuisances and limiting the spread of communicable disease. The need for housing codes to protect the inhabitants themselves is a fairly recent phenomenon of the growth of cities.

"A few large eastern cities passed housing codes near the turn of the century. Prior to 1954 there had been some 56 housing codes enacted in the entire country. In 1954, in an effort to safeguard federal funds spent on local redevelopment programs which could not succeed in providing adequate housing without a related community-wide effort, Congress enacted the 'workable program requirement' requiring the community to develop a 'workable program . . . to eliminate and prevent the development or spread of slums and urban blight.' Certification of a workable program by the HHFA Administrator was made a statutory condition to urban renewal loan and capital grant assistance, public housing aid, and FHA mortgage insurance. Housing Act of 1954, §303, 68 Stat. 623, as amended, 42 U.S.C. §1451 (c) (Supp. I, 1965). The Administrator prescribed several requirements for a workable program, including the adoption of local housing codes and preparation of plans for their enforcement. The 1964 Housing Act amendments directed the Administrator to make the workable program as effective as possible and also directed that, beginning in 1967, he could not certify or recertify a workable program unless the locality has had in effect a housing code for at least 6 months and the Administrator was satisfied that it is carrying out an effective program of enforcement. As a result of the workable program requirement, more than 1,000 communities have enacted housing codes since 1954." [Gribetz and Grad, Housing Code Enforcement: Sanctions and Remedies, 66 Colum. L. Rev. 1254, 1259-1260 (1966) (most footnotes omitted; one has been worked into the text)]

2. "The essential contents (though not the standards) of housing codes . . . have remained unchanged since the Model Tenement House Act developed by Veiller, which formed the basis for the New York Tenement House Law enacted in 1901. Although housing codes may regulate other, additional matters, their core content consists of 1) requirements for proper maintenance, including cleanliness and repair; 2) requirements for lighting and ventilation; 3) requirements for fire safety; 4) requirements for equipment and facilities, including sanitary facilities, water supply, sewerage and drainage, heating and electrical equipment; and 5) requirements respecting minimum space and maximum occupancy. Finally, housing codes contain provisions for administration and enforcement, including a delineation of responsibilities for compliance by the owner and by the occupant.

"A review of standards in existing housing codes indicates broad similarities in the codes of different municipalities, with most, if not all, of the newer codes (adopted after the 1954 workable program requirement came into being) following one of four or five model housing ordinances to a considerable extent. The Model Codes, in turn, show considerable similarity among themselves. The relatively few housing codes that preceded the 1954 workable program requirement were generally adopted in the early years of this century, and generally appear to be adaptations—with updating amendments—of Veiller's Model Tenement House Act or of its New York counterpart.

"In addition to the Model Codes and the municipal codes frequently derived from them, there are several state housing codes. Some of these apply statewide, generally permitting municipalities to adopt more stringent requirements, while others have been promulgated as optional codes that municipalities within the state may, but need not, adopt as they see fit. The general coverage of the state codes is not substantially different from that of the codes or their derivatives." [Legislative Drafting Research Fund of Columbia University, Housing Codes and their Enforcement 195-196 (Oct. 1966)]

3. It was widely believed that the housing code duties of landlords created no reciprocal *contract* rights in tenants, and that only the municipality could seek redress if landlords failed to meet code standards. Cf. Davar Holdings Inc. v. Cohen, 255 A.D. 445, 7 N.Y.S.2d 911 (1st Dept. 1938); Saunders v. First National Realty Corp., 245 A.2d 836 (D.C. Ct. App. 1968). The *Saunders* case, on appeal, led to one of the most influential decisions in modern property law, Javins v. First National Realty Corp., 428 F.2d 1071 (D.C. Cir. 1970). The federal court, in a decision written by J. Skelley Wright, ruled that the housing code of the District of Columbia required that a warranty of habitability be implied in the leases of all housing that it covered, and that the landlord's material breach of this warranty would give rise to a suspension of some or all of the reserved rental. Within a few years, state courts and legislatures, in droves, embraced the implied warranty of habitability. Green v. Superior Court, *infra*, typifies that development in the courts.

GREEN v. THE SUPERIOR COURT OF THE CITY AND COUNTY OF SAN FRANCISCO

10 Cal. 3d 616, 517 P.2d 1168, 111 Cal. Rptr. 704 (1974)

Tobriner, J. Under traditional common law doctrine, long followed in California, a landlord was under no duty to maintain leased dwellings in habitable condition during the term of the lease. In the past several years, however, the highest courts of a rapidly growing number of states and the District of Columbia have reexamined the bases of the old common law rule and have uniformly determined that it no longer corresponds to the realities of the modern urban landlord-tenant relationship. Accordingly, each of these jurisdictions has discarded the old common law rule and has adopted an implied warranty of habitability for residential leases.[1] In June 1972, the California Court of Appeal reviewed this emerging out-of-state precedent in the case of Hinson v. Delis (1972) 26 Cal. App. 3d 62, 102 Cal. Rptr. 661, and, persuaded by the reasoning of these decisions, held that a warranty of habitability is implied by law in residential leases in California. We granted a hearing in the instant case, and a companion case, to consider the *Hinson*

1. See Pines v. Perssion (1961) 14 Wis. 2d 590, 111 N.W.2d 409; Lemle v. Breeden (1969) 51 Haw. 426, 462 P.2d 470; Javins v. First National Realty Corp. (1970) 138 U.S. App. D.C. 369, 428 F.2d 1071, *cert. den.* 400 U.S. 925, 91S. Ct. 186, 27 L. Ed. 2d 185; Marini v. Ireland (1970) 56 N.J. 130, 265 A.2d 526; Kline v. Burns (1971) 111 N.H. 87, 276 A.2d 248; Jack Spring, Inc. v. Little (1972) 50 Ill. 2d 351, 280 N.E.2d 208; Mease v. Fox (1972) Iowa, 200 N.W.2d 791; Boston Housing Authority v. Hemingway (1973) Mass., 293 N.E.2d 831.

decision and to determine whether the breach of such implied warranty may be raised as a defense by a tenant in an unlawful detainer action.

For the reasons discussed below, we have determined that the *Hinson* court properly recognized a common law implied warranty of habitability in residential leases in California, and we conclude that the breach of such warranty may be raised as a defense in an unlawful detainer action.

First, as the recent line of out-of-state cases comprehensively demonstrates, the factual and legal premises underlying the original common law rule in this area have long ceased to exist; continued adherence to the time-worn doctrine conflicts with the expectations and demands of the contemporary landlord-tenant relationship and with modern legal principles in analogous fields. To remain viable, the common law must reflect the realities of present day society; an implied warranty of habitability in residential leases must therefore be recognized.

Second, we shall point out that the statutory "repair and deduct" provisions of Civil Code section 1941 et seq. do not preclude this development in the common law, for such enactments were never intended to be the exclusive remedy for tenants but have always have viewed as complementary to existing common law rights.

Finally, we have concluded that a landlord's breach of this warranty of habitability may be raised as a defense in an unlawful detainer action. Past California cases have established that a defendant in an unlawful detainer action may raise any affirmative defense which, if established, will preserve the tenant's possession of the premises. As we shall explain, a landlord's breach of a warranty of habitability directly relates to whether any rent is "due and owing" by the tenant; hence, such breach may be determinative of whether the landlord or tenant is entitled to possession of the premises upon nonpayment of rent. Accordingly, the tenant may properly raise the issue of warranty of habitability in an unlawful detainer action.

We begin with a brief review of the facts of the instant case, which reveal a somewhat typical unlawful detainer action. On September 27, 1972, the landlord Jack Sumski commenced an unlawful detainer action in the San Francisco Small Claims Court seeking possession of the leased premises and $300 in back rent. The tenant admitted non-payment of rent but defended the action on the ground that the landlord had failed to maintain the leased premises in a habitable condition. Some of the more serious defects described by the tenants included (1) the collapse and non-repair of the bathroom ceiling, (2) the continued presence of rats, mice, and cockroaches on the premises, (3) the lack of any heat in four of the apartment's rooms, (4) plumbing blockages, (5) exposed and faulty wiring, and (6) an illegally installed and dangerous stove. [3] The landlord apparently did not attempt to contest the presence of

---

3. The instant record contains no allegations—by either the landlord or tenant—that the premises were in an uninhabitable condition at the time they were first rented by petitioner. Consequently we have no occasion in the instant case to pass on the question of whether a lease of such premises constitutes an "illegal contract" (see Shephard v. Lerner (1960) 182 Cal. App. 2d

serious defects in the leased premises, but instead claimed that such defects afforded the tenant no defense in an unlawful detainer action.

The superior court judge ultimately agreed with the landlord's contention, holding that the "repair and deduct" provisions of Civil Code section 1941 et seq. constituted the tenant's exclusive remedy under these circumstances. Accordingly, the superior court entered judgment for the landlord, awarding him $225 and possession of the premises.

The tenant thereafter sought certification and transfer of the case to the Court of Appeal (see Cal. Rules of Court, rules 62, 63), but the superior court denied the request. The tenant then sought a writ of mandate or prohibition from the Court of Appeal, contending that the trial court had erroneously failed to follow the *Hinson* decision. The Court of Appeal denied the writ summarily; the tenant thereafter sought a hearing in this court, because of the statewide importance of the general issues presented we exercised our discretion and issued an alternative writ of mandate, staying the execution of judgment conditioned upon the tenant's payment into court of all rent which had accrued since the superior court judgment and all future rent as it became due. We now turn to the general legal issues presented.

At common law, the real estate lease developed in the field of real property law, not contract law. Under property law concepts, a lease was considered a conveyance or sale of the premises for a term of years, subject to the ancient doctrine of caveat emptor. Thus, under traditional common law rules, the landlord owed no duty to place leased premises in a habitable condition and no obligation to repair the premises. (3 Holdsworth, A History of English Law (5th ed. 1966) pp. 122-123; see, e.g., Brewster v. DeFremery (1867) 33 Cal. 341, 345-346.) These original common law precepts perhaps suited the agrarianism of the early Middle Ages which was their matrix; at such time, the primary value of a lease lay in the land itself and whatever simple living structures may have been included in the leasehold were of secondary importance and were readily repairable by the typical "jack-of-all-trades" lessee farmer. Furthermore, because the law of property crystallized before the development of mutually dependent covenants in contract law, a lessee's covenant to pay rent was considered at common law as independent of the lessor's covenants. Thus even when a lessor expressly covenanted to make repairs, the lessor's breach did not justify the lessee's withholding of the rent. (See 6 Williston, Contracts (3d ed. 1962) §890, pp. 580-589; Arnold v. Krigbaum (1912) 169 Cal. 143, 145, 146 P. 423.)

In recent years, however, a growing number of courts have begun to re-examine these "settled" common law rules in light of contemporary conditions, and, after thorough analysis, all of these courts have discarded the tradi-

---

746, 6 Cal. Rptr. 433: Brown v. Southall Realty Co. (D.C. Mun. App. (1968) 237 A.2d 834) or, conversely, whether the tenant should be considered to have "assumed the risk" of uninhabitable premises. On the present record, the case at bar involves only an allegation that the landlord failed to maintain the leased premises in a habitable condition. (Cf. Javins v. First National Realty Corp. (1970) 138 U.S. App. D.C. 369, 428 F.2d 1071, 1079.)

tional doctrine as incompatible with contemporary social conditions and modern legal values. This emerging line of decisions, along with a veritable flood of academic commentaries,[7] demonstrates the obsolescence of the traditional common law rule absolving a landlord of any duty to maintain leased premises in a habitable condition during the term of the lease.

The recent decisions recognize initially that the geographic and economic conditions that characterized the agrarian lessor-lessee transaction have been entirely transformed in the modern urban landlord-tenant relationship. The typical city dweller, who frequently leases an apartment several stories above the actual plot of land on which an apartment building rests, cannot realistically be viewed as acquiring an interest in land; rather, he has contracted for a place to live. As the Court of Appeal for the District of Columbia observed in Javins v. First National Realty Corp. (1970) 138 U.S. App. D.C. 369, 428 F.2d 1071, 1074: "When American city dwellers, both rich and poor, seek 'shelter' today, they seek a well known package of goods and services—a package which includes not merely walls and ceilings, but also adequate heat, light and ventilation, serviceable plumbing facilities, secure windows and doors, proper sanitation, and proper maintenance." [Fn. omitted.]

Modern urbanization has not only undermined the validity of utilizing general property concepts in analyzing landlord-tenant relations, but it has also significantly altered the factual setting directly relevant to the more specific duty of maintaining leased premises. As noted above, at the inception of the common law rule, any structure on the leased premises was likely to be of the most simple nature, easily inspected by the lessee to determine if it fit his needs, and easily repairable by the typically versatile tenant farmer. Contemporary urban housing and the contemporary urban tenant stand in marked contrast to this agrarian model.

First, the increasing complexity of modern apartment buildings not only renders them much more difficult and expensive to repair than the living quarters of earlier days, but also makes adequate inspection of the premises by a prospective tenant a virtual impossibility; complex heating, electrical and plumbing systems are hidden from view, and the landlord, who has had experience with the building, is certainly in a much better position to discover and to cure dilapidations in the premises. Moreover, in a multiple-unit dwelling repair will frequently require access to equipment and areas solely in the control of the landlord.

Second, unlike the multi-skilled lessee of old, today's city dweller generally has a single, specialized skill unrelated to maintenance work. Further-

7. The list of recent law review articles on this subject, uniformly advocating the adoption of an implied warranty of habitability as a more realistic approach to contemporary conditions, is virtually endless. (E.g., Lesar, Landlord and Tenant Reform (1969) 35 N.Y.U.L. Rev. 1279; Quinn & Phillips, The Law of Landlord-Tenant: A Critical Evaluation of the Past With Guidelines for the Future (1969) 38 Fordham L. Rev. 225; Schoskinski, Remedies of the Indigent Tenant: Proposal for Change (1966) 54 Geo. L.J. 519; Loeb, Low Income Tenant in California: A Study in Frustration (1970) 21 Hastings L.J. 287; Moskovitz, Rent Withholding and the Implied Warranty of Habitability (1970) 4 Clearinghouse Rev. 49; Note, Repairing the Duty to Repair (1971) 11 Santa Clara Law. 298.)

more, whereas an agrarian lessee frequently remained on a single plot of land for his entire life, today's urban tenant is more mobile than ever; a tenant's limited tenure in a specific apartment will frequently not justify efforts at extensive repairs. Finally, the expense of needed repairs will often be outside the reach of many tenants for "[l]ow and middle income tenants, even if they were interested in making repairs, would be unable to obtain any financing for major repairs since they have no long-term interest in the property." (Javins v. First National Realty Corp. (1970) 138 U.S. App. D.C. 369, 428 F.2d 1071, 1078-1079.)

In addition to these significant changes, urbanization and population growth have wrought an enormous transformation in the contemporary housing market, creating a scarcity of adequate low cost housing in virtually every urban setting. This current state of the housing market is by no means unrelated to the common law duty to maintain habitable premises. For one thing, the severe shortage of low and moderate cost housing has left tenants with little bargaining power through which they might gain express warranties of habitability from landlords, and thus the mechanism of the "free market" no longer serves as a viable means for fairly allocating the duty to repair leased premises between landlord and tenant.[9] For another, the scarcity of adequate housing has limited further the adequacy of the tenant's right to inspect the premises; even when defects are apparent the low income tenant frequently has no realistic alternative but to accept such housing with the expectation that the landlord will make the necessary repairs. Finally, the shortage of available low cost housing has rendered inadequate the few remedies that common law courts previously have developed to ameliorate the harsh consequences of the traditional "no duty to repair" rule.[10]

These enormous factual changes in the landlord-tenant field have been paralleled by equally dramatic changes in the prevailing legal doctrines governing commercial transactions. Whereas the traditional common law "no

9. In light of this inequality of bargaining power, the Massachusetts Supreme Judicial Court, in recently recognizing a warranty of habitability for residential leases, held that such warranty generally could not be waived by any provision in the lease or rental agreement. (See Boston Housing Authority v. Hemingway (1973) Mass., 293 N.E.2d 831, 843.) We agree that public policy requires that landlords generally not be permitted to use their superior bargaining power to negate the warranty of habitability rule. The Legislature has recently reached a similar conclusion with respect to tenants' rights under Civil Code section 1941 et seq. (See Civ. Code, §1942.1.)

10. Thus, for example, the doctrine of "constructive eviction," which expanded the traditional "covenant of quiet enjoyment" from simply a guarantee of the tenant's possession of the premises (see Connor v. Bernheimer (N.Y. Com. Pleas 1875) 6 Daly 295, 299; Georgeous v. Lewis (1912) 20 Cal. App. 255, 258, 128 P. 768) to a protection of his "beneficial enjoyment" of the premises through the maintenance of basic, necessary services (Groh v. Kover's Bull Pen, Inc. (1963) 221 Cal. App. 2d 611, 614, 34 Cal. Rptr. 637; Sierad v. Lilly (1962) 204 Cal. App. 2d 770, 773, 22 Cal. Rptr. 580), gives little help to the typical low income tenant today because to avail himself of the doctrine a tenant must vacate the premises. (See, e.g., Veysey v. Moriyama (1921) 184 Cal. 802, 805-806, 195 P. 662; Lori Ltd. v. Wolfe (1948) 85 Cal. App. 2d 54, 65, 192 P.2d 112.) In the present housing market many tenants cannot find any alternative housing which they can afford, and thus this reform of the common law rules has in reality provided little comfort to most needy tenants. (See Loeb, The Low Income Tenant in California: A Study in Frustration (1970) 21 Hastings L.J. 287, 304.)

duty to maintain or repair" rule was steeped in the caveat emptor ethic of an earlier commercial era (see, e.g., Nelson v. Myers (1928) 94 Cal. App. 66, 75-76, 270 P. 719), modern legal decisions have recognized that the consumer in an industrial society should be entitled to rely on the skill of the supplier to assure that goods and services are of adequate quality. In seeking to protect the reasonable expectations of consumers, judicial decisions, discarding the caveat emptor approach, have for some time implied a warranty of fitness and merchantability in the case of the sale of goods. [Citations omitted.] (See generally Jaeger, Warranties of Merchantability and Fitness for Use (1962) 16 Rutgers L. Rev. 493.) In recent years, moreover, California courts have increasingly recognized the applicability of this implied warranty theory to real estate transactions; prior cases have found a warranty of fitness implied by law with respect to the construction of new housing units. [11] [Citations omitted.] In most significant respects, the modern urban tenant is in the same position as any other normal consumer of goods. (See Note, The Tenant as Consumer (1971) 3 U.C. Davis L. Rev. 59.) Through a residential lease, a tenant seeks to purchase "housing" from his landlord for a specified period of time. The landlord "sells" housing, enjoying a much greater opportunity, incentive and capacity than a tenant to inspect and maintain the condition of his apartment building. A tenant may reasonably expect that the product he is purchasing is fit for the purpose for which it is obtained, that is, a living unit. Moreover, since a lease contract specifies a designated period of time during which the tenant has a right to inhabit the premises, the tenant may legitimately expect that the premises will be fit for such habitation for the duration of the term of the lease. It is just such reasonable expectations of consumers which the modern "implied warranty" decisions endow with formal, legal protection. (Cf. Gray v. Zurich Insurance Co. (1966) 65 Cal. 2d 263, 269-271, 54 Cal. Rptr.

---

11. Indeed, even before the turn of the century, common law courts had recognized an implied warranty of habitability in leases of furnished rooms or furnished houses. In the seminal case of Ingalls v. Hobbs (1892) 156 Mass. 348, 350, 31 N.E. 286, 286) the Supreme Judicial Court of Massachusetts explained why the traditional no warranty of habitability rule did not apply to such rentals:

> [T]here are good reasons why a different rule should apply to one who hires a furnished room, or a furnished house. . . . Its fitness for immediate use . . . is a far more important element entering into the contract than when there is a mere lease of real estate. . . . An important part of what the hirer pays for is the opportunity to enjoy it without delay, and without the expense of preparing it for use. It is very difficult, and often impossible, for one to determine on inspection whether the house and its appointments are fit for the use for which they are immediately wanted, and the doctrine of caveat emptor, which is ordinarily applicable to a lessee of real estate, would often work injustice if applied to cases of this kind. It would be unreasonable to hold, under such circumstances, that the landlord does not impliedly agree that what he is letting is a house suitable for occupation in its condition at the time.

Recent cases have recognized that the rationale underlying the *Ingalls* court's adoption of an implied warranty of habitability in the rental of furnished dwellings is now applicable to urban residential leases generally. (See, e.g., Boston Housing Authority v. Hemingway (1973) Mass., 293 N.E.2d 831, 841; Javins v. First National Realty Corp. (1970) 138 U.S. App. D.C. 369, 428 F.2d 1071, 1078.) Our decision today may be seen as a logical development of the common law principles embodied in the *Ingalls* decision.

104, 419 P.2d 168. See generally Leff, Contract as a Thing (1970) 19 Am. U.L. Rev. 131.)

Finally, an additional legal development casts significant light upon the continued vitality of the traditional common law rule. The past half century has brought the widespread enactment of comprehensive housing codes throughout the nation; in California, the Department of Housing and Community Development has established detailed, statewide housing regulations (see Health & Saf. Code, §17921; Cal. Admin. Code, tit. 25, §§1000-1090), and the Legislature has expressly authorized local entities to impose even more stringent regulations. (See Health & Saf. Code, §17951.) These comprehensive housing codes affirm that, under contemporary conditions, public policy compels landlords to bear the primary responsibility for maintaining safe, clean and habitable housing in our state. As the Supreme Court of Wisconsin declared with respect to that state's housing code:

> [T]he legislature has made a policy judgment—that it is socially (and politically) desirable to impose these duties on a property owner—which has rendered the old common law rule obsolete. To follow the old rule of no implied warranty of habitability in leases would, in our opinion, be inconsistent with the current legislative policy concerning housing standards. [Pines v. Perssion (1961) 14 Wis. 2d 590, 596, 111 N.W.2d 409, 412-413; see Buckner v. Azulai (1967) 251 Cal. App. Supp. 2d 1013, 1015, 59 Cal. Rptr. 806.) . . .]

For the reasons discussed at length above, we believe that the traditional common law rule has outlived its usefulness; we agree with the *Hinson* court's determination that modern conditions compel the recognition of a common law implied warranty of habitability in residential leases.

[The court then concludes that tenants' statutory "repair and deduct" remedy was not intended to be tenants' exclusive remedy where premises were not habitable.]

The landlord in a companion case contends, however, that even if we should uphold such a warranty, we could never permit a tenant to raise a landlord's breach of it in an unlawful detainer action. Relying initially on the fact that the *Hinson* decision itself involved a declaratory judgment action and not an unlawful detainer action, the landlord maintains that the trial court's refusal to permit the defense of a "warranty of habitability" in the instant case fully conforms with *Hinson*. We cannot agree.

In the first place, nothing in the *Hinson* decision supports such a distinction. Second, and more fundamentally, we have concluded that even apart from the *Hinson* decision, no legal doctrine bars a tenant from raising such a critical defense in an unlawful detainer action. We note initially that absolutely nothing in the statutory provisions governing unlawful detainer proceedings prohibits the assertion of any defense. [16]

---

16. Section 1170 of the Code of Civil Procedure provides that in summary unlawful detainer proceedings "the defendant may appear and *answer* or demur" (emphasis added), and under section 431.30, an "answer" may contain "[a] statement of any new matter constituting a defense" but may not claim affirmative relief. Thus, nothing in the statutory scheme precludes a defendant from interposing an affirmative defense in an unlawful detainer proceeding.

The crucial issue in this case thus becomes whether a landlord's breach of a warranty of habitability directly relates to the issue of possession. Holding that such breach was irrelevant to the question of possession, early California cases refused to permit a defense that the landlord had breached a covenant to repair premises. (See, e.g., Arnold v. Krigbaum (1915) 169 Cal. 143, 145, 146 P. 423; Frasier v. Witt (1923) 62 Cal. App. 309, 315, 217 P. 114.) These decisions, however, rested primarily upon the ancient property doctrine of "independent covenants," under which a tenant's obligation to pay rent was viewed as a continuing obligation which was not excused by the landlord's failure to fulfill any covenant of repair he may have assumed. As indicated earlier in this opinion, the entire foundation of the "independent covenants" doctrine rested on the central role played by land in the lease transaction of the Middle Ages; the doctrine simply reflected the fact that in those early times covenants regarding the maintenance of buildings were generally "incidental" to the furnishing of land, and did not go to the root of the consideration for the lease. In that setting, a landlord's breach of such an "incidental" covenant to repair was reasonably considered insufficient to justify the tenant's refusal to pay rent, the tenant's main obligation under the lease.[20]

The transformation which the residential lease has undergone since the Middle Ages, however, has completely eroded the underpinnings of the "independent covenant" rule. Today the habitability of the dwelling unit has become the very essence of the residential lease; the landlord can as materially frustrate the purpose of such a lease by permitting the premises to become uninhabitable as by withdrawing the use of a portion of the premises. (See fn. 20, supra.) Thus, in keeping with the contemporary trend to analyze urban residential leases under modern contractual principles, we now conclude that the tenant's duty to pay rent is "mutually dependent" upon the landlord's fulfillment of his implied warranty of habitability.

Once we recognize that the tenant's obligation to pay rent and the landlord's warranty of habitability are mutually dependent, it becomes clear that the landlord's breach of such warranty may be directly relevant to the issue of possession. If the tenant can prove such a breach by the landlord, he may demonstrate that his nonpayment of rent was justified and that no rent is in fact "due and owing" to the landlord. Under such circumstances, of course, the landlord would not be entitled to possession of the premises. (See Skaggs v. Emerson (1875) 50 Cal. 3, 6; Giraud v. Milovich (1938) 29 Cal. App. 2d 543, 547-549, 85 P.2d 182.)

The landlord contends, however, that the recognition of such a defense

20. The traditional "independent covenant" rule only applied to convenants, such as the covenant to repair buildings, which were "collateral" to the landlord's obligation to provide the land to the tenant; because of the importance of land in early leases, the common law generally recognized that the tenant's obligation to pay rent was mutually dependent upon the landlord's fulfillment of his covenant to furnish the land. Thus, if the landlord deeded away even a small portion of the leased land, the common law considered this a "partial actual eviction" and relieved the tenant of his rental obligation. (See Giraud v. Milovich (1938) 29 Cal. App. 2d 543, 547-549, 85 P.2d 182.)

will completely undermine the speedy procedure contemplated for unlawful detainer actions. In the first place, however, while the state does have a significant interest in preserving a speedy repossession remedy, that interest cannot justify the exclusion of matters which are essential to a just resolution of the question of possession at issue. As the Court of Appeal observed in Abstract Investment Co. v. Hutchinson (1962) 204 Cal. App. 2d 242, 249, 22 Cal. Rptr. 309, 314: "Certainly the interest in preserving the summary nature of an action cannot outweigh the interest of doing substantial justice. To hold the preservation of the summary proceeding of paramount importance would be analogous to the 'tail wagging the dog.' "

Second, we believe the landlord's contention greatly exaggerates the detrimental effect of the recognition of this defense on the summary unlawful detainer procedure.

. . . [D]efendants in unlawful detainer actions have long been permitted to raise those affirmative defenses—both legal and equitable—that are directly relevant to the issue of possession; over the years, the unlawful detainer action has remained an efficient, summary procedure. We see no reason why the availability of a warranty of habitability defense should frustrate the summary procedure when the availability of these other defenses has not.

Moreover, as the *Hinson* court indicated, sound procedural safeguards suffice to protect the landlord's economic interests without depriving the tenant of a meaningful opportunity to raise the breach of warranty issue. The *Hinson* court, elaborating on a procedural mechanism suggested by the Court of Appeal for the District of Columbia in the *Javins* opinion (428 F.2d at p. 1083, fn. 67), stated:

> If the tenant claims that all or a part of the rent is not due because of the defects in the premises, the trial court may, during the pendency of the action and at the request of either party, require the tenant to make the rental payments at the contract rate into court as they become due for as long as the tenant remains in possession. At the trial of the action the court can then determine how the rent paid into court should be distributed. [26 Cal. App. 3d at p. 71, 102 Cal. Rptr. at p. 666.]

Such a procedure can serve as a fair means of protection of landlords from potential abuses of the proposed warranty of habitability defense. (See National Conference of Commissioners on Uniform State Laws, Uniform Residential Landlord and Tenant Act (1972) §4.105.)

CONCLUSION

We have concluded that a warranty of habitability is implied by law in residential leases in this state and that the breach of such a warranty may be raised as a defense in an unlawful detainer action. Under the implied warranty which we recognize, a residential landlord covenants that premises he leases for living quarters will be maintained in a habitable state for the duration of the lease. This implied warranty of habitability does not require that a landlord ensure that leased premises are in perfect, aesthetically pleasing condition, but it does mean that "bare living requirements" must be maintained. [22] In most cases substantial compliance with those applicable building and housing code standards which materially affect health and safety will suffice to meet the landlord's obligations under the common law implied warranty of habitability we now recognize. As the *Hinson* court observed: "[m]inor housing code violations standing alone which do not affect habitability must be considered de minimis and will not entitle the tenant to reduction in rent. . . ." (26 Cal. App. 2d at p. 70, 102 Cal. Rptr. at p. 666.)

If the trial court does find a breach of implied warranty, the court must then determine the extent of the damages flowing from this breach. Recent decisions have suggested that in these circumstances the "tenant's damages shall be measured by the difference between the fair rental value of the premises if they had been as warranted and the fair rental value of the premises as they were during occupancy by the tenant in the unsafe or unsanitary condition." (Mease v. Fox (1972) Iowa, 200 N.W.2d 791, 797; Boston Housing Authority v. Hemingway (1973) Mass., 293 N.E.2d 831, 845; Academy Spires, Inc. v. Jones (1970) 108 N.J. Super. 395, 261 A.2d 413, 417.)

We recognize that the ascertainment of appropriate damages in such cases will often be a difficult task, not susceptible of precise determination, but in this respect these cases do not differ significantly from a host of analogous situations, in both contract and tort law, in which damages cannot be computed with complete certainty. [Citations omitted.] In these situations, trial courts must do the best they can and use all available facts to approximate the fair and reasonable damages under all of the circumstances. (See McGregor, Damages (13th ed. 1972) §258, p. 184; McCormick, Damages (1935) §27, p. 101.) [24]

---

22. The recent case of Academy Spires, Inc. v. Brown (1970) 111 N.J. Super. 477, 268 A.2d 556 gives a good indication of the general scope of the warranty of habitability. In that case, a tenant in a multi-story apartment building complained of a series of defects, including (1) the periodic failure to supply heat and water, (2) the malfunctioning of an incinerator, (3) the failure in hot water supply, (4) several leaks in the bathroom, (5) defective venetian blinds, (6) cracks in plaster walls, (7) unpainted condition of walls and (8) a nonfunctioning elevator. The *Academy Spires* court held:

> Some of these clearly go to the bare living requirements. In a modern society one cannot be expected to live in a multi-storied apartment building without heat, hot water, garbage disposal or elevator service. Failure to supply such things is a breach of the implied covenant of habitability. Malfunction of venetian blinds, water leaks, wall cracks, lack of painting, at least of the magnitude presented here, go to what may be called "amenities." Living with lack of painting, water leaks and defective venetian blinds may be unpleasant, aesthetically unsatisfying, but does not come within the category of uninhabitability. Such things will not be considered in diminution of the rent. (268 A.2d at p. 559.) (See also Gillette v. Anderson (1972) 4 Ill. App. 3d 838, 282 N.E. 2d 149 (warranty of habitability breached by failure to provide adequate bathing facilities).)

24. The case of Academy Spires, Inc. v. Brown (1970) 111 N.J. Super. 477, 268 A.2d 556, 561-562 demonstrates one reasonable response to the problem. The *Academy Spires* court, after fully acknowledging the difficulty of precisely determining damages resulting from a landlord's breach of an implied warranty of habitability, assessed damages by a "percentage reduction of use"

In the instant case, the tenant has already quit the premises and thus the only matter to be determined on remand is the question of money damages owing to the landlord. In unlawful detainer actions generally, however, if the trial court determines that the landlord's breach of warranty is total, and that the tenant owes no rent whatsoever, the court should, of course, enter judgment for the tenant in the unlawful detainer action. If the court determines, however, that the damages from the breach of warranty justify only a partial reduction in rent, the tenant may maintain possession of the premises only if he pays that portion of the back rent that is owing, as directed by the trial court. (See Code Civ. Proc., §1174; cf. Academy Spires, Inc. v. Brown (1970) 111 N.J. Super. 447 [268 A.2d 556, 562]; Javins v. First National Realty Corp. (1970) 138 U.S. App. D.C. 369, 428 F.2d 1071, 1083.) If the tenant fails to pay such sum, the landlord is entitled to a judgment for possession. Finally, of course, if the trial court finds that the landlord has not breached the warranty of habitability, it should immediately enter judgment in favor of the landlord.

In summary, we have concluded that the traditional common law rule which imposed no warranty of habitability in residential leases is a product of an earlier, land-oriented era, which bears no reasonable relation to the social or legal realities of the landlord-tenant relationship of today. The United States Supreme Court has observed that "the body of private property law . . . , more than almost any other branch, of law, has been shaped by distinctions whose validity is largely historical," (Jones v. United States (1960) 362 U.S. 257, 266, 80 S. Ct. 725, 733, 4 L. Ed. 2d 697), and on previous occasions in recent years our own court has responded to the changes wrought by modern conditions by discarding outworn common law property doctrines. (See Rowland v. Christian (1968) 69 Cal. 2d 108, 70 Cal. Rptr. 97, 443 P.2d 561.) In taking a similar step today, we do not exercise a novel prerogative, but merely follow the well-established duty of common law courts to reflect contemporary social values and ethics. As Justice Cardozo wrote in his celebrated eassy "The Growth of the Law" chapter V, pages 136-137:

> A rule which in its origin was the creation of the courts themselves, and was supposed in the making to express the *mores* of the day, may be abrogated by courts when the *mores* have so changed that perpetration of the rule would do violence to the social conscience. . . . This is not usurpation. It is not even innovation. It is the reservation for ourselves of the same power of creation that built up the common law through its exercise by the judges of the past.

---

approach, under which the court reduced the tenant's rental obligation by a percentage corresponding to the relative reduction of use of the leased premises caused by the landlord's breach. In applying this approach, the *Academy Spires* court carefully reviewed both the importance of the particular defects in the premises (including failure to supply heat, hot water, elevator service and a working incinerator) and the length of time such defects had existed (from one or two days to several weeks), and finally concluded that under all the circumstances "the diminution of rent of 25% is a fair amount." (268 A.2d at p. 562.) (See also Samuelson v. Quinones (1972) 119 N.J. Super. 338, 291 A.2d 580, 583; Morbeth Realty Corp. v. Rosenshine (1971) 67 Misc. 2d 325 [323 N.Y.S.2d 363, 366-367].)

Let a peremptory writ of mandate issue directing the superior court to vacate the San Francisco Superior Court judgment entered in the case of Sumski v. Green, S.C.A. No. 11836 on January 3, 1973, and instructing the court to proceed with the trial of the unlawful detainer action in accordance with the views expressed herein.

NOTES AND QUESTIONS

1. Restatement (Second) of Property §5.5 (1977) contains an implied warranty of habitability for residential quarters. It reads:

(1) Except to the extent the parties to a lease validly agree otherwise, the landlord, under a lease of property for residential use, is obligated to the tenant to keep the leased property in a condition that meets the requirements of governing health, safety, and housing codes, unless the failure to meet those requirements is the fault of the tenant or is the consequence of a sudden non-manmade force or the conduct of third parties.

(2) Except to the extent the parties to a lease validly agree otherwise, the landlord is obligated to the tenant to keep safe and in repair the areas remaining under his control that are maintained for the use and benefit of his tenants. . . .

Notice the qualifications:

a. "except to the extent the parties to a lease validly agree otherwise"

Examine carefully the Model Apartment Lease, *supra*, ¶¶3 (first two sentences), 6, and 16. How do these provisions change the basic Restatement rule?

The Restatement (Second) of Property §5.6 (1977) would allow the parties to a lease to increase or decrease what would otherwise be the obligations of the landlord with respect to the condition of the leased property [and similarly with respect to the tenant's remedies] unless the agreement is "unconscionable or significantly against public policy." Many states which have created a statutory warranty of habitability bar any contrary agreement, see, e.g., N.Y. Real Prop. L. §235-b (McKinney Supp. 1980); Ohio Rev. Code Ann. §§5321.04, 5321.06 and 5321.07 (Page Supp. 1975), or permit only limited change, see, e.g., Michigan Comp. Laws Ann. §554.139 (Supp. 1976) (contrary agreement allowed only for leases longer than one year); Virginia Code Ann. §§55-248.13 and 55-248.21 (Supp. 1975) (contrary agreement allowed only when landlord's purpose is not to evade his primary obligations).

Under what circumstances might a residential tenant knowingly agree to relinquish some of her rights to habitability?

b. "a lease of property for residential use"

What are the arguments for and against extending the warranty of habitability to nonresidential premises? See Note, Commercial Leases: Behind the *Green* Door, 12 Pacific L.J. 1067, 1091-97 (1981); Restatement (Second) of

Property §5.1, Rep. Note 2 (1977) ("The present state of the statutory development and judicial development does not warrant taking a position one way or the other as to non-residental property . . . The Reporter is of the opinion that the rule of this section should be extended to non-residential property. The small commercial tenant particularly needs its protection.")

If you believe that some, but not all, nonresidential tenants deserve the protection of an implied warranty of habitability, how would you cast a statute (or draft a common-law rule) that would separate the two classes?

To date, state courts have been reluctant to extend the implied warranty into the nonresidential area. Cf. Yuan Kane Ing v. Levy, 26 Ill. App. 3d 889, 892, 326 N.E.2d 51, 54 (1975); Van Ness Industries v. Clairemont Painting & Decorating Co., 129 N.J. Super. 507, 324 A.2d 102 (1974). But cf. Four Seas Investment Corp. v. Int'l Hotel Tenant's Ass'n, 81 Cal. App. 3d 604, 613, 146 Cal. Rptr. 531, 535 (1978) (dicta).

c. "in a condition that meets the requirements of governing health, safety, and housing codes"

Some communities remain without housing codes, and many housing codes exempt one-family dwellings or owner-occupied two-family units. Does any justification exist for curtailing the warranty in such instances? Cf. Graham v. Wisenburn, 39 A.D.2d 334, 334 N.Y.S.2d 81 (1972) (pre-statutory decision: court refuses to extend implied warranty to tenant-occupied one-family house).

d. "unless the failure to meet those requirements . . . is the consequence of a sudden non-manmade force or the conduct of third parties"

The Restatement neither cites any supporting authority nor gives any explanation. Except with respect to matters of notice and reasonable opportunity to make the repairs, should the warranty of habitability be so qualified?

2. Notwithstanding its many qualifications, the Restatement proviso was adopted on the floor of the American Law Institute only after a stormy debate led by those who argued that the implied warranty was (a) not yet fully supported by court decisions, (b) likely to be wholly ineffectual, and (c) certain to reduce the supply of affordable housing for lower-income tenants. These criticisms are elaborated in Meyers, Covenant of Habitability and the American Law Institute, 27 Stan. L. Rev. 879 (1975).

3. In the *Green* opinion, the court draws heavily upon the sale-of-goods analogy: "In most significant respects, the modern urban tenant is in the same position as any other normal consumer of goods." [page 306, *supra*]

Are there any factors militating against treating the lease of an apartment and the sale of an auto in the same way?

4. According to the *Green* opinion, page 310, *supra, minor* housing code violations standing alone might not affect habitability so as to entitle the tenant to a rent reduction. In that event, tenant's defense fails and the landlord gets judgment for possession. Should tenants (or their lawyers) have to risk guessing wrong as to what violations are minor and what violations are not? If you were lawyer for the tenant and wanted to protect him (and your own inner peace) against a bad guess, what procedural steps might accom-

pany your *Green*-type defense? When a state court adopts the *Green* rule, should code enforcement officials then promulgate a list of violations affecting habitability? If this were done, however, might someone then argue against the validity of any code provision whose violation did not affect habitability, the argument being that the regulatory power rests on dangers to health, safety, etc.? To examine this issue differently: what constitutes habitability (or unhabitability)?

5. The court remanded *Green* for trial, principally to allow proof as to what portion of the tenant's obligation to pay rent was suspended by the landlord's breach. The court explicitly recognized that the landlord might be entitled to some of the rent. At the trial, which party has the burden of coming forward to establish the (reduced) rental value of the premises? What form of proof is required? It is realistic to expect that poor tenants can present the (expert?) testimony that will establish (or contradict the owner's evidence of) rental value? Do you see any solution to this procedural difficulty? Cf. New York Real Prop. L. §235-b (McKinney Supp. 1980-81) ("In determining the amount of damages [for breach of implied warranty of habitability], the court did not require any expert testimony.")

6. "[I]f the trial court determines that the landlord's breach of warranty is total . . . the tenant owes no rent whatsoever). . . ." [page 311, *supra*]

What does total breach mean? Doesn't every apartment have some rental value? Suppose that Green had bought a new auto that had a top speed of only seventeen miles an hour. Could he keep the auto, use it as best he can, and refuse all payment? Cf. U.C.C. §2-602(2)(a).

7. Suppose that the trial jury finds that the tenant's entire rental obligation has been extinguished by the landlord's breach; if the landlord refuses to repair, may the tenant remain indefinitely and pay no rent? Cf. Robinson v. Diamond Housing Corp., 257 A.2d 492 (D.C. Ct. App. 1969) (where code violations existed when the lease began, the lease "illegal," void ab initio, and unenforceable). However, when landlord then sought to evict tenant as an occupant at sufferance, court directed to determine whether the landlord's action was "retaliatory" against the tenant for previously raising the "illegality" defense). 463 F.2d 853 (D.C. Cir. 1972).

8. Suppose that the trial jury finds that a tenant's entire rental is extinguished by the landlord's breach; thereafter, landlord undertakes a repair program requiring six months to complete. Is the landlord entitled to collect any rent before the end of six months? Do you see any feasible scheme for gradual restoration of the tenant's rent as repairs proceed?

9. *Green* was a landlord-initiated suit to recover possession. The court found an implied covenant of habitability. Is this promise one that the tenant can sue specifically to enforce? In short: is there any way that tenants can compel their landlords to provide habitable quarters (other than through muncipal code enforcement proceedings)? Suppose that tenant obtains a mandatory injunction requiring landlord to make specified repairs? Will the landlord go to jail if he refuses? If he cannot afford the repairs? May the landlord,

instead of obeying the injunction, withdraw the apartment from the rental market?

    10.   Landlord sues for nonpayment of rent. Tenant interposes the un-habitability defense.

   (a) Landlord acknowledges that the premises were without heat and hot water throughout October but argues that he should be excused because he had to replace an inefficient boiler. Persuasive argument? See Leris Realty Co. v. Robbins, 95 Misc. 2d 712, 408 N.Y.S.2d 166 (Civ. Ct. 1978).

   (b) Landlord acknowledges that tenants suffered a seventeen-day deprivation of garbage disposal, janitorial, and repair services but argues that he should be excused because all his employees were on strike. Persuasive argument? Park West Management Corp. v. Mitchell, 47 N.Y.2d 316, 391 N.E.2d 1288, 418 N.Y.S.2d 310 (1979).

   (c) Landlord acknowledges that tenants suffered noise and dust irritation from his demolition and construction activity on an adjacent parcel, but argues that he should be excused because the work was done in a lawful and reasonable manner. Persuasive argument? Mantica R. Corp. NV v. Malone, 106 Misc. 2d 953, 436 N.Y.S.2d 797 (Civ. Ct. 1981).

    11.   May tenants take the initiative and sue to recover part or all of the rent previously paid, on grounds that landlord has breached the covenant of habitability? Cf. Berzito v. Gambino, 63 N.J. 460, 469, 308 A.2d 17, 22 (1973). Must landlords first be given fair warning of the breach?

    12.   Consider very carefully what you think the impact will be on housing conditions and shelter costs generally if all rental agreements are deemed to include an implied covenant of habitability (fitness).

    13.   Should there be serious concern that the remedy of summary dispossess may become even less summary if tenants can routinely assert an unhabitability defense? Will the caseload in landlord-tenant courts become unmanageable if the issue of habitability is raised routinely? And is there (should there be) any way to screen the tenant genuinely trying to improve his environment from the tenant who has the intention neither to stay nor to pay?

§5.9   The Remedy of Repair and Offset

MARINI v. IRELAND

56 N.J. 130, 265 A.2d 526 (1970)

HANEMAN, J. This matter concerns the appealability of County District Court landlord and tenant dispossess judgments; the scope of a landlord's duty to make repairs; and the right to offset the cost of such repairs against accruing rent on the failure of the landlord to make same, if found to be required.

On or about April 2, 1969, plaintiff, landlord, and defendant, tenant, entered into a one-year lease for an apartment located in a two-family duplex building at 503-B Rand Street, Camden, New Jersey. The annual rent of $1,140 was agreed to be paid in monthly installments of $95. The lease incorporated a covenant of quiet enjoyment but did not include a specific covenant for repairs.

On or about June 25, 1969, defendant alleges that she discovered that the toilet in the leased apartment was cracked and water was leaking onto the bathroom floor. She further alleges that repeated attempts to inform plaintiff of this condition were unsuccessful. On or about June 27, 1969, defendant hired one Karl T. Bittner, a registered plumber, to repair the toilet. Bittner repaired the toilet at a cost of $85.72, which the tenant paid.

On July 15, 1969, defendant mailed plaintiff a check for $9.28 together with the receipt for $85.72 in payment of the July rent. Plaintiff challenged the offsetting of the cost of the repair and demanded the outstanding $85.72.

When his demands were refused, plaintiff instituted a summary dispossess action for nonpayment of rent in the Camden County District Court pursuant to N.J.S.A. 2A:18-53(b) alleging the nonpayment of the July rent in the amount of $85.72 and August rent of $95. A hearing was had on August 15, 1969. Plaintiff argued that he was entitled to the $85.72 because he had no duty to make repairs and consequently, defendant's payment of the cost of repair could not be offset against rent.

The judge conceived the issue as entirely a legal one and determined that the facts which defendant alleged did not create a duty upon the landlord to make repairs. Thus, without trying out the issues tendered by defendant, he found a default in payment of rent of $85.72 (July) and $95 (August) plus costs and rendered a judgment for possession. Defendant appealed to the Appellate Division.

On August 29, 1969, a judge of the Appellate Division granted a temporary stay of the judgment for possession and the warrant of eviction. The Appellate Division granted a stay pending appeal on September 23, 1969 and ordered defendant to pay all the rents then due except the contested July rent. The Appellate Division also then denied plaintiff's cross-motion to dismiss the appeal. Before the Appellate Division heard argument, this Court certified the case on its own motion. R. 2:12-1.

The issues which evolve on this appeal are: Did defendant's claimed right to offset her cost of repairs against rent raise a "jurisdictional" issue? If the answer to that query is in the affirmative, did the landlord have a duty to repair and may the issue of failure to comply with such duty be raised in a dispossess action? Also involved in the latter question is the right of the tenant to make repairs upon the landlord's failure to so do and the right to offset the cost thereof against rent.

N.J.S.A. 2A:18-53 provides in part:

> Any lessee or tenant . . . of any houses, buildings, lands or tenements, . . .
> may be removed from such premises by the county district court of the county
> within which such premises are situated, in an action in the following cases: . . .
> b.   Where such persons shall hold over after a default in the payment of
> rent, pursuant to the agreement under which the premises are held.

N.J.S.A. 2A: 18-59 reads:

> Proceedings had by virtue of this article shall not be appealable except on
> the ground of lack of jurisdiction. The landlord, however, shall remain liable in
> a civil action for unlawful proceedings under this article. . . .

. . . We hold, therefore, that equitable as well as legal defenses asserting
payment or absolution from payment in whole or part are available to a
tenant in a dispossess action and must be considered by the court. Denial of a
motion by defendant directed at the complaint for failure to make adequate
factual allegations, or of a motion at the conclusion of the trial for failure to
supply proof that the amount of rent alleged in the complaint is in default,
both going to the question of jurisdiction, are each appealable.

Insofar as Peters v. Kelly, 98 N.J. Super. 441 (App. Div. 1968), conflicts
with the foregoing it is overruled.

It becomes necessary to consider the merits of defendant's equitable defense that the failure of the landlord to repair the toilet constituted a breach of
the covenant of habitability or quiet enjoyment and gave rise to defendant's
entitlement to self-help, permitting her to repair the toilet and offset the cost
thereof against her rent. We need not concern ourselves with the covenant of
quiet enjoyment as will hereafter become apparent.

We are here concerned with the lease of premises for residential purposes. The lease provides:

> WITNESSETH, that the said party of the first part hath let, and by these
> present doth grant, demise and to farm let unto the said property of the second
> part, all that contains 4 rooms and bath, apartment situated in the city and
> county of camden [sic], state [sic] of New Jersey, known and designated as 503-
> B Rand Street. . . . [N]or use or permit any part thereof to be used for any other
> purpose than dwelling. . . .

As the lease contains no express covenant to repair we are obliged to
determine whether there arises an implied covenant, however categorized,
which would require the landlord to make repairs. . . .

A covenant in a lease can arise only by necessary implication from
specific language of the lease or because it is indispensable to carry into effect
the purpose of the lease. In determining, under contract law, what covenants

are implied, the object which the parties had in view and intended to be accomplished, is of primary importance. . . .

So here, the lease expressly described the leased premise as "4 rooms and bath, apartment" and restricted the use thereof for one purpose,—"dwelling." Patently, "the effect which the parties, as fair and reasonable men, presumably would have agreed on," was that the premises were habitable and fit for living. The very object of the letting was to furnish the defendant with quarters suitable for living purposes. This is what the landlord at least impliedly (if not expressly) represented he had available and what the tenant was seeking. In a modern setting, the landlord should, in residential letting, be held to an implied covenant against latent defects, which is another manner of saying, habitability and livability fitness. See Hyland v. Parkside Investment Co., Inc., 10 N.J. Misc. 1148 (Sup. Ct. 1932). It is a mere matter of semantics whether we designate this covenant one "to repair" or "of habitability and livability fitness." Actually it is a covenant that at the inception of the lease, there are no latent defects in facilities vital to the use of the premises for residential purposes because of faulty original construction or deterioration from age or normal usage. And further it is a covenant that these facilities will remain in usable condition during the entire term of the lease. In performance of this covenant the landlord is required to maintain those facilities in a condition which renders the property livable.

It is eminently fair and just to charge a landlord with the duty of warranting that a building or part thereof rented for residential purpose is fit for that purpose at the inception of the term and will remain so during the entire term. Of course, ancillary to such understanding it must be implied that he has further agreed to repair damage to vital facilities caused by ordinary wear and tear during said term. Where damage has been caused maliciously or by abnormal or unusual use, the tenant is conversely liable for repair. The nature of vital facilities and the extent and type of maintenance and repair required is limited and governed by the type of property rented and the amount of rent reserved. Failure to so maintain the property would constitute a constructive eviction.

It becomes necessary to consider the respective rights and duties which accompany such an implied covenant. We must recognize that historically, the landlord's covenant to alter or repair premises and the tenant's covenant to pay rent were generally regarded as independent covenants. The landlord's failure to perform did not entitle the tenant to make the repair and offset the cost thereof against future rent. It only gave rise to a separate cause of action for breach of covenant. Duncan Development Co. v. Duncan Hardware, Inc., 34 N.J. Super. 293 at 298 (App. Div. 1955), *cert. denied*, 19 N.J. 328 (1955); Stewart v. Childs Co., 86 N.J.L. 648 (E. & A. 1914). This result also eventuated from the application of the law of real estate rather than of contract. The concept of mutually dependent promises was not originally applied to the ascertainment of whether covenants in leases were dependent or independent.

However, presently we recognize that covenants are dependent or independent according to the intention of the parties and the good sense of the case. Higgins v. Whiting, 102 N.J.L. 279 (Sup. Ct. 1925); 3 Thompson on Real Property, §1115 (1959 Replacement).

In Higgins v. Whiting, *supra,* the court said at pp. 280 and 281 concerning the test of dependency of express covenants:

> In 24 Cyc. 918, it is said that covenants are to be construed as dependent or independent according to the intention and meaning of the parties and the good sense of the case. Technical words should give way to such intention. 7 R.C.L. 1090 §7. So, the rule is thus stated; where the acts or covenants of the parties are concurrent, and to be done or performed at the same time, the covenants are dependent, and neither party can maintain an action against the other, without averring and proving performance on his part. 13 Corpus Juris 567. . . .
>
> In the present case, the covenant to pay rent and the covenant to heat the apartment are mutual and dependent. In the modern apartment house equipped for heating from a central plant, entirely under the control of the landlord or his agent, heat is one of the things for which the tenant pays under the name "rent."

Our courts have on a case by case basis held various lease covenants and covenants to pay rent as dependent and under the guise of a constructive eviction have considered breach of the former as giving the right to the tenant to remove from the premises and terminate his obligation to pay rent. See McCurdy v. Wyckoff, 73 N.J.L. 368 (Sup. Ct. 1906); Weiler v. Pancoast, 71 N.J.L. 414 (Sup. Ct. 1904); Higgins v. Whiting, 102 N.J.L. 279 (Sup. Ct. 1925); Stevenson Stanoyevich Fund v. Steinacher, 125 N.J.L. 326 (Sup. Ct. 1940).

It is of little comfort to a tenant in these days of housing shortage to accord him the right, upon a constructive eviction, to vacate the premises and end his obligation to pay rent. Rather he should be accorded the alternative remedy of terminating the cause of the constructive eviction where as here the cause is the failure to make reasonable repairs. See Reste Realty Corporation v. Cooper, . . . 53 N.J. pp. 462, 463. This latter course of action is accompanied by the right to offset the cost of such repairs as are reasonable in the light of the value of the leasehold against the rent. His pursuit of the latter form of relief should of course be circumscribed by the aforementioned conditions.

If, therefore, a landlord fails to make the repairs and replacements of vital facilities necessary to maintain the premises in a livable condition for a period of time adequate to accomplish such repair and replacements, the tenant may cause the same to be done and deduct the cost thereof from future rents. The tenant's recourse to such self-help must be preceded by timely and adequate notice to the landlord of the faulty condition in order to accord him the opportunity to make the necessary replacement or repair. If the tenant is unable to give such notice after a reasonable attempt, he may nonetheless proceed to repair or replace. This does not mean that the tenant is relieved from the payment of rent so long as the landlord fails to repair. The tenant has only the alternative remedies of making the repairs or removing from the premises upon such a constructive eviction.[14]

We realize that the foregoing may increase the trials and appeals in landlord and tenant dispossess cases and thus increase the burden of the judiciary. By way of warning, however, it should be noted that the foregoing does not constitute an invitation to obstruct the recovery of possession by a landlord legitimately entitled thereto. It is therefore suggested that if the trial of the matter is delayed the defendant may be required to deposit the full amount of unpaid rent in order to protect the landlord if he prevails. Also, an application for a stay of an order of removal on appeal should be critically analyzed and not automatically granted.

In the light of the foregoing we find it unnecessary to pass on defendant's other grounds of appeal.

Reversed and remanded for trial in accordance with the above.

For reversal and remandment—CHIEF JUSTICE WEINTRAUB and JUSTICES JACOBS, FRANCIS, PROCTOR, HALL, SCHETTINO and HANEMAN—7.

For affirmance—None.

NOTES AND QUESTIONS

1. In Garcia v. Freeland Realty, Inc., 63 Misc. 2d 937, 314 N.Y.S.2d 215 (Civ. Ct. 1970), tenant sued to recover (1) the cost of plaster and paint needed to repair his apartment's walls, and (2) the reasonable value of his labor, computed at $7.00 an hour for ten hours. The record established that the tenant's two very young children had been ingesting plaster and paint flakes from walls that the landlord had refused to repair.

Although the court gave judgment to the tenant and cited the *Marini* decision, the court narrowed the *Marini* rationale. Judicial notice was taken that New York City slum children often suffered serious lead poisoning (and sometimes mental retardation) from eating plaster and paint flakes. (The New York Times had reported 25,000 to 35,000 cases yearly.) Calling the condition of the tenant's walls one of emergency, the court held that the tenant could remove this menace to his children's health and charge the cost to the landlord, since the landlord (under New York law) might well be liable in tort if any child was poisoned. In other words, the tenant was free to head off an actionable tort resulting from the landlord's inaction. Why might the landlord have been liable in tort? In Altz v. Leiberson, 233 N.Y. 16, 134 N.E. 703 (1922), a tenant, injured when a ceiling fell in his apartment, sued and recovered judgment from a landlord who had breached the statutory duty to repair.

14. Does this contradict *Green?*—ED.

In the *Garcia* case, Judge Goodell, by permitting "repair and offset" whenever a tenant's health was jeopardized, moved the common law several inches forward. A few months later, a different trial judge (Sandler of *East Haven Associates* "fame," page 286, *supra*) took the next foot. See Jackson v. Rivera, 65 Misc. 2d 468, 318 N.Y.S.2d 7 (Civ. Ct. 1970) (tenant able to make and offset a $22 "emergency" repair of a toilet that did not work).

2. Some states, by statute, have long given the tenant either a limited or an open-ended privilege to repair and offset. Below are two examples.

(a) California Civil Code §1942 (West 1954):

> If within a reasonable time after notice to the lessor, of dilapidations which he ought to repair, he neglects to do so, the lessee may repair the same himself, where the cost of such repairs do not require an expenditure greater than one month's rent of the premises, and deduct the expenses of such repairs from the rent, or the lessee may vacate the premises, in which case he shall be discharged from further payment of rent, or performance of other conditions.

(b) Oklahoma Statutes Annotated title 41, §32:

> If within a reasonable time after notice to the lessor of dilapidations which he ought to repair, he neglects to do so, the lessee may repair the same himself and deduct the expense of such repairs from the rent, or otherwise recover it from the lessor; or the lessor may vacate the premises, in which case he shall be discharged from further payment of rent, or performance of other conditions.

Is there any practical justification for denying tenants the privilege of repair and offset? Or, as in the California statute, limiting the expenditure for which offset is available?

3. Assume that the state recognizes a repair and offset rule:

(a) May the tenant, who performs the work himself, charge for his time? If so, at what rate? Cf. Garcia v. Freeland Realty Inc., note 1, *supra*.

(b) Before embarking on the repairs, must tenant first give landlord a reasonable chance to do the work? If so, what is reasonable? Might "reasonable" depend upon the degree of tenant's inconvenience if the work remains undone, or on the peril to the tenant's health, or on the landlord's previous record of making repairs? Should tenant be reimbursed if he goes ahead without first giving landlord notice and a fair chance to do the work? In that connection, suppose that the tenant does the work perfectly and at a cost no greater than the landlord would have incurred?

(c) Suppose that the tenant does the work perfectly—after landlord refuses to act—but at a cost greater than "the fair and reasonable value" of the labor and materials (alternatively, at a cost greater than the landlord would have incurred). May the tenant recoup his entire outlay? Suppose that the tenant imperfectly does the work. What then are his risks?

(d)   In the name of "repairs," what work may the tenant order? Suppose, for example, there is an electrical short that requires urgent attention, and also a long-standing incapacity in the electrical wiring system preventing tenant from using major appliances. May tenant, while the electrician is repairing the short, also order the rewiring even though the installation of heavier wiring is a form of capital improvement?

(e)   Realistically, how valuable is the repair and offset remedy for low-income tenants who are not able to do much of the repair work themselves? What if tenant orders the work, but does not pay for it; may the unpaid artisan file a mechanic's lien against the property? Cf. 79 A.L.R. 962 (1932); 163 A.L.R. 992 (1946); 4 A.L.R. 685, 687 (1919). What new financing, maintenance, and security mechanisms seem called for to insure a steady level of repairs as part of a code enforcement program?

(f)   The *Marini* and (to a lesser extent) *Garcia* decisions privilege the tenant to make the repairs when landlord refuses to act. Might it be argued that the privilege is coupled with a duty—i.e., the tenant *must* act (if he can reasonably do so) to eliminate conditions perilous to his health and safety, and that tenant assumes the risk of his failure to act?

(g)   The common law imposed no duty upon landlords to repair, but if the landlord undertook to make repairs voluntarily (or by covenant), he was liable to his tenants for injuries caused by his negligence or unskillfulness in making repairs, or in leaving the premises in an unsafe condition. Marks v. Nambil Realty Co., 245 N.Y. 256, 157 N.E. 129 (1927), 150 A.L.R. 1373 (1944). Compare May v. 11 1/2 East 49th St. Co., 269 A.D. 180, 54 N.Y.S.2d 860 (1945), *aff'd,* 296 N.Y. 599, 68 N.E.2d 881 (1946) (*Marks* rule does not apply where work done by independent contractor). Should tenant who voluntarily makes repairs also be subject to liability if he completes the repairs negligently? To take a specific case: Suppose that tenant, while repairing hallway stairs, fails to properly tack down the carpeting and a second tenant trips and injures himself. Does the injured tenant have a claim against the tenant who repaired? Since a fellow tenant may very well be uninsured and totally unable to pay any judgment rendered against him, what value has the suit? Can it be argued successfully that the "repairing" tenant—for the purpose of these repairs—acted as landlord's agent?

(h)   The cases that we have seen deal with repairs within the tenant's own apartment. Are there any reasons why the doctrine should not extend to repairs in the common areas or in an apartment of a neighboring tenant (1) where the condition threatens the acting tenant's health or safety, (2) where the condition threatens the acting tenant's property, and (3) where the condition interferes with the acting tenant's comfort? In short, can we have a tenant (or a tenant's association) acting as a building "ombudsman," curing code violations as they occur and applying all expenditures against future rent? Would we need a statute to achieve this? How would you draft the statute?

§5.10　The Economics of Rental Housing

G. STERNLIEB AND J. HUGHES, THE FUTURE OF RENTAL HOUSING

3-5, 8-11, 12-13, 83-91 (1981)

HOUSING DEMAND: THE EVOLVING PROFILE OF RENTAL HOUSING CONSUMERS

Throughout the 1970s, the profile of renter household types evolved considerably. In part, this was a concomitant of national demographic shifts, of marked growth in single person and nonmodular households. But it was also the consequence of a process that we have labeled the "cream skimming" of the rental market: the withdrawal of the more affluent household types—particularly husband-wife tenants—into ownership status. With income showing wide variation in accordance with household configuration, the household formats dominating rental housing portend an ominous lag in rent paying capacity in the future. The maturation of the "post-shelter" society—housing as investment as well as shelter—has made homeownership virtually a mandatory strategy for coping in an inflationary milieu. Only the truly affluent (or those too poor to care) can afford to ignore the tax and investment benefits of ownership tenure.

1. A major determinant of housing demand is the evolution of both the number and composition of the nation's households. Between 1970 and 1979, the total number of households increased by almost 14 million, an increment comparable to that of the growth in total population (approximately 15-million people) for the corresponding time interval.

2. The gains accruing to individual household types varied significantly, however. Husband-wife configurations represented the slowest growing household type, one parent families and nonfamily households the fastest. America's population is rapidly partitioning itself into an increasing number of varied, once considered "atypical," household arrangements.

3. When changing household profiles are sectored by tenure, sharp differentials are evident between owner and renter occupied sectors. Over the 1970 to 1978 time period, the following trends were operative:

   a. Of the total gains in owner households (10.9 million), 5.7 million were husband-wife configurations.
   b. The second largest growth sector comprised one-person households (2.8 million). However, the rate of increase (59.1 percent) of the latter was more than triple that of husband-wife households (18.4 percent).
   c. While "other male head" and "female head" configurations experienced smaller absolute growth increments, their rates of increase (44.6 and 44.3 percent, respectively) were also far greater than that registered by husband-wife households.

4.   The rental sector, over the 1970 to 1978 period, exhibited tendencies of a substantially different nature:

   a. While the total number of rental households increased by 3.3 million, a loss of 2.6 million husband-wife households was concurrently experienced (-20.2 percent).

   b. One-person households, in contrast, increased by 3.2 million, or 50.0 percent. The growth rates for "other male head" (75.1 percent) and "female head" (56.5 percent) configurations were even higher, but their absolute growth increments were somewhat smaller in magnitude.

5.   As a result of these household shifts, rental housing has assumed a much more limited and much more sharply defined functional role within the United States than held true in earlier years. With the declining presence of husband-wife households, rental facilities have become increasingly focused on nonmodular households. The rental sector has lost market penetration in areas that have been viewed as its traditional heartland—pre- and post-child rearing stages of the family life cycle.

6.   When black central city renter households are isolated, the preceding phenomena are even more accentuated. While the number of husband-wife formats declined by one in four (25 percent) in the rental sector, female headed households increased by 56.9 percent and one-person households by 55 percent. By 1978, female headed households evolved into the dominant (37.4 percent of total) sector of the black central city rental market. The following profiles illustrate the overall contours of the phenomena:

Household Configurations	Total U.S. Households		Total U.S. Renter Households		Central City Black Renter Households	
	1970	1978	1970	1978	1970	1978
Total Households	100.0	100.0	100.0	100.0	100.0	100.0
2-or-More Person Households	82.4	77.8	72.9	64.4	74.7	68.1
Male Head, Wife Present	68.7	60.5	54.1	37.9	40.1	24.6
Other Male Head	3.8	5.0	4.9	7.4	5.5	6.1
Female Head	9.9	12.3	13.9	19.0	29.1	37.4
1-Person Households	17.6	22.2	27.1	35.6	25.2	31.9

7.   Attendant to the changing profiles of renter/owner household configurations are sharp distinctions in fiscal capacities and income levels, Husband-wife configurations, particularly when the wife is in the paid labor force,

is the most affluent household type; however, it is this precise market sector that is vacating rental housing. Female and male headed households without spouse, and one-person households, are characterized by much lower income resources; these are the household types that are increasingly dominating the rental market.

8. The following income ratios are illustrative of the income differentials that are developing:

	1973	1978	1973	1978
	Renter/	*Renter/*	*Black Renter/*	*Black Renter/*
Household	*Owner*	*Owner*	*Total Renter*	*Total Renter*
Configuration	*Ratio*	*Ratio*	*Ratio*	*Ratio*
Total Households	.63	.55	.88	.70
2-or-More Person				
Households	.68	.58	.76	.69
Male Head, Wife				
Present	.73	.69	.88	.90
Other Male Head	.69	.63	.69	.91
Female Head	.73	.57	.91	.85
1-Person				
Households	1.13	1.09	.78	.77

By 1978, the income of all renter households was only 55 percent of owner income; concurrently, the income of black central city renters was only 70 percent of that of all renter households. The most competitive renter income household male head, wife present is rapidly withdrawing from rental tenure. This is particularly the case for black central city residents.

HOUSING SUPPLY: CHANGING INVENTORY PARAMETERS

The rapid pace of household formation in the 1970s could only have proceeded in the context of a conplementary expansion in the nation's supply. As the accounts of housing production over the decade are examined, it indeed becomes clear that record net inventory gains—both in terms of rental and owner housing—were achieved. It is difficult to avoid the impression, however, that whatever the scale of supply expansion, it was immediately matched by corresponding rates of household formation, i.e., population immediately diffuses into any inventory enlargement. The consumption, on a per-capita base, of increasing quantities of housing throughout the past decade has been unprecedented in the nation's housing annals. *Inexpensive housing supply begets households!*

1. From 1970 to 1978, over 15 million year-round housing units were added to the nation's housing inventory, an increment far greater than the 11-million net additions recorded over the *entire* 1960 to 1970 decade.

2.   While the 1970 to 1978 gains of the renter occupied sector (3.3-million units) were but one-third of those registered by owner occupied units (10.4-million units), their absolute magnitude approached that of the entire preceding decade (3.3-million units). It is highly probable that the net rental gains of the 1970s will exceed that of any preceding intercensal decade, at least since 1920.

3.   Thus, rental housing's declining share of the total inventory is not due to the lack of growth in this sector. It is the result of unparalleled expansion in homeownership during a decade that has been the most prolific housing period in America's history.

4.   Indeed, the 1970s recorded an acceleration of long-term trends toward homeownershp. As late as 1940, renter occupied units accounted for 56.4 percent of the total occupied housing stock. By 1978, the rental share declined to 34.8 percent. This long-term shift has been marked across all geographic partitions and racial groups.

5.   The expansion of the rental sector has taken place principally in the suburban areas of SMSAs and in nonmetropolitan areas. By 1978, central cities accounted for only 43.9 percent of all renter occupied units. On a regional base, the South and West secured the largest shares of new construction, the Northeast the smallest share. Within the latter region, only one out of ten (9.9 percent) renter occupied units was built from 1970 to 1978. In the South and West, the corresponding share was roughly one in five (22.1 and 20.0 percent, respectively).

6.   As of 1978, the bulk of the nation's rental units (26.9-million total units) were located in 2- to 4-unit structures (7.4-million units) and one-family detached structures (7.2 million units). Only 2.5-million units were located in buildings containing 50 or more units. Thus, the supply of rental housing is far more heterogeneous than is sometimes understood.

7.   At the same time, the actual scale of individual rental units is much more consistent than the structural configuration in which they are incorporated. The vast majority of rental units contain three to five rooms, with the median (4.0 rooms) remaining constant over the 1970 to 1978 period.

8.   The 1970s also witnessed the increasing presence of full amenities in the rental inventory, at least as measured by complete kitchens, bathrooms, and full plumbing facilities.

9.   Concurrently, however, the median monthly gross rent increased from $108 in 1970 to $200 by 1978, an 80.5 percent increase. The number of units renting for under $150 contracted sharply, while over 11.5-million units surged above the $200 per-month threshold.

THE CHANGING RENTAL MARKET: DEMAND AND SUPPLY INTERRELATIONSHIPS

The intersection of the demand and supply sectors of the rental market is revealed by a select, but limited, set of indicators revealing the interaction of corresponding demand and supply variables: rent-income ratios, persons per-room measures (overcrowding), and vacancy rates. Changes in these indices provide some insight into the satisfactory functioning of the housing market.

The decade of the 1970s was one in which the housing buying power of all Americans came under sustained pressures of erosion. The increasing share of the family budget that must be devoted to shelter costs has relegated to the history text older guidelines and sets of expectations, e.g., by 1980 a clear majority of all renter households expended considerably more than 25 percent of their income for rent payments. Thus, what appears to be certain levels of degeneration in the rental housing market may not be indicative of a rental housing problem *per se,* but a symbol of much more significant problems of American society. Nonetheless, while there are distressing elements, changes of a more positive kind should be noted.

1. As a result of lower income households gaining increased penetration in the rental market—in the context of steadily increasing rents—the overall median rent-income ratio shifted from 20 percent in 1970 to 25 percent by 1978.

2. This pattern of deterioration is evident across the basic profile of renter households:

Median Annual Rent as a Percent
of Median Annual Income

	Total U.S. Renters		Black Central City Renters	
	1973	*1978*	*1973*	*1978*
2-or More Person Households	19.6	23.8	21.8	27.5
Male Head, Wife Present	18.2	19.4	18.1	18.2
Other Male Head	21.0	27.8	24.2	23.7
Female Head	26.9	35.8	24.9	34.1
1-Person Households	30.7	30.3	31.9	30.6

The household type with the most favorable ratios—male head, wife present (husband-wife families)—is precisely that format which is being lost to the rental market. Female headed households, as would be expected, exhibit the most ominous ratios. To reiterate, the latter represent a major growth sector in the rental market.

3. The lack of sharp differentiation between total renters and black central city renters in the preceding tabulation is mainly the result of lower rent levels attendant to the central city inventory. As has been documented previously, the latters' income resources fall far below those of their total renter counterparts.

4. While not mitigating the severity of escalating rent-income relationships, a concurrent phenomenon has been the vast reduction in overcrowding, a continuation of a trend of long-standing note. The age old vision of overcrowding while still leaving a remnant, has largely been overcome.

5. In general, vacancy rates were far lower at the end of the decade of the 1970s than at the beginning, suggesting that rental demand was growing faster than supply. However, the last two years (1979 and 1980) have seen a rise in vacancy rates, suggesting a reversal of the decade long pattern. . . .

ISSUES AND DILEMMAS

A number of issues and considerations emanate from the preceding analyses, as well as from further investigations concerning the financing, construction, and operation of rental facilities.

1. The costs of operating rental housing have surged over the decade of the 1970s; the entire spectrum of expenditure requirements was buffeted by sustained inflation. It is difficult to envision any substantial reductions in these pressures in the 1980s, particularly in the energy cost operating components.

2. Shifts in the costs of capital (financing) have been equally severe. Renegotiable mortgages have long been used de facto in multifamily rental housing, typically written for short periods of time, though based upon long-term amortization. This permitted lending institutions to review the satisfactoriness of the payment experience as well as interest rates. While historically (pre-1970) this was a relatively passive process in terms of rates, it presently means the negotiation process is much more onerous than those accustomed to long-term fixed rate borrowing may appreciate.

3. At the same time, the limitations on expanding rents are severe. They are exacerbated, but far from limited to the constraints of rent control. Much more formidable, much more widespread, and much more chronic is the increasing paucity of rent paying capacity among the primary consumers of rental housing.

4. Thus, the substitution of government lending for multifamily rental housing purposes is in part a tribute to its availability; it also reflects on the necessity for fixed interest rates over long periods of time—and these are available only from the nonprivate sector.

5. As a result, the public sector has become not merely the lender of last resort, typically limited to the specifically impacted, but rather the primary source of multifamily rental housing finance. In the absence of such government instrumentalities, it is difficult to foresee a capacity on the part of the private market to deliver the required rental facilities.

THE ISSUE OF OPERATING COSTS

There is an unusual void in the nation's standardized data accounts in regard to the composition and changes in the operating cost structures of multifamily rental housing facilities. Despite the endemic crisis of growing imbalances between renter incomes and the costs of shelter, this situation has been permitted to continue. FHA operating cost data for rental structures, while informally accumulated in individual FHA offices, has yet to be coordinated, leaving the field with all too limited baselines.

Within this relative vacuum, there are two basic sources of operating information that provide some insight into the problem. The first is the "Price Index of Operating Costs for Rent Stabilized Apartment Houses," conducted for New York City and its Rent Stabilization Association by the Bureau of Labor Statistics. This index comprises a finite market basket of specifically defined operating elements; the changing prices of each element are tracked overtime, and by appropriately weighting each element—the fixed quantities of which were defined as of the time of the inception of this study in 1967—an overall price index is secured. While, by very definition the index is somewhat limited in its geographic range, its findings tend to be confirmed by the second study derived on a national base, which will be described later in this chapter.

[Tables 5 and 6] summarize the experiences of the New York City "Price Index." From a base of 100 in 1967, the index experienced rapid increases to 132.2 by 1971 [Table 6]. The next five years, which incorporated the first energy crisis (1974), showed the index breaking the 200 level (203.5). Thus, by 1976, the terminal point of the first ten years of the index, a doubling of prices had been recorded. The ensuing four years, which once again incorporated an energy crisis, saw the index soar to the 270.3 level, despite a period of relative tranquility in 1978.

Thus, within a pattern of general increases, there were three distinct

[TABLE 5]
Price Index of Operating Costs for Rent Stabilized Apartment Houses,
New York City: 1975 to 1980
(1967 = 100)

			Change: 1975 to 1980	
Group	1975	1980	Number	Percent
All items	191.3	270.3	79.0	41.3%
Taxes, fees, and permits	153.6	169.4	15.8	10.3
Labor costs	208.4	291.6	83.2	39.9
Fuel and utilities	345.1	648.5	303.4	87.9
Contractor services	180.3	255.1	74.8	41.5
Administrative costs	142.5	200.4	57.9	40.6
Insurance costs	206.8	330.6	123.8	59.9
Parts and supplies	181.7	267.2	85.5	47.1
Replacement costs	148.0	212.5	64.5	43.6

Source: U.S. Department of Labor, Bureau of Labor Statistics, Middle Atlantic Regional Office. *1980 Price Index of Operating Costs for Rent Stabilized Apartment Houses in New York City,* Annual.

price surges: 1970 and 1971, 1973 and 1974, and most recently the 1979 to 1980 period. Interspersed between these surges are years of relatively mild price increases.

However, the latter often represent—at least within the political milieu of New York City—the politically feasible limits on rent increases. When exceptional increases are registered—such as 19.2 percent in 1974—the increment is often so large as to make it infeasible to adjust rents accordingly. Yet, it is virtually impossible (politically) to secure rent "catch-ups" in subsequent years, even ignoring limited rent paying capacities.

In [Table 5], the data are further dissected for the most recent five-year period, 1975 to 1980. It is noteworthy in this context to observe that even though taxes remained relatively constant with an increment of only 10.3

[TABLE 6]
Price Index of Operating Costs for Rent Stabilized Apartment Houses, New York City: 1967 to 1980

Year (As of April)	Index	Percent Change
1967	100.0	—
1968	103.5	3.5
1969	107.6	4.0
1970	116.6	8.4
1971	132.2	13.4
1972	139.7	5.7
1973	150.8	7.9
1974	179.7	19.2
1975	191.3	6.5
1976	203.5	6.4
1977	219.5	7.9
1978	220.5	0.5
1979	238.6	8.2
1980	270.3	13.3

The 1975 to 1978 Period

		Change: 1975 to 1978	
1975	*1978*	*Number*	*Percent*
191.3	220.5	29.2	15.3%

The 1978 to 1980 Period

		Change: 1978 to 1980	
1978	*1980*	*Number*	*Percent*
220.5	270.3	49.8	22.6%

Source: U.S Department of Labor, Bureau of Labor Statistics, Middle Atlantic Regional Office. *1980 Price Index of Operating Costs for Rent Stablized Apartment Houses in New York City,* Annual.

percent, every other element increased by nearly 40 percent or more. Fuel and utilities, as would be anticipated, nearly doubled (87.9 percent); insurance costs were the second most significant element, exhibiting an increase of nearly 60 percent.

The second set of data available on rental housing operating cost structures is provided by the Institute for Real Estate Management (IREM). This is an actual cost index rather than a price index. Since a fixed market basket is not adhered to, a cost index reflects actual operating experience, i.e., undoubtedly mirroring efforts of owners to reduce, or find substitutes for, specifically costly operational elements. Unfortunately, at this writing, the most current data are available only from 1975 through 1978. (In order to provide comparability, note that on the bottom of [Table 6] the New York City experience from 1975 to 1978 is also isolated.) Nonetheless, as shown in Exhibit 3, over the four-year period—regardless of specific configuration, whether elevator, low rise, or garden—the cost experience reflected double digit inflation roughly comparable to the price increases gauged in New York City [Table 6]. Garden apartment units were the least impacted, but even here there was an increase of 13.2 percent.

Table 7 further details a comparison of changes in gross rents per square foot that took place using the IREM sample in the same period from 1975 to 1978. Rent gains, in general, exceeded the increments in costs. This is detailed at the bottom of the exhibit that isolates changes in the annual operating ratios from 1975 to 1978—operating expenses divided by rent collections.

But, this was the result of a number of years in which operating costs were decidedly restrained. Referring back again to the 1975 to 1978 period, as shown in [Table 6], the cumulative impact of inflation in those several years averaged out to less than 5-percent per year. If, on the other hand, the 1978 to 1980 period is examined [Table 6], the hammer blow of inflation in costs— increasing 22.6 percent in New York City in this brief period—becomes evident.

The specific components of the cost increases from 1975 to 1978 are shown in subsequent exhibits. Without going into detail on the individual elements, it is evident that they represent a very broad spectrum of expenditure requirements.

Thus, in sum, operating costs, assuming a finite market basket, have nearly tripled (following the New York experience) from 1967 through 1980. Despite landlords' efforts to alter the market basket of expense items, and thus minimize the impact of individual item cost increments, the national data (IREM) tend to suggest that the New York experience is not atypical.

The last three years, 1978 to 1980, have shown the most marked increment. Earlier shocks of cost surges were typically confined to a single year. We now suffer from a cumulative impact. Landlords in the broad, from 1975 to 1978, were able to raise rents in a fashion more than adequate to cope with expense inflation in these years. However, given the income characteristic of renters, particularly in the central city, the stresses of most recent years need

[TABLE 7]
General Operating Parameters:
1975 to 1978

Median Operating Expenses Per Square Foot,
1975 to 1978: USA and Canada

Building Type	1975	1978	Change: 1975 to 1978	
			Number	Percent
Elevator	$1.92	$2.26	$.34	17.7%
Low Rise, 25+ Units	1.40	1.76	.36	25.7
Low Rise, 12 to 24 Units	1.37	1.59	.22	16.1
Garden	1.29	1.46	.17	13.2

Gross Rent Per Square Foot,
1975 to 1978: USA and Canada

Building Type	1975	1978	Change: 1975 to 1978	
			Number	Percent
Elevator	$3.32	$4.11	$.79	23.7%
Low Rise, 25+ Units	2.93	3.55	.62	21.2
Low Rise, 12 to 24 Units	2.87	3.50	.63	22.0
Garden	2.57	3.09	.52	20.2

Annual Operating Ratio 1975 to 1978:
USA and Canada
(Operating Expenses ÷ Rent Collections)

Building Type	1975	1978	Change: 1975 to 1978	
			Number	Percent
Elevator	55.8%	53.7%	2.1%	−3.8%
Low Rise, 25+ Units	49.3	48.6	0.7	−1.4
Low Rise, 12 to 24 Units	49.3	45.3	4.0	−8.1
Garden	51.8	47.6	4.2	−8.1

Source: IREM, *Income/Expense Analysis.* Chicago: Institute of Real Estate Management, 1979.

little elaboration. But, even this measure of rent gains probably overstates their salubrious effect. Rents tend to lag behind expenses—note very specifically the enormous level of increment in the latter in the 1973 to 1974 period. To that degree the improvement in operating ratios from 1975 to 1978 (shown on the bottom of [Table 7]) probably is illusory.

THE PROBLEM OF FINANCING COSTS

The expenditure patterns described above refer only to operating costs. They do not take into account the enormous shifts that have taken place in capital costs. And these have been even more brutal in their impact both on investor interest in extant apartment houses as well as the development of new ones. The old rule of thumb of a new building being worth somewhere on the order of seven times the rent roll clearly can make very little sense when the mortgage costs of the finished structure exceed the 14-percent level—and that is effectively the case today. Owners of older buildings, even with much lower rate mortgages, find themselves—and their equity—trapped by the increments in interest rates, unless very substantial rent increases are forthcoming. If, for example, we assume an older building only valued at five times the rent roll, the situation becomes clear. If the owner wishes to remortgage a paid down indenture, which may have been written at the 9-percent mark, at a time when interest rates are at the 13-percent level, the increment in interest costs is roughly equal to 20 percent of the rent roll (i.e., 4 percent multiplied by five times the building's rent roll). In conversations with developers, the phrase very frequently used that there is no more "leverage" in building finance: that the yields on equity for new multifamily residential facilities may not exceed that given to debt.

The limitations on expending rents are severe. They are exacerbated, but far from limited to the constraints of rent control. Much more formidable, much more widespread, and much more chronic, is the increasing paucity of rent paying capacity of renter households as shown earlier in this study.

Indeed, if one were to use current mortgage costs, there is very little real equity left in the field of conventional rental ownership. It has been implicitly wiped out by the increases in the effective costs of debt required for sale or refinancing.

While certainly nonresidential facilities have been impacted by the same phenomenon, typically there is either a much greater capacity to pass on rent increments to their ultimate customers—as, for example, in a shopping center—or it represents a relatively small part of the overall operating statement of the firm—the prestige office headquarters building. There is no such buffer when we turn to the bulk of the residential renter market.

In addition, it should be noted that the concept of the renegotiable mortgage, while something of a novelty in private residential financing, has long been used de facto in multifamily housing. Thus, nongovernmental mortgages in the field have been typically written for relatively short periods of time, though based upon long-term amortization. This permitted lending institutions to review the satisfactoriness of the payment experience as well as interest rates. While, historically, this was a relatively passive process, in terms of rates, it currently means that the renegotiation process is much more onerous than those accustomed to long-term fixed rate borrowing may appreciate.

Thus, the substitution of government lending for these purposes is in part a tribute to the availability of the latter; it also reflects on the necessity for fixed interest rates over long periods of time—and these are largely available only from the nonprivate sector.

For the sake of brevity, we have not discussed here the changing balanced cost of capital as equity is further squeezed. It should be noted, however, that in general the proportion of total value that will be covered by a mortgage lender on a multifamily residential facility has shown some signs of decreasing over time, i.e., requiring much more in the way of relatively expensive equity participation. In general, government lending has been much more generous in terms of its coverage.

In sum, therefore, the construction of new multifamily residential facilities is substantially hindered by a rate of inflation in operating costs that is not matched by the rent paying capacity of the tenantry. It is further accentuated by the increased costs of capital and borrowing. Again, these latter two elements have little in the way of buffering potential (except for luxury buildings), in terms of pass through to the tenantry. Government has become not merely the lender of the last resort, typically limited to the specifically impacted, but rather the primary source of multifamily rental structure finance. And, this will not change.

NOTES AND QUESTIONS

1.   Professor Sternlieb is one of the nation's foremost housing economists. In a seminal study, The Tenement Landlord (1969), he closely examined the operating returns on thirty-two slum properties in Newark, New Jersey, and analyzed the effect upon slum area investment, of high vacancy rates, vandalism, and the market's inability to absorb rental increases. One year later, Professor Sternlieb turned his spotlight on New York City properties and produced a massive tome, The Urban Dilemma (1970). His sample of more than 600 buildings showed that fewer than half were earning a 6 percent return for their owners in 1967. Id. at 290.

2.   Professor Sternlieb revisited the Newark tenement landlord in Residential Abandonment (1973) (with Burchell). The authors concluded (id. at xxii-xxvi):

The Participants in Abandonment

The "Abandoners": The Tenement Landlords

The whole web of governmental intervention in the private housing sphere, as well as a substantial part of private investment, operates in great measure through the matrix of the landlord. With the exception of public housing, alternative approaches to the ownership and management of low income housing have been much more frequent in the verbal than in the physical, i.e., much more talked about than built. Low income housing cooperatives are just beginning to make a significant impact on the market; the vast bulk of central city housing remains in forms of ownership and management which have changed little over the last hundred years.

One of the more satisfying folk figures of our time is that of the slumlord. This is an individual who popularly is supposed to dominate the low income private housing stock, and who has not only grown wealthy historically because of his tenure, but is currently securing a more than adequate return on his properties. The myth is satisfying because it leads to the belief that the major input necessary to provide more adequate standards of maintenance and operating behavior is to get this overfed individual to disgorge some of his excess earnings; the basic pie of rents is adequate both to support owner interests in holding on to his parcels and continuing their operation while still providing the tenants with adequate service inputs. The bulk of governmental measures in the older housing sphere has revolved around this concept, whether it is tax abatement in order to assure the owner that improvements will not be overassessed, long-term inexpensive loans for essential repairs in line with code enforcement efforts, or any of the more localized activities along these same lines. All of them essentially are based on the belief in the desirability, not only from a social point of view but also from the owner's economic point of view, of holding onto his properties. They presume a basic economic viability in operating low income housing. Thus governmental intervention has essentially been enabling legislation not to change present yields, but rather to permit better services and improved structures without altering the basic rent/expense ratios. . . .

While the large-scale, nonresident slumlords are far from an insignificant proportion of total ownership, as previous research indicates, the degree of concentration is much overstated.

In reality the changes in form and function of the older city and the folkways of its inhabitants, the great migration patterns which have dominated the demographic considerations in and about the United States metropolitan areas for decades, and, more recently, urban racial unrest, have occasioned a housing market situation of virtual stagnation. The combination of risk, decreasing profitability, and loss of potential for capital gains has substantially restricted the kinds of professional owners who are willing to invest in slum properties. It takes a highly insensitive individual to become a professional nonresident owner of slum property, in the light of present societal attitudes. This is not an individual who is easily influenced to invest his money unless an appropriate return can be secured.

There is as yet, however, no adequate replacement for these hard core tenement owners. The minority owner (to be discussed subsequently), frequently buying for residence rather than income purposes, is avoiding the worst areas of the city. This leaves a definite gap as to who will manage hard core, urban realty. City-employed bureaucrats have characteristically done a poor job at housing management. The condition and solvency of housing run by local authorities attest to this. . . .

Those Who Remain: The New Minority Landlords

One of the most provocative and potentially important developments of our time is the increased level of minority group ownership of central city real property. This is a trend which parallels that of all the other earlier immigrant groups into the city—first as tenants, then as owners, typically of the most marginal of parcels, then with the formation of capital, the movement into the middle class mainstream. Will this sequence be replicated for our present minority group owners, both Spanish and black?

From the overall society's point of view the most crucial question of all is whether the new owners can make it, whether there is a potential for capital accumulation and for success in the future through this type of acquisition. The vigor of private ownership in a decaying city clearly is dependent upon the future growth of such activity. How then do these minority group owners view the future? What are their problems and are there any ways that society can optimize the turnover mechanisms?

Certainly for many of the minority group homeowners interviewed in the Newark study, the suburban one-family house typically is much too expensive an investment. They rather require income producing properties: the three-family house and the small tenement of Newark—these are the possible alternatives. If the sweat and savings of these kinds of familis are to be utilized by society to stabilize the city, how can we insure an appropriate reward mechanism? If we do not, the results will be very evident.

The new owners of the sixties may have little romance about their prospects, but they had great confidence in their capacity to maintain and improve the properties which they had acquired, to secure good living within them, both for themselves and their children. These same owners of the early 1970s still preserve some level of spark. Their buildings are better maintained, their hopes for the future still more considerable than for longer-term white holders in the same areas, but this positive feeling is fast ebbing, based on experience within the city.

This experience is several-fold. On the one hand, the basic parameters are degenerating: fear of crime, fire, and drugs may be far from abstractions to suburbanites, but to the central cityite and particularly in parts of the city dominated by minority group home buyers, they are deadly realities. In addition, the minority home buyer of a decade ago now finds his investment at a dead end—there are no potential buyers. How can society cope with this?

The problem is not merely one of equity, it is rather central to the preservation of the city. If a new, stable, middle class resident operating group cannot be secured—then the private residential market in the city is doomed. But, as yet, governmental action in this frontier has been confined to the awkward giant of acquisition—providing financing for the purchase of a property, and in that very act often inflating the costs—rather than necessarily imparting the skill for successful operation or, even more important, ensuring a take-out mechanism, a resale after a period of years which will serve as a reward for sustained care and demonstrably competent operating procedures.

One thing is clear, it must be governmental intervention in this frontier. Primary lenders in urban areas—commercial and mutual savings banks, savings and loan associations, insurance companies, and even individuals—are getting out of the inner city mortgage lending business. They are replaced by mortgage companies which deal almost exclusively in insured loans. Given the excesses which have been attributed to some of the procedures under the latter, even the mortgage companies may soon be leaving the scene.

The substantial default rates that are characteristic of the urban real estate market are, within conventional lending procedures, only encompassed with great difficulty. Given the risks involved and the potential for abandonment, normal profit standards and limited operating and supervisory margins may be inappropriate. What is required are completely new financial operating mechanisms, new means of property acquisition from the reluctant to new operating owners, from the owner by default to one of positive intent. Again, for this, there must be a reward mechanism—a take-out mechanism—after a period of years of good operation for the new owner operator.

Minority home ownership appears to be increasing within urban areas. In 1972 for many secondary, older industrial cities, there were probably more minority home purchasers than white ones. These new owners frequently differ from their predecessors in that their equity is low, their financial capacities limited. But their relative youth and a high level of resident ownership, the latter several times the proportion of white buyers, tend to yield better operation and maintenance of structures.

But where is public policy to be directed in this regard? *While minority home ownership is good for the building and for the municipality, is it good for the owner?* This group typically is buying for the purpose of residence rather than business; it provides stability for the neighborhood and unquestionably is invaluable to the city, but certainly in terms of the individual the situation is more complex.

One of the primary functions of home ownership in our society over the last generation has been for the purpose of capital accumulation. For most of the lower and even middle socio-economic groups, it is the long-term holding of a house, the paying down of a mortgage and the building up of equity, coupled with increasing value through inflation, which has provided the major form of securing a nest egg. The black home buyer in Newark of the 1960s has seen his investment at a standstill, while suburban equivalents doubled and tripled over the same length of time.

3.   The argument for more assertive code enforcement, even at the cost of forcing many slum landlords from the market, appears in Ackerman, Regulating Slum Housing Markets on Behalf of the Poor: Of Housing Codes, Housing Subsidies and Income Redistribution Policy, 80 Yale L.J. 1093 (1971). Answer and reply appear in Komesar, Return to Slumville: A Critique of the Ackerman Analysis of Housing Code Enforcement and the Poor, 82 Yale L.J. 1175 (1973), and Ackerman, More on Slum Housing and Redistribution Policy: A Reply to Professor Komesar, 82 Yale L.J. 1194 (1973).

4.   Against this empirical and analytical background, of what consequence is the warranty of habitability in furthering housing maintenance?

§5.11   Tenant's Right to Safe Premises

Under the common law, absent any statutory or contract duty, lessors generally were not responsible for a tenant's physical injury resulting from a defective condition within the leased premises. Bowles v. Mahoney, 202 F.2d 320, 323 (D.C. Cir. 1952). By the early 1960s, however, courts *inferred* a statutory duty when the condition was one that violated an applicable housing code and when landlord, in the exercise of reasonable care, should have known the condition existed. See, e.g., Whetzel v. Jess Fisher Management Co., 282 F.2d 943 (D.C. Cir. 1960) (tenant injured when bedroom ceiling fell). Contra: Thrash v. Hill, 63 Ohio St. 2d 178, 407 N.E.2d 495 (1980). Liability based upon a contract duty ensued when landlord's breach of an express repair agreement led proximately to the tenant's injury. Other exceptions from the general rule of nonliability involved the landlord who concealed a dangerous condition present when the tenancy began, the landlord who negligently failed to maintain parts of the building within her control, and the landlord who negligently made repairs. 2 Restatement (Second) of Torts §357.

A second decision from the U.S. Court of Appeals for the District of Columbia, decided shortly after Javins v. First National Realty Corp., page 301, *supra*, has similarly seeded the law of landlord and tenant. Kline v. 1500 Massachusetts Avenue Apartment Corp., 439 F.2d 477 (D.C. Cir. 1970), involved a tenant whom an intruder assaulted and robbed in the hallway of her apartment building. *Kline* became the first significant case placing liability upon a landlord for failing to take steps to protect tenants from foreseeable criminal acts committed by third parties. Unlike *Javins*, however, which led overnight to countrywide adoption of a warranty of habitability directed at the tenant's use and enjoyment, the *Kline* decision, directed at the tenant's physical security, influenced the law far more slowly. Courts, both for practical and conceptual reasons, were uncertain (and divided) as to whether (or how far) to hold landlords responsible when tenants suffered criminal harm, and on this issue legislatures gave little guidance.

Trentacost v. Brussel, which follows, completes one court's efforts to establish some ruling principle.

TRENTACOST v. BRUSSEL
82 N.J. 214, 412 A.2d 436 (1980)

PASHMAN, J. Once again this Court is asked to examine the contours of the relationship between residential landlords and their tenants. Specifically, the question is whether a landlord who provides inadequate security for common areas of rental premises may be liable for failing to prevent a criminal assault upon a tenant. The trial court entered judgment for the tenant upon a jury's award of damages. The Appellate Division affirmed. 164 N.J. Super. 9, 395 A.2d 540 (App. Div. 1978). We granted defendant's petition for certification, 81 N.J. 48, 404 A.2d 1148 (1979), to consider whether the landlord was obligated to secure the entrance to the common areas of plaintiff's building. We now affirm.

I. FACTS

On the afternoon of December 21, 1973, plaintiff, Florence Trentacost, returned to her apartment at 273 Monroe Street, Passaic, New Jersey, from an afternoon of shopping. After she had entered her building and reached the top of a flight of stairs leading to her apartment, someone grabbed her ankles from behind and dragged her down the stairs. Her attacker, who remains unknown, left her bleeding in the ground floor hallway but returned almost immediately to steal her purse. Conscious yet unable to speak, she lay helpless for several minutes until a tenant leaving the building noticed her. Another neighbor then called the police, who took plaintiff to a nearby hospital.

Mrs. Trentacost was hospitalized for 15 days. Her injuries included a dislocated right shoulder, fractures of the left shoulder, left ankle and jaw, lacerations about the mouth and broken teeth. She wore casts on her arms and leg for about a month and a half, and at the time of trial in late 1976 still suffered from pain and loss of mobility.

At the time of the attack, plaintiff was 61 years old and a widow. She had rented her four-room apartment for more than ten years from defendant, Dr. Nathan T. Brussel. The building consisted of eight dwelling units located over street level stores with access provided by front and rear entrances. A padlock secured the back entrance, but there was no lock on the front door, which both plaintiff and apparently her assailant had used to enter the premises.

There was considerable evidence at trial regarding criminal and other suspicious activity in the vicinity of plaintiff's residence. A Passaic city detective testified that in the three years preceding the incident, the police had investigated from 75 to 100 crimes in the neighborhood, mostly burglaries and street muggings. Another policeman stated that "civil disturbances" had occurred in the area between 1969 and 1971. Two months before she was attacked, Mrs. Trentacost had herself reported to defendant an attempt to break into the building's cellar. At other times she had notified the landlord of the presence of unauthorized persons in the hallways. Plaintiff claimed the defendant had promised to install a lock on the front door, but he denied ever discussing the subject prior to the assault on plaintiff.

At the close of evidence, the trial court granted plaintiff's motion to strike the defense of contributory negligence. The judge instructed the jury in part as follows:

> A landlord owes to his tenants the duty of exercising reasonable care to guard against foreseeable dangers arising from the use of premises in connection with those portions which remain within the landlord's control. . . . The relationship between a landlord and his tenant does not impose upon the landlord the duty to protect a tenant from the crime of third persons. Only upon proper proof that the landlord unreasonably enhanced the risk of the criminal activity by failing to take reasonable measures to safeguard the tenants from foreseeable criminal conduct and a showing of suitable notice of existing defects to the landlord can a tenant recover damages from his landlord.

After the jury returned a verdict for plaintiff of $3,000, the trial court denied defendant's motion for judgment notwithstanding the verdict. R. 4:40-

2. When defendant refused to consent to an additur of $15,000, the court granted plaintiff's motion for a new trial as to damages. A second jury found damages in the sum of $25,000. Defendant then appealed.

In discussing the extent of the landlord's obligation to provide security measures for his tenants, the Appellate Division found our decision in Braitman v. Overlook Terrace Corp., 68 N.J. 368, 346 A.2d 76 (1975), to be controlling. 164 N.J. Super. at 14, 395 A.2d 540, 543. According to the court, "[t]he keynote of the decision in *Braitman* was simply that the liability of the landlord was properly posited upon familiar negligence concepts." Id. Examining the evidence, the court concluded there was sufficient support for finding that the absence of a lock on the entrance to the building, which was located in a high-crime neighborhood, created a foreseeable risk of harm to tenants. It was therefore a jury question whether the landlord had failed to take reasonable security measures to protect the tenant. Id. at 16, 395 A.2d 540. Rejecting defendant's other arguments regarding the sufficiency and admissibility of evidence, the Appellate Division affirmed.

II. LIABILITY FOR FORESEEABLE CRIMINAL CONDUCT

As the Appellate Division correctly recognized, *Braitman* supplies the focal point of controversy regarding the landlord's duty. In that case the tenants had suffered property loss resulting from theft because of a defective "dead bolt" lock on the apartment door. See 68 N.J. at 371-372, 346 A.2d 76. The trial court found that the remaining slip lock had not provided adequate security and that the landlord had received sufficient notice of the defective dead lock. Id. at 373, 346, A.2d 76. Since the robbery was within the scope of the foreseeable risks created by the inadequate security, the court found the landlord liable for negligence.

After the Appellate Division affirmed judgment for the tenants, 132 N.J. Super. 51, 332 A.2d 212 (App. Div. 1974), this Court examined in detail the various evolving theories concerning the responsibilities of a landlord. We began by noting the traditional rule: "[T]he relationship between a landlord and his tenant does not, without more, impose upon the landlord a duty to protect the tenant from the crime of third persons." 68 N.J. at 374, 346 A.2d at 79 (citations omitted). We went on, however, to cite with approval Kline v. 1500 Massachusetts Ave. Apartment Corp., 141 U.S. App. D.C. 370, 439 F.2d 477 (D.C. Cir. 1970), as the leading case in the trend away from that tradition.

In fashioning a duty to provide tenant security, the court in *Kline* drew upon three sources. The first, described as "the logic of the situation itself," id. at 376, 439 F.2d at 483, was the recognition that the landlord was in a better economic position than the tenant to take precautionary measures. The court adopted this as a predicate for the landlord's tort liability. Id. at 377, 439 F.2d at 484. Relying on existing law in the District of Columbia, the court noted as a second source an implied contractual undertaking to maintain those protective measures in effect at the beginning of the lease term. Id. at 378, 439 F.2d at 485. A third source was the law governing an innkeeper's duties towards his guests. The court thought this doctrine provided a more appropriate analogy than that of a medieval agrarian lease—the formal predecessor of the modern urban residential lease—for determining the landlord's obligations. See id. at 375, 378, 439 F.2d at 482, 485; see also Javins v. First Nat'l Realty Corp., 138 U.S. App. D.C. 369, 375-377, 428 F.2d 1071, 1077-1079 (D.C. Cir. 1970), *cert. den.,* 400 U.S. 925, 91 S. Ct. 186, 27 L. Ed. 2d 185 (1970). These three bases provided a foundation for enlarging the landlord's duty to maintain common areas of rental premises so as to safeguard tenants from foreseeable criminal conduct of third parties. *Kline,* 141 U.S. App. D.C. at 380, 439 F.2d at 487.

 Although a majority of the Court in *Braitman* did not embrace the reasoning of *Kline,* see *Braitman,* 68 N.J. at 387-388, 346 A.2d 76 (separate views of Hughes, C. J., Sullivan and Pashman, JJ.), we did acknowledge "a developing judicial reluctance to allow landlords to insulate themselves from liability to their tenants for the criminal conduct of third parties," id. at 378, 346 A.2d at 81.[3] We then turned to the development of negligence liability for foreseeable criminal conduct in New Jersey. We held that "upon a logical extension of the principles of our own case law," a landlord could be held liable for creating an "unreasonably enhanced" risk of loss resulting from foreseeable criminal conduct. Id. at 382-383, 346 A.2d 76, 84. See Zinck v. Whelan, 120 N.J. Super. 432, 445, 294 A.2d 727 (App. Div. 1972). As in *Braitman,* here the landlord was confronted with the existence of a high level of crime in the neighborhood, see *ante* at 218-219. Yet he failed to install a lock on the front door leading in to the building's lobby. By failing to do anything to arrest or even reduce the risk of criminal harm to his tenants, the landlord effectively and unreasonably enhanced that risk. See *Braitman,* 68 N.J. at 381-382, 346 A.2d 76.

 We reiterate that our holding in *Braitman* lies well within traditional principles of negligence law. "Negligence is tested by whether the reasonably prudent person at the time and place should recognize and foresee an unreasonable risk or likelihood of harm or danger to others." Rappaport v. Nichols, 31 N.J. 188, 201, 156 A.2d 1, 8 (1959). If the reasonably prudent person would foresee danger resulting from another's voluntary, criminal acts, the fact that another's actions are beyond defendant's control does not preclude liability. [Citations omitted.] Foreseeability of harm, not the fact of another's intervention, is the crucial factor in determining "whether a *duty* exists to take measures to guard against [criminal activity]." *Goldberg,* 38 N.J. at 583, 186 A.2d at 293.

 Application of these principles in *Braitman* led to the imposition of liability for a landlord's failure to provide adequate security against foreseeable criminal conduct. [Citations omitted.] They also support affirmance of plain-

---

3. We also noted cases decided after *Kline* which were part of this trend. E.g., Warner v. Arnold, 133 Ga. App. 174, 210 S.E.2d 350 (Ct. App. 1974); Johnston v. Harris, 387 Mich. 569, 198 N.W.2d 409 (Sup. Ct. 1972); Sherman v. Concourse Realty Corp., 47 A.D.2d 134, 365 N.Y.S.2d 239 (App. Div. 1975); see *Braitman,* 68 N.J. at 376-378, 346 A.2d 76.

tiff's judgment in the present case. There was ample evidence that criminal activity affecting the Monroe Street building was reasonably foreseeable. More than one witness testified to the high incidence of crime in the neighborhood. Plaintiff's own, unchallenged testimony related an attempted theft within the building. Against this background, the jury could readily view the absence of a lock on the front entrance—an area outside an individual tenant's control—as exemplifying a callous disregard for the residents' safety in violation of ordinary standards of care. Since there was sufficient evidence for concluding that the mugging was a foreseeable result of the landlord's negligence, the jury's finding of liability was warranted.

III.   THEORIES OF LANDLORD LIABILITY

Although we need go no further to affirm the judgment for the tenant, we choose not to ignore the alternative theories of landlord liability discussed in *Braitman*. A majority of that Court found that a violation of an administrative regulation governing the condition of multiple dwellings was independent evidence of negligence, 68 N.J. at 385-386, 346 A.2d 76, while two members considered that breach to establish negligence conclusively, id. at 389, 346 A.2d 76 (Clifford and Schreiber, JJ., concurring). Three members raised the possibility of imposing liability for unsafe premises based on the landlord's implied warranty of habitability. Id. at 387-388, 346 A.2d 76 (separate views of Hughes, C.J., Sullivan and Pashman, JJ.). There was also mention of liability based on a covenant implied in fact to furnish adequate security. Id. at 389, 346 A.2d 76 (Clifford and Schreiber, JJ., concurring).

Over four years have passed since we decided *Braitman*. During this period the need for judicial guidance regarding landlord liability has grown. See generally Note, "The 1975-1976 New Jersey Supreme Court Term," 30 Rut. L. Rev. 492, 692-702 (1977). Although we need not reconcile the alternative theories of *Braitman* to resolve this case, we nevertheless take this opportunity to clarify the scope of a residential landlord's duty to his tenant. This approach is in keeping with the traditional practice of common-law adjudication followed by this Court. We recall the statement of Chief Justice Weintraub:

> [T]here is no constitutional mandate that a court may not go beyond what is necessary to decide a case at hand. Whether an issue will be dealt with narrowly or expansively calls for a judge's evaluation of many things, including the need for guidance for the bar or agencies of government or the general public. To that end, the Court may express doubts upon existing doctrines, thereby inviting litigation, or may itself raise an issue it thinks should be resolved in the public interest, or may deliberately decide issues which need not be decided when it believes that course is warranted. [Busik v. Levine, 63 N.J. 351, 363-364, 307 A.2d 571, 578 (1973), *app. dism.*, 414 U.S. 1106, 94, S. Ct. 831, 38 L. Ed. 2d 733 (1973)]

In the spirit of this judicial philosophy, we conclude that it is necessary to reconsider "the general principle that the mere relationship of landlord and tenant imposes no duty on the landlord to safeguard the tenant from crime." *Braitman*, 68 N.J. at 387, 346 A.2d 76.

A.   IMPLIED WARRANTY OF HABITABILITY

This Court has long recognized that traditional principles of property law, when applied in the context of a residential lease, have "lagged behind changes in dwelling habits and economic realities." Michaels v. Brookchester, Inc., 26 N.J. 379, 382, 140 A.2d 199, 201 (1958). Leases acquired the character of conveyances of real property when their primary function was to govern the relationship between landowners and farmers. Unlike the original, medieval tenant, the modern apartment dweller rents not for profit but for shelter.

When engaged in the business of providing shelter, present-day landlords do not furnish merely four walls, a floor and a ceiling. They have come to supply, and tenants now expect, the physical requisites of a home. An apartment today consists of a variety of goods and services. At a minimum, the necessities of a habitable residence include sufficient heat and ventilation, adequate light, plumbing and sanitation and proper security and maintenance.

It is undisputed that maintaining minimum conditions of habitability including security is beyond an individual tenant's control. Where the task involves the common areas of a multiple-dwelling building, tenants' efforts are entirely precluded. See *Michaels*, 26 N.J. at 382, 140 A.2d 199; Dubonowski v. Howard Savings Institution, 124 N.J.L. 368, 12 A.2d 384 (E & A 1940). Nor in this highly mobile society should tenants be required to invest substantial sums in improvements that might outlast their tenancy. The landlord, however, can spread the cost of maintenance over an extended period of time among all residents enjoying its benefits.

Recognizing the landlord's "greater opportunity, incentive and capacity . . . to inspect and maintain," Green v. Superior Ct., 10 Cal. 3d at 627, 517 P.2d at 1175, 111 Cal. Rptr. at 711, as well as the tenant's lack of bargaining power, this Court has endeavored to give effect to the legitimate expectations which characterize the modern residential tenancy. Since our decision in Marini v. Ireland, 56 N.J. 130, 265 A.2d 526 (1970), we have imposed upon the landlord an implied warranty of habitability which arises from his economic and social relationship with his tenants. The scope of this warranty extends to all "facilities vital to the use of the premises for residential purposes." *Marini*, 56 N.J. at 144, 265 A.2d at 534. A breach of the warranty gives the tenant the right to deduct the reasonable cost of repairs to a vital facility from his monthly rent, id. at 146, 265 A.2d 526, and a right of action for the return or reduction of rent. . . .

Among the "facilities vital to the use of the premises" are the provisions for the tenant's security. Unfortunately, crime against person and property is an inescapable fact of modern life. Its presence threatens the suburban enclave as well as the the inner city. Tenants universally expect some effective means of excluding intruders from multiple dwellings; without a minimum of security, their well-being is as precarious as if they had no heat or sanitation. Recognizing that a safer and more secure apartment is truly more livable, landlords frequently offer superior protective measures as an inducement for entering into premium lease agreements. Under modern living conditions, an apartment is clearly not habitable unless it provides a reasonable measure of security from the risk of criminal intrusion.

In *Braitman* we considered but declined to resolve whether the implied warranty is "flexible enough to encompass appropriate security devices." 68 N.J. at 388, 346 A.2d at 87 (separate opinion of Hughes, C.J., Sullivan and Pashman, JJ.). We now conclude that it is and therefore hold that the landlord's implied warranty of habitability obliges him to furnish reasonable safeguards to protect tenants from foreseeable criminal activity on the premises.

The "premises" which the landlord must secure necessarily encompass the common areas of multiple dwellings. There is no doubt that the rent charged by a landlord includes a portion for maintaining such areas. That these areas are used by all the tenants does not require a different result. Viewing "premises" as restricted to the individual dwelling units would render common areas a "no man's land" for the purposes of assessing habitability. We consider the provision of some measure of security in these areas to be "vital to the use of the premises."

Examining the facts of this case, we find that defendant breached his implied warranty by failing to secure in any way the front entrance of the building. The absence of even a simple slip lock—the most elementary of safeguards—permitted the halls and stairwells to become virtually public ways, completely accessible to the criminal element. Defendant did nothing to protect against the threat of crime which seriously impaired the quality of residential life in his building. Since the landlord's implied undertaking to provide adequate security exists independently of his knowledge of any risks, there is no need to prove notice of such a defective and unsafe condition to establish the landlord's contractual duty. It is enough that defendant did not take measures which were in fact reasonable for maintaining a habitable residence.

By failing to provide adequate security, the landlord has impaired the habitability of the tenant's apartment. He has therefore breached his implied warranty of habitability and is liable to the tenant for the injuries attributable to that breach.

B.   VIOLATIONS OF ADMINISTRATIVE REGULATIONS

In *Braitman* we noted that "the violation of a statutory duty of care is not conclusive on the issue of negligence . . . but it is a circumstance which the trier of fact should consider in assessing liability." 68 N.J. at 385, 346 A.2d at 85. It is entirely appropriate in an action to establish civil liability to consider the landlord's statutory and administrative responsibilities to his tenants to furnish habitable residential premises. As we stated in *Michaels,* 26 N.J. at 386, 140 A.2d 199, and reiterated in *Braitman,* 68 N.J. at 383-386, 346 A.2d 76, the statutory and regulatory scheme governing the habitability of multifamily dwellings establishes a standard of conduct for landlords. It is thus available as evidence for determining the duty owed by landlords to tenants. Defendant's eight-unit building was a "multiple dwelling" subject to the requirements of the regulations.[6] Regulation 602.3(f)(2)(i) of the "Regulations for the Construction and Maintenance of Motels and Multiple Dwellings" effective July 19, 1968, provided that "building entrance doors and exterior exit doors shall be equipped with heavy duty lock sets." The absence of a lock at the time of Mrs. Trentacost's assault was contrary to the Legislature's standard of care. Since the violation was clearly established it constitutes evidence of defendant's negligence.

IV.   CONCLUSION

We have been presented with the opportunity to delineate the responsibilities of residential landlords for the living conditions of their tenants. Changes in the social and economic environment have caused the character of that responsibility to evolve from its origin in medieval property law. Although he is not an insurer of his tenants' safety, a landlord is definitely no mere bystander. See *Kline,* 141 U.S. App. D.C. at 374, 439 F.2d at 481. All three branches of government have recognized this development, and have expressed in varying ways the content of a new landlord-tenant estate. Its paramount concern is with health and safety. Accordingly, the expense involved in making a dwelling secure and habitable does not diminish the landlord's responsibility.

Our analysis has led to the conclusion that a landlord has a legal duty to take reasonable security measures for tenant protection on the premises. His obligation to provide safe and habitable premises gives rise to potential liability on alternative grounds of conventional negligence and the implied warranty of habitability. Together these theories will serve to protect the otherwise precarious position of the individual tenant in a manner consistent with modern conceptions of public policy.

For the foregoing reasons, the judgment of the Appellate Division is affirmed.

CHIEF JUSTICE WILENTZ, JUSTICE SULLIVAN and JUSTICE HANDLER join in this opinion in its entirety.

JUSTICE POLLOCK joins in all but Part IIIA of this opinion.

---

6. The statute defines "multiple dwelling" to include all structures "in which three or more units of dwelling space are occupied . . . by three or more persons who live independently of each other." N.J.S.A. 55:13A-3(k).

JUSTICES CLIFFORD and SCHREIBER concur in the result and have filed separate opinions.

SCHREIBER, J., concurring in the result.

CLIFFORD, J., concurring in the result and dissenting in part.

For affirmance: CHIEF JUSTICE WILENTZ and JUSTICES SULLIVAN, PASHMAN, CLIFFORD, SCHREIBER, HANDLER and POLLOCK—7.

For reversal: None.

SCHREIBER, J., concurring. The narrow question presented in our order granting certification in this case is "whether there was a duty on the part of the landlord to provide a lock for the door which opened into the common access area of the building where the attack on the tenant occurred." I would answer affirmatively based on a traditional tort theory.

The Legislature has declared that the Hotel and Multiple Dwelling Law, N.J.S.A. 55:13A-1 et seq. "being . . . remedial legislation necessary for the protection of the health and welfare of the residents of this State in order to assure the provision therefor of decent, standard and safe units of dwelling space, shall be liberally construed to effectuate the purposes and intent thereof." That underlying policy was furthered when the Commissioner of Community Affairs adopted regulation N.J.A.C. 5:10-605.3(f)(2), which provided in pertinent part:

> Security Requirements—The following provisions shall apply to all buildings heretofor [*sic*] or hereafter erected that may be classified in residential occupancy group L-2. Existing buildings shall comply with the requirements of this Section within two years after the effective date of these regulations.
>
> (i) Building entrance doors and other exterior exit doors shall be equipped with heavy duty lock sets. Latch sets shall have stop-work in the inside cylinder controlled by a master key only. Outside cylinders of main entrance door locks shall be operated by the tenant's key, which shall not be keyed to also open the tenant's apartment entrance door. Main entrance door locks shall be kept in the locked position and shall be freely openable from the inside at all times. Other exterior exit doors shall be locked to prevent entry and shall be freely openable from the inside at all times.

This regulation, having the effect of law, N.J.S.A. 55:13A-6(e) and N.J.A.C. 5:10-1.7, prescribed a standard of conduct for owners of multiple dwellings (buildings with three or more housing units, N.J.S.A. 55:13A-3(k)) with respect to a part of the premises under the landlord's control. A tenant may have a cause of action in negligence for failure of the landlord to comply with that standard. Chief Justice Weintraub wrote in Michaels v. Brookchester, Inc., 26 N.J. 349, 140 A.2d 199 (1958), referring to the Tenement House Act, N.J.S.A. 55:1-1 et seq., the predecessor of the Hotel and Multiple Dwelling Law:

> Our statute does not expressly authorize a suit by one injured by reason of a landlord's violation and hence does not create a statutory cause of action as that term is understood. Rather, in harmony with our usual approach to statutes

of this kind, the act is deemed to establish a standard of conduct, and to permit the intended beneficiaries to rely upon a negligent failure to meet that standard in a common law action for negligence. Evers v. Davis, 86 N.J.L. 196, 90 A. 677 (E. & A. 1914); Daniels v. Brunton, *supra* (7 N.J. 102, 80 A.2d 547). [at 386, 140 A.2d at 203]

The principle enunciated in *Michaels* is equally applicable here.

I find "no need to search for or rely upon any doctrine" to respond to the question certified. See Braitman v. Overlook Terrace Corp., 68 N.J. 368, 388, 346 A.2d 76, 87 (1975) (Clifford and Schreiber, JJ., concurring).

JUSTICE CLIFFORD joins in this opinion.

CLIFFORD, J., dissenting in part. The sense of conviction which prompted my agreement with Justice Schreiber in Braitman v. Overlook Terrace Corp., 68 N.J. 368, 388, 346 A.2d 76 (1975) (concurring opinion), remains undiminished by time, events, or any development in landlord-tenant law. I therefore join fully in his concurring opinion today.

In addition, I take this opportunity to register disagreement with the notion that liability can be imposed on the defendant landlord on the theory of implied warranty of habitability. Emphasizing the growing presence of crime in society the Court declares today that "the landlord's implied warranty of habitability obliges him to furnish reasonable safeguards to protect tenants from foreseeable criminal activity on the premises", *ante* at 218; and that "[s]ince [this] undertaking exists independently of [the landlord's] knowledge of any risks, there is no need to prove notice of a defective and unsafe condition." *Ante* at 218.

The harsh realities of modern life are all too well-known. I share the majority's concern with them. But novel application of the implied warranty of habitability to the baleful conditions reflected in those realities is unwarranted and ill-advised. In practical effect this exercise predicates what amounts to absolute liability solely upon the relationship between the landlord and tenant and upon loose notions of foreseeability. In my view the existence of a duty here should not be grounded simply on a special relationship between the parties but rather should arise from the particular circumstances of the case, including foreseeability. [Citations omitted.] Clearly the inquiry must involve a fair balancing of the relative interests of the parties, the nature of the risk, and the public interest in the proposed solution. *Goldberg, supra,* 38 N.J. at 583, 186 A.2d 291. This process has been well served in the past through the application of traditional negligence principles. I perceive no compelling reason for departing from that practice.

NOTES AND QUESTIONS

1. Compare Gulf Reston, Inc. v. Rogers, 215 Va. 155, 206 S.E.2d 841 (1974). Tenant died of a heart attack allegedly caused when an unknown intruder climbed to the roof while decedent was cooking steaks on his patio

below and threw aluminum paint on him. In an action for wrongful death against the landlord, plaintiff established many instances known to defendant of unauthorized access to the apartment building's roof. The jury returned a verdict against the landlord, which the appellate court reversed:

> Since no special relationship existed between defendant and plaintiff, defendant was under no duty to protect plaintiff from an intentional criminal act committed by an unknown third person. Although some risk of injury was involved, this did not impose a duty on defendant. To hold otherwise under the circumstances of this case would make the landlord an insurer of his tenant's safety. [215 Va. at 159, 207 S.E.2d at 845]

Under what circumstances might a "special relationship" exist between landlord and tenant, so as to create some protective duty in the landlord? When the landlord can reasonably foresee *criminal* activity? When the housing code commands the landlord to install security devices? When a warranty of habitability affects the premises?

When the court denies a special relationship, is that short-hand for saying that conditions have not yet arisen which impose any responsibility in the landlord for the tenant's safety?

2. Haines, Landlords or Tenants: Who Bears the Costs of Crime, 2 Cardozo L. Rev. 299, 340-343 (1981):

> There appears to be a modest but growing judicial trend toward imposing some duty on landlords to protect tenants from third party criminal acts on the leased premises. In cases where courts have found an obligation, they have either determined that landlord-tenant is a special relationship creating a duty on the part of the landlord to use reasonable care for tenant protection, extended the landlord's duty to safely maintain common areas to include an obligation to keep those areas reasonably safe from foreseeable criminal activity, ruled that the landlord had assumed a protective duty, or imposed a duty on the landlord based on the foreseeability of criminal conduct.
>
> In light of changed societal conditions, landlord-tenant should be treated as a special relationship, requiring the landlord to take reasonable steps to protect tenants from foreseeable criminal acts of third parties. The modern landlord-tenant relationship fits into the mold of other relationships in which similar protective duties have been imposed, relations in which the ability of one party to provide for his own protection has been limited by his partial submission to the control of another. The special relationship categorization does not make the landlord an insurer of his tenant's safety, but rather requires him to provide protective measures that are reasonable under the circumstances.

3. We might readily agree that the landlord should have foreseen the harm to Ms. Trentacost from the failure to provide adequate locks, but does this prescience, per se, create the duty to install the locks? Why should it? Suppose that no measures short of around-the-clock attendants at the building entrances would have fully protected his tenants, and both the landlord *and* the tenants recognized this peril. What then is the landlord's duty?

4.　The court in Kline v. 1500 Massachusetts Avenue Apartment Corp., *supra,* page 338, expressed an alternative contract theory to support tenant's cause of action. According to the opinion, the landlord had implicitly contracted to maintain the level of protection that existed when the tenancy began. Note that this duty may be sometimes broader, sometimes narrower, than the duty based upon the implied warranty of habitability.

If a court were to adopt the *Kline* theory of contractual duty, what of the landlord's argument that the implied duty to furnish protection must be recast against the levels of protection currently existing each time the tenant renews her lease?

Suppose that A becomes a tenant in 1980 and B becomes a tenant in 1981. During 1982, the level of protection declines. In 1983, B is assaulted. Can B hold landlord to the level of protection that landlord implicitly agreed to furnish A? What if A's tenancy had already expired when B's injury occurred?

Might the level of protection remain steady while the degree of security drop (or rise)? Should the implied covenant be stated in terms of protection or security? If the latter, are we not really saying that habitability includes security?

Under a contract theory, whether based on the warranty of habitability or a *Kline*-like implied promise, may a tenant sue the landlord for specific performance (or damages) before suffering any injury?

5.　More on the alternative contract and tort theories of landlord liability:

(a)　Measure of damages. Contract law limits recovery to general damages (here, the diminution in rental value resulting from the breach) and to special damages flowing naturally from the breach or specifically contemplated by the parties. Hadley v. Baxendale, 156 Eng. Rep. 145 (Ex. 1854). In practice, would the injured tenant's potential recovery be any less (greater) under contract theory than would be possible under tort theory?

(b)　Statute of limitations. When does the statute begin to run under a contract theory? Under a tort theory?

(c)　Protected parties. A tenant's guest suffers injury due to a defective condition within the apartment. Does the injured guest have a cause of action against the landlord in both contract and tort?

6.　Liability insurance rates: The most significant factor in the setting of premium rates is geographical location. Rates for the same category of structure (no elevators, some commercial tenants) on Manhattan's "decaying" lower East Side are 4.27 times greater than on the borough's "fashionable" East Side. These differences do not reflect the existence of a *Kline* duty. Comment, 71 Colum. L. Rev. 275, 300 (1971). What is the likely effect of a *Kline* rule on liability insurance rates? Will insurers even be willing to insure in high crime areas? If not, what then?

7. The economic impact of the *Kline* rule:

It would seem that the most effective direct measure for protecting tenants is to provide guard or doorman service. This would also be the most costly measure, as may be readily illustrated. In New York City, for example, the average salary for service employees and doormen is rapidly approaching $140 per week; the minimum annual cost of providing round-the-clock doorman or guard service in that city would, then, be approximately $22,000. It seems reasonable to assume that costs in other metropolitan areas would not be significantly less. Consequently, in a middle-income apartment house with 100 apartment units and an average monthly rental of $200 per unit, the cost of providing twenty-four hour guard or doorman service would consume almost 10 percent of the annual rent roll of $240,000. If the landlord passed on the entire cost to the tenants, the increase in the monthly rental rate would be about $18.50 per apartment unit. A far greater per-apartment burden would be imposed on those smaller structures in which lower income tenants normally live. For example, if the owner of a 25-unit structure with an average monthly rental of $125 per unit were to provide a comparable level of protection, the $22,000 cost figure would consume nearly 60 percent of the annual rental income. To cover this cost completely, the landlord would have to increase the monthly unit rental rate by approximately $73. [Comment, 71 Colum. L. Rev. 275, 298 (1971)]

8. In crime-ridden areas, where foreseeable risks are greatest, how can protection be given that is not prohibitively expensive? Will the real impact of the *Kline* rule be felt only in higher-income buildings?

9. Suppose that tenant is assaulted while residing in a low-rent public housing project. To what degree do doctrines of sovereign immunity disable tenant from bringing suit on either a tort or an implied contract theory? Is it a defense that subsidies do not allow for adequate security protection? Cf. Knox Hill Tenant Council v. Washington, 448 F.2d 1045 (D.C. Cir. 1971).

§5.12 Fair Dealing

Consider, as you read the following case, whether courts ought to read into every lease an implied covenant that each party shall deal fairly with the other.

MOBIL OIL CORP. v. LIONE
66 Misc. 2d 599, 322 N.Y.S.2d 82 (Dist. Ct. 1971)

MAUCERI, J. This is an action by the landlord for possession of the premises based upon a termination of a lease.

The Respondent operates a gasoline station in the Town of Huntington, State of New York, pursuant to an annual lease with the Petitioner. He also has a retail dealer's contract to sell the Petitioner's products (Petitioner's exhibit #1). The Respondent has had this lease with the Petitioner for the past 19 years and on each occasion, the lease has been renewed. The end of the last term of the lease was February 28th, 1971, and after having been renewed for the past 19 years, he received, pursuant to the terms of the lease, a 90 day notice terminating his lease (Petitioner's exhibit #2). The Respondent still remains in possession. . . .

A registered letter, dated November 30th, 1970, was allegedly mailed to respondent on November 30th, 1970.

To compute the 90 day period, the first day is excluded and the last day is included (General Construction Law, Sec. 20). Ninety days from November 30th, 1970 falls on February 28th, 1971, the termination date of the lease. The Court finds that the registered letter was not mailed on November 30th, 1970 and therefore was untimely. The return receipt requested was not introduced into evidence and Respondent has testified that he received the letter around December 5, 1970. Petitioner has not sustained its burden of proof concerning the timely mailing of notice to terminate. The notice, being late, was ineffective and therefore could not terminate the lease.

With regard to the counterclaim asking for equitable relief, the Court must say at the outset "every man is presumed to be capable of managing his own affairs, and whether his bargains are wise or unwise, is not ordinarily a legitimate subject of inquiry in a court of either legal or equitable jurisdiction" (Parmelee v. Cameron, 41 N.Y. 392, 395). Where a contract gives either party thereto the absolute unqualified right to terminate upon notice, the court need not look to the reason behind the notice to terminate (Brown v. Retsof Mining Co., 127 App. Div. 368, 111 N.Y.S. 594). [15] In the Matter of Sinkoff Beverage Co., Inc. v. Jos. Schlitz Brewing Company, 51 Misc. 2d 446, 273 N.Y.S.2d 364, the Court determined the question of unreasonable termination in a contract. It held that it must view the situation as of the time when the contract was entered into, and from that viewpoint, the termination clause was not unconscionable (Uniform Commercial Code, Sections 2-302; 2-309(3)). The Court, in Division of Triple T Service, Inc. v. Mobil Oil Corp., 60 Misc. 2d 720, 304 N.Y.S.2d 191, aff'd 34 A.D.2d 618, 311 N.Y.S.2d 961, which is a case directly in point, held that reasonable notice of termination was given and that such termination without cause, is in good faith and is not unconscionable. This Court, as well as the court in the case of Triple T Service, Inc. was aware of the legislation (S 4915, 1969) that was passed by the New York State Legislature in amending the General Business Law (new article 9-c). The legislation had a short life span as the governor vetoed the bill. It provided that franchisors (the petitioners) deal fairly and equitably with their franchisees (the respondent) with reference to all aspects of the franchise relationship. Such legislation is sorely needed and although no bill has been

---

15. A universal statement? Cf. Edwards v. Habib, page 378, *infra.*—ED.

introduced in the present session of the Legislature, this Court feels that it should be done as quickly as possible. This Court is constrained to follow the law of the State of New York as it exists, although it believes that this matter should not be laid to rest. The oil and gasoline companies of this country, in this day and age, no longer provide a luxury product but are almost a public utility, for without the easy flow of this product to the consumers, a calamity would strike this great nation which happens to be a nation on wheels. Yet, this quasi-public utility is allowed to function as a monolithic giant without regard to our citizens who contract with them and perform services for them. It is for our Legislature to protect our people from this type of action.

It is unconscionable, although legal at present, for the Petitioner to be allowed, without cause, to terminate this lease after 19 years of annual renewal. The only salient reason that was given by the Petitioner was the following: although this Respondent did increase his sales approximately 25 percent, the company believes they can make more money with someone else as an operator. These operators are neither fish nor fowl, neither employees nor joint venturers, upon termination regardless of their length of service, they are not even entitled to receive the time honored "solid gold watch." To say that the operator has no stake in the business is ludicrous. The Petitioner would have this Court believe that the regular customers of any service station go there because of the product. I think it would be hard to deny that regular customers go to a particular station because of the service and friendliness of the operator of that station, not because of the product alone. To say that this does not give rise to a property right on behalf of the operator is without solid foundation. To say that the operator is not entitled to a consideration for the good will developed over the years is not accurate and to allow terminations without cause, stripping the Respondent of his property rights without recompense, harks back to the early days of our nation's industrial development when corporations were king and the workers were only to be used. This Court hopes fervently that it could grant equitable relief but as previously stated it is precluded but it also fervently hopes that the Legislature and the Governor of this State will see fit to enact, again, legislation which will protect this vast number of our citizens.

NOTES AND QUESTIONS

1. Contrast the court's attitude expressed in *Lione* with that of another judge in a case raising similar issues:

> The court in this case will not indulge itself in such fantasies. It is not its function to guarantee every businessman's success in his enterprise, or to protect him from entering into improvident or ill-advised contracts, or to relieve him from contracts freely negotiated, that prove to be onerous. It cannot be denied that the vitality of our marketplace is derived to a great degree from the time-

honored caveat that the individual must enjoy the right of "freedom of contract" subject only to the obvious limitations of legality, fraud and lack of capacity. [Texaco, Inc. v. A.A. Gold, Inc., 78 Misc. 2d 1050, 1054, 357 N.Y.S.2d 951, 956 (Sup. Ct. 1974)]

2. Two states, at least, have passed laws regulating the franchise relationship. A California statute somewhat restricts the power of a franchisor to refuse renewal of the franchise agreement [Cal. Bus. & Prof. Code §20000 (West Supp. 1981)]. A Connecticut statute prohibits the franchisor from terminating, cancelling, or failing to renew a franchise except for good cause. If the franchise involves a lease, good cause would not include, without other factors present, the leasing of the site to another operator [Conn. Gen. Stat. Ann. §42-133l (Supp. 1981)].

3. Compare the *Lione* case with Lippman v. Sears, Roebuck & Co., 44 Cal. 2d 136, 280 P.2d 775 (1955). There tenant had signed a ten-year lease to operate a retail sales business. The lease required a fixed rental plus a percentage rental based upon "net sales upon the leased premises." After several years, tenant transferred its sales business to another location, using the original space for merchandise storage only. Although tenant continued to pay the fixed rental, the court held that the landlord was also entitled to damages. The opinion stated that where the rental for use of a building is based upon a percentage of sales, the lessee reasonably may be said to covenant implicitly that he will use good faith to insure that the sales continue. Accord: Cissna Loan Co. v. Baron, 149 Wash. 386, 270 P. 1022 (1928) (implied covenant of fair dealing). How should damages be measured?

4. Rowe v. Great A & P Tea Co., 46 N.Y.2d 62, 385 N.E.2d 566 (1978) also involved a long-term percentage lease. Although the lease did not bar assignment, landlord sued for rescission and damages after tenant assigned the lease to Gristedes, a lower-volume (ergo: lower percentage base) supermarket chain. The court of appeals, reversing the appellate division, held unanimously that an implied covenant limiting the right to assign should not be read into the lease, even though the landlord would suffer a percentage rental drop after the assignment.

A lease agreement, like any other contract, essentially involves a bargained-for exchange between the parties. Absent some violation of law or transgression of a strong public policy, the parties to a contract are basically free to make whatever agreement they wish, no matter how unwise it might appear to a third party. It is, of course, far too late in the day to seriously suggest that the law has not made substantial inroads into such freedom of private contracts. There exists an unavoidable tension between the concept of freedom to contract, which has long been basic to our socioeconomic system, and the equally fundamental belief that an enlightened society must to some extent protect its members from the potentially harsh effects of an unchecked free market system. Thus, rightly or wrongly, society has chosen to intervene in various ways in the dealings between private parties. This intervention is perhaps best exemplified by statutes mandating the express or implicit inclusion of certain substantive or procedural provisions in various types of contracts (e.g., Insurance Law, §167; Real Property Law, §§226-b, 234, 235-b). It is also illustrated by judicial decisions to the effect that there exists in every contract certain implied-by-law covenants, such as the promise to act with good faith in the course of performance (e.g., Kirke La Shelle Co. v. Armstrong Co., 263 N.Y. 79, 87). In a similar vein, the law has developed the concept of unconscionability so as to prevent the unjust enforcement of onerous contractual terms which one party is able to impose under [*sic*] the other because of a significant disparity in bargaining power (e.g., Uniform Commercial Code, §2-302). Despite all this, there yet remains substantial room for bargaining by the parties.

5.   From your study of contract law, can you cite any parallel for requiring fair dealing between two contracting parties? Cf. U.C.C. §1-203. Do you believe that the law *should* bind the leasing parties to a course of fair dealing? If the *Lione* court had read fair dealing into the Mobil Oil franchise-lease agreement, would tenant have received a life tenancy after nineteen years? What would have been fair on the facts given? Suppose that the tenant had refused to renew the lease and had taken his good will to the Exxon location across the street? Unfair dealing?

6.   Do you understand the difference between unconscionability and unfair dealing?

§5.13   Transferability of Leasehold Interests

In an earlier section, *supra*, §2.4(d), we saw the law's preference for freely alienable fee interests in land. This attitude carries over initially to leasehold interests as well. Thus, if the lease does not mention alienability, the tenant may assign the lease or sublet the premises without restriction. (The distinction between assignment and subletting comes later, *infra*, pages 578-587.) In long-term commercial leases, either free transferability is the practice or, if restrictions on transferability do appear, they usually result from hard bargaining between the landlord and tenant. By contrast, however, in most residential situations, as well as in business lettings involving relatively weak or unsophisticated tenants, the boiler-plate lease bars transferability without the landlord's consent. Moreover, where such language appears, courts have generally upheld it, even though the landlord might withhold her consent for good reason or bad, or for no reason at all.[16] Consequently, the landlord could, if she wished, exercise virtual autonomy over who would be present to discharge the leasehold duties.

16. Unless the reason is one that violates some statutory antidiscrimination law, *supra*, §1.4.—ED.

In keeping with the current mood of rethinking the landlord and tenant relationship, some courts have begun to question their easy acceptance of restricted leasehold transferability. The case which follows illustrates that development.

HOMA-GOFF INTERIORS, INC. v. COWDEN
350 So. 2d 1035 (Ala. 1977)

JONES, J. This summary judgment case involves a counterclaim filed by the appellants, Homa-Goff Interiors, Inc., against Geraldine Cowden, the appellee, claiming interference with a contractual relationship and unlawful refusal, by Mrs. Cowden, to grant consent to a sublease agreement between Homa-Goff and certain named prospective subtenants.

In February of 1974, a lease was entered into by Mrs. Cowden and Homa-Goff, John Goff, Pal Shoemaker, Henry Goff, and Thomas Gallion for a ten-year period. The lease was negotiated by Ted Cason, Mrs. Cowden's son-in-law. The lease contained a clause which restricted the lessees' power to sublet subject to the landlord's written consent.

In October, Homa-Goff opened a furniture store on the leased premises. After several months in business, however, it became apparent to the appellants that, because of financial problems, they could not continue their operation. Therefore, they began seeking a subtenant. After some negotiation with the State of Alabama, the appellants, according to their counterclaim, reached a tentative agreement with the State to sublease the premises at a rental rate in excess of the rate paid by the lessees. Mrs. Cowden, exercising her option provided in the lease, refused to approve the State as a sublessee.

Homa-Goff also attempted to sublease the property to James Rudd, Jr. The appellants and Rudd, Jr., had several meetings and set up a meeting at the leased premises. Upon arriving at the premises, John Goff discovered Ted Cason talking with Rudd's father. Appellants charged in their counterclaim that Cason informed Rudd, Sr., that John Goff was without authority to rent the building, but that he, Cason, on behalf of Mrs. Cowden, could lease the building to Rudd, immediately, at a lower rental rate.

Rudd, Jr., testified at deposition that he had no intention of subleasing. John Goff testified at deposition that Rudd, indeed, was interested in subleasing and had inquired about prices. In any event, the building was eventually leased to Rudd, by Cason, for the same amount of rent paid by Homa-Goff.

Mrs. Cowden filed suit against the appellants claiming breach of the terms and conditions of the lease, consisting of failure to pay the November, 1975, rent installment. After Homa-Goff counterclaimed, Mrs. Cowden filed a motion for summary judgment as to the counterclaim, which was granted by the trial Judge.

The trial Judge based his ruling upon two legal principles. First, the trial Judge ruled: "Alabama is one State that does not recognize in general a cause of action for interference with a contractual relationship." Secondly, the trial Judge ruled: "[t]he landlord's withholding of consent can be arbitrary and unreasonable." From the order based on these rulings, Homa-Goff appeals. We reverse.

The threshold question is whether Mrs. Cowden, pursuant to ¶15(a) of the lease, may arbitrarily and capriciously reject a subtenant proposed by the lessee. This question, apparently, has never been considered by this Court. If we hold that the trial Judge was correct in ruling in the affirmative on this issue, we need not deal with the allegations concerning interference with a contractual relationship. And this for the reason that, if Mrs. Cowden may arbitrarily reject proposed subtenants, Homa-Goff was powerless to enter into any contractual relationship with the State or Rudd, Jr., without Mrs. Cowden's approval.

It should be noted at the outset that, in the absence of a restrictive clause as set out in ¶15(a), the lessee generally has the right, without consent of the lessor, to assign his interest under the lease, or to sublet the premises, because the law looks with disfavor on restraints on alienation. 49 Am. Jur. 2d, Landlord and Tenant, §§398, 481. ¶15(a) of the lease states:

> The Lessee shall not assign or sublease all or any part of the demised premises except by and with approval of the Lessor in writing. Should such approval be given, the assignment or sublease of said leased premises shall not release the Lessee of its obligation hereunder.

The general rule throughout the country has been that, when a lease contains an approval clause, the landlord may arbitrarily and capriciously reject proposed subtenants. See 49 Am. Jur. 2d, Landlord and Tenant, §423; 51C C.J.S. Landlord and Tenant §36(1); 31 A.L.R.2d 821. This rule, however, has been under steady attack in several states in the past twenty years; and this for the reason that, in recent times, the necessity of reasonable alienation of commercial building space has become paramount in our ever-increasing urban society.

Ohio has expressly rejected the general rule. Shaker Building Co. v. Federal Lime and Stone Co., 28 Ohio Misc. 246, 277 N.E.2d 584 (1971). In *Shaker,* the lease provision permitted assignment and subletting only with the permission of the landlord. The Ohio Court, in ruling on whether the landlord could arbitrarily withhold consent, stated:

> (W)here provision is made in a lease permitting assignment of rights thereunder, limited only by the requirement of prior consent of the lessor, such consent may not be withheld unless the prospective assignee is unacceptable, using the same standards applied in the acceptance of the original lessee. 277 N.E.2d at 587.

The arbitrary and capricious rule has also been rejected in Illinois. Arrington v. Walter E. Heller International Corp., 30 Ill. App. 3d 631, 333

N.E.2d 50 (1975). In *Arrington,* the situation was somewhat reversed in that the lessee had the right to refuse to consent to the occupation of the building by another lessee. The defendant leased the top fifteen floors from the plaintiff. The lease contained a provision which stated: "Landlord covenants and agrees that it will not enter into any lease or other arrangement respecting the use of space on the ground floor, mezzanine and lower concourse of the building without the written consent of tenant, which consent shall not be unreasonably withheld."

The Appellate Court points out that, in *Arrington,* the tenant expressly provided that he would not unreasonably withhold consent. The Court adds, however, that this was a mere recital of the law of Illinois which is:

> Where the lease merely contains a provision—without more—granting a person, normally a landlord, the power to withhold consent, *regardless of whether explicitly qualified to reasonable exercises of that power* . . . the courts have held the person's refusal to consent to a person acceptable by reasonable commercial standards to be an unreasonable exercise and thus violative of the lease. 333 N.E.2d at 58. [Emphasis added.]

Guided by this rationale, we hold that, even where the lease provides an approval clause, a landlord may not unreasonably and capriciously withhold his consent to a sublease agreement. The landlord's rejection should be judged under a test applying a reasonable commercial standard.

This question, of course, becomes a question of fact to be determined by the jury. Therefore, we hold that the trial Judge erred in granting a summary judgment in favor of Mrs. Cowden regarding appellant's claim alleging Mrs. Cowden was arbitrary and capricious in rejecting the prospective subtenants. It is a jury question whether Mrs. Cowden acted reasonably, and there is sufficient conflict of material fact to mandate a reversal.

While our decision is not limited to the particular facts before us, we can perceive no set of circumstances which would more dramatically support the reasons behind this rule, and the moral need for it, than the facts of this case. The tenant sought and secured a potential subtenant. Before a sublease agreement was consummated, Mrs. Cowden exercised her "right" under the lease to disapprove the proffered subtenant. Thereafter, however, she proceeded immediately to lease the same premises to the same person previously rejected. To accept as a tenant the very party rejected as a subtenant is, at the very least, evidence of extreme bad faith, for, in this instance, the act of disapproval became the act of approval.

Because we have ruled that a landlord may not arbitrarily and capriciously reject a subtenant when the landlord reserves the right of approval of sublessees, we must now address the issue whether Alabama law recognizes a cause of action for tortious interference with a contractual relation. The trial Judge is correct in stating that generally Alabama does not recognize a cause of action for the tortious interference with a contract. There are, however, two important exceptions to this rule which are set forth in Erswell v. Ford, 208 Ala. 101, 94 So. 67 (1922): The first involves employer-employee relationships; and the second occurs when a party to a lease has been induced, by fraud or coercion, to breach his contract. See McCluskey v. Steele, 18 Ala. App. 31, 88 So. 367 (1920). Appellants specifically allege, "Ted Cason . . . intentionally, fraudulently, maliciously and wrongfully made statements to James Rudd. . . ." Thus, under the exceptions enunciated in *Erswell*, the appellants have properly set forth a cause of action, and the trial Judge erred in granting summary judgment.

Reversed and remanded.

FAULKNER, J., concurs.

MADDOX, SHORES, EMBRY and BEATTY, JJ., concur specially.

TORBERT, C.J., and BLOODWORTH and ALMON, JJ., dissent.

BEATTY, J. (concurring specially). I concur with the majority opinion of Justice Jones in which he maintains that the lessor may not arbitrarily reject a sublessee chosen by the lessee. In my opinion, clauses which restrict subleasing should be interpreted to call for the application of reasonable commercial standards unless the parties themselves expressly agree that the lessor's decision, for whatever reason, is binding. This is so because it is probable that when contracting the parties expect each other to act reasonably.

I express no opinion upon the other aspects of the majority opinion, particularly regarding the reference to the effect of the moral point of view upon the decision in this case. The prospect of this Court's (or any court) deciding individual cases upon the Court's own moral assessments is something which might be useful in frightening little children into proper behavior, but its utility in decision-making deserves much study.

MADDOX, SHORES and EMBRY, JJ., concur.

BLOODWORTH, J. (dissenting).

I respectfully dissent. Since 1853, this Court has upheld lease provisions which provide that there shall be no subletting without the express consent of the lessor.

To overturn a century and a quarter of existing real estate law without giving contracting parties "fair notice" is my principal complaint with the majority's opinion. At the very least, I think the majority ought to make the rule they have adopted "prospective."

There must be literally tens of thousands of existing leases with similar "consent" provisions as to subletting as those in this case. Lawyers and judges should have a right to rely on existing well-settled property law interpretations by our courts. See my special concurrence in Nunn v. Keith, 289 Ala. 518, 524, 268 So. 2d 792 (1972).

As Mr. Justice Almon points out in his dissent, in quoting from Mr. Justice Bouldin's opinion in *Faucett, supra,* parties have a right to contract as they see fit so long as their contracts are not violative of the law, and I would add, or against public policy. Here, the parties made their contract; they ought to be bound by it. I would add that I concur in the other views expressed in Justice Almon's dissent.

TORBERT, C.J., and ALMON, J., concur.

ALMON, J. (dissenting). I would adhere to the view adopted by a majority of jurisdictions in this country. Citizens should have the right to contract. Art. 1, Sec. 22, Constitution of Alabama, 1901.

In my judgment, the court has rewritten this contract so as to rid it of its alleged moral harshness. There are many valid reasons why a lessor would insist that a lease-contract contain a provision to prevent subletting without the consent of the lessor. Why should a lessor be obligated to accept a subtenant chosen by a defaulting original tenant on the basis of "commercial standards," (whatever they may be) when the lessor's contract plainly gives him a contrary right?

Moreover, the leasing of real property for a term of years conveys an estate. The majority has enlarged that estate.

> Under the plenary power to make contracts, not violative of law, the lessor and lessee may stipulate there shall be no subletting of the property nor any portion of same without advance consent of the lessor evidenced by written endorsement on the lease. This is said to be restrictive of the estate which would otherwise pass to the lessee. Annotation 117 Am. St. Rep. 92 et seq.; 32 Am. Jur. 333; Maddox v. Westcott, 156 Ala. 492, 47 So. 170, 16 Ann. Cas. 604. Faucett v. Provident Mut. Life Ins. Co. of Philadelphia, 244 Ala. 308, 13 So.2d 182 (1943).

I respectfully disagree with the judgment of the Court.

TORBERT, C.J., and BLOODWORTH, J., concur. . . .

NOTES AND QUESTIONS

1.   Restatement (Second) of Property §15.2(2)(1977) would also qualify the landlord's absolute power over alienation. It reads:

> A restraint on alienation without the consent of the landlord of the tenant's interest in the leased property is valid, but the landlord's consent to an alienation by the tenant cannot be withheld unreasonably, unless a freely negotiated provision in the lease gives the landlord an absolute right to withhold consent.

The Reporter acknowledges that the rule is contrary to the established common-law. Id., Reporter's Note 7.

The Restatement fails to amplify "freely negotiated provision," an exception that would give landlord the absolute right to withhold consent. Presumably, this would not cover the typical situation in which an apartment tenant signs a boiler-plate lease. Suppose, however, that the prospective apartment tenant asks that the "no assignment" clause be deleted or modified, and the landlord flatly refuses. Has there been free negotiation?

2. A few states have statutorily limited the privilege of landlords to restrain alienation. Consider, for example, N.Y. Real Prop. L. §226-(b) (McKinney Supp. 1981):

> A tenant renting a residence in a dwelling having four or more residential units shall have the right to sublease or assign his premises [sic], subject to the written consent of the landlord given in advance of the sublease or assignment. Such consent shall not be unreasonably withheld. If the landlord unreasonably withholds consent for such sublease or assignment, the landlord must release the tenant from the lease upon request of the tenant.

The statute then sets forth procedures that tenants must follow to solicit their landlord's consent.

Although §226-b strengthens the tenant's situation somewhat, how does it fall short of the Restatement position?

A New York tenant covered by the statute has two years remaining on her lease. She would like to sublet her apartment for the six months she will be away from the city. Landlord refuses unreasonably to give his consent. What, under the statute, are the tenant's options? See Grayshaw v. New Amsterdam Apartments Co., 106 Misc. 2d 936, 436 N.Y.S.2d 804 (Sup. Ct. 1981).

3. British landlords are required by statute to refrain from withholding their consent unreasonably to an assignment or subletting. The Landlord and Tenant Act of 1927, 17-18 Geo. 5, c. 36, §19(1). Discussion of the British experience appears in Arnold, Covenants to Leases and Tenancy Agreements, c. 4 (1930), and in a series of articles in 72 So. J. 96, 655, 722, 817 (1929).

4. Assume that the lease itself requires the landlord not to withhold his consent unreasonably to a proposed assignment. In each of the following instances, would you think a landlord unreasonable should he withold his consent?

(a) The landlord wishes to sell the building and believes that a vacant unit (should the tenant move out) betters his prospects of sale. Compare Wohl v. Yelen, 22 Ill. App. 2d 455, 161 N.E.2d 339 (1959).

(b) The unit has become more valuable, and the landlord wishes to relet the unit himself at a higher rental. Compare Equity Funding Corp. v. Carol Management Corp., 66 Misc. 2d 1020, 322 N.Y.S.2d 965 (Sup. Ct. 1972).

(c) There are several vacancies in the building. The landlord would rather have the proposed assignee move into one of the vacant units.

(d) The proposed assignee is in the same business as another tenant. Although he has no legal obligation to do so, the landlord wants to protect his present tenant against competition.

The proposed assignee is in the same business as another tenant. Although he has no legal obligation to do so, the landlord wants to protect his present tenant against competition.

(e) The landlord wishes the apartment for his personal use. Compare Matter of Cedarhurst Park Apartments, Inc. v. Milgrim, 55 Misc. 2d 118, 284 N.Y.S.2d 330 (Dist. Ct. 1967).

(f) The proposed assignee is a law student. The landlord dislikes law student tenants because they insist on the letter of their rights—and then some. Compare Kramarsky v. Stahl Management, 92 Misc. 2d 1030, 42 N.Y.S.2d 943 (Sup. Ct. 1977).

(g) The landlord, a religious organization, objects to the activity of the proposed assignee, a family planning organization. Compare American Books Co. v. Yeshiva University Development Foundation, Inc., 59 Misc. 2d, 31, 297 N.Y.S.2d, 156 (Sup. Ct. 1969).

5. Where the lease fails to restrain alienation, the tenant may freely assign or mortgage the lease and sublet the premises. Exceptions to this general rule of free alienability involve a tenancy at will and the lease that "requires significant personal services from either party [,] and a transfer of the party's interest would substantially impair the other party's chances of obtaining those services." Restatement (Second) of Property §15.1 (1977). Does an assignment relieve the original tenant of his leasehold duties? Does a subletting of the premises? See Amco Trust, Inc. v. Naylor, page 580, *infra.*

6. Despite their validity, clauses limiting the tenant's power to alienate are construed with great strictness. Thus, a bar against assignment will not usually prevent a subletting or a mortgaging of the term. See 2 Powell, Real Property ¶246[1] (Rohan ed. 1973).

7. A curiosity of the common law is the Rule in Dumpor's Case. 4 Coke 119b, 76 Eng. Rep. 1110 (K.B. 1603). Under the rule, once a landlord approves an assignment of the lease, he relinquishes his power to restrict future assignments. The rule does not apply to approved sublettings. This is one more instance of the courts' attempt to weaken, yet not repudiate, a questionable doctrine—the power of a landlord to restrain alienation. Burby, Real Property 200-201 (2d ed. 1953). The rule may yet linger in a few states. See Powell, Real Property 163 n. 16 (Powell & Rohan abr. ed. 1968). Cf. Model Apartment Lease ¶11, page 241, *supra.*

8. What is the effect of an assignment made without the landlord's consent when such consent is required? Cf., e.g., Model Apartment Lease ¶9, page 240, *supra.*

Chapter 6

Landlord and Tenant: Landlord Remedies

In this chapter we examine how the landlord proceeds when tenant defaults. As you study the following materials, consider the growing fusion of property and contract law. Recall also the materials on holdover tenancies covered in Chapter 4.

Independently of any provision of the lease, the tenant's failure at common law to pay the rent due (or perform any other lease term) did not work a forfeiture of the tenant's estate. Cf. Brown's Administrator v. Bragg, 22 Ind. 122, 123 (1864). The court there wrote: "As well might a man who sells a horse to be paid for in the future, claim to recover him back on failure of the purchaser to pay according to his stipulation, as the lessor of real estate to recover it from his tenant because of his failure to pay rent, there being no stipulation that such failure should work a forfeiture."

But, of course, landlords early learned—in written leases, anyway—to couple tenant's breach with a forfeiture of the estate.[1] Cf., e.g., Model Apartment Lease ¶9, page 240, *supra*. And even if the lease agreement is silent (often the case with oral lettings), statutes now provide for termination where tenant fails to pay rent or uses the premises illegally. See, e.g., N.Y. Real Prop. Acts. Law §§711(2), 711(5) (1963).

§6.1 Self-Help

JORDAN v. TALBOT
55 Cal. 2d 597, 361 P.2d 20, 12 Cal. Rptr. 488 (1961)

TRAYNOR, J. Plaintiff was a tenant in defendant's apartment house. The lease provided that the lessor had a right of re-entry upon the breach of any

---

1. Disputes sometimes arise as to whether the defeasance clause works automatically or requires the landlord's election—by analogy to the difference between fee on a limitation and fee on a condition. Contrast, for example, Hayman v. Butler Bros., 196 Misc. 641, 92 N.Y.S.2d 148 (Mun. Ct. 1949) (condition, not a limitation), with Remedco Corp. v. Bryn Mawr Hotel, 45 Misc. 2d 586, 257 N.Y.S.2d 525 (Civ. Ct. 1965) (limitation, not a condition).

condition in the lease and a lien upon all personal effects, furniture, and baggage in the tenant's apartment to secure the rents and other charges. One of the conditions was the payment of $132.50 rent on the first of each month. Plaintiff paid the rent for eight months. After she was two months in arrears in rent, defendant, without her consent and during her temporary absence, unlocked the door of her apartment, entered and removed her furniture to a warehouse, and refused to allow her to re-occupy the apartment. Thereupon plaintiff filed this action for forcible entry and detainer[1] and for conversion of her furniture and other personal property.

The jury returned a verdict of $6500 for forcible entry and detainer and for conversion and $3000 punitive damages. Plaintiff appeals from an order granting defendant's motion for a new trial. . . .

Defendant contends that there is no evidence that he violated either section 1159 or 1160 of the Code of Civil Procedure and that the evidence is therefore insufficient as a matter of law to sustain a verdict for forcible entry and detainer. He bases this contention on the grounds that (1) his entry was not unlawful, since he had a right of re-entry; (2) he did not violate subdivision 1 of section 1159, since he did not use force to enter the premises . . . and that (5) in any case his entry was privileged by virtue of his lien on the property in the apartment.

DEFENDANT'S RIGHT OF RE-ENTRY IS NOT A DEFENSE TO AN ACTION FOR FORCIBLE ENTRY

In defining forcible entry section 1159 of the Code of Civil Procedure refers to "every person," thereby including owners as well as strangers to the title. Under section 1172 of the Code of Civil Procedure the plaintiff "shall only be required to show, in addition to the forcible entry or forcible detainer complained of, that he was peaceably in the actual possession at the time of the forcible entry, or was entitled to the possession at the time of the forcible

---

1. Section 1159 of the Code of Civil Procedure defines a forcible entry as follows:

> Every person is guilty of a forcible entry who either:
> 1. By breaking open doors, windows, or other parts of a house, or by any kind of violence or circumstance of terror enters upon or into any real property; or,
> 2. Who, after entering peaceably upon real property, turns out by force, threats, or menacing conduct, the party in possession.

Section 1160 of the Code of Civil Procedure defines a forcible detainer as follows:

> Every person is guilty of a forcible detainer who either:
> 1. By force, or by menaces and threats of violence, unlawfully holds and keeps the possession of any real property, whether the same was acquired peaceably or otherwise; or,
> 2. Who, in the night-time, or during the absence of the occupant of any lands, unlawfully enters upon real property, and who, after demand made for the surrender thereof, for the period of five days, refuses to surrender the same to such former occupant.
>   The occupant of real property, within the meaning of this subdivision, is one who, within five days preceding such unlawful entry, was in the peaceable and undisturbed possession of such lands.

detainer. The defendant may show in his defense that he or his ancestors, or those whose interest in such premises he claims, have been in the quiet possession thereof for the space of one whole year together next before the commencement of the proceedings, and that his interest therein is not ended or determined; and such showing is a bar to the proceedings." Nowhere is it stated that a right of re-entry is a defense to an action for forcible entry or detainer.

Nor can such a defense be implied from the historical background or purpose of the statute. [2]

Both before and after the enactment of the present forcible entry and detainer statutes this court held that ownership or right of possession to the property was not a defense to an action for forcible entry. In McCauley v. Weller, 1859, 12 Cal. 500, 524 [decided before the enactment of sections 1159-1179a of the Code of Civil Procedure] and in Voll v. Hollis, 1882, 60 Cal. 569, 573 [decided after the enactment of the foregoing sections] it was held that evidence of defendant's ownership of the land was irrelevant to the question of liability for a forcible entry and detainer.

"[T]he action of forcible entry and detainer is a summary proceeding to recover possession of premises forcibly or unlawfully detained. The inquiry in such cases is confined to the actual peaceable possession of the plaintiff and the unlawful or forcible ouster or detention by defendant—the object of the law being to prevent the disturbance of the public peace, by the forcible assertion of a private right. Questions of title or right of possession cannot arise; a forcible entry upon the actual possession of plaintiff being proven, he would be entitled to restitution, though the fee-simple title and present right of possession are shown to be in the defendant. The authorities on this point are numerous and uniform." [Citations omitted.]

[In four of the cases, *supra*,] the landlord entered pursuant to a lease granting him a right of re-entry similar to defendant's right of re-entry in the present case. In each case the court held that absent a voluntary surrender of the premises by the tenant, the landlord could enforce his right of re-entry only by judicial process, not by self-help. Under section 1161 of the Code of Civil Procedure a lessor may summarily obtain possession of his real property within three days. This remedy is a complete answer to any claim that self-help is necessary.

As in the foregoing cases, the lease herein is silent as to the method of enforcing the right of re-entry. In any event a provision in the lease expressly permitting a forcible entry would be void as contrary to the public policy set forth in section 1159. . . .

2. The original forcible entry and detainer statute, enacted in England in 1381 (5 Richard II c. 7; see Dickinson v. Maguire, 9 Cal. 46, 50-51), provided only criminal sanctions for its breach. The purpose of the statute was to preserve the peace by preventing disturbances that frequently accompanied struggles for the possession of land. See 2 Taylor, Landlord and Tenant 412 (9th ed.); Dickinson v. Maguire, *supra*. This early prohibition against self-help extended to persons having a right to possession and thus fostered recourse to orderly court process. See 1 Harper and James, The Law of Torts, 260.

Regardless of who has the right to possession, orderly procedure and preservation of the peace require that the actual possession shall not be disturbed except by legal process.

DEFENDANT WAS GUILTY OF FORCIBLE ENTRY

Section 1159, subdivision 1, prohibits an entry by means of breaking open doors or windows. Defendant violated this section when he unlocked plaintiff's apartment without her consent and entered with the storage company employees to remove her furniture, even though there was no physical damage to the premises or actual violence. . . .

Even if we were to interpret the first subdivision of section 1159 as being inapplicable unless a door or window was physically damaged or threats of violence actually occurred, the evidence in the instant case would nevertheless support a finding of forcible entry as defined by subdivision 2 of section 1159. Under that subdivision a forcible entry is completed if, after a peaceable entry, the occupant is excluded from possession by force or threats of violence. The removal of plaintiff's furniture without her consent rendered the apartment unsuitable for residence and forced her to seek shelter elsewhere. Moreover, when plaintiff returned to her apartment at 1:30 A.M. and inquired about her belongings defendant's employee ordered her to "Get the hell out of here. You're out of this place. Don't talk to me about it. Call Mr. Talbot." The jury could reasonably conclude that plaintiff was justified in believing that any attempt on her part to reinstall her furniture would be met by force. It has long been settled that there is a forcible entry under subdivision 2 if a show of force is made that causes the occupant to refrain from re-entering. . . .

DEFENDANT WAS NOT AUTHORIZED TO ENFORCE HIS LIEN BY ENTERING PLAINTIFF'S HOME

The provision in the lease granting defendant a lien does not specify a means of enforcement. In Childs etc. Co. v. Shelburne Realty Co., 23 Cal. 2d 263, 268, [143 P.2d 697], 699, where the lessor had a similar lien, we stated "in the absence of provisions in the lease for enforcement, equitable action would be necessary to make the lien operative [citations]." Even if the lease had authorized a forcible entry it would be invalid as violating the policy of the forcible entry and detainer statutes. . . .

We conclude therefore that the evidence supports the verdict of forcible entry and detainer. There was evidence that defendant entered plaintiff's apartment without her consent. Such an entry violates section 1159 of the Code of Civil Procedure. There was evidence that defendant refused to allow plaintiff to re-enter her apartment. Such conduct violates section 1160 of the Code of Civil Procedure. Since the policy of these sections is the preservation of the peace, the rights thereunder may not be contracted away; thus defendant's right of re-entry and his lien on personal property in the apartment did not justify his entry into the apartment.

DEFENDANT DID NOT CONVERT PLAINTIFF'S GOODS

Defendant stored most of the items removed from plaintiff's apartment in a warehouse in plaintiff's name. The items that the warehousemen had difficulty removing were stored in the lessor's basement and held for the plaintiff. The lessor did not use any of plaintiff's belongings or make any claim of ownership to them. In Zaslow v. Kroenert, 29 Cal. 2d 541, 551 [176 P.2d 1], we held that the removal of another's property and storing it in the owner's name without any other exercise of dominion or control is not a conversion. We there stated that "[w]here the conduct complained of does not amount to a substantial interference with the possession of the right thereto, but consists of intermeddling with or use of or damages to the personal property, the owner has a cause of action for trespass or case, and may recover only the actual damages suffered by reason of the impairment of the property or the loss of its use." Zaslow v. Kroenert, *supra*, at page 551; see Prosser on Torts [2d ed.] pp. 102-107; Fleming on Torts, p. 58.

Plaintiff is therefore entitled only to actual damages in an amount sufficient to compensate her for any impairment of the property or loss of its use.

The verdict for conversion was as a matter of law unsupported by the evidence. The new trial was therefore properly granted.

The purported appeal from the order granting judgment notwithstanding the verdict is dismissed. The order granting a new trial is affirmed. Each side is to bear its own costs on appeal.

GIBSON, C.J., and PETERS, J., and DOOLING, J., concurred.

SCHAUER, J., dissenting. It appears to me that upon a review of the entire record the evidence on the points at issue here should be held to be, as a matter of law, insufficient to support a judgment for the plaintiff and that affirmance of the order granting defendant's motion for a new trial should be placed upon that ground. . . .

It should be recognized that it is still presumably lawful for adult persons, not convicted of felony, to own real property, contract for its rental, require the tenant to pay the agreed value of occupancy, and provide for security therefor, including a right of peaceful re-entry upon any default of the tenant. Tenants and property owners may agree that the latter shall have some rights as against defaulting tenants, short of the time and expense required by court proceedings, and where such rights can be exercised peaceably, as was done here, it seems to me only common and elementary justice that the courts uphold them. It may be further observed that the import and effect of the majority holding in refusing to sustain those rights appears to constitute state action impairing the obligation of a contract in violation of section 10 (clause 1) of article I of the Constitution of the United States and section 16 of article I of the Constitution of California.

Finally, and most distressing in my view, is the seeming alignment of the court on the side of the person who not only breached a contract but, according to the undisputed evidence, appears to have compounded the civil wrong by issuing and passing a check without sufficient funds or credit, to the end of extending her unlawful taking of the owner's property (the use and occupation of his premises) for a further period without compensation. To reward such a person for such conduct at the expense of the innocent party to the contract (whose only wrong consisted in believing that a contract, admittedly executed by competent parties with a lawful object and for a valuable consideration, would be upheld) appears to me to pervert law and subvert justice.

In the circumstances I would hold that as a matter of law plaintiff is not entitled to judgment against defendant for forcible entry and detainer.

McComb, J., and White, J., concurred.

NOTES AND QUESTIONS

1. After Jordan v. Talbot, how would you advise a California landlord who wishes to reacquire the premises from a delinquent tenant without judicial process and whose lease agreement contains this privilege? Contrast the decision with Drinkhouse v. Parka Corp., 3 N.Y.2d 82, 143 N.E.2d 767, 164 N.Y.S.2d 1 (1957), which says (3 N.Y.2d at 91) that New York's forcible entry or detainer statute only applies "where the force employed to oust a tenant is unusual, tends to bring about a breach of peace, and the entry is with a strong hand, or by a multitude of people, or in a riotous manner, or with personal violence, or with threat and menace to life and limb under circumstances which would naturally inspire fear and lead one to apprehend danger of personal injury if he stood up in defense of his possession. . . . Mere trespass does not give rise to such an action, even when it is accompanied by 'wrenching off the lock.' " See also Pine Hill Associates v. Malveaux, 93 Misc. 2d 63, 403 N.Y.S.2d 399 (Sup. Ct. 1978) (lease clause authorizing re-entry without legal process not unconscionable). But see Yates v. Kaplan, 75 Misc. 2d 259, 347 N.Y.S.2d 543 (Civ. Ct. 1973) (padlocking of holdover tenant's door to prevent her return after a brief absence held wrongful detainer; treble damages awarded).

2. As the decision in Jordan v. Talbot notes, forcible entry or detainer laws have an ancient lineage. The original forcible entry statute, 5 Rich. 2, c. 7 (1381), provided that "none from henceforth shall make any Entry into any Lands and Tenements, but in Case where Entry is given by Law; and in such Case not with strong Hand, nor with Multitude of People, but only in a peaceable and easy manner. And if any man from henceforth do to the contrary, and thereof be duly convict, he shall be punished by Imprisonment of his Body and thereof ransomed at the King's Will."

Forcible detainer also was made a crime ten years later. 15 Rich. 2, c. 2 (1391). Then followed a civil remedy (treble damages) if a tenant was damaged by either act. 8 Hen. 6, c. 9 (1429).

3. Landlord who employs self-help, even when such action is not forcible, may later be sued on a theory of wrongful eviction if landlord was not entitled to possession. In Lopez v. City of New York, 78 Misc. 2d 575, 357 N.Y.S.2d 659 (Civ. Ct. 1974), the tenant's award for wrongful eviction included $1,000 for mental anguish.

4. Restatement (Second) of Property §§14.2-14.3 (1977) preserves the use of self-help where "controlling law permits." It would require, however, that recovery be accomplished

(a) within a reasonable time after the lease termination;
(b) without causing physical harm, or the reasonable expectation of physical harm; and
(c) with reasonable care to avoid damage to the tenant's property.

§6.2   Distraint and Statutory Lien

Some states still allow landlord to seize tenant's goods in lieu of unpaid rent. This common-law remedy of distraint may violate the tenant's due process, as appears in the following case.

HALL v. GARSON
468 F.2d 845 (5th Cir. 1972)

Before DYER, SIMPSON and MORGAN, J.J.

SIMPSON, J. Beginning May 23, 1967, plaintiff-appellant Hall was a tenant of the Cosmopolitan Apartments in Houston, Texas, which were operated by defendants-appellees Garson, Kaplan and Sud. On September 24, 1969, Hall was in arrears in her rent, although the amount of the arrearage was in dispute. Because of this due and unpaid rent, defendants-appellees' agent was sent to Hall's apartment and, on their instructions, entered Hall's apartment and took therefrom a portable television set owned by Hall and delivered it to defendants-appellees. Neither the entry upon the premises nor the seizure of the television set was consented to by plaintiff-appellant Hall nor by any member of her household; nor was the entry or seizure authorized by any judicial or administrative officer.

Upon demand by Hall, defendant-appellee Garson or her agent, acting on behalf of all named defendants-appellees, refused to return the television set under authority of Vernon's Tex. Rev. Civ. Stat. Ann. Art. 5238a, which grants to the operator of any apartment a lien upon certain personal property found within the tenant's dwelling for all rents due and unpaid by the tenant thereof and grants to the operator the right to enforce that lien by peremptory seizure and retention of such property until the amount of unpaid rent is paid. Art. 5238a makes no provision for any kind of prior hearing.[2]

Subsequent to the taking of Hall's television set, defendants-appellees notified Hall that her television set was being held for the past due rent owed and that it would be returned upon her paying the arrearage. Appellant Hall has never paid nor tendered payment of the rent due and defendants-appellees have indicated they are ready and willing to return the television set to Hall at the time such payment is made.

Hall brought a class action under Rule 23, F.R. Civ. P. on behalf of herself and all other persons similarly situated, challenging the constitutionality of this statutory authority under the Due Process Clause of the Fourteenth Amendment of the U.S. Constitution and for appropriate injunctive relief against defendants-appellees. The district court dismissed the action as jurisdictionally premature, but we reversed and found that Title 28, U.S.C. Section 1343, provided the requisite jurisdiction and that plaintiffs-appellants stated a claim for which relief could be granted under Title 42, U.S.C. Section 1983. Hall, et al. v. Garson, et al., 5 Cir. 1970, 430 F.2d 430. On remand, the district court denied the injunctive relief requested and dismissed the complaint by an unreported memorandum decision.

Fuentes v. Shevin, 1972, 407 U.S. 67, was decided by the Supreme Court subsequent to the instant appeal, but before oral argument. That case was a logical extension of the constitutional principles applied in Goldberg v. Kelly, 1970, 397 U.S. 254, and Sniadach v. Family Finance Corp., 1969, 395 U.S. 337. On the authority of *Fuentes* we hold that Tex. Rev. Stat. Ann. Art. 5238a works "a deprivation of property without due process of law insofar as [it denies] the right to a prior opportunity to be heard before chattels are taken from their possessor." 407 U.S. at 96.

    2. Tex. Rev. Civ. Stat. Ann. Art. 5238a:

        Art. 5238a. Baggage lien for rent
        Section 1. The operator of any residential house, apartment, duplex or other single or multi-family dwelling, shall have a lien upon all baggage and all other property found within the tenant's dwelling for all rents due and unpaid by the tenant thereof; and said operator shall have the right to take and retain possession of such baggage and other property until the amount of such unpaid rent is paid. . . .
        Sec. 2. In any sale to satisfy said lien, said operator shall be subject to the same duties and shall follow the same procedures as set our for proprietors of hotels, boarding houses, inns, tourist courts, and motels, in Article 4595, Revised Civil Statutes of Texas, 1925, as amended.
        Sec. 3. Notwithstanding any provisions to the contrary contained in Article 3840. Revised Civil Statutes of Texas, 1925, as amended, there shall be exempt from the lien set out in Section 1 of this Act, the following: (1) all wearing apparel and (2) all tools, apparatus and books belonging to any trade or profession. Additionally, the following shall be exempt from such lien when said house, duplex or apartment is occupied by a family, defined as a person and others whom he is under a legal or moral obligation to support: (1) one automobile and one truck, (2) family library and all family portraits and pictures, (3) household furniture to the extent of one couch, two living room chairs, dining table and chairs, all beds and bedding, and all kitchen furniture and utensils, (4) all agricultural implements, saddles, and bridles, and, (5) good subject to a recorded mortgage lien or financing agreement.

In *Fuentes* the Supreme Court invalidated Florida and Pennsylvania statutes which provided for the summary seizure of goods in a person's possession
under a writ of replevin to be issued upon the ex parte application of any other
person who claimed a right to them and posted a security bond. The Court
found the constitutional infirmity to be the complete absence of prior notice
and opportunity to be heard to the party in possession of the property, and
held that such violation of due process could be cured only by providing
adequate safeguards at a meaningful time and in a meaningful manner so as
to obviate the danger of an unfair or mistaken deprivation of property.

Here we have no such protections. Art. 5238a clothes the apartment
operator with clear statutory authority to enter into another's home and seize
property contained therein. This makes his actions those of the State. Screws v.
United States, 1945, 325 U.S. 91, 110-111; United States v. Classic, 1941, 313
U.S. 299, 326; Ex parte Virginia, 1880, 100 U.S. 339, 346-347; Hall v. Garson, *supra*, 430 F.2d at 439-440. There is no requirement that the landlord first
have the validity or the accuracy of his claim impartially determined, or that
a need for immediate seizure be present. Those decisions are left to the operator himself to act upon with no prior opportunity for challenge by the possessor of the property. "The constitutional right to be heard is a basic aspect of
the duty of government to follow a fair process of decisionmaking when it acts
to deprive a person of his possessions." 407 U.S. at 80, 92 S. Ct. at 1994, 32 L.
Ed. 2d at 570. And: "If the right to notice and a hearing is to serve its full
purpose, then, it is clear that it must be granted at a time when the deprivation can still be prevented." 407 U.S. at 81, 92 S Ct. at 1994, 32 L. Ed. 2d at
570.

We reverse the judgment of the district court and remand for further
proceedings consistent with this opinion.

NOTES AND QUESTIONS

1.   Accord: Culbertson v. Leland, 528 F.2d 426 (9th Cir. 1975). Contra: Davis v. Richmond, 512 F.2d 201 (1st Cir. 1975); Anastasia v. Cosmopolitan National Bank of Chicago, 527 F.2d 150 (7th Cir. 1975). The Seventh
Circuit, in dealing with the precedent of Hall v. Garson, wrote:

> Perhaps distinctions can be drawn between this case and *Hall,* but we do
> not think that they would be very satisfactory ones. For example, the Texas
> statute in *Hall* expressly granted landlords the right to enter a dwelling by
> authorizing them "to take and retain possession" of "property found within the
> dwelling." Id. at 432 n.1. Ch. 71, §2 does not contain the same language, cf.
> Calderon v. United Furniture Co., 505 F.2d 950 (5th Cir. 1974), but the right to
> enter a room may be implicit in the statute. Also, involved in this case is a hotel
> room, rather than an apartment or house. But there is no question that the

plaintiffs in this case used the hotels as their principal long-term residences. Thus, the distinctions do not cut very deeply. Fundamentally, we simply disagree with the result in *Hall*. The historical accuracy of that case's assertion that the execution of liens was traditionally a state function has been questioned. Burke & Reber, State Action, Congressional Power and Creditors' Rights: An Essay on the Fourteenth Amendment, 47 S. Cal. L. Rev. 1, 50 (1973). And this assessment seems correct, except insofar as *Hall* may have relied on particular characteristics of prior Texas law. Plaintiffs freely acknowledge the hoary nature of the innkeepers' lien, and a landlord's right to seize property of a tenant whose rent is in arrears has common law roots as well. Thus, while the sheriff unquestionably is often the party who executes a lien, the function can hardly be said to be traditionally and exclusively that of the state. At most it is one that has been shared by the state with private persons. We see little similarity between this case and the public function cases decided by the Supreme Court and therefore find no basis for concluding that there is state action here.

Because we hold that there is no state action, we have no occasion to consider whether the actions of the hotel proprietors would be violative of the Fourth or Fourteenth Amendment had state action been present. [Id. at 157-58]

Despite the split among the circuit courts, the Supreme Court has not yet dealt directly with the issue. The Supreme Court, however, has decided an analogous case adversely to the debtor. Flagg Bros., Inc. v. Brooks, 436 U.S. 149, 98 S. Ct. 1729, 56 L. Ed. 2d 185 (1978). At issue was the validity of New York's Uniform Commercial Code provision, which gave warehousemen the power to sell stored goods to satisfy unpaid charges. Ironically, the debtor in *Flagg Bros.* was a former tenant who had been evicted from her apartment for unpaid rent and whose household belongings had been placed in storage by the city marshall following the eviction.

2. Since the decision in Hall v. Garson, the United States Supreme Court has watered down its holding in Fuentes v. Shevin, 407 U.S. 67 (1972), on which the *Hall* court partly relied. Mitchell v. W. T. Grant Co., 416 U.S. 600, 94 S. Ct. 1895, 40 L. Ed. 2d 406 (1974).

Consider also the related case of Jackson v. Metropolitan Edison Co., 419 U.S. 345, 95 S. Ct. 449, 42 L. Ed. 2d 477 (1974). There the Supreme Court rejected the claim that a homeowner must receive a due process hearing before a regulated utility may cut off electrical service for alleged nonpayment.

3. Without taking a position on the validity of distraint, Restatement (Second) of Property (1977) lists twenty-four states that have no provision for or have expressly abolished restraint. Id. at §12.1 (statutory note 5(c)). U.R.L.T.A. §4.205 (1972) also abolishes the remedy.

4. What policies argue for allowing (or denying) landlords the remedy of distraint when tenants fail to pay rent or otherwise breach their leases? Do the arguments apply similarly to the forfeiture of a security deposit without a prior court hearing? to private repossessions when debtors fail to meet their installment obligations? to repossession of an apartment without a court warrant?

5. Notice that the Texas statute in *Hall* exempted much of the tenant's

personal belongings from distraint. State homestead laws (8.6, *infra*), which extend their protection to tenants as well as homeowners, would similarly weaken the usefulness of distraint.

6.   Compare Sharrock v. Dell Buick-Cadillac, Inc., 45 N.Y.2d 152, 379 N.E.2d 1169, 408 N.Y.S.2d 39 (1978). New York gave garagemen a statutory lien on their customers' cars for repair and storage charges, and if the charges were unpaid, the power to conduct an ex parte sale of the bailed automobile. The court of appeals held that the statute failed to meet the procedural due process requirements of the *state* constitution by depriving the car owner of a significant property interest without a prior hearing.

> As noted, common law afforded the garageman only the right to posses-
> sion; it was the State which authorized enforcement of the lien by means of ex
> parte sale of the vehicle without first affording its owner an opportunity to be
> heard (see L. 1909, ch. 38, as amd.). Thus, New York has done more than simply
> furnish its statutory imprimatur to purely private action. Rather, it has entwined
> itself into the debtor-creditor relationship arising out of otherwise regular con-
> sumer transactions. The enactment of substantive provisions of law which autho-
> rize the creditor to bypass the courts to carry out the foreclosure sale encourages
> him to adopt this procedure rather than to rely on more cumbersome methods
> which might comport with constitutional due process guarantees. Indeed, not
> only does the State encourage adoption of this patently unfair procedure, it
> insulates the garageman from civil or criminal liability arising out of the sale and
> requires one of its agencies, the Department of Motor Vehicles, to recognize and
> record the transfer of title (see Vehicle and Traffic Law, §401), thus enabling the
> garageman to transfer title to a vehicle he would not otherwise be deemed to own
> (Adams v. Department of Motor Vehicles, 11 Cal. 3d 146, 150-151; cf. Ceasar v.
> Kiser, 387 F. Supp. 645; Barber v. Rader, 350 F. Supp. 183; Dielen v. Levine,
> 344 F. Supp. 823).
>
> Even more fundamentally, the underlying purpose of the sale provisions of
> the Lien Law—that of conflict resolution—has always been deemed one of the
> essential attributes of sovereignty. Absent consent of the debtor, the power to
> fashion the means to order legally binding surrenders of property has always
> been exclusively vested in the State. Implementation of dispute settlement, irre-
> spective of the strength of the competing interests of the parties, is the function of
> the judiciary, and is not dependent "on custom or the will of strategically placed
> individuals, but on the common-law model" (Boddie v. Connecticut, 401 U.S.
> 371, 375). But by permitting the possessory lienor to take those steps necessary to
> foreclose his lien in a nonjudicial setting where the power of sale is premised on
> possession alone, the State has permitted the garageman to arrogate to himself
> the exclusive power of the sovereign to resolve disputes. However strong the
> interest of the garageman in the vehicle may be, his power of foreclosure has no
> vitality until it is sanctioned by the State. It follows, then, that such a person
> vested by the State with the power to resolve unilaterally an otherwise judicially
> cognizable controversy, is nothing more than a delegate of an exclusively gov-
> ernmental function (cf. North Ga. Finishing v. Di-Chem, 419 U.S. 601, *supra;*
> Fuentes v. Shevin, 407 U.S. 67, 93, *supra*). For this reason, the debtor must be
> provided with that measure of due process as would be afforded in a court of law.
> [45 N.Y.2d at 161-162, 379 N.E.2d at 1174-1175, 408 N.Y.S.2d 45]

Keep in mind that state courts may read protections found in their own constitution more expansively than federal courts would construe parallel provisions in the United States Constitution. Compare Pruneyard Shopping Center v. Robins, *supra,* page 31.

7. Tenant vacates the apartment but fails to take all his personal belongings. What steps should a prudent landlord take as to the goods that tenant leaves behind? Cf. Boston Educational Research Co. v. American Machine & Foundry Co., 488 F.2d 344, 348-349 (1st Cir. 1973).

§6.3 Criminal Process

In at least one state, after a default landlords may elect to terminate a tenancy and, without first obtaining a civil order of dispossess, initiate criminal proceedings against the holdover tenant. The validity of the Arkansas statute is at issue below.

POOLE v. STATE
244 Ark. 1222, 428 S.W.2d 628 (1968)

JONES, J. Appellant, Patricia Poole, was charged in Little Rock Municipal Court with the offense of failure to vacate under Ark. Stat. Ann. §50-523 (1947). After her plea of not guilty was entered, appellant was tried and found guilty in municipal court and was assessed a fine of $15.00 and costs of $10.50. Upon appeal to the Pulaski County Circuit Court, appellant's motion to dismiss was denied and the judgment of the Little Rock Municipal Court was affirmed. On appeal to this court, appellant relies on the following point for reversal:

> Appellant's conviction should be reversed and Ark. Stat. Ann. 50-523 declared to be unconstitutional since it constitutes an invalid and unreasonable exercise of the police power of the State of Arkansas in that the subject matter thereof is outside the scope of the public health, safety and general welfare and interest, and consequently the enforcement of Ark. Stat. Ann. 50-523 deprives appellant of rights secured to her by the due process clause of the Fourteenth Amendment to the United States Constitution.

The facts are stipulated and not in dispute. On April 14, 1967, appellant entered into an oral agreement with Mr. Frank Seymour to rent an apartment located at 4408 West 28 Street in Little Rock on a weekly basis at the rate of $22.00 per week. On June 23, 1967, at which time appellant was one week and six days behind in her rent, she was served with a ten day notice to vacate the apartment for nonpayment of rent. Only July 20, 1967, some 28 days after service of the notice to vacate, appellant had still not moved and was charged under Ark. Stat. Ann. §50-523 (1947), which is as follows:

> Any person who shall rent any dwelling house, or other building or any land, situated in the State of Arkansas, and who shall refuse or fail to pay the rent therefor, when due, according to contract, shall at once forfeit all right to longer occupy said dwelling house or other building or land. And if, after ten [10] days notice in writing shall have been given by the landlord, his agent or attorney, to said tenant, to vacate said dwelling house or other building or land, said tenant shall wilfully refuse to vacate and surrender the possession of said premises to said landlord, his agent or attorney, said tenant shall be guilty of a misdemeanor and upon conviction thereof before any justice of the peace, or other court of competent jurisdiction, in the County where said premises are situated, shall be fined in any sum not less than one dollar [$1.00], nor more than twenty-five dollars [$25.00] for each offense, and each day said tenant shall wilfully and unnecessarily hold said dwelling house or other building or land after the expiration of notice to vacate, shall constitute a separate offense.

We cannot agree with appellant that §50-523, *supra*, is unconstitutional. Its provisions have been the law in this state since 1901 and its constitutionality has never been judicially questioned. The courts may not review the wisdom, discretion, or expediency of the legislature in the exercise of the powers it possesses, Berry v. Gordon, 237 Ark. 547, 376 S.W.2d 279; Dabbs v. State, 39 Ark. 353, and a statute will not be struck down by the courts unless it is obviously unconstitutional. All reasonable doubt must be resolved in favor of such constitutionality, there being a presumption in favor of validity. Berry v. Gordon, *supra;* McEachin v. Martin, 193 Ark. 787, 102 S.W.2d 864. Furthermore, a statute effective over a long period of time, with its validity being unquestioned by bench or bar, although not conclusive, is highly persuasive of the validity of such statute. McEachin v. Martin, *supra;* 16 C.J.S. Constitutional Law §99, p. 443.

It seems clear to us that §50-523, *supra*, was enacted as a valid exercise of the police power of this state. The right of an individual to acquire and possess and protect property is inherent and inalienable and declared higher than any constitutional sanction in Arkansas, Young v. City of Gurdon, 169 Ark. 399, 275 S.W. 890, and the public health, safety and welfare is always threatened when a person wrongfully trespasses upon another person's property in Arkansas. Especially is this true when the trespasser persists in the trespass and defies the owner's right to possession. Whether such trespass may become a matter of regulation through the police power depends upon the exercise of that power bearing a real and substantial relationship to an end which promotes or protects the public health, safety or welfare.

In the case at bar appellant's right to possession of the property terminated upon the expiration of the week for which she had it rented. Appellant claims no title or right in the property and claims no right to retain its possession. She does not base her continued possession upon any claim of right whatever, except a right to force the owner to the expense of bond, attorney's fee, and irrecoverable court costs in civil litigation. The option in pursuing a civil remedy lies with the property owner and any defense available to appellant in a civil action is still available under the penal code. Section 50-523, *supra*, by its provisions, relates only to one who "shall refuse or fail to pay the rent therefor, when due, according to contract" *and after ten days notice to vacate, "shall wilfully refuse"* to do so. Thus limited in its scope, §50-523 relates only to one who has become a trespasser on property as a result of giving up all legal rights to its possession and after ten days notice wilfully refusing to remove therefrom with the necessary criminal intent to deprive the rightful owner of his property.

No one can seriously argue that wrongful trespass does not come within the police power of the state, and the use of the police power to prevent such wrongful acts which disrupt the well-being, peace, happiness, and prosperity of people, surely bears a real and substantial relationship to an end which promotes the public health, safety and welfare. The use of police power in dealing with unlawful trespass is not so unreasonable as to amount to a violation of substantive due process, and ten days notice to vacate premises one holds wrongfully is more than liberal in keeping with our standards of procedural due process.

We cannot say that §50-523 is unconstitutional as an invalid exercise of the police power of this state or that it deprives appellant of her right of due process. Therefore, the judgment of the trial court is affirmed.

NOTES AND QUESTIONS

1. Several years after the decision in State v. Poole, a tenant class sued to enjoin a local prosecutor from enforcing the statute. The tenants contended that criminal proceedings were brought arbitrarily, without the intent of obtaining convictions but to assist landlords in evicting persons who failed to pay rent. The plaintiffs further asserted that tenants were forced to risk criminal conviction and fine as a result of what they considered to be a justified refusal to pay rent. The federal district judge issued an injunction, which the appeals court reversed. Manson v. Gilliam, 543 F.2d 48 (8th Cir. 1976). The record failed to convince the appeals judges that the prosecutor had been acting in bad faith. Moreover, on the substantive merits of the law, the court wrote:

> That a tenant who fails, without justification, to pay rent is in effect stealing property from the landlord and should be criminally punished, is a conclusion available to the state under the Constitution. [Id. at 53]

In your opinion, is the failure to pay rent without justification the equivalent of theft?

2.   The Arkansas statute allows for any civil defense to be asserted in the criminal proceeding. Would a tenant's attorney prefer to argue nonhabitability in a civil or in a criminal proceeding?

§6.4 Summary Proceedings

At common law, the action in ejectment was the landlord's chief judicial remedy for the removal of a tenant. It was (and is) an expensive and often dilatory proceeding, especially if one considers that a landlord's expenses (taxes, insurance, debt service, etc.) continue to accrue whether the tenant pays his rent or not. The nineteenth century witnessed a new remedy, the so-called summary proceeding, of which an 1820 New York statute was typical (2 Rev. Stat. c. 8, tit. 10, art. 2, §29). The remedy was originally limited to cases where the conventional relation of landlord and tenant, created by agreement, existed between the parties, but its availability has gradually been extended. Among those in New York who may employ the present law are the purchaser at a tax or foreclosure sale, the licensor after expiration of a license, and the buyer after a conveyance when the seller holds over. N.Y. Real Prop. Acts. Law §713 (1979).

What is summary about the proceeding is the speed with which a matter can be placed on the trial docket. The New York statute serves as illustration. Suppose that the tenant's rent is due on the first of the month and is unpaid. The landlord, after making a demand for the rent, begins the action by serving a petition and notice of petition. Id. §731. Personal service is unnecessary. Id. §735. The petition can be made returnable in five days. Id. §733. Thus, it is theoretically possible for the claim to be heard six days after the rent is due.

If the tenant neither answers nor appears, the landlord is entitled to an order of eviction and, if the tenant has been served personally, to a judgment for the rent due. Since the order is not self-executing, the landlord must also obtain a warrant of eviction and place it with a court officer (the county sheriff, a town constable, or a city constable or marshall). Id. §749. The tenant is then given an additional seventy-two hours of notice before the warrant can be executed. Id.

But, unless the tenant chooses to vacate voluntarily, the bringing of a summary proceeding does not usually result in so swift a recovery of the premises. The tenant will often make a rent tender on or before the return date, which the landlord must accept unless rescission has already taken place.[2] Alternatively, the tenant is entitled to file an answer, which may con-

---

2. In this regard, contrast N.Y. Real Prop. Acts. Law §§711(1), 711(2): "A special proceeding may be maintained under this article upon the following grounds: 1. The tenant continues in possession of any portion of the premises after the expiration of his term, without the permission of the landlord. . . . 2. The tenant has defaulted in the payment of rent. . . ."

tain any legal or equitable defense, or counterclaim. Id. §743.[3] As the rent covenant becomes increasingly interdependent, as tenants receive new statutory defenses, and as the jurisdictional limits of the lower level trial courts are enlarged, the tenant who believes he has good reason to withold his rent should find it easier to get a hearing coincident with the hearing on the landlord's claim for possession.

Finally, the New York law gives courts broad power to stay the issuance or execution of a warrant, under some circumstances for as long as six months. Id. §§751, 753.

New York provides for a court trial of issues of fact unless either party demands a trial by jury. Id. §745. Most standard form leases contain, however, a waiver-of-jury clause. New York courts have divided on the validity of such waiver. See note 5(a), *supra*, page 257.

Like many other state codes, the summary proceeding law for the District of Columbia did not provide for a jury. The United States Supreme Court recently held that the Seventh Amendment guarantee of jury trial "in suits at common law, where the value in controversy shall exceed twenty dollars" did apply to a suit to recover real property in a congressionally established court, such as those in the District of Columbia. Pernell v. Southall Realty, 416 U.S. 363, 94 S. Ct. 1723, 40 L. Ed. 2d 198 (1974). The Supreme Court has ruled consistently, however, that the Seventh Amendment guarantee does not apply to the state courts. Pearson v. Yewdall, 95 U.S. 294, 296 (1878).

§6.5   Bridling the Landlord: The Defense of Retaliatory Eviction

EDWARDS v. HABIB

397 F.2d 687 (D.C. Cir. 1968); cert. denied, 393 U.S. 1016 (1969)

Before DANAHER, WRIGHT and McGOWAN, J.J.

WRIGHT, J. In March 1965 the appellant, Mrs. Yvonne Edwards, rented housing property from the appellee, Nathan Habib, on a month-to-month basis. Shortly thereafter she complained to the Department of Licenses and Inspections of sanitary code violations which her landlord had failed to remedy. In the course of the ensuing inspection, more than 40 such violations were discovered which the Department ordered the landlord to correct. Habib then gave Mrs. Edwards a 30-day statutory notice[1] to vacate and obtained a default judgment for possession of the premises. Mrs. Edwards promptly moved

probably used a summary proceeding; she didn't appear and was in default

3. In the past, the courts in New York State have been singularly erratic in their views as to what this section allows. Some have construed it narrowly, others have not. Generalization is risky. The annotations appear at book 49½, McKinney's Consolidated Laws 178-186 (1963).

1. 45 D.C. Code §902 (1967), Notices to quit—Month to month: "A tenancy from month to month, or from quarter to quarter, may be terminated by a thirty days' notice in writing from the landlord to the tenant to quit, or by such a notice from the tenant to the landlord of his intention to quit, said notice to expire, in either case, on the day of the month from which such tenancy commenced to run."

to reopen this judgment, alleging excusable neglect for the default and also alleging as a defense that the notice to quit was given in retaliation for her complaints to the housing authorities. Judge Greene, sitting on motions in the Court of General Sessions, set aside the default judgment and, in a very thoughtful opinion, concluded that a retaliatory motive, if proved, would constitute a defense to the action for possession. At the trial itself, however, a different judge apparently deemed evidence of retaliatory motive irrelevant and directed a verdict for the landlord.

Mrs. Edwards then appealed to this court for a stay pending her appeal to the District of Columbia Court of Appeals, and on December 3, 1965, we granted the stay, provided only that Mrs. Edwards continue to pay her rent. Edwards v. Habib, 125 U.S. App. D.C. 49, 366 F.2d 628 (1965). She then appealed to the DCCA, which affirmed the judgment of the trial court. 227 A.2d 388 (1967). In reaching its decision the DCCA relied on a series of its earlier decisions holding that a private landlord was not required, under the District of Columbia Code, to give a reason for evicting a month-to-month tenant and was free to do so for any reason or for no reason at all. The court acknowledged that the landlord's right to terminate a tenancy is not absolute, but felt that any limitation on his prerogative had to be based on specific statutes or very special circumstances. Here, the court concluded, the tenant's right to report violations of law and to petition for redress of grievances was not protected by specific legislation and that any change in the relative rights of tenants and landlords should be undertaken by the legislature, not the courts. We granted appellant leave to appeal that decision to this court. We hold that the promulgation of the housing code by the District of Columbia Commissioners at the direction of Congress impliedly effected just such a change in the relative rights of landlords and tenants and that proof of a retaliatory motive does constitute a defense to an action of eviction. Accordingly, we reverse the decision of the DCCA with directions that it remand to the Court of General Sessions for a new trial where Mrs. Edwards will be permitted to try to prove to a jury that her landlord who seeks to evict her harbors a retaliatory intent. . . .

45 D.C. Code §910, in pertinent part provides: "Whenever . . . any tenancy shall be terminated by notice as aforesaid [45 D.C. Code §902, see Note 1 *supra*], and the tenant shall fail or refuse to surrender possession of the leased premises, . . . the landlord may bring an action to recover possession before the District of Columbia Court of General Sessions, as provided in sections 11-701 to 11-749."

And 16 D.C. Code §1501, in pertinent part, provides: "When a person detains possession of real property . . . after his right to possession has ceased, the District of Columbia Court of General Sessions . . . may issue a summons to the party complained of to appear and show cause why judgment should not be given against him for restitution of possession."

These provisions are simply procedural. They neither say nor imply anything about whether evidence of retaliation or other improper motive should be unavailable as a defense to a possessory action brought under them.

It is true that in making his affirmative case for possession the landlord need only show that his tenant has been given the 30-day statutory notice and he need not assign any reason for evicting a tenant who does not occupy the premises under a lease. But while the landlord may evict for any legal reason or for no reason at all, he is not, we hold, free to evict in retaliation for his tenant's report of housing code violations to the authorities. As a matter of statutory construction and for reasons of public policy, such an eviction cannot be permitted.

The housing and sanitary codes, especially in light of Congress' explicit direction for their enactment, indicate a strong and pervasive congressional concern to secure for the city's slum dwellers decent, or at least safe and sanitary, places to live. Effective implementation and enforcement of the codes obviously depend in part on private initiative in the reporting of violations. Though there is no official procedure for the filing of such complaints, the bureaucratic structure of the Department of Licenses and Inspections establishes such a procedure, and for fiscal year 1966 nearly a third of the cases handled by the Department arose from private complaints. To permit retaliatory evictions, then, would clearly frustrate the effectiveness of the housing code as a means of upgrading the quality of housing in Washington.

As judges, "we cannot shut our eyes to matters of public notoriety and general cognizance. When we take our seats on the bench we are not struck with blindness, and forbidden to know as judges what we see as men." Ho Ah Kow v. Nunan, C.C.D. Cal., 12 Fed. Cas. 252, 255 (No. 6546) (1879). In trying to effect the will of Congress and as a court of equity we have the responsibility to consider the social context in which our decisions will have operational effect. In light of the appalling condition and shortage of housing in Washington, the expense of moving, the inequality of bargaining power between tenant and landlord, and the social and economic importance of assuring at least minimum standards in housing conditions, we do not hesitate to declare that retaliatory eviction cannot be tolerated. There can be no doubt that the slum dweller, even though his home be marred by housing code violations, will pause long before he complains of them if he fears eviction as a consequence. Hence an eviction under the circumstances of this case would not only punish appellant for making a complaint which she had a constitutional right to make, a result which we would not impute to the will of Congress simply on the basis of an essentially procedural enactment, but also would stand as a warning to others that they dare not be so bold, a result which, from the authorization of the housing code, we think Congress affirmatively sought to avoid.

The notion that the effectiveness of remedial legislation will be inhibited if those reporting violations of it can legally be intimidated is so fundamental that a presumption against the legality of such intimidation can be inferred as inherent in the legislation even if it is not expressed in the statute itself. Such an inference was recently drawn by the Supreme Court from the federal labor statutes to strike down under the supremacy clause a Florida statute denying unemployment insurance to workers discharged in retaliation for filing complaints of federally defined unfair labor practices. While we are not confronted with a possible conflict between federal policy and state law, we do have the task of reconciling and harmonizing two federal statutes so as to best effectuate the purposes of each. The proper balance can only be struck by interpreting 45 D.C. Code §§902 and 910 as inapplicable where the court's aid is invoked to effect an eviction in retaliation for reporting housing code violations.

This is not, of course, to say that even if the tenant can prove a retaliatory purpose she is entitled to remain in possession in perpetuity. If this illegal purpose is dissipated, the landlord can, in the absence of legislation or a binding contract, evict his tenants or raise their rents for economic or for other legitimate reasons, or even for no reason at all. The question of permissible or impermissible purpose is one of fact for the court or jury, and while such a determination is not easy, it is not significantly different from problems with which the courts must deal in a host of other contexts, such as when they must decide whether the employer who discharges a worker has committed an unfair labor practice because he has done so on account of the employee's union activities. As Judge Greene said, "There is no reason why similar factual judgments cannot be made by courts and juries in the context of economic retaliation [against tenants by landlords] for providing information to the government."

Reversed and remanded.

NOTES AND QUESTIONS

1. Compare McQueen v. Druker, 438 F.2d 781 (1st Cir. 1971). Tenants resided in a 500-unit apartment complex built and operated under a federal subsidy. Landlord, a private entity, notified tenants that he would not renew their leases. Tenants sought an injunction against their threatened eviction, alleging that the landlord's "chief reason" for his action was resentment at the tenants' effort to organize their fellow residents into a tenants' association. Landlord did not deny that at least in part his motive was retaliatory.

After finding that the landlord, through the federal subsidy and various other connections, had sufficient relationship with the state to expose his activities to the Fourteenth Amendment, the court held that tenants were protected from eviction where the landlord's "dominant and primary motive" was one of retaliation against tenants for their exercise of First Amendment rights.

Notice that McQueen v. Druker deals constitutionally with the tenant's plea of constructive eviction, while the decision in Edwards v. Habib goes off on statutory grounds and vague allusions to public policy. This still leaves unanswered the following case: L, a *private* landlord, serves a 30-day notice upon T, a month-to-month tenant, for joining a tenant's association. But at least three courts have refused to protect T against retaliation. Seidelman v. Kouvacus, 57 Ill. App. 3d 350, 373 N.E.2d 53 (1978); Lincoln Financial

Corp. v. Ferrier, 567 P.2d 1102 (Utah 1977); Aluli v. Trusdell, 54 Haw. 417, 508 P.2d 1217 (1973).

The court in Edwards v. Habib refuses to find the requisite state action for invoking the Fourteenth Amendment; in short, a private landlord's use of state courts to punish a tenant for speaking out or associating does not become the action of the state itself. The limits of state action in this context have been debated hotly since the landmark Supreme Court decisions in Shelley v. Kraemer, 334 U.S. 1, 68 S. Ct. 836, 92 L. Ed. 1161 (1948), and Barrows v. Jackson, 346 U.S. 249, 73 S. Ct. 1031, 97 L. Ed. 1586 (1953), which held that courts could not enforce racially restrictive covenants either injunctively or via damages. See, e.g., Henkin, Shelley v. Kraemer: Notes for a Revised Opinion, 110 U. Pa. L. Rev. 473 (1962); G. Gunther and N. Dowling, Constitutional Law 475-481 (8th ed. 1970).

2.   What can L show to overcome T's defense of retaliatory eviction, i.e., to show that L has not retaliated (where T has complained of code violations):

(a) that L cannot afford to make the repairs at the current rental?
(b) that L intends to withdraw the unit from the rental market?
(c) that L intends to rent the unit to another T at a higher rental?
(d) that T has violated some substantial condition of the tenancy?
(e) that L no longer wishes to rent the unit to any tenant with four children?
(f) that L no longer wishes to rent the unit to any tenant receiving welfare?
(g) that L *has* no reason for terminating the lease? Cf. Robinson v. Diamond Housing Corp., 463 F.2d 853, 861 (1972)

3.   Where does (should) the burden of persuasion lie? Upon the tenant who claims retaliatory eviction? Or upon the landlord who seeks to rebut the claim? Cf. Restatement (Second) of Property §14.8; Comment f (1977). Since the defense deals with the landlord's subjective state of mind, is it evidentiarily harder to prove or to disprove a retaliatory motive?

4.   Suppose, after a T's complaint, L makes the repairs but then raises the rent: if T does not want to pay the increase, might the plea of retaliatory eviction be heard?

5.   The leases in McQueen v. Druker, *supra,* Note 1, were for a term of years that expired on July 31, 1970. Although the leases required landlord to notify the tenants formally that the term would end and that they would have to leave by July 31, the landlord's "election" is technically very different from the election in a month-to-month tenancy, as in Edwards v. Habib. A term of years ends automatically unless both parties elect to renew the term; a periodic tenancy continues automatically unless one party or both elects to end the tenancy. Is this a technical difference that the court in McQueen v. Druker should have considered?

6. After validating the tenant's defense of retaliatory eviction in Markese v. Cooper, 70 Misc. 2d 478, 333 N.Y.S.2d 63 (County Ct. 1972), the judge continued:

> Unfortunately, the matter does not rest here. I recognize the myriad problems which now confront a trial court. For example, what remedy shall it permit the tenant here if she is successful? It is precisely here that legislation, if it existed, would set forth definite remedial standards that would apply uniformly throughout the State. Unfortunately, any remedy must now be applied on a case-by-case basis that guarantees considerable diversity until, ultimately, there has emerged a pattern which all courts can follow.
>
> Another problem which the trial court must face is the standard of proof that will be required to prove the tenant's defense and the criteria to be employed. For example, how does one go about proving a retaliatory motive, and must it be the dominant or paramount motive, or need it be only a substantial one? . . .
>
> As to the remedy to be afforded, it is clear that a tenant may not remain upon the premises indefinitely solely by reason of a successful defense of retaliatory eviction. In Edwards v. Habib (397 F.2d 687, *supra*), the court cautioned that even if a tenant can prove a retaliatory purpose he would not be entitled to remain in possession in perpetuity. "If this illegal purpose is dissipated, the landlord can, in the absence of legislation or a binding contract, evict his tenants or raise their rents for economic or other legitimate reasons, or even for no reason at all." (p. 702)
>
> Unfortunately, Judge Wright did not set forth how or when such illegal purpose is "dissipated" nor did he define the outer limits of its baneful influence. Here again the trial court has been left with a principle, but without a palpable, tangible procedure. . . .
>
> And since the eviction proceedings would be tainted by an unlawful motive, damages should be made available to the tenant. These would be compensatory and special damages . . .,[11] and, in a proper case, could be exemplary or punitive as well. . . .
>
> Unfortunately, unless the Legislature acts, these admittedly incomplete standards will have to suffice until the slow hand of experience shapes new and better ones. . . . [70 Misc. 2d at 489, 333 N.Y.S.2d at 74]

7. The Uniform Residential Landlord and Tenant Act, drafted and approved by the National Conference of Commissioners on Uniform State Laws (1972), contains the following article:

Article V. Retaliatory Conduct

Section 5.101. Retaliatory Conduct Prohibited
(a) Except as provided in this section, a landlord may not retaliate by increasing rent or decreasing services or by bringing or threatening to bring an action for possession after:

---

11. See, e.g., Aweeka v. Bonds, 20 Cal. App. 3d 278, 97 Cal. Rptr. 650 (1971) (T may sue to recover damages for "intentional infliction of mental distress").—ED.

(1) the tenant has complained to a governmental agency charged with responsibility for enforcement of a building or housing code of a violation applicable to the premises materially affecting health and safety; or

(2) the tenant has complained to the landlord of a violation under Section 2.104 [landlord to maintain premises]; or

(3) the tenant has organized or become a member of a tenant's union or similar organization.

(b)   If the landlord acts in violation of subsection (a), the tenant is entitled to the remedies provided in Section 4.107 [the greater of treble damages or 3 months' rent] and has a defense in any retaliatory action against him for possession. In an action by or against the tenant, evidence of a complaint within [1] year before the alleged act of retaliation creates a presumption that the landlord's conduct was in retaliation. The presumption does not arise if the tenant made the complaint after notice of a proposed rent increase or diminution of services. "Presumption" means that the trier of fact must find the existence of the fact presumed unless and until evidence is introduced which would support a finding of its nonexistence.

(c)   Notwithstanding subsections (a) and (b), a landlord may bring an action for possession if:

(1) the violation of the applicable building or housing code was caused primarily by lack of reasonable care by the tenant, a member of his family, or other person on the premises with his consent; or

(2) the tenant is in default in rent; or

(3) compliance with the applicable building or housing code requires alteration, remodeling, or demolition which would effectively deprive the tenant of use of the dwelling unit. . . .

Discuss the proposal in the light of the foregoing questions.

8.   Restatement (Second) of Property §§14.8-14.9 (1977) offers tenants a more limited defense of retaliatory eviction than would be available under URLTA. It applies to a termination or refusal to renew where the leased premises are subject to a housing code, the landlord "is in the business of renting residential property," the tenant is not "materially in default," the landlord's primary motive in so acting is because tenant has complained about a code violation, and the tenant's complaint "was made in good faith and with reasonable cause."

9.   The statutory note to Restatement §§14.8-14.9, *supra*, lists more than twenty jurisdictions having some protection against retaliation for residential (and in a few cases, commercial) tenants. See, e.g., Cal. Civ. Code §1942.5 (West Supp. 1979); Conn. Gen. Stat. §47a-33 (Supp. 1979); N.J. Stat. Ann. tit. 2A, §§42:10-10, 42:10-12 (Supp. 1980). Florida law makes retaliatory eviction an unfair trade practice, which is a criminal offense. Cf. Bowles v. Blue Lake Development Corp., 504 F.2d 1094, 1097 (5th Cir. 1974).

10.   Might the defense of retaliatory eviction also be available to protect tenants who exercise other forms of legal rights: for example, the tenant who complains to landlord (or brings suit) based upon an alleged eviction or other interference with the tenant's quiet enjoyment; the retail tenant who opposes the landlord's variance application that would permit expansion of a shopping center and bring about increased competition?

11.   What of the argument that retaliatory eviction is an abuse of process? Cf. Note, Abuse of Rights Doctrine in the Civil Law, 36 La. L. Rev. 813 (1976).

§6.6   Bridling the Landlord: The Tenant's Right to a "Due Process" Hearing

ESCALERA v. NEW YORK CITY HOUSING AUTHORITY
425 F.2d 853 (2d Cir.), cert. denied, 400 U.S. 853 (1970)

SMITH, CIRCUIT JUDGE. Appellants are tenants in New York City public housing projects. They brought four suits in the United States District Court for the Southern District of New York against the New York City Housing Authority [hereinafter cited as "HA"] and certain individuals as officers of the HA, in the form of class actions on behalf of themselves and all tenants similarly situated. The complaints invoked jurisdiction under the Civil Rights Act, 28 U.S.C.A. §1343(3) (1962), and alleged the deprivation of appellants' right to due process secured by the Fourteenth Amendment to the Constitution and of their rights under the United States Housing Act of 1937, 42 U.S.C.A. §1401 et seq. (1962). They sought injunctive and declaratory relief against certain alleged practices of the HA, 28 U.S.C.A. §§2201, 2202 (1962), 42 U.S.C.A. 1983 (1970), and in two instances (Haywood and Lockman) a money judgment for additional rents which had been paid.

Appellants sought a preliminary injunction by filing an order to show cause. Defendant then moved pursuant to Rule 12(b) of the Federal Rules of Civil Procedure to dismiss the actions for, inter alia, failure to state a claim upon which relief could be granted, lack of jurisdiction, lack of substantial federal question, and failure to exhaust administrative remedies, and because the federal courts should abstain from considering these actions pending a determination by New York state courts in the first instance.

After the parties submitted affidavits, argument on the motions was heard before District Judge Sylvester J. Ryan. Thereafter by an opinion of October 31, 1968 (67 Civ. 4236, 4306, 4307, 4414 S.D.N.Y.), and judgment of the next day, Judge Ryan granted defendants' motion, and dismissed the actions on the merits. We find error in the dismissal of these actions and remand to the district court to consider appellants' application for preliminary relief and to hold a trial on the merits.

The instant class actions challenge the constitutionality of the procedures used by the HA in three different types of actions: (1) termination of tenancy on the ground of non-desirability; (2) termination of tenancy for violation of HA rules and regulations; and (3) assessment of "additional rent" charges under the HA lease for undesirable acts by tenants. The HA, a corporate governmental agency financed by federal, state and city funds, administers the largest public housing program in the country, housing more than 144,000 families.

I

A.   TERMINATION FOR NON-DESIRABILITY

Tenants in HA projects are required to sign month-to-month automatically renewable leases which can be terminated at the end of any month by either party upon the giving of one month's notice. Leases are terminated by the giving of one month's notice if the tenant is found to be non-desirable. [1]

If a tenant's undesirable acts persist to the point where the project manager decides he should recommend the termination of the tenancy on the ground of non-desirability, the manager has a meeting with the tenant at which he informs the tenant of his proposed recommendation, reviews with the tenant the information in the tenant's folder (which contains the entire history of the tenancy), and discusses the undesirable activity in question. The tenant is given a chance to explain his activity.

If after the meeting the project manager still wishes to recommend termination for non-desirability, the tenant is notified that he may submit a written statement to be sent with the project manager's recommendation and the tenant's folder to the HA Tenant Review Board [hereinafter cited "TRB"].

The TRB consists of eight officers of the HA. They consider the tenant's folder and the project manager's recommendation, and if they make a preliminary determination of the tenant's non-desirability, they inform the tenant in writing that they are "considering a recommendation" of termination, that he may appear before the TRB to tell his side of the case if he requests an appearance in 10 days, and that if he so requests an appearance he will be informed of the nature of the conduct under consideration. If the tenant fails to request an appearance within 10 days, the preliminary determination of non-desirability is made final by the TRB Chairman.

If the tenant makes a timely request for an appearance, he is sent a form letter telling him the time and place of the scheduled hearing, the general

---

1. A family is non-desirable if it constitutes ". . . a detriment to health, safety or morals of its neighbors or the community; an adverse influence upon sound family and community life; a source of danger or a cause of damage to the property of the Authority; a source of danger to the peaceful occupation of other tenants, or a nuisance." Tenant Review Handbook, Ch. VII, ¶, Appendix B at 4.

definition of a non-desirable tenant (as set out in footnote 1, *supra*), a short, often one-sentence, statement of the nature of the particular non-desirable conduct under consideration,[2] and the fact that he may bring any person to help represent him at the hearing.

A panel of two or more, usually three, of the TRB members is present at the hearing. The HA ordinarily presents no witnesses, but rather has a panel member read a summary of the entries in the tenant's folder. The tenant or his representative is permitted to comment about the entries or question witncsscs in that regard. The tenant is generally not permitted to see the contents of the folder, the names of those who complained of his non-desirable activity, or the summary of the entries.[3] The rules and regulations governing the TRB and its panels in non-desirability cases, set out in the TRB "Handbook" are not made available to the tenant, even upon request. No transcript of the hearing is maintained.

Despite the summary notification to the tenant prior to hearing of the conduct under consideration, the panel decides whether the tenant is non-desirable on the basis of the tenant's entire folder; thus the decision may be based in whole or in part on entries in the folder although the tenant received no notification prior to the hearing that the TRB was considering these entries, or indeed the decision may rest in some part on items in the folder about which the tenant is not notified even at the hearing.

If the panel decides that the tenant is non-desirable, the Chairman of the TRB notifies the tenant that the panel has determined that the tenant is ineligible. No findings or reasons grounding the panel's determination are released. Thereafter the HA gives the tenant the required one month's notice under lease to terminate the tenancy, and notifies the tenant that he should vacate. If the tenant does not vacate, a holdover proceeding is commenced in the New York City Civil Court. The only issue in such a proceeding is the validity of the notice to terminate under the lease, and the determination of non-desirability cannot be put in question. . . .

The facts as to the instant plaintiffs may be quickly summarized. Proceedings were begun against the Rolles because of the alleged anti-social acts (such as statutory rape) of their son Fred, and against the Humphreys because Mr. Humphrey had been arrested on a narcotics charge several miles from the

2. The plaintiffs in the instant cases received the following notification of their non-desirable conduct.

Mr. and Mrs. Rolle: "Record of antisocial activities and arrests of your son, Fred, Jr., constituting a threat to the peace and safety of the community."

Mr. and Mrs. Humphrey: "Illegal acts of Mr. Humphrey, having an adverse effect on the project and its tenants."

3. In the case of plaintiff Rolle, upon demand of counsel, the TRB panel permitted counsel to inspect the folder at the premises of the hearing, and offered to grant an adjournment of the hearing if one were requested. In the case of plaintiff Humphrey, however, the folder and the summary of its contents were not made available to the tenant despite repeated requests. Affidavits submitted on behalf of plaintiffs indicate that other tenants, not named in this suit, have been unable to gain access to their folders.

project. Both requested hearings. Counsel for Rolle demanded a variety of procedural safeguards sought in the present action, such as advance notice of the complete charge, a transcript of the hearing, confrontation and cross-examination of witnesses, an impartial hearing examiner, etc. Although the panel permitted Rolle's counsel to inspect the folder, it did not grant the other requests and Rolle refused to go forward with the hearing. Any further action by the HA with respect to Rolle was voluntarily postponed pending the outcome of this litigation. The Humphreys went through with the hearing although they were not permitted to inspect the folder, and were found to be non-desirable, and were given notice of termination and to vacate. No holdover action was brought due to the intervention of this action.

As to the procedures for termination on the ground of non-desirability, the appellants seek the following relief: (1) an injunction against evictions on this ground unless the following safeguards are afforded in connection with the hearing: (a) written notice prior to the hearing of all the grounds to be relied on in the decision; (b) notice of the rules and regulations governing the TRB panel at the hearing; (c) inspection of the tenant folder; (d) exclusion of items about which advance notice was not given; (e) confrontation and cross-examination of witnesses; (f) exclusion of hearsay items; (g) right to compel attendance of witnesses; (h) the keeping of a written record of the hearing; (i) impartial hearing examiner; (j) written decision with findings of facts and reasons; and (k) access to prior decisions as precedent; (2) an injunction against using a lease which permits the HA to evict simply by giving one month's notice and thus which permits the HA to evict without the above safeguards; (3) an injunction against the failure of the HA to negotiate new leases which provide safeguards which are constitutionally required; (4) a declaratory judgment that the present procedures are constitutionally deficient; and (5) an injunction against the termination of tenancies on grounds not set out in the lease or otherwise made known and which are too vague.

B.   TERMINATION FOR BREACH OF RULES AND REGULATIONS. . . .

C.   "ADDITIONAL RENT" CHARGES OR FINES. . . .

II

Appellants challenge the constitutionality of the HA procedures for terminating tenancies on the grounds of non-desirability and breach of the rules and regulations and for assessing "additional rent" charges, contending that these procedures deny members of their classes their rights to due process of law. Although the termination of tenancy procedures afforded by the HA in this case admittedly satisfy the requirements of the Department of Housing and Urban Development circular of February 7, 1967, considered by the Supreme Court in Thorpe v. Housing Authority of City of Durham, 393 U.S.

268, 89 S. Ct. 518, 21 L. Ed. 2d 474 (1969), this is not dispositive of the question of whether the procedures satisfy the due process requirements of the Fourteenth Amendment. . . .

Nor is it conclusive in the consideration of appellant's constitutional claims to argue that there is no constitutional right to continue living in public housing projects. See Chicago Housing Authority v. Blackman, 4 Ill. 2d 319, 122 N.E.2d 522, 524 (1954). . . . The government cannot deprive a private citizen of his continued tenancy, without affording him adequate procedural safeguards even if public housing could be deemed to be a privilege. See Goldberg v. Kelly, 397 U.S. 254, 262-63, 90 S. Ct. 1011, 1017, 25 L. Ed. 2d 285 (March 23, 1970); . . . Van Alstyne, The Demise of the Right-Privilege Distinction in Constitutional Law, 81 Harv. L. Rev. 1439, 1451-54 (1968); Note, Another Look at Unconstitutional Conditions, 117 U. Pa. L. Rev. 144 (1968).

Since these actions were dismissed at the pleadings stage, we must view the allegations in the complaints and supporting affidavits in the light most favorable to the appellants, see p. 857 *supra;* in this light we find that appellants have a claim for relief. Certain aspects of the alleged present HA procedures cannot stand without a convincing showing at trial that the HA has a compelling need for procedural expedition.

"The very nature of due process negates any concept of inflexible procedures universally applicable to every imaginable situation." Cafeteria & Restaurant Workers Union, Local 473 v. McElroy, 367 U.S. 886, 895, 81 S. Ct. 1743, 1748, 6 L. Ed. 2d 1230 (1961); Dixon v. Alabama State Bd. of Education, 294 F.2d 150, 155 (5 Cir. 1961). The minimum procedural safeguards required by due process in each situation, depend on the nature of the governmental function involved and the substance of the private interest which is affected by the governmental action. Goldberg v. Kelly, *supra,* 397 U.S. at 263, 90 S. Ct. at 1017; see Joint Anti-Fascist Refugee Committee v. McGrath, 341 U.S. 123, 162-163, 71 S. Ct. 624, 95 L. Ed. 817 (1951) (Frankfurter, J., concurring). Since these competing interests have not been fully developed at the trial level, it is not now appropriate for this court to prescribe the minimum necessary procedural requirements. However, if appellants can show at trial the existence of certain of the pleaded HA procedures, we hold that they will have made out a prima facie case for relief; the exact nature and extent of that relief can only be determined after trial.

A

We consider first the procedures for terminating tenancies on the ground of non-desirability. We find this procedure may be deficient in four respects. First, summary notice such as that sent to the tenants here of the non-desirable conduct under consideration by the TRB is inadequate. See In re Williams, *supra,* 309 N.Y.S.2d [454,] 460. The one-sentence notices sent to the present appellants were insufficient to notify them even of the particular conduct thought by the TRB to be most serious. But since the TRB bases its decisions on the tenant's entire folder, detailed notice as to the particular conduct thought to be most serious would be inadequate to give the tenant advance notice of all the items which might be considered against him so that he might challenge these items.

The purpose of requiring that notice be given to the tenant before the hearing is to insure that the tenant is adequately informed of the nature of the evidence against him so that he can effectively rebut that evidence. The instant one-sentence summary notices are inadequate for this purpose. Willner v. Committee on Character & Fitness, 373 U.S. 96, 105, 107, 83 S. Ct. 1175, 10 L. Ed. 2d 224 (1963); Dixon, *supra,* 294 F.2d at 158-159. Nor does the conference between the project manager and the tenant cure the deficiency in the notice, see Goldberg v. Kelly, *supra,* 397 U.S. at 270, 90 S. Ct. at 1020, since the manager does not divulge all entries in the folder some of which may influence the TRB's decision.

Second, denying tenants access to the material in their folders, when the entire folder is considered by the TRB in its determination of eligibility, deprives the tenants of due process. Goldberg v. Kelly, *supra,* 397 U.S. at 270, 90 S. Ct. at 1021. A hearing at which the tenant can rebut evidence against him would be of little value if the TRB's ultimate decision can rest on items in the tenant's folder of which he has no knowledge and hence has had no opportunity to challenge. Willner, *supra,* 373 U.S. at 107, 83 S. Ct. 1175 (Goldberg, J., concurring).

If secrecy must be preserved as to some items in the tenant's folder, then these items may not be relied on in the decision of the HA. The decision must be based solely on the evidence adduced at the hearing. Goldberg v. Kelly, *supra,* 397 U.S. at 271, 90 S. Ct. at 1022. Although it is unnecessary to write a full judicial opinion, the HA should "demonstrate compliance with this elementary requirement" and "state the reasons for [its] determination and indicate the evidence [it] relied on." Id. at 271, 90 S. Ct. at 1022. . . .

Third, denying the tenant the opportunity to confront and cross-examine persons who supplied information on the tenant's folder upon which HA action is grounded is improper. Goldberg v. Kelly, *supra,* 397 U.S. at 270, 90 S. Ct. at 1021; Willner, *supra,* 373 U.S. at 107, 83 S. Ct. 1175 (Goldberg, J., concurring). . . . "In almost every setting where important decisions turn on questions of fact, due process requires an opportunity to confront and cross-examine adverse witnesses." Goldberg v. Kelly, *supra,* 397 U.S. at 269, 90 S. Ct. at 1021.

Under the present procedures, it appears that often the tenant is not even advised as to the source of many of the entries in his folder; preliminary disclosure of this information is, of course, necessary before the tenant can decide whether to confront the person supplying the damaging entry in his folder. If disclosure of the names of persons supplying information in the folder, or the subsequent confrontation at a hearing between the tenant and such persons is deemed to be undesirable because of possible hostility amongst housing project neighbors, the HA may not base its determination on such information. Goldberg v. Kelly, *supra,* at 270, 90 S. Ct. at 1022; see Alderman v. United States, 394 U.S. 165, 89 S. Ct. 961, 22 L. Ed. 2d 176 (1969); Silverthorne Lumber Co. v. United States, 251 U.S. 385, 40 S. Ct. 182, 64 L. Ed. 319 (1920).

Finally, we find that the HA's failure to disclose the rules and regulations in the TRB Handbook governing the TRB panel at the hearing concerning termination for non-desirability may be found to be improper. See Goldberg v. Kelly, *supra,* 397 U.S. at 271, 90 S. Ct. at 1022 ("The decision maker's conclusion . . . must rely solely on the *legal rules* and evidence adduced at the hearing" [emphasis added]). Appellants allege that this information is necessary to adequate preparation of the tenant's substantive case before the TRB. If this is established at trial, these regulations must be made generally available prior to the hearing. The HA's argument, that the regulations contained in the Handbook are merely internal procedural guidelines, may be considered by the trial court in determining whether, in fact, the Handbook is necessary in preparing a tenant's case before the TRB.

[The parts of the opinion that deal with breach of rules and regulations, additional rent, jurisdiction, substantiality, case or controversy, abstention, state review and exhaustion of administrative remedies have been omitted.]

IV

The minimum procedural requirements of due process under the Fourteenth Amendment must reflect the balance between the government's interest in efficient administration and the nature of the individual's interest being affected by governmental action. We hold only that granting every favorable inference to plaintiffs' complaints and affidavits, it appears that the HA's procedures are deficient in several specific aspects. Upon trial, the HA may be able to show great need for expedited procedures, or the plaintiffs may fail to substantiate all of their allegations. Therefore the fashioning of a remedy or a declaratory judgment must await the full trial of these actions.

Reversed and remanded for consideration of plaintiff's motion for preliminary relief and for trial on the merits.

NOTES AND QUESTIONS

1. The opinion speaks of the HUD circular of February 7, 1967, discussed by the Supreme Court in Thorpe v. Housing Authority of City of Durham, 393 U.S. 268 (1969). This circular directed local authorities to inform any tenant facing eviction of "the specific reason(s) for [the] notice to vacate; thereupon, the tenant was to be given an opportunity to make such reply or explanation as he wished."

Previously, even this simple procedural safeguard was denied public housing tenants, who could be summarily evicted, without explanation, when their month-to-month (the standard) tenancy ended. See, e.g., Walton v. City of Phoenix, 69 Ariz. 26, 208 P.2d 309 (1949).

2. Prior to *Escalera,* a state court had directed a local authority to give reasons for terminating a month-to-month tenancy; otherwise the summary proceeding would fail. Affirming the lower court order, a divided (3 to 2) appellate division in Vinson v. Greenburgh Housing Authority, 29 A.D.2d 338, 288 N.Y.S. 2d 159 (2d Dept. 1968), wrote as follows:

> The Authority's return alleges no reason for the termination of the lease; it admits that the petitioners' attorney spoke to its attorney, who informed the former that the Authority was not required to give a reason for the eviction. The Authority claims as a defense that the notice validity terminated the lease and that its determination was neither a judicial nor a quasi-judicial act and hence not reviewable by the court.
>
> Special Term in effect granted the relief sought by the petitioners, unless the Authority submit an appropriate return stating the grounds for its determination. Special Term reasoned that the petitioners had asserted grave charges of irresponsibility by the Authority and that the latter's contention that its exercise of discretion to terminate the lease was absolute could not be sustained. By permission of Special Term, the Authority appeals (CPLR 5701, subd. [c]).
>
> The Authority argues that the provisions in the lease for its termination are plain and binding on both parties and cannot be modified by the court. To interfere with its determination by requiring an explanation, the Authority urges, imposes a burden not demanded from other landlords and thus discriminates unfairly and invalidly against it. On the other hand, the petitioners press on us the contention that the Authority may not act arbitrarily toward its tenants, for otherwise a tenant might be evicted without cause or justification.
>
> We meet, then, the question of the nature of the relationship between a housing authority and its tenants. Ordinarily, provisions in a lease permitting its termination upon the service of a notice of a stated period are enforcible by the landlord at will (Zule v. Zule, 24 Wend. 76; cf. Metropolitan Life Ins. Co. v. Carroll, 43 Misc. 2d 639, 251 N.Y.S.2d 693). The relationship between landlord and tenant is considered contractual simply; and the terms of the lease for termination, unless calling for a reasonable basis for action, may be exercised without explanation. But a housing authority is not an ordinary landlord, nor its lessees ordinary tenants.
>
> Our Constitution recognizes low rent housing as a proper governmental function (N.Y. Const., art. XVIII). The Legislature, in response to its direction, has enacted the Public Housing Law. . . .
>
> Thus, our State has distinguished low rent housing as a human need to be satisfied through governmental action and has created by specific statutory provisions the structure of the relationship between the housing authority and the tenant. The statute consequently enters into and becomes a part of the lease; and its spirit and intent must be the guiding beacon in the interpretation of the terms of the lease.

" 'Due process of law' is not confined to judicial proceedings, but extends to every case which may deprive a citizen of life, liberty, or property, whether the proceeding be judicial, administrative, or executive in its nature" (Stuart v. Palmer, 74 N.Y. 183, 190-191). Once the State embarks into the area of housing as a function of government, necessarily that function, like other governmental functions, is subject to the constitutional commands. Low rent housing is not the leasing of government-owned property originally acquired for a different purpose, but now surplus or not required for that purpose, on a sporadic or temporary basis (cf. United States v. Blumenthal, 3 Cir., 315 F.2d 351), where the traditional notions of private property might well be applied; rather, it imports a status of a continuous character, based on the need of the tenants for decent housing at a cost proportionate to their income, subject to the compliance by the tenants with reasonable regulations and the payment of rent when due. "The Government as landlord is still the government. It must not act arbitrarily, for, unlike private landlords, it is subject to the requirements of due process of law" (Rudder v. United States, 96 U.S. App. D.C. 329, 226 F.2d 51, 53). . . . We think that a housing authority cannot arbitrarily deprive a tenant of his right to continue occupancy through the exercise of a contractual provision to terminate the lease. In other words, the action of the housing authority must not rest on mere whim or caprice or an arbitrary reason.

Several considerations combine to justify the difference in treatment between governmental agencies and private individuals. Realistically, it must be acknowledged that the housing authority prescribes the terms of the lease and that the tenant does not negotiate with the authority in the usual sense (see, Reich, The New Property, 73 Yale L.J. 733, 749-752; Friedman, Public Housing and the Poor: An Overview, 54 Cal. L. Rev. 643, 660; Note, Government Housing Assistance to the Poor, 76 Yale L.J. 508, 512). In this condition of affairs, to impose a requirement of good faith and reasonableness on the party in the stronger bargaining position when he exerts a contractual option is but a reflection of simple justice (cf. New York Cent. Iron Works Co. v. United States Radiator Co., 174 N.Y. 331, 66 N.E. 967; Wood v. Duff-Gordon, 222 N.Y. 88, 118 N.E. 214). . . .

Moreover, in balancing the interests of the State against the interests of the individual, the advantages to the State are outweighed by the detriment to the individual, if we were to deny the tenant protection from an arbitrary termination of the lease. The eviction of a family in the income bracket eligible under the standards of public housing from its household is a serious blow. If, in fact, a mistake has been made in the accusation against the tenant of improper conduct or a violation of regulations, or if the reason for the ouster has no better basis than dislike or unjustified discipline, the requirement of the disclosure of the ground for the termination of the lease affords the tenant the opportunity to protest its exercise. On the other hand, the authority will suffer no more than delay in the ultimate eviction in the event the termination of the lease is made on reasonable grounds; and in the meantime the authority may control excessive misbehavior of the tenant through police action.

The declared purpose of the statute makes clear that low rent housing was considered to be permanent and not transitory and that, so long as the tenants remain qualified and do not violate the reasonable regulations of the State agency, they would not be evicted for grounds extrinsic to these requirements. So, the State policy was established in contemplation of "insanitary and substandard housing conditions owing to overcrowding and concentration of the population," as a result of which "the construction of new housing facilities, under public supervision in accord with proper standards of sanitation and safety and at a cost which will permit monthly rentals which persons of low income can afford to pay" is necessary; and it was acknowledged that "these conditions require the creation of the agencies, instrumentalities and corporations hereinafter prescribed, which are declared to be agencies and instrumentalities of the state for the purpose of attaining the ends herein recited" (Public Housing Law, §2). . . .

Once the field of housing as a utility has been encompassed by the State, we think that the traditional protection against the caprice of State agencies must be preserved. "Discretionary administrative power over individual rights . . . is undesirable per se, and should be avoided as far as may be, for discretion is unstandardized power and to lodge in an official such power over person or property is hardly conformable to the 'Rule of Law' " (Freund, Historical Survey in Growth of American Administrative Law, pp. 22-23).

The dissenting justices in *Vinson* agreed that public housing tenants do have a property right, which governmental agencies could not arbitrarily take from them. But the dissenters insisted that it was a property right circumscribed by the terms and conditions of the lease upon which it was founded.

The Illinois Supreme Court distinguished between governmental activities (arbitrariness not allowed) and proprietary activities (arbitrariness tolerated), and held that the Chicago Housing Authority was a "proprietary" landlord. Chicago Housing Authority v. Stewart, 40 Ill. 2d 23, 237 N.E.2d 463 (1968). But can one find the governmental-proprietary distinction in the Constitution? And is housing management less "governmental" than, let us say, insuring mortgages or paying urban renewal write-downs?

3. Shortly after the *Thorpe* decision, tenants' groups asked to negotiate with HUD on the rights of public housing tenants. With the National Associations of Housing and Redevelopment Officials (NAHRO) joining the discussions as an active third party, the negotiations resulted in two tentative drafts, one on leases and the other on grievance procedures. HUD has since issued circulars that generally embody these agreements. The circular on grievance procedures compels a hearing—if a tenant wishes—before an impartial official or a hearing panel. If representatives of managements are on the panel, tenants must be represented in equal numbers. A tenant is entitled to see the evidence against him, cross-examine witnesses, have the proceedings open or closed, and be represented by counsel. The final decision, which must be in writing, must contain the reasons and evidence relied on. Renewal & Housing Management §§7465.8, 7465.9 (Feb. 22, 1971).

The fair hearing safeguards of *Escalera* and the HUD circulars resemble those constitutionally required in Goldberg v. Kelly, 397 U.S. 254 (1970), for the termination of welfare benefits. Is it a serious argument that equally rigorous administrative procedures are not needed to terminate welfare payments and public housing tenancies, since the tenant will always have his day in court before he is evicted? Cf. Caulder v. Housing Authority, 433 F.2d 998 (4th Cir. 1970) (dissenting opinion). Can it be argued, conversely, that a public housing tenancy—in view of the urgent shortage of standard, low-rent facilities—should be protected even more jealously than a welfare benefit? The loss of welfare frequently implies alternative income; but the loss of public housing (as a nondesirable) usually implies a return to squalor or unbearably higher rentals.

4. The HUD circular states that the tenant may invoke the formal hearing procedures for "any LHA [Local Housing Authority] action or failure to act in accordance with the lease requirements, or . . . involving interpretation or application of LHA's regulations, policies or procedures which adversely affect the tenant's rights, duties, welfare or status." Renewal & Housing Management §7465.9 (Feb. 22, 1971). Presumably this would include an eviction for any cause, including nonpayment of rent; or the levying of a fine for rule violation. Would the hearing procedure be suitable for a tenant's complaint of poor maintenance or lack of services?

5. Do the due process procedures described in *Escalera* cover tenants facing eviction from all other forms of *state-aided* housing? And if so, when is housing state-aided? On that issue the cases are still in disarray. Compare Lopez v. Henry Phipps Plaza South, Inc., 498 F.2d 937 (2d Cir. 1974) (§236 project), and McQueen v. Druker, 438 F.2d 781 (1st Cir. 1971), or Keller v. Romney, 504 F.2d 483 (9th Cir. 1974), or Appel v. Beyer, 114 Cal. Rptr. 336, 39 P.3d S7 (Sup. Ct. 1974) (§221(d)(3) projects), where the Fourteenth Amendment did apply, with Weigand v. Afton View Apartments, 473 F.2d 545 (8th Cir. 1973) (§236 project), and McGuane v. Chenango Court, Inc., 431 F.2d 1189 (2d Cir. 1971) (§221(d)(3) project), where the amendment did not apply. See Procedural Due Process in Government-Subsidized Housing, 86 Harv. L. Rev. 880 (1972).

Section 221(d)(3) projects receive direct federal 3 percent mortgages. Section 236 projects receive federal interest-reduction payments. These subsidies reduce the rental cost to the low-income occupant. Congress has also funded a housing allowance experiment that pays the subsidy directly to the tenant, who then competes with nonsubsidized families for private housing. Should we stretch the Fourteenth Amendment to give prior hearing rights to housing allowance recipients as well?

6. Having gained important procedural rights, do tenants in state-aided projects also enjoy greater substantive protection against removal than do tenants in private housing? Take the following case: management, after a due process hearing, terminates the tenancy of a low-income family because their teenage son has burglarized a store in the state-aided project. Charged as a juvenile delinquent, the son has entered a work camp and no longer lives at home. Should the court reinstate the tenancy? Cf. Lopez v. Henry Phipps

Plaza South, Inc., 498 F.2d 937 (2d Cir. 1974). Cf. also Tyson v. New York City Housing Authority, 369 F. Supp. 513 (S.D.N.Y. 1974).

Can it be argued that the Constitution protects tenants in state-aided housing from removal except for *good cause?* Make the argument.

7. Should *all* tenancies be protected against arbitrary termination, as long as housing remains in short supply? Or, to put the question somewhat differently, should all private landlords be deemed public utilities, regulated both as to their rates and their manner of dealing with customers (tenants)? Can the courts do this?

Is the tenant also entitled to a fair hearing when faced with a rent increase or a higher service charge? Cf. Burr v. New Rochelle Municipal Housing Authority, 479 F.2d 1165 (2d Cir. 1973). HUD now requires that the local Housing Authority give tenants thirty days' notice of any proposed rent increases, that tenants be permitted to inspect and copy any documents supporting the increase, and that any written comments submitted by tenants opposing the increase be forwarded to HUD, where the power to approve the increase lies. 24 CFR 861.

§6.7 Tenant Abandons the Premises

Suppose that tenant wants to break his lease before the term ends. He may find that landlord is happy to let him do so. The premises have become more valuable; the landlord wants to use the premises himself; the landlord can readily relet the premises to a "better" tenant. When landlord and tenant wish the same end, landlord will usually agree to release tenant from his unmatured duties under the lease. We say then that tenant has surrendered his unexpired term and that landlord has accepted the surrender. An express surrender[4] is subject to the Statute of Frauds. Whether the statute applies depends on the term remaining at the time of surrender. See, e.g., N.Y. Gen. Oblig. Law §5-703 (writing required if unexpired term more than one year).

Suppose, however, that landlord is unwilling to release tenant, but that tenant abandons the premises anyway. When then are the options left to landlord?

SOMMER v. KRIDEL
74 N.J. 446, 378 A.2d 767 (1977)

PASHMAN, J. We granted certification in these cases to consider whether a landlord seeking damages from a defaulting tenant is under a duty to miti-

---

4. Shortly you will see surrender by operation of law, page 411, *infra.*

gate damages by making reasonable efforts to re-let an apartment wrongfully vacated by the tenant. Separate parts of the Appellate Division held that, in accordance with their respective leases, the landlords in both cases could recover rents due under the leases regardless of whether they had attempted to re-let the vacated apartments. Although they were of different minds as to the fairness of this result, both parts agreed that it was dictated by Joyce v. Bauman, 113 N.J.L. 438, 174 A. 693 (E. & A. 1934), a decision by the former Court of Errors and Appeals. We now reverse and hold that a landlord does have an obligation to make a reasonable effort to mitigate damages in such a situation. We therefore overrule Joyce v. Bauman to the extent that it is inconsistent with our decision today.

I

A. SOMMER V. KRIDEL

This case was tried on stipulated facts. On March 10, 1972 the defendant, James Kridel, entered into a lease with the plaintiff, Abraham Sommer, owner of the "Pierre Apartments" in Hackensack, to rent apartment 6-L in that building.[1] The term of the lease was from May 1, 1972 until April 30, 1974, with a rent concession for the first six weeks, so that the first month's rent was not due until June 15, 1972.

One week after signing the agreement, Kridel paid Sommer $690. Half of that sum was used to satisfy the first month's rent. The remainder was paid under the lease provision requiring a security deposit of $345. Although defendant had expected to begin occupancy around May 1, his plans were changed. He wrote to Sommer on May 19, 1972, explaining

> I was to be married on June 3, 1972. Unhappily the engagement was broken and the wedding plans cancelled. Both parents were to assume responsibility for the rent after our marriage. I was discharged from the U.S. Army in October 1971 and am now a student. I have no funds of my own, and am supported by my stepfather.
>
> In view of the above, I cannot take possession of the apartment and am surrendering all rights to it. Never having received a key, I cannot return same to you.
>
> I beg your understanding and compassion in releasing me from the lease, and will of course, in consideration thereof, forfeit the 2 month's rent already paid.
>
> Please notify me at your earliest convenience.

Plaintiff did not answer the letter.

Subsequently, a third party went to the apartment house and inquired about renting apartment 6-L. Although the parties agreed that she was ready,

---

1. Among other provisions, the lease prohibited the tenant from assigning or transferring the lease without the consent of the landlord. If the tenant defaulted, the lease gave the landlord the option of re-entering or re-letting, but stipulated that failure to re-let or to recover the full rental would not discharge the tenant's liability for rent.

willing and able to rent the apartment, the person in charge told her that the apartment was not being shown since it was already rented to Kridel. In fact, the landlord did not re-enter the apartment or exhibit it to anyone until August 1, 1973. At that time it was rented to a new tenant for a term beginning on September 1, 1973. The new rental was for $345 per month with a six week concession similar to that granted Kridel.

Prior to re-letting the new premises, plaintiff sued Kridel in August 1972, demanding $7,590, the total amount due for the full two-year term of the lease. Following a mistrial, plaintiff filed an amended complaint asking for $5,865, the amount due between May 1, 1972 and September 1, 1973. The amended complaint included no reduction in the claim to reflect the six week concession provided for in the lease or the $690 payment made to plaintiff after signing the agreement. Defendant filed an amended answer to the complaint, alleging that plaintiff breached the contract, failed to mitigate damages and accepted defendant's surrender of the premises. He also counterclaimed to demand repayment of the $345 paid as a security deposit.

The trial judge ruled in favor of defendant. Despite his conclusion that the lease had been drawn to reflect "the 'settled law' of this state," he found that "justice and fair dealing" imposed upon the landlord the duty to attempt to re-let the premises and thereby mitigate damages. He also held that plaintiff's failure to make any response to defendant's unequivocal offer of surrender was tantamount to an acceptance, thereby terminating the tenancy and any obligation to pay rent. As a result, he dismissed both the complaint and the counterclaim. The Appellate Division reversed in a per curiam opinion, 153 N.J. Super. 1 (1976), and we granted certification. 69 N.J. 395, 354 A.2d 323 (1976).

B.   RIVERVIEW REALTY CO. V. PEROSIO

This controversy arose in a similar manner. On December 27, 1972, Carlos Perosio entered into a written lease with plaintiff Riverview Realty Co. The agreement covered the rental of apartment 5-G in a building owned by the realty company at 2175 Hudson Terrace in Fort Lee. As in the companion case, the lease prohibited the tenant from subletting or assigning the apartment without the consent of the landlord. It was to run for a two-year term, from February 1, 1973 until January 31, 1975, and provided for a monthly rental of $450. The defendant took possession of the apartment and occupied it until February 1974. At that time he vacated the premises, after having paid the rent through January 31, 1974.

The landlord filed a complaint on October 31, 1974, demanding $4,500 in payment for the monthly rental from February 1, 1974 through October 31, 1974. Defendant answered the complaint by alleging that there had been a valid surrender of the premises and that plaintiff failed to mitigate damages.

The trial court granted the landlord's motion for summary judgment against the defendant, fixing the damages at $4,050 plus $182.25 interest.[2]

The Appellate Division affirmed the trial court, holding that it was bound by prior precedents, including Joyce v. Bauman, *supra.* 138 N.J. Super. 270, 350 A.2d 517 (App. Div. 1976). Nevertheless, it freely criticized the rule which it found itself obliged to follow:

> There appears to be no reason in equity or justice to perpetuate such an unrealistic and uneconomic rule of law which encourages an owner to let valuable rented space lie fallow because he is assured of full recovery from a defaulting tenant. Since courts in New Jersey and elsewhere have abandoned ancient real property concepts and applied ordinary contract principles in other conflicts between landlord and tenant there is no sound reason for continuation of a special real property rule to the issue of mitigation. . . . [138 N.J. Super. at 273-74, 350 A.2d at 519; citations omitted]

We granted certification. 70 N.J. 145, 358 A.2d 191 (1976).

II

As the lower courts in both appeals found, the weight of authority in this State supports the rule that a landlord is under no duty to mitigate damages caused by a defaulting tenant. [Citations omitted.] This rule has been followed in a majority of states, Annot. 21 A.L.R.3d 534, §2[a] at 541 (1968), and has been tentatively adopted in the American Law Institute's Restatement of Property. Restatement (Second) of Property, §11.1(3) (Tent. Draft No. 3, 1975).

Nevertheless, while there is still a split of authority over this question, the trend among recent cases appears to be in favor of a mitigation requirement. [Citations omitted.] The majority rule is based on principles of property law which equate a lease with a transfer of a property interest in the owner's estate. Under this rationale the lease conveys to a tenant an interest in the property which forecloses any control by the landlord; thus, it would be anomalous to require the landlord to concern himself with the tenant's abandonment of his own property. Wright v. Baumann, 239 Or. 410, 398 P.2d 119, 120-21, 21 A.L.R.3d 527 (1965).

For instance, in Muller v. Beck, 94 N.J.L. 311, 110 A. 831 (1920), where essentially the same issue was posed, the court clearly treated the lease as governed by property, as opposed to contract, precepts.[3] The court there ob-

---

2. The trial court noted that damages had been erroneously calculated in the complaint to reflect ten months rent. As to the interest awarded to plaintiff, the parties have not raised this issue before this Court. Since we hold that the landlord had a duty to attempt to mitigate damages, we need not reach this question.

3. It is well settled that a party claiming damages for a breach of contract has a duty to mitigate his loss. See Frank Stamato & Co. v. Borough of Lodi, 4 N.J. 14, 71 A.2d 336 (1950);

served that the "tenant had an estate for years, but it was an estate qualified by this right of the landlord to prevent its transfer," 94 N.J.L. at 313, 110 A. at 832, and that "the tenant has an estate with which the landlord may not interfere." Id. at 314, 110 A. at 832. . . .

Yet the distinction between a lease for ordinary residential purposes and an ordinary contract can no longer be considered viable. As Professor Powell observed, evolving "social factors have exerted increasing influence on the law of estates for years." 2 Powell on Real Property (1977 ed.), §221[1] at 180-81. The result has been that

> [t]he complexities of city life, and the proliferated problems of modern society in general, have created new problems for lessors and lessees and these have been commonly handled by specific clauses in leases. This growth in the number and detail of specific lease covenants has reintroduced into the law of estates for years a predominantly contractual ingredient. [Id. at 181]

Thus in 6 Williston on Contracts (3 ed. 1962), §890A at 592, it is stated: There is a clearly discernible tendency on the part of courts to cast aside technicalities in the interpretation of leases and to concentrate their attention, as in the case of other contracts, on the intention of the parties. . . . [Citations omitted.]

Application of the contract rule requiring mitigation of damages to a residential lease may be justified as a matter of basic fairness.[4] Professor McCormick first commented upon the inequity under the majority rule when he predicted in 1925 that eventually

> the logic, inescapable according to the standards of a "jurisprudence of conceptions" which permits the landlord to stand idly by the vacant, abandoned premises and treat them as the property of the tenant to recover full rent, [will] yield to the more realistic notions of social advantage which in other fields of the law have forbidden recovery for damages which the plaintiff by reasonable efforts could have avoided. [McCormick, "The Rights of the Landlord Upon Abandonment of the Premises by the Tenant," 23 Mich. L. Rev. 211, 221-22 (1925)]

Various courts have adopted this position.

The pre-existing rule cannot be predicated upon the possibility that a landlord may lose the opportunity to rent another empty apartment because he must first rent the apartment vacated by the defaulting tenant. Even where the breach occurs in a multi-dwelling building, each apartment may have

---

Sandler v. Lawn-A-Mat Chem. & Equip. Corp., 141 N.J. Super. 437, 455, 358 A.2d 805 (App. Div. 1976); Wolf v. Marlton Corp., 57 N.J. Super. 278, 154 A.2d 625 (App. Div. 1956); 5 Corbin on Contracts (1964 ed.), §1039 at 241 et seq.; McCormick, Damages, §33 at 127 (1935). See also N.J.S.A. 12A:2-708.

4. We see no distinction between the leases involved in the instant appeals and those which might arise in other types of residential housing. However, we reserve for another day the question of whether a landlord must mitigate damages in a commercial setting. Cf. Kruvant v. Sunrise Market, Inc., 58 N.J. 452, 456, 279 A.2d 104 (1971), modified on other grounds, 59 N.J. 330, 282 A.2d 746 (1971).

unique qualities which make it attractive to certain individuals. Significantly, in Sommer v. Kridel, there was a specific request to rent the apartment vacated by the defendant; there is no reason to believe that absent this vacancy the landlord could have succeeded in renting a different apartment to this individual.

We therefore hold that antiquated real property concepts which served as the basis for the pre-existing rule, shall no longer be controlling where there is a claim for damages under a residential lease. Such claims must be governed by more modern notions of fairness and equity. A landlord has a duty to mitigate damages where he seeks to recover rents due from a defaulting tenant.

If the landlord has other vacant apartments besides the one which the tenant has abandoned, the landlord's duty to mitigate consists of making reasonable efforts to re-let the apartment. In such cases he must treat the apartment in question as if it was one of his vacant stock.

As part of his cause of action, the landlord shall be required to carry the burden of proving that he used reasonable diligence in attempting to re-let the premises. We note that there has been a divergence of opinion concerning the allocation of the burden of proof on this issue. See Annot., 21 A.L.R.3d 534, §12 at 577 (1968). While generally in contract actions the breaching party has the burden of proving that damages are capable of mitigation, see Sandler v. Lawn-A-Mat Chem. & Equip. Corp., 141 N.J. Super. 437, 455, 358 A.2d 805 (App. Div. 1976); McCormick, Damages, §33 at 130 (1935), here the landlord will be in a better position to demonstrate whether he exercised reasonable diligence in attempting to re-let the premises. Cf. Kulm v. Coast to Coast Stores Central Org., 248 Or. 436, 432 P.2d 1006 (1967)(burden on lessor in contract to renew a lease).

III

The Sommer v. Kridel case presents a classic example of the unfairness which occurs when a landlord has no responsibility to minimize damages. Sommer waited 15 months and allowed $4658.50 in damages to accrue before attempting to re-let the apartment. Despite the availability of a tenant who was ready, willing and able to rent the apartment, the landlord needlessly increased the damages by turning her away. While a tenant will not necessarily be excused from his obligations under a lease simply by finding another person who is willing to rent the vacated premises, see, e.g., Reget v. Dempsey-Tegler & Co., 70 Ill. App. 2d 32, 216 N.E.2d 500 (Ill. App. 1966) (new tenant insisted on leasing the premises under different terms); Edmands v. Rust & Richardson Drug Co., 191 Mass. 123, 77 N.E. 713 (1906) (landlord need not accept insolvent tenant), here there has been no showing that the new tenant would not have been suitable. We therefore find that plaintiff could have avoided the damages which eventually accrued, and that the defendant was relieved of his duty to continue paying rent. Ordinarily we would require the tenant to bear the cost of any reasonable expenses incurred by a landlord in attempting to re-let the premises, see Ross v. Smigelski, *supra,* 166 N.W.2d at 248-49; 22 Am. Jur. 2d, Damages, §169 at 238, but no such expenses were incurred in this case.[5]

In Riverview Realty Co. v. Perosio, no factual determination was made regarding the landlord's efforts to mitigate damages, and defendant contends that plaintiff never answered his interrogatories. Consequently, the judgment is reversed and the case remanded for a new trial. Upon remand and after discovery has been completed, R. 4:17 et seq., the trial court shall determine whether plaintiff attempted to mitigate damages with reasonable diligence, see Wilson v. Ruhl, *supra,* 356 A.2d at 546, and if so, the extent of damages remaining and assessable to the tenant. As we have held above, the burden of proving that reasonable diligence was used to re-let the premises shall be upon the plaintiff. See Annot., *supra,* §11 at 575.

In assessing whether the landlord has satisfactorily carried his burden, the trial court shall consider, among other factors, whether the landlord, either personally or through an agency, offered or showed the apartment to any prospective tenants, or advertised it in local newspapers. Additionally, the tenant may attempt to rebut such evidence by showing that he proffered suitable tenants who were rejected. However, there is no standard formula for measuring whether the landlord has utilized satisfactory efforts in attempting to mitigate damages, and each case must be judged upon its own facts. Compare Hershorin v. La Vista, Inc., 110 Ga. App. 435, 138 S.E.2d 703 (App. 1964) ("reasonable effort" of landlord by showing the apartment to all prospective tenants); Carpenter v. Wisniewski, 139 Ind. App. 325, 215 N.E.2d 882 (App. 1966) (duty satisfied where landlord advertised the premises through a newspaper, placed a sign in the window, and employed a realtor); Re Garment Center Capitol, Inc., 93 F.2d 667, 115 A.L.R. 202 (2 Cir. 1938) (landlord's duty not breached where higher rental was asked since it was known that this was merely a basis for negotiations); Foggia v. Dix, 265 Or. 315, 509 P.2d 412, 414 (1973) (in mitigating damages, landlord need not accept less than fair market value or "substantially alter his obligations as established in the pre-existing lease"); with Anderson v. Andy Darling Pontiac, Inc., 257 Wis. 371, 43 N.W.2d 362 (1950) (reasonable diligence not established where newspaper advertisement placed in one issue of local paper by a broker); Scheinfeld v. Muntz T. V., Inc., 67 Ill. App. 2d 8, 214 N.E.2d 506 (Ill. App. 1966) (duty breached where landlord refused to accept suitable subtenant); Consolidated Sun Ray, Inc. v. Oppenstein, 335 F.2d 801, 811 (8 Cir. 1964) (dictum) (demand for rent which is "far greater than the provisions of the lease called for" negates landlord's assertion that he acted in good faith in seeking a new tenant).

5. As to defendant's counterclaim for $345, representing the amount deposited with the landlord as a security deposit, we note that this issue has not been briefed or argued before this Court, and apparently has been abandoned. Because we hold that plaintiff breached his duty to attempt to mitigate damages, we do not address defendant's argument that the landlord accepted a surrender of the premises.

IV

The judgment in Sommer v. Kridel is reversed. In Riverview Realty Co. v. Perosio, the judgment is reversed and the case is remanded to the trial court for proceedings in accordance with this opinion.

NOTES AND QUESTIONS

1. Gruman v. Investors Diversified Services, Inc., 247 Minn. 502, 78 N.W.2d 377 (1956) typifies the more prevalent view. Defendant rented commercial premises for a seven-year term. The lease barred any assignment or subletting without the landlord's consent. With fourteen months remaining on the term, defendant vacated the premises, but tendered for landlord's consent a subtenant, the United States postmaster general, who would use the space for a regional office. Although landlord conceded the government's suitability as a subtenant, he refused his consent. Defendant vacated the premises and landlord brought suit for the full rentals due under the unexpired term of the lease.

In holding for the landlord, the court wrote:

> In foreign jurisdictions, where the question has been presented, a majority of the courts have held that in a lease such as this the lessor does not have the duty of mitigating damages; may arbitrarily refuse to accept a subtenant suitable and otherwise responsible; and may recover from the lessee the full rentals due under the lease as and when they become due. [Citations from 22 jurisdictions omitted.]
>
> The reasons expressed in support of this rule are that, since the lessor has exercised a personal choice in the selection of a tenant for a definite term and has expressly provided that no substitute shall be acceptable without his written consent, no obligation rests upon him to look to anyone but the lessee for his rent, Stern v. Thayer, 56 Minn. 93, 57 N.W. 329; White v. Huber Drug Co., 190 Mich. 212, 157 N.W. 60; that a lease is a conveyance of an interest in real property and, when a lessor has delivered the premises to his lessee, the latter is bound to him by privity of estate as well as by privity of contract, Davidson v. Minnesota Loan & Trust Co., 158 Minn. 411, 197 N.W. 833, 32 A.L.R. 1418; cf. W. C. Hines Co. v. Angell, 188 Minn. 387, 247 N.W. 387; that a lessor's right to reenter the premises upon lessee's default or abandonment thereof is at the lessor's option and not the lessee's, Kulawitz v. Pacific Woodenware & Paper Co., 25 Cal.(2d) 664, 155 P.(2d) 24; Rau v. Baker, 118 Ill. App. 150; and that a lessee's unilateral action in abandoning leased premises, *unless accepted by his lessor,* does not terminate the lease or forfeit the estate conveyed thereby, nor the lessee's right to use and possess the leased premises and, by the same token, his obligation to pay the rent due therefor. Haycock v. Johnston, 81 Minn. 49, 83 N.W. 494, 1118; id. 97 Minn. 289, 106 N.W. 304. . . .
>
> A number of writers have advanced the theory that a more modern and just viewpoint should be applied in situations such as the present; that the rule

applicable in ordinary breach of contract cases, requiring efforts to mitigate damages after breach, should be applied to leases; and in furtherance of this view that a lessor should be obligated to accept a suitable subtenant offered by the lessee. See 2 Powell, Real Property, par. 229, note 79; McCormick, Rights of Landlord upon Abandonment, 23 Mich. L. Rev. 211, 222; 44 Harv. L. Rev. 993; 34 Harv. L. Rev. 217. Defendant also cites decisions from the Supreme Courts of Iowa, Kansas and Wisconsin as giving support to this viewpoint.

We feel that we must adhere to the majority rule. In reaching this conclusion we are motivated by the fact that the language of the assignment provision is clear and unambiguous and that many leases now in effect covering a substantial amount of real property and creating valuable property rights were carefully prepared by competent counsel in reliance upon the majority viewpoint. It would seem clear from the language adopted in all such cases that the lessors therein are entitled to place full reliance upon the responsibility of their respective lessees for the rentals they have contracted to pay. Should a lessee desire the right to assign or sublet to a suitable tenant, a clause might readily be inserted in the lease similar to those now included in many leases to the effect that the lessor's written consent to the assignment or subletting of the leased premises should not be unreasonably withheld. There being no clause in the present lease to such effect, we are compelled to give its terms their full force and effect as have the courts of a majority of other jurisdictions.

2.   Restatement (Second) of Property §12.1, Comment i (1977) clings to the majority rule. In justification, the comment reads:

> If the tenant has abandoned the leased property and the landlord stands by and does nothing, the lease is not terminated. A tenant who abandons leased property is not entitled to insist on action by the landlord to mitigate the damages, absent an agreement otherwise. Abandonment of property is an invitation to vandalism, and the law should not encourage such conduct by putting a duty of mitigation of damages on the landlord.

Have you been convinced?

3.   If landlord proceeds on the *Gruman* majority rule basis, suing for the unpaid rent as it becomes due, may the defaulted tenant change his mind about abandonment and retake possession of the leased premises?

4.   Notice carefully the interplay between an absence of the landlord's duty to mitigate and a restriction on the tenant's power to assign her lease or sublet the premises.

5.   Suppose that the lease in a nonmitigation jurisdiction were to provide: "In default of the payment of the rent in monthly installments, as herein provided, the whole of the rent remaining unpaid for the balance of the leasehold term shall at once become due and payable." Would this form of acceleration clause be enforceable?

Compare Fifty States Management Corp. v. Pioneer Auto Parks, Inc., 46 N.Y.2d 573, 389 N.E.2d 113, 415 N.Y.2d 800 (1979) (acceleration clause valid by analogy with similar provisions in mortgage bonds), with Ricker v.

Rombough, 120 Cal. App. 2d 912, 261 P.2d 328 (1953) (acceleration clause invalid as being either a penalty or an agreement for liquidated damages when the damages are readily ascertainable). Also compare Fifty States Management Corp. v. Pioneer Auto Parks, Inc., *supra*, with Seidlitz v. Auerbach, 230 N.Y. 167, 129 N.E. 461 (1920) (acceleration clause invalid as penalty where landlord sought to accelerate $7,500 on rental after tenant failed to pay $17 insurance premium).

Even if the landlord may accelerate the unpaid rental installments, should his claim be limited to the present value of those installments?

FIRST WISCONSIN TRUST CO. v. L. WIEMANN CO.

93 Wis. 2d 258, 286 N.W.2d 360 (1980)

HANSEN, J. The defendant entered into a 28 year lease for the ground floor of a building in Milwaukee in which to operate a retail variety store. The term of the lease was from June 1, 1953, to May 31, 1981. The rent was $1,000 per month, plus a percentage of the net sales in excess of $200,000 per year, and $166.66 per month to repay a $25,000 loan from the lessor for the financing of improvements. The defendant also agreed to pay one-half of the real estate taxes in excess of $4,000 per year.

Subsequent to the time the lease was entered into, the plaintiffs purchased the property from the former owners for $257,500 and expended $60,000 for improvements, making a total investment of $317,500.

On October 4, 1972, the plaintiff lessors commenced an action against the defendant lessee alleging that the defendant had failed to pay rent for the month of October, 1972, and demanding the sum of $1,166.67 as damages. The defendant answered and alleged as an affirmative defense that the plaintiffs breached the covenant of quiet enjoyment and the covenant to repair contained in the lease, and that the action of the plaintiffs constituted constructive eviction. The defendant also alleged that prior to September 28, 1972, the defendant vacated the leased premises, and on that date it mailed a notice of termination to the plaintiffs and delivered possession of the premises to the plaintiffs; therefore the defendant was not liable for the payment of rent.

On June 26, 1973, the plaintiffs commenced a second action against the defendant alleging three causes of action. In their first cause of action the plaintiffs sought damages in excess of $139,000 for the defendant's abandonment of the premises and failure to pay rent from September, 1972, through the end of the lease term, May, 1981, and for the defendant's failure to pay real estate taxes which it was obligated to pay under the terms of the lease. In their second cause of action the plaintiffs alleged that the defendant negligently caused damage to the premises in the amount of $1,200. The third cause of action alleged that the plaintiffs sold the property for $100,000; that they had invested $317,500 in the property; and that by breaching the lease the defendant had caused the plaintiffs damages in the amount of $217,500.

The trial court ordered the two cases consolidated for trial, and the issues were tried to the court.

At the conclusion of the trial, the trial judge made extensive findings of fact and pronounced the following conclusions of law:

1. Plaintiffs' claim for $1,200 for damages to the leased premises, objected to by defendant, is allowed for the sum of $1,200 plus interest from the date of this Court's decision, February 28, 1977.

2. Plaintiffs' claim for real estate taxes, objected to by defendant, is allowed for the sum of $3,019.68 plus interest at the rate of 5% per annum from September 28, 1972, the date of the breach of the lease, to February 28, 1977, the date of this Court's decision, said interest being in the sum of $666.84, for a total sum of $3,686.52

3. Plaintiff's loss of rental under the lease from October 1972 through February 1973, objected to by the defendant, at the rate of $800.00 per month in a total sum of $4,000.00, with interest from February 1st, 1973 to February 28th, 1977, the date of this Court's decision, at the rate of 5% per annum, said interest being in the sum of $814.79, for a total of $4,814.79.[1]

4. For breach of the lease, objected to by the defendant, in the sum of $91,586.00 with interest from February 28, 1977, the date of this Court's decision.

5. That in total, including interest as above specified, the plaintiffs are entitled to Judgment in the sum of $101,287.31. In addition thereto, the plaintiffs are entitled to interest on said sum of $101,287.31 at the rate of 7% per annum from the date of this Court's decision on February 28, 1977 to the date that Judgment is entered. Further, that the plaintiffs are entitled to Judgment for their statutory costs and disbursements.

Judgment was thereupon entered, awarding the plaintiffs damages in the sum of $101,287.31, together with interest in the sum of $2,599.70, plus costs and disbursements of the action in the sum of $219.08, all of which totaled $104,108.09.

We are of the opinion that the following facts are also relevant to the issues raised on this appeal.

The lease contained a covenant for quiet enjoyment of the leased premises which provides as follows:

> *Quiet Enjoyment.* The landlord covenants that the Tenant, on payment of the rent herein reserved and the performance of agreements, covenants and conditions on the part of the Tenant to be performed and observed herein contained, shall and may, peaceably and quietly, have, hold and enjoy the premises demised herein throughout the term hereof and of any renewal thereof, free from molestation, eviction or disturbance by the landlords or any person or persons claiming by, through or under the landlord, or by any other person or persons whomsoever.

1. The base rent for the leasehold premises was $1,000 a month and a portion thereof was rented by the plaintiffs for the period set forth in conclusion *3* for $200 per month.

It was for an alleged breach of this covenant by the plaintiffs that the defendant terminated the lease in September, 1972.

There was testimony that during the term of the lease the area near 27th and Center streets, where the leasehold property was located, declined as a business area when it became part of the "inner core." Many businesses closed, many businesses had trouble with shoplifting, vandalism and break-ins, and as result of these incidents and because of attacks on clerks and office help, merchants were having trouble keeping employees. The defendant also experienced these problems.

The defendant sustained repeated water damage from water that came from the second floor tenants. However, there is no evidence as to how much damage was sustained.

In 1962, there was a fire in the leased premises which resulted in damage. In 1965, an automobile smashed into the building and caused a business interruption. The plaintiffs expended $120,000 to repair the building. On May 22, 1971, there was another substantial fire loss and break-in which caused another serious interruption in the defendant's business.

On September 28, 1972, the defendant sent a letter to the plaintiffs which informed them that the defendant was terminating the lease "for a number of good and sufficient reasons, among which are the following":

> 1. Constant breaches of the quiet enjoyment provisions contained in Par. 17 of said Lease, committed by tenants of the upper floors of the said building, which have destroyed the Company's ability to make proper use of the store premises.
> 2. Various other improper acts of upper floor tenants in said building which have been disturbing and destroying the Company's ability to continue to operate the leased premises for its retail store business.
> 3. Failure of the Landlords to make necessary repairs of constant damage to the leased premises.
> 4. The foregoing constitute a constructive eviction of the L. Wiemann Company from the leased premises.

The defendant had removed all its property from the premises and it sent the keys to the premises with the letter.

After the defendant vacated the premises, the plaintiffs inspected the property and found that the wall paneling was removed from the wall, three windows were broken, the electrical outlets in the floor were pulled up and exposed, and there was a hole approximately 3 by 5 feet cut through the floor. The plaintiffs expended $1,200 in repairing the damage.

After the defendant terminated the lease, the plaintiffs attempted to relet the premises. They advertised, placed signs in the windows and contacted people who they thought would be interested in renting the premises. The plaintiffs rented a portion of the premises to another company on a month-to-month tenancy at $200 per month commencing in October, 1972.

On February 28, 1973, the plaintiffs sold the property for $100,000, and conveyed title to the property and delivered possession thereof to the purchaser free and clear of all encumbrances, and free of the lease. The conveyances contained the following provision: "Seller reserves the right to sue the Wiemann Company for breach of its lease at subject premises, and the proceeds resulting from such action or judgment rendered thereupon shall belong to seller."

A real estate appraiser testified that the lease had a present value of $91,586 assuming that the lease was in force and effect. He capitalized the future monthly rent of $1,166.66 with a factor of eight percent for eight years and eight months, from October 1, 1972, to May 31, 1981. On cross-examination he stated that when he made his evaluation he was unaware that the plaintiffs had sold the property and turned over possession on February 28, 1973, and that if the plaintiffs were not entitled to collect rent under the lease, the lease had no value.

We are of the opinion that this case presents the following issues:

1.   Was the defendant justified in terminating the lease?
2.   Was the defendant liable for future rent to the end of the term of the lease? . . .

[The court holds that the defendant presented no evidence to justify its termination of the lease.]

The defendant alleges that the trial court erred in awarding the plaintiffs damages for future rent for the balance of the term of the lease. The defendant argues that the plaintiffs accepted its surrender of the property when they sold the property and thus terminated the obligation of the defendant under the lease.

When a tenant vacates or abandons the leased premises before the end of the lease term, the landlord has a right to elect (1) to accept the surrender and terminate the lease or (2) to enter and take possession for the purpose of mitigating the damages for which the tenant is liable because of his breach of the lease. Ross v. Smigelski, 42 Wis. 2d 185, 193, 166 N.W.2d 243 (1969); Galvin v. Lovell, 257 Wis. 82, 90, 91, 42 N.W.2d 456 (1950); Weinsklar Realty Co. v. Dooley, 200 Wis. 412, 415, 228 N.W. 515 (1930).

> . . . The election to enter for the purpose of mitigating damages may be evidenced by formal notice or by other proper means constituting such unequivocal act as would amount to an election of remedies in a proper case.
>
> The mere entry and taking possession of the premises for the purpose of leasing the same does not constitute such an election, because it is an equivocal act—something to be done by the landlord regardless of whether his purpose be to terminate the lease or merely to perform his legal duty to mitigate damages.
>
> The right to elect which course he will pursue remains with the landlord until he makes his election by taking some step which clearly evidences an intent to make a choice between the two inconsistent remedies that are open to him. . . .
> Weinsklar Realty Co. v. Dooley, *supra*, at 415, 228 N.W. at 517.

Upon the tenant's surrender of the leased premises, the landlord has a duty to exercise reasonable diligence to re-rent the premises in order to mitigate damages. Sprecher v. Weston's Bar, Inc., 78 Wis. 2d 26, 42, 253 N.W.2d 493 (1977); Patton v. Milwaukee Commercial Bank, 222 Wis. 167, 171, 268 N.W. 124 (1936); Strauss v. Turck, 197 Wis. 586, 587, 222 N.W. 811 (1929); sec. 704.29, Stats.

In this case the evidence shows that the plaintiffs made reasonable attempts to find another tenant between October, 1972, and the sale of the property in February, 1973. Entry and taking possession of the premises for the purpose of leasing does not constitute an election of remedies because it is an equivocal act. Richter v. Fassett, 253 Wis. 101, 103, 33 N.W.2d 230 (1948); Weinsklar Realty Co. v. Dooley, *supra,* 200 Wis. at 415, 228 N.W. 515. Re-renting a portion of the premises for these five months did not constitute such an unequivocal act of the landlord as to constitute acceptance of the surrender of the premises. Sec. 704.29(4)(b), Stats. Specifically sec. 704.29(4), states:

> *(4) Acts privileged in mitigation of rent or damages.* The following acts by the landlord do not defeat his right to recover rent and damages and do not constitute an acceptance of surrender of the premises:
>
> (a) Entry, with or without notice, for the purpose of inspecting, preserving, repairing, remodeling and showing the premises;
>
> (b) Rerenting the premises or a part thereof, with or without notice, with rent applied against the damages caused by the original tenant and in reduction of rent accruing under the original lease;
>
> (c) Use of the premises by the landlord until such time as rerenting at a reasonable rent is practical, not to exceed one year, if the landlord gives prompt written notice to the tenant that the landlord is using the premises pursuant to this section and that he will credit the tenant with the reasonable value of the use of the premises to the landlord for such a period;
>
> (d) Any other act which is reasonably subject to interpretation as being in mitigation of rent or damages and which does not unequivocally demonstrate an intent to release the defaulting tenant.

This court has held that when the landlord occupies the premises for his own use or takes exclusive possession, he accepts the tenant's surrender and terminates the lease, and he cannot collect rent which would have accrued under the lease subsequent to the surrender. Galvin v. Lovell, *supra,* 257 Wis. at 92, 42 N.W.2d 456; Richter v. Fassett, *supra,* 253 Wis. at 104, 33 N.W.2d 230; Mahonna v. Chaimson, 214 Wis. 396, 400, 253 N.W. 391 (1934); West Concord Milling Co. v. Hosmer, 129 Wis. 8, 13, 107 N.W. 12 (1906).

In Anderson v. Andy Darling Pontiac, Inc., 257 Wis. 371, 43 N.W.2d 362 (1950), after the lessee vacated the premises the lessors took possession and resumed operation of a business on their own account. The lessors gave a written notice to the lessee which stated that they "... 'will ... re-enter the premises described in said lease and will re-possess said premises for the purpose of mitigation of damages thereunder, and will not waive any of their rights, legal or equitable, to any cause of action they may have by virtue of the said breach of said agreement.' " Id. at 373, 43 N.W.2d at 363. The court held that the lessors accepted the lessee's surrender, stating:

> Plaintiffs contend that their re-entry does not constitute an acceptance of defendant's surrender of the leased premises; that their purpose to the contrary is expressed in the notice served upon defendant which recites that the re-entry was made only for the purpose of mitigating damages. Their expression is not consistent with their conduct. An intention to re-enter for the purpose of minimizing damages must be made clear at the time of re-entry. Mahonna v. Chaimson, 214 Wis. 396, 253 N.W. 391. Re-entry for the purpose of minimizing damages only must be read out of all the circumstances, from the conduct as well as from the expression of the landlord. Immediately upon surrender the plaintiffs took possession of the premises and by a newspaper advertisement announced their intention to resume the same character of business on their own account which they and the defendant had previously conducted therein. They made no effort to obtain a new tenant until nearly two months after the surrender and after this action was commenced. Their conduct indicates their intention to take possession for the purpose of resuming the business which they had previously conducted on the premises. Id. at 374, 43 N.W.2d at 364.

In the instant case, the plaintiffs made reasonable efforts to re-rent the premises after the defendant vacated and they were able to re-rent a part of the premises for a period of five months. In February, 1973, they sold the premises free and clear of all encumbrances, including the lease. The fact that the plaintiffs reserved the right to sue the defendant for breach of the lease and hold it liable for rent for the balance of the lease term is inconsistent with the sale of the property.

The act of selling the property in February, 1973, evidences a clear intent to make the election between accepting the surrender and terminating the lease, and entering and taking possession of the premises for the purpose of mitigating damages.

We conclude that the plaintiffs accepted the surrender of the premises and terminated the lease, and therefore they are deprived of the right to recover damages for future rent after they sold the premises.

Since we determine that the actions of the plaintiffs constituted acceptance of the surrender of the premises and termination of the lease, we do not reach the issue of whether the trial court denied the defendant the benefit of a finding regarding mitigation of damages. . . .

Judgment reversed in part; affirmed in part.

NOTES AND QUESTIONS

1. Notice that Wisconsin adheres to the minority view requiring that landlord either accept the tenant's surrender or re-enter for the purpose of

mitigating damages. Compare Gruman v. Investors Diversified Services, Inc., *supra,* page 403, Note 1. We call the latter alternative reletting the premises *for the tenant's account.* In that event, tenant is relieved of future liabilities under the lease, including liability for future rent, to the extent the same are performed as a result of a reletting on terms that are reasonable. Restatement (Second) of Property §12.1(3)(b) (1977). In legal shorthand: on the tenant's account theory, landlord has a damages claim (respecting rent) measured by the difference (for the unexpired term of the lease) between the reserved rental and the rents collected on any reletting.

2. *Landlord's implied acceptance of the tenant's surrender:* As the main case indicates, the landlord who elects a tenant's account theory is vulnerable to the claim of an accepted surrender. Adding to the landlord's difficulty is the timing of the claim, which usually is made only after the landlord sues for his loss of rental. By then, it is too late for the landlord to retrace his steps, either to make his conduct less vulnerable to the tenant's claim or to manage the premises differently so as to minimize the rental loss.

What practical steps might a landlord take to avoid the finding of an accepted surrender?

How might the landlord, who has *expressly* accepted a tenant's surrender, deal with the premises differently from one who has re-entered the premises on a tenant's account theory?

Is a landlord who sues for the rent after the tenant vacates also vulnerable to the claim of an accepted surrender?

In each of the following cases, tenant claimed an accepted surrender. How should the cases have been decided?

(a) On March 1, 1952, tenant vacated, but continued to pay rent through June 1952. In July 1952, tenant returned the keys. Landlord placed "For Rent" signs in the windows and advertisements in the newspapers. In September 1952, landlord, without notice to the tenant, allowed an appliance house to store furniture in the premises free of charge. This arrangement continued for eight months, when the appliance house became a permanent tenant. John L. Cutler Assn. v. De Jay Stores, 3 Utah 2d 107, 279 P.2d 700 (1955).

(b) On March 15, 1958, tenant vacated and returned the keys, after having notified landlord in May 1957 that he would do so. At that time, tenant received an oral assurance that he would be relieved of his leasehold duties if a replacement tenant could be secured. In September 1957, landlord's agent placed a "For Rent" sign in front of the building, stating its availability as of March 15, 1958. After tenant vacated, landlord re-entered the premises, made various repairs and alterations, and in December 1958 relet the premises for a five-year term (tenant's lease expired in October 1959). Wiese v. Steinauer, 201 Cal. App. 2d 651, 20 Cal. Rptr. 295 (1962).

(c) Tenant wrote to landlord, September 20, 1965, stating that for reasons of health it was imperative that he move by October 15 (8½ months prematurely). Landlord did not reply, but, on October 13, 1965, landlord advertised the apartment for rent at a higher rental, having re-entered on or about that date. The lease provided for reletting for the account of tenant. Building Supervision Corp. v. Skolinsky, 50 Misc. 2d 375, 270 N.Y.S.2d 454 (Civ. Ct. 1966).

3. *When may the landlord sue for his rental losses?* In Hermitage Co. v. Levine, 248 N.Y. 333, 162 N.E. 97 (1928), the facts were these: Plaintiff leased to defendant a seven-story building for a term of twenty-one years and two months, commencing August 1, 1924, and ending October 1, 1945. Defendant paid rent for only a few months and was dispossessed in summary proceedings on December 31, 1924. by August 1, 1925, plaintiff had relet the entire building in three separate leases: three-and-a-half floors were relet for 15 years; two-and-a-half, for ten years; and one, for three years. The plaintiff sued in March 1926 for the rental deficiencies computed to that time. Held: the action is premature; ascertainment of plaintiff's damages will be impossible until October 1, 1945.

> No doubt, a damage clause can be drawn in such a way as to make a tenant responsible for monthly deficits after the re-entry of his landlord, and this without charging the landlord with a duty to account for a surplus in other seasons. Such a clause will be found in McCready v. Lindenborn (172 N.Y. 400), where the lease was to the effect that the tenant would pay the difference in rent "in equal monthly payments as the amount of such difference shall from time to time be ascertained." A clause similar in effect, though more uncertain in its terms, will be found in Mann v. Munch Brewery (225 N.Y. 189), where the tenant was to "continue liable for the payment of the rent and the performance of all the other conditions herein contained." None the less, in the absence of a provision that points with reasonable clearness to a different construction, a liability for damages resulting from a reletting is single and entire, not multiple and several. The deficiency is to be ascertained when the term is at an end. . . .
>
> We do not overlook the hardship to the landlord in postponing the cause of action until October, 1945. The hardship is so great as to give force to the argument that postponement to a date so distant may not reasonably be held to have been intended by the parties. There is no reason to suppose, however, that the landlord was expectant of so early a default or so heavy a deficiency. It had in its possession a deposit of cash security in the sum of $30,000. Very likely this was supposed to be enough to make default improbable and the risk of loss remote. If the damage clause as drawn gives inadequate protection, the fault is with the draftsman. The courts are not at liberty to supply its omissions at the expense of a tenant whose liability for the future ended with the cancellation of the lease except in so far as he bound himself by covenant to liability thereafter. [248 N.Y. 333, 337-339, 162 N.E. 97, 98]

As landlord's attorney, draft a lease clause that avoids the rule of Hermitage Co. v. Levine. See, e.g., Bedford Myrtle Corp. v. Martin, 28 Misc. 2d 33, 209 N.Y.S.2d 201 (Sup. Ct. 1960).

4. Tenant abandons the premises. Landlord proceeds on a tenant's account theory. Landlord finds a replacement tenant who enters into a lease for a higher rental and longer term than the original lease provided. However, the replacement tenant soon defaults. Who bears the risk of any uncollected rental under the original lease, the original tenant or the landlord? Cf. U.S. Nat'l Bank of Oregon v. Homeland, Inc., 291 Or. 374, 631 P.2d 761 (1981) (the original tenant similar to one who assigns a lease, yet remains responsible for the rent if the assignee fails to pay).

5. If in reletting the premises on a tenant's account theory a landlord collects more than the reserved rental, is tenant entitled to the surplus? Cf. A & J Realty Corp. v. Kent Dry Cleaners, Inc., 61 Misc. 2d 887, 307 N.Y.S.2d 99 (Dist. Ct. 1969).

6. Tenant abandons the premises. Landlord proceeds on a tenant's account theory. Before landlord finds a new tenant, defaulted tenant seeks to return. Must landlord accept him? Cf. Howard Stores Corp. v. Robinson Rayon Co., 64 Misc. 2d 913, 315 N.Y.S.2d 720 (App. T. 1970).

7. Landlord *must* mitigate damages if he elects a tenant's account theory. What steps should prudent landlord take to avoid ruling, after the fact, that he failed to mitigate properly?

SAGAMORE CORP. v. WILLCUTT
120 Conn. 315, 180 A. 464 (1935)

BANKS, J. The complaint alleged that on October 1st, 1934, the plaintiff leased to the defendant for the term of one year from that date certain premises for the annual rental of $480 payable at the rate of $40 a month on the first day of each month in advance, that the defendant occupied the premises until February 1st, 1935, on which day he moved out and thereafter notified the plaintiff that he would no longer comply with the terms of the lease and would pay no further rent, and that as a result of the defendant's breach of the lease the plaintiff has suffered as damages the difference between the rental specified in the lease and the reasonable rental value of the premises for the remainder of the term. The defendant's demurrer to the complaint, stated in four paragraphs, makes a single claim: that the breach of a covenant to pay rent creates no debt until the time stipulated for payment arrives, that the defendant owes the plaintiff no duty except to pay the rent on the first of each month during the remainder of the term, and consequently the plaintiff is not entitled, in an action brought before the expiration of the term of the lease, to recover damages for the defendant's anticipatory breach of his covenant to pay rent.

The lessee has abandoned the leased premises and refused to pay any further rent. The lessor in such a situation has two courses of action open to him. He may accept the surrender of the premises, thereby terminating the lease and effecting a rescission of the contract, or he may refuse to accept the surrender. In the latter case he may let the property lie idle and collect the balance of the rent due under the lease, or he may take possession of the property and lease it to others; in which case he may recover from the original lessee the balance of the rent due under his lease less the rent received from the new lessee. Whether the taking possession of the premises constitutes a rescission of the contract depends upon his intent. . . . By bringing this action for damages for breach of contract the plaintiff has manifested its intention to accept the surrender of the premises, and has acquiesced in the termination of the lease, and the rescission of the contract. Its action is one for damages for the breach by the defendant of his covenant to pay rent.

The arguments and briefs of counsel appear to have proceeded largely upon the assumption that the breach arose out of the repudiation by the defendant of his obligation to pay rent which would accrue in the future and therefore constituted an anticipatory breach, or more accurately, a breach by anticipatory repudiation of his contract. A positive statement to the promisee that the promisor will not perform his contract constitutes an anticipatory repudiation which is a total breach of contract, except in cases of a contract originally unilateral and not conditional on some future performance by the promisee and of a contract originally bilateral that has become unilateral and similarly unconditional by full performance by one party. Amer. Law Institute Restatement, Contracts, Vol. 1, §318. Where the contract was originally unilateral or has become so by the performance of one party, no breach can arise before the time fixed in the contract for some performance. There must be some dependency of performance in order to make anticipatory breach possible. Restatement, op. cit., Comment e. A lease is primarily a conveyance of an interest in land and its execution by the lessor may be said to constitute performance on his part, making the instrument, when considered as a contract, a unilateral agreement with no dependency of performance which would make an anticipatory breach possible. This, we take it, is the basis of the distinction which the defendant claims to exist between a covenant to pay rent in a lease of real estate and an ordinary executory contract.

But the plaintiff is not obliged to rely solely upon the rules controlling a right to recover for an anticipatory breach arising out of the defendant's repudiation of his obligation to pay rent to accrue in the future. The complaint alleges that the rent was payable on the first day of each month in advance, that the defendant moved out on the first day of February, 1935, and thereafter notified the plaintiff that he would pay no further rent. This can only be construed as an allegation of a refusal to pay the rent which had fallen due on that date as well as that to accrue in the future. This constituted a present breach of his covenant to pay rent then due. Granting the defendant's contention that a covenant to pay rent creates no debt until the time stipulated for payment arrives, that time had arrived, so far as the rent due February 1st was concerned, and his failure to pay that rent constituted a breach of the covenants of his lease. The question remains whether this was a total or only a partial breach. If the former, the plaintiff would be entitled to maintain this action to recover the damages alleged in its complaint; if the latter, it would be limited to those resulting from the refusal to pay the rent due on February 1st. Considering a lease as a unilateral contract, or a bilateral contract that has been wholly performed by the lessor, the covenant to pay rent at certain fixed periods is a contract for the payment of money in installments, and the failure to pay any installment of rent as it falls due would constitute a partial breach of the lessee's contract. Restatement, Contracts, Vol. 1, §316. But when such a partial breach is accompanied or followed by a repudiation of the entire contract, the promisee may treat it as a total breach. Restatement, Contracts, Vol. 1, §317, Comment b; Connecticut Annotations, p. 214; 13 C.J., p. 658, §736, and cases cited; 3 Williston, Contracts, §1317; Armsby v. Grays Harbor Commercial Co., 62 Ore. 173, 123 Pac. 32; Peters Grocery Co. v. Collins Bag Co., 142 N.C. 174, 55 S.E. 90. Defendant's failure to pay the rent due on February 1st, considered alone, constituted a breach only of his agreement to pay that particular installment of rent. His subsequent statement to the plaintiff that he would no longer comply with the terms of the lease and would pay no further rent was a repudiation of his entire contract. The breach thereupon became a total one justifying an immediate action by the plaintiff to recover the damages which would naturally follow from such a breach. . . .

There is no error.

In this opinion the other judges concurred.

NOTES AND QUESTIONS

1. Discussion of the case appears in Note, 34 Mich. L. Rev. 430 (1936).

2. "Other items which have been held recoverable by landlords after breach by tenants are taxes which the tenant agreed to pay, the value of improvements which tenant failed to make after agreeing to do so, the cost of removal of tenant's property from the premises, the value of reasonable expenses necessary to get a new tenant, but not the value of extensive alterations made to facilitate re-renting." Id. at 432-433 (footnotes omitted).

3. "It is well settled that the proper measure of damages presently recoverable by a lessor under a lease for years, from the lessee therein, on an abandonment constituting a breach thereof by the lessee, is the *present value* of the difference between the fair rental value, at the time of such breach, of the leased premises for the balance of the unexpired term and the total agreed rent for such unexpired term." Leo v. Pearce Stores Co., 57 F.2d 340, 341 (6th Cir. 1932) (emphasis added).

4. When the tenant's breach occurred, the lease had a remaining term of sixty-seven years. Landlord sued on the theory of Sagamore v. Willcutt.

Held: the trial court did not err in fixing the determinable or predictable period of damages at ten years. Hawkinson v. Johnston, 122 F.2d 724 (8th Cir. 1941), *cert. denied,* 314 U.S. 694 (1941).

> There was competent evidence from which it could be inferred with reasonable certainty or probability that the rental value of the property . . . under community conditions and locational situation for the next ten years could be expected to remain fairly stable.
>
> . . . It will of course generally be argued in a case of this character, as it is here, that any period of definite forecast or certain predictability attempted to be fixed by the trial court is arbitrary and excessive. But the rule for determining the damages in such a situation is no different than in any other case. The damages are not speculative merely because they cannot be computed with mathematical exactness, if under the evidence they are capable of reasonable approximation. Obviously there is not, nor can there be a fixed, uniform period for which damages should be allowed in every case of total breach of a long term lease, but the period for which the damages can be reasonably forecast or soundly predicted in such a situation must depend upon the circumstances and evidence of the particular case. [Id. at 730-731]

5.   *The bankrupt tenant:* in 1978, Congress enacted a substantially revised bankruptcy act overhauling a law that had seen no significant change since 1938. Under the earlier law, the tenant's trustee in bankruptcy might reject an unexpired lease, which would reduce the landlord's claim to the amount of reserved rental, without acceleration, for one year (three years in the case of a corporate reorganization) from the date of the tenant's "surrender," plus unpaid rental prior to surrender. The revised act deals far more extensively with the rights both of landlords and of the tenant's estate. Section 365(a) of the act (all references are to Title 11 of the U.S. Code) allows the trustee to assume or reject any unexpired lease of the tenant debtor. In the event of rejection, the landlord may recover any unpaid rent at the time of the bankruptcy petition as well as the greater of (1) the rent reserved, without acceleration, for one year, or (2) 15 percent of the rent reserved for the unexpired term, not to exceed the rent reserved for three years. Id. at 502. Before the trustee may assume the lease, however, the landlord is entitled to various assurances of future performance. Id. at §365(b).

6.   As counsel for a landlord, draft a lease clause that would obviate the risk of a court not adhering to the Sagamore v. Willcutt rule of anticipatory breach. See, e.g., Oldden v. Tonto Realty Corp., 143 F.2d 916 (2d Cir. 1944).

7.   Given a wide choice of remedies from which she must make an election, how does the landlady decide whether to accept a tenant's surrender (if tendered), to treat the lease as still in force, to relet for the tenant's account, or to sue on the theory of Sagamore Corp. v. Willcutt?

Chapter 7

Concurrent Interests

§7.1 The Joint Tenancy and the Tenancy in Common

Suppose that two individuals, A and B, agree to buy a 1,000-acre farm, each to contribute equally to the purchase price. One necessary decision, usually made before the closing of title, is in whose name and in what form title will be taken. The parties might decide to subdivide the farm into halves (assuming they were of equal value), each party taking title to 500 acres in his own name. Were this their decision, absent further agreement, A would enjoy the exclusive possessory interest in one parcel, B in the other. We would say that each owned his parcel "in severalty."

If A and B would rather continue together, title to the farm might be taken in one of several different ways. The parties might want to operate or subdivide the farm as a business venture and might form a business entity such as a partnership or corporation, which could then take title. If A and B wanted instead to hold the land directly (either for personal or business purposes), they might choose either the joint tenancy or the tenancy in common, so-called concurrent interests. Whatever the form of concurrent interest, we would speak generically of the interested parties as *cotenants*.

What characterizes all concurrent interests is the so-called unity of possession: each cotenant is entitled to possess and enjoy the total parcel, and while it is often not feasible for two persons to utilize the same plot of ground at once, each has a legal right to be there. (This will become clearer when we reach the *Newman* case, page 445, *infra*.) Thus, it would be said of A and B, as cotenants, that each has an undivided one-half interest in the 1,000-acre farm.

a. The Joint Tenant's Right of Survivorship

A cotenant's death is the critical event distinguishing a joint tenancy from a tenancy in common. In the joint tenancy, the surviving cotenant becomes the owner, in severalty, of the *entire* parcel. This right of survivorship ("jus accrescendi")—the salient feature of the joint tenancy—might seem somewhat unusual to modern lawyers, since one cotenant stands to lose his full investment by the accident of prior death. By contrast, when one tenant in common dies, his undivided one-half interest either descends or passes by will, and his heirs or devisees become tenants in common with the surviving cotenant. Problem: A and B are tenants in common. A dies intestate, leaving equal heirs, X, Y, and Z. How is title now held? (As you see, tenancy in common tends to multiply the number of cotenants.)

In feudal law the joint tenancy was greatly preferred to the tenancy in common; for in a system depending heavily upon the rendition of services to lord and master, the fewer the cotenants the easier to account for responsibility.[1] Thus, if a transfer to A and B did not specify the form of cotenancy, feudal law treated A and B as joint tenants. One exception to the presumption of joint tenancy was an inheritance by female heirs, who took a cotenancy estate known as coparcenary. Like the tenancy in common, coparcenary did not carry with it the right of survivorship.

Today, the joint tenancy still has widespread importance: in the ownership of bank accounts;[2] in the ownership of land by husband and wife; in the holding of legal title by coexecutors and cotrustees. But in most other cases where land is held jointly, it is presumed that the cotenants hold as tenants in common, a turnabout from the feudal law.

b.   How to Destroy the Survivorship Right

One thing more about the joint tenancy before you read the next several cases. The right of survivorship is a brittle affair; it is quite easily destroyed: consensually, by agreement among the joint tenants; unilaterally, by the act before his death of a joint tenant; and, in some instances, by the acts of strangers to the joint tenancy.

For example, if A and B, joint tenants, wish to convert their interests into a tenancy in common, they have the power to do so. A simple agreement is enough, or alternatively, A and B might jointly execute a deed naming themselves "tenants in common."

But A need not await B's joinder to convert their joint tenancy. If A wishes to sell or donate his interest to a stranger, X, he may do so, and when the transfer occurs, X joins B, not as a joint tenant but as a tenant in common. Even if X (or A) predeceases B, the latter does not gain, by reason of his cotenancy, the outstanding title. In short, A, by his unilateral act, can destroy B's survivorship right (as well as his own); we speak of this as a severance. But

---

1. Transfer tax avoidance may also have encouraged the preferred status of the joint tenancy.

2. Special statutory rules often govern the interests of cotenants in a joint bank account. See, e.g., N.Y. Banking Law §675 (McKinney 1973).

A must act before his death to convert the joint tenancy. At the instant of his death, A's title inures to the surviving cotenant, and any attempt by A to dispose of his interest by will would be futile.

This power that each joint tenant has to destroy the survivorship right comes from the common-law requirement of the four unities, integral to every joint tenancy. Description of the four unities appears at note 5, page 429, *infra*. The cases generally agree that a mortgage,[3] partition decree, or even executory sales contract will effect a severance. The effect of a lease, given by one cotenant to a stranger, remains somewhat unsettled. The English rule supports a conversion to a tenancy in common; the American rule does not. See, e.g., Tenhet v. Boswell, 18 Cal. 3d 150, 445 P.2d 330, 133 Cal. Rptr. 10 (1976). Can you think of any reason why the giving of a deed and a lease should not produce the same result? See Annot., 64 A.L.R.2d 919 (1959) (exhaustive case presentation); Sevenson and Degnan, Severance of Joint Tenancies, 38 Minn. L. Rev. 466 (1954); see also Estate of Faring, 93 Cal. App. 2d 577, 209 P.2d 642 (1949) (condemnation proceeds retain joint tenancy form).

NOTE PROBLEMS

1.   Suppose that A wishes to convert the joint tenancy unilaterally into a tenancy in common between himself and his fellow cotenant. Can A accomplish this? At common law, if A wished to make *himself* B's tenant-in-common, it was necessary to use a straw man. A had first to destroy B's survivorship right by an inter vivos conveyance to a confederate, X, who could then reconvey his tenancy in common interest to A.[4] Since the old livery of seisin required two parties, so, too, did paper transfers long after the ceremonial event became obsolete.

Quite recently, the California Supreme Court held that joint tenant A could unilaterally sever a joint tenancy without use of a intermediary device. Thus A, shortly before her death, executed a grant deed conveying an undivided one-half interest to herself, and in doing so, successfully terminated a

---

3. See Annot., 67 A.L.R.2d 999 (1959). People v. Nogarr, 164 Cal. App. 2d 591, 330 P.2d 858 (1958), is contrary; there the court reasons from the so-called lien theory of mortgages. Since the mortgage does not transfer legal title, or the right to possession, none of the four unities is destroyed. Apart from possible flaws in the reasoning, what are the practical consequences of a rule that would make it impossible for the lender to enforce its lien against a surviving joint tenant who did not sign the mortgage instrument? Cf. also Mattis, Severance of Joint Tenancies by Mortgages: A Contextual Approach, 1977 S. Ill. U.L.J. 27.

4. This straw man requirement was a throwback to the feudal livery of seisin ceremony that accompanied early transfers of title. The grantor and grantee would stand together upon the land being conveyed. The grantor would hand a symbol of the land, such as a lump of earth or a twig, to the grantee and incant ceremonial words of conveyance: "With this twig I do enfeoff (grant)."

The modern term "straw man" is said to come from the former practice of individuals— usually hangers-on around the county seat—placing straw in their shoes if they would agree to act as conduits.

joint tenancy between herself and her husband, B. Riddle v. Harmon, 102 Cal. App. 3d 524, 162 Cal. Rptr. 530 (1980). Accord: Hendrickson v. Minneapolis Fed. Sav. and Loan Ass'n, 281 Minn. 452, 161 N.W.2d 688 (1968).

2. A, B, and C are joint tenants. A conveys his interest to X. A dies intestate, leaving an heir, AH. How is title now held?

X then dies intestate, leaving an heir, XH. How is title now held?

B then dies intestate, leaving an heir, BH. How is title now held?

C then dies intestate, leaving an heir, CH. How is title now held? Cf. Giles v. Sheridan, 179 Neb. 257, 137 N.W.2d 828 (1965).

3. A and B are joint tenants. A murders B, then commits suicide. Each leaves an heir, AH and BH. How is title now held? Compare Bierbrauer v. Moran, 279 N.Y.S. 176 (App. Div. 1935), with Bradley v. Fox, 7 Ill. 2d 106, 129 N.E.2d 699 (1955), and with Welsh v. James, 408 Ill. 18, 95 N.E.2d 872 (1951). See also Note, Joint Tenant Kills His Co-Tenant: A New Answer to an Old Problem, 1953 Wis. L. Rev. 567.

4. A and B are joint tenants. A and B die together in an airplane crash. Each leaves an heir, AH and BH. How is title now held? See Matter of Strong, 171 Misc. 445, 12 N.Y.S.2d 544 (Sur. Ct. 1939). The Uniform Simultaneous Death Act, which has been widely adopted, provides:

> Where there is no sufficient evidence that two joint tenants or tenants by the entirety have died otherwise than simultaneously the property so held shall be distributed one half as if one had survived and one half as if the other had survived. If there are more than two joint tenants and all of them have so died the property then distributed shall be in the proportion that one bears to the whole number of joint tenants.

See also Note, Estate Planning for the Common Disaster, 38 B.U.L. Rev. 257 (1958).

c. Nature of the Interest Created: Joint Tenancy or Tenancy in Common?

GAGNON v. PRONOVOST

96 N.H. 154, 71 A.2d 747, aff'd on rehearing,
96 N.H. 158, 71 A.2d 750 (1950)

Bill in equity, to remove a cloud on the title to real estate claimed to be owned by the plaintiff. The dispute involves the construction of a warranty deed under seal from Anthony Grady to Jules Letourneau and Georgiana Turgeon which read in part as follows:

> Know All Men By These Presents
> That I, Anthony Grady of Manchester, in the County of Hillsborough and State of New Hampshire, for and in consideration of the sum of One Dollar and

other valuable consideration, to me in hand, before the delivery hereof, well and truly paid by Jules Letourneau and Georgiana Turgeon *and to the survivors of them,* the receipt whereof I do thereby acknowledge, have given granted, bargained, sold, and by these presents do give, grant, bargain, sell, alien, enfeoff, convey and confirm unto the grantees, their heirs and assigns forever.

The italicized words to not appear elsewhere in the body of the deed.

The plaintiff, as the successor in interest of Georgiana Turgeon, who survived Jules Letourneau, claims the deed created a joint tenancy and that she has the title to the whole. The defendants, as the heirs of Jules Letourneau, claim the deed created a tenancy in common and that they have title to an undivided one-half interest therein.

The Presiding Justice decreed the plaintiff to be the owner of the premises described in the deed. . . . The defendants' exceptions to the decree were reserved and transferred by Goodnow, C.J.

LAMPRON, J. This bill in equity to remove a cloud on title presents the question whether a joint tenancy or a tenancy in common was created by the deed. If the former, the plaintiff prevails and the appeal is dismissed; if the latter, the defendants prevail to the extent of an undivided one-half interest in common and the appeal is granted. The controlling statute, R.L. c. 259, §17, provides:

> Tenants in Common. Every conveyance or devise of real estate made to two or more persons shall be construed to create an estate in common and not in joint tenancy, unless it shall be expressed therein that the estate is to be holden by the grantees or devises as joint tenants, or to them and the survivor of them, or unless other words are used clearly expressing an intention to create a joint tenancy.

The purpose of the statute was to require that the intention to create a joint tenancy should be clearly expressed. Laws ed. 1830, p. 110; Stilphen v. Stilphen, 65 N.H. 126, 138, 23 A. 79. The use of the phrase "and to the survivors of them" in the clause of the deed which recites the consideration and names the grantees is too sketchy and speculative to comply with the statutory requirement of a clear expression to create a joint tenancy. In no other clause of the deed are there words which suggest any estate other than a tenancy in common. It is difficult to believe that the quoted phrase can qualify as an expression that the estate is "to be holden . . . (to thé grantees) and the survivor of them." At most it was an obscure and inaccurate use of the statutory language and consequently insufficient to come within the statute.

While we are not bound by technical common law rules of construction, . . . we are not committed to a rule that may discourage the use of accurate and clear expressions in legal instruments. The phrase used in this case and its location in the deed is more indicative of lack of comprehension on the part of the draftsman as to the effect of the words used than it is indicative of an intent and purpose to create a joint tenancy. The deed created a tenancy in common and the order must be

Exceptions sustained.

JOHNSTON, C.J., and KENISON, J., dissented; the others concurred.

KENISON, J. (dissenting). The quoted statute as construed in this state is not a legislative expression of hostility to the creation of joint tenancies for "the purpose of the statute is not to forbid or prevent the creation of estates in joint tenancy, but to make certain that effect is given to the intention of the grantor." . . . If a joint tenancy is intended, it will be so construed even though it is contrary to common law rules of construction. . . . "It has been many years since the technicalities of real estate conveyancing have been much regarded here." Newmarket Mfg. Co. v. Nottingham, 86 N.H. 321, 324, 168 A. 892, 895.

Upon analysis it appears that the statute provides three ways to create a joint tenancy. The first method is an express statement in the deed that the grantees shall take as joint tenant. The second method calls for express statement of the grantees "and the survivor of them." The third method is the use of any other words "clearly expressing an intention to create a joint tenancy." The deed in question is not within the first and third methods enumerated above. The question remains whether it is a substantial compliance with the second.

There is considerable authority for the proposition that the use of the word "survivor" or "survivors" in deeds and wills is sufficient to negative the statutory presumption of a tenancy in common. . . . "There is no substantial difference between deeding or devising land to two persons, and the survivor of them, and deeding or devising land to two persons to be held in joint tenancy." 4 Thompson, Real Property, Perm. Ed. §1790. In Massachusetts, which has a statute similar to ours, it appears that words of survivorship in the singular or the plural will create a joint tenancy in the absence of other limiting or qualifying phrases. . . .

It may be conceded that the deed in dispute is not a model form to create a joint tenancy and that the notary public who prepared it was not a model draftsman. That is not fatal, however, if it can be fairly said that the intent was expressed in reasonably clear terms. "If the intent to create a right of survivorship is expressed, it is to be given effect." Burns v. Nolette, 83 N.H. 489, 496, 144 A. 848, 852, 67 A.L.R. 1051. The defendants argue that there can be no "survivors" of two grantees and that this is not the singular use of the word provided by the statute. We are content with the construction placed upon the word by the Trial Court as a substantial compliance with the statutes. "The law has outgrown its primitive stage of formalism when the principal word was the sovereign talisman, and every slip was fatal." Cardozo, J., Wood v. Lucy Lady Duff-Gordon, 222 N.Y. 88, 118 N.E. 214. It is a well established rule in this state in considering written instruments and pleadings that their expressed intent will be enforced even though inarticulately worded. . . .

Objection is made that the words of survivorship do not appear in other parts of the deed and are therefore ineffective. The relative weight to be given words appearing in different sections of the deed as developed at common law has never been followed in this jurisdiction. The intent of the grantor is to be gathered from all parts of the deed without resorting to presumption of law in determining their effect. It is finally suggested that the construction placed upon this deed discourages clearness of expression and the better forms of conveying. This argument has been considered many times in the last half a century but it has not been considered as important as the principle of carrying out of the expressed intent of written documents regardless of the method of their expression. Lawyers and judges sometimes have difficulty when they attempt to make a fortress out of the dictionary and we should impose no higher standards upon the layman. . . .

JOHNSTON, C.J., concurs in this opinion. . . .

NOTES AND QUESTIONS

1. Do Justices Lampron and Kenison view differently the statute's purpose? If so, is conflict between them unavoidable?

2. The modern presumption in favor of the tenancy in common, except for some instances noted *infra,* has become universal, in many states by statute, in the remaining states by court decision. What policy factors underlie today's presumption?

To overcome the presumption requires a fairly strong showing that a joint tenancy was intended. Ordinarily, a conveyance "to A and B, jointly" is not enough. See, e.g., Montgomery v. Clarkson, 585 S.W.2d 483 (Mo. 1979); contra: Householter v. Householter, 160 Kan. 614, 164 P.2d 101 (1945). See also Riggs v. Snell, 186 Kan. 355, 350 P.2d 54 (1960), *rehearing denied,* 186 Kan. 725, 352 P.2d 1056 (1960), where the court refused to find a joint tenancy created by a deed "to A and B, or to the survivor of either" because other language in the deed read: "the said parties of the second part, their heirs and assigns." But cf. Germaine v. Delaine, 294 Ala. 443, 318 So. 2d 681 (1975) ("to A & B, jointly, as tenants in common and to the survivor thereof"; held: joint tenancy created).

Suppose that the word "jointly" appears in an instrument that a layman has prepared. Does this strengthen or weaken the argument for a joint tenancy? Compare Overheiser v. Lackey, 207 N.Y. 229, 100 N.E. 738 (1913), with Kurpiel v. Kurpiel, 50 Misc. 2d 604, 271 N.Y.S.2d 114 (Sup. Ct. 1966). For an even wilder example, see Walter v. Ham, 68 A.D. 381, 75 N.Y.S. 185 (2d Dept. 1902), where the disputed clause read "to A and B, as joint tenants and tenants in common." The court held that a joint tenancy had been created, finding the necessary intent largely in the fact that the draftsman was an experienced (?) lawyer!

For a general discussion and collection of cases, see Annot., 46 A.L.R.2d 519 (1956).

3.　The presumption against joint tenancies does not apply to grantees who are husband and wife, coexecutors, or cotrustees; and in a disputed case, a survivorship interest is usually the result. 4 Thompson, Real Property §1782 (1961 ed.). What policy factors underlie these exceptions?

4.　Hines, Real Property Joint Tenancies: Law, Fact, and Fancy, 51 Iowa L. Rev. 582 (1966), is an excellent example of empirical research. The author examined the land records in five well-scattered Iowa counties to determine the distribution of sole and concurrent ownership, and the breakdown in concurrent ownership between tenancies in common and joint tenancies in common and joint tenancies (Iowa does not recognize the tenancy by the entirety, *infra*). Other variables that were tabulated included the relationship, if any, of concurrent owners; the location of the property—urban vs. rural; and the value of the property.

The findings reveal that the usage of joint tenancy rose sharply after 1933 and leveled off in the late 1950s. The following figures represent joint tenancy as a percentage of all transfers for the years examined. (Hines at 586, 607.)

1864	0%	1944	31%
1914	0.25%	1946	35%
1933	0.25%	1950	42%
1938	6%	1954	46%
1940	10%	1959	53%
1942	13%	1964	51%

If transfers to corporate and fiduciary grantees are excluded, the prevalence of joint tenancy is even more impressive. (Hines at 608.)

	1954	*1959*	*1964*	*Overall*
Total Transfers	2902	2995	3266	9163
Joint tenancy	49.0%	58.3%	57.4%	55.1%
Sole	41.0	31.4	31.9	34.6
Ambiguous[5]	9.5	9.5	9.3	9.5
Tenancy in common	0.5	0.8	1.4	0.9

The proportion of urban joint tenancies (58.3 percent) for the years 1954, 1959, and 1964 greatly exceeded the proportion of farm joint tenancies (37.9 percent) (Hines at 610); also, the larger the farm, the less likely a joint tenancy (ibid.).

The most significant findings concern the relationship of concurrent grantees. (Hines at 617.)

---

5. If nothing was said concerning the form of ownership, or if the deed provisions were unclear, the cotenancy was classed as ambiguous.

	Joint Tenancy	Ambiguous	Tenancy in Common
Total Transfers	5045	867	83
Husband and Wife	98.4%	68.4%	75.9%
Related	1.1	20.9	15.7
Unrelated	0.4	10.7	8.4

Hines also speculates (at 587-591) as to what has caused the resurgence of the joint tenancy.

Query: suppose that the grantees in *Gagnon* were husband and wife. Is there any way that the lawyer for plaintiff could use the Hines data?

5.   The deed reads: "to A, unmarried, and B and C, his wife, as joint tenants and not as tenants in common." What is A's interest? See Fulton v. Katsowney, 342 Mass. 503, 174 N.E.2d 366 (1961).

d.   **Nature of the Interest Created: Tenancy in Common During Joint Lives with Indestructible Right of Survivorship**

HASS v. HASS

248 Wis. 212, 21 N.W.2d 398 (1945), motions for rehearing denied, 248 Wis. 224a, 22 N.W.2d 151 (1946)

[This action was commenced on January 25, 1945, by Walter H. Hass, administrator of the estate of Bertha Hass, deceased, Walter H. Hass, Erna Haehlke, and Lavine Hass Krause and Gerald Hass, minors, by Leona Saeger, their guardian ad litem, plaintiffs, against Herbert W. Hass, Julius Hass, and Arnold Hass, defendants, to see aside a deed given by Bertha Hass to herself and Herbert W. Hass, dated February 8, 1944, and for a construction thereof. The court dismissed the first cause of action on the merits and rendered judgment construing the deed which was entered July 6, 1945. The defendant, Herbert W. Hass, appeals from that part of the judgment construing the deed. Other facts will be stated in the opinion.]

ROSENBERRY, C.J. The facts may be briefly stated as follows: On February 8, 1944, Bertha Hass, an elderly widow, was the owner of a one-hundred-twenty-acre farm and the personal property thereon. Her son, Herbert, was about thirty-seven years of age and had lived and worked on the farm all his life. Mrs. Hass had previously made a will bequeathing and devising the property to Herbert. During the winter of 1943-1944 she was in poor health and fearful that the son Walter might cause trouble, she asked her son Arnold to procure someone to draw a deed so that she could deed the farm to Herbert in such a way that it would be his after her death but would be hers in case Herbert should predecease her. After the execution of the deed in question the will was destroyed.

The deed was prepared on a printed form bearing across its top the label "Warranty Deed To Husband and Wife as Joint Tenants." The scrivener who drafted the instrument had been an abstractor and real-estate broker for more than twenty-five years but was not an attorney at law. The appropriate blanks, the description, the names of the parties to the instrument, and the recitation thereon below the description were all written in longhand by the scrivener in pen and ink. In the deed Bertha Hass, widow, was described as the party of the first part. The parties of the second part were described as— "Bertha Hass and Herbert W. Hass of Marathon county, mother and son, and the survivor of them in his or her own right."

The granting clause provided that the said party of the first part for a consideration, gives, grants, etc.,—"unto the said parties of the second part, a life estate as joint tenants during their joint lives and an absolute fee forever in the remainder to the survivor of them, his or her heirs and assigns, in and to the following-described real estate [description]."

After the description is the following:

"The purpose of this conveyance is to vest the title to the above-described property in the grantees herein named as joint tenants and none other." . . .

The law relating to the creation of joint tenancies was modified by sec. 230.45 (2) and (3), Stats., ch. 437, Laws of 1933, which provides:

> (2) Any deed from husband to wife or from wife to husband which conveys an interest in the grantor's lands and by its terms evinces an intent on the part of the grantor to create a joint tenancy between grantor and grantee shall be held and construed to create such joint tenancy, and any husband and wife who are grantor and grantee in any such deed heretofore given shall hold the premises described in such deed as joint tenants.
> (3) Any deed to two or more grantees which, by the method of describing such grantees or by the language of the granting or habendum clause therein evinces an intent to create a joint tenancy in grantees shall be held and construed to create such joint tenancy.

The trial court was of the view that if the deed in question had been given by a husband to his wife or by a wife to her husband, it would have created a joint tenancy in the husband and wife, but this only because of the express language contained in sub. (2), but that the parties to this deed not being husband and wife, only sub. (3) applies.

The court was further of the view that if the language of sub. (3) was broad enough to include a deed from an owner to himself and another as joint tenants, sub. (2) would be meaningless. The court further said:

> I do not think that it was the intent of this deed to create a mere life estate [in the grantor], as we think of the creating of a life estate.[6] It is true that they

---

6. Query: who made this argument, and why?—ED.

used language in here which is language that is customarily used, or at least is properly used, in creating a joint tenancy, but I don't think it was the intent of this instrument, "Exhibit A," to reserve a life estate merely, to the grantor, Bertha Hass. I think it was her clear intent that she should get this property in the event her son should die ahead of her. The express language written in pen and ink is as follows: "The purpose of this conveyance is to vest title to the above-described property in the grantees herein as joint tenants and none other." . . .

We agree with the trial court that sub. (3) does not apply but that does not dispose of the case. We have set out the material parts of the conveyance and while no doubt it was the intent of the scrivener to draft an instrument which would create a joint tenancy as between the mother and her son, the fact that the instrument as drawn did not accomplish that purpose does not make it void and the trial court so held. In the granting clause the following language is employed: The mother granted—"unto the said parties of the second part, a life estate as joint tenants during their joint lives and an absolute fee forever in the remainder to the survivor of them, his or her heirs and assigns, in and to the following-described real estate [description]."

Inasmuch as the conveyance was not effective to convey any interest or estate from the grantor to herself, the effective part of the conveyance is that which relates to the grant to the son. We can reach no other conclusion from the language employed than that the instrument created in the parties a tenancy in common for their joint lives and conveyed an estate in fee to the son if he survived his mother. If he predeceased his mother, his death terminated his interest in the estate. In that event the condition upon which the remainder was to pass to him could not happen and the entire title to the property would be in the grantor.

It is clear from the language of the deed that the conveyance was intended to create a tenancy for the joint lives of the parties with the remainder in the survivor. That it created a tenancy in common rather than a joint tenancy is also beyond question. We see no reason why this type of survivorship may not be created by deed. It has one advantage over the right of survivorship incident to joint tenancy, it cannot be destroyed by the act of one of the parties. A conveyance by one joint tenant of his interest in the property destroys the right of survivorship. . . .

In this case a joint tenancy was not created during the joint lives for the reason that the unities of time and title were absent. The result was there was a tenancy in common during their joint lives with the survivor to take the remainder in fee. . . .

By the Court. That part of the judgment appealed from is reversed on the defendant's appeal . . . with directions to the lower court to enter judgment adjudging the defendant to be the sole owner of real property in fee and the owner of the personal property described in the deed. . . .

ROSENBERRY, C.J. (on motion for rehearing). The defendants [*sic*] [7] have made a motion for rehearing in this case which appears to be based upon a misconception of what the court decided. Counsel say:

> We feel that the court has created a legal oddity and has so unsettled the rules of tenancies as known by the bar in this state that the decision, if allowed to stand, will produce much unnecessary litigation. It, therefore, seems important not only to our clients but also to the court, the bar in general, and the public at large, that the court again examine into this matter before letting this decision become final. . . .
>
> The court has created a tenancy in common with right of survivorship, although the court found the intent was to create a joint tenancy, and even though this court has always been committed to the doctrine that the only estate having the right of survivorship is a joint tenancy.

The term "survivorship" is used mainly in three classes of cases: (1) Those involving joint tenancy, an incident of which is the right of survivorship, where the instrument creating the joint tenancy "evinces an intention to create a joint tenancy in the grantees." In this class of cases survivorship is dependent upon the nature of the tenancy.

(2) Estates by the entirety which are abolished by the laws of this state. In this class of cases survivorship is dependent upon the status of the parties as it can exist only where the grantees are husband and wife. [Cf. §7.2, *infra*.]

(3) Cases where a surviving tenant in common by virtue of the express terms of the instrument creating the tenancy takes the remainder. This species of survivorship is referred to in the opinion as a type. Perhaps it would be more accurate to say that such an instrument creates an indestructible remainder rather than a type of survivorship. In this class the right of the survivor to take the remainder does not depend upon the nature of the tenancies or the status of the parties, but upon the express provisions of the instrument creating the remainder. The case under consideration falls in the third class.

With this explanation it ought to be perfectly clear that the court has done no violence to existing law.

BY THE COURT. Motion denied with $25 costs.

NOTES AND QUESTIONS

1. See also Holbrook v. Holbrook, 240 Or. 567, 403 P.2d 12 (1965) (concurrent life estates with contingent remainders in the life tenants, the remainder to vest in the survivor, will result from attempt to create joint tenancy

---

7. Even Chief Judges err! The plaintiffs sought the rehearing, according to the motion papers on file with the clerk of the court.—ED.

after statute abolishes it). The *Hass* case is commented upon in Notes: 1947 Wis. L. Rev. 117 (best of the lot), 30 Marq. L. Rev. 182 (1946), 44 Mich. L. Rev. 1144 (1946), 23 Notre Dame Law. 103 (1947).

2. The Wisconsin legislature acted promptly after the *Hass* decision to amend §230.45(3) to read:

> Any deed to two or more grantees, including any deed in which the grantor is also one of the grantees, which by the method of describing such grantees or by the language of the granting or habendum clause herein evinces an intent to create a joint tenancy in grantees shall be held and construed to create such joint tenancy. [Wis. Stat. Ann. §230.45(3) (1957)]

Having amended §230.45(3), should the legislature also have repealed §230.45(2)? For the possibility that §230.45(2) may have an unexpected force of its own, suppose that A now makes a conveyance to B "as joint tenant with A." What is the nature of the estate created?

If the legislature has acted to remove a common-law anachronism, should the courts read the curative statute narrowly, or construe it liberally so as to advance the legislature's apparent goal?

3. What language would you, as a draftsman, use to create an indestructible survivorship right in a cotenancy? If a grantor wants to create a cotenancy with right of survivorship, what factors should she weigh in choosing between a destructible and indestructible right? Should courts indiscriminately allow parties to create an indestructible right of survivorship?

4. Why was it necessary, at common law, to use two pieces of paper to achieve what Bertha Hass tried (and failed) to achieve with one? For Bertha could have averted the issues raised in this suit had she transferred her land to a third person who would then have granted it "to Bertha and her son, Herbert, as joint tenants." This "stranger" to the title, whose only service is to execute a conveyance satisfying the four unities, *infra*, is the straw man (see p. 419 *supra*). In choosing a straw man, what precautions must the landowner take? For what other purposes might a straw man be used today? See Cook, Straw Men in Real Estate Transactions, 25 Wash. U.L.Q. 232 (1940); Note, The Use of Straw Men in Massachusetts Real Estate Transactions, 44 B.U.L. Rev. 187 (1964).

5. The four unities, which the common law required of a joint tenancy, are detailed by Blackstone in the following passage. Since generations of lawyers cut their legal teeth on Blackstone, no present-day law students should escape entirely the chance to sample what law study must once have been like. Therefore, place yourselves in the early nineteenth century, light the candles, take a deep breath, and read on.

PROPERTIES OF JOINT ESTATE—The properties of a joint estate are derived from its unity, which is fourfold; the unity of interest, the unity of title, the unity of time, and the unity of possession: or, in other words, joint tenants have one and the same interest, accruing by one and the same convey-ance, commencing at one and the same time, and held by one and the same undivided possession.

UNITY OF INTEREST—First, they must have one and the same inter-est. One joint tenant cannot be entitled to one period of duration or quantity of interest in lands, and the other to a different; one cannot be tenant for life, and the other for years: one cannot be tenant in fee, and the other in tail. If land be limited to A and B for their lives, this makes them joint tenants of the freehold; if to A and B and their heirs, it makes them joint tenants of the inheritance. If land be granted to A and B for their lives, and to the heirs of A; here A and B are joint tenants of the freehold during their respective lives, and A has the remainder of the fee in severalty: or, if land be given to A and B, and the heirs of the body of A; here both have a joint estate for life, and A hath a several remainder in tail.

UNITY OF TITLE—Secondly, joint tenants must also have a unity of title: their estate must be created by one and the same act, whether legal or illegal; as by one and the same grant, or by one and the same diseisin. Joint tenancy cannot arise by descent or act of law; but merely by purchase, or acqui-sition by the act of the party: and, unless that act be one and the same, the two tenants would have different titles; and if they had different titles, one might prove good, and the other bad, which would absolutely destroy the jointure.

UNITY OF TIME—Thirdly, there must also be a unity of time: their estates must be vested at one and the same period, as well as by one and the same title. As in case of a present estate made to A and B; or a remainder in fee to A and B after a particular estate; in either case B and A are joint tenants of this present estate, or this vested remainder. But if, after a lease for life, the remainder be limited to the heirs of A and B; and during the continuance of the particular estate A dies, which vests the remainder of one moiety in his heirs; and then B dies, whereby the other moiety becomes vested in the heir of B; now A's heir and B's heir are not joint tenants of this remainder, but tenants in common; for one moiety vested at one time, and the other moiety vested at another. . . .

UNITY OF POSSESSION—Lastly, in joint tenancy, there must be a unity of possession. Joint tenants are said to be seised by the half and by all; that is, they each of them have the entire possession, as well of every parcel as of the whole. They have not, one of them a seisin of one-half, and the other of the other half; neither can one be exclusively seised of one acre, and his companion of another; but each as an undivided part of the whole. [Blackstone, Commentaries 230-231 (Ehrlich ed. 1959)]

If you have read Note 1, page 419 supra, you should understand why a conveyance from A "to A and B, as joint tenants," would not satisfy the unities of title and time, even though A and B *qua* "joint tenants" seem to acquire their estate in the same grant (unity of title), and at the same time (unity of time).

6. The Wisconsin Supreme Court faced a similar case three years after its decision in Hass v. Hass. In 1942, Emil A. Moe executed a deed to his 168-acre farm naming as joint tenants himself and his sister, Emma Moe. Emma predeceased her brother and, before long, Emil and his sister's heirs were

disputing ownership of the farm. Relying heavily on the *Hass* decision, Emil argued for a survivorship interest even if the 1942 conveyance failed to create a common-law joint tenancy. The trial court, also relying on *Hass,* agreed. In reversing the judgment, the supreme court excoriated the court below:

> The trial court made a so-called first alternative conclusion that if the deed did not create a joint tenancy it created a tenancy in common during the lives of Emil A. Moe and Emma Moe, and that under such deed Emil A. Moe succeeded to the entire title in fee simple upon the death of Emma Moe. Just how the trial court arrived at this conclusion we are not informed. It appears to be a tour de force to make a survivorship an incident to a tenancy in common. It is considered that the court had no such power. [Moe v. Krupke, 255 Wis. 33, 40-41, 37 N.W.2d 865, 868 (1949)]

The author of the opinion? Rosenberry, C.J.

To distinguish its earlier decision, the court stressed that the Hass deed had contained the words "and an absolute fee forever in the remainder to the survivor, etc.," while no such words appeared in the Moe deed. But, how is this phrase relevant except as further evidence that the grantor intended to create a survivorship interest? Having stated this intention once by describing the grantees as "joint tenants," why should Moe's case collapse because he did not say it again?

Emma Moe was not exactly a gratuitous grantee. In consideration for the cotenancy interest, Emma had released a $10,000 mortgage that she held against her brother's farm. The court noted that Emma's rights as mortgagee were more valuable than her rights as a tenant in common. On what theory might this evidence be admissible?

7. Many states have followed the Wisconsin example, Note 2, *supra,* and have legislated away the need for a straw man. See, e.g., N.Y. Real Prop. Law. §240-b (1980); Cal. Civ. Code §683 (1980); Ill. Rev. Stat. c. 76, §2.1 (1966). Some courts have not awaited a statute to reject the straw man anachronism. See, e.g., Miller v Riegler, 243 Ark. 251, 419 S.W.2d 599 (1967); Switzer v. Pratt, 237 Iowa 788, 23 N.W.2d 837 (1946); Lipps v. Crowe, 28 N.J. Super. 131, 100 A.2d 361 (1953); Colson v. Baker, 42 Misc. 407, 87 N.Y.S. 238 (Kings County Ct. 1904) (a compelling opinion); Annot., 44 A.L.R.2d 595, 605-608 (1955) (cases collected).

When should the courts discard a shopworn common-law principle rather than await legislative action? The opposing views are sharply stated in the following extracts:

> It is essential that titles and estates in land be definite and certain. It is not a field in which the court should undertake to establish that it is liberal and modernistic in keeping pace with changing conditions. The creation of hybrid estates unknown to the common law is to be deplored. It can only bring about uncertainty, confusion and want of stability in estates and their attributes. Carried to an absurd conclusion, there would eventually be as many different kinds

of estates as there are tracts of land. The plan duty of this court is in the opposite direction. Many states have made changes by legislative action and this is entirely proper. Other states have made such changes by judicial fiat which have resulted in all the varied and conflicting decisions cited in the dissent. I submit that it is the obligation of this court to adhere to the landmarks of the common law [requirements of four unities] on this subject until we are directed by competent authority to deviate therefrom. [Stuehm v. Mikulski, 139 Neb. 374, 409-410, 297 N.W. 595, 603 (1941) (concurring opinion)]

In the absence of a contrary public policy or prohibitory legislation express or implied, it is the rule in this State that the expressed intention of the grantor will override, whenever possible, purely formalistic objections to real estate conveyancing based on shadowy, subtle and arbitrary distinctions and niceties of the feudal common law. . . . "It is revolting to have no better reason for a rule of law than that so it was laid down in the time of Henry IV. It is still revolting if the grounds upon which it was laid down have vanished long since, and the rule simply persists from blind imitation of the past." Holmes, Collected Legal Papers (1920) 187. [Therrien v. Therrien, 94 N.H. 66, 67, 46 A.2d 538, 539 (1946)]

What if the legislature has considered the "nicety" and has failed to act?

8. Where a statute purports to overturn the existing case law, how would it affect a prior grant from A "to A and B, as joint tenants"? See, e.g., Anson v. Murphy, 149 Neb. 716, 32 N.W.2d 271 (1948); Moe v. Krupke, *supra.*

§7.2 The Tenancy by the Entirety

In less than half the states and the District of Columbia,[8] a husband and wife may jointly acquire real property as "tenants by the entirety." Closely related to the joint tenancy, the tenancy by the entirety also features a right of survivorship (in the decedent's spouse) and is sometimes subject to the four unities test.[9] What distinguishes the tenancy by the entirety is the far greater durabil-

---

8. One treatise regards the tenancy by the entirety as having real importance in not more than twenty-two states: Alaska, Arkansas, Delaware, Florida, Indiana, Kentucky, Maryland, Massachusetts, Michigan, Missouri, New Jersey, New York, North Carolina, Oklahoma, Oregon, Pennsylvania, Rhode Island, Tennessee, Vermont, Virginia, Wisconsin, and Wyoming. 4A Powell, Real Property ¶621 n.7 (Rohan ed. 1977). Hawaii also recognizes the entirety. Sawada v. Endo, 57 Haw. 608, 561 P.2d 1291 (1977).

9. Thus, a conveyance from H "to H and W, as tenants by the entirety" might not realize the grantor's goal. See, e.g., Pegg v. Pegg, 165 Mich. 228, 130 N.W. 617 (1911); In re Walker's Estate, 340 Pa. 13, 16 A.2d 38 (1940).

Some courts, while adhering to the four unities test, have found a way to get around its application for husband and wife. See, e.g., the statement of Judge Collin, in Matter of Klatzl, 216 N.Y. 83, 94, 110 N.E. 181 (1915): "The husband did not convey to himself, but to a legal unity

ity of its survivorship right. You have seen how easily one joint tenant, prior to death, can sever the joint tenancy. In comparison, neither husband nor wife, as tenant by the entirety, may unilaterally deprive his/her spouse of the benefit of survival. Only the marriage's end or the spouses' combined action will destroy the survivorship right.

(Problem: H and W are tenants by the entirety. H deeds his interest to X. W does not join in the deed. H predeceases W, leaving a sole heir, HH. How is the title now held? Assume instead that W predeceases H, leaving a sole heir, WH. How is the title now held? See King v. Greene, *infra*.)

At early common law, a conveyance to husband and wife was presumptively a tenancy by the entirety, for the reason that husband and wife were "but one person in the law." Littleton, Tenures §291 (Wambaugh ed. 1903). Although its theoretical basis is gone, this presumption remains in most states recognizing the entirety. Hoag v. Hoag, 213 Mass. 50, 99 N.E. 521 (1912), is an extreme example: "To H and W, . . . as joint tenants in joint tenancy . . ."; held: tenancy by the entirety created. Why do you suppose the presumption persists? What societal values, if any, does the entirety serve?

a. Notes on the Creation and Termination of Tenancy by the Entirety

1. The grantees must be husband and wife when the entirety estate is created, and even if they subsequently intermarry, an entirety will not arise nunc pro tunc. Hiles v. Fisher, 144 N.Y. 306, 39 N.E. 337 (1895). The deed need not recite that the grantees are husband and wife so long as the intent to create an entirety is clear. Parol evidence is later admissible to establish the parties' intermarriage at the time of the conveyance. Dowling v. Salliotte, 83 Mich. 131, 47 N.W. 225 (1890). Parol evidence is equally admissible to rebut a statement of intermarriage appearing in the deed. Kent v. O'Neil, 53 So. 2d 779 (Fla. 1951).

A troublesome issue has been the treatment of an attempted entirety where the prerequisite marriage did not exist. Most courts have treated the parties as tenants in common, see, e.g., Collins v. Norris, 314 Mich. 145, 22 N.W.2d 249 (1946), yet this result disregards the parties' implied or stated preference for a survivorship right. Since the issue usually arises after one party has died, the survivor loses a half interest in favor of the decedent's creditors or heirs—the deserved fruit, some might say, of having pretended to be what one was not. Alternatively, the same court has sometimes found a joint tenancy, see, e.g., Jackson City Bank & Trust Co. v. Frederick, 271 Mich. 538, 260 N.W. 908 (1935). See also Kepner, Effect of Attempted Creation of Estate by Entirety in Unmarried Grantees, 6 Rutgers L. Rev. 550 (1952).

---

or entity which was the consolidation of himself and another." Although the judge wrote this in a dissenting opinion, the court of appeals (in a stunning circumlocution) later adopted it as the rule of the case. Boehringer v. Schmid, 254 N.Y. 355, 173 N.E. 220 (1930).

2. A final decree of divorce terminates the interspousal unity and with it the tenancy by the entirety. Millar v. Millar, 200 Md. 14, 87 A.2d 838 (1952); Bernatarvicius v. Bernatarvicius, 259 Mass. 486, 156 N.E. 685 (1927). Unless the decree makes other provision, the parties hold thereafter as tenants in common, ibid. Cf. Corder v. Corder, 546 S.W.2d 798 (Mo. Ct. App. 1977).

But the District of Columbia, by statute, recognizes an entirety in property even after divorce if the divorced couple held the property by the entirety during marriage and agreed prior to divorce to continue this form of ownership afterwards. What policy might support this statute? Cf. Benson v. United States, 442 F.2d 1221 (D.C. Cir. 1971).

Many lawyers can recall instances of de facto separations involving a couple who would not cooperate in the management of an entirety parcel. Neither could sell or mortgage the premises without the other's consent; sometimes the other was nowhere to be found. Yet partition [10] seemed technically impossible as long as the marriage continued. In this instance, should not an equity court exercise its power to order partition? Compare Tendrick v. Tendrick, 193 F.2d 368 (D.C. App. 1951) (partition embodied in a decree of separation).

3. H and W are tenants by the entirety. The real estate is sold and the sales proceeds are placed in a joint bank account. Does the entirety continue? Compare Hawthorne v. Hawthorne, 13 N.Y.2d 82, 192 N.E.2d 20 (1963) (no entirety in fire insurance proceeds after entirety property destroyed) with Est. of Siegel, 350 So. 2d 89 (Fla. Dist. Ct. App. 1977) (entirety in purchase money mortgage held by sellers after entirety property sold).

4. H and W are tenants by the entirety. H deliberately sets fire to the real estate. W is an innocent party. The insurance company refuses to pay either spouse; it argues that each spouse has a joint obligation to preserve the property and if either spouse violates such duty, breach is chargeable to both spouses. Convincing? Compare Rockingham Mutual Insurance Co. v. Hummel, 250 S.E.2d 774, 219 Va. 803 (1979) (spouse denied recovery) with Steigler v. Insurance Company North America, 384 A.2d 398 (Del. 1978) (spouse granted recovery).

b. Creditor's Rights in Tenancy by the Entirety

H, an uninsured motorist, causes an automobile accident that results in a recovery against him of $25,000. C, the injured party, establishes that H has only one asset—a $100,000 home that he owns with W, his wife, as a tenant by the entirety. What difficulties confront C in attempting to satisfy his $25,000 judgment?

---

10. Partition, to be more fully treated *infra*, page 443 is the property's conversion from a cotenancy into shares held in severalty (partition in kind), or the property's public sale and the division of the sale proceeds into separate shares (partition by sale). Partition by sale always requires a court decree, and partition in kind usually does.

KING v. GREENE

30 N.J. 395, 153 A.2d 49 (1959)

BURLING, J. This is an action seeking possession of lands, damages for mesne profits [11] and a declaration that a mortgage encumbrance held by defendant Margaretta P. W. Harrison is a nullity and directing its discharge of record. The Superior Court, Law Division, hearing the matter on stipulated facts, granted plaintiff's motion for summary judgment. Defendants appealed, and while pending and prior to argument in the Appellate Division, we certified the cause on our motion. After argument in this court, we directed that the cause be reargued and requested that the New Jersey Title Insurance Association appear as amicus curiae.

The following facts are stipulated: In 1913 plaintiff, Marie King, acquired the title to three lots on Patterson Avenue in the Borough of Shrewsbury, New Jersey. In 1931 her husband, Philip King, brought an action against her in the Court of Chancery which resulted in a decree being entered that plaintiff owed him $1225. It was further ordered that plaintiff execute a conveyance of the three lots to herself and her husband as tenants by the entirety. While the conveyance was never made, the decree was recorded, the self-operative effect which was to make Marie and Philip King become seized of the premises as tenants by the entirety. R.S. 2:29-61 (now N.J.S. 2a: 16-7, N.J.S.A.).

In 1932 execution was issued to satisfy the 1931 money judgment and a sheriff's deed was made to John V. Crowell of all plaintiff's right, title and interest in the property. In 1933 Philip King conveyed his right, title and interest in the three lots to Martin Van Buren Smock. John V. Crowell and his wife joined in the deed to Smock, conveying their interest acquired by virtue of the sheriff's deed. Philip King died in 1938. In 1946 Smock conveyed his interest to defendants Joseph and Mabel Greene.

In 1957 plaintiff, as surviving spouse of Philip King, instituted the present action for possession, contending that she is the sole owner of the property and that the 1932 sheriff's deed conveyed only one-half the rents, issues and profits of the property during the joint lives of the spouses and did not convey her right of survivorship. She alleges that when her husband died in 1938 the life estate for the joint lives of the spouses terminated and she became entitled to the fee. Defendants' contention is that the sheriff's deed conveyed plaintiff's right of survivorship as well as a life interest.

The trial court concluded that the sheriff's deed did not include the right of survivorship and entered a summary judgment for plaintiff which declared that she is the present holder of a fee simple in the premises; that a mortgage upon the premises held by defendant Margaretta Harrison and given by the defendants Joseph and Mabel Greene is discharged; that defendants John and Elaine Cusick, the Greenes' tenants, must vacate the premises and the plaintiff

---

11. The rental value, i.e., the value of the use and occupation of land.—ED.

is entitled to mesne profits for six years prior to the commencement of this action.

The question at issue is whether the purchaser at an execution sale under a judgment entered against the wife in a tenancy by the entirety acquires the wife's right of survivorship. . . .

Involved are two fundamental problems: (A) the nature of an estate by the entirety at common law, and (B) the effect upon the estate by the entirety of the Married Women's Act (L. 1852, p. 407, now R.S. 37:2-12 et seq., N.J.S.A.)

A—ESTATES BY THE ENTIRETY AT COMMON LAW

At the outset we note that the industry of counsel and our own independent research have failed to reveal any English case decided prior to 1776, touching upon the question of whether a voluntary or involuntary conveyance of a husband's interest in a tenancy by the entirety carries with it his right of survivorship.

The unique form of concurrent ownership at common law, labeled estates by the entirety, may be traced into antiquity at least as far back as the 14th and 15th Centuries. 3 Holdsworth, History of the English Law (3d ed. 1923), 128; Kepner, "The Effect of an Attempted Creation of an Estate by the Entirety in Unmarried Grantees," 6 Rutgers L. Rev. 550 (1952). The estate was unique because of the common-law concept of unity of husband and wife and the positing of that unity in the person of the husband during coverture. Putnam, "The Theory of Estates by the Entirety," 4 Southern L. Rev. 91 (1879). A husband and wife cannot hold by moieties or in severalty, said Littleton, "and the cause is, for that the husband and wife are but one person in law. . . ." Coke on Littleton, sec. 29. Blackstone, in his judicial capacity noted: "This estate [entirety] differs from joint-tenancy, because joint-tenants take by moieties, and are each seised of an undivided moiety of the whole, per my et per tout, which draws after it the incident of survivorship or jus accrescendi, unless either party chooses in his life-time to sever the jointure. But husband and wife, being considered in law as one person, they cannot, during the coverture take separate estates; and therefore upon a purchase made by them both, they cannot be seised by moieties, but both and each has the entirety. . . . they are seised per tout and not per my." Green v. King, 2 Wm. Blackstone 1211, 1214, 96 Eng. Rep. 713, 714 (C.P. 1777). To the same effect see the opinion of Chancellor Kent in Rogers v. Benson, 5 Johns. Ch. 431 (N.Y. 1821).

The unity of the spouses theory was early recognized in New Jersey as the foundation upon which estates by the entirety rested. Den ex dem. Hardenbergh v. Hardenbergh, 10 N.J.L. 42 (Sup. Ct. 1828).

By virtue of the jus mariti and jure uxoris [12] the husband was the domi-

---

12. See §8.1, *infra.*—ED.

nant figure in the marital unity. Thus, in an estate by the entirety the husband had absolute dominion and control over the property during the joint lives. The husband was entitled to the rents, issues and profits during the joint lives of himself and his wife, with the right to use and alienate the property as he desired, and the property was subject to execution for his debts. Washburn v. Burns, 34 N.J.L. 18 (Sup. Ct. 1869) (it should be noted that although *Washburn* was decided after the Married Women's Act, the court overlooked the effect of the act and decided the case on common-law principles); Freeman, Co-Tenancy and Partition (2d ed. 1888) 140; 2 American Law of Property, §6.6 p. 28 (1952); Phipps, "Tenancy by Entireties," 25 Temple L.Q. 24, 25 (1951). As stated by the court in Washburn v. Burns, *supra*:

> . . . [T]he husband has an interest which does not flow from the unity of the estate, and in which the wife has no concern. He is entitled to the use and possession of the property during the joint lives of himself and wife. During this period the wife has no interest in or control over the property. It is no invasion of her rights, therefore, for him to dispose of it at his pleasure. The limit of this right of the husband is, that he cannot do any act to the prejudice of the ulterior rights of his wife. (34 N.J.L. at page 20).

The remaining question is, could the husband unilaterally alienate his right of survivorship at common law? Our study of the authorities convinces us that he could. The entire thrust of the authorities on the common law, with one notable exception, is to the effect that the only distinction between a joint tenancy and a tenancy by the entirety at common law was that survivorship could not be affected by unilateral action in the latter estate.

It was settled in England as early as the 14th Century that the husband could not defeat the wife's right of survivorship. In that case, reported in 2 Coke on Littleton, sec. 291, William Ocle was found guilty of treason (he murdered Edward II) and his estate was forfeited. Edward III granted the forfeited lands (owned jointly with his wife) to someone else. It was held that the husband's act of treason could not deprive the wife of her right of survivorship. Back v. Andrew, 2 Vern. 120 (1690), stands for the same proposition. But to say that the husband cannot by his voluntary or involuntary act defeat the wife's right of survivorship is not to say that his own right of survivorship, subject to wife's right of survivorship, should he predecease her, cannot be alienated. . . .

No prejudice would result to the wife's interest at common law by the husband's alienation of his right of survivorship. If he predeceased her, she would take a fee. If she predeceased him, her interests were cut off anyway. During his lifetime she had no interest in the estate. . . .

Most courts and commentators have taken the position that at common law the husband's right of survivorship was alienable, so that the purchaser or grantee would take the entire fee in the event the wife predeceased the husband and the interest was subject to execution for his debts. [Citations omitted.]

It is our view [also] that the husband could, at common law, alienate his right of survivorship, or, more properly, his fee simple subject to defeasance. . . .

B—Effect of the Married Women's Act of 1852 (L. 1852, p. 407, Now R.S. 37:2-12 et seq., N.J.S.A.) Upon Estates by the Entirety

R.S. 37:2-12, N.J.S.A. provides:

"The real and personal property of a woman which she owns at the time of her marriage, and the real and personal property, and rents, issues and profits thereof, of a married woman, which she receives or obtains in any manner whatsoever after her marriage, shall be her separate property as if she were a feme sole."

At least nine jurisdictions took the view that the Married Women's Act, having destroyed the spousal unity, destroyed the foundation upon which estates by the entirety rested, and therefore such concurrent ownership could no longer arise. Phipps, *supra*, 25 Temple L.Q., at pp. 28-29. This was the view originally taken in New Jersey, Kip v. Kip, 33 N.J. Eq. 213 (Ch. 1880), and was the view taken by the lower court in Rosenblath v. Buttlar, 7 N.J.L.J. 143 (Ch. 1884). It might be noted that presently tenancy by the entirety does not exist in 29 states. Phipps, *supra*, 25 Temple L.Q., at p. 32. In the absence of legislation abolishing or altering estates by the entirety, our role, in light of the settled precedent that they do exist in New Jersey, is merely to define their incidents.

The Court of Errors and Appeals in Buttlar v. Rosenblath, 42 N.J. Eq. 651, 9 A. 695 (E. & A. 1887), settled the question of the effect of the Married Women's Act upon estates by the entirety. After holding that the act does not destroy the estate, it was held that the effect and purpose of the act was to put the wife on a par with the husband. It was held:

> There is nothing in the married woman's act which indicates an intention to exclude this estate wholly from its operation. I think, therefore, that the just construction of this legislation, and the one in harmony with its spirit and general purpose, is that the wife is endowed with the capacity, during the joint lives, to hold in her possession, as a single female, one-half of the estate in common with her husband, and that the right of survivorship still exists as at common law. (42 N.J. Eq., at page 657, 9 A at page 698.)

Subsequent decisions have confirmed that presently husband and wife, by virtue of the Married Women's Act, hold as tenants in common for their joint lives; that survivorship exists as at common law and is indestructible by unilateral action; and that the rights of each spouse in the estate are alienable,

voluntarily or involuntarily, the purchaser becoming a tenant in common with
the remaining spouse for the joint lives of the husband and wife. [Citations
omitted.]

It is clear that the Married Women's Act created an equality between
the spouses in New Jersey, insofar as tenancies by the entirety are concerned.
If, as we have previously concluded, the husband could alienate his right of
survivorship at common law, the wife, by virtue of the act, can alienate her
right of survivorship. And it follows, that if the wife takes equal rights with the
husband in the estate, she must take equal disabilities. Such are the dictates of
complete equality. Thus, the judgment creditors of either spouse may levy and
execute upon their separate rights of survivorship. . . .

It might be argued that the involuntary sale of right of survivorship will
not bring a fair price. However, the creditor [under a prior decision] can
receive a one-half interest in the life estate for the joint lives. It seems to us that
if this interest were coupled with the debtor-spouse's right of survivorship the
whole would command a substantially higher price and the creditor may
thereby realize some present satisfaction out of the debtor-spouse's assets.

Moreover, to hold that a sheriff's deed does not pass the debtor-spouse's
right of survivorship compels the creditor to maintain a constant vigilance
over the estate. This is particularly true where the purchaser at execution sale
of the debtor-spouse's life interest is someone other than the judgment creditor.[13] There is, in short, no compelling policy reason why a judgment creditor
should be inordinately delayed, or, in some instances completely deprived of
his right to satisfaction out of the debtor-spouse's assets.

The judgment appealed from is reversed and the cause is remanded for
the entry of a judgment in accordance with the views expressed in this opinion.

For reversal: JUSTICES BURLING, JACOBS, FRANCIS, PROCTOR, and SCHET-
TINO—5.

For affirmance: CHIEF JUSTICE WEINTRAUB and JUSTICE HALL—2.

WEINTRAUB, C.J. (dissenting). The estate by the entirety is a remnant of
other times. It rests upon the fiction of a oneness of husband and wife. Neither
owns a separate, distinct interest in the fee; rather each and both as an entity
own the entire interest. Neither takes anything by survivorship; there is nothing to pass because the survivor always had the entirety. To me the conception
is quite incomprehensible. The inherent incongruity permeates the problem
before use.

Presumably the estate by the entirety was designed to serve a social
purpose favorable to the parties to the marriage. We are asked to recognize
incidents more compatible with present thinking. Specifically, we are asked to
subject a spouse's interest in the *fee* to execution sale. I am not sure that I can
identify just what is being sold. In theory there is no right of survivorship;
nothing accrues on death. And during coverture neither spouse has a separate

---

13. Why is that?—ED.

interest in the fee. Whatever the nature of the "fee" interest a purchaser receives, he can to nothing with it except wait and hope. What he buys is the chance that the non-debtor spouse will expire before the judgment debtor.

I do not seriously urge such academic difficulties; indeed, one cannot confidently make deductions from a premise that is fictional. My objection is a practical one, to wit, that so long as we adhere to the concept of an estate by the entirety, an execution sale will result in the sacrifice of economic interests. Since the purchaser at the sale does not acquire a one-half interest in the fee with a right to partition the fee, the execution sale can be but a gambling event, yielding virtually nothing to the debtor, or for that matter to the creditor either unless he is the successful wagerer at the sale and in the waiting game to follow.

I concede that earlier decisions recognizing a right to sell the *life interest* of the debtor presented the same problem in theory, but the practical consequences were negligible. I think it has been the general experience of the bar that judgments obtained against a spouse have not been followed by execution sales of the life interest. And in bankruptcy proceedings the interest of the debtor regularly has been sold for a nominal sum to the other spouse or a representative of both. The general assumption, I believe, has been that the fee was not involved; and the life interest for one reason or another was not regarded by outsiders as sufficiently attractive. But if the purchaser at an execution or bankruptcy sale may one day reap the harvest of a full title, there will be an invitation to speculators.

If public policy demands that a creditor's interest be respected (I have no quarrel with the thought), the basis should be just to both the creditor and the debtor. It cannot be unless what is offered for sale is a non-contingent, non-speculative one-half interest which would support a partition suit. In that setting, bidders would know what is being sold and the sale could yield a fair price. An equitable solution can be achieved only by a statute abolishing the estate by the entirety in favor of a joint tenancy, or at least entitling the purchaser at an involuntary sale to have partition. In my judgment, a halfway approach will prove unjust. It will appreciably turn against the husband and wife a fictional concept that doubtless was originated for their benefit. . . .

The impact upon the free movement of property in the market-place may also be noted. In effect, the purchaser at the involuntary sale becomes a member of the entity for title purposes. In the hands of a husband and wife, property will be sold when the common economic interests of the family will be furthered. But when the power to alienate the whole is divided between a spouse and a stranger with unrelated economic motivations, property will not be moved unless those diverse interests can come to terms. Neither can compel a sale. In practical effect, there is a new restraint upon alienability to the disservice of the public interest.

I accordingly vote to affirm.

HALL, J. (dissenting). . . .

NOTES AND QUESTIONS

1. Discussion of King v. Greene appears in Notes: 73 Harv. L. Rev. 792 (1960), 58 Mich. L. Rev. 601 (1960), 14 Rutgers L. Rev. 457 (1960), 5 Vill. L. Rev. 154 (1959).

2. Nowhere is the law in wilder disarray than in the handling of creditors' claims against entirety assets. The New Jersey rule is followed in Alaska, Arkansas, New York, and Oregon. Its disadvantages are well stated by Chief Justice Weintraub's dissenting opinion in King v. Greene.

In Massachusetts prior to 1980, the Married Women's Property Act had left the tenancy by the entirety essentially untouched. Courts there had ruled consistently that a statute protective of the *separate* rights of married women did not alter the spousal "unity" of the estate by the entirety. Translated, this view created quite a disparity between the creditors of husband and wife. A husband's creditor could levy execution against the entire property for the duration of the marriage, and if the husband survived, the purchaser at the execution sale would acquire absolute title.[14] Raptes v. Pappas, 259 Mass. 37, 155 N.E. 787 (1927). By contrast, the wife's creditor could not, during the marriage, subject any interest in the property to attachment, levy, and sale. Licker v. Gluskin, 256 Mass. 403, 164 N.E. 613 (1929).

No other state in recent years followed the "Massachusetts rule," which lost much of its force statutorily in 1979. Mass. Ann. Laws, ch. 209. §1 (1981). The Bay State, as to the *principal residence*[15] of the nondebtor spouse, now takes the majority lead, next paragraph *infra*.

Most states do not permit the separate creditor of husband or wife to reach any part of the entirety during coverture. The underlying rationale is that neither spouse has a divisible interest in the property (it is owned by the marital unity), and that because of the Married Women's Property Acts neither spouse alone can receive the income and profits of, nor alone transfer any interest in, the property. To permit the creditor of the debtor-spouse to reach his/her interest would interfere with the right of the other spouse to full enjoyment.

More so than does either the "late" Massachusetts or New Jersey rule, this majority rule sets forth a logical interaction between the common-law tenancy by the entirety and the Married Women's Property Acts but, while protective of husband and wife, unduly deprives their separate creditors.[16] This

---

14. One writer had likened the husband's interest to a determinable fee simple. Huber, Creditors' Rights in Tenancies by the Entireties, 1 B.C. Ind. & Com. L. Rev. 197, 200 (1960).

15. It remains uncertain whether the husband-wife dichotomy continues to govern other forms of real property. If so, is this impermissible, gender-based discrimination? Who would have standing to raise this issue: the wife's creditors, the wife, or the husband? Cf. Friedman v. Harold, 638 F.2d 262 (1st Cir. 1981).

16. The recent Massachusetts statute excepts "debts incurred on account of necessaries furnished to either spouse or to a member of either family." With respect to such debts, the creditor of either spouse may levy against all of the entirety property. Mass. Ann. Laws, ch. 209, §1 (1981).

logic carried beyond its ultimate conclusion has denied creditors not only access to income and principal but also power to levy execution against the debtor's right of survivorship. Thus (except for Tennessee and Kentucky among this group of majority states), the debtor and spouse may join in a conveyance of entirety assets completely free of the creditor's lien. For an elaborate state-by-state comparison, see Phipps, Tenancy by Entireties, 25 Temple L.Q. 24, 46-57 (1951).

3.   To test your understanding of the several rules, consider the following: H and W own as tenants by the entirety a two-family dwelling worth $100,000. They occupy one unit and rent out the other unit for $500 monthly. (The units are of equal value.) X obtains a judgment against H for $20,000, and levies execution against H's interest in the real estate. What price might P bid at the execution sale if the combined expectancy of H and W is 10 years and if H has a 40 percent chance of surviving W? In Florida (majority rule)? In New Jersey? In Tennessee? Should P consider whether H and W are happily married?

4.   After reviewing the present situation, one author concluded:

> The retention of the tenancy by the entirety has resulted, except in a few states, in a partial or nearly total exemption of the property from the claims of creditors. Is this a desirable social and legal result? The only apparent direct benefit is that the marital community is assured of some available resources for support. The state is thus pro tanto free of the obligation to support an indigent family. This may be particularly important to the wife who thus has an assured amount of property on her husband's death. In a broader sense, the exemption reflects a policy favoring the preservation of property interests over commercial use of property as a base for credit or as an article of commerce itself. But even if it is granted that these policies are sound, does the exemption of the tenancy from the claims of creditors accomplish the desired results? It is believed not. Any amount of property may be put into this form of holding, free from creditors' claims although its value well exceeds any reasonable amounts necessary for support. While, of course, many persons may be aware of the benefit of this type of ownership and act accordingly, many others having a greater need for protection will not be so guided. Thus there can be no assurance of equality of treatment since much depends upon whether the spouses were sufficiently foresighted to take property in this form. As to the elimination of property so held as a base for commercial credit, the general effect of many such ownerships in a state will be to reduce credit and hence limit commercial activity.
>
> Are there means readily available by which the valid portion of the policies favoring restrictions on creditors' rights in property held by a marital community may be effectuated while avoiding excessive restrictions on their rights? ... Those states retaining the tenancy by the entirety but permitting creditors of each spouse to reach his half possessory interest and his right of survivorship have at least partly solved the problem. There the non-debtor-spouse's interest is protected while the debtor-spouse is still able to use his interest in the estate as a base for credit. But the rule of these states is unsatisfactory in other respects: the non-debtor-spouse's exempt interest is not limited in amount or value; the appli-

cation of the exemption depends upon the accident of the form of ownership rather than upon any direct social policy of preserving some exempt marital assets; the debtor-spouse is not protected at all if he is the survivor and as such the one who requires some protection from the claims of his creditors.

The social policy favoring protection of the marital community from creditors can best be obtained by the use of devices other than the tenancy by the entirety. The tenancy no longer serves a useful social function and the legal consequences of its use are, in many cases, difficult to justify. It should be abolished. Protection of the marital community could be more readily assured by other existing although presently somewhat inadequate devices. Homestead and personal property exemption statutes, modernized as to content and values, should provide protection for the marital community during its existence. Upon its termination by death, the widow and possibly the widower should be given priority over creditors in the assets of the estate, up to a reasonable support value determined in part by other assets available to the survivor, the number of dependents, and the earning capacity of the survivors. . . . It is believed that with appropriate legislation drawn with particular attention to these and other special problems better protection could be afforded the surviving members of the family of the decedent without undue prejudice to the just claims of creditors and the needs of the commercial community. [Huber, Creditors' Rights in Tenancies by the Entireties, 1 B.C. Ind. & Com. L. Rev. 197, 205-207 (1960)]

5.   Consider a state having the King v. Greene rule if the entirety asset is a couple's one-family residence. The husband's interest is levied against and sold at judgment sale. Is the purchaser entitled, during the husband's lifetime, to share the premises with the debtor's wife? Faced with this question, a New York court ruled that the purchaser was entitled to a shared possession, if he wanted this. The purchaser, Arnold Lover, preferred the value of such possession. Lover v. Fennell, 14 Misc. 2d 874, 879, 179 N.Y.S.2d 1017, 1022 (Sup. Ct. 1958). Compare also Matter of Berlin v. Herbert, 48 Misc. 2d 393, 265 N.Y.S.2d 25 (Dist. Ct. 1965); Newman v. Chase, page 445, *infra*.

§7.3   The Cotenant's Rights, Duties, and Liabilities

a.   Partition

Suppose that cotenants A and B have a falling-out and can no longer agree as to the use or management of the common property. They might agree to disagree and voluntarily divide the assets so that each thereafter owns his share in severalty. Alternatively, but less likely, they might themselves sell the assets and divide the sales proceeds. But if they cannot dissolve their cotenancy by joint action, either cotenant may sue for partition and obtain a decree ending the cotenancy.

The device of partition dates from the thirteenth century, originating in disputes among coparceners. By 1540, the remedy was extended to joint tenants and tenants in common, but to this day, partition remains unavailable to tenants by the entirety. In the United States, every state has a partition statute which sets out the procedure for obtaining this remedy. See, e.g. Cal. Civ. Proc. Code §§752 et seq. (West 1955); N.Y. Real Prop. Acts. Law §§901 et seq. (McKinney 1963).

The court may order either division in kind or a public sale and division of the sales proceeds. Division in kind was at one time the only mode of partition; thus if A and B owned 100 acres of farmland as cotenants, the court would divide the farm into two parts, each representing the value of A and B's cotenancy interest. To this day, partition in kind is said to be preferred over partition by sale, and statutes regularly pay lip service to that preference. [17] But the realities of real estate development in a nonrural society usually make it unfeasible to divide improved property in kind, so that forced sale usually results from a partition suit.

Although the right to partition (more precisely, a privilege) adheres to every joint tenancy and tenancy in common, cotenants by agreement may restrict their right, and if the restraint is not perpetual or unreasonably long, courts generally will allow the restraint. See Annot., 37 A.L.R. 3d 962 (1971). Typical of this restraint is the *statutory* bar against partition of the common area of a condominium while the property remains subject to the condominium regime. But a restraint otherwise valid may be set aside when circumstances between the parties have so changed as to make enforcement unduly harsh. See, e.g., Michalski v. Michalski, 50 N.J. Super. 454, 142 A.2d 645 (1958) (suit for partition between estranged husband and wife, tenants in common). And, conversely, equity has occasionally (but rarely) refused to allow partition "in the interest of justice." See Newman v. Chase, *infra.*

b. Possession and the Duty to Account

The unity of possession entitles each cotenant to occupy and enjoy the common property. The rule at common law would allow A to enjoy the property free of any duty to account for its value to cotenant B, unless B objected to A's possession and wished to use the property himself. In an agrarian society, this rule made good sense, for it encouraged the productive use of land (which might otherwise be damaged by neglect); furthermore, disputes

---

17. "Sale if partition cannot be made.

"If the court shall find that the land or any portion thereof is so situated that partition cannot be made without greater prejudice to the owners, it may order the sheriff to sell the premises so situated at public auction. . . ." Wis. Stat. §276.20 (1958).

Note that the Wisconsin statute (as do others) treats partition synonymously with division in kind, and public sale as a different remedy—a throwback to partition's earliest form.

over use or management could readily be resolved by partition in kind. Present-day difficulties arise, however, where the jointly held asset does not submit to shared possession by the two cotenants. Consider, for example, the following case involving a one-family house, in which the husband's entirety interest was acquired at a bankruptcy sale.

NEWMAN v. CHASE
70 N.J. 254, 359 A.2d 474 (1976)

MOUNTAIN, J. Plaintiff, Howard C. Newman, purchased from the trustee in bankruptcy of defendant, Arthur D. Chase, all of the latter's interest in certain property owned by Chase and his wife, Dorothy A. Chase, as tenants by the entirety. Mrs. Chase is also a defendant in this action. The property is the home of the defendants. Plaintiff seeks partition of the estate for the joint lives of Mr. and Mrs. Chase, of which he is now tenant in common with Mrs. Chase. The trial court, on the authority of the Appellate Division's treatment of a parallel situation in Silver Bay Homes v. Herrmann, 128 N.J. Super. 114, 319 A.2d 243 (App. Div. 1974) granted the relief sought, ordering a partition sale of the estate for the joint lives of the defendants, husband and wife. . . .

For the reason hereinafter set forth we now reverse

The facts of the case are not in dispute. Defendants, Arthur and Dorothy Chase, took title as tenants by the entirety to a one-family house in Toms River, in November 1971, having obtained a mortgage for the full purchase price of $25,990 from the Lincoln Savings Bank. With their two small children, they have occupied the home since January 5, 1973. Defendant, Arthur D. Chase filed a petition in bankruptcy on October 2, 1972, and was discharged in bankruptcy on February 5, 1973. On November 20, 1972, plaintiff purchased from the trustee in bankruptcy all Mr. Chase's interest in the premises for a consideration of $1,000, and thereupon received a trustee's deed. Mrs. Chase, with her family, continued to occupy the property, denying access to Mr. Newman. Consequently, on October 22, 1974, Newman instituted this partition action, seeking in addition an accounting from Mrs. Chase for one-half the rental value of the premises from January 5, 1973. On motion for summary judgment, the trial court found for plaintiff and ordered a partition sale of the tenancy in common for the joint lives of Mr. and Mrs. Chase, specifying that the sale would not affect in any way rights of survivorship. A stay of the order was granted pending this appeal. . . .

Since the decision in King v. Greene, 30 N.J. 395, 153 A.2d 49 (1959) it has been the law of this State that the purchaser at an execution sale under a judgment entered against a tenant by the entirety acquires the right of survivorship of the debtor spouse as well as the interest of the latter in the life estate for the joint lives of husband and wife. This statement rests upon the assumption that the levy under the judgment and the ensuing sale purport to reach and include all of the right, title and interest of the debtor spouse. The purchaser from a trustee in bankruptcy, such as the plaintiff here, acquires the same interest in the real estate of the bankrupt spouse as does the purchaser at judicial sale mentioned above. 11 U.S.C.A. §110; In Re Ved Elva, Inc., 260 F. Supp. 978 (D.N.J. 1966). Hence Mr. Newman, at the time he instituted this action, had succeeded to both Mr. Chase's interest as tenant in common for the joint lives of Mr. and Mrs. Chase, and also the interest of which Mr. Chase would come into full possession and enjoyment should he survive his wife. It is solely as owner of the former interest that plaintiff here seeks relief by way of partition.

It is conceded that there may be no partition with respect to lands held by spouses as tenants by the entirety. [Citations omitted.]

It is equally well settled that as between or among tenants in common partition may normally be had as of course. [Citations omitted.]

As we have said, plaintiff and defendant, Dorothy A. Chase, are now tenants in common of the estate for the joint lives of Arthur and Dorothy Chase. Yet despite their being tenants in common of this estate, we think that here the remedy of partition should not be available as a matter of right. . . .

Partition is . . . an ancient head of equity jurisdiction, an inherent power of the court independent of statutory grant. 4 Pomeroy, Equity Jurisprudence §§1387-90 (5th ed. 1941). [Other citations omitted.]

In the exercise of this power our courts of equity have not hesitated to exercise discretion as to the particular manner in which partition is effected between the parties.

> It is an established principle that a court of equity, in decreeing partition, does not act ministerially and in obedience to the call of those who have a right to the partition, but founds itself on its general jurisdiction as a court of equity, and administers its relief ex aequo et bono, according to its own notions of general justice and equity between the parties. [Woolston v. Pullen, 88 N.J. Eq. 35, 40, 102 A. 461, 462 (Ch. 1917)] [Other citations omitted.]

No case in this state has hitherto gone so far as to deny absolutely the right of partition to a petitioning cotenant, at least in the absence of a prior agreement not to partition. Yglesias v. Dewey, 60 N.J. Eq. 62, 47 A. 59 (Ch. 1900); cf. Michalski v. Michalski, 50 N.J. Super. at 462-63, 142 A.2d 645. In other jurisdictions, however, courts have allowed equitable defenses to be raised to defeat relief by way of partition. In Craig v. Maher, 158 Or. 40, 74 P.2d 396 (1937), for instance, the petitioning cotenant was a lawyer who had acquired a one-fifteenth interest in real property as a consideration for professional services. The court found that partition, whether in kind or by sale, would be unduly prejudicial to the defendant, and granted instead a monetary award. Many jurisdictions have adopted a similar rule with respect to cotenants of minerals in place, including oil and gas rights. With respect to such interests one court said

[A] court of equity is vested with sufficient discretion in awarding or denying relief [by way of partition] to prevent the remedy from becoming an instrument of fraud or oppression. [Shell Oil Co. v. Seeligson, 231 F.2d 14, 17 (10th Cir. 1955)]

See also Sadler v. Public Nat. Bank & Trust Co., 172 F.2d 870, 876 (10th Cir. 1949); Holland v. Shaffer, 162 Kan. 474, 178 P.2d 235, 173 A.L.R. 845 (1947).

In the case of partition sought by a transferee of the interest of one spouse in the family home, considerations of policy persuade us that a court should be permitted to exercise its equitable discretion in deciding whether or not to allow the remedy. While the original reason for the peculiar characteristics of a tenancy by the entirety was no doubt the common-law concept of the unity of husband and wife, 2 American Law of Property, §6.6, the fact that the Legislature has preserved these characteristics indicates that they continue to serve the ends of public policy. In Sanders v. Sanders, 118 N.J. Super. 327, 330, 287 A.2d 464, 466 (Ch. Div. 1972), the court characterized a tenancy by the entirety as

[A] protection of the parties to a marriage as security to both spouses during coverture of marital assets that were the work products of their marital economic life and the additional security to the surviving spouse upon the termination of their union by death of the other.

See also Ten Eyck v. Walsh, 139 N.J. Eq. 533, 540, 52 A.2d 445 (Prerog. Ct. 1947).

In effect, the special treatment of tenancies by the entirety in New Jersey serves the purposes which are achieved in many states by statutory or constittutional homestead laws. See Haskins, Homestead Exemptions, 63 Harv. L. Rev. 1289 (1950). Just as the homestead exemptions effect a balance between two competing social policies—on the one hand, that a debtor's assets should be available to his creditors; on the other, that the family of a debtor should not become a charge upon the state—so can an equitable treatment of the rights of a purchaser of one spouse's interest in a tenancy by the entirety serve to achieve a similar balance.

The life interest in residential real property for the joint lives of two spouses is a speculative asset, lively to bring only a low price and hence to be of little avail to a creditor seeking satisfaction of a spouse's debt. This consideration alone might not operate to deny to a purchaser the right of partition, especially as it has long been held that life estates are partible. Buckis v. Townsend, 100 N.J. Eq. 374, 136 A. 432 (Ch. 1927). But when the creditor's interest in the dwelling is weighed against that of the debtor's family, equitable principles persuade us that the creditor should not, as of right, be granted such minimal relief at the cost of dispossessing the family of its home.

We do not go so far as to hold that a purchaser at an execution sale or from a receiver or trustee in bankruptcy may never be entitled to partition. There is no limit to the value of real property which can be held by husband and wife as tenants by the entirety. Were partition to be automatically denied, there might well be situations in which a debtor would thus be afforded "opportunity to sequester substantial assets from just liabilities." Way v. Root, 174 Mich. 418, 140 N.W. 577, 579 (1913). But where, as in the present case, a bankrupt husband lives with his young family in a modest home, we hold that it is within the equitable discretion of the court to deny partition to a purchaser of the husband's interest, leaving the creditor to resort to some other remedy.

Nevertheless, despite the equities in favor of defendants, plaintiff has, after all, legitimately succeeded to Mr. Chase's interest in the property. While in this case we hold that policy considerations preclude partition either in kind or by sale, plaintiff is nonetheless entitled to the alternative equitable remedy of an accounting from his cotennat, Mrs. Chase. Lohmann v. Lohmann, 50 N.J. Super. 37, 141 A.2d 84 (App. Div. 1958); Nobile v. Bartletta, 109 N.J. Eq. 119, 156 A. 483 (E. & A. 1931); Neubeck v. Neubeck, 94 N.J. Eq. 167, 119 A. 26 (E. & A. 1922); O'Connell v. O'Connell, 93 N.J. Eq. 603, 117 A. 634 (E. & A. 1922); Bilder v. Robinson, 73 N.J. Eq. 169, 67 A. 828 (Ch. 1907).

The cited cases involve for the most part commercial properties with respect to which rents paid by third parties were collected by the cotenant in possession. It is settled law in New Jersey that in such circumstances the cotenants out of possession are entitled to an accounting for their share of the rents, issues and profis. Lohmann v. Lohmann, *supra,* and cases there cited. With respect to the residential property involved in this case, the situation is different. The only benefit inuring to the tenant in possession is the value of her use and occupation of the property—in effect, the imputed rental value of the house. A a general rule, since each cotenant has an undivided interest in the whole estate, each is entitled to occupy the entire property. Thus, absent ouster of the other cotenants, a cotenant in possession is not required to account to them for the value of use and occupation. Baird v. Moore, 50 N.J. Super. 156, 166-68, 141 A.2d 324 (App. Div. 1958); Mastbaum v. Mastbaum, 126 N.J. Eq 366, 9 A.2d 51 (Ch. 1939). We think, however, that where one cotenant, with her family, remains in possession of a one-family house which is not susceptible of joint occupancy, and refuses to accede to plaintiff's demands for access to the property, such conduct clearly constitutes an ouster. Mastbaum v. Mastbaum, *supra;* Maxwell v. Eckert, 109 A. 730 (Ch. 1920); Rowden v. Murphy, 20 A. 379 (Ch. 1890); Edsall v. Merrill, 37 N.J. Eq. 114 (Ch. 1883). Mrs. Chase is thus accountable to Mr. Newman for one-half the imputed rental value of the house.

This conclusion does not end the calculation, however, for the property is encumbered by a mortgage the principal amount of which was $24,150.98 on January 1, 1973. Mrs. Chase asserts that since then she has been making mortgage, tax, and insurance payments and undertaking necessary repairs to the house. Absent ouster, a cotenant in possession is entitled to contribution from cotenants out of possession for payments made to preserve the common property; see the discussion of the development of this doctrine by Judge Conford in Baird v. Moore, *supra,* 50 N.J. Super. at 165-66, 141 A.2d 324. When, as here, there has been an ouster but the ousted cotenant receives an accounting based on the value of the use and occupation by the cotenant in possession, equity requires that appropriate payments made by the cotenant in possession be credited in calculating what is due the cotenant out of possession.

Plaintiff in his prayer for partition included a demand for one-half the rental value of the premises dating from January 5, 1973, when defendants first occupied the property. To this he is entitled. This sum, subject to an offset, pro rata, for appropriate payments made by Mrs. Chase, will be included in the final judgment.

The judgment of the trial court is reversed and the cause is remanded to it for further proceedings not inconsistent with this opinion.

SULLIVAN, J. (concurring and dissenting). In Mueller v. Mueller, 95 N.J. Super. 244, 248, 230 A.2d 534, 536 (App. Div. 1967), I noted that the estate of tenancy by the entirety "spawns numerous title problems and disputes." This is but another example. I agree that plaintiff is not entitled to partition. However, although I recognize that it follows established case law, I disagree with that part of the majority decision which holds that plaintiff has a present possessory interest in the homestead property as a tenant in common with the other spouse during the coverture and is entitled to an accounting of that spouse's possession.

We are here concerned with the family homestead owned by the husband and wife as tenants by the entirety. Each, and both as an entity, own the entire interest. Each, and both, are entitled to the entire possession. While the husband and wife are considered tenants in common during their joint lives, this is solely by virtue of their being married to each other

A purchaser at a bankruptcy sale, even though the interest of the debtor spouse is purchased, cannot step into the spouse's shoes as a tenant in common with the other spouse. That smacks of the bankruptcy sale reaching into the marital union itself.

I would hold that the bankruptcy sale purchaser of a debtor-spouse's interest in the marital homestead owned by the entirety does not acquire a present possessory interest in such property as a tenant in common with the other spouse and is not entitled to an accounting from the other spouse of that spouse's possession during the coverture.

Should the debtor-spouse survive the other spouse, the purchaser would then become the owner of the property. If the marriage is terminated by divorce, the purchaser would then own an undivided one-half interest in the property as a tenant in common. He is entitled to no more.

PASHMAN, J. (concurring in part and dissenting in part). I concur in the result reached by the majority with respect to plaintiff's request for partition of the Chase family home. I must dissent, however, from that part of the majority opinion which provides plaintiff with a right to an accounting as a tenant in common in this property during the joint lives of Mr. and Mrs. Chase.

The right to an accounting, like the action for partition, is essentially an equitable remedy. [Citations omitted.] Consequently, the same equitable considerations which warrant the denial of a partition in this case must also be measured against the necessity for an accounting. An assessment of these factors impels me to conclude that *both* partition and accounting should be denied. Plaintiff should retain only the possibility of a fee simple interest (the so-called "right of survivorship") subject to defeasance should Mrs. Chase survive her husband. . . .

Protection of the marital home when a family has suffered financial reversals, as in the present case, is throughly consistent with federal bankruptcy principles which extend a "fresh start" in life to honest but unfortunate debtors and their families. [Citations omitted.] Requiring Mrs. Chase to make an accounting in this case would contradict the "fresh start" sought by her husband through the bankruptcy proceedings. Mrs. Chase, though not a party to the bankruptcy proceedings, would be directly and unfairly subject to its "penalties." Moreover, the imposition of this additional burden on the family might result in dispossession of the family, forcing it to become a "charge upon the state" and thereby defeating one of the salient purposes of this tenancy. Finally, there is something offensive about an outside bidder at a bankruptcy sale intruding upon the privacy of a marital home and obtaining a substantial right for an inordinately low bid. In this respect, I join with my Brother Sullivan who observes that the accounting ordered by the Court today "smacks of the bankruptcy sale reaching into the marital union itself." As a matter of equity, I would not permit it. . . .

NOTES AND QUESTIONS

1. "It is settled law . . . that [with respect to rents paid by third parties collected by the cotenant in possession], the cotenants out of possession are entitled to an accounting." [Newman v. Chase, p. 445, *supra*.]

Prior to the Statute of Anne, 4 & 5 Anne, c. 16, §27 (1705), the law was otherwise. Unless he had agreed to account, cotenant A could lease the premises to X, and keep all of the rents collected prior to the time that cotenant B might demand his share. With enactment of the statute, A's duty to account begins upon the making of the lease. Is it any more unfair to let A pocket without accounting the rents paid by third persons than enjoy without accounting the premises himself?

Most states have adopted statutes similar to the Statute of Anne, or have treated it as part of the received law.

2. The facts in Seesholts v. Beers, 270 So. 2d 434 (Fla. Dist. Ct. App. 1972) were these. In 1969, Charles and Elizabeth were divorced. The decree converted the tenancy by the entirety in their former marital home into a tenancy in common. Charles took possession. Elizabeth sought an accounting for one-half of the rental value. In denying the accounting, the court reaffirmed the long-standing Florida (perhaps majority) rule:

> Where one cotenant has exclusive possession of lands owned as tenant in common with another and uses those lands for his own benefit and does not receive rents or profits therefrom, such cotenant is not liable or accountable to his cotenant out of possession *unless* such cotenant in exclusive possession holds adversely or as the result of ouster or the equivalent thereof. [270 So. 2d at 435-436]

While continuing to adhere to this rule, the New Jersey court in Newman v. Chase, *supra*, held that an ouster had occurred, thereby touching off the duty to account, Note 3 *infra*.

But consider, however, the facts in Cohen v. Cohen, 157 Ohio St. 503, 106 N.E.2d 77 (1952). In 1925, Lena Wolfson, a widow, married Joseph Cohen, a widower with five children. The newlyweds acquired a one-family house as tenants in common, and lived there together until Joseph's death in 1941. Joseph devised his one-half interest to his five children, who allowed Lena to occupy the premises without demanding access until 1948, when a dispute arose. The children then sought an accounting for the period beginning with their father's death.

The Ohio court required Lena to account for the reasonable rental value of her entire occupancy. Recognizing this was a departure from the common law, the court relied on the following statute: "One tenant in common, or coparcener, may recover from another tenant in common, or coparcener his share of rents and profits received by such tenant in common or coparcener from the estate, according to the justice and equity of the case." Ohio Rev. Code §5307.21 (1964).

Can it be said that the statute squarely supports the decision in *Cohen?*

Suppose, in *Cohen*, that the premises had been a two-family house, that Lena had occupied one unit, and that the second unit had remained vacant. How would you have argued this case for Lena? For her cotenants?

What policies underlie the *Seesholts* rule or the *Cohen* alternative? In Hohfeldian terms, both Charles Seesholts and Lena Cohen enjoyed the privilege of possession as attributes of cotenancy, but Lena's privilege carried with it a duty to pay rental value while Charles was entitled to stay on rent-free. Neither Lena's duty nor Charles's nonduty follows inexorably from their possessory interests; that a cotenant is privileged to use and enjoy the whole property does not require the conclusion that he may do so "rent-free."

Although the decisions speak in other terms, presumption and burden of proof are ultimately involved. To indicative why: under the *Seesholts* rule, if the occupant has agreed to pay rent, his duty is clear; conversely, under the *Cohen* rule, if the occupant has been permitted to remain rent-free, he need not account. Controversy is most likely to erupt when the cotenants have acted ambiguously in defining their relation. If litigation results, the *Seesholts* rule requires that the cotenant not in possession prove an agreement (or ouster); the *Cohen* rule shifts that burden—as to an agreement at least—to the occupant. In general, which should be the easier of parol proof: an agreement by an occupant to pay, or a consent to rent-free occupancy? If you practiced law in a *Seesholts* jurisdiction and represented a cotenant who wished rent-free occupancy, what, if anything, would you advise him to get in writing? What considerations would be relevant in shaping your advice?

3. "If one tenant in common occupies the whole estate, claiming it as his own, it is an ouster of his co-tenant, who must first establish his right at law, and then recover his mesne profits. . . ." Izard v. Bodine, 11 N.J. Eq. 403, 404 (1857).

There is universal agreement as to the statement of this rule, but considerable confusion in the cases as to two of its aspects: (1) What is an "ouster"? (2) Is the aggrieved cotenant ever entitled to more than mesne profits (rental value)?

Because one does not usually eject a cotenant bodily, most claims of ouster do not involve assaults. Suppose instead that cotenant A, in possession, receives a demand from cotenant B, out of possession, that B be permitted to share the premises, and A refuses. Or that B demands that A vacate in favor of himself, or in favor of some third person to whom B would like to lease the premises. What if A ignores the demand and some months elapse before B decides to act?

Can ouster be inferred from cotenant A's express refusal pay his share of the rental value? From A's nonreply to a demand for payment? Compare Matter of Holt, 14 Misc. 2d 971, 177 N.Y.S.2d 192 (Sur. Ct. 1958) (A liable), with Utah Oil Refining Co. v. Leigh, 98 Utah 149, 96 P.2d 1100 (1939) (A not liable).

As to the "ousted" cotenant's measure of damages, consider the following case: A and B are cotenants of a rental building with an annual rental value of $20,000. A "ousts" B and establishes a laundry in the building. At the end of the year A shows a net profit of $100,000 before deduction for rent. How much can B recover from A? $10,000? $40,000? $60,000? Compare Simkin v. New York Cent. R.R., 138 Ind. App. 668, 214 N.E.2d 661 (1966), with White v. Smyth, *infra*.

PROBLEMS

1. A and B own a two-family house as equal cotenants. A resided in the lower-floor apartment rent-free throughout 1982. This apartment had a $500

monthly rental value. A leased out the upper floor apartment, and in 1982 collected $6,000—the agreed-upon rental—from the tenant. For the year, A spent the following sums attributable to the property:

(a)	Real estates taxes*	$1600
(b)	Fire insurance*	400
(c)	Fuel*	1000
(d)	Utilities*	1200
(e)	Mortgage interest*	3000
(f)	Reduction of mortgage principal*	600
(g)	Repair of downstairs toilet	200

* These items cover both units. Assume an equal allocation.

(1)   The court orders A to account for the year 1982, but does not require him to include the rental value of his unit. What does A owe B? (Suggested answer: B owes A $350.)

(2)   Recompute this debt if A must account for his use and occupancy. (Suggested answer: A owes B $2000.)

2.   Suppose that in 1982 A installed central air conditioning at a cost of $2,000, and did so without B''s knowledge or consent. On these facts, is A entitled to a contribution? If so, what should measure contribution: the actual outlay? the enhanced value of the premises? the actual outlay or the enhanced value of the premises, whichever is smaller? Cf. Buschmeyer v. Eikermann, 378 S.W.2d 468 (Mo. 1964). See also 4A Powell, Real Property, §604 at 617-618 (Rohan ed. 1973); Note, Right of Cotenant to Contribution from Other Cotenants for Unauthorized Repairs and Improvements Made to the Common Property, 32 Notre Dame Law. 493 (1957).

3.   A and B are cotenants of a tract of undeveloped land with a rental value of $1,000. Without obtaining B's consent, A drills for oil and invests $10,000 in dry wells the first year. B refuses to contribute to the cost. The second year A spends another $10,000, strikes oil, and sells the crude oil for a net profit of $100,000 before deduction for rent or the cost of the first year's drilling. B, of course, sues for an accounting. How much should B recover? Compare Dabney-Johnston Oil Corp. v. Walden, 4 Cal. 2d 367, 52 P.2d 237 (1935), with Aldrich v. Stevers, 115 Vt. 379, 61 A.2d 551 (1948). See generally American Law of Property §§6.14-6.18 (Casner ed. 1952).

4.   Suppose that B recovers a share of the profits in the preceding problem. In the third year, crude oil prices fall sharply, and A loses $20,000. A sues B for contribution. What result? Compare Delta Cotton Oil Co. v. Lovelace, 189 Miss. 113, 196 So. 644 (1940), and Edsall v. Merrill, 37 N.J. Eq. 114 (1883), with Cobbett v. Gallagher, 339 Pa. 231, 13 A.2d 403 (1940). See generally 51 A.L.R.2d 388 (1958) for an exhaustive discussion of the accountability of cotenants for rents and profits.

c. The Cotenant as a Double-Dealer

Should the bare fact that A and B are cotenants invest them with any fiduciary duties arising out the property's use or potential value? Consider this question when you read the next case and the problems that follow it.

WHITE v. SMYTH
147 Tex. 272, 214 S.W.2d 967 (1948)

[The Smyth ranch contained 30,000 acres of land valuable for its rock asphalt deposits. On the death of J. G. Smyth, the ranch passed in undivided interests to his nine children, one of whom was the wife of the defendant, R. L. White. In 1923, the cotenants leased the ranch to the defendant for mining the rock asphalt, White agreeing to pay royalties of 25 cents (and lesser amounts) per ton of rock asphalt taken. The lease term was 99 years but was terminable at the defendant's option on payment of $14,222.22. White operated under the lease until 1941, when he exercised his power to terminate and advised that he would vacate the property shortly. Before leaving, however, White acquired his wife's one-ninth interest. The defendant then wrote to his newly acquired cotenants (and former lessors) that he would "now want to take out such part of my share of the rock as is practical before I move my machinery." Over his cotenants' objections, White continued mining. After several years, the cotenants sued White for a partition of the rock asphalt and also for an accounting for rock asphalt removed by him without their consent. The trial court found (a) that the rock asphalt was incapable of division in kind; (b) that the defendant had not mined more than one-ninth of the value of the rock asphalt still unmined when his cotenancy began; (c) that the value of the rock asphalt in the ground which was mined during the dispute was $99,334.53; and (d) that the net profit realized was $250,180.56. The trail court decreed that the property be sold and the proceeds distributed among the common owners and awarded plaintiffs a judgment against White for $222,382.72 (eight-ninths of his net profit). White appealed. (In preparing this summary of the facts, the editor has tampered with them slightly, but not significantly, in the hope that he has made the controversy more understandable.)]

MR. JUSTICE SMEDLEY delivered the opinion of the court. . . .

The application for writ of error presents under several points three principal contentions: First, the petitioner White owes no duty to account to respondents, because he has not taken more than his fair share of the rock asphalt in place, has not excluded respondents from the premises, and in mining has made merely normal use of the property, it having already been devoted to the mining of rock asphalt at the time petitioner acquired his undivided interest therein; second, that if he owes a duty to account, he is liable only for eight-ninths of the value in the ground of the rock asphalt he has mined and not for profits which he has realized; and third, that the jury's findings that the rock asphalt in certain surveys in the ranch and in all of the property outside of certain surveys cannot be equitably partitioned in kind are without evidence to support them. We consider first the points pertaining to partition, since the question whether the property is or is not capable of partition in kind has an important bearing upon the other questions.

The record contains many pages of testimony as to the nature, location, quantity and quality of the rock asphalt in the lands. [After summarizing this testimony, the court rules it sufficient to support the finding below that the mineral deposits were not susceptible of fair division by metes and bounds, and upholds the trial court's direction that the lands be sold and the proceeds be distributed.]

The amount of the trial court's judgment in favor of respondents against petitioner represents eight-ninths of the net profits realized by petitioner from mining, processing and selling 397,381.11 tons of rock asphalt taken from the land during the period from October 29, 1942, to September 30, 1945. This amount of net profits was found by the jury after deducting from the gross proceeds all expenses incurred by petitioner, together with a reasonable compensation for his personal services and the reasonable value of the use of his plant and other property in the operation of the mine. . . .

It seems that there are no decisions in this state as to the duty of a co-owner who takes solid minerals from the property to account to his cotenant. It is held, however, as in most of the other states that one who takes oil without the consent of his cotenants must account to them for their share of the proceeds of the oil less the necessary and reasonable cost of producing and marketing it. . . .

Petitioner contends that the rule above stated does not apply to this case, and that he need not account to his cotenants, because he has mined no more than his fair share of the rock asphalt in place and has not excluded them from the premises. He relies primarily upon Kirby Lumber Co. v. Temple Lumber Co., 125 Texas 284, 83 S.W. (2d) 638. . . .

In the *Kirby Lumber Company* case the Temple Company owned an undivided two-thirds interest and the Kirby Company owned an undivided one-third interest in a 640 acre tract of land on which there was valuable standing timber. The Temple Company, believing that it owned the entire title to a specific 427 acres of the land, cut all of the timber standing on that tract, amounting to ten million feet, and manufactured it into lumber. There remained uncut on the 640 acres, 2,783,325 feet of timber. The court's opinion states that the 640 acres was generally of uniform value as to timber and otherwise. The Kirby Company sued the Temple Company to recover the manufactured value of one-third of the timber that had been cut. The trial court found that the total amount of timber standing on the land before the cutting was 12,783,325 feet, of which the Kirby Company's one-third amounted to 4,261,108 feet, and that the amount left standing was 2,783,325 feet, which was treated as belonging to the Kirby Company, and that thus the Temple Company had cut 1,477,783 feet more than its share. Its judgment awarded to the Kirby Company $43,372.93, being the manufactured value of the 1,477,783 feet. The Court of Civil Appeals reversed and rendered the trial court's judgment, after holding that the Kirby Company was charged with notice that its predecessor in title had cut timber from part of the land. 42 S.W. (2) 1070. The Supreme Court reversed the judgments of the two lower courts and rendered judgment in favor of the Kirby Company against the Temple Company for the stumpage value, $5.00 per thousand feet, of the 1,477,783 feet of excess timber cut by the Temple Company. Most of the Court's opinion is devoted to a discussion of the question whether the Kirby Company should be charged with notice that timber had been cut by its predecessor in title and of the question as to the amount of the recovery, that is whether stumpage value or manufactured value. Little is said in the approval of that part of the trial court's judgment which charged the Temple Company with only the amount of the timber cut in excess of its share. The authorities there cited relate to timber and to the question whether stumpage value or manufacture value may be recovered.

The important distinction between the *Kirby Lumber Company* case and the instant case, in respect to the ruling that the Temple Company need not account for the timber cut not in excess of its two-thirds share, is that in that case, as shown by the Court's statement that "the 640 acres was generally of uniform value as to timber and otherwise," the timber was fairly subject to partition in kind, whereas in the instant case the rock asphalt is not. The Temple Company's action in cutting the timber up to its share and the Court's approval of that action by the judgment rendered worked in effect a partition of the timber. Here there has not been, and there could not be consistently with the finding that the rock asphalt is not capable of partition in kind, an approval by the court of White's action in taking for himself and disposing of a part of the rock asphalt. The ownership of all of the cotenants extends to all of the rock asphalt, and White was not authorized to make partition of it. . . .

The facts of this case attest the obvious soundness of the rule that a cotenant cannot select and take for himself part of the property jointly owned and thus make partition. While he was lessee under the lease that covered the entire ranch, White selected the site for and developed the present pit, making extensive improvements, including the construction of roads, excavations and grading for private tracks, other excavations and grading, all at great cost and of very substantial value. The location of the plant site was favorable and valuable. . . .

When White exercised the right to terminate the lease . . . he had no further right or interest in the rock asphalt in the lands, the mine or the mine site, except that he was given by the lease the right to remove his machinery, tools, houses and implements. The rock asphalt estate in all of the lands belonged to all of the cotenants, as did also the added advantages and values to the entire mineral estate created and existing by reason of the developed pit and mine site; but White, taking advantage for himself of the added values, after acquiring the one-ninth interest of his wife [and his wife's sister] mined from the pit about four hundred thousand tons of the rich, valuable and readily accessible rock asphalt. . . .

Kirby Lumber Co. v. Temple Lumber Co. [*supra*] is cited by petitioner to sustain his assignment of error that if he owes respondents the duty to account, he must account only for the value in the ground of the rock asphalt mined by him. That case is not an authority for this point. The plaintiff did not ask for an accounting for profits. There were no allegations as to profits and no issue as to profits was submitted. There is nothing to show that any profits were made. The question before the court was whether the defendant should be required to pay for the stumpage value of the timber cut or for its value after having been manufactured into lumber and without deduction for expenditures. The court held that the former, that is stumpage value, was the measure of recovery because the defendant had acted in good faith, believing that it owned all of the timber that it had cut. A fundamental difference between the facts of the *Kirby* case and the instant case, which has been noted herein, has an important bearing here. It is that in the *Kirby* case the standing timber was of uniform value and could readily be partitioned in kind, whereas in this case the rock asphalt cannot be fairly and equitably partitioned in kind.

Three cases are cited by petitioner in which the cotenant who had taken minerals was charged with their value in place: Appeal of Fulmer, 128 Pa. 24, 18 Atl. 49, 15 Am. St. Rep. 662; McGowan v. Bailey, 179 Pa. 470, 36 Atl. 325; and Clowser v. Joplin (W.D. Mo.) 4 Dill. 469n, Fed. Cas. No. 2908a. While the opinions in the two Pennsylvania cases contain reasoning to justify the use of that measure, they also indicate that it was deemed just and equitable under the peculiar facts, and that it might not be applicable to all cases. In the Federal case a memorandum opinion adopts the measure of liability stated in the two Pennsylvania cases as appropriate under the Missouri statute. The three cases depart from the majority rule, supported by the authorities cited and discussed herein, which majority rule is stated in American Jurisprudence as follows:

> Since any co-owner of a mine or mineral property is at liberty to work it, some courts have intimated that a co-owner who does not choose to avail himself of this right should have no claim upon the production of one who has elected to do so. But this view seems to be contrary to the weight of authority, and the prevailing rule appears to be that the producer must account to his cotenant for all profits made to the extent of his interest in the property. (14 Am. Jur., p. 104, §36.) . . .

It is argued by petitioner that his receipts have been from sales of a manufactured product, and that respondents should not be permitted, by sharing in the profits, to obtain the benefits of his personal skill and industry and of the flux oil and water used and the machinery, apparatus and equipment belonging to petitioner. We believe that the preparation of the rock asphalt for market, as described by petitioner's testimony and by that of other witnesses, is a processing rather than a manufacturing. The rock asphalt is rock asphalt in the ground, that is, limestone rock impregnated with asphalt. To make it ready for the market and for use in the building of roads it is mixed and crushed, and oil is mixed with it to give the small particles of rock a film of oil, and water is put in the mixture so that it will not become solid in transit. It is rock asphalt when it is sold and when it is used on the roads. The producing tenant is required to account to his cotenants for net profits realized from mining, smelting, crushing, processing or marketing solid minerals taken from the land. . . .

The judgments of the district court and the Court of Civil Appeals are affirmed. . . .

MR. JUSTICE SIMPSON, with whom JUSTICES SHARP, BREWSTER and FOLLEY concur, dissenting.

It is respectfully submitted that the measure of recovery allowed the respondents by the majority ruling is wrong, and is contrary to the applicable precedents under the established facts. It results in what is earnestly urged to be an unjust exaction of the petitioner White, who should have been required to account for $99,334.53, the value in place of the rock asphalt taken, and not $222,382.72, its net manufactured value.

Petitioner White had spent practically a lifetime in the rock asphalt business. He worked the asphalt deposits on the Smyth ranch from 1923 until 1941 under a contract with the landowers, which he then terminated, as he had the right to do. He had acquired one-ninth . . . of the rock asphalt under some 30,000 acres of the Smyth ranch, and continued working the deposits after the contract with his cotenants ended. He notified them what he was doing. He had a complete legal and moral right to be on the land and to mine the rock.

This rock, after mining, has to be manufactured into paving material before it is of any practicable use. It is blasted from its beds in large pieces, which are broken up by further blasting. It is then scooped onto trucks by steam shovels and hauled to and further pulverized by a crushing machine. It is then taken to a storage bin where the rock with high asphaltic content is placed at one end, that with a low content at the other. This bin is equipped with vibrating feeders which drop the rock in proper portions on a conveyor belt which takes it to other grinders for further processing. After the final crushing, the rock, by means of a screen, is separated into three bins according to the size of the particles into which it has been crushed. Then the rock, sizes kept separate, is weighed, dropped into a mixer known as a "pug mill" and oil is introduced into the product under pressures running from 75 to 100 pounds. Powerful paddles churn the material so the oil is thoroughly fused into it. . . . Suitable quantities of water are added and milled into the product. The resulting mixture is a manufactured paving material which petitioner has been selling under the registered name of "Valdemix."

The plant and equipment investment of the petitioner exceeded $500,000.00.

The asphalt business is highly competitive. So competitive in fact that petitioner's Uvalde Mines and Uvalde Asphalt Company are the only survivors among all who have tried. One adequately capitalized concern, for instance, abandoned the business after losing at least $1,000,000.00.

In addition to the manufacturing of crude rock asphalt into a finished paving product, petitioner employed his skill and experience in selling it. He would agree in advance with contractors bidding on road work that if the contractor should be the successful bidder he would deliver "Valdemix" in given quantities and at certain prices and times. His lifetime of experience in the business enabled him to succeed where others had failed. He knew how to mine, how to manufacture, and how to sell.

What the complaining cotenants are entitled to get is the value of that which was taken, that is, crude rock asphalt. Any higher figure would no longer be compensatory but punitive. . . .

NOTES AND QUESTIONS

1. This decision is discussed critically in Notes, 1 Baylor L. Rev. 364 (1949), and 27 Texas L. Rev. 863 (1949).

2. Having held that White took only his fair share of the rock asphalt in place, should not the trial court have regarded his activity as partition in kind? Although the opinion speaks of White's mined rock asphalt as being "rich, valuable and readily accessible," these are the very factors which, together with volume, must be applied to the unmined rock to determine its value. Whatever the superior advantages of White's rock, the court's initial finding as to the value of remaining rock carries with it an estimate that at least eight-ninths of the potential extraction profits were yet to be realized.

3. A, B, and C are heirs of D, a life tenant who has the power to encroach upon the corpus. Upon D's death, they are to become cotenants of whatever property D has not transferred. Nine days before she dies, D executes a forty-year coal-mining lease to A. Is the lease valid? If so, do the operating profits from the lease inure to B and C as well? See Givens v. Givens, 387 S.W.2d 851 (Ky. 1965).

4. A and B are tenants in common. The property is sold for unpaid taxes. May A acquire the property for his own account? Cf. Gavin v. Hosey, 230 So. 2d 570 (Miss. 1970) (purchase of tax title by cotenant inures to the benefit of other cotenants). May A wait until after the redemption period has expired and then acquire the property from a stranger who purchased the property at the tax foreclosure sale? Compare Spencer v. Spencer, 160 Fla. 749, 36 So. 2d 424 (1948), with Pease v. Snyder, 169 Kan. 628, 220 P.2d 151 (1950). May A acquire the property for his own account at a partition sale? See 20 Am. Jur. 2d §74 (1965).

Chapter 8

Marital Property Interests

Early in the feudal era, the common law gave each of the parties to a marriage vital interests in the lands owned by the other. In part, this was born of solicitude: for the guardianship of children after a mother's untimely death (viz., curtesy); for economic well-being of a surviving widow after her husband's death (viz., dower). In part, this was built upon notions of male primacy: when she became a spouse, the married woman lost more than her maidenhood; in the law's eyes (and who but men made the law), she also lost her legal competency—a state of affairs that gave her parity with infants, idiots, and felons, although she could end this disability by outlasting her husband (or the marriage).

The common-law marital estates have little present-day standing, and even this is disappearing. Yet, they have continuing interest for law students for several principal reasons: (1) as examples of legal life estates—that is, life estates created by operation of law; (2) as forerunners of the modern law of marital property; (3) as potential title problems in states where they once existed, or may still exist; (4) as further examples of the law's response to changing social attitudes and economic needs.

§8.1   Estate by the Marital Right (Jure Uxoris)

At the moment of marriage, the husband acquired immediate control over his wife's property. He was entitled to the rents and profits of her freehold estates.[1] He could enjoy them without an accounting, transfer them as he wished, and permit his creditors to reach them by execution. The wife was powerless to protest. Except as it was transformed by curtesy, this utter dominion ended with the end of the marriage. Thus, the husband actually received a life estate

---

1. Personalty and nonfreehold estates also were subject to this dominion. As to these interests, the husband might dissipate or transfer not only the income but also the corpus.

(measured by the joint lives of husband and wife *qua* husband and wife), and this was all that his transferees would be allowed to take. Chancery steadily weakened the husband's unilateral control, and the Married Women's Acts of the nineteenth century brought it virtually to an end.

§8.2   Curtesy

At the birth of live issue[2] who were qualified to inherit their mother's estate,[3] the husband's jure uxoris was expanded to a life estate *for his life*[4] in *all of* his wife's inheritable, freehold lands. This newly formed estate, called *curtesy initiate,* was said to be granted "by the curtesy of England,"[5] since it treated the husband more generously than did an earlier civil law prototype. If a man's wife predeceased him, his estate was renamed *curtesy consummate,* but its attributes were left unchanged. Both before and after his wife's death, the husband continued his plenary control over the rents and profits that had been his to enjoy under jure uxoris. So tenuous did the law regard the wife's status in her own lands that adverse possession *could not* begin to run against the married woman during her husband's lifetime. Can you explain why?

§8.3   Dower

The best known and the most enduring of the legal life estates is the dower interest of a wife in the lands of her husband. Its sources are Teutonic; the groom by custom promised the family of his bride to leave her an endowment should she survive him. In England, provision for a widow became a legal incident of marriage; a widow was entitled, as a matter of law, to a life estate in *one third* of the inheritable, freehold lands of which her husband was seized[6] during coverture. Before the husband's death, the wife's interest was *dower inchoate;* at his death, the widow's interest became *dower prior to assignment* until the courts decided which lands should be set aside to meet the one-third

2. An infant's survival was often touch and go in an era of high infant mortality. Accordingly, the criteria for a live birth were in keeping with the hazards of childbirth. The mother need not survive the child; and as for the child, it was enough for its heartbeat to have been felt, or its cry to have been heard.

3. Thus, if the wife's estate was an estate tail female, the birth of a male child would not suffice.

4. A life estate that would still be cut short, however, by divorce.

5. Curtesy, perhaps, but courtesy, no! Neither a husband's adultery, not his desertion, nor the two in combination, would bar curtesy.

6. What "seisin" is within the context of dower has caused endless controversy. For a discussion and citation of cases, see 2 Powell, Real Property ¶209[1], at 141-149 (Rohan ed. 1973).

requirement. In the lands assigned to her, the widow then had *dower consummate,* a life estate ending with her death. In an era when land was the chief form of wealth, dower gave a measure of security both to the widow and to those of her children who, because of primogeniture and male preference, received no interest in their father's lands.

Whatever his feelings for his wife, the husband could not, without the wife's cooperation, strip her of dower. Any transfer or mortgage of his lands, or any levy of execution by his creditors, was subject to his wife's inchoate interest, unless the mortgage was given in a purchase money transaction or the creditor's claim preceded the husband's marriage. The wife might join, however, in the transfer or mortgage—for the sole purpose of relinquishing her dower interest. [7] And she might agree, before marriage, to accept some substitute for dower; as might be expected, such agreements were closely scrutinized for their essential fairness. [8]

For many reasons, including those advanced in the following opinion, dower and curtesy have been either whittled down or eliminated in most states. The Massachusetts statute, *infra,* typifies this process, and raises anew the pervasive issues of "due process" whenever property institutions get "reformed."

OPINION OF THE JUSTICES
337 Mass. 786, 151 N.E.2d 475 (1958)

On June 27, 1958, the Justices submitted the following answers to questions propounded to them by the Senate.

To the Honorable the Senate of the Commonwealth of Massachusetts:

The undersigned Justices of the Supreme Judicial Court respectfully submit these answers to the questions set forth in an order of the Senate dated June 18, 1958, and transmitted to us on June 20. The order refers to a pending bill, Senate No. 388, entitled "An Act to restrict dower and curtesy claims to land owned at the death of the claimant's spouse."

The bill has three sections. Section 1 seeks to amend by striking out G.L. (Ter. Ed.) c. 189, §1, and substituting the following: "A husband shall upon the death of his wife hold for his life one third of all land owned by her at the time of her death. Such estate shall be known as his tenancy by curtesy, and the law relative to dower shall be applicable to curtesy. A wife shall, upon the death of her husband, hold her dower at common law in land owned by him at the time of his death. Such estate shall be known as her tenancy by dower. Any encumbrances on land at the time of the owner's death shall have precedence over curtesy or dower. To be entitled to such curtesy or dower the surviving husband or wife shall file his or her election and claim therefor in the

---

7. Courts will sometimes transfer inchoate dower to the proceeds of sale when a wife refuses to join in her husband's transfer. In such event, either the entire sum realized or, more properly, the discounted value of the wife's expectancy interest is deposited into court. Id. ¶209[2], at 154.

8. Id. ¶212[3], at 170.8-170.9.

registry of probate within six months after the date of the approval of the bond of the executor or administrator of the deceased, and shall thereupon hold instead of the interest in real property given in section one in chapter one hundred and ninety,[9] curtesy or dower, respectively, otherwise such estate shall be held to be waived.[10] Such curtesy and dower may be assigned by the probate court in the same manner as dower is now assigned, and the tenant by curtesy or dower shall be entitled to the possession and profits of one undivided third of the real estate of the deceased from her or his death until the assignment of curtesy or dower. . . . Except as preserved herein, dower and curtesy are abolished."

Section 2 reads: "If it should be held that this act cannot constitutionally apply to rights of dower or curtesy as they existed prior to the effective date of this act, it shall nevertheless be fully effective except as to such rights." Section 3 provides that the act shall take effect on January 1, 1959.

The questions are as follows:

"1. Can said pending bill, if enacted into law, constitutionally apply to inchoate rights of dower or curtesy as they existed prior to the effective date thereof under Article X of the Declaration of Rights of the Constitution of Massachusetts, section 10 of Article I of the Constitution of the United States in so far as said section forbids any state to make any law impairing the obligation of contracts, or the Fourteenth Amendment to the Constitution of the United States?

"2. Can said pending bill, if enacted into law, constitutionally empower a person after the effective date thereof to deprive his spouse of such inchoate rights of dower or curtesy of such spouse as were in existence prior to said effective date under Article X of the Declaration of Rights of the Constitution of Massachusetts, section 10 of Article I of the Constitution of the United States in so far as said section forbids any state to make any law impairing the obligation of contracts, or the Fourteenth Amendment to the Constitution of the United States?"[11]

The order recites that a substantially identical bill, Senate No. 274 of 1956, was referred to the Judicial Council by c. 10 of the Resolves of 1956; and that a majority of the Judicial Council in its thirty-second report in 1956, at pages 24-28, recommended passage but suggested the possibility of an advisory opinion of the Justices. In that report we read that the purpose of the bill "is to reduce the title problems affecting the marketability of land whether by sale or mortgage" (page 25). We there are told that these problems have two

---

9. Chapter 190 is part of the state's law of intestate succession. After the decedent's debts and funeral expenses are all paid, the surviving spouse will receive: (a) where the decedent leaves kindred but no issue, $25,000 and one-half of the remaining estate; (b) where the decedent leaves issue, one-third of the estate; (c) where the decedent leaves no kindred and no issue, the entire estate.—ED.

10. If husband dies intestate, under what conditions will wife elect dower, rather than waive it?—ED.

11. How are the questions different?—ED.

chief causes: (1) The omission of a husband or wife to declare an existing marriage and to obtain the signature of the spouse to a deed. (2) The ever growing number of migratory divorces with the attendant doubt as to their validity and the consequent uncertainty as to the legality of remarriage. The result might be described as a conveyancer's nightmare.

Under §1 as now in effect, curtesy is a life estate of a surviving husband in one third of all land owned by his wife during marriage unless he had joined in a deed of conveyance or "otherwise" released his right to claim curtesy; and dower is a similar life estate of a surviving wife in one third of land owned by the husband. And see G.L. (Ter. Ed.) c. 189, §1A. Either curtesy or dower may be "otherwise" released by a deed subsequent to the deed of conveyance executed either separately or jointly with the spouse. G.L. (Ter. Ed). c. 189, §5. Of course, neither can exist without a valid marriage. By statute neither survives divorce. G.L. c. 208, §7 (as amended through St. 1949, c. 76, §2). This, of course, means a valid divorce. During marriage the right to claim curtesy or dower is said to be inchoate. (At common law the phrase was curtesy initiate.) Upon the death of the spouse, or, at any rate, after the later assignment of a specified one third of the land, it is said to be consummate. Curtesy and dower, under §1 in its present form, are superior to the rights of creditors. It should be noted that nothing like curtesy or dower exists as to personal property, which a husband or wife may dispose of freely without the consent of the spouse. . . .

That the bill would violate no provision of the Federal Constitution is settled by decisions of the Supreme Court of the United States. In Randall v. Kreiger, 23 Wall. 137, decided in 1874, it was said, at page 148: "During the life of the husband the right [of dower] is a mere expectancy or possibility. In that condition of things, the lawmaking power may deal with it as may be deemed proper. It is not a natural right. It is wholly given by law, and the power that gave it may increase, diminish, or otherwise alter it, or wholly take it away. It is upon the same footing with the expectancy of heirs, apparent or presumptive, before the death of the ancestor. Until that event occurs the law of descent and distribution may be moulded according to the will of the legislature." In Ferry v. Spokane, Portland & Seattle Ry., 258 U.S. 314, decided in 1922, the court upheld a decision of the Circuit Court of Appeals for the Ninth Circuit, 268 Fed. 117, to the effect that an Oregon statute limiting the right of dower of a nonresident to land of which the husband died seised was not unconstitutional. In the *Ferry* case the Supreme Court of the United States said, at pages 318-319: "Dower is not a privilege or immunity of citizenship, either state or federal, within the meaning of the provisions relied on [§2 of art. 4 and the Fourteenth Amendment]. At most it is a right which, while it exists, is attached to the marital contract or relation; and it always has been deemed subject to regulation by each State as respects property within its limits. Conner v. Elliott, 18 How. 491. . . . The cases recognize that the limitation of the dower right is to remove an impediment to the transfer of real estate and to assure titles against absent and probably unknown wives."

Turning to art. 10 of the Declaration of Rights of the Constitution of the Commonwealth, we observe in the thirty-second report of the Judicial Council that the doubt as to the validity of the bill springs from statements in several earlier decisions of the Supreme Judicial Court, in none of which, however, was the question before us presented. The question here is whether the bill if enacted would amount to a taking of property without due process of law. . . .

Dower and curtesy are of much less importance than formerly. This diminution in value is due to the great increase in the amount of personal property and in the superior alternative rights in the estate of a deceased husband or wife accorded by statute to a surviving spouse. The thirty-second report of the Judicial Council points to St. 1854, c. 406, as a source of such rights. These rights have been gradually increased by legislation. . . .

According to the thirty-second report of the Judicial Council claims of dower or curtesy in this Commonwealth have almost ceased to be made; and, in fact, a claim of neither is advisable except under two special circumstances: "(1) if the deceased owned real estate, but died insolvent or so nearly so that the bulk of the real estate must be sold to pay the debts and expenses; and (2) if the deceased during his or her lifetime conveyed a considerable amount of real estate without procuring a release of curtesy or dower in the deed." Newhall, Settlement of Estates (4th ed.) §213. It may be noted that statutory changes in dower as a common law incident of marriage have been made in this Commonwealth without making an exception of existing marriages. See 40 Mass. L.Q. No. 4, p. 36.

We are not surprised to learn that dower and curtesy either no longer exist or are of little practical importance in more than half the States. Powell, Real Property, §§217-218. . . .

In the light of the shrinking significance of curtesy or dower as alternatives which must be elected by a surviving husband or wife in the estate of a deceased spouse, we cannot regard the statements quoted from our cases as precluding inchoate curtesy and inchoate dower from being viewed in this Commonwealth in the same way as in a majority of the States. We are of opinion that as a matter of public policy the Legislature can restrict them in the manner proposed. Let it be conceded that each is a valuable interest and more than a possibility. Yet each is only a contingency—a contingency of waning value—which in the usual estate today is of slight importance. We think that inchoate curtesy and inchoate dower, as contingencies before the death of the predeceasing spouse, are subject to action by the Legislature, which may make an evaluation in the public interest, and determine that any slight advantage in their retention in a relatively few cases is outweighed by the far greater benefit to the general good accruing from their restriction.

To question 1, we answer, "Yes."

Believing that this answer covers all that is intended to be asked by question 2, we respectfully request that we be excused from making a separate answer to question 2.

NOTES AND QUESTIONS

1. How did Senate No. 388 change the prior dower and curtesy statute? How did the prior statute change the common law?

2. The Massachusetts legislature passes a bill converting all fees on special limitation and fees on condition into fee simple absolutes. The accompanying report states that the bill's purposes are to reduce title problems and restrict dead-hand control. Your client is the present holder of a possibility of reverter. Can you distinguish the decision above?

3. Contrast the Massachusetts bill with the New York statute that abolished curtesy outright, but retained dower as to real estate owned by a husband prior to the statute's effective date—September 1, 1930. Another law now sets a two-year limitation (after husband's death) for an action to assign dower. N.Y. Real Prop. Law §§189, 190 (McKinney 1968); N.Y. Real Prop. Actions Law §1001 (McKinney 1963). When must a New York title examiner worry about dower?

4. At latest count, dower survives in its pristine form in nine or ten jurisdictions, curtesy in two. See 2 Powell, Real Property ¶213[1] at 170.17, ¶213[2] at 170.21-170.22 (Rohan ed. 1973). In the eight community property states, *infra,* the common-law marital estates never were recognized.

5. The statutory substitutes for dower or curtesy are extremely varied. They include:

    (a) The surviving wife (husband) receives a share, not restricted to a life estate, in all of the assets owned by the husband (wife) at death.

    (b) The surviving wife (husband) receives a share, not restricted to a life estate, in all of the land owned by the husband (wife) during coverture.

    (c) The surviving wife (husband) is given an election, as against common-law dower (curtesy), to receive an intestate share in the husband's (wife's) estate.

6. Several articles by Professor Haskins provide us with a rich lode on the common-law marital interests: Curtesy at Common Law, 29 B.U.L. Rev. 228 (1949); The Development of Common Law Dower, 62 Harv. L. Rev. 42 (1948); Curtesy in the United States, 100 U. Pa. L. Rev. 196 (1951); The Estate by Marital Right, 97 U. Pa. L. Rev. 345 (1949).

§8.4   Community Property

a.   Background and Significance

Community property is a civil-law system brought to this continent by France and Spain and introduced into the territories they at one time controlled or claimed. Today, there are eight community property states: Arizona, California, Idaho, Louisiana, Nevada, New Mexico, Texas, and

Washington. In these states, the system is the touchstone for defining the property rights of husband and wife who, together, are the so-called marital community.

During the 1940s, community property caused a brief flurry of excitement elsewhere, after it was discovered that the system offered unique tax benefits. The advantage ended in 1948 with an amendment to the Internal Revenue Code enabling husband and wife to file a joint return. Before Congress acted, however, five additional states and one territory had passed community property laws. All were later repealed or declared unconstitutional. See Note, 50 Colum. L. Rev. 332 (1950).

Nevertheless, the study of community property is of more than parochial interest. The following is a routine problem that the lawyer in a noncommunity property state might expect to handle:

H and W are married in California. While living there, they buy real estate that they later sell for cash and a purchase-money mortgage. Then they move to New York, separate, and agree to obtain a divorce. Before a property settlement can be arranged, the attorney must determine who owns the sales proceeds, and this requires that he consult California law.

Because of its civilian background, community property law is largely statutory in content. Thus, there are really eight community property systems in the United States, and any generalization must be checked out against the laws of each of the eight states.

b. How the System Works

The wealth of husband and wife is divided into two categories, separate property and community property. Statutes specifically define separate property. In general, the property that each spouse brings to the marriage is separate. So, too, is property that either receives during marriage by gift, devise, or descent. By contrast, whatever is gained during marriage by the toil or talent of either spouse is community property. For example, a husband's (wife's) salary, or the stock purchases made from his (her) earnings, are common forms of community property.[12] In three states (Idaho, Louisiana, and Texas), the earnings from separate property belong to the community. Elsewhere, whether such earnings are regarded as separate or community property will depend upon how the earnings arise. Cf. Beam v. Bank of America, *infra*.

The rarely stated premise of community property is that the wife who labors in the home contributes as much to the family wealth as the husband who labors in the office.

Not all states treat personal injury damage awards alike. Four states treat the entire award as community property. The four other states split the

---

12. H deposits ten percent of his salary in mutual funds. Even if the shares are registered in H's name, they are regarded as community property. Similarly, any dividend or interest receipts derived from such funds are community property.

award to compensate the injured spouse separately for his (her) pain and suffering, and the community for medical expenses, lost wages, and the like. See W. DeFuniak and M. Vaughn, Principles of Community Property §§82-83.1 (2d ed. 1971).

A recurring theme is the status of property located outside the state and acquired with community assets. If the parties are already domiciled in a community property state when acquisition occurs, any personalty they acquire belongs to the community. Cf. In re Estate of Perry, 480 S.W.2d 893 (Mo. 1972). Not so realty, unless its situs is in a state also recognizing community property. The law is more varied as to personalty acquired before husband and wife move their domicile to a community property state. At least one state, California, has attempted by recent statute to bring these assets within its system also.[13] If the parties move away from a community property state, community assets that the couple take with them keep that identity. Cf. 14 A.L.R.3d 404 (1967).

After property is defined as either separate or community, we apply the incidents of ownership. With respect to separate property, each spouse has undisputed control over his or her wealth; the married woman never suffered—as did her counterpart in the common-law system prior to curative statutes—any disability as to what was exclusively hers. Until very recently, however, community assets were handled quite differently. There, the husband was in charge, although even this dominion was less autocratic than that possible under the common law's jure uxoris. The husband was more nearly a trustee—typically, he was accountable for mismanagement, unable to sell personalty without valuable consideration (unless his wife gave written consent), and unable to make any long-term conveyance of realty unless his wife joined him in the transfer. Cf. Campbell v. Sandy, 190 Wash. 528, 69 P.2d 808 (1937).

During the 1970s, all eight community property states modified their laws regarding management of community assets. Although the details vary, they share a common thrust: toward creating management equality between the spouses.[14] In California, for example, either spouse may manage the couple's nonbusiness assets (business personalty becomes—or remains—the province of the spouse operating the business); both spouses must join in any mortgage or conveyance of community realty.

---

13. The statute designates personalty acquired by the parties while domiciled elsewhere as quasi-community property if the parties move to California and if the personalty would have been community property under California law. Quasi-community property may be dealt with as community property in any action for divorce and maintenance. Cal. Civ. Code §§4801, 4803 (1970). The statute survived constitutional attack. Addison v. Addison, 62 Cal. 2d 558, 399 P.2d 897, 43 Cal. Rptr. 97 (1965). An earlier law, treating such personalty as community property for all purposes, was struck down as a taking of property without due process. In re Thornton, 1 Cal. 2d 1, 33 P.2d 1 (1934).

14. The women's movement and constitutionality doubts led to the change. As to the latter, evidently none too soon. The United States Supreme Court has invalidated, as a denial of equal protection, the earlier version of the Louisiana law giving husband exclusive managerial control over community wealth. Kirchberg v. Feenstra, 101 S. Ct. 1195 (1981).

The claims of third persons against community assets, once treated quite disparately, now seem to follow a fairly common pattern. Debts incurred for community benefit are collectible from community property; so too are claims against the spouse who, when the claim arose, had been managing the community assets.

Divorce (or judicial separation) terminates the community. At that time separate property is returned to the owner. In California, if a spouse obtains a judgment for separate maintenance or a divorce because of adultery, extreme cruelty, or incurable insanity, the community property will be apportioned as the court deems just. If the judgment is granted for any other reason, or if the court grants both parties a divorce, the community property will be divided evenly.

Death, quite obviously, also terminates the community. The survivor succeeds to one-half of the community property. The other half passes by devise or descent along with the decedent's separate property.

Community property disputes arise generally when the community ends. The issue of first importance in many disputes is whether various assets are to be treated as separate or community property. The materials that follow indicate some of the difficulties that attend that issue.

SMITH v. LEWIS

13 Cal. 3d 349, 530 P.2d 589, 118 Cal. Rptr. 621 (1975)

Mosk, J. Defendant Jerome R. Lewis, an attorney, appeals from a judgment entered upon a jury verdict for plaintiff Rosemary E. Smith in an action for legal malpractice. The action arises as a result of legal services rendered by defendant to plaintiff in a prior divorce proceeding. The gist of plaintiff's complaint is that defendant negligently failed in the divorce action to assert her community interest in the retirement benefits of her husband.

Defendant principally contends, inter alia, that the law with regard to the characterization of retirement benefits was so unclear at the time he represented plaintiff as to insulate him from liability for failing to assert a claim therefor on behalf of his client.[1] We conclude defendant's appeal is without merit, and therefore affirm the judgment.

In 1943 plaintiff married General Clarence D. Smith. Between 1945 and his retirement in 1966 General Smith was employed by the California National Guard. As plaintiff testified, she informed defendant her husband "was paid by the state . . . it was a job just like anyone else goes to." For the first 16 years of that period the husband belonged to the State Employees' Retirement

---

1. Defendant alternatively contends the state and federal military retirement benefits in question cannot properly be characterized as community property, and hence his advice to plaintiff was correct. As will appear, the contention is manifestly untenable in light of recent decisions by this court.

System, a contributory plan.[2] Between 1961 and the date of his retirement he belonged to the California National Guard retirement program, a noncontributory plan. In addition, by attending National Guard reserve drills he qualified for separate retirement benefits from the federal government, also through a noncontributory plan. The state and federal retirement program each provide lifetime monthly benefits which terminate upon the death of the retiree. The programs make an allowance for the retiree's widow.

On January 1, 1967, the State of California began to pay General Smith gross retirement benefits of $796.26 per month. Payments under the federal program, however, will not begin until 1983, i.e., 17 years after his actual retirement, when General Smith reaches the age of 60. All benefits which General Smith is entitled to receive were earned during the time he was married to plaintiff.

On February 17, 1967, plaintiff retained defendant to represent her in a divorce action against General Smith. According to plaintiff's testimony, defendant advised her that her husband's retirement benefits were not community property. Three days later defendant filed plaintiff's complaint for divorce. General Smith's retirement benefits were not pleaded as items of community property, and therefore were not considered in the litigation or apportioned by the trial court. The divorce was uncontested and the interlocutory decree divided the minimal described community property and awarded Mrs. Smith $400 per month in alimony and child support. The final decree was entered on February 27, 1968.

On July 17, 1968, pursuant to a request by plaintiff, defendant filed on her behalf a motion to amend the decree, alleging under oath that because of his mistake, inadvertence, and excusable neglect (Code Civ. Proc., §473) the retirement benefits of General Smith had been omitted from the list of community assets owned by the parties, and that such benefits were in fact community property. The motion was denied on the ground of untimeliness. Plaintiff consulted other counsel, and shortly thereafter filed this malpractice action against defendant.

Defendant admits in his testimony that he assumed General Smith's retirement benefits were separate property when he assessed plaintiff's community property rights. It is his position that as a matter of law an attorney is not liable for mistaken advice when well informed lawyers in the community entertain reasonable doubt as to the proper resolution of the particular legal question involved. Because, he asserts, the law defining the character of retirement benefits was uncertain at the time of his legal services to plaintiff, defendant contends the trial court committed error in refusing to grant his motions for nonsuit and judgment notwithstanding the verdict and in submitting the issue of negligence to the jury under appropriate instructions.[3]

2. A contributory plan is one in which the member contributes to his retirement fund, normally through payroll deductions. A noncontributory plan is one in which no such contributions are made.

3. The jury was instructed as follows:

In performing legal services for a client in a divorce action an attorney has the duty

The law is now settled in California that "retirement benefits which flow from the employment relationship, to the extent they have vested, are community property subject to equal division between the spouses in the event the marriage is dissolved." [Citations omitted.] Because such benefits are part of the consideration earned by the employee, they are accorded community treatment regardless of whether they derive from a state, federal, or private source, or from a contributory or noncontributory plan. (10 Cal. 3d at p. 596, 111 Cal. Rptr. 369, 517 P.2d 449.) In light of these principles, it becomes apparent that General Smith's retirement pay must properly be characterized as community property.[4]

We cannot, however, evaluate the quality of defendant's professional services on the basis of the law as it appears today. In determining whether defendant exhibited the requisite degree of competence in his handling of plaintiff's divorce action, the crucial inquiry is whether his advice was so legally deficient when it was given that he may be found to have failed to use "such skill, prudence, and diligence as lawyers of ordinary skill and capacity commonly possess and exercise in the performance of the tasks which they undertake." (Lucas v. Hamm (1961) 56 Cal. 2d 583, 591, 15 Cal. Rptr. 821, 825, 364 P.2d 685, 689.) We must, therefore examine the indicia of the law which were readily available to defendant at the time he performed the legal services in question.

The major authoritative reference works which attorneys routinely consult for a brief and reliable exposition of the law relevant to a specific problem uniformly indicated in 1967 that vested retirement benefits earned during marriage were generally subject to community treatment.[5] (See, e.g., Note, Pensions, and Reserve or Retired Pay, as Community Property, 134 A.L.R. 368; 15 Am. Jur. 2d, Community Property, §46, p. 859; 38 Cal. Jur. 2d, Pensions, §12, p. 325; 10 Cal. Jur. 2d, Community Property, §25, p. 692; 1 Cal. Family Lawyer (Cont. Ed. Bar 1962) p. 111; 4 Witkin, Summary of Cal. Law (1960) pp. 2723-2724; cf. 41 C.J.S. Husband and Wife §475, p. 1010 & fn. 69 and 1967 Supp. p. 1011.) A typical statement appeared in The Califor-

---

to have that degree of learning and skill ordinarily possessed by attorneys of good standing, practicing in the same or similar locality and under similar circumstances.

It is his further duty to use the care and skill ordinarily exercised in like cases by reputable members of his profession practicing in the same or a similar locality under similar circumstances, and to use reasonable diligence and his best judgment in the exercise of his skill and the accomplishment of his learning, in an effort to accomplish the best possible result for his client.

A failure to perform any such duty is negligence.

An attorney is not liable for every mistake he may make in his practice; he is not, in the absence of an express agreement, an insurer of the soundness of his opinions.

4. The fact General Smith will not receive any portion of the federal benefits until he reaches the age of 60 does not affect their community character. Though his right to the payments remained unmatured at the time of the divorce, it had fully vested.

5. In evaluating the competence of an attorney's services, we may justifiably consider his failure to consult familiar encyclopedias of the law. (People v. Ibarra (1963) 60 Cal. 2d 460, 465, 34 Cal. Rptr. 863, 386 P.2d 487.)

nia Family Lawyer, a work with which defendant admitted general familiarity: "Of increasing importance is the fact that pensions or retirement benefits are community property, even though they are not paid or payable until after termination of the marriage by death or divorce." (1 Cal. Family Lawyer, *supra*, at p. 111.)

Although it is true this court had not foreclosed all conflicts on some aspects of the issue at that time, the community character of retirement benefits had been reported in a number of appellate opinions often cited in the literature and readily accessible to defendant. . . .

We are aware, moreover, of no significant authority existing in 1967 which proposed a result contrary to that suggested by the cases and the literature, or which purported to rebut the general statutory presumption, as it applies to retirement benefits, that all property acquired by either spouse during marriage belongs to the community. (Civ. Code, §5110, as amended Jan. 1, 1970; formerly Civ. Code §164.)

On the other hand, substantial uncertainty may have existed in 1967 with regard to the community character of General Smith's *federal* pension. The above-discussed treatises reveal a debate which lingered among members of the legal community at that time concerning the point at which retirement benefits actually vest.[6] (See also Kent, Pension Funds and Problems Under California Community Property Laws (1950) 2 Stan. L. Rev. 447; Note, Community Property: Division of Expectancies as Community Property at Time of Divorce (1942) 30 Cal. L. Rev. 469.) Because the federal payments were contingent upon General Smith's survival to age 60, 17 years subsequent to the divorce, it could have been argued with some force that plaintiff and General Smith shared a mere expectancy interest in the future benefits. (See French v. French (1941) *supra*, 17 Cal. 2d 775, 778, 112 P.2d 235; but see fn. 4, *ante*.) Alternatively, a reasonable contention could have been advanced in 1967 that federal retirement benefits were the personal entitlement of the employee spouse and were not subject to community division upon divorce in the absence of express congressional approval. In fact, such was the conclusion reached in 1973 by Judge B. Abbott Goldberg in his scholarly article Is Armed Services Retired Pay Really Community Property? (1973) 48 State Bar Journal 12. Although we rejected Judge Goldberg's analysis in In re Marriage of Fithian (1974) *supra*, 10 Cal. 3d 592, 597, 111 Cal. Rptr. 369; 517 P.2d 449, footnote 2, the issue was clearly an arguable one upon which reasonable lawyers could differ. (See Sprague v. Morgan (1960) 185 Cal. App. 2d 519, 523, 8 Cal. Rptr. 347; Annot., 45 A.L.R.2d 5, 15.)

Of course, the fact that in 1967 a reasonable argument could have been offered to support the characterization of General Smith's federal benefits as separate property does not indicate the trial court erred in submitting the issue of defendant's malpractice to the jury. The *state* benefits, the large majority of the payments at issue, were unquestionably community property according to

---

6. Indeed this debate may, to some extent, continue today. See, e.g., In re Marriage of Wilson (1974) 10 Cal. 3d 851, 112 Cal. Rptr. 405, 519 P.2d 165.

all available authority and should have been claimed as such. As for the *federal* benefits, the record documents defendant's failure to conduct any reasonable research into their proper characterization under community property law.[7] Instead, he dogmatically asserted his theory, which he was unable to support with authority and later recanted, that all noncontributory military retirement benefits, whether state or federal, were immune from community treatment upon divorce. The jury could well have found defendant's refusal to educate himself to the applicable principles of law constituted negligence which prevented him from exercising informed discretion with regard to his client's rights.

As the jury was correctly instructed, an attorney does not ordinarily guarantee the soundness of his opinions and, accordingly, is not liable for every mistake he may make in his practice. He is expected, however, to possess knowledge of those plain and elementary principles of law which are commonly known by well informed attorneys, and to discover those additional rules of law which, although not commonly known, may readily be found by standard research techniques. [Citations omitted.] If the law on a particular subject is doubtful or debatable, an attorney will not be held responsible for failing to anticipate the manner in which the uncertainty will be resolved. [Citation omitted.] But even with respect to an unsettled area of the law, we believe an attorney assumes an obligation to his client to undertake reasonable research in an effort to ascertain relevant legal principles and to make an informed decision as to a course of conduct based upon an intelligent assessment of the problem. In the instant case, ample evidence was introduced to support a jury finding that defendant failed to perform such adequate research into the question of the community character of retirement benefits and thus was unable to exercise the informed judgment to which his client was entitled. (See fn. 7, *infra.*)

We recognize, of course, that an attorney engaging in litigation may have occasion to choose among various alternative strategies available to his client, one of which may be to refrain from pressing a debatable point because potential benefit may not equal detriment in terms of expenditure at time and resources or because of calculated tactics to the advantage of his client. But, as the Ninth Circuit put it somewhat brutally in Pineda v. Craven (9th Cir. 1970) 424 F.2d 369, 372: "There is nothing strategic or tactical about igno-

---

7. At trial defendant testified that prior to the division of property in the divorce action, he had assumed the retirement benefits were not subject to community treatment, despite the fact General Smith had already begun to receive payments from the state: that he did not at that time undertake any research on the point nor did he discuss the matter with plaintiff; that subsequent to the divorce plaintiff asked defendant to research the question whereupon defendant discovered the *French* case which contained dictum in support of plaintiff's position; that the *French* decision caused him to change his opinion and conclude "that the Supreme Court, when it was confronted with this [the language in *French*] may hold that it [vested military retirement pay] is community property." On the basis of *French* defendant filed his unsuccessful motion to amend the final decree of divorce to allow plaintiff an interest in the retirement benefits. Defendant admitted at trial. "I would have been very willing to assert it [a community interest] on her behalf had I known of the dictum in the *French* case at the time."

rance. . . ." In the case before us it is difficult to conceive of tactical advantage which could have been served by neglecting to advance a claim so clearly in plaintiff's best interest, nor does defendant suggest any. The decision to forego litigation on the issue of plaintiff's community property right to a share of General Smith's retirement benefits was apparently the product of a culpable misconception of the relevant princples of law, and the jury could have so found.

Furtheremore, no lawyer would suggest the property characterization of General Smith's retirement benefits to be so esoteric an issue that defendant could not reasonably have been expected to be aware of it or its probable resolution. (Lucas v. Hamm (1961) *supra,* 56 Cal. 2d 583, 15 Cal. Rptr. 821, 364 P.2d 685.) In *Lucas* we held that the rule against perpetuities poses such complex and difficult problems for the draftsman that even careful and competent attorneys occasionally fall prey to its traps. The situation before us is not analogous. Certainly one of the central issues in any divorce proceeding is the extent and division of the community property. In this case the question reached monumental proportions, since General Smith's retirement benefits constituted the only significant asset available to the community.[8] In undertaking professional representation of plaintiff, defendant assumed the duty to familiarize himself with the law defining the character of retirement benefits; instead, he rendered erroneous advice contrary to the best interests of his client without the guidance through research of readily available authority. . . .

Having concluded the issue of negligence was property placed before the jury, we now consider defendant's claims that the verdict was excessive and unsupported by the evidence and that the trial court used an incorrect measure of damages in making a unitary award of $100,000. An economist appearing on plaintiff's behalf as an expert witness testified to the actuarial current value of the benefits payable under the state and federal retirement plans. His assessment was based upon General Smith's life expectancy of approximately 29 years, the total amount of future monthly payments from the pensions, including estimated cost of living increases, and an assumed average rate of interest. It was the witness' opinion that the state retirement benefits had a present value of $272,954 and the federal benefits were currently worth $49,078. Thus the estimated total value was $322,032, one-half of which is $161,016.

Defendant, on the other hand, presented no evidence on the issue of damages. His cross-examination of plaintiff's expert on questions such as General Smith's physical condition relative to his life expectancy and whether taxes were improperly omitted from his computation bears on the weight to be accorded the witness' conclusions, but does not prevent the testimony from supporting the verdict. Valuation is a question of fact for the jury, and its

---

8. It is undisputed that the only assets the parties had to show as community property after 24 years of marriage, aside from General Smith's retirement benefits, were an equity of $1,800 in a house, some furniture, shares of stock worth $2,800, and two automobiles on which money was owing.

award of $100,000 in this case was well within the range of damages suggested by substantial evidence.

The Judgment is affirmed.

CLARK, J. (dissenting).

I dissent.

The evidence is insufficient to prove plaintiff lost $100,000 from her lawyer's negligence in 1967. There is no direct evidence a well-informed lawyer would have obtained an award of the husband's pensions in the wife's divorce, nor does the record provide such inference. Rather, the state of the law and the circumstances of the parties reveal lawyer Lewis reached a reasonable result for his client in 1967.

To establish liability for negligence, a plaintiff must show defendant's negligence contributed to injury so that "but for" the negligence the injury would not have been sustained. If the injury would have occurred anyway—whether or not the defendant was negligent—the negligence was not a cause in fact. (4 Witkin, Summary of Cal. Law (8th ed. 1970) §622, pp. 2903-2904; Rest. 2d Torts (1966) §432; Prosser, The Law of Torts (4th ed. 1971) p. 236 et seq.) "It is not enough merely to show that the probabilities were evenly divided. The evidence must be such that it could be found the balance of probabilities was in plaintiff's favor. (Prosser, 'Proximate Cause in California,' 38 Cal. L. Rev. 369, 378-379.)" (Singh v. Frye (1960) 177 Cal. App. 2d 590, 593, 2 Cal. Rptr. 372, 374.)

This fundmental principle is reflected in legal malpractice cases. Prior to today's majority opinion, a lawyer was "not liable for being in error as to a question of law on which reasonable doubt may be entertained by well-informed lawyers. [Citations.]" (Lucas v. Hamm (1961) 56 Cal. 2d 583, 591, 15 Cal. Rptr. 821, 825, 364 P.2d 685, 689.) The rule has been variously stated: "It has frequently been held that a lawyer is not liable for lack of knowledge as to the true state of the law where a doubtful or debatable point is involved." (Sprague v. Morgan (1960) 185 Cal. App. 2d 519, 523, 8 Cal. Rptr. 347, 350.) Or, a lawyer "is not holden for errors in judgment nor in cases where well-informed attorneys entertain different views concerning a proposition of law which has not been settled." (Floro v. Lawton (1967) 187 Cal. App. 2d 657, 673, 10 Cal. Rptr. 98, 108, quoting from 69 N.J.L.J. 265.) It should be noted the foregoing statements go beyond lawyer *negligence*, going to the ultimate question of *liability*—he shall not be "liable" or "holden" for the errors.

The advice or services performed by the lawyer may be rendered erroneous by subsequent decisions, but if his contemporaries could reasonably have been expected to have performed in the same manner, it is illogical to assume the client would have gained more by having chosen another lawyer. The point is illustrated by the reasoning in Lucas v. Hamm, *supra*, 56 Cal. 2d 583, 593, 15 Cal. Rptr. 821, 826, 364 P.2d 685, 690, involving a lawyer who prepared a will violating the rule against perpetuities. The court compared his position with that of a nonnegligent lawyer, stating there was no liability because "an attorney of ordinary skill acting under the same circumstances might well have 'fallen into the net which the Rule spreads for the unwary' and failed to recognize the danger."

When we consider the law existing in 1967 and the circumstances of the parties, it cannot be concluded on the record before us that it was probable another lawyer would have obtained pension rights for plaintiff in addition to the award obtained for her by defendant.

As the majority opinion points out, when defendant was employed to procure the divorce in 1967, the law was clear that, other than military retirement payments, pension *payments* constituted community property. (E.g., Benson v. City of Los Angeles (1963) 60 Cal. 2d 355, 359, 33 Cal. Rptr. 257, 384 P.2d 689; 4 Witkin, Summary of Cal. Law (7th ed. 1960) pp. 2733-2734.) However, *no reported California case prior to 1967 stated that a court was empowered to award on employee's future pension benefits to his spouse in a divorce action.* To the contrary, there were strong indications from statutory and case authorities that such an award could not be obtained. Further, in every reported case where a spouse sought award of the employee's pension, that spouse lost.

Let us examine the hurdles faced by a 1967 lawyer seeking the pensions now claimed by plaintiff.

INTEREST IS MERE EXPECTANCY

The first hurdle for a spouse seeking to recover an employee's pension in 1967 was the doctrine enunciated in Williamson v. Williamson (1962) 203 Cal. App. 2d 8, 11, 21 Cal. Rptr. 164, 167, that in a divorce action pensions could be taken into account only to the extent that the employee had received benefits or was certain to receive benefits. The court stated:

> The principle established by these cases [citations omitted] is that pensions become community property, subject to the division in a divorce, when and *to the extent* that the party is *certain* to receive some payment or recovery of funds. To the extent that payment is, at the time of the divorce, subject to conditions which may or may not occur, the pension is an *expectancy,* not subject to division as community property. (Italics added.)

In earlier discussion, the court quoted language in Cheney v. City & County of San Franscisco, 7 Cal. 2d 565, 61 P.2d 754, referring to the contingent event of death. (203 Cal. App. 2d at p. 10, 21 Cal. Rptr. 164.) Reading the two statements together, it appears the divorce court could not award future pension payments if they were conditioned on the employee's survival. In the instant case, such a rule would mean the divorce court could have awarded only an amount equal to the first two state pension payments received before the divorce decree. Future payments were apparently subject to the contingency of survival. The first two payments were approximately $1,300, far less than the $100,000 award. . . .

FEDERAL LAW

The majority concedes that in 1967 there was substantial doubt whether federal military pensions constituted community property, awardable in a divorce action.

Aside from the questions discussed above, the principal argument that military pensions were not community property was based on the cases relating to National Service Life Insurance benefits. Wissner v. Wissner (1949) 89 Cal. App. 2d 759, 764-771, 201 P.2d 837, had held that where the premiums were paid by community funds, the insurance proceeds became community property and the widow would be entitled to half the benefits. (Petition for hearing denied with Schauer, J., voting for a hearing.) The United States Supreme Court reversed, holding that because federal statute specified the insured could designate and change the beneficiary, an award of a share of the policy proceeds to the widow when another was designated as beneficiary, would frustrate the intention of Congress. (Wissner v. Wissner (1950) 338 U.S. 655, 658, 70 S. Ct. 398, 94 L. Ed. 424 et. seq.; see Estate of Allie (1958), 50 Cal. 2d 794, 798, 329 P.2d 903 et seq.)

The principle enunciated by the United States Supreme Court in *Wissner* of giving effect to the statutory provision governing the benefit at the expense of the community property system was applied under California law in Benson v. City of Los Angeles, 60 Cal. 2d 355, 33 Cal. Rptr. 257, 384 P.2d 689. This court held that the *widow's* benefit under a Los Angeles Charter provision, concededly community property of a first marriage, was payable in its entirety to the widowed second wife to the exclusion of the first wife.

In the light of *Wissner* and *Benson,* there existed strong reason to believe statutory provisions for payment to the retiree would be interpreted literally to effectuate congressional and legislative intent, thereby excluding community property claims. Additional legal problems inherent in an award of a military pension to a spouse, typical of those faced by counsel in 1967, are discussed In re Marriage of Fithian (1974) 10 Cal. 3d 592, 597-604, 111 Cal. Rptr. 369, 517 P.2d 449.

Although conceding this troubling federal question applied to the federal pension, the majority *incorrectly* implies the *Wissner* rule could not apply to the state pension. The majority opinion fails to recognize that the husband retired under section 228 of the Military and Veterans Code which is in accordance with "federal law, statutes, rules and regulations which . . . govern the retirement of commissioned officers and warrant officers of the reserve components of the Army of the United States on extended active duty; . . ." (Mil. & Vet. Code, §228, see also §§100-104.) Certainly well-informed counsel in 1967 could reasonably have concluded that by appropriating federal law, the Legislature intended it determinative of the character of the pensions.

Assuming defendant fully researched the question whether the pensions could be obtained and further assuming his analysis of the authorities led him to forecast this court's later decisions . . . it does not follow that he should have pursued an award of the pensions. Although defendant by litigating the awardability of pensions would perhaps have performed a valuable service to the State of California by attempting to settle the law, the lawyer's first duty is to his client's best interest—not to the resolution of uncertain legal questions.

Considering the circumstances of this case, including the alimony obtained, expensive litigation by counsel to recover pensions would have gained the client little—if anything—above that obtained in the uncontested action. And, in view of the uncertainty in the law and the risk that the litigation might result in a net loss, pursuit of the pensions would have been an unrealistic alternative. After his retirement, the husband worked as an automobile salesman receiving commissions of approximately $300 per month. Plaintiff had been earning the same amount shortly before. Plaintiff informed defendant that her husband received $645 monthly pension from the National Guard. Under the divorce decree, plaintiff obtained substantially all of the community property for herself and her son, and was awarded $300 per month alimony and $100 per month child support for her son who was then 18. It is apparent the plaintiff would receive more than one-half of the expected joint incomes of the spouses from the pension payment and salaries.

Setting aside alimony awards because of error in the division of community property, this court has recognized the direct relationship between the two awards. [Citations omitted.] The relationship is emphasized in Kinsey v. Kinsey, 231 Cal. App. 2d 219, 222, 41 Cal. Rptr. 802, 805, in the pension context:

> Manifestly, it would be grossly inequitable to permit plaintiff to retain the benefits of the property settlement and the alimony payments as provided by the terms of the interlocutory judgment entered after the default hearing that resulted from the stipulation of the parties, and also now to permit her to "modify" this agreement in such fashion as to entitle her as a matter of right to one-half of defendant's future income in the event of his retirement. Plaintiff's present alimony award is subject to future modification and is ample protection for her future right to share in any income her husband may receive by reason of his pension payments.

Because of the relationship between community property and alimony awards, it was to be anticipated that had defendant succeeded through litigation in establishing a right to assignment of the pensions, the alimony award would have been *greatly reduced* or *eliminated altogether* and the award of the remaining community property possibly altered. Although an award of part of the pension would no doubt have been more valuable than an alimony award of equal amount, the benefit pales in significance when viewed in light of the uncertainty of the law and the large expense required to establish the right to assignment. Further, litigation would have created the risk that a court might conclude not only that pensions did not constitute awardable community property but also, based on the relative earning abilities of the spouses, alimony should be less than $300.

CONCLUSION

Given the uncertain status of the law, the circumstances of the parties, and the close relationship between property division and alimony payment, an ethical, diligent and careful lawyer would have avoided litigation over pension rights and instead would have sought a compensating alimony award for any inequity. [Citations omitted.] So far as appears, defendant secured such compensating award.

Accordingly, even assuming that defendant was negligent in failing to research the pension questions, the record does not furnish a balance of probabilities that his negligence—rather than the uncertain status of the law and the availability of uncontested alimony—caused plaintiff to lose a $100,000 pension award.

I would adhere to the rule of Lucas v. Hamm, *supra*, 56 Cal. 2d 583, 591, 15 Cal. Rptr. 821, 825, 364 P.2d 685, 689, that an attorney is not liable for errors on issues "on which reasonable doubt may be entertained by well-informed lawyers." As shown above, such an issue was presented Attorney Lewis in 1967 concerning recovery of unpaid pension benefits in a divorce action. Further, the law applicable to federal pension benefits also presented such an issue, applicable not only to the federal pension but also to the state pension by section 228 of the Military and Veterans Code.

The majority limits *Lucas* to "esoteric" cases. (Ditto Op., p. 628 of 118 Cal. Rptr., p.— of —P.2d.) Even assuming *Lucas* to be so limited, the hurdles discussed above certainly make the instant case as "esoteric" as *Lucas*. As pointed out by Professor Leach in his classic 1938 article, Perpetuities in a Nutshell, 51 Harv. L. Rev. 638, 669-670, violation of the rule against perpetuities—the claimed malpractice in *Lucas*—may be avoided by use of a simple standard clause placed in every will. The 22 pages of legal discussion since 1967 by this court establishing awardability of pensions generally, of statutory pensions, and of military pensions [citations omitted] attest to the complexity of the pension issues.

I would reverse the judgment.

McCOMB, J., concurs.

NOTES AND QUESTIONS

1. Within a few years after Smith v. Lewis, *supra*, the California Supreme Court returned several times to the issue of the nonworking spouse's rights in the working spouse's postemployment benefits. See especially In re Marriage of Jones, 13 Cal. 3d 456, 531 P.2d 420 (1975) (serviceman's right to disability income is not a community asset); In re Marriage of Brown, 15 Cal. 3d 838, 544 P.2d 561 (1976) (employee's *nonvested* pension rights are a community asset) (overruling French v. French, decided in 1941); In re Marriage of Stenquist, 21 Cal. 3d 779, 582 P.2d 96 (1978) (the "retirement component" of a serviceman's disability income is a community asset, modifying In re Mar-

riage of Jones, *supra.*). The court's decisions led inter alia to (a) abandonment
of a long-standing precedent, (b) major qualification of a decision made only
three years earlier, and (c) subsequent reversal by the United States Supreme
Court, Note 2, *infra.*

2.   Lawyer Lewis may well have been correct about the status of the
federal pension. Compare Hisquierdo v. Hisquierdo, 439 U.S. 752, 99 S. Ct.
802, 59 L. Ed. 2d 1 (1979), which overturned a California ruling that would
have treated benefits under the federal Railroad Retirement Act as a community asset. Husband, a fifty-five-year-old railroad machinist, was within five
years of retirement when his marriage terminated. Wife claimed half the retirement benefits attributable to the husband's labor during the fourteen years
of their marriage. In holding for the husband, the United States Supreme
Court relied upon its reading of the Congressional intent that such benefits not
be shared with the worker's spouse in the event of divorce. Justices Rehnquist
and Stewart, dissenting, failed to see that Congress meant to pre-empt California law.

Two later U.S. Supreme Court decisions have further weakened the
"community" claim of a nonemployee spouse in federal employee benefit programs. McCarty v. McCarty, 101 S. Ct. 2728 (1981) (military retirement
pay); Ridgway v. Ridgway, 102 S. Ct. 49 (1981) (military Servicemen's
Group Life Insurance benefits).

3.   On the malpractice issue, consider the following questions:

(a) Suppose that lawyer Lewis had treated the matter of retirement
    benefits less cavalierly, that is, he had researched the matter but had
    concluded, albeit erroneously, that a court would be unlikely to
    direct that the benefits be shared. Is it still malpractice?
(b) The court acknowledged that it had not yet settled the status of
    prospective military retirement benefits. As the dissenters pointed
    out, "no reported California case prior to 1967 stated that a court
    was empowered to award an employee's *future* pension benefits to his
    spouse in a divorce action." Where the employee and his spouse
    have reached an amicable settlement, as they did in this uncontested
    divorce action, should the lawyer stir the waters by suggesting to his
    client that they litigate an issue in order to advance the law?
(c) Are you satisfied that the court correctly measured the plaintiff's
    damages?

BEAM v. BANK OF AMERICA

6 Cal. 3d 12, 490 P.2d 257, 98 Cal. Rptr. 137 (1971)

TOBRINER, J. Mrs. Mary Beam, defendant in this divorce action, appeals
from an interlocutory judgment awarding a divorce to both husband and wife
on grounds of extreme cruelty. The trial court determined that the only com-

munity property existing at the time of trial was a promissory note for $38,000, and, upon the husband's stipulation, awarded this note to the wife; the court found all other property to be the separate property of the party possessing it. The court additionally awarded Mrs. Beam $1,500 per month as alimony and granted custody of the Beam's two minor children to both parents, instructing the husband to pay $250 per month for the support of each child so long as the child remained within the wife's care.

On this appeal, Mrs. Beam attacks the judgment primarily on the grounds that the trial court (1) failed adequately to compensate the community for income attributable to the husband's skill, efforts and labors expended in the handling of his sizable separate estate during the marriage, and (2) erred in suggesting that community living expenses, paid from the income of the husband's separate estate, should be charged against community income in determining the balance of community funds. In addition, the wife challenges the court's categorization of several specific assets as separate property of her husband. For the reasons discussed below, we have concluded that substantial precedent and evidence support the various conclusions under attack; thus we conclude that the judgment must be affirmed.

I. THE FACTS

Mr. and Mrs. Beam were married on January 31, 1939; the instant divorce was granted in 1968, after 29 years of marriage. Prior to and during the early years of the marriage, Mr. Beam inherited a total of $1,629,129 in cash and securities, and, except for brief and insignificant intervals in the early 1940's, he was not employed at all during the marriage but instead devoted his time to handling his separate estate and engaging in private ventures with his own capital. Mr. Beam spent the major part of his time studying the stock market and actively trading in stocks and bonds; he also undertook several real estate ventures, including the construction of two hotel resorts, Cabana Holiday I at Piercy, California, and Cabana Holiday II at Prunedale, California. Apparently, Mr. Beam was not particularly successful in these efforts, however, for, according to Mrs. Beam's own calculations, over the lengthy marriage her husband's total estate enjoyed only a very modest increase to $1,850,507.33.

Evidence introduced at trial clearly demonstrated that the only moneys received and spent by the parties during their marriage were derived from the husband's separate estate; throughout the 29 years of marriage Mrs. Beam's sole occupation was that of housewife and mother (the Beams have four children). According to the testimony of both parties, the ordinary living expenses of the family throughout the marriage amounted to $2,000 per month and, in addition, after 1960, the family incurred extraordinary expenses (for travel, weddings, gifts) of $22,000 per year. Since the family's income derived solely from Mr. Beam's separate estate, all of these household and extraordinary expenses were naturally paid from that source.

During the greater part of the marriage (1946 to 1963) the Beams resided in a home on Spencer Lane in Atherton, California. In 1963 the family sold the Spencer Lane house and acquired a smaller residence in Atherton, on Selby Lane. This home was sold in 1966 for a cash down payment, which was apparently divided between the parties, and for a promissory note in the sum of $38,000, payable in monthly installments of $262.56. The trial court concluded that this note was community property but, upon Mr. Beam's stipulation, awarded the entire proceeds of the note to the wife.

On this appeal, Mrs. Beam of course does not question the disposition of the promissory note, but does attack the trial court's conclusion that this asset was the only community property existing at the time of the divorce. Initially, and most importantly, the wife contends that the trial court erred in failing to find any community property resulting from the industry, efforts and skill expended by her husband over the 29 years of marriage. We address this issue first.

Section 5108 of the Civil Code provides generally that the profits accruing from a husband's separate property are also separate property. Nevertheless, long ago our courts recognized that, since income arising from the husband's skill, efforts and industry is community property, the community should receive a fair share of the profits which derive from the husband's devotion of more than minimal time and effort to the handling of his separate property. (Pereira v. Pereira (1909) 156 Cal. 1, 7, 103 P. 488; see Millington v. Millington (1968) 259 Cal. App. 2d 896, 907-908, 67 Cal. Rptr. 128 and cases cited therein.) Furthermore, while this principle first took root in cases involving a husband's efforts expended in connection with a separately owned farm or business . . . our courts now uniformly hold that "[a]n apportionment of profits is required not only when the husband conducts a commercial enterprise but also when he invests separate funds in real estate or securities. [Citations.]" . . .

Without question, Mr. Beam's efforts in managing his separate property throughout the marriage were more than minimal . . . and thus the trial court was compelled to determine what proportion of the total profits should properly be apportioned as community income.

Over the years our courts have evolved two quite distinct, alternative approaches to allocating earnings between separate and community income in such cases. One method of apportionment, first applied in Pereira v. *Pereira* (1909) 156 Cal. 1, 7, 103 P. 488 and commonly referrred to as the *Pereira* approach, "is to allocate a fair return on the [husband's separate property] investment [as separate income] and to allocate any excess to the community property as arising from the husband's efforts." (Estate of Neilson (1962) 57 Cal. 2d 733, 740, 22 Cal. Rptr. 1, 4, 371 P.2d 745, 748.) The alternative apportionment approach, which traces its derivation to Van Camp v. Van Camp (1921) 53 Cal. App. 17, 27-28, 199 P.2d 885, is "to determine the reasonable value of the husband's services . . . , allocate that amount as community property, and treat the balance as separate property attributable to the normal earnings of the [separate estate]." (Tassi v. Tassi (1958) 160 Cal. App. 2d 680, 690, 325 P.2d 872, 878.)

The trial court in the instant case was well aware of these apportionment formulas and concluded from all the circumstances that the *Pereira* approach should be utilized. As stated above, under the *Pereira* test, community income is defined as the amount by which the actual income of the separate estate exceeds the return which the initial capital investment could have been expected to earn absent the spouse's personal management. In applying the *Pereira* formula the trial court adopted the legal interest rate of 7 percent simple interest as the "reasonable rate of return" on Mr. Beam's separate property. . . .

Testimony at trial indicated that, based upon this 7 percent simple interest growth factor. Mr. Beam's separate property would have been worth approximately 4.2 million dollars at the time of trial if no expenditures had been made during the marriage. Since Mrs. Beam's own calculations indicate that the present estate, plus all expenditures during marriage, would not amount to even 4 million dollars, it appears that, under *Pereira,* the entire increase in the estate's value over the 29-year period would be attributable to the normal growth factor of the property itself, and, thus, using this formula, all income would be designated as separate property. . . . In other words, under the *Pereira* analysis, none of the increased valuation of the husband's separate property during the marriage would be attributable to Mr. Beam's efforts, time or skill and, as a result, no community income would have been received and, consequently, no community property could presently be in existence.

The wife concedes that the use of the *Pereira* formula does sustain the trial court's conclusion that the present remainder of the husband's estate is entirely his separate property, but she contends that, under the circumstances, the *Pereira* test cannot be said to "achieve substantial justice between the parties" (Logan v. Forster (1952) 114 Cal. App. 2d 587, 600, 250 P.2d 730, 738) and thus that the trial court erred in not utilizing the *Van Camp* approach. Although the trial judge did not explicitly articulate his reasons for employing the *Pereira* rather than the *Van Camp* analysis, we cannot under the facts before us condemn as unreasonable the judge's implicit decision that the modest increment of Mr. Beam's estate was more probably attributable to the "character of the capital investment" than to the "personal activity, ability, and capacity of the spouse." (Cf. Estate of Ney (1963) 212 Cal. App. 2d 891, 898, 28 Cal. Rptr. 442.) In any event, however, we need not decide whether the court erred in applying the *Pereira* test because we conclude, as did the trial court, that even under the *Van Camp* approach, the evidence sufficiently demonstrates that all the remaining assets in the estate constitute separate property.

Under the *Van Camp* test community income is determined by designating a reasonable value to the services performed by the husband in connection with his separate property. At trial Mrs. Beam introduced evidence that a professional investment manager, performing similar functions as those undertaken by Mr. Beam during the marriage, would have charged an annual fee of 1 percent of the corpus of the funds he was managing; Mrs. Beam contends that such a fee would amount to $17,000 per year (1 percent of the 1.7 million dollars corpus) and that, computed over the full term of their marriage, this annual "salary" would amount to $357,000 of community income. Mrs. Beam asserts that under the *Van Camp* approach she is now entitled to one-half of this $357,000.

Mrs. Beam's contention, however, overlooks the fundamental distinction between the total community *income* of the marriage, i.e., the figure derived from the *Van Camp* formula, and the community *estate* existing at the dissolution of the marriage. The resulting community estate is not equivalent to total community income so long as there are any community *expenditures* to be charged against the community income. A long line of California decisions has established that "it is presumed that the expenses of the family are paid from community rather than separate funds [citations] [and] thus, in the absence of any evidence showing a different practice the community earnings are chargeable with these expenses. [Citations.]" Under these precedents, once a court ascertains the amount of community income, through either the *Pereira* or the *Van Camp* approach, it deducts the community's living expenses from community income to determine the balance of the community property.

If the "family expense" presumption is applied in the present case, clearly no part of the remaining estate can be considered to be community property. Both parties testified at trial that the family's *normal* living expenses were $2,000 per month, or $24,000 per year, and if those expenditures are charged against the annual community income, $17,000 under the *Van Camp* accounting approach, quite obviously there was never any positive balance of community property which could have been built up throughout the marriage. . . .

Mrs. Beam contends that the evidence clearly establishes that her husband transmuted the two resort business enterprises, Cabana Holiday I and Cabana Holiday II, concededly financed with his separate property, into community property, and thus that the trial court erred in concluding that the enterprises remained her husband's separate property. We believe that sufficient evidence in the record supports the trial court's characterization of the business as separate property.

Mrs. Beam testified at trial that in 1959, when the plans for the resorts were first initiated, her husband gathered the family together and presented the idea of the Cabana projects as a "family project," in which husband and wife were to be "partners." Thereafter, Mrs. Beam stated, she assisted in the plans for the resorts' construction and helped with the management of the project; she declared at trial that she believed these resorts were to be a "community project."

At trial Mr. Beam did not deny that his wife did expend some effort in connection with these resort projects, but he did dispute her claim that he intended to transmute the Cabana Holiday enterprises, worth almost one-half million dollars, into community property. The husband testified that at various times throughout the marriage he and his wife discussed the manner in which title was to be held on his property and, while his wife wanted some property held in joint tenancy, he consistently stated that he desired to keep his separate property in his name alone. The evidence reveals that whereas the family's residences were held in the names of both husband and wife, the Cabana properties remained in Mr. Beam's name alone.

We recognize, of course, that a husband or wife may orally transmute separate property into community property . . . and, even in the absence of an explicit agreement, written or oral, a court may find a transmutation of property if the circumstances clearly demonstrate that one spouse intended to effect a change in the status of his separate property. . . . Thus the wife's testimony in the instant case would clearly be sufficient to support a finding that a transmutation did occur.

The trial court, however, found that no such transmutation did take place and that the Cabana project remained separate property; such a finding will normally be upheld on appeal. . . .

Examining the instant record as a whole, we find that substantial evidence supports the trial court's conclusion. Mr. Beam testified that he entertained no intention of changing the status of the Cabana properties from separate to community property. Although he did not contradict the wife's declaration that some casual references to the enterprises as "family projects" had occurred, he did establish that the formal title of the property continued to be held in his name alone. The court heard testimony as to the total history of the family finances and could conclude, on the basis of the above evidence, that no transmutation of the resort properties occurred. . . .

The judgment is affirmed.

NOTES AND QUESTIONS

1. By her own calculations, Mrs. Beam claimed approximately $180,000 as her share of the "community" assets. By the court's calculation, there was no community property to be divided, but Mrs. Beam would still receive *qua* alimony $18,000 yearly. That (rapid calculation!) works out to the equivalent of a 10 percent yield on a putative $180,000 investment. Did Mrs. Beam get indirectly what the court refused her directly? What *are* the differences between alimony and property division? Should (would) a spouse's own wealth (including any community property) be considered in fixing her/his alimony award?

2. Problem: To test your understanding of Beam v. Bank of America, consider the following facts. Prior to his marriage, husband acquires a pharmacy, for which he pays $20,000. At the time of his marriage, the business is worth $30,000. During ten years of marriage, husband's annual withdrawals average $20,000. All of the withdrawn money is devoted to family living

expenses. At the time of divorce, husband's business is worth $100,000. You are the husband's (wife's) attorney. At issue is whether any part of the pharmacy business is community property. How would you prepare your case? What additional information would you seek?

3.   The limitations period is ten years. Five years before his marriage, H begins an adverse occupancy that he completes five years after his marriage. Separate or community property? Compare Crouch v. Richardson, 158 La. 822, 104 So. 728 (1925) (community), with Siddal v. Haight, 132 Cal. 320, 64 P. 410 (1901) (separate).

4.   H and W, California residents, take title to real estate as "joint tenants." H transfers the real estate to X. Does X acquire a tenancy in common with W? Cf. Launer v. Griffin, 60 Cal. App. 2d 659, 141 P.2d 236 (1943) (conveyance to H and W as joint tenants destroys presumption that property is community).

§8.5   "Equitable" Distribution of Property

In an era when nearly one marriage in two will end in divorce and every second wife holds a job, the common-law treatment of property acquired during the marriage can often work quite an injustice upon one of the spouses. When a marriage ends in death, common-law states (through dower, curtesy, intestacy, right of election) have to some degree recognized that marriage itself creates mutual interests in property acquired during the marriage, even though legal title is held only by one partner. However, if the marriage ends in divorce, the emphasis on legal title generally has meant, for example, that if one spouse (usually the husband) has taken title to real estate in his own name, what he holds remains with him after the divorce unless the other spouse can show that she (he) helped pay for the asset. The community law recognition that marriage was an economic relationship, even when only one of the spouses was a bread-winner, was absent at common-law.

All that has changed quite dramatically within the past decade. By 1980, when New York reluctantly joined the ranks, virtually every common-law state [15] had provided for the "equitable distribution" of property in the event of marriage dissolution. Stated simply, this requires that property accumulated during the marriage be distributed in a manner that reflects the individual needs and circumstances of the parties regardless of the name in which property is held. Paralleling the community property system, equitable distribution laws distinguish between separate and marital property. With respect to the latter, courts are required to distribute it equitably between the

15. At the end of 1981, only Mississippi and Virginia remained outside the fold.

parties. The New York statute typifies the factors that judges are expected to consider in the name of equity:

    (1)   the income and property of each party at the time of marriage, and at the time of the commencement of the action;

    (2)   the duration of the marriage and the age and health of both parties;

    (3)   the need of a custodial parent to occupy or own the marital residence and to use or own its household effects;

    (4)   the loss of inheritance and pension rights upon dissolution of the marriage as of the date of dissolution;

    (5)   any award of maintenance under subdivision six of this part;

    (6)   any equitable claim to, interest in, or direct or indirect contribution made to the acquisition of such marital property by the party not having title, including joint efforts or expenditures and contributions and services as a spouse, parent, wage earner and homemaker, and to the career or career potential of the other party;

    (7)   the liquid or non-liquid character of all marital property;

    (8)   the probable future financial circumstances of each party;

    (9)   the impossibility or difficulty of evaluating any component asset or any interest in a business, corporation or profession, and the economic desirability of retaining such asset or interest intact and free from any claim or interference by the other party;

    (10)   any other factor which the court shall expressly find to be just and proper.

Still in its infancy, equitable distribution is bound to provoke much litigation, commentary, and statutory change. In time, attorneys and judges will gain some facility in advising clients and deciding cases; until then, we will have much to learn. Your own learning must largely await later courses. However, the following decision is an interesting sample.

IN RE MARRIAGE OF McMANAMA
399 N.E.2d 371,—Ind.—(1980)

PIVARNIK, J. This cause comes to us on a petition to transfer from the Third District Court of Appeals by Respondent-Appellant, Patrick J. McManama.

Petitioner Patrick J. McManama was respondent in the trial court in a cause of action for dissolution of marriage brought by Gertrude Figura McManama. The sole issue raised in the appeal was whether the trial court erred in awarding Gertrude thirty-six hundred dollars ($3600) in furtherance of the property settlement. The facts showed, without dispute, that both of the parties pursued higher education during their marriage, as well as contributing to the income in the home. Appellee wife performed the homemaking duties as well as contributing a larger share of the income, particularly in the last year of the marriage when the parties moved from Connecticut to South Bend, Indiana. At that time they had six thousand dollars ($6,000) in savings. During that last year, appellee-wife earned fourteen thousand seven-hundred and eight-five dollars ($14,785) and appellant-husband went to law school full time, contributing only twelve-hundred and fifty dollars ($1,250) of income. At the time of the separation on August 12, 1976, the only remaining amount in the six-thousand dollar savings account was ninety-six dollars ($96) which was retained by appellant-husband, Patrick. Payments for tuition and books for law school for Patrick amounted to thirty-two hundred dollars ($3,200) and a past due bill for Patrick's tuition while in Connecticut was also paid after they came to South Bend.

The trial court distributed the property of the parties by granting sole ownership, possession and use of the real estate owned by them to appellee-wife, together with any equity and ordering her to hold the husband harmless as to the presently existing mortgage obligation. All personal property was divided between the parties and the husband was held to be responsible for certain remaining financial liabilities of the parties which totalled one-thousand and eighty dollars ($1,080).

The court then made the following entry in its judgment: "In furtherance of this property disposition, and in recognition of the Wife's contribution as a homemaker, as well as her contribution, by way of employment, to the satisfaction of liabilities during the course of the marriage, and contributions toward the legal education of the Husband, the Wife is awarded a judgment against the Husband, in the amount of Three Thousand Six Hundred ($3,600.00) Dollars, to be paid in installments of One Hundred ($100.00) Dollars per month, first payment September 1, 1978, and subsequent payments to be made on the first of each month thereafter until paid in full."

The Court of Appeals, Third District, in an opinion by Hoffman, J., with Chipman, P. J., concurring, affirmed the decision of the trial court. In Re Marriage of McManama, (1979) Ind. App., 386 N.E.2d 953.

Appellant-petitioner contends in his petition to transfer that the trial court erred in awarding Gertrude thirty-six hundred dollars ($3,600) as part of the property settlement. Relying on Wilcox v. Wilcox, (1977) Ind. App., 365 N.E.2d 792, he claims that any award over the value of the marital assets must represent some form of maintenance and since there was no showing of physical or mental incapacitation of appellee-wife pursuant to Ind. Code §31-1-11.5-9(c) (1977 Burns Supp.) the court had no power or authority to make the award. We agree with petitioner-appellant's contention and accordingly vacate the opinion of the Court of Appeals.

The statute providing for disposition of marital assets by the trial court in effect at that time was Ind. Code §31-1-11.5-11 (Burns Supp. 1977) (amended 1979) which read as follows:

Disposition of property.—In an action pursuant to section 3(a) [subsection (a) of 31-1-11.5-3], the court shall divide the property of the parties, whether owned by either spouse prior to the marriage, acquired by either spouse in his or her own right after the marriage and prior to final separation of the parties, or acquired by their joint efforts, in a just and reasonable manner, either by division of the property in kind, or by setting the same or parts thereof over to one [1] of the spouses and requiring either to pay such sum as may be just and proper, or by ordering the sale of the same under such conditions as the court may prescribe and dividing the proceeds of such sale.

In determining what is just and reasonable the court shall consider the following factors:

(a) the contribution of each spouse to the acquisition of the property, including the contribution of a spouse as homemaker;

(b) the extent to which the property was acquired by each spouse prior to the marriage or through inheritance or gift;

(c) the economic circumstances of the spouse at the time the disposition of the property is to become effective, including the desirability of award-ing the family residence or the right to dwell therein for such periods as the court may deem just to the spouse having custody of any children;

(d) the conduct of the parties during the marriage as related to the disposition or dissipation of their property;

(e) the earnings or earning ability of the parties as related to a final division of property and final determination of the property right of the parties."

In 1979, Ind. Code §31-1-11.5-11 was amended and subsection (b) was added which reads as follows:

(b) When the court finds there is little or no marital property, it may award either spouse a money judgment not limited to the existing property. However, this award may be made only for the financial contribution of one [1] spouse toward tuition, books, and laboratory fees for the higher eduction of the other spouse.

However, this subsection was not in effect at the time of this order of August 5, 1977, and cannot apply here.

The trial court and the Court of Appeals apparently interpreted section (d) of Ind. Code §31-1-11.5-11 (Burns Supp. 1977) quoted above to authorize the trial court to repay an aggrieved party in a dissolution judgment for property that had been dissipated by the other partner. This is a misinterpre-tation of that section. The statute clearly sets out factors the court is to use in determining what is a just and reasonable distribution of the property owned by the parties at the time of dissolution. Section (d) was one of the factors the court was to use in making a distribution of the parties' property. In interpret-ing this statute, the First District Court of Appeals in Wilcox v. Wilcox, *supra,* held that the factors set out in the statute can only affect the marital assets in which a vested present interest exists at the time of the dissolution, and do not lend themselves to the interpretation that future income is property and therefore divisible. The thirty-six hundred dollar ($3,600) award to the wife is above the total value of the marital assets as shown by the evidence at trial. It is apparent in the judgment of the trial court that this amount would be paid as an award of the husband's future income. The only way the trial court could have given any additional amounts to the wife at that time, would have been by way of an award of either support or maintenance pursuant to other sections of the statute which authorize the court to do so when there is evidence that the wife is physically or mentally incapacitated. There is no evidence in this cause, nor any finding by the trial court in its judgment, that the wife was physically or mentally incapacitated to the extent that her ability to support herself was materially affected. In fact, the evidence was to the contrary.

Therefore, transfer is granted and the opinions of the Court of Appeals are vacated. The judgment of the trial court is reversed to the extent that it awarded the appellee-wife judgment for thirty-six hundred dollars ($3,600) from the appellant-husband's future income and above the total value of the marital assets. The judgment is ordered amended accordingly.

HUNTER, J., dissenting.

I respectfully dissent. The majority opinion has too narrowly construed the plain meaning of the statute, Ind. Code §31-1-11.5-11 (Burns Supp. 1977) in refusing to find that a professional degree is an intangible asset and therefore part of the marital property. The fact is that the law degree obtained by the husband in this case is *something of value* in which he had a present vested interest at the time of the dissolution and which was obtained as a result of the efforts and sacrifices of both parties. To flatly refuse to find any sort of protected property interest in the degree under the present circumstances would denigrate the very concept of equity.

It is true that a professional degree lacks many of the attributes of tangible property. It does not have an exchange value on the open market, and since it is personal to the holder, it cannot be inherited, assigned, sold, transferred, or conveyed. However, many courts have found that intangible and nontransferable items should be treated as property for some purposes. As Justice Marshall of the United States Supreme Court has said:

> The decisions of this Court have given constitutional recognition to the fact that in our complex modern society, wealth and property take many forms. We have said that property interests requiring constitutional protection "extend well beyond actual ownership of real estate, chattels, or money." Arnett v. Kennedy, (1974) 416 U.S. 134, 207-08, 94 S. Ct. 1633, 1670-71, 40 L. Ed. 2d 15, 64 [footnotes and citation omitted.]

It was further noted: ". . . today more and more of our wealth takes the form of rights or status rather than of tangible goods. . . . A profession or job is frequently far more valuable than a house or bank account. . . ." Arnett v. Kennedy, *supra*, 416 U.S. at 207, n.2, 94 S. Ct. at 1670, n.2, 40 L. Ed. 2d at 64, n.2.

The United States Supreme Court has found that there is a property interest for constitutional purposes in such items as tenured federal employment, Arnett v. Kennedy, *supra;* welfare benefits, Goldberg v. Kelly, (1970) 397 U.S. 254, 90 S. Ct. 1011, 25 L. Ed. 2d 287; and possession of a driver's license, Bell v. Burson, (1971) 402 U.S. 535, 91 S. Ct. 1586, 29 L. Ed. 2d 90. Other courts have divided such items as pension benefits, McGrew v. McGrew, (1977) 151 N.J. Super. 515, 377 A.2d 697; Hutchins v. Hutchins, (1976) 71 Mich. App. 361, 248 N.W.2d 272, and goodwill, In re Marriage of Lopez, (1974) 38 Cal. App. 3d 93, 113 Cal. Rptr. 58. In our own state, it has been held that an interest in a profit-sharing pension plan which was held solely in the name of *one* spouse was an asset to be taken into consideration by the court in determining the amount of the award in a property settlement. Stigall v. Stigall, (1972) 151 Ind. App. 26, 277 N.E.2d 802.

The majority overly narrows the statute by concluding that a professional degree cannot be considered as "property." It is clear that the statute speaks about the division of "marital property" without any attempt to define what property that includes. In fact, it has been expressly stated that ". . . no guidance is given as to precisely what constitutes 'property' within the meaning of the statute." Savage v. Savage, (1978) Ind. App., 374 N.E.2d 536, 538. The majority turns to cases dealing with future interests for guidance and concludes that there must be a vested present interest in an item before it can come within the ambit of "property of the parties." Ind. Code §31-1-11.5-11; Savage v. Savage, *supra,* Wilcox v. Wilcox, (1977) Ind. App., 365 N.E.2d 792. I feel it is clear that the holder of the degree has a present vested interest in the professional degree and only one party must have the present vested interest in the item before it is considered an asset. Stigall v. Stigall, *supra.*

This degree is an intangible asset which was in the nature of an equitable debt extended and expended by the wife to the husband during coverture and the trial court was correct in considering it as an asset in making the division of property.

It is not necessary to consider future earnings in order to determine the value of the degree as an asset. The economic reality is clear that the degree was acquired through the expenditure of time and money on the part of both parties. Had the money spent for the degree bought tangible goods there is no doubt that the trial court had power to divide those goods. There is no reason that the court cannot look to the amount of money expended in achieving the degree and use that as a basis for determining its present value as a marital asset.

In fact, it is very reasonable for courts of equity to have the power to find that since a professional degree is an asset it must be taken into consideration in fashioning a full and just relief for both parties. Nothing in the statute or our prior case law prevents this result in this case. There is no award of maintenance here since the monetary award is based entirely on a division of marital property.

The majority concludes that the monetary award here must be a distribution of the husband's future income and that this is improper since there is no present vested interest in the future income. However, I feel the trial court correctly considered previously expended and dissipated assets in fashioning a division of present assets in this case, since the statute clearly provided that the conduct of the parties could be considered. If a tangible item had been purchased with the expended assets of one party, the court could order it to be sold in order to fairly divide its value between the parties. Since the degree could not be divided, the court fashioned equitable relief through a monetary award repaying the wife for her share in the acquisition of the asset. This is not an award of future income based upon a right of the wife in that income, or an enlargement of the marital estate beyond that property in which the parties maintain a present vested interest, but is a repayment of expended assets which is entirely proper for a court of equity to order.

In order to prevent an inequitable result under these circumstances, some monetary award must be made. To deny that the degree is part of the marital assets in this case, is to give one spouse a windfall of contribution to his or her increased earning capacity while penalizing the other spouse for being a "breadwinner." Courts in several states have found that some monetary award must be made to the working spouse under similar situations although these awards have been upheld on a variety of theories. In re Marriage of Horstmann, (Iowa 1978) 263 N.W.2d 885; Inman v. Inman, (Ky. Ct. App. 1979) 578 S.W.2d 266; Moss v. Moss, (1978) 80 Mich. App. 693, 264 N.W.2d 97; Daniels v. Daniels, (1961) Ohio App., 20 Ohio Op. 2d 458, 185 N.E.2d 773.

The trial court was correct in the instant case in determining that the degree was a marital asset and fashioned a just and equitable relief in the form of a monetary award to the party who was unjustly deprived of a present share in that asset. The intent of the legislature in this area has been made clear in the new code and this code *expressly* approves the relief granted by the trial court in this case.

I would deny transfer and affirm the trial court.

NOTES AND QUESTIONS

1. Compare Inman v. Inman, 578 S.W.2d 266 (Ky. Ct. App. 1979) (dental license is marital property when that is the "only way in which a court can achieve an equitable result"; where wife had contributed financially to husband's professional training, she was entitled to the amount spent for direct support and school expenses, plus reasonable interest and adjustments for inflation; otherwise, wife would have been left "empty handed"), and Hub-

bard v. Hubbard, 603 P.2d 751 (Okla. 1979) (professional license is marital property); with DeWitt v. DeWitt, 98 Wis. 2d 44, 296 N.W.2d 760 (Wis. App. 1980), Frausto v. Frausto, 611 S.W.2d 659 (Tex. Ct. Civ. App. 1980), and In re Marriage of Graham, 194 Colo. 429, 574 P.2d 75 (Colo. 1978), all holding that professional license is not marital property.

2. Prior to their marriage, a man and woman may sign a contract that provides for different property arrangements, in the event of the parties' divorce or one of the parties' death, from those that govern state law. Courts will usually recognize antenuptial agreements that are fair and reasonable or based upon full disclosure of the parties' assets. See generally Clark, Antenuptial Contracts, 50 U. Colo. L. Rev. 141 (1979).

3. In what situation, should divorce occur, might the nonworking spouse fare better (worse) under an equitable distribution statute than would his or her counterpart under a community property system? Note, though, that some community property states have also enacted equitable distribution laws.

4. The National Conference of Commissioners on Uniform State Laws has under review (January 1982) a draft Uniform Marital Property Act (UMPA). In draft version, UMPA would divide assets into "individual property," "marital property," and "quasi-marital property." Individual property would include those assets either party brought into the marriage, or acquired donatively during marriage, as well as any appreciation on such assets. Marital property would include the earnings of individual property, the spouse's interest in any employee benefit plan attributable to his or her earnings, and all nonindividual property that either spouse acquires. In the case of marital property, each spouse would have an undivided one-half interest. Quasi-marital property would include any wealth brought into the UMPA state from a non-UMPA state, which under UMPA would have been marital property. It remains individual property for all purposes prior to a marital termination or a spouse's death. It is then divided like marital property. With respect to all property, however, the parties may, if they wish, own their wealth in any concurrent or survivorship form, and more importantly, may enter into a marital property agreement classifying their wealth and future earnings and income however they choose. The parties' mutual promises would support such agreements, which could be made both before and during marriage, and modified at any time.

The UMPA proposal has several unusual features. For example, management and control of marital property would follow title, which would allow one spouse to transfer ownership without the nontitled spouse's joinder. However, for any donative transfer, the joinder of both spouses would be necessary unless the gift is "normal and usual," given family circumstances. Moreover, to guard against possible abusive transfers, the act contains an "add-a-name" process, whereby a marital property declaration when appropriately filed would inform both the transferee and the transferor spouse that both spouses must sign off.

The drafters of UMPA were undecided as of January, 1982, which of three marital property divisions to recommend in the event of the spouses' separation. The three possibilities were:

(1) Very strong presumption of 50/50 division of marital property, and no division of individual property except under extraordinary circumstances and only after marital property exhausted.
(2) Marital property presumed to be 50/50, but equitable apportionment possible in other ratios based upon relative facts and circumstances. No division of individual property absent extraordinary circumstances.
(3) Absolute 50/50 division of marital property. No division of individual property. No discretion.

5. Although this course is not the place to learn the specifics, you should be aware that federal tax law treats spousal support payments under a divorce or separation decree quite differently from property distributions, and that tax considerations often inform the arrangements to which the separating spouses agree. For a recent instance in which the spousal support/property distribution distinction made a considerable difference, see Beard v. Comm'r., 77 T.C. No. 94 (1981).

§8.6   The Homestead Exemption: More Absolute Than a Fee Simple

The settler who moved into Texas in the early 1800s was often a man of ten-gallon debts. Seeking to protect this new arrival from the claims of his unappeased creditors, the Republic of Texas in 1829 exempted all land from execution for presettlement debts. This law spawned an 1839 statute of the Republic exempting the family home from execution for any unsecured debt. Following the Texas example, most states have since established homestead exemptions by constitution or statute.

The exemption seeks "to assure a permanent common home to members of a family by setting apart property belonging to the head of a family . . . and immunizing this property from the claims of general creditors and from the misfortunes or improvidence of the person who is the head of the family." 2 Powell, Real Property ¶263 (Rohan ed. 1973). Underlying the exemption was the lawmakers' attitude "that an economy containing a debtor living and working and a creditor partly unpaid was more satisfactory than one harbouring the destitute beggar and the complacent banker." Milner, Homestead Act for England? 22 Modern L. Rev. 458, 462 (1959).

To protect the family home against creditors, the states have usually chosen either to exempt the value of the property up to a certain fixed amount or to limit the exemption to a defined quantum of land. (Some laws do both.) Where the exemption is stated solely in terms of dollar value, there is no uniform pattern of protection. For example, Maryland grants a $100 exemption which may be claimed in real property; Maine allows a $3,000 exemption; and California permits a $15,000 exemption.

The inadequacy of the fixed-sum approach, especially when the limits remain unchanged for years, has occasioned much criticism.

> In step with current economic and social realizations, the exemption laws should insofar as possible be flexible in nature so that with economic changes the same real exemptions will continue to be available to debtors. The old crystallized exemption provisions which become outmoded in a few short years should, as far as possible, be abandoned. The risk of fluid exemption laws to creditors seeking a future certainty is recognized. A more extensive use of some intermediate type of exemption law which gives fluidity in the changing economic picture and still gives the creditor reasonable grounds for forecasting available assets is the present need. Escalator and percentage exemption provisions should be more extensively utilized and experimentation with current, reliable indices to which exemption values could be tied is advisable. [Joslin, Debtor's Exemption Laws: Time for Modernization, 34 Ind. L.J. 355, 375-376 (1959)]

In states such as Kansas and Minnesota the homestead is limited only by area, but a distinction is made between urban and rural land, with a larger allowance for the latter. Other jurisdictions, including Arkansas, Mississippi, and North Dakota, establish both a dollar and an area limitation on the homestead exemption. Virginia permits the family debtor who does not hold an interest in land protected by the homestead statute to apply the exemption to personal property.

A head of a family need not own a fee simple interest in his land to avail himself of the homestead exemption. Nor must the homestead property be used exclusively for residential purposes; states may allow a homestead exemption even where the property is primarily used for the operation of a business. See, e.g., Phelps v. Loop, 64 Cal. App. 2d 332, 148 P.2d 674 (1944) (owner of 18-unit apartment house allowed a homestead exemption on the entire property although he occupied only one unit).

Generally, debts incurred for the acquisition of the homestead or for repairs and improvements to the homestead property do not fall within the homestead exemption. The rationale for these exceptions is clear—a "debtor should not be able to acquire a free home by means of the exemption." [16]

---

16. Other "preferred" obligations include taxes and assessments. Some jurisdictions distinguish between obligations founded on contract and those arising from tort or criminal fine, the latter being free of the exemption. Where property is held by cotenants, one cotenant may not set up the homestead exemption to restrict the interest of the other. See Banner v. Welch, 115 Kan. 868, 225 P. 98 (1924).

Some states require a formal declaration in order to establish a homestead, and a few of these states apply the homestead exemption only to liabilities incurred after declaration. Although this type of statute does serve to protect creditors against fraud, ignorance of the requirement by homeowners or their lawyers may deprive many families of the exemption's benefit. In other states the homestead exemption takes effect automatically upon acquisition of the property, or may apply even to antecedent liabilities.

Because of the relatively small dollar exemption allowed in many states, often a residence will be considerably more valuable than the maximum exemption permitted. In such cases the excess value can usually be reached by creditors of the record owners, either through partition in kind, if practicable, or by sale of the entire property with the proceeds of the sale above the exemption amount available to the creditor.

The homestead laws also serve the goal of family protection by vesting some interest in the homestead property in the surviving spouse and minor children.[17] While most states limit the power of a spouse to devise the homestead, some require a surviving spouse to elect between the homestead and the provisions of the decedent's will.

Similar to homestead exemption laws are the constitutional and statutory provisions protecting certain personal property from execution. These laws also vary widely among the states, and may exempt specific property

---

Under the Bankruptcy Act, the bankrupt is entitled to the "exemptions which are prescribed by . . . the State laws in force at the time of the filing of the petition. . . ." 30 Stat. 548 (1898), as amended, 11 U.S.C. §24 (1964). Thus state homestead laws are applicable in bankruptcy proceedings. This is particularly important because of the frequency of petitions in bankruptcy. For example, in fiscal 1963 there were 27,608 bankruptcies filed in California alone. Rifkind, Archaic Exemption Laws, 39 Cal. St. B.J. 370 (1964).

17. See Haskins, Homestead Rights of a Surviving Spouse, 37 Iowa L. Rev. 36, 37-38 (1951):

The degree of protection to which the surviving spouse is entitled under the homestead statutes varies considerably from state to state. The property interest may take the form of a right to rents and profits, a right of occupancy, a life estate, or an interest in fee. Its continuance is sometimes conditioned upon occupancy or widowhood. Its extent may depend on such factors as the existence of children or upon the ownership of property in which the homestead during coverture was established. Generally, the survivor's interest is subject to the same limitations in value as those imposed upon the homestead during coverture, so that the excess is not within the exemption and may be reached by creditors, but it has occasionally been held that the survivor may hold the entire homestead exempt even when it exceeds the specified value.

ranging from a spinning wheel to a television set,[18] or property necessary for a particular trade or profession, or a percentage of wages.

---

18. See, e.g., §34.26 of the Virginia Code (Supp. 1981):

> *§34-26. Exempt articles enumerated.*—In addition to the estate, not exceeding in value five thousand dollars, which every householder residing in this State shall be entitled to hold exempt, as provided in chapter 2 (§34-4 et seq.) of this title, he shall also be entitled to hold exempt from levy or distress the following articles or so much or so many thereof as he may have, to be selected by him or his agents:
>
> (1) The family Bible.
> (1a) Wedding and engagement rings.
> (2) Family pictures, schoolbooks and library for the use of the family.
> (3) A lot in a burial ground.
> (4) All necessary wearing apparel of the debtor and his family, all beds, bedsteads and bedding necessary for the use of such family, two dressers or two dressing tables, wardrobes, chifforobes or chests of drawers or a dresser and a dressing table; carpets, rugs, linoleum or other floor covering; and all stoves and appendages put up and kept for the use of the family not exceeding three.
> (5) All cats, dogs, birds, squirrels, rabbits and other pets not kept or raised for sale; one cow and her calf until one year old, one horse, six chairs, six plates, one table, twelve knives, twelve forks, two dozen spoons, twelve dishes, or if the family consists of more than twelve, then a plate, knife, fork and two spoons and a dish for each member thereof; two basins, one pot, one oven, six pieces of wooden or earthenware; one dining room table, one buffet, china press, one icebox, freezer or refrigerator of any construction, one washing machine, one clothes dryer not to exceed one hundred fifty dollars in value, one loom and its appurtenances, one kitchen safe or one kitchen cabinet or press, one spinning wheel, one pair of cards, one axe and provisions other than those hereinafter set out of the value of fifty dollars; two hoes; fifty bushels of shelled corn, or, in lieu thereof, twenty-five bushels of rye or buckwheat; five bushels of wheat, or one barrel of flour; twenty bushels of potatoes, two hundred pounds of bacon or pork, three hogs, fowl not exceeding in value twenty-five dollars, all canned and frozen goods, canned fruits, preserved fruits or home-prepared food put up and prepared for use and consumption of the family, twenty-five dollars in value of forage or hay, one cooking stove and utensils for cooking therewith, one sewing machine, and in case of a mechanic, the tools and utensils of his trade, and in case of an oysterman or fisherman his boat and tackle, not exceeding one thousand five hundred dollars in value; if the boat and tackle exceed fifteen hundred dollars in value the same shall be sold, and out of the proceeds the oysterman or fisherman shall first receive one thousand five hundred dollars in lieu of such boat and tackle.
>
> No officer or other person shall levy or distrain upon, or attach, such articles, or otherwise seek to subject such articles to any lien or process. (Code 1919, §6552; 1934, p. 371; 1936, p. 322; 1956, c. 637; 1970, c. 428; 1975, c. 466; 1976, c. 150; 1977, cc. 253, 496.)

Chapter 9

Adverse Possession and Prescription

By now you have seen that voluntary transfer is not the only way land interests are created. While sale or lease, mortgage, and testamentary devise are the primary means by which landowner A confers property interests in B, they are not exclusive methods, and often B acquires rights in A's land without regard to the expressed wishes of A, i.e., involuntarily or by operation of law. Thus, if A dies intestate leaving sole heir B, it matters not that A would have given everything to charity rather than let B enjoy a single blade of grass. Or, if B becomes A's judgment creditor, B may levy execution against A's assets and force their sale at public auction. Or, if a community adopts rent control, B may become A's statutory tenant even though his original lease has expired.

This chapter examines still another method for gaining property interests by operation of law. Adverse possession and its near relative, prescription, enjoy an ancient lineage, yet remain an essential part of modern land law. As you ponder the materials ahead, think especially about the policies that the doctrines of adverse possession and prescription seem to further and whether the law as "writ" seems in step with policy.

§9.1 Elements of Title by Adverse Possession

Take the following case. A owns a parcel of land. Neighbor B builds a fence that encroaches on A's land. A may sue to enjoin the fence and recover possession of his entire parcel. A's suit to recover possession, like legal remedies generally, must begin before the governing statute of limitations has run. A's penalty for delaying his suit may be loss of title, *by adverse possession,* of the strip B occupies.

Statutes of limitation governing the recovery of land have very early origins that culminate in 21 Jac. 1, c. 16, §§1, 2 (1623), which created a twenty-year limitations period. Significantly, this statute did more than bar the remedy; its expressed goals were the "avoiding of Suits" [1] *and* the "quieting of Man's Estates." Thus, once the action was barred, the original owner could not recover title simply by regaining possession.

Most American jurisdictions first adopted the English model of a twenty-year limitation. See, e.g., Mass. Gen. Laws Ann. c. 260 §21 (West 1968). But the trend is toward shorter limitations periods (why should this be?) and for greater diversity of treatment. For example, Michigan now has a basic fifteen-year statute, but reduces the term to ten years if possession is pursuant to a tax foreclosure, and to five years if pursuant to a court order, a fiduciary's deed, or a sheriff's deed. Mich. Comp. Laws Ann. §600.5801 (1968). New York has twice lowered its limitations period to the present ten years. N.Y. Real Prop. Act. Law §§511, 512, 521, 522 (McKinney 1963). California has a five-year statute. Cal. Civ. Proc. Code §§324, 325 (West 1954). [2]

Not every occupancy of another's land gives rise to a cause of action. In fact, most occupancies do not. Before the cause of action accrues, so that the occupancy can begin to ripen into title by adverse possession, the occupancy must satisfy certain criteria. The following opinion discusses them.

WEST v. TILLEY

33 A.D.2d 228, 306 N.Y.S.2d 591 (4th Dept. 1970)

Bastow, J. Plaintiff's appeal brings before us for review a judgment which among other things, decreed that respondent was the owner by adverse possession as against plaintiff of a triangular parcel of land with dimensions of approximately 55 by 40 by 23 feet fronting on Conesus Lake in Livingston County.

For many years respondent and members of her family have owned lands bounded on the west by the shore of that lake and on the east by a highway known as East Lake Road. In 1959 appellant acquired a tract of land on the east side of East Lake Road none of which abutted on the lake. The conveyance to him, however, also included a parcel of land on the west side of the highway which adjoined respondent's land on the northerly side thereof. This strip had frontages on the highway and Conesus Lake, respectively, of 10.44 feet. The other two sides of the quadrangle measured about 135 feet.

---

1. Very often, the adverse party claiming title sues *after* the original owner's suit is barred. Does the doctrine "avoid" suits, or simply switch parties? Consider how litigation might sometimes be avoided.

2. A 1978 survey of state adverse possession laws reported that the basic limitations period ranged from 5 years (four states) to 30 years (two states and Puerto Rico). Other limitations periods were: 7 years (5 states); 10 years (15 states); 15 years (8 states and District of Columbia); 18 years (1 state); 20 years (12 states); 21 years (2 states); 25 years (1 state). National Law Journal, Dec. 25, 1978, at 16.

In 1925 respondent's father constructed a cement wall (to serve as a breakwater) along the westerly (shore) line of his property. This wall not only extended along all the frontage then owned by respondent's father but included the frontage (10.44 feet) subsequently acquired by appellant and an additional 12 or 13 feet in a northerly direction. Dirt was then filled in behind the wall bringing it to a level with the adjacent lands. In 1925 and for many years thereafter the shoreline at the northerly extremity of this wall curved in a generally southeasterly direction to form a cove or bay. In 1936 another concrete wall (forming another breakwater) was constructed by respondent's husband. This commenced at the northerly end of the first wall and extended along the then shoreline in a southeasterly direction across the 10-foot strip now owned by appellant to a concrete monument set on the northerly line of respondent's property. It is these two concrete walls and the northerly line of respondent's land that form the three sides of the triangle containing the land to which respondent has been adjudged to be the owner by adverse possession.

The character of the second concrete breakwater constructed in 1936 was drastically changed, however, in 1963 when one Pope (the owner of lands to the north of the 10-foot strip owned by appellant) constructed an extension of the north-south wall along the lake front, which had been built by respondent's father in 1925. Pope then land-filled behind (and to the east) of this wall and obliterated a portion of the bay.

To sustain her claim of title by adverse possession respondent, of course, was required to establish the five essential elements that first, the possession was hostile and under claim of right; second, it was actual; third, it was open and notorious; fourth, it was exclusive; and fifth, it was continuous. (Belotti v. Bickhardt, 228 N.Y. 296, 302.) Furthermore, inasmuch as respondent's claim of title was not based on a written instrument, she was by statute limited in her claim to "the premises so actually occupied, and no others," and to land that "has been usually cultivated or improved" or "has been protected by a substantial inclosure." (Real Property Actions and Proceedings Law, §§521, 522; formerly Civ. Prac. Act, §§39, 40; Code Civ. Pro., §§371, 372.)

We conclude, that except for the requirement that the possession was hostile and under a claim of right, which will be hereinafter discussed, the proof establishes all of these essential common-law and statutory requirements. Not only was the triangular parcel, which included the westerly portion of appellant's strip of land, enclosed (from 1936 to 1963) with two cement walls, but continuously for more than 25 years respondent and members of her family openly and exclusively occupied, dominated and controlled the parcel. In 1939 a concrete shuffleboard was constructed partially on respondent's land and the remainder on a portion of the land forming the triangle and owned by appellant's predecessor in title. The reminder of the triangular parcel was made into a lawn and shrubs planted thereon. Through the ensuing years the grass planted thereon was regularly cut during the summer months and the shrubbery pruned. On the trial appellant conceded that respondent had used the land in dispute.

Appellant contends, however, that respondent's occupation was not open and notorious because his 10-feet strip was wild, overgrown and little used; that it was not until Pope cleared out and improved his lake front property that respondent's occupation of his land became apparent from the highway. The short answer is that even a casual inspection by appellant in 1959 of the boundary lines of the property he proposed to purchase would have revealed respondent's occupation and use of the westerly portion thereof, which was then enclosed on two sides with concrete walls.

Appellant further, and vigorously, argues that respondent's possession was not hostile and under a claim of right. This contention is based on Mrs. Tilley's testimony. Thus, when asked if by the construction of the east-west wall in 1936 it was her intention to intrude on appellant's land, her reply was "we were only enclosing our own property." Later she testified that it had always been her claim that she owned appellant's land; that since 1935 she had treated it as an owner—"I claim title to everything that is within the walls." The documentary proof, however, establishes that she was mistaken in her views and claims.

This presents the issue as to whether the necessary element of hostile possession may exist although such possession is taken by the mistaken view of a claimant thereto that it was within his true boundary lines or, on the other hand, whether such a mistake prevents the existence of the requisite hostility and claim of right.

Professor Powell in discussing this question has written that "The leading case holding the mistake to be of no importance was French v. Pearce [8 Conn. 439] decided in Connecticut in 1931. In this case the court said: 'Into the recesses of his [the adverse claimant's] mind, his motives or purposes, his guilt or innocence, no inquiry is made. . . . The very nature of the act (entry and possession) is an assertion of his own title, and the denial of the title of all others. It matters not that the possessor was mistaken and that had he been better informed, would not have entered on the land. . . .' This viewpoint has gained increasingly widespread acceptance. The more subjectively oriented view regards the 'mistake' as necessarily preventing the existence of the required claim of right. The leading case on this position is Preble v. Maine Central R.R. Co. [85 Me. 260] decided in 1893. This position is still followed in a few states. It has been strongly criticized as unsound historically, inexpedient practically, and as resulting in better treatment for a ruthless wrongdoer than for the honest landowner. Its harshness is substantially mitigated by a judicially accepted presumption of hostility. . . . On the whole the law is simplified, in the direction of real justice, by a following of the Connecticut leadership on this point." (6 Powell, Real Property, §1015.)

The majority, or so-called Connecticut rule, that the necessary element of hostile possession may exist although possession was taken by mistake has been recognized and restated by modern text writers. (3 Am. Jur. 2d, Adverse Possession, §§39-42; 2 N.Y. Jur., Adverse Possession, §15; 3 American Law of Property, §15.5; Ann. 80 A.L.R.2d 1171, 1183; 10 Univ. of Florida L. Rev., 245, 253-260.)

In this jurisdiction the majority rule has been recognized, at least where a building is erected partially on adjacent property by reason of mistake as to the location of the true boundary line. (Belotti v. Bickhardt, 228 N.Y. 296, *supra;* Smith v. Egan, 225 App. Div. 586.) In Belotti (*supra,* p. 302) the rule was thus stated: "Adverse possession, even when held by a mistake or through inadvertence, may ripen into a prescriptive right after twenty years of such possession [citing cases], the actual physical occupation and improvement being, in a proper case, sufficient evidence of the contention to hold adversely [citing cases]." . . .

We conclude that although respondent, or her predecessors in interest, took possession of appellant's land through mistake, it was not the less adverse for the reason that "It is the visible and adverse possession, with an intention to possess land occupied under a belief that it is the possessor's own, that constitutes its adverse character, and not the remote view or belief of the possessor." (2 N.Y. Jur., Adverse Possession, §15.)

We further conclude, as stated, that the proof sustains a finding pursuant to statute (Real Property Actions and Proceedings Law, §522) that appellant's land so possessed by respondent had been "usually cultivated or improved" if not "protected by a substantial inclosure." (Cf. Barnes v. Light, 116 N.Y. 34; Connolly v. Merz, 201 N.Y.S.2d 401 [Meyer, J.].) In Connolly (*supra,* p. 404) it was written: "Cultivation and improvement consistent with the nature of the property and such as to indicate exclusive ownership of the property is all that is required [citing cases] and while 'occasional forays' or the cutting and removal of 'a load or two of thatch' are not sufficient [citing case] a regular and consistent use has been shown here."

The judgment should be affirmed.

MARSH, J.P., WITMER and MOULE, JJ., concur.

Judgment unanimously affirmed, with costs.

NOTES AND QUESTIONS

1. The *West* opinion sets out the common-law elements for "adverse" possession. The possession must be "hostile and under claim of right," "actual," "open and notorious," and "exclusive." It is one thing to state the criteria, quite another to determine whether they are present in a given controversy. Once all are present, the cause of action accrues, and if "adverse" possession remains "continuous" for the statutory period, title by adverse possession is the result.

(a)   *"Hostile and under claim of right":*

(1) In Preble v. Maine Cent. R. Co., 85 Me. 260, 27 A. 149 (1893), the plaintiff testified that he had continuously occupied the land to the fence (inside his neighbor's lot) in the belief that it marked the true line. The court refused to find title by adverse possession, since plaintiff had mistakenly occupied his neighbor's land "with no intention to claim title beyond his actual boundary wherever that may be." Contrast *Preble* with the court's treatment of hostility in *West*. Should "animus" be essential for possession to ripen into title? If so, how can the occupier prove that "animus" existed; how can the original owner prove that it did not? Might one view the requirement of "animus" differently in a dispute over a boundary in a central city than in a dispute over the boundary between two farms? The *Preble* doctrine is no longer widely held. 6 Powell, Real Property, ¶1015 at 726 (Rohan ed. 1973). One court has even refused to extend the benefits of adverse possession to "bad faith" possessors. Roy v. Elmer, 153 So. 2d 209 (La. App. 1963).

(2) The original owner, O, testifies that he knew of A's possession, but since he had no immediate plans to use the property, he did not object. How relevant is this testimony?

(3) If one enters possession as of right, as a lessee or a cotenant, for example, may she ever acquire title adversely against her landlord or her fellow cotenant? Cf. N.Y. Real Prop. Actions Law §531 (McKinney 1963) (landlord and tenant) (occupation presumed permissive for 10 years after rent stops or term ends; presumption rebuttable); id. §541 (cotenants). What steps should such an occupier take to manifest his "hostility"? See, e.g., Graham v. Graham, 45 Misc. 2d 298, 256 N.Y.S.2d 888 (Sup. Ct. 1965); McKnight v. Basilides, 19 Wash. 2d 391, 143 P.2d 307 (1943); West v. Evans, 29 Cal. 2d 414, 175 P.2d 219 (1946).

(b)   *"Actual":*

The New York statute specifies quite exactly how the occupier must use the land if he is to gain title by adverse possession. Thus, if A does not have "color of title" (see §9.2 *infra*), New York requires that the parcel claimed be either protected by a "substantial inclosure" or "usually cultivated or improved." N.Y. Real Prop. Actions Law §522 (McKinney 1963). See also Cal. Civ. Proc. Code §§324, 325 (West 1954).

(c)   *"Open and notorious":*

(1) Construction of a sixteen-story apartment building began in 1960. While excavating for the foundation, the plaintiff discovered that the Sixth Avenue subway had been encroaching (thirty feet beneath the surface) since its construction twenty-one years before. In a suit for trespass, the plaintiff denied any knowledge of the encroachment

prior to 1960. Has the defendant acquired an interest by operation of law? 509 Sixth Avenue Corp. v. New York City Transit Auth., 15 N.Y.2d 48, 203 N.E.2d 486 (1964).

(2) Plaintiff and defendant were adjoining landowners. In 1883 a cave opening was discovered on defendant's land, and almost at once Marengo's Cave, as it was called, became a popular attraction. The plaintiff learned only in 1932, twenty-five years after he had acquired title, that part of the cave extended beneath his land, yet he was well acquainted with the cave throughout this period. Plaintiff sues to quiet his title. Result? Marengo Cave Co. v. Ross, 212 Ind. 624, 10 N.E.2d 917 (1937).

(d) *"Exclusive":*

Cases hold that the claimant's possession must be exclusive and that a "scrambled" possession is not enough. But the cases rather scramble the doctrine. One thing that "exclusive" will mean is that A's occupancy must be to the exclusion of O, the original owner—not entirely self-evident even when A claims adversely to O. (Why should an occasional *use* by O interrupt A's claim?) But "exclusive" seems (usually) not to mean that only one person at a time may acquire an adverse interest. For example. if A and B together occupy O's parcel and are acting in concert, they may obtain a cotenancy interest. (Different result if A and B are acting adversely to each other, as well as to O.) Nor will A's occupancy be nullified if he overlooks an occasional trespass by strangers or gives a permissive use to others, so long as his occupancy remains consistent with a claim of ownership.

(e) *"Continuous":*

Continuous means something less than unbroken physical presence for every instant of the limitations period. For example, where the premises were vacant for various intervals between tenancies, a court wrote:

> While no principle of law of adverse possession is more firmly settled in Kentucky than that requiring continuous and uninterrupted possession for the full statutory period in order to ripen an adverse claim into a legal title, an exception to the rule is just as well recognized; that a temporary break or interruption, not of unreasonable duration, does not destroy the continuity of the adverse possession and where the periods of vacancy are occasioned by change of possession or by the substitution and possession of one tenant for another which are not of longer duration than is reasonable in view of the character of the land and the uses to which it is adopted and devoted, they do not constitute interruption of possession destroying its continuity in legal contemplation where there is no intention to abandon. [Gillis v. Curd, 117 F.2d 705 (6th Cir. 1941)]

2. *Tacking:* This term, well known to sailors, tailors, and carpet layers, also has its meaning for the property lawyer. Suppose that A enters Blackacre and remains in possession, adversely and continuously for nineteen of the statutory twenty years. A dies, and his heir, AH, replaces him in possession.

Must AH complete a twenty-year term in his own right, or may he avail himself of the ancestor's prior occupancy? Although Blackacre's owner has a theoretical argument for insisting that the statute run anew, the courts have allowed the two periods of occupancy to be joined, or *tacked* together. Can you explain why?

Tacking occurs whenever the successive occupiers are said to be in "privity of estate." Privity of estate is a term that recurs often, and, to the dismay of law students, is not always blessed with quite the same content. Here, however, privity would be satisfied if the relationship between the first and second occupier were: grantor-grantee; landlord-tenant; testator-devisee; decedent-heir; mortgagor-mortgagee. In each instance, either a consensual or a legally formed nexus exists to join the two occupiers. Not so if A is forcibly ousted by B. See, e.g., Doe, ex dem. Harlan v. Brown, 4 Ind. 143, 145 (1853). What policy goals does the privy requirement serve here?

Suppose that the adverse claim depends upon the tacking between A and B, grantor-grantee, but that A's deed to B fails to describe the parcel claimed. Has tacking occurred? Compare Bradt v. Giovannone, 35 A.D.2d 322, 315 N.Y.S.2d 961 (3d Dept. 1970), with Marquis v. Drost, 155 Conn. 327, 231 A.2d (1967).

3. *Disability:* One other factor must be present before the statute of limitations can begin to run: the claimant must have capacity to sue. If the aggrieved person is disabled when the cause of action accrues, the statute is tolled. The 1623 statute, page 499 *supra*, set an early pattern for listing the conditions of disability and their relationship to the limitations period:

> II. Provided nevertheless, That if any Person or Persons . . . entitled to such Writ . . . or (having) such Right . . . of Entry . . . shall be at the Time . . . the said Right . . . first . . . accrued . . . within the Age of one and twenty years, Feme Covert, Non Compos Mentis, imprisoned or beyond the Seas, that then such Person and Persons . . . shall or may, notwithstanding the said twenty Years be expired, bring his Action, or make his Entry, as he might have done before this Act; (2) so as such Person and Persons . . . shall within ten Years next after his and their full Age, Discoverture, coming of sound Mind, Enlargement out of Prison, or coming into this Realm, or Death, take Benefit of and sue forth the same, and at no time after the said ten Years.

Foreign travel or a woman's equally venturesome journey into marriage are no longer legally disabling events, nor is imprisonment in most jurisdictions. But infancy and, less often, mental incapacity remain so.

To understand their effect in states having adopted the English model, work through the following problems:

(a) A enters Blackacre in 1960 and remains in possession, adversely and continuously thereafter. In 1960, the Blackacre owner, O, is five years old. When does the statute of limitations expire?

(b) A enters Blackacre in 1960 and remains in possession, adversely and continuously thereafter. In 1960, Blackacre's owner, O, is legally incompetent. O dies in 1975. When does the statute of limitations expire?

(c) A enters Blackacre in 1960 and remains in possession, adversely and continuously thereafter. In 1960 Blackacre's owner, O, is 15 years old and also legally incompetent. In 1970, O is declared legally competent. When does the statute of limitations expire? *doesn't start*

running

(d) A enters Blackacre in 1960 and remains in possession, adversely and *until O* continuously thereafter. In 1970, Blackacre's owner, O, is declared *is of age* legally incompetent. O dies in 1980. When does the statute of limi- *or legally* tations expire? *competent*

(e) A enters Blackacre in 1960 and remains in possession, adversely and continuously thereafter. In 1960, Blackacre is owned by O and P, as tenants in common. O is legally incompetent. In 1976, O is declared legally competent. When does the statute of limitations expire?

In some states, the limitations period runs for its full term after the disability ends. In a few others, the statute expires after a given interval even if the disability remains.

Of the three statutory approaches to disability, which one do you prefer? Is there any policy justification for retaining the disability feature?

In its relation to adverse possession, disability may appear in a rather distinctive form. Suppose that the ownership of Blackacre is divided into present and future interests when the adverse occupancy begins. Does possession ripen into title at one time against both sets of interest holders? Remember that the cited statute speaks of persons "entitled" to the writ of entry. Take these examples:

(f) A enters Blackacre in 1960 and remains in possession, adversely and continuously thereafter. In 1960, Blackacre is owned by O, for life, remainder in P. O dies in 1980. Given a twenty-year limitations period, who owns Blackacre in 1982? What if O were still alive? 6 Powell, Real Property ¶1024 at 762.6 (Rohan ed. 1973).

(g) A enters Blackacre in 1960 and remains in possession, adversely and continuously therafter. In 1960, Blackacre is owned by O, for life, remainder in those persons whom O shall appoint by will. Given a twenty-year limitations period, who owns Blackacre in 1980?

(h) A enters Blackacre in 1960 and remains in possession, adversely and continuously thereafter. In 1950, Blackacre was leased to O for a term of ninety-nine years, reversion in P. Given a twenty-year limi- tations period, who owns Blackacre in 1980?

(i) A enters Blackacre in 1960 and remains in possession, adversely and continuously thereafter. In 1969, O transfers Blackacre to P, for life,

remainder to Q. Given a twenty-year limitations period, who owns
Blackacre in 1980?

If these were cases of first impression, what factors might the court consider in reaching its decision?

4.   In many jurisdictions, the limitations period for an action in contract (or quasi contract) is six years. If A's possession ripens into title in 1980,
may the original owner, D, still recover the rental value of the premises for A's
occupancy between 1974 and 1980? Cf. Counce v. Yount-Lee Oil Co., 87 F.2d
572 (5th Cir. 1937), *cert. denied sub nom.* Wilkinson v. Yount-Lee Oil Co., 302
U.S. 693 (1937).

5.   X is a judgment creditor of the original owner, D. If A's adverse
possession of D's land ripens into title, does A take free of X's judgment lien?
Cf. American Employers Ins. Co. v. Texas, 153 S.W.2d 501 (Tex. Civ. App.
1941). Does A take subject to outstanding mortgages, easements, and tract
restrictions? Cf. 6 Powell, Real Property ¶1025 at 762.9 (Rohan ed. 1973).

§9.2   Occupancy Under Color of Title

Many states give favored treatment to an occupancy that begins under "color
of title"—that is, under a writing (deed, mortgage, decree, etc.) professing to
pass title, but not doing so, usually because of a procedural defect or a want in
the grantor's title. While color of title is rarely a necessary element of adverse
possession, the claimant having a semblance of title often enjoys two statutory
benefits: (1) a shorter limitations period; (2) use of the doctrine of "constructive possession." The Illinois statute, for one, requires only a seven-year occupancy under color of title against ten years for other occupancies. Ill. Ann.
Stat. ch. 83, §§1, 6 (Smith-Hurd 1966). [3]

Constructive possession permits the occupant to gain title to the entire
parcel described in the written instrument, even though his occupancy extends
only to some of the parcel. (Compare *actual* possession, page 504, *supra.*) Thus,
the New York statute provides:

> For the purpose of constituting an adverse possession by a person claiming a title
> founded upon a written instrument or a judgment or decree, . . . where a known
> farm or a single lot has been partly improved, the portion of the farm or lot that
> has been left not cleared or not inclosed, according to the usual course and
> custom of the adjoining country, is deemed to have been occupied for the same

3. Most color of title statutes require the occupant to pay real estate taxes during the
occupancy period on the parcel claimed. California imposes a tax-paying requirement upon all
claims of adverse possession. Cal. Civ. Proc. Code §325 (West 1954).

length of time as the part improved and cultivated. [N.Y. Real Prop. Actions Law §512 (McKinney 1963)]

Lawmakers invented the doctrine of constructive possession to meet the problem of poor title records that plagued the westward movement. Settlers would invest their energies in clearing land, then learn they had faulty title. Conventional adverse possession doctrine would have secured title only to the land actually worked.

As courts have fleshed out the doctrine, they have generally refused to extend title to a noncontiguous parcel, to a contiguous parcel separately owned, or even, in some cases, to a contiguous parcel held by the same original owner.

§9.3   The "Agreed Boundaries" Doctrine

The "agreed boundaries" doctrine often arises in the same context as a dispute over title by adverse possession. Sometimes a claimant, unable to prove the necessary elements for adverse possession, may turn to an agreed boundaries theory in an effort to establish title. Consider the use of agreed boundaries in the following case.

JOAQUIN v. SHILOH ORCHARDS
84 Cal. App. 3d 192, 148 Cal. Rptr. 495 (1978)

FRANSON, J. The fundamental question presented by this quiet title action is the extent of the trial court's obligation to fix the location of an agreed boundary between contiguous owners of land where the monument fixing the line (a fence) has been removed without a survey or other marking to identify its precise location. As we shall explain, the trial court is required to fix the location of the agreed boundary according to the evidence presented at trial if it is reasonably possible to do so. Thus, in the present case the court erred in refusing to determine the location of the agreed boundary and in quieting title in respondents according to their complaint.

Prior to 1942 the Bank of America was the common owner of the adjoining parcels of real property now owned by appellant and respondents, the boundary line of which is the subject of this controversy. On April 6, 1942, the bank sold one parcel to the respondents' predecessors in interest and on March 1, 1943, sold the other parcel to the appellant's predecessor in interest. The deed to both parcels described their common boundary as the quarter section line separating the southwest quarter section from the northwest quarter section of section 19, in township 4 south, range 8 east, Mount Diablo Base and Meridian, in the County of Stanislaus. There is a 5-inch diameter concrete monument located in Shiloh Road marking the western quarter section corner, which the federal government established in 1854. The monument set at the easterly corner of the section line in 1854 has never been located, but a surveyor reestablished this point in 1974 for a survey of nearby property.

At sometime prior to 1944, a fence was constructed which divided one portion of the property from the other, and the two portions were separately farmed and utilized up to the fence. In addition, the separate farming practices of the adjoining owners over the years created a line demarcing the differing cultural practices, evidenced by a change in elevation or "bench" between the two farms at the fence line, ranging from 12 to 36 inches in height. The fence was located at the top of this bench. The area between the fence line and the quarter section line is approximately 2.4 acres.

Respondents acquired their parcel on September 5, 1967, and appellant acquired its parcel on December 28, 1973. At the date of appellant's acquisition, appellant and its predecessors in interest accepted and understood the fence to be the boundary between the respective parcels. Appellant entered into possession of its parcel to the fence and dealt with the property as if the fence constituted the boundary, cultivating and improving its parcel, including the now disputed piece.

In 1974 appellant removed the fence to establish an almond orchard on the property, which it accomplished in 1975. The fence line was removed to help control weeds that had grown along the fence. Appellant used a disc to control the weeds on the old fence line. The effect of the discing was to "round" the bench somewhat, but not enough to extinguish the original line. Appellant leveled the property, installed a sprinkler system, and planted an almond orchard, at the cost of approximately $2,100 per acre. . . .

In the course of constructing a power line project, respondents began to suspect that the former fence line might not be the boundary described in the deeds to the respective parcels. Respondents commissioned a land survey, which indicated that the boundary described in the deeds was some distance to the north of the newly planted almond orchard, leaving ownership of a portion of the orchard in dispute and leading to this action.

The trial court found that although a fence had been in existence for many years south of the quarter section line, and the parties and their predecessors had each farmed the land to the fence, causing the formation of an embankment of soil along the fence line, the removal of the fence without a survey or other method of marking its exact location resulted in a loss of appellant's title in the land to the fence. In support of this conclusion, the court found that appellant had disced and broadened the bank after the fence had been removed; that neither the top nor the bottom of the bank as it existed prior to 1974 had been established; and that no remnants of the fence post remaining below ground had been shown. From these findings the court concluded that "[t]he only ascertainable boundary which can be defined in words and which can be translated into monuments on the ground is the common quarter section line as used and described in the recorded deed of each property." It then quieted title in respondents according to the prayer of their complaint.

The doctrine of acquiescence to a boundary line is referred to in California as the doctrine of title by agreed boundary. (See Ernie v. Trinity Lutheran Church (1959) 51 Cal. 2d 702, 707, 336 P.2d 525.) It is a mixture of implied agreement and estoppel. (Miller and Starr, Current Law of California Real Estate (1977) §21:27, pp. 552-559.) The elements of the doctrine are an uncertainty as to the true boundary line, an agreement between the adjacent owners establishing the line, and acceptance and acquiescence in that line. (Ernie v. Trinity Lutheran Church, *supra;* Duncan v. Peterson (1970) 3 Cal. App. 3d 607, 611, 83 Cal. Rptr. 744.)

The doctrine clearly applies to this case. The inability to locate the eastern quarter section monument demonstrates the requisite uncertainty. The evidence shows that the owners had accepted the fence as the boundary line. "A longstanding acceptance of a fence as a boundary line gives rise to an inference that there was, in fact, a boundary agreement between the coterminous owners resulting from an uncertainty or dispute as to the location of the true line." (Current Law of California Real Estate, *supra,* §21:31, p. 562; Ernie v. Trinity Lutheran Church, *supra,* 51 Cal. 2d 702, 708, 336 P.2d 525.)

The trial court apparently misunderstood the full legal consequences of the agreed boundary.

> . . . [W]hen such owners, being uncertain of the true position of the boundaries so described, agree upon its true location, mark it upon the ground, or build up to it, occupy on each side up to the place thus fixed, and acquiesce in such location for a period equal to the statute of limitations, or under such circumstances that substantial loss would be caused by a change of its position, *such line becomes, in law, the true line called for by the respective descriptions, regardless of the accuracy of the agreed location, as it may appear by subsequent measurements.* [Emphasis added. Young v. Blakeman (1908) 153 Cal. 477, 481, 95 P. 888, 889; Duncan v. Peterson, *supra,* 3 Cal. App. 3d 607, 611, 83 Cal. Rptr. 744.]

Once an agreement between parties over an uncertain boundary line is established according to law, the agreement is conclusive as to the correctness of the boundary. (Martin v. Lopes (1946) 28 Cal. 2d 618, 622, 170 P.2d 881; 2 Cal. Jur. 3d, Adjoining Landowners, §93, p. 146.) The agreement establishes the true boundary line which the parties are estopped to deny. If more land is given to one than the description of his deed actually requires, he holds the excess by legal and not merely equitable title. (Sneed v. Osborn (1864) 25 Cal. 619, 631; 2 Cal. Jur. 3d, *supra,* §93, p. 146.) Thus, once appellant proved by uncontradicted evidence that the fence line was the agreed boundary separating the two properties, respondent lost their right to quiet title to the quarter section line.

The decree quieting title in respondents to the real property described in their complaint is reversed. The matter is remanded to the trial court with directions to receive such additional evidence as either party shall desire to produce and determine the location of the agreed line according to the evidence available.

NOTES AND QUESTIONS

1. The defendant had not pressed a claim to the disputed 2.4 acres based upon title by adverse possession. Were any of the elements for such a claim missing?

2. California requires a successful claimant in adverse possession to have paid the real estate taxes on a disputed parcel for a five-year period (the statute of limitations term). In practice, on the facts given, to whom would the 2.4 acre parcel have been assessed? If the defendant had tried to pay taxes on the disputed parcel, what problems would it have faced? As an element of adverse possession, does the tax-paying requirement serve any valid purpose? See Comment, The Payment of Taxes Requirement in Adverse Possession Statutes, 37 Cal. L. Rev. 477, 478-81 (1949). The Comment listed seventeen states as then having some tax-paying requirement, id. at 482-83, although nine of the states also had an alternative mode of adverse possession not requiring tax payment, id. at 484. Frequently the tax-paying requirement seems to be coupled with a shorter limitations period or with adverse possession claims based upon color of title.

3. Does the agreed boundaries doctrine serve any of the same policy goals as those of the adverse possession doctrine? Cf. Minson v. Aviation Finance, 113 Cal. Rptr. 223, 226, 38 Cal. App. 3d 489, 484 (Ct. App. 1974).

4. A and B are adjoining landowners. They agree orally to relocate their boundary line; they then build a fence marking the new line. Each cultivates up to the fence on his side. Some years later A and B have a dispute and seek to rescind their agreement. Are they bound?

5. Could the New York court have decided the *West* case, §9.1 *supra,* on an agreed boundaries theory?

6. Having formulated the agreed boundaries doctrine, should the courts liberally apply it? Discretion centers on two key elements: whether there was both "uncertainty" and "agreement" as to the boundary line. The court in Minson v. Aviation Finance, Note 4, *supra,* found the key elements in the 1883 decision of two neighbors to ask the county to build a road between their parcels and to accept the county survey, which located the road, as fixing the boundary.

§9.4   Squatting and Squatters

C. ABRAMS, MAN'S STRUGGLE FOR SHELTER IN AN URBANIZING WORLD

12-14, 21-22 (1964)

SQUATTING AND SQUATTERS

Human history has been an endless struggle for control of the earth's surface; and conquest, or the acquisition of property by force, has been one of its more ruthless expedients. With the surge of population from the rural lands to the cities, a new type of conquest has been manifesting itself in the cities of the developing world. Its form is squatting, and it is evidencing itself in the forcible preemption of land by landless and homeless people in search of a haven. Unlike other forms of conquest that were propelled by the pursuit of glory, trade routes, or revenues, squatting is part of a desperate contest for shelter and land. Of all forms of illegal seizure, squatting is the most condonable.

The old frontier areas of the more developed nations were once also the scenes of squatting, but in time titles were established, the land was often granted or sold to the squatters, and the law of force was supplanted by the force of law. Squatting, however, was rarely carried over into the cities of America or Europe, because law and property rights in cities were too firmly rooted. Members of the British privileged classes who had acquiesced in rural squatting until the time of the enclosures would not long allow the same indulgences for urban property. The urban slum, not the squatter's shack, became the mark of industrialization in Europe and later in America.

Squatting in the cities of the underdeveloped world today is usually open and defiant, tempting more squatting by its successes. It has affected not only government-owned land but private land as well, including tracts provided with costly facilities. When squatting is prevalent, orderly development and expansion are impeded, investment in greatly needed urban enterprises may be discouraged, and the political stabilization of government may be delayed.

The squatting problem exists in many parts of Asia, Latin America, and Africa—in fact, wherever there has been a mass movement of people to cities and insufficient shelter. There are now some 240,000 squatter units *(gececondu)* in Turkey. Squatters make up about 45 percent of the population of Ankara, where some land has had to be turned over to them. They are 21 percent of Istanbul's population and 18 percent of Izmir's. In 1951, they numbered sixty thousand in Baghdad and twenty thousand in Basra, Iraq; in Karachi, squatters represented about a third of the population. Squatters account for at least 20 percent of Manila's population, and in Davao squatters have taken possession of the whole parkway area running from the city hall to the retail center. Urban centers in South America are also experiencing a flood of migrant squatters. In Venezuela the proportion of squatters (rural and urban) is more than 65 percent of the total population, with a 35 percent rate for Caracas and 50 percent for Maracaibo. Cali, Colombia, has a squatter population that makes up about 30 percent of the total figure. In Santiago, Chile, squatters represent an estimated 25 percent of the population. They constitute 15 percent in Singapore and 12 percent in Kingston, Jamaica.

Though usually primitive, the appearance of squatting colonies varies somewhat according to the availability of building materials, the financial status of the squatters, and the prospects of continued possession. Little one-room shacks built of adobe and scrap are cropping up in Medellín, Barranquilla, and Cali, Colombia, and in fact throughout Latin America. The colonies lack paved streets, a sewerage system, and a water supply. Havana has a profusion of rude huts without sanitary facilities. In Algiers, tin-can towns, or *bidonvilles*, stand just five minutes away from the center of the city in almost any direction. The tightly packed shanties with only narrow alleys for passage are built of old oil drums, scrap metal, tin cans, and odd boards. Each hut, about 10 by 10 feet, houses an average of four or more persons and often a goat. In Tunis, the squatters live in caves dug out of hillsides. Around the edges of Johannesburg, South Africa, sprawl squatter colonies that are a chaos of shacks and hovels pieced together by the homeless and destitute. In India's larger cities, squatters can be found hanging on to their precarious hovels in old forts or wherever they can acquire a foothold. They include not only the unemployed but also construction workers, some 250,000 of whom move from zone to zone as they finish one job and start another. Their tin and rag shanties remain long after they have left for other places. Almost 150,000 squatters live in Delhi, about 90,000 of whom are on public land.

Squatting is triggered by many factors—enforced migration of refugees because of fear, hunger, or rural depression, the quest for subsistence in the burgeoning urban areas, and simple opportunism. Usually it is the by-product of urban landlessness and housing famine. Surplus rural labor and the need for labor in the towns combine to speed migrations. When there is no housing for the migrants, they do the only thing they can—they appropriate land, more often publicly owned land, from which there is less fear of being dislodged. Sympathy with the squatters' movements or lack of a consistent official policy encourages further squatting. Existing settlements spread, and new settlements mushroom. Many of Delhi's squatters put up shacks during the 1962 political campaign when they thought that politicians had assured them they would not be harassed. Their shacks were demolished after the election. . . .

TYPES OF SQUATTERS

The types of buildings erected by squatters vary with the materials available, but most are one-story makeshifts made of mud, scrap lumber, or tin. Sometimes there are substantial houses. In Lima, Peru, squatter groups have even been said to hire surveyors to lay out sites. Some houses are built so that the owners can take them to other sites if official or private owners persevere in harassing them.

The types of squatter tenure are not uniform and may generally be classified as follows:

The *owner squatter* owns his shack, though not the land; he erects the shack on any vacant plot he can find. Public lands and those of absentee owners are the most prized. The owner squatter is the most common variety.

The *squatter tenant* is in the poorest class, does not own or build a shack, but pays rent to another squatter. Many new in-migrants start as squatter tenants, hoping to advance to squatter ownership.

The *squatter holdover* is a former tenant who has ceased paying rent and whom the landlord fears to evict.

The *squatter landlord* is usually a squatter of long standing who has rooms or huts to rent, often at exorbitant profit.

The *speculator squatter* is usually a professional to whom squatting is a sound business venture. He squats for the tribute he expects the government or the private owner to grant him sooner or later. He is often the most eloquent in his protests and the most stubborn in resisting eviction.

The *store squatter or occupational squatter* establishes his small lockup store on land he does not own, and he may do a thriving business without paying rent or taxes. Sometimes his family sleeps in the shop. A citizen of Davao, in the Philippines, can get a dental cavity filled by a squatter dentist, his appendix removed by a squatter surgeon, or his soul sent on to a more enduring tenure by a squatter clergyman.

The *semi-squatter* has surreptitiously built his hut on private land and subsequently come to terms with the owner. The semi-squatter, strictly speaking, has ceased to be a squatter and has become a tenant. In constructing his house, he usually flouts the building codes.

The *floating squatter* lives in an old hulk or junk which is floated or sailed into the city's harbor. It serves as the family home and often the workship. It may be owned or rented, and the stay may be temporary or permanent. In Hong Kong, there are so many thousand of junks and sampans in one area that one is no longer aware of the water on which they rest.

The *squatter "cooperator"* is part of the group that shares the common foothold and protects it against intruders, public and private. The members may be from the same village, family, or tribe or may share a common trade, as in the case of groups of weavers on evacuee land in Pakistan.

§9.5 Adverse Possession Against State-Owned Lands

HINKLEY v. STATE OF NEW YORK
234 N.Y. 309, 137 N.E. 599 (1922)

CRANE, J. Chapter 555 of the Laws of 1918 provides for the construction of a barge canal terminal at Poughkeepsie, New York, and for the entry upon and acquisition of land needed for the site. The title states the purpose to be "with a view of improving the commerce of the state, and making an appropriation therefor."

Part of the land selected has been the subject of this litigation before the Court of Claims. It consists of property purchased on the water front of the Hudson river in 1818 by Matthew Vassar. Part of the land is upland, and the rest, as it exists today, is filled-in land. For the land under water, with the exception of that known as parcel T 192 (appropriation map), patents were granted by the state. Parcel T 192, which is in question, consists of land bulkheaded and filled in, about 0.615 acres. How early this land, for which there was no patent, was filled in is not definitely known, but it must have been done shortly after the acquisition of the property by Vassar. It appears as filled-in land, docked and bulkheaded, on a map of the incorporated village of Poughkeepsie, dated September, 1834.

Vassar was a brewer, and on this filled-in land was erected a malt house and other buildings. To the north and to the south of parcel T 192 the land under water has been filled in under grants from the state to the respective upland owners. The water front along all of his property has been well bulkheaded and presents a straight and even frontage. The entire land appropriated, therefore, consists of upland and filled-in land, one parcel on the water front having been filled in without authority from the state, other than that which the law may give to riparian owners. For this parcel in question there could be found no grant or patent.

The property which the state has sought to appropriate for the barge canal terminal, including the parcel in question, T 192, was owned or claimed at the time of this proceeding by Etheline H. Hinkley, who received it through mesne conveyances from Matthew Vassar.

The state and the owner entered into negotiations for the purchase of this property, the state offering for the whole tract the sum of $35,000. On examination of the title it was for the first time discovered by the parties that no water grant for parcel T 192 could be found. This, as before stated, was land under water filled in level with the upland. Negotiations were entered into between the state, the city of Poughkeepsie and Mrs. Hinkley, which need not here be referred to at length, and which resulted in Mrs. Hinkley transferring to the state of New York all the upland which she owned at this point, together with the filled-in land for which there had been patents granted, reserving under stipulation parcel T 192, appropriation map, for submission to the Court of Claims. Mrs. Hinkley claimed the fee of this parcel by reason of adverse possession for a period of seventy or eighty years. The state claimed that she had no title, and that, in the interest of navigation, the state could take it without compensation for the barge canal terminal.

In accordance with the stipulation Mrs. Hinkley submitted her claim known as claim No. 16,427 to the Court of Claims on the 15th day of October, 1920, in which she stated her rights to be as follows: "The claimant was at the time of the appropriation the sole owner in fee of the premises appropriated. The plaintiff claims a good and sufficient title to the lands appropriated by and through an uninterrupted adverse possession of the same by her and her preceding grantors for over fifty years before the date of said appropriation and before the filing of her said claim in this court. The plaintiff further claims and alleges that neither the said claimant herein or her preceding grantors, during a period of at least fifty years before said appropriation, or at any time prior thereto, paid any rentals or profits for the use or occupation of the premises so appropriated to the state of New York or to any of its officers or authorities."

By the stipulation of submission previously signed by Mrs. Hinkley it was expressly understood that for the parcel in question she would receive a sum not to exceed $5000 as the value of her right, interest or estate in the property.

The Court of Claims found for the claimant in the sum of $5000, holding that she had established her title by adverse possession. The Appellate Division reversed this award and dismissed the case. The finding of fact that the possession of Mrs. Hinkley and her predecessors in title had been exclusive and adverse to any claim of title on the part of the people of the state of New York was set aside. It is necessary for us, therefore, to determine from the record whether there be any evidence of adverse possession tending to establish title as against the state.

The situation presented is this: An upland owner has certain riparian rights in the Hudson river. In the exercise of those rights he bulkheads and fills in the land under water using the made land as a dock and for the erection of buildings thereon. This possession and use continues for nearly seventy-five years without any interference or claim of authority by the state. No grant or patent has been given to the upland owner for the lands under water which he has filled in. What are the rights of the respective parties?

Section 31 of the Civil Practice Act (L. 1920, ch. 925), formerly section 362 of the Code of Civil Procedure, provides:

> §31. When the people will not sue. The people of the state will not sue a person for or with respect to real property, or the issues or profits thereof, by reason of the right or title of the people to the same, unless either:
> 1. The cause of action accrued within forty years before the action is commenced; or
> 2. The people, or those from whom they claim, have received the rents and profits of the real property or of some part thereof, within the same period of time.

It may be that there is a distinction in the class of property owned by the state, and that there can be no adverse possession whatever as against the property which the state holds in trust for the public, as distinguished from such property as it may hold in a private or proprietary character. No time, for instance, can run against the state as to property which it could not grant to private individuals, such as forest lands set aside for a park (People v.

Baldwin, 197 App. Div. 285; *affd.*, 233 N.Y. 672), or as to canal property, . . .
(Donahue v. State of New York, 112 N.Y. 145). . . .

Whether title can be gained by adverse possession as to lands under
water which the state could have granted by patent we need not now decide as
in our opinion the evidence does not jusify the conclusion that the possession of
Mrs. Hinkley and her predecessors back to Matthew Vassar has been adverse.

Adverse possession must be exclusive, under no permission or license or
favor upon the part of the owner; the claim must be under color of independent title, exclusive of any right derived from the actual owner. . . .

When the entry upon land has been by permission or under some right
or authority derived from the owner, adverse possession does not commence
until such permission or authority has been repudiated and renounced and the
possessor thereafter has assumed the attitude of hostility to any right in the real
owner.

> Occupation must not only be hostile in its *inception,* but it must continue hostile,
> and at all times, during the required period of twenty years, challenge the right
> of the true owner in order to found title by adverse possession upon it. The *entry*
> must be strictly adverse to the title of the rightful owner, *for if the first possession is
> by permission it is presumed to so continue until the contrary appears.* If the occupation
> begins with the recognition of the real owner's estate it is presumed to be subser-
> vient, and that the one making the entry intends to hold honestly and not
> tortiously. The character of the possession depends on the intention with which
> entry is made and occupation continued. There is no disseisin until there is
> occupation with intention to claim title, and the fact of entry and the quo animo
> fix the character of the possession. The burden of proving all the facts necessary
> to constitute adverse possession is upon the one who asserts it, for in the absence
> of such proof possession is presumed to be in subordination to the true title.
> (Lewis v. New York & Harlem R.R. Co., 162 N.Y. 202, 220.)

Excessive use or violation of the right or privilege granted by the owner
cannot create adverse possession until it amounts to a claim openly distinct
from any claim of ownership on the part of the original proprietor.

"The object of the statute defining the acts essential to constitute an
adverse possession is that the real owner may, by unequivocal acts of the
usurper, have notice of the hostile claim and be thereby called upon to assert
his legal title." (Monnot v. Murphy, 207 N.Y. 240, 245.) See, also, Culver v.
Rhodes, 87 N.Y. 348; Flora v. Carbean, 38 N.Y. 111.

Matthew Vassar as riparian owner had certain rights which involved the
land under water. These were given to him by law and may be considered as
a permission or license from the people of the state of New York. The right of
a riparian owner was fully considered in Town of Brookhaven v. Smith (188
N.Y. 74, 84) and in Thousand Island Steamboat Co. v. Visger (179 N.Y. 206).
He has the right of access to the channel or the navigable part of the river for
navigation, fishing and such other uses as commonly belong to riparian ownership, the right to make a landing wharf or pier, for his own use, or for that
of the public, with the right of passage to and from the same with reasonable

safety and convenience. A pier may be constructed without a grant from the state of the land under water upon which it rests. In this country it has generally been held that the upland owner has the right of constructing a proper pier, or landing, for the use of himself and the public, subject to the general regulations prescribed by the state or the United States. What form or shape or size the pier may take varies with use and necessity. The upland owner has no right to fill in the land under water for purposes foreign to commerce and navigation. (Barnes v. Midland R.R. Terminal Co., 193 N.Y. 378.)

Vassar, the upland owner, in 1835 and thereafter, as well as his successors in title, had the right to wharf or pier out to the navigable part of the Hudson river. They could build piers which would rest upon the land under water, or they could build wharves and erect bulkheads. They also could fill in marshy ground and erect a substantial wharf for use of navigation and commerce connected with their business. (People v. Mould, 37 App. Div. 35.) All these things could be done under the implied permission of the people of the state of New York by reason of the law pertaining to upland owners, i.e., the law of riparian rights. When Vassar built his pier or bulkheaded and erected his wharf he did not act adversely to the interests or title of the people of the state of New York, but acted under a right given to him by the people through the law. His user may have been excessive. It may be that he had no right to fill in this land and build thereon a malt house or manufacturing plant, as distinguished from structures connected with navigation, but this abuse of his privilege could not of itself make the use adverse. What was the state to do? There are many miles of water front upon the waterways of the state of New York. The upland owners have, as above stated, the right to build wharves and piers for use in navigation. Such user is not adverse. Must the state keep a body of paid employees to constantly inspect all its waterways to see that riparian rights are not pushed beyond lawful limitations and the occupation ripen into adverse possession? Such a demand upon the resources of the state would be unreasonable. "Who is to watch," said the court in Jersey City v. Hall (79 N.J.L. 559, 574), "so as to detect within a certain period all encroachments upon the innumerable public highways in the state, or who is to keep similar guard over all parts of its extensive harbors and navigable rivers?" . . .

There may be circumstances which would justify the running of the Statute of Limitations against the state, and we refrain from holding that in no instance can title be acquired by adverse possession where the state in the first instance could have made a grant of the land to private individuals. (Matter of City of New York, 217 N.Y. 1, 13; 2 Corpus Juris, p. 214, note 38B.) The cases referred to by Judge Cullen in Fulton Light, H. & P. Co. v. State of New York (200 N.Y. 400, 422) are cases where the state had no right at any time to make a grant of the property or privilege claimed. We leave that question open. We do hold, however, that where, as in this case, an upland owner enters upon the land under water for the purpose of erecting piers, wharves or filling in for bulkhead and wharf purposes, his user does not become adverse merely by the erection of a building thereon. Something more must have been done or claimed to make this lawful entry adverse as against the state. . . .

The judgment appealed from should be affirmed, with costs.

HOGAN, CARDOZO, POUND and McLAUGHLIN, J., concur; ANDREWS, J., concurs in result; HISCOCK, CH. J., not voting.

Judgment affirmed.

NOTES AND QUESTIONS

1. At common law the Latin epigram "nullum tempus occurrit regi" (time does not run against the king) said it succinctly: adverse possession could not defeat the state's title. Even today, many states have retained the tradition, relying on rationales such as the state is "trustee" for all its citizens (a trustee's power to alienate is often circumscribed), or, state lands that have been made inalienable or whose mode of conveyance has been prescribed by constitution or statute cannot be transferred by operation of law. Often, the bar against adverse possession has been formalized by statute. See, e.g., Fla. Stat. §95.15 (1960); N.H. Rev. Stat. Ann. §§477.34 (1955), 539.6 (1968).

In several states, the contrary doctrine has gained an insecure toehold. Thus, as in New York, statutes have opened up state-owned lands to the claim of adverse possession, although the limitations period tends to exceed that for privately held lands. Several courts (and statutes) have embraced a distinction between "public lands," which are not subject to adverse possession, and "private or proprietary lands," which are. See, e.g., Brown v. Trustees of Schools, 224 Ill. 184, 79 N.E. 579 (1906); Herndon v. Board of Commrs. of Pontotoc County, 158 Okla. 14, 11 P.2d 939 (1932). Occasionally, the doctrine of estoppel has been brought to the aid of a private claimant. See, e.g., Bridges v. Incorporated Town of Grand View, 158 Iowa 402, 139 N.W. 917 (1913).

But, in general, the courts have yielded the state's dominion reluctantly, even when a statute has freed them to do so. In this respect, the *Hinkley* case is quite typical. Moreover, if one can sense a trend, legislators are themselves becoming more jealous of the state's resources. In Delaware, for example, a century-old statute allowing adverse possession was repealed in 1953, 49 Del. Laws, c. 386 (1953). Other states also have re-established the earlier common-law immunity. See, e.g., Mich. Comp. Laws Ann. §317.294 (1967) (swamp lands along Great Lakes, etc.); Ore. Rev. Stat. §12.250 (Supp. 1971).

Looking behind the easy generalizations, do you see any basis for giving state-owned lands an immunity that is not available to lands privately held? Should it make a difference whether the lands in question are the boundaries of a schoolyard, tidal lands that have been farmed and grazed by upland owners, a highway right-of-way that has been only partly used, or a state forest?

2. Congress has carved some exceptions from the immunity from adverse possession that federal lands once enjoyed. U.S.C.A. Title 43, §1068 (1964), is the most inclusive, directing the Secretary of the Interior to issue patents for up to 160 acres of public land, where the claimant can show:

(a) peaceful, adverse possession,
(b) under claim or color of title,
(c) in good faith,
(d) for more than twenty years, and
(e) improvements or partial cultivation.

The Secretary must charge for the patent not less than $1.25 per acre.

This section also gives the Secretary *discretionary* power to issue a patent where the claimant's possession dates from 1901 or before, and the claimant has paid state or local taxes levied against the parcel; under this provision, the claimant need not have built improvements or have cultivated the soil. Ibid.

The Mining Claim Occupancy Act, 30 U.S.C.A. §§701-709 (1971), and the Public Land Sale Act of 1968, 43 U.S.C.A. §§1431-35 (Supp. 1974), also authorize federal patents in limited situations to parties lacking valid title.

Unless a claimant can bring himself within one of these statutory exceptions, he cannot assert title by adverse possession or prescription against the United States. See United States v. 1,629.6 Acres of Land, County of Sussex, Del., 503 F.2d 764, 767 (3d Cir. 1974).

The Public Land Law Review Commission has recommended to the president and the Congress an expanded doctrine of adverse possession operating against the government. Report, One Third of the Nation's Land 15,260-15,262 (1970). At least one commentator has angrily attacked the proposal. Million, Adverse Possession Against the United States—A Treasure for Trespassers, 26 Ark. L. Rev. 467 (1973).

3. One might note that in England, adverse possession is now available against state-owned lands. Thirty years of occupancy is required generally, sixty years for shorelands. Limitations Act, 1939, 2 & 3 Geo. 6, c. 21, §4(1).

§9.6 Elements of Easements by Prescription

The adverse use of another's land for the limitations period may establish an *easement* by prescription. In reading the case that follows, consider which of the requirements for *title* by adverse possession are lacking.

HUNT LAND HOLDING CO. v. SCHRAMM
121 So. 2d 697 (Fla. 1960)

KANNER, J. A mandatory injunction sought by and granted to the plaintiffs in the suit below required that the defendants remove a dam which they had constructed across an outfall drainage ditch. The appeal has been advanced upon the sole proposition that there was no proof of adverse user and hence there could be created no easement by prescription.

Located near the northern city limits of Fort Lauderdale, the outfall ditch in question, thirty feet wide at its east end, extends from U.S. Highway 1 on the west, thence about 1300 feet in an easterly direction to the intracoastal waterway. Coursing through the lands of both the plaintiffs and the defendants, the ditch is in township 49 south, range 43 east, between sections 12 and 13, of which the plaintiffs are subdivision developers and individual lot owners on both sides of the ditch's westerly portion, and between sections 7 and 18, of which the defendants are rival subdivision developers of both sides of the easterly portion of the ditch. The plaintiffs' property is somewhat higher than that of the defendants and has already been subdivided, the ditch being utilized for drainage. Defendants' lands, consisting largely of mangrove swamp, are to be developed when made usable by the digging of canals and the supplying of fill. The natural drainage in the area concerned is easterly and southerly into the intracoastal waterway, and in this respect the plaintiffs have the dominant estate. Passage of the ditch through the low-lying swamp lands now owned by the defendants was shown as having been necessary.

In 1929 U.S. Highway 1 was constructed, running north and south along the west side of the plaintiffs' land. A culvert six feet wide and three feet high was built by the road department under the original road bed, this having been extended to pass under the new highway when U.S. 1 was widened in 1952. At both times the road department constructed drainage ditches west and east of U.S. 1 for drainage of surface and rain waters from the north and west into the culvert, thence to the intracoastal waterway via the drainage ditch here involved. The road department has periodically cleaned the ditch and maintained it from the time U.S. 1 was constructed to the time of the instant suit. The use of the ditch is for drainage, not only of the land surrounding it but of 320 acres of land situated to the west of U.S. 1, under which the culvert was constructed for that purpose by the road department.

Artificial at its inception, the ditch existed and functioned to provide drainage for surrounding lands in excess of forty-five years, although it was constructed at a time and under circumstances and by persons not now ascertainable. It has through the years been used without objection by anyone concerned and all have thus acquiesced in its use. Lands which it drained were used previously for farming purposes, except for those of the defendants, which were too low. This ditch was never closed but was always open to drain the area, and all earlier persons had considered it to be a permanent means of drainage.

Damming of the drainage ditch by the defendants proceeded despite the fact that throughout its existence the ditch has been in open, notorious, and continuous use. This is conceded by the defendants. It is also conceded that the ditch is considered as necessary by the county commission, the county engineer, the planning and zoning board, and the county health department.

Grievance of the plaintiffs commenced when the defendants built a prior dam across the ditch, preventing drainage from plaintiffs' lands. This dam was washed out by natural causes, following which the defendants supplanted it with a permanent dam. The Broward County Health Department refused to approve building permits on plaintiffs' lands because it deemed it necessary that the ditch be kept open and maintained for sanitary and health purposes.

The chancellor found the equities to be with the plaintiffs and held their right to relief to be based upon three legal propositions, (1) the theory of "mutual drain," (2) the theory that the legal character of the artificial ditch has changed to that of a natural water course by virtue of its long use,[4] and (3) the theory that easement by prescription has been created.

The defendants confine their appeal to a single point of whether an easement by prescription can be created without showing of adverse use. Their contention is that the evidence shows the use of the outfall ditch was not exclusive but was for the mutual benefit of all the adjoining lands and therefore not adverse, and, further, that they are favored with the presumption that the use was permissive rather than adverse. Because of this, they assert that they are entitled to prevail.

Florida has aligned herself with the more contemporary authorities whose trend is to abandon the theory that prescriptive rights are based on the presumption of a prior grant and to treat the acquisition of such prescriptive rights as having been acquired by methods substantially similar to those by which title is acquired by adverse possession. Downing v. Bird, Fla. 1958, 100 So. 2d 57.

In order to establish an easement by prescription, a claimant must prove actual, continuous, uninterrupted use for a period of twenty years. In acquisition of such an easement the use must be adverse under claim of right and must either be with the knowledge of the owner or by a use so open, notorious, visible, and uninterrupted that knowledge of the use by an adverse claimant is imputed to the owner. Moreover, the use must be inconsistent with the owner's use and enjoyment of his lands and also must not be a permissive use; for the use is required to be such that the owner has a right to a legal remedy to stop it. Downing v. Bird, *supra,* and J. C. Vereen & Sons v. Houser, 1936, 123 Fla. 641, 167 So. 45.

There is a distinction between acquiring of title by adverse possession and the acquiring of a prescriptive right. In the former, title must be through possession. In the latter, a prescriptive right is through the use of the privilege without actual possession.[5] In acquisition of the title by adverse possession, the possession must be exclusive, while in acquisition of a prescriptive right, the use may be in common with the owner or the public. Downing v. Bird, *supra.*

In either prescription or adverse possession, the use or possession is presumed to be in subordination to the title and thus is presumed to be permissive. However, the presumption of permissive use or possession is not conclusive and is ineffectual in the face of facts which cause its dissipation.

Declarations or assertions by a claimant are not essential to possession or use under claim of right, the adverse character of possession or use is a ques-

---

4. The owner of land bordering a natural watercourse enjoys, under Florida law, the reasonable use of the watercourse, which may not be interfered with by other riparian owners.—ED.

5. Can you explain the difference between possession and use?—ED.

tion discoverable and determinable from all the circumstances of the case. Stetson v. Youngquist, 1926, 76 Mont. 600, 248 P. 196.

Thus we see that the presumption of permissive use may be overcome by knowledge imputed to the owner of adverse use by the party claiming the prescriptive right, that it is not necessary that this be done by declarations or assertions but it may be effectuated by use inconsistent with the owner's use and enjoyment of his lands, and, further, that the use need not be exclusive but may be in common with the owner or the public.

Here the long, continuous, uninterrupted, open and notorious use of the ditch for drainage of farm lands is conceded to have existed more than forty-five years without any objection until the present dispute; the use was accepted, acquiesced in, and was treated as necessary [6] and permanent for drainage of the area through the years, up to the present time. It was improved and serviced by the state road department and has served to drain surface waters from the public highway as well as the lands involved. It was declared as necessary by the county health department, the county commission, the county engineer, and the planning and zoning board.

At the hearing for the taking of testimony the defendants offered no evidence to show that their predecessors in title had given consent to the user, but as indicated they place their reliance on the presumption that the use was permissive. We conclude that the plaintiffs proved by clear and positive evidence that the use was so continuous, uninterrupted, open, and notorious as to impute to the owners of the lands that the claimants were exercising their privilege under a claim of right adverse to the owners for the required period, and that the use was inconsistent with the rights of the owners to their use and enjoyment of the lands. By such proof the plaintiffs have surmounted the defendants' claim as to presumption that the use was permissive rather than adverse, and they are entitled to prevail.

The chancellor found the plaintiffs were entitled to relief under three supporting theories. Since the appeal is on the single point, "Can an easement by prescription be created without showing of adverse user?", we have no comment to make as to the other theories. The decree is affirmed.

NOTES AND QUESTIONS

1. The close analogy of prescriptive easements with title by adverse possession is now orthodox legal doctrine, as is seen in the instant case. This equivalence is relatively new; the claim of a prescriptive easement once rested upon quite a different theory—the fiction of a lost grant.

As early as Bracton, the law had begun to recognize the right to an easement, even though unsupported by a grant from the servient owner. " . . . [I]f there has been any user extending over considerable time, exercised in

---

6. Might this case have been decided on some other theory, not advanced by defendants? Cf. Easement by Necessity, pages 552-560 *infra.*—ED.

peace, without any interruption and not by violence or stealth or by virtue of a request . . . the person enjoying the right cannot be ousted of it, at all events without the judgment of the court." (Lib. IV, cap. 37, fol. 220b.)

In order to establish his prescriptive interest, the claimant had to introduce proof of use from "time immemorial." Seeking to put fixed content into that phrase, the law settled on the year 1189 (the start of Richard I's reign) as the year from which proof of use should begin. In time, the testimonial difficulties of proving use from 1189 onward became unmanageable, and a new test for prescription—similar to the earliest formulation—was introduced. Testimony of usage, continuing for as long as living witnesses could recall, would create a presumption that the use had originated by 1189. But new difficulties for the claimant arose at once, for the presumption of continued user was easily rebutted; to defeat the claim, the servient owner need only show a time interval when user could not have occurred, or when ownership of the dominant and servient estates was merged.

In 1623 the writ of entry became subject to a twenty-year statute of limitations, which, as we saw, not only barred the landowner's remedy but also established the occupant's title. Although the statute did not apply to incorporeal interests, courts eventually adopted its twenty-year measure as the period of use that would ripen into a prescriptive right. But to regard twenty years as the factual equivalent of use stretching backward for more than four centuries was so transparent a fiction that the courts saw fit to concoct a more plausible fiction and, in doing so, to alter the theoretical basis for prescriptive rights. Hence, a claimant who could prove twenty years or more of uninterrupted use was presumed to have begun his use pursuant to a grant from the servient owner, which grant (instrument) had later disappeared. This, then, was the doctrine of the lost (or mislaid) grant.

If the 1623 statute of limitations had been construed to apply to incorporeal interests, the lost grant fiction would have been unnecessary, since the statute barring the remedy would also have established the prescriptive interest. In making available to the prescriptive claimant the twenty-year analogy, the courts certainly lightened the claimant's testimonial load, but it was not an entirely happy accommodation even at that. For the courts could find no consensus as to how the doctrine worked. If the claimant could show the requisite period of uninterrupted use, had he created an irrefutable presumption of a lost grant, or might the owner offer proof that the use initiated under a revocable license or an easement for ten years, or in an openly *hostile* manner? If the claimant attempted to show the requisite period of uninterrupted use, what form of proof would dispute this—a letter from the servient owner demanding that the use cease? A letter from the servient owner privileging the use to continue until the privilege was revoked? For a brief exposure to the operational complexities of the lost grant theory, see Parker & Edgarton v. Foote, 19 Wend. 309 (N.Y. Sup. Ct. of Jud. 1838).

The British attempted statutory reform in 1832, but nearly one century later a commentator wrote that "no branch of English law is in a more unsatisfactory state than the law of prescription." Holdsworth, Historical Introduction of the Land Law 286 (1927). By then, however, the fiction of the lost grant had already become unwelcome in American courts, as prescription and adverse possession were being regarded as two expressions of a similar truth.

2.   "The satisfaction of the . . . prerequisites for 'adversity,' namely, that the user has been made not in subordination to the rights of the claimed servient owner, but, rather, has been made under claim of right is commonly inferred, rather than directly proved. Thus, proof that a particular use of another's land has in fact occurred normally justifies, in most states, a finding that the use has been adverse until this presumption is challenged by rebutting evidence. When, however, rebutting evidence has been produced, the burden of establishing the fact of adversity rests upon the claimant of the easement. In three special situations this presumption of adversity is inapplicable. The first of these situations exists where the landowner and the claimant have such a relationship to each other that the landowner is reasonably entitled to regard the user as permissive unless specifically informed of the contrary fact, as, for example, when they are closely related by blood or a prior license of the use in question is being repudiated. The second of these three situations exists when the land over which the easement is claimed is open, unenclosed and unimproved. Since the land is not being actively used by its owner, the claimant's use can be better regarded as permissive until affirmatively shown to be adverse. The third of these three situations exists when the established user by the claimant is not exclusive. . . . If the claimant is only one of two, or several, or many, who make the user in question, it is perhaps inferrable that all of these uses are permissive. In such case the claimant must affirmatively prove the adverse character of his user." Powell, Real Property 566 (Powell and Rohan abr. ed. 1968).

3.   In general, the states that require the payment of taxes as an element of adverse possession do not extend the requirement to prescription. See, e.g., Reinsch v. City of Los Angeles, 243 Cal. App. 2d 737, 52 Cal. Rptr. 613 (1966); Hahn v. Curtis, 73 Cal. App. 2d 382, 166 P.2d 611 (1946).

4.   Plaintiff owned and operated a movie theatre. Defendant owned and operated a bank adjacent to the theatre. For more than thirty years (prescriptive period: twenty-one years), plaintiff and its predecessors used the public sidewalk in front of the bank to change signs on the movie theatre marquee. The city vacated the sidewalk and defendant planned to construct a new, larger building that would occupy the former sidewalk. This would physically block one side of plaintiff's marquee from public view and would prevent plaintiff from changing the marquee signs.

Before its vacation, the public sidewalk was held in fee by defendant, subject only to the "public's easement of passage." Recognizing that it could not (in this case) gain a prescriptive right against the city, plaintiff claimed, instead, that it had acquired such right against the fee owner.

The court held that plaintiff's complaint, seeking to enjoin defendant from blocking off the marquee, stated a cause of action:

Easements by prescription are created by adverse, open, notorious, continuous, and uninterrupted use of land for 21 years. . . . The complaint thus alleges that all of the requirements necessary to establish a prescriptive easement are present. The difficulty posed by this case is the presence of the public easement. Any use of the sidewalk within the scope of the public easement is not adverse to Mellon Bank and cannot serve as the basis for the acquisition of a prescriptive easement. . . .

While the abutting fee owner may have power to impose frequent temporary obstructions on the public way in order to serve his own reasonable commercial needs, the Pennsylvania decisions clearly establish that an abutting fee owner may not obstruct the public sidewalk owned by another abutting fee owner on a recurring basis in order to serve commercial needs. Such use of the public sidewalk would amount to an appropriation of another's property for private commercial purposes. . . .

Easements against the abutting owner can be established by prescription in a sidewalk, so long as the use is outside the scope of the public easement. The abutting fee owner retains certain primary rights in the sidewalk, and those rights can be lost by prescription. The public policy which prevents the acquisition of rights against a municipality or the public by prescription does not prevent the acquisition of rights by prescription against a private entity. [RKO-Stanley Warner Theatres, Inc. v. Mellon National Bank and Trust Co., 436 F.2d 1297, 1300-1303 (3d Cir. 1970)]

5.   The limitations period is ten years. In each of the following cases, has a prescriptive right been obtained?

(a) *Open and notorious.* B installs an underground drainage sewer that encroaches on A's parcel without his knowledge. B uses the sewer for ten years. Cf. Wolek v. Di Feo, 60 N.J. Super. 324, 159 A.2d 127 (1960). Compare with Van Sandt v. Royster, page 538, *infra.*

(b) *Exclusive.* The entire neighborhood beats a path across A's parcel for ten years without his permission.

(c) *Continuous.* B travels across A's parcel for nine years without his permission. A blocks off the path. Two weeks later, B removes the barrier and resumes his use through the tenth year. Compare Voorhies v. Pratt, 200 Mich. 91, 166 N.W. 844 (1918) (spasmodic interruption of drain flowage—continuity not broken), with Dartnell v. Bidwell, 115 Me. 227, 98 A. 743 (1916) (written notice forbidding further use—continuity broken). Can you reconcile these holdings? If not, which is the better rule?

(d) *Continuous.* B travels across the easterly portion of A's parcel for five years without his permission. Still without permission, B travels across the westerly portion of A's parcel for five more years. Cf. Riggs v. Springfield, 344 Mo. 420, 126 S.W.2d 1144 (1939).

(e) *Continuous.* B travels across A's parcel for five years without his permission. A then sells his parcel to B, who leases it to C for one year.

When the lease expires, B sells the parcel to C. B continues to use the right of way during his ownership and, thereafter, during C's—without C's permission. The combined periods of use total ten years. Cf. Scott v. Powers, 140 Colo. 14, 342 P.2d 664 (1959).

(f) *Continuous.* B travels across A's parcel for five years without his permission. B sells his parcel to C, but the deed fails to include the right of way. C travels across A's parcel for another five years without his permission. Cf. Jacobs v. Lewicki, 12 A.D.2d 625, 208 N.Y.S.2d 140 (1960), *aff'd* 10 N.Y.2d 778, 177 N.E.2d 58, 219 N.Y.S.2d 619 (1961) (C cannot "tack" his use onto the time accumulated by B where the deed did not include the alleged easement and there was no proof the grantor intended to include it). Why is there a more rigorous requirement for prescription than for adverse possession? What evidence might C introduce on the issue of B's intent?

PART IV

ALLOCATION AND DEVELOPMENT OF LAND RESOURCES

Until now we have discussed land with some abstraction. In learning to classify estates, in stressing the "right to possession," we have tended to regard Blackacre wholly apart from the process of shaping and sharing this vital resource to the ends of man. Blackacre may have been 1,000 acres of Iowa cornfield, a tract house in Los Angeles County, a blockfront in mid-Manhattan—but its identity mattered little for purposes of describing a cotenancy or of choosing between the defeasible estates.

For the remainder of this course, the use of land, rather than its title, will be our chief concern. Given that land is one of the resources upon which all life depends, how have we put it to work? Who decides the use of land? How are the decisions made? What goals do decisionmakers seek through the use of land? What goals should they seek? How are goals formulated? How well have decisionmakers achieved their goals? How has property doctrine evolved to meet out changing demands on land? What old concepts have been sloughed off or modified? What new ones have gained status? What others, still untested, lie in the wings awaiting their chance? What new nondoctrinal institutions are being developed to help achieve land-use goals?

Until the early twentieth century, legislatures gave little attention to land consumption, and when they did act, it was mostly to encourage favored activity, not to discourage unfavored venture. Thus, land grants to homesteaders, railroads, or mining companies far more typified the nineteenth-century legislative response than did the occasional measure directed at the unsafe or unsanitary multiple dwelling. For their part, the courts played a key role (which still continues) in resolving land use disputes between adjoining owners (viz., nuisance, lateral support) or between present and future owners (viz., waste).

Much has changed since the advent of zoning in New York City in 1916. Today, public control over land use through zoning, mapping, subdivision regulations, building and housing codes, fair housing laws, conservation measures, and air pollution standards is extensive and expanding. Governmental spending for slum clearance, highway construction, public housing, reclamation, and community facilities has become a major force in shaping land resources. The government has also found ways to stimulate worthy private investment; thus, programs of urban renewal, mortgage insurance, low-interest direct loans, property tax abatement, income tax shelter, and zoning incentive all are designed to spur the private sector into making preferred land-use decisions.

For, after all, private choice remains both an essential value and the principal contributing force in the allocation of our land resources. We will watch that choice at work: the lot owner who permits a neighbor to share his driveway, the high-rise builder who seeks to preserve an unobstructed view of the surrounding area, the tract developer who strives for harmony of style. You will soon discover, however, that private choice is not unfettered, that landowners are not free to fix the patterns of land use wholly without regard to the values of a larger community. What those values are, or how the community is defined, is part of our concern.

In the next two chapters, you will witness the struggling efforts of courts—and legislatures—to determine when private arrangements should be legally enforced, and when they should not.

Chapter 10

Creating the Private Arrangement

§10.1 Coming to Terms with Easements

You have already met the easement once or twice along the way, but we will now examine this interest and its various siblings with more than passing concern, because this family has long offered, and still provides, a principal technique for realizing private wishes about the use of land.

Here, as elsewhere in this course, vocabulary is important, and since there is a fair amount to assimilate, we will first illustrate and discuss the most widely used terms.

Maintaining the nebulous distinction between possession and use, the Restatement of Property describes an easement as an interest in land that is in the possession of another, permitting a "limited use or enjoyment of the land in which the interest exists." Restatement of Property §450.[1] Consider, for example, the following common situation: A owns Lot 1, B owns the adjoining Lot 2; a two-car garage and connecting driveway straddle the two lots. The two neighbors agree that each is to have "perpetual" use of the driveway for getting to or from the garage. The interest that each one has in the other's land is called an *affirmative* easement, which, in Hohfeldian terms, privileges A (B) to enter and make affirmative use of B's (A's) land, and bars B (A) from interfering with that use. Most easements are affirmative, generally occurring as rights-of-way, public utility easements (for example, telegraph poles and wires), drainage easements, and profits à prendre, a subcategory we will examine shortly. An easement is also described as affirmative when it privileges its holder—for example, A—to make use of his own land in a way that interferes with the enjoyment of someone else's land. For example, B might agree to let A operate a backyard piggery even though B finds the odors offensive and, had he never consented, B might seek to enjoin the odors as a nuisance. Compare Waldrop v. Town of Brevard, §11.5 *infra*.

---

1. The Restatement emphasizes that an easement is not terminable at the will of the possessor of the land, thus distinguishing it from the "revocable" license.

Negative easements can be illustrated by an agreement between neighbors A and B wherein A agrees, in order to protect B's view of the surrounding countryside, not to build any structure on her lot higher than two stories. In Hohfeldian terms this interest privileges B to enjoy the view and bars A from interfering with that view—a privilege that A would otherwise have (in the absence of zoning).

Unlike the holder of an affirmative easement, the holder of a negative easement receives an advantage that does not contemplate his physical, or quasi-physical, movement onto another's land. At early common law, negative easements were fairly uncommon, limited almost exclusively to easements for *light, air, or view, or for greater lateral support or benefit from a stream* than the easement holder would otherwise be entitled to receive.

The land that is subject to, or burdened by, *any* restriction upon its use is called the *servient* estate.

Running of the easement's burden. Suppose that, in the first illustration above, B, the coholder of the driveway easement, sells Lot 2 to Y and Y seeks to bar A from any further use of the Lot 2 strip of driveway. Is Y privileged to do so? Putting the question differently: when the servient estate is conveyed, does the new owner automatically bear the easement's burden? The answer is yes if two conditions are met: (1) the creating parties intended the easement to bind a succeeding owner, or other interest holder,[2] of the servient estate; (2) the new owner, if a purchaser for value, has notice of the easement when he acquires the premises.[3] Public records usually supply the notice, but if the easement is "apparent" on visual inspection (see, e.g., Van Sandt v. Royster, page 538, *infra*), it is as if the new owner has actual knowledge; he is deemed to have notice whether or not record notice is also present.

Running of the easement's benefit. Suppose that, in the first illustration above, B, the coholder of the driveway easement, sells Lot 2 to Y and Y continues the driveway use. Is he privileged to do so? The answer will require us to examine the original agreement between A and B and possibly, depending upon what we find, the agreement between B and Y.

It is quite likely, but not certain, that B bargained for an interest that would benefit not only himself but would continue to benefit Lot 2 regardless of who became its owner (or occupier). If so, then the easement is said to be *appurtenant* to Lot 2, that is, its benefit is regarded as an incident to the ownership of Lot 2 and passes automatically from one owner to the next.[4] (At least one case has held that if B were to sell Lot 2 and try to keep an appurtenant easement for himself, the easement would be extinguished; see Cadwalader v. Bailey, 17 R.I. 495, 23 A. 20 (1891).) The benefited land, Lot 2, is called the *dominant* estate, and Y as the new owner may enjoy the easement. (We would

2. For example, a tenant would ordinarily be bound if the owner—his landlord—were bound.

3. A donee is bound, regardless of notice.

4. The B-Y deed need not even refer to the easement for Y to enjoy the *benefit* of an easement appurtenant. Compare, however, the tacking discussion for prescriptive easements, pages 527-528, *supra*.

make the same analysis of A's interest in that part of the driveway lying on Lot 2; thus, in a common driveway arrangement, both lots are servient, and quite probably dominant.)

In the unlikely event that A and B intended that the cross-easements benefit themselves personally, apart from any land they might happen to own, the interests are said to be *in gross,* and there is no dominant estate. Whether or not B's successor, Y, may now use the driveway depends on two factors: (1) Is the easement assignable? (2) Was an assignment made?

The early common law was most unrelenting about easements in gross: they could not be assigned. Underlying this attitude was a weighing of the relative inutility of easements in gross against their potential for title-clogging if assignability were freely permitted. But the balance began to shift as nonappurtenant grants were made increasingly for railroad and public utility rights-of-way. The Restatement of Property, reacting to this development, divided easements in gross into "commercial" and "noncommercial" types, making assignable only those easements that "result primarily in economic benefit rather than personal satisfaction." Id. §489, Comment c. To the critics of the Restatement, this was simply further reason for cavil. See, e.g., C. Clark, Real Covenants and Other Interests Which "Run with Land" 80-84 (1947).

The trend is toward free assignability of any easement in gross, if the original parties wish it.[5] "To A, his heirs and assigns" is the draftsman's style for asserting this preference.

§10.2   Is the Easement Appurtenant or in Gross?

Because instruments creating easements are often silent or unclear on the point, disputes sometimes arise as to whether the parties intended an easement appurtenant or in gross. A constructional preference for the former is very strong, as the following case illustrates.

MARTIN v. MUSIC
254 S.W.2d 701 (Ky. 1953)

CULLEN, COMMR. This action involves the construction of the following agreement:

> This mutual agreement, made and entered into by and between Marvin Music, of Prestonsburg, Kentucky, party of the first part, and Fred Martin, of Prestonsburg, Kentucky, party of the second part.

5. Simes, The Assignability of Easements in Gross in American Law, 22 Mich. L. Rev. 521 (1924), is the leading statement for free assignability.

Witnesseth: That for and in consideration of the sum of One ($1.00) Dollar, and other considerations hereinafter set out, parties of the first and second part mutually agree:

Party of the first part gives and grants to second party[6] the right to construct and maintain a sewer line under and through his property located in the Layne Heirs addition to the City of Prestonsburg, Kentucky, in the Garfield Bottom, and being lots Nos. 17 through 24 inc. of said addition.

In consideration of said right, second party agrees to lay said sewer line at sufficient depth to not interfere with first party's use and enjoyment of said property; and to place an intake connection in said line for use of said party at a point to be designated by him; and further agrees to pay to first party any damage which may result to his property by reason of the laying, maintaining, repairing and operation of said sewer line.

Given under our hands, this December 3, 1949.

At the time the agreement was executed, the eight lots owned by Music were unoccupied, except for a garage building used by Music for the vehicles operated by him in his business as a bulk distributor of oil and gasoline. Martin constructed his sewer across the lots, and thereafter Music sold six of the lots to one Moore, who in turn sold three each to the appellees Wells and Allen. [See Figure 1.] Wells and Allen each commenced the construction of a dwelling house on his lots, and prepared to connect with Martin's sewer. Martin then brought this action for a declaration of rights, maintaining that the right to connect with the sewer was personal to Music alone, for the purpose of serving a dwelling house which Music had planned to build, and that the right did not accrue to Wells and Allen. The court adjudged that Music, Wells and Allen each had the right to connect with the sewer, provided that the connection was made through the one intake connection provided for in the written contract. Martin appeals.

Considerable evidence was introduced concerning the circumstances surrounding the execution of the agreement, and the situation that existed at the time the agreement was made. It appears that the lots owned by Music had a depth of 120 feet, from east to west, and a width of 25 feet each, fronting on a street on the west and an alley on the east. Across the alley to the east, Martin owned six lots on which he had his private residence and a motel. Martin's northernmost lot was opposite Music's southernmost lot. The Big Sandy River lies some 600 feet west of Martin's property, and he desired to run the sewer line from his property to the river.

Martin's evidence was that he first proposed to construct his sewer down the alley between his lots and those of Music, but that Music, upon learning of this plan, offered to let the sewer cross his lots, in return for an intake connection privilege. Martin testified that the understanding was that Music was to build a home on his lots, and that the sewer connection was for that purpose.

Music's evidence was that Martin did not want to run his sewer down

6. Note that the agreement does not mention "assigns." Is this significant?—ED.

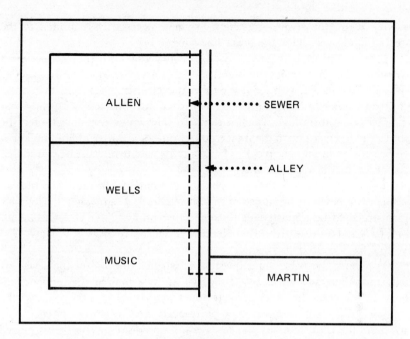

FIGURE 1

the alley, for fear that it then would be classified as a public sewer, to which anyone could connect; that Music offered to let the sewer go across his lots in return for a connection privilege; that there was no understanding that the intake was to be limited to one dwelling to be erected by Music, but on the contrary it was clearly understood that the intake was to be available for each of the eight lots.

Martin's sewer is a six-inch main, which the appellees' evidence tends to show is capable of handling the sewage from their buildings, in addition to that from Martin's properties, with no difficulty. On the other hand, Martin testified that the sewer line had a low grade of descent, and that in times of heavy rains, when the river was high, there would be danger of the sewer backing up into his basement. He complains particularly of the proposal of the appellees to connect their eaves and downspouts to the sewer, which he claims will create too great a flow of water for the sewer line to accommodate.

Martin maintains that the agreement provides for an easement in gross, rather than one running with the land. He relies upon Mannin v. Adkins, 199 Ky. 241, 250 S.W. 974, which we do not consider to be in point. In that case, the grantor of a piece of property reserved the right to "have, use, and get coal off the lands hereby conveyed for fuel for his own purposes or home consumption as fuel." The court held that the reservation was personal to the grantor, and did not run with the adjoining land which he occupied as his home place at the time of the conveyance. There, the reserved privilege was not related to a particular piece of property as a dominant estate, and it necessarily was personal. Here, the sewer connection privilege necessarily is limited to the parcel of land over which the sewer line runs.

If an easement is to be exercised in connection with the occupancy of particular land, then ordinarily it is classified as an easement appurtenant. 28 C.J.S., Easements, §4(b), p. 635. We think it is clear that the right to connect to Martin's sewer line was to be exercised only in connection with the occupancy of the land through which it ran, and that Music was not granted the right to run a sewer line to the intake point from some parcel of land he might own or acquire in another block. Therefore, the easement must be considered to be an easement appurtenant.

It is the general rule that easements in gross are not favored, and that an easement will never be presumed to be a mere personal right when it can fairly be construed to be appurtenant to some other estate. 28 C.J.S., Easements, §4(c), p. 638. This rule prevails in Kentucky. Buck Creek R. Co. v. Haws, 253 Ky. 203, 69 S.W.2d 333.

We think the controlling question is whether the use of the sewer by Wells and Allen, as well as by Music, will unduly burden the servient tenement (in this case, the sewer line). It appears to be the general rule that the dominant estate may be divided or partitioned, and the owner of each part may claim the right to enjoy the easement, if no additional burden is placed upon the servient estate. 17 Am. Jur., Easements, sec. 126, p. 1014.

Here, it cannot be ascertained from the written agreement, nor can it be ascertained with certainty from the evidence of the circumstances and conditions surrounding the execution of the agreement just what burden it was contemplated might be imposed by way of connection with the sewer line. As far as the face of the agreement is concerned, Music could have built an apartment house, a hotel, or even a factory, upon his lots, and connected them with the sewer. Either of these would have required only one intake connection. The agreement does not limit the kind of use that Music was to make of the sewer. Since, under the words of the agreement, Music could have placed a much greater burden upon Martin's sewer we do not believe that two or three dwellings will increase the burden contemplated by the parties as expressed in their agreement.

If we go beyond the words of the agreement, and accept all of the evidence as to what the parties intended, then we find a conflict of evidence, upon which we could not say that the chancellor erred.

The judgment is affirmed.

COMBS, J., not sitting.

NOTES AND QUESTIONS

1. Why is a constructional preference given to an appurtenant easement?

2. Given the decision, what dominant and servient estates resulted from the 1949 agreement? Were they created by reservation or by grant? Cf. §10.3 (a), *infra*.

3. What language in the original agreement might have strengthened the argument for easement in gross? For limiting the burden on the easement as Martin sought? For indemnifying Martin against damages from sewer backup?

4. The *profit à prendre* is a form of affirmative easement that privileges its holder to enter the servient estate to appropriate something of value. Early forms of profit, prevalent in a rural society, included "turbary" (the right to cut turf for fuel), "estover" (the right to cut timber for fuel), "piscary" (the right to take fish), and the right of pasture. More recently, profits have sometimes been used as an arrangement for the extraction of mineral wealth, such as coal, iron, oil, and gas. 3 Powell, Real Property ¶405 (Rohan ed. 1979). Unlike the right of way, the profit tends to be *in gross*. (So, too, does the public utility easement.)

§10.3   Modes of Creating the Easement

a.   Creation by Express Agreement

Most easements (and profits) are the result of an express arrangement between the benefited party and the owner of the servient estate. At early common law, livery of seisin was regarded as inappropriate for the transfer of an easement; instead, a sealed writing called a "grant" was used. Paradoxically, the law required a writing for the creation of an easement before one became necessary for a lease or the transfer of a fee.[7] Today, we still speak of the *grant* of an easement—whenever the owner of the servient estate creates this burden on his land. Sometimes, the easement arises not by grant, but by *reservation*. This would occur if B, the owner of adjoining Lots 1 and 2, transferred the fee in Lot 1 to A, but reserved a right of way, or some other easement interest, as a burden on Lot 1. (One might also think of an easement by reservation as a legal short cut to avoid a two-step process whereby B would transfer the unencumbered fee to A, and A would then grant the easement to B.) Easements also arise contractually. Two common examples are the reciprocal driveway agreement (adjoining owners A and B agree to share the common driveway straddling their lots) and the easement for light and air (A, the owner of the servient estate, "promises" his neighbor, B, not to build within ten feet of the lot line or higher than two stories).

7. An oral agreement to grant an easement is unenforceable. See, e.g., Gracie Sq. Realty Corp. v. Choice Realty Corp., 305 N.Y. 271, 113 N.E.2d 416 (1953).

Easements sometimes arise not from express arrangement but from "operation of law"—the courtroom creation of an easement to reconcile a dispute over the use of land. The next four cases illustrate this concept.

b.   Easement by Implication

VAN SANDT v. ROYSTER
148 Kan. 495, 83 P.2d 698 (1938)

The opinion of the court was delivered by ALLEN, J. The action was brought to enjoin defendants from using and maintaining an underground lateral sewer drain through and across plaintiff's land. The case was tried by the court, judgment was rendered in favor of defendants, and plaintiff appeals.

In the city of Chanute, Highland avenue, running north and south, intersects Tenth street running east and west. In the early part of 1904 Laura A. J. Bailey was the owner of a plot of ground lying east of Highland avenue and south of Tenth street. Running east from Highland avenue and facing north on Tenth street the lots are numbered respectively, 19, 20 and 4. [See Figure 2.] In 1904 the residence of Mrs. Bailey was on lot 4 on the east part of her land.

In the latter part of 1903 or the early part of 1904, the city of Chanute constructed a public sewer in Highland avenue, west of lot 19. About the same time a private lateral drain was constructed from the Bailey residence on lot 4 running in a westerly direction through and across lots 20 and 19 to the public sewer.

On January 15, 1904, Laura A. J. Bailey conveyed lot 19 to John J. Jones, by general warranty deed with usual covenants against encumbrances,

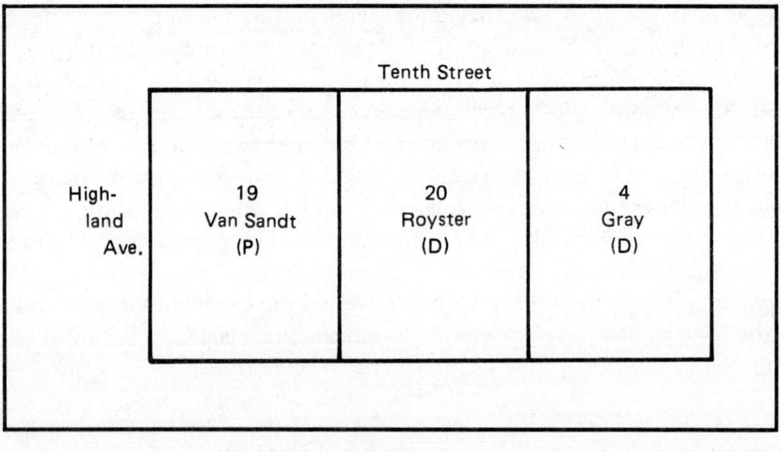

FIGURE 2

and containing no exceptions or reservations. Jones erected a dwelling on the north part of the lot. In 1920 Jones conveyed the north 156 feet of lot 19 to Carl D. Reynolds; in 1924 Reynolds conveyed to the plaintiff, who has owned and occupied the premises since that time.

In 1904 Laura A. J. Bailey conveyed lot 20 to one Murphy, who built a house thereon, and by mesne conveyances the title passed to the defendant, Louis H. Royster. The deed to Murphy was a general warranty deed without exceptions or reservations. The defendant Gray has succeeded to the title to lot 4 upon which the old Bailey home stood at the time Laura A. J. Bailey sold lots 19 and 20.

In March, 1936, plaintiff discovered his basement flooded with sewage and filth to a depth of six or eight inches, and upon investigation he found for the first time that there existed on and across his property a sewer drain extending in an easterly direction across the property of Royster to the property of Gray. The refusal of defendants to cease draining and discharging their sewage across plaintiff's land resulted in this lawsuit.

The trial court returned findings of fact, from which we quote: . . .

> 8. There is not now and was not at the time plaintiff purchased his property anything on record in the office of the register of deeds of the county pertaining to the private sewer above referred to.[8]
>
> 9. At the time plaintiff purchased his property he and his wife made a careful and thorough inspection of the same, knew that the house they were buying was equipped with modern plumbing and knew that the plumbing had to drain into a sewer, but otherwise had no further knowledge of the existence of said lateral sewer.
>
> 10. That the lateral sewer in controversy was installed prior to the sale of the property by Mrs. Laura A. J. Bailey to John J. Jones on January 15, 1904; but if not, the said lateral sewer certainly was installed shortly after the sale to John J. Jones and with the knowledge and acquiescence of said John J. Jones, and that the said John J. Jones paid the said Laura A. J. Bailey one third of the cost of the installation of the said sewer.[9]
>
> 11. That . . . the said lateral sewer was an appurtenance to the properties belonging to plaintiff and Louise Royster, and the same is necessary to the reasonable use and enjoyment of the said properties of the parties.

The drain pipe in the lateral sewer was several feet under the surface of the ground. There was nothing visible on the ground in the rear of the houses to indicate the existence of the drain or the connection of the drain with the houses.

As a conclusion of law the court found that "an appurtenant easement existed in the said lateral sewer as to all three of the properties involved in the controversy here." Plaintiff's prayer for relief was denied and it was decreed

8. Of what significance?—ED.
9. Is there a Statute of Frauds problem if the sewer was installed after the sale from Bailey to Jones?—ED.

that plaintiff be restrained from interfering in any way with the lateral drain or sewer.

Plaintiff contends that the evidence fails to show that an easement was ever created in his land, and, assuming there was an easement created as alleged, that he took the premises free from the burden of the easement for the reason that he was a bona fide purchaser, without notice, actual or constructive.

Defendants contend: (1) That an easement was created by implied reservation on the severance of the servient from the dominant estate of the deed from Mrs. Bailey to Jones; (2) there is a valid easement by prescription.

In finding No. 11, the court found that the lateral sewer "was an appurtenance to the properties belonging to plaintiff and Louise Royster, and the same is necessary to the reasonable use and enjoyment of the said properties of the parties."

As an easement is an interest which a person has in land in the possession of another, it necessarily follows that an owner cannot have an easement in his own land. (Johnston v. City of Kingman, 141 Kan. 131, 39 P.2d 924; Ferguson v. Ferguson, 106 Kan. 823, 189 Pac. 925).

However, an owner may make use of one part of his land for the benefit of another part, and this is very frequently spoken of as a quasi easement.

> When one thus utilizes part of his land for the benefit of another part, it is frequently said that a quasi easement exists, the part of the land which is benefited being referred to as the "quasi dominant tenement" and the part which is utilized for the benefit of the other part being referred to as the "quasi servient tenement." The so-called quasi easement is evidently not a legal relation in any sense, but the expression is a convenient one to describe the particular mode in which the owner utilizes one part of the land for the benefit of the other. . . .
>
> If the owner of land, one part of which is subject to a quasi easement in favor of another part, conveys the quasi dominant tenement, an easement corresponding to such quasi easement is ordinarily regarded as thereby vested in the grantee of the land, provided, it is said, the quasi easement is of an apparent continuous and necessary character. [2 Tiffany on Real Property, 2d ed., 1272, 1273]

Following the famous case of Pyer v. Carter, 1 Hurl. & Nor. 916, some of the English cases and many early American cases held that upon the transfer of the quasi-servient tenement there was an implied reservation of an easement in favor of the conveyor. Under the doctrine of Pyer v. Carter, no distinction was made between an implied reservation and an implied grant.

The case, however, was overthrown in England by Suffield v. Brown, 4 De G. J. & S. 185, and Wheeldon v. Burrows, L.R. 12 Ch. D. 31. In the former case the court said:

> It seems to me more reasonable and just to hold that if the grantor intends to reserve any right over the property granted, it is his duty to reserve it expressly

in the grant, rather than to limit and cut down the operation of a plain grant (which is not pretended to be otherwise than in conformity with the contract between the parties), by the fiction of an implied reservation. If this plain rule be adhered to, men will know what they have to trust, and will place confidence in the language of their contracts and assurances. . . . But I cannot agree that the grantor can derogate from his own absolute grant so as to claim rights over the thing granted, even if they were at the time of the grant continuous and apparent easements enjoyed by an adjoining tenement which remains the property of him the grantor. [pp. 190, 194]

Many American courts of high standing assert that the rule regarding implied grants and implied reservations is reciprocal and that the rule applies with equal force and in like circumstances to both grants and reservations. (Washburn on Easements, 4th ed. 75; Miller v. Skaggs, 79 W. Va. 645, 91 S.E. 536, Ann. Cas. 1918 D 929).

On the other hand, perhaps a majority of the cases hold that in order to establish an easement by implied reservation in favor of the grantor the easement must be one of strict necessity, even when there was an existing drain or sewer at the time of the severance. . . .

We are inclined to the view that the circumstance that the claimant of the easement is the grantor instead of the grantee, is but one of many factors to be considered in determining whether an easement will arise by implication. An easement created by implication arises as an inference of the intentions of the parties to a conveyance of land. The inference is drawn from the circumstances under which the conveyance was made rather than from the language of the conveyance. The easement may arise in favor of the conveyor or the conveyee. In the Restatement of Property, tentative draft No. 8, section 28, the factors determining the implication of an easement are stated:

Sec. 28. Factors Determining Implication of Easements or Profits

In determining whether the circumstances under which a conveyance of land is made imply an easement or a profit, the following factors are important: (a) whether the claimant is the conveyor or the conveyee, (b) the terms of the conveyance, (c) the consideration given for it, (d) whether the claim is made against a simultaneous conveyee, (e) the extent of necessity of the easement or the profit to the claimant, (f) whether reciprocal benefits result to the conveyor and the conveyee, (g) the manner in which the land was used prior to its conveyance, and (h) the extent to which the manner of prior use was or might have been known to the parties. [10] . . .

At the time John J. Jones purchased lot 19 he was aware of the lateral sewer, and knew that it was installed for the benefit of the lots owned by Mrs. Bailey, the common owner. The easement was necessary to the comfortable

10. Except for the allusion to profits, which was removed, this language appears unchanged in the final draft. Restatement of Property §47b.—ED.

enjoyment of the grantor's property. If land may be used without an easement, but cannot be used without disproportionate effort and expense, an easement may still be implied in favor of either the grantor or grantee on the basis of necessity alone. This is the situation as found by the trial court.

Neither can it be claimed that plaintiff purchased without notice. At the time plaintiff purchased the property he and his wife made a careful and thorough inspection of the property. They knew the house was equipped with modern plumbing and that the plumbing had to drain into a sewer. Under the facts as found by the court, we think the purchaser was charged with notice of the lateral sewer. It was an apparent easement as that term is used in the books. (Wiesel v. Smira, 49 R.I. 246, 142 Atl. 148, 58 A.L.R. 818; 19 C.J. 868.)

The author of the annotation on Easements by Implication in 58 A.L.R. 832, states the rule as follows:

> While there is some conflict of authority as to whether existing drains, pipes, and sewers may be properly characterized as apparent, within the rule as to apparent or visible easements, the majority of the cases which have considered the question have taken the view that appearance and visibility are not synonymous, and that the fact that the pipe, sewer, or drain may be hidden underground does not negative its character as an apparent condition; at least, where the appliances connected with and leading to it are obvious.

As we are clear that an easement by implication was created under the facts as found by the trial court, it is unnecessary to discuss the question of prescription.

The judgment is affirmed.

HARVEY, J., concurs in the order of affirmance, but not in all that is said in the opinion.

[Query: What might he have disagreed with?]

NOTES AND QUESTIONS

1. Discussion of the case appears at 13 S. Cal. L. Rev. 525 (1940), 25 Va. L. Rev. 626 (1939). General discussion of implied easements can be found in Leesman, The Rationale of the Quasi-easement in Illinois, 30 Ill. L. Rev. 963 (1936).

2. On the facts in this case, could defendant have obtained an easement by prescription?

3. *Is the use "apparent"?* Whether a particular use is "apparent" depends upon an answer to the question: How complete an inspection and inquiry should we require of the purchaser? The facts in Sievers v. Flynn, 305 Ky. 325, 204 S.W.2d 364 (1947), resembled those in the main case. A manhole in the street and a slight depression in the ground were the only signs of a private

sewer line, but the court ruled that the line was "apparent" so as to bind the lot owner who had had no other notice (305 Ky. at 329): "It may be that appellee did not recognize the manhole and the depression as visible signs of a sewer line; but certainly a person conversant with sewer lines and sewer connections could not fail to recognize them as such." Should a purchaser be expected to have a plumber, electrician, etc., at her side when making her inspection?

In Heatherdell Farms, Inc. v. Huntley Estates at Greenburg No. 3 Corp., 130 N.Y.S.2d 335 (Sup. Ct. 1954), defendant acquired a wooded 120-acre tract adjoining plaintiff's 25-acre parcel that housed a sanitarium. Plaintiff claimed an implied easement to maintain a septic tank and drainage field 100 feet inside defendant's tract. The tank had a concrete slab top, roughly twelve feet by ten feet, set flush with the ground, with four or five manhole covers therein. The top and covers were so obscured, however, by tall grass and underbrush that one would not notice them until he had approached within twenty-five feet. In refusing to find an implied easement, the court wrote (130 N.Y.S.2d at 338):

> It is not reasonable to require a purchaser of large acreage in its natural state to thoroughly inspect every rod or acre or to have it inspected by a title company or its agents. It is a well-known fact that the on-the-ground inspection by an ordinary prudent purchaser of such land consists of looking at it from one or more vantage points with a general locating of the boundaries. Such a purchaser will also generally examine a map or plotting of the acreage, but it is not expected that he will thoroughly inspect the land to search out possible servitudes or encumbrances not ordinarily to be expected on such land.

Suppose that the defendant had chanced upon the concrete slab while inspecting the terrain, but had not made further inquiry before purchasing the tract. Would he then be subject to the easement?

FONTAINEBLEAU HOTEL CORP. v. FORTY-FIVE
TWENTY-FIVE, INC.

114 So. 2d 357 (Fla. Dist. Ct. App. 1959)

PER CURIAM. This is an interlocutory appeal from an order temporarily enjoining the appellants from continuing with the construction of a fourteen-story addition to the Fontainebleau Hotel, owned and operated by the appellants. Appellee, plaintiff below, owns the Eden Roc Hotel, which was constructed in 1955, about a year after the Fontainebleau, and adjoins the Fontainebleau on the north. Both are luxury hotels, facing the Atlantic Ocean. The proposed addition to the Fontainebleau is being constructed twenty feet from its north property line, 130 feet from the mean high water mark of the Atlantic Ocean, and 76 feet 8 inches from the ocean bulkhead line. The 14-

story tower will extend 160 feet above grade in height and is 416 feet long from east to west. During the winter months, from around two o'clock in the afternoon for the remainder of the day, the shadow of the addition will extend over the cabana, swimming pool, and sunbathing areas of the Eden Roc, which are located in the southern portion of its property.

In this action, plaintiff-appellee sought to enjoin the defendants-appellants from proceeding with the construction of the addition to the Fontainebleau (it appears to have been roughly eight stories high at the time suit was filed), alleging that the construction would interfere with the light and air on the beach in front of the Eden Roc and cast a shadow of such size as to render the beach wholly unfitted for the use and enjoyment of its guests, to the irreparable injury of the plaintiff; further, that the construction of such addition on the north side of defendants' property, rather than the south side, was actuated by malice and ill will on the part of the defendants' president toward the plaintiff's president; and that the construction was in violation of a building ordinance requiring a 100-foot setback from the ocean. It was also alleged that the construction would interfere with the easements of light and air enjoyed by plaintiff and its predecessors in title for more than twenty years and "impliedly granted by virtue of the acts of the plaintiff's predecessors in title, as well as under the common law and the express recognition of such rights by virtue of Chapter 9837, Laws of Florida 1923. . . ." Some attempt was also made to allege an easement by implication in favor of the plaintiff's property, as the dominant, and against the defendants' property, as the servient, tenement.

The defendants' answer denied the material allegations of the complaint, pleaded laches and estoppel by judgment.

The chancellor heard considerable testimony on the issues made by the complaint and the answer and, as noted, entered a temporary injunction restraining the defendants from continuing with the construction of the addition. His reason for so doing was stated by him, in a memorandum opinion, as follows:

> In granting the temporary injunction in this case the Court wishes to make several things very clear. The ruling is not based on any alleged presumptive title nor prescriptive right of the plaintiff to light and air nor is it based on any deed restrictions nor recorded plats in the title of the plaintiff nor of the defendant nor of any plat of record. It is not based on any zoning ordinance nor on any provision of the building code of the City of Miami Beach nor on the decision of any court, nisi prius or appellate. It is based solely on the proposition that no one has a right to use his property to the injury of another. In this case it is clear from the evidence that the proposed use by the Fontainebleau will materially damage the Eden Roc. There is evidence indicating that the construction of the proposed annex by the Fontainebleau is malicious or deliberate for the purpose of injuring the Eden Roc, but it is scarcely sufficient, standing alone, to afford a basis for equitable relief.

This is indeed a novel application of the maxim *sic utere tuo ut alienum non laedas*. This maxim does not mean that one must never use his own property in such a way as to do any injury to his neighbor. Beckman v. Marshall, Fla. 1956, 85 So. 2d 552. It means only that one must use his property so as not to injure the lawful *rights* of another. Cason v. Florida Power Co., 74 Fla. 1, 76 So. 535, L.R.A. 1918A, 1034. In Reaver v. Martin Theatres, Fla. 1951, 52 So. 2d 682, 683, 25 A.L.R.2d 1451, under this maxim, it was stated that "it is well settled that a property owner may put his own property to any reasonable and lawful use, so long as he does not thereby deprive the adjoining landowner of any right of enjoyment of his property *which is recognized and protected by law, and so long as his use is not such a one as the law will pronounce a nuisance."* [Emphasis supplied.]

No American decision has been cited, and independent research has revealed none, in which it has been held that—in the absence of some contractual or statutory obligation—a landowner has a legal right to the free flow of light and air across the adjoining land of his neighbor. Even at common law, the landowner had no legal right, in the absence of an easement or uninterrupted use and enjoyment for a period of 20 years, to unobstructed light and air from the adjoining land. Blumberg v. Weiss, 1941, 129 N.J. Eq. 34, 17 A.2d 823; 1 Am. Jur., Adjoining Landowners, §51. And the English doctrine of "ancient lights" has been unanimously repudiated in this country. 1 Am. Jur., Adjoining Landowners, §49, p. 533; Lynch v. Hill, 1939, 24 Del. Ch. 86, 6 A.2d 614, overruling Clawson v. Primrose, 4 Del. Ch. 643.

There being, then, no legal right to the free flow of light and air from the adjoining land, it is universally held that where a structure serves a useful and beneficial purpose, it does not give rise to a cause of action, either for damages or for an injunction under the maxim *sic utere tuo ut alienum non laedas,* even though it causes injury to another by cutting off the light and air and interfering with the view that would otherwise be available over adjoining land in its natural state, regardless of the fact that the structure may have been erected partly for spite. . . .

We see no reason for departing from this universal rule. If, as contended on behalf of plaintiff, public policy demands that a landowner in the Miami Beach area refrain from constructing buildings on his premises that will cast a shadow on the adjoining premises, an amendment of its comprehensive planning and zoning ordinance, applicable to the public as a whole, is the means by which such purpose should be achieved. (No opinion is expressed here as to the validity of such an ordinance, if one should be enacted pursuant to the requirements of law. Cf. City of Miami Beach v. State ex rel. Fontainebleau Hotel Corp., Fla. App. 1959, 108 So. 2d 614, 619; *certiorari denied,* Fla. 1959, 111 So. 2d 437.) But to change the universal rule—and the custom followed in this state since its inception—that adjoining landowners have an equal right under the law to build to the line of their respective tracts and to such a height as is desired by them (in the absence, of course, of building restrictions or regulations) amounts, in our opinion, to judicial legislation. As stated in Musumeci v. Leonardo, supra [77 R.I. 255, 75 A.2d 177], "So use your own as not to injure another's property is, indeed, a sound and salutary principle for the promotion of justice, but it may not and should not be applied so as gratuitously to confer upon an adjacent property owner incorporeal rights incidental to his ownership of land which the law does not sanction."

We have also considered whether the order here reviewed may be sustained upon any other reasoning, conformable to and consistent with the pleadings, regardless of the erroneous reasoning upon which the order was actually based. See McGregor v. Provident Trust Co. of Philadelphia, 119 Fla. 718, 162 So. 323. We have concluded that it cannot.

The record affirmatively shows that no statutory basis for the right sought to be enforced by plaintiff exists. The so-called Shadow Ordinance enacted by the City of Miami Beach at plaintiff's behest was held invalid in City of Miami Beach v. State ex rel. Fontainebleau Hotel Corp., *supra*. It also affirmatively appears that there is no possible basis for holding that plaintiff has an easement for light and air, either express or implied, across defendants' property, nor any prescriptive right thereto—even if it be assumed, arguendo, that the common-law right of prescription as to "ancient lights" is in effect in this state. And from what we have said heretofore in this opinion, it is perhaps superfluous to add that we have no desire to dissent from the unanimous holding in this country repudiating the English doctrine of ancient lights.

NOTES AND QUESTIONS

1.   Are there any sets of facts that would have supported plaintiff's assertion of an implied easement?

2.   An easement for light and air may restrict the servient estate in one of several respects: as to building location, building height, or percentage of lot coverage. Such restrictions have begun serving an additional purpose in the high-density areas of Manhattan and other commercial centers where zoning laws limit a building's floor space to a specified multiple of the lot area. See page 779, *infra*. A developer can obtain the equivalent of more land (thus permitting a bulkier building) if his neighbor will agree to under-use his lot. The developer then applies for a building permit based on the combined floor area limits for his lot and the unused capacity of the servient lot. The law seems to have sanctioned this device. See Hotel Taft Assoc. v. Summer, 34 Misc. 2d 367, 374, 226 N.Y.S.2d 155 (Sup. Ct. 1962), *aff'd mem.*, 18 A.D.2d 796, 236 N.Y.S.2d 939 (1963).

How much should the developer be willing to pay for this easement?

For a striking proposal to transfer unused air rights to nonneighborhood owners as a vehicle for landmark preservation, see Costonis, The Chicago Plan: Incentive Zoning and the Preservation of Urban Landmarks, 85 Harv. L. Rev. 574 (1972), §13.2, *infra*.

NOTE ON THE ENGLISH DOCTRINE OF ANCIENT LIGHTS

"Early in its history the common law recognized a landowner's right to the enjoyment of light, air and view unobstructed by buildings on a neighboring estate. Nonetheless, equity would not vindicate the landowner's right unless the deprivation was in such a degree as to render occupation of his home uncomfortable or exercise of his business less beneficial. Under the common law doctrine of 'ancient lights,' the right to light, air and view was acquired by unobstructed enjoyment, first throughout 'immemorial use' and later for a period of twenty years fixed by the statute of limitations." Note, 34 Tul. L. Rev. 599 (1960).

"By the English common law if one opened windows overlooking his neighbor's property, the latter had the right to erect barriers to obstruct the view; and his motives in doing so were wholly immaterial. But there was a reason for this which does not exist [in the United States]. That rule was a necessary corollary to the doctrine of ancient lights, whereby one enjoying the uninterrupted use of a window for a given period . . . acquired an easement in the adjoining land which the owner could neither gainsay nor deny. Hence to open a window overlooking a neighbor's land was regarded as an encroachment, though no action lay therefor. The only remedy was to build a barrier opposite the offending window. The adjoining proprietor not only had the right to erect such barrier; but was obliged to do so to pretect the title to his land. This was the only method whereby he could prevent the user into a right." Rumble, Limitations on the Use of Property by Its Owner, 5 Va. L. Rev. 297, 306 (1918).

However well the doctrine of ancient lights may have suited England's one-time agrarian society, its survival to this day is surprising indeed. See, e.g., McGrath v. Munster & Leinster Bank, 94 Ir. L.T.R. 110 (1960) (tenant recovered damages from neighboring landowner whose remodeled building darkened tenant's office).

The Rights of Light Act of 1959 (7 & 8 Eliz. 2, c. 56), although reaffirming the doctrine, made two important concessions to urban life: (1) the prescriptive period was lengthened to twenty-seven years; (2) the filing of a simple notice became a legally sufficient substitute for an opaque barrier.

A major impetus for the reform law was the difficulty in obtaining planning permission to erect an unsightly screen. Greene, Securing Rights of Light, 112 L.J. 744 (1962).

NOTE ON SPITE FENCES

Should a court ever enjoin a structure, not otherwise unlawful, simply because it was built to spite or harass a neighboring landowner? As a useful corollary to the doctrine of ancient lights, English courts refused to consider the builder's motives; prior to 1959, the law gave him no other way in which he could unilaterally protect his land against the easement.

One might expect that when the doctrine of ancient lights was rejected in the United States its corollary would also fail. But, on the contrary, some American courts still refuse to examine the builder's motive. For example, Pennsylvania is among the states that have adopted the English position that refuses to enjoin a spite fence. Cohen v. Perrino, 355 Pa. 455, 50 A.2d 348 (1947).

In his well-researched opinion for the Pennsylvania court, Justice Stearne quoted from two decisions that embody the opposing rationales:

> [T]o prohibit him [an adjoining landowner] from causing [injury to his neighbor] in case the structure is neither beneficial nor ornamental, but erected from motives of pure malice, is not protecting a legal right, but is controlling his moral conduct. In this state a man is free to direct his moral conduct as he pleases, in so far as he is not restrained by statute. . . . There is no conflict between law and equity in our practice, and what a man may lawfully do cannot be prohibited as inequitable. It may be immoral, and shock our notion of fairness, but what the law permits equity tolerates. It would be much more inequitable and intolerable to allow a man's neighbors to question his motives every time that he should undertake to erect a structure upon his own premises. . . . [Letts v. Kessler, 54 Ohio St. 73, 81-82, 42 N.E. 765, 766 (1896)]

> . . . Malicious use of property resulting in injury to another is never a "lawful use" but is in every case unlawful. The right to the use of property is therefore a qualified rather than absolute right. When one acting solely from malevolent motives does injury to his neighbor, to call such conduct the exercise of an absolute legal right is a perversion of terms. . . . The use of one's own property for the sole purpose of injuring another is not a right that a good citizen would desire nor one that a bad citizen should have. [Hornsby v. Smith, 191 Ga. 491, 499, 13 S.E.2d 20, 24 (1941)]

If a head count of decisions were taken today, the latter view would predominate; equity, even in the absence of a statute, will usually enjoin as a private nuisance a spite structure serving no useful purpose. Furthermore, several states have supplied a statutory support, e.g., Mass. Ann. Laws c. 49, §21 (Michie/Law. Co-op 1966); Conn. Gen. Stat. Ann. §§52-480, 52-570 (1960); N.Y. Real Prop. Acts. Law §843 (McKinney 1963). Rideout v. Knox, 148 Mass. 368, 19 N.E. 390 (1889), is the leading case approving such statutes as a valid exercise of the police power. With his usual aplomb, Justice Holmes wrote for the court (148 Mass. at 372-373):

> Some small limitations of previously existing rights incident to property may be imposed for the sake of preventing a manifest evil; larger ones could not be except by eminent domain . . . The statute is confined to fences and structures in the nature of fences, and to such fences only as unnecessarily exceed six feet in height. It is hard to imagine a more insignificant curtailment of rights of prop-

erty. Even the right to build a fence above six feet is not denied, when any convenience of the owner would be served by building higher.

The requirements for injunctive relief under a typical statute are:

(1) malicious erection of a structure on defendant's land that is intended to injure plaintiff's enjoyment of his land;
(2) impairment, in fact, of plaintiff's enjoyment;
(3) a structure otherwise useless to defendant. United Petroleum Corp. v. Atlantic Refining Co., 3 Conn. Cir. Ct. 255, 212 A.2d 589 (1965).

Malice may be inferred solely from the objective facts. See Rapuano v. Ames, 21 Conn. Supp. 110, 145 A.2d 384 (1958).

Two recent cases illustrate the leaven of good sense that a court must add to the statutory recipe. Sitting in equity, would you have granted an injunction to either plaintiff?

(a) Plaintiff A operated a gasoline station along the southbound lane of a divided highway. Defendant built an Atlantic station to the immediate north and erected a 12' × 25' sign that blocked off plaintiff's advertising from the view of southbound drivers. Plaintiff carried a non-brand-name gasoline, which he sold more cheaply than Atlantic. See United Petroleum Corp. v. Atlantic Refining Co., *supra*.

(b) Plaintiff B owned a building one-quarter mile from the site of the 1964-1965 New York World's Fair. Before the fair began, plaintiff erected a 250'-long red neon advertising sign atop its building. The defendant fair in turn planted a screen of shrubbery that blocked off plaintiff's advertising from the view of fairgoers. See A. & P. Tea Co. v. New York World's Fair, 42 Misc. 2d 855, 249 N.Y.S.2d 256 (Sup. Ct. 1964).

ZILLMAN AND DEENY, LEGAL ASPECTS OF SOLAR ENERGY DEVELOPMENT

25 Ariz. St. L.J. 25, 28-29, 33-35 (1976)

Because approximately one-quarter to one-third of all American energy use is dedicated to heating water and to heating and cooling homes, offices, and factories, the prominent short-term use of solar energy will be to heat water, and to heat and cool buildings. Installation of solar equipment in all new structures and converting (retrofitting) a significant number of existing structures for the use of solar energy can provide a fossil fuel savings sufficient to allay fears of over-dependence on foreign oil for decades to come. The technology is developed for water and space heating, but is not well advanced in the cooling area.

Solar building design has been consistently innovative, creating a diversity of solar energy devices and homes. Nevertheless, there is substantial agreement on the basics of a working solar energy system. Even without actual solar equipment, attention to design and energy conservation can provide substantial savings in heating and cooling costs. As any resident of the southern United States knows, the solar heat input from a southern exposure can be substantial. In the winter this is desirable, but in the summer it is not. By simply constructing an appropriate roof overhang, a significant energy saving occurs. In summer, when the sun is high in the sky, the overhang deflects heat. In winter, when the sun is low on the horizon, heat enters the house without deflection. Similarly, use of curtains, screens, and foliage can admit the sun's rays when desired, trap them for use at night, and exclude them in summer when the sun's heat is a bane rather than a boon. This is solar architecture in its most primitive form—the conscious design of structures to maximize their use of the sun's energy.

Basic solar architecture can save substantial energy. But by no means does it exhaust solar potential. Greater heating efficiency is obtained by using a system which collects solar radiation that falls on a building, stores the heat collected, and circulates it throughout the building when needed. The system begins with the solar collector typically mounted on the building's roof. The most common collecting device has been the flat plate collector. A single collector resembles a shallow rectangular box. A metal receiving surface is painted black for maximum sun absorption and placed within a frame. The frame and metal sheet are covered with glass or plastic to prevent re-radiation, and a heat trap results in which temperatures can approach 200° Fahrenheit. The trapped heat is transferred to air or water circulated just beneath the metallic sheet. When a large number of individual collectors are placed together, the energy absorbed can supply a considerable percentage of the heating needs of a structure. The captured heat is circulated through a closed system to a central storage area. A large rock-filled cylinder often serves this purpose. The rocks will retain the heat for up to several days. As heat is needed, a pump or fan can circulate it throughout the building.

The solar homeowner needs the protection of a negative easement. He must be able to prevent the owner of the servient estate from blocking his access to direct sunlight. An express agreement between landowners can solve the problem.

Another significant aspect of easement law is the distinction between express easements and implied or prescriptive easements. The express easement is a product of agreement between landowners. The prescriptive or implied easement arises by operation of law as either a matter of necessity (one landowner's estate is worthless without the easement) or long usage.

With respect to long usage, a particular difficulty in the United States has been the courts' refusal to recognize implied easement rights to light and air. The English doctrine of "ancient lights" has never been adopted by jurisdictions of this country. While the English doctrine is concerned with access to fresh air and light, rather than direct access to sun rays, it provides an analogy which might be used to protect solar energy devices.

If a court were willing to recognize a prescriptive easement for solar access, it would probably date the prescription from the initial installation of the solar collector. This raises practical problems. The party installing the solar collector would like to have his right to perpetual solar access decreed immediately. Yet he may face a ten-year period before his easement is secure. During this time the initial servient owner or his successor would be free to impede solar access as he wished. Possibly he might find it legally desirable to impede solar access solely for the purpose of preserving his future rights.

In the area of easements by necessity, the law again raises problems for the prospective solar energy user. In classic easement law, a unity of ownership is required to establish an easement by necessity. Such an easement arises, for example, when A owns two parcels of land and conveys one to B, but leaves B no means of egress. B is thus landlocked and his property is far less valuable. In such circumstances, B's easement can be created by necessity.

There are differing views on the degree of necessity required to establish the easement. Some cases hold that "absolute necessity" must be shown where light and air are involved. Others rely on a "reasonable necessity" argument. Bydlon v. United States [69] illustrates the latter category. That case involved air space for airplane travel. In allowing the easement, the court noted changes in technological conditions. Such an argument has obvious relevance to the promotion of solar easements.

Under any set of circumstances it would seem desirable to secure an express or consensual easement. But the newness of solar technology may work against the landowner. His neighbor, who may be quite willing to grant a portion of his land for a footpath or a driveway, may be unsure of the consequences of relinquishing rights to a portion of the airspace over his land. The servient owner may be giving up the right to construct a second story to his residence or to plant trees. His offer of a short-term easement may not be encouraging to the solar energy user contemplating a $10,000 investment. The solar energy user must also consider the types of uses to which he may later put the property. If initially he wishes only to provide sufficient paneling for water heating, he may need to renegotiate the easement if he later converts to solar space heating and cooling. The solar energy user must also consider how many separate landowners must join in the easement. The construction of a 14-story building two lots over may nullify easement agreements with the immediately adjoining neighbor. The easement's virtue, of course, may be its relative permanency. A properly drafted solar easement can benefit subsequent owners of the solar house and bind subsequent owners of the servient property. While the easement may be lost through abandonment, this seems

69. 175 F. Supp. 891 (U.S. Ct. Claims 1959).

unlikely. Most probably the person selling a solar house will have to find another solar-inclined purchaser in view of the substantial investment in solar equipment and concomitant increase in resale prices.

Overall, the burdens facing the potential solar energy user seeking an easement may be substantial. But if adjoining property owners are not forbidden by other means (restrictive covenants, zoning) from screening the solar user's property, resort to easements may be necessary. One possible way to avoid the painstaking individual agreement approach would be to create statutory easements. Such easements have been legislated for power companies and cable television.

c. Easement by Necessity

BERKELEY DEVELOPMENT CORP. v. HUTZLER
229 S.E.2d 732 (W. Va. 1976)

BERRY, C. J. The appellant, Hunter Hutzler, seeks a reversal of a judgment of the Circuit Court of Berkeley County permanently enjoining him from entering on or across the lands of the appellee, Berkeley Development Corporation.

The parties are owners of adjacent tracts of real estate located in Gerrardstown District, Berkeley County, West Virginia. In 1972, the Berkeley Development Corporation acquired its 550 acre tract and began to develop it as a recreational, residential subdivision. By deed dated August 10, 1943, Mr. Hunter Hutzler purchased his 105 acre tract which, subsequent to its acquisition, has been used primarily as a source of timber or pulp wood. Hutzler does not reside on this land.

In 1974, the Berkeley Development Corporation initiated an action in the Circuit Court of Berkeley County to obtain an injunction against Hutzler to prohibit Hutzler from entering on the 550 acre tract and from interfering with the surface of that land. The appellee's complaint recited that Hutzler had entered on the land with equipment to cut trees and grade the surface. By way of defense to the appellee's action, Hutzler contended that he had a prescriptive easement, or, in the alternative, a private way of necessity across an existing road which ran from his land over the plaintiff's land and onto a public road.

At trial, it was stipulated that the tracts of the respective parties shared a common source of title, the two tracts having been originally owned by one Moses S. Grantham. It was further stipulated there were no express easements in any of the conveyances in the line of title of either party.

On behalf of the Berkeley Development Corporation, Mr. Gilbert R. Clarke, the organization's president, testified that prior to purchasing the 550 acres he spent a great deal of time examining the property. He stated that he walked over the common boundary and that he saw a faint trail which he assumed to be a logging trail. He stated that the inspection revealed no indication of any travel on the trail and that there was substantial growth in the way. Mr. Clarke also observed that a small stream which crossed the trail had eroded its banks making passage impossible. It was Mr. Clarke's estimate that the trail had not been used for twelve to fifteen years prior to his inspection.

In advance of its purchase, the appellee had the 550 acre tract and some of the surrounding properties surveyed by a licensed land surveyor, Galtjo Geertsema. Geertsema, called as a witness on behalf of the appellee, described his survey and indicated that he observed the road in question at the time. Geertsema described the road as an old road, averaging approximately ten feet wide and running a thousand feet over the property of the Berkeley Development Corporation, from the point where it crossed the common boundary. The surveyor indicated that he did not observe any evidence of the use of the road although he stated that it was passable.

With reference to alternate ways of ingress and egress, neither Clarke or Geertsema could say with any degree of certainty that there were other roads from the Hutzler property to a public road.

The evidence adduced on behalf of the appellant was that the 105 acre tract had previously been an orchard and for a number of years the roadway in question was used by Hutzler's predecessor in title as a route for hauling fruit to a public road. Walker Brannon, the son of one of the appellee's predecessors in title, testified that the road had been in continuous use to his recollection for more than seventy years. Brannon stated that the road was first used to haul fruit and later to haul timber from the Hutzler property. Brannon indicated that the road followed substantially the same route as it did in 1901 and was in substantially the same condition except for the natural vegetative growth in the roadway. Brannon further testified that there was no other means of access to the Hutzler property except across a precipitous and difficult route which went across the property of others and which was passable only by horse and rider.

The appellant, Hunter Hutzler, testified that prior to his purchase of the tract, he had worked on the orchard and had hauled fruit over the road in question for a number of years. Hutzler indicated that the road had been used for a period of fifty years to his recollection, with the acquiescence of the previous owners of the Berkeley Development tract. In addition, Hutzler had, himself, hauled lumber across the road in the years following his purchase of the orchard tract. Finally, the appellant indicated that the road in question was the only means to get in and out of his property.

Elwood Hutzler, the son of the appellant, confirmed his father's testimony concerning the use of the road, the acquiescence of the previous owner of the adjacent land and the absence of any other way to a public road. In addition Elwood Hutzler stated that he had personally used the road during the previous year.

On the evidence adduced, the circuit court held that the appellant had neither a prescriptive easement nor a way of necessity across the Berkeley

Development tract. In accordance with this ruling, the court permanently enjoined Hutzler from entering on or across the appellee's land. Hutzler contends that the trial court erred in holding that he did not have an easement or right-of-way either by prescription or necessity over the land of the appellee. The appellee counters by arguing that the trial court was correct, but if either a prescriptive easement or a way of necessity was established, it was lost by virtue of the fact that the appellee obtained the property in question as a bona fide purchaser for value without notice of the existence of any easement over the land.

The burden of proving an easement rests on the party claiming such right and must be established by clear and convincing proof. [Citations omitted.] It is abundantly clear that the appellant established, by the requisite degree of proof in this case, an easement over the land of the appellee. This conclusion is supported by the evidence presented by both the appellant and the appellee.

First, there is no doubt about the existence of the roadway in question. While the parties have used different terms to characterize this road, the basic facts of its presence and location were confirmed by the statements of all witnesses, including the appellee's president and its surveyor, as well as the appellant and his corroborating witnesses. In addition, Hutzler, his son and others familiar with the tracts involved, testified, without contradiction, to the continuous use of the road for more than seventy years. Finally, it was virtually stipulated that the private way connected with a public road and the appellee offered nothing to rebut the appellant's unequivocal proof that there was no other reasonable means of ingress and egress to the 105 acre tract. These circumstances patently establish the essential elements of both an easement by prescription and a way of necessity. However, the general rule is that these two easements are distinguished one from the other since they arise by virtue of different and mutually exclusive conditions. Thus, the existence of a prescriptive easement negates the requisite necessity for a way of necessity. Similarly, if a way of necessity exists, its use is not adverse so as to confer a prescriptive right. 25 Am. Jur. 2d Easements and Licenses §§34 & 47 (1966).

In order to establish an easement by prescription, the use of a private way over the land of another must be continuous and uninterrupted for a period of ten years under a bona fide claim of right, adverse to the owner of the land, and with his knowledge and silence. [Citations omitted.] It is apparent from the authorities that, in the absence of a higher right, the evidence of the case at bar pertaining to an easement by prescription clearly establishes the appellant's right to such easement for the use of a private way over the land of the appellant.

Notwithstanding the fact that the record developed below is sufficient to support the finding of a prescriptive easement in favor of the appellant the evidence also establishes a way of necessity. As was noted above, it was essentially stipulated that the tracts owned by the parties were at a prior time a part of a larger tract owned by the same person. Thus, by definition, the parties derived their respective titles from a common source. This fact is essential to demonstrate a way of necessity inasmuch as it cannot exist if the two tracts had never shared common ownership. 2 Thompson, Real Property §363 (1961 Repl. Vol.).

The rationale behind the way of necessity is that the law implies an easement over the servient estate when the grantor owns and conveys a portion of the original lands without expressly providing a means of ingress and egress. This reasoning is reflected in Syllabus point 2 in Gwinn v. Gwinn, 77 W. Va. 281, 87 S.E. 371 (1915): "A way of necessity exists where land granted is completely environed by land of the grantor, or partially by his land and the land of strangers. The law implies from these facts that a private right of way over the grantor's land was granted to the grantee as appurtenant to the estate." In order for a way of necessity to be created or established there must be a reasonable necessity for an easement over the lands of a grantor for the grantee or his successors to have access to a public road and to thereby have full use of the lands conveyed. [Citations omitted.]

A way of necessity having been created by implication for the benefit of the grantee of the dominant estate or his successors, thereafter, it cannot be extinguished so long as the necessity continues to exist. [Citations omitted.]

Applying the applicable principles outlined above to the evidence developed in the trial court, this Court concludes that the appellant has demonstrated the requisite elements of a way of necessity over the land of the appellee. It is not questioned that the parties derived their title to the lands in question from a common source and all the evidence introduced by both the plaintiff and the defendant confirms the fact that there is no reasonable way for the appellant to obtain access to a public way except over the road in question.

It is contended by the appellee that it purchased the 550 acre tract of land without any notice of the existence of an easement over such land, and as a consequence, any easement which the appellant may have had was therefore extinguished. We reject this argument. In the first place, the evidence indicates that the appellee, through its president and its surveyor, was aware of the existence of the roadway in question. The statements of both of these witnesses clearly showed their knowledge that there was a trail or old road on the line where the appellant claimed his easement to be. On this set of facts, it is apparent that the appellee had actual notice of the existence of the easement and there was no extinguishment by virtue of the purchase of the servient estate. Even if it were assumed that the appellee had no notice of the existence of the roadway, it could not prevail. The rule that a bona fide purchaser for value who takes the servient estate without knowledge of an existing easement is relieved of a prescriptive easement does not apply to a way of necessity. A way of necessity exists in favor of a dominant estate whether it is used or not, since, as has been previously stated, the implied easement continues so long as the necessity exists. [Citations omitted.]

Having determined that the record of the trial court below sustains the conclusion that the appellant demonstrated an easement, either by prescription or by necessity, and that the appellee acquired its land with actual notice of the easement, it remains only to determine, as between the two possibilities, which easement is most consonant with the evidence. We are of the opinion that the proof, taken as a whole, more directly supports the implied easement than the prescriptive right. Therefore, we hold that the appellant is entitled to use the roadway across the appellee's land as a way of necessity to and from his 105 acre tract.

The judgment of the Circuit Court of Berkeley County is, therefore, reversed and judgment is entered here for the appellant.

Reversed and judgment entered here.

NOTES AND QUESTIONS

1. After this decision, the defendant wishes to develop his 105–acre tract into an industrial park. This would increase several fold the volume of traffic along the right-of-way across plaintiff's parcel. Would plaintiff be able to halt that added burden? Might your answer depend upon whether defendant held a private way of necessity or a prescriptive easement?

2. Why, in order to establish an easement by necessity, was defendent required to prove that his tract and the plaintiff's once shared common ownership? Suppose that the common owner, Moses Grantham, had barred any passage across the 550 acres that Grantham retained when he sold the 105 acres to defendant's predecessor: would this have changed the result? Compare Note, 9 Md. L. Rev. 84 (1948). Suppose the Grantham deed had given defendant's predecessor a revocable license to cross the 550 acres.

3. Compare Finn v. Williams, 376 Ill. 95, 33 N.E.2d 226 (1941). In 1895, Charles Williams owned a 140-acre tract. He sold off a 40-acre parcel to the plaintiff's predecessor. At the time, this parcel had passage across other lands to a public highway. Forty years later this access was lost. Plaintiff thereupon sued to establish a right-of-way by necessity across the 100-acre parcel that Williams had retained. Held: an easement by necessity was necessarily implied in the 1895 conveyance. That the grantee had other passage to a highway across strangers' lands was immaterial. When the passage was lost, grantee (and his successors) might avail themselves of the *dormant* easement implied in the deed severing the dominant and servient estates.

4. One writer traces the doctrine of easement by necessity at least as far back as the time of Edward I (1272-1307), citing a contemporary text as stating: "Note that the law is that anyone who grants a thing to someone is understood to grant that without which the thing cannot be or exist." For a leisurely journey through the centuries, see Simonton, Ways by Necessity, 25 Colum. L. Rev. 571 (1925).

5. Courts have voiced two quite different theories to support the easement by necessity doctrine. One view regards the easement by necessity as a form of implied easement, a carrying out of the parties' presumed intent when the landlocked parcel was first conveyed: "And although it is called a way of

necessity, yet in strictness the necessity does not create the way, but merely furnishes evidence as to the real intent of the parties. For the law will not presume that it was the intention of the parties, that one should convey land to the other, in such a manner that the grantee could derive no benefit from the conveyance; nor that he should so convey a portion as to deprive himself of the enjoyment of the remainder. The law, under such circumstances, will give effect to the grant according to the presumed intent of the parties." Collins v. Prentice, 15 Conn. 39, 44 (1842).

The second view regards presumed intent as unessential: "[The foundation of this rule regarding ways of necessity is said to be] a fiction of the law [wherein] there is an implied reservation or grant to meet a special emergency, on grounds of public policy . . . in order that no land should be left inaccessible for purposes of cultivation." Buss v. Dyer, 125 Mass. 287, 291 (1878).

Which theory better expresses the reasoning in Berkeley Development Corp. v. Hutzler? Which theory do you prefer?

6.   Should an easement by necessity ever be granted without payment to the servient owner for the loss in his estate's value? Would it matter whether the underlying rationale is "implied easement" or "public policy"?

Article 917 of the German Civil Code of 1900 provided that a land-locked owner without access to a highway might compel adjoining owners to grant him a way on payment of a reasonable rental. Article 918 provided that, if as a result of a conveyance, "the part alienated or the part retained is cut off from the connection with the public road, the owner of the part over which the connection formerly existed must permit a way of necessity." See Simonton, Note 4 *supra*, at 577-578.

7.   Whether the easement by necessity doctrine applies to lands acquired by federal grants remains confused. See Note, 35 Wash. L. Rev. 105 (1960).

8.   Many states have legislated easements by necessity. Until it was struck down, *infra*, a Texas statute was typical:

> 1.   . . . (b)   1.   A person who claims the right to use land which is either wholly or partially surrounded by land owned by another person shall have the right to enter the surrounding land for purposes of ingress and egress to such land that is wholly or partially surrounded. Such person shall follow for purpose of ingress and egress to such land, a reasonable route designated by the owner, proprietor, lessee or person in charge of the surrounding land. Such person who claims a right to use land wholly or partially surrounded, shall furnish the owner, proprietor, lessee, or person in charge of the surrounding land, with a description of the location and boundaries of the land wholly or partially surrounded, and if requested by the owner, proprietor, lessee or person in charge of the surrounding land, shall go upon the wholly or partially surrounded land and point out the boundaries of such land so as to enable the owner, proprietor, lessee or person in charge of the surrounding land to designate a reasonable route for ingress and egress to such wholly surrounded or partially surrounded land. In the event the owner of the surrounded land shall not have a survey of his claim

and should the owner of the surrounding land demand the boundaries of the surrounded land, then the expenses of surveying the surrounded land shall be borne and paid by the owner of the surrounding land demanding the same.

    2. The owner, proprietor, lessee or person in charge of surrounding land shall designate a reasonable route for purposes of ingress and egress to land wholly or partially surrounded by such surrounding land within thirty (30) days after being notified in writing by the owner or surface lessee of the surrounded lands that such a route is needed, and if such route is not designated in writing within such thirty (30) days the owner or surface lessee of the surrounded lands shall have the right to select the shortest route to the said surrounded lands, having due regard to selecting the route which will lease damage such surrounding lands and which will cause the lease inconvenience to the owner or surface lessee of the surrounding lands. The owner or surface lessee of such surrounded lands shall notify the owner or surface lessee of the surrounding lands in writing of the route that he proposes to use, and he shall be confined to such route. [Tex. Prob. Code Ann. art. 13776 (Vernon 1953, Supp. 1965)]

ESTATE OF WAGGONER v. GLEGHORN
378 S.W.2d 47 (Tex. 1964)

WALKER, J. Wilmer Gleghorn, respondent, owns 1600 acres of land completely surrounded by land of the W. T. Waggoner Estate, petitioner. The Wichita River meanders through respondent's property in a general easterly and westerly direction. About 900 acres of his land are north of the river, and respondent's residence is located on the 700 acres lying south of the river. He has a recognized roadway from such residence across Waggoner land to a public road on the south. Respondent brought this suit to establish his right to a roadway from the public road across Waggoner land to the north portion of the 1600 acres, contending that he is entitled to the same: (1) as a way of necessity, and (2) by virtue of the provisions of Article 1377b. Vernon's Ann. P.C. After a trial to the court without a jury, judgment was rendered awarding respondent the road he sought, and the Court of Civil Appeals affirmed. 370 S.W.2d 786.

As pointed out by the Court of Civil Appeals, the three requisites for a way of necessity are: (1) unity of ownership of the alleged dominant and servient estates; (2) that the roadway is a necessity; and (3) that the necessity existed at the time of the severance of the two estates. See Duff v. Matthews, 158 Tex. 333, 311 S.W.2d 637; Othen v. Rosier, 148 Tex. 485, 226 S.W.2d 622. There is no evidence that respondent's property and that of petitioner were ever under common ownership, and we agree with the intermediate court that the judgment in his favor cannot be upheld on the theory that he is entitled to an easement by necessity.

Section 2 of Article 1377b . . . purports to grant to anyone who claims the right to use land which is wholly or partially surrounded by land of another person the right to an easement over the surrounding land for ingress and egress to and from the surrounded property. Petitioner attacks this statute on a number of different constitutional grounds. As we view the case, it is necessary for us to consider only one of these questions.

Section 17 of Article 1 of the Constitution of Texas, Vernon's Ann. St., provides that "No person's property shall be taken, damaged or destroyed for or applied to public use without adequate compensation being made, unless by consent of such person. . . . " That provision not only requires the payment of adequate compensation for property taken for public use, it prohibits the taking of property for *private* use. Marrs v. Railroad Commission, 142 Tex. 293, 177 S.W.2d 941, 949; Coastal States Gas Producing Co. v. Pate, 158 Tex. 171, 309 S.W.2d 828, 833. The provision operates as a limitation on the power of the Legislature as well as a limitation on the power of governmental agencies and public and private corporations. McInnis v. Brown County Water Imp. Dist., Tex. Civ. App., 41 S.W.2d 741, 744, *writ refused.* The Legislature may not authorize that which the Constitution prohibits. Maher v. Lasater, 163 Tex. 356, 354 S.W.2d 923.

Respondent bought all of his land as one tract and in one transaction. Part of the property lying north of the river is in a government soil conservation program, and it is necessary for respondent to keep down all noxious weeds thereon. The remainder of his land north of the river is leased as pasture. All of the ranch is in a game preserve, but commercial hunting is not permitted on the land which is in the government program. At different seasons of the year the Wichita River varies in depth from six inches to eight feet. Respondent and his lessees have crossed the same frequently, but it is impossible to cross during periods of flood and always inconvenient to do so. The roadway here in question extends from the public highway east across petitioner's land for some six miles to the north-west corner of respondent's property. While respondent needs the same for his own convenience and that of his tenants and others who have occasion to be on the land north of the river, no one else will receive any direct benefit from the road. The economic use of such property will undoubtedly be facilitated by a ready means of access from the highway, but the public interest is not otherwise served in any way by the right of way which respondent seeks. . . .

Respondent contends that Article 1377b should be upheld as a valid exercise of the police power. We recognize the rule that damage to or loss of property resulting from a proper exercise of the police power does not constitute a taking under the power of eminent domain, and that compensation is not required to be paid therefor. See State v. Richards, 157 Tex. 166, 301 S.W.2d 597, and authorities there cited. It seems clear to us, however, that the permanent appropriation of an easement for a right of way for travel across a tract of land constitutes a "taking" within the purview of Article 1, Section 17, of the Constitution. In our opinion Article 1377b is unconstitutional and void to the extent that it purports to authorize the taking of private property for a private purpose. . . .

NOTES

1. For the Oregon and Alabama experience with similar statutes, see Notes, 19 Ore. L. Rev. 171 (1940), 11 Ala. L. Rev. 182 (1959). See also Houston v. Hanby, 149 Ark. 486, 232 S.W. 930 (1921), construing what is now Ark. Stat. Ann. §76-110 (1947) and Morgan v. Culpepper, 324 So. 2d 598 (La. Ct. App. 1975), *aff'd,* 326 So. 2d 377 (La. 1976), construing what is now La. Civ. Code Ann. arts. 699-700.

2. Leo Sheep Co. v. United States, 440 U.S. 668, 99 S. Ct. 1403, 59 L. Ed. 2d 677 (1979) offers a touch of Rehnquist whimsy, while teaching both a history lesson and some easement by necessity law. To help subsidize the expansion of the nation's railroads, Congress designed the "checkerboard" land-grant scheme. Land for twenty miles surrounding railway rights-of-way was divided into "checkerboard" lots. Odd-numbered lots were granted to the railroad; even-numbered lots were kept by the government.

The plaintiff sheep company, Wyoming livestock grazers, acquired some odd-numbered lots, lying to the east of the Seminoe Reservoir, a public recreational area. To provide access to the reservoir, the federal government cleared a connecting road from a local county road across the plaintiff's land. The government refused to pay compensation, however, insisting that it had implicitly reserved an easement (by necessity) across the odd-numbered lots in order to provide access between the even-numbered lots that it had retained.

The Supreme Court was unimpressed with the government's claim and awarded plaintiff compensation:

> Where a private landowner conveys to another individual a portion of his lands in a certain area and retains the rest, it is presumed at common law that the grantor has reserved an easement to pass over the granted property if such passage is necessary to reach the retained property. These rights of way are referred to as "easements by necessity." There are two problems with the Government's reliance on that notion in this case. First of all, whatever right of passage a private landowner might have, it is not at all clear that it would include the right to construct a road for public access to a recreational area. More importantly, the easement is not actually a matter of necessity in this case because the Government has the power of eminent domain. Jurisdictions have generally seen eminent domain and easements by necessity as alternative ways to effect the same result. For example, the State of Wyoming no longer recognizes the common-law easement by necessity in cases involving landlocked estates. It provides instead for a procedure whereby the landlocked owner can have an access route condemned on his behalf upon payment of the necessary compensation to the owner of the servient estate. For similar reasons other state courts have held that the "easement by necessity" doctrine is not available to the sovereign. [440 U.S. at 679-680, 99 S. Ct. at 1409-1410, 59 L. Ed. 2d 686-687]

    d.   **Easement by Prescription (see §9.6 and Berkeley Development Corp. v. Hutzler, *supra*)**

§10.4   The Real Covenant (Covenant That "Runs with the Land")

a.   Affirmative Covenants Described

Suppose that in the driveway agreement with which this chapter opens, A and B both promise to keep that strip of driveway lying within their respective lots free of ice and snow. Subsequently, A neglects his promise; and when a midwinter storm dumps several feet of snow, B cannot remove his car from the garage. If we assume B is damaged, what are his rights against A?

Notice A's promise. Although it concerns land, it is analytically different from A's earlier agreement permitting B the use of the driveway. That agreement, though fixing a duty on A (not to interfere with B's access), requires no affirmative action; A can perform his duty doing nothing. As to the snow removal agreement, however, A must take steps to perform.

This distinction, which may seem labored to you, matters not at all when B seeks damages from A. Since they are both original parties to the snow removal agreement, contract principles will decide the outcome. What these principles are we leave to another course.

Suppose, now, that A sells Lot 1 to X, that X also neglects the promise, and that B's damages occur during X's ownership. Ignoring for now whether B might still recover against A,[11] what are B's rights against X?[12] We have already stated that when an easement exists, the succeeding owner of the servient estate bears its burden whenever two conditions are met, intention and notice. Therefore, if the snow removal agreement *is* an easement, B (assuming intention and notice) would be able to proceed against X for the agreement's breach. In doing so, he would be asserting a right in land.

Had the law taken this turn, generations of law students would have been spared the agony (and, who can say, perhaps denied the ecstasy) of becoming acquainted with real covenants. But this was not to be. The distinction we have noted between an affirmative easement (including one created by words of promise) and a promise to perform an affirmative act, even though it concerns land, was formulated early in the common law and persists still.[13]

Prior to the sixteenth century, landholders often gave such "affirmative"

---

11. For further discussion, see pages 596-598, *infra*.

12. We assume here that X did not expressly agree to keep the promise when he became the owner. The rights of A against a *promising* X are discussed later. See page 586, *infra*.

13. Curiously, early courts did treat several forms of affirmative covenants indistinguishably from easements. Included among these were the covenant to have a convent sing in the manor chapel and the covenant to build a boundary fence. The covenantee's rights were regarded as interests in property and as an appropriate subject for a grant. Holmes, The Common Law 392-393 (1881). (Note that in the first example, the *burden* of the covenant is in gross.)

Just how and why such affirmative obligations came to be treated as easements is shrouded by the language of the early opinions. In his classic work on the English law of easement, Gale referred to the landowner's obligation to build and maintain a fence as a "spurious kind of easement." C. Gale, Easements 465 (8th ed. 1908).

covenants. A tenant's assurances to his feudal lord or a lessee's covenant to pay rent are two early examples. The common law at first regarded these promises as personal undertakings, binding on the covenantor (when sued by the covenantee), not binding on the covenantor's successor unless he renewed the promise. Slowly the tradition changed, first as to the obligations of feudal tenure, next as to some of the promises contained in a lease. Where it could be shown that the covenant's burden was intended to pass with the estate, the succeeding owner was sometimes bound whether or not he had given new assurances. By no means, however, was it every affirmative covenant whose burden was said "to run with the land." To sort out those covenants that ran, the "real covenants," from those covenants that did not, the common law devised a set of technical guidelines that will seem baffling and, at times, oppressive. Yet, before we judge too harshly, we must realize the law's concern. Feudalism had taught how readily landholders gave promises related to their tenure and how ingeniousiy new breeds of commitment were formed, and in an era when commerce in land was expanding, burdens attending ownership were to be discouraged.[14] What you are about to see, the common law regulation of affirmative covenants, is wholly consistent with that objective and with the doctrinal apparatus at hand.

This is not to say that the guidelines were all inspired: some were silly, others became outmoded. Yet, once it had given birth to an idea, the common law doted on and nourished its mistakes with undiscriminating ardor.

b. Negative Covenants Described

Suppose that A and B enter into still another agreement, each promising the other not to let his parcel be used for business purposes. Note, analytically, that this mutual promise, which we call a *negative* covenant, resembles an earlier agreement wherein each promised not to build his house higher than two stories. We called that agreement a negative easement, privileging each to enjoy some interest in the other's land—(an unobstructed view) without physically entering that land—and imposing upon each, as owner of a servient estate, the duty not to deny his neighbor's privilege. So, too, A's (B's) promise barring commercial use creates in B (A) a privilege analytically akin to a clear view across A's (B's) land.

Seeking to protect residential neighborhoods against being overrun by the grimier aspects of urban industrial life, nineteenth-century landowners began to restrict their holdings against various forms of hitherto unregulated development. Typical among the negative covenants were bars against business, factories, the raising of livestock, and, much later, sales to "undesirable" persons.

Once again the law might have looked at these (nonactivity) promises as a subform of (negative) easement, enforcing them against subsequent owners

---

14. For a fair sample of the judicial attitude, albeit expressed several centuries later, see Keppell v. Bailey, 2 My. & K. 517, 535, 39 Eng. Rep. 1042, 1049 (Ch. 1834); "[I]t must not therefore be supposed that incidents of a novel can be devised and attached to property, at the fancy or caprice of any owner."

of the servient estate where there was requisite intention and notice. That was not to be the case, however, as the English courts stoutly held to the five kinds of negative easements we listed before (page 532, *supra*), applying easement doctrine only to them and subjecting negative covenants to the technical restraints on affirmative covenants.

In time, equity intervened (see Tulk v. Moxhay, page 587, *infra*). First with negative covenants and then with affirmative covenants, equity helped to break down the rigid formalism of the common-law treatment of all "noneasement" promises tied to land.

Affirmative and negative covenants abound nowadays. They are regularly found embodied in leases, in schemes of neighborhood development, in the bylaws of condominiums, and in agreements between an urban renewal agency and a private redeveloper. Examples of these covenants—which are likely to run—and of several others whose capacity to run is more uncertain, follow.

1. A tenant covenants to pay rent, carry fire insurance, and construct a $1,000,000 fireproof addition to an existing structure.

2. Each of the lot owners in a residential subdivision covenants to pay an annual assessment for the upkeep of the swimming pool and tennis courts.

3. Each of the unit owners in a condominium agrees to submit any bona fide offer for the purchase of his unit to the condominium board of managers so that the board may match the offer if it wishes to.

4. A private redeveloper acquires land from an urban renewal agency and agrees to landscape and maintain the plaza area shown on his plans.

5. The owner of a building agrees to maintain an auxiliary electric generator for his own and his neighbor's use in the event of power failure.

6. A lot owner covenants with his neighbors to fly the Confederate flag every year to celebrate the birthday of Stonewall Jackson.

7. The purchaser of an office building covenants with his seller, who is in the fuel business, to give seller an opportunity to bid competitively for all of the building's fuel oil requirements.

8. The owner of a shopping center agrees not to rent space to the tenant's competitors in any building owned by him within one mile of the center.

§10.5 The Essentials of a Real Covenant—The Running of the Burden (Is R' Liable?) [15]

a. Intent

Spencer's Case, which follows, is truly a landmark. At issue is whether the burden of a covenant is enforceable against a subsequent owner of the

---

15. R' succeeds to the original promisor (R) in the burdened estate without making a new promise to become liable.

servient estate who did not expressly agree to become liable. The decision, which denies recovery, establishes two criteria, although the second (historically, by far the more important) appears as dictum. First, the court adds a gloss to the requirement of intent (that the burden run). Second, the court, for the first time, speaks of the need that the covenant "touch or concern" the servient estate. This phrase has become inextricably related to covenants—for good *and* for bad.

SPENCER'S CASE

5 Co. Rep. 16a, 77 Eng. Rep. 72 (K.B. 1583)

Spencer and his wife brought an action of covenant against Clark, assignee to J. assignee to S. and the case was such: Spencer and his wife by deed indented demised a house and certain land (in the right of the wife) to S. for term of 21 years, by which indenture S. covenanted for him, his executors, and administrators, with the plaintiffs, that he, his executors, administrators, or assigns, would build a brick wall upon part of the land demised, &c. S. assigned over his term to J. and J. to the defendant; *and for not making of the brick wall the plaintiff brought the action of covenant against the defendant as assignee:* and after many arguments at the Bar, the case was excellently argued and debated by the Justices at the Bench: and in this case these points were unanimously resolved by Sir Christopher Wray, Chief Justice, Sir Thomas Gawdy, and the whole Court. And many differences taken and agreed concerning express covenants and covenants in law, and which of them run with the land, and which of them are collateral, and do not go with the land, and where the assignee shall be bound without naming him, and where not: and where he shall not be bound although he be expressly named, and where not.

1. When the covenant extends to a thing in esse, parcel of the demise, the thing to be done by force of the covenant is quodammodo annexed and appurtenant to the thing demised, and shall go with the land, and shall bind the assignee although he be not bound by express words: but when the covenant extends to a thing which is not in being at the time of the demise made, it cannot be appurtenant or annexed to the thing which hath no being: as if the lessee covenants to repair the houses demised to him during the term, that is parcel of the contract, and extends to the support of the thing demised, and therefore is quodammodo annexed appurtenant to houses, and shall bind the assignee although he be not bound expressly by the covenant: but in the case at Bar, the covenant concerns a thing which was not in esse at the time of the demise made, but to be newly built after and therefore shall bind the covenantor, his executors, or administrators, and not the assignee, for the law will not annex the covenant to a thing which hath no being. . . . [The opinion continues, following the note.]

NOTE

The first principle of Spencer's Case, that the assigns must be <u>expressly</u> bound where the promise is to do acts concerning something not in esse, had an early following in this country—see, e.g., Lametti v. Anderson, 6 Cow. 302 (N.Y. 1826); Gulf, C. & S.F. Ry. v. Smith, 72 Tex. 122, 9 S.W. 865 (1888)— and even made its way into David Dudley Field's draft code (§695) and into the state codes that Field influenced; see, e.g., Cal. Civ. Code §1464 (West 1954). See also Abbot, Covenants in a Lease Which Runs with the Land, 31 Yale L.J. 127, 144 (1921); Bordwell, English Property Reform and Its American Aspects, 37 Yale L.J. 1, 25-27 (1927). But it is a principle that should have been stillborn, for it serves no rational basis, and traps only the unwary or slovenly draftsman. Most courts either have repudiated the doctrine or have ignored it. See, e.g., Purvis v. Shurman, 273 Ill. 286, 112 N.E. 679 (1916); Bald Eagle Valley R.R. v. Nittany Ry., 171 Pa. 284, 294, 33 A. 239, 241 (1895). Except for the remnants of the "not in esse" distinction, no technical words are indispensable to establish intent. With respect to some of the more usual covenants (e.g., covenant to pay rent), intention usually is presumed. Otherwise, the courts may infer intent from the nature of the covenant, the relation of the parties, the other aspects of the original transaction. Cf., e.g., Silverstein v. Shell Oil Co., 40 A.D.2d 34, 337 N.Y.S.2d 442 (3d Dept. 1972) (grantor agrees for 50 years not to use parcel for sale of products competitive with grantees'; since grantor in his middle fifties, not realistic to assume that parties intended a personal covenant only).

In a much earlier landmark decision, Packenham's Case, Y.B. Hil. 42 Edw. 3, f. 3, pl. 14 (1368), the absence of the phrase "assigns" was not even noticed. See Woodbine, Packenham's Case, 38 Yale L.J. 775, 780 (1929).

b. "Touch or Concern"

SPENCER'S CASE
5 Co. Rep. 16a, 77 Eng. Rep. 72 (K.B. 1583)

2. It was resolved that in this case, if the lessee had covenanted for him and his assigns, that they would make a new wall upon some part of the thing demised, that for as much as it is to be done upon the land demised, that it should bind the assignee; for although the covenant doth extend to a thing to be newly made, yet it is to be made upon the thing demised, and the assignee is to take the benefit of it, and therefore shall bind the assignee by express words. . . . But although the covenant be for him and his assigns, yet if the thing to be done be merely collateral to the land, and doth not touch or concern the thing demised in any sort, there the assignee shall not be charged. As if the lessee covenants for him and his assigns to build a house upon the land of the lessor which is no parcel of the demise, or to pay any collateral sum

to the lessor, or to a stranger, it shall not bind the assignee, because it is merely collateral, and in no manner touches or concerns the thing that was demised, or that is assigned over; and therefore in such case the assignee of the thing demised cannot be charged with it, no more than any other stranger. [16]

NOTE

The second principle of Spencer's Case, that the covenant must "touch or concern" the premises, survives as one of the essentials of a real covenant. See C. Clark, Covenants and Interests Running with Land 96 (2d ed. 1947). Although formulated by Lord Coke in a controversy over a lease, the rule has been extended to fee situations. Courts and legal scholars have achieved little success, however, in framing a test to determine what covenants do, in fact, "touch or concern" so that the burden will run. Consider, for instance, the following case.

EAGLE ENTERPRISES, INC. v. GROSS
39 N.Y.2d 505, 349 N.E. 2d 816, 384 N.Y.S.2d 717 (1976)

Moglen doesn't like this opinion or test

GABRIELLI, J. In 1951, Orchard Hill Realties, Inc., a subdivider and developer, conveyed certain property in the subdivision of Orchard Hill in Orange County to William and Pauline Baum. The deed to the Baums contained the following provision:

> The party of the first part shall supply to the party of the second part, seasonably, from May 1st to October 1st, of each year, water for domestic use only, from the well located on other property of the party of the first part, and the party of the second part agrees to take said water and to pay the party of the first part, a fee of Thirty-five ($35.00) dollars per year, for said water so supplied.

In addition, the deed also contained the following:

> It is expressly provided that the covenants herein contained shall run with the land . . . and shall bind and shall enure to the benefit of the heirs, distributees, successors, legal representatives and assigns of the respective parties hereto.

Appellant is the successor in interest of Orchard Hill Realties, Inc., and respondent, after a series of intervening conveyances, is the successor in interest of the Baums. The deed conveying title to respondent does not contain the afore-mentioned covenant to purchase water and, in fact, none of the deeds

---

16. The notes accompanying Spencer's Case, id. at 73, list many early English cases where controverted covenants (in leaseholds) were held to run. These include the lessor's covenant to renew, and the lessee's covenants to insure against fire and to repair.—ED.

following the original deed to the Baums contained the mutual promises regarding water supply. While some of the deeds in the chain of title from Baum contained a provision that they were made subject to the restrictions in the deed from Orchard Hill Realties to Baum, the deed to respondents contained no such covenants, restrictions or "subject to" clause.

According to the stipulated facts, respondent has refused to accept and pay for water offered by appellant since he has constructed his own well to service what is now a year-round dwelling. Appellant, therefore, instituted this action to collect the fee specified in the covenant (contained only in the original deed to Baum) for the supply of water which, appellant contends, respondent is bound to accept. The action was styled as one "for goods sold and delivered" even though respondent did not utilize any of appellant's water. Two of the lower courts found that the covenant "ran" with the land and, hence, was binding upon respondent as successor to the Baums, but the Appellate Division reversed and held that the covenant could not be enforced against respondent. We must now decide whether the promise of the original grantees to accept and make payment for a seasonal water supply from the well of their grantor is enforceable against subsequent grantees and may be said to "run with the land." We agree with the determination of the Appellate Division and affirm its order.

Regardless of the express recital in a deed that a covenant will run with the land, a promise to do an affirmative act contained in a deed is generally not binding upon subsequent grantees of the promisor unless certain well-defined and long-established legal requisites are satisfied (Nicholson v. 300 Broadway Realty Corp., 7 N.Y.2d 240, 244; Neponsit Prop. Owners' Assn. v. Emigrant Ind. Sav. Bank, 278 N.Y. 248, 254-255; see, also, Morgan Lake Co. v. New York, New Haven & Hartford R. R. Co., 262 N.Y. 234, 239; Miller v. Clary, 210 N.Y. 127; Mygatt v. Coe, 147 N.Y. 456; 13 N.Y. Jur., Covenants and Restrictions, §12, pp. 252-253). In the landmark *Neponsit* case *(supra)*, we adopted and clarified the following test, originating in the early English decisions, for the enforceability of affirmative covenants (cf. Spencer's Case, 77 Eng. Rep. 72 [1583]), and reaffirmed the requirements that in order for a covenant to run with the land, it must be shown that:

(1) The original grantee and grantor must have intended that the covenant run with the land.

(2) There must exist "privity of estate" between the party claiming the benefit of the covenant and the right to enforce it and the party upon whom the burden of the covenant is to be imposed.

(3) The covenant must be deemed to "touch and concern" the land with which it runs. (See, also, Nicholson v. 300 Broadway Realty Corp., *supra;* Restatement Property, §§531, 534, 537, 538; 13 N.Y. Jur. Covenants and Restrictions, §8, p. 248.)

Even though the parties to the original deed expressly state in the instrument that the covenant will run with the land, such a recital is insufficient to render the covenant enforceable against subsequent grantees if the other requirements for the running of an affirmative covenant are not met. The rule is settled that "[r]egardless of the intention of the parties, a covenant will run with the land and will be enforceable against a subsequent purchaser of the land at the suit of one who claims the benefit of the covenant, only if the covenant complies with certain legal requirements" (*Neponsit, supra,* p. 254; see, also, Morgan Lake Co. v. New York, New Haven & Hartford R. R. Co., *supra,* p. 238). Thus, although the intention of the original parties here is clear and privity of estate exists, the covenant must still satisfy the requirement that it "touch and concern" the land.

It is this third prong of the tripartite rule which presents the obstacle to appellant's position and which was the focus of our decisions in *Neponsit* and Nicholson v. 300 Broadway Realty Corp. (7 N.Y.2d 240, 244, *supra*). *Neponsit* first sought to breathe substance and meaning into the ritualistic rubric that an affirmative covenant must "touch and concern" the land in order to be enforceable against subsequent grantees. Observing that it would be difficult to devise a rule which would operate mechanically to resolve all situations which might arise, Judge Lehman observed that "the distinction between covenants which run with land and covenants which are personal, must depend upon the effect of the covenant on the legal rights which otherwise would flow from the ownership of land and which are connected with the land" (*Neponsit, supra,* p. 258). Thus, he posed as the key question whether "the covenant in purpose and effect substantially alter[s] these rights" (p. 258). In *Nicholson,* this court reaffirmed the soundness of the reasoning in *Neponsit* as "a more realistic and pragmatic approach" (*supra,* p. 245).

The covenants in issue in *Neponsit* required the owners of property in a development to pay an annual charge for the maintenance of roads, paths, parks, beaches, sewers, and other public improvements. The court concluded that the covenant substantially affected the promisor's legal interest in his property since the latter received an easement in common and a right of enjoyment in the public improvements for which contribution was received by all the landowners in the subdivision (*supra,* pp. 259-260).

A close examination of the covenant in the case before us leads to the conclusion that it does not substantially affect the ownership interest of land-owners in the Orchard Hill subdivision. The covenant provides for the supplying of water for only six months of the year; no claim has been advanced by appellant that the lands in the subdivision would be waterless without the water it supplies. Indeed, the facts here point to the converse conclusion since respondent has obtained his own source of water. The record, based on and consisting of an agreed stipulation of facts, does not demonstrate that other property owners in the subdivision would be deprived of water from appellant or that the price of water would become prohibitive for other property owners if respondent terminated appellant's service. Thus, the agreement for the seasonal supply of water does not seem to us to relate in any significant degree to the ownership rights of respondent and the other property owners in the subdivision of Orchard Hill. The landowners in *Neponsit* received an easement in common to utilize public areas in the subdivision; this interest was in the nature of a property right attached to their respective properties. The obligation to receive water from appellant resembles a personal, contractual promise ← to purchase water rather than a significant interest attaching to respondent's property. It should be emphasized that the question whether a covenant is so closely related to the use of the land that it should be deemed to "run" with the land is one of degree, dependent on the particular circumstances of a case *(Neponsit, supra,* p. 258). Here, the meager record before us is lacking and woefully insufficient to establish that the covenant "touches and concerns" the land, as we have interpreted that requirement.

There is an additional reason why we are reluctant to enforce this covenant for the seasonal supply of water. The affirmative covenant is disfavored in the law because of the fear that this type of obligation imposes an "undue restriction on alienation or an onerous burden in perpetuity" (Nicholson v. 300 Broadway Realty Corp., 7 N.Y.2d 240, 246, *supra*). In *Nicholson,* the covenant to supply heat was not interdicted by this concern because it was conditioned upon the continued existence of the buildings on both the promisor's and the promisee's properties. Similarly, in *Neponsit,* the original 1917 deed containing the covenant to pay an annual charge for the maintenance of public areas expressly provided for its own lapse in 1940. Here, no outside limitation has been placed on the obligation to purchase water from appellant. Thus, the covenant falls prey to the criticism that it creates a burden in perpetuity, and purports to bind all future owners, regardless of the use to which the land is put. Such a result militates strongly against its enforcement. On this ground also, we are of the opinion that the covenant should not be enforced as an exception to the general rule prohibiting the "running" of affirmative covenants.

Accordingly, the order of the Appellate Division should be affirmed, with costs.

NOTES AND QUESTIONS

1. "The distinction between covenants which run with land and covenants which are personal, must depend upon the effect of the covenant on the legal rights which otherwise would flow from the ownership of land and which are connected with the land." Eagle Enterprises v. Gross, *supra,* quoting Neponsit Prop. Owners' Assn. v. Emigrant Industrial Savings Bank, 278 N.Y. at 258.

What *does* that mean? Do you understand why a covenant to purchase water does not affect the promiser's legal rights, see Eagle Enterprises v. Gross, whereas a covenant to supply heat, as in Nicholson v. 300 Broadway Realty Corp., 7 N.Y.2d 240, 164 N.E.2d 832, 196 N.Y.S.2d 945 (1959), was held to be effective? Suppose, in *Eagle Enterprises,* that plaintiff had decided that it no longer wanted to supply water to the defendant. If the dispute had taken that stance, is it clear that plaintiff would have prevailed?

2.   The Restatement of Property (1944) uses a different formulation for touch and concern.

> *§537.   Relation to Benefit and Burden*
>
> The successors in title to land respecting the use of which the owner has made a promise can be found as promisors only if
>> (a)   the performance of the promise will benefit the promisee or other beneficiary of the promise in the physical use or enjoyment of the land possessed by him, or
>> (b)   the consummation of the transaction of which the promise is a part will operate to benefit and is for the benefit of the promisor in the physical use or enjoyment of land possessed by him,
>
> and the burden on the land of the promisor bears a reasonable relation to the benefit received by the person benefited.

If the New York court had applied this litmus to the water in Eagle Enterprises v. Gross, *supra,* what conclusion would the court have reached?

3.   Courts have sometimes also required "touch or concern" of negative covenants. See, e.g., Norcross v. James, 140 Mass. 188, 2 N.E. 946 (1885).

4.   Judge Charles Clark, whose writing on real covenants more than a generation ago remains the classic statement, said of "touch or concern," in effect, that a layman knows it when he sees it: "Where the parties, as laymen and not as lawyers, would rationally regard the covenant as intimately bound up with the land, aiding the promisee as landowner or hampering the promisor in similar capacity, the requirement should be held fulfilled." Clark, Real Covenants and Other Interests Which "Run With the Land" 99 (2d ed. 1947).

More to the point, is there a reasonable basis for having a "touch or concern" or an equivalent concept?

Here is a further sampling of cases where courts have found that the covenant did (or did not) touch or concern so as to bind a successor to CR:

(a)   CR promised to tear his building down after five years. Covenant did not touch or concern. Town of North Hempstead v. Eckerman, 30 Misc. 2d 798, 216 N.Y.S.2d 566 (Sup. Ct. 1961), *aff'd,* 252 N.Y.S.2d 232, 21 A.2d 751 (1964).

(b)   CR promised to pay annual levy to Property Owners' Association for maintenance of roads and parks. Covenant did touch or concern. Neponsit Property Owners' Assn. v. Emigrant Industrial Savings Bank, 278 N.Y. 248, 15 N.E.2d 793 (1938). But cf. Nassau County v. Kensington Assn., 21 N.Y.S.2d 208 (Sup. Ct. 1940); University Gardens Property Owners Assn. v. Steinberg, 41 Misc. 2d 816, 244 N.Y.S.2d 208 (Nassau Dist. Ct. 1963).

(c) CR (tenant) covenanted to arbitrate any controversy arising under the lease. Covenant did touch or concern. Abbott v. Bob's U-Drive, 222 Or. 147, 352 P.2d 598 (1960).

For an analysis of the factual contexts in which *lease* covenants have been held to "touch or concern," see Bigelow, The Content of Covenants in Leases, 12 Mich. L. Rev. 639 (1914).

PROBLEMS

1. The bylaws of the St. Tropez, a New York City condominium, provide:

Article VII. Sales, Leases and Mortgages of Units.

§1. *Sales and Leases.* No unit owner may sell or lease his apartment unit or any interest therein except by complying with the following provisions:

Any unit owner who receives a bona fide offer for the sale of his apartment unit . . . or a bona fide offer for a lease of his apartment unit, (hereinafter called an "Outside Offer"), which he intends to accept, shall give notice to the Board of Managers of such offer and of such intention, the name and address of the proposed purchaser or lessee, the terms of the proposed transaction and such other information as the Board of Managers may reasonably require, and shall offer to sell such apartment unit, together with the Appurtenant Interests, or to lease such apartment unit, to the Board of Managers, or its designee, corporate or otherwise, on behalf of the owners of all other apartment units, on the same terms and conditions as contained in such Outside Offer. The giving of such notice shall constitute a warranty and representation by the unit owner who has received such offer, to the Board of Managers on behalf of the other unit owners, that such unit owner believes the Outside Offer to be bona fide in all respects. Within thirty days after receipt of such notice, the Board of Managers may elect, by notice to such unit owner, to purchase such apartment unit, together with the Appurtenant Interests, or to lease such apartment unit, as the case may be, (or to cause the same to be purchased or leased by its designee, corporate or otherwise), on behalf of all other unit owners, on the same terms and conditions as contained in the Outside Offer and as stated in the notice from the offering unit owner. . . .

In the event the Board of Managers or its designee shall fail to accept such offer within thirty days as aforesaid, the offering unit owner shall be free to contract to sell such apartment unit, together with the Appurtenant Interests, or to lease such apartment unit, as the case may be. . . .

Any purported sale or lease of an apartment unit in violation of this section shall be voidable at the election of the Board of Managers.

Why does this provision appear? See Berger, Condominium: Shelter on a Statutory Foundation, 63 Colum. L. Rev. 987, 1017–1019 (1963).

2. X is a unit owner who has not subscribed to the bylaws. Absent the statute in paragraph 3 below, can it be said, after *Eagle Enterprises*, that X must submit a bona fide offer to the board of managers?

3. New York's Condominium Act, Real Prop. Law art. 9-B (McKinney 1964), provides at §339-j: "Every unit owner shall comply strictly with the by-laws and with rules, regulations, resolutions and decisions adopted pursuant thereto. . . ." Does this language entirely put to rest the "running of the burden" issue?

4. Suppose that each deed in a residential tract gives to the tract developer a right of first refusal similar to that provided in the St. Tropez bylaws. May she enforce the right against a nonpromising grantee? Is it relevant why the right appears?

c. Privity of Estate Between Covenantor and Covenantee—The So-Called Horizontal Privity

By every reckoning, the next of the common-law requirements for a real covenant is indefensible, and its grip, which may never have been quite as great as the following case and the Restatement of Property §534 indicate, seems to have little remaining force. What this requirement entailed was a nexus between *promisor* and *promisee* that one could find in only a few relationships: viz., landlord and tenant, grantor and grantee, easement holder and servient owner. Wheeler v. Schad is a grotesque example of the "horizontal privity" requirement.

WHEELER v. SCHAD
7 Nev. 204 (1871)

By the Court, Lewis, C.J. On the fifth day of June, A.D. 1862, M. S. Hurd, Ferdinand Dunker and Peter Bossell, being the owners and in possession of a certain mill-site and water privilege, regularly conveyed to Charles Doscher, Charles Itgen, Charles D. McWilliams and William C. Duval a portion thereof, together with the water privilege connected therewith. The grantees entered into possession and erected a quartz mill on the premises thus conveyed. The stream was first conducted to the mill of Hurd and associates, and thence to that of their grantees. On the eleventh day of the same month, the respective parties entered into an agreement which, after reciting the necessity of constructing a dam across the river and a flume to conduct the water to their several mills, provided that the dam and flume should be constructed at their joint expense, Hurd and his associates, however, agreeing to pay five hundred dollars more than one-half the cost, and the other parties the balance; the dam and flume, when completed, to be owned and enjoyed jointly in equal shares. It was also agreed that they should be kept in good order and repair at the joint and equal expense of the respective parties. Some time after the construction of these works, Wheeler succeeded to the interest of Bossell, and he, together with Hurd and Dunker, continued in the ownership and remained in possession of the first mill, known as the Eureka.

Doscher and his associates having mortgaged their mill some time between January and March, 1868, put the assignee of the mortgage (defendant) in possession, who continued to hold the property under the mortgage until he obtained the absolute title by virtue of foreclosure and sale under his mortgage, which occurred in October A.D. 1868. Early in the year 1868, while the defendant was in possession under the mortgage, the dam and flume were damaged to such an extent that it became necessary to make extensive repairs upon them. Before proceeding with the work, the plaintiffs notified the defendant of their damaged condition, and requested him to unite with them in making the proper repairs. The defendant agreed that the work should proceed, and requested the plaintiff Wheeler to superintend it and "take charge of the workmen." The repairs were made in due time, at an expense of three thousand five hundred dollars, one-half of which is now sought to be recovered. Judgment for defendant; plaintiffs appeal; and it is argued on their behalf: first, that the defendant is liable on the agreement entered into between the defendant's grantors and the plaintiffs; and secondly, if not, that he is so upon his own agreement with the plaintiffs, authorizing the work to be done.

To maintain the first point, it is contended that the deed of conveyance of the mill-site to the grantors of the defendant, and the agreement referred to, should be held to be one instrument; that the stipulations of the latter should be engrafted upon the deed and held to be covenants running with the land. But nothing is clearer than that the two instruments are utterly disconnected, as completely independent of each other as they possibly could be. The deed was executed on the fifth day of June, at which time it does not appear that there was any thought of an agreement to construct or keep in repair any dam or flume. There is no evidence that such a project was in contemplation even by any of the parties, much less that any agreement of this character was in view. It was not, in fact, executed until six days afterwards, and there can be no presumption other than that it was not contemplated until such time. Had it entered into the transaction; had it been understood between the parties at the time of the conveyance that such contract should be executed, there might be some ground for the claim that the agreement and deed constituted but one transaction, and therefore should be construed as one instrument; but unfortunately for the appellants, there is no such showing in the case. If, in fact, the agreement did not enter into the conveyance, or was not contemplated at the time, it is of no consequence how soon afterwards it may have been executed; a day or an hour would as completely separate the instruments and make them independent of each other, as a year. It is impossible, under the evidence in this case, to merge the deed and agreement into one instrument, and construe them as if executed simultaneously.

Unless they constituted one instrument or transaction, it cannot be claimed that the covenants of the agreement run with the land so as to charge the grantee of the covenantor. To make a covenant run with the land, it is necessary, first, that it should relate to and concern the land; and secondly, a covenant imposing a burden on the land can only be created where there is privity of estate between the covenantor and covenantee. Whether a covenant for the benefit of land can be created where there is no privity is still questioned by some authorities; but it was held in Packenham's case, determined as early as the time of Edward III, that a stranger might covenant with the owner in such manner as to attach the benefit of a covenant to the land and have it run in favor of the assignees of the covenanteee; and the rule there established has since been frequently recognized as law, although questioned by text writers, and the broad doctrine sought to be maintained that privity of estate is absolutely essential in all cases, to give one man a right of action against another upon a covenant, when there is no privity of contract.

Whether the rule announced in Packenham's case be law or not, is not necessary to determine here, for all the courts hold that the *burden* of a covenant can only be imposed upon land so as to run with it when there is privity of estate between the covenantor and covenantee. It was said by Lord Kenyon, in Webb v. Russell, 3 Term, 393, that "it is not sufficient that a covenant is concerning the land, but in order to make it run with the land there must be a privity of estate between the covenanting parties." That was the law long prior to the time of Kenyon, and has never been doubted, although perhaps cases may be found where an erroneous application of the rule has been made. To render a covenant binding on the assignee of the covenantor, it must therefore not only be meant to bind his estate as well as his person, but the relation between the parties must be such as to render the intention effectual— that is, there must be privity of estate between the covenanting parties. To constitute such relation, they must both have an interest in the land sought to be charged by the covenant. It is said their position must be such as would formerly have given rise to the relation of tenure. A covenant real is, and can only be, an incident to land. It cannot pass independent of it. It adheres to the land, is maintained by it, is in fact a legal parasite, created out of and deriving life from the land to which it adheres. It follows, that the person in whose favor a covenant is made must have an interest in the land charged with it; for he can only get the covenant through, and as an incident to, the land to which it is attached. . . .

Did the plaintiffs in this case have any estate in the land owned by the defendant at the time this agreement was entered into? It is not even claimed they had. Nor did the agreement itself create any such interest. There is no attempt in it to convey any estate to them, nor a word of grant in the whole instrument. It is a mere contract for the erection of a dam, which does not appear to be on the premises either of the plaintiffs or defendant, and a flume to conduct water to their respective mills, and to maintain them in good order. Suppose the grantors of the defendant had entered into an agreement binding themselves to build the dam and flume for the benefit of the plaintiffs, for a stipulated sum of money; will it be claimed that such an agreement could be held a covenant running with land owned by such grantors, and which was entirely distinct from that upon which the work was to be performed? We apprehend not. Where the distinction, as to its capacity to run with the land, between such a covenant and that entered into here, where instead of compensation in money the defendant's grantors were to receive a benefit from the improvement itself?

As the grantors had no estate in the land owned by the defendant when the agreement was entered into, but were mere strangers to it, the case comes directly within the rule announced by Lord Coke, and very uniformly followed both by the English and American courts since his time. Webb v. Russell, 3 Term, and Stokes v. Russell, Id.; Hurd v. Curtis, 19 Pick. 459; Plymouth v. Carver, 16 Pick. 183. See also an elaborate review of the question in 1 Smith's Leading Cases, note to Spencer's Case; 2 Washburn on Real Property, 16 Pick. 183. . . .

There being no privity of estate, or of contract between the parties, it only remains to determine whether the defendant is holden on his own promise made to the plaintiffs. First, the action is not based on any such promise or contract. The complaint is framed with reference exclusively to the written agreement, and upon that alone relief is sought. Nothing is charged in the complaint tending to charge the defendant with any personal obligation, except that the repairs were made with his knowledge. As the complaint does not allege any personal promise or contract on the part of the defendant, it would hardly be conformable to the rules of law to award relief upon assumption of its existence. No personal promise or agreement by the defendant could properly be proven under the complaint; for proof is only admissable to establish the case made by the allegations of the pleading.

But again, if any such promise was made, it is undoubtedly barred by the statute of limitations, not being evidenced by writing. It cannot be said that the defendant adopted the written agreement as his own, and thereby bound himself to it, for it is not shown that he knew of its existence. But even if he knew it, the only evidence of his obligation upon it was in parol, and therefore it cannot with any degree of reason be said that if he had directly adopted the contract by a parol promise, his obligation would not be barred by the limitation prescribed for parol contracts.

The judgment below must be affirmed.

NOTES AND QUESTIONS

1. In the much-quoted Real Covenants and Other Interests Which "Run With the Land" (2d ed. 1947), Judge Charles Clark termed the require-

ment of privity between the covenantor and covenantee a "barren formality" and the decision in Wheeler v. Schad one that "surely cannot be justified." (Id. at 117.) Should it ever be impossible to accomplish with two pieces of paper what the parties assuredly would have accomplished with one? Should it ever be possible to accomplish with three pieces of paper what the parties could not accomplish with two?

2. As the main opinion indicates, Lord Kenyon is usually credited(?) with an early statement of the rule requiring privity between covenantor and covenantee. Webb v. Russell, 3 T.R. 393, 402, 100 Eng. Rep. 639, 644 (K.B. 1789). But a careful reading of the *Webb* case discloses that its holding rested chiefly on other grounds, for the court would have refused to enforce the covenant even if privity had been present. Moreover, the English law courts, before (and after) the *Webb* decision, have been reluctant to enforce affirmative promises, other than covenants for title and those covenants that accompany a landlord-tenant relation; the latter would, of course, satisfy Lord Kenyon's "dictum" on the need for privity. American courts, by contrast, have seemed quite willing to give covenants a wider range for their use; in no jurisdiction is their availability limited to leases. Having accepted in principle the greater utility of covenants, the Nevada court should have given Lord Kenyon a closer reading before attributing to him *its* privity requirement; after all, Lord Kenyon would have been startled by the inference that the Hurd-to-Doscher conveyance, had it included the promise, would have satisfied his notions of privity.

3. Although the Wheeler v. Schad requirement of privity (for nonlease covenants) has been frequently reaffirmed by the text writers, see, e.g., 3 Tiffany, Real Property §851 (3d ed. 1939), Judge Clark was able to find, after a meticulous survey of the reported opinions, only a handful of instances where courts actually had insisted upon it. Clark, *supra*, at 116 n.71. (Keep in mind that it is one thing for a court to *state* the requirement, quite something else for a court to deny relief because the requirement is not met.) A survey of the post-1947 cases is almost equally barren in this regard, although the author knows of at least one case where a court actually refused to enforce a covenant because it failed to satisfy the horizontal privity requirements of the Restatement of Property §534. Clear Lake Apartments, Inc. v. Clear Lake Utilities Co., 537 S.W.2d 48 (Tex. Civ. App. 1976), *aff'd*, 549 S.W.2d 385 (Tex. 1977) (service contract between utility company and landowner; homeowner refuses to accept service agreed to by covenantor).

4. The Restatement of Property §534 (1944) incorporated the Wheeler v. Schad requirement of privity of estate, expanding it to cover situations in which the promise concerns an easement held by one of the promising parties in the land of the other.

§534. *Privity Between Promisee and Promisor.* The successors in title to land respecting the use of which the owner has made a promise are not bound as promisors upon the promise unless

(a) the transaction of which the promise is a part includes a transfer of an interest either in the land benefited by or in the land burdened by the performance of the promise; or

(b) the promise is made in the adjustment of the mutual relationships arising out of the existence of an easement held by one of the parties to the promise in the land of the other. [See, e.g., Morse v. Aldrich, 19 Pick. 449 (Mass. 1837)]

5. Professor Powell wrote:

Ultimately the decision to continue the prerequisite of privity in a substantial form (as the Restatement does on the topic of burdens) or to eliminate it by diluting its content (as Judge Clark believes to have been done) depends on the decision of the question of social value. If one believes these burdens to be generally objectionable, since they impose restrictions on persons who never made a promise, and since they restrict the free use and alienability of land, the continuance of a prerequisite of privity will lessen their importance. If, on the other hand, one believes that these burdens generally serve socially useful ends, and aid rather than hinder the alienability of land, the result will be a readiness to minimize or to emasculate the prerequisite of privity, so that more can run as to burden. [5 Powell, Real Property 181 (Rohan ed. 1974)]

Even if one were to agree that affirmative covenants should be curtailed because they restrict the use and alienability of land, does the horizontal privity of estate test offer a rational basis for determining which covenants shall run and which shall not?

6. Holmes, The Common Law 404 (1881):

According to the general opinion there must be a privity of estate between the covenantor and covenantee . . . in order to bind the assigns of the covenantor. Some have supposed this privity to be tenure; some, an interest of the covenantee in the land of the covenantor; and so on.[1] The first notion is false, the second misleading, and the proposition to which they are applied is unfounded. Privity of estate, as used in connection with covenants at common law, does not mean tenure or easement; it means succession to a title.[2] It is never necessary between covenantor and covenantee. . . .

7. Review the *Eagle Enterprises* case, *supra*. Notice how the opinion speaks of privity of estate. To underline the confusion in this area, that requirement—second of the three listed—does not appear in the earlier court of appeals decision in Nicholson v. 300 Broadway Realty Corp., 7 N.Y.2d 240, 164 N.E.2d 832, 196 N.Y.S.2d 945 (1959), *supra*, page 569, Note 1. In its stead, the *Nicholson* opinion requires that there be "a continuous succession of convey-

---

1. 4 Kent (12th ed.), 480, n.l.

2. It is used in a somewhat different sense in describing the relation between a tenant for life or years and reversioner. Privity between them follows as an accidental consequence of their being as one tenant, and sustaining a single *persona* between them.

ances between the original covenantor and the party now sought to be burdened," 7 N.Y.2d at 245, 196 N.Y.S.2d at 950, 164 N.E.2d at 835. This is the so-called vertical privity, discussed below.

d.   Privity of Estate Between Covenantor and Successor to the Servient Land—The So-Called Vertical Privity

In our survey of easements, we saw that if intent and notice were present, each new owner of the servient estate took subject to its burden. In the opening example, if A, who together with B shares a common driveway, transfers his fee to X, the latter must respect B's interest. Suppose, however, that X takes possession of Lot 1 under a lease from A; as a tenant, is X still subject to the easement (assuming that the lease is silent)? If you answer "yes," your intuition is sound; it would be unthinkable if X, as a tenant, were allowed to barricade B's passage.

Consider now A's promise to keep his part of the driveway free of ice and snow. If A transfers his fee to X, and if all other requirements for a real covenant are met, B may enforce the promise against X. This is because X has succeeded to A's identical interest, thus satisfying vertical privity—another of the common-law requirements for the running of the burden of a covenant real. Cf. Restatement of Property §535, *infra*. Suppose, however, that X occupies Lot 1 as a tenant under a one-year lease. If X has not bound himself contractually, can he be liable on the covenant? The Restatement of Property offers its answer:

> §535. *Privity as Between Promisor and Successor.* The successors in title to land respecting the use of which the owner has made a promise are not bound as promisors upon the promise unless by succession they hold
>
> (a)   the estate or interest held by the promisor at the time the promise was made, or
>
> (b)   an estate or interest corresponding in duration to the estate or interest held by the promisor at the time. [17]

One strength of this position is its ease of application. A second is its logic: if we regard a real covenant not as an interest in the servient land but as a limitation on the covenantor's estate, a nonpromisor should be bound only if he succeeds to the identical estate. In general, the courts have adopted the Restatement position. A conspicuous example is the relative immunity enjoyed by a subtenant from the claims of the landlord. See Amco Trust, Inc. v. Naylor, *infra*.

---

17. The Restatement Comment gives the example of a promisor easement-holder who carves out a short-term easement from his holding and transfers it to CR: in this case, CR' would not be charged. Id. §535, Comment f.—ED.

However, there is a third factor, apart from convenience and logic, which may have overriding importance. Is it ever reasonable to require the nonpromisor's performance if he doesn't succeed to CR's exact estate? An answer might well depend upon the weighing of several variables: the nature of the nonpromisor's interest and method of acquisition; the cost of performance and the offsetting benefits, if any; the injury to the covenantee if denied enforcement. Consider the following examples, all involving fee covenants:

(a) X acquires the fee to Lot 1 by adverse possession (no succession); the covenant requires payment of an annual assessment for the upkeep of neighborhood park facilities.
(b) Y occupies Lot 1 on a week-to-week tenancy; the covenant requires installation of a retaining wall costing $500.
(c) Z occupies Lot 1 on a 99-year lease; the covenant requires suitable landscaping.

Under the Restatement view, "vertical" privity of estate does not exist; therefore the parties cannot be charged. Under a more flexible formula, X would pay the tract assessment; Y would not build the wall: Z would landscape.

The most difficult applications of the vertical privity requirement arise, however, where the original covenant appears in a *lease,* and CR' has taken possession from the original promising tenant. To give a common example: L and T enter into a two-year lease, T agreeing to pay $500 monthly. With six months remaining, T transfers his premises to CR', who completes the term. May L sue CR' as the rent becomes due? The conventional wisdom (and simple answer) is that L may sue CR' if CR' acquires *all* of T's unexpired interest in the lease. To explain our answer we would reason that vertical privity exists between T and CR' (succession to identical interest—the unexpired six months) and that rent promises otherwise satisfy the essential of real covenants. Courts also say (to show that privity has another, somewhat confusing, shade of meaning) that if vertical privity exists between T and CR', privity of estate also exists between L and CR'. We are speaking of horizontal privity now, the link between landlord and tenant that seems partly to blame for the mostly repudiated common-law view that real covenants could not run unless horizontal privity existed between promisor and promisee. Cf. pages 572-578, *supra.*

When CR' succeeds to all of T's unexpired interest in the lease, we call the transaction an *assignment* of lease. The tenant T is the assignor, CR' is the assignee. As we shall see shortly, CR' may either be an assuming assignee or a naked assignee, which adds another face to the issue of L against CR'.

Suppose, however, that with six months remaining, T transfers only a three-month interst to CR'. May L still sue CR' as the rent becomes due? Here the conventional wisdom is that L may not sue CR', since CR' did not acquire all of T's unexpired interest in the lease. We would explain that the absence of vertical privity between T and CR' prevents any running of the burden of a real covenant. Courts also say (horizontal privity again) that privity of estate does not exist between L and CR' so as to render CR' liable, in estate theory, on the lease covenants. [18]

Where CR' succeeds to part of T's unexpired interest in the lease, we call the transaction a *sublease*, or a subletting of the premises. The tenant T is the sublessor, CR' is the sublessee. A landlord and tenant relation exists between T and CR'. No landlord and tenant relation exists between L and CR'; but the original relation of landlord and tenant between L and T survives.

Few things are simple, and this neat dichotomy between assignment and subletting poses two serious and very difficult kinds of issues. The first appears openly in the *Amco* case: how do we tell, where parties act ambiguously, whether the transaction is an assignment or subletting? The second pervades our entire discussion: when, if ever, should the subtenant owe duties to the prime landlord arising from the original lease?

AMCO TRUST, INC. v. NAYLOR
159 Tex. 146, 317 S.W.2d 47 (1958)

WALKER, J. On the principal question in this case, we hold that the owner of a security interest in a leasehold estate who takes possession of the leased premises does not thereby become an assignee and liable as such to the lessor for the payment of rent under the terms of the lease.

P. C. Naylor, respondent, leased a one story building in San Antonio to South Texas Kitchens, Inc., hereinafter referred to as Kitchens, and its president, C. P. Ernster, for a term of five years, beginning December 15, 1953, at a rental of $225 per month. Kitchens went into possession of the property and there engaged in the business of selling and installing kitchen cabinets on a contract basis. During the ensuing two years, Amco Trust, Inc., petitioner, made sundry loans to Kitchens, secured by pledges of the latter's kitchen installation contracts.

Early in 1956 the aggregate balance unpaid on such loans exceeded $37,000, and Kitchens was unable to meet these or its other obligations. Kitch-

---

18. The foregoing discussions may prompt another view of the essentials of real covenants, which would treat the requirement of vertical privity as a manifestation of horizontal privity. Thus, when the English courts indicated that only leasehold promises would be enforceable against remote parties and that CR' must succeed to the identical estate of the original promisor, the courts were speaking of substituted liability—that is, the assignee CR' would replace the original tenant both in privity of estate and in the performance of the leasehold duties. Where CR' had a lesser interest than the original promisor, substitution did not occur and there was no liability on the part of CR'. In moving over to cases of promises between fee owners, the courts, even after scrapping the essential of horizontal privity, persisted in their view that CR' must acquire the identical estate of the original promisor—unwittingly treating the duty of CR' as a substitute for that of CR.

ens and its stockholders thereupon entered into a contract with petitioner, effective as of March 1, 1956, under the terms of which all assets and stock of Kitchens were assigned to petitioner as additional security for its loans and petitioner was authorized to take over, manage and operate the business until its indebtedness was satisfied. Petitioner was given the right to complete existing contracts, negotiate new contracts, collect and disburse money, and use the proceeds of the business to discharge Kitchens' debts. The instrument further provided that petitioner did not assume any of such obligations, and that the agreement would terminate upon the final payment and discharge of Kitchens' indebtedness to petitioner.

Petitioner went into possession of the leased premises and there operated the business for a period of some six months, paying the rent regularly during most of that period. On September 6, 1956, it vacated the property and removed and sold the office furniture and equipment and display kitchen units which Kitchens had placed therein. The building has not been occupied, and no rent has been paid, by either the original lessees or petitioner since that date.

This suit was brought by respondent against Kitchens, Ernster, and petitioner to recover the rent payable under the terms of the lease. . . .

The case was tried to the court without a jury and judgment was entered in favor of respondent and against Kitchens, Ernster and petitioner, jointly and severally, for the rent due and to become due for the remainder of the lease term. From this judgment petitioner alone appealed. The Court of Civil Appeals concluded that petitioner is liable as an assignee for the rent throughout the term, but since the lease contains no acceleration clause, the judgment of the trial court was reformed so as to allow respondent to recover only the unpaid installments accrued up to the date of trial. 311 S.W.2d 257.

The Court of Civil Appeals reasoned that the contract between Kitchens and petitioner gave the latter a security interest in the leasehold estate, and with this conclusion we agree. Its holding that petitioner upon entering into possession became liable as an assignee is undoubtedly a correct application of the rule adopted in Cockrell v. Houston Packing Co., 105 Tex. 283, 147 S.W. 1145, 1151, where it was said:

> The mortgagee of a lease, who takes possession of the leased premises, is in the attitude of an assignee of such lease, and is therefore liable to the landlord for the rent. It seems to be a well-settled rule, applicable to our law, that the mortgagee of a lease, not in possession of the leased property, cannot be considered as an assignee; but if he takes possession of the leased premises he becomes, in law, the assignee of the lease, and is liable for the rents to the landlord. . . .[19]

---

19. Although the court rejects the *Cockrell* rule, a few other states still cling to it. Compare Williams v. Safe Deposit & Trust Co., 167 Md. 499, 175 A. 331 (1934) (tenant's mortgagee had to perform leasehold covenants as an "assignee" after tenant defaulted on mortgage, even though foreclosure had not yet occurred). The leasehold mortgagee's duty rests on whether the state follows the "title," "intermediate," or (as in Texas and most other states) the "lien" theory of mortgages. The difference in the mortgage theories, and a state's classification as "title," "interme-

Our investigation discloses that this rule is neither as well settled nor as well grounded as might be supposed from reading the *Cockrell* case. Liability to the original lessor for the payment of rent or the performance of other lease covenants may arise from either privity of contract or privity of estate. When the lessee voluntarily transfers part or all of his interest under the lease to another, the transaction is accordingly treated as either an assignment or a sublease for the purpose of determining the rights and liabilities of the parties. In order to constitute an assignment, the lessee must part with his entire interest in all or part of the demised premises without retaining any reversionary interest. One who thus acquires the entire leasehold estate becomes the tenant in place of the lessee and is in privity of estate with the lessor. An assignee is accordingly liable for the rent reserved in the lease and for the performance of covenants which run with the land. If, on the other hand, the lessee retains any reversionary interest, no matter how small it may be, his transferee is not in privity of estate with the lessor and is regarded as a sublessee. There is no privity of contract between the lessor and a sublessee, and the latter is not liable to the lessor on the covenants of the lease, unless he assumes or otherwise binds himself to perform the same. See Davis v. Vidal, 105 Tex. 444, 151 S.W. 290, 42 L.R.A., N.S., 1084. . . .

In the present case the lease was assigned to petitioner solely as security, and there is nothing in the record to suggest that the lien was ever foreclosed or that petitioner acquired Kitchens' entire interest in the leasehold estate in any other manner. Under the terms of the agreement petitioner was entitled to possession of the premises but could not use the same for its own exclusive benefit. The property was to be used only as a place to operate the business for Kitchens, and petitioner was under a duty to apply any profits arising therefrom to the lessee's debts. It was expressly provided, moreover, that the contract would terminate upon payment of the amount owing to petitioner. When that occurred, all of petitioner's rights in the leasehold estate would revert to Kitchens.

The lessee thus retained a reversionary interest in the leased premises, which might come back to it upon the happening of a contingency, and the transaction clearly constitutes a subletting rather than an assignment. . . .

Since petitioner did not assume the obligations of the lease and is not chargeable as an assignee, it is not liable to respondent for rent accruing after it vacated the premises. We do not attempt to determine whether there is any other theory upon which it might be responsible for either the stipulated or a reasonable rental during the time it occupied the property, because that question is not briefed by the parties. This probably is due to the fact that respondent was paid the rent for most of that period. . . .

---

diate," or "lien," were once prominent features in the law school course in mortgages. The theories matter far less today, and most writers are sharply critical whenever the relationship of the parties to a mortgage transaction, or the rights and duties of interested third persons, seem to depend on the state's choice of theory.—ED.

NOTES AND QUESTIONS

1. Discussion of the *Amco* case appears in Note, 58 Mich. L. Rev. 140 (1959).

2. In view of the court's rationale, did Kitchens needlessly pay rent to the landlord while it occupied the premises?

3. In Davis v. Vidal, 105 Tex. 444, 151 S.W. 293 (1912), the facts were these: L (Mrs. Davis) gave T (Dallas Brewery) a three-year lease, expiring April 30, 1910. Five months later, T transferred its remaining term to Vidal, who agreed to pay the lease rental of $100 monthly. T reserved the power to terminate Vidal's possession if the latter did not pay him the rent promptly. Thereafter, it appears that T became insolvent, whereupon L sought to recover $1,200—the rent then owing on the original lease—directly from Vidal.

The court decided that the transaction between T and Vidal was not an assignment, which would have supported L's claim, but was instead a subletting of the premises.

[T]he conclusion must be reached that the instrument executed by the Dallas Brewery to Vidal was a sub-lease and not an assignment. The instrument speaks for itself. By its terms the whole estate granted to the Dallas Brewery by its lease from Mrs. Davis is not conveyed, for the reason there is reserved to the Dallas Brewery, a contingent reversionary interest in the estate, to be resumed summarily upon the failure of Vidal to pay rent. More than this, and of equal significance, by the terms of the instrument the Dallas Brewery reserved the right to pay the rent to the original lessor, and thereby the right was reserved to forestall Mrs. Davis, upon the failure of Vidal to pay the rent, from exercising the right to re-enter and possess the premises. That right was reserved to the Dallas Brewery and gave it the power to control the estate in the premises upon failure by Vidal to pay it the rent. . . .

We are aware that there is great conflict of authority upon this subject, and that it would be futile to attempt to reconcile such conflict. Many of the authors of the text books on the subject of the assignment of leases and subletting under leases, and the decisions of a great many of the States in this Union hold that the fact that the right of re-entry is reserved in the assignment to the assignor upon failure of the assignee to pay rent does not change the instrument of assignment from such to a sub-lease. The holding of such authors and decisions is based upon the theory that the right of re-entry is not an estate or interest in land, nor the reservation of a reversion. They hold that the reservation of the right of re-entry upon failure to pay rent is neither an estate nor interest in land, but a mere chose in action, and when exercised the grantor comes into possession of the premises through the breach of the condition and not by reverter. . . .

We are not able to discern why there may not be a contingent reversionary estate or interest in land, as well as any other contingent estate or interest. It certainly cannot be contended upon sound principle that because the right of re-entry and resumption of possession of land is contingent that it is thereby any the less an estate or interest in land. The very definition of a contingent estate as distinguished from a *vested* estate is that "*the right to its* enjoyment is to accrue on an event which is dubious and uncertain." 1 Washburn on Real Property, 38. . . .

If by any limitation or condition in the conveyance the entire term, which embraces the estate conveyed in the contract of lease as well as the length of time for which the tenancy is created, may by construction be said not to have passed from the original tenant, but that a contingent reversionary estate is retained in the premises the subject of the reversion, the instrument must be said to constitute a sub-letting and not an assignment. . . .

The court in Davis v. Vidal adhered to the so-called Massachusetts rule. See Dunlap v. Bullard, 131 Mass. 161 (1881). For a good statement of the contrary rule, see Sexton v. Chicago Storage Co., 129 Ill. 318, 21 N.E. 920 (1889); Thomas v. United States, 505 F.2d 1282, 1286-1287 (Ct. Cl. 1974).

Is it sound that the outcome of the landlord's cause of action should depend upon whether a court regards the power of termination as a reversionary interest in land? Under what circumstances *should* the landlord be able to collect his rent directly from the party in possession? As counsel to a landlord, what leasehold adjustments would you advise in response to Davis v. Vidal?

Why should a tenant, having agreed to transfer his remaining term, wish to reserve a power of termination if the transferee does not pay the rent? In a Davis v. Vidal jurisdiction, can the original tenant make an assignment without relinquishing all right to regain possession?

4. "As a general proposition, the courts of both England and the United States agree that a transfer of a tenant's entire interest in the premises is an assignment, not a sublease, and that the transferee is substituted as the tenant of the landlord in place of the transferor. Conversely, a transfer of an estate in the premises less than that which the transferor himself has, with a reversion left in him, is not an assignment, but a sublease, making the transferee the tenant of the transferor. . . .

"Unfortunately, these basic principles, so firmly intrenched, so unfailingly reiterated in our law, are applied, especially in this country, only to the most obvious and simple situations. . . . The difficulty is: What have the courts regarded as a sufficient retention to constitute a reversionary estate?" Wallace, Assignment and Sublease, 8 Ind. L.J. 359 (1933).

Consider, in each of the following instances, whether a court is more likely to call the transaction an assignment or a sublease.

(a) T is a tenant for a term of years. T lets the premises to another who holds at will. See Austin v. Thomson, 45 N.H. 113 (1863).

(b) T holds a twenty-one-year lease expiring at midnight, December 31, 1995. T lets the premises to another for a term expiring at 11:59 P.M., December 31, 1995.

(c) T occupies a house and garage under a two-year lease. T lets the garage to another for the remaining term. Compare New Amsterdam Casualty Co. v. National Union Fire Ins. Co., 266 N.Y. 254, 194 N.E. 745 (1935), with Shannon v. Grindstaff, 11 Wash. 536, 40 P. 123 (1895). Cf. 1 American Law of Property §3.57 (Casner ed. 1952).

(d) T is a tenant for a term of years, paying a monthly rental of $100. T lets the premises to another for the remaining term ·at a monthly rental of $90. At a rental of $150.

5. The original Restatement of Property did not, as a discrete body of law, cover the relationship between landlord and tenant. When the American Law Institute adopted the first chapters of Restatement (Second) of Property, which repair the earlier omission, the Institute had an opportunity to consider whether to retain the privity of estate requirement for leasehold promises running with the land. Without much discussion, the requirement survived. Id. at §16.1. The Restatement gives this illustration:

> L leases to T for five years. T subleases to T-1 the leased property for the next two years. T-1 is not in privity of estate with L. Hence, T-1, as a transferee, is not liable on the promissory obligations of T to L. [Id. at Comment e, Illus. 21]

6. In Davis v. Vidal, *supra,* the subtenant agreed to pay the leasehold rent. Although the agreement was made with the original tenant, isn't there a theory (or two) that might support the landlord's direct claim for the rent against the subtenant? See Note, 40 Colum. L. Rev. 1049, 1055 n.48, 1058 n.69 (1940) (somewhat dated, but still useful); cf. Goldberg v. L. H. Realty Corp., 227 Miss. 345, 86 So. 2d 326 (1956).

7. The landlord's ultimate weapon against the recalcitrant subtenant is termination of the main lease and re-entry of the premises, if the landlord has reserved these remedies for nonperformance of the lease terms. But consider now the subtenant's risk. Suppose that he has dutifully paid the sublease rental to the tenant, who, in turn, has failed to pay *his* rental. Or suppose that the tenant becomes insolvent, and this is a material breach of the main lease. Are there any practical steps a subtenant might take to reduce these risks to his possession? See, e.g., Friedman, Preparation of Leases 37-41 (1962).

8. T assigns its lease. T-1 assumes all leasehold terms, covenants, and conditions. The lease calls for termination on tenant's bankruptcy. T becomes bankrupt. T-1 is solvent and fully performing the lease. L declares the lease terminated and sues to recover possession. Result? Inip Co. v. Bailey, Green & Elger, Inc., 78 Misc. 2d 235, 356 N.Y.S.2d 436 (Dist. Ct. 1974).

PROBLEM

The full text of Restatement (Second) of Property §16.1 (1977) appears below:

§16.1   Obligation Created by an Express Promise—Burden of Performance After Transfer

(1) A transferor of an interest in leased property, who immediately before the transfer is obligated to perform an express promise contained in the lease that touches and concerns the transferred interest, continues to be obligated after the transfer if:

   (a) the obligation rests on privity of contract, and he is not relieved of the obligation by the person entitled to enforce it; or

   (b) the obligation rests solely on privity of estate and the transfer does not terminate his privity of estate with the person entitled to enforce the obligation, and that person does not relieve him of the obligation.

(2) A transferee of an interest in leased property is obligated to perform an express promise contained in the lease if:

   (a) the promise creates a burden that touches and concerns the transferred interest;

   (b) the promisor and promisee intend that the burden is to run with the transferred interest;

   (c) the transferee is not relieved of the obligation by the person entitled to enforce it; and

   (d) the transfer brings the transferee into privity of estate with the person entitled to enforce the promise.

(3) The transferee will not be liable for any breach of the promise which occurred before the transfer to him.

(4) If the transferee promises to perform an express promise contained in the lease, the transferee's liability rests on privity of contract and his liability after a subsequent transfer is governed by subsection (1) (a).

In the light of the above provision, consider the following:

On January 1, 1980, L leased offices to T for three years ending December 31, 1982. The annual rental was $12,000. The lease did not restrict assignment or subletting. Thereafter, the following occurred:

   (a) On January 1, 1981, T assigned his lease to X. The assignment agreement contained this clause: "X covenants to perform the terms and conditions [of the original lease]."

   (b) On July 1, 1981, X sublet the premises to Y for three months ending September 30, 1981. The subletting agreement contained this clause: "Y covenants to pay $1,000 monthly for the use of the premises."

   (c) On October 1, 1981, the AAA Corporation acquired X's leasehold interest at a judgment execution sale.

   (d) On January 1, 1982, the AAA Corporation assigned the lease to Z. The assignment agreement contained this clause: "Z covenants to perform the terms and conditions [of the original lease].

L, having received no rent for the years 1980, 1981, and 1982, finally decides to sue. Discuss the potential liability of T, X, Y, Z, and the AAA Corporation.

Suppose that L agreed, on January 1, 1982, to excuse X from any rent he might owe. Would this in any way change L's rights aginst T? Cf. Gerber v. Pecht, 15 N.J. 29, 104 A.2d 41 (1954) (after assignment, relationship between landlord and original tenant comparable to that of principal and surety); Restatement (Second) of Property §16.1, Comment e (1977).

Suppose that the lease gives tenant an option to renew for three years at the same annual rental. While in possession, Z elected to renew. Discuss T's potential liability for the renewal term. See Annot., 10 A.L.R.3d 818 (1966).

check on this!

e. Notice

Occasionally one finds statements, unsupported by authority, that a real covenant binds a purchaser for value even without notice. See, e.g., Abbot, Covenants in a Lease Which Run with the Land, 31 Yale L.J. 127, 131 (1921). One should not believe everything that is in print! Notice is as essential to the running of a covenant's burden as it would be for an easement. But, as the implied easement cases illustrated, whether notice has been acquired is sometimes disputed. See also Sanborn v. McLean, page 621, *infra*.

§10.6 The Intervention of Equity—The Covenant Enforceable in Equity

Spencer's Case was 265 years old when a new landmark, Tulk v. Moxhay, *infra*, appeared on the covenant scene. As we have seen, the common law had formulated a set of five criteria against which it measured covenants whose enforcement was sought against nonpromising successors to the servient estate. (For the sake of clarity, we repeat the criteria: intent, touch-or-concern, horizontal privity, vertical privity, notice.) Tulk v. Moxhay breaks sharply with the past, as you are about to learn.

TULK v. MOXHAY
2 Ph. 774, 41 Eng. Rep. 1143 (Ch. 1848)

In the year 1808 the Plaintiff, being then the owner in fee of the vacant piece of ground in Leicester Square, as well as of several of the houses forming the Square, sold the piece of ground by the description of "Leicester Square garden or pleasure ground, with the equestrian statue then standing in the centre thereof, and the iron railing and stone work round the same," to one Elms in fee: and the deed of conveyance contained a covenant by Elms, for himself, his heirs, and assigns, with the Plaintiff, his heirs, executors, and administrators, "that Elms, his heirs, and assigns should, and would from time to time, and at all times thereafter at his and their own costs and charges, keep and maintain the said piece of ground and square garden, and the iron railing round the same in its then form, and in sufficient and proper repair as a square garden and pleasure ground, in an open state, uncovered with any buildings, in neat and ornamental order; and that it should be lawful for the inhabitants of Leicester Square, tenants of the Plaintiff, on payment of a reasonable rent for the same, to have keys at their own expense and the privilege of admission therewith at any time or times into the said square garden and pleasure ground."

The piece of land so conveyed passed by divers mesne conveyances into the hands of the Defendant, whose purchase deed contained no similar covenant with his vendor: but he admitted that that he had purchased with notice of the covenant in the deed of 1808.

The Defendant having manifested an intention to alter the character of the square garden, and asserted a right, if he thought fit, to build upon it, the Plaintiff, who still remained owner of several houses in the square, filed this bill for an injunction; and an injunction was granted by the Master of the Rolls to restrain the Defendant from converting or using the piece of ground and square garden, and the iron railing round the same, to or for any other purpose than as a square garden and pleasure ground in an open state, and uncovered with buildings.

On a motion, now made, to discharge that order, . . .

THE LORD CHANCELLOR [COTTENHAM], (without calling upon the other side). That this Court has jurisdiction to enforce a contract between the owner of land and his neighbour purchasing a part of it, that the latter shall either use or abstain from using the land purchased in a particular way, is what I never knew disputed. Here there is no question about the contract: the owner of certain houses in the square sells the land adjoining, with a covenant from the purchaser not to use it for any other purpose than as a square garden. And it is now contended, not that the vendee could violate that contract, but that he might sell the piece of land, and that the purchaser from him may violate it without this Court having any power to interfere. If that were so, it would be impossible for an owner of land to sell part of it without incurring the risk of rendering what he retains worthless. It is said that, the covenant being one which does not run with the land, this Court cannot enforce it; but the question is, not whether the covenant runs with the land, but whether a party shall be permitted to use the land in a manner inconsistent with the contract entered into by his vendor, and with notice of which he purchased. Of course, the price would be affected by the covenant, and nothing could be more inequitable than that the original purchaser should be able to sell the property the next day for a greater price, in consideration of the assignee being allowed to escape from the liability which he had himself undertaken.

[handwritten margin note: Knocks out requirement of horiz. privity]

[handwritten margin note: Similar to unjust enrichment]

That the question does not depend upon whether the covenant runs with the land is evident from this, that if there was a mere agreement and no covenant, this Court would enforce it against a party purchasing with notice of it; for if an equity is attached to the property by the owner, no one purchasing with notice of that equity can stand in a different situation from the party from whom he purchased. . . .

treating this like a contract case

I think the cases cited before the Vice-Chancellor and this decision of the Master of the Rolls perfectly right, and, therefore, that this motion must be refused, with costs.

NOTES AND QUESTIONS

1. As to the covenant at issue in Tulk v. Moxhay, which of the common-law requirements for the running of a covenant's burden had been satisfied? Which had not been?

2. Which of the common-law requirements for the running of the covenant's burden seemed to have survived the decision in Tulk v. Moxhay to grant equitable relief? Which seem not to have survived? *← horiz. privity*

3. In the context of the question above, consider the following: Does the court hold that if notice is present, any interest-holder in the servient estate must bear the covenant's burden? Suppose that Moxhay had held a ninety-nine-year lease? Or a month-to-month tenancy? Or had acquired the estate by adverse possession? Would the outcome have been the same? Should it have been the same? Putting the question more broadly: where a covenant *bars* activity in the servient estate, should equitable relief be had against anyone acquiring some interest in the servient estate? Compare Amco Trust, Inc. v. Naylor, *supra* (landlord may not compel subtenant to pay rent), with Century Paramount Hotel v. Rock Land Corp., 68 Misc. 2d 603, 327 N.Y.S.2d 695 (Civ. Ct. 1971) (landlord may enjoin subtenant from showing burlesque where lease bars such activity). Do you see any analogies to the enforceability, via injunction, of affirmative and negative easements?

4. In the context of question 2, does Tulk v. Moxhay stand for the enforcement of any covenant, regardless of its content, where notice is present? Cf. §10.10 (a) *infra*.

5. Note the similarity between the covenant not to build (to keep the garden open) and a negative easement for light and air. Remember, though, that the English courts curtailed the forms of negative easement; the restriction at issue in Tulk v. Moxhay was not one of the traditional forms. See page 532 *supra*. Accordingly, the court did not treat this as a negative easement case. Suppose, however, that the court had done so. How might this have changed the opinion?

6. *Affirmative covenants in equity:* Of what importance is it that the covenant at issue in Tulk v. Moxhay barred activity rather than compelled it? Suppose defendant, after the decision in Tulk v. Moxhay, refuses to keep the

garden and the iron railing in good repair, and plaintiff seeks equitable relief. Will he recover?

Beginning with the decision in Haywood v. Brunswick Permanent Building Soc., 8 Q.B. 403 (C.A. 1881), the English courts have refused enforcement in equity of affirmative covenants unenforceable at law. "The covenant to repair can only be enforced by making the owner put his hand into his pockets, and there is nothing that would justify us in going that length." Id. at 409.

By contrast, American courts generally have not limited Tulk v. Moxhay to negative covenants. Affirmative covenants—even if they are technically defective at law—are frequently enforceable via injunction under the Tulk v. Moxhay rationale. Reno, The Enforcement of Equitable Servitudes in Land, 28 Va. L. Rev. 951, 972 (1942). See, e.g., Fitzstephens v. Watson, 218 Or. 185, 344 P.2d 221 (1959) (covenant to supply water; defendants enjoined from interfering with the supply); Petersen v. Beekmore, Inc., 117 N.J. Super. 155, 283 A.2d 911 (1971) (covenant to purchase stock in community association; affirmative covenant enforceable in equity, whether or not enforceable at law; plaintiffs, however, failed to establish *their* right to enforce).

Why should equity courts be marginally more loath to enforce affirmative covenants than they are to enforce negative covenants? Is it because mandatory injunctions are more difficult to supervise than prohibiting injunctions would be? Or is it because a mandatory injunction puts the court's hand in the defendant's pocket, so to speak?

7. *Negative covenants at law:* Reciprocity suggests that if Tulk v. Moxhay has eased the enforceability of affirmative covenants in equity, negative covenants might now be more readily enforceable at law, with less homage paid to technical perfection. To illustrate: A and B, neighboring landowners, agree not to use their premises for competing business purposes; B leases his premises to B′ who opens a competing business. Instead of seeking an injunction, A sues B′ for damages. The lack of vertical privity between B and B′ would not be a bar to equitable relief. Should it remain a bar in a suit at law?

We have now entered the realm of speculation, since courts are less likely than are law teachers to sort things out neatly. It would seem foolish for courts to persist in a double standard, especially in the modern era when the same judges administer both the law and equity sides of the docket. To apply the general principle to the concrete case, it would seem surprising if A could gain an injunction—the more drastic remedy—while being denied damages. Plaintiffs must often settle for damages as a second choice to an injunction.

Another consideration is the way lawyers now view the negative covenant. The court in Tulk v. Moxhay treated the covenant as a form of contract. The opinion reads: "If there was a mere agreement and no covenant, this Court would enforce it against a party purchasing with notice of it. . . ." Contract principles explain the outcome of Tulk v. Moxhay. We have seen (Note 5, *supra*) that the English courts refused to regard negative covenants as a species of negative easement. (Remember that common law required only intent and notice for the enforcement of negative easements.) However, the

Tulk v. Moxhay "contract" rationale has since been superseded, in many American courts, by a property view which treats some negative covenants as if they were a latter-day easement. Note, in the opinion that follows, the various labels placed on the covenant at issue.

TRUSTEES OF COLUMBIA COLLEGE v. LYNCH

70 N.Y. 440 (1877)

[handwritten margin note: court throws out horizontal privity as a requirement also acts as a court of equity, not of law]

This action was brought to restrain the carrying on of business in certain premises situated on the north-east corner of Fiftieth street and Sixth avenue in the city of New York, of which the defendant Lynch was owner and the other defendants tenants, upon the ground that the premises were subject to a covenant reserving the property exclusively for dwelling houses.

The westerly portion of the block in question, prior to 1860, belonged to Joseph D. Beers, from whom defendant Lynch acquired title, and the portion adjoining on the east belonged to the plaintiffs.

On the 25th day of July, 1859, an agreement was executed by the parties, whereby the said Beers, in consideration of similar reciprocal covenants therein contained on the part of the plaintiffs, did for himself, his heirs and assigns, in respect to the lands which he then owned, covenant and agree to and with the plaintiffs, their successors and assigns, that his lands above mentioned, and every part thereof, should be subject to the following covenants, among others, namely: That the said Beers, his heirs or assigns, his or their tenants, and others occupying his lands, above described, or any part thereof, should not permit, grant, erect, establish or carry on in any manner on any part of said lands any stable, schoolhouse, engine-house or manufactory, or business whatsover; or erect or build, or commence to erect or build, any building or edifice, with intent to use the same, or any part thereof, for any of the purposes aforesaid.

And it was mutually covenanted and agreed between the parties, that the grants, covenants and agreements therein contained should not only be binding upon the parties, their heirs and successors, but that the same should be binding upon all persons who might thereby become interested in the lands, or any part or parts thereof, as owners, tenants or occupants, or otherwise claiming under or through the said Beers, or as lessees of the plaintiffs, or as assignees, under tenants, occupants or otherwise under such lessees, and might be enforced by or against any of such persons as occasion might require.

The agreement was duly recorded, and the defendant Lynch took her lot expressly subject to the conditions and restrictions of the agreement of Beers and the plaintiffs.

Before the action was commenced, the defendant Lynch erected a four-story dwelling house upon that part of the premises conveyed to her, between Sixth avenue and a line distant twenty-two feet eastwardly therefrom, and running to the center of the block, between Fiftieth and Fifty-first streets, of the full width thereof, fronting on and entered by a high stoop from Fiftieth street, and in width on Sixth avenue sixty-four feet. On the basement story, in front, by the side of the stoop, and on the side opening on Sixth avenue, were two French windows, and one on Fiftieth street, which were used as entrance doors to the basement.

Yates, one of the defendants, occupied a portion of the basement of said building as a dwelling for himself and family, having in one room thereof a real estate office, and using it for that business, with a business sign; and the defendants, William A. Blaisdell and Harrison A. Blaisdell, occupied a room in said office for receiving orders for painting, to be done by them, with a business sign.

The court found these facts, and also that the opposite side of Sixth avenue, between Fiftieth and Fifty-first streets, is entirely occupied by the Broadway Railroad stables; that there is a grocery store on the southeast corner and a liquor store on the southwest corner of Sixth avenue and Fiftieth street; and that Sixth avenue, in that vicinity, is occupied as a business street.

As conclusions of law, the court found: _horizontal privity_

no conveyance "1. That there was no privity of estate between the plaintiffs and Beers.

"2. That the covenant sought to be enforced in this action does not run with the land.

"3. That the defendants' land is not bound by the covenant sought to be enforced in this action.

"4. That the restrictions imposed by the agreement between the plaintiffs and Beers did not mutually and reciprocally bind the plaintiffs and their assigns and Beers and his assigns.

"5. That the covenant against carrying on any business is one liable to conflict with the public welfare, and retards the advancement of the community."

And directed judgment dismissing the complaint.

Judgment was entered accordingly.

ALLEN, J. . . . The agreement itself is not void, as in restraint of trade or as imposing undue restrictions upon the use of property. Covenants, conditions and reservations, imposing like restrictions upon urban property, for the benefit of adjacent lands, having respect to light, air, ornamentation, or the exclusion of occupations which would render the entire property unsuitable for the purposes to which it could be most advantageously devoted, have been sustained, and have never been regarded as impolitic. They have been enforced at law and in equity without question. The restrictions are deemed wise by the owners, who alone are interested, and they rest upon and withdraw from general and unrestricted use but a small portion of territory within the corporate limits of any city or municipality, and neither public or private interest can suffer. It is not alleged in the answer, nor was it proved upon the hearing, that there has been any change in the character of the locality, the surroundings of the premises, or the occupation of contiguous property, or the business of the vicinage, which has rendered it inexpedient to observe the covenant, or made a disregard of it indispensable to the practical and profitable use and occupation of the premises, so that it might be inequitable to compel a specific performance of the agreement. [20] If such a defense could avail, it has not been interposed, so that the facts found by the learned trial judge, in respect of the character of the buildings, and the business carried on at this time in the Sixth avenue, are immaterial and cannot affect the result.

The purpose and intent of the parties to the agreement is apparent from its terms preceded by the recital. The agreement recites the ownership by the respective parties of adjacent premises particularly described, and these constitute the subject-matter of the mutual covenants. There was no privity of estate, or community of interest between the parties, but each could, by grant, create an easement in his own lands for the benefit of the lands owned by the other, and the purpose of the agreement was to create mutual easements, negative in their character, for the benefit of the lands of each. It was the design to impose mutual and corresponding restrictions upon the premises belonging to each, and thus to secure a uniformity in the structure and position of buildings upon the entire premises, and to reserve the lots for, and confine their use to, first-class dwellings, to the exclusion of trades and all business, and all structures which would derogate from their value for private residences. The purpose clearly disclosed was, by the restrictions mutually imposed by the owners respectively upon the use of their several properties, to make the lots more available and desirable as sites for residences, and the agreement professes to, and does in terms, impose, for the common benefit, the restrictions in perpetuity, and to bind the heirs and assigns of the respective covenantors. This should be construed as a grant by each to the other in fee of a negative easement in the lands owned by the covenantors. An easement in favor of, and for the benefit of lands owned by third persons, can be created by grant, and a covenant by the owner, upon a good consideration, to use, or to refrain from using, his premises in a particular manner, for the benefit of premises owned by the covenantor, is, in effect, the grant of an easement, and the right to the enjoyment of it will pass as appurtenant to the premises in respect of which it was created. Reciprocal easements of this character may be created upon the division and conveyances in severalty to different grantees of an entire tract, and they may be created by a reservation in a conveyance, by a condition annexed to a grant, or by a covenant, and even a parol agreement of the grantees. . . . The right sought to be enforced here is an easement, or, as it is sometimes called, an amenity, and consists in restraining the owner from doing that with, and upon, his property which, but for the grant or covenant, he might lawfully have done, and hence is called a negative easement, as distinguished from that class of easements which compels the owner to suffer something to be done upon his property by another. (Wash. on Easements, 5.) Easements of all kinds may be created and exist in favor of any third person,

---

20. The sequel appears in Trustees of Columbia College v. Thacher, 87 N.Y. 311 (1882), page 649, *infra.*—ED.

irrespective of any privity of estate or community of interest between the parties; and, in this respect, there is no distinction between negative easements and those rights that are more generally known as easements as a way, etc.

A covenant by the owner with A. B., his heirs and assigns, that it should be lawful for them at all times afterwards to have and to use a way by and through a close, etc., was held to be an actual grant of a way and not a covenant only for the enjoyment of such right. . . . A negative easement, by which the owner of lands is restricted in their use, can only be created by covenant in favor of other lands not owned by the grantor and covenantor. The covenant made by Beers was valid and binding upon him, and had he retained the ownership of the premises, it would have been specially enforced by a court of equity. Upon a disturbance of the easement by him, it was capable of being enforced by the appropriate remedies at law or in equity at the suit of the owner of the dominant tenement, at the time of the violation of the covenant. The plaintiffs appear to retain the ownership of the premises to which the easement is appurtenant, and therefore this action is properly brought by them. Equity has jurisdiction to compel the observance of covenants made for the mutual benefit and protection of all the owners of lands, by those owning different parcels of the lands, and to secure to those entitled the enjoyment of easements or servitudes annexed by grant, covenant, or otherwise to private estates. . . .

It is strenuously urged, in behalf of the defendants and respondents, that there was no privity of estate between the mutual covenantors and covenantees, in respect of the premises owned by them respectively, and which were the subjects of the covenants and agreements, and that the covenants did not therefore run with the lands, binding the grantees, and subjecting them to a personal liability thereon. This may be conceded for all the purposes of this action. It is of no importance whether an action at law could be maintained against the grantees of Beers, as upon a covenant running with the land and binding them. Whether it was a covenant running with the land or a collateral covenant, or a covenant in gross, or whether an action at law could be sustained upon it, is not material as affecting the jurisdiction of a court of equity, or the right of the owners of the dominant tenement to relief upon a disturbance of the easements.

The covenantor, Beers, bound himself, and in equity charged the premises with the observance of the covenant, and thus impressed this easement upon the lands then owned by him in favor of the lands then and now owned by the plaintiffs. A right, in respect of the defendants' lands, and affecting the use in behalf of the plaintiffs and their lands, existed, which, while Beers continued the owner, equity would have enforced, and this right was a right in perpetuity, going with and attaching to, the lands in the hands of all subsequent grantees taking title, with notice of its existence. An owner may subject his lands to any servitude,[21] and transmit them to others charged with the

---

21. Too sweeping an assertion? Cf. §10.10(a), *infra.*—ED.

same; and one taking title to lands, with notice of any equity attached thereto, or any outstanding right or claim affecting the title or the use and enjoyment of the lands, takes subject to such equities, and such right or claim, and stands, in the place of his grantor, bound to do or forbear to do whatever he would have been bound to do or forbear to do. . . . Here each successive grantee, from Beers, the covenantor, down to and including the defendant Lynch, the present owner, not only had notice of the covenant, and all equities growing out of the same, but took their title in terms subject to it, and impliedly agreeing to observe it. It would be unreasonable and unconscientious to hold the grantees absolved from the covenant in equity for the technical reason assigned, that it did not run with the land, so as to give an action at law. A distinguished judge answered a like objection in a similar case by saying, in substance, that, if an action at law could not be maintained, that was an additional reason for entertaining jurisdiction in equity and preventing injustice. The action can be maintained for the establishment and enforcement of a negative easement created by the deed of the original proprietor, affecting the use of the premises now owned and occupied by the defendants, of which they had notice, and subject to which they took title. There is no equity or reason for making a servitude of the character of that claimed by the plaintiffs in the lands of the defendant, an exception to the general rule which charges lands in the hands of a purchaser with notice with all existing equities, easements, and servitudes. . . .

The author of the American note to Spencer's Case (1 Smith's Leading Cases [6th Am. ed.], 167), recognizes the distinction between the binding obligation at law of covenants not running with the lands and the equitable rights recognized and enforced in equity in such cases. He says, speaking of such a covenant: "But although the covenant, when regarded as a contract, is binding only between the original parties, yet, in order to give effect to their intention, it may be construed by equity as creating an incorporeal hereditament (in the form of an easement) out of the unconveyed estate, and rendering it appurtenant to the estate conveyed; and when this is the case, subsequent assignees will have the right and be subject to the obligations which the title or liability to such an easement creates." . . .

Judgment reversed.

RENO, THE ENFORCEMENT OF EQUITABLE SERVITUDES IN LAND

28 Va. L. Rev. 951, 972-977 (1942)

Although the doctrine of equitable servitudes has now received wide acceptance in this country, there is no substantial agreement among the courts as to the theoretical basis for enforcing the burden of an agreement respecting land against subsequent possessors or users with notice. A few early cases intimated that equity was merely extending the doctrine of covenants running with the land. However, this is clearly not the basis since lack of privity of estate, either between the promisor and promisee or between the promisor and the present possessor of the land, has been no deterrent to the enforcement of the agreement. Enforcement has been granted upon the basis of notice against an underlessee, a mere occupant of the land, and even against an adverse possessor. A relationship between the parties to the suit, an element which courts of law required in covenants running with the land and found in the concept of privity of estate, seems never to have been considered necessary in equity if the defendant is charged with notice. One writer has described the necessary relationship as merely the "equitable principle of privity of conscience."

Most discussions of the theoretical basis for the doctrine center around one or the other of two widely different theories: one, that the doctrine of Tulk v. Moxhay, is merely an application by equity of its principle of specific performance of contracts concerning land, and the other, that it is the recognition of the existence in equity of equitable easements not recognized and enforceable at law. Under the first theory the enforcement rests on a contractual obligation only, and under the second it is based on a property interest in the burdened land in many respects similar to legal easements. . . .

The [second] theory, which has gained wide acceptance among property writers, is that equity is enforcing the agreement against possessors with notice not as a contractual obligation but as one arising from an equitable easement in the burdened land. These writers refer to the doctrine of Tulk v. Moxhay as the doctrine of equitable easements or servitudes. Under this theory a contract by the owner of land that he will use or abstain from using his land in a particular way creates in the promisee an equitable property interest in the burdened land. The existence of a property interest means that the promisee holds certain equitable rights in rem against the entire world in respect to the use of this land. Since rights in rem can create only correlative negative duties in members of the public, every third person whether in possession of the burdened land or not is under a negative duty to abstain from using the land in a manner inconsistent with the contract, unless he can bring himself within the equitable defense of purchaser without notice. Such a theory fully explains the enforcement of restrictive equitable servitudes as merely an extension of the legal doctrine of negative easements to new and novel situations.

However, the existence of equitable rights in rem against the public will not explain the basis of enforcement of an affirmative equitable servitude against a purchaser with notice. In order for him to be subject to an affirmative duty there must be a correlative right in personam existing in the promisee in addition to his rights in rem. The contract theory of equitable servitudes finds such a "right-duty" relationship under the equitable principles of specific performance of contracts, while the property theory finds such a relationship as a primary relationship based upon the concept of a real obligation attaching to the land and passing with the land to all subsequent possessors. This is the same basis for the enforcement of "spurious easements." [22] In addition to the rights in rem against the public, there arises a primary right in personam against the possessor of the land. The correlative duty of this latter right, whether affirmative or negative, attaches to the land as a real obligation and passes with it to all subsequent possessors, who cannot set up the equitable defense of purchaser without notice.

Under such a theory of treating the agreement as creating a property interest consisting of both rights in rem and rights in personam, we find that equity has developed the concept of a real obligation, which attaches to the land itself and not as in the case of covenants running with the land merely to an estate in the land. This permits the enforcement of affirmative agreements against any possessor of the burdened land without respect to any question of privity of estate. . . .

NOTE: THE CONTINUING OBLIGATION OF THE ORIGINAL COVENANTOR

A and B enter into reciprocal covenants to maintain their respective properties. B transfers his parcel to B', who breaches. May A recover judgment against B?

We have already seen (Problem, pages 585-586, *supra*) that where covenants appear in a lease, privity of contract exists between promisor and promisee, so that the tenant, who covenants to pay rent, for example, remains liable in contract (as a surety) even after he assigns the lease. Should this principle of contract privity also apply to covenants between fee holders?

If we think of the A-B promise in contract terms, then B's liability would continue even after the transfer to B'. Unless the promisee accepts a novation, a promisor may not delegate his contract duties to another. If, however, we think of the A-B promise as the conveyance of an interest in land only, then contract rules should not govern the transaction. For example, if B covenants to give A a right of way, or if B covenants not to compete, we might view the covenants as creating an affirmative easement and an equitable (easement) servitude, respectively, fully analogous to the *grant* of a right of way or a covenant not to block A's light and air, which we regard as property transactions not subject to contract rules. As property events, the duties of the holder of the servient estate come to an end when he transfers title. Thus B, having once granted a right of way to A, does not forever carry the burden of personal obligation should his successors, years hence, violate the terms of the easement. We might say that B has personal duties to A only while there is a "privity of estate" between them.

This property theorem of one-generation liability makes good sense in the cases of affirmative or negative easements and negative covenants, since

22. Recall n.13, page 561, *supra*.—ED.

the interest holder will usually be able to protect his rights by in rem relief. Since A may seek a prohibitory injunction if B′ blocks off the right of way or builds so as to block off A's view or competes where competition is barred, it is only of secondary importance to A that he may also be able to get a money judgment for damages.

The difficult problem area surrounds the question with which we began: how do we deal with the affirmative covenantor? When a covenant to repair or to supply electrical power or to pay assessments is breached, the promisee may gain only an uncollectable judgment for his enforcement efforts. Why shouldn't he then be able to seek redress against the party whose promise originally created the right?

In thinking about this question, for which a solid answer does not exist, consider the following factors:

(a)   Would affirmative covenants be less freely given if the original promisor remained contingently liable after she transferred the servient estate? If so, do we want to discourage the creation of affirmative covenants?

(b)   Isn't it better to have some rules, whatever they may be, rather than continued ambiguity, since the parties can then decide either to adopt the rule or to structure the transaction differently?

(c)   Should we treat *all* affirmative covenants alike? (We have already applied contract rules to leasehold covenants.) If we distinguish between leasehold and fee covenants, might we want to distinguish further among the varieties of the covenants? For example, contrast a covenant to pay a subdivision assessment, where enforcement might have been secured originally through a lien on the servient estate (cf. the *Neponsit* case, §10.8, *infra*), with a covenant to build a sewerage treatment plant, where the personal credit of the original promisor may be all that would give value to a judgment.

§10.7   The Essentials of a Real Covenant—The Running of the Benefit (May E′ Enforce?)

We have spent much time on the burden side of covenants. Happily, much less need be said on the benefit side, although courts have not left the benefit issue free of confusion and semantic garble either. To return to our opening example of the adjoining owners A and B who have agreed to keep their driveways cleared as part of a common-driveway agreement: A sells Lot 1 to A′; B the original promisor breaches; A′ sues B for damages.

The abstract issue is whether B's promise benefits not only its original promisee but also A's successor in interest: in short, does the *benefit* of B's promise to maintain Lot 2 run with Lot 1? To recall easement law: the benefit of an easement runs automatically with succession of the dominant estate. There need be only succession (no identity of interest) and a dominant estate.

While disputes sometimes erupt over whether the easement is linked to a dominant estate (easement appurtenant) or remains personal (in gross), cf. Martin v. Music, §10.2 *supra,* once a court finds a dominant estate, anyone validly interested in that estate may enforce the easement against the holder of the servient estate.

As we are about to see, even the best of the commentators on covenants, *[can't, because he is bound by N.Y. law]* as he sought to simplify analysis, failed to grasp the opportunity to apply easement wisdom to covenant law. The commentator was Charles Clark,[23] by then a circuit judge. The case was 165 Broadway Building v. City Investing Co., and the issue was whether the benefit of a covenant between landowners, in which A agreed to pay B $10,000 on the happening of an event, ran to B's successor. In deciding that the benefit ran, Judge Clark wrote for a divided court.

165 BROADWAY BUILDING v. CITY INVESTING CO.

120 F.2d 813, 817-819 (2d Cir. 1941) *[following state law because of Erie]*
[this is an interpleader case]

. . . It is now well settled that no particular formula is necessary for the expression of intent that a covenant shall "run with land" and pass with the conveyance of an estate therein, so long as the parties have made their desires clear. Denman v. Prince, 40 Barb., N.Y., 213, 217; Murphy v. Kerr, 8 Cir., 5 F.2d 908, 910, 41 A.L.R. 1359; Fowler v. Kent, 71 N.H. 388, 52 A. 554. The parties here made their intent clearly manifest—in paragraph tenth, as to the benefit of repayment of construction costs to the owner, "its successors or assigns." . . .

As to the requirement of "privity of estate," the master thought that it was lacking because of no conveyance of an interest in the premises between the parties at the time of the making of the covenant. This particular requirement is probably the greatest source of confusion in the subject, because an understandable policy against title encumbrances (carried, however, to an unreal extreme in these days of modern community land developments) has been buttressed by privity doctrines of seemingly authentic, but actually dubious, historicity. That the parties to an action to enforce a covenant, if not themselves makers of the contract, must each have succeeded by privity to the estate of one of such makers is good enough sense; it is why we say a covenant runs with such estate. But to go further and require that there must be some such succession between the covenanting parties themselves—that there must have been a grant or conveyance between them at the time of the covenant or possibly some continuing interest of tenure, easement, or otherwise—is supported neither by ancient land law nor by modern policy. . . . That a requirement so anomalous should exist at all is therefore doubtful; the authorities

[Knocking out horiz. privity]

23. As a Yale law professor, Clark wrote Real Covenants and Other Interests Which "Run With the Land" (2d ed. 1947).

tend to show that, if it is not to be rejected altogether, it is not applicable in any event to the running of the benefit of covenants, as here. . . .

We turn, therefore, to the final requirement that the promises in question must "touch" or "concern" appellant's real property, the 165 Broadway Building, before appellant can claim their benefit. This question, too, has been the subject of conflicting decisions and learned discourse, as the *Neponsit* case points out. But there we have the realistic modern view, at page 258 of 278 N.Y., at page 796 of 15 N.E.2d, 118 A.L.R. 973, that "unless we exalt technical form over substance, the distinction between covenants which run with land and covenants which are personal, must depend upon the effect of the covenant on the legal rights which otherwise would flow from ownership of land and which are connected with the land. The problem then is: Does the covenant in purpose and effect substantially alter these rights?" And the learned court considers particularly promises to pay money, stating that, while they may be entirely disconnected with the use of land and hence quite personal, yet a promise to pay for something to be done in connection with the promisor's land does not differ essentially from a promise, to do the thing itself. Hence the court, stressing the intent and substantial effect of the promise there in issue—one made to a realty company to pay an annual charge to a property owner's association (a different entity) for the maintenance of roads, paths, parks, beach, sewer, and other public purposes in the area then being developed by the realty company—holds that its burden runs even though it calls for money to be expended on land other than that now owned by the defendant.

We think this poses the problem, as well as affords means for its solution. A promise to refund viewed merely as a promise to pay on condition, i.e., a windfall refund, is personal; while a promise to pay money for land development, or to do something about the land which if the promisor did it in person would clearly benefit such land, may run. Here had the refunds been definitely stated as for the repair and restoration of the building upon the demolition of the elevated station (or as agreements to pay for such restoration not to exceed the amounts originally advanced), there could be no question of the running of the covenant benefits. Our real question is how far such an intent shall be deduced from the circumstances here present. . . . Perhaps the best we can say is that prima facie promises to refund should be considered as not for the benefit of land, but that the *Neponsit* case warns us to be pragmatic and realistic in looking to the real, rather than the formal, effect of the agreement on the parties' relation to the land and to proper and natural commerce in land.

Thus cautioned, it appears to us that, viewing the agreement as a whole, it would be unreal to consider these refunds as a windfall payment for the benefit of persons having no present interest in the land, rather than as a component part of a rather carefully thought-out plan of land utilization. The reason and the desire of the building owner here to obtain direct access from its building to a then effective means of transportation are clear and natural. That this arrangement in all its details was a desirable, even a necessary, one for the purpose also seems obvious. It was made for this building; it could not be effected with anything other than this building. The refunding provisions were intimately tied together in common sense. Thus the company assumed no obligation for repairs and restoration of the premises, thereby avoiding an uncertain and unlimited obligation in the remote future; but it did agree to return the money it had received for the original construction, as well as the subsidy for the ticket chopper. Note that conversely and when discontinuance came at the instance of the owner—and obviously the then owner who alone could serve notice of discontinuance—he must pay for such restoration and repair to the company. Here there was no refund to provide a fund, and obviously repair to the platform when the bridge was taken down would be comparatively slight. Mutuality of obligation and of right was secured by the plan (which the parties, as we have seen, conceived of as freely running); it would be destroyed on appellee's contention when the refund goes to a stranger while the owner has to restore its building with a hole in its front and without assistance from anyone.

NOTES AND QUESTIONS

1. The Restatement of Property accepted Judge Clark's view that horizontal privity was not required on the benefit side:

> §548. *Privity Between Promisor and Promisee.* It is not essential to the running of the benefit of a promise respecting the use of land of the promisee or other person entitled to the benefit of the promise that there be any privity between the promisor and the promisee other than that arising out of the promise.

2. While Judge Clark rings the death knell for horizontal privity, which of the four other burden requirements seem to remain on the benefit side: intent, touch or concern, vertical privity, notice?

3. *Running of the benefit—intent and touch or concern.* Do you see any relationship between the requirements of intent and touch or concern, as Judge Clark discusses them, and the discussion in Martin v. Music, §10.2 *supra,* as to whether an easement is appurtenant or in gross? Could it be said that Judge Clark is simply using covenant terms to ask whether the benefit is personal to the original promisee ("in gross") or attached to a dominant estate ("appurtenant")?

4. May the benefit of a real covenant be held in gross? Cf. Neponsit Property Owners' Assn. v. Emigrant Industrial Savings Bank, §10.8 *infra.*

5. Running of the benefit—vertical privity. The Restatement of Property sets forth the following:

§547. *Privity Between Beneficiary and Successor.* The benefit of a promise respecting the use of land of the beneficiary of the promise can run with the land only to one who succeeds to some interest of the beneficiary in the land respecting the use of which the promise was made.

Is the paragraph restrictive (that is, one may not claim a benefit unless he has succeeded to some interest held by the promisee), or expansive (that is, anyone may claim a benefit who has succeeded to some interest held by the promisee)? Which reading seems preferable? By analogy to easement, what interest in a dominant estate must one enjoy to enforce an easement? Should the same requirement (or absence thereof) apply to real covenants?

Under the Restatement view, may a party who acquires title to the benefited estate by adverse possession enforce the covenant? Should he be permitted to? May the adverse occupier enforce an easement after he acquires title to the dominant estate? Before he acquires title? Should he be permitted to?

Does §547 state or imply whether the benefit of a real covenant may be held in gross?

6. Landlord covenants to maintain the premises in good repair. The premises are subleased to S. May S sue the landlord for failure to repair?

A close reading of §547 would indicate that such a claim is possible since S has succeeded to "some interest" of the tenant promisee. Is this result anomalous since the landlord has no claim against a subtenant who has violated a tenant's covenant?

Restatement (Second) of Property (1977) partly avoids this disparity in cases where tenant has not assigned the benefit of his covenants to the subtenant. The Restatement would permit the benefit to run, in the absence of assignment, only where "the transfer brings the transferee into privity of estate with the person obligated to perform the promise." Id. at §16.2; id. at example 6.

7. In some states the landlord and subtenant are by statute given the same rights against each other as those existing between the landlord and head tenant. See, e.g., Ind. Ann. Stat. §32-7-1-11 (1933); Kan. Stat. Ann. §58-2515 (1964). Also the landlord's statutory lien or power of distress, where they exist, have sometimes enabled the landlord to enforce the rent obligation against the subtenant's belongings. See, e.g., Peak v. Gaddy, 152 Okla. 138, 3 P.2d 1042 (1931); Bernard v. McClanahan, 115 Va. 453, 79 S.E. 1059 (1913); contra: Gray v. Rawson, 11 Ill. 527 (1850).

Does the doctrine of equitable servitude, §10.6 *infra,* also help to erase any disparity? See Note, The Scope of Liability Between Landlord and Subtenant, 16 Colum. J.L. & Soc. Prob. 365 (1981).

8. The facts are these: X and Y are adjoining owners of Lots 1 and 2. X covenants that Lot 1 will be devoted to private dwellings only; Y gives the same covenant covering Lot 2. Thereafter X subdivides his Lot into Lots 1-A and 1-B, conveying the subdivided lots—subject to the covenants—to P and

[handwritten notes in margin: only Y was intended to benefit from X's promise, not 1-A against 1-B]

[handwritten diagram: covenant X ⟷ Y with X branching to P (1-A) and (1-B)]

D. D begins construction of a school on Lot 1-B, and P seeks an injunction. Is P entitled to injunctive relief? Held: no. Benford v. Board of Education of Mamaroneck, N.Y.L.J., Feb. 14, 1967, at 20, col. 7 (Sup. Ct. Westchester Co.). Why this result? See also Korn v. Campbell, 192 N.Y. 490, 495-496, 85 N.E. 687, 689 (1908).

9.   There are two other situations that our analysis should account for. The first of these is a benefit that runs with the land while the land remains unsubdivided, but terminates when subdivision of the dominant estate occurs. Compare Martin v. Music, §10.2 *supra.* Levy v. Blue Ridge Construction Co., 74 Misc. 2d 676, 345 N.Y.S.2d 314 (Sup. Ct. 1973), illustrates this situation. R, owner of 100 acres, grants 95.3 acres to E. The deed gives E an option of first refusal to purchase the excepted 4.7 acres for $45,000. E then breaks the 95.3-acre tract into smaller parcels. R-1 sues to bar present owners of the subdivided tract from enforcing the purchase option.

In granting relief, the court found that the original parties intended that the promise would not survive the subdivision of the dominant estate.

Closely related to the situation above is a covenant that benefits E alone, and only while E remains the owner of benefited land. In the *Levy* case, the court hints that E-1 might not have been able to enforce the covenant even if E had not subdivided the tract. Language in the opinion speaks of the personal nature of the covenant.

10.   *Running of the benefit—notice.* There is no requirement that a party seeking to enforce the covenant shall have had notice of the benefit when he acquired his interest in the benefited estate. Why is that?

§10.8   May the Benefit of a Covenant Be Held in Gross?

NEPONSIT PROPERTY OWNERS' ASSN. v. EMIGRANT INDUSTRIAL SAVINGS BANK

278 N.Y. 248, 15 N.E.2d 793 (1938)

LEHMAN, J. The plaintiff, as assignee of Neponsit Realty Company, has brought this action to foreclose a lien upon land which the defendant owns. The lien, it is alleged, arises from a covenant, condition or charge contained in a deed of conveyance of the land from Neponsit Realty Company to a predecessor in title of the defendant. The defendant purchased the land at a judicial sale. The referee's deed to the defendant and every deed in the defendant's chain of title since the conveyance of the land by Neponsit Realty Company purports to convey the property subject to the covenant, condition or charge contained in the original deed. . . .

It appears that in January, 1911, Neponsit Realty Company, as owner of a tract of land in Queens county, caused to be filed in the office of the clerk of the county a map of the land. The tract was developed for a strictly residential community, and Neponsit Realty Company conveyed lots in the tract to purchasers, describing such lots by reference to the filed map and to roads and streets shown thereon. In 1917, Neponsit Realty Company conveyed the land now owned by the defendant to Robert Oldner Deyer and his wife by deed which contained the covenant upon which the plaintiff's cause of action is based.

That covenant provides:

> And the party of the second part for the party of the second part and the heirs, successors and assigns of the party of the second part further covenants that the property conveyed by this deed shall be subject to an annual charge in such an amount as will be fixed by the party of the first part, its successors and assigns, not, however, exceeding in any year the sum of four ($4.00) Dollars per lot 20 × 100 feet. The assigns of the party of the first part may include a Property Owners' Association which may hereafter be organized for the purposes referred to in this paragraph, and in case such association is organized the sums in this paragraph provided for shall be payable to such association. The party of the second part for the party of the second part and the heirs, successors and assigns of the party of the second part covenants that they will pay this charge to the party of the first part, its successors and assigns on the first day of May in each and every year, and further covenants that said charge shall on said date in each year become a lien on the land and shall continue to be such lien until fully paid. Such charge shall be payable to the party of the first part or its successors or assigns, and shall be devoted to the maintenance of the roads, paths, parks, beach, sewers and such other public purposes as shall from time to time be determined by the party of the first part, its successors or assigns. And the party of the second part by the acceptance of this deed hereby expressly vests in the party of the first part, its successors or assigns, the right and power to bring all actions against the owner of the premises hereby conveyed or any part thereof for the collection of such charge and to enforce the aforesaid lien therefor.
>
> These covenants shall run with the land and shall be construed as real covenants running with the land until January 31st, 1940, when they shall cease and determine.

Every subsequent deed of conveyance of the property in the defendant's chain of title, including the deed from the referee to the defendant, contained, as we have said, a provision that they were made subject to covenants and restrictions of former deeds of record.

There can be no doubt that Neponsit Realty Company intended that the covenant should run with the land and should be enforceable by a property owners association against every owner of property in the residential tract which the realty company was then developing. [The court holds, after extended analysis, that the burden runs to the defendant.]

. . . Another difficulty remains. Though between the grantor and the grantee there was a privity of estate, the covenant provides that its benefit shall run to the assigns of the grantor who "may include a Property Owners' Association which may hereafter be organized for the purposes referred to in this paragraph." The plaintiff has been organized to receive the sums payable by the property owners and to expend them for the benefit of such owners. Various definitions have been formulated of "privity of estate" in connection with covenants that run with the land, but none of such definitions seems to cover the relationship between the plaintiff and the defendant in this case. The plaintiff has not succeeded to the ownership of any property of the grantor. It does not appear that it ever had title to the streets or public places upon which charges which are payable to it must be expended. It does not appear that it owns any other property in the residential tract to which any easement or right of enjoyment in such property is appurtenant. It is created solely to act as the assignee of the benefit of the covenant, and it has no interest of its own in the enforcement of the covenant.

The arguments that under such circumstances the plaintiff has no right of action to enforce a covenant running with the land are all based upon a distinction between the corporate property owners' association and the property owners for whose benefit the association has been formed. If that distinction may be ignored, then the basis of the arguments is destroyed. How far privity of estate in technical form is necessary to enforce in equity a restrictive covenant upon the use of land, presents an interesting question. Enforcement of such covenants rests upon equitable principles (Tulk v. Moxhay, 2 Phillips, 774; Trustees of Columbia College v. Lynch, 70 N.Y. 440; Korn v. Campbell, 192 N.Y. 490), and at times, at least, the violation "of the restrictive covenant may be restrained at the suit of one who owns property, or for whose benefit the restriction was established, irrespective of whether there were privity either of estate or of contract between the parties, or whether an action at law were maintainable." (Cheseboro v. Moers, 233 N.Y. 75, 80.) The covenant in this case does not fall exactly within any classification of "restrictive" covenants, which have been enforced in this State (cf. Korn v. Campbell, 192 N.Y. 490), and no right to enforce even a restrictive covenant has been sustained in this State where the plaintiff did not own property which would benefit by such enforcement so that some of the elements of an equitable servitude are present. In some jurisdictions, it has been held that no action may be maintained without such elements. (But cf. Van Sant v. Rose, 260 Ill. 401.) We do not attempt to decide now how far the rule of Trustees of Columbia College v. Lynch (*supra*) will be carried, or to formulate a definite rule as to when, or even whether, covenants in a deed will be enforced, upon equitable principles, against subsequent purchasers with notice, at the suit of a party without privity of contract or estate. (Cf. "Equitable Rights and Liabilities of Strangers to a Contract," by Harlan F. Stone, 18 Columbia Law Review, 291.) There is no need to resort to such a rule if the courts may look behind the corporate form of the plaintiff.

The corporate plaintiff has been formed as a convenient instrument by which the property owners may advance their common interest. . . . Only blind adherence to an ancient formula devised to meet entirely different conditions could constrain the court to hold that a corporation formed as a medium for the enjoyment of common rights of property owners owns no property which would benefit by enforcement of common rights and has no cause of action in equity to enforce the covenant upon which such common rights depend. . . . In substance, if not in form, the covenant is a restrictive covenant which touches and concerns the defendant's land, and in substance, if not in form, there is privity of estate between the plaintiff and the defendant. . . .

    The order should be affirmed. . . .

    CRANE, C.J., O'BRIEN, LOUGHRAN, FINCH and RIPPEY, JJ., concur; HUBBS, J., taking no part.

    Order affirmed, etc.

NOTES AND QUESTIONS

    1. "In substance, if not in form, there is privity of estate between the plaintiff and the defendant [*sic*] . . ." 278 N.Y. 248, 262, 15 N.E.2d 793, 798.

    Note that the *Neponsit* court has blurred horizontal and vertical privity. Having held that the property owners' association is the alter ego of the owners themselves, the court implies that each parcel is a dominant estate whose owner might himself enforce the assessment against a delinquent owner. If this defines the court's logic, the privity of estate in dispute is the link between the original promisee and the present plaintiff. Is it true, however, that the owner of Lot 1 may enforce the assessment against the owner of Lot 2? And if Lot 1 has been leased, may the tenant enforce the assessment? Cf. Restatement of Property §547, page 602 *supra*. Does the answer to the two previous questions depend on whether the developer actually forms a property owners' association to which it then transfers the enforcement powers? In short, would a property owners' association, once formed, have exclusive power to enforce the assessment? Should it have exclusive power? If it does enjoy exclusive power, does the association hold that power as the "attorney" of the individual lot owners—supporting a position that each lot is a dominant estate whose owners have implicitly executed an irrevocable power of attorney to the association? Or alternatively, does the association hold its power as the "assignee" of the developer—supporting a position that the benefit is held in gross? Does it make any difference which view the courts take? Suppose, for example, that in the *Neponsit* case the developer had not formed a property owners' association and had sued to enforce the assessment: could the developer recover? Or suppose that the delinquent owner had acquired his lot after every other lot had been transferred: would he be subject to suit by the association or by his neighbors who obtained their lots earlier? Cf. Sanborn v. McLean, page 621 *infra*.

    2. In Britain, a covenant does not run against a nonpromisor unless the covenantee owns land that can benefit from the covenant—in short, the benefit may not be held in gross. The classic exposition of this doctrine appears in

London County Council v. Allen, 3 K.B. 642 (1914). Allen had agreed with the Council to procure its prior consent before erecting any structure on two plots which he owned (the plots were reserved for roads). Thereafter, Allen transferred one plot to his wife. Ignoring the agreement, Allen built a wall and Mrs. Allen built three houses on their respective plots. The Council obtained a mandatory injunction against Allen, but was denied relief against Mrs. Allen.

The defendant argued that "the London County Council were not neighboring landowners . . . that to affect [defendant] the right must be in the nature of a negative easement; that an easement required both a dominant and servient tenement; and that as the council had no land to which the benefit of the covenant could attach, there could be no dominant tenement, and therefore no negative easement binding on a servient tenement, but only an easement in gross, which did not bind assigns of the land." The court adopted this argument, not without discomfort (id. at 673): "I regret that I do not see my way to depriving Mrs. Allen of her costs, as, whatever may be her equitable rights, I am not at all favourably impressed with her conduct as a good citizen."

Might the reasoning in the *Neponsit* case, *supra*, have supported an injunction against Mrs. Allen? On what theory could the council enjoin Mr. Allen?

3.   In Van Sant v. Rose, 260 Ill. 401, 103 N.E. 194 (1913), V conveyed a lot to R who covenanted not to erect an apartment house on the site for a period of twenty years. R conveyed to his wife; together they planned an apartment house. V sought and obtained an injunction. The defendant urged that V did not own other property in the neighborhood. Held: injunction granted:

> True, a bill to enjoin the breach of restrictive covenants cannot be maintained by one having no connection with or interest in their enforcement; but we cannot agree that complainants had no interest. They were the original covenantees, and by their conveyance of the property reserved an interest in it. They conveyed the property subject to that interest. They had a right to reserve such interest, and this right was not dependent upon the covenantees having other property in the vicinity that would be affected by a breach of the covenants, or that they should in any other manner sustain damages thereby. This court has held, in harmony with the prevailing rule in other jurisdictions, that the right to enjoin the breach of restrictive covenants does not depend upon whether the covenantee will be damaged by the breach; but the mere breach is sufficient ground for interference by injunction. [Citations omitted.] It would seem inconsistent, then, to say, as the covenantees had no other land in the neighborhood, they had no interest in the performance of the covenants. The only purpose their having other land in the vicinity could serve would be to show that they would be injuriously affected—that is, damaged—by a violation of contract. But, as their right does not necessarily depend upon their being damaged by the breach, it would seem it would not necessarily depend upon their owning other land in the vicinity. . . . [I]t is no answer to an action of this kind to say the breach will

inflict no injury upon the complainant, or even that it will be a positive benefit. [Id. at 406-407, 103 N.E. at 196]

Van Sant and *London County Council* represent the polar views on the enforceability of a covenant in gross. Is either view satisfactory?

§10.9   Homes Associations

The use of a homes association to own and maintain common areas had its beginnings in two neighborhoods that survive virtually unchanged after 100 years. In 1831, Samuel Ruggles drained a crooked little swamp in Manhattan, laid out a square, surrounded it with an eight-foot fence, and installed gates which only neighboring residents could unlock. Title to the park was vested in trustees for the benefit of the owners of the sixty-six surrounding plots. The area's name: Gramercy Park. Urban Land Institute, The Homes Association Handbook 39 (TB-50, Oct. 1964).

Boston's famed Louisburg Square, once a pasture belonging to artist John Singleton Copley, was developed in 1826. Its originators made no provision, however, to maintain the neighborhood park. In 1844, owners of the twenty-eight homesites organized a three-man "Committee of the Proprietors of Louisburg Square," levied an initial assessment not to exceed $150 per lot, and invested the committee with responsibility for improving and maintaining the park area. Over the years, the committee's annual business (and social) meeting has become something of a state occasion.

In the spring of 1962, the Urban Land Institute began a nationwide study of homes associations, receiving data on 233 residential developments. The Institute inventoried the facilities that were being managed by the respondent associations. Id. at 21.

Common Facility	Percentage of Associations That Had the Common Facility
Landscaped parks and natural preserves	50
Larger recreation areas	47
Neighborhood entrance ways	42
Swimming pools	27
Buffer fence or plantings	27
Recreation areas of less than one-half acre	23
Off-street walkways for access to common areas	21
Trash and garbage disposal	20
Common halls, room or gym	18
Streets serving home sites	13
Off-street storm drainage	13

In discussing the factors contributing to the development's success or failure, the study noted:

> Three legal factors were stressed as crucial to association success. First, the developer should set up an automatic homes association before selling the first lot; covenants running with the land should make the assessments collectible as liens. Second, the developer should retain voting control in the association, until most of the lots are sold, at least until enough units have been sold to spread the costs of the common properties and to assure successful merchandising of the remainder without major change in the plans. Third, the assessment maximum must be based on a flexible formula in order that the purchasing power of the maximum assessment may remain constant in spite of inflation. . . .
>
> The most frequent complaint was that the developer failed to set up correct legal provisions for the automatic association and its assessment, particularly in respect to the enforcement of assessments. [Id. at 24]

This complaint, voiced by approximately ten percent of the builders, realtors, and lenders whom the Institute interviewed, was disavowed by all of the attorney respondents. (Id. at 27)

§10.10   A Few (More) Problem Areas

a.   What Covenants Will (Should) Equity Refuse to Enforce Against a Successor with Notice?

HALL v. AMERICAN OIL CO.
504 S.W.2d 313 (Mo. Ct. App. 1973)

GUNN, J. Plaintiffs-appellants appeal from an order of the trial court dismissing both counts of plaintiffs' petition for failure to state a claim upon which relief could be granted. Count I of plaintiffs' petition sought a declaration of plaintiffs' rights in a parcel of land encumbered by a restrictive covenant. Count II of the petition sought money damages by reason of defendants' alleged restraint of trade in violation of Chapter 416 R.S.Mo. 1969, V.A.M.S. The issues to be resolved are whether plaintiffs' petition did state a cause of action against defendants and whether the restrictive covenant imposed is valid. We find that we are unable to determine the rights of all the parties to the action until the matter is put at issue by defendants' answers and evidence presented. We reverse and remand.

The facts are not in dispute. In 1972, plaintiffs filed their petition in the Circuit Court of St. Louis County alleging in Count I that they were owners of certain land which had been conveyed to them by general warranty deed in 1969. Defendant-respondent American Oil Company is the owner of a parcel of land adjacent to plaintiffs' property. Defendants Fred and Estelle Schuepfer had at one time owned the two adjoining parcels of property—that which plaintiffs now own and that which American Oil Company now owns. American Oil Company received its parcel from the Schuepfers by general warranty deed dated October 18, 1965. On October 20, 1965, two days after the conveyance to American Oil Company, an instrument purporting to impose a restriction on the adjacent lot now owned by the Halls, but which at the time was owned by the Schuepfers, was recorded in the office of the St. Louis County Recorder of Deeds. [1] The apparent intent was that when American Oil Company purchased its lot from the Schuepfers, the use of the adjoining lot retained by the Schuepfers and ultimately conveyed to the plaintiffs and the subject of this suit was to be restricted against a gasoline service station. In 1966, the Schuepfers conveyed their property containing the restricted lot to . . . John and Jean Sgonina by general warranty deed. In 1969, the Sgoninas conveyed the restricted lot to the plaintiffs. None of the deeds of conveyance referred to the declaration of restriction, and plaintiffs allege that when they took their property they had no knowledge of any restriction.

Plaintiffs allege that in 1971, as they were preparing to execute a lease on their land to Shell Oil Company for construction of a gasoline service station, they discovered the restriction on their lot. It was further alleged that plaintiffs contacted American Oil Company concerning the restriction and were advised that the restriction had been bargained for as a part of its initial purchase of the adjoining property; that American Oil Company considered the restriction binding on all subsequent grantees of the lot adjacent to its property and refused its release.

American Oil Company has claimed an interest in plaintiffs' lot by reason of the restriction. Plaintiffs allege that American Oil Company's claim is without merit and prayed for the circuit court to try, ascertain and determine the estate, title and interest of the parties in the real estate. The prayer also included a request that plaintiffs be declared fee simple owners and that defendants be enjoined and restrained from asserting any right, title or interest in the property.

Count II of plaintiffs' petition alleged that the Schuepfers and American Oil Company had violated the Missouri Anti-Trust Statutes by their agreement to restrict the lot which plaintiffs now own. [2] Plaintiffs allege that the

---

1. The purported restriction reads as follows:

> Land use hereby restricted against the erection and operation of an Auto Gas Filling Station and the dispensing and sale of Petroleum Products—all conveyances, agreements, leases and options made or given by Fred C. Schuepfer and Estelle H. Schuepfer, his wife, their heirs or assigns of any of the Real Estate herein above described, or any resurvey or subdivision thereof, or any part thereof, is made subject to the aforesaid restrictive covenant, which shall be deemed to run with the land to be kept, observed and performed by said Fred C. Schuepfer and Estelle H. Schuepfer, his wife, their grantees, heirs, executors and assigns and by their respective grantees and assigns for as long as an Auto Filling Station shall be operated on the following described property. . . .

Thereafter follows a description of the property conveyed to American Oil Company.

2. Specifically, plaintiffs allege violation of §416.010 R.S.Mo. 1959, V.A.M.S., which provides:

effect of the restriction prohibits them from leasing their property to Shell Oil Company; that by American Oil Company's refusal to release the restriction, the Halls are restrained in the use of their property in violation of the Missouri anti-trust statutes; that the restriction agreed to by the Schuepfers and American Oil Company, since it is in violation of the anti-trust statutes, is invalid and unenforceable.

In May, 1972, American Oil Company filed a motion to dismiss both counts of plaintiffs' petition for failure to state a claim of action. . . .

On July 31, 1972, the motion to dismiss counts I and II of plaintiffs' petition was sustained, and this appeal followed. . . .

. . . The pivotal underlying issue in this case . . . is whether the covenant purporting to restrict the use of the plaintiffs' property against an automobile gasoline service station is binding upon plaintiffs as subsequent grantees of the property by reason of the covenant being real or personal.[3] We do not have before us sufficient information on which to rest a decision as to the validity of the covenant.

In this case, as to plaintiffs, if the restrictive covenant is ultimately determined to be valid, it is inconsequential whether it is denominated real or personal. If it is a valid real restrictive covenant, it would run with the land and thus bind plaintiffs. If it is to be designated a personal covenant, it would likewise bind plaintiffs, since by its recordation plaintiffs are presumed to have constructive notice of its existence and would be bound thereby; that plaintiffs disavowed knowledge of the existence of the covenant is of no significance. Toothaker v. Pleasant, 315 Mo. 1239, 288 S.W. 38 (1926); Cook v. Tide Water Associated Oil Company, 281 S.W.2d 415 (Mo. App. 1955).

The free and untrammeled use of land is favored and restrictive covenants are to be strictly construed and any doubt as to their validity is to be resolved in favor of the free use of the property. Steve Vogli & Co. v. Lane,

---

Any person who shall create, enter into, become a member of or participate in any pool, trust, agreement, combination, confederation or understanding with any person or persons in restraint of trade or competition in the importation, transportation, manufacture, purchase or sale of any product or commodity in this state, or any article or thing bought or sold whatsoever, shall be deemed and adjudged guilty of a conspiracy in restraint of trade, and shall be punished as provided in sections 416.010 to 416.100, 416.240, 416.260 to 416.290 and 416.400.

3. The distinction is made between real and personal restrictive covenants, the former being those which "touch and concern" or benefit the land and which may run with the land; the latter are those which, as recognized in Tulk v. Moxhay, 2 Phil. C.H. 774, 41 Eng. Rep. 1143 (1848), are personal regarding the use or restriction upon the land between the grantor and grantee, not attaching to the land but binding upon a successor purchaser who purchases with notice, actual or constructive, of the covenant. We forbear the adventure of a full discussion on equitable servitudes and restrictive covenants, as we believe sufficient guidelines have been specified for the trial court to follow in determining the issues in this case. But we note that the trend in other jurisdictions is toward a more liberalized approach in upholding reasonable restrictive covenants as to business enterprises. See Oliver v. Hewitt, 191 Va. 163, 60 S.E.2d 1 (Va. 1950). Cf. Shell Oil Co. v. Henry Ouellette & Sons, Inc., 352 Mass. 725, 227 N.E.2d 509 (Mass. 1967). For detailed discussions on equitable servitudes and personal and real covenants, see 3 Tiffany, Real Property §§848-857 (3rd ed. 1939); 9 Ariz. L. Rev. 441 (1967-68); 41 Va. L. Rev. 675 (1955); Annot., 23 A.L.R.2d 520-531 (1952).

405 S.W.2d 885 (Mo. 1966); Pellegrini v. Fournie, 501 S.W.2d 564 (Mo. App. 1973) (No. 34,859). But that is not to say that a covenant of the type in this case, ostensibly imposing a land restriction upon subsequent grantees of the land so encumbered, would necessarily be invalid, particularly where the covenant has been recorded. Such was the case in Cook v. Tide Water Associated Oil Company, *supra.* However, in order for such a covenant to be valid in Missouri, it must not transgress certain standards, for restrictions in derogation of the fee are not favored. Kerrick v. Schoenberg, 328 S.W.2d 595 (Mo. 1959); Dean v. Monteil, 361 Mo. 1204, 239 S.W.2d 337 (1951). Dean v. Monteil, *supra,* found that a restrictive covenant protecting business interests was void as against public policy and did not run with the land or apply to subsequent purchasers of the property upon which the restrictive covenant was to have attached. The court, in quoting from Mallinckrodt Chemical Works v. Nemnich, 83 Mo. App. 6 (1899), at pages 14 and 16, stated:

> "The general doctrine is that agreements in restriction of trade will be upheld when the restriction does not go beyond some particular locality, is founded on a sufficient consideration, and is limited as to time, place and person." . . . "This class of contracts is always regarded with suspicion by the courts, as their effect usually is to create a monopoly, and before any one of them will be upheld, it should clearly appear that no monopoly is created by it; that its enforcement will not prejudice the public; that it is reasonable as to time, space and person, not oppressive or injurious, and that the contract is founded on a good consideration, and that its enforcement will be useful and beneficial to the promisee." [4]

This same principle was adopted in Kerrick v. Schoenberg, *supra,* where a restrictive covenant similar to that involved in this case recited: "The seller agrees not to sell any of the present holdings of land in this area for other gasoline filling stations." The same standards as set forth in Mallinckrodt Chemical Works v. Nemnich, *supra,* and Dean v. Monteil, *supra,* were repeated with the court in *Kerrick* finding:

> We deem the provision in the contract under consideration, purporting indefinitely to restrict against any sale of any part of defendants' adjoining lands for

---

4. An update and more definite portrayal of the standards recited in Mallinckrodt Chemical Works v. Nemnich, *supra,* can be found in the California case of Doo v. Packwood, 265 Cal. App. 2d 752, 71 Cal. Rptr. 477, 480 (Dist. Ct. App. 1962):

> "While the courts have manifested some disfavor of covenants restricting the use of property, they have generally sustained them where reasonable, not contrary to public policy or to law, and not in restraint of trade or for the purpose of creating a monopoly. Restrictions per se are not violative of the public good, inimical to public policy, or subversive of the public interests, and it has been said that building restrictions have never been regarded as impolitic. However, a restriction imposed on property conveyed may be invalid if it contravenes some constitutional or statutory provision, or where it is of no benefit to anyone and its enforcement might seriously interfere with the proper development of the community, and restrictions which amount to a prohibition of use of the property are void. Subject to these limitations, the court will enforce restrictions to the same extent that it would lend judicial sanction to any other valid contractual relationship. So long as the beneficial enjoyment of the estate is not materially impaired and the public good and interests are not violated, such restrictions are valid."

use of any other filling station, to be void as in restraint of trade and as against public policy, and that it is not a covenant running with the adjoining land of the defendants, nor any charge or encumbrance thereon, and has no place in the contract or in the deed to which plaintiff is entitled. (1. c. 602 of 328 S.W.2d)

Thus, from the *Mallinckrodt* case, Dean v. Monteil and Kerrick v. Schoenberg,[5] we have standards set forth upon which a court may determine whether a covenant of the type in this case may be valid. We cannot in this complex case on the naked pleading before us make determination whether the restrictive covenant can stand. It is essential that there be evidence touching on each of the criterion elicited. The guidelines set forth in the early Missouri case of Skrainka v. Scharringhausen, 8 Mo. App. 522, 525 (1880), are also appropriate:

> . . . Where the contract injures the parties making it by diminishing their means for supporting their families, tends to deprive the public of the services of useful men, discourages industry, diminishes production, prevents competition, enhances prices, and, being made by large companies or corporations, excludes rivalry and engrosses the market . . . it is against the policy of the law. But restraints upon trade imposed by agreement, under limitations as to locality, time, and persons, are not necessarily restraints of trade in the general sense which is objectionable.

Also, from Kerrick v. Schoenberg, *supra,* is the required finding that the contract establishing the restrictive covenant be based on good consideration. We have no evidence of a contract before us in this case, and this facet should be developed.

The time factor requires comment. We do not regard the time limitation "so long as an auto filling station shall be operated on" American Oil Company's property necessarily oppressive. Such a time limitation can be compatible with the purposes of the covenant and in many instances less onerous as a burden on property than a restriction for years where the purpose of the restriction ceases to exist and the restriction would be no longer purposeful. Shepherd v. Spurgeon, 365 Mo. 989, 291 S.W.2d 162 (1956) (100 Year Restriction ruled unreasonable). An indefinite time restriction was approved in Cook v. Tide Water Associated Oil Co., *supra.* Whether the type of time limitation sought to be imposed in this case would be proper will depend on the facts developed. If the indefinite time limitation is approved, but it should later develop that it has become unreasonable or burdensome, the property owner of the servient tenement would not be precluded from bringing an action for the removal of the condition based on a change of circumstances. Marks v. Bettendorf's Inc., 337 S.W.2d 585 (Mo. App. 1960).

Thus, using the patterns referred to in the recited cases, such as contract consideration, reasonableness as to time, space and person, monopolistic con-

---

5. The *Dean* and *Kerrick* cases involved attempted restrictions on 35 and 600 acres of land, respectively.

siderations and usefulness and benefit to the benefactor of the covenant, surrounding business and competitive conditions, and effect on public policy, the case should be referred to the trial court for evidence on such guidelines. Without such evidence, we are unable to determine how this case harmonizes with the standards of Dean v. Monteil, *supra,* Kerrick v. Schoenberg, *supra,* Cook v. Tide Water Associated Oil Company, and Mallinckrodt Chemical Works v. Nemnich, *supra.* More is needed.

It is charged in Count II of plaintiffs' petition—although, as confessed by plaintiffs, inelegantly drawn—that American Oil Company bargained for the restriction on plaintiffs' property, the effect of which was to violate the Missouri anti-trust statutes by restricting the use of plaintiffs' property against a gasoline filling station when plaintiffs had a lessee available for such purpose. The facts alleged are marginally sufficient to establish a cause of action. Reisenbichler v. Marquette Cement Co., 341 Mo. 744, 108 S.W.2d 343 (1937). Plaintiffs should be permitted to develop their anti-trust case also, and whether a violation exists will depend on the evidence presented.

The judgment is, accordingly, reversed and remanded for trial.

SMITH, P.J., and SIMEONE and KELLY, JJ., concur.

NOTES AND QUESTIONS

1. At the retrial, you are the plaintiffs' (defendant's) attorney. What forms of evidence would you present to persuade the court that the restriction is invalid (valid)?

2. If the court were to deem the restriction invalid as it concerned the plaintiff who acquired the servient estate with notice, would the restriction have been similarly unenforceable against Schuepfer, the original covenantor?

3. In Norcross v. James, 140 Mass. 188, 2 N.E. 946 (1885), Justice Holmes, writing for the court, described a covenant (in favor of a quarry operator) that barred a fee owner from quarrying on his farm, as seeking to create "an easement of monopoly"; his court denied enforcement. Antagonism to such covenants, treating them as invalid per se, persisted. See Shade v. M. O'Keefe, Inc., 260 Mass. 180, 156 N.E. 867 (1927) (covenant barring fee owner from carrying on grocery business). The opinion in Shell Oil Co. v. Henry Ouellette & Sons, 352 Mass. 725, 731, 227 N.E.2d 509, 513 (1967), first questioned the absolutist view, and the court in Whitinsville Plaza, Inc. v. Kotseas, 390 N.E.2d 243, 250 (Mass. 1979), finally overruled *Norcross* and *Shade,* bringing Massachusetts in line with her sister states.

4. A sells land to B and covenants not to sell petroleum products for fifty years on any other land A still owns within a radius of 2500 feet. In a suit to enforce the covenant, A's successor—after an unsuccessful argument that the promise binds only A—contends that the restriction bars competition and offends public policy. The court rejects the contention, citing the rule that a restriction reasonable with respect both to territory involved and to duration is

not monopolistic. What is reasonable territory? Reasonable time? Silverstein v. Shell Oil Co., 40 A.D.2d 34, 337 N.Y.S.2d 442 (3d Dept. 1972), *aff'd*, 33 N.Y.2d 950 (1974).

5. As you saw earlier, leasehold covenants restricting competition appear routinely. Should their enforceability be governed by standards any different from those that restrict the owner of a fee? Compare Restatement (Second) of Property §13.2, Comment b (1977).

PRATTE v. BALATSOS

99 N.H. 430, 113 A.2d 492 (1955)

Bill in Equity, seeking "a decree permanently enjoining the defendant from breaching an agreement" between the plaintiff and Albert Larochelle, former proprietor of a business now conducted by the defendant in Manchester, which related to the use and operation of the plaintiff's coin-operated record player and related equipment in the place of business. The bill also sought a temporary order restraining the defendant from removing the record player from the premises.

A temporary injunction was issued. Thereafter, following a hearing on the merits before Grant, J. the injunction was dissolved and the bill dismissed. . . . The Court ruled that the defendant "was not bound by the terms of the contract . . . and that [the plaintiff's] remedy lies against Larochelle."

To this ruling the plaintiff duly excepted. . . .

DUNCAN, J. The terms of the contract between the plaintiff and Larochelle are not in dispute. It provided that in return for payment of forty percent of the income from the record player the plaintiff might install it in "a permanent and convenient part of [Larochelle's] place of business" and that "said machine shall be operated during the term of this Agreement [14 years and six months] and that no similar equipment nor any other kind of coin-operated machine will be installed or operated on said premises by anyone else." Thus it was intended by the parties to the agreement that the plaintiff should have exclusive rights to operate such a record player at the location in question in connection with the conduct of Larochelle's business there.

Neither the bill of sale from Larochelle to the defendant under date of November 2, 1953, nor the contract of purchase and sale which preceded it, referred to the record player or the contract with Larochelle of September 19, 1952, relating to it. The bill of sale purported to convey "an assignment of the lease [of the premises] dated April 1, 1947." No attempt was made to assign the Larochelle contract to the defendant nor did the defendant expressly assume Larochelle's obligations under it.

On the other hand, the defendant conceded at the trial that he knew that the record player was under contract with the plaintiff and that he took it into account as a source of income in evaluating the business. He testified that some fifteen days after the sale he learned for the first time that the plaintiff would allow him only forty percent of the income. Under date of November 20, 1953, he notified the plaintiff to remove the machine within seven days, and a like notice was given by his attorneys on February 3, 1954.

The plaintiff takes the position that because of the finding that the defendant had notice of the existence of a contract with the former owner when he bought the business, the defendant is bound by the agreement. . . . The extent to which the defendant may be charged with obligations arising out of the contract made by his predecessor in the business depends upon the nature of the rights created by the contract. No claim is made that the contract constituted a lease to the plaintiff. He hired no specific space within the premises leased to Larochelle, and no intention to create the relationship of landlord and tenant is suggested by the language of the document. . . . Neither can it be said that the parties intended a revocable license, for the obvious purpose was to confer rights to operate the machine for a specified term. If as a matter of law the plaintiff acquired only a revocable license, specific performance would be futile and the plaintiff was properly remitted to his action for damages for breach of contract. [24]

"The alternative antithesis of 'licenses' and 'leases' tends to cause a court to feel bound to label the transaction before it one or the other of the two, rather than to realize it has three choices, namely, lease, license or easement." 3 Powell on Real Property, 430. . . .

By reason of the agreement with Larochelle, the plaintiff may be considered to have acquired a right that he specifically perform. The question is presented whether that right which is in the nature of an equitable servitude is enforceable against the defendant as successor to Larochelle's interest with notice of the existence of the contract. Equitable restrictions are recognized in this jurisdiction and held to be binding upon a purchaser of the servient tenement with notice. . . . No decisions of this court involving restrictions in gross, and personal to the covenantee have come or been called to our attention. The defendant contends that the contract in question cannot be enforced as a restrictive covenant because it plainly does not run with the land and is essentially affirmative rather than negative in its undertaking. The plaintiff contends that it is in the nature of a covenant running with the business and should be binding on that account, even though the contract was never assigned to the defendant. The situation is analogous to that presented by the early English cases involving "tied" houses, and holding that covenants for the purchase of beverages exclusively from one brewer were "for the benefit of the business" and enforceable against an underlessee with notice. John Brothers etc. Co. v. Holmes [1900] 1 Ch. 188; Luker v. Dennis, 7 Ch. D. 227; Catt v. Tourle, L.R. 4 Ch. App. 654. It has been pointed out that these decisions would not be followed in England today in view of the decision in London County Council v. Allen [1914] 3 K.B. 642. See II American Law of Property, 428, s. 9.32. However this result has been criticized as "illogical," and the

---

24. When would a licensee be entitled to damages from the licensor based upon license revocation?—Ed.

enforcement in this country of equitable servitudes in gross is "commended" by the author of the cited text. Id., 430. See also, Clark, Covenants and Interests Running with Land (2nd ed.) 104, note 36, 181, 182. In an article entitled "Equitable Liabilities of Strangers," the late Chief Justice Stone, then Dean Stone, viewed the English tendency as "unfortunate," (19 Col. L.R. 191) and earlier reached the conclusion that if the plaintiff has an equitable right which equity will enforce by compelling the covenantor to perform, thus giving the plaintiff a property right, then "equity should not deny relief merely because the result of a specific performance does not fall within one of the categories of property recognized as such by the courts of common law." 18 Col. L.R. 291, 313-314. In Pomeroy, Equity Jurisprudence, s. 1295, it is said that the doctrine that a purchaser with notice of a covenant with respect to the use of land takes subject to the covenant may be explained "by regarding the covenant as creating an equitable easement." The doctrine extends to affirmative covenants (Id., pp. 851, 852), and restrictive covenants creating equitable easements may be "specifically enforced in equity by means of an injunction, not only between the immediate parties, but also against subsequent purchasers with notice, even when the covenants are not of the kind which technically run with the land." Id., s. 1342.

The absence of any finding by the Trial Court concerning the effect of the defendant's knowledge of the existence of the Larochelle contract suggests that the ruling that the defendant was not bound by it was made as a matter of law. On the other hand, the decree may imply a finding that the defendant was not chargeable with notice of its terms. Under these circumstances the case will be returned to the Superior Court for an amendment, or for a new trial the extent of which will be for the Trial Court. . . .

Whether the defendant had such notice as to put him upon inquiry as to the terms of the contract, see Rochester Poster Advertising Co. v. Smithers, 224 App. Div. 435, 231 N.Y.S. 315, *supra,* and what such inquiry would probably have disclosed, Janvrin v. Janvrin, 60 N.H. 169; Dame v. Fernald, 86 N.H. 468, 472, 171 A. 369, must be determined before the defendant's responsibility with respect to the contract can be fixed. If the Court intended by its decree to imply a finding that the notice was insufficient to subject the defendant to the plaintiff's rights, the decree may stand. If not, the facts should be found; and if the defendant is bound by the agreement, an injunction may issue in the Court's discretion. . . .

Remanded.

All concurred except KENISON, C.J., who was of the opinion that the plaintiff's exceptions should be overruled.

NOTE

The late Zechariah Chafee was appalled by the *Pratte* decision and excoriated it in Chafee, The Music Goes Round and Round: Equitable Servitudes and Chattels, 69 Harv. L. Rev. 1250 (1956). In Professor Chafee's view, the servitude was not a restriction on the use of land, to which the policies (query: what are these?) of Tulk v. Moxhay might apply, but was, instead, a restriction on the defendant's business, to which other policies should apply (69 Harv. L. Rev. at 1258):

> [I]s it desirable for their agreement to be carried out to the extent of making it bind a man who never signed it? . . . The big point is that the imposition of a novel burden, either on land or a chattel or both, ought not to depend solely on the will of the parties. The validity or invalidity of the burden they want to create ought to depend on considerations of public policy. Do business needs make it desirable to create this novel burden? Does its enforcement involve such grave possibilities of annoyance, inconvenience, and useless expenditure of money that it should not be allowed? In other words, is the game worth the candle?
>
> The real issue is whether there are strong reasons for requiring the occupant of a restaurant or similar place of business to keep a juke box there for fourteen and a half years if he does not want it. Would it not be a good idea for judges to get away for a time from old learning about easements or servitudes and instead imagine that they are listening to a juke box? Suppose that it is in a restaurant conveniently close to the courthouse where the judges like to lunch because of the good food. Will they have to go on listening to popular music for years and years when the proprietor would be delighted to get rid of the juke box and give the judges and other diners a chance to talk with each other? If for fourteen and a half years, why stop there? Does the Rule Against Perpetuities apply? Why not a hundred years? Let us assume that a man starts a restaurant on a small scale and puts in a juke box for the enjoyment of patrons of such establishments. He sells out. The new owner does better and better. He wants to redecorate and have his place the best restaurant in town. A juke box is a fatal obstacle to his ambition. So long as it stays there many of the kind of people whom he wants will stay away. Now that the United States Supreme Court holds that we are obliged to listen to music we dislike in trolley cars and busses, can't we at lease enjoy the luxury of a peaceful meal? I confess that I see no strong public policy in permitting the manufacturer of these raucous devices to prevent an enterprising American citizen from creating the kind of restaurant which he wants and which a good many consumers of food would be delighted to have.

One should never treat too lightly the influence of the professorial pen. On the remand of Pratte v. Balatsos, the trial court rendered judgment for plaintiff, after finding that defendant should have been on inquiry notice as to the terms of the original contract. By this time, the Chafee article was in print, and defendant relied heavily upon it in arguing his appeal. 101 N.H. 48, 49, 132 A.2d 142, 143 (1957): "The defendant urged in effect that we overrule our previous opinion . . . and in so doing he relies mainly on an article on 'Equitable Servitudes and Chattels'. . . . Reexamination of (the) decision in the light of the article convinces us there is no reason to do so."

TUCKERTON BEACH CLUB V. BENDER
91 N.J. Super. 167, 219 A.2d 529 (1966)

SULLIVAN, S.J.A.D. This case, in essence, involves the validity of certain restrictions and covenants contained in the deeds of some 500 property owners in a development known as Tuckerton Beach, Ocean County, New Jersey. The covenants and restrictions are as follows:

> All property owners in this development are required to be members of a property owners' association known or to be known as "Tuckerton Beach Club" or similar name and to faithfully abide by its rules. No sale, resale or rental of any property in Tuckerton Beach shall be made to any person or group of persons who are, have been, or would be disapproved for membership by the said club.
>
> Being a private club, the Tuckerton Beach Club shall make such rules as it deems necessary pertaining to persons eligible for membership and any other rules or regulations it chooses.
>
> The Tuckerton Beach Club shall each year collect from its bona fide member lot owners or lot lessees the sum of Twenty Five ($25.00) Dollars per lot owned or leased by each member, except as modified by Charter membership privilege as hereinafter defined.
>
> One half the yearly charges thus made are to be paid yearly to Tuckerton Beach, a corporation, the beach owners, as yearly consideration and payment for the use of the Club House and bathing beach and lagoon to be leased to the Tuckerton Beach Club.
>
> The use of the Club House and bathing beaches designated on plan of Tuckerton Beach are for the exclusive use of members in good standing of the Tuckerton Beach Club and/or guests, and/or tenants of such members.
>
> The Tuckerton Beach Club shall lease on long term the bathing beaches, Club House area and Club House designated on plan of Tuckerton Beach, from the owners of said beaches, areas and buildings. . . .
>
> All covenants contained herein are to run with the land and shall be binding on all parties and persons claiming under them until January 1, 2000, at which time the said covenants shall automatically extend for an additional period of fifty (50) years, unless by vote of the majority of the members of the Tuckerton Beach Club it is agreed to change said covenants in whole or in part.

Under the original by-laws of the club, the membership committee, consisting of three club members, had absolute discretion to admit or reject any application for club membership. In July 1964, during the pendency of the present suit, the club adopted or attempted to adopt an amendment to the by-laws which would make merely a properly completed application to the club and the payment of the first year's dues the sole requirement for membership.

The Tuckerton Beach development was commenced in 1955 and continued until 1960 when the various developers went into bankruptcy. In 1961 a group of property owners took over the club and since then have attempted to revitalize the project. It is asserted that the success or failure of the club and its ability to furnish beach facilities, club house and other improvements, depend on each property owner in the development being required to belong to the club and pay the annual dues specified in the covenants and restrictions set forth in the deeds. When defendants refused to become members of the club and to pay the annual dues of $25, the instant suit was commenced to enforce the aforesaid deed provisions. Defendants counterclaimed to have said provisions declared void.

The trial court held that the covenants and restrictions under the original club by-laws would be clearly void. The court also expressed doubts as to the efficacy of the July 1964 attempted amendment. However, the court determined that it would declare the deed covenants and restrictions to be valid "provided" that plaintiff club within 60 days amended its constitution and by-laws to provide that admission to the club could be had by anyone who filed an application and paid the first year's dues; "membership shall not in any wise be conditioned upon any vote on any other factor or any approval by any membership committee or otherwise." This was done, and a final judgment was then entered declaring the covenants and restrictions in the deed to be valid and binding and requiring defendants to pay to plaintiff club the sum of $25 per year for each year since 1961.

We conclude that the covenants and restrictions are void on their face. They prohibit sale, resale or rental to anyone who "would be disapproved for membership" in the club. They provide that the club shall make such rules as it deems necessary "pertaining to persons eligible for membership." Manifestly, these provisions indicate that the property may be conveyed only to persons who would be approved for membership and eligible for membership under such rules as the club might in its discretion see fit to adopt. These provisions, as written, contain an unreasonable restraint on alienation, are against public policy and are void. Mountain Springs Association of New Jersey, Inc. v. Wilson, 81 N.J. Super. 564, 196 A.2d 270 (Ch. Div. 1963). The amendments attempted in 1964 while suit was pending, and in 1965 pursuant to the court's ruling, cannot breathe life into them. The provision requiring payment of $25 annual dues is so inextricably interwoven with the invalid restraints upon alienation that it must likewise fall.

The judgment herein in favor of plaintiff is reversed and the matter remanded for entry of judgment in favor of defendants declaring the covenants and restrictions in question to be null and void. No costs on this appeal.

NOTES AND QUESTIONS

1. Would the membership requirements have been enforceable if the 1964 and 1965 amendments had been in effect when the beach club brought its suit?

2. Would the covenants have been enforceable had they conditioned membership solely upon the property owner's financial responsibility? Suppose that Tuckerton Beach were a condominium development.

3. Compare White Egret Condominium, Inc. v. Franklin, 379 So. 2d 346 (Fla. 1979). The condominium agreement restricted residency by children under the age of twelve. Does such a restriction violate a purchaser's constitutional rights to marriage, procreation, and association? See Doyle, Retirement Communities: The Nature and Enforceability of Residential Segregation by Age, 76 Mich. L. Rev. 64 (1977).

4. In 1908, six lots are restricted to private residential use. In 1971, a religious group buys a dwelling house on a restricted lot and converts it into a parochial school for sixty students. In a neighbor's suit to enforce the restriction, the defendant argues that a state court injunction would prevent the free exercise of religion and, on the analogy to Shelley v. Kraemer, would violate the Fourteenth Amendment. Result? Ginsberg v. Yeshiva of Far Rockaway, 45 A.D.2d 334, 358 N.Y.S.2d 477 (2d Dept. 1974), aff'd, 36 N.Y.2d 706, 325 N.E.2d 876 (1975).

b. May a Covenant Be Implied?

SANBORN v. McLEAN
233 Mich. 227, 206 N.W. 496 (1925)

Wiest, J. Defendant Christina McLean owns the west 35 feet of lot 86 of Green Lawn subdivision, at the northwest corner of Collingwood avenue and Second boulevard, in the city of Detroit, upon which there is a dwelling house, occupied by herself and her husband, defendant John A. McLean. The house fronts Collingwood avenue. At the rear of the lot is an alley. Mrs. McLean derived title from her husband, and, in the course of the opinion, we will speak of both as defendants. Mr. and Mrs. McLean started to erect a gasoline filling station at the rear end of their lot, and they and their contractor, William S. Weir, were enjoined by decree from doing so and bring the issues before us by appeal. Mr. Weir will not be further mentioned in the opinion.

Collingwood avenue is a high grade residence street between Woodward avenue and Hamilton boulevard, with single, double, and apartment houses, and plaintiffs, who are owners of land adjoining and in the vicinity of defendants' land, and who trace title, as do defendants, to the proprietors of the subdivision, claim that the proposed gasoline station will be a nuisance per se, is in violation of the general plan fixed for use of all lots on the street for residence purposes only, as evidenced by restrictions upon 53 of the 91 lots fronting on Collingwood avenue, and that defendants' lot is subject to a reciprocal negative easement barring a use so detrimental to the enjoyment and value of its neighbors. Defendants insist that no restrictions appear in their chain of title and they purchased without notice of any reciprocal negative easement, and deny that a gasoline station is a nuisance per se. We find no occasion to pass upon the question of nuisance, as the case can be decided under the rule of reciprocal negative easement.

This subdivision was planned strictly for residence purposes, except lots fronting Woodward avenue and Hamilton boulevard. The 91 lots on Collingwood avenue were platted in 1891, designed for and each one sold solely for residence purposes, and residences have been erected upon all of the lots. Is defendants' lot subject to a reciprocal negative easement? If the owner of two or more lots, so situated as to bear the relation, sells one with restrictions of benefit to the land retained, the servitude becomes mutual, and, during the period of restraint, the owner of the lot or lots retained can do nothing forbidden to the owner of the lot sold. For want of a better descriptive term this is styled a reciprocal negative easement. It runs with the land sold by virtue of express fastening and abides with the land retained until loosened by expiration of its period of service or by events working its destruction. It is not personal to owners, but operative upon use of the land by any owner having actual or constructive notice thereof. It is an easement passing its benefits and carrying its obligations to all purchasers of land, subject to its affirmative or negative mandates. It originates for mutual benefit and exists with vigor sufficient to work its ends. It must start with a common owner. Reciprocal negative easements are never retroactive; the very nature of their origin forbids. They arise, if at all, out of a benefit accorded land retained, by restrictions upon neighboring land sold by a common owner. Such a scheme of restriction must start with a common owner; it cannot arise and fasten upon one lot by reason of other lot owners conforming to a general plan. If a reciprocal negative easement attached to defendants' lot, it was fastened thereto while in the hands of the common owner of it and neighboring lots by way of sale of other lots with restrictions beneficial at that time to it. This leads to inquiry as to what lots, if any, were sold with restrictions by the common owner before the sale of defendants' lot. While the proofs cover another avenue, we need consider sales only on Collingwood.

December 28, 1892, Robert J. and Joseph R. McLaughlin, who were then evidently owners of the lots on Collingwood avenue, deeded lots 37 to 41 and 58 to 62, inclusive, with the following restrictions: "No residence shall be erected upon said premises which shall cost less than $2500, and nothing but residences shall be erected upon said premises. Said residences shall front on Helene (now Collingwood) avenue and be placed no nearer than 20 feet from the front street line."

July 24, 1893, the McLaughlins conveyed lots 17 to 21 and 78 to 82, both inclusive, and lot 98 with the same restrictions. Such restrictions were imposed for the benefit of the lands held by the grantors to carry out the scheme of a residential district, and a restrictive negative easement attached to the lots retained, and title to lot 86 was then in the McLaughlins. Defendants' title, through mesne conveyances, runs back to a deed by the McLaughlins dated September 7, 1893, without restrictions mentioned therein. Subsequent deeds to other lots were executed by the McLaughlins, some with restrictions and some without. Previous to September 7, 1893, a reciprocal negative easement had attached to lot 86 by acts of the owners, as before mentioned, and such easement is still attached and may now be enforced by plaintiffs, provided defendants, at the time of their purchase, had knowledge, actual or constructive, thereof. The plaintiffs run back with their title, as do defendants, to a common owner. This common owner, as before stated, by restrictions upon lots sold, had burdened all the lots retained with reciprocal restrictions. Defendants' lot and plaintiff Sanborn's lot, next thereto, were held by such common owner, burdened with a reciprocal negative easement, and, when later sold to separate parties, remained burdened therewith, and right to demand observance thereof passed to each purchaser with notice of the easement. The restrictions were upon defendants' lot while it was in the hands of the common owners, and abstract of title to defendants' lot showed the common owners, and the record showed deeds of lots in the plat restricted to perfect and carry out the general plan and resulting in a reciprocal negative easement upon defendants' lot and all lots within its scope, and defendants and their predecessors in title were bound by constructive notice under our recording acts. The original plan was repeatedly declared in subsequent sales of lots by restrictions in the deeds, and, while some lots sold were not so restricted, the purchasers thereof, in every instance, observed the general plan and purpose of the restrictions in building residences. For upward of 30 years the united efforts of all persons interested have carried out the common purpose of making and keeping all the lots strictly for residences, and defendants are the first to depart therefrom.

When Mr. McLean purchased on contract in 1910 or 1911, there was a partly built dwelling house on lot 86, which he completed and now occupies. He had an abstract of title which he examined and claims he was told by the grantor that the lot was unrestricted. Considering the character of use made of all the lots open to a view of Mr. McLean when he purchased, we think, he was put thereby to inquiry, beyond asking his grantor, whether there were restrictions. He had an abstract showing the subdivision and that lot 86 had 97 companions. He could not avoid noticing the strictly uniform residence character given the lots by the expensive dwellings thereon, and the least inquiry would have quickly developed the fact that lot 86 was subjected to a reciprocal negative easement, and he could finish his house, and, like the others, enjoy the benefits of the easement. We do not say Mr. McLean should have asked his neighbors about restrictions, but we do say that with the notice he had from a view of the premises on the street, clearly indicating the residences were built and the lots occupied in strict accordance with a general plan, he was put to inquiry, and, had he inquired, he would have found of record the reason for such general conformation, and the benefits thereof serving the owners of lot 86 and the obligations running with such service and available to adjacent lot owners to prevent a departure from the general plan by an owner of lot 86. . . .

We notice the decree in the circuit directed that the work done on the building be torn down. If the portion of the building constructed can be utilized for any purpose within the restrictions, it need not be destroyed.

With this modification, the decree in the circuit is affirmed, with costs to plaintiffs.

NOTES AND QUESTIONS

1. Under the reasoning of Sanborn v. McLean, is it necessary for the residential scheme to have been decided upon when the first lot is sold? Compare Bristol v. Woodward, 251 N.Y. 275, 283, 167 N.E. 441, 444 (1929) ("A scheme for uniform improvement, if it is to lay the basis for the implication of reciprocal restrictions on the part of a grantor, must at least have been made known to the [first] grantee, and that definitely and clearly.").

2. Compare Sanborn v. McLean with Steinmann v. Silverman, 14 N.Y.2d 243, 200 N.E.2d 192, 251 N.Y.S.2d 1 (1964). Between 1947 and 1955, O conveyed twenty parcels adjoining Treasure Lake to various persons, including plaintiff. Each deed restricted the plot to a single residence. In 1957, O sold a nearby parcel to defendant, whose deed carried the same restriction. Defendant's parcel already held a house and barn. When defendant began to convert the barn into the second dwelling on the parcel, plaintiff sued to enforce the restriction. The court of appeals (three judges dissenting) overturned the lower court injunction, finding no common scheme with respect to the covenant.

O had never filed a map in the county clerk's office, although he had prepared a map showing the development of numerous parcels. Evidently O did not show the map to any purchaser. The court stressed that only four of O's deeds referred to a development plan, that the parcels were of varying shapes and sizes and spread out in no discernible pattern, and that (concurring opinion) O retained the privilege to decide as he went along where to fix the lot lines.

See also Lewis v. Spies, 43 A.D.2d 714, 350 N.Y.S.2d 14 (2d Dept. 1973).

§10.11   The Neighborhood Scheme

Protective covenants in subdivision development. One of the early privately planned subdivisions, as we would use that term today, appeared at Riverside, Illinois, in 1871. Land there was sold "only to an absolute settler who [would] agree to build immediately or within one year from the time of purchase, a home costing at least $3000, to be located thirty feet back from the front of the lot line, which thirty feet [was to] be retained as an open court or dooryard." By the 1910s, with tract development now the fashion, deed restrictions based on the developer's plan were appearing routinely: understandably so, for public controls such as zoning and subdivision approval did not yet exist. As late as 1925, a widely regarded city planner wrote: "It is the Realtor subdivider who is really planning our cities today, who is the actual city planner in practice." City Planning and Unbuilt Outlying Areas, 3 Annals of Real Estate Practice

[TABLE 8]

Form of Restriction		Number of Restricted Subdivisions (of 84)
Business or Trade Prohibited		48
All business barred	31	
Business on specified lots	16	
Manufacturing barred	1	
Type of Residential Improvement		73
Single-family residences only	45	
Single-family residences except on specified lots	8	
"Dwellings"	4	
"Private dwellings"	2	
Various on specified lots	3	
Apartments on specified lots	4	
Single- and two-family residences	3	
Other	4	
Height of Buildings		18
Approval of Building Plans		41
Required by seller	33	
Required by homes assn.	3	
Required by art jury & homes assn.	1	
Other	4	
Minimum Cost of Buildings		61
Building Lines		70
Lot Frontage		7
30–35 foot minimum	1	
40–45 foot minimum	3	
50 foot minimum	2	
60 foot minimum	1	
Public Areas		18
Title reserved by seller	16	
Seller will improve and maintain	1	
Riparian rights reserved	1	
Restrictions on Alienation		39*
"Caucasians only" (covenant)	19	
"Caucasians only" (condition)	8	
Negroes barred	4	
Africans, Mongolians barred	3	
Seller must approve	2	
Others	3	

[Cont.]

[TABLE 8 continued]

Form of Restriction		Number of Restricted Subdivisions (of 84)
Restrictions on Occupancy		37
"Caucasians only" (covenant)	18	
"Caucasians only" (condition)	7	
Negroes barred	4	
Africans, Mongolians barred	2	
Seller must approve	2	
Others	4	
Duration of Restrictions		
Original term		52
Average duration		
Ante-1920 cases—39.7 years		
Post-1920 cases—31.1 years		
Provisions for extensions		23
Maintenance Charges		26
Administered by seller	6	
Owners' assn.	6	
Other or not shown	14	

*Of the 55 cases post-1920, 38 contained restrictions; of the 29 cases ante-1920, 1 contained restrictions.

Source: Adapted from Monchow, The Use of Deed Restrictions in Subdivision Development (Inst. for Research in Land Economics and Public Utilities 1928).

247 (1925). Substitute the word "Builder" for "Realtor," and move the scene to suburban America, and one might fairly ask to what extent this statement would still be true today.

In 1928, the Institute for Research in Land Economics and Public Utilities published an analysis of the restrictions appearing in eighty-four residential subdivisions located throughout the country, including such distinguished tracts as Roland Park (Baltimore), Shaker Heights (Cleveland), St. Frances Wood (San Francisco), and Palos Verdes Estates (near Los Angeles). About one third of the tract examples antedated 1920; the remaining tracts were developed during the 1920s. A summary of their deed provisions appears in Table 8, and permits comparison with the controls suggested in a recent FHA model of protective covenants, *infra.* H. Monchow, The Use of Deed Restrictions in Subdivision Development (1928). Despite its age, this study may still be the latest well-publicized attempt to examine the actual content of neighborhood restrictions.

Model subdivision covenant provisions. "Attractive developments are not assured of continuing appeal and stability unless protective covenants prevent inharmonious or injurious future use of individual properties." These words, appearing in an FHA-prepared guidebook for developers, express an official view that few builders or homeowners would dissent from. Today, standard equipment for a residential subdivision (or an industrial park) includes not only roads and water mains, but also an elaborately drawn (boiler-plate?) set of tract restrictions. A sample version approved by the FHA follows, along with that agency's commentary. As you examine the covenants, consider also what is meant by the FHA's further assertion:

> In zoned communities protective covenants are an important supplementary aid in maintaining neighborhood character and values. The extent of zoning protection is limited to governmental exercise of police powers of maintaining and promoting public health, safety, and welfare. Protective covenants being agreements between private parties can go much further in meeting the needs of a particular neighborhood and in providing maximum possible protection.

What are the respective roles of private agreement (developer's will?) and public control in fixing patterns of land use? What should be their roles? You will have occasion to reconsider the paragraph above as you move into Chapters 13 et seq.

F.H.A., LAND PLANNING BULLETIN NO. 3
(rev. April 1959)

PROTECTIVE COVENANTS FOR DEVELOPMENTS OF SINGLE-FAMILY DETACHED DWELLINGS

This information is offered as a general guide to sponsors who desire to obtain for individual properties maximum protection against inharmonious land uses.

Protective covenants are essential to the sound development of proposed residential areas. Covenants properly prepared and legally sound contribute to the establishment of the character of a neighborhood and to the maintenance of value levels through the regulation of type, size and placement of buildings, lot sizes, reservation of easements, and prohibition of nuisances and other land uses that might affect the desirability of a residential area. . . .

Development sponsors should have their protective covenants drafted by legal counsel. The preliminary draft of the covenants should be submitted to FHA for comment at the same time the sponsor presents his preliminary subdivision plan to FHA for comment.

The proper form of protective covenants varies in the different states. A generally acceptable and enforceable form is written declaration by the owner of the entire tract which is recorded in land office records. Frequently in smaller complete developments, the covenants and conditions are stated on the recorded map. When a separate declaration is made it is good practive to record it simultaneously with the recordation of the subdivision map.

The written declaration of covenants is a preferable form of establishing a uniform scheme for the development and protection of the entire area. Piecemeal control by inserting covenants in individual deeds at the time properties are conveyed is not conducive to harmonious development.

Sample Clauses and Detail Covenants

Part A. Preamble
(Include the date, purposes, names and addresses of all parties and legal descriptions of all lands involved.)

Part B. Area of Application
B-1.   Fully-protected Residential Area. The residential area covenants in Part C in their entirety shall apply to _____ (Include entire subdivision or suitable portion of it. Include any adjoining land in other ownership to which all residential covenants are to apply.)

B-2.   Partially-protected Adjoining Residential Area. The residential area covenants numbered _____ *and* _____ *in part C shall apply to* _____

B-3.   Park Area. The park area covenants in Part D shall apply to

_____

B-4.   Civic Area. The civic area covenants in Part E shall apply to
_____ (Areas, if any, for churches, community buildings, schools, etc.)

B-5.   Business Area. The business area covenants in Part F shall apply to

_____

Area of Application

In small developments complete protective covenants usually should be applied to the entire development area and, in addition, to any adjacent area which would possibly affect the properties within the development if put to a nonconforming use. Adjoining or nearby lands should be made subject at least to covenants regulating land use and type of building, lot size, and prohibition of nuisances and temporary structures.

For large tracts of land to be developed by sections it is desirable to establish protective covenants over the entire area in connection with the development of the first section, particularly with respect to land use, type of building, lot size, and prohibition of nuisances and temporary structures. Where only a section of a large development is to be made subject to all covenants, the protection should extend to and include a buffer area immediately adjacent to the section. When subsequent sections of the development are opened, complete protective covenants are extended to new sections and adjoining buffers in the same manner.

Where nonresidential uses such as parks or business are to be provided special covenants applying to specific locations should be included. The degree of the effect upon fully protected properties may then be anticipated.

Part C. Residential Area Covenants

C-1. Land Use and Building Type. No lot shall be used except for residential purposes. No building shall be erected, altered, placed, or permitted to remain on any lot other than one detached single-family dwelling not to exceed two and one-half stories in height and a private garage for not more than two cars.

C-2. Architectural Control. No building shall be erected, placed, or altered on any lot until the construction plans and specifications and a plan showing the location of the structure have been approved by the Architectural Control Committee as to quality of workmanship and materials, harmony of external design with existing structures, and as to location with respect to topography and finish grade elevation. No fence or wall shall be erected, placed or altered on any lot nearer to any street than the minimum building setback line unless similarly approved. Approval shall be as provided in part G.

ARCHITECTURAL CONTROL

This is best accomplished by establishing an architectural control committee to review plans and specifications of buildings, fences, walls and planting as to location and exterior design. The covenant should apply both to new construction and to future alterations.

C-3. Dwelling Cost, Quality and Size. No dwelling shall be permitted on any lot at a cost of less than $_____ based upon the cost levels prevailing on the date these covenants are recorded, it being the intention and purpose of the covenant to assure that all dwellings shall be of a quality of workmanship and materials substantially the same or better than that which can be produced on the date these covenants are recorded at the minimum cost stated herein for the minimum permitted dwelling size. The ground floor area of the main structure, exclusive of one-story open porches and garages, shall be not less than _____ square feet for a one-story dwelling, nor less than _____ square feet for a dwelling of more than one story.

DWELLING QUALITY AND SIZE

A protective covenant establishing a minimum dwelling cost or quality and size is important in maintaining property values because protection is afforded to desirable dwellings from the encroachment of buildings below the standards of residential character originally established.

C-4. Building Location. (a) No building shall be located on any lot nearer to the front line or nearer to the side street line than the minimum building setback lines shown on the recorded plat.

(b) No building shall be located nearer than _____ feet to an interior lot line. . . .
No dwelling shall be located on any interior lot nearer than _____ feet to rear lot
line. . . .

BUILDING LOCATION

The most satisfactory method of regulating the depth of front yards is by
reference to building setback lines shown on the recorded plat as it is sometimes desirable to vary the setback because of topographic conditions.

On corner lots there should be little if any difference in setback distances
from both streets. This prevents projection of the side or rear of a corner
dwelling beyond the building lines of adjacent dwellings.

A minimum side yard regulation for principal buildings is essential to
provide necessary light, air and privacy. Occasionally this covenant also establishes a minimum aggregate total of both side yards.

Generally, dwellings at rear of lots have had an adverse effect on the
successful use of the remaining land in a subdivision and in maintaining its
highest desirable value.

C-5.   Lot Area and Width. No dwelling shall be erected or placed on any lot
having a width of less than _____ feet at the minimum building setback line nor shall any
dwelling be erected or placed on any lot having an area of less than _____ square feet. . . .

LOT AREA AND WIDTH

Unless the protective covenants specifically prohibit the resubdivision of
lots, which is not considered advisable, as some allowance should be made for
adjustment of location of buildings to fit exceptional topographic conditions, a
covenant establishing minimum lot area and width should be included. Generally, there is no need of resubdividing if the development plan is properly
prepared.

C-6.   Easements. Easements for installation and maintenance of utilities and
drainage facilities are reserved as shown on the recorded plat and over the rear five feet of
each lot. Within these easements, no structure, planting or other material shall be placed or
permitted to remain which may damage or interfere with the installation and maintenance
of utilities, or which may change the direction of flow of drainage channels in the ease-
ments, or which may obstruct or retard the flow of water through drainage channels in the
easements. The easements area of each lot and all improvements in it shall be maintained
continuously by the owner of the lot, except for those improvements for which a public
authority or utility company is responsible.

EASEMENTS

It is preferable that electric and telephone pole lines be erected along
rear or side lot lines to avoid the unsightly appearance of these utilities with

lead-in wires along streets. To provide for immediate or future installation and maintenance, the protective covenants should reserve easements for poles and wires along interior lot lines. Sometimes it is advantageous because of topography or subsurface conditions to also install sewer lines or other utilities along these easements.

C-7. Nuisances. No obnoxious or offensive activity shall be carried on upon any lot, nor shall anything be done thereon which may be or may become an annoyance or nuisance to the neighborhood.

C-8. Temporary Structures. No structure of a temporary character, trailer, basement, tent, shack, garage, barn, or other outbuilding shall be used on any lot at any time as a residence either temporarily or permanently.

Nuisances

Protective covenants should prohibit trade or business, any activity obnoxious or offensive to residential use, and shacks or other structures for temporary occupancy.

Part D. Park Area Covenants
(Include appropriate covenants for any designated area.)
Part E. Civic Area Covenants
(Include appropriate covenants for any designated area.)
Part F. Business Area Covenants
(Include appropriate covenants for any designated area.)

Park, Civic and Business Area Covenants

If the subdivision plan includes a park or recreation area, business site, sites for social or civic activities, or other nonresidential uses, covenants should be included at least for front and side yards, height of buildings, and land uses.

Once the need for a local shopping area has been determined to be economically justified, particularly where the small local shopping area is concerned, it may become a great asset or a blight for its neighborhood. Experience indicates that business area covenants help assure success of the shopping center and the protection of the neighborhood.

A minimum-size neighborhood shopping center typically contains a food market, a drug store, variety store and several small shops and offices. A filling station may or may not be appropriate for the small center. Large shopping centers need covenants permitting two-story buildings, theatres, gasoline stations and other appropriate uses.

Covenants for all shopping centers abutting residential areas should contain appropriate provisions regulating types of business uses, building locations and size, architectural control, amount of parking, signs and other features related to safety and neighborhood protection. Covenants for a business area should be an integral part of the legal instrument which contains the covenants for the residential areas in a development.

Part G. Architectural Control Committee

G-1. Membership. The Architectural Control Committee is composed of _____ (names and addresses of three members). A majority of the committee may designate a representative to act for it. In the event of death or resignation of any member of the committee, the remaining members shall have full authority to designate a successor. Neither the members of the committee, nor its designated representative shall be entitled to any compensation for services performed pursuant to this covenant. At any time, the then record owners of a majority of the lots shall have the power through a duly recorded written instrument to change the membership of the committee or to withdraw from the committee or restore to it any of its powers and duties.

G-2. Procedure. The committee's approval or disapproval as required in these covenants shall be in writing. In the event the committee, or its designated representative, fails to approve or disapprove within 30 days after plans and specifications have been submitted to it, or in any event, if no suit to enjoin the construction has been commenced prior to the completion thereof, approval will not be required and the related covenants shall be deemed to have been fully complied with.

ARCHITECTURAL CONTROL COMMITTEE

Initially the committee is selected by the developer, but as the development nears completion and the builder's interests lessen, the membership of the committee should be selected by property owners enjoying the protection of the covenants. Experience has indicated that the control of this function usually should be retained by the developer through membership appointed by him until the development is substantially built up. It is usually advisable for the developer to designate a membership of disinterested persons including an architect and possibly a landscape architect to pass on the technical as well as aesthetic qualities of the plans.

In developments where adequate public maintenance of park areas, streets or other facilities is not available, it is advisable to establish a property owners' maintenance association or other acceptable community maintenance organization with adequate powers to provide maintenance and to assess the benefiting property owners at a reasonable rate and collect such assessments. Establishment of a property owners' association is also advisable to provide an effective means of obtaining adherence to protective covenants. The architectural control committee may be a part of the association.

Part H. General Provisions

H-1. Term. These covenants are to run with the land and shall be binding on all parties and all persons claiming under them for a period of thirty years from the date these covenants are recorded, after which time said covenants shall be automatically extended for successive periods of 10 years unless an instrument signed by a majority of the then owners of the lots has been recorded, agreeing to change said covenants in whole or in part.

H-2. Enforcement. Enforcement shall be by proceedings at law or in equity against any person or persons violating or attempting to violate any covenant either to restrain violation or to recover damages.

H-3. Severability. Invalidation of any one of these covenants by judgment or court order shall in no wise affect any of the other provisions which shall remain in full force and effect.

GENERAL PROVISIONS

Protective covenants to be effective should run with the land and be binding on all property owners in the protected area. They should be effective for a stipulated time, after which they are to be automatically extended for successive stated periods unless a change is agreed upon by a stipulated proportion of property owners affected by the instrument.

The periods for which covenants are to run without change should be sufficiently long to protect the original investments and permit amortization of the capital. Rights to modify should never be reserved to one individual.

The covenants should contain a general provision for prosecuting any proceedings in law or in equity against violations of any covenant.

Part J. Attest

(Include the date and signatures of all parties. Include signatures of prior lien holders to evidence consent to subordination of existing lien to covenants.)

Chapter 11

Modifying or Terminating the Arrangement

§11.1 By Agreement, Release, or Merger

Agreement. Generally, unless statutory limitations exist, §11.6 *infra,* the parties creating an easement, covenant, or equitable servitude have complete initial control over the duration and scope of their agreement. Thus, they may agree that it will be perpetual, or that it will terminate in X years, when a stated event occurs, when a specified purpose is accomplished, or, as is often done in residential subdivisions, when a stated percentage of the benefited landowners agree.

Release. The parties need not await the scheduled termination if the dominant owner chooses to execute a release. Such a release probably should satisfy whatever requirements the Statute of Frauds imposed on the original agreement.[1]

Merger. Unity of title of the dominant and servient parcels in the same person will terminate an easement, covenant, or equitable servitude. Professor Powell explained this doctrine of merger in the case of easements. "An easement, by definition, is a right to land which is in the possession of another. This prerequisite situation ceases to exist . . . when the dominant and servient estates of an . . . easement come into the same ownership. . . . [T]he owner of the easement, having become the owner of the servient estate, has, as such owner of the servient estate, right of user greater than those comprised in the easement itself. The lesser is swallowed by the greater and the easement is permanently terminated by this merger." 3 Powell, Real Property ¶425 at 34-264 (Rohan ed. 1979).

---

1. Restatement of Property §557 (1936), Comment e, suggests, however, that an oral release might be sufficient as there is no actual grant to the servient owner, merely an elimination of a restriction on her use of land.

Merger operates only when both tenements are held in fee. Thus, if the dominant owner acquires a life estate or an estate for years in the servient tenement, the easement, covenant, or equitable servitude is merely suspended while common ownership continues. Similarly, if less than all of the area of the two estates is held in common ownership, the agreement is extinguished only as to that area commonly owned. Also, as you have already seen, Note 3, page 556 *supra,* courts have grafted the quasi (or dormant) easement exception onto the doctrine of merger in order to explain analytically some implied easement decisions.

Although an agreement, release, or merger can relieve the servient owner of his duties to one dominant party, the duties to any other dominant persons remain in force. Thus if A grants easements of access to B, C, D, and E, and also covenants with all of them not to build a multi-unit dwelling on his property, and subsequently obtains a release from B or purchases B's land, A's duties to C, D, and E are unchanged.

The rules above speak of the usual situation where interests change or terminate much as the parties intend. But courts sometimes face disputes where one party is urging that the arrangement be ended (or modified) even though it remains—by its own terms—still intact. Such cases appear in this chapter.

In reading this group of cases, notice something that they all share—the high-intensity concentration on facts. By now, it should hardly surprise you that facts do matter, and that much of a litigator's success lies in his or her ability to amass and present facts clearly and powerfully, stressing and organizing those details that put a client's case to best advantage. Land use disputes are particularly fact-laden and, of course, what appears in the appellate opinion is only the final crystallization.

§11.2   By Misuse of the Benefit

CRIMMINS v. GOULD

149 Cal. App. 2d 383, 308 P.2d 786 (1957)

BRAY, J. Plaintiff sued in declaratory and injunctive relief primarily to determine that defendants have no rights in a certain roadway. Defendants cross-complained for like relief primarily to establish their rights in said roadway. From a judgment in favor of plaintiff and against defendants and cross-complainants, the latter appeal.

Questions Presented.

1. Did "McCormick Lane" become a public way?
2. Was the easement in said lane extinguished by misuse?

3.   Should lesser relief have been granted plaintiff? . . .

5.   Was the court's determination unconstitutional?

Evidence.

In 1929 McCormick owned a tract of land in Atherton. It was bounded on the north by Watkins Avenue and on the south by Fair Oaks Lane. That year McCormick built McCormick Lane to give access to Fair Oaks Lane. The lane runs northerly from Fair Oaks Lane to the junction of the southerly lines of parcels 1 and 2. Adjoining parcel 1 on the west is parcel 2. Only the southeasterly point of parcel 2 touches McCormick Lane. At the time the lane was first constructed parcel 1 as well as the land through which the lane ran was owned by McCormick. Parcel 2 never was. The McCormick land other than parcel 1 has been subdivided and is now owned by Hecker, Hans, Crimmins, Gould and Baxter. Express rights of way over McCormick Lane were deeded to all of these owners except Baxter who was given an oral right of way. In 1931 McCormick deeded the lane to Crimmins in fee. Crimmins later deeded the Crimmins property and the lane to plaintiff, his wife.

The map [Figure 3] shows McCormick Lane as originally maintained, and the extension thereof and Burns Avenue as constructed by defendants.

The lane is paved, with a red rock fill entrance to parcels 1 and 2. Both parcels 1 and 2 now belong to defendants Walton and Emelia Gould. In 1926 McCormick conveyed parcel 1 to a predecessor of the Goulds together with "an easement of Right of Way for ingress and egress," such easement to commence five years thereafter.

At the time of trial, the Goulds, of record, appeared to own two portions of the McCormick property—the former Gibbs place with its easement over McCormick Lane, and parcel 1, which had an easement of ingress and egress to and from McCormick Lane. In addition they now own parcel 2. In 1954 they subdivided parcels 1 and 2 into 29 residential lots. Six of these are wholly within parcel 1 and two other lots lie substantially within it. By a roadway dedicated to the public and accepted by the town, defendants extended McCormick Lane northerly across parcel 1 to its junction with Watkins Avenue. They also constructed "Burns Avenue," a public road, across parcel 2 connecting it to the extension of McCormick Lane on parcel 1.

At the entrance to McCormick Lane on Fair Oaks Avenue there has been continuously posted a sign reading "McCormick Lane." At one time a sign stated "Not a Through Street" or "Dead End Street." No other signs have been posted there. About 1925, parcels 1 and 2 were planted with pear and walnut trees. During the early years the orchard and the lane were separated by a wire fence which the orchardist removed in 1941. There has been no obstruction since. From 1931 through 1954 the orchard was operated by tenants who used the lane as a means of ingress and egress in their orchard operations. The peak of the use was in harvesting season when for about three and a half days fruit pickers and trucks hauling fruit used the lane. Otherwise the use by the orchardists was an average of at least once a week. Some fruit went out over Watkins Avenue.

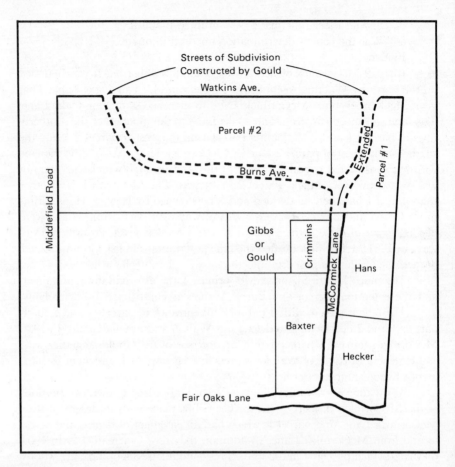

FIGURE 3

Sometime between 1940 and 1942 Crimmins quarrelled with an orchardist and put cardboard signs at the orchard end of the lane and at a place about midpoint on the lane, saying that it was a private road, permission to pass revocable. The signs were directed at the orchardist and were torn down and thrown away. None have been posted since, nor has there ever been any barricade at the Fair Oaks Lane entrance. Prior to 1948 no taxes were assessed against the lane. Since 1948 taxes for plaintiff's residence and the lane have been assessed together to plaintiff.

In 1935 Mr. Crimmins offered to deed the lane to Atherton but the offer was refused unless the road was rebuilt to specifications. Instead, Crimmins resurfaced the road, the cost being borne by then property owners, McCormick, Gibbs' predecessor, Baxter and Crimmins. The other property owners, including the owner of parcel 1, refused to pay. Thereafter the road was maintained solely at the expense of the four above mentioned property owners.

The lane was used by others not connected with the properties surrounding the lane. The Atherton police patrolled it occasionally. Sightseers and those who thought the lane was a public street would drive in and out. Groups would drive to the orchard end for a picnic or to park. "Necking" couples drove in. A few cars were abandoned on the road. Public utilities were granted rights of way in the lane. In 1952 sanitary district inspectors and workers used it in connection with the installation of a sewer outfall system across the parcels. About twenty years ago at its junction with Fair Oaks Lane Atherton installed guard rails on each side of the lane, and has maintained them since. At Mr. Crimmins' request in 1935, the town installed an electric street light at midpoint in the lane. Ever since, the town has supplied the current and upkeep of the light. Chuckholes in the lane were repaired from time to time by the town just as any other street would be repaired. In 1946 Mr. Crimmins in a letter to defendants' predecessor claimed ownership of the lane and objected to the manner in which the tenant farmer was using the lane and several discussions were had between them in which Crimmins disputed the use of the lane. Crimmins notified defendants' predecessors that he was opposed to the proposed subdivision extending McCormick Lane into it. On learning of the new subdivision Crimmins notified defendants that the lane was not to be connected to the subdivision. Since the connection was made in 1954 the use of the lane and the wear and tear thereon has greatly increased.

On this evidence, the court found that the lane had never become a public way; that the lane was subject to an easement "as a private means of ingress and egress for Parcel One;" that no easement or right of way in or over the lane ever existed as to parcel 2; that by defendants' acts in subdividing parcel 2 and in laying out public roads on parcels 1 and 2 connecting McCormick Lane with Watkins Avenue the burden on the lane has been substantially increased by the public and by occupants of parcel 2 and their invitees, causing substantial damage to plaintiff. The burden of maintenance on McCormick Lane was slight as compared to what it will be; that the acts of defendants are incompatible with the nature and exercise of the servitude appurtenant to parcel 1 granted in 1926 over the lane; it is impossible to use the easement granted in 1926 as it was intended to be used or to segregate the use of the lane by the owners of parcel 1 or 2, from its use by the general public; that because of defendants' acts they no longer have any right to use, occupy or pass over the lane. The court concluded that defendants had not acquired as appurtenant to parcel 2 any easement or right of way; that the easement appurtenant to parcel 1 has been extinguished and thereupon enjoined defendants from using it.

1. Public Way.

The foregoing recital shows that the lane never became a public way. Such use of it as was made by the public was permissive only. The small amount of improvement and repair made by the town did not constitute an adverse use or an acceptance by the town of the lane as a public way. The only offer of it as such was rejected by the town. There are only two methods by which private property may become a public way other than by purchase: (1) By an offer of dedication by the owner and a formal acceptance by a public authority or long continued use by the public itself. This did not exist here. (2) Where no express offer of dedication is made by the owner, by long continued adverse use by the public. In such event offer of dedication by the owner is presumed. The evidence showed no such situation here. See Union Transp. Co. v. Sacramento County, 42 Cal. 2d 235, 240, 267 P.2d 10, for discussion of these two methods. . . .

  2. Extinguishment of Easement.

The evidence clearly shows that parcel 2 neither by grant nor prescription acquired any right to use McCormick Lane. The small use of it made by the owners or occupants of parcel 2 over the years until recently was not an adverse one. The most serious question in the case is whether the easement of ingress and egress to and from the lane appurtenant to parcel 1 was lost by the attempted change in use. Plaintiff concedes that the change from orchard to residential estates did not extinguish the easement. It is the acts of defendants in extending McCormick Lane to Watkins Avenue dedicating it as a public street, and in allowing the owners of parcel 2 to connect with McCormick Lane as extended, a public street, which runs across parcel 2 and connects with Watkins Avenue, which plaintiff claims extinguished the easement of parcel 1. Defendants thereby attempted to use the easement appurtenant to parcel 1 for the benefit of all owners in parcel 2 and the public generally. This caused the court to declare the easement abandoned by misuse.

Civil Code, §811, subdivision 3, provides that a servitude is extinguished by "the performance of any act upon either tenement, by the owner of the servitude, or with his assent, which is incompatible with its nature or exercise. . . ."

However, here the question is not the propriety of an injunction but rather the propriety of an extinguishment. There do not seem to be any California cases on extinguishment for excessive use by non-dominant property where the right given to the dominant estate was by grant. But there are a number of out-of-state cases. The general rule is that misuse or excessive use is not sufficient for abandonment or forfeiture, but an injunction is the proper remedy. (16 A.L.R.2d 610.) But where the burden of the servient estate is increased through changes in the dominant estate which increase the use and subject it to use of non-dominant property, a forfeiture will be justified if the unauthorized use may not be severed and prohibited. (16 A.L.R.2d 613.) See also Penn Bowling Recreation Center v. Hot Shoppes, 1949, 86 U.S. App. D.C. 58, 179, 16 A.L.R.2d 602, 179 F.2d 64.

The situation here is different than that in Tarpey v. Lynch, 155 Cal. 407, 101 P. 10. There a water ditch easement appurtenant to 80 acres of land under single ownership was held to accrue to each portion thereof divided among plural ownership. Thus in our case the easement of ingress and egress appurtenant to parcel 1, although acquired at a time of single ownership of that parcel, would be extended to the subdivided portions of that parcel. But not content with that, defendants here attempted to extend it to all parts of parcel 2 which had no easement therein and also attempted to extend it to two public streets. It is not a question of merely "some increase in burden" upon a servient tenement by permitting an easement appurtenant to attach to each of the parts into which a dominant tenement may be subdivided, which comment (b) to section 488, Restatement of Property, and a number of cases cited by defendants, state is permissible. Rather it is one of the performance of acts by the owner of the servitude "which is incompatible with its nature or exercise." Civ. Code §811, subd. 3.

The California cases holding that injunctive relief is a proper remedy of the servient owner for unauthorized or excessive uses of an easement do not hold that it is the exclusive remedy. As hereafter pointed out an injunction could not grant plaintiff real relief where defendants have attempted to tie two public streets into their easement.

The fact that the cases which to date have interpreted section 811, subdivision 3, were ones not of misuse or overuse of an easement but were ones where a change in conditions of either the dominant or servient estates made the easement impossible of use, does not mean that the application of the section is limited to such situations. Certainly here the situation which defendants deliberately brought about is "incompatible with" the "nature or exercise" of the easement. Defendants quote 28 C.J.S., Easements, §62, p. 729:

> The right to an easement is not lost by using it in an unauthorized manner or to an unauthorized extent, *unless it is impossible to sever the increased burden so as to preserve to the owner of the dominant tenement that to which he is entitled, and yet impose on the servient tenement only that burden which was originally imposed on it without the obligation attempted to be imposed on it by alterations.* The rule is especially applicable where the servitude is not materially increased. Such a misuser does not authorize the owner of the servient estate to prevent a further use of the easement by erecting obstructions, or by restraining the owner of the easement by force or violence, the proper remedy being an action for damages, or for an injunction if the remedy at law is inadequate. (Emphasis added.)

The situation here meets the one covered by the exception described by the [italicized] portion of the above quotation.

3. Lesser Relief.

Defendants' contention that lesser relief than a declaration that defendants no longer had any right to use McCormick Lane is without merit. A sign as suggested by defendants to the effect that the lane was restricted to the use of residents of McCormick Lane alone would not protect plaintiff's rights. Nor would an injunction attempting to restrain all persons from using McCormick Lane other than owners or residents fronting on the lane or their invitees be practicable or enforceable. Defendants have extended the lane in a sort of an inverted "Y." The northerly ends of each section of the Y join Watkins Avenue, so that what is equal to two through streets run into McCormick Lane. Such a sign and injunction would not prevent all or any of the residents of parcel 2 as well as the general public from using McCormick Lane. The only practical way of preventing this is to close McCormick Lane at its junction with parcels 1 and 2.[3] This compels the extinguishment of defendants' easement therein. By causing McCormick Lane as extended by defendants and Burns Avenue as joined to it to become dedicated public streets, defendants have made it impossible for the portion of McCormick Lane belonging to plaintiff to be used in a limited way. Unless a fence is built across McCormick Lane at its intersection with the southerly line of parcel 1, there is no feasible way of keeping the general public as well as the residents of parcel 2 out of McCormick Lane. . . .

    5. Constitutionality.

While of course defendants' easement appurtenant to parcel 1 was a valuable right, the fact that the court held that by their misuse of it they had abandoned that right, is not taking defendants' property without due process. It is not taking their property at all. It is merely determining that their own acts were such as the law determines constitutes an extinguishment of the easement. By their own acts they have made it impossible for either themselves or plaintiff to confine the use of the easement to the owners of lots in parcel 1 only.

    The judgment is affirmed.

    PETERS, P.J., and WOOD, J., concur.

NOTES AND QUESTIONS

    1. In the *Crimmins* case, the plaintiff conceded that the change of parcel 1 from orchard to residential use did not extinguish the easement. Why not? Suppose that the defendant had built a shopping center on parcel 1: same concession? If A gives B "an easement of right of way for ingress and egress" without qualifying the easement, may B develop his parcel (the dominant estate) without limitation?

    2. Might the defendants in *Crimmins* have acquired via *prescription* an additional burden on the right of way? If so, on your reading of the facts, when (if at all) did the defendants' activity become hostile? What steps might the owner of the servient estate take, short of suing for equitable relief, to bar the prescription?

    3. Suppose that you represented the defendants before the trial and believed that the court on the known facts would extinguish your clients' right of way. (In short, the outcome would not have surprised you.) What would be your negotiation or litigation strategy to try to prevent total extinguishment?

---

3. It should be pointed out that in doing this defendants and the owners of lots in parcels 1 and 2 are not deprived in any way of access to Watkins Avenue. Actually they continue to have two ways of reaching it from their lots. They are only deprived of direct access to Fair Oaks Lane, which they can reach by going around the block.

§11.3   By Abandonment

FLANAGAN v. SAN MARCOS SILK CO.
106 Cal. App. 2d 458, 235 P.2d 107 (1951)

GRIFFIN, J. Plaintiffs and respondents brought this action to quiet title to a parcel of land described as Lots 2 and 5 [see Figure 4] of Rancho Los Valecitos de San Marcos, located near San Marcos, and it is directed to a claim by these appealing defendants to an easement for the maintenance of a pipe line over a portion of the real property owned by plaintiff. . . .

Plaintiffs concede that defendants' predecessor in interest, American Silk Factors, Inc., a corporation (hereinafter referred to as the Silk Company) owned a large parcel of land south of Lots 2 and 5, which lots were at that time owned by a Mr. and Mrs. Brambley; that by written grant deed, duly recorded in 1927, the Brambleys deeded to the Silk Company a "perpetual easement or right-of-way" for the construction of pipe lines over and across their property which is now owned by plaintiffs. A similar easement was obtained from the Akermans, who owned a parcel of land lying between that owned by the Silk Company and the parcel owned by the Brambleys. The Vista Irrigation District operated a water distributing ditch just north of plaintiffs' property. A pipe line was laid over and across plaintiff's land, across the Akerman property, and across the Silk Company's property to the silk plant, and was the means by which the Silk Company was to obtain its water, operate its silk mills, and grow mulberry trees. The Silk Company's property was not in the irrigation district but in 1927 it obtained an agreement whereby

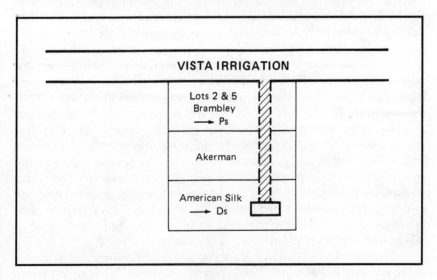

FIGURE 4

the district would furnish water to it through their pipe line. During the operation of the plant, from 1927 to 1933, there was delivered to it each year in excess of 100 cubic feet. Shortly before 1933 the Silk Company became bankrupt. In February of that year the trustee in bankruptcy executed a trustee's deed and bill of sale to one Poulsen, conveying all property owned by the Silk Company, and specifically conveying the Brambley easement involved in this action. Received in evidence (Exhibit 10) is a commissioner's deed, dated November 19, 1933, being the result of a judgment of foreclosure dated October 18, 1932, on the Silk Company's property conveying to one Evans the property and all appurtenances thereunto belonging. By mesne conveyances thereafter a portion of the property originally owned by the Silk Company was transferred to and is now owned by defendant American Real Silk, Inc., subject to certain liens and trust deeds held by the other appealing defendants.

The court specifically found and concluded that "The common predecessor in interest of the defendants sometime during the year 1933 abandoned any interest which such predecessor in interest ever had in the easement in, over and upon a portion of plaintiffs' lands," and ordered plaintiffs' title quieted accordingly.

The main question on this appeal is the sufficiency of the evidence to support the finding of abandonment. In this connection the court found that in 1933 the pipe line in question was broken or blocked at its northerly end where it had previously been connected to the supply line of the irrigation district, and thereafter no water could or did run through it until 1944; that in 1933 the predecessor in interest of defendants drilled certain wells upon portions of the property now owned by the defendants and irrigated their premises; that no water was ever carried through the pipe line here in dispute to any lands of defendants since 1933; that no water has been available for such delivery to defendants or their predecessors in interest since 1933; that this pipe line has been incapable of conducting water by reason of severance thereof; that after plaintiffs acquired their property, they caused the pipe line to be reconnected to the irrigation district system to supply water to their lands; that prior thereto the line was cut off and blocked at the south end of the easement; that in 1946, it was broken at a point on the McCandless property, being a group of lots south of plaintiffs' property and that these owners connected, with defendants' consent, to water from a reservoir pumped from wells on defendants' property and were using that portion of the pipe line as a system wholly separate from the pipe line here involved. (Thereafter McCandless blocked off both ends of the pipe line on their property, dug their own well, and continued to use that portion of the pipe line on their property to carry water to it.) The evidence supports these particular findings and there is very little conflict in the evidence in this respect.

It is defendants' position that they acquired their interest and ownership in the property in 1943, in reliance upon the provisions in the several instruments conveying the easement across plaintiffs' land to them, and in reliance upon the statements of the seller that such easement was still in existence for the benefit of the property of defendants; that they had no knowledge of any purported abandonment at any time, and that they were innocent purchasers for value; that neither defendants nor their predecessors in interest ever ordered the pipe line disconnected or authorized its use by plaintiffs and that since no written notice of abandonment of the easement was ever recorded by defendants or their predecessors in interest, the easement is still in existence.

It is true that plaintiffs purchased their property in April, 1935, and soon thereafter learned about the pipe line and the easement of record across their property. [2] They testified they had no consent of the Silk Company or its successors in interest to connect the pipe line to the irrigation district ditch but since their property was in the district they applied for and received consent from the district to establish a meter and receive water through those pipes. The evidence further shows that on September 28, 1948, defendant American Real Silk Company wrote plaintiffs that it had come to its attention that plaintiffs were using the pipe line belonging to that company and located on the easement in question; that since the company had no present use for it, it would be satisfactory for them to continue using it until such time as the defendant company had a need for it. The source of defendants' claimed title thereto was set forth in the letter. . . .

Defendants contend that although the pipe line in dispute was not being used by defendants to carry water, it was being held by the company as a "stand-by" source of supply to supplement the wells drilled on the property. It is its argument that the evidence shows nothing more than nonuse of the easement and pipe line in question since 1932, and that mere "nonuser," without more, is not sufficient evidence of abandonment or intent to abandon. . . . It cites the rule stated in Smith v. Worn, 93 Cal. 206, 213 [28 P. 944], that "The acts of the owner of the dominant tenement in case of nonuser, or to prevent him from obtaining an *easement acquired by grant,* must be of a character so decisive and conclusive as to indicate a clear intent to abandon the easement."

As to this general proposition of law plaintiffs do not quarrel with defendants but strongly maintain that "nonuser," accompanied by an intention, either express or implied, to abandon the easement is sufficient, citing . . . Moon v. Rollins, 36 Cal. 333 [95 Am. Dec. 181], where it is said: ". . . lapse of time does not of itself constitute an abandonment, but that is only a circumstance for the jury to consider in determining the question whether there was an abandonment. . . . It is a question of *intention,* and has been so held over and over again, and *not* a question of time. . . ."

In Home Real Estate Co. v. Los Angeles Pacific Co., 163 Cal. 710 [126 P. 972], the rule is stated that while nonuser alone does not extinguish the easement, a long continued nonuser is some evidence of an intent to abandon, and that an intention with which an act is done is a question of fact to be determined by the trial court from a consideration of the conduct of the parties

2. Why did plaintiffs learn about the pipeline only after they bought the land?—Ed.

and the surrounding circumstances, and that where evidence is such that a finding either way might reasonably be made, the conclusion of the trial court must be upheld under the familiar rule protecting from review on appeal findings based on conflicting evidence.

In the instant case there is no question about the discontinuance of the use of the pipe line in question in the year 1932 or 1933, when the Silk Company went bankrupt. It was not subsequently used by it or its successors in interest. The trial court apparently fixed the year 1933 as the one in which abandonment occurred. Standing alone, this evidence of nonuse may not have been sufficient to support a finding of intent to abandon. . . . It is defendants' argument that any evidence of the conduct of the Silk Company and its successors in interest thereafter was inadmissible and should not be considered for any purpose. The authorities cited by defendants do not support this argument. Since abandonment involves intent, evidence of actions after 1932 by the several successors in interest was relevant as bearing on the question. As pointed out by counsel for plaintiffs, suppose a husband left his wife in 1933 and went to another city and did not return. Evidence as to his subsequent actions would be relevant to determine whether he left her in 1933 with the intent to desert her. . . . Therefore, in connection with the fact of nonuser, there is the additional evidence, as exemplified by pictures in evidence, that the pipe line easement had grown over with thick underbrush, the pipe became exposed, and gulches washed from under it. There is some evidence that it needed repair and that it would soon need replacing due to leaks and deterioration. The grant of easement contained a clause that the grantee and its successors were bound to maintain the pipe line upon plaintiffs' property "as free from leaks as possible." In 17 Am. Jur. 1027, section 142, the rule is stated to be that: "Ordinarily, failure to repair does not constitute an abandonment, but an abandonment may be predicated upon facts showing that the means of enjoyment of an easement have been in a state of disrepair for a long period of time." . . .

The facts here show: (1) Nonuser by defendants and their successors in interest for over 16 years; (2) affirmative acts of these parties in obtaining a new and different source of supply of water by means of digging wells in the year 1934; (3) the sale and grant by defendants' predecessors in interest to a stranger in 1933 of a portion of the Silk Company's original property over which the pipe line passed and lying between the plant and plaintiffs' property without a special reservation of an easement of right-of-way for this particular pipe line contained in the grant; (4) permitting the blocking of a portion of the pipe line for the private use of the McCandless property; (5) the apparent adverse use of a blocked portion of the easement pipe line by plaintiffs since 1944; and (6) failure to maintain the easement line in question free from leaks.

Had the trial court found that there had been no abandonment the finding might be supported by the evidence produced. Defendants bring this case before us upon a finding which is against them as to both the question of abandonment and intent. We cannot say that the finding of the trial court lacks evidentiary support. . . .

Judgment affirmed.

BARNARD, P.J., and MUSSELL, J., concurred.

NOTES AND QUESTIONS

1. Consider whether plaintiffs in *Flanagan* might also have won on a theory of adverse possession.

2. Andrien v. Heffernan, 299 Pa. 284, 149 A. 184 (1930), is as striking a case as one might find for the rule that proof of nonuser will not by itself destroy an easement. A right of way that had been reserved more than 125 years earlier, that had not been used for at least forty years, and that was overgrown with trees and shrubbery was treated as unextinguished and a cloud on title, in a suit for specific performance of a sales contract. Might the *Flanagan* case have been decided differently had planitiffs been trying to enforce an executory sales contract against a reluctant vendee, whose argument was that the outstanding easement rendered title unmarketable?

3. California Civ. Proc. Code §1971 (West 1955) reads: "No estate or interest in real property . . . can be created, granted, assigned, surrendered, or declared, otherwise than by operation of law, or a conveyance or other instrument in writing. . . ." Could the defendants in *Flanagan* have invoked this version of the Statute of Frauds to defeat the claim of abandonment? Why not?

4. While an easement created by grant is not lost by mere nonuse, intent to abandon being an essential element, one created by prescription may be lost if the nonuse is for the prescriptive period. Zimmer v. Dykstra, 39 Cal. App. 3d 422, 114 Cal. Rptr. 380 (1974). Why is there a different, less secure, status for prescriptive easements?

5. Owner "abandonment" of slum properties has worsened in recent years as these holdings become unprofitable. See generally G. Sternlieb and R. Burchell, Residential Abandonment: The Tenement Landlord Revisited (1974).

In legal terms, what happens when the owner of a building "abandons" it and the underlying land? Does your answer depend upon the nature of the operator's interest in the land and building? Compare, for example, someone who owns the land and building in fee simple with someone who runs the building on a fifty-year lease. Consider also what happens if the real estate taxes or the mortgage installments remain unpaid.

In short: can the rules that govern the abandonment of easements also apply to corporeal interests in land and building improvements?

6. A chattel may be abandoned, it is said, when its owner "with the specific intent of desertion and relinquishment casts away or leaves behind his property, or when after a casual and unintentional loss all purpose further to

seek and reclaim the lost property is given up." R. Brown, Personal Property 8 (3d ed. 1975). He who first takes possession of abandoned personalty ordinarily becomes its new owner. Eads v. Brazelton, 22 Ark. 499, 79 Am. Dec. 88 (1861).

7.   Statutes in most states provide for the escheat of abandoned or unclaimed bank accounts, life insurance funds, condemnation awards, and the like. See, e.g., N.Y. Aband. Prop. Law §§300-305, 700-706, 1000-1003 (1976). As the following newspaper article indicates, escheat has become a surprisingly fruitful source of state revenue. N.Y. Times, March 30, 1964, at 44, cols. 2-5:

> An informal survey last week disclosed that only one person in 25 polled— a lawyer—was aware of escheat, state seizure of property that has no apparent owner. Yet anyone may be subject to its ill effects, unless precautions are taken.
>
> Escheat is practiced, to a greater or lesser degree, by all states. The oldest and most common form is Government acquisition of the estate of a person who dies intestate—without heirs. The next most common, and perhaps most familiar, form is escheat of unclaimed bank deposits. Depending on the state, other property may be affected, such as unclaimed stock dividends, securities, insurance proceeds and wages.
>
> With the exception of the lawyer, initial reaction of those interviewed was indifference. Typically, an advertising executive said:
>
> "Escheat—how do you spell it?—it doesn't apply to me. I certainly keep track of all I own, and it's absolutely inconceivable that anything of mine could be declared ownerless and taken by the state."
>
> However, that indifference faded, in most cases, during a discussion of several of the situations in which escheat laws would apply.
>
> For example, . . . many married people . . . secretly put aside (money) for special purposes.
>
> These investments or bank accounts might be held by husbands or wives building private nest eggs, or mothers saving, as a future surprise, the weekly room-and-board payments made by children just beginning their careers.
>
> Such secret assets could ultimately be taken by the Government, should the owner die. Survivors, unaware of them, would not file claims. Further, if the family relocated, the bank or corporation might not be able to trace them, and the state would get the property after the prescribed waiting period. . . .
>
> There are many other situations in which property could be exposed to escheat. A gift of a savings account or securities to a grandchild may, with the passing years, fade from memory. A savings account, considered safe, might be left unattended for years, without even one visit to have accumulated interest entered in the passbook—or a letter to notify the bank of a change of address.
>
> A paid-up life insurance policy may be buried in a pile of "valuable" papers and eventually lost, with no claim ever being filed on it.
>
> In New York State, there must be no communication with, or payment to, an owner of a corporate security, bank account or other personal property for 10 years before it can be declared abandoned and escheatable.
>
> In general, banks and other holders of the personal property of missing owners are required to reach them by mail at their last-known address, through advertisements and by posting notices.

Among such holders may be corporations that have issued stock, or brokerage houses that hold unpaid dividends, securities and other assets in the investors' accounts.

The nonpayment period varies from state to state, and sometimes with the type of property. A holder of a winning parimutuel ticket, for example, had better not wait too long before cashing it in. . . .

State legislatures, it is said, look to escheat laws primarily for revenue. The public value of such laws is that they use ownerless property for the common good, rather than leave it with whoever happens to hold it.

Escheat related under early common law to the passage of real property to the crown upon death of its owner without heirs. In feudal times, escheat occurred when an owner of land died without heirs capable of serving his feudal lord, or when he was convicted of a felony or treason.

In the United States, escheat has been steadily broadened to include a wide range of personal property, especially since 1940, the period in which most states enacted escheat legislation. Before that, common law prevailed in all states but Pennsylvania, which has had escheat statutes since 1913.

In a study, "Modern Rationales of Escheat," in last November's University of Pennsylvania Law Review,[3] David C. Auten noted that the "most significant rationale of modern escheat is that the state's custody protects the owner." This applies to states, such as New York, that take custody of property, rather than confiscate it, and thus allow an owner to reclaim it.

It usually is less expensive and difficult to recover property from a government than from a private individual. However, the claimant still must prove his ownership often by winning a court judgment.

That raises another point that was well made by Mr. Auten. Many states sell escheated property, and pay a recognized owner the sale price, less costs. Thus, in an inflationary period, the owner would be out not only his and the state's expenses, but also the amount the property might have increased in value, had it not been sold. Of course, in a period of deflation or market decline, he would be ahead, if the property had been sold at a price above the then current level.

The percentage of refunds is small. In the 1961-62 fiscal year, New York collected $12.65 million and refunded only $574,000. . . .

§11.4 By Neighborhood Change

TRUSTEES OF COLUMBIA COLLEGE v. THACHER
87 N.Y. 311 (1882)

Appeal from judgment of the General Term of the Superior Court of the city of New York, entered upon an order made June, 1880, which affirmed a judgment in favor of plaintiff, entered upon a decision of the court on trial at Special Term.

3. 112 U. Pa. L. Rev. 95 (1963).—Ed.

The action was brought to enforce the observance of certain covenants in an agreement made on the 25th of July, 1859, between the plaintiffs and Joseph D. Beers, who then owned adjacent portions of the block of land between Fifth and Sixth avenues and Fiftieth and Fifty-first streets, New York, in respect to the mode of improvement and the future occupation of their respective portions.

The case upon a former appeal is reported in 70 N.Y. 440.[4] . . . During the pendency of this action the defendant Thacher became the owner of the said premises, having purchased the same with notice of said agreement and of this action, and he was made a defendant herein by an order of the court, upon his own application. The court found that said

> Thacher permits certain parts of the house upon said premises to be occupied by his tenants for the purpose of trade and business; that is to say, apartments in the first story of said house for the business of a tailor and for that of a milliner, and apartments in the basement of the said house for the business of an insurance agent, of a newspaper dealer, of two express carriers, and of a tobacconist, which trades or businesses were carried on in the said house at the time of the trial. That the several trades or businesses carried on as aforesaid by the defendants Yates and Blaisdell, at the time of the commencement of the action, and by the tenants of the defendant Thacher at the time of trial, were violations of the agreement above set forth, and of the spirit as well as the letter thereof. That since the action was begun an elevated railway has been built in the Sixth avenue, running by the said premises, and a station thereof established at the intersection of Fiftieth street and the Sixth avenue, in front of said premises, and that the said railway and station affect the said premises injuriously, and render them less profitable for the purpose of a dwelling-house, but do not render their use for business purposes indispensable to their practicable and profitable use and occupation. The said railway and station, however, do not injuriously affect all the property fronting on Fiftieth street and included in the said covenant, but only a comparatively small part thereof.

Further facts appear in the opinion. . . .

DANFORTH, J. The validity and binding obligation of the covenant cannot be questioned by the defendant Thacher. (Trustees of Columbia College v. Lynch, 70 N.Y. 440.) Moreover it appears that he bought with notice, not only of the agreement, but of this action. He, therefore, could not take the property without performing the obligation attached to it, and must be deemed to have taken it at his peril, to the extent of such judgment as might be rendered in the action. . . . We have no doubt that the conclusion of the trial judge was right upon the point presented, and agree with him, that these several trades or occupations were violations, not only of the spirit, but also of the letter of the covenant.

Now having before us a covenant binding the defendant, and his breach of it, if there is nothing more, the usual result must follow, viz.: an injunction

4. See page 591 *supra.*—Ed.

to keep within the terms of the agreement. . . . Indeed, this has in substance been recognized in the decision before made by us (70 N.Y. *supra*). It was then, however, suggested, that another trial might disclose objections not before us, and it is now claimed by the appellant, that there has been such an entire change in the character of the neighborhood of the premises, as to defeat the object and purpose of the agreement, and that it would be inequitable to deprive the defendant of the privilege of conforming his property to that character, so that he could use it to his greater advantage, and in no respect to the detriment of the plaintiff. The agreement before us recites, that the object which the parties to the covenant had in view was "to provide for the better improvement of the lands, and to secure their permanent value." It certainly is not the doctrine of courts of equity, to enforce, by its peculiar mandate, every contract, in all cases, even where specific execution is found to be its legal intention and effect. It gives or withholds such decree according to its discretion, in view of the circumstances of the case, and the plaintiff's prayer for relief is not answered, where, under those circumstances, the relief he seeks would be inequitable. (Peters v. Delaplaine, 49 N.Y. 362; Margraf v. Muir, 57 id. 155; Mathews v. Terwilliger, 3 Barb. 51; Radcliffe v. Warrington, 12 Vesey 331.) If for any reason, therefore, not referable to the defendant, an enforcement of the covenant would defeat either of the ends contemplated by the parties, a court of equity might well refuse to interfere, or if in fact the condition of the property by which the premises are surrounded has been so altered "that the terms and restrictions" of the covenant are no longer applicable to the existing state of things. (1 Story's Eq. Jur. [10th ed.], §750.) And so though the contract was fair and just when made, the interference of the court should be denied, if subsequent events have made performance by the defendant so onerous, that its enforcement would impose great hardship upon him, and cause little or no benefit to the plaintiff. . . .

In the case before us, the plaintiffs rely upon no circumstance of equity, but put their claim to relief upon the covenant and the violation of its conditions by the defendant. They have established, by their complaint and proof, a clear legal cause of action. If damages have been sustained, they must, in any proper action, be allowed. But on the other hand, the defendant has exhibited such change in the condition of the adjacent property, and its character for use, as leaves no ground for equitable interference, if the discretion of the court is to be governed by the principles I have stated, or the cases which those principles have controlled. The general current of business affairs has reached and covered the entire premises fronting on Sixth avenue, both above and below the lot in question. If this was all, however, the plaintiffs would be justified in their claim, for it is apparent from the agreement that such encroachment was anticipated, and that the parties to it intended to secure the property in question from the disturbance which business would necessarily produce. But the trial court has found that since the action was begun, an elevated railway has been built in the Sixth avenue. It runs past the premises, and a station has been established in front of them, at the intersection of Fiftieth street. He finds that "the railway and station affect the premises injuriously and render them less profitable for the purpose of a dwelling-house, but do not render their use for business purposes indispensable to their practicable and profitable use and occupation." The evidence sustains the finding. The premises may still be used for dwellings, but the occupants are not likely to be those whose convenience and wishes were to be promoted by the covenant, persons of less pecuniary ability, and willing to sacrifice some degree of comfort for economy, transient tenants of still another class, whose presence would be more offensive to quiet and orderly people who might reside in the neighborhood. Not only large depreciation in rents when occupied, but also frequent vacancies have followed the construction of the road. Its trains, propelled by steam, run at intervals of a few minutes, until midnight. The station covers from fifteen to twenty feet of the street opposite the defendant's premises. Half the width of the sidewalk is occupied by its elevated platform. From it, persons waiting for the trains, or there for other purposes, can look directly into the windows. Noise from its trains can be heard from one avenue to the other.

It is obvious, without further detail, that the construction of this road and its management have rendered privacy and quiet in the adjacent buildings impossible, and so affected the premises of the defendant, and all those originally owned by him, who, with the plaintiff, entered into the covenant, that neither their better improvement nor permanent value can be promoted by enforcing its observance. Nor are the causes of this depreciation transient. The platform of the railroad station, which renders inspection of the interior of the house easy to all observers; the stairs, which render the road accessible, must remain so long as the road is operated; and the noise and smoke are now, at least, an apparent necessity, consequent upon its operation. It is true, the covenant is without exception or limitation, but I think this contingency which has happened was not within the contemplation of the parties. The road was authorized by the legislature, and, by reason of it, there has been imposed upon the property a condition of things which frustrates the scheme devised by the parties, and deprives the property of the benefit which might otherwise accrue from its observance. This new condition has already affected, in various ways and degrees, the uses of property in its neighborhood, and property values. It has made the defendant's property unsuitable for the use to which, by the covenant of his grantor, it was appropriated, and if, in face of its enactment and the contingencies flowing from it, the covenant can stand anywhere, it surely cannot in a court of equity. The land in question furnishes an ill seat for dwelling-houses, and it cannot be supposed that the parties to the covenant would now select it for a residence, or expect others to prefer it for that purpose. . . .

It is apparent that the original design of the parties has been broken up by acts for which neither the defendant nor his grantors are responsible, that the object of the covenant has been, so far as the defendant is concerned, defeated, and that to enforce it would work oppression, and not equity.

To avoid this result the judgment appealed from should be reversed; and the complaint dismissed, but as this result is made necessary by reason of events occurring since the commencement of the action, it should be without costs.

All concur.

Judgment reversed, and complaint dismissed.

ALBINO v. PACIFIC FIRST FEDERAL SAVINGS & LOAN ASSN.

257 Or. 473, 479 P.2d 760 (1971)

TONGUE, J. This is a suit in which plaintiffs seek a declaratory judgment that building restrictions in deeds to all lots in a residential subdivision in Eugene do not prohibit the construction of "multiple family or apartment housing" on two of such lots. Plaintiffs, who proposed the construction of so-called "garden court" apartments on these lots, appeal from an adverse judgment.

Two contentions are made by plaintiffs: (1) That a deed restriction prohibiting all buildings except "a private dwelling house" does not prohibit the construction of "multiple family or apartment housing"; and (2) That due to a "substantial and radical change in the character of the area," such restrictions are no longer enforceable to prohibit the construction of "multiple family or apartment housing" on such lots.

In support of the contention that construction of "multiple family or apartment" housing is not prohibited by deed restrictions prohibiting all buildings except "a private dwelling house," plaintiffs concede that the authorities are in conflict. Plaintiffs contend, however, that the better rule is as stated in Leverich v. Roy, 338 Ill. App. 248, 87 N.E.2d 226, 228-229 (1949). In that case it was held that the words "one dwelling house" did not prohibit a "house" from being occupied by two families "living separate and apart from each other."

On the contrary, in Schmidt v. Culhane, 223 Or. 130, 134, 354 P.2d 75, 76 (1960), we held that restrictions providing that "not more than one dwelling may be erected on a single tract of land conveyed" prohibits the construction of "multiple dwellings." Although the terms of the deed restrictions in this case are not identical, we believe that the intent and effect of such terms is the same. Thus, we hold that a deed restriction providing that no building shall be erected except "a private dwelling house" prohibits the construction of "multiple family or apartment housing," including "garden court" apartments, as proposed in this case. See also Taylor v. Lambert, 279 Pa. 514, 124 A. 169 (1924), involving a restriction prohibiting buildings other than "a private dwelling house."

In support of the contention that the deed restrictions are no longer enforceable to prohibit "multiple family or apartment housing" because of a "substantial and radical change in the area justifying removal of said restrictions," plaintiffs offered testimony that since the sale of lots in Alpha Place Addition began in 1940 there has been an "enormous increase" in traffic on

Willamette Street, adjacent to the addition; that apartments and business offices have been built along that street in the immediate area of the addition; that what was formerly a high school ball park across Willamette Street from the addition has been developed into a Civic Stadium for professional baseball, with a large "planned unit development" adjacent to the stadium, and that in recognition of these developments the zoning classification for lots fronting on Willamette Street in that area, including seven lots in Alpha Addition, has been changed from R-1 (single family residential) to R-G3 (garden apartments).

Plaintiffs also offered testimony that although the two lots in question, also fronting on Willamette Street, were originally purchased by plaintiff Albino with the intent of building a home, he then purchased a home elsewhere, and since 1955 had attempted to sell the two lots; that he had been unable to sell them for residential purposes; that the only offers for the purchase of the lots had been for the construction of apartments, conditioned upon the removal of the restrictions; that if the restrictions were removed plaintiffs Weaver would purchase the lots and build "garden apartments," to include eight living units; that the constructions of "garden apartments" on these lots was considered by planning experts to be an appropriate "transitional use" or "buffer" between Willamette Street, including the activity along that street, and the R-1 residential property to the west of that street, but not fronting on it, and would benefit the remaining lots in Alpha Addition, rather than harm them. Plaintiffs also contended that homes fronting on Willamette Street in that area had "deteriorated," with a shift from owner-occupied dwellings to rental use; that the existing restrictions were no longer of any substantial benefit to the 24 remaining lots in Alpha Addition or to the individual owners of such lots, and that unless the restrictions are removed plaintiffs will be "unable to use the property for any beneficial purpose," so as to "confiscate" plaintiffs' property.

In opposition to this testimony and these contentions defendants testified that despite changes in the area along Willamette Street, Alpha Addition itself, including the homes in that subdivision, had not deteriorated, but had remained substantially the same during the past 25 years, except for the addition of a few new homes, as a "very nice residential area" of well-maintained homes; and that the increase in traffic noise and the lights and noise from Civic Stadium had not been serious annoyances.

Most of the individual defendants, as well as a realtor, also testified that, in their opinions, the removal of the building restrictions on plaintiffs' two lots and the construction of even "garden apartments" on those lots would decrease the value of the remaining lots in the subdivision. The individual owners most concerned were those adjacent to plaintiffs' lots and those adjacent to an alleyway which provided access to the rear of seven lots fronting on Willamette Street (including plaintiffs' two lots). The concern of the owners of the lots fronting on Willamette Street was due in part to the location of such lots on a bank above the street and banning of parking on that street. As a result, the principal access to these lots was by an alley running parallel to Willamette Street. That alley also provided access to the rear of eight lots to the west of that alley, although fronting on another street.

The owners of all of these lots expressed concern that the construction of even eight apartment units on plaintiffs' two lots, as proposed for the "garden court" apartments, would substantially increase traffic through that somewhat narrow and partially improved alleyway and would also result in a substantial increase in noise, to the annoyance of nearby private home owners. Thus, defendants offered testimony that the construction of apartments on plaintiffs' two lots would cause a decrease in the value of adjacent lots and that this, in turn, would adversely affect the value of lots adjacent to them, so as to also result in a substantial decrease in values of other lots in the subdivision. Conversely, defendants also offered testimony that the existing building restrictions were still of benefit to owners of property in Alpha Place Addition.

In addition, defendants' realtor witness also testified that, in his opinion, plaintiffs' lots could still be sold for residential use, depending on the price. It is thus of interest to note that plaintiffs' testimony was somewhat vague as to the price at which the lots had been offered for sale during the entire period of ownership by plaintiff Albino. Apparently, however, plaintiff Albino expected to recover the price originally paid by him, plus taxes paid by him since then. Thus, the price at which he eventually sold the lots to plaintiff Weaver subject to removal of the building restrictions, was double the original purchase price, "plus you pick up . . . four or five years back taxes." Plaintiff Weaver, a realtor and apartment house operator, also had no detailed plans or specifications for the projected "garden apartments."

After considering the evidence and briefs offered by both plaintiffs and defendants, the trial court held that plaintiffs had failed to sustain the allegations of their complaint by a preponderance of the evidence and that the deed restrictions were still valid and binding and prohibited plaintiffs from erecting multiple family housing on plaintiffs' lots. After reading the entire record, we agree with that decision.

Where the contention is made, as in this case, that such restrictive covenants are no longer binding and enforceable because of a "radical change" in the character of the neighborhood and because enforcement would be "oppressive," it is well established in Oregon that a court of equity will not refuse to enforce such restrictions unless the effect of the change upon the restricted area is such as to "clearly neutralize the benefits of the restrictions to the point of defeating the object and purpose of the covenant." Ludgate v. Somerville, 121 Or. 643, 651, 256 P. 1043, 1046 (1927), quoted with approval in Blair v. Allen C. Edwards Realty Co., 241 Or. 257, 260, 405 P.2d 538 (1965). As also held in *Ludgate,* and approved in *Blair,* it is not sufficient that there have been changes outside the restricted area, unless there have also been changes in the area itself, nor is it sufficient that, as a result of changes outside the area the property within a restricted residential area may be more valuable for business purposes.

To the same effect, as held by this court in Crawford v. Senosky, 128 Or. 229, 235, 274 P. 306 (1929), also approved in *Blair,* 241 Or. at p. 261, 405 P.2d at p. 540, the test is whether, notwithstanding such changes, the restrictive covenant is "still of substantial value to a dominant estate." See also 4 A.L.R.2d 1111, 1160, and 5 Restatement of the Law, Property §564.

In applying these established rules in *Blair,* this court went on to hold, at p. 261, 405 P.2d at p. 540:

> . . . If defendant's lot and others adjacent to the highway are permitted business uses, plaintiffs' residences are that much closer to commercial encroachment. For that reason plaintiffs are deprived of some of the benefit of the restriction upon which they relied when they purchased their properties. If the restriction is not enforced, their first line of defense will have fallen. The erosion will have commenced and there will, in turn, be grounds for removing the restrictions from all adjacent properties.

Thus, this court held in *Blair* that the restrictive covenant in that case was still of substantial value to the properties subject in the restricted area, with the result that it was held to be valid and enforceable. For the same reasons, we hold that the deed restrictions in this case are valid and enforceable.

Plaintiffs contend, however, that under the rule of *Blair* it is necessary to find that the restrictive covenant is still of substantial value to the *property* intended to be benefited, despite the changed use of land in the vicinity, and that benefit to the *owners* of such property is not sufficient. [1]

We do not so construe *Blair,* in which this court, at pp. 260-261, 405 P.2d at p. 540, expressly quoted with approval from its previous decision in *Ludgate* (in which plaintiff brought suit to enjoin violation of deed restrictions by defendant) that:

> . . . We are not prepared to say, in view of the evidence, that the maintenance of this part of Laurelhurst as a residential district is of no substantial benefit to plaintiff. It is true that it might be more valuable for business purposes, but there are some things in this strenuous age of commercialism that count more than cash. It is her home.

In any event, there was ample evidence in this case that removal of the building restrictions on plaintiffs lots, so as to permit the construction of "garden apartments" on those lots, would have adversely affected the value of others lots in Alpha Addition. Conversely, it follows that there was sufficient evidence in this case to support the finding and conclusion that the mainte-

---

1. Plaintiffs also offered evidence that on one of the adjacent lots there was an apartment over the garage, in addition to a house, and that plaintiff's vacant lots had been used by some of the neighbors for the dumping of clippings and for other similar purposes. It appears, however, that the garage apartment was used by a member of the family of the owner of the lot and no contention is made by plaintiffs that the building restrictions had been waived by defendants.

nance of such restrictions upon the property in Alpha Addition was still of substantial value to other property in that addition as of the date of the trial in this case, as well as to the owners of such property.

Affirmed.

NOTES AND QUESTIONS

1. The *Thacher* case marks one of the earliest statements of the doctrine of neighborhood change. The *Albino* case, nearly ninety years later, suggests that the doctrine remains actively litigated as landowners chafe from covenants that bar a more profitable use of their land. Indeed, the very neighborhood change that creates the profit opportunity usually serves as the legal excuse for grabbing the opportunity.

As a threshold question: on the logic of Tulk v. Moxhay, should not the landowner who bought with notice of the restrictions, and who may have paid less because of them, always lose when he claims that neighborhood change makes the covenant unenforceable? Should courts be party to a windfall gain?

2. Examine and compare carefully the rationales of the *Thacher* and *Albino* decisions. How do you explain the different outcomes? Are the courts stating different versions of the same rule? Or are there *significant* factual differences between the two cases? Or do the courts not only look at changes past but also (without saying so) try to predict changes future? (You should know that Radio City Music Hall now graces the easterly Sixth Avenue blockfront between West 50th and West 51st Streets).

3. Both courts agree, inter alia, that covenants of no benefit to the covenantee will not be injunctively enforced. Why is that?

If the covenantee cannot prove any pecuniary loss from the lifting of the restrictions, might the expected loss of psychic, or sentimental, or aesthetic benefits be enough to keep the restrictions intact? Cf. Evangelical Lutheran Church of the Ascension of Snyder v. Sahlem, 254 N.Y. 161, 166, 172 N.E. 455, 457 (1930).

4. Do these cases illustrate or ignore the old-fashioned equitable rule that chancery will not grant injunctive relief when an adequate remedy in damages exists? Putting this question in perspective, note that equity is more likely to enforce the restriction when lifting it would cause significant, measurable damage to the benefited owner, and more likely to refuse the injunction when the benefited owner is not able readily to measure his injury. Is this getting things backward? Or is there another equitable rule involved here— the balancing of hardships and benefits, and the principle that equity will not act unless the magnitude of the asserted hardship and benefit are roughly balanced?

5. In any event, if the restriction is lifted, may the injured neighbors turn around and sue for whatever damages they can prove? As a condition for lifting the restrictions, might equity itself require the windfall gainer to com-

pensate his neighbors? Cf. Wicks v. Pat Pallone Co., 48 Misc. 2d 734, 265 N.Y.S.2d 732 (Sup. Ct. 1965), *rev'd on other grounds*, 29 A.D.2d 626, 285 N.Y.S.2d 1008 (4th Dept. 1967).

6.   Suppose that A and B sue to enforce a covenant against neighbor X. Their suit fails. To what extent does the outcome bind neighbors C, D, etc., who are not parties to the suit? See 10 A.L.R.2d 357 (1949).

7.   On a claim of neighborhood change, X lifts a restriction from Lot 1, which he owns. Y, owner of adjoining Lot 2, opposed the claim. Three months later, Y claims neighborhood change vis-à-vis his lot, and Y's neighbor, Z, resists. Would there be any basis for rejecting Y's claim? Compare Wolff v. Fallon, 44 Cal. 2d 695, 284 P.2d 802 (1955). Can courts draw distinctions within a subdivision, or must a restriction go down for all lots if it goes down for one lot?

8.   Notice that the Willamette Street lots in the *Albino* case were zoned R-G3, permitting garden apartments. Why wasn't this conclusive for the plaintiffs who wanted to build garden apartments? Is it significant that single-family houses were also a permitted use in an R-G3 zone?

The general rule states that a valid restriction is not superseded by the adoption of a zoning ordinance. For a review of the cases and a criticism of the courts' failure to state why this should be, see Berger, Conflicts Between Zoning Ordinances and Restrictive Covenants, 43 Neb. L. Rev. 449 (1964). Would private restrictions that are created after the zoning ordinance also gain primacy?

Do you see any legally significant difference between the following cases:

(a) *Restriction:* single-family residence only.
    Zoning ordinance: R-G3 zone—garden apartments *and* single-family residences permitted uses.
(b) *Restriction:* single-family residence only.
    Zoning ordinance: R-G3 zone—garden apartments only permitted use.

9.   In a suit to nullify restrictions because of neighborhood change, what evidentiary weight should be given to a zoning ordinance that allows a use that the restriction bars?

10.   The *Albino* case raises another much-litigated issue: what is the scope or coverage of a restriction? Wherever any slight ambiguity exists, a landowner hoping to escape the restrictions may have another trump card. Because restrictions under attack tend to be middle-aged, prepared from boiler plate, and not particularly forward-looking, ambiguity is a common trait.

Where ambiguity is in issue, which of the following constructional rules makes the most sense to you? (You may choose more than one, or write your own rules.)

(a) The court should construe any ambiguity against the draftsman (usually the subdivider).

(b) The court should seek to carry out the intent of the draftsman.
(c) The court should seek to reinforce the expectations of those land-owners benefiting most directly from the restrictions.
(d) Since restrictions are a restraint on land use, the court should read generously the uses permitted and narrowly the uses banned.
(e) The court should construe any ambiguity to allow landowners to build whatever the zoning ordinance allows.

§11.5   Does the Doctrine of Neighborhood Change Apply Also to Noncovenant Arrangements?

One might expect that an equitable doctrine that seeks to accommodate con-flicting claims over the use of land would ignore any differences in the legal forms by which these claims arise, yet consider the following material.

WALDROP v. TOWN OF BREVARD
233 N.C. 26, 62 S.E.2d 512 (1950)

This is an action in which the plaintiffs seek to have abated as a private and public nuisance the presently maintained garbage dump of the Town of Brevard, and to recover special damages resulting from its operation since October 1, 1946.

In 1938 the Town of Brevard purchased from I. F. Shipman and wife a tract of land, consisting of five acres, for a garbage dump. The land purchased was near the middle of a 120-acre tract owned by the grantors. At the time the appellees purchased this land, only the grantors and one family lived on the Shipman lands.

The duly recorded deed from Shipman and wife to the Town of Brevard, in addition to conveying the five-acre tract of land, contains the following provisions:

> Together with a right of way across the lands of the parties of the first part 16 feet in width. . . .
>
> It is understood and agreed that the party of the second part is purchasing the property hereinabove described for use as a dumping ground for garbage, waste, trash, refuse, and other materials and products which the party of the second part desires to dispose of. And as a part of this conveyance the parties of the first part do hereby grant and convey unto the said party of the second part, its successors and assigns, the right, without limit as to time and quantity, to use the lands hereinabove described as a dumping ground for the Town of Brevard for garbage, waste, trash, refuse and other materials and products of any and every kind which the said party of the second part desires to dispose of by

dumping on said lands and burning or leaving thereon, and the said parties of the first part do hereby release, discharge, waive and convey unto the said party of the second part, its successors or assigns, any or all rights of action, either legal or equitable which they have or ever might or may have by reason of any action of the party of the second part in using the lands hereinabove described as a dumping ground for the Town of Brevard, or by reason of any fumes, odors, vapors, smoke or other discharges into the atmosphere by reason of such location and use of a dumping ground on the lands hereinabove described.

The agreements and waiver hereinabove set out shall be covenants running with the remainder of the lands owned by the parties of the first part, and binding on said parties as the owners of said lands, and their heirs and assigns, and anyone claiming under them, or any of them, as owners or occupants thereof.

After the Town of Brevard began using the land referred to herein as a garbage dump, I. F. Shipman and wife began selling other portions of the original 120-acre tract. Now some 35 or 40 families live in the neighborhood.

In 1939 Van R. Tinsley and wife purchased a lot from I. F. Shipman and wife, the lot being a portion of the original 120-acre tract and situated approximately 300 yards or more from the land used by the defendant as a garbage dump. The Tinsleys constructed a house on the lot and conveyed the property to the plaintiffs in 1940. They have owned and resided on the premises since that time.

The plaintiffs offered evidence which they contend supports the allegations of their complaint, to the effect that the garbage dump as maintained by the defendant is a public and private nuisance, and that they have suffered special damages as a result thereof. . . .

At the close of plaintiffs' evidence, the defendant moved for judgment as of nonsuit. The motion was denied, but upon renewal thereof at the close of all the evidence, the motion was allowed. Plaintiffs except, appeal and assign error. . . .

DENNY, J. If it be conceded that the normal operation of the defendant's garbage dump in a reasonably careful and prudent manner constitutes a nuisance, in our opinion these plaintiffs are estopped from asserting any claim for damages or for other relief by reason thereof, in view of the grant and covenants contained in the conveyance from I. F. Shipman and wife to the Town of Brevard.

It was stated in the conveyance to the Town of Brevard, that the property was to be used as a garbage dump, and I. F. Shipman and wife expressly granted to it the right, without limit as to time and quantity, to use the premises conveyed as a dumping ground for the Town of Brevard, for garbage, waste, etc., and for themselves, their heirs and assigns, they released, discharged and waived any or all rights of action, either legal or equitable which they have or might have by reason of any action of the Town of Brevard in using the lands conveyed to it as a dumping ground for said town, or by reason of any fumes, odors, vapors, smoke or other discharges into the atmosphere by reason of the use of the premises as a garbage dumping ground. The parties further stipulated that the agreements and waiver set forth in the deed shall be covenants running with the remainder of the lands owned by the grantors and binding on them "as the owners of said lands, and their heirs and assigns, and anyone claiming under them, as owners or occupants thereof."

"A covenant or agreement may operate as a grant of an easement if it is necessary to give it that effect in order to carry out the manifest intention of the parties." 17 Am. Jur. Sec. 27, p. 940.

The grant and release or waiver contained in the deed from I. F. Shipman and wife to the Town of Brevard, in our opinion, created a right in the nature of an easement in favor of the Town of Brevard, upon the remainder of the lands owned by the grantors. And the waiver or release of any right to make a future claim for damages or other relief, resulting from the use of the premises conveyed to the defendant as a garbage dump, constitutes a covenant not to sue and is binding on the grantors, their heirs and assigns. [Citations omitted.]

The appellants contend they are not bound by the covenants in the deed from I. F. Shipman and wife to the Town of Brevard, because . . . there has been such a change in the neighborhood it would be unconscionable and inequitable, and against public policy to enforce the covenants in the defendant's deed. . . .

The plaintiffs' contention that conditions have changed to such an extent, in the neighborhood adjacent to the defendant's garbage dump, that the covenants in the defendant's deed should not be enforced, is without merit. Changed conditions may, under certain circumstances, justify the non-enforcement of restrictive covenants, but a change, such as that suggested by the plaintiffs here, will not in any manner affect a duly recorded easement previously granted.

We do not construe the plaintiffs' complaint to allege that the nuisance complained of was the result of negligent conduct on the part of the defendant, its agents or employees. Therefore, in view of the interpretation we have given to the provisions contained in the defendant's conveyance from I. F. Shipman and wife, plaintiffs' predecessors in title, the judgment as a nonsuit entered below should be upheld.

Affirmed.

NOTES AND QUESTIONS

1. Is there any reason for the result in *Waldrop* other than the court's unwillingness to apply the neighborhood change doctrine to an easement? If the court *had* applied the doctrine to these facts, would plaintiffs have certainly won?

2. Consider also Sakansky v. Wein, 86 N.H. 337, 169 A. 1 (1933). In 1849, plaintiff's ancestors received an eighteen-foot right of way across defen-

dant's land. Defendant, nearly a century later, sought to erect a building over the right of way. He proposed to allow headroom of eight feet where the way would pass under his building and to lay out a new way over level ground around one end of the building, giving plaintiff easy access to his commercial property for vehicles needing more than the 8-foot headroom.

Plaintiff objected to this new arrangement and the court, applying a "rule of reason," decreed the status quo:

> In this state the respective rights of dominant and servient owners are not determined by reference to some technical and more or less arbitrary rule of property law as expressed in some ancient maxim, . . . but are determined by reference to the rule of reason. The application of this rule raises a question of fact to be determined by consideration of all the surrounding circumstances, including the location and uses of both dominant and servient estates, and taking into consideration the advantage to be derived by one and the disadvantage to be suffered by the other owner. . . .

> The rule of reason is a rule of interpretation. . . . [It] does not prevent the parties from making any contract regarding their respective rights which they may wish, regardless of the reasonableness of their wishes on the subject. The rule merely refuses to give unreasonable rights, or to impose unreasonable burdens, when the parties, either actually or by legal implication, have spoken generally.

> In the case at bar the parties are bound by a contract which not only gave the dominant owner a way across the servient estate for the purpose of access to the rear of its premises, but also, gave that way definite location upon the ground. The use which the plaintiff may make of the way is limited by the bounds of reason, but within those bounds its has the unlimited right to travel over the land set apart for a way. It has no right to insist upon the use of any other land of the defendants for a way, regardless of how necessary such other land may be to it, and regardless of how little damage or inconvenience such use of the defendants' land might occasion to them. No more may the defendants compel the plaintiff to detour over other land of theirs. . . .

> The argument advanced that what is reasonable must be considered in the light of the situation as it was at the time the way was granted in 1849 is without merit. What is or is not a reasonable use of a way does not become crystallized at any particular moment of time. Changing needs of either owner may operate to make unreasonable a use of the way previously reasonable, or to make reasonable a use previously unreasonable. There is an element of time as well as of space in this question of reasonableness. In the absence of contract on the subject the owner of the dominant estate is not limited in his use of the way to such vehicles only as were known at the time the way was created, but he may use the way for any vehicle which his reasonable needs may require in the development of his estate. . . .

> Case discharged.

> All concurred.

3. If plaintiff today can use a right of way for vehicles not known to his ancestor in 1849, why, for the defendant's benefit, should not the court fix a

slightly different route to accommodate building design or neighborhood conditions not imagined in 1849?

Conversely, should a court alter the route to meet the plaintiff's changing needs when no harm is caused the defendant?

4.   A two-story brick building occupied Lot 5 (owned by plaintiffs) and Lot 7 (owned by defendants). A party wall divided the building. Sole access to the building's second floor was furnished by an interior stairway situated wholly within Lot 5. A written easement gave use of the stairway to the owners of Lot 7 "so long as the lot on which said stairway is now built is occupied by the building now on said lot."

When the building was about thirty-five years old, plaintiffs sought a declaratory judgment that would allow them to destroy the building on Lot 5 and erect a modern building in its stead. The trial court found that depreciation and obsolescence had so far progressed as to make it "economically advantageous" to plaintiffs to carry out their plans.

Were plaintiffs entitled to a decree permitting destruction of the easement? See Rothschild v. Wolf, 20 Cal. 2d 17, 123 P.2d 483 (1942).

5.   *Does the doctrine of neighborhood change apply to defeasible estates?* Letteau v. Ellis, 122 Cal. App. 584, 10 P.2d 496 (1932), is cited frequently as standing for the doctrine's applicability. Here the court refused to enforce a condition (against black occupancy) where the restricted tract and the surrounding locality had become thickly settled with blacks. In the appellate court opinion (at 588) there appear these words:

> We find it needless to follow appellants' arguments on the technical rules and distinctions made between conditions, covenants, and mere restrictions. In many, if not all, of the cases dealing with changed conditions, the terms have been used with apparent disregard of the niceties of differentiation, and the reasons advanced would have application to a resulting situation, regardless of the means of its creation.

But there was also a trial court finding that plaintiffs had waived their rights to enforcement by allowing the change to occur without acting earlier.

Although Goldstein, Rights of Entry and Possibilities of Reverter as Devices to Restrict the Use of Land, 54 Harv. L. Rev. 248, 266-271 (1940), cites several other decisions for the proposition that neighborhood change will prevent forfeiture, Letteau v. Ellis, *supra,* is alone among the cases cited where the issue was even plausibly before the court. Nor did a more recent investigation add to the instances. Note, 53 Mich. L. Rev. 246, 251 (1954). And in Murray v. Trustees of the Lane Seminary, 140 N.E.2d 577 (Ohio Ct. C.P. 1956), the court flatly refused to apply the doctrine to a defeasible estate.

Can you think of any reasons why the doctrine of neighborhood change should not apply to a defeasible estate?

§11.6   By Legislative Action

Earlier in the text, we examined statutory limits on those defeasible estates that curbed the free use of land. This section deals with statutory limits on covenants that restrict the use of land. As you read the following materials, consider whether efforts to regulate covenants present the same issues for a legislature as would efforts to curb defeasible estates. To help you crystallize your thoughts, be sure to ask yourself:

(a) who the winners and the losers are when a covenant (condition) is unenforceable.
(b) the purposes for which covenants (conditions) are usually created.
(c) whether covenants (conditions) usually arise from donative or commercial transactions.
(d) to what extent covenants (conditions) are already subject to "regulation" by the courts.
(e) how the public interest is served by the regulation of covenants (conditions).

MOHAWK CONTAINERS, INC. v. HANCOCK
43 Misc. 2d 716, 252 N.Y.S.2d 148 (Sup. Ct. 1964)

CARDAMONE, J. The plaintiff, Mohawk Containers, Inc., has previously instituted an action for a declaratory judgment against the defendants to extinguish certain restrictions on the use of their land, pursuant to the provisions of section 1951 of the Real Property Actions and Proceedings Law.

The plaintiff now moves for an order determining that the restrictions are of no actual and substantial benefit to the defendants by reason of changed conditions. The plaintiff further requests judgment that the said restrictions be completely extinguished upon payment to the defendants of such damages, if any, which defendants may sustain.

Mohawk Containers, Inc., (hereinafter called Mohawk) is a manufacturer of corrugated boxes, with a plant located in the Village of New Hartford, Oneida County, New York. Its property, industrially zoned, fronts on Campion Road. The rear of Mohawk's property, which was previously zoned residential, abuts on a residential area comprised of one-family dwelling houses located on Colonial Drive, also located in the said Village. The defendants in this action are property owners who reside on Colonial Drive. In its complaint, Mohawk alleges that it owns, "in fee simple", certain property which is subject to a restrictive covenant that it "shall be used only for residential purposes . . .", and for "single-family dwellings". On November 14, 1963, the zoning of the premises in question was changed to industrial. Subsequent to the zoning change, seven of the eleven owners bound by the restrictions released their rights voluntarily and without financial consideration. One of the owners has remained neutral and the remaining three property owners affected are the defendants in this action. Each of them insists that his property will sustain loss in value if the restrictions on the plaintiff's land are extinguished. In his affidavit, the vice-president of the plaintiff corporation conceded that "these defendants sincerely believed that they will suffer financial loss if this restriction is released". Mohawk proposes to add an extension to its existing building to accommodate new and necessary equipment. There is a natural boundary line between the plaintiff's residential property (where the proposed addition would be located) and the Colonial Manor residential property, consisting of a natural ridge twenty-five (25) feet high. The Zoning Board of Appeals of the Town of New Hartford at the time that it granted the zoning change, did so subject to eleven conditions designed to protect the residential character of the area. There has been no change in the character of the residential lots comprising the Colonial Manor development. All of the property has been and still is used strictly for residential purposes, the price range of the homes starting at $20,000.00

Section 1951 of the Real Property Actions and Proceedings Law provides as follows: [5]

> 2. When relief against such a restriction is sought in an action to quiet title or to obtain a declaration with respect to enforceability of the restriction . . ., if the court shall find that the restriction is of no actual and substantial benefit to the persons seeking its enforcement or seeking a declaration or determination of its enforceability, either because the purpose of the restriction has already been accomplished or, by reason of changed conditions or other cause, its purpose is not capable of accomplishment, or for any other reason, it may adjudge that the restriction is not enforceable by injunction . . . and that it shall be completely extinguished upon payment, to the person or persons who would otherwise be entitled to enforce it in the event of a breach at the time of the action, of such damages, if any, as such person or persons will sustain from the extinguishment of the restriction.

This Statute (eff. Sept. 1, 1963) codifies the doctrine of balancing interests (sometimes referred to as the doctrine of relative hardship), long recognized in Evangelical Lutheran Church of the Ascension of Snyder v. Sahlem, 254 N.Y. 161, 172 N.E. 455 (1930). Ordinarily, where the residential area itself has not changed or deteriorated (and such is conceded here) the covenant is enforceable. (Cummins v. Colgate Properties Corp., 2 Misc. 2d 301, 305, 153 N.Y.S.2d 321, 325-326 (1956), *affd.* 2 A.D.2d 749, 153 N.Y.S.2d 608 (Second Dep't 1956); Kiernan v. Snowden, 123 N.Y.S.2d 895 (Sup. Ct. Westchester Co. 1953); Bull v. Burton, 227 N.Y. 101, 124 N.E. 111 (1919). Still, the Courts of Equity give or withhold decrees according to their discretion in view of the

5. For some legislative background on §1951, see N.Y. Law Review Commission, 1958 Report Recommendations and Studies 211-374.—Ed.

circumstances of each case. Trustees of Columbia College v. Thacher, 87 N.Y. 311, 316 (1882)). A Court of Equity will not enforce a restrictive covenant when it appears that the injury to the defendant is not serious or substantial, and when enforcing it would subject the plaintiff to great inconvenience and loss. . . .

While the action instituted by the plaintiff before the Town Zoning Board of Appeals was appropriate, and the action of that Board was proper in the imposition of reasonable conditions upon the plaintiff (Church v. Town of Islip, 8 N.Y.2d 254, 203 N.Y.S.2d 866, 168 N.E.2d 680 (1960)), despite the change of zoning, the defendants still "have the right to insist upon adherence to the covenant". (Lefferts Manor Ass'n v. Fass, 28 Misc. 2d 1005, 1007, 211 N.Y.S.2d 18, 20 (Sup. Ct. Kings County, 1960); Nemet v. Edgemere Garage & Sales Co., 73 N.Y.S.2d 921 (Sup. Ct. Queens Co. 1947)). In the *Nemet* case, the then Justice Froessel, (later a judge of the Court of Appeals) wrote at page 924:

> I do not find in the statute the legislative intention ascribed by the defendants, and if construed as urged by them, Section 35, in my opinion, would, assuming plaintiff had an easement in the street, deprive him of property without due process of law, *and be an unconstitutional exercise of the legislative power. The Board of Standards and Appeals may, within its powers, grant a permit to an owner, but it may not determine rights in real property.* (emphasis supplied)

The outcome of this controversy must be determined then under the equitable principles of law enunciated by Judge Cardozo in Evangelical Lutheran Church of the Ascension of Snyder v. Sahlem, (254 N.Y. 161, 172 N.E. 455, *supra*). Both the plaintiff and defendants have cited this case in their briefs as supporting their respective contentions. Judge Cardozo wrote at page 166 of 254 N.Y., at page 457 of 172 N.E.: "By the settled doctrine of equity, restrictive covenants in respect of land will be enforced by preventive remedies while the violation is still in prospect, *unless the attitude of the complaining owner in standing on his covenant is unconscionable or oppressive. . . .*" (emphasis supplied) The plaintiff concedes that there are no "unconscionable or oppressive" motives on the defendants' part when it admits that "these defendants *sincerely believe* that they will suffer financial loss if this restriction is released." Since the " 'parties had the right to determine for themselves in what way and for what purposes their lands should be occupied irrespective of pecuniary gain or loss' ", (Evangelical Lutheran Church v. Sahlem, 254 N.Y. 161, 167, 172 N.E. 455, 457), since the defendants "insist upon adherence to a covenant which is now as valid and binding as at the hour of its making" (Ibid., at 168, 172 N.E. at 457), even though some of the "neighbors are willing to modify the restriction and forego a portion of their rights" (Ibid., at 168, 172 N.E. at 457) and since the defendants believe "that the comfort of (their) dwelling will be imperiled by the change, and so (they chose) to abide by the covenant as framed . . ." (Ibid., at 168, 172 N.E. at 457), the choice is for them only. Further, in this case, as in the *Sahlem* case, "the building is yet a plan, the work on it preliminary . . .", (Ibid., at 169, 172 N.E. at 458). Finally, "In the award of equitable remedies there is often an element of discretion, but . . . 'Discretion . . . "must be regulated upon grounds that will make it judicial".' " (Ibid., at 167, 172 N.E. at 457). Since these defendants are "satisfied with the existing state of things" and refuse to disturb it, they "will be protected in (their) refusal by all the power of the law". (Ibid., at 168, 172 N.E. at 457).

Accordingly, the motion of the plaintiff is denied and the complaint is dismissed.

NOTES AND QUESTIONS

1. What weight, if any, should the court in *Mohawk Containers* have given to the following testimony, had plaintiff introduced it:

(a) plaintiff occupied the only industrially zoned parcel in the village.
(b) the village had rezoned to industrial the balance of plaintiff's parcel after conducting a study on the need for industrial expansion within the locality.
(c) plaintiff will close down its plant and move elsewhere if it cannot enlarge the present facility. One hundred persons now work at the plant.
(d) the three homeowners who defended the suit each had asked $50,000 for a release of the tract restrictions.
(e) the restrictions were filed and the Colonial Drive houses were built after plaintiff had built its plant.

2. Refer to question 1(d) above. This is a common occurrence—that is, a landowner seeking more for a release than the developer is ready (able) to pay. Where the court believes that a holdup situation is present, should the court treat §1951 as a mandate to award damages and lift the restriction? Even in the absence of a §1951, might the clean-hands doctrine permit equity to lift the restriction where the court believes one party is behaving badly?

3. Might the village still rescue the situation by condemning the defendants' interest in the plaintiff's property, paying the defendants just compensation, and reselling the interest to the plaintiff? What exactly is the defendants' interest? How would the compensation be fixed? Compare §18.2 *infra*.

4. Section 1951 applies to restrictions on the use of land created at any time "by covenant, promise or negative easement." In Bardach v. Mayfair-Flushing Corp., 49 Misc. 2d 380, 267 N.Y.S.2d 609 (Sup. Ct. 1966), *aff'd mem.*, 26 A.D.2d 620, 272 N.Y.S.2d 969 (2d Dept. 1966), the court relied on §1951 to declare an easement unenforceable. The easement gave the defendants, tenants of an adjacent apartment house, access to plaintiff's vacant lot for

ingress and egress of vehicles and pedestrians, and for a garden, recreation, and play area. Is it clear that §1951 covers this case?

5.   A Georgia statute provides that no privately held restriction shall be enforceable after twenty years if it conflicts with a zoning law. Ga. Code Ann. §29-301 (1935) (exception for interests held by a corporation or a trust for the "public use"). Do you see any problem construing this statute? Compare Note 8, page 658 *supra.*

6.   In 1965 a British commission headed by Leslie Searman began a study on restrictive covenants and on January 31, 1967, filed its report. Law Cmnd. No. 11, pursuant to §3(2) of the Law Commissions Act of 1965. The commission would give to the country's Lands Tribunal clear power to modify or discharge a land obligation where two requirements were satisfied, "first, that the restriction was, or unless modified or discharged would be, detrimental to the public interest by impeding the reasonable uses of land for public or private purposes, second, that the persons entitled to the benefit of the restriction could be adequately compensated in money for any disadvantage that they might suffer."

Slightly altered, this proposal has become law: Law of Property Act 1969, §28. How does the English law differ from §1951? Will Britain be nationalizing certain private interests in land? Would you welcome a similar law to your state?

PART V

THE ALLOCATION AND DEVELOPMENT OF LAND RESOURCES THROUGH RELIANCE ON THE COURTS

Chapter 12

The Judicial Doctrines

§12.1   The Doctrine of Waste

BROKAW v. FAIRCHILD

135 Misc. 70, 237 N.Y.S. 6 (Sup. Ct. 1929), aff'd, 231 A.D. 704, 254 N.Y.S. 402 (1st Dept. 1930), aff'd, 256 N.Y. 670, 177 N.E. 186 (1931)

HAMMER J. . . . In the year 1886 the late Isaac V. Brokaw bought for $199,000 a plot of ground in the borough of Manhattan, city of New York, opposite Central Park, having a frontage of 102 feet 2 inches on the easterly side of Fifth avenue and a depth of 150 feet on the northerly side of Seventy-ninth street. Opposite there is an entrance to the park and Seventy-ninth street is a wide crosstown street running through the park. Upon the corner portion, a plot of ground 51 feet 2 inches on Fifth avenue and a depth of 110 feet on Seventy-fifth street, Mr. Brokaw erected in the year 1887, for his own occupancy, a residence known as No. 1 East Seventy-ninth street, at a cost of $300,000. That residence and corner plot is the subject-matter of this action. The residence, a three-story, mansard and basement granite front building, occupies the entire width of the lot. The mansard roof is of tile. On the first floor are two large drawing rooms on the Fifth avenue side and there are also a large hallway running through from south to north, a reception room, dining room and pantry. The dining room is paneled with carved wood. The hallway is in Italian marble and mosaic. There are murals and ceiling panels. There is a small elevator to the upper portion of the house. On the second floor are a large library, a large bedroom with bath on the Fifth avenue side and there are also four other bedrooms and baths. The third floor has bedrooms and baths. The fourth floor has servants' quarters, bath and storage rooms. The building has steam heat installed by the plaintiff, electric light and current, hardwood floors and all usual conveniences. It is an exceedingly fine house, in construction and general condition as fine as anything in New York. It is contended by plaintiff that the decorations are heavy, not of a type now required by similar residences, and did not appeal to the people to whom it was endeavored to rent the building.

Since 1913, the year of the death of Isaac V. Brokaw and the commencement of the life estate of plaintiff, there has been a change of circumstances and conditions in connection with Fifth avenue properties. Apartments were erected with great rapidity and the building of private residences has practically ceased. Forty-four apartments and only two private residences have been erected on Fifth avenue from Fifty-ninth street to One Hundred and Tenth street. There are to-day but eight of these fifty-one blocks devoted exclusively to private residences. (Exhibits 11 and 12.) Plaintiff's expert testified:

> It is not possible to get an adequate return on the value of that land by any type of improvement other than an apartment house. The structure proposed in the plans of plaintiff is proper and suitable for the site and show 172 rooms which would rent for $1,000 per room. There is an excellent demand for such apartments. . . . There is no corner in the City of New York as fine for an apartment house as that particular corner.

The plaintiff testified also that his expenses in operating the residence which is unproductive would be at least $70,542 greater than if he resided in an apartment. He claims such difference constitutes a loss and contends that the erected apartment house would change this loss into an income or profit of $30,000. Plaintiff claims that under the facts and changed conditions shown the demolition of the building and erection of the proposed apartment is for the best interests of himself as life tenant, the inheritance, and the remaindermen. The defendants deny these contentions and assert certain affirmative defenses. (1) That the proposed demolition of the residence is waste, which against the objection of the adult defendant remaindermen plaintiff cannot be permitted to accomplish. . . .

Coming, therefore, to plaintiff's claimed right to demolish the present residence and to erect in its place the proposed apartment, I am of the opinion that such demolition would result in such an injury to the inheritance as under the authorities would constitute waste. The life estate given to plaintiff under the terms of the will and codicil is not merely in the corner plot of ground with improvements thereon, but, without question, in the residence of the testator. Four times in the devising clause the testator used the words "my residence." This emphasis makes misunderstanding impossible. The identical building which was erected and occupied by the testator in his lifetime and the plot of ground upon which it was built constitute that residence. By no stretch of the imagination could "my residence" be in existence at the end of the life tenancy were the present building demolished and any other structure, even the proposed thirteen-story apartment, erected on the site.

It has been generally recognized that any act of the life tenant which does permanent injury to the inheritance is waste. The law intends that the life tenant shall enjoy his estate in such a reasonable manner that the land shall pass to the reversioner or remainderman as nearly as practicable unimpaired in its nature, character and improvements. The general rule in this country is that the life tenant may do whatever is required for the general use and enjoyment of his estate as he received it. The use of the estate he received is contemplated and not the exercise of an act of dominion or ownership. What the life tenant may do in the future in the way of improving or adding value to the estate is not the test of what constitutes waste. The act of the tenant in changing the estate, and whether or not such act is lawful or unlawful, i.e., whether the estate is so changed as to be an injury to the inheritance, is the sole question involved. The tenant has no right to exercise an act of ownership. In the instant case the inheritance was the residence of the testator—"my residence"—consisting of the present building on a plot of ground fifty-one feet two inches on Fifth avenue by one hundred and ten feet on Seventy-ninth street. "My residence"—such is what the plaintiff under the testator's will has the use of for life. He is entitled to use the building and plot reasonably for his own convenience or profit. To demolish that building and erect upon the land another building, even one such as the contemplated thirteen-story apartment house, would be the exercise of an act of ownership and dominion. It would change the inheritance or thing, the use of which was given to the plaintiff as tenant for life, so that the inheritance or thing could not be delivered to the remaindermen or reversioners at the end of the life estate. The receipt by them at the end of the life estate of a thirteen-story $900,000 apartment house might be more beneficial to them. Financially, the objecting adults may be unwise in not consenting to the proposed change. They may be selfish and unmindful that in the normal course of time and events they probably will not receive the fee. With motives and purposes the court is not concerned. . . .

[U]pon the present facts, circumstances and conditions as they exist and are shown in this case, regardless of the proposed security and the expressed purpose of erecting the proposed thirteen-story apartment, or any other structure, the plaintiff has no right and is not authorized to remove the present structures on or affecting the real estate in question. . . .

ENNIS, LANDMARK MANSION ON 79TH ST. TO BE RAZED
N.Y. Times, Sept. 17, 1964, at 1, cols. 2-5

A chateau at Fifth Avenue and 79th Street that had been designated by the city as a landmark is to be torn down along with two other mansions adjoining it to make way for a new commercial building. The City's Landmarks Preservation Commission said it would protest the move although it lacks the legal power to stop it.

The houses are on the property on the northeast corner of Fifth Avenue and 79th Street, at 984 Fifth Avenue, 1 East 79th Street, and 7 East 79th Street. The chateau-like structure at 1 East 79th Street, known as the Brokaw mansion, has been designated by the Landmarks Commission as worthy of preservation.

James Grote Van Derpool, the Commission's executive director, when he was told of the plan yesterday, deplored it as "the threatened loss of still another example of New York in the Age of Elegance precisely at a time when new interest and understanding of that period is so strongly present."

"Architecture throws light on history," Mr. Van Derpool said, and added that "we need such structures in order to understand in a meaningful way how people lived at a time so very different from our own." . . .

The Fifth Avenue houses are under contract of sale to Anthony Campagna and his son John, builders of many apartment houses here. John Campagna said yesterday that he and his father planned a new building, but would give no further details.[1] The corner site, one of the city's choicest, consists of about 12,500 square feet of land, whose value is estimated at $2.5 million.

The property is being sold by the Institute of Electrical and Electronics Engineers through the Cross & Brown Company, real estate brokers. The institute has occupied the three houses for a number of years, and will move to the United Engineering Center, 345 East 47th Street at the United Nations Plaza, when the buyers take title to the Fifth Avenue property, probably next spring.

No expense was spared in constructing the palatial houses, and architects provided every conceivable luxury available at the time. The house at 1 East 79th Street, which was built for Isaac Vail Brokaw from 1887 to 1890, has huge, airy and well-lighted rooms.

Its grandiose entrance hall is of Italian marble and mosaic and huge murals line the walls. The ceilings are paneled in stone and wood and no two of them are alike. The library has a seven-foot-tall safe concealed behind a panel opened by pressing a hidden catch in a molding.

Mr. Brokaw, realty operator and head of Brokaw Brothers, men's clothing manufacturers, died in 1913. His youngest of three sons, George, occupied the mansion at the time of his marriage in 1923 to Clare Boothe, now Mrs. Henry Luce. Mrs. Luce, who divorced Mr. Brokaw in 1929, inherited a half interest in the house from her daughter, Ann Clare Brokaw, who was killed in an automobile accident. Mrs. Luce, who reportedly disliked the house, sold her share to Mr. Luce.

George Brokaw lived in the mansion until shortly before his death in 1935. He was said to have never liked the house because of its size and cost of its upkeep.

In 1926 he filed suit in the Supreme Court for permission to raze the mansion and erect an apartment house. He asked that his brothers Irving and Howard, who occupied adjoining houses and who opposed the demolition plans, be enjoined from interfering with the proposal for the new building.

---

1. The Brokaw site now has a new multistory stock cooperative, said to contain some of Manhattan's most expensive apartments.—ED.

George Brokaw won his suit and in November, 1926, filed plans for a 13-story building. However, the Supreme Court, on appeal, reversed its decision and the building plans were dropped.

He sued again in 1928 for permission to raze the mansion, but lost that suit on the ground that Isaac Brokaw's will would be violated. . . .

NOTES AND QUESTIONS

1. Criticism of the decision appears in Notes, 15 Cornell L.Q. 501 (1930), 43 Harv. L. Rev. 506 (1930), 30 Mich. L. Rev. 784 (1932), and 7 N.Y.U.L. Rev. 761 (1930).

2. Before the advent of recording acts and the use of metes and bounds description, property was described by its physical appearance with heavy reliance on natural landmarks. Thus, the ancient doctrine of waste was based not only on the reversioner's or remainderman's right to receive the property as it was conveyed to the tenant, but also on the quite understandable fear that if the property were significantly altered, even though improved, proof of title would be more difficult. What policies, if any, remain for putting some check on a life tenant's plans to improve (meliorate) the premises?

3. Following the *Brokaw* decision, the New York Legislature enacted a law "which release[d] whatever hold the English medieval law had on the New York law of waste." Note, 38 Colum. L. Rev. 532, 533 (1938). N.Y. Real Prop. Acts. Law §803 (1963). This section allows a tenant with an expectancy or unexpired term of at least five years to alter the premises without liability for waste if he fulfills the statutory conditions. Before looking, what conditions would you expect to find? Is it clear that the statute would have changed the *Brokaw* decision?

4. The English antecedents to the law of waste begin no later than the thirteenth century. The Statute of Marlbridge, 52 Hen. 3, c. 23, §2 (1267), subjected life tenants and tenants for a term of years who "make waste" to the payment of full damages. The Statute of Gloucester, 6 Edw. 1, c. 5 (1278), upped the penalty to treble damages and forfeiture of the thing wasted.

"Punishment" for waste, although ended in Britian in the nineteenth century, has survived in many American states. A 1968 treatise lists twenty-two states and the District of Columbia as still having statutes permitting the recovery of multiple damages. Nearly as many states forfeiture. Powell, Real Property 698-699 (Powell & Rohan abr. ed. 1968).

Is there any present-day need to treat wasters more harshly than we treat most persons who break contracts?

5. The *Brokaw* case is an atypical waste dispute, in that the life tenant there was seeking to improve the premises. Allegations of waste are usually heard when the party in possession is stripping the land of its resources—e.g.,

timber or minerals—or is failing to maintain the premises as the future inter-est-holder would like.

Professors Powell and Rohan list five forms of waste (id. at 684).

(1) voluntary acts of commission that are *ameliorative* in effect (the *Brokaw* case)

(2) voluntary acts of commission that are destructive in effect (*active waste*)

(3) voluntary inactions that are injurious in effect (*permissive* waste)

(4) failures to prevent conduct of an outsider that is injurious in effect

(5) equitable waste

The authors criticize courts for allowing waste recoveries of the fourth type, where the holder of the future interest can sue the wrongdoing third party directly. Id. at 689; accord, Restatement of Property §146.

So-called equitable waste traces its roots deep into sixteenth century chancery. Before then, present-interest holders sometimes obtained their interests "without impeachment for waste," which the law courts saw as giving total freedom to the party in possession. At the plea of the future-interest holder, chancery stepped in to prevent willful and unconscionable plunder of the property. There has evolved, where someone holds "without impeachment for waste," a duty which chancery will enforce "not to strip the future interest owner of his asset with impunity." Powell, *supra*, at 689-690.

6.   In resolving waste disputes, American courts generally apply the "good husbandry" or "prudent owner" test. For a discussion of the underlying rationale and the difficulties in application, see 5 American Law of Property 75-93 (Casner ed. 1952).

7.   Mortgages frequently contain the mortgagor's covenant not to commit waste. Might the criteria for waste depend on whether it is a mortgagee or some future interest-holder who has complained? Consider, for example, whether a mortgagee holding a $10,000 mortgage may enjoin timber-cutting that would reduce the value of the mortgaged property from $50,000 to $25,000. Cf. Cal. Civ. Code §2929 (West 1974). May a remainderman?

§12.2   The Doctrines of Lateral and Subjacent Support

a.   Lateral Support

X and Y are adjoining landowners. X has built an apartment house whose foundation is only a few inches from the X-Y boundary. Y now decides to build an apartment house. In digging the foundation on his lot, Y withdraws ground support from his neighbor's land, causing severe injury (crumbling and buckling) to X's building. May X recover his damages?

Y's liability to X at common law depended upon the doctrine of lateral support, that is, upon a landowner's duty not to act on his own land so as to impair the soil integrity of his neighbor's land. The general rule gave each landowner the right that his land, *in its natural state,* receive lateral support from the land of his neighbor. In the case at hand, X would be deemed either to have a (negative) easement in Y's land or something akin to an implied (by operation of law) contract right to soil integrity. And, of course, Y would have corresponding rights against X.

The common-law doctrine may have worked quite well in an agrarian setting, but when carried into areas of intensive development, the doctrine fared badly. Since it protects only land in its natural state, the doctrine caused confusion and frequent dispute when the supported land contained a structure. There was, first of all, a factual question: did the weight of the structure contribute to the subsidence or, given the depth and manner of excavation, would subsidence have occurred even without the structure? Technical experts often battled over that one. Second, there were the legal issues. If the weight of the structure did not help cause subsidence, the injured landowner could always recover for the damage to his soil, but could he also recover for any *structural* damage? In all states, the excavator's negligence led to full recovery for the damage to land *and* building, provided, of course, that the building's weight was not a contributing factor. Where the excavator had not preceeded negligently, however, two lines of authority emerged. The "American" rule barred recovery, cf. Moellering v. Evans, 121 Ind. 195, 22 N.E. 989 (1889) ("The owner of the house is without remedy. It was his own folly to put it there."). The "English" rule, increasingly popular in the United States, gave recovery, cf. Prete v. Cray, 49 R.I. 209, 141 A. 609 (1928). Query: which rule better suits rapid urban expansion? Why?

Difficult issues remained, however, centering on the negligence of the excavator's conduct. One writer has listed six forms of excavator negligence.

(1) an unnecessary excavation is made by one who foresees that it will cause a neighbor's land to subside

(2) the excavation serves a useful purpose, but is made without giving notice to the adjoining possessors in sufficient time to permit them to take the steps necessary to prevent subsidence

(3) the excavator assumes responsibility for safeguarding his neighbor's land but is negligent in executing the task

(4) the excavator informs his neighbor of the precautions that he plans to take but thereafter changes his procedure without informing his neighbor of the facts of these changes

(5) the excavator fails to ascertain in advance, by customary methods, whether the proposed excavation is likely to endanger the adjoining land and buildings

(6) departure from the accepted methods of excavation. Powell, Real Property 765-766 (Powell & Rohan abr. ed. 1968)

Many state legislatures have sought to rationalize lateral support. The California law, *infra*, typifies the most frequent statutory approach. The legislature in 1968 reduced from twelve feet to nine feet the depth prescribed in paragraph 4. What interests might that change serve?

> *Lateral and subjacent support; excavations; degree of care; damages; protection of other structures.* Each coterminous owner is entitled to the lateral and subjacent support which his land receives from the adjoining land, subject to the right of the owner of the adjoining land to make proper and usual excavations on the same for purposes of construction or improvement, under the following conditions:
>
>   1. Any owner of land or his lessee intending to make or to permit an excavation shall give reasonable notice to the owner or owners of adjoining lands and of buildings or other structures, stating the depth to which such excavation is intended to be made, and when the excavating will begin.
>
>   2. In making any excavation, ordinary care and skill shall be used, and reasonable precautions taken to sustain the adjoining land as such, without regard to any building or other structure which may be thereon, and there shall be no liability for damage done to any such building or other structure by reason of the excavation, except as otherwise provided or allowed by law.
>
>   3. If at any time it appears that the excavation is to be of a greater depth than are the walls or foundations of any adjoining building or other structure, and is to be so close as to endanger the building or other structure in any way, then the owner of the building or other structure must be allowed at least thirty days, if he so desires, in which to take measures to protect the same from any damage, or in which to extend the foundations thereof, and he must be given for the same purposes reasonable license to enter on the land on which the excavation is to be or is being made.
>
>   4. If the excavation is intended to be or is deeper than the standard depth of foundations, which depth is defined to be a depth of nine feet below the adjacent curb level, at the point where the joint property line intersects the curb and if on the land of the coterminous owner there is any building or other structure the wall or foundation of which goes to standard depth or deeper then the owner of the land on which the excavation is being made shall, if given the necessary license to enter on the adjoining land, protect the said adjoining land and any such building or other structure thereon without cost to the owner thereof, from any damage by reason of the excavation, and shall be liable to the owner of such property for any such damage, excepting only for minor settlement cracks in buildings or other structures. [Cal. Civ. Code §832]

Cf. also N.Y. City Admin. Code §C26-1903.1 (1969) (ten-foot depth controls duties).

NOTES AND QUESTIONS

1. How does the California statute change the English (American) common-law rule? The statute, notwithstanding litigation, still occurs regu-

larly. How might the disputes arise? See, e.g., the annotations to Cal. Civ. Code §832 (West).

    2. At least two other statutory formulae exist:

(a) In a few states, the owner of the already improved land obtains support neither for his building nor his land if the excavator observes the statutory requirements.

(b) In some cities, the excavator is liable absolutely for any damage to his neighbor's land or building. Cf. 5 Powell, Real Property ¶702 at 305 (Rohan ed. 1980).

What are the pros and cons of each statutory type?

    3. Returning to the illustrative case, how would you fix X's damages if X can establish a claim against Y?

(a) the cost of restoration or the diminution in value, whichever is the smaller
(b) the cost of restoration
(c) the decrease in market value Cf. 5 Powell, Real Property ¶701 at 302-304 (Rohan ed. 1980).

b. Subjacent Support

Subjacent support involves the rights and duties of two parties whose holdings lie one above the other. This often occurs in mining areas where one party owns the surface and a second party holds subsurface privileges.

The common law treated subjacent support by analogy to lateral support. Thus the surface owner had the absolute right to subjacent support for his soil in its natural state. If there were structures, too, problems arose as to whether the structural weight contributed to the subsidence and if it did not, whether the surface owner must still prove the miner's negligence to recover for structural damage. There was a practical difference, however, from the lateral support cases. It was relatively easy for the surface owner to show that subsidence would have occurred regardless of the structures. This meant, in practice, that in "English" rule jurisdictions, surface owners could usually recover for all their damage on a theory of absolute liability.

Statutes have tended to enlarge the surface owner's rights, sometimes by requiring that the underground operator give security before he continues mining, see, e.g., Pa. Stat. Ann. tit. 52, §1406.5 (Supp. 1981), sometimes by creating an agency to regulate mining, see, e.g., Pa. Stat. Ann. tit. 52, §1406.7 (Supp. 1981), sometimes by flatly barring any mining that causes subsidence to dwelling places and specified other structures, see, e.g., Pa. Stat. Ann. tit. 52, §661 (1966); id. at §1407 (bars only *negligent* mining in bituminous areas).

Often as part of the deed or lease that creates the mining privilege, the operator will bargain for a release of the surface owner's rights to subjacent support. You will shortly read one of the most cited cases in the Supreme Court annals, which involved a state law that sought to regulate such releases, Pennsylvania Coal Co. v. Mahon, page 712, *infra.*

§12.3   The Doctrine of Nuisance

a.   Private Nuisance

In an era of rising environmental awareness, the phrase "sic utere tuo ut alienum non laedas" has far-reaching consequences for the life quality that we and our children will enjoy. Even if you have already met nuisance in your torts course, it seems worthwhile to examine this doctrine within the context of land use.

What we see is an inevitable tension between the demands resulting from industrial society, energy shortage, and population growth on one side, and the delicate balance between man and nature on the other side. State and federal laws dealing with the problem abound, and we shall examine in a later chapter (§16.4) some of these statutes and the legal issues that result. But courts also play a common-law role as they fashion doctrine in those frequent disputes that arise between neighbors.

Bove v. Donner-Hanna Coke Corp., *infra,* is an old-line decision that gives counterpoint to Boomer v. Atlantic Cement Co., which follows. *Boomer* typifies the new breed of nuisance case, in which lawyers and judges deal sophisticatedly with industrial technology, economic theory, and environmental science. In reading and comparing *Bove* and *Boomer,* consider whether a private dispute carried to the courtroom is the best way to shape the use of land.

BOVE v. DONNER-HANNA COKE CORP.
236 A.D. 37, 258 N.Y.S. 229 (4th Dept. 1932)

EDGCOMB, J. The question involved upon this appeal is whether the use to which the defendant has recently put its property constitutes a private nuisance, which a court of equity should abate.

In 1910 plaintiff purchased two vacant lots at the corner of Abby and Baraga streets in the city of Buffalo, and two years later built a house thereon. The front of the building was converted into a grocery store, and plaintiff occupied the rear as a dwelling. She rented the two apartments on the second floor.

Defendant operates a large coke oven on the opposite side of Abby street. The plant runs twenty-four hours in the day, and three hundred and sixty-five days in the year. Of necessity, the operation has to be continuous, because the ovens would be ruined if they were allowed to cool off. The coke is heated to a temperature of around 2000 degrees F., and is taken out of the ovens and run under a "quencher," where 500 or 600 gallons of water are poured onto it at one time. This is a necessary operation in the manufacture of coke. The result is a tremendous cloud of steam which rises in a shaft and escapes into the air, carrying with it minute portions of coke and more or less gas. This steam and the accompanying particles of dirt, as well as the dust which come from a hugh coal pile necessarily kept on the premises, and the gases and odors which emanate from the plant are carried by the wind in various directions, and frequently find their way onto the plaintiff's premises and into her house and store. According to the plaintiff this results in an unusual amount of dirt and soot accumulating in her house, and prevents her opening the windows on the street side; she also claims that she suffers severe headaches by breathing the impure air occasioned by this dust and these offensive odors, and that her health and that of her family has been impaired, all to her very great discomfort and annoyance; she also asserts that this condition has lessened the rental value of her property, and has made it impossible at times to rent her apartments.

Claiming that such use of its plant by the defendant deprives her of the full enjoyment of her home, invades her property rights, and constitutes a private nuisance, plaintiff brings this action in equity to enjoin the defendant from the further maintenance of said nuisance, and to recover the damages which she asserts she has already sustained.

As a general rule, an owner is at liberty to use his property as he sees fit, without objection or interference from his neighbor provided such use does not violate an ordinance or statute. There is, however, a limitation to this rule; one made necessary by the intricate complex and changing life of to-day. The old and familiar maxim that one must so use his property as not to injure that of another (sic utere tuo ut alienum non laedas) is deeply imbedded in our law. An owner will not be permitted to make an unreasonable use of his premises to the material annoyance of his neighbor if the latter's enjoyment of life or property is materially lessened thereby. This principle is aptly stated by Andrews, Ch. J., in Booth v. R., W. & O.T.R.R. Co. (140 N.Y. 267, 274) as follows:

> The general rule that no one has absolute freedom in the use of his property, but is restrained by the co-existence of equal rights in his neighbor to the use of his property, so that each in exercising his right must do no act which causes injury to his neighbor, is so well understood, is so universally recognized, and stands so impregnably in the necessities of the social state, that is vindication by argument would be superfluous. The maxim which embodies it is sometimes loosely interpreted as forbidding all use by one of his own property, which annoys or disturbs

his neighbor in the enjoyment of his property. The real meaning of the rule is that one may not use his own property to the injury of any legal right of another.

Such a rule is imperative, or life to-day in our congested centers would be intolerable. If a citizen was given no protection against unjust harassment arising from the use to which the property of his neighbor was put, the comfort and value of his home could easily be destroyed by any one who chose to erect an annoyance nearby, and no one would be safe, unless he was rich enough to buy sufficient land about his home to render such disturbance impossible. When conflicting rights arise, a general rule must be worked out which, so far as possible, will preserve to each party that to which he has a just claim.

While the law will not permit a person to be driven from his home, or to be compelled to live in it in positive distress or discomfort because of the use to which other property nearby has been put, it is not every annoyance connected with business which will be enjoined. Many a loss arises from acts or conditions which do not create a ground for legal redress. Damnum absque injuria is a familiar maxim. Factories, stores and mercantile establishments are essential to the prosperity of the nation. They necessarily invade our cities, and interfere more or less with the peace and tranquillity of the neighborhood in which they are located.

One who chooses to live in the large centers of population cannot expect the quiet of the country. Congested centers are seldom free from smoke, odors and other pollution from houses, shops and factories, and one who moves into such a region cannot hope to find the pure air of the village or outlying district. A person who prefers the advantages of community life must expect to experience some of the resulting inconveniences. Residents of industrial centers must endure without redress a certain amount of annoyance and discomfiture which is incident to life in such a locality. Such inconvenience is of minor importance compared with the general good of the community. . . .

Whether the particular use to which one puts his property constitutes a nuisance or not is generally a question of fact, and depends upon whether such use is reasonable under all the surrounding circumstances. What would distress and annoy one person would have little or no effect upon another; what would be deemed a disturbance and a torment in one locality would be unnoticed in some other place; a condition which would cause little or no vexation in a business, manufacturing or industrial district might be extremely tantalizing to those living in a restricted and beautiful residential zone; what would be unreasonable under one set of circumstances would be deemed fair and just under another. Each case is unique. No hard and fast rule can be laid down which will apply in all instances. . . .

The inconvenience, if such it be, must not be fanciful, slight or theoretical, but certain and substantial, and must interfere with the physical comfort of the ordinarily reasonable person. . . .

Applying these general rules to the facts before us, it is apparent that defendant's plant is not a nuisance per se, and that the court was amply justified in holding that it had not become one by reason of the manner in which it had been conducted. Any annoyance to plaintiff is due to the nature of the business which the defendant conducts, and not to any defect in the mill, machinery or apparatus. The plant is modern and up to date in every particular. It was built under a contract with the Federal government, the details of which are not important here. The plans were drawn by the Kopperas Construction Company, one of the largest and best known manufacturers of coke plants in the world, and the work was done under the supervision of the War Department. No reasonable change or improvement in the property can be made which will eliminate any of the things complained of. If coke is made, coal must be used. Gas always follows the burning of coal, and steam is occasioned by throwing cold water on red hot coals.

The cases are legion in this and other States where a defendant has been held guilty of maintaining a nuisance because of the annoyance which he has caused his neighbor by reason of noise, smoke, dust, noxious gases and disagreeable smells which have emanated from his property. But smoke and noisome odors do not always constitute a nuisance. I find none of these cases controlling here; they all differ in some particular from the facts in the case at bar.

It is true that the appellant was a resident of this locality for several years before the defendant came on the scene of action, and that, when the plaintiff built her house, the land on which these coke ovens now stand was a hickory grove. But in a growing community changes are inevitable. This region was never fitted for a residential district; for years it has been peculiarly adapted for factory sites. This was apparent when plaintiff bought her lots and when she built her house. The land is low and lies adjacent to the Buffalo river, a navigable stream connecting with Lake Erie. Seven different railroads run through this area. Freight tracks and yards can be seen in every direction. Railroads naturally follow the low levels in passing through a city. Cheap transportation is an attraction which always draws factories and industrial plants to a locality. It is common knowledge that a combination of rail and water terminal facilities will stamp a section as a site suitable for industries of the heavier type, rather than for residential purposes. In 1910 there were at least eight industrial plants, with a total assessed valuation of over a million dollars, within a radius of a mile from plaintiff's house.

With all the dirt, smoke and gas which necessarily come from factory chimneys, trains and boats, and with full knowledge that this region was especially adapted for industrial rather than residential purposes, and that factories would increase in the future, plaintiff selected this locality as the site of her future home. She voluntarily moved into this district, fully aware of the fact that the atmosphere would constantly be contaminated by dirt, gas and foul odors; and that she could not hope to find in this locality the pure air of a strictly residential zone. She evidently saw certain advantages in living in this congested center. This is not the case of an industry, with its attendant noise and dirt, invading a quiet, residential district. It is just the opposite. Here a residence is built in an area naturally adapted for industrial purposes and already dedicated to that use. Plaintiff can hardly be heard to complain at this late date that her peace and comfort have been disturbed by a situation which existed, to some extent at least, at the very time she bought her property, and which condition she must have known would grow worse rather than better as the years went by.

To-day there are twenty industrial plants within a radius of less than a mile and three-quarters from appellant's house, with more than sixty-five smokestacks rising in the air, and belching forth clouds of smoke; every day there are 148 passenger trains, and 225 freight trains, to say nothing of switch engines, passing over these various railroad tracks near to the plaintiff's property; over 10,000 boats, a large portion of which burn soft coal, pass up and down the Buffalo river every season. Across the street, and within 300 feet from plaintiff's house, is a large tank of the Iroquois Gas Company which is used for the storage of gas.

The utter abandonment of this locality for residential purposes, and its universal use as an industrial center, becomes manifest when one considers that in 1929 the assessed valuation of the twenty industrial plants above referred to aggregated over $20,000,000, and that the city in 1925 passed a zoning ordinance putting this area in the third industrial district, a zone in which stockyards, glue factories, coke ovens, steel furnaces, rolling mills and other similar enterprises were permitted to be located.

One has only to mention these facts to visualize the condition of the atmosphere in this locality. It is quite easy to imagine that many of the things of which the plaintiff complains are due to causes over which the defendant has no control. At any rate, if appellant is immune from the annoyance occasioned by the smoke and odor which must necessarily come from these various sources, it would hardly seem that she could consistently claim that her health has been impaired, and that the use and enjoyment of her home have been seriously interfered with solely because of the dirt, gas and stench which have reached her from defendant's plant.

It is very true that the law is no respecter of persons, and that the most humble citizen in the land is entitled to identically the same protection accorded to the master of the most gorgeous palace. However, the fact that the plaintiff has voluntarily chosen to live in the smoke and turmoil of this industrial zone is some evidence, at least, that any annoyance which she has suffered from the dirt, gas and odor which have emanated from defendant's plant is more imaginary and theoretical than it is real and substantial.

I think that the trial court was amply justified in refusing to interfere with the operation of the defendant's coke ovens. No consideration of public policy or private rights demands any such sacrifice of this industry.

Plaintiff is not entitled to the relief which she seeks for another reason.

Subdivision 25 of section of the General City Law (added by Laws of 1917, chap. 483) gives to the cities of this State authority to regulate the location of industries and to district the city for that purpose. Pursuant to such authority the common council of the city of Buffalo adopted an ordinance setting aside the particular area in which defendant's plant is situated as a zone in which coke ovens might lawfully be located.

After years of study and agitation it has been found that development in conformity with some well-considered and comprehensive plan is necessary to the welfare of any growing municipality. The larger the community the greater becomes the need of such plan. Haphazard city building is ruinous to any city. Certain areas must be given over to industry, without which the country cannot long exist. Other sections must be kept free from the intrusion of trade and the distraction of business, and be set aside for homes, where one may live in a wholesome environment. Property owners, as well as the public, have come to recognize the absolute necessity of reasonable regulations of this character in the interest of public health, safety and general welfare, as well as for the conservation of property values. Such is the purpose of our zoning laws.

After due consideration the common council of Buffalo decreed that an enterprise similar to that carried on by the defendant might properly be located at the site of this particular coke oven. It is not for the court to step in and override such decision, and condemn as a nuisance a business which is being conducted in an approved and expert manner, at the very spot where the council said that it might be located. A court of equity will not ordinarily assume to set itself above officials to whom the law commits a decision, and reverse their discretion and judgment, unless bad faith is involved. No such charge is made here. (Morgan v. City of Binghamton, 102 N.Y. 500; Matter of Union Bank of Brooklyn, 176 App. Div. 477, 486.)

Other defenses have been urged by the defendant, which it is unnecessary to discuss, in view of the conclusion which has already been reached.

I see no good reason why the decision of the Special Term should be disturbed. I think that the judgment appealed from should be affirmed.

All concur.

Judgment affirmed, with costs.

BOOMER v. ATLANTIC CEMENT CO.

26 N.Y.2d 219, 257 N.E.2d 870, 309 N.Y.S.2d 312 (1970)

BERGAN, J. Defendant operates a large cement plant near Albany. These are actions for injunction and damages by neighboring land owners alleging injury to property from dirt, smoke and vibration emanating from the plant. A nuisance has been found after trial, temporary damages have been allowed; but an injunction has been denied.

The public concern with air pollution arising from many sources in industry and in transportation is currently accorded ever wider recognition accompanied by a growing sense of responsibility in State and Federal Governments to control it. Cement plants are obvious sources of air pollution in the neighborhoods where they operate. . . .

Effective control of air pollution is a problem presently far from solution even with the full public and financial powers of government. In large measure adequate technical procedures are yet to be developed and some that appear possible may be economically impracticable.

It seems apparent that the amelioration of air pollution will depend on technical research in great depth; on a carefully balanced consideration of the economic impact of close regulation; and of the actual effect on public health. It is likely to require massive public expenditure and to demand more than any local community can accomplish and to depend on regional and interstate controls.

A court should not try to do this on its own as a by-product of private litigation and it seems manifest that the judicial establishment is neither equipped in the limited nature of any judgment it can pronounce nor prepared to lay down and implement an effective policy for the elimination of air pollution. This is an area beyond the circumference of one private lawsuit. It is a direct responsibility for government and should not thus be undertaken as an incident to solving a dispute between property owners and a single cement plant—one of many—in the Hudson River valley.

The cement making operations of defendant have been found by the court at Special Term to have damaged the nearby properties of plaintiffs in these two actions. That court, as it has been noted, accordingly found defendant maintained a nuisance and this has been affirmed at the Appellate Division. The total damage to plaintiffs' properties is, however, relatively small in comparison with the value of defendant's operation and with the consequences of the injunction which plaintiffs seek.

The ground for the denial of injunction, notwithstanding the finding both that there is a nuisance and that plaintiffs have been damaged substantially, is the large disparity in economic consequences of the nuisance and of the injunction. This theory cannot, however, be sustained without overruling a doctrine which has been consistently reaffirmed in several leading cases in this court and which has never been disavowed here, namely that where a nuisance has been found and where there has been any substantial damage shown by the party complaining an injunction will be granted.

The rule in New York has been that such a nuisance will be enjoined although marked disparity be shown in economic consequence between the effect of the injunction and the effect of the nuisance.

The problem of disparity in economic consequence was sharply in focus in Whalen v. Union Bag & Paper Co. (208 N.Y. 1). A pulp mill entailing an investment of more than a million dollars polluted a stream in which plaintiff, who owned a farm, was "a lower riparian owner". The economic loss to plaintiff from this pollution was small. This court, reversing the Appellate Division, reinstated the injunction granted by the Special Term against the argument of the mill owner that in view of "the slight advantage to plaintiff and the great loss that will be inflicted on defendant" an injunction should not be granted

(p. 2). "Such a balancing of injuries cannot be justified by the circumstances of this case", Judge Werner noted (p. 4). He continued: "Although the damage to the plaintiff may be slight as compared with the defendant's expense of abating the condition, that is not a good reason for refusing an injunction" (p. 5).

Thus the unconditional injunction granted at Special Term was reinstated. The rule laid down in that case, then, is that whenever the damage resulting from a nuisance is found not "unsubstantial", viz., $100 a year, injunction would follow. This states a rule that had been followed in this court with marked consistency (McCarthy v. Natural Carbonic Gas Co., 189 N.Y. 40; Strobel v. Kerr Salt Co., 164 N.Y. 303; Campbell v. Seaman, 63 N.Y. 658). . . .

Although the court at Special Term and the Appellate Division held that injunction should be denied, it was found that plaintiffs had been damaged in various specific amounts up to the time of the trial and damages to the respective plaintiffs were awarded for those amounts. The effect of this was, injunction having been denied, plaintiffs could maintain successive actions at law for damages thereafter as further damage was incurred.

The court at Special Term also found the amount of permanent damage attributable to each plaintiff, for the guidance of the parties of such permanent damage as a settlement of all the controversies among the parties. The total of permanent damages to all plaintiffs thus found was $185,000. This basis of adjustment has not resulted in any stipulation by the parties.

This result at Special Term and at the Appellate Division is a departure from a rule that has become settled; but to follow the rule literally in these cases would be to close down the plant at once. This court is fully agreed to avoid that immediately drastic remedy; the difference in view is how best to avoid it.[1]

One alternative is to grant the injunction but postpone its effect to a specified future date to give opportunity for technical advances to permit defendant to eliminate the nuisance; another is to grant the injunction conditioned on the payment of permanent damages to plaintiffs which would compensate them for the total economic loss to their property present and future caused by defendant's operations. For reasons which will be developed the court chooses the latter alternative.

If the injunction were to be granted[,] unless within a short period—e.g., 18 months—the nuisance be abated by improved methods, there would be no assurance that any significant technical improvement would occur.

The parties could settle this private litigation at any time if defendant paid enough money and the imminent threat of closing the plant would build up the pressure on defendant. If there were no improved techniques found,

---

1. Respondent's investment in the plant is in excess of $45,000,000. There are over 300 people employed there.

there would inevitably be applications to the court at Special Term for extensions of time to perform on showing of good faith efforts to find such techniques.

Moreover, techniques to eliminate dust and other annoying by-products of cement making are unlikely to be developed by any research the defendant can undertake within any short period, but will depend on the total resources of the cement industry Nationwide and throughout the world. The problem is universal wherever cement is made.

For obvious reasons the rate of the research is beyond control of defendant. If at the end of 18 months the whole industry has not found a technical solution a court would be hard put to close down this one cement plant if due regard be given to equitable principles.

On the other hand, to grant the injunction unless defendant pays plaintiffs such permanent damages as may be fixed by the court seems to do justice between the contending parties. All of the attributions of economic loss to the properties on which plaintiffs' complaints are based will have been redressed.

The nuisance complained of by these plaintiffs may have other public or private consequences, but these particular parties are the only ones who have sought remedies and the judgment proposed will fully redress them. The limitation of relief granted is a limitation only within the four corners of these actions and does not foreclose public health or other public agencies from seeking proper relief in a proper court.

It seems reasonable to think that the risk of being required to pay permanent damages to injured property owners by cement plant owners would itself be a reasonably effective spur to research for improved techniques to minimize nuisance.

The power of the court to condition on equitable grounds the continuance of an injunction on the payment of permanent damages seems undoubted. (See, e.g., the alternatives considered in McCarthy v. Natural Carbonic Gas Co., *supra*, as well as Strobel v. Kerr Salt Co., *supra*).

The damage base here suggested is consistent with the general rule in those nuisance cases where damages are allowed. "Where a nuisance is of such a permanent and unabatable character that a single recovery can be had, including the whole damage past and future resulting therefrom, there can be but one recovery" (66 C.J.S., Nuisances, §140, p. 947). It has been said that permanent damages are allowed where the loss recoverable would obviously be small compared with the cost of removal of the nuisance (Kentucky-Ohio Gas Co. v. Bowling, 264 Ky. 470, 477). . . .

Thus it seems fair to both sides to grant permanent damages to plaintiffs which will terminate this private litigation. The theory of damage is the "servitude on land" of plaintiffs imposed by defendant's nuisance. (See United States v. Causby, 328 U.S. 256, 261, 262, 267, where the term "servitude" addressed to the land was used by Justice Douglas relating to the effect of airplane noise on property near an airport.)

The judgment, by allowance of permanent damages imposing a servitude on land, which is the basis of the actions, would preclude future recovery by plaintiffs or their grantees (see Northern Indiana Public Serv. Co. v. Vesey, [210 Ind. 338, 351]).

This should be placed beyond debate by a provision of the judgment that the payment by defendant and the acceptance by plaintiffs of permanent damages found by the court shall be in compensation for a servitude on the land.

Although the Trial Term has found permanent damages as a possible basis of settlement of the litigation, on remission the court should be entirely free to reexamine this subject. It may again find the permanent damage already found; or make new findings.

The orders should be reversed, without costs, and the cases remitted to Supreme Court, Albany Court to grant an injunction which shall be vacated upon payment by defendant of such amounts of permanent damage to the respective plaintiffs as shall for this purpose be determined by the court.

JASEN, J. (dissenting). I agree with the majority that a reversal is required here, but I do not subscribe to the newly enunciated doctrine of assessment of permanent damages, in lieu of an injunction, where substantial property rights have been impaired by the creation of a nuisance.

It has long been the rule in this State, as the majority acknowledges, that a nuisance which results in substantial continuing damage to neighbors must be enjoined. (Whalen v. Union Bag & Paper Co., 208 N.Y. 1; Campbell v. Seaman, 63 N.Y. 568; see, also, Kennedy v. Moog Servocontrols, 21 N.Y.2d 966.) To now change the rule to permit the cement company to continue polluting the air indefinitely upon the payment of permanent damages is, in my opinion, compounding the magnitude of a very serious problem in our State and Nation today.

In recognition of this problem, the Legislature of this State has enacted the Air Pollution Control Act (Public Health Law, §§1264-1299-m) declaring that it is the State policy to require the use of all available and reasonable methods to prevent and control air pollution (Public Health Law, §1265 [1]).

The harmful nature and widespread occurrence of air pollution have been extensively documented. Congressional hearings have revealed that air pollution causes substantial property damage, as well as being a contributing factor to a rising incidence of lung cancer, emphysema, bronchitis and asthma. [2]

The specific problem faced here is known as particulate contamination because of the fine dust particles emanating from defendant's cement plant.

1. See, also, Air Quality Act of 1967, 81 U.S. Stat. 485 (1967) [42 U.S.C. §§1857 et seq.].
2. See U.S. Cong., Senate Comm. on Public Works, Special Subcomm. on Air and Water Pollution, Air Pollution 1966, 89th Cong., 2d Sess., 1966, at pp. 22-24; U.S. Cong., Senate Comm. on Public Works, Special Subcomm. on Air and Water Pollution, Air Pollution 1968, 90th Cong., 2d Sess., 1968, at pp. 850, 1084.

The particular type of nuisance is not new, having appeared in many cases for at least the past 60 years. (See Hulbert v. California Portland Cement Co., 161 Cal. 239 [1911].) It is interesting to note that cement production has recently been identified as a significant source of particulate contamination in the Hudson Valley.[3] This type of pollution, wherein very small particles escape and stay in the atmosphere, has been denominated as the type of air pollution which produces the greatest hazard to human health.[4] We have thus a nuisance which not only is damaging to the plaintiffs,[5] but also is decidedly harmful to the general public.

I see grave dangers in overruling our long-established rule of granting an injunction where a nuisance results in substantial continuing damage. In permitting the injunction to become inoperative upon the payment of permanent damages, the majority is, in effect, licensing a continuing wrong. It is the same as saying to the cement company, you may continue to do harm to your neighbors so long as you pay a fee for it. Furthermore, once such permanent damages are assessed and paid, the incentive to alleviate the wrong would be eliminated, thereby continuing air pollution of an area without abatement.

It is true that some courts have sanctioned the remedy here proposed by the majority in a number of cases,[6] but none of the authorities relied upon by the majority are analogous to the situation before us. In those cases, the courts, in denying an injunction and awarding money damages, grounded their decision on a showing that the use to which the property was intended to be put was primarily for the public benefit. Here, on the other hand, it is clearly established that the cement company is creating a continuing air pollution nuisance primarily for its own private interest with no public benefit.

This kind of inverse condemnation (Ferguson v. Village of Hamburg, 272 N.Y. 234) may not be invoked by a private person or corporation for private gain or advantage. Inverse condemnation should only be permitted when the public is primarily served in the taking or impairment of property. (Matter of New York City Housing Auth. v. Muller, 270 N.Y. 333, 343; Pocantico Water Works Co. v. Bird, 130 N.Y. 249, 258.) The promotion of the interests of the polluting cement company has, in my opinion, no public use or benefit.

Nor is it constitutionally permissible to impose servitude on land, without consent of the owner, by payment of permanent damages where the con-

3. New York State Bureau of Air Pollution Control Services, Air Pollution Capital District, 1968, at p. 8.

4. J. Ludwig, Air Pollution Control Technology: Research and Development on New and Improved Systems, 33 Law & Contemp. Prob., 217, 219 (1968).

5. There are seven plaintiffs here who have been substantially damaged by the maintenance of this nuisance. The trial court found their total permanent damages to equal $185,000.

6. See United States v. Causby (328 U.S. 256); Kentucky-Ohio Gas Co. v. Bowling (Ky. 470, 477); Northern Indiana Public Service Co. v. Vesey (210 Ind. 338); City of Amarillo v. Ware (120 Tex. 456); Pappenheim v. Metropolitan El. Ry. Co. (128 N.Y. 436); Ferguson v. Village of Hamburg (272 N.Y. 234).

tinuing impairment of the land is for a private use. (See Fifth Ave. Coach Lines v. City of New York, 11 N.Y.2d 342, 347; Walker v. City of Hutchison, 352 U.S. 112.) This is made clear by the State Constitution (art. I, §7, subd. [a]) which provides that "[p]rivate property shall not be taken for *public use* without just compensation" (emphasis added). It is, of course, significant that the section makes no mention of taking for a *private* use.

In sum, then, by constitutional mandate as well as by judicial pronouncement, the permanent impairment of private property for private purposes is not authorized in the absence of clearly demonstrated public benefit and use.

I would enjoin the defendant cement company from continuing the discharge of dust particles upon its neighbors' properties unless, within 18 months, the cement company abated this nuisance.[7]

It is not my intention to cause the removal of the cement plant from the Albany area, but to recognize the urgency of the problem stemming from this stationary source of air pollution, and to allow the company a specified period of time to develop a means to alleviate this nuisance.

I am aware that the trial court found that the most modern dust control devices available have been installed in defendant's plant, but, I submit, this does not mean that *better* and more effective dust control devices could not be developed within the time allowed to abate the pollution.

Moreover, I believe it is incumbent upon the defendant to develop such devices, since the cement company, at the time the plant commenced production (1962), was well aware of the plaintiffs' presence in the area, as well as the probable consequences of its contemplated operation. Yet, it still chose to build and operate the plant at this site.

In a day when there is a growing concern for clean air, highly developed industry should not expect acquiescence by the courts, but should, instead, plan its operations to eliminate contamination of our air and damage to its neighbors.

Accordingly, the orders of the Appellate Division, insofar as they denied the injunction, should be reversed, and the actions remitted to Supreme Court, Albany County to grant an injunction to take effect 18 months hence, unless the nuisance is abated by improved techniques prior to said date.

CHIEF JUDGE FULD and JUDGES BURKE and SCILEPPI concur with JUDGE BERGAN; JUDGE JASEN dissents in part and votes to reverse in a separate opinion; JUDGES BREITEL and GIBSON taking no part.

In each action: Order reversed, without costs, and the case remitted to Supreme Court, Albany County, for further proceedings in accordance with the opinion herein.

---

7. The issuance of an injunction to become effective in the future is not an entirely new concept. For instance, in Schwarzenbach v. Oneonta Light & Power Co. (207 N.Y. 671), an injunction against the maintenance of a dam spilling water on plaintiff's property was issued to become effective one year hence.

NOTES AND QUESTIONS

1. Eight property owners joined in the suit against the Atlantic Cement Company. In each case, the trial court found that the plaintiff had suffered at least a 50 percent loss of market value because of defendant's operations. 55 Misc. 2d 1023, 1026, 287 N.Y.S.2d 112, 115 (Sup. Ct. 1967).

The $185,000 award of permanent damages (as of 1967) compares with the finding of temporary damages (loss of usable value) of $6,420 per year. Which would plaintiffs rather receive, $185,000 now or $6,420 per year indefinitely? Do you see any contradiction between the two findings?

2. At the retrial to fix permanent damages (as of 1971), the plaintiffs argued that standard valuation rules for just compensation should not apply. Instead of the "willing buyer, willing seller, negotiated price" standard, plaintiffs asked the court to use a "contract price" theory, i.e., the amount that a buyer would agree to pay where it needed a servitude to stay in business as against a seller unwilling to sell his land. The court rejected this theory, which might have doubled or tripled the plaintiffs' recovery. Was the court correct in doing so?

Even as to standard valuation, the opposing experts were poles apart, as Table 9 shows. For comparison, the table also shows the "contract price" claims.

Settlement negotiations continued even after trial, and plaintiffs Boomer and Meilak finally accepted an undisclosed amount from the defendant. Faced with the irreconcilable testimony on the Kinley parcel, the court fixed permanent damages at $175,000. Boomer v. Atlantic Cement Co., 72 Misc. 2d 834, 340 N.Y.S.2d 97 (Sup. Ct. 1972).

In commenting on the expert testimony, the court recalled a passage from Ferguson v. Hubbell, 97 N.Y. 507, 514 (1884): "Better results will generally be reached by taking the impartial, unbiased judgments of twelve jurors

TABLE 9

	Value Without Nuisance	Value with Nuisance	Standard Damage	"Contract Price" Damage
Boomer Parcel				
Plaintiff's expert	97,700	5,000	92,700	250,000
Defendant's expert	36,000	27,000	9,000	—
Meilak Parcel				
Plaintiff's expert	90,000	4,000	86,000	—
Defendant's expert	48,000	40,800	7,200	—
Kinley Parcel				
Plaintiff's expert	420,500	25,000	395,500	918,900
Defendant's expert	210,000	185,250	24,750	—

of common sense and common experience than can be obtained by taking the opinions of experts, if not generally hired, at least friendly, whose opinions cannot fail generally to be warped by a desire to promote the cause in which they are enlisted."

3. The opinion does not say so, but the Atlantic Cement plant was located in an industrial zone. 35 Albany L. Rev. 48, 149 n.7 (1970). Should plaintiffs still have recovered? Can you reconcile the *Bove* and *Boomer* decisions?

More directly, what survives (or should survive) of the common-law doctrine of nuisance where the defendant can show conformity with the zoning ordinance? Compare Sweet v. Campbell, 282 N.Y. 146, 25 N.E.2d (1940).

4. The state legislature has the following bill before it: "Cement companies shall have the power upon payment of just compensation to acquire privately owned land whenever needed to expand the company's industrial operation." Would passage of this law raise the constitutional objection that Judge Jasen worries about in his *Boomer* dissent? Is there any difference between legislating a private taking and decreeing one, as in *Boomer?*

What other instances have you already seen where either the courts or legislatures have allowed a landowner to acquire a property interest from his unwilling neighbor?

5. Do you see any contradiction between a court's refusal to enjoin the cement works in *Boomer* and a court's refusal to allow the plant expansion in *Mohawk Containers*, §11.6 *supra?* In the second case, the neighbors successfully claimed a contract-property right that the plant not expand. Is this a higher order of right than the "mere" property right that the *Boomer* plaintiffs asserted?

6. Suppose that the *Boomer* plaintiffs had sued five years earlier to enjoin construction of the plant on grounds that the plant's operation would become a nuisance. Would this suit have created a balance different from the one that the court actually faced? How should the hypothetical case be decided?

7. Neither the *Bove* nor the *Boomer* court gave much importance to the fact that the plaintiff homeowners had been there first. What weight, if any, should courts give to the date of the parties' arrival in the neighborhood?

8. X and Y are adjoining landowners. Y constructs an office building that encroaches 6 inches on X's parcel. It would cost Y $200,000 to remove the encroachment. The value of X's 6-inch strip is $35,000. X sues Y for an injunction. Would the reasoning in the *Boomer* case compel the denial of the injunction? Should it? Would your answer change if you were told that Y deliberately encroached? Cf. Annot., 28 A.L.R.2d 679, 705 (1953); Stuart v. Lake Washington Realty Corp., 141 W. Va. 627, 652-653, 92 S.E.2d 891, 905 (1956). Cf. also N.Y. Real Prop. Acts. Law §611 (1963) (where exterior wall encroachment not more than 6 inches, owner must sue within one year from

building completion to recover possession or within two years to recover damages).

9. Doesn't the decision in the *Boomer* case substitute judicial price-fixing for private negotiations between the parties? To put this question differently, what would be likely to happen if the court said it would issue an injunction in six months unless the defendant acquired the plaintiffs' parcels (or obtain the plaintiffs' release) by negotiated settlement?

Do you see an unfolding paradox? By agreeing to award damages in lieu of an injunction, the court is forcing plaintiffs to accept a fair price for their injury, since they cannot "hold up" the defendant too unreasonably. This is one of the chief reasons for eminent domain. If government had to negotiate every acquisition down to the last parcel, the cost of public improvements in this country would be vastly inflated. Why so? Yet eminent domain presupposes a public good, and statutes giving private landowners the equivalent power (pages 1027-1028 *infra*) also assume that the hospital, or university, or low-income housing developer is serving the public good. In *Boomer*, however, plaintiffs must show that defendant is committing a social harm, i.e., a nuisance, or they won't collect anything. Can you resolve the paradox?

CALABRESI AND MELAMED, PROPERTY RULES, LIABILITY RULES, AND INALIENABILITY

85 Harv. L. Rev. 1089-1093, 1115-1124 (1972)

I. INTRODUCTION

Only rarely are Property and Torts approached from a unified perspective. Recent writings by lawyers concerned with economics and by economists concerned with law suggest, however, that an attempt at integrating the various legal relationships treated by these subjects would be useful both for the beginning student and the sophisticated scholar. By articulating a concept of "entitlements" which are protected by property, liability, or inalienability rules, we present one framework for such an approach. We then analyze aspects of the pollution problem to demonstrate how the model enables us to perceive relationships which have been ignored by writers in those fields.

The first issue which must be faced by any legal system is one we call the problem of "entitlement." Whenever a state is presented with the conflicting interests of two or more people, or two or more groups of people, it must decide which side to favor. Absent such a decision, access to goods, services, and life itself will be decided on the basis of "might makes right"—whoever is stronger or shrewder will win. Hence the fundamental thing that law does is to decide which of the conflicting parties will be entitled to prevail. The entitlement to make noise versus the entitlement to have silence, the entitlement to pollute versus the entitlement to breathe clean air, the entitlement to have children versus the entitlement to forbid them—these are the first order of legal decisions.

Having made its initial choice, society must enforce that choice. Simply setting the entitlement does not avoid the problem of "might makes right"; a minimum of state intervention is always necessary. Our conventional notions make this easy to comprehend with respect to private property. If Taney owns a cabbage patch and Marshall, who is bigger, wants a cabbage, he will get it unless the state intervenes. But it is not so obvious that the state must also intervene if it chooses the opposite entitlement, communal property. If large Marshall has grown some communal cabbages and chooses to deny them to small Taney, it will take state action to enforce Taney's entitlement to the communal cabbages. The same symmetry applies with respect to bodily integrity. Consider the plight of the unwilling ninety-eight-pound weakling in a state which nominally entitles him to bodily integrity but will not intervene to enforce the entitlement against a lustful Juno. Consider then the plight—absent state intervention—of the ninety-eight-pounder who desires an unwilling Juno in a state which nominally entitles everyone to use everyone else's body. The need for intervention applies in a slightly more complicated way to injuries. When a loss is left where it falls in an auto accident, it is not because God so ordained it. Rather it is because the state has granted the injurer an entitlement to be free of liability and will intervene to prevent the victim's friends, if they are stronger, from taking compensation from the injurer. The loss is shifted in other cases because the state has granted an entitlement to compensation and will intervene to prevent the stronger injurer from rebuffing the victim's request for compensation.

The state not only has to decide whom to entitle, but it must also simultaneously make a series of equally difficult second order decisions. These decisions go to the manner in which entitlements are protected and to whether an individual is allowed to sell or trade the entitlement. In any given dispute, for example, the state must decide not only which side wins but also the kind of protection to grant. It is with the latter decisions, decisions which shape the subsequent relationship between the winner and the loser, that this article is primarily concerned. We shall consider three types of entitlements—entitlements protected by property rules, entitlements protected by liability rules, and inalienable entitlements. The categories are not, of course, absolutely distinct; but the categorization is useful since it reveals some of the reasons which lead us to protect certain entitlements in certain ways.

An entitlement is protected by a property rule to the extent that someone who wishes to remove the entitlement from its holder must buy it from him in a voluntary transaction in which the value of the entitlement is agreed upon by the seller. It is the form of entitlement which gives rise to the least amount of state intervention: once the original entitlement is decided upon, the state does not try to decide its value. It lets each of the parties say how much the entitlement is worth to him, and gives the seller a veto if the buyer does not offer enough. Property rules involve a collective decision as to who is to be given an initial entitlement but not as to the value of the entitlement.

Whenever someone may destroy the initial entitlement if he is willing to pay an objectively determined value for it, an entitlement is protected by a liability rule. This value may be what it is thought the original holder of the entitlement would have sold it for. But the holder's complaint that he would have demanded more will not avail him once the objectively determined value is set. Obviously, liability rules involve an additional stage intervention: not only are entitlements protected, but their transfer or destruction is allowed on the basis of a value determined by some organ of the state rather than by the parties themselves.

An entitlement is inalienable to the extant that its transfer is not permitted between a willing buyer and a willing seller. The state intervenes not only to determine who is initially entitled and to determine the compensation that must be paid if the entitlement is taken or destroyed, but also to forbid its sale under some or all circumstances. Inalienability rules are thus quite different from property and liability rules. Unlike those rules, rules of inalienability not not "protect" the entitlement; they may also be viewed as limiting or regulating the grant of the entitlement itself.

It should be clear that most entitlements to most goods are mixed. Taney's house may be protected by a property rule in situations where Marshall wishes to purchase it, by a liability rule where the government decides to take it by eminent domain, and by a rule of inalienability in situations where Taney is drunk or incompetent. This article will explore two primary questions: (1) In what circumstances should we grant a particular entitlement? and (2) In what circumstances should we decide to protect that entitlement by using a property, liability, or inalienability rule? . . .

IV. THE FRAMEWORK AND POLLUTION CONTROL RULES

Nuisance or pollution is one of the most interesting areas where the question of who will be given an entitlement, and how it will be protected, is in frequent issue. Traditionally, and very ably in the recent article by Professor Michelman, the nuisance-pollution problem is viewed in terms of three rules. [6] First, Taney may not pollute unless his neighbor (his only neighbor let us assume), Marshall, allows it (Marshall may enjoin Taney's nuisance). Second, Taney may pollute but must compensate Marshall for damages caused (nuisance is found but the remedy is limited to damages). Third, Taney may pollute at will and can only be stopped by Marshall if Marshall pays him off (Taney's pollution is not held to be a nuisance to Marshall). In our terminology rules one and two (nuisance with injunction, and with damages only) are

---

6. Michelman, Pollution as a Tort: A Non-Accidental Perspective on Calabresi's Costs, 80 Yale L.J. 647 (1971).

entitlements to Marshall. The first is an entitlement to be free from pollution and is protected by a property rule; the second is also an entitlement to be free from pollution but is protected only by a liability rule. Rule three (no nuisance) is instead an entitlement to Taney protected by a property rule, for only by buying Taney out at Taney's price can Marshall end the pollution.

The very statement of these rules in the context of our framework suggests that something is missing. Missing is a fourth rule repesenting an entitlement in Taney to pollute, but an entitlement which is protected only by a liability rule. The fourth rule, really a kind of partial eminent domain coupled with a benefits tax, can be stated as follows: Marshall may stop Taney from polluting, but if he does he must compensate Taney.

As a practical matter it will be easy to see why even legal writers as astute as Professor Michelman have ignored this rule. Unlike the first three it does not often lend itself to judicial imposition for a number of good legal process reasons. For example, even if Taney's injuries could practicably be measured, apportionment of the duty of compensation among many Marshalls would present problems for which courts are not well suited. If only those Marshalls who voluntarily asserted the right to enjoin Taney's pollution were required to pay the compensation, there would be insuperable freeloader problems. If, on the other hand, the liability rule entitled one of the Marshalls alone to enjoin the pollution and required all the benefited Marshalls to pay their share of the compensation, the courts would be faced with the immensely difficult task of determining who was benefited how much and imposing a benefits tax accordingly, all the while observing procedural limits within which courts are expected to function.

The fourth rule is thus not part of the cases legal scholars read when they study nuisance law, and is therefore easily ignored by them. But it is available, and may sometimes make more sense than any of the three competing approaches. Indeed, in one form or another, it may well be the most frequent device employed. To appreciate the utility of the fourth rule and to compare it with the other three rules, we will examine why we might choose any of the given rules.

We would employ rule one (entitlement to be free from pollution protected by a property rule) from an economic efficiency point of view if we believed that the polluter, Taney, could avoid or reduce the costs of pollution more cheaply than the pollutee, Marshall. Or to put it another way, Taney would be enjoinable if he were in a better position to balance the costs of polluting against the costs of not polluting. We would employ rule three (entitlement to pollute protected by a property rule) again solely from an economic efficiency standpoint, if we made the converse judgment on who could best balance the harm of pollution against its avoidance costs. If we were wrong in our judgments and if transactions between Marshall and Taney were costless or even very cheap, the entitlement under rules one or three would be traded and an economically efficient result would occur in either case. If we entitled Taney to pollute and Marshall valued clean air more than Taney valued the pollution, Marshall would pay Taney to stop polluting even though no nuisance was found. If we entitled Marshall to enjoin the pollution and the right to pollute was worth more to Taney than freedom from pollution was to Marshall, Taney would pay Marshall not to seek an injunction or would buy Marshall's land and sell it to someone who would agree not to seek an injunction. As we have asssumed no one else was hurt by the pollution, Taney could now pollute even though the initial entitlement, based on a wrong guess of who was the cheapest avoider of the costs involved, allowed the pollution to be enjoined. Wherever transactions between Taney and Marshall are easy, and wherever economic efficiency is our goal, we could employ entitlements protected by property rules even though we would not be sure that the entitlement chosen was the right one. Transactions as described above would cure the error. While the entitlement might have important distributional effects, it would not substantially undercut economic efficiency.

The moment we assume, however, that transactions are not cheap, the situation changes dramatically. Assume we enjoin Taney and there are 10,000 injured Marshalls. Now *even* if the right to pollute is worth more to Taney than the right to be free from pollution is to the sum of the Marshalls, the injunction will probably stand. The cost of buying out all the Marshalls, given holdout problems, is likely to be too great, and an equivalent of eminent domain in Taney would be needed to alter the initial injunction. Conversely, if we denied a nuisance remedy, the 10,000 Marshalls could only with enormous difficulty, given freeloader problems, get together to buy out even one Taney and prevent the pollution. This would be so even if the pollution harm was greater than the value to Taney of the right to pollute.

If, however, transaction costs are not symmetrical, we may still be able to use the property rule. Assume that Taney can buy the Marshalls' entitlements easily because holdouts are for some reason absent, but that the Marshalls have great freeloader problems in buying out Taney. In this situation the entitlement should be granted to the Marshalls unless we are sure the Marshalls are the cheapest avoiders of pollution costs. Where we do not know the identity of the cheapest cost avoider it is better to entitle the Marshalls to be free of pollution because, even if we are wrong in our initial placement of the entitlement, that is, even if the Marshalls are the cheapest cost avoiders, Taney will buy out the Marshalls and economic efficiency will be achieved. Had we chosen the converse entitlement and been wrong, the Marshalls could not have bought out Taney. Unfortunately, transaction costs are often high on both sides and an initial entitlement, though incorrect in terms of economic efficiency, will not be altered in the market place.

Under these circumstances—and they are normal ones in the pollution area—we are likely to turn to liability rules whenever we are uncertain whether the polluter or the pollutees can most cheaply avoid the cost of pollution. We are only likely to use liability rules where we are uncertain because, if we are certain, the costs of liability rules—essentially the costs of collectively valuing the damages to all concerned plus the cost in coercion to those who would not sell at the collectively determined figure—are unnecessary. They are unnecessary because transaction costs and bargaining barriers become irrelevant when we are certain who is the cheapest cost avoider; economic efficiency will be attained without transactions by making the correct initial entitlement.

As a practical matter we often are uncertain who the cheapest cost avoider is. In such cases, traditional legal doctrine tends to find a nuisance but imposes only damages on Taney payable to the Marshalls. This way, if the amount of damages Taney is made to pay is close to the injury caused, economic efficiency will have had its due; if he cannot make a go of it, the nuisance was not worth its costs. The entitlement to the Marshalls to be free from pollution unless compensated, however, will have been given *not* because it was thought that polluting was probably worth less to Taney than freedom from pollution was worth to the Marshalls, nor even because on some distributional basis we preferred to charge the cost to Taney rather than to the Marshalls. It was so placed *simply because we did not know* whether Taney desired to pollute more than the Marshalls desired to be free from pollution, and the only way we thought we could test out the value of the pollution was by the only liability rule we thought we had. This was rule two, the imposition of nuisance damages on Taney. At least this would be the position of a court concerned with economic efficiency which believed itself limited to rules one, two, and three.

Rule four gives at least the possibility that the opposite entitlement may also lead to economic efficiency in a situation of uncertainty. Suppose for the moment that a mechanism exists for collectively assessing the damage resulting to Taney from being stopped from polluting by the Marshalls, and a mechanism also exists for collectively assessing the benefit to each of the Marshalls from such cessation. Then—assuming the same degree of accuracy in collective valuation as exists in rule two (the nuisance damage rule)—the Marshalls would stop the pollution if it harmed them more than it benefited Taney. If this is possible, then even if we thought it necessary to use a liability rule, we would still be free to give the entitlement to Taney or Marshall for whatever reasons, efficiency or distributional, we desired.

Actually, the issue is still somewhat more complicated. For just as transaction costs are not necessarily symmetrical under the two converse property rule entitlements, so also the liability rule equivalents of transaction costs—the cost of valuing collectively and of coercing compliance with that valuation—may not be symmetrical under the two converse liability rules. Nuisance damages may be very hard to value, and the costs of informing all the injured of their rights and getting them into court may be prohibitive. Instead, the assessment of the objective damage to Taney from foregoing his pollution may be cheap and so might the assessment of the relative benefits to all Marshalls of such freedom from pollution. But the opposite may also be the case. As a result, just as the choice of which property entitlement may be based on the asymmetry of transaction costs and hence on the greater amenability of one property entitlement to market corrections, so might the choice between liability entitlements be based on the asymmetry of the costs of collective determination.

The introduction of distributional considerations makes the existence of the fourth possibility even more significant. One does not need to go into all the permutations of the possible tradeoffs between efficiency and distributional goals under the four rules to show this. A simple example should suffice. Assume a factory which, by using cheap coal, pollutes a very wealthy section of town and employs many low income workers to produce a product purchased primarily by the poor; assume also a distributional goal that favors equality of wealth. Rule one—enjoin the nuisance—would possibly have desirable economic efficiency results (if the pollution hurt the homeowners more than it saved the factory in coal costs), but it would have disastrous distribution effects. It would also have undesirable efficiency effects if the initial judgment on costs of avoidance had been wrong and transaction costs were high. Rule two—nuisance damages—would allow a testing of the economic efficiency of eliminating the pollution, even in the presence of high transaction costs, but would quite possibly put the factory out of business or diminish output and thus have the same income distribution effects as rule one. Rule three—no nuisance—would have favorable distributional effects since it might protect the income of the workers. But if the pollution harm was greater to the homeowners than the cost of avoiding it by using a better coal, and if transaction costs—holdout problems—were such that homeowners could not unite to pay the factory to use better coal, rule three would have unsatisfactory efficiency effects. Rule four—payment of damages to the factory after allowing the homeowners to compel it to use better coal, and assessment of the cost of these damages to the homeowners—would be the only one which would accomplish both the distributional and efficiency goals.

An equally good hypothetical for any of the rules can be constructed. Moreover, the problems of coercion may as a practical matter be extremely severe under rule four. How do the homeowners decide to stop the factory's use of low grade coal? How do we assess the damages and their proportional allocation in terms of benefits to the homeowner? But equivalent problems may often be as great for rule two. How do we value the damages to each of the many homeowners? How do we inform the homeowners of their rights to damages? How do we evaluate and limit the administrative expenses of the court actions this solution implies?

The seriousness of the problem depends under each of the liability rules on the number of people whose "benefits" or "damages" one is assessing and the expense and likelihood of error in such assessment. A judgment on these questions is necessary to an evaluation of the possible economic efficiency benefits of employing one rule rather than another. The relative ease of making such assessments through different institutions may explain why we often employ the courts for rule two and get to rule four—when we do get there—only through political bodies which may, for example, prohibit pollution, or

"take" the entitlement to build a supersonic plane by a kind of eminent domain, paying compensation to those injured by these decisions. But all this
does not, in any sense, diminish the importance of the fact that an awareness of
the possibility of an entitlement to pollute, but one protected only by a liability rule, may in some instances allow us best to combine our distributional and
efficiency goals.

We have said that we would say little about justice, and so we shall. But
it should be clear that if rule four might enable us best to combine efficiency
goals with distributional goals, it might also enable us best to combine those
same efficiency goals with other goals that are often described in justice language. For example, assume that the factory in our hypothetical was using
cheap coal *before* any of the wealthy homes were built. In these circumstances,
rule four will not only achieve the desirable efficiency and distributional results mentioned above, but it will also accord with any "justice" significance
which is attached to being there first. And this is so whether we view this
justice significance as part of a distributional goal, as part of a long run
efficiency goal based on protecting expectancies, or as part of an independent
concept of justice.

Thus far in this section we have ignored the possibility of employing
rules of inalienability to solve pollution problems. A general policy of barring
pollution does seem unrealistic. But rules of inalienability can appropriately
be used to limit the levels of pollution and to control the levels of activities
which cause pollution.

One argument for inalienability may be the widespread existence of
moralisms against pollution. Thus it may hurt the Marshalls—gentlemen
farmers—to see Taney, a smoke-choked city dweller, sell his entitlement to be
free of pollution. A different kind of externality or moralism may be even more
important. The Marshalls may be hurt by the expectation that, while the
present generation might withstand present pollution levels with no serious
health damages, future generations may well face a despoiled, hazardous environmental condition which they are powerless to reverse. And this ground for
inalienability might be strengthened if a similar conclusion were reached on
grounds of self-paternalism. Finally, society might restrict alienability on paternalistic grounds. The Marshalls might feel that although Taney himself
does not know it, Taney will be better off if he really can see the stars at night,
or if he can breathe smogless air.

Whatever the grounds for inalienability, we should reemphasize that
distributional effects should be carefully evaluated in making the choice for or
against inalienability. Thus the citizens of a town may be granted an entitlement to be free of water pollution caused by the waste discharges of a chemical
factory; and the entitlement might be made inalienable on the grounds that
the town's citizens really would be better off in the long run to have access to
clean beaches. But the entitlement might also be made inalienable to assure
the maintenance of a beautiful resort area for the very wealthy, at the same
time putting the town's citizens out of work.

NOTES

1. In quite a remarkable decision, the Supreme Court of Arizona—apparently without having first read the above article—has adopted the Calabresi-Melamed fourth possibility. Spur Industries, Inc. v. Del E. Webb Development Co., 108 Ariz. 178, 494 P.2d 700 (1972). Spur Industries had operated a feedlot lawfully since 1956. In 1959, Del E. Webb began to develop Sun City, a residential community, within a few miles of the feedlot. As the community expanded toward the feedlot, drifting odors and the persistent presence of flies (30,000 feeding cattle generated one million pounds of wet manure daily) became quite unpleasant, and the developer sued to enjoin the feedlot as a public and private nuisance.

The supreme court affirmed the trial court's judgment, which permanently enjoined the feedlot operation on both theories of nuisance. The appellate court refused, however, to place the financial burden of its decision upon the operator. Instead, it required Webb to indemnify Spur for a "reasonable amount of the cost" of moving or shutting down.

> It does not seem harsh to require a developer, who has taken advantage of the lesser land values in a rural area as well as the availability of large tracts of land on which to build and develop a new town or city in the area, to indemnify those who are forced to leave as a result. [108 Ariz. 186, 494 P.2d 708]

2. Polinsky, Resolving Nuisance Disputes: The Simple Economics of Injunctive and Damage Remedies, 32 Stan. L. Rev. 1075 (1980), extends the Calabresi and Melamed analysis by re-examining when the alternative remedies of injunction and damages would better serve the dual goals of economic efficiency and distributional equity.

b. Public Nuisance

UNITED STATES v. COUNTY BD. OF ARLINGTON COUNTY
487 F. Supp. 137 (E.D. Va. 1979)

LEWIS, S. D. J. The United States brought this suit for declaratory and injunctive relief against Arlington County, Virginia; Arland Towers Company; Rosslyn Center Development Corporation; Twin Development Corporation; and Theodore B. Gould, to prevent the construction of four high-rise office buildings and one hotel in the Rosslyn section of the County—on the grounds of illegal zoning and federal common law nuisance.

The complaint alleges that the Secretary of the Interior is charged by law to conserve the scenery and the natural and historical objects [in the parks and monuments] and to provide for the enjoyment of the same in such manner and by such means as will leave them unimpaired for the enjoyment of future generations and—

As guardian of our national parks, the Secretary has a constitutionally and Congressionally-based mandate to protect the rights of the public in the parks which he deems threatened by this commercial development in Arlington County.

That through the National Capital Planning Commission the United States is charged with preserving the historical and natural features thereof by, among other things, maintaining the open space requirements along the Virginia shoreline that L'Enfant intended as a most important segment of the green backdrop of the monuments of the Capital.

That the United States owns property in both Arlington County, Virginia and the District of Columbia upon which are memorials and monuments revered by all American citizens.

That the buildings for which the site plans were unlawfully approved will soar high above the present Rosslyn skyline.

That they will present visual intrusions to the enjoyment of such areas as the Lincoln Memorial, the Washington Monument, the Theodore Roosevelt Memorial, the John F. Kennedy Center, and other park lands in the District of Columbia, and the Arlington National Cemetery and the Iwo Jima Marine Memorial in Arlington County, Virginia.

That the traffic generated as a result of the density and building heights greater than permitted under the Arlington County Ordinances will also have an adverse impact on traffic conditions on the George Washington Memorial Parkway located, in part, in Arlington County.

That by reason of the foregoing, the interests of the United States and its people have been and will be injured through the visual intrusion of the defendants' buildings on the memorials, monuments and parks of our Nation's Capital, and by the increased traffic and congestion resulting from the use of the buildings constructed under the unlawful site plans of development and in violation of the zoning ordinance of Arlington County, and the laws of the State of Virginia.

Jurisdiction pursuant to 28 U.S.C. §1345 was not seriously questioned. . . .

The question for determination in this case is—whether or not the United States can limit the height and bulk of buildings in Rosslyn on the theory of public nuisance. The Department of Justice contends that any building [in Rosslyn] over 290 feet above sea level or 20 stories would be a visual intrusion on the monumental core of the Nation's Capital—it would seriously impair the beauty of the Nation's Capital as defined in its horizontal nature and its major vistas of major public monuments—both in and from the monumental core.

The material facts are not in dispute—only the inferences to be drawn therefrom. The monumental core of the Nation's Capital is located on the dominant axis of the federal city, centering on the Mall area. The seven major monuments, the memorials and edifices in the monumental core are the Capitol building to the east; the Washington Monument, the Lincoln Memorial and the White House to the north; the Jefferson Memorial to the south; and the Arlington Cemetery and the Iwo Jima Memorial to the west.

Washington is a horizontal city; its buildings are of a relatively low, uniform height that follow the contour of the land. Major visual corridors were created and preserved, such as various specific avenues, the Mall, West Potomac Park and the Ellipse area. The McMillan Plan of 1901 proposed, in part, that the Mall concept of the L'Enfant Plan be strengthened and expanded by the introduction of the Lincoln Memorial at the terminus of the Mall.

In 1928, the National Capital Parks and Planning Commission proposed a plan for Potomac River parks to be implemented not only in the District of Columbia, but also on the Virginia-Maryland shoreline.

Some forty million people visit the monuments, memorials and public buildings in the monumental core annually.

The original ten-mile square area designated by George Washington as the place for the seat of the national government included what is now known as Arlington County—the land south of the Potomac has been ceded back to Virginia.

The Rosslyn high-rise office buildings are located between Nash Street, Arlington Boulevard, Interstate Route 66 and Arlington Ridge Road on the Virginia side of the Potomac River, facing Georgetown and Roosevelt Island. The nearest building is some 600 feet from the River. I-66, Arlington Ridge Road and the George Washington Parkway lie between the high-rises and the River—The AM Building is the tallest building in Rosslyn; it is 333 feet above mean sea level. When completed, the Rosslyn Center Building will be 351 feet above mean sea level. The office towers in the Arland Complex are 380 feet above mean sea level, and the Twin Development Building is 362 feet above mean sea level. The Arland Hotel will be 300 feet above mean sea level, 33 feet lower than the present AM Building, and 51 feet below the Rosslyn Center Building. The Arland office building will be 29 feet taller than the Rosslyn Center Building. The Twin Development Building will be 11 feet taller.

Both sides introduced a number of photographs taken from different sections of the monumental core looking toward the Rosslyn skyline—many were taken by long-range lenses. Both sides called expert witnesses—the Government's experts premised their opinions on the height and bulk of the buildings protruding over the tree line on the Virginia Ridge—one said the [high buildings] tend to interfere with the perception of the general visitor to Washington and its immediate area in terms of its historical role as a horizontal city dominated by the dome of the Capitol, and as a pilgrimage site for the great national memorials of this Nation. Another said they would detract from the enjoyment of the basic principal of the plan developed over the last 100 years, which was, essentially, the radial vistas, the radial street plan, and the horizontal nature of the Capital as a whole within the region. Another said they would dominate the background—all said they would be visual intrusions on the monumental core. The defendants' experts said the buildings would be unobtrusive and opined that the buildings would not be a public nuisance. All of the witnesses agreed you could see the tops of the buildings, looking west from the Kennedy Center and Roosevelt Island—looking northwest from the Lincoln Memorial, up river from the Jefferson Memorial and north from Iwo Jima.

The Government offered no evidence to support their public nuisance theory, except the height and bulk of the buildings. They abandoned their allegations of increased traffic congestion and other environmental damage.

A nuisance case is a proceeding in equity—each case involves two inquiries; first, whether the condition complained of is, in fact, a nuisance; and, if a nuisance is found, whether an injunction is the appropriate remedy. See Harrisonville v. Dickey Clay Co., 289 U.S. 334, 53 S. Ct. 602, 77 L. Ed. 1208 (1933). The term "nuisance" is incapable of an exhaustive definition which will fit all cases—it is very comprehensive—it includes everything that endangers life or health, gives offense to the senses, violates the laws of decency, or obstructs the reasonable and comfortable use of property. The difference between a public and a private nuisance is that the former affects the public at large while the latter affects the individual or a limited number of individuals only. A public nuisance has been defined as the doing of or the failure to do something that injuriously affects the safety, health, or morals of the public, or works some substantial annoyance, inconvenience or injury to the public generally—see Nuisances, 58 Am. Jur. 2d.

Height alone is not enough—unsightliness or offense to the esthetic senses is not sufficient to constitute a public nuisance. See City of Newport News v. Hertzler, 216 Va. 587, 221 S.E.2d 146 (1976), where the appearance of portable toilets and other items of park maintenance distasteful to adjacent residents was an insufficient basis to create a nuisance.

Florida ex rel. Gardner v. Sailboat Key, Inc., 295 So. 2d 658 (Fla. App. 1974) relied on by the Government to support their theory of esthetic nuisance, states only that a building could be a public nuisance.

The imposition of general restrictions on the height of buildings for the safety and convenience of the public is a valid exercise of the police power; but in some instances the erection of high buildings or other ugly objects has been prohibited so that a park or a beautiful public building would not be disfigured by the proximity of such structures. To sustain such an interference with the use of private land without compensation as an exercise of the police power has been farther than the courts have been willing to go. When, however, compensation is provided, such restrictions may be looked upon as easements, created by statute for the benefit of the land on which the park or public building lies, and which have been taken by the public by eminent domain. See 2A J. Sackman Nichols, The Law of Eminent Domain, Section 7.516[1] at 7-239 (rev. 3d ed. 1976).

These buildings are more than a mile and a half from the Lincoln Memorial and from two to three and a half miles from the White House, Washington Monument and the Capitol Building. Viewing them from inside the monumental core, one would not see the Rosslyn high-rise buildings unless he looked in a northwesterly direction. He would first see the intervening buildings and parks in the District, then the broad expanse of the Potomac and the George Washington Parkway on the Virginia shore. He could see the buildings from the Iwo Jima Memorial if he turned around and looked toward Rosslyn.

The maximum additional height of any of these buildings over the existing Rosslyn skyline is less than thirty feet. The Court is satisfied from the evidence presented and from on-site views of Rosslyn from various places in the monumental core, that these buildings would not detract from the average visitor's view of the memorials, monuments and parks of our Nation's Capital.

The United States has failed to prove, that the visual intrusion complained of is, in fact, a public nuisance.

Therefore, the suit should be dismissed, and

It Is So Ordered.

If a public nuisance were found, the propriety of an injunction would depend first of all on a showing of substantial injury to the public. Often, even when substantial injury is shown, a balancing of the harm or inconvenience to those injured by the nuisance with the overall harm which would occur if the injunction is granted is undertaken by the courts. See United States v. Reserve Mining Company, 380 F. Supp. 11 (D.C. Minn. 1974), and cases cited therein.

The harm to the defendants would be great as construction on the Gould Building is well underway—excavation on the Arland Towers property has begun. It is debatable, to say the least, whether an order enjoining the completion of these buildings would be the appropriate remedy.

The Constitution of the United States prohibits the taking of private land for public purposes without just compensation.

Prior to the filing of this suit, the Court has been advised that the Department of Justice has never attempted to control the height or bulk of the buildings erected on private land adjacent to or near National parks or monuments on a public nuisance theory—heretofore, the United States has always controlled the height of the buildings on the Virginia side of the Potomac River by condemning scenic easements. When a former Secretary of the Interior objected to the height of a proposed building on the Merrywood property, the Government did just that. . . .

NOTES AND QUESTIONS

1. What, other than the plaintiff's identity, distinguishes a suit based on public nuisance from its private nuisance counterpart? Suppose that the

government had gained injunctive relief in the *Arlington County* case. To draw upon the Calabresi and Melamed analysis, what kind of entitlement would the government have enjoyed: property, liability, or inalienability?

2.   Having lost its suit, the government might then consider whether to condemn a scenic easement (as to those parcels on which construction was not already well under way). To draw again upon the Calabresi and Melamed analysis, what kind of entitlement do the landowners enjoy?

3.   Suppose that the County Board of Arlington County, believing that the Rosslyn skyline should not intrude visually upon Washington's public monuments, had placed suitable height restrictions on Rosslyn buildings. Is it clear that such restrictions would have exceeded the county's regulatory power? See generally Chapter 13, *infra;* see also City of St. Paul v. Chicago, St. Paul, Minneapolis & Omaha County, 413 F.2d 762 (8th Cir. 1969).

4.   Consider also Puritan Holding Co., Inc. v. Holloschitz, 82 Misc. 2d 905, 372 N.Y.S.2d 500 (Sup. Ct. 1975). Defendant owned an abandoned building almost directly across the street from plaintiff's newly renovated apartment house. Plaintiff claimed that defendant had created a nuisance by allowing her building to become unsightly and occupied by derelicts. The court agreed and awarded damages based upon the difference between the market value of plaintiff's property before and after the nuisance. The opinion stressed that "one bad building may eventually destroy an entire neighborhood."

PART VI

THE ALLOCATION AND
DEVELOPMENT OF LAND
RESOURCES THROUGH
COMMUNITY PLANNING

Chapter 13

When Is Regulation a Taking? How Do Courts Decide?

§13.1 A Landmark Decision: Pennsylvania Coal Co. v. Mahon

Before we enter Chapter 14, dealing with the planning process, we should face head-on a question that has intrigued some of the finest legal minds of this century: when is regulation a taking? The dichotomy between a valid regulation, which permits government to inflict economic loss without compensation, and a taking, which requires government to pay "just" compensation, is easily stated. Yet, when applied to specific cases, the distinction often results in furious disagreement between the parties and the judges themselves. The effort to analyze court decisions and to express a rational overview has produced a literature of its own: sophisticated, profound, provoking—and utterly in conflict. Perhaps we should concede at the outset that there are some questions for which there are no easy answers, and that "When is regulation a taking?" is such a question.

The importance of the question lies in the options that are enjoyed by legislatures to achieve land use planning goals. For example: a community decides that it needs more off-street parking in its downtown district. Several legal tools are at hand. The community might acquire land, then build and operate public garages throughout the business area; the community would pay for the land it acquired, and it would finance the land purchase and the garage by taxes and operating revenue. Alternatively, the community might force all building owners within the business area to take immediate steps, at their own expense, to create specified numbers of off-street parking spaces, or—somewhat less drastically—require such spaces as a condition to the granting of a building or renovating permit. The acquisition choice, via the medium of eminent domain, involves public outlays whose burden would be quite broadly shared. By contrast, the regulatory choice, via the media of zoning and building codes, places the initial burden, which may be quite heavy, upon a relatively small group of property owners. Regulation may not always achieve planning goals with the speed of a formal taking; but regulation costs much less (to the taxpayer), and this often makes it an attractive choice. At issue is the question of when it is also a constitutionally acceptable choice.

With this brief background, we consider first the *Pennsylvania Coal Co.* case, in which two of America's great jurists, Justices Holmes and Brandeis, debate the issue of regulation versus taking. Courts still quote from that decision whenever the issue is joined. Then we look at the problem in a current context, that of landmark preservation. Decided more than a half-century after the *Pennsylvania Coal Co.* case, Penn Central Transportation Co. v. City of New York, *infra,* illustrates how intractable the taking issue remains.

PENNSYLVANIA COAL CO. v. MAHON
260 U.S. 393, 43 S. Ct. 158, 67 L. Ed. 322 (1922)

MR. JUSTICE HOLMES delivered the opinion of the Court. This is a bill in equity brought by the defendants in error to prevent the Pennsylvania Coal Company from mining under their property in such way as to remove the supports and cause a subsidence of the surface and of their house. The bill sets out a deed executed by the Coal Company in 1878, under which the plaintiffs claim. The deed conveys the surface, but in express terms reserves the right to remove all the coal under the same, and the grantee takes the premises with the risk, and waives all claim for damages that may arise from mining out the coal. But the plaintiffs say that whatever may have been the Coal Company's rights, they were taken away by an Act of Pennsylvania, approved May 27, 1921, P.L. 1198, commonly known there as the Kohler Act. . . .

The statute forbids the mining of anthracite coal in such way as to cause the subsidence of, among other things, any structure used as a human habitation. . . . As applied to this case the statute is admitted to destroy previously existing rights or property and contract. The question is whether the police power can be stretched so far.

Government hardly could go on if to some extent values incident to property could not be diminished without paying for every such change in the general law. As long recognized, some values are enjoyed under an implied limitation and must yield to the police power. But obviously the implied limitation must have its limits, or the contract and due process clauses are gone. One fact for consideration in determining such limits is the extent of the diminution. When it reaches a certain magnitude, in most if not in all cases there must be an exercise of eminent domain and compensation to sustain the act. So the question depends upon the particular facts. The greatest weight is given to the judgment of the legislature, but it always is open to interested parties to contend that the legislature has gone beyond its constitutional power.

This is the case of a single private house. No doubt there is a public interest even in this, as there is in every purchase and sale and in all that happens within the commonwealth. Some existing rights may be modified even in such a case. Rideout v. Knox, 148 Mass. 368. But usually in ordinary private affairs the public interest does not warrant much of this kind of interference. A source of damage to such a house is not a public nuisance even if similar damage is inflicted on others in different places. The damage is not common or public. Wesson v. Washburn Iron Co., 13 Allen, 95, 103. The extent of the public interest is shown by the statute to be limited, since the statute ordinarily does not apply to land when the surface is owned by the owner of the coal. Furthermore, it is not justified as a protection of personal safety. That could be provided for by notice. Indeed the very foundation of this bill is that the defendant gave timely notice of its intent to mine under the house. On the other hand the extent of the taking is great. It purports to abolish what is recognized in Pennsylvania as an estate in land—a very valuable estate—and what is declared by the Court below to be a contract hitherto binding the plaintiffs. If we were called upon to deal with the plaintiffs' position alone, we should think it clear that the statute does not disclose a public interest sufficient to warrant so extensive a destruction of the defendant's constitutionally protected rights.

But the case has been treated as one in which the general validity of the act should be discussed. . . .

It is our opinion that the act cannot be sustained as an exercise of the police power, so far as it affects the mining of coal under streets or cities in places where the right to mine such coal has been reserved. As said in a Pennsylvania case, "For practical purposes, the right to coal consists in the right to mine it." Commonwealth v. Clearview Coal Co., 256 Pa. St. 328, 331. What makes the right to mine coal valuable is that it can be exercised with profit. To make it commercially impracticable to mine certain coal has very nearly the same effect for constitutional purposes as appropriating or destroying it. This we think that we are warranted in assuming that the statute does.

It is true that in Plymouth Coal Co. v. Pennsylvania, 232 U.S. 531, it was held competent for the legislature to require a pillar of coal to be left along the line of adjoining property, that, with the pillar on the other side of the line, would be a barrier sufficient for the safety of the employees of either mine in case the other should be abandoned and allowed to fill with water. But that was a requirement for the safety of employees invited into the mine, and secured an average reciprocity of advantage that has been recognized as a justification of various laws.

The rights of the public in a street purchased or laid out by eminent domain are those that it has paid for. If in any case its representatives have been so short sighted as to acquire only surface rights without the right of support, we see no more authority for supplying the latter without compensation than there was for taking the right of way in the first place and refusing to pay for it because the public wanted it very much. The protection of private property in the Fifth Amendment presupposes that it is wanted for public use, but provides that it shall not be taken for such use without compensation. A similar assumption is made in the decisions upon the Fourteenth Amendment. Hairston v. Danville & Western Ry. Co., 208 U.S. 598, 605. When this seemingly absolute protection is found to be qualified by the police power, the natural tendency of human nature is to extend the qualification more and more until at last private property disappears. But that cannot be accomplished in this way under the Constitution of the United States.

The general rule at least is, that while property may be regulated to a certain extent, if regulation goes too far it will be recognized as a taking. It may be doubted how far exceptional cases, like the blowing up of a house to stop a conflagration, go—and if they go beyond the general rule, whether they do not stand as much upon tradition as upon principle. Bowditch v. Boston, 101 U.S. 16. In general it is not plain that a man's misfortunes or necessities will justify his shifting the damages to his neighbor's shoulders. Spade v. Lynn & Boston R.R. Co., 172 Mass. 488, 489. We are in danger of forgetting that a strong public desire to improve the public condition is not enough to warrant achieving the desire by a shorter cut than the constitutional way of paying for the change. As we already have said, this is a question of degree—and therefore cannot be disposed of by general propositions. But we regard this as going beyond any of the cases decided by this Court. The late decisions upon laws dealing with the congestion of Washington and New York, caused by the war, dealt with laws intended to meet a temporary emergency and providing for compensation determined to be reasonable by an impartial board. They went to the verge of the law but fell far short of the present act. Block v. Hirsh, 256 U.S. 135. Marcus Brown Holding Co. v. Feldman, 256 U.S. 170. Levy Leasing Co. v. Siegel, 258 U.S. 242.

We assume, of course, that the statute was passed upon the conviction that an exigency existed that would warrant it, and we assume that an exigency exists that would warrant the exercise of eminent domain. But the question at bottom is upon whom the loss of the changes desired should fall. So far as private persons or communities have seen fit to take the risk of acquiring only surface rights, we cannot see that the fact that their risk has become a danger warrants the giving to them greater rights than they bought.

Decree reversed.

MR. JUSTICE BRANDEIS, dissenting. . . . Coal in place is land; and the right of the owner to use his land is not absolute. He may not so use it as to create a public nuisance; and uses, once harmless, may, owing to changed conditions, seriously threaten the public welfare. Whenever they do, the legislature has power to prohibit such uses without paying compensation; and the power to prohibit extends alike to the manner, the character and the purpose of the use. Are we justified in declaring that the Legislature of Pennsylvania has, in restricting the right to mine anthracite, exercised this power so arbitrarily as to violate the Fourteenth Amendment?

Every restriction upon the use of property imposed in the exercise of the police power deprives the owner of some right theretofore enjoyed, and is, in that sense, an abridgment by the States of rights in property without making compensation. But restriction imposed to protect the public health, safety or morals from dangers threatened is not a taking. The restriction here in question is merely the prohibition of a noxious use. The property so restricted remains in the possession of its owner. The State does not appropriate it or make any use of it. The State merely prevents the owner from making a use which interferes with paramount rights of the public. Whenever the use prohibited ceases to be noxious,—as it may because of further change in local or social conditions,—the restriction will have to be removed and the owner will again be free to enjoy his property as heretofore.

The restriction upon the use of this property can not, of course, be lawfully imposed, unless its purpose is to protect the public. But the purpose of a restriction does not cease to be public, because incidentally some private persons may thereby receive gratuitously valuable special benefits. Thus, owners of low buildings may obtain, through statutory restrictions upon the height of neighboring structures, benefits equivalent to an easement of light and air. Welch v. Swasey, 214 U.S. 91. Compare Lindsley v. Natural Carbonic Gas Co., 220 U.S. 61; Walls v. Midland Carbon Co., 254 U.S. 300. Furthermore, a restriction, though imposed for a public purpose, will not be lawful, unless the restriction is an appropriate means to the public end. But to keep coal in place is surely an appropriate means of preventing subsidence of the surface; and ordinarily it is the only available means. Restriction upon use does not become inappropriate as a means, merely because it deprives the owner of the only use to which the property can then be profitably put. The liquor and the oleomargarine cases settled that. Mugler v. Kansas, 123 U.S. 623, 668, 669; Powell v. Pennsylvania, 127 U.S. 678, 682. See also Hadacheck v. Los Angeles, 239 U.S. 394; Pierce Oil Corporation v. City of Hope, 248 U.S. 498. Nor is a restriction imposed through exercise of the police power inappropriate as a means, merely because the same end might be effected through exercise of the power of eminent domain, or otherwise at public expense. Every restriction upon the height of buildings might be secured through acquiring by eminent domain the right of each owner to build above the limiting height; but it is settled that the State need not resort to that power. Compare Laurel Hill Cemetery v. San Francisco, 216 U.S. 358; Missouri Pacific Ry. Co. v. Omaha, 235 U.S. 121. If by mining anthracite coal the owner would necessarily unloose poisonous gasses, I suppose no one would doubt the power of the State to prevent the mining, without buying his coal fields. And why may not the State, likewise, without paying compensation, prohibit one from digging so deep or excavating so near the surface, as to expose the community to like dangers? In the latter case, as in the former, carrying on the business would be a public nuisance. . . .

NOTES AND QUESTIONS

1. Read carefully the Holmes opinion. What standard does the justice enunciate for testing whether the regulation satisfies the Constitution? Similarly, examine the Brandeis dissent. What is his benchmark? Has either justice supplied more than rhetoric to courts having to struggle with the taking issue?

2. The Court assumes that the Kohler Act, if applied in this case, would make it "commercially impracticable to mine certain coal." What does that mean? Is it clear that the coal company would have no choice other than to cease its operation beneath the Mahon parcel? Notice that the statute forbids the mining of coal as to cause subsidence *of any structure* used as a human habitation. Consider also Boomer v. Atlantic Cement Co., page 685 *supra*.

3. Is the rub in the *Mahon* case that the coal company should not be forced to reacquire an entitlement in 1922 after paying for it originally in 1878?

4. The liquor and oleomargarine cases, which Justice Brandeis cites, validated state prohibition and regulatory laws that wiped out certain businessmen (i.e., made their operations "commercially impracticable"). Are John Barleycorn and (in a dairy-farming state) grain-based butter of a different order of public menace than a landslide would be?

5. Suppose that the Pennsylvania legislature had not enacted the Kohler Act and that the Mahons had sued the coal company to enjoin a nuisance: judgment for the defendant? Suppose that the city of Seranton, where the Mahons lived, had sued the coal company to enjoin a nuisance: judgment for the defendant?

6. To add to your frame of reference, be aware of two situations where, under classical doctrine, the outcome is certain:

(a) The "invasion" theory—government physically occupies privately held land. All agree that this is a "taking," for which the Fifth and Fourteenth Amendments compel compensation. Ordinarily, government acts formally to compensate via eminent domain, but if government fails to offer compensation, the landowner may proceed in inverse condemnation. Cf. United States v. Causby, 328 U.S. 256 (1946). Where nontangible invasions occur, such as from noise or vibration, the courts may refuse to compensate the landowner by holding that no taking has occurred. Cf. Batten v. United States, 306 F.2d 580 (10th Cir. 1962), §18.3 *infra*.

One other aspect of the invasion theory appears in partial condemnation cases. Suppose that a town acquires a ten-foot strip on either side of an existing road. The landowners whose frontage is taken will receive compensation not only for the value of the lost strip, but also for the consequential or severance damage to the rest of their land. Such damage can include the deleterious impact of increased roadway noise and odors on the remainder. Cf. Dennison v. State, 22 N.Y.2d 409, 239 N.E.2d 708, 293 N.Y.S.2d 68 (1968). By contrast, if the town acquires a twenty-foot strip on one side of the road, and no land on the other side, property owners who do not suffer a taking must suffer their discomfort and economic injury without compensation.

Many *state* constitutions provide that no property may be taken *or damaged* without compensation. What does this language add to the invasion theory?

(b) The "noxious use" theory—government may abate a noxious use, that is, a use that is deleterious to the health and safety of others, without paying the landowner anything for the economic injury that follows abatement. We have seen the "noxious use" theory operate in the nuisance cases, and again in housing codes, where measures designed to protect the physical well-being of tenants can cause uncompensated economic injury to building owners. In extreme cases, where a "noxious" use affects health or safety, the nuisance decision or regulation may reduce land value to zero without entitling the landowner to recover his losses. See, e.g., Goldblatt v. Town of Hempstead, 369 U.S. 590 (1962).

Between these extreme situations lies the wide range of governmental activity where privately held values suffer, and the legal system must decide where the loss should fall.

7. Within the disputed range lie cases where courts have upheld a regulation as barring a noxious use, even though the regulated use seemed only marginally related to health or safety. An early illustration appears in Commonwealth v. Alger, 61 Mass. (7 Cush.) 53 (1851), where the court upheld a law barring the erection of a wharf beyond specified lines in Boston Harbor: "But he is restrained . . . because it would be a noxious use, contrary to the maxim, *sic utere tuo ut alienum non laedas.* . . . It is therefore not within the principle of property taken under the right of eminent domain." And, as we shall see, the landmark decision in Village of Euclid v. Ambler Realty Co., 272 U.S. 365 (1926), page 780 *infra,* depends heavily upon the nuisance analogy to validate public restrictions on land use via zoning.

8. Here are four proposals for reconciling the "police power vs. taking" dilemma. As to each, consider first how courts would have decided the *Pennsylvania Coal Co.* case under the enumerated tests. Then consider whether that outcome seems right to you.

(a) Measures that prevent a landowner from imposing a harm upon his neighbors may be enacted under the police power; measures that compel him to confer a benefit upon the community must be enacted under the condemnation power. Cf. Dunham, A Legal and Economic Basis for City Planning, 58 Colum. L. Rev. 650, 651 (1958).

(b) Government activity should be divided into two categories, enterprise and mediation. When government seems to be acting as an enterprise (building highways, parks, etc.), private parties who incur economic loss are entitled to just compensation. In contrast, when government seems to be settling a conflict between two private claimants, the party suffering loss may not demand compensation. Sax, Takings and the Police Power, 74 Yale L.J. 36 (1964).

The author later repudiated this view, *infra.*

(c) The privilege to use property so as to cause *spillover* effect may constitutionally be restrained, however severe the economic loss on the property owner, without compensation. Any use of property not having spillover effect may not be restricted without just compensation. Spillover effect comes in three forms:

(1) A's use of land physically restricts B's use. Illustration: A owns strip mine midway up a hillside. B owns lower parcel. A's mining would

carry wastes onto B's land. (Conversely, B's desire for waste-free parcel restricts A's use).

(2) A uses a common to which B has an equal right. Illustration: A's factory emits smoke into the air (the common) over B's land. (Conversely, B's demand for smoke-free air inhibits A's use of the common). Waterways and visual prospects also are commons.

(3) A's use of land harms the health or well-being of community members who may or may not be landowners, or it imposes an affirmative obligation on the community—e.g., to supply police protection to a remotely located residential subdivision. Sax, Takings, Private Property and Public Rights, 81 Yale L.J. 149 (1971).

(d) "The only 'test' for compensability which is 'correct' in the sense of being directly responsive to society's purpose in engaging in a compensation practice is the test of fairness; is it fair to effectuate this social measure without granting this claim to compensation for private loss thereby inflicted?" Michelman, Property, Utility, and Fairness: Comments on the Ethical Foundations of "Just Compensation" Law, 80 Harv. L. Rev. 1165, 1171-1172 (1968).

§13.2   Another Landmark Decision: The Grand Central Terminal Case

> America's approaching Bicentennial will be a bittersweet affair. The nation will celebrate, but it will also mourn. . . . It will mourn the countless . . . landmarks, sites, and buildings that have been swept away over its 200-year history. . . . A single statistic points up the problem: over a third of the 16,000 structures listed in the Historic American Buildings Survey (commenced by the federal government in 1933) are gone. More distressing than this cold statistic is the identity of the victims. The roster reads like a catalog of the nation's—and world's—most distinguished buildings, including, for example, such gems as the Old Stock Exchange building and the Garrick Theatre in Chicago and New York's Pennsylvania Station. Because these buildings enriched, indeed defined the very character of the urban fabric of which they were a part, theirs is truly a grievous loss. Ominously, the forces that claimed them continue to assault the ever smaller company of remaining landmarks. [J. Costonis, Space Adrift 3, 4 (1974)]

Professor Costonis then identifies four forces that together threaten the survival of this nation's most distinguished landmarks:

1. Real estate economics, especially in downtown areas, where most urban landmarks appear. The sites usually can earn a greater return when redeveloped with larger modern structures.

2. The "pursuit of progress" syndrome, in which real estate interests

and government officials join to sacrifice the sentiment of preservation for the practical necessity of change.

    3.   Constitutional and property law doctrines, which favor private gain over the community benefit in preservation.

    4.   The failure of city, state, and federal government to devise landmark programs that "grapple realistically with the overriding preference of the legal system for private property rights." (Id. at 4)

PENN CENTRAL TRANSPORTATION CO. v. CITY OF NEW YORK

438 U.S. 104, 98 S. Ct. 2646, 57 L. Ed. 2d 631 (1978)   *Grand Central Terminal case*

    Mr. Justice Brennan delivered the opinion of the Court. The question presented is whether a city may, as part of a comprehensive program to preserve historic landmarks and historic districts, place restrictions on the development of individual historic landmarks—in addition to those imposed by applicable zoning ordinances—without effecting a "taking" requiring the payment of "just compensation." Specifically, we must decide whether the application of New York City's Landmarks Preservation Law to the parcel of land occupied by Grand Central Terminal has "taken" its owners' property in violation of the Fifth and Fourteenth Amendments. . . .

    This case involves the application of New York City's Landmarks Preservation Law to Grand Central Terminal (Terminal). The Terminal, which is owned by the Penn Central Transportation Co. and its affiliates (Penn Central), is one of New York City's most famous buildings. Opened in 1913, it is regarded not only as providing an ingenious engineering solution to the problems presented by urban railroad stations, but also as a magnificent example of the French beaux arts style.

    The Terminal is located in midtown Manhattan. Its south facade faces 42d Street and that street's intersection with Park Avenue. . . . The Terminal itself is an eight-story structure which Penn Central uses as a railroad station and in which it rents space not needed for railroad purposes to a variety of commercial interests. The Terminal is one of a number of properties owned by appellant Penn Central in this area of midtown Manhattan. . . . At least eight of these are eligible to be recipients of development rights afforded the Terminal by virtue of landmark designation.

    On August 2, 1967, following a public hearing, the Landmarks Preservation Commission designated the Terminal a "landmark" and designated the "city tax block" it occupies a "landmark site." [16] The Board of Estimate con-

---

16. The Commission's report stated:

> Grand Central Station, one of the great buildings of America, evokes a spirit that is unique in this City. It combines distinguished architecture with a brilliant engineering solution, wedded to one of the most fabulous railroad terminals of our time. Monumental in scale, this great building functions as well today as it did when built. In style, it represents the best of the French Beaux Arts. (Record 2240.)

firmed this action on September 21, 1967. Although appellant Penn Central had opposed the designation before the Commission, it did not seek judicial review of the final designation decision.

On January 22, 1968, appellant Penn Central, to increase its income, entered into a renewable 50-year lease and sublease agreement with appellant UGP Properties, Inc. (UGP), a wholly owned subsidiary of Union General Properties, Ltd. a United Kingdom corporation. Under the terms of the agreement, UGP was to construct a multistory office building above the Terminal. UGP promised to pay Penn Central $1 million annually during construction and at least $3 million annually thereafter. The rentals would be offset in part by a loss of some $700,000 to $1 million in net rentals presently received from concessionaires displaced by the new building.

Appellants UGP and Penn Central then applied to the Commission for permission to construct an office building atop the Terminal. Two separate plans, both designed by architect Marcel Breuer and both apparently satisfying the terms of the applicable zoning ordinance, were submitted to the Commission for approval. The first, Breuer I, provided for the construction of a 55-story office building, to be cantilevered above the existing facade and to rest on the roof of the Terminal. The second, Breuer II Revised, [17] called for tearing down a portion of the Terminal that included the 42d Street facade, stripping off some of the remaining features of the Terminal's facade, and constructing a 53-story office building. . . .

After four days of hearings at which over 80 witnesses testified, the Commission denied this application as to both proposals. . . .

Appellants did not seek judicial review.

. . . Instead, appellants filed suit in New York Supreme Court, Trial Term, claiming, inter alia, that the application of the Landmarks Preservation Law had "taken" their property without just compensation in violation of the Fifth and Fourteenth Amendments and arbitrarily deprived them of their property without due process of law in violation of the Fourteenth Amendment. Appellants sought a declaratory judgment, injunctive relief barring the city from using the Landmarks Law to impede the construction of any structure that might otherwise lawfully be constructed on the Terminal site, and damages for the "temporary taking" that occurred between August 2, 1967, the designation date, and the date when the restrictions arising from the Landmarks Law would be lifted. The trial court granted the injunctive and declaratory relief, but severed the question of damages for a "temporary taking." [20]

---

17. Appellants also submitted a plan, denominated Breuer II, to the Commission. However, because appellants learned that Breuer II would have violated existing easements, they substituted Breuer II Revised for Breuer II, and the Commission evaluated the appropriateness only of Breuer II Revised.

20. Although that court suggested that any regulation of private property to protect landmark values was unconstitutional if "just compensation" were not afforded, it also appeared to rely upon its findings: first, that the cost to Penn Central of operating the Terminal building itself, exclusive of purely railroad operations, exceeded the revenues received from concessionaires and tenants in the Terminal; and second, that the special transferable development rights afforded

Appellees appealed, and the New York Supreme Court, Appellate Division, reversed. 50 App. Div. 2d 265, 377 N.Y.S.2d 20 (1975). . . .

The New York Court of Appeals affirmed. 42 N.Y.2d 324, 366 N.E.2d 1271 (1977). That court summarily rejected any claim that the Landmarks Law had "taken" property without "just compensation," id., at 329, 366 N.E.2d 1274, indicating that there could be no "taking" since the law had not transferred control of the property to the city, but only restricted appellants' exploitation of it. In that circumstance, the Court of Appeals held that appellants' attack on the law could prevail only if the law deprived appellants of their property in violation of the Due Process Clause of the Fourteenth Amendment. Whether or not there was a denial of substantive due process turned on whether the restrictions deprived Penn Central of a "reasonable return" on the "privately created and privately managed ingredient" of the Terminal. Id., at 328, 366 N.E.2d, at 1273. [23] The Court of Appeals concluded that the Landmarks Law had not effected a denial of due process because: (1) the landmark regulation permitted the same use as had been made of the Terminal for more than half a century; (2) the appellants had failed to show that they could not earn a reasonable return on their investment in the Terminal itself; (3) even if the Terminal proper could never operate at a reasonable profit, some of the income from Penn Central's extensive real estate holdings in the area, which include hotels and office buildings, must realistically be imputed to the Terminal; and (4) the development rights above the Terminal, which had been made transferable to numerous sites in the vicinity of the Terminal, one or two of which were suitable for the construction of office buildings, were valuable to appellants and provided "significant, perhaps 'fair', compensation for the loss of rights above the terminal itself." Id., at 333-336, 366 N.E.2d, at 1276-1278. . . .

[Appellants] filed a notice of appeal in this Court. We noted probable jurisdiction. 434 U.S. 983, 54 L. Ed. 2d 477, 98 S. Ct. 607 (1977). We affirm.

The issues presented by appellants are (1) whether the restrictions imposed by New York City's law upon appellants' exploitation of the Terminal site effect a "taking" of appellants' property for a public use within the meaning of the Fifth Amendment, which of course is made applicable to the States through the Fourteenth Amendment, see Chicago, B. & Q. R. Co. v. Chicago,

---

Penn Central as an owner of a landmark site did not "provide compensation to plaintiffs or minimize the harm suffered by plaintiffs due to the designation of the Terminal as a landmark."

23. The Court of Appeals suggested that in calculating the value of the property upon which appellants were entitled to earn a reasonable return, the "publicly created" components of the value of the property—i.e., those elements of its value attributable to the "efforts of organized society" or to the "social complex" in which the Terminal is located—had to be excluded. However, since the record upon which the Court of Appeals decided the case did not, as that court recognized, contain a basis for segregating the privately created from the publicly created elements of the value of the Terminal site and since the judgment of the Court of Appeals in any event rests upon bases that support our affirmance, see infra, this page and 122, 57 L. Ed. 2d, at 647, we have no occasion to address the question whether it is permissible or feasible to separate out the "social increments" of the value of property. See Costonis, The Disparity Issue: A Context for the Grand Central Terminal Decision, 91 Harv. L. Rev. 402, 416-417 (1977).

166 U.S. 226, 239, 41 L. Ed. 979, 17 S. Ct. 581 (1897), and, (2), if so, whether the transferable development rights afforded appellants constitute "just compensation" within the meaning of the Fifth Amendment. [24] We need only address the question whether a "taking" has occurred. [25]

Before considering appellants' specific contentions, it will be useful to review the factors that have shaped the jurisprudence of the Fifth Amendment injunction "nor shall private property be taken for public use, without just compensation." The question of what constitutes a "taking" for purposes of the Fifth Amendment has proved to be a problem of considerable difficulty. While this Court has recognized that the "Fifth Amendment's guarantee . . . [is] designed to bar Government from forcing some people alone to bear public burdens which, in all fairness and justice, should be borne by the public as a whole," Armstrong v. United States, 364 U.S. 40, 49, 4 L. Ed. 2d 1554, 80 S. Ct. 1563 (1960), this Court, quite simply, has been unable to develop any "set formula" for determining when "justice and fairness" require that economic injuries caused by public action be compensated by the government, rather than remain disproportionately concentrated on a few persons. See Goldblatt v. Hempstead, 369 U.S. 590, 594, 8 L. Ed. 2d 130, 82 S. Ct. 987 (1962). Indeed, we have frequently observed that whether a particular restriction will be rendered invalid by the government's failure to pay for any losses proximately caused by it depends largely "upon the particular circumstances [in that] case." United States v. Central Eureka Mining Co., 357 U.S. 155, 168, 2

---

24. Our statement of the issues is a distillation of four questions presented in the jurisdictional statement:

> Does the social and cultural desirability of preserving historical landmarks through government regulation derogate from the constitutional requirement that just compensation be paid for private property taken for public use?
> Is Penn Central entitled to no compensation for that large but unmeasurable portion of the value of its rights to construct an office building over the Grand Central Terminal that is said to have been created by the efforts of "society as an organized entity"?
> Does a finding that Penn Central has failed to establish that there is no possibility, without exercising its development rights, of earning a reasonable return on all of its remaining properties that benefit in any way from the operations of the Grand Central Terminal warrant the conclusion that no compensation need be paid for the taking of those rights?
> Does the possibility accorded to Penn Central, under the landmark-preservation regulation, of realizing some value at some time by transferring the Terminal development rights to other buildings, under a procedure that is conceded to be defective, severely limited, procedurally complex and speculative, and that requires ultimate discretionary approval by governmental authorities, meet the constitutional requirements of just compensation as applied to landmarks? (Jurisdictional Statement 3-4.)

The first and fourth questions assume that there has been a taking and raise the problem whether, under the circumstances of this case, the transferable development rights constitute "just compensation." The second and third questions, on the other hand, are directed to the issue whether a taking has occurred.

25. As is implicit in our opinion, we do not embrace the proposition that a "taking" can never occur unless government has transferred physical control over a portion of a parcel.

L. Ed. 2d 1228, 78 S. Ct. 1097 (1958), see United States v. Caltex, Inc., 344 U.S. 149, 156, 97 L. Ed. 157, 73 S. Ct. 200 (1952).

In engaging in these essentially ad hoc, factual inquiries, the Court's decisions have identified several factors that have particular significance. The economic impact of the regulation on the claimant and, particularly, the extent to which the regulation has interfered with distinct investment-backed expectations are, of course, relevant considerations. See Goldblatt v. Hempstead, *supra,* at 594, 8 L. Ed. 2d 130, 82 S. Ct. 987. So, too, is the character of the governmental action. A "taking" may more readily be found when the interference with property can be characterized as a physical invasion by government, see, e.g., United States v. Causby, 328 U.S. 256, 90 L. Ed. 1206, 66 S. Ct. 1062 (1946), than when interference arises from some public program adjusting the benefits and burdens of economic life to promote the common good.

"Government hardly could go on if to some extent values incident to property could not be diminished without paying for every such change in the general law," Pennsylvania Coal Co. v. Mahon, 260 U.S. 393, 413, 67 L. Ed. 322, 43 S. Ct. 158, 28 A.L.R. 1321 (1922), and this Court has accordingly recognized, in a wide variety of contexts, that government may execute laws or programs that adversely affect recognized economic values. Exercises of the taxing power are one obvious example. A second are the decisions in which this Court has dismissed "taking" challenges on the ground that, while the challenged government action caused economic harm, it did not interfere with interests that were sufficiently bound up with the reasonable expectations of the claimant to constitute "property" for Fifth Amendment purposes. See, e.g., United States v. Willow River Power Co., 324 U.S. 499, 89 L. Ed. 1101, 65 S. Ct. 761 (1945) (interest in high-water level of river for runoff for tailwaters to maintain power head is not property); United States v. Chandler-Dunbar Water Power Co., 229 U.S. 53, 57 L. Ed. 1063, 33 S. Ct. 667 (1913) (no property interest can exist in navigable waters) [citations omitted].

More importantly for the present case, in instances in which a state tribunal reasonably concluded that "the health, safety, morals, or general welfare" would be promoted by prohibiting particular contemplated uses of land, this Court has upheld land-use regulations that destroyed or adversely affected recognized real property interests. [Citations omitted.] Zoning laws are, of course, the classic example, see Euclid v. Ambler Realty Co., 272 U.S. 365, 71 L. Ed. 303, 47 S. Ct. 114, 4 Ohio L. Abs. 816, 54 A.L.R. 1016 (1926) (prohibition of industrial use). . . . In contending that the New York City law has "taken" their property in violation of the Fifth and Fourteenth Amendments, appellants make a series of arguments, which, while tailored to the facts of this case, essentially urge that any substantial restriction imposed pursuant to a landmark law must be accompanied by just compensation if it is to be constitutional. Before considering these, we emphasize what is not in dispute. Because this Court has recognized, in a number of settings, that States and cities may enact land-use restrictions or controls to enhance the quality of life by preserving the character and desirable aesthetic features of a city, [citations omitted] appellants do not contest that New York City's objective of preserving structures and areas with special historic, architectural, or cultural significance is an entirely permissible governmental goal. They also do not dispute that the restrictions imposed on its parcel are appropriate means of securing the purposes of the New York City law. Finally, appellants do not challenge any of the specific factual premises of the decision below. They accept for present purposes both that the parcel of land occupied by Grand Central Terminal must, in its present state, be regarded as capable of earning a reasonable return, and that the transferable development rights afforded appellants by virtue of the Terminal's designation as a landmark are valuable, even if not as valuable as the rights to construct above the Terminal. In appellants' view none of these factors derogate from their claim that New York City's law has effected a "taking."

They first observe that the airspace above the Terminal is a valuable property interest, citing United States v. Causby, *supra*. They urge that the Landmarks Law has deprived them of any gainful use of their "air rights" above the Terminal and that, irrespective of the value of the remainder of their parcel, the city has "taken" their right to this superadjacent airspace, thus entitling them to "just compensation" measured by the fair market value of these air rights. . . .

Stated baldly, appellants' position appears to be that the only means of ensuring that selected owners are not singled out to endure financial hardship for no reason is to hold that any restriction imposed on individual landmarks pursuant to the New York City scheme is a "taking" requiring the payment of "just compensation." Agreement with this argument would, of course, invalidate not just New York City's law, but all comparable landmark legislation in the Nation. We find no merit in it. . . .

In any event, appellants' repeated suggestions that they are solely burdened and unbenefited is factually inaccurate. This contention overlooks the fact that the New York City law applies to vast numbers of structures in the city in addition to the Terminal—all the structures contained in the 31 historic districts and over 400 individual landmarks, many of which are close to the Terminal. [31] Unless we are to reject the judgment of the New York City Council that the preservation of landmarks benefits all New York citizens and all structures, both economically and by improving the quality of life in the city as a whole—which we are unwilling to do—we cannot conclude that the owners of the Terminal have in no sense been benefited by the Landmarks Law.

Rejection of appellants' broad arguments is not, however, the end of our inquiry, for all we thus far have established is that the New York City law is not rendered invalid by its failure to provide "just compensation" whenever a

---

31. There are some 53 designated landmarks and five historic districts or scenic landmarks in Manhattan between 14th and 59th Streets. See Landmarks Preservation Commission, Landmarks and Historic Districts (1977).

landmark owner is restricted in the exploitation of property interests, such as air rights, to a greater extent than provided for under applicable zoning laws. We now must consider whether the interference with appellants' property is of such a magnitude that "there must be an exercise of eminent domain and compensation to sustain [it]." Pennsylvania Coal Co. v. Mahon, 260 U.S. at 413, 67 L. Ed. 322, 43 S. Ct. 158, 28 A.L.R. 1321. That inquiry may be narrowed to the question of the severity of the impact of the law on appellants' parcel, and its resolution in turn requires a careful assessment of the impact of the regulation on the Terminal site. . . .

The New York City law does not interfere in any way with the present uses of the Terminal. Its designation as a landmark not only permits but contemplates that appellants may continue to use the property precisely as it has been used for the past 65 years: as a railroad terminal containing office space and concessions. So the law does not interfere with what must be regarded as Penn Central's primary expectation concerning the use of the parcel. More importantly, on this record, we must regard the New York City law as permitting Penn Central not only to profit from the Terminal but also to obtain a "reasonable return" on its investment.

Appellants, moreover, exaggerate the effect of the law on their ability to make use of the air rights above the Terminal in two respects.[33] First, it simply cannot be maintained, on this record, that appellants have been prohibited from occupying *any* portion of the airspace above the Terminal. While the Commission's actions in denying applications to construct an office building in excess of 50 stories above the Terminal may indicate that it will refuse to issue a certificate of appropriateness for any comparably sized structure, nothing the Commission has said or done suggests an intention to prohibit *any* construction above the Terminal. The Commission's report emphasized that whether any construction would be allowed depended upon whether the proposed addition "would harmonize in scale, material and character with [the Terminal]." Record 2251. Since appellants have not sought approval for the construction of a smaller structure, we do not know that appellants will be denied any use of any portion of the airspace above the Terminal.[34]

Second, to the extent appellants have been denied the right to build above the Terminal, it is not literally accurate to say that they have been denied *all* use of even those pre-existing air rights. Their ability to use these rights has not been abrogated; they are made transferable to at least eight parcels in the vicinity of the Terminal, one or two of which have been found suitable for the construction of new office buildings. Although appellants and others have argued that New York City's transferable development-rights program is far from ideal, the New York courts here supportably found that, at least in the case of the Terminal, the rights afforded are valuable. While these

33. Appellants, of course, argue at length that the transferable development rights, while valuable, do not constitute "just compensation." Brief for Appellants 36-43.

34. Counsel for appellants admitted at oral argument that the Commission has not suggested that it would not, for example, approve a 20-story office tower along the lines of that which was part of the original plan for the Terminal. See Tr. of Oral Arg. 19.

rights may well not have constituted "just compensation" if a "taking" had occurred, the rights nevertheless undoubtedly mitigate whatever financial burdens the law has imposed on appellants and, for that reason, are to be taken into account in considering the impact of regulation. Cf. Goldblatt v. Hempstead, 369 U.S., at 594 n.3, 8 L. Ed. 2d 130, 82 S. Ct. 987.

On this record, we conclude that the application of New York City's Landmarks Law has not effected a "taking" of appellants' property. The restrictions imposed are substantially related to the promotion of the general welfare and not only permit reasonable beneficial use of the landmark site but also afford appellants opportunities further to enhance not only the Terminal site proper but also other properties. [36]

Affirmed.

Mr. Justice Rehnquist, with whom The Chief Justice and Mr. Justice Stevens join, dissenting.

Of the over one million buildings and structures in the city of New York, appellees have singled out 400 for designation as official landmarks. [1] The owner of a building might initially be pleased that his property has been chosen by a distinguished committee of architects, historians, and city planners for such a singular distinction. But he may well discover, as appellant Penn Central Transportation Co. did here, that the landmark designation imposes upon him a substantial cost, with little or no offsetting benefit except for the honor of the designation. The question in this case is whether the cost associated with the city of New York's desire to preserve a limited number of "landmarks" within its borders must be borne by all of its taxpayers or whether it can instead be imposed entirely on the owners of the individual properties.

Only in the most superficial sense of the word can this case be said to involve "zoning." [2] Typical zoning restrictions may, it is true, so limit the

---

36. We emphasize that our holding today is on the present record, which in turn is based on Penn Central's present ability to use the Terminal for its intended purposes and in a gainful fashion. The city conceded at oral argument that if appellants can demonstrate at some point in the future that circumstances have so changed that the Terminal ceases to be "economically viable," appellants may obtain relief. See Tr. of Oral. Arg. 42-43.

1. A large percentage of the designated landmarks are public structures (such as the Brooklyn Bridge, City Hall, the Statue of Liberty and the Municipal Asphalt Plant) and thus do not raise Fifth Amendment taking questions. See Landmarks Preservation Commission of the City of New York, Landmarks and Historic Districts (1977 and Jan. 10, 1978 Supplement). Although the Court refers to the New York ordinance as a *comprehensive* program to preserve *historic* landmarks, *ante,* at 107, 57 L. Ed. 2d, at 638, the ordinance is not limited to historic buildings and gives little guidance to the Landmarks Preservation Commission in its selection of landmark sites. Section 207-1.0(n) of the Landmarks Preservation Law, as set forth in N.Y.C. Admin. Code ch. 8-A (1976), requires only that the selected landmark be at least 30 years old and possess "a special character or special historical or aesthetic interest or value as part of the development, heritage or cultural characteristics of the city, state or nation."

2. Even the New York Court of Appeals conceded that

[t]his is not a zoning case. . . . Zoning restrictions operate to advance a comprehensive community plan for the common good. Each property owner in the zone is both benefited and restricted from exploitation, presumably without discrimination, except for permitted continuing nonconforming uses. The restrictions may be designed to maintain the general

prospective uses of a piece of property as to diminish the value of that property in the abstract because it may not be used for the forbidden purposes. But any such abstract decrease in value will more than likely be at least partially offset by an increase in value which flows from similar restrictions as to use on neighboring properties. All property owners in a designated area are placed under the same restrictions, not only for the benefit of the municipality as a whole but for the common benefit of one another. In the words of Mr. Justice Holmes, speaking for the Court in Pennsylvania Coal Co. v. Mahon, 260 U.S. 393, 415, 67 L. Ed. 322, 43 S. Ct. 158, 28 A.L.R. 1321 (1922), there is "an average reciprocity of advantage."

Where a relatively few individual buildings, all separated from one another, are singled out and treated differently from surrounding buildings, no such reciprocity exists. The cost to the property owner which results from the imposition of restrictions applicable only to his property and not that of his neighbors may be substantial—in this case, several million dollars—with no comparable reciprocal benefits. . . .

The Fifth Amendment provides in part: "nor shall private property be taken for public use, without just compensation."[3] In a very literal sense, the actions of appellees violated this constitutional prohibition. Before the city of New York declared Grand Central Terminal to be a landmark, Penn Central could have used its "air rights" over the Terminal to build a multistory office building, at an apparent value of several million dollars per year. Today, the Terminal cannot be modified in *any* form, including the erection of additional stories, without the permission of the Landmark Preservation Commission, a permission which appellants, despite good-faith attempts, have so far been unable to obtain. Because the Taking Clause of the Fifth Amendment has not always been read literally, however, the constitutionality of appellees' actions requires a closer scrutiny of this Court's interpretation of the three key words in the Taking Clause—"property," "taken," and "just compensation."[4]

---

character of the area, or to assure orderly development, objectives inuring to the benefit of all, which property owners acting individually would find difficult or impossible to achieve. . . .

Nor does this case involve landmark regulation of a historic district. . . . [In historic districting, as in traditional zoning,] owners although burdened by the restrictions also benefit, to some extent, from the furtherance of a general community plan. . . .

Restrictions on alteration of individual landmarks are not designed to further a general community plan. Landmark restrictions are designed to prevent alteration or demolition of a single piece of property. To this extent, such restrictions resemble "discriminatory" zoning restrictions, properly condemned. . . ." 42 N.Y.2d 324, 329-330, 366 N.E.2d 1271, 1274 (1977).

3. The guarantee that private property shall not be taken for public use without just compensation is applicable to the States through the Fourteenth Amendment. Although the state "legislature may prescribe a form of procedure to be observed in the taking of private property for public use, . . . it is not due process of law if provision be not made for compensation." Chicago, B. & Q. R. Co. v. Chicago, 166 U.S. 226, 236, 41 L. Ed. 979, 17 S. Ct. 581 (1897).

4. The Court's opinion touches base with, or at least attempts to touch base with, most of the major eminent domain cases decided by this Court. Its use of them, however, is anything but meticulous. In citing to United States v. Caltex, Inc., 344 U.S. 149, 156, 97 L. Ed. 157, 73 S. Ct.

Appellees do not dispute that valuable property rights have been destroyed. And the Court has frequently emphasized that the term "property" as used in the Taking Clause includes the entire "group of rights inhering in the citizen's [ownership]." United States v. General Motors Corp., 323 U.S. 373, 89 L. Ed. 311, 65 S. Ct. 357, 156 A.L.R. 390 (1945). The term is not used in the

> vulgar and untechnical sense of the physical thing with respect to which the citizen exercises rights recognized by law. [Instead, it] . . . denote[s] the *group of rights* inhering in the citizen's relation to the physical thing, *as the right to possess, use and dispose of it.* . . . The constitutional provision is addressed to *every sort of interest* the citizen may possess. Id., at 377-378, 89 L. Ed. 311, 65 S. Ct. 357, 156 A.L.R. 390 (emphasis added).

While neighboring landowners are free to use their land and "air rights" in any way consistent with the broad boundaries of New York zoning, Penn Central, absent the permission of appellees, must forever maintain its property in its present state.[5] The property has been thus subjected to a nonconsensual servitude not borne by any neighboring or similar properties.[6] . . .

As early as 1887, the Court recognized that the government can prevent a property owner from using his property to injure others without having to compensate the owner for the value of the forbidden use. . . . Thus, there is no "taking" where a city prohibits the operation of a brickyard within a residential city, see Hadacheck v. Sebastian, 239 U.S. 394, 60 L. Ed. 349, 36 S. Ct. 143 (1915), or forbids excavation for sand and gravel below the water line, see Goldblatt v. Hempstead, 369 U.S. 590, 8 L. Ed. 2d 130, 82 S. Ct. 987 (1962). Nor is it relevant, where the government is merely prohibiting a noxious use of property, that the government would seem to be singling out a particular property owner. Hadacheck, *supra,* at 413, 60 L. Ed. 348, 36 S. Ct. 143.[8] . . .

---

200 (1952), for example, *ante,* at 124, 57 L. Ed. 2, at 648, the only language remotely applicable to eminent domain is stated in terms of "the destruction of respondents' terminals by a trained team of engineers in the face of their impending seizure by the enemy." 344 U.S., at 156, 97 L. Ed. 157, 73 S. Ct. 200.

    5. In particular, Penn Central cannot increase the height of the Terminal. This Court has previously held that the "air rights" over an area of land are "property" for purposes of the Fifth Amendment. See United States v. Causby, 328 U.S. 256, 90 L. Ed. 1206, 66 S. Ct. 1062 (1946) ("air rights" taken by low-flying airplanes); Griggs v. Allegheny County, 369 U.S. 84, 7 L. Ed. 2d 585, 82 S. Ct. 531 (1962) (same); Portsmouth Harbor Land & Hotel Co. v. United States, 260 U.S. 327, 67 L. Ed. 287, 43 S. Ct. 135 (1922) (firing of projectiles over summer resort can constitute taking). See also Butler v. Frontier Telephone Co., 186 N.Y. 486, 79 N.E. 716 (1906) (stringing of telephone wire across property constitutes a taking).

    6. It is, of course, irrelevant that appellees interfered with or destroyed property rights that Penn Central had not yet physically used. The Fifth Amendment must be applied with "reference to the uses for which the property is suitable, having regard to the existing business or wants of the community, *or such as may be reasonably expected in the immediate future.*" Boom Co. v. Patterson, 98 U.S. 403, 408, 25 L. Ed. 206 (1879) (emphasis added).

    8. Each of the cases cited by the Court for the proposition that legislation which severely affects some landowners but not others does not effect a "taking" involved noxious uses of property. See Hadacheck; Miller v. Schoene, 276 U.S. 272, 72 L. Ed. 568, 48 S. Ct. 246 (1928); Goldblatt. See *ante,* at 125-127, 133, 57 L. Ed. 2d, at 649-650, 654.

Appellees are not prohibiting a nuisance. The record is clear that the proposed addition to the Grand Central Terminal would be in full compliance with zoning, height limitations, and other health and safety requirements. Instead, appellees are seeking to preserve what they believe to be an outstanding example of beaux arts architecture. Penn Central is prevented from further developing its property basically because *too good* a job was done in designing and building it. The city of New York, because of its unadorned admiration for the design, has decided that the owners of the building must preserve it unchanged for the benefit of sightseeing New Yorkers and tourists. . . .

Even where the government prohibits a noninjurious use, the Court has ruled that a taking does not take place if the prohibition applies over a broad cross section of land and thereby "secure[s] an average reciprocity of advantage." Pennsylvania Coal Co. v. Mahon, 260 U.S. at 415, 67 L. Ed. 322, 43 S. Ct. 158, 28 A.L.R. 1321.[10] It is for this reason that zoning does not constitute a "taking." While zoning at times reduces *individual* property values, the burden is shared relatively evenly and it is reasonable to conclude that on the whole an individual who is harmed by one aspect of the zoning will be benefited by another.

Here, however, a multimillion dollar loss has been imposed on appellants; it is uniquely felt and is not offset by any benefits flowing from the preservation of some 400 other "landmarks" in New York City. Appellees have imposed a substantial cost on less than one-tenth of one percent of the buildings in New York City for the general benefit of all its people. It is exactly this imposition of general costs on a few individuals at which the "taking" protection is directed. . . .

As Mr. Justice Holmes pointed out in Pennsylvania Coal Co. v. Mahon, "the question at bottom" in an eminent domain case "is upon whom the loss of the changes desired should fall." 260 U.S., at 416, 67 L. Ed. 322, 43 S. Ct. 158, 28 A.L.R. 1321. The benefits that appellees believe will flow from preservation of the Grand Central Terminal will accrue to all the citizens of New York City. There is no reason to believe that appellants will enjoy a substantially greater share of these benefits. If the cost of preserving Grand Central Terminal were spread evenly across the entire population of the city of New York, the burden per person would be in cents per year—a minor cost appellees would surely concede for the benefit accrued. Instead, however, appellees would impose the entire cost of several million dollars per year on Penn Central. But it is precisely this sort of discrimination that the Fifth Amendment prohibits.

Appellees in response would argue that a taking only occurs where a

---

10. Appellants concede that the preservation of buildings of historical or aesthetic importance is a permissible objective of state action. Brief for Appellants 12. Cf. Berman v. Parker, 348 U.S. 26, 99 L. Ed. 27, 75 S. Ct. 98 (1954); United States v. Gettysburg Electric R. Co., 160 U.S. 668, 40 L. Ed. 576, 16 S. Ct. 427 (1896).

For the reasons noted in the text, historic *zoning*, as has been undertaken by cities such as New Orleans, may well not require compensation under the Fifth Amendment.

property owner is denied *all* reasonable value of his property.[13] The Court has frequently held that, even where a destruction of property rights would not *otherwise* constitute a taking, the inability of the owner to make a reasonable return on his property requires compensation under the Fifth Amendment. See, e.g., United States v. Lynah, 188 U.S., at 470, 47 L. Ed. 539, 23 S. Ct. 349. But the converse is not true. A taking does not become a noncompensable exercise of police power simply because the government in its grace allows the owner to make some "reasonable" use of his property. "[I]t is the character of the invasion, not the amount of damage resulting from it, so long as the damage is substantial, that determines the question whether it is a taking." United States v. Cress, 243 U.S. 316, 328, 61 L. Ed. 746, 37 S. Ct. 380 (1917); United States v. Causby, 328 U.S., at 266, 90 L. Ed. 1206, 66 S. Ct. 1062. See also Goldblatt v. Hempstead, 369 U.S., at 594, 8 L. Ed. 2d 130, 82 S. Ct. 987.

Appellees, apparently recognizing that the constraints imposed on a landmark site constitute a taking for Fifth Amendment purposes, do not leave the property owner empty-handed. As the Court notes, *ante,* at 113-114, 57 L. Ed. 2d, at 642, the property owner may theoretically "transfer" his previous right to develop the landmark property to adjacent properties if they are under his control. Appellees have coined this system "Transfer Development Rights," or TDRs.

Of all the terms used in the Taking Clause, "just compensation" has the strictest meaning. The Fifth Amendment does not allow simply an approximate compensation but requires "a full and perfect equivalent for the property taken." Monongahela Navigation Co. v. United States, 148 U.S., at 326, 37 L. Ed. 463, 13 S. Ct. 622. . . .

Appellees contend that, even if they have "taken" appellants' property, TDRs constitute "just compensation." Appellants, of course, argue that TDRs are highly imperfect compensation. Because the lower courts held that there was no "taking," they did not have to reach the question of whether or not just compensation has already been awarded. The New York Court of Appeals' discussion of TDRs gives some support to appellants: "The many defects in New York City's program for development rights transfers have been detailed elsewhere. . . . The area to which transfer is permitted is severely limited [and] complex procedures are required to obtain a transfer permit." 42 N.Y.2d 324,

---

13. Difficult conceptual and legal problems are posed by a rule that a taking only occurs where the property owner is denied all reasonable return on his property. Not only must the Court define "reasonable return" for a variety of types of property (farmlands, residential properties, commercial and industrial areas), but the Court must define the particular property unit that should be examined. For example, in this case, if appellees are viewed as having restricted Penn Central's use of its "air rights," *all* return has been denied. See Pennsylvania Coal Co. v. Mahon, 260 U.S. 393, 67 L. Ed. 322, 43 S. Ct. 158, 28 A.L.R. 1321 (1922). The Court does little to resolve these questions in its opinion. Thus, at one point, the Court implies that the question is whether the restrictions have "an unduly harsh impact upon the owner's use of the property," *ante,* at 127, 57 L. Ed. 2d, at 650; at another point, the question is phrased as whether Penn Central can obtain "a 'reasonable return' on its investment," *ante,* at 136, 57 L. Ed. 2d, at 656; and, at yet another point, the question becomes whether the landmark is "economically viable," *ante,* at 138 n.36, 57 L. Ed., at 657.

334-335, 366 N.E.2d 1271, 1277 (1977). And in other cases the Court of Appeals has noted that TDRs have an "uncertain and contingent market value" and do "not adequately preserve" the value lost when a building is declared to be a landmark. French Investing Co. v. City of New York, 39 N.Y.2d 587, 591 350 N.E.2d 381, 383, appeal dismissed, 429 U.S. 990, 50 L. Ed. 2d 602, 97 S. Ct. 515 (1976). On the other hand, there is evidence in the record that Penn Central has been offered substantial amounts for its TDRs. Because the record on appeal is relatively slim, I would remand to the Court of Appeals for a determination of whether TDRs constitute a "full and perfect equivalent for the property taken."

Over 50 years ago, Mr. Justice Holmes, speaking for the Court, warned that the courts were "in danger of forgetting that a strong public desire to improve the public condition is not enough to warrant achieving the desire by a shorter cut than the constitutional way of paying for the change." Pennsylvania Coal Co. v. Mahon, 260 U.S., at 416, 67 L. Ed. 322, 43 S. Ct. 158, 28 A.L.R. 1321. The Court's opinion in this case demonstrates that the danger thus foreseen has not abated. The city of New York is in a precarious financial state, and some may believe that the costs of landmark preservation will be more easily borne by corporations such as Penn Central than the overburdened individual taxpayers of New York. But these concerns do not allow us to ignore past precedents construing the Eminent Domain Clause to the end that the desire to improve the public condition is, indeed, achieved by a shorter cut than the constitutional way of paying for the change.

NOTES AND QUESTIONS

1. The New York City preservation ordinance, which the Court validated, is fairly typical of its genre. It contains this sequence of procedures:

   (a) After public hearing, the City Landmarks Commission designates a building as an individual landmark.
   (b) Thereafter, the property owner must obtain commission approval to demolish or alter the exterior structure. If the commission finds that the proposed work will impair the building's character, the commission may deny the permit, provided that this action does not subject the owner to "undue economic hardship." The ordinance defines hardship as less than 6 percent return on assessed valuation. (Because assessed valuation rarely reaches true value, the "true" return would actually be less.)
   (c) Where hardship will result from permit denial, the commission may devise a scheme, usually involving real estate tax relief, to bring the return up to the 6 percent level.
   (d) If the commission is unable to devise a suitable scheme, or if the building owner rejects the scheme, then the city must acquire the

property by condemnation or purchase within 90 days. Otherwise, the building owner may proceed with demolition or alteration. New York City Admin. Code ch. 8A (1971).

If the structure enjoys tax exemption (as did the Grand Central Terminal), it becomes eligible for special treatment only if four preconditions are satisfied: (1) the owner has agreed to sell the parcel contingent upon issuance of a certificate of approval; (2) the property, as it exists, cannot earn a reasonable return; (3) the structure is no longer suitable to its past or present purposes; and (4) the prospective buyer plans to alter the structure. In that event, the commission must either find another buyer or allow the sale and construction to proceed.

2.   The New York Court of Appeals, in concluding that landmark designation had not deprived the terminal owners of due process, noted that the development rights above the terminal might be transferred to other sites and, in their transferable state, provide "significant" compensation for the loss of rights above the terminal itself.

Professor John Costonis was an early champion of the development rights transfer (DRT). Cf. Costonis, Development Rights Transfer: An Exploratory Essay, 83 Yale L.J. 75 (1973); Space Adrift (1974). Recognizing that landmark owners may constitutionally demand an "acceptable" investment return, the DRT plan offers an ingenious bailout for strapped city treasuries unable to afford the condemnation alternative. Inasmuch as landmark sites (like Grand Central) can often be redeveloped with larger structures, Costonis would permit the landmark owner to sell his unused development rights to developers elsewhere in the city. The sale proceeds would lower the landmark owner's investment base, and together with some further tax relief, would enable the owner to earn an acceptable yield.

To illustrate the transferrable development rights concept: a landmark building occupies a plot of 20,000 square feet in an FAR 14 zone (see p. 779; §16.4, *infra*). This would allow 280,000 square feet of rentable space. The present structure contains only 128,000 square feet. The landmark owner could sell to developers in "transfer districts" the aggregate right to build an additional 152,000 square feet beyond their zoned-for capacity (see Table 10).

TABLE 10

	Size of Plot (sq. ft.)	FAR	Allowable Floor Area (sq. ft.)	Development Right Acquired (sq. ft.)	Revised Allowable Floor Area (sq. ft.)
Developer X	10,000	10	100,000	20,000	120,000
Developer Y	20,000	12	240,000	48,000	288,000
Developer Z	30,000	14	420,000	84,000	504,000
				152,000	

New York City currently allows landmark owners to transfer their unused rights to an *adjacent* lot. New York, N.Y., Zoning Resolution Act VII, ch. 4, §§74-79 to 74-793 (1975). A makeshift effort to broaden the transfer district solely in behalf of one (reluctant) owner, whose landmark parcel elsewhere was to be retained partly as open space, failed to satisfy the requirement of comprehensive planning. Fred F. French Investing Co. v. City of New York, 39 N.Y.2d 587, 350 N.E.2d 381, 385 N.Y.S.2d 5 (1976), *appeal dismissed,* 429 U.S. 990 (1976).

The DRT scheme is no panacea and raises difficult problems of valuation, defining transfer districts, and interim financing (when the development rights supply exceeds the demand for them). Cf. Berger, The Accommodation Power in Land Use Controversies: A Reply to Professor Costonis, 76 Colum. L. Rev. 799, 802-812 (1976).

Paradoxically, the DRT scheme may have even wider utility for environmentalists. Cf. Costonis, Development Rights Transfer: An Exploratory Essay, 83 Yale L.J. 75 (1973); Chapter 16.4, *infra.*

3. Read carefully the Brennan opinion. What standard does the justice formulate for testing whether the regulation satisfies the Constitution? Similarly, examine the Rehnquist dissent. What is his benchmark? Has he enunciated a different standard or is his disagreement with Justice Brennan one of application? Has the court, or any of its justices, made real headway in helping one to decide when a regulation goes "too far"?

4. Re-examine the four tests that appear in footnote 24, page 722 *supra.* Consider how a court would decide the *Grand Central* case in light of each test.

5. Historic preservation also extends to entire neighborhoods. Outstanding examples include New Orleans's Vieux Carré (Old Quarter), Washington, D.C.'s Georgetown, and Boston's Louisburg Square. Property owners within a historic neighborhood must usually obtain prior approval for demolition or exterior alterations, and new structures must show compatible design. Courts are basically sympathetic with neighborhood preservation efforts. See, e.g., Maher v. City of New Orleans, 516 F.2d 1051 (5th Cir. 1975) (ordinance valid as applied even though cottage in question allegedly enjoyed no historical or architectural values).

Are the economic, legal, or political problems present in preserving a historic neighborhood different from those faced in preserving a landmark building? What societal values underlie neighborhood preservation? See generally Note, The Police Power, Eminent Domain, and the Preservation of Historic Property, 63 Colum. L. Rev. 708 (1963).

6. European cities have long been jealous of their architectural heritage, and have not hesitated to use the legal and financial resources of government to forestall change. In France, the Ministry for Cultural Affairs and the Ministry of Housing have, by agreement, marked out in each department "sensitive zones," within which special architectural regulations apply. In Britain, the Town and Country Planning Act of 1947, supplemented by the 1962 Act, give local planning agencies explicit tools with which to preserve

historically important districts. In both countries, the government's role is strengthened by the energetic efforts of private bodies (e.g., England's National Trust). See Preservation and Development of Ancient Buildings and Historic or Artistic Sites, Council of Europe (Strasbourg 1963).

7.   Below are several other disputes between the landowner and the state as to whether the regulation was, in fact, a taking. Consider how—and by what criteria—you would resolve them.

(a) A owns 16 acres zoned residential. As A readies to develop her parcel, a city ordinance designates 4.0 acres of the parcel as potential parkland. The ordinance further bars any building on the 4.0 acres for three years. At the end of this period, the city must either buy the 4.0 acres or allow A to build. A challenges the ordinance. Miller v. Beaver Falls, 368 Pa. 189, 82 A.2d 34 (1951). Compare Headley v. City of Rochester, 272 N.Y. 197, 5 N.E.2d 198 (1936). Compare also Golden v. Planning Board of Town of Ramapo, §16.5 *infra.*

(b) B owns a 2-acre parcel next to a railroad station rezoned so as to permit only the parking and storage of automobiles. The parcel has been used profitably for this purpose for thirty years. All the surrounding land has been zoned and developed for even more profitable business use. B challenges the zoning classification of his parcel. The city asserts the need for off-street parking at this site. Vernon Park Realty v. City of Mount Vernon, 307 N.Y. 493, 121 N.E.2d 517 (1954).

(c) The state legislature asks for an advisory opinion on a proposed bill that would create (possibly without compensation) a "public on-foot free right-of-passage" during daylight hours along the state's entire coastline between the mean high-water and the extreme low-water lines. By virtue of a colonial ordinance, title to this tidal land is held by the upland owner. Is the proposal valid? In re Opinion of the Justices, 365 Mass. 681, 313 N.E.2d 561 (1974).

(d) A 1973 state law bars without compensation strip mining within state-owned lands. Through a series of earlier transactions, C has obtained mining rights within a state forest. C challenges the new law. Bureau of Mines of Maryland v. George's Creek Coal and Land Co., 272 Md. 143, 321 A.2d 748 (1974).

Chapter 14

The Planning Process

Although America is not a tight little island, it has become a highly interdependent community. Even the most ardent believer in laissez-faire would agree that government must exercise some guidance and control over land-use decisions if the nation and its citizens are to prosper. Thus, few would deny that the government should build roads, enact housing codes, provide clean water, control air pollution, and maintain beaches and parks, to cite just a few of the land-use roles that we freely assign to government.

When we speak of how these roles are decided upon, we usually refer to the political process, the tug-and-pull between various interest groups all striving for the ends dearest to them. But there is another process, planning, which co-exists with politics and is itself often intensely political, and which property students can ignore only at the risk of an incomplete understanding of how land allocation and development choices result.

Yet in seeking to learn what planning is and how planning works, you should prepare for frustration, frustration that is born of several factors. At the theoretical level, planning still suffers an identity crisis. Despite its claim to be an intellectual discipline, planning has evoked almost as many theoretical self-expressions as there are persons who practice the craft. On the pragmatic side, planners are caught between the nation's ambivalence towards long-range governmental planning, which still smacks of despised socialism to many, and the first reality: planning underlies major investment and allocation decisions in every realm of personal, corporate, and administrative life. Planners are further buffeted between their wish to practice apolitically as true professionals free of any voter pressure, and the second reality: planning decisions rarely occur in a political vacuum.

There is the further issue of where the planning is done. In the realm of land use, America has cherished home rule; units of local government—village, town, and city—all make land allocation choices within their corporate four walls. Yet that tradition is under fire and faces retreat. Inevitably, we shall have far greater planning direction from the county, state, and nation.

The significance of this chapter is implicit in its location in the text. It comes before the chapters on zoning and eminent domain. Although the layman usually confuses it with planning, zoning is simply one way for government to execute a plan. Eminent domain is another, nor should you forget that taxes and the capital budget are also powerful tools for achieving a governmental plan.

§14.1 Several Views of the Planning Process

WILLIAMS, PLANNING LAW AND DEMOCRATIC LIVING
20 Law & Contemp. Prob. 317-318 (1955)

. . . As used here, "planning" means the process of consciously exercising rational control over the development of the physical environment, and of certain aspects of the social environment, in the light of a common scheme of values, goals, and assumptions. Planning is concerned with guiding both public and private action, and may be on a local, metropolitan, or regional basis.

In planning, primary emphasis is on the physical environment; yet the social environment is also involved in many ways. First, intelligent correlation of decisions on the development of the physical environment necessarily involves having consistent assumptions and policies derived from the social environment, as for example on the size and characteristics of the population, even though such matters are left generally to individual decisions. Second, in some instances attempts are made to influence individual decisions on such matters, as for example population migration and the birth rate—although here there is a wide difference of opinion on how far planning should go.[1] Finally, the distinction between the physical and the social environment is really an artificial and untenable one anyway, since the arrangement of the physical environment has a decided impact upon social conditions, and vice versa.

This process of conscious and purposeful control over the development of the physical and social environment in a relatively free society is something rather new in history. Moreover, in such a society the development of techniques to forecast probable future trends, and thus to ascertain and evaluate the range of possibilities within which control may be exercised, is a difficult process at best. The development of effective methods of exercising such control is even more difficult. Any consideration of planning techniques must therefore start with a realization that planning for the future environment is still in the experimental stage, and that the techniques available, while extremely useful, are still rather crude. It is a truism to say that even the best plans must be subject to constant review in the light of changing conditions. Moreover, what techniques are available have generally not been thought out in terms of all their implications for the whole environment. . . .

---

1. The one point on which there is universal agreement is that the precise outer limits of urban and regional planning are not easy to define. However, we are not concerned here with over-all economic planning in the socialist or collectivist sense.

OZBEKIAN, "CAN" IMPLIES "OUGHT"

Planning for Diversity and Choice 208 (Anderson ed. 1968)

I think much of what I have said up to this point shows my own conception of planning to consist of three interrelated and interactive approaches. . . . These are: The "normative plan," which deals with the *oughts* and defines the goals on which all policy rests; the "strategic plan," which formulates what in the light of elected oughts, or chosen policies, we *can* actually do; and finally the "operational plan," which establishes how, when, and in what sequence of action we *will* implement the strategies that have been accepted as capable of satisfying the policies. . . .

Strategic planning and operational planning fit quite well into current practice. Normative planning, to my knowledge, is not seriously considered yet as an integral element of that same practice. Policy considerations still remain outside the planning process and enter into it as exogenous givens. In the system I have just outlined such a differentiation would not exist. Policy making, strategy definition, and the determination of implementing steps would be viewed as parts of a single integrated and iterative process. . . .

[I]n normative planning the important thing is not to be surpassed or overcome by current events. This always tends to happen. Whenever it happens, planning reverts to becoming mainly responsive to current situations rather than creative of futures, and as long as planning is not futures-creative, it must be an after-the-fact ordering exercise dominated by present events. Such an exercise is obviously not planning but something else.

DUHL, THE PARAMETERS OF URBAN PLANNING

Planning for Diversity and Choice 34 (Anderson ed. 1968)

Many architects and city planners (technicians who have grandiose notions as to the impact of their efforts upon the future) still do not realize that the real *planning* is taking place in some of society's basic political processes. Planning grows out of the confrontations between people and between those in the community and those who are making the decisions. Planning is affected by the way budgets are allocated, the way we write our governmental rules and regulations. . . . [M]ost architects, planners, and technicians . . . don't understand this game at all. . . .

THE CASE FOR REGIONAL PLANNING

Directive Comm. on Regional Planning, Yale Univ. 77-79 (1947)

It has been the genius of the American people to work out a happy balance between total planlessness and total planning—to effect that balance between governmental and voluntary action, between the different branches of government (executive, legislative, and judicial), and between the different levels of government (federal, state, local) which is appropriate to the maintenance of a free society, to the liberation of the widest possible zones for private action. If planning be thus understood as the rational adaptation of appropriate means to the liberation of the maximum creative energies of our people, the Constitution, as has often been remarked, was the first great plan in the United States, and it has since been continuously implemented by myriads of lesser plans, at all levels of government. . . .

. . . Timid and uninformed prophets even now cry through the land that there is an irreconcilable contradiction between planning and freedom, that there is no middle road between anarchy and regimentation, and that any nation or community which consciously sets out to clarify its goals, including freedom, and to adopt rational means to their achievement is already on the road to serfdom. Their argument is an evolving one. It is impossible, we are told first, for our citizens to agree on any goals more precise than those of the Declaration of Independence; even if agreement could be reached on relatively precise goals in the common interest, we are told next, the technical means for the achievement of such goals are not within human knowledge; or even if the technical means might be devised, we are told again, the processes of democratic government are not amenable to administering tasks which require any more detailed supervision than the maintenance of public order; and so on. The main thesis of this prophecy of doom seems to be, in sum, that the best way to achieve social goals is by some mysterious indirection; a people or a community must back its way into freedom and abundance!

Happily there is no such antinomy as is alleged between planning and freedom. Its existence is refuted by the whole of our national history. It is as false as the purely verbal dichotomy, the spurious psychology, and the distorted notions of democratic government upon which it is based. Simple dichotomies, created by an uncritical use of polar words, are seldom adequate representations of the continuum of reality. It is a particularly meretricious combination of confusions and perversions to contrapose planning and freedom.

Freedom, as the late Bronislaw Malinowski insisted after surveying many societies, primitive and contemporary, is both meaningless and unattainable except as a function of planning and organization.

To the question how men can plan and still remain free the appropriate answer is: How can men remain free if they do not plan? In Malinowski's words, "the concept of freedom" must "first and foremost" be referred always "to the increase in range, diversity and power in human planning." It is "the ability to foresee and plan ahead," "the ability to use past experience in order to establish future conditions corresponding to the needs, the desires and the aspirations of man," that "is the first essential prerequisite to freedom." It is, furthermore, contrary to fact to suggest that there is not in this country today a fundamental agreement, which transcends all groups and occupations, about the basic democratic values involved in sharing power, respect, knowledge, health, income, and safety and an agreement which can be reduced to relatively concrete goals in terms of voting, nondiscrimination, schools, medical care, nutrition, homes, clothing, and so on. Indeed, it would be contrary to all that modern science tells us about the formation of individual conscience and character to expect our nation, without its being subjected to a change in conditions that would portend its imminent destruction, suddenly to produce a host of moral mavericks denying all its basic values. The mere fact that we do not have complete knowledge of all possible techniques of social engineering should not, again, prevent us from making the best use of what knowledge we do have, which is not inconsiderable; it cannot, with safety to freedom, be left to the enemies of freedom alone to use science in the pursuit of values. It is, finally, democratic government which of all forms of government is most amenable to the planning process. It alone can secure that delicate adjustment of claims of right and acknowledgements of duty which is necessary in any group or institution to inspire men to their fullest, most spontaneous, and most rational exertions. It is as we have seen, the most efficient form of government yet devised for securing that balance between government and voluntary action and between the different branches and levels of government which is necessary to insure a society of both freedom and abundance. It is the planning process in action.

§14.2   The Role of the Local Planning Agency

Two quite different views exist as to where, within the hierarchy of city government, the planning agency belongs. Originally, many believed in an independent commission (usually of laymen), its members chosen by the chief executive but expected to regard the public as its client. The Standard City Planning Enabling Act (SEPA) (U.S. Dept. of Commerce 1928) chose this model, and most communities followed suit. At the root of this belief was an elitist doubt that elected officials could withstand political and corrupting pressures. It foresaw, instead, a body of fearless and public-spirited citizens, often serving without pay, with the technical backup of equally courageous professionals, who together would stand above the fray while creating the urban dream.

That vision, now fifty years old, was neither prophetic nor sound. The independent commission idea has been called a dodo, denounced as undemocratic, and described as not having worked in *any* city in America. While planning directors themselves seem unwilling to forsake the concept entirely, executive responsibility for both planning and program is well under way, particularly in larger communities.

The weaknesses of the independent commission model appear to be many. To begin with, the commissions have enjoyed limited power. As we shall see shortly, the planning body can advise, plead, and sometimes veto; but except for subdivision approval and the granting of special exceptions, it can seldom enact. Thus, the drafting of a proposed capital budget or a revised zoning ordinance makes little sense if it ignores the political attitudes, priority systems, and idiosyncracies of the men and women who must act on the proposal. This link between the planner and other government officials becomes even more inextricable as the tie between physical and social planning fastens tightly, and as local budgets increasingly depend upon federal and state money infusions. And even in smaller communities, where life problems still remain manageable, and where the power to approve subdivisions and special exceptions still matters, the image of a public-spirited planning gentry is often tarnished by cronyism, narrow-mindedness, and greed.

Figure 5 typifies a large city department of planning, from which the planning commission draws its technical competence. Notice the scope and complexity. It would take only one organizational change, however, to replace the planning commission with a departmental chief executive, who like other

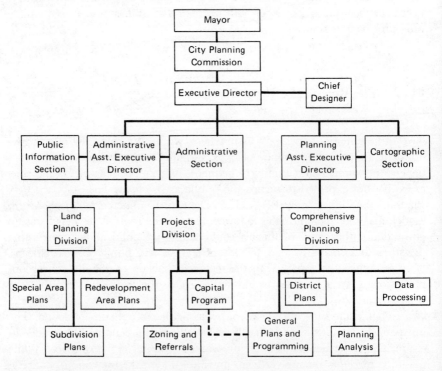

Source: Principles and Practice of Urban Planning 537 (Goodman ed. 1968).

[FIGURE 5]
City Planning Organization Chart

agency heads would become part of an administrative team. (In communities having a managerial form of government, the city manager would replace the mayor in the hierarchy). It would take much more sweeping change, however, to assure the cooperativeness between the planning agency and a host of other city agencies and independent bodies (e.g., local public housing authorities and publicly elected school boards) that is needed for a coordinated attack on a community's physical, economic, and social problems.

NEW YORK CITY CHARTER
(Rev. 1976) (Supp. 1980)

THE DUTIES OF THE CITY PLANNING AGENCY

§191. *Department and director of city planning.*—a. There shall be a department of city planning, the head of which shall be the director of city planning. He shall be chairman and a member of the city planning commission.

§192. *City planning commission.*—a. There shall be a city planning commission to consist of the chairman and six members to be appointed by the mayor.

§197-a. *Plans.*—a. The city planning commission shall be responsible for the conduct of planning relating to the orderly growth and improvement and future development of the city, including adequate and appropriate resources for the housing, business, industry, transportation, distribution, recreation, comfort, convenience, health and welfare of its population. Plans for the development, growth, and improvement of the city and of its boroughs and community districts may be initiated by (1) the mayor, (2) the city planning commission, (3) a borough board with respect to land located within two or more community districts, or (4) a community board with respect to land located within its community district. A community board or borough board that initiates any such plan shall conduct a public hearing on it and submit a written recommendation to the city planning commission. Plans initiated by the mayor or the city planning commission shall be referred to the affected community board or boards and, if land located within two or more community districts is included, to the affected borough board or boards for review and recommendation after public hearing. . . .

b. The city planning commission shall review any plan initiated pursuant to subdivision a of this section, hold a public hearing on it and recommend to the board of estimate approval, modification or disapproval of the plan. The board of estimate shall hold a public hearing on the plan and the recommendation of the city planning commission, and thereafter take final action of approval, modification or disapproval. The board may by a three-fourths vote override any action of the city planning commission which disapproved a plan. If the city planning commission has approved a plan with or without modification, the board of estimate may take final action on it by majority vote. Copies of approved plans shall be filed with the city clerk, the department of city planning and every borough president and the borough boards and community boards affected. . . .

§197-c. *Uniform land use review procedure.*—a. Except as otherwise provided in this charter, proposals and applications by any person or agency for changes, approvals, contracts, consents, permits or authorization thereof, respecting the use, development or improvement of real property subject to city regulation shall be reviewed pursuant to a uniform review procedure in the following categories:

(1) The city map pursuant to section one hundred ninety-eight and section one hundred ninety-nine; . . .
(3) Designations of zoning districts under the zoning resolution, including conversion from one land use to another land use, pursuant to section two hundred;
(4) Special permits within the jurisdiction of the city planning commission under the zoning resolution, pursuant to section two hundred; . . .
(6) Franchises and revocable consents involving residential, industrial, commercial, transportation or community facility projects pursuant to chapter fourteen; . . .
(8) Housing and urban renewal plans. . . .

b.   Each proposal or application shall be filed with the department of city planning, which shall forward a copy within five days to the community board for each community district in which the land involved, or any part thereof, is located, and to the borough board if the proposal or application involves land located in two or more districts in a borough.

c.   Each such community board shall, not later than sixty days after receipt of the proposal or application . . . (2) conduct a public hearing thereon and (3) prepare and submit a written recommendation directly to the city planning commission. . . .

e.   Not later than sixty days after the filing of a recommendation with it by a community board or borough board or the latest filing if there is more than one within the time allowed, the city planning commission shall approve, modify, or disapprove, the proposal or application and shall file its decision with the board of estimate.

§198. *City map.*—a. The city map, as the same shall exist at the time when this charter goes into effect, is hereby continued.

b.   The director of city planning shall be the custodian of the city map, and it shall be his duty to complete and maintain the same and to register thereon all changes resulting from action authorized by law.

§199. *Projects and changes in city map.*—a. No improvement or project affecting the master plan or the city map and no addition to or change in the city map shall be authorized otherwise than as provided in this charter.

b.   The review of any proposed addition to or change in the city map initiated by or referred to the city planning commission shall be made pursuant to section one hundred ninety-seven-c except that if the city planning commission (1) does not recommend approval or recommends a modification of the proposed addition to or change in the city map which is not acceptable to the board of estimate or (2) fails to act within the time limit specified in subdivision e of section one hundred ninety-seven-c, the board of estimate nevertheless may approve or modify the proposed addition to or change in the city map by a three-fourths vote.

§200. *Zoning regulations.*—a. Except as provided in subdivision b, any existing resolution or regulation of the board of estimate or of the city planning commission to regulate and limit the height and bulk of buildings, to regulate and determine the area of yards, courts and other open spaces, to regulate density of population or to regulate and restrict the locations of trades and industries and location of buildings designed for specific uses or creating districts for any such purpose, including any such regulation which provides that the board of standards and appeals may determine and vary the application of such resolutions or regulations in harmony with their general purpose and intent and in accordance with general or specific rules contained in such regulations, may be amended, repealed or added to only in the following manner:

(1) The city planning commission may upon its own initiative at any time or upon application as provided in section two hundred one, adopt a resolution for any such purpose subject to the limitations provided by law.

(2) Approval, disapproval or modification by the board of estimate of a recommendation by the commission for a change in the zoning resolution must occur within sixty days from the date of filing of the recommendation of the commission with the board. In case the board shall fail to act on such affirmative resolution within such period of sixty days, such change shall be deemed approved and effective on the sixty-first day after the date of filing unless a protest of owners of affected property shall have been filed in accordance with the provisions of subdivision three. Any resolution for a zoning change which the mayor shall have certified to the planning commission as necessary, and which has been disapproved by the commission, may be adopted by the board of estimate by a three-fourths vote and after a public hearing. The foregoing limitation of sixty days shall be inapplicable to such an adoption and the change shall become effective at a time fixed by the board of estimate.

(3) In case a protest against a proposed resolution shall have been presented to the secretary of the board of estimate within thirty days from the date of such filing, duly signed and acknowledged by the owners of twenty per centum or more of the area of

   (1) the land included in changes proposed in such proposed resolution, or

(2) the land immediately adjacent extending one hundred feet therefrom, or

(3) the land, if any, directly opposite thereto extending one hundred feet from the street frontage of such opposite land,

such resolution shall not be effective after the filing of such protest unless approved by the board of estimate, either in the form in which it was filed or as modified by the board, by a three-fourths vote of the board within one hundred eighty days after the filing of said resolution with the secretary of the board of estimate. . . .

b. Designations of zoning districts under the zoning resolution and the issuance of special permits which under the terms of the zoning resolution are within the jurisdiction of the city planning commission shall conform to the procedures provided in section one hundred ninety-seven-c, except that whenever the city planning commission has not recommended approval of a proposed change in the designation of a zoning district or the issuance of a special permit under the zoning resolution or has failed to act on such a matter within the time specified in section one hundred ninety-seven-c, the board of estimate by a three-fourths vote may approve such change or the issuance of such permit only if the mayor shall have certified to the city planning commission that such change or issuance is necessary.

§201. *Applications for zoning changes.*—Applications for changes in zoning resolutions or regulations or for the issuance of special permits within the jurisdiction of the city planning commission under the zoning resolution may be filed by any taxpayer, community board, or borough board with the city planning commission. For applications involving changes in the designation of zoning districts or the issuance of special permits under the zoning resolution, the review and hearing procedure in section one hundred ninety-seven-c, as modified by subdivision b of section two hundred, shall be applicable. For applications involving other changes in zoning resolutions and regulations, the commission prior to taking action upon any such application shall refer it to the affected community boards or borough boards for a public hearing and
· recommendation.

§202. *Platting of land and dedication of streets and public places.*—a. No map of a subdivision or platting of land into streets, avenues or public places and blocks within the limits of the city shall be received for filing in the office in which instruments affecting real property are required to be recorded in the county in which the land is situated, unless such map shall have been submitted to the board of estimate and approved by such board, after transmittal to the city planning commission for report, by the same procedure as provided in subdivision b of section one hundred ninety-nine for changes in the city map. If such map is disapproved by the board of estimate, the secretary of the board shall certify such fact in writing upon such map, and such map shall be received only for record without such approval.

[In many communities elsewhere, the planning commission is delegated plenary power over the approval of subdivision plats.]

b.   No street, avenue, highway or public place, the layout of which has not been approved as provided in this section, shall be deemed to have been accepted by the city as a street, avenue, highway or public place, unless such street, avenue, highway or public place shall lie within the lines of a street, avenue, highway or public place upon the city map.

[Why might it matter whether a street has been accepted?]

§14.3   Elements of a Land-Use Plan

California is one of several states that now require comprehensive land-use planning at the local level.[1] A 1965 law provides that within each city and county the planning agency shall prepare and the legislative body shall adopt "a comprehensive, long-term general plan for the physical development of the county or city, and of any land outside its boundaries which in the planning agency's judgment bears relation to its planning." Cal. Govt. Code §65300 (1966).

Before looking carefully at the statutory excerpts below, pause to consider what a "physical" plan should consist of. List the chief areas of private and governmental activity—e.g., highway building, housing, etc.—that employ land resources and for which, you believe, planning is essential. Then see what the California statute has included.

CALIFORNIA GOVERNMENT CODE
(West Supp. 1973)

§65302. *Elements required to be included in plan.*
The general plan shall consist of a statement of development policies and shall include a diagram or diagrams and text setting forth objectives, principles, standards, and plan proposals. The plan shall include the following elements:

(a)   A land-use element which designates the proposed general distribution and general location and extent of the uses of the land for housing, business, industry, open space, including agriculture, natural resources, recreation, and enjoyment of scenic beauty, education, public buildings and grounds, solid and liquid waste disposal facilities, and other categories of public and private uses of land. The land-use element shall include a statement of the standards of population density and building intensity recommended for the various districts and other territory covered by the plan. The land-use element shall also identify areas covered by the plan which are subject to flooding and shall be reviewed annually with respect to such areas.

---

1. Similar laws now exist in Washington State, Wash. Rev. Code §36.70.010 (1964), and Oregon, Or. Rev. Stat. §215.050 (Supp. 1977) (county plans).

(b) A circulation element consisting of the general location and extent of existing and proposed major thoroughfares, transportation routes, terminals, and other local public utilities and facilities, all correlated with the land-use element of the plan.

(c) A housing element as provided in Section 65580 et seq.

(d) A conservation element for the conservation, development, and utilization of natural resources including water and its hydraulic force, forests, soils, rivers and other waters, harbors, fisheries, wildlife, minerals, and other natural resources. That portion of the conservation element including waters shall be developed in coordination with any countrywide water agency and with all district and city agencies which have developed, served, controlled or conserved water for any purpose for the county or city for which the plan is prepared. The conservation element may also cover:

(1) The reclamation of land and waters.

(2) Flood control.

(3) Prevention and control of the pollution of streams and other waters.

(4) Regulation of the use of land in stream channels and other areas required for the accomplishment of the conservation plan.

(5) Prevention, control, and correction of the erosion of soils, beaches, and shores.

(6) Protection of watersheds.

(7) The location, quantity and quality of rock, sand and gravel resources.

The conservation element shall be prepared and adopted no later than December 31, 1973.

(e) An open-space element as provided in Article 10.5 (commencing with Section 65560) of this chapter.

(f) A seismic safety element consisting of an identification and appraisal of seismic hazards such as susceptibility to surface ruptures from faulting, to ground shaking, to ground failures, or to effects of seismically induced waves such as tsunamis and seiches.

The seismic safety element shall also include an appraisal of mudslides, landslides, and slope stability as necessary geologic hazards that must be considered simultaneously with other hazards such as possible surface ruptures from faulting, ground shaking, ground failure and seismically induced waves. . . .

(g) A noise element, which shall recognize guidelines adopted by the Office of Noise Control . . . and which quantifies the community noise environment in terms of noise exposure contours for both near- and long-term levels of growth and traffic activity. . . . The noise exposure information shall become a guideline for use in development of the land use element to achieve noise-compatible land-use and also to provide baseline levels and noise source identification for local noise ordinance enforcement.

The sources of environmental noise considered in this analysis shall include, but are not limited to, all of the following:

(1) Highways and freeways.
(2) Primary arterials and major local streets.
(3) Passenger and freight on-line railroad operations and ground rapid transit systems.
(4) Commercial, general aviation, heliport, helistop, and military airport operations, aircraft overflights, jet engine test stands, and all other ground facilities and maintenance functions related to airport operation.
(5) Local industrial plants, including, but not limited to, railroad classification yards.
(6) Other ground stationary noise sources identified by local agencies as contributing to the community noise environment.

The noise exposure information shall be presented in terms of noise contours expressed in community noise equivalent level (CNEL) or day-night average level (L_{dn}). CNEL means the average equivalent A-weighted sound level during a 24-hour day, obtained after addition of five decibels to sound levels in the evening from 7 P.M. to 10 P.M. and after addition of 10 decibels to sound levels in the night before 7 A.M. and after 10 P.M. L_{dn} means the average equivalent A-weighted sound level during a 24-hour day, obtained after addition of 10 decibels to sound levels in the night before 7 A.M. and after 10 P.M.

The contours shall be shown in minimum increments of 5db and shall continue down to 60db. For areas deemed noise sensitive, including, but not limited to, areas containing schools, hospitals, rest homes, long-term medical or mental care facilities, or any other land-use areas deemed noise sensitive by the local jurisdiction, the noise exposure shall be determined by monitoring.

A part of the noise element shall also include the preparation of a community noise exposure inventory, current and projected, which identifies the number of persons exposed to various levels of noise throughout the community.

The noise element shall also recommend mitigating measures and possible solutions to existing and foreseeable noise problems.

(h) A scenic highway element for the development, establishment, and protection of scenic highways pursuant to the provisions of Article 2.5 (commencing with Section 260) of Chapter 2 of Division 1 of the Streets and Highways Code.

(i) A safety element for the protection of the community from fires and geologic hazards including features necessary for such protection as evacuation routes, peak load water supply requirements, minimum road widths, clearances around structures, and geologic hazard mapping in areas of known geologic hazards.

The requirements of this section shall apply to charter cities.

§65303. *Elements permitted as part of plan.*

The general plan may include the following elements or any part or phase thereof:

(a)   A recreation element showing a comprehensive system of areas and public sites for recreation, including the following, and, when practicable, their locations and proposed development:

(1) Natural reservations.
(2) Parks.
(3) Parkways.
(4) Beaches.
(5) Playgrounds.
(6) Recreational community gardens.
(7) Other recreation areas.

(b)   The circulation element provided for in Section 65302(b) may also include recommendations concerning parking facilities and building setback lines and the delineations of such systems on the land; a system of street naming, house and building numbering; and such other matters as may be related to the improvement of circulation of traffic.

(c)   A transportation element showing a comprehensive transportation system, including locations of rights-of-way, terminals, viaducts, and grade separations. This element of the plan may also include port, harbor, aviation, and related facilities.

(d)   A transit element showing a proposed system of transit lines, including rapid transit, streetcar, motor coach and trolley coach lines, and related facilities.

(e)   A public services and facilities element shoing general plans for sewerage, refuse disposal, drainage, and local utilities, and rights-of-way, easements, and facilities for them.

(f)   A public building element showing locations and arrangements of civic and community centers, public schools, libraries, police and fire stations, and other public buildings, including their architecture and the landscape treatment of their grounds.

(g)   A community design element consisting of standards and principles governing the subdivision of land, and showing recommended designs for community and neighborhood development and redevelopment, including sites for schools, parks, playgrounds and other uses.

(h)   A housing element consisting of standards and plans for the elimination of substandard dwelling conditions.

(i)   A redevelopment element consisting of plans and programs for the elimination of slums and blighted areas and for community redevelopment, including housing sites, business and industrial sites, public building sites, and for other purposes authorized by law.

(j)   A historical preservation element for the identification, establishment, and protection of sites and structures of architectural, historical, archeological or cultural significance, including significant trees, hedgerows and other plant materials. The historical preservation element shall include a program which develops actions to be taken in accomplishing the policies set forth in this element.

Guidelines shall be developed by the Office of Planning and Research by February 1, 1976 in consultation with appropriate public and private organizations concerned with historical preservation.

(k) Such additional elements dealing with other subjects which in the judgment of the planning agency relate to the physical development of the county or city.

ARTICLE 10.6 HOUSING ELEMENTS

§65580. *Legislative finding and declaration.*
The Legislature finds and declares as follows:

(a) The availability of housing is of vital statewide importance, and the early attainment of decent housing and a suitable living environment for every California family is a priority of the highest order.

(b) The early attainment of this goal requires the cooperative participation of government and the private sector in an effort to expand housing opportunities and accommodate the housing needs of Californians of all economic levels. . . .

§65581. *Intent of legislature.*
It is the intent of the Legislature in enacting this article:

(a) To assure that counties and cities recognize their responsibilities in contributing to the attainment of the state housing goal.

(b) To assure that counties and cities will prepare and implement housing elements which, along with federal and state programs, will move toward attainment of the state housing goal.

(c) To recognize that each locality is best capable of determining what efforts are required by it to contribute to the attainment of the state housing goal, provided such a determination is compatible with the state housing goal and regional housing needs. . . .

§65583. *Contents of housing element.*
The housing element shall consist of an identification and analysis of existing and projected housing needs and a statement of goals, policies, quantified objectives, and scheduled programs for the preservation, improvement, and development of housing. The housing element shall identify adequate sites for housing, including rental housing, factory-built housing, and mobilehomes, and shall make adequate provision for the existing and projected needs of all economic segments of the community. The element shall contain all of the following:

(a) An assessment of housing needs and an inventory of resources and constraints relevant to the meeting of these needs. The assessment and inventory shall include the following:

(1) Analysis of population and employment trends and documentation of projections and a quantification of the locality's existing and projected housing needs for all income levels. Such existing and projected needs shall include the locality's share of the regional housing need in accordance with Section 65584.

(2) Analysis and documentation of household characteristics, including level of payment compared to ability to pay, housing characteristics, including overcrowding, and housing stock condition.

(3) An inventory of land suitable for residential development, including vacant sites and sites having potential for redevelopment, and an analysis of the relationship of zoning and public facilities and services to these sites.

(4) Analysis of potential and actual governmental constraints upon the maintenance, improvement, or development of housing for all income levels, including land use controls, building codes and their enforcement, site improvements, fees and other exactions required of developers, and local processing and permit procedures.

(5) Analysis of potential and actual nongovernmental constraints upon the maintenance, improvement, or development of housing for all income levels, including the availability of financing, the price of land, and the cost of construction.

(6) Analysis of any special housing needs, such as those of the handicapped, elderly, large families, farmworkers, and families with female heads of households.

(7) Analysis of opportunities for energy conservation with respect to residential development.

(b) A statement of the community's goals, quantified objectives, and policies relative to the maintenance, improvement, and development of housing.

It is recognized that the total housing needs identified pursuant to subdivision (a) may exceed available resources and the community's ability to satisfy this need within the content of the general plan requirements outlined in Article 5 (commencing with Section 65300). Under these circumstances, the quantified objectives need not be identical to the identified existing housing needs, but should establish the maximum number of housing units that can be constructed, rehabilitated, and conserved over a five-year time frame.

(c) A program which sets forth a five-year schedule of actions the local government is undertaking or intends to undertake to implement the policies and achieve the goals and objectives of the housing element through the administration of land use and development controls, provision of regulatory concessions and incentives, and the utilization of appropriate federal and state financing and subsidy programs when available. In order to make adequate provision for the housing needs of all economic segments of the community, the program shall do all of the following:

(1) Identify adequate sites which will be made available through appropriate zoning and development standards and with public services and facilities needed to facilitate and encourage the development of a variety of types of housing for all income levels, including rental housing, factory-built housing and mobilehomes, in order to meet the community's housing goals as identified in subdivision (b).

(2) Assist in the development of adequate housing to meet the needs of low- and moderate-income households.

(3) Address and, where appropriate and legally possible, remove governmental constraints to the maintenance, improvement, and development of housing.

(4) Conserve and improve the condition of the existing affordable housing stock.

(5) Promote housing opportunities for all persons regardless of race, religion, sex, marital status, ancestry, national origin, or color.

The program shall include an identification of the agencies and officials responsible for the implementation of the various actions and the means by which consistency will be achieved with other general plan elements and community goals. The local government shall make a diligent effort to achieve public participation of all economic segments of the community in the development of the housing element, and the program shall describe this effort.

§65584. *Locality's share of regional housing needs; determination and distribution; revision.*

(a) For purposes of subdivision (a) of Section 65583, a locality's share of the regional housing needs includes that share of the housing need of persons at all income levels within the area significantly affected by a jurisdiction's general plan. The distribution of regional housing needs shall, based upon available data, take into consideration market demand for housing, employment opportunities, the availability of suitable sites and public facilities, commuting patterns, type and tenure of housing need, and the housing needs of farmworkers. The distribution shall seek to avoid further impaction of localities with relatively high proportions of lower income households. Based upon data provided by the Department of Housing and Community Development relative to the statewide need for housing, each council of governments shall determine the existing and projected housing need for its region. The Department of Housing and Community Development shall ensure that this determination is consistent with the statewide housing need and may revise the determination of the council of governments if necessary to obtain this consistency.

§65589. *Construction of article.*

(a) Nothing in this article shall require a city, county, or city and county to do any of the following:

(1) Expend local revenues for the construction of housing, housing subsidies, or land acquisition.

(2) Disapprove any residential development which is consistent with the general plan.

(b)   Nothing in this article shall be construed to be a grant of authority or a repeal of any authority which may exist of a local government to impose rent controls or restrictions on the sale of real property.

(c)   Nothing in this article shall be construed to be a grant of authority or a repeal of any authority which may exist of a local government with respect to measures that may be undertaken or required by a local government to be undertaken to implement the housing element of the local general plan.

(d)   The provisions of this article shall be construed consistent with, and in promotion of, the statewide goal of a sufficient supply of decent housing to meet the needs of all Californians.

NOTES AND QUESTIONS

1.   Section 65302 originally prescribed only the land-use and circulation elements. The legislative history of this section traces a growing awareness of the possibilities for comprehensive planning.

> 1967 amendment: added "natural resources" to subd. (a) and added the housing element.
> 1969 amendment: added "flooding" sentence to subd. (a).
> 1970 amendment: added "open space" and "enjoyment of scenic beauty" to subd. (a) and added the conservation and open-space elements.
> 1971 amendment: added the seismic safety (it *is* California!), noise, and scenic highway elements.
> 1972 amendment: added the "mudslide, etc." paragraph to subd. (f).

2. Notice also the division between prescribed and optional elements of the plan. Can you think of any reasons for the two categories? Are some elements more "important" than others? If so, by what criteria does a legislator decide?

Here again, the legislative history of §65303 shows changing attitudes. The conservation element (1970) and the safety element (1971) were both removed from the optional list and made mandatory.

3. Prior to 1972, the California law placed no time limit on compliance with any part of its planning code. That year, the legislature directed all cities and counties to submit a local open-space plan (cf. §65302(e)) to the Secretary of the State Resources Agencies by June 30, 1973. Also, the conservation element (cf. §65302(d)) became subject to a June 30, 1973 deadline, later delayed to December 31.

While the California law carries no direct sanction for a city or county failing to follow these provisions, the indirect cost of noncompliance comes very high. Section 65860 directs that all county or city zoning ordinances be consistent with the general plan by January 1, 1973 (which assumes adoption of a general plan), and authorizes any resident or property owner within a city or county to bring suit to enforce compliance. The state legislature has also directed that all subdivisions satisfy the community's general plan. Cal. Gov't. Code §66473.5 (Supp. 1981).

The California legislature, finding that "the growth, development, and redevelopment of its counties and cities requires a more comprehensive framework than that provided by the existing state-mandated local planning process," authorized in 1978 a demonstration project in which three cities and not more than three counties were to be selected to develop and test an alternative "integrated legal planning process." Cal. Gov't. Code §§65420 et seq. (Supp. 1981).

4.   Another model for forcing a plan from the local community is to make eligibility for state or federal benefit programs dependent upon a plan. For example, conformity to a comprehensive or regional plan has become a requirement for more and more federal programs. Compare the Demonstration Cities and Metropolitan Development Act of 1966, 42 U.S.C.A. §§3301, 3335 (1977) (grants for water and sewerage treatment plants, highways, and for open-space projects conditioned upon submission of local grant application to a metropolitan or regional planning body for review). Compare also the environmental impact requirement for a proposed major federal action, which the National Environmental Policy Act now mandates. 42 U.S.C.A. §§4321, 4332 (1977), page 861 *infra*.

5.   Alternatively, the state itself might step in, and either reassert on a statewide basis the planning powers previously delegated to local units, or establish metropolitan or regional bodies with plenary planning powers. Vermont illustrates the statewide approach. "Act 250," passed in 1969, created a nine-member Environmental Board having the duty to adopt a land-use plan for the entire state, taking into full account, however, duly adopted regional and town plans, capital programs, and municipal land-use bylaws. An interim step—adoption by the board and the state legislature of a statewide capability and development plan—occurred in 1973. 10 Vt. Stat. Ann. §§6001 et seq. (Supp. 1980). See especially id. §6042. The Adirondack Park Agency Act, N.Y. Exec. Law §§800 et seq. (1976) illustrates regionalism. The agency had to prepare and submit—for ultimate legislative approval—a land use and development plan for 9,470 square miles of parkland spread across portions of thirteen counties.

6.   The Ninety-third Congress failed to enact a proposed "Land Use Policy and Planning Assistance Act," which would have given state land-use planning a strong boost. Senate Bill 268, which passed the Senate, would have authorized the Secretary of the Interior to make annual planning grants to each state to develop and administer a land-use program (§201). After receiving a grant, the state would have three years to develop an adequate statewide land-use planning *process* (§202) and five years to develop an adequate state

land-use *program* (§203). Continuing eligibility for planning grants would require that these goals be achieved and maintained. Where a state failed to become eligible for a planning grant or lost its eligibility, no major federal action significantly affecting the use of nonfederal lands could go forward until the responsible federal agency looked substantively at the land-use impact of the proposed action (§208). Within states maintaining their eligibility, federal activities were to conform to state land-use programs (§207).

7. The ALI Model Land Development Code would permit, but not require, local governments to adopt a "Local Land Development Plan" (LLDP). Section 3-101 (1975). Adoption of an LLDP would enable the government to exercise certain powers that would otherwise be denied to the locale. These additional powers would include:

(a) providing for planned unit development, cf. §17.6 *infra;*
(b) reserving land for future acquisition by public agencies, cf. Miller v. Beaver Falls, 368 Pa. 189, 82 A.2d 34 (1951), page 734 *supra;*
(c) designating "specially planned areas" within which *no* development could ensue without express approval from a land development agency, cf. §16.4 *infra.*

Cf. ALI Model Land Development Code, Note to §3-101 (1975). The drafters of the code hope that the granting of these additional powers would "create an incentive for local governments to engage in the planning process." Ibid.

8. The ALI's Local Land Development Plan (LLDP) would contain "statements of trends, objectives, policies, and standards" (§3-104) and a short-term (one to five years) program of specific public actions to achieve the §3-104 ambitions (§3-105). It "envisions sequential proposals for actions such as urban renewal in one location, the creation of a park in another, the amendment of the regulatory ordinances in some particular, the construction of a hospital and a school, etc." Section 3-103 enumerates the various planning studies, e.g., population, housing, transportation, etc., upon which the LLDP shall be based. What differences seem to emerge between the purposes and scope of the ALI model and the plans prescribed by the California statute?

9. What protects the development "objectives" of Town A from disruption by the discordant plans of neighboring Town B? Note, below, California's recognition of the problem. Is there any way to solve it?

§ 65305. *City planning agencies; reference of plan to other municipalities.*

Whenever a city planning agency is considering a general plan or any part or element thereof it shall be referred to the planning agency of the county in which the city is located, every other county which abuts upon such city, every city which abuts upon such city, the local agency formation commission of each county in which the city is located or which abuts upon the city, and every county or city in the territory of which is included in said plan or part or element thereof, for the purpose of informing such planning agency or agencies of said plan or part or element thereof and receiving its or their comments thereon. The provisions of this section are directory, not mandatory, and the failure to refer such plan or any part or element thereof as herein provided shall not in any manner affect its validity.

Section 65306 contains a similar provision for county plans.

Should courts entertain suits by Town B complaining of the discordant development activity that is proposed within Town A? Compare Village of Barrington Hills v. Village of Hoffman Estates, 410 N.E.2d 37 (Ill. 1980) (standing given if town B has "real interest"), with Town of No. Hempstead v. Vill. of No. Hills, 38 N.Y.2d 792, 342 N.E.2d 566, 379 N.Y.S.2d 792 (1975) (absent statutory grant of standing, town A may not challenge zoning action of village B).

10. More importantly, what protects the "objectives, principles and standards" of a larger community, e.g., the citizens of the entire state or a metropolitan area, from the discordant plans of Town A? See, e.g., objectives in the Master Plan of Parsippany-Troy Hills, New Jersey (1954), a community less than twenty-five miles from Manhattan: ". . . 2. To maintain the exclusively one-family character of the residential development of the Township, and at an over-all low density. . . . 4(a). [To] encourage the building of houses of a value that will contribute substantially to the tax base in relation to the cost of required municipal services. . . ." Compare Southern Burlington County NAACP v. Township of Mount Laurel, 67 N.J. 151, 336 A.2d 713 (1975).

11. The drafters of the ALI Model Land Development Code would adopt an intermediate stance between uncontrolled local autonomy and assertive state involvement in land-use decisions. Article 7 would give a state land-planning agency the power to establish policies and review local regulations in "areas of critical state concern," such as a tidelands marsh, a major highway interchange, or the appoaches to an airport. Also, developments of "regional impact," such as airports, major highways, etc., would be subject to state control regardless of their location.

In arguing against a more pervasive state control, the drafters remark:

> [I]t is important to channel this (State) concern into areas where it will be effective in dealing with important problems without unnecessarily increasing the cost of the land development process. A time-consuming and inefficient procedure requiring the approval of state or federal agencies for decisions of minor importance could have serious social consequences, especially for development in which cost is a key factor, such as housing. [Id. at 286]

Consider this attitude in the light of the paragraphs quoted from the Parsippany-Troy Hills plan, Note 10 *supra.* Also compare it with the attitude implied in Cal. Govt. Code §65580, *supra.*

§14.4   The Plan's Legal Effect

COCHRANE v. PLANNING BD. OF CITY OF SUMMIT
87 N.J. Super. 526, 210 A.2d 99 (1965)

FELLER, J.S.C. This is an action in lieu of prerogative writs challenging the adoption of a master plan by the Planning Board of the City of Summit and seeking to enjoin the city and its agencies, boards and officials from implementing the master plan in any way. In particular, plaintiffs object to that part of the plan which would permit an expansion of the Ciba Corporation's parking area and research and office space into the residential area which adjoins the rear of plaintiffs' property.

Plaintiffs are citizens, taxpayers and owners of lands located at 249 Kent Place Boulevard in Summit. Their property is adjacent and contiguous to property owned by the Ciba Corporation (hereinafter Ciba). Plaintiffs' premises and that portion of the Ciba tract in question are presently in the A-15 zoning district, which is limited to one-family residences with a minimum lot area of 15,000 square feet. Prior to 1958 the Ciba tract was in an A-10 zone, which was limited to one-family residences with a minimum lot area of 10,000 square feet. The tract is bordered on three sides by one-family residences and is presently subject to enforceable deed restrictions which limit the use of the tract to the erection of one-family residences until 1975.

On December 9, 1963 the defendant planning board adopted a master plan for the city, which provided in part that the Ciba tract, namely, 63½ acres in the A-15 zone, should be rezoned for parking areas and research and office building use. This rezoning is for the purpose of providing for the eventual expansion therein of Ciba's existing operations. The plan requires a 125-foot buffer zone, which would separate the rear line of plaintiffs' property from the proposed Ciba construction. This zone would contain trees, shrubs, and a screen, all of them calculated to preserve the existing residential atmosphere of the area. . . .

Plaintiffs also contend that the master plan is confiscatory in that it destroys existing property values to the special damage of plaintiffs, in violation of N.J.S.A. 40:55-1.12, which requires that a master plan preserve property values previously established. The action of the board was allegedly based on insufficient and incompetent facts and findings and on insufficient surveys and studies, in violation of N.J.S.A. 40:55-1.12. Plaintiffs claim that their personal and property rights have been violated in contravention of the New Jersey and Federal Constitutions. . . .

Defendants contend that plaintiffs' failure to allege and prove injury to their property rights results in the presentation of legal questions which are premature and which do not present justiciable controversies. . . .

The crux of this problem is clear when it is remembered that a master plan is of no force and effect until it is adopted by the governing body of the municipality. Thus, the master plan under consideration in the City of Summit is of no effect until it is adopted by the municipal governing body.

The master plan represents at a given time the best judgment of the planning agency as to the proper course of action to be followed. In this stage the plan for community development remains flexible and is not binding, either on government or individual. See Webster, Urban Planning & Municipal Policy 265 (1958). A master plan is not a straitjacket delimiting the discretion of the legislative body, but only a guide for the city, Rhyne, Municipal Law, sec. 32-59, p. 977 (1957); furthermore, a master plan is nothing more than the easily changed instrumentality which will show a commission from day to day the progress it has made. Haar, Land Use Planning 693 (1959).

The mere adoption and recording of a master plan has no legal consequence. The plan is merely a declaration of policy and a disclosure of an intention which must thereafter be implemented by the adoption of various ordinances. Horack & Nolan, Land Use Controls 36 (1955).

In New Jersey the fact that a master plan adopted by a planning board has no legal consequences is substantiated, not only by the absence of statutory language to that effect, but also by the necessity of a municipality's adoption of the master plan by the governing body before the plan takes effect. See N.J.S.A. 40:55-1.13; Wollen v. Fort Lee, 27 N.J. 408, 424 (1958), where the court said that "the master plan is not conclusive on the governing body." . . .

Professor Cunningham, in his "Controls of Land Use in New Jersey," 15 Rutg. L. Rev. 1, 19 (1960), said:

> The statute does not require that the governing body shall accept the recommendation of the planning board nor does it require a vote of more than a majority of the governing body to adopt an official map . . . which is inconsistent with the planning board's recommendation. *It would thus appear that even after the planning board has adopted a master plan, the governing body is free to ignore the recommendation of the planning board based on the master plan when the governing body adopts or amends an official map.* (Emphasis added.)

It is clear that a master plan is only a plan, and that it requires legislative implementation before its proposals have binding effect and legal consequences. If the necessary legislative implementation is taken—and, of course, such implementation must be taken according to the applicable statutes—then a zoning ordinance and not a master plan would be before the court. Until appropriate municipal legislative action is taken, however, the municipality has only a dormant plan which differs from proposals that may be under consideration by any municipal board or citizen of the municipality in that it is comprehensive and has been reduced to printed form. . . .

The plaintiffs have alleged that the adoption of the master plan destroys property values. To support this thesis they called as witnesses George Goldstein, who is a real estate appraiser and a consultant for the Federal Government and many public agencies, as well as for many of the largest industrial companies in the country, and Norman Lemcke, who is a retired vice-president of the Prudential Mortgage Loan Department. Goldstein testified that the adoption of the master plan had diminished adjacent property values up to 25%, as in the case of plaintiffs' home. Lemcke testified that before the plan he would have granted a 66% mortgage on the plaintiffs' house, but after its adoption he would only grant a 50% mortgage. He further testified that for financing purposes lending institutions take into account whether there is a master plan affecting the property, and the manner in which it is affected. . . .

The contentions of plaintiffs' two experts are disputed by several witnesses for the defense; but without considering the relative merits of the contentions raised by the conflicting views, this court feels that the testimony, taken in the light most favorable to plaintiffs, is at best mere conjecture. There has been no attempted sale by plaintiffs of their property, and the damages which they claim they will sustain if and when they do try to sell their property, is at this point a matter of speculation. . . .

It is the opinion of this court that plaintiffs' suit is premature. Not until their property is actually taken or damaged will they be in a position to establish that its value will be destroyed or diminished.

Plaintiffs question the soundness of the master plan on the ground that it is arbitrary, capricious and unreasonable. In view of the position taken by this court that plaintiffs are premature in their suit, it is not necessary to discuss this issue. However, the court feels that even if the reasonableness of the master plan were properly before it, the result would be the same. The action of a planning board is only an initial step; it is not even required by law, Kozesnik v. Montgomery Township, [24 N.J. 154 (1957)] ; it is only the manifestation of an advisory step in connection with *quasi*-judicial action the board may take in the future. As stated by Horack & Nolan, Land Use Controls 36 (1955): "[The master plan] is merely a declaration of policy and a disclosure of an intention which must thereafter be implemented." Since this master plan may never be adopted by the governing body of Summit, there is at present no justiciable controversy before the court. There may be such a controversy if and when the proposed plan is adopted by the governing body. Until implementation of the proposal is attempted, there can be no purpose in an adjudication by this court at this time. . . .

NOTES AND QUESTIONS

1. The New Jersey statute is typical. Not until the legislative enactment does the plan gain "legal effect."

Why is it that the legislature must act before the plan can operate? Recall again the distinction between the plan (statement of objectives, standards, etc.; supporting studies; program alternatives) and measures to implement the plan—viz., regulation, taxation, eminent domain, etc. Only the legislature can exercise police power, levy taxes, or authorize condemnation. Without the implementing measures, the plan *theoretically* is only a preparatory study—a legislative prelude.

2. Yet doesn't the *Cochran* case present a real dilemma for the courts? Land economists know well the plague of "planning blight." This is the depre-

ciating impact on land and building values that occurs during the interval between the first announcement of a plan and the appropriate legislative response. A singular example appears in urban renewal areas: buildings marked for renewal may lose all their tenants before the city council finally adopts the plan and votes to condemn the properties. Cf. pages 1053-1061 *infra*.

Where condemnation occurs, the landowner will argue (sometimes successfully) that he should realize the earlier, higher value existing at the plan's announcement. But suppose that the city council never adopts the plan. Can the landowner claim successfully that the overhang of condemnation, which depressed his property's value, entitles him to compensation nevertheless? This brings us close to the claim in *Cochran,* where the lowered land values allegedly resulted from the fear that government would endorse the plan.

3.   Perhaps the court in *Cochran* was unconvinced because the plaintiffs could not have won even if the Summit City Council had rezoned their lots. Suppose, however, that plaintiffs owned vacant, undeveloped land which the yet-unapproved plan would set aside for a permanent green belt, to be gained by rezoning the plaintiffs' land from "residential" to "open space": must plaintiffs' relief, if any, still await plan adoption although they can show that the market for their land, which was based on development potential, has disappeared?

Chapter 15

Zoning

Of the many ways to carry out a community's physical plan, zoning should be dealt with first. Several factors explain this choice. The practicing lawyer is more likely to meet a zoning problem than a problem involving any other plan-execution device. Technically, zoning has become far more intricate and sophisticated than the early ordinances that first tested the concept. Doctrinally, zoning disputes are once again raising difficult and far-reaching issues of constitutional law that the United States Supreme Court no longer seems able to avoid. (And while ours is not a course in constitutional law, we can not escape these issues either; nor should we want to.) Finally, and philosophically, zoning forces us to consider tough resource allocation choices: who should live where (and who decides); whether we should produce more energy or a cleaner environment; whether we should build new apartments or preserve landmarks. And the issues multiply.

In this chapter we will first distill the zoning ordinance into its components. Then we shall see how the Supreme Court met the challenge to zoning and established certain doctrines that are with us today. In the next chapter, we shall look at zoning in a half-dozen highly controversial contexts.

§15.1 The Elements of a Zoning Law

a. The Enabling Statute

The U.S. Department of Commerce, in September 1921, appointed an Advisory Committee on Zoning. Two lawyers, three engineers, two housing consultants, one realtor, one landscape architect, and one "civic investigator" composed its membership. In August 1922, the committee sponsored a model enabling law, which gained immediate and lasting acceptance. By 1925, nineteen states had already adopted the model wholly or in part, and today enabling laws exist in every state. All states allow municipalities to zone, and three quarters of the states now enable countywide zoning. For a comprehensive survey of the enabling laws, see Cunningham, Land-Use Control—The State and Local Programs, 50 Iowa L. Rev. 367, 268-380 (1965).

A half-century later, the texts of most enabling statutes still show their ancestry, despite enormous changes in zoning theory and practice. This may mean that the committee did its job well, combining a sound intuition about the future with an uncommon skill in drafting. Or, alternatively, this durability may simply reflect legislative inertia—a failure to re-examine first premises and to modify them as needed. Perhaps, as you go through these materials, you will form your own ideas as to which it is.

A STANDARD STATE ZONING ENABLING ACT

U.S. Department of Commerce (1926 rev.)*

§1. *Grant of power.* For the purpose of promoting health, safety, morals, or the general welfare[1] of the community, the legislative body of cities and incorporated villages is hereby empowered to regulate and restrict the height, number of stories, and size of buildings and other structures, the percentage of lot that may be occupied, the size of yards, courts, and other open spaces, the density of population,[2] and the location and use of buildings, structures, and land for trade, industry, residence, or other purposes.

§2. *Districts.* For any or all of said purposes the local legislative body may divide the municipality into districts of such number, shape, and area as may be deemed best suited to carry out the purposes of this act; and within such districts it may regulate and restrict the erection, construction, reconstruction, alteration, repair, or use of buildings, structures, or land. All such regulations shall be uniform for each class or kind of buildings throughout each district[3] but the regulations in one district may differ from those in other districts.

---

* The general explanatory notes, page 766 *infra,* also derive from the Standard Act.—ED.

1. *"general welfare":* The main pillars on which the police power rests are these four, viz., health, safety, morals, and general welfare. It is wise, therefore, to limit the purposes of this enactment to these four. There may be danger in adding others, as "prosperity," "comfort," "convenience," "order," "growth of the city," etc., and nothing is to be gained thereby. . . . [Footnotes renumbered.—ED.]

2. *"density of population":* The power to regulate density of population is comparatively new in zoning practice. It is, however, highly desirable. Many different methods may be employed. For this reason the phrase "density of population" is a better phrase to use than one giving the power to "limit the number of people to the acre," as this is only *one* method of limiting density of population. It may be more desirable to limit the number of families to the acre or the number of families to a given house, etc. The expression "number of people to the acre" is therefore limited in its meaning and describes only one way of reducing congestion of population, while the phrase "limiting density of population" is all-embracing. It is believed that, with proper restrictions, this provision will make possible the creation of one-family residence districts. . . .

3. *"uniform for each class or kind of buildings throughout each district":* This is important, not so much for legal reasons as because it gives notice to property owners that there shall be no improper discriminations, but that all in the same class shall be treated alike. . . .

§3. *Purposes in view.*[4] Such regulations shall be made in accordance with a comprehensive plan[5] and designed to lessen congestion in the streets; to secure safety from fire, panic, and other dangers; to promote health and the general welfare; to provide adequate light and air; to prevent the overcrowding of land; to avoid undue concentration of population; to facilitate the adequate provision of transportation, water, sewerage, schools, parks, and other public requirements. Such regulations shall be made with reasonable consideration among other things, to the character of the district and its peculiar suitability for particular uses, and with a view to conserving the value of buildings[6] and encouraging the most appropriate use of land throughout such municipality.

§4. *Method of procedure.* The legislative body of such municipality shall provide for the manner in which such regulations and restrictions and the boundaries of such districts shall be determined, established, and enforced, and from time to time amended, supplemented, or changed. However, no such regulation, restriction, or boundary shall become effective until after a public hearing in relation thereto, at which parties in interest and citizens[7] shall have an opportunity to be heard. At least 15 days' notice of the time and place of such hearing shall be published in an official paper, or a paper of general circulation, in such municipality.

§5. *Changes.* Such regulations, restrictions, and boundaries may from time to time be amended, supplemented, changed, modified, or repealed. In case, however, of a protest against such change[8] signed by the owners of 20

---

4. *"Purposes in view":* This section should be clearly differentiated from the statement of purpose (under the police power) contained in the first sentence of section 1. *That* defined and limited the powers created by the legislature to the municipality under the police power. *This* section contains practically a direction from the legislative body as to the purposes in view in establishing a zoning ordinance and the manner in which the work of preparing such an ordinance shall be done. It may be said, in brief, to constitute the "atmosphere" under which the zoning is to be done.

5. *"with a comprehensive plan":* This will prevent haphazard or piecemeal zoning. No zoning should be done without such a comprehensive study. . . .

6. *"conserving the value of buildings":* It should be noted that zoning is not intended to enhance the value of buildings but to conserve that value—that is, to prevent depreciation of values such as come in "blighted districts," for instance—but it *is* to encourage the most appropriate use of land.

7. *"and citizens":* This permits any person to be heard, and not merely property owners whose property interests may be adversely affected by the proposed ordinance. It is right that every citizen should be able to make his voice heard and protest against any ordinance that might be detrimental to the best interest of the city. . . .

8. *"change":* This term, as here used, it is believed will be construed by the courts to include "amendments, supplements, modifications, and repeal," in view of the language which it follows. These words might be added after the word "change," but have been omitted for the sake of brevity. On the other hand, there must be stability for zoning ordinances if they are to be of value. For this reason the practice has been rather generally adopted of permitting ordinary routine changes to be adopted by a majority vote of the local legislative body but requiring a three-fourths vote in the event of a protest from a substantial proportion of property owners whose interests are affected. This has proved in practice to be a sound procedure and has tended to stabilize the ordinance. . . .

percent or more either of the area of the lots included in such proposed change, or of those immediately adjacent in the rear thereof extending _____ feet thereform, or of those directly opposite thereto extending _____ feet from the street frontage of such opposite lots, such amendment shall not become effective except by the favorable vote of three-fourths of all the members of the legislative body of such municipality. The provisions of the previous section relative to public hearings and official notice shall apply equally to all changes or amendments.

§6. *Zoning commission.* In order to avail itself of the powers conferred by this act, such legislative body shall appoint a commission, to be known as the zoning commission, to recommend the boundaries of the various original districts and appropriate regulations to be enforced therein. Such commission shall make a preliminary report and hold public hearings thereon before submitting its final report, and such legislative body shall not hold its public hearings or take action until it has received the final report of such commission. Where a city plan commission already exists, it may be appointed as the zoning commission.

§7. *Board of adjustment.* Such local legislative body may provide for the appointment of a board of adjustment, and in the regulations and restrictions adopted pursuant to the authority of this act may provide that the said board of adjustment may, in appropriate cases and subject to appropriate conditions and safeguards, make special exceptions to the terms of the ordinance in harmony with its general purpose and intent and in accordance with general or specific rules therein contained. . . .

All meetings of the board shall be open to the public. . . .

Appeals to the board of adjustment may be taken by any person aggrieved or by any officer, department, board, or bureau of the municipality affected by any decision of the administrative officer. Such appeal shall be taken within a reasonable time, as provided by the rules of the board, by filing with the officer from whom the appeal is taken and with the board of adjustment a notice of appeal specifying the grounds thereof. The officer from whom the appeal is taken shall forthwith transmit to the board all the papers constituting the record upon which the action appealed from was taken.

The board of adjustment shall fix a reasonable time for the hearing of the appeal, give public notice thereof, as well as due notice to the parties in interest, and decide the same within a reasonable time. Upon the hearing any part may appear in person or by agent or by attorney.

The board of adjustment shall have the following powers:

1.   To hear and decide appeals where is is alleged there is error in any order, requirement, decision, or determination made by an administrative official in the enforcement of this act or of any ordinance adopted pursuant thereto.

2.   To hear and decide special exceptions to the terms of the ordinance upon which such board is required to pass under such ordinance.

3. To authorize upon appeal in specific cases such variance from the terms of the ordinance as will not be contrary to the public interest, where, owing to special conditions, a literal enforcement of the provisions of the ordinance will result in unnecessary hardship, and so that the spirit of the ordinance shall be observed and substantial justice done.

In exercising the above-mentioned powers such board may, in conformity with the provisions of this act, reverse or affirm, wholly or partly, or may modify the order, requirement, decision, or determination appealed from and may make such order, requirement, decision, or determination as ought to be made, and to that end shall have all the powers of the officer from whom the appeal is taken. . . .

Any person or persons, jointly or severally, aggrieved by any decision of the board of adjustment, or any taxpayer, or any officer, department, board, or bureau of the municipality, may present to a court of record a petition, duly verified, setting forth that such decision is illegal, in whole or in part, specifying the grounds of the illegality. Such petition shall be presented to the court within 30 days after the filing of the decision in the office of the board.

Upon the presentation of such petition the court may allow a writ of certiorari directed to the board of adjustment to review such decision of the board of adjustment. . . . The court may reverse or affirm, wholly or partly, or may modify the decision brought up for review.

§8. *Enforcement and remedies.* [9] The local legislative body may provide by ordinance for the enforcement of this act and of any ordinance or regulation made thereunder. A violation of this act or of such ordinance or regulation is hereby declared to be a misdemeanor, and such local legislative body may provide for the punishment thereof by fine or imprisonment or both. It is also empowered to provide civil penalties for such violation.

In case any building or structure is erected, constructed, reconstructed, altered, repaired, converted, or maintained, or any building, structure, or land is used in violation of this act or of any ordinance or other regulation made under authority conferred hereby, the proper local authorities of the municipality, in addition to other remedies, may institute any appropriate action or

---

9. *"Enforcement and remedies":* This section is vital. Without it the local authorities, as a rule, will be powerless to do more than inflict a fine or penalty for violation of the zoning ordinance. It is obvious that a person desiring undue privileges will be glad to pay a few hundred dollars in fines or penalties if thereby he can obtain a privilege to build in a manner forbidden by law, or use his building in an unlawful manner, when he may profit thereby to the extent of many thousands of dollars. What is necessary is that the authorities shall be able to stop promptly the construction of an unlawful building before it is erected and restrain and prohibit an unlawful use.

(Many communities cannot provide for comprehensive inspection of properties to insure continuing compliance with the zoning laws. As a result, violations may be widespread and enforcement proceedings brought only fitfully. In some places, until someone complains, the violation goes officially unnoticed. At least one state court, however, has condemned the practice of making zoning law enforcement entirely dependent upon citizen complaints. People v. T.S. Klein Corp., 86 Misc. 2d 354, 381 N.Y.S.2d 787 (City Ct. 1976); cf. also People v. Acme Markets, 37 N.Y.2d 326, 334 N.E.2d 555, 372 N.Y.S.2d 590 (1975).—Ed.)

proceedings[10] to prevent such unlawful erection, construction, reconstruction, alteration, repair, conversion, maintenance, or use, to restrain, correct, or abate such violation, to prevent the occupancy of said building, structure, or land, or to prevent any illegal act, conduct, business, or use in or about such premises. . . .

EXPLANATORY NOTES IN GENERAL

1. *An enabling act is advisable in all cases.* A general State enabling act is always advisable, and while the power to zone may, in some States, be derived from constitutional as distinguished from statutory home rule, still it is seldom that the home-rule powers will cover all the necessary provisions for successful zoning.

2. *Constitutional amendments not required.* No amendment to the State constitution, as a rule, is necessary. Zoning is undertaken under the police power and is well within the powers granted to the legislature by the constitutions of the various States. . . .

14. *Note to revised edition, 1926.* . . . In this [revision] section 8, dealing with enforcement and remedies, has been revised in order to give the municipality more effective means of obtaining conformance to the zoning ordinance. . . .

NOTES AND QUESTIONS

1. *Density of population:* Would the language in §1 seem to give local government the power to enact the following measures?

(a) In order to regulate the city's rate of growth, the council fixes an annual quota limiting construction to 500 dwelling units. Cf. Construction Industry Assn. of Sonoma County v. City of Petaluma, 522 F.2d 897 (9th Cir. 1975), page 880 *infra;* Albrecht Realty Co. v.

---

10. *"any appropriate action or proceedings":* Under the provisions of this section the local authorities may use any or all of the following methods in trying to bring about compliance with the law: They may sue the responsible person for a penalty in a civil suit; they may arrest the offender and put him in jail; they may stop the work in the case of a new building and prevent its going on; they may prevent the occupancy of a building and keep it vacant until such time as the conditions complained of are remedied; they can evict the occupants of a building when the conditions are contrary to law and prevent its reoccupancy until the conditions have been cured. All of these things the local authorities should be given power to do if zoning laws are to be effective.

(For discussion on the availability of mandamus to cancel permits erroneously granted in violation of a local zoning ordinance, see 68 A.L.R.3d 166 (1976).—ED.)

Town of New Castle, 8 Misc. 2d 255, 167 N.Y.S.2d 843 (Sup. Ct. 1957), page 880 *infra*.

(b) The council rezones all undeveloped residential acreage to a maximum density of one dwelling unit per four acres. Cf. National Land and Investment Co. v. Kohn, 419 Pa. 504, 215 A.2d 597 (1965), page 891 *infra*.

(c) The council limits occupancy in residential districts to families— defined as those related by blood, marriage, or adoption. Cf. Village of Belle Terre v. Boraas, 416 U.S. 1 (1974), page 906 *infra*.

2. "In accordance with a comprehensive plan" (§3): By this language, were the draftsmen of the act expecting each community to have a plan like that which the California statute, §14.3 *supra,* now prescribes?

It is more likely that their intent was unformed. City planning was a new profession, and while planning implied ambitious master plans of community development, few communities had either the manpower or the organization to produce such plans. Moreover, there was little agreement—then as now—as to the content of a master plan. Thus the drafters may have hoped that communities would evolve toward master planning, but—in the short run—as zoning laws were written, the "comprehensive plan" requirement implied much less than a master plan.

How *much* less a plan could be before it no longer fulfilled the requirement became a frequently litigated issue. Many of the earliest zoning ordinances had no planning input; the zoning law was, literally, the plan. Faced with the comprehensive plan requirement, courts often examined such a zoning ordinance to see whether it had a rational basis—one that a planning expert, after the fact, could justify. If so, the ordinance survived. Otherwise, the court struck down the ordinance as arbitrary, unreasonable, capricious, and not in accordance with a comprehensive plan. Compare Bartram v. Zoning Commn. of City of Bridgeport, 136 Conn. 89, 68 A.2d 308 (1949), §17.3 *infra*.

More recently, courts have been demanding a higher degree of planning input in the legislative process. The planning must precede, not follow, the enactment of a zoning law. See, e.g., Udell v. Haas, 21 N.Y.2d 463, 235 N.E.2d 897, 288 N.Y.S.2d 888 (1968); compare Levine v. Town of Oyster Bay, 46 Misc. 2d 106, 259 N.Y.S.2d 247 (Sup. Ct. 1964) ("To say that the Town's 'comprehensive zoning plan' is interchangeable with 'comprehensive plan' is to say that zoning regulations . . . must be in 'accordance' with themselves. This Court cannot believe that the Legislature intended or contemplated such a meaningless interpretation of these provisions." Id. at 113, 259 N.Y.S.2d at 254.) Yet there need not be a master plan. Planning studies which support the classification, or the district change, or the use prohibition, and on which the legislature has relied, meet the enabling law requirement of "comprehensive plan." Cf. generally, Haar, In Accordance With a Comprehensive Plan, 68 Harv. L. Rev. 1154 (1955).

The judicial approach conforms to the reality. Most communities still do not have a master plan and are unlikely to produce one until someone other than a court forces them to. New York City, to cite the most striking example, still has no plan, although this is where zoning began—in 1916. In 1969, a "Blue Ribbon" staff, after spending many years and $1.5 million, produced a six-volume, handsomely printed, lavishly illustrated draft of a plan for New York City. The proposal excited discussion and endless disagreement. Five years later, the chairman of the New York City Planning Commission quietly shelved the proposal. N.Y. Times, Nov. 29, 1974, at 54, col. 2.

   3.   The American Law Institute in 1975 approved a Model Land Development Code (MLDC), which was intended to supplant the model zoning (and planning) enabling acts of the 1920s. MLDC would regulate not only structural use, but also such land-based activities as mining, tree removal, refuse disposal, outdoor advertising, and flood plain alteration. The phrase "development ordinance" would describe the local law enacted pursuant to MLDC; zoning, subdivision, and other land use controls would be gathered together within the development ordinance.

   Section 1.101 of the Model Land Development Code enumerates its purposes. Compare this provision with sections 1 and 3 of the Standard Zoning Enabling Act. How would you summarize the conceptual differences?

Section 1-101.   Purposes

   It is the legislative purpose to protect the land, air, water, natural resources and environment of this State, to encourage their use in a socially and economically desirable manner, and to provide a mechanism by which the state may establish and carry out a state land use policy, including

   (1)   The designation of the local governments of this State as the primary authorities for planning and regulating development in this State according to a system of uniform statewide procedural standards;

   (2)   authorization of the acquisition and disposition of land and interests therein to promote desirable patterns of land use;

   (3)   provision for state review of decisions involving land development having a significant impact beyond the boundaries of a single local government or affecting an area of critical state concern;

   (4)   encouragement for the adoption of local and state Land Development Plans to guide the use of land, water and natural resources of this State;

   (5)   establishment of a system of administrative and judicial review of local and state land use decisions which encourages both effective citizen participation and prompt resolution of disputes;

   (6)   provision of fair and efficient means for enforcement of land development regulations including the discontinuance of existing uses;

   (7)   establishment of a system for permanently recording development regulations and decisions in a manner that will enable the most efficient and accurate dissemination of this information;

   (8)   the encouragement of cooperation among governmental agencies to help achieve land use policy goals; and

   (9)   provision that financial support for capital improvements be made in accordance with state and local land use policy.

b. The Zoning Ordinance

The Euclid, Ohio, ordinance, at issue in Village of Euclid v. Ambler Realty Co., page 780 *infra,* is a good example of the generation of zoning laws enacted during the twenty-five years before the onset of World War II. Gradually these ordinances are yielding to a modernized series of measures, as functional obsolescence besets the earlier model. While the newer ordinances are still recognizable to lawyers of the Village of Euclid era, they depart significantly from their lineal ancestors in key respects:

(a) Far more detailed and sophisticated planning analysis underlies their preparation.

(b) Uses previously thought inharmonious are now allowed to coexist.

(c) Industrial and commercial districts have gained protection against incompatible uses ("noncumulative" zoning, §15.3 *infra*).

(d) Bulk controls—on height, setback, lot coverage, floor space—have reached a complexity understood best (and perhaps only) by architects and engineers. (Where such provisions exist, a lawyer should hesitate to express *his* opinion as to a building's compliance.)

(e) Traffic congestion has led to stiff off-street parking requirements.

To illustrate the new breed of zoning law, the text reproduces sections of the 1960 San Francisco ordinance which, significantly, is not even called a zoning ordinance, but is styled instead a "City Planning Code."

SAN FRANCISCO CITY PLANNING CODE

(Effective 1960, with amendments to and including July 10, 1964)

I. THE TEXT

§101. *Purposes.* This City Planning Code is adopted to promote and protect the public health, safety, peace, morals, comfort, convenience and general welfare, and for the following more particularly specified purposes:

(a) To guide, control and regulate future growth and development in accordance with the Master Plan of the City and County of San Francisco;

(b) To protect the character and the stability of residential, commercial and industrial areas within the City, and to promote the orderly and beneficial development of such areas;

(c) To provide adequate light, air, privacy and convenience of access to property, and to secure safety from fire and other dangers;

(d) To prevent overcrowding the land and undue congestion of population;

(e) To regulate the location of buildings and the use of buildings and land adjacent to streets and thoroughfares, in such manner as to obviate the danger to public safety caused by undue interference with existing or prospective traffic movements on such streets and thoroughfares.

§104. *Classes of Use Districts.* In order to carry out the purposes and provisions of this Code, the City is hereby divided into the following classes of use districts:

P	Public Use Districts
R-1-D	One-Family Residential Districts (Detached Dwellings)
R-1	One-Family Residential Districts
R-2	Two-Family Residential Districts
R-3	Low-Medium Density Multiple Residential Districts
R-3.5	High-Medium Density Multiple Residential Districts
R-4	High Density Multiple Residential Districts
R-5	Highest Density Multiple Residential Districts
C-1	Neighborhood Shopping Districts
C-2	Community Business Districts
C-3	Central Business Districts
C-M	General Commercial Districts
M-1	Light Industrial Districts
M-2	Heavy Industrial Districts

106. *Permits of Occupancy.* Except as otherwise provided herein, land, buildings and premises in any district shall hereafter be used only for the purposes listed herein as permitted in that district, and in accordance with the regulations herein established for that district. A Permit of Occupancy shall be issued by the Department of Public Works (Central Permit Bureau) to the effect that the use or proposed use of a building or premises conforms to the provisions of this and related ordinances, prior to the occupancy of any building hereafter erected, enlarged or structurally altered, or where any vacant land is hereafter proposed to be occupied or used except for permitted agricultural uses. Such a permit shall also be issued whenever the character of use of any building or land is proposed to be changed from a use first permitted in any district to a use first permitted in a less restricted district. Upon written request from the owner, such a permit shall also be issued covering any lawful use of a building or premises existing on the effective date of this Code, including non-conforming buildings and uses.

§107. *Approval of Permits.* No application for a building permit or other permit or license, or for a Permit of Occupancy, shall be approved by the Department of City Planning, and no permit or license shall be issued by any City department, which would authorize the use or change in use of any land or building contrary to the provisions of this Code, or for the erection, moving, alteration, enlargement or occupancy of any building designed or intended to be used for a purpose or in a manner contrary to the provisions of this Code.

§120. *Height and Bulk, General Provisions.* No building or structure or part thereof shall be constructed, reconstructed, altered, relocated or otherwise permitted to exceed the height and bulk regulations set forth herein for the use and height districts in which it is located. An existing building which conforms to the use regulations but exceeds the height or floor area ratio limitations of this Code shall not be deemed to be a non-conforming building, but no such building shall hereafter be enlarged or structurally altered so as to further increase its height or bulk.

§122. *Floor Area Ratio.* No building in any R-3, R-3.5, R-4, R-5, C or M district shall exceed the floor area ration specified in [Table 11] for the district in which the building is located.

[TABLE 11]
Maximum Permitted Floor Area Ratio

District	Floor Area Ratio
R-3, R-3.5 (except dwellings)	1.8 to 1
R-4 (all buildings)	4.8 to 1
R-5 (all buildings)	10.0 to 1
C-1, C-2 (all buildings)	3.6 to 1
C-3 (all buildings)	16.0 to 1
C-M (all buildings)	9.0 to 1
M-1, M-2 (all buildings)	5.0 to 1

Provided that in a C-2 district on a lot which is nearer to an R-5 district than to any other R district, the floor area ratio shall be 10 to 1. The distance to the nearest R district shall be measured from the midpoint of the front lot line, or from a point directly across the street therefrom, whichever gives the greater ratio.

§124. *Minimum Lot Width and Area.* (a) No dwelling shall be constructed or relocated upon any lot in a new subdivision, other than a lot of record as hereinafter provided, which has a width at the front line of the building of less than thirty-three (33) feet and an area less than twenty-six hundred forty (2640) square feet, or such greater width and area as may be required to conform to the pattern established by the residential development of the immediately adjacent area as determined by the City Planning Commission; provided, however, than in an R-1-D district the area required shall not be less than four thousand (4000) square feet. . . .

(c) Any lot existing and recorded as a separate parcel in the office of the Assessor or the Recorder at the effective date of this Code, herein termed a lot of record, which has lesser dimensions than required by this Code, may nevertheless be occupied by a dwelling if all other requirements of this Code are met. The same exception shall apply to a lot created by the merger of such existing lots of record or parts thereof in such a manner as to establish a lesser number of lots each having an increased area. . . .

§125. *Lot Coverage.* No building in an R district, other than a public building in conformity with the Master Plan, shall be constructed or enlarged so as to cover a greater percentage of the area of the lot than is indicated in [Table 12] for the district in which the lot is located.

[TABLE 12]
Maximum Permitted Lot Coverage

District	On Corner Lots	On Other Lots
R-1-D	60%	55%
R-1	75%	60%
R-2	75%	65%
R-3, R-3.5	70%	65%
R-4	80%	75%
R-5	90%	75%

§135. *Automobile Parking Spaces, General.* Hereafter there shall be provided at the time of construction of any main building, or of any major addition to a main building, off-street parking spaces for automobiles except in C-3 districts, and off-street loading spaces in all districts, in accordance with these regulations. . . .

§136. *Required Parking Spaces, Residential Buildings.* The number of off-street parking spaces required for residential buildings hereafter constructed shall be as follows:

(a)   One (1) for each dwelling unit in a one-family, two-family or three-family dwelling; except where the lot upon which any such dwelling is located is entirely inaccessible by automobile because of topographic conditions;

(b)   For multiple dwellings containing four (4) or more dwelling units: one (1) for each dwelling unit. . . .

§138. *Required Parking Spaces, Other Business Uses.* When the total floor area used for any other business use or uses in a building exceeds five thousand (5000) square feet, the number of off-street parking spaces required shall be as set forth in [Table 13]. For this purpose the floor area shall be deemed to mean the gross area of space so used or available for such use within the building, exclusive of that designed for automobile parking or for non-public purposes such as utilities, repairs, processing, packaging, incidental storage, show windows, store management or building maintenance offices, dressing rooms or rest rooms.

§309. *Enforcement.* . . .

(d)   *Methods of Enforcement.* In addition to the regulations of this Code and provisions of the Charter which govern the approval or disapproval of applications for building permits or other permits or licenses affecting the use of land or buildings, the Zoning Administrator shall have the authority to implement the enforcement thereof by any of the following means:

1. He may serve notice requiring the removal of any use in violation of this Code upon the owner, agent or tenant of the building or land, or upon the architect, builder, contractor or other person who commits or assists in any such violation;

[TABLE 13]
Minimum Number of Parking Spaces Required

Use	Number of Spaces
Medical or dental office building or clinic	One for each 300 square feet
Other business offices	One for each 500 square feet
Service or repair shops, wholesale stores, and retail stores which handle only bulky merchandise including motor vehicles, machinery or furniture	One for each 1000 square feet
Other retail stores	One for each 500 square feet up to 20,000, plus one for each additional 250 square feet
Mortuary establishments	Five, unless a greater number is required by the Commission in approving a conditional use
Motels	One for each rental unit
Storage buildings; wholesale warehouses; any use first permitted in an M-2 district	One for each 2000 square feet where the floor area exceeds 10,000 square feet
Other manufacturing and industrial uses	One for each 1500 square feet, where the floor area exceeds 7500 square feet

2. He may call upon the District Attorney to institute any necessary legal proceedings to enforce the provisions of this Code, and the District Attorney is hereby authorized to institute appropriate actions to that end;

3. He may call upon the Chief of Police and his authorized agents to assist in the enforcement of this Code.

In addition to any of the foregoing remedies, the City Attorney may maintain an action for injunction to restrain or abatement to cause the correction or removal of any violation of this Code.

§310. *Penalties.* Any person, firm or corporation violating any of the provisions of this Code shall be deemed guilty of a misdemeanor and upon conviction thereof shall be fined in an amount not exceeding Five Hundred ($500.00) Dollars or be imprisoned for a period not exceeding six (6) months or be both so fined and imprisoned. Each day such violation is committed or permitted to continue, shall constitute a separate offense and shall be punishable as such hereunder.

§105. *Zoning Map.* The designations, locations and boundaries of the districts established by this Code shall be shown upon the "Zoning Map of the City and County of San Francisco" which shall consist of a series of numbered sectional maps. . . .

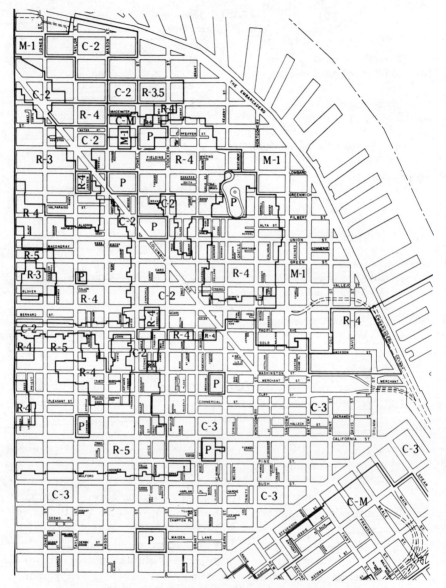

San Francisco Munic. Code, Pt. ii, C. ii, § 105 (effective date May 2,
1960, with amendments to and including Oct. 1, 1965).

[FIGURE 6]
Zoning Map of the City and County of San Francisco

§105.1. *Zoning Map Incorporated Herein.* The Zoning Map of the City and County of San Francisco referred to in Section 105, the original of which is on file with the Clerk of the Board of Supervisors under File No. 4608, is hereby incorporated herein as though fully set forth . . . [see Figure 6].

[For summary of planning code, see Table 14.]

[TABLE 14]
Summary of Basic Provisions of the San Francisco City Planning Code

*Note: **This summary chart is an aid to use of the City Planning Code but is not part of the adopted ordinance. The City Planning Code should be consulted for complete and official provisions.***

Zoning District	Principal Uses Permitted	Transitional Uses (Permitted on Lots Adjacent to or Facing a C or M District)	Conditional Uses (Subject to Commission Approval)
R-1-D	Sec. 201.1 One-family detached dwelling; church; nonprofit elementary or secondary school.	Secs. 201.1(j), 118 One-family row house; two-family dwelling.	Sec. 201.2 Private school operated for profit; nursery school; institution of higher learning; private noncommercial open recreation; community club house; community garage; utility installation; planned unit development; greenhouse or plant nursery (no retail sales).
R-1	Sec. 202.1 All principal uses permitted in R-1-D district. One-family row dwelling.	Secs. 202.1(d), 118 Two-family dwelling; professional office for one person; private club or lodge (noncommercial).	Sec. 202.2 Same as for R-1-D, plus parking lot; access driveway to C or M district.
R-2	Sec. 203.1 All principal uses permitted in R-1 district. Two-family dwelling; home for aged (not to exceed six persons).	Multiple dwelling as regulated in R-3 districts; private club or lodge (noncommercial); boarding house; prof. office for 1 person; fraternity; each according to specific regulations.	Secs. 203.1(d), 118 Sec. 203.2 Same as for R-1, plus hospital; sanitarium; rest home, if more than 6 patients; philanthropic institution; dwelling (in certain multiple-family situations).

[*Cont.*]

[TABLE 14] continued

Zoning District	Principal Uses Permitted	Transitional Uses (Permitted on Lots Adjacent to or Facing a C or M District)	Conditional Uses (Subject to Commission Approval)
R-3	Sec. 204.1 All principal uses permitted in R-2 district. Multiple-family dwelling not more than 3 stories; boarding house; fraternity.	Secs. 204.1(e), 118 All R-3.5 principal uses. All R-2 transitional uses.	Sec. 204.2 Same as for R-2, plus institution primarily for treatment of contagious diseases or drug or liquor addicts if occupying entire city block or lot not less than 3 acres in area; hotel, private club or lodge building, according to specific regulations.
R-3.5	Sec. 204.4 All principal uses permitted in R-3 district	Secs. 204.4(b), 118 All R-4 principal uses. All R-2 transitional uses.	Sec. 204.5 Same as for R-3.
R-4	Sec. 205.1 All principal uses permitted in R-3 district. Multiple-story multiple-family dwelling; private club or lodge (non-commercial).	Secs. 205.1(d), 206, 118 Professional office building or office of single firm; restaurant, personal service shop, newsstand, where not more than 5 persons employed; storage garage; some R-1-D conditional uses; in R-4, multiple dwelling as regulated in R-5 if adjacent to C-3 district.	Secs. 205.2, 206 Same as for R-3, plus professional offices according to specific regulations.
R-5	Sec. 206 All principal uses permitted in R-4 district.		

[Cont.]

[TABLE 14] continued

Zoning District	Principal Uses Permitted	Transitional Uses (Permitted on Lots Adjacent to or Facing a C or M District)	Conditional Uses (Subject to Commission Approval)
C-1	Sec. 207.1 Neighborhood retail business; personal service; business or professional office; service station; parking lot; advertising sign; dwelling.	Does not apply.	Sec. 207.2 Planned unit development; aircraft landing field; wireless transmission tower; railroad; institution primarily for treatment of contagious diseases or for the treatment or care of drug or liquor addicts; storage garage according to specific regulations.
C-2	Sec. 208.1 Community retail business and service; dwelling.	Does not apply.	Secs. 208.2, 209.2 Same as for C-1, plus animal hospital in enclosed building; mortuary; parcel delivery service in enclosed building; minor automobile repair in enclosed building; automobile sales lot; storage building for household goods.
C-3	Sec. 209.1 Central business and shopping; dwelling.	Does not apply.	
C-M	Sec. 210.1 General commercial; wholesale storage; mortuary; automobile sales lot; dwelling other than a one- or two-family dwelling.	Does not apply.	Sec. 210.2 Same as for C-2, plus experimental laboratory; dairy products distribution plant in enclosed building.

[Cont.]

[TABLE 14] continued

Zoning District	Principal Uses Permitted	Transitional Uses (Permitted on Lots Adjacent to or Facing a C or M District)	Conditional Uses (Subject to Commission Approval)
M-1	Sec. 211.1 Light industry and manufacturing. (No dwelling, hotel, motel or boarding house.)	Does not apply.	Sec. 211.2 Planned unit development; truck terminal if not less than 200 feet from any R district; institution primarily for treatment of contagious diseases, or for the treatment or care of drug or liquor addicts.
M-2	Secs. 212.1, 212.2 Heavy industry; food processing. (No dwelling, hotel, motel, boarding house, school or institution for human habitation or care.)	Does not apply.	Sec. 212.3 Same as for M-1, plus smelter; garbage incineration; manufacture of corrosive acid or alkali, cement, gypsum, explosives; petroleum refining; abattoir.
P	Sec. 215 Land owned by governmental agency and in some form of public use.	Does not apply.	Sec. 215.2 Same as for R-1-D, plus church.

NOTES AND QUESTIONS

1. Compare the statement of purposes (§101) in the San Francisco ordinance with the paragraph on purposes (§3) in the standard enabling act. How are they similar? Different?

2. Examine the permit provisions of §§106 and 107. These express a two-stage permit procedure, which most communities have established. Before any construction can begin, the developer must obtain a *building permit,* which a buildings department must issue routinely if the proposed structure satisfies

the zoning law, building code, and any other relevant regulation. (Conversely, if the proposed structure would violate any law, the buildings department must deny the permit routinely.) When construction has ended, the developer must then obtain an *occupancy* permit before persons can use the structure. Again, granting or denying the permit is a ministerial decision.

3. The floor area ratio (FAR) provision of §122, together with the lot coverage provisions of §125, regulate the bulk and height of a structure. FAR sets a maximum on the rentable square feet within the structure, which one calculates by multiplying the lot size times the FAR for the district. A landowner with a plot of 20,000 square feet in an R-4 zone (FAR = 4.8) could construct a multiply dwelling containing 96,000 square feet of rentable space. If he owned a corner lot (maximum lot coverage = 80 percent), no floor could contain more than 16,000 square feet. Thus, the building might be six stories high and cover 80 percent of the lot, or twelve stories high and cover 40 percent of the lot, or any other combination of height and per-floor area that does not exceed the FAR and lot coverage ceilings.

What considerations help determine FAR and lot coverage limits?

4. To test your ability to work with a zoning code, advise each of the following clients:

(a) X owns a parcel 100′ × 150′ at the southeast corner of California Street and Jones Street. He wishes to build an apartment house with maximum lot coverage. How high can X build? If apartments average 1000 square feet, how many parking spaces are required?

(b) Y owns a parcel 100′ × 200′ at the northeast corner of Washington Street and Battery Street. He wishes to build professional offices on the site. Using 40 percent of lot coverage, how high can Y build? How many parking spaces are required?

(c) Z owns the entire easterly blockfront of Sansome Street between Green and Vallejo Streets. Which of the following uses is Z permitted?

(1) high-rise apartment house
(2) truck terminal
(3) food processing plant
(4) shopping center

5. The ALI Model Land Development Code (1975) does not, as did the Standard Zoning Enabling Act §2, specify in detail how zoning districts are to be regulated. The ALI model code simply provides: "A development ordinance may divide the jurisdiction of the local government into districts . . ." (§2-101[3]). The drafters explain this nonspecificity thus: "As the courts have enlarged the limits of permissible regulation the need for detailed specification has diminished." Note to §2-101.

§15.2 The Supreme Court Validates "Euclidian" Zoning

By the time the Supreme Court heard the appeal in Village of Euclid v. Ambler, *infra*, zoning was already ten years old, and many state courts (but not all that considered the issue) had validated the concept. The Euclid ordinance, however, was not the first local land-use control tested in the Supreme Court. Welch v. Swasey, 214 U.S. 91 (1909), upheld a Massachusetts "fire control" measure fixing height limits in certain residential areas of the city of Boston. Three cases—Reinman v. City of Little Rock, 237 U.S. 171 (1915) (livery stable), Hadacheck v. Sebastian, 239 U.S. 394 (1915) (brickmaking), and Pierce Oil Co. v. City of Hope, 248 U.S. 498 (1919) (petroleum storage)— sustained ordinances that prevented an already established business from remaining in certain areas; the analogy to nuisance underlay the decisions. In losing, the owner of the brickyard in the *Hadacheck* case expected a reduction in land value from $800,000 to $60,000. In two other cases, which were concerned with billboard regulation, the nuisance analogy was badly strained but the ordinances were upheld. Thomas Cusack Co. v. City of Chicago, 242 U.S. 526 (1917), and St. Louis Poster Advertising Co. v. City of St. Louis, 249 U.S. 269 (1919).

Only once during the pre-*Euclid* era had the Court refused to sustain a local land-control measure. Eubank v. City of Richmond, 226 U.S. 137 (1912). This involved a Richmond, Virginia, ordinance allowing the owners of two-thirds of the property abutting any street to determine a minimum building line not less than five feet nor more than thirty feet from the street line. It was the blockfront democracy that seemed to bother the Court even more than the dubious relation between a minimum setback and the community welfare, for fifteen years later, the Court upheld a Roanoke, Virginia, ordinance that *required* a setback as great as that of 60 percent of the existing houses on a block, Gorieb v. Fox, 274 U.S. 603 (1927).

Despite this fairly unbroken precedent in behalf of local land-use control, the Euclid ordinance almost failed its test. The Supreme Court heard oral argument not once, but twice; and two justices may have switched their votes after the second argument to give the ordinance its 6 to 3 margin. See McCormack, A Law-Clerk's Recollections, 46 Colum. L. Rev. 710 (1946). At least two things distinguished the Euclid ordinance from the earlier measures: its comprehensiveness and its curbs on apartments and businesses, uses not previously viewed as noxious.

VILLAGE OF EUCLID v. AMBLER REALTY CO.
272 U.S. 365, 47 S. Ct. 114, 71 L. Ed. 303 (1926)

MR. JUSTICE SUTHERLAND delivered the opinion of the Court. The Village of Euclid is an Ohio municipal corporation. It adjoins and practically is a suburb of the City of Cleveland. Its estimated population is between 5000 and 10,000, and its area from twelve to fourteen square miles, the greater part of which is farm lands or unimproved acreage. It lies, roughly, in the form of a parallelogram measuring approximately three and one-half miles each way. East and west it is traversed by three principal highways: Euclid Avenue, through the southerly border, St. Clair Avenue, through the central portion, and Lake Shore Boulevard, through the northerly border in close proximity to the shore of Lake Erie. The Nickel Plate railroad lies from 1500 to 1800 feet north of Euclid Avenue, and the Lake Shore railroad 1600 feet farther to the north. The three highways and the two railroads are substantially parallel.

Appellee is the owner of a tract of land containing 68 acres, situated in the westerly end of the village, abutting on Euclid Avenue to the south and the Nickel Plate railroad to the north. Adjoining this tract, both on the east and on the west, there have been laid out restricted residential plats upon which residences have been erected.

On November 13, 1922, an ordinance was adopted by the Village Council, establishing a comprehensive zoning plan for regulating and restricting the location of trades, industries, apartment houses, two-family houses, single-family houses, etc., the lot area to be built upon, the size and height of buildings, etc.

The entire area of the village is divided by the ordinance into six classes of use districts, denominated U-1 to U-6, inclusive; three classes of height districts, denominated H-1 to H-3, inclusive; and four classes of area districts, denominated A-1 to A-4, inclusive. The use districts are classified in respect of the buildings which may be erected within their respective limits, as follows: U-1 is restricted to single-family dwellings, public parks, water towers and reservoirs, suburban and interurban electric railway passenger stations and rights of way, and farming, noncommercial greenhouse nurseries and truck gardening; U-2 is extended to include two-family dwellings; U-3 is further extended to include apartment houses, hotels, churches, schools, public libraries, museums, private clubs, community center buildings, hospitals, sanitariums, public playgrounds and recreation buildings, and a city hall and courthouse; U-4 is further extended to include banks, offices, studios, telephone exchanges, fire and police stations, restaurants, theatres and moving picture shows, retail stores and shops, sales offices, sample rooms, wholesale stores for hardware, drugs and groceries, stations for gasoline and oil (not exceeding 1000 gallons storage) and for ice delivery, skating rinks and dance halls, electric substations, job and newspaper printing, public garages for motor vehicles, stables and wagon sheds (not exceeding five horses, wagons or motor trucks) and distributing stations for central store and commercial enterprises; U-5 is further extended to include billboards and advertising signs (if permitted), warehouses, ice and ice cream manufacturing and cold storage plants, bottling works, milk bottling and central distribution stations, laundries, carpet cleaning, dry cleaning and dyeing establishments, blacksmith, horseshoeing, wagon and motor vehicle repair shops, freight stations, street car

barns, stables and wagon sheds (for more than five horses, wagons or motor
trucks), and wholesale produce markets and salesrooms; U-6 is further extended to include plants for sewage disposal and for producing gas, garbage
and refuse incineration, scrap iron, junk, scrap paper and rag storage, aviation
fields, cemeteries, crematories, penal and correctional institutions, insane and
feeble minded institutions, storage of oil and gasoline (not to exceed 25,000
gallons), and manufacturing and industrial operations of any kind other than,
and any public utility not included in, a class U-1, U-2, U-3, U-4 or U-5 use.
There is a seventh class of uses which is prohibited altogether.

Class U-1 is the only district in which buildings are restricted to those
enumerated. In the other classes the uses are cumulative; that is to say, uses in
class U-2 include those enumerated in the preceding class, U-1; class U-3
includes uses enumerated in the preceding classes, U-2 and U-1; and so on. In
addition to the enumerated uses, the ordinance provides for accessory uses,
that is, for uses customarily incident to the principal use, such as private
garages. Many regulations are provided in respect of such accessory uses.

The height districts are classified as follows: In class H-1, buildings are
limited to a height of two and one-half stories or thirty-five feet; in class H-2,
to four stories or fifty feet; in class H-3, to eighty feet. To all of these, certain
exceptions are made, as in the case of church spires, water tanks, etc.

The classification of area districts is:[2] In A-1 districts, dwellings or
apartment houses to accommodate more than one family must have at least
5000 square feet for interior lots and at least 4000 square feet for corner lots;
in A-2 districts, the area must be at least 2500 square feet for interior lots, and
2000 square feet for corner lots; in A-3 districts, the limits are 1250 and 1000
square feet, respectively; in A-4 districts, the limits are 900 and 700 square
feet, respectively. The ordinance contains, in great variety and detail, provisions in respect of width of lots, front, side and rear yards, and other matters,
including restrictions and regulations as to the use of billboards, sign boards
and advertising signs. . . .

Appellee's tract of land comes under U-2, U-3 and U-6. The first strip of
620 feet immediately north of Euclid Avenue falls in class U-2, the next 130
feet to the north, in U-3, and the remainder in U-6. . . .

Annexed to the ordinance, and made a part of it, is a zone map, showing
the location and limits of various use, height and area districts. . . .

The enforcement of the ordinance is entrusted to the inspector of buildings, under rules and regulations of the board of zoning appeals. Meetings of
the board are public, and minutes of its proceedings are kept. It is authorized
to adopt rules and regulations to carry into effect provisions of the ordinance.
Decisions of the inspector of buildings may be appealed to the board by any
person claiming to be adversely affected by any such decision. The board is

2. Note that the minimum lot sizes in this early ordinance range *downward* from an approximate one-ninth of an acre. Compare these lot sizes with those that prevail today. Cf. page
889 *infra*.—ED.

given power in specific cases of practical difficulty or unnecessary hardship to interpret the ordinance in harmony with its general purpose and intent, so that the public health, safety and general welfare may be secure and substantial justice done. Penalties are prescribed for violations, and it is provided that the various provisions are to be regarded as independent and the holding of any provision to be unconstitutional, void or ineffective shall not affect any of the others.

The ordinance is assailed on the grounds that it is in derogation of §1 of the Fourteenth Amendment to the Federal Constitution in that it deprives appellee of liberty and property without due process of law and denies it the equal protection of the law, and that it offends against certain provisions of the Constitution of the State of Ohio. The prayer of the bill is for an injunction restraining the enforcement of the ordinance and all attempts to impose or maintain as to appellee's property any of the restrictions, limitations or conditions. The court below held the ordinance to be unconstitutional and void, and enjoined its enforcement. 297 Fed. 307.

Before proceeding to a consideration of the case, it is necessary to determine the scope of the inquiry. The bill alleges that the tract of land in question is vacant and has been held for years for the purpose of selling and developing it for industrial uses, for which it is especially adapted, being immediately in the path of progressive industrial development; that for such uses it has a market value of about $10,000 per acre, but if the use be limited to residential purposes the market value is not in excess of $2500 per acre; that the first 200 feet of the parcel back from Euclid Avenue, if unrestricted in respect of use, has a value of $150 per front foot, but if limited to residential uses, and ordinary mercantile business be excluded therefrom, its value is not in excess of $50 per front foot. . . .

The record goes no farther than to show, as the lower court found, that the normal, and reasonably to be expected, use and development of that part of appellee's land adjoining Euclid Avenue is for general trade and commercial purposes, particularly retail stores and like establishments, and that the normal, and reasonably to be expected, use and development of the residue of the land is for industrial and trade purposes. Whatever injury is inflicted by the mere existence and threatened enforcement of the ordinance is due to restrictions in respect of these and similar uses; to which perhaps should be added—if not included in the foregoing—restrictions in respect of apartment houses. . . .

We proceed, then, to a consideration of those provisions of the ordinance to which the case as it is made relates, first disposing of a preliminary matter.

A motion was made in the court below to dismiss the bill on the ground that, because complainant [appellee] had made no effort to obtain a building permit or apply to the zoning board of appeals for relief as it might have done under the terms of the ordinance, the suit was premature. The motion was properly overruled. The effect of the allegations of the bill is that the ordinance of its own force operates greatly to reduce the value of appellee's lands and destroy their marketability for industrial, commercial and residential uses; and the attack is directed, not against any specific provision or provisions, but against the ordinance as an entirety. Assuming the premises, the existence and maintenance of the ordinance, in effect, constitutes a present invasion of appellee's property rights and a threat to continue it. Under these circumstances, the equitable jurisdiction is clear. See Terrace v. Thompson, 263 U.S. 197, 215; Pierce v. Society of Sisters, 268 U.S. 510, 535. . . .

Building zone laws are of modern origin. They began in this country about twenty-five years ago. Until recent years, urban life was comparatively simple; but with the great increase and concentration of population, problems have developed, and constantly are developing, which require, and will continue to require, additional restrictions in respect of the use and occupation of private lands in urban communities. Regulations, the wisdom, necessity and validity of which, as applied to existing conditions, are so apparent that they are now uniformly sustained, a century ago, or even half a century ago, probably would have been rejected as arbitrary and oppressive. Such regulations are sustained, under the complex conditions of our day, for reasons analogous to those which justify traffic regulations, which, before the advent of automobiles and rapid transit street railways, would have been condemned as fatally arbitrary and unreasonable. And in this there is no inconsistency, for while the meaning of constitutional guaranties never varies, the scope of their application must expand or contract to meet the new and different conditions which are constantly coming within the field of their operation. In a changing world, it is impossible that it should be otherwise. But although a degree of elasticity is thus imparted, not to the *meaning*, but to the *application* of constitutional principles, statutes and ordinances, which, after giving due weight to the new conditions, are found clearly not to conform to the Constitution, of course, must fall.

The ordinance now under review, and all similar laws and regulations, must find their justification in some aspect of the police power, asserted for the public welfare. The line which in this field separates the legitimate from the illegitimate assumption of power is not capable of precise delimitation. It varies with circumstances and conditions. A regulatory zoning ordinance, which would be clearly valid as applied to the great cities, might be clearly invalid as applied to rural communities. In solving doubts, the maxim sic utere tuo ut alienum non laedas, which lies at the foundation of so much of the common law of nuisances, ordinarily will furnish a fairly helpful clew. And the law of nuisances, likewise, may be consulted, not for the purpose of controlling, but for the helpful aid of its analogies in the process of ascertaining the scope of, the power. Thus the question whether the power exists to forbid the erection of a building of a particular kind or for a particular use like the question whether a particular thing is a nuisance, is to be determined, not by an abstract consideration of the building or of the thing considered apart, but by considering it in connection with the circumstances and the locality. Sturgis v. Bridgeman, L.R. 11 Ch. 852, 865. A nuisance may be merely a right thing in the wrong place—like a pig in the parlor instead of the barnyard.[3] If the validity of the legislative classification for zoning purposes be fairly debatable, the legislative judgment must be allowed to control. Radice v. New York, 264 U.S. 292, 294.

There is no serious difference of opinion in respect of the validity of laws and regulations fixing the height of buildings within reasonable limits, the character of materials and methods of construction, and the adjoining area which must be left open, in order to minimize the danger of fire or collapse, the evils of overcrowding, and the like, and excluding from residential sections offensive trades, industries and structures likely to create nuisances. See Welch v. Swasey, 214 U.S. 91; Hadacheck v. Los Angeles, 29 U.S. 394; Reinman v. Little Rock, 237 U.S. 171; Cusack Co. v. City of Chicago, 242 U.S. 526, 529-530.

Here, however, the exclusion is in general terms of all industrial establishments, and it may thereby happen that not only offensive or dangerous industries will be excluded, but those which are neither offensive nor dangerous will share the same fate. But this is no more than happens in respect of many practice-forbidding laws which this Court has upheld although drawn in general terms so as to include individual cases that may turn out to be innocuous in themselves. Hebe Co. v. Shaw, 248 U.S. 297, 303; Pierce Oil Corp. v. City of Hope, 248 U.S. 498, 500. The inclusion of a reasonable margin to insure effective enforcement, will not put upon a law, otherwise valid, the stamp of invalidity. Such laws may also find their justification in the fact that, in some fields, the bad fades into the good by such insensible degrees that the two are not capable of being readily distinguished and separated in terms of legislation. In the light of these considerations, we are not prepared to say that the end in view was not sufficient to justify the general rule of the ordinance, although some industries of an innocent character might fall within the proscribed class. It can not be said that the ordinance in this respect "passes the bounds of reason and assumes the character of a merely arbitrary fiat." Purity Extract Co. v. Lynch, 226 U.S. 192, 204. Moreover, the restrictive provisions of the ordinance in this particular may be sustained upon the principles applicable to the broader exclusion from residential districts of all business and trade structures, presently to be discussed.

It is said that the Village of Euclid is a mere suburb of the City of Cleveland; that the industrial development of that city has now reached and

3. Shades of Dr. Johnson! His biographer, James Boswell, reported this conversation:

Boswell: . . . I talked of the recent expulsion of six students from the University of Oxford, who were methodists, and would not desist from publickly praying and exhorting.
Johnson: Sir, that expulsion was extremely just and proper. What have they to do at an University, who are not willing to be taught, but will presume to teach? . . .
Boswell: But, was it not hard, Sir, to expel them, for I am told they were good beings?
Johnson: I believe they might be good beings; but they were not fit to be in the University of Oxford. A cow is a very good animal in the field; but we turn her out of a garden.

[1 Boswell, The Life of Dr. Johnson 436 (Everyman's ed. 1960)]—Ed.

in some degree extended into the village and, in the obvious course of things, will soon absorb the entire area for industrial enterprises; that the effect of the ordinance is to divert this natural development elsewhere with the consequent loss of increased values to the owners of the lands within the village borders. But the village, though physically a suburb of Cleveland, is politically a separate municipality, with powers of its own and authority to govern itself as it sees fit within the limits of the organic law of its creation and the State and Federal Constitutions. Its governing authorities, presumably representing a majority of its inhabitants and voicing their will, have determined, not that industrial development shall cease at its boundaries, but that the course of such development shall proceed within definitely fixed lines. If it be a proper exercise of the police power to relegate industrial establishments to localities separated from residential sections, it is not easy to find a sufficient reason for denying the power because the effect of its exercise is to divert an industrial flow from the course which it would follow, to the injury of the residential public if left alone, to another course where such injury will be obviated. It is not meant by this, however, to exclude the possibility of cases where the general public interest would so far outweigh the interest of the municipality that the municipality would not be allowed to stand in the way.

We find no difficulty in sustaining restrictions of the kind thus far reviewed. The serious question in the case arises over the provisions of the ordinance excluding from residential districts, apartment houses, business houses, retail stores and shops, and other like establishments. This question involves the validity of what is really the crux of the more recent zoning legislation, namely, the creation and maintenance of residential districts, from which business and trade of every sort, including hotels and apartment houses, are excluded. Upon that question this Court has not thus far spoken. . . .

The matter of zoning has received much attention at the hands of commissions and experts, and the results of their investigations have been set forth in comprehensive reports. These reports, which bear every evidence of painstaking consideration, concur in the view that the segregation of residential, business, and industrial buildings will make it easier to provide fire apparatus suitable for the character and intensity of the development in each section; that it will increase the safety and security of home life; greatly tend to prevent street accidents, especially to children, by reducing the traffic and resulting confusion in residential sections; decrease noise and other conditions which produce or intensify nervous disorders; preserve a more favorable environment in which to rear children, etc. With particular reference to apartment houses, it is pointed out that the development of detached house sections is greatly retarded by the coming of apartment houses, which has sometimes resulted in destroying the entire section for private purposes; that in such sections very often the apartment house is a mere parasite, constructed in order to take advantage of the open spaces and attractive surroundings created by the residential character of the district. Moreover, the coming of one apartment house is followed by others, interfering by their height and bulk with the free circulation of air and monopolizing the rays of the sun which otherwise would fall upon the smaller homes, and bringing, as their necessary accompaniments, the disturbing noises incident to increased traffic and business, and the occupation, by means of moving and parked automobiles, of larger portions of the streets, thus detracting from their safety and depriving children of the privilege of quiet and open spaces for play, enjoyed by those in more favored localities,—until finally, the residential character of the neighborhood and its desirability as a place of detached residences are utterly destroyed. Under these circumstances, apartment houses, which in a different environment would be not only entirely unobjectionable but highly desirable, come very near to being nuisances.

If these reasons, thus summarized, do not demonstrate the wisdom or sound policy in all respects of those restrictions which we have indicated as pertinent to the inquiry, at least, the reasons are sufficiently cogent to preclude us from saying, as it must be said before the ordinance can be declared unconstitutional, that such provisions are clearly arbitrary and unreasonable, having no substantial relation to the public health, safety, morals or general welfare. . . .

It is true that when, if ever, the provisions set forth in the ordinance in tedious and minute detail, come to be concretely applied to particular premises, including those of the appellee, or to particular conditions, or to be considered in connection with specific complaints, some of them, or even many of them, may be found to be clearly arbitrary and unreasonable. But where the equitable remedy of injunction is sought, as it is here, not upon the ground of a present infringement or denial of a specific right, or of a particular injury in process of actual execution, but upon the broad ground that the mere existence and threatened enforcement of the ordinance, by materially and adversely affecting values and curtailing the opportunities of the market, constitute a present and irreparable injury, the court will not scrutinize its provisions, sentence by sentence, to ascertain by a process of piecemeal dissection whether there may be, here and there, provisions of a minor character, or relating to matters of administration, or not shown to contribute to the injury complained of, which, if attacked separately, might not withstand the test of constitutionality. . . .

. . . What would be the effect of a restraint imposed by one or more of the innumerable provisions of the ordinance, considered apart, upon the value or marketability of the lands is neither disclosed by the bill nor by the evidence, and we are afforded no basis, apart from mere speculation, upon which to rest a conclusion that it or they would have any appreciable effect upon these matters. Under these circumstances, therefore, it is enough for us to determine, as we do, that the ordinance in its general scope and dominant features, so far as its provisions are here involved, is a valid exercise of authority, leaving other provisions to be dealt with as cases arise directly involving them. . . .

Decree reversed.

Mr. Justice Van Devanter, Mr. Justice McReynolds and Mr. Justice Butler, dissent.

NOTES AND QUESTIONS

1. The one-time Secretary of War (1916-1921) Newton D. Baker represented the Ambler Realty Company. His adversary was a Cleveland lawyer, James Metzenbaum. Several years later, Metzenbaum wrote a colorful account of the lawsuit, replete with reports of Taftian humor, dubious oral argument, and early-morning adventures on a snowbound train. J. Metzenbaum, The Law of Zoning (1930).

Metzenbaum's enthusiasm for his cause leaps from the page (id. at 121-122):

> Once more the keys of the newspaper offices clicked. This time to tell to American cities, that neither the limitations in the particular ordinance nor the fundamental and underlying philosophy of zoning were deemed to be unconstitutional, but that, on the contrary, the municipalities of this country might feel themselves free, within the bounds of reasonable and proper limits, to so zone and regulate their territories, that conditions in the future might be livable and tolerable.
>
> The rejoicing with which the news was received from coast to coast, was evidence of the relief of the citizenry who had been looking forward to the right to aid in making our cities worth while.
>
> The public had begun to realize the lasting character which the decision would have, had come to sense the importance of the results of the movement and to visualize the possibilities for the betterment of conditions, not only for the present but for the oncoming generations as well.
>
> The American home too, had found shelter and protection.
>
> Here was the reward for four years of unbroken effort.

2. The trial court, which had invalidated the Euclid ordinance, wrote:

> The plain truth is that the true object of the ordinance in question is to place all the property in an undeveloped area of 16 square miles in a strait-jacket. The purpose to be accomplished is really to regulate the mode of living of persons who may hereafter inhabit it. In the last analysis, the result to be accomplished is to classify the population and segregate them according to their income or situation in life. The true reason why some persons live in a mansion and others in a shack, why some live in a single-family dwelling and others in a double-family dwelling, why some live in a two-family dwelling and others in an apartment, or why some live in a well-kept apartment and others in a tenement, is primarily economic. It is a matter of income and wealth, plus the labor and difficulty of procuring adequate domestic service. Aside from contributing to these results and furthering such class tendencies, the ordinance has also an esthetic purpose; that is to say, to make this village develop into a city along

lines now conceived by the village council to be attractive and beautiful. The assertion that this ordinance may tend to prevent congestion, and thereby contribute to the health and safety, would be more substantial if provision had been or could be made for adequate east and west and north and south street highways. Whether these purposes and objects would justify the taking of plaintiff's property as and for a public use need not be considered. It is sufficient to say that, in our opinion, and as applied to plaintiff's property, it may not be done without compensation under the guise of exercising the police power. [Ambler Realty Co. v. Village of Euclid, 297 F. 307, 316 (N.D. Ohio 1924)]

Looking back at this argument from the vantage of a half-century, what do you think of it?

3. The "parasitic" image of apartment houses (page 786 *supra;* cf. also page 899 *infra*) has had a pervasive influence on the zoning of American suburbs. For example, at one time only 0.7 percent of the vacant land zoned "residential" in the New York metropolitan region permitted multifamily construction. Regional Plan Association, Spread City 40 (1962). Ignoring Justice Sutherland's explanation, if you wish, how do you account for this antipathy? Are the factors aesthetic, economic, social, fiscal?

4. Justice Sutherland notes "the possibility of cases where the general public interest would so far outweigh the interest of the municipality that the municipality would not be allowed to stand in the way" (page 786 *supra*). Does this dictum have present-day relevance?

5. Is the *Euclid* decision authority for either of the following principles?

(a) The community may limit the height of residential buildings.
(b) A zoning curb may be valid even though it depresses the worth of land from $10,000 to $2,500 an acre.

6. Although the Supreme Court did uphold the community's power to regulate the use of land by creating districts within which various uses would or would not be allowed, Justice Sutherland carefully refused to rule on the validity of the Euclid ordinance as it applied to the Ambler property. Can you locate this language? Why did the Court stop short? Had you represented Ambler Realty Co., how might you have proceeded after the *Euclid* decision?

NECTOW v. CITY OF CAMBRIDGE
277 U.S. 183, 48 S. Ct. 447, 72 L. Ed. 842 (1928)

MR. JUSTICE SUTHERLAND delivered the opinion of the Court. A zoning ordinance of the City of Cambridge divides the city into three kinds of districts: residential, business and unrestricted. Each of these districts is subclassified in respect of the kind of buildings which may be erected. The ordinance is an elaborate one, and of the same general character as that considered by this Court in Euclid v. Ambler Co., 272 U.S. 365. In its general scope it is conceded to be constitutional within that decision. The land of plaintiff in error was put in district R-3, in which are permitted only dwellings, hotels, clubs, churches, schools, philanthropic institutions, greenhouses and gardening, with customary incidental accessories. The attack upon the ordinance is that, as specifically applied to plaintiff in error, it deprived him of his property without due process of law in contravention of the Fourteenth Amendment.

The suit was for a mandatory injunction directing the city and its inspector of buildings to pass upon an application of the plaintiff in error for a permit to erect any lawful buildings upon a tract of land without regard to the provisions of the ordinance including such tract within a residential district. The case was referred to a master to make and report findings of fact. After a view of the premises and the surrounding territory, and a hearing, the master made and reported his findings. The case came on to be heard by a justice of the court, who, after confirming the master's report, reported the case for the determination of the full court. Upon consideration, that court sustained the ordinance as applied to plaintiff in error, and dismissed the bill. 260 Mass. 441.

A condensed statement of facts, taken from the master's report, is all that is necessary. When the zoning ordinance was enacted, plaintiff in error was and still is the owner of a tract of land containing 140,000 square feet, of which the locus here in question is a part. The locus contains about 29,000 square feet, with a frontage on Brookline street, lying west, of 304.75 feet, on Henry street, lying north, of 100 feet, on the other land of the plaintiff in error, lying east, of 264 feet, and on land of the Ford Motor Company, lying southerly, of 75 feet. The territory lying east and south is unrestricted. The lands beyond Henry street to the north and beyond Brookline street to the west are within a restricted residential district. The effect of the zoning is to separate from the west end of plaintiff in error's tract a strip 100 feet in width. The Ford Motor Company has a large auto assembling factory south of the locus; and a soap factory and the tracks of the Boston & Albany Railroad lie near. Opposite the locus, on Brookline street, and included in the same district, there are some residences; and opposite the locus, on Henry street, and in the same district, are other residences. The locus is now vacant, although it was once occupied by a mansion house. Before the passage of the ordinance in question, plaintiff in error had outstanding a contract for the sale of the greater part of his entire tract of land for the sum of $63,000. Because of the zoning restrictions, the purchaser refused to comply with the contract. Under the ordinance, business and industry of all sorts are excluded from the locus, while the remainder of the tract is unrestricted. It further appears that provision has been made for widening Brookline street, the effect of which, if carried out, will be to reduce the depth of the locus to 65 feet. After a statement at length of further facts, the master finds "that no practical use can be made of the land in question for residential purposes, because among other reasons herein related, there would not be adequate return on the amount of any investment for the development of the property." The last finding of the master is:

> I am satisfied that the districting of the plaintiff's land in a residence district would not promote the health, safety, convenience and general welfare of the inhabitants of that part of the defendant City, taking into account the natural development thereof and the character of the district and the resulting benefit to accrue to the whole City and I so find.

It is made pretty clear that because of the industrial and railroad purposes to which the immediately adjoining lands to the south and east have been devoted and for which they are zoned, the locus is of comparatively little value for the limited uses permitted by the ordinance.

We quite agree with the opinion expressed below that a court should not set aside the determination of public officers in such a matter unless it is clear that their action "has no foundation in reason and is a mere arbitrary or irrational exercise of power having no substantial relation to the public health, the public morals, the public safety or the public welfare in its proper sense." Euclid v. Ambler Co., *supra*, p. 395.

An inspection of a plat of the city upon which the zoning districts are outlined, taken in connection with the master's findings, shows with reasonable certainty that the inclusion of the locus in question is not indispensable to the general plan. The boundary line of the residential district before reaching the locus runs for some distance along the streets, and to exlude the locus from the residential district requires only that such line shall be continued 100 feet further along Henry street and thence south along Brookline street. There does not appear to be any reason why this should not be done. Nevertheless, if that were all, we should not be warranted in substituting our judgment for that of the zoning authorities primarily charged with the duty and responsibility of determining the question. Zahn v. Bd. of Public Works, 274 U.S. 325, 328, and cases cited. But that is not all. The governmental power to interfere by zoning regulations with the general rights of the land owner by restricting the character of his use, is not unlimited, and other questions aside, such restriction cannot be imposed if it does not bear a substantial relation to the public health, safety, morals, or general welfare. Euclid v. Ambler Co., *supra*, p. 395. Here, the express finding of the master, already quoted, confirmed by the court below, is that the health, safety, convenience and general welfare of the inhabitants of the part of the city affected will not be promoted by the disposition made by the ordinance of the locus in question. This finding of the master, after a hearing and an inspection of the entire area affected, supported, as we think it is, by other findings of fact, is determinative of the case. That the invasion of the property of plaintiff in error was serious and highly injurious is clearly established; and, since a necessary basis for the support of that invasion is wanting, the action of the zoning authorities comes within the ban of the Fourteenth Amendment and cannot be sustained.

Judgment reversed.

NOTES AND QUESTIONS

1.   What litmus does Justice Sutherland use for testing the ordinance when the landowner claims that *as applied* the ordinance deprives him of property without due process:

(a) Does the ordinance promote the general welfare of the landowner's neighbors? (Of the entire city?)
(b) Does the ordinance bear a substantial relationship to the general welfare?
(c) Does the ordinance deny the landowner an adequate return on his investment?

2.   Putting aside the semantic difficulty with Justice Sutherland's opinion, be aware that the reports burst with successful due process attacks on zoning laws as applied. Moreover, you can find cases asserting each of the Nectow tests or some recognizable variant thereof. The first and second tests measure the law's soundness, with courts ready to disagree with a legislature's judgment (implicit in any regulation) that the act promotes the general welfare, or bears some substantial relation thereto.

Yet an entire generation of law students has grown up learning that courts do (should) not undo social or economic regulation in the name of substantive due process simply because judges question a legislature's wisdom. Is there something about zoning that gives it special vulnerability to substantive due process assaults? In this regard, should an ordinance that requires every employer to pay a minimum wage, which may bankrupt some marginal shopkeepers, have a different (and higher) presumption of validity from an ordinance that limits every parcel along Brookline Street to residential use, which may cause some landowners economic injury?

3.   Test (c) assumes that the regulation will promote the general welfare but refuses enforcement because of severe hardship to the landowner. Despite the frequency with which courts utter "no adequate return on investment," the concept remains shadowy. On a purely technical level, there are the problems both of procedure and appropriateness of remedy. All zoning laws entitle the landowner to a variance (see Standard State Zoning Enabling Act §7, page 764 *supra*) where the restriction visits "unnecessary hardship" because of special conditions. In such a case, the appropriate remedy for the landowner is to seek a variance, an administrative procedure; and, if the zoning board refuses the variance, the landowner may then seek judicial review. At issue on review is the soundness of administrative discretion, not the validity of the ordinance.

See generally pages 931-956, *infra.* Not every claim of hardship is grist for a variance. As we shall see, the courts do try to distinguish between a hardship that is special to this landowner, because of something about *his* parcel (e.g., an irregularly shaped plot), for which variance is the proper remedy, and a hardship that extends to an entire group of landowners (e.g., all downtown owners required to provide off-street parking), for which a zoning attack is proper. Clear-cut lines do not always separate the two situations, and courts and zoning boards often blur or ignore the lines, but you as a lawyer should recognize this distinction. From your still-limited vantage, do you believe that the facts in *Nectow* would indicate a variance?

4.   There is also a technical problem of substance. What is an adequate return on investment? Courts rarely reveal the arithmetic of their decisions concerning this matter, and the zoning laws give no direct guidance.[4] The adequacy of investment return has two components, the normative yield and the investment base against which one calculates that yield. I know of no case where a court has made explicit what percentage it deemed an adequate rate of return. If you were a landowner's attorney, faced with the courts' inscrutability, what steps would you take to design a normative percentage yield?

No less troublesome than fixing the normative yield is determining the investment base. In each of the following cases, what value should the court use in measuring the adequacy of return?

(a) X paid $10,000 for her residentially zoned parcel ten years ago. The parcel is currently worth $12,000. Unrestricted, the parcel would sell for $25,000.

(b) X paid $12,000 for her residentially zoned parcel ten years ago. The parcel is currently worth $10,000. Unrestricted, the parcel would sell for $25,000.

(c) X paid $25,000 for her parcel six months ago. The zoning then permitted business use. Rezoned for residential use, the parcel would sell for $15,000.

5.   At the very root of the "no adequate return" test is the philosophical issue we saw earlier: when does a regulation become a "taking"? We know that a law confiscating all land value may sometimes survive attack, cf. Consolidated Rock Products Co. v. City of Los Angeles, 57 Cal. 2d 515, 370 P.2d 342 (1962), *appeal dismissed,* 371 U.S. 36 (1962), and that a law causing only moderate harm to the landowner may sometimes fail, cf. Vernon Park Realty v. City of Mount Vernon, 307 N.Y. 493, 121 N.E.2d 517 (1954), page 734 *supra.* With this loose frame of reference, consider the regulation that the court

---

4. Statutes in other areas do express a standard. Landmark preservation laws offer a fairly relevant comparison. The owner of a designated landmark may typically obtain relief if his property does not yield a specified return. See, e.g., New York, N.Y.; Admin. Code Ann. ch. 8A, §§207-1.0q, 207-8.0 (1971) (6 percent of assessed valuation).

struck down in the *Nectow* case. Of what purpose was the transitional R-3 zone in which plaintiff's property was placed? Do you find significant the court's comment that there does not appear to be any reason why the zonal boundary should not be moved 100 feet further west? Does the court seem to downgrade the purpose of the zone? Or alternatively, the means taken to achieve the purpose?

Perhaps some principle may be emerging that connects the "legislative soundness" tests with the "no adequate return" test. Try this one out: where a landowner attacks a zoning law as applied, the hardship he must prove rises in some proportion to the urgency (or the soundness) of the regulation he attacks, and the burden falls in converse proportion. Could this principle help explain why courts fudge on the arithmetic of adequate return?

6.   If the court seems to be saying that boundaries, particularly in built-up areas, can often be moved a short distance without defeating the plan, should courts leave the boundaries alone and direct the landowner to his administrative remedy? In sustaining the *Nectow* ordinance, the Massachusetts Supreme Court had written:

> If there is to be zoning at all, the dividing line must be drawn somewhere. There cannot be a twilight zone. If residence districts are to exist, they must be bounded. In the nature of things, the location of the precise limits of the several districts demands the exercise of judgment and sagacity. There can be no standard susceptible of mathematical exactness in its application. Opinions of the wise and good well may differ as to the place to put the separation between different districts. . . . Courts cannot set aside the decisions of public officers in such a matter unless compelled to the conclusion that it has no foundation in reason and is a mere arbitrary or irrational exercise of power having no substantial relation to the public health, the public morals, the public safety or the public welfare in its proper sense. These considerations cannot be weighed with exactness. That they demand the placing of the boundary of a zone 100 feet one way or the other in land having similar material features would be hard to say as a matter of law. . . . [Nectow v. City of Cambridge, 260 Mass. 441, 447, 448, 157 N.E. 618, 620 (1927)]

7.   Before the *Nectow* decision, X buys a residence on the north side of Henry Street (or the west side of Brookline Street), expecting Nectow's R-3 designation to continue. If the R-3 designation is removed, X's property value will drop. Should this be considered on the issues of (a) X's standing to intervene in the *Nectow* suit; (b) the continuing validity of the R-3 designation? Should a landowner, who enjoys zoning "protection," be able to block any change in a neighbor's zoning status? Consider by analogy a landowner's rights to the continuing enforcement of restrictive covenants (Mohawk Containers, Inc. v. Hancock, §11.6 *supra*). Is the analogy a good one? Is it feasible to develop a compensation and assessment system that will reflect the economic impact of zoning regulation, including zoning changes?

8. After this decision, may the plaintiff develop his land without restriction? Suppose that the city of Cambridge acted at once to rezone plaintiff's land for business.

§15.3   Cumulative Zoning and Beyond

The Euclid ordinance featured a zoning practice that all of the early ordinances adopted. Notice how Euclid described the six use districts. It did so pyramidically. The U-1 district occupied the apex; herein, only single-family dwellings and a few related uses were allowed. The U-2 district, once removed, added two-family dwellings to the uses permitted in U-1. The U-3 district further extended the permitted uses, while continuing to allow all of the more highly restricted uses. And so on down to the pyramid base, where in the U-6 district, gasoline storage tanks and one-family homes could *theoretically* exist side-by-side.

Cumulative zoning, as this practice has been called, eventually proved unsound. As one court wrote: "Experience has satisfied many that, for example, homes are no more appropriate in an industrial district than industry in a residential one. In both situations the baleful influences upon residences are the same." Cf. Kozenick v. Township of Montgomery, 24 N.J. 154, 169, 131 A.2d 1, 9 (1957). Moreover, it was a two-way friction. Factories, even when zoned for, did not gain complete immunity from nuisance claims, thus discouraging location or expansion within any industrial zone that also allowed dwellings. Again, it was more difficult to prepare for industrial development within mixed-use zones. Homes and factories require a different infrastructure of roads, sewers, and utilities. And the pockmarking of an industrial zone with homes often defeated assembly of the large contiguous tract that a factory would need.

These conditions led to the practice of noncumulative zoning, the barring of dwellings and sometimes businesses from industrial districts. See, e.g., the San Francisco City Planning Code, page 775 *supra*. Suits attacking the practice arose quite frequently during the 1950s, and the plaintiffs sometimes prevailed. See, e.g., Opgal, Inc. v. Burns, 20 Misc. 2d 803, 189 N.Y.S.2d 606 (Sup. Ct. 1959), *aff'd without opinion*, 9 N.Y.2d 659, 173 N.E.2d 50 (1961) (ordinance barred residences from light industrial zone; held: ordinance invalid, as applied to plaintiff's parcel, where much other industrially zoned land still lying vacant, and where finding that zoning would lower plaintiff's land value from $18,000 to $7,000 per acre); Comer v. City of Dearborn, 342 Mich. 471, 70 N.W.2d 813 (1955) (ordinance barred dwellings, including motels, from industrial zone; held: ordinance invalid, as applied to plaintiff's parcel, where the immediate neighborhood already contained some residences, several business places, but very few industrial enterprises); Katobimar Realty Co. v. Webster, 20 N.J. 114, 118 A.2d 824 (1955) (ordinance barred dwellings and retail stores from industrial zone; held: ordinance invalid; no reasonable basis for exclusion of retail uses from industrial zone).

Today, noncumulative zoning is widely sanctioned, and cases abound where courts have approved both principle *and* its application. Cf., e.g., Lamb v. City of Monroe, 358 Mich. 136, 99 N.W.2d 566 (1959) (residences excluded from industrial zone); Roney v. Board of Supervisors [of Contra Costa County], 138 Cal. App. 2d 740, 292 P.2d 529 (1956) (same); State v. Iten, 259 Minn. 77, 106 N.W.2d 366 (1960) (same).

For general discussion, see Note, Industrial Zoning to Exclude Higher Uses, 32 N.Y.U.L. Rev. 1261 (1957); Mott and Wehrly, The Prohibition of Residential Developments in Industrial Districts (Urban Land Institute Technical Bulletin No. 10, Nov. 1948).

As counterpoint to noncumulative zoning, planners have come to understand that sensible mixtures of land use, which Euclidian zoning barred, may also improve the quality of urban life. We shall see, in the section on zoning flexibility (§17.6 *infra*), how planned unit development (PUD) has entered the modern ordinance.

§15.4   Zoning and the Antitrust Laws

The Sherman Act proscribes contracts, combinations or conspiracies in restraint of trade. The Supreme Court has read the Act as creating an antitrust immunity for state action, Parker v. Brown, 317 U.S. 341 (1943), but has refused to extend that immunity automatically to actions of local governments, City of Lafayette v. Louisiana Power & Light Co., 435 U.S. 389 (1978). This refusal becomes germane in the light of two recent lower court decisions where cities were alleged to have conspired through their zoning laws with private persons to restrain trade. In Whitworth v. Perkins, 559 F.2d 378 (5th Cir. 1977), *vacated and remanded sub nom.* City of Impact v. Whitworth, 435 U.S. 992 (1978), *opinion reinstated and case remanded per curiam sub nom.* Whitworth v. Perkins, 576 F.2d 696 (5th Cir. 1978), the court upheld a complaint alleging that the zoning ordinance protected an existing liquor dealer by foreclosing competitors from entering the community.

> The mere presence of the zoning ordinance does not necessarily insulate the defendants from antitrust liability where, as here, the plaintiff asserts that the enactment of the ordinance was itself part of the alleged conspiracy to restrain trade. [559 F.2d at 379]

In Mason City Center Associates v. City of Mason City, 468 F. Supp. 737

(N.D. Iowa 1979), the validated complaint alleged that the city denied plaintiffs the rezoning needed to build a regional shopping center, in order that it could protect existing downtown merchants.

One writer suggests that this expanded view of the antitrust laws may have serious relevance in the exclusionary zoning and growth management contexts, §§16.5, 16.6 *infra*. Blumstein, A Prolegomenon to Growth Management and Exclusionary Zoning Issues, 43 Law and Contemp. Prob. 5, 109-110 (Spring 1979).

Even if the antitrust laws were not to apply (for example, no conspiracy shown), how might an aggrieved businessman successfully attack a local measure that sharply constricted competition?

Chapter 16

Problems of Zoning Application

In this chapter, zoning appears in the context of several tough, controversial community development issues.

§16.1   Elimination of Nonconforming Uses

Nonconforming uses appear wherever an existing activity violates the restrictions of a newly enacted or amended zoning law. The early zoning ordinances often were superimposed upon well-established neighborhoods. Not uncommonly, a gasoline station or corner grocery occupied a parcel within a residential zone, from which all *new* nondwelling uses were barred. Dealing with these incongruities was at once recognized as a troublesome issue. If a *new* auto repair shop was an unsuitable neighbor for the one-family house, so, too, was an existing shop.

The most direct response would simply have been to outlaw all nonconforming uses: in short, the auto repair shop must shut down. It may surprise you that at least one city (New Orleans) took this tack, that the state courts upheld the law, and that the United States Supreme Court denied certiorari. State ex rel. Dema Realty Co. v. McDonald, 168 La. 172, 121 So. 613 (1929), *cert. denied*, 280 U.S. 556 (1929). Moreover, the Supreme Court had previously upheld nonzoning laws that had forced a stable, a brickyard, and petroleum storage facilities from their existing locations. Reinman v. Little Rock, 237 U.S. 171 (1915); Hadacheck v. Sebastian, 239 U.S. 394 (1915); Pierce Oil Co. v. City of Hope, 248 U.S. 498 (1919), page 780 *supra*.

But most writers agreed that except for uses that the common law would deem nuisancelike, the elimination of all nonconforming uses would raise serious due process objections in the genre of Pennsylvania Coal Co. v. Mahon. See, e.g., Retroactive Zoning and Nuisances, 41 Colum. L. Rev. 457 (1941);

O'Reilly, Nonconforming Uses and Due Process of Law, 23 Ga. L. Rev. 218 (1934). Furthermore, the political objections to a law that failed to recognize any vested right in existing businesses demanded a less drastic approach. Cf. E. Basset, Zoning 115-116 (1st ed. 1936).

The scheme most ordinances adopted was to validate existing noncon-forming uses, but to curtail their ability to expand, modernize, rebuild after a fire, reopen after a shutdown, or change to another nonconforming use. In this way, planners believed, time and obsolescence would force most of these busi-nesses—in the manner of the proletarian state—to wither away. Unhappily, planners guessed wrong, for they overlooked both the durability of a monop-oly location (the only grocery in the neighborhood) and the laxity of zoning administration. For example, zoning boards issued variances quite generously to allow the rebuilding or expansion of nonconforming uses. See generally Anderson, The Nonconforming Use—A Product of Euclidian Zoning, 10 Syracuse L. Rev. 214 (1959); Norton, Elimination of Incompatible Uses and Structures, 20 Law and Contemp. Prob. 305 (1955).

Given this failure, and the persistent presence of the nonconforming use, some communities have tried a technique based upon the principle of "amor-tization." This device would allow the owner to operate long enough to recoup his original investment. Then he would shut the nonconforming use down or move it elsewhere. The next cases examine the legality of this device.

HARBISON v. CITY OF BUFFALO
4 N.Y.2d 553, 152 N.E.2d 42, 176 N.Y.S.2d 598 (1958)

FROESSEL, J. Petitioner Andrew Harbison, Sr., purchased certain real property located at 35 Cumberland Avenue in the city of Buffalo on January 5, 1924. Shortly thereafter he erected a 30- by 40-foot-frame building thereon, and commenced operating a cooperage business, which, with his son, he has continued to date. The building has not been enlarged, and the volume of petitioners' business is stated to be the same now as then. The only difference is that, whereas petitioners formerly dealt mainly with wooden barrels, they now recondition, clean and paint "used" steel drums or barrels. No issue of that difference is made here. These drums, or barrels, are stacked to a height of about 10 feet in the yard, and on an average day about 600 or 700 barrels are stored there.

When petitioner Andrew Harbison, Sr., established his business in 1924, the street upon which it was located was an unpaved extension of an existing street, the city operated a dump in the area, and there was a glue factory in the vicinity. At the present time, the glue factory has gone, and there are residences adjoining both sides of petitioners' property and across the street. The change in the surrounding area is reflected by the fact that in 1924 the land was unzoned, but since 1926 (except for the period between 1949 and

1953, when it was zoned for business), the land has been zoned for residential use; and it is presently in an "R3" dwelling district.

Thus it is clear that at the time of the enactment of the first zoning ordinance affecting the premises, petitioners had an existing nonconforming use, that is, the conduct of a cooperage business in a residential zone. In 1936, under an ordinance which included the operations of petitioners in a definition of "junk dealers," petitioners applied for and received a license to carry on their business. Licenses were obtained by petitioners every year from 1936 through the fiscal year of 1956.

However, the ordinances of the City of Buffalo were amended, effective as of July 30, 1953, so as to state in chapter LXX (§18):

> 1. Continuing existing uses: Except as provided in this section, any non-conforming use of any building, structure, land or premises may be continued. Provided, however, that on premises situated in any "R" district each use which is not a conforming use in the "R5" district and which falls into one of the categories hereinafter enumerated shall cease or shall be changed to a conforming use within 3 years from the effective date of this amended chapter. The requirements of this subdivision for the termination of non-conforming uses shall apply in each of the following cases: . . . (d) Any junk yard. (Defined in §23, subd. 24.)

On November 27, 1956 the director of licenses of the City of Buffalo sent a letter to petitioners stating: "At a meeting of the Common Council under date of November 13, 1956 . . . [it] evinced its intention not to amend or modify the provisions of [Section] 18, Subdivision I of Chapter LXX of the Ordinances relating to non-conforming uses by junk yards . . . in 'R' districts. . . . You are hereby notified to discontinue the operation of your junk yard . . . at once." A subsequent application by petitioners for a wholesale junk license and one for a "drum reconditioning license" were refused on the ground that "said premises lie within an area zoned as 'R3' Dwelling Distict . . . and the operation of a junk yard and the outside storage of used materials is prohibited therein." Petitioners then brought this article 78 proceeding in the nature of mandamus in which they sought an order directing the city to issue a whole-sale junk license to them, and the lower courts sustained them. . . .

In the major point involved on this appeal, the city argues that the ordinance requiring the termination of petitioners' nonconforming use of the premises as a junk yard within three years of the date of said ordinance is a valid exercise of its police power. Its claim is not based on the theory of nuisance (see People v. Miller, 304 N.Y. 105, 107, and cases there cited; Noel, Retroactive Zoning and Nuisances, 41 Col. L. Rev. 457), and indeed this record contains little evidence as to the manner of operation of petitioners' business and the nature of the surrounding neighborhood. Rather, in this case, the city bases its claim largely on out-of-State decisions which have sustained ordinances requiring the termination of nonconforming uses or structures after a period of permitted continuance, where such "amortization" period was held reasonable.

When zoning ordinances are initially adopted to limit permissible uses of property, or when property is rezoned so as to prevent uses of property previously allowed, a degree of protection is constitutionally required to be given owners of property then using their premises in a manner forbidden by the ordinance. Thus we have held that, where substantial expenditures were made in the commencement of the erection of a building, a zoning ordinance may not deprive the owner of the "vested right" to complete the structure. [Citations omitted.] So, where the owner already has structures on the premises, he cannot be directed to cease using them [citations omitted], just as he has the right to continue a prior business carried on there. [citations omitted.]

However, where the benefit to the public has been deemed of greater moment than the detriment to the property owner, we have sustained the prohibition of continuation of prior nonconforming uses. These cases involved the prior use of property for parking lots. [Citations omitted.] We have also upheld the restriction of projected uses of the property where, at the time of passage of the ordinance, there had been no substantial investment in the nonconforming uses. [Citations omitted.] In these cases, there is no doubt that the property owners incurred a loss in the value of their property and otherwise a result of the fact thay they were unable to carry out their prospective uses; but we held that such a deprivation was not violative of the owners' constitutional rights. In People v. Miller (*supra*, p. 108), we explained these cases by stating that they involved situations in which the property owners would sustain only a "relatively slight and insubstantial" loss.

It should be noted that even where the zoning authorities may not prohibit a prior nonconforming use, they may adopt regulations which restrict the right of the property owner to enlarge or extend the use or to rebuild or make alterations to the structures on the property. [Citations omitted.]

As these cases indicate, our approach to the problem of permissible restrictions on nonconforming uses has recognized that, while the benefit accruing to the public in terms of more complete and effective zoning does not justify the immediate destruction of substantial businesses or structures developed or built prior to the ordinance (People v. Miller, *supra*, p. 108), the policy of zoning embraces the concept of the ultimate elimination of nonconforming uses, and thus the courts favor reasonable restriction of them. But, where the zoning ordinance could have required the cessation of a sand and gravel business on one year's notice, we have held it unconstitutional (Town of Somers v. Camarco, 308 N.Y. 537, *supra*).

The development of the policy that nonconforming uses should be protected and their existence preserved at the stage of development existing at the time of passage of the ordinance seems to have been based upon the assumption that the ultimate ends of zoning would be accomplished as the nonconforming use terminated with time. But this has not proven to be the case, as commentators have noted that the tendency of many of these uses is to flourish, capitalizing on the fact that no new use of that nature could be begun in the area (see, e.g., 9 U. Chi. L. Rev. 477, 479, 481; 102 U. Pa. L. Rev. 91, 94; 35 Va. L. Rev. 348, 352-353; 1951 Wis. L. Rev. 685). Because of this situation, communities have sought new forms of ordinances restricting nonconforming uses, and in particular have turned to provisions which require termination after a given period of time. . . .

Leaving aside eminent domain and nuisance, we have often stated in our decisions that the owner of land devoted to a prior nonconforming use, or on which a prior nonconforming structure exists (or has been substantially commenced), has the right to continue such use, but we have never held that this right may continue virtually in perpetuity. Now that we are for the first time squarely faced with the problem as to whether or not this right may be terminated after a reasonable period, during which the owner may have a fair opportunity to amortize his investment and to make future plans, we conclude that it may be, in accordance with the overwhelming weight of authority found in the courts of our sister States, as well as with the textwriters and commentators who have expressed themselves upon the subject.

With regard to prior nonconforming *structures,* reasonable termination periods based upon the amortized life of the structure are not, in our opinion, unconstitutional. They do not compel the immediate destruction of the improvements, but envision and allow for their normal life without extensive alterations or repairs. Such a regulation is akin to those we have sustained relating to restrictions upon the extension or substantial repair or replacement of prior nonconforming structures. . . .

If, therefore, a zoning ordinance provides a sufficient period of permitted nonconformity, it may further provide that at the end of such period the use must cease. This rule is analogous to that with respect to nonconforming structures. In ascertaining the reasonable period during which an owner of property must be allowed to continue a nonconforming use, a balance must be found between social harm and private injury. We cannot say that a legislative body may not in any case, after consideration of the factors involved, conclude that the termination of a use after a period of time sufficient to allow a property owner an opportunity to amortize his investment and make other plans is a valid method of solving the problem.

To enunciate a contrary rule would mean that the use of land for such purposes as a tennis court, an open air skating rink, a junk yard or a parking lot—readily transferable to another site—at the date of the enactment of a zoning ordinance vests the owner thereof with the right to utilize the land in that manner in perpetuity, regardless of the changes in the neighborhood over the course of time. In the light of our ever expanding urban communities, such a rule appears to us to constitute an unwarranted restriction upon the Legislature in dealing with what has been described as "One of the major problems in effective administration of modern zoning ordinances" (1951 Wis. L. Rev. 685). When the termination provisions are reasonable in the light of the nature of the business of the property owner, the improvements erected on the land, the character of the neighborhood, and the detriment caused the property owner, we may not hold them constitutionally invalid.

In the present case, the two lower courts have expressed the view that, "Whatever the law may be in California or Florida or other jurisdictions, in this State" no regulation infringing at any time the perpetual right of an owner to continue a prior nonconforming use is valid. Accordingly, neither court considered the question of whether the particular period prescribed by the ordinance was reasonable under the facts of this case.

Their conclusion is not in accord with the general rule applicable to protection of nonconforming uses as stated in People v. Miller (304 N.Y. 105, *supra*). In that case we decided that where the enforcement of an ordinance requiring the termination of a prior nonconforming use caused "relatively slight and insubstantial" loss to the property owner, it would be constitutional. While it is true that the ordinance there involved did not have an "amortization" provision, nevertheless the general test enunciated is no less germane when such a provision is included in the ordinance. As previously pointed out, the period of "amortization" allowed by the ordinance is a crucial factor in determining whether the ordinance has been constitutionally applied in a given case.

Here, petitioners are engaged in the business of reconditioning barrels or used steel drums. We are told that the value of the property together with the improvements is $20,000; but there is no indication of the relative value of the land and improvements separately. It was further alleged that the improvements consists of a 30- by 40-foot-frame building erected in 1924, and, in addition thereto, petitioners claim that at the insistence of the City of Buffalo, three years before the ordinance went into effect, they were obliged to install a special sewage system at a cost of $2000 and a boiler at a cost of $700.

Material triable issues of fact thus remain, and a further hearing should adduce evidence relating to the nature of the surrounding neighborhood, the value and condition of the improvements on the premises, the nearest area to which petitioners might relocate, the cost of such relocation, as well as any other reasonable costs which bear upon the kind and amount of damages which petitioners might sustain, and whether petitioners might be able to continue operation of their business if not allowed to continue storage of barrels or steel drums outside their frame building. It is only upon such evidence that it may be ascertained whether the resultant injury to petitioners would be so substantial that the ordinance would be unconstitutional as applied to the particular facts of this case.

The order of the Appellate Division should be reversed, without costs, and the matter remanded to Special Term for a trial of the material issues and further proceedings as outlined in this opinion.

VAN VOORHIS, J. (dissenting). [Dissent omitted.]

JUDGE BURKE concurs with JUDGE FROESSEL; JUDGES DESMOND and FULD concur in result upon the principles stated in People v. Miller (304 N.Y.

105, 108, 109); JUDGE VAN VOORHIS dissents in an opinion in which CHIEF JUDGE CONWAY and JUDGE DYE concur.

Order reversed, etc.

POSTSCRIPT TO HARBISON

Real estate experts gave the following testimony when *Harbison* was retried at Special Term: The buildings and fixtures were worth $10,747; the land alone was worth $5,347. The only other suitable site reasonably nearby would cost $32,000. Moving expenses were estimated at $2,025. Within 300 yards of the Harbison parcel was a "mercantile area" occupied by used car lots and a storage place for concrete blocks.

The lower court concluded that a move would cost the petitioners approximately $20,000, and that the ordinance was "unconstitutional as applied to the particular facts of this case." There was no appeal from this decision. Note, 44 Cornell L.Q. 450, 451 (1959).

TOWN OF HEMPSTEAD v. ROMANO
33 Misc. 2d 315, 226 N.Y.S.2d 291 (Sup. Ct. 1963)

BRENNAN, J. The plaintiff township seeks through the injunctive process to enforce an amortization provision in its building zone ordinance against the nonconforming use by the defendants of their land as a junk yard and automobile wrecking business. At issue by way of defense is the constitutionality of the ordinance.

Since January 20, 1930, the ordinance has prohibited the use of any land in the town for a junk yard or automobile wrecking business. It has also provided (art. 14, §G-3.0): "Notwithstanding any other provision of this Ordinance any automobile or other junk yard in existence at the effective date of this Ordinance in a residence district shall at the expiration of three years from such date be discontinued."

The facts have either been stipulated or are not in dispute. In 1922, Giuseppi Romano and his wife Filomena acquired title to land designated as Section 32, Block 591, lots 15 through 29 and lots 35 through 44, on the Nassau County Land Map. In 1949, Filomena conveyed all her interest in said lots to Giuseppi who died testate on December 5, 1958.

From 1926 to April, 1956, he had conducted a junk yard and automobile wrecking business on lots 15 through 29, and thereafter he and his son Joseph, a defendant herein, continued said business thereon. By his will, the decedent devised his real property to his three sons, the defendants herein, and bequeathed his interest in the junk-yard business to the defendants Frank and John Romano with the direction and request that the three defendants conduct the junk yard and automobile wrecking business jointly, as they have in fact done since his death.

The property involved (lots 15 through 29) has been zoned Residence C since January 20, 1930. No effort has previously been made to terminate the nonconforming use which began in 1926, when the land was unzoned.

There is no question that in this State nonconforming uses and structures in existence when a prohibitory zoning ordinance is enacted are allowed to continue if, and only if, enforcement of the ordinance would, by rendering valueless substantial improvements or businesses built up over the years, cause serious financial harm to the property owner. (People v. Miller, 304 N.Y. 105, 109). In the cited case the court noted that this rule placed "its emphasis upon pecuniary and economic loss" (p. 109) and said: "The destruction of substantial businesses or structures developed or built prior to the adoption of a zoning ordinance is not deemed to be balanced or justified by the advantage to the public, in terms of more complete and effective zoning, accruing from the cessation of such uses" (p. 108).

In 1958, the Court of Appeals indicated that its approach to the problem of permissible restrictions on nonconforming uses has recognized that, while the benefit accruing to the public in terms of more complete and effective zoning does not justify the immediate destruction of substantial business or structures developed or built prior to the ordinance, the policy of zoning embraces the concept of the ultimate elimination of nonconforming uses and thus of reasonable restriction of them (Matter of Harbison v. City of Buffalo, 4 N.Y.2d 553, 559, 560). However, the permissible boundaries within which the concept may operate were not established, nor did the prevailing 4 to 3 opinion promulgating the concept have the unqualified support of the entire majority. . . .

It is against this background of applicable authority that we can now proceed to review the facts in the case at bar.

The premises are improved with a one-story dwelling used as such since its erection prior to 1930 and separate building, 18 feet by 18 feet, also erected prior to 1930 and at all times since used in connection with the junk yard and auto-wrecking business. It is not adapted to any use permitted in a Residence C District. The dwelling had a value of $4,756 in 1930 and $8,036 in 1961; the separate building had a value of $1,044 in 1930 and $1,764 in 1961. The land value increased from $5,300 in 1930 to $8,100 in 1961. It is also found that the value of the equipment now on the premises used in the defendants' business is $28,000 to which must be added $10,000 of inventory and stock in trade. This property cannot readily be moved nor can the good will of the business estimated at $22,000 be salvaged because there is *no* land in the county available for the present business (junk yard and automobile wrecking) by virtue of local zoning except in the Town of Oyster Bay where such use is permitted as a special exception in an industrial district. The cost of relocation of the business to any area within a radius of 10 miles of the present location would be at least $10,000.

The recital of the facts demonstrates the substantial loss that would attach were the ordinance now enforced against the defendants. As a matter of fact, application of the ordinance would be tantamount to terminating the business of the defendants without compensation. The loss is not lessened by the failure of the plaintiff to act for more than 18 years upon its alleged rights which accrued in 1933 under the ordinance, a failure which permitted the defendants, within the proper limits of their rights of nonconforming user, to make substantial investments in business.

As pointed out in a note in the Cornell Law Quarterly (vol. 44, pp. 450, 458) after discussing the *Harbison* case (4 N.Y.2d 553, *supra*): "Municipalities have a legitimate interest in preventing the perpetual continuance of prior nonconforming uses. However, constitutional protections should not be lightly cast aside nor should the desire for complete conformity demand unreasonable individual sacrifices." The defendants herein have well-recognized legal property rights which must be protected by this court. Accordingly, the complaint is dismissed, without costs.

NOTES AND QUESTIONS

1.   The Commentary to the ALI Model Land Development code 146-148 (1975) states that "for the most part the courts have been sympathetic to the idea of amortization." It then lists thirty decisions from fifteen states upholding amortization laws. The uses amortized include:

billboards and advertising signs (10 cases)
commercial uses (5 cases)
junkyards (3 cases)
gasoline stations (3 cases)
auto wrecking yards (2 cases)
dog kennel, riding stable, pigeon loft, cement plant, check-cashing
    agency, salvage yard (1 case each)
"any nonconforming use which is not in a building" (1 case)

The amortization periods were as short as six months (riding stable) and as long as twenty-five years (gasoline station, commercial building).

Harbison v. City of Buffalo, *supra,* does not appear on the ALI list.

The Commentary cites the decisions of two states (Ohio and Missouri) treating amortization as unconstitutional, and the decisions of two other states (Michigan and New Jersey) treating amortization as beyond the powers given to local bodies by the zoning enabling act. Re-examine the Standard State Zoning Enabling Act, page 762 *supra,* to see if it deals with the elimination of nonconforming uses.

2.   In 1971 the American Society of Planning Officials surveyed the extent to which local laws contained amortization procedures. Of 489 cities

and countries responding, 159 reported some amortization, but only 27 applied the technique against buildings and structures! Amortization usually has affected only uses, such as billboards, having a modest capital investment. See Scott, The Effect of Nonconforming Land-Use Amortization (Planning Advisory Service Report No. 280, May 1972).

3.   *Harbison* and *Romano* typify cases where courts have accepted amortization in principle only to find it wanting as applied. See also James v. City of Greenville, 227 S.C. 565, 88 S.E.2d 661 (1955); City of Corpus Christi v. Allen, 152 Tex. 137, 254 S.W.2d 759 (1953); Village of Oak Park v. Gordon, 32 Ill. 2d 295, 205 N.E.2d 464 (1965); Art Neon Co. v. City and County of Denver, 357 F. Supp. 466 (D. Colo. 1973).

4.   How should a lawyer or a judge quantify a claim that an amortization statute *as applied* deprives the owner of the nonconforming use of property without due process? In putting a dollar value on the property owner's damages, which of the following items, or parts thereof, should the court consider?

  (a) business building and fixtures
  (b) land
  (c) cost of suitably zoned site
  (d) moving expenses
  (e) stock-in-trade and inventory
  (f) locational goodwill
  (g) business goodwill

5.   The concept of amortization derives from the tax and accounting fields, where taxpayers and businesses "write down" or depreciate their investments over the asset's estimated useful life. With respect to tangible assets, such as structures, the tax and accounting view is that these assets will have become worthless, except for salvage value, at the end of their estimated useful lives. Yet, experience teaches that assets frequently retain much value even after they have been written down to zero on the balance sheet. Should courts consider the balance sheet or the market value of a tangible asset when the owner has attacked an amortization law as applied to his property? Cf. Metromedia, Inc. v. City of San Diego, 26 Cal.3d 848, 883, 610 P.2d 407, 428, 164 Cal. Rptr. 510, 531 (1980) (1-4 year amortization period, linked to depreciated value of advertising signs, not unreasonable), *rev'd on other grounds*, 101 S. Ct. 2882 (1981).

6.   With respect to intangible assets, such as business or locational good will, tax law seldom allows the taxpayer to amortize his investment, and accounting theory also presumes against the practice. If a businessman has paid $5,000 for the locational advantage or good will of a business, how—via amortization—can he recoup this expenditure?

7.   Communities might also seek to eliminate nonconforming uses via the power of eminent domain. See, e.g., Mich. Comp. Laws §125.583a (Supp. 1981). If the Town of Hempstead were to condemn Romano's rights in the

junkyard, which of the items of value, listed in Note 4 *supra,* would be compensable under existing doctrine? See §18.2, *infra.* Would the answer partly depend upon whether the town acquired the Romano parcel or only Romano's right to operate a junkyard on the site?

In Great Britain the power of eminent domain is used extensively to remove nonconforming uses. Also, planning permission on one parcel is sometimes conditioned on the owner's promise to remove an existing nonconforming use from some other parcel belonging to him. Pooley, The Evolution of British Planning Legislation 71, 81 (1960). Professor Pooley questions the propriety of this practice. Ibid.

8. Where a property owner challenges the validity of an amortization law as applied, can the court make any response other than to approve or disapprove the ordinance unconditionally? For example, in the *Harbison* remand, the lower court rejected Buffalo's three-year amortization law as applied to the petitioner, who would lose $20,000 in the shutdown. Instead, might the court have approved the law conditionally upon Buffalo giving Harbison some period longer than three years to leave the premises? Or are courts unable to recast a specifically drawn statute, even for the sake of saving the law? Alternatively, might an amortization law be written for an indeterminate grace period, for example, from three to ten years, letting an administrator in each case fix the period pursuant to statutory standards, and making the administrative decision subject to judicial review for possible discretionary abuse? Cf. Village of Oak Park v. Gordon, 32 Ill. 2d 295, 205 N.E.2d 464 (1965).

9. We have skirted the constitutional issue as to the vestedness of an existing use. Compare the following cases. Can you think of any reasons why a zoning challenge should not yield the same outcome in all?

(a) X operates a gasoline station on a site that is rezoned from business to residential. The station becomes a nonconforming use. X will lose 30 percent of his investment if forced to move. The ordinance gives X one year to eliminate the nonconforming use.

(b) X owns vacant land that is rezoned from business to residential, defeating his plans to operate a gasoline station on the site. The value of X's parcel declines 30 percent.

(c) X owns vacant land on which he has obtained a building permit for a gasoline station. Before construction begins, the site is rezoned from business to residential and the building permit is rescinded. The value of X's parcel declines 30 percent. In addition, X has spent $5,000 for engineering, architectural, and legal fees.

In general, courts have treated more protectively the status of an existing activity than that of a proposed activity. Ordinarily, landowners do not gain vestedness in the original zoning until they have made a significant expenditure, beyond the land cost, to develop the parcel. What *is* a significant expenditure is the grist of endless litigation. See Annot., 6 A.L.R.2d 960 (1949).

10. The ALI Model Land Development Code devotes its entire Article IV to "Discontinuance of Existing Land Uses." In general, the code would treat differently nonconforming uses in an area with a well-defined character from those in an area where development was yet to unfold fully. In a developing area, unless a use was "offensive and performing no essential public function," it could remain. In a built-up area, a law could provide for elimination of a nonconforming use, but only if the loss of property value did not constitute a taking or, alternatively, if the landowner received compensation. Offensive uses could be eliminated in any area, but—as with nonoffensive uses—the regulation must provide for compensation if it results in a taking.

To avoid such takings, the code embraces a flexible amortization concept, in which a local land development agency would allow a "reasonable time" for discontinuance of an incompatible use. Factors that the agency would weigh in fixing the time would include: (a) the probable extent of the economic usefulness of the land use; (b) the urgency of the public purpose requiring discontinuance; and (c) the cost to the owner of discontinuance.

11. There is no shortage of literature on the subject of nonconforming uses. See, e.g., Graham, Legislative Techniques for the Amortization of the Nonconforming Use: A Suggested Formula, 12 Wayne L. Rev. 435 (1966); Anderson, The Nonconforming Use—A Product of Euclidean Zoning, 10 Syracuse L. Rev. 214 (1959); Norton, Elimination of Incompatible Uses and Structures, 20 Law & Contemp. Prob. 305 (1955); Notes, 55 Iowa L. Rev. 998 (1970), 57 Nw. U.L. Rev. 323 (1962), 26 U. Chi. L. Rev. 442 (1959), 27 Stan. L. Rev. 1325 (1975); Annot., 22 A.L.R.3d 1134 (1968); Comment, Conforming the Nonconforming Use: Proposed Legislative Relief for a Zoning Dilemma, 33 Sw. L.J. 855 (1979).

§16.2 Control of Aesthetics

The police power . . . is based upon public necessity. . . . This is the reason why mere aesthetic considerations cannot justify the use of the police power. [Citation omitted.] It is commendable and desirable, but not essential to the public need, that our aesthetic desires be gratified. Moreover, authorities in general agree as to the essentials of a public health program, while the public view as to what is necessary for aesthetic progress greatly varies. Certain Legislatures might consider that it was more important to cultivate a taste for jazz than for Beethoven, for posters than for Rembrandt and for limericks than for Keats. Successive city councils might never agree as to what the public needs from an aesthetic standpoint, and this fact makes the aesthetic standard impractical as a standard for use restriction upon property. The world would be at continual seesaw if aesthetic considerations were permitted to govern the use of the police power. We are therefore remitted to the porposition that the police power is based upon public necessity, and that the public health, morals, or safety, and not merely aesthetic interest, must be in danger in order to justify its use. [City of Youngstown v. Kahn Bros. Bldg. Co., 112 Ohio St. 654, 661-662, 148 N.E. 842, 844 (1925)]

The above quotation appears in a decision striking down a local law whose height limits would have barred apartments from a one-family zone. Decided before Village of Euclid v. Ambler Realty Co., this case two years later might have ended differently in view of Justice Sutherland's image about the "parasitic" nature of apartment houses. But the views expressed about the use of the police power to regulate appearance are as provocative today as they were then, and the problems of aesthetic control cannot be lightly sloughed off.

The *Reid* case, *infra*, involves a fairly typical control—the use of an architectural board to review and approve plans before a building permit can issue. As you read the *Reid* case, begin thinking about the following questions:

(a) What objective(s) does the legislation seek?
(b) How do the objectives relate to the "general welfare"?
(c) Are the means chosen rationally related to the objectives sought?
(d) Does the legislation contain sufficient standards to reduce administrative arbitrariness or to expose it to meaningful judicial review?
(e) Can the objectives be gained in any other way?

REID v. ARCHITECTURAL BOARD OF REVIEW
119 Ohio App. 67, 192 N.E.2d 74 (1963)

KOVACHY, P.J. This is an appeal on questions of law from a judgment rendered by the Court of Common Pleas in favor of the defendant appellee, The Architectural Board of the City of Cleveland Heights, Ohio.

Donna S. Reid, plaintiff appellant, hereinafter designated applicant, applied to the Building Commissioner of the City of Cleveland Heights for a permit to build a residence on a lot owned by her and her husband on North Park Boulevard in Cleveland Heights. As required by ordinance, the plans and specifications were referred to the Architectural Board of Review, which Board, after due consideration, made the following order: "This plan is for a single-story building and is submitted for a site in a multi-story residential neighborhood. The Board disapproves this project for the reason that it does not maintain the high character of community development in that it does not conform to the character of the houses in the area."

Upon appeal to the Court of Common Pleas, that court rendered a judgment in favor of the Board, holding (1) that the Codified Ordinances were constitutional enactments under the police power of the City; (2) that the Board had the power and authority to render the decision appealed from; (3) that the Board did not abuse its discretion; and (4) that due process was accorded applicant.

The Board is composed of three architects registered and authorized to practice architecture under Ohio laws with ten years of general practice as such.

Section 137.05 of the Codified Ordinances of the City of Cleveland Heights, titled "Purpose" reads as follows:

> The purposes of the Architectural Board of Review are to protect property on which buildings are constructed or altered, to maintain the high character of community development, and to protect real estate within this City from impairment or destruction of value, by regulating according to proper architectural principles the design, use of materials, finished grade lines and orientation of all new buildings, hereafter erected, and the moving, alteration, improvement, repair, adding to or razing in whole or in part of all existing buildings, and said Board shall exercise its powers and perform its duties for the accomplishment of said purposes only.

This ordinance is intended to:

1. protect property,
2. maintain high character of community development,
3. protect real estate from impairment or destruction of value, and the Board's powers are restricted "for the accomplishment of said purposes only."

These objectives are sought to be accomplished by regulating:

1. design,
2. use of material,
3. finished grade lines,
4. orientation (new buildings).

The City of Cleveland Heights is a suburb of the City of Cleveland and was organized to provide suitable and comfortable home surroundings for residents employed in Cleveland and its environs. It has no industry or railroads within its confines and is a well-regulated and carefully groomed community, primarily residential in character. An ordinance designed to protect values and to maintain "a high character of community development" is in the public interest and contributes to the general welfare. Moreover, the employment of highly trained personages such as architects for the purpose of applying their knowledge and experience in helping to maintain high standards of the community is laudable and salutary and serves the public good.

We determine and hold that Ordinance 137.05 is a constitutional exercise of the police power by the City Council and is, therefore, valid. . . .

Section 137.05, as outlined above, sets out criteria and standards for the Board to follow in passing upon an application for the building of a new home which are definite as to the objective to be attained—to protect property, to maintain high character of community development, to protect real estate from impairment and destruction of value; specific as to matters to be considered and regulated—design, use of material, finished grade lines, orientation; instructive as to the method by which the matters specified are to be adjudged—"proper architectural principles" and informative as to the bounds within which it is to exercise these powers—"for the accomplishment of said purposes only."

When borne in mind that the members of the Board are highly trained experts in the field of architecture, the instruction that they resolve these questions on "proper architectural principles" is profoundly reasonable since such expression has reference to the basic knowledge on which their profession is founded.

It is our view, therefore, that Section 137.05 contains all the criteria and standards reasonably necessary for the Board to carry on the duties conferred upon it.

In 1 Ohio Jurisprudence 2d 431, Administrative Law and Procedure, Section 28, it is stated that: "The discretion conferred on administrative agencies must not be unconfined and vagrant but must be canalized within banks that keep it from overflowing."

We have read the bill of exceptions filled in this case carefully. It discloses that North Park Boulevard is in a district zoned for Class 1A residences not to exceed thirty-five feet in height or two and one-half stories, whichever is lesser, and which are required to cover not less than fifteen thousand square feet of lot space. This district extends through a park area with buildings on the north side and trees, ravines, and bushes hundreds of feet wide on its south side. The buildings on this Boulevard are, in the main, dignified, stately and conventional structures, two and one-half stories high.

The house designed for the applicant, as described by applicant, is a flat-roofed complex of twenty modules, each of which is ten feet high, twelve feet square and arranged in a loosely formed "U" which winds its way through a grove of trees. About sixty percent of the wall area of the house is glass and opens on an enclosed garden; the rest of the walls are of cement panels. A garage of the same modular construction stands off from the house, and these two structures, with their associated garden walls, trellises and courts, form a series of interior and exterior spaces, all under a canopy of trees and baffled from the street by a garden wall.

A wall ten feet high is part of the front structure of the house and garage and extends all around the garden area. It has no windows. Since the wall is of the same height as the structure of the house, no part of the house can be seen from the street. From all appearances, it is just a high wall with no indication of what is behind it. Not only does the house fail to conform in any manner with the other buildings but presents no identification that it is a structure for people to live in.

The Board, as well as the architect for the applicant, concede that this structure would be a very interesting home placed in a different environment. It is obvious that placed on North Park Boulevard, it would not only be out of keeping with and a radical departure from the structures now standing but would be most detrimental to the further development of the area since there are two vacant lots immediately to the west and a third vacant lot on the street bordering the westernmost lot.

Esthetics was a consideration that played a part in the ruling of the Board, but there were many other factors that influenced its decision. The structure designed is a single-story home in a multi-story neighborhood; it does not conform to general character of other houses; it would affect adjacent homes and three vacant lots; it is of such a radical concept that any design not conforming to the general character of the neighborhood would have to be thereafter approved; when viewed from the street, it could indicate a commercial building; it does not conform to standards of the neighborhood; it does not preserve high character of neighborhood; it does not preserve property values; it would be detrimental to neighborhood on the lot where proposed and it would be detrimental to the future development of the neighborhood.

16 C.J.S. Constitutional Law §195, Esthetic Conditions, p. 939, states:

> The concept of the public welfare is broad and inclusive. The values it represents are spiritual as well as physical, esthetic as well as monetary. It is within the power of the legislature to determine that the community should be beautiful as well as healthy, spacious as well as clean, well-balanced as well as carefully patrolled. Nevertheless, it is held that esthetic conditions alone are insufficient to support the invocation of the police power, although if a regulation finds a reasonable justification in serving a generally recognized ground for the exercise of that power, the fact that esthetic considerations play a part in its adoption does not affect its validity.

It is our determination and we hold that the record in this case discloses ample evidence to support the judgment of the trial court that the Board did not abuse its discretion in its decision in this matter.

We conclude, therefore, that no error prejudicial to the substantial rights of the applicant intervened in the trial of this cause and, consequently, overrule applicant's assignments of error and affirm the judgment.

Judgment affirmed.

SILBERT, J., concurs.

CORRIGAN, J. (dissenting). . . .

In this dissent it is deemed necessary merely to consider appellant's first assignment of error, namely that the Board's denial of a permit was contrary to law in that it was based exclusively on an aesthetic consideration. That the Board's determination was based entirely on such a consideration is, to this member of the court, conclusively established by the record before us. Take for example these questions and answers in connection with the interrogation of the witness, Russell Ralph Peck, a registered architect, who is a member of the

Board of Architectural Review, at the trial in the Common Pleas Court. It should be remembered that it was stipulated by counsel for both parties that, if the other two members of the Board of Architectural Review would have testified, their testimony would be the same as the testimony of Mr. Peck. It is to be remembered also that both of these other members are likewise registered architects.

. . . Q. Now the Board never took the position that this house would hurt property values along North Park Boulevard, did it?

A. Our issue was the fact that it was a single story house in a multi-story neighborhood. . . .

Q. In other words, you were concerned . . .

A. . . . *and it did not conform to the aesthetics of the neighborhood.* (Emphasis added.)

Q. Your objection was grounded upon the appearance of this house and not upon any market value depreciation possibility?

A. There is no question that the house would be in a class cost-wise with those in the neighborhood. . . .

Q. The application for the permit was denied solely on the ground that the house did not conform to the character of the other houses along North Park Boulevard; is that correct?

A. Yes.

Q. And the application wasn't denied because of any purported or existing violation of technical requirements of the building code?

A. Oh, no. . . .

Q. At the meeting of January 2nd and February 6th, was there any evidence before the Board that this house, if built, would threaten, endanger or impair the public health or public safety?

A. No.

Q. Any evidence before the Board that if that house were built it would adversely affect the public welfare, Mr. Peck?

A. It might affect public opinion.

Q. Might affect public opinion?

A. Yes, but not welfare.

Q. But not welfare?

A. Yes. . . .

One of the sixteen stipulations entered into between the parties in the trial court was to the effect that neither the Zoning Code nor the Building Code of the Codified Ordinances of the City of Cleveland Heights establishes a minimum height in terms of stories or of feet to which residences must conform.

Another stipulation between the parties was that Architect Kelly's design for the appellant's proposed home satisfies the Cleveland Heights Zoning and Building Code requirements as to size, height, mass and setback.

Further, it was stipulated that most residences in the City of Cleveland Heights were built prior to World War II.

Therefore, the question presented under this assignment of error is: does the Board have the right to prohibit a citizen from building a house that does not conform to the other houses in the neighborhood, as Mr. Peck testified, *supra,* or in other words, on aesthetic considerations alone, where the design and plans of such house meet the zoning and building code requirements and will not threaten, endanger or impair the public health, safety or welfare, and will not impair property values in the neighborhood?

This member of the court is of the opinion that the answer is an emphatic negative in the light of the law that is applicable to the situation.

First, to take up the decision of the Board: what answers do *[sic]* the evidence provide as to "the character of the houses in the area," as stated in the Board's decision. North Park Boulevard is an important motor vehicle thoroughfare running generally east and west. On the south side of the boulevard, there is a park area. There are no sidewalks on either side of the boulevard in the block, at least, where appellant's site is located. The homes along North Park Boulevard show examples of Tudor, flat-roofed contemporary or modern, Spanish Colonial, and other types. Some are two and one-half or three storied homes. The plaintiff's lot abuts to the north on the south end of lots on Colchester Road. This latter street on both sides presents a prosaic succession of two family homes, some of brick construction, some of wood, and some of a combination of both, all of two and one-half stories in height. Two lots west of the plaintiff's property and clearly within view from her lot are the modest frame single homes of two stories on both sides of Woodmere Drive. So here in one small area in Cleveland Heights we find a melange of architectural styles and of obviously varying lot sizes and price values. Then the question occurs as to what is the "character of the houses in the area." A fair definition would appear to consider "character" as the sum of qualities or features by which the area is distinguished from others or a sum of traits conferring distinctiveness. But, is there any distinctiveness to this area? It seems to reflect the result observable in any American suburb of the age of Cleveland Heights with localities of residences constituted of a mixture of architectural designs and of varying price values, most of which were obviously constructed at least from twenty-five to forty years ago. This is not the new suburbia, the packaged villages that are becoming the barracks of the new generation.

The residence proposed to be constructed on her lot by appellant does have character, in the opinion of this member of the court, judging from the description of the plans given by the architect and the model of the proposed construction introduced as an exhibit. It does have attributes conferring distinctiveness. It is one story with a flat roof. But there are other one story modern homes on North Park Boulevard with flat roofs. The plans include a wall to be built at the setback line, 106 feet from North Park Boulevard, approximately seven feet high with walls describing irregular courses on the easterly and westerly sides and a wall on north line. If appellant does not wish to be bothered with a view of the "round the clock" vehicular traffic swishing past on North Park Boulevard to and from the marts of trade, she should be permitted this peace. If she wishes to screen out the view of the neighboring mixture of architectural styles and enjoy her trees and garden and other beauties of nature and whatever decoration she introduces within her walls and her home, these should be permitted to her. She feels that the plan submitted calls for a residence of beauty and utility and so does her architect.

It should be borne in mind that there is an important principle of eclecticism in architecture which implies freedom on the part of the architect or client or both to choose among the styles of the past and present that which seems to them most appropriate.

Should the appellant be required to sacrifice her choice of architectural plan for her property under the official municipal juggernaut of conformity in this case? Should her aesthetic sensibilities in connection with her selection of design for her proposed home be stifled because of the apparent belief in this community of the group as a source of creativity? Is she to sublimate herself in this group and suffer the frustration of individual creative aspirations? Is her artistic spirit to be imprisoned by the apparent beneficence of community life in Cleveland Heights? This member of the court thinks not under the record in this case and the pertinent legal principles applicable thereto.

The proposition that the regulatory powers of a municipality cannot be exercised for purely aesthetic reasons unrelated to the requirements of public health, safety or welfare is well settled in Ohio. . . .

Accordingly, the Board's disapproval of the issuance of a permit for aesthetic reasons alone is contrary to law and the claim of error is well taken.

For these reasons, it is my view that the judgment of the Court of Common Pleas should be reversed and the cause remanded with instructions to return the cause to the Board of Architectural Review of Cleveland Heights directing that body to approve the issuance of a building permit to appellant.

NOTES AND QUESTIONS

1. State the objectives (purposes) of the Cleveland Heights ordinance. Now re-examine the Standard State Zoning Enabling Act. Does §3, page 763 *supra*, contain language fitting this case? Make the same comparison between §1 of the standard act and the means chosen by Cleveland Heights to achieve its purposes. On the assumption that the Ohio enabling law parallels the standard act on these issues, is the Cleveland Heights ordinance ultra vires? Compare State ex rel. Stoyanoff v. Berkeley, 458 S.W.2d 305 (Mo. 1970), with Piscitelli v. Township Committee, 103 N.J. Super. 589, 248 A.2d 274 (1968).

2. Do you agree with the Court that the Cleveland Heights ordinance did not confer "unconfined and vagrant" discretion upon the Architectural Board of Review? Compare the zoning ordinance of Bernardsville, New Jersey, which also established a design review committee. The stated purposes of

design review were to enhance borough desirability as a place of employment and residence, to preserve property values, and to promote the general welfare. A citizens' committee was to examine all site and building plans and to make recommendations to the planning board, where power to approve or reject the plans ultimately rested. In reviewing plans, the committee and the board were to use nine enumerated (in some detail) "design standards," including landscape preservation, relation of proposed buildings to environment, design similarity and dissimilarity, open space, circulation, and parking. One of the standards reads in full:

Relation of Proposed Buildings to Environment

Proposed structures shall be related harmoniously to the terrain and to existing buildings in the vicinity that have a visual relationship to the proposed buildings. Such relationship shall be achieved by:

> Architectural design which is harmonious with the character of existing development;
> The use of exterior colors, facade or roof materials or the combination of colors and materials that are harmonious;
> The relationship of design features such as height and mass, building proportions, roof lines, building projections and ornamental features that will create a coordinated and harmonious appearance.

The New Jersey court sustained a facial attack on the ordinance on the grounds that the enumerated standards were so broad and vague as to be incapable of being objectively applied, thereby permitting arbitrary action by the reviewing agencies. Morristown Road Associates v. Mayor of Bernardsville, 163 N.J. Super. 58, 394 A.2d 153 (1978).

> No definitions of the terms "harmonious," "displeasing" or "appropriate" are given in the ordinance. It may be that, regarding architectural design, there are "concepts of congruity held so widely that they are inseparable from the enjoyment and hence the value of property." United Advertising Corp. v. Metuchen, 42 N.J. 1, 5 (1964). However, the standards set forth in the present ordinance are not limited to such concepts. The basic criterion for design review under the ordinance is harmony with existing structures and terrain. This standard does not adequately circumscribe the process of administrative decision nor does it provide an understandable criterion for judicial review. It vests the design review committee, as well as the planning board, with too broad a discretion, and permits determinations based upon whim, caprice or subjective considerations. Harmony of design and appearance is conceptual. A proposal which is considered harmonious and appropriate by one person may be deemed displeasing by another. A standard which permits such evaluations does not meet the test of certainty and definiteness required of zoning regulations. [Id. at 67]

Can harmony of design and appearance be tested by "proper architectural principles," which were said to inform the Cleveland Heights board?

3.   Do you see any difference between a law whose sole expressed goal is to enhance the visual appeal of an area and a law whose goals are partly aesthetic and partly more traditional (e.g., safety)? For example, a community bars all billboards from high-speed roads. It does so partly to preserve the landscape and partly to eliminate distractions for the passing motorist. Do you see any objection to this safety-aesthetic measure? Compare New York State Thruway Auth. v. Ashley Motor Court, Inc., 10 N.Y.2d 151, 176 N.E.2d 566, 218 N.Y.S.2d 640 (1961) (bar against advertising signs within 660 feet of the Thomas E. Dewey Thruway upheld) with Metromedia, Inc. v. City of San Diego, 101 S. Ct. 2882 (1981) (ban on only *commercial* advertising signs held unconstitutional).

As a rule, courts have approved laws having a second, nonaesthetic purpose, and—so as not to approve solely on aesthetic grounds—have often stretched to find that second nonaesthetic purpose. Thus, courts have upheld antibillboard ordinances not only because billboards are unsightly, but also because billboards encourage the accumulation of rubbish, shield immoral practices, and attract loiterers and criminals. See, e.g., Thomas Cusack Co. v. City of Chicago, 242 U.S. 526 (1917); United Advertising Corp. v. Borough of Raritan, 11 N.J. 144, 93 A.2d 362 (1952). An extreme example appears below:

> [B]illboards . . . endanger the public health, promote immorality, constitute hiding places and retreats for criminals and all classes of miscreants. They are also inartistic and unsightly. In cases of fire they often cause their spread and constitute barriers against their extinction; and in cases of high wind, their temporary character, frail structure and broad surface, render them liable to be blown down and to fall upon and injure those who may happen to be in their vicinity. The evidence shows and common observation teaches us that the ground in the rear thereof is being constantly used as privies and dumping ground for all kinds of waste and deleterious matters, and thereby creating public nuisances and jeopardizing public health; the evidence also shows that behind these obstructions the lowest form of prostitution and other acts of immorality are frequently carried on, almost under public gaze; they offer shelter and concealment for the criminal while lying in wait for his victim; and last, but not least, they obstruct the light, sunshine, and air, which are so conducive to health and comfort. [St. Louis Gunning Advertising Co. v. St. Louis, 235 Mo. 99, 145, 137 S.W. 929, 942 (1911), *app. dismissed,* 231 U.S. 761 (1913)]

4.   The City of Rye, New York, passed an ordinance barring property owners from hanging clothes in the front yard. Concededly, the city directed the law against Stover, a disgruntled resident who had filled his front yard clotheslines with old clothes, scarecrows, and rags as a "peaceful protest" against high property taxes. When Stover refused to obey the new law, the city prosecuted him, and Stover's challenge—on due process and free speech grounds—reached the New York Court of Appeals. People v. Stover, 12 N.Y.2d 462, 191 N.E.2d 272, 240 N.Y.S.2d 734 (1963).

Faced with earlier decisions in New York and elsewhere that aesthetic considerations alone did not justify exercise of the police power, the city of Rye argued that the ordinance would reduce distractions and improve visibility, thereby avoiding accidents, and would also give better access in the event of fires. The court, however, doubted that the city could show a reasonable relationship between the *stated* objectives and the ban on front yard clotheslines. Instead, the court held that aesthetics was a valid subject of legislative concern and that reasonable regulation to achieve that end came validly within the police power. The Rye ordinance was such a reasonable regulation. [1]

Yet, despite the court's open support of aesthetic control, a close reading of the opinion leaves one uncertain as to the standard by which reasonableness should be tested. As to the Rye ordinance, the court holds that the city has acted reasonably because:

(a)   The law proscribes conduct which offends the sensibilities *and* tends to depress property values.

But the opinion also refers to, without quite embracing, two other less demanding standards, to wit:

(b)   The law proscribes conduct which unnecessarily offends the visual sensibilities of the average man.

(c)   The law helps to achieve an attractive, efficiently functioning, prosperous community.

Would you agree that conduct exists that offends the visual sensibilities of the average man? Does the hanging out of dirty clothes do so? Of clean clothes? Can you give some (other) examples? If it is settled that certain conduct offends the senses of *hearing* and *smell* and may be validly regulated, why does the visual sense seem a more elusive area for protection? Should a law that is patently aesthetic also be required to satisfy an objective criterion—for example, the proscribed conduct tends to depress property values? Examine again the Cleveland Heights ordinance for its statement of purposes: in turning down a proposal, must the board show that, if built, the structure would impair property value?

5.   The third test above first appeared in a seminal article by J. J. Dukeminier, Zoning for Aesthetic Objectives: A Reappraisal, 20 Law and Contemp. Prob. 218, 231 (1955):

---

1. Dr. Webster Stover, 61-year-old former president of Arnold College, went to jail today in the latest chapter of his long-standing feud with authorities here.

He had spent the last few days in a Manhattan hotel room "working on my income taxes, due today" while Westchester County deputy sheriffs had sought him since Friday. . . . He chose to surrender today to serve the 19 remaining days (of a 30 day sentence), rather than pay a $100 fine.

His wife, Marion, 62 years old, paraded in front of their big red brick colonial house today carrying picket signs protesting taxes in Rye and her husband's arrest.

"False arrest in Rye" one sign read. "I put up the clotheslines to protest three illegal tax increases but Rye sends my husband to jail."

"Let them try to find a law against this," the slim gray-haired woman snapped. "I'll march with these signs every day my husband is in jail." [N.Y. Times, Jan. 16, 1964, at 46, col. 2]

Our communities need to achieve an environment that is emotionally satisfactory, that effects a reduction in purposeless nervous and physical tensions of the inhabitants. When the inner life of an individual is out of balance, anxiety occurs, expressing itself in a number of socially destructive ways. Architecture, indeed every object in the individual's aesthetic continuum, has a direct effect upon the equilibrium of his personality and upon the happiness and richness of his life. Community officials need to become more aware of the significance design holds for each individual and thus for society.

Zoning restrictions which implement a policy of neighborhood amenity should be voided, if at all, not because they are for aesthetic objectives, but only because the restrictions are unreasonable devices of implementing community policy. Whether an ordinance of this type should be declared invalid should depend upon whether in the particular institutional context the restriction was an arbitrary and irrational method of achieving an attractive, efficiently functioning, prosperous community—and *not* upon whether the objectives were primarily aesthetic.

Are these views irreconcilable with those that opened this section, page 810 *supra?*

6. "The concept of the public welfare is broad and inclusive. . . . The values it represents are spiritual as well as physical, aesthetic as well as monetary. It is within the power of the legislature to determine that the community should be beautiful as well as healthy, spacious as well as clean, well-balanced as well as carefully patrolled. . . . If those who govern the District of Columbia decide that the Nation's Capital should be beautiful as well as sanitary, there is nothing in the Fifth Amendment that stands in the way." Berman v. Parker, 348 U.S. 26, 33 (1954) (quoted in Reid v. Architectural Bd. of Rev., *supra,* page 811).

This frank approval of aesthetic values appears in an opinion of Justice Douglas's upholding the use of eminent domain to acquire land in an urban renewal project. Should it be any easier constitutionally to achieve purely aesthetic goals by eminent domain, which implies paying for them, than by regulation, which implies getting them for free? To put this question in context: the community condemns two narrow strips of land along the sides of a highway, which it plants with shade trees. If the community is ready to pay for the land (and the trees), the action is valid if it meets the public purpose or welfare test. Berman v. Parker makes clear that the test is met. Alternatively, the community forbids any improvements along the narrow strips, which remain in private ownership, and requires each owner to plant and maintain shade trees, which the community will supply. Is it as clear that this action will (should) be validated? Suppose that the property owners must supply their own saplings? Do these questions suggest a substantive difference between the concept of "general welfare," which validates regulation, and the concept of "public purpose," which validates eminent domain?

7. Might there not be one other consideration that we and courts should keep in sight—the economic burden of the aesthetic regulations? The

opinion in People v. Stover, Note 4 *supra,* alludes to this passingly when it remarks that the Rye ordinance causes no undue hardship to any property owner. Would this not be generally true also of architectural review in cases where the landowner wants to put up a house that costs no less to build than do the more traditional homes of his neighbors? Cf. Reid v. Architectural Board of Review, *supra.* If the regulation seemed of dubious validity, could the community condemn a development easement, acquiring the landowner's privilege of building a house not approved by the architectural board? How would a court value this development easement?

On the other hand, suppose that architectural review forces landowners to build more expensively then they might otherwise choose. Does this weaken the case for valid regulation?

8.   Aren't there also some noneconomic considerations affecting the rights of the regulated owner? We might refer to these generically as freedom of expression, autonomy, individuality, privacy. To what extent did the court consider these interests in Reid v. Architectural Board of Review? Shouldn't more have been said about them? Cf. Williams, Subjectivity, Expression, and Privacy: Problems of Aesthetic Regulation, 62 Minn. L. Rev. 1 (1977).

9.   In People v. Stover, Note 4 *supra,* the property owner argued that the laundry display was a protest; therefore, the Rye ordinance infringed his right of free speech. While agreeing that nonverbal protest enjoys constitutional protection, the court, nevertheless, upheld the Rye law. "Speech" that works an injury on property is subject to reasonable regulation, 12 N.Y.2d 462, 469, 191 N.E.2d 272, 276, 240 N.Y.S.2d 734 (1963). The need to meet the First Amendment argument may partly explain why the court coupled the "property value" to the "offensiveness" tests, see Note 11 *infra.* But cf. Williams, Note 8 *supra,* who argues that a "threshold requirement of expressive character seems clearly fatal to the Stovers' claim," since nothing in the nature of a clothesline expresses a "particularized message" of tax protest. Id. at 48-49.

Yet if hanging a clothesline sends no *particular* message, a clothesline laden with scarecrows and rags is nonetheless expressive. So, too, is the way one dresses, or cuts his hair, or—as with *Reid*—designs her home. Shouldn't a public school that imposes a dress code, a public employer that insists upon short hair and close shaves, and a municipality that enacts architectural review all be required to show some compelling governmental interest before the regulation can be upheld?

10.   Cleveland Heights was trying to preserve the character of a middle-aged neighborhood. Architectural review often arises in other, quite different settings. How do the factual differences in the situations below shape analysis of the legal and policy issues that underlie architectural review?

(a) The city council of Columbus, Ohio, creates a historical district known as German Village, in order to restore the charm of the nineteenth-century homes that predominate in the area. No owner in German Village may alter the exterior architectural features of his dwelling without first getting a "certificate of appropriateness" from the German Village Commission.

(b) The village of Scarsdale, New York, requires that all residential subdivisions obtain prior approval from the Village Planning Commission. Before gaining approval, the developer must satisfy the commission as to site design, which includes the placement of houses on lots so as to maximize sight lines, the varying of front elevations so as to avoid monotony, and the retention of trees and other landscaping features so as to preserve a well-settled appearance.

(c) The purchaser of a condominium dwelling agrees not to alter the exterior features of his unit without obtaining the prior approval of an architectural board, chosen by the condominium association.

11. In the light of the foregoing questions, discuss the validity of the following:

(a) A zoning law that bars front-yard fences in a residential district. Cf. Norris v. Bradford, 204 Tenn. 319, 321 S.W.2d 543 (1958) (law invalid).

(b) A zoning law that bars any sign larger than four square feet in a commerical zone. Cf. People v. Goodman, 31 N.Y.2d 262, 290 N.E.2d 139, 338 N.Y.S.2d 97 (1972) (law valid).

(c) A zoning board that refuses to issue a variance for the construction of a twenty-foot-wide residence that the board views as an "aesthetic abomination." De Sena v. Bd. of Zoning Appeals, 45 N.Y.2d 105, 379 N.E.2d 1144, 408 N.Y.S.2d 14 (1978) (action invalid).

(d) A zoning law that requires residential owners to park their recreational vehicles within enclosures. City of Euclid v. Fitzhum, 48 Ohio App. 2d 297, 357 N.E.2d 402 (1976) (law invalid). Cf. also Williams, Subjectivity, Expression, and Privacy: Problems of Aesthetic Regulation, 62 Minn. L. Rev. 1, 49-50 (1977) (decision criticized).

12. As early as 1909, the British embraced the concept of "amenity" as an appropriate planning goal. In that year local authorities were empowered to make a "town planning scheme . . . as respects any land which is in course of development or appears likely to be used for building purposes, with the general object of securing proper sanitary conditions, amenity and convenience in connection with the laying out and use of the land, and of any neighboring lands." 9 Edw. 7, c. 44, §54(1). The term still appears in planning legislation, although it is nowhere defined by statute. The Minister of Local Government and Planning, in attempting to give the phrase further content, describes amenity as "that element in the appearance and layout of town and country which makes for a comfortable and pleasant life rather than a mere existence. It is quality which a well-designed building estate or neighborhood

will have and which streets of solid but uninspired 'bye-law' housing conspicuously lack." Minister of Local Government & Planning, Town and Country Planning, 1943-1951, Cmd. No. 8204 at 139 (1951). ("Bye-law" housing was built principally for the working classes under a succession of laws dating from 1890.)

The *Reid* case and the material that followed dealt tangentially with the tension between aesthetic regulation and First Amendment values. That conflict becomes sharper when the First Amendment claim involves verbal expression, rather than nonverbal. The next case reviews a sign regulation, a fairly common "aesthetic" control.

STATE v. MILLER
83 N.J. 402, 416 A.2d 821 (1980)

CLIFFORD, J. This case questions the extent to which a municipality may constitutionally regulate signs in a residential neighborhood.

In August, 1976 defendant, Donald L. Miller, placed a four by eight foot sign on the lawn in front of his home, located in a residentially zoned district of the Borough of Milltown. The sign contained the following message:

WELCOME!!

PROSPECTIVE RESIDENTS OF

LAWRENCE BROOK GLEN

THIS RESIDENT AND OTHERS

OF RIVA AVE.

WANT TO WELCOME YOU TO THIS

FLOOD HAZARD AREA.

GOOD LUCK!!

INFORMATION AVAILABLE.

Defendant was charged with violating section 20-9.1(a) of the Borough of Milltown's zoning ordinance, which permitted only the following types of signs in residential zones:

1. A decorative sign showing name or address of house or family, no larger than two square feet in area.
2. Signs advertising the prospective sale or rental of the premises upon which it is maintained, or signs identifying firms working at a site

(one sign per firm), or indicating the future use of the site. Sale or rental signs shall be removed within one month after the new construction has been occupied. Maximum sign area per sign in square feet shall not exceed 15 percent of the frontage of the lot along the street [which the] sign is to be located[,] measured in feet.

3. A sign erected by the borough, county, state or federal government.
4. Identification signs for and signs announcing events of churches, schools, playgrounds, parks and public utility installations. Total area of signs shall not exceed 25 feet in area on each lot.

Subsection 20-9.1(d)(4), which applies to signs in business and industrial zones as well as in residential zones, states that "[a]ll signs with an area exceeding six square feet shall require a permit." The complaint filed by the building inspector charged defendant with erecting a sign exceeding six square feet in a residential zone without first obtaining a permit. The Borough stipulated that a permit would have been denied because the sign did not fall within any of the categories set out in Section 20-9.1(a) above.

Defendant was convicted in municipal court and again after a trial de novo in the Middlesex County Court. The Appellate Division reversed, holding that the municipal ordinance violated the first amendment by absolutely prohibiting "political and public interest expression" and was unconstitutional as applied to this defendant's sign. 162 N.J. Super. 333, 339, 392 A.2d 1222 (1978). The Borough appealed as of right under R. 2:2-1(a)(1). We now affirm.

I

The goals of the Borough sign ordinance here are the maintenance of aesthetic charm in the residential neighborhoods and the preservation of property values. [2] The Borough pursues these goals under the zoning component of the police power to promote the general health, safety and welfare of the community.

Under early case law in this state, such goals would have been improper as beyond legitimate municipal powers. [Citations omitted.] The general rule was enunciated by the Court of Errors and Appeals in 1905: "Aesthetic considerations are a matter of luxury and indulgence rather than of necessity, and it is necessity alone which justifies the exercise of the police power to take private property without compensation." Passaic v. Paterson Bill Posting Co., 72 N.J.L. 285, 287, 62 A. 267, 268 (municipal ordinance regulating size and location of signs held invalid).

More recently, however, our courts have acknowledged the value and

---

2. Defendant does not question the statutory authority of the municipality to regulate signs. Such authority is found when N.J.S.A. 40:55D-62(a) is read with N.J.S.A. 40:55D-65(a). Cf. United Advertising Corp. v. Borough of Raritan, 11 N.J. 144, 93 A.2d 362 (1952) (municipalities have right to legislate on subject of billboards).

importance of aesthetic concerns in municipal land use law. . . . [Citations omitted.] Consideration of aesthetics in municipal land use and planning is no longer a matter of luxury or indulgence. To the extent that our earlier cases may hold to the contrary, they no longer represent sound zoning law. The development and preservation of natural resources and clean, salubrious neighborhoods contribute to psychological and emotional stability and well-being as well as stimulate a sense of civic pride.[3] We therefore hold that a zoning ordinance may accommodate aesthetic concerns. As has been recognized by the United States Supreme Court, consideration of aesthetics may be a legitimate pursuit of the police power of a state:

> The concept of the public welfare is broad and inclusive. . . . The values it represents are spiritual as well as physical, aesthetic as well as monetary. It is within the power of the legislature to determine that the community should be beautiful as well as healthy, spacious as well as clean, well-balanced as well as carefully patrolled. [Berman v. Parker, 348 U.S. 26, 33, 75 S. Ct. 98, 102, 99 L. Ed. 27, 38 (1954) (citations omitted)]

Accordingly, we have recently recognized that the preservation of family-style living, the " 'blessings of quiet seclusion' " and " 'refreshment of repose and tranquility of solitude' " are legitimate zoning goals. State v. Baker, 81 N.J. 99, 106, 405 A.2d 368 (1979) (quoting Berger v. State, 71 N.J. 206, 223, 364 A.2d 993 (1976)).

Concern with aesthetics has been a subject of legislative activity as well. Among the purposes of Municipal Land Use Law, N.J.S.A. 40:55D-1 to -92, are the provision of "adequate light, air, and open space", N.J.S.A. 40:55D-2(c), and the promotion of "a desirable visual environment through creative development techniques and good civic design and arrangements", N.J.S.A. 40:55D-2(i). See Home Builders League v. Township of Berlin, 81 N.J. 127, 145, 405 A.2d 381 (1979). The conversation of property values is subsumed within the purposes of the Law, N.J.S.A. 40:55D-2(a), (e) and (i). Home Builders League v. Township of Berlin, *supra*, 81 N.J. at 145, 405 A.2d 381. Indeed, at least one state court has noted that considerations of aesthetics and economics are intimately related in this context, Metromedia, Inc. v. San Diego, 592 P.2d 728, 735, 154 Cal. Rptr., 212, 219 (1979), and that "[t]o hold that a city cannot prohibit off-site commercial billboards for the purpose of

---

3. Over a century ago Henry David Thoreau gave voice to an aspect of this notion:

Shall that dirty roll of bunting in the gunhouse be all the colors a village can display? A village is not complete, unless it have [these] trees to mark the season in it. They are important, like the town clock. A village that has them not will not be found to work well. It has a screw loose, an essential part is wanting. . . . Of course, there is not a picture-gallery in the country which would be worth so much to us as is the western view at sunset under the elms of our main street. . . .

A village needs these innocent stimulants of bright and cheering prospects to keep off melancholy and superstition. [Thoreau, "Autumnal Tints" (Atlantic Monthly, October 1862)]

protecting and preserving the beauty of the environment is to succumb to a bleak materialism." Id. at 748, 592 P.2d at 748, 154 Cal. Rptr. at 232. The California court went on to quote Ogden Nash:

> I think that I shall never see
> A billboard lovely as a tree.
> Indeed, unless the billboards fall,
> I'll never see a tree at all. [Id.]

However, the injection of aesthetic considerations and values into the zoning law process is not without problems. See generally Williams, "Subjectivity, Expression, and Privacy: Problems of Aesthetic Regulation," 62 Minn. L. Rev. 1 (1977). Nor is the power to zone based on aesthetics a limitless one. Cf. Home Builders League v. Berlin Twp., *supra,* (minimum floor area requirements unrelated to legitimate zoning purposes); State v. Baker, *supra* (zoning regulation limiting residency based on number of unrelated persons in single housekeeping unit unconstitutional). The case before us now is a fine illustration of the problems in and the limits to aesthetic zoning, particularly when it conflicts with beauty of a different sort—free speech.

II

The only signs allowed in the residential zones here are those expressly set forth in Section 20-9.1(a) of the Borough's ordinance, i.e., (1) decorative name and address plates; (2) "for sale" or "for rent" signs, signs indicating future use, and signs identifying firms doing work on the premises; (3) signs maintained by the local, state or federal government; and (4) identification signs for churches, schools, playgrounds, parks, and public utility installations. Although the defendant was cited for erecting a sign exceeding six square feet without first obtaining a permit, in violation of Section 20-9.1(d)(4), it is apparent that the sign violated the provisions of Section 20-9.1(a) irrespective of its size.

So construed, and as conceded before us by the Borough, the ordinance precludes a residential property owner from communicating any other than an extremely limited message by the use of stationary signs on his or her property. In particular, the ordinance's restrictions on the manner and place of defendant's speech, so severe as to amount to an absolute ban on political speech, offend the First Amendment.

The message on the defendant's sign concerned a matter of public interest. As such, it is political speech and occupies a preferred position in our system of constitutionally-protected interests. Murdock v. Pennsylvania, 319 U.S. 105, 115, 63 S. Ct. 870, 876, 87 L. Ed 1292, 1300 (1943). As the Appellate Division here correctly noted: "Political expression obviously includes any fair comment on any matter of public interest, whether or not the subject of an election campaign, whether or not embarrassing to the local governing body, and whether or not irritating to one's neighbors." 162 N.J. Super. at 338, 392 A.2d at 1225.[5] Where political speech is involved, our tradition insists that government "allow the widest room for discussion, the narrowest range for its restriction." Thomas v. Collins, 323 U.S. 516, 530, 65 S. Ct. 315, 323, 89 L. Ed. 430, 440 (1945). As a result a regulation restricting the time, place or manner of speech will survive constitutional scrutiny only if it (1) can be justified without reference to the content of the regulated speech; (2) serves a significant government interest; and (3) leaves open ample alternative channels for the communication of the information. See, e.g., Virginia State Bd. of Pharmacy v. Virginia Citizens Consumer Council, Inc., 425 U.S. 748, 771, 96 S. Ct. 1817, 1830, 48 L. Ed. 2d 346, 363-64 (1976). The governmental interest to be protected must be balanced against the effect of the restriction on protected activities. See, e.g., Schneider v. New Jersey, 308 U.S. 147, 60 S. Ct. 146, 84 L. Ed. 155 (1939). In such situations

> the courts should be astute to examine the effect of the challenged legislation. Mere legislative preferences or beliefs respecting matters of public convenience may well support regulation directed at other personal activities, but be insufficient to justify such as diminishes the exercise of rights so vital to the maintenance of democratic institutions. [Id. at 161, 60 S. Ct. at 151, 84 L. Ed. at 165]

During the last ten years many states have enacted statutes regulating and even banning signs and billboards as part of zoning laws designed to further aesthetics, preserve property values and promote traffic safety. See, e.g., Markam Advertising Co. v. State, 73 Wash. 2d 405, 439 P.2d 248 (1968) (Washington State Highway Advertising Control Act of 1961) (cited with approval in Young v. American Mini Theaters, 427 U.S. 50, 96 S. Ct. 2440, 49 L. Ed. 2d 310, reh. den., 429 U.S. 873, 97 S. Ct. 191, 50 L. Ed. 2d 155 (1976)). The constitutionality of such statutes has generally been sustained where political speech is exempted from the ban. [Citations omitted.] However, ordinances which exclude political signs from residential districts have uniformly been held unconstitutional. Baldwin v. Redwood City, 540 F.2d 1360 (9th Cir. 1976), cert. den., sub nom. Leipzig v. Baldwin, 431 U.S. 913, 97 S. Ct. 2173, 53 L. Ed. 2d 223 (1977); Ross v. Goshi, 351 F. Supp. 949 (D. Haw. 1972); Peltz v. South Euclid, 11 Ohio St. 2d 128, 228 N.E.2d 320 (1967).

---

5. Political speech may be distinguished from commercial speech, defined by the United States Supreme Court as follows:

Our pharmacist does not wish to editorialize on any subject, cultural, philosophical, or political. He does not wish to report any particularly newsworthy fact, or to make generalized observations even about commercial matters. The "idea" he wishes to communicate is simply this: "I will sell you the X prescription drug at the Y price." [Virginia State Bd. of Pharmacy v. Virginia Citizens Consumer Council, Inc., 425 U.S. 748, 761, 96 S. Ct. 1817, 1825, 48 L. Ed. 2d 346, 358 (1976)] Although commercial speech is protected under the First Amendment, there is a "commonsense" distinction between speech proposing a commercial transaction and other varieties of speech, including political speech, and thus the constitutional protection accorded to commercial speech is less than is provided to other constitutionally guaranteed expression. Central Hudson Gas & Electric Corp. v. New York Public Service Commission,—U.S.—, 100 S. Ct. 2343, 65 L. Ed. 2d 341 (1980).

The constitutionality of the ordinance here cannot be sustained. Significant First Amendment interests are at stake. Adequate alternative means of political communication are not available to owners who are precluded from putting signs and posters in their yards.

> [M]eans of political communication are not entirely fungible; political posters have unique advantages. Their use may be localized to a degree that radio and newspaper advertising may not. With exception of handbills, they are the least expensive means by which a candidate may achieve name recognition among voters in a local election. [Baldwin v. Redwood City, *supra*, 540 F.2d at 1368 (footnote omitted)]

As defendant points out, the most effective and least expensive way to reach his intended audience—prospective Riva Avenue home purchasers and his neighbors—was to place a sign in front of his house. While personal contact with neighbors might have been an alternative means of communication, even that would not be a realistic alternative for reaching prospective purchasers of homes in the affected area.

III

Because the ordinance so directly cuts to the heart of the First Amendment, we decline to perform judicial surgery or to adopt a narrow construction in an effort to save it. The ordinance is unconstitutional on its face. However, for the benefit of municipalities concerned with the impact of community aesthetics on zoning, we offer for guidance the following comments on the permissible scope of sign regulation.

As noted below, some regulation of signs in municipalities may be permissible if within constitutional limits. The United States Supreme Court has recognized that "[p]reserving the sanctity of the home, the one retreat to which men and women can repair to escape from tribulations of their daily pursuits, is surely an important value." Carey v. Brown,—U.S.—,—, 100 S. Ct. 2286, 2295, 65 L. Ed. 2d 263,—, (1980).

To withstand the strict constitutional scrutiny required here, the restriction on signs must be tied to a compelling municipal interest as well as to the uses permitted in a given zone. Schoen v. Hillside, 155 N.J. Super. 296, 297, 382 A.2d 704. This is illustrated in a different context by Taxpayers Assoc. v. Weymouth Twp., 80 N.J. 6, 364 A.2d 1016 (1976), *appeal dismissed; cert. den., sub nom.* Feldman v. Weymouth, 430 U.S. 977, 97 S. Ct. 1672, 52 L. Ed. 2d 373 (1977), where this Court upheld zoning of a mobile home park exclusively for the elderly. In that case Justice Pashman, writing for the Court, held that ordinances adopted under the zoning enabling act "must bear a real and substantial relationship to the regulation of land within the municipality." 80 N.J. at 21, 364 A.2d at 1024. While recognizing the municipality's desire to satisfy the social and psychological needs of the elderly, id. at 28-31, 364 A.2d

1016, we required the municipality to articulate tangible, specific objectives promoted by the zoning measure—there the unusual physical and economic needs of the elderly. Id. at 31, 364 A.2d 1016. We then carefully examine the factual bases of the municipality's conclusion that reserving mobile homes for the elderly in fact served those specific ends. Id. at 33-37, 364 A.2d 1016. See generally "Developments—Zoning", 91 Harv. L. Rev. 1427, 1456-57 (1978).

As we have announced herein, preservation of aesthetics and property values is a legitimate end for a municipal zoning ordinance. However, to satisfy the analysis called for by *Weymouth Twp.*, described above, the municipality must demonstrate more than a mere desire to preserve property values. It must show that the particular restrictions on signs in fact relate to the stated goal.

In keeping with this analysis a municipality may distinguish between commercial and political speech in imposing restrictions on signs. See Lehman v. Shaker Heights, 418 U.S. 298, 94 S. Ct. 2714, 41 L. Ed. 2d 770 (1974); Railway Express Agency, Inc. v. New York, 336 U.S. 106, 69 S. Ct. 463, 93 L. Ed. 533 (1949). Certain commercial enterprises may be excluded from residential zones, see, e.g., Pierro v. Baxendale, *supra*, and residents should therefore not be compelled to live with commercial advertisements in the form of signs publicizing those excluded uses. [6] This distinction has been endorsed by the United States Supreme Court in Young v. American Mini Theaters, *supra:*

> We have recently held that the First Amendment affords some protection to commercial speech. We have also made it clear, however, that the content of a particular advertisement may determine the extent of its protection. . . . A state statute may permit highway billboards to advertise businesses located in the neighborhood but not elsewhere . . . The measure of constitutional protection to be afforded commercial speech will surely be governed largely by the content of the communication. [427 U.S. at 68-69, 96 S. Ct. 2440, 49 L. Ed. 2d at 325 (footnotes omitted)]

See also n.5 *supra.*

It should be emphasized, however, that the regulation of sign content must be limited to a general distinction between commercial speech as tied to commercial uses permitted in a given zone, and political speech which is and must be permitted everywhere. Specific types of speech or particular messages may not be prohibited. Consolidated Edison Co. v. New York Public Service Commission,—U.S.—, 100 S. Ct. 2326, 65 L. Ed. 2d 319, (1980). [Citations omitted.] However, they may of course be subjected to reasonable restrictions on their time, place and manner.

Limitations on the size of a sign may be imposed if the allowable square

---

6. Thus, "for sale" signs, although commercial in character, may not be excluded from a residential neighborhood, see Linmark Assoc., Inc. v. Willingboro, 431 U.S. 85, 97 S. Ct. 1614, 52 L. Ed. 2d 155 (1977), inasmuch as they relate to a use permitted in a residential zone. By contrast the commercial signs of contractors working on homes may be excluded in keeping with the analysis described above. State v. J. & J. Painting, *supra.*

footage is not determined in an arbitrary manner. The size limits, if any, must be large enough to permit viewing from the road, both by persons in vehicles and on foot. Inadequate sign dimensions may strongly impair the free flow of protected speech. Schoen v. Hillside, *supra,* 155 N.J. Super. at 298, 382 A.2d 704. In the context of the Milltown Borough ordinance here, the limitation to six square feet imposed in Section 20-9.1(d)(4) is probably inadequate. See Baldwin v. Redwood City, *supra* (16 square foot limitation on signs does not offend First Amendment); Ross v. Goshi, *supra* (18 square foot limitation upheld).

Other restrictions commonly placed on signs include durational limitations, setback restrictions and restrictions on the aggregate number of signs permissible on a given piece of property. See, e.g., Metromedia, Inc. v. San Diego, *supra;* Ross v. Goshi, *supra.* At least one court has held that no duration limitation on the posting of pre-election campaign signs is constitutional. Orazio v. North Hempstead, 426 F. Supp. 1144 (E.D.N.Y. 1977). We are not faced with such restrictions today and specifically decline to determine their constitutionality, emphasizing only that restrictions upon the time, place and manner of signs must serve a significant government interest and be tied to the uses permitted in that zone.

Affirmed.

NOTES AND QUESTIONS

1. "Although commercial speech is protected under the First Amendment, there is a 'commonsense' distinction between speech proposing a commercial transaction and other varieties of speech, including political speech, and thus the constitutional protection accorded to commercial speech is less than is provided to other constitutionally guaranteed expression." State v. Miller, *supra,* footnote 5.

How clear is the "commonsense" distinction between commercial and other varieties of speech? Consider the view of Justice Brennan (shared by Justice Blackmun) as it appears in his concurring opinion in Metromedia, Inc. v. City of San Diego, 101 S. Ct. 2882, 2907 (1981):

> . . . Of course the plurality is correct when it observes that "our cases have consistently distinguished between the constitutional protection afforded commercial as opposed to noncommercial speech," *ante,* at 2891, but it errs in assuming that a *governmental unit* may be put in the position in the first instance of deciding whether the proposed speech is commercial or noncommercial. In individual cases, this distinction is anything but clear. Because making such determinations would entail a substantial exercise of discretion by city's officials, it presents a real danger of curtailing noncommercial speech in the guise of regulating commercial speech. . . .
>
> It is one thing for a court to classify in specific cases whether commercial or noncommercial speech is involved, but quite another—and for me disposi-

tively so—for a city to do so regularly for the purpose of deciding what messages may be communicated by way of billboards. Cities are equipped to make traditional police power decisions, see Saia v. New York, *supra,* 334 U.S., at 564, 565, 68 S. Ct., at 1151-1152 (Frankfurter, J., dissenting), not decisions based on the content of speech. I would be unhappy to see city officials dealing with the following series of billboards and deciding which ones to permit: the first billboard contains the message "Visit Joe's Ice Cream Shoppe"; the second, "Joe's Ice Cream Shoppe uses only the highest quality dairy products"; the third, "Because Joe thinks that dairy products are good for you, please shop at Joe's Shoppe"; and the fourth, "Joe says to support dairy price supports; they mean lower prices for you at his Shoppe." Or how about some San Diego Padres baseball fans—with no connection to the team—who together rent a billboard and communicate the message "Support the San Diego Padres, a great baseball team." May the city decide that a United Automobile Workers billboard with the message "Be a patriot—do not buy Japanese-manufactured cars" is "commercial" and therefore forbid it? What if the same sign is placed by Chrysler?

2.   Metromedia, Inc. v. City of San Diego, Note 1, *supra,* invalidated a local ordinance barring "outdoor advertising display signs," a measure that the California Supreme Court had previously upheld, 26 Cal. 3d 848, 164 Cal. Rptr. 510, 610 P.2d 407 (1980).

The San Diego regulation provided two kinds of exceptions to the general prohibition: on-site commercial signs, and signs falling within twelve specified categories. The exempted categories included government signs and "temporary political campaign signs."

Plaintiffs, who were engaged in the outdoor advertising business and who owned many outdoor displays, challenged the law on due process, taking, and First Amendment grounds. The city defended the ordinance as being within the legitimate exercise of the regulatory power, specifically, as promoting appearance and traffic safety; the city also denied that a taking had occurred, inasmuch as plaintiffs were allowed a reasonable period to amortize their investments.

Justice White wrote a plurality opinion, which received the support only of Justices Marshall, Powell, and Stewart. The four justices accepted as reasonable the local judgment that billboards are real and substantial hazards to traffic safety and that billboards by their very nature, wherever located and however constructed, can be perceived as an "esthetic harm." But the justices thought this ordinance defective for containing a broad exception for *on-site* commercial advertisements, but lacking a similar exception for noncommercial speech.

> As indicated above, our recent commercial speech cases have consistently accorded noncommerical speech a greater degree of protection than commercial speech. San Diego effectively inverts this judgment, by affording a greater degree of protection to commercial than to noncommercial speech. [101 S. Ct. at 2895]

Justices Brennan and Blackmun helped to form a six-justice majority against the ordinance. However, they rejected the plurality distinction between commercial and noncommercial speech in favor of extending equally strong constitutional protection to both modes.

> In the case of billboards, I would hold that a city may totally ban them if it can show that a sufficiently substantial governmental interest is directly furthered by the total ban, and that any more narrowly drawn restriction, i.e., anything less than a total ban, would promote less well the achievement of that goal. Applying that test to the instant case, I would invalidate the San Diego ordinance. [Id. at 2903]

The concurring justices then explained that the city had failed to demonstrate (a) that billboards actually impaired traffic safety or (b) that its asserted interest in aesthetics was sufficiently substantial in commercial and industrial areas.

> A billboard is not *necessarily* inconsistent with oil storage tanks, blighted areas, or strip development. Of course, it is not for a court to impose its own notion of beauty on San Diego. But before deferring to a city's judgment, a court must be convinced that the city is seriously and comprehensively addressing aesthetic concerns with respect to its environment. Here, San Diego has failed to demonstrate a comprehensive coordinated effort in its commercial and industrial areas to address other obvious contributors to an unattractive environment. In this sense the ordinance is underinclusive. See Erznoznik v. City of Jacksonville, 422 U.S. 205, 214, 95 S. Ct. 2268, 2275, 45 L. Ed. 2d 125 (1975). Of course, this is not to say that the city must address all aesthetic problems at the same time, or none at all. Indeed, from a planning point of view, attacking the problem incrementally and sequentially may represent the most sensible solution. On the other hand, if billboards alone are banned and no further steps are contemplated or likely, the commitment of the city to improving its physical environment is placed in doubt. By showing a comprehensive commitment to making its physical environment in commercial and industrial areas more attractive, and by allowing only narrowly tailored exceptions, if any, San Diego could demonstrate that its interest in creating an aesthetically pleasing environment is genuine and substantial. This is a requirement where, as here, there is an infringement of important constitutional consequence.

In his dissenting opinion, Justice Stevens reasoned that a city might impose a total ban on billboards.

> I believe a community has the right to decide that its interests in protecting property from damaging trespasses and in securing beautiful surroundings outweigh the countervailing interest in uninhibited expression by means of words and pictures in public places. If the First Amendment categorically protected the marketplace of ideas from any quantitative restraint, a municipality could not outlaw graffiti. . . . [Id. at 2914]

Having accepted in principal a total ban, Justice Stevens is unpersuaded that the exceptions in the San Diego ordinance "present any additional threat to the interests protected by the First Amendment."

Without indicating whether he, too, would approve a total ban, Chief Justice Burger castigates the plurality for upsetting the city's effort to minimize traffic hazards and eyesores "simply because, in exercising rational legislative judgment, it has chosen to permit a narrow class of signs that serve special needs." Id. at 2917.

Finally, Justice Rehnquist would allow a total prohibition of billboards within a community on "aesthetic justification alone." Moreover, unlike Justice Brennan, he would not require a city to convince a local judge "that the elimination of billboards would have more than a negligible impact on aesthetics." Id. at 2925.

With which of these views, if any, do you associate?

§16.3   Restrictions Against "Adult" Uses

SCHAD v. BOROUGH OF MOUNT EPHRAIM
101 S. Ct. 2176 (1981)

JUSTICE WHITE delivered the opinion of the Court. In 1973, appellants began operating an adult bookstore in the commercial zone in the Borough of Mount Ephraim in Camden County, N.J. The store sold adult books, magazines and films. Amusement licenses shortly issued, permitting the store to install coin-operated devices by virtue of which a customer could sit in a booth, insert a coin and watch an adult film. In 1976, the store introduced an additional coin-operated mechanism permitting the customer to watch a live dancer, usually nude, performing behind a glass panel. Complaints were soon filed against appellants charging that the bookstore's exhibition of live dancing violated §99-15B of Mount Ephraim's zoning ordinance, which described the permitted uses in a commercial zone, in which the store was located, as follows:

B. Principal permitted uses on the land and in buildings.

(1)   Offices and banks; taverns; restaurants and luncheonettes for sit-down dinners only and with no drive-in facilities; automobile sales; retail stores, such as but not limited to food, wearing apparel, millinery, fabrics, hardware, lumber, jewelry, paint, wallpaper, appliances, flowers, gifts, books, stationery, pharmacy, liquors, cleaners, novelties, hobbies and toys; repair shops for shoes, jewels, clothes and appliances; barbershops and beauty salons; cleaners and laundries; pet stores; and nurseries. Offices may, in addition, be permitted to a group of four (4) stores or more without additional parking, provided the offices

do not exceed the equivalent of twenty percent (20%) of the gross floor area of the stores.

    (2) Motels.

Section 99-4 of the Borough's code provided that "[a]ll uses not expressly permitted in this chapter are prohibited."

Appellants were found guilty in the municipal court and fines were imposed. Appeal was taken to the Camden County Court, where a trial de novo was held on the record made in the municipal court and appellants were again found guilty. The County Court first rejected appellants' claim that the ordinance was being selectively and improperly enforced against them because other establishments offering live entertainment were permitted in the commercial zones. Those establishments, the court held, were permitted, nonconforming uses that had existed prior to the passage of the ordinance. In response to appellants' defense based on the First and Fourteenth Amendments, the court recognized that "live nude dancing is protected by the First Amendment" but was of the view that "First Amendment guarantees are not involved" since the case "involves solely a zoning ordinance" under which "[l]ive entertainment is simply not a permitted use in any establishment" whether the entertainment is a nude dance or some other form of live presentation. App. to Juris. Statement 8a, 12a. Reliance was placed on the statement in Young v. American Mini Theatres, Inc., 427 U.S. 50, 62, 96 S. Ct. 2440, 2448, 49 L. Ed. 2d 310 (1976), that "[t]he mere fact that the commercial exploitation of material protected by the First Amendment is subject to zoning and other licensing requirements is not a sufficient reason for invalidating these ordinances." The Appellate Division of the Superior Court of New Jersey affirmed appellants' convictions in a per curiam opinion "essentially for the reasons" given by the County Court. App. to Juris. Statement 14a. The Supreme Court of New Jersey denied further review, 82 N.J. 287, 412 A.2d 793. Id., at 17a, 18a.

Appellants appealed to this Court. Their principal claim is that the imposition of criminal penalties under an ordinance prohibiting all live entertainment, including nonobscene, nude dancing, violated their rights of free expression guaranteed by the First and Fourteenth Amendments of the United States Constitution.[4] We noted probable jurisdiction,—U.S.—, 101 S. Ct. 264, 66 L. Ed. 2d 127 (1980) and now set aside appellants' convictions.

I

As the Mount Ephraim code has been construed by the New Jersey courts—a construction that is binding upon us—"live entertainment," includ-

---

4. Appellants also contend that the zoning ordinance, as applied to them, violates due process and equal protection, since the Borough has acted arbitrarily and irrationally in prohibiting booths in which customers can view live nude dancing while permitting coin-operated movie booths. Since we sustain appellants' First Amendment challenge to the ordinance, we do not address these additional claims.

ing nude dancing, is "not a permitted use in any establishment" in the Borough of Mount Ephraim. App. to Juris. Statement 12a. By excluding live entertainment throughout the Borough, the Mount Ephraim ordinance prohibits a wide range of expression that has long been held to be within the protections of the First and Fourteenth Amendments. Entertainment, as well as political and ideological speech, is protected; motion pictures, programs broadcast by radio and television and live entertainment, such as musical and dramatic works fall within the First Amendment guarantee. [Citations omitted.] Nor may an entertainment program be prohibited solely because it displays the nude human figure. "Nudity alone" does not place otherwise protected material outside the mantle of the First Amendment. [Citations omitted.] Furthermore, as the state courts in this case recognized, nude dancing is not without its First Amendment protections from official regulation. [Citations omitted.] Whatever First Amendment protection should be extended to nude dancing, live or on film, however, the Mount Ephraim ordinance prohibits all live entertainment in the Borough: no property in the Borough may be principally used for the commercial production of plays, concerts, musicals, dance or any other form of live entertainment.[5] Because appellants' claims are rooted in the First Amendment, they are entitled to rely on the impact of the ordinance on the expressive activities of others as well as their own. "Because overbroad laws, like vague ones, deter privileged activities, our cases firmly establish appellant's standing to raise an overbreadth challenge." Grayned v. City of Rockford, 408 U.S. 104, 114, 92 S. Ct. 2294, 2302, 33 L. Ed. 2d 222 (1972).

II

The First Amendment requires that there be sufficient justification for the exclusion of a broad category of protected expression as one of the permitted commercial uses in the Borough. The justification does not appear on the face of the ordinance since the ordinance itself is ambiguous with respect to whether live entertainment is permitted: §99-15B purports to specify only the "principal" permitted uses in commercial establishments, and its listing of permitted retail establishments is expressly nonexclusive; yet, §99-4 declares that all uses not expressly permitted are forbidden. The state courts at least partially resolved the ambiguity by declaring live entertainment to be an impermissible commercial use. In doing so, the County Court, whose opinion was adopted by the Appellate Division of the Superior Court, sought to avoid or to meet the First Amendment issue only by declaring that the restriction on the use of appellants' property was contained in a zoning ordinance that

---

5. The Borough's counsel asserted at oral argument that the ordinance would not prohibit noncommercial live entertainment, such as singing Christmas carols at an office party. Tr. of Oral Arg., at 33. Apparently a high school could perform a play if it did not charge admission. However, the ordinance prohibits the production of plays in commercial theaters. Tr. of Oral Arg., at 34.

excluded all live entertainment from the Borough, including live nude dancing.

The power of local governments to zone and control land use is undoubtedly broad and its proper exercise is an essential aspect of achieving a satisfactory quality of life in both urban and rural communities. But the zoning power is not infinite and unchallengeable; it "must be exercised within constitutional limits." Moore v. City of East Cleveland, 431 U.S. 494, 514, 97 S. Ct. 1932, 1943, 52 L. Ed. 2d 531 (1977) (Stevens, J., concurring). Accordingly, it is subject to judicial review; and is most often the case, the standard of review is determined by the nature of the right assertedly threatened or violated rather than by the power being exercised or the specific limitation imposed. Thomas v. Collins, 323 U.S. 516, 529-530, 65 S. Ct. 315, 322, 89 L. Ed. 430 (1945).

Where property interests are adversely affected by zoning, the courts generally have emphasized the breadth of municipal power to control land use and have sustained the regulation if it is rationally related to legitimate state concerns and does not deprive the owner of economically viable use of his property. Agins v. City of Tiburon, 447 U.S. 255, 260, 100 S. Ct. 2138, 2141, 65 L. Ed. 2d 106 (1980); Village of Belle Terre v. Boraas, 416 U.S. 1, 94 S. Ct. 1536, 39 L. Ed. 2d 797 (1974); Euclid v. Ambler Realty Co., 272 U.S. 365, 395, 47 S. Ct. 114, 121, 71 L. Ed. 303 (1926). But an ordinance may fail even under that limited standard of review. Moore v. City of East Cleveland, 431 U.S. 494, 520, 97 S. Ct. 1932, 1946, 52 L. Ed. 2d 531 (1977) (Stevens, J., concurring); Nectow v. Cambridge, 277 U.S. 183, 48 S. Ct. 447, 72 L. Ed. 842 (1928).

Beyond that, as is true of other ordinances, when a zoning law infringes upon a protected liberty, it must be narrowly drawn and must further a sufficiently substantial government interest. . . . Because the ordinance challenged in this case significantly limits communicative activity within the Borough, we must scrutinize both the interests advanced by the Borough to justify this limitation on protected expression and the means chosen to further those interests.

As an initial matter, this case is not controlled by Young v. American Mini Theatres, Inc., *supra,* the decision relied upon by the Camden County Court. Although the Court there stated that a zoning ordinance is not invalid merely because it regulates activity protected under the First Amendment, it emphasized that the challenged restriction on the location of adult movie theaters imposed a minimal burden on protected speech. 427 U.S., at 62, 96 S. Ct., at 2448. The restriction did not affect the number of adult movie theaters that could operate in the city; it merely dispersed them. The Court did not imply that a municipality could ban all adult theaters—much less all live entertainment or all nude dancing—from its commercial districts citywide. Moreover, it was emphasized in that case that the evidence presented to the Detroit Common Council indicated that the concentration of adult movie theaters in limited areas led to deterioration of surrounding neighborhoods, and it was concluded that the city had justified the incidental burden on First Amendment interests resulting from merely dispersing, but not excluding, adult theaters.

In this case, however, Mount Ephraim has not adequately justified its substantial restriction of protected activity. [12] None of the justifications asserted in this Court was articulated by the state courts and none of them withstands scrutiny. First, the Borough contends that permitting live entertainment would conflict with its plan to create a commercial area that caters only to the "immediate needs" of its residents and that would enable them to purchase at local stores the few items they occasionally forgot to buy outside the Borough. No evidence was introduced below to support this assertion, and it is difficult to reconcile this characterization of the Borough's commercial zones with the provisions of the ordinance. Section 99-15A expressly states that the purpose of creating commercial zones was to provide areas for "local and *regional* commercial operations." (Emphasis added.) The range of permitted uses goes far beyond providing for the "immediate needs" of the residents. Motels, hardware stores, lumber stores, banks, offices, and car showrooms are permitted in commercial zones. The list of permitted "retail stores" is nonexclusive, and it includes such services as beauty salons, barber shops, cleaners, and restaurants. Virtually the only item or service that may not be sold in a commercial zone is entertainment, or at least live entertainment. The Borough's first justification is patently insufficient.

Second, Mount Ephraim contends that it may selectively exclude commercial live entertainment from the broad range of commercial uses permitted in the Borough for reasons normally associated with zoning in commercial districts, that is, to avoid the problems that may be associated with live entertainment, such as parking, trash, police protection, and medical facilities. The Borough has presented no evidence, and it is not immediately apparent as a matter of experience, that live entertainment poses problems of this nature more significant than those associated with various permitted uses; nor does it appear that the Borough's zoning authority has arrived at a defensible conclusion that unusual problems are presented by live entertainment. Cf. Young v. American Mini Theatres, Inc., 427 U.S., at 54-55, and n.6, 96 S. Ct., at 2444, and n.6. [15] We do not find it self-evident that a theater, for example, would

12. If the New Jersey courts had expressly interpreted this ordinance as banning all entertainment, we would reach the same result.

15. Mount Ephraim also speculates that the Borough may have concluded that live nude dancing is undesirable. Brief for Appellee 20. It is noted that in California v. LaRue, 409 U.S. 109, 93 S. Ct. 390, 34 L. Ed. 2d 342 (1972), this Court identified a number of problems that California sought to eliminate by prohibiting certain explicitly sexual entertainment in bars and in nightclubs licensed to serve liquor. This speculation lends no support to the challenged ordinance. First, §99-15B excludes all live entertainment, not just live nude dancing. Even if Mount Ephraim might validly place restrictions on certain forms of live nude dancing under a narrowly drawn ordinance, this would not justify the exclusion of all live entertainment or, insofar as this record reveals, even the nude dancing involved in this case. Second, the regulation challenged in California v. LaRue was adopted only after the Department of Alcoholic Beverage Control had deter-

create greater parking problems than would a restaurant. Even less apparent is what unique problems would be posed by exhibiting live nude dancing in connection with the sale of adult books and films, particularly since the bookstore is licensed to exhibit nude dancing on films. It may be that some forms of live entertainment would create problems that are not associated with the commercial uses presently permitted in Mount Ephraim. Yet this ordinance is not narrowly drawn to respond to what might be the distinctive problems arising from certain types of live entertainment, and it is not clear that a more selective approach would fail to address those unique problems if any there are. The Borough has not established that its interests could not be met by restrictions that are less intrusive on protected forms of expression.

The Borough also suggests that §99-15B is a reasonable "time, place and manner" restriction; yet it does not identify the municipal interests making it reasonable to exclude all commercial live entertainment but to allow a variety of other commercial uses in the Borough.[17] In Grayned v. City of Rockford, 408 U.S. 104, 92 S. Ct. 2294, 33 L. Ed. 2d 222 (1972), we stated:

> The nature of a place, "the pattern of its normal activities, dictate the kinds of regulations of time, place, and manner that are reasonable." . . . The crucial question is whether the manner of expression is basically incompatible with the normal activity of a particular place at a particular time. Our cases made clear that in assessing the reasonableness of a regulation, we must weigh heavily the fact that communication is involved; the regulation must be narrowly tailored to further the State's legitimate interest. 408 U.S., at 116-117, 92 S. Ct., at 2303 (footnotes omitted).

Thus, the initial question in determining the validity of the exclusion as a time, place and manner restriction is whether live entertainment is "basically incompatible with the normal activity [in the commercial zones.]" As discussed above, no evidence has been presented to establish that live entertainment is incompatible with the uses presently permitted by the Borough. Mount Ephraim asserts that it could have chosen to eliminate all commercial uses within its boundaries. Yet we must assess the exclusion of live entertainment in light of the commercial uses Mount Ephraim allows, not in light of what the Borough might have done.[18]

---

mined that significant problems were linked to the activity that was later regulated. Third, in California v. LaRue the Court relied heavily on the State's power under the Twenty-first Amendment. Cf. Doran v. Salem Inn, Inc., 422 U.S. 922, 95 S. Ct. 2561, 45 L. Ed. 2d 648 (1975).

17. Mount Ephraim argued in its brief that nonlive entertainment is an adequate substitute for live entertainment. Brief for Appellees 20-21. This contention was apparently abandoned at oral argument, since the Borough's counsel stated that the ordinance bans all commercial entertainment. At any rate, the argument is an inadequate response to the fact that live entertainment, which the ordinance bans, is protected by the First Amendment.

18. Thus, our decision today does not establish that every unit of local government entrusted with zoning responsibilities must provide a commercial zone in which live entertainment is permitted.

To be reasonable, time, place and manner restrictions not only must serve significant state interests but also must leave open adequate alternative channels of communication. Grayned v. City of Rockford, *supra,* at 116, 118, 92 S. Ct., at 2303, 2304; [other citations omitted.] Here, the Borough totally excludes all live entertainment, including nonobscene nude dancing that is otherwise protected by the First Amendment. As we have observed, Young v. American Mini Theatres, Inc., *supra,* did not purport to approve the total exclusion from the city of theaters showing adult, but not obscene, materials. It was carefully noted in that case that the number of regulated establishments was not limited and that "[t]he situation would be quite different if the ordinance had the effect of suppressing, or greatly restricting access to, lawful speech." 427 U.S., at 71, n.35, 96 S. Ct., at 2453, n.35.

The Borough nevertheless contends that live entertainment in general and nude dancing in particular are amply available in close-by areas outside the limits of the Borough. Its position suggests the argument that if there were countywide zoning, it would be quite legal to allow live entertainment in only selected areas of the county and to exclude it from primarily residential communities, such as the Borough of Mount Ephraim. This may very well be true, but the Borough cannot avail itself of that argument in this case. There is no countywide zoning in Camden County, and Mount Ephraim is free under state law to impose its own zoning restrictions, within constitutional limits. Furthermore, there is no evidence in this record to support the proposition that the kind of entertainment appellants wish to provide is available in reasonably nearby areas. The courts below made no such findings; and at least in their absence, the ordinance excluding live entertainment from the commercial zone cannot constitutionally be applied to appellants so as to criminalize the activities for which they have been fined. "[O]ne is not to have the exercise of his liberty of expression in appropriate places abridged on the plea that it may be exercised in some other place." Schneider v. State, 308 U.S. 147, 163, 60 S. Ct. 146, 151, 84 L. Ed. 155 (1939).

Accordingly, the convictions of these appellants are infirm and the judgment of the Appellate Division of the Superior Court of New Jersey is reversed and the case is remanded for further proceedings not inconsistent with this opinion.

So ordered.

JUSTICE BLACKMUN, concurring. I join the Court's opinion, but write separately to address two points that I believe are sources of some ambiguity in this still emerging area of law.

First, I would emphasize that the presumption of validity that traditionally attends a local government's exercise of its zoning powers carries little, if any, weight where the zoning regulation trenches on rights of expression protected under the First Amendment. In order for a reviewing court to determine whether a zoning restriction that impinges on free speech is "narrowly drawn [to] further a sufficiently substantial governmental interest," *ante,* at 2182-2183, the zoning authority must be prepared to articulate, and support, a reasoned and significant basis for its decision. This burden is by no means insurmountable, but neither should it be viewed as de minimis. In this case, Mount Ephraim evidently assumed that because the challenged ordinance was intended as a land-use regulation, it need survive only the minimal scru-tiny of a rational relationship test, and that once rationality was established, appellants then carried the burden of proving the regulation invalid on First Amendment grounds. Brief for Appellee 11-12. After today's decision, it should be clear that where protected First Amendment interests are at stake, zoning regulations have no such "talismanic immunity from constitutional challenge." Young v. American Mini Theatres, Inc., 427 U.S. 50, 75, 96 S. Ct. 2440, 2454, 49 L. Ed. 2d 310 (1976) (concurring opinion).

My other observation concerns the suggestion that a local community should be free to eliminate a particular form of expression so long as that form is available in areas reasonably nearby. In *Mini Theatres* the Court dealt with locational restrictions imposed by a political subdivision, the city of Detroit, that preserved reasonable access to the regulated form of expression within the boundaries of that same subdivision. It would be a substantial step beyond *Mini Theatres* to conclude that a town or county may legislatively prevent its citizens from engaging in or having access to forms of protected expression that are incompatible with its majority's conception of the "decent life" solely be-cause these activities are sufficiently available in other locales. I do not read the Court's opinion to reach, nor would I endorse, that conclusion.

Were I a resident of Mount Ephraim, I would not expect my right to attend the theater or to purchase a novel to be contingent upon the availabil-ity of such opportunities in "nearby" Philadelphia, a community in whose decisions I would have no political voice. Cf. Southeastern Promotions, Ltd. v. Conrad, 420 U.S. 546, 556, 95 S. Ct. 1239, 1245, 43 L. Ed. 2d 448 (1975) (" '[O]ne is not to have the exercise of his liberty of expression in appropriate places abridged on the plea that it may be exercised in some other place,' " quoting Schneider v. State, 308 U.S. 147, 163, 60 S. Ct. 146, 151, 84 L. Ed. 155 (1939)). Similarly, I would not expect the citizens of Philadelphia to be under any obligation to provide me with access to theaters and bookstores simply because Mount Ephraim previously had acted to ban these forms of "entertainment." This case does not require articulation of a rule for evaluat-ing the meaning of "reasonable access" in different contexts. The scope of relevant zoning authority varies widely across our country, as do geographic configurations and types of commerce among neighboring communities, and this issue will doubtless be resolved on a case-by-case basis. For now, it is sufficient to observe that in attempting to accommodate a locality's concern to protect the character of its community life, the court must remain attentive to the guarantees of the First Amendment, and in particular to the protection they afford to minorities against the "standardization of ideas . . . by . . . dominate [*sic*] political or community groups." Terminiello v. Chicago, 337 U.S. 1, 4-5, 69 S. Ct. 894, 895-896, 93 L. Ed. 1131 (1979).

JUSTICE POWELL, with whom JUSTICE STEWART joins, concurring. I join the Court's opinion as I agree that Mt. Ephraim has failed altogether to justify its broad restriction of protected expression. This is not to say, however, that some communities are not free—by a more carefully drawn ordinance—to regulate or ban all commercial public entertainment. In my opinion, such an ordinance could be appropriate and valid in a residential community where all commercial activity is excluded. Similarly, a residential community should be able to limit establishments to essential "neighborhood" services permitted in a narrowly zoned area.

But the Borough of Mt. Ephraim failed to follow these paths. The ordinance before us was not carefully drawn and, as the Court points out, it is sufficiently over- and under-inclusive that any argument about the need to maintain the residential nature of this community fails as a justification.

JUSTICE STEVENS, concurring in the judgment. The record in this case leaves so many relevant questions unanswered that the outcome, in my judgment, depends on the allocation of the burden of persuasion. If the case is viewed as a simple attempt by a small residential community to exclude the commercial exploitation of nude dancing from a "setting of tranquility," *post*, at 2191 (Burger, C.J., dissenting), it would seem reasonable to require appellants to overcome the usual presumption that a municipality's zoning enactments are constitutionally valid. To prevail in this case, appellants at least would be required to show that the exclusion was applied selectively, or perhaps that comparable expressive activity is not "amply available in close-by areas outside the limits of the Borough." *Ante,* at 2186-2187 (opinion of the Court). On the other hand, if one starts, as the Court does, from the premise that "appellants' claims are rooted in the First Amendment," *ante,* at 2181, it would seem reasonable to require the Borough to overcome a presumption of invalidity. The Borough could carry this burden by showing that its ordinances were narrowly drawn and furthered "a sufficiently substantial government interest." *Ante,* at 2183 (opinion of the Court) (footnote omitted).

Neither of these characterizations provides me with a satisfactory approach to this case. For appellants' business is located in a commercial zone, and the character of that zone is not unequivocally identified either by the text of the Borough's zoning ordinance or by the evidence in the record. And even though the foliage of the First Amendment may cast protective shadows over some forms of nude dancing, its roots were germinated by more serious concerns that are not necessarily implicated by a content-neutral zoning ordinance banning commercial exploitation of live entertainment. Cf. Young v. American Mini Theatres, Inc., 427 U.S. 50, 60-61, 96 S. Ct. 2440, 2447, 49 L. Ed. 2d 310.

One of the puzzling features of this case is that the character of the prohibition the Borough seeks to enforce is so hard to ascertain. Because the written zoning ordinance purports to ban all commercial uses except those that are specifically listed—and because no form of entertainment is listed— literally it prohibits the commerical exploitation not only of live entertainment, but of motion pictures and inanimate forms as well. But the record indicates that what actually happens in this commercial zone may bear little resemblance to what is described in the text of the zoning ordinance.

The commercial zone in which appellants' adult bookstore is located is situated along the Black Horse Pike, a north-south artery on the eastern fringe of the Borough. The parties seem to agree that this commercial zone is relatively small; presumably, therefore, it contains only a handful of commercial establishments. Among these establishments are Al-Jo's, also known as the Club Al-Jo, My Dad's, and Capriotti's, all of which offer live entertainment. In addition, the zone contains the Mount Ephraim Democratic Club, the Spread Eagle Inn, and Guiseppi's. The record also contains isolated references to establishments known as the Villa Picasso and Millie's. Although not mentioned in the record, Mount Ephraim apparently also supports a commercial motion picture theater.

The record reveals very little about the character of most of these establishments, and it reveals nothing at all about the motion picture theater. The one fact that does appear with clarity from the present record is that, in 1973, appellants were issued an amusement license that authorized them to exhibit adult motion pictures which their patrons viewed in private booths in their adult bookstore. Borough officials apparently regarded this business as lawful under the zoning ordinance and compatible with the immediate neighborhood until July of 1976 when appellants repainted their exterior sign and modified their interior exhibition.

Without more information about this commercial enclave on Black Horse Pike, one cannot know whether the change in appellants' business in 1976 introduced cacophony into a tranquil setting or merely a new refrain in a local replica of Place Pigalle. If I were convinced that the former is the correct appraisal of this commercial zone, I would have no hesitation in agreeing with the Chief Justice that even if the live nude dancing is a form of expressive activity protected by the First Amendment, the Borough may prohibit it. But when the record is opaque, as this record is, I believe the Borough must shoulder the burden of demonstrating that appellants' introduction of live entertainment had an identifiable adverse impact on the neighborhood or on the Borough as a whole. It might be appropriate to presume that such an adverse impact would occur if the zoning plan itself were narrowly drawn to create categories of commercial uses that unambiguously differentiated this entertainment from permitted uses. However, this open-ended ordinance affords no basis for any such presumption.

The difficulty in this case is that we are left to speculate as to the Borough's reasons for proceeding against appellants' business, and as to the justification for the distinction the Borough has drawn between live and other forms of entertainment. While a municipality need not persuade a federal court that its zoning decisions are correct as a matter of policy, when First Amendment interests are implicated it must at least be able to demonstrate that a uniform policy in fact exists and is applied in a content-neutral fashion. Presumably, municipalities may regulate expressive activity—even protected activity—pursuant to narrowly-drawn content-neutral standards; however, they may not regulate protected activity when the only standard provided is the unbridled discretion of a municipal official. Compare Saia v. New York, 334 U.S. 558, 68 S. Ct. 1148, 92 L. Ed. 1574, with Kovacs v. Cooper, 336 U.S. 77, 69 S. Ct. 448, 93 L. Ed. 513. Because neither the text of the zoning ordinance, nor the evidence in the record, indicates that Mount Ephraim applied narrowly-drawn content-neutral standards to the appellants' business, for me this case involves a criminal prosecution of appellants simply because one of their employees has engaged in expressive activity that has been assumed arguendo to be protected by the First Amendment. Accordingly, and without endorsing the overbreadth analysis employed by the Court, I concur in its judgment.

CHIEF JUSTICE BURGER, with whom JUSTICE REHNQUIST joins, dissenting. The Borough of Mount Ephraim is a small borough in Camden County, New Jersey. It is located on the Black Horse Turnpike, the main artery connecting Atlantic City with two major cities, Camden and Philadelphia. Mount Ephraim is about 17 miles from the city of Camden and about the same distance from the river that separates New Jersey from the State of Pennsylvania.

The Black Horse Turnpike cuts through the center of Mount Ephraim. For 250 feet on either side of the turnpike, the Borough has established a commercial zone. The rest of the community is zoned for residential use, with either single- or multi-family units permitted. Most of the inhabitants of Mount Ephraim commute to either Camden or Philadelphia for work.

The residents of this small enclave chose to maintain their town as a placid, "bedroom" community of a few thousand people. To that end, they passed an admittedly broad regulation prohibiting certain forms of entertainment. Because I believe that a community of people are—within limits—masters of their own environment, I would hold that, as applied, the ordinance is valid.

At issue here is the right of a small community to ban an activity incompatible with a quiet, residential atmosphere. The Borough of Mount Ephraim did nothing more than employ traditional police power to provide a setting of tranquility. This Court has often upheld the power of a community "to determine that the community should be beautiful as well as healthy, spacious as well as clean, well-balanced as well as carefully patrolled." Berman v. Parker, 348 U.S. 26, 32-33, 75 S. Ct. 98, 102, 99 L. Ed. 27 (1954). Justice Douglas, speaking for the Court, sustained the power to zone as "ample to lay out zones where family values, youth values, and the blessings of quiet seclusion and clean air make the area a sanctuary for people." (Village of Belle Terre v. Boraas, 416 U.S. 1, 9, 94 S. Ct. 1536, 1541, 39 L. Ed. 2d 797 (1979).)

Here we have nothing more than a variation on that theme.

The Court depicts Mount Ephraim's ordinance as a ban on live entertainment. But, in terms, it does not mention any kind of entertainment. As applied, it operates as a ban on nude dancing in appellants' "adult" book store, and for that reason alone it is here. Thus, the issue *in the case that we have before us* is not whether Mount Ephraim may ban traditional live entertainment, but whether it may ban nude dancing, which is used as the "bait" to induce customers into the appellants' book store. When, and if, this ordinance is used to prevent a high school performance of "The Sound of Music," for example, the Court can deal with that problem.

An overconcern about draftsmanship and overbreadth should not be allowed to obscure the central question before us. It is clear that, in passing the statute challenged here, the citizens of the Borough of Mount Ephraim meant only to preserve the basic character of their community. It is just as clear that, by thrusting its live nude dancing shows on this community, the appellant alters and damages that community over its objections. As applied in this case, therefore, the statute speaks directly and unequivocally. It may be that, as applied in some other case, this statute would violate the First Amendment, but, since such a case is not before us, we should not decide it.

Even assuming that the "expression" manifested in the nude dancing that is involved here is somehow protected speech under the First Amendment, the Borough of Mount Ephraim is entitled to regulate it. In Young v. American Mini Theatres, we said: "The mere fact that the commercial exploitation of material protected by the First Amendment is subject to zoning and other licensing requirements is not a sufficient reason for invalidating these ordinances." (427 U.S. 50, 62, 96 S. Ct. 2440, 2448, 49 L. Ed. 2d 310 (1972).)

Here, as in *American Mini Theatres,* the zoning ordinance imposes a minimal intrusion on genuine rights of expression; only by contortions of logic can it be made otherwise. Mount Ephraim is a small community on the periphery of two major urban centers where this kind of entertainment may be found acceptable. The fact that nude dancing has been totally banned in this community is irrelevant. "Chilling" this kind of show business in this tiny residential enclave can hardly be thought to show that the appellants' "message" will be prohibited in nearby—and more sophisticated—cities.

The fact that a form of expression enjoys some constitutional protection does not mean that there are not times and places inappropriate for its exercise. The towns and villages of this nation are not, and should not be forced into a mold cast by this Court. Citizens should be free to choose to shape their community so that it embodies their conception of the "decent life." This will sometimes mean deciding that certain forms of activity—factories, gas stations, sports stadia, bookstores, and surely live nude shows—will not be allowed. That a community is willing to tolerate such a commercial use as a convenience store, a gas station, a pharmacy, or a delicatessen does not compel it also to tolerate every other "commercial use," including pornography peddlers and live nude shows.

In Federalist Paper No. 5, Madison observed:

> In framing a government which is to be administered by men over men, the
> great difficulty lies in this: you must first enable a government to control the
> governed; and in the next place oblige it to control itself.

This expresses the balancing indispensable in all governing, and the Bill of
Rights is one of the checks to control overreaching by government. But it is a
check to be exercised sparingly by federal authority over local expressions of
choice going to essentially local concerns.

    I am constrained to note that some of the concurring views exhibit an
understandable discomfort with the idea of denying this small residential enclave the power to keep this kind of show business from its very doorsteps. The
Borough of Mount Ephraim has not attempted to suppress the point of view of
anyone or to stifle any category of ideas. To say that there is a First Amendment right to impose every form of expression on every community, including
the kind of "expression" involved here, is sheer nonsense. To enshrine such a
notion in the Constitution ignores fundamental values that the Constitution
ought to protect. To invoke the first Amendment to protect the activity involved in this case trivializes and demeans that great Amendment.

NOTES AND QUESTIONS

    1. Four of the five opinions cite Young v. American Mini Theatres,
Inc., 427 U.S. 50, 96 S. Ct. 2440, 49 L. Ed. 2d 310 (1976), in which the Court
narrowly upheld (5 to 4) a Detroit ordinance that greatly restricted the display
of sexually explicit "adult" movies. The Detroit law sought to disperse adult
theaters by barring their location within 1000 feet of any two other "regulated
uses" (such as cabarets, hotels or motels, bars, public lodging houses, other
adult theaters) or within 500 feet of a residential area. When enacting the
ordinance, the city council had found that the concentration of some uses was
especially injurious to a neighborhood: that close proximity of adult theaters
to the various other regulated uses attracted an undesirable run of transients,
increased prostitution and other crimes, and encouraged residents and businesses to move elsewhere. During the five years that preceded the ordinance,
there had been an increase in the number of adult theaters in Detroit from two
to twenty-five, and a comparable increase in the number of adult book stores
and other "adult-type businesses."
    The operators of two motion picture theaters attacked the ordinance on
grounds of vagueness, violation of Equal Protection, and suppression of free
speech. The district court granted defendants' motion for summary judgment;
the court called the ordinance a rational attempt to preserve the city's neighborhoods and it rejected the plaintiffs' various claims. 373 F. Supp. 363 (E.D.
Mich. 1974). The Sixth Circuit reversed, concluding that the ordinance imposed a prior restraint on constitutionally protected communication. 518 F.2d
1014 (6th Cir. 1975). The Supreme Court granted certiorari and, in turn,
upheld the regulation.

In delivering the Court's opinion, Justice Stevens gave little weight to the prior restraint claim. He reasoned that the city's zoning laws required all motion picture theaters to satisfy locational restrictions, such as confinement to certain specified commercial districts, and that even if "adult" theaters had to satisfy an additional restriction, this would not per se be deemed an impermissible prior restraint. Reasonable regulation of time, place, or manner of protected speech is not akin to censorship.

But the plaintiffs argued that even if the regulation were not a prior restraint, the city's content-based distinction would offend the First Amendment, and, via incorporation, the Equal Protection clause. Justice Stevens continued to disagree:

> Moreover, even though we recognize that the First Amendment will not tolerate the total suppression of erotic materials that have some arguably artistic value, it is manifest that society's interest in protecting this type of expression is of a wholly different, and lesser, magnitude than the interest in untrammeled political debate. . . . Whether political oratory or philosophical discussion moves us to applaud or to despise what is said, every school child can understand why our duty to defend the right to speak remains the same. But few of us would march our sons and daughters off to war to preserve the citizen's rights to see "Specified Sexual Activities" exhibited in theatres of our choice. Even though the First Amendment protects communication in this area from total suppression, we hold that the State may legitimately use the content of these materials as the basis for placing them in a different classification from other motion pictures. [427 U.S. at 70-71]

The four dissenting justices saw the matter quite differently. In his dissenting opinion, Justice Stewart (joined by Justices Brennan, Marshall, and Blackmun) wrote:

> What this case does involve is the constitutional permissibility of selective interference with protected speech whose content is thought to produce distasteful effects. It is elementary that a prime function of the First Amendment is to guard against just such interference. By refusing to invalidate Detroit's ordinance the Court rides roughshod over cardinal principles of First Amendment law, which require that time, place, and manner regulations that affect protected expression be content neutral except in the limited context of a captive or juvenile audience. . . . Since "few of us would march our sons and daughters off to war to see 'Specified Sexual Activities' " . . . the Court implies that these films are not entitled to the full protection of the Constitution. . . . The guarantees of the Bill of Rights were designed to protect against precisely such majoritarian limitations on individual liberty. [Id. at 85-86]

The dissenters also joined in an opinion of Justice Blackmun's attacking the law's vagueness.

Justice Powell wrote a separate opinion concurring with the result and with some, but not all, of the Court's opinion. Excerpts from the concurrence appear below:

This is the first case in this Court in which the interests in free expression protected by the First and Fourteenth Amendments have been implicated by a municipality's commercial zoning ordinances. Respondents would have us mechanically apply the doctrines developed in other contexts. But this situation is not analogous to cases involving expression in public forums or to those involving individual expression or, indeed, to any other prior case. The unique situation presented by this ordinance calls, as cases in this area so often do, for a careful inquiry into the competing concerns of the State and the interests protected by the guarantee of free expression.

Because a substantial burden rests upon the State when it would limit in any way First Amendment rights, it is necessary to identify with specificity the nature of the infringement in each case. The primary concern of the free speech guarantee is that there be full opportunity for expression in all of its varied forms to convey a desired message. Vital to this concern is the corollary that there be full opportunity for everyone to receive the message. . . .

In this case, there is no indication that the application of the Anti-Skid Row Ordinance to adult theaters has the effect of suppressing production of or, to any significant degree, restricting access to adult movies. Nortown concededly will not be able to exhibit adult movies at its present location, and the ordinance limits the potential location of the proposed Pussy Cat. The constraints of the ordinance with respect to location may indeed create economic loss for some who are engaged in this business. But in this respect they are affected no differently from any other commercial enterprise that suffers economic detriment as a result of land-use regulation. The cases are legion that sustained zoning against claims of serious economic damage. See, e.g., Zahn v. Board of Public Works, 274 U.S. 325, 71 L. Ed. 1074, 47 S. Ct. 594 (1927).

The inquiry for First Amendment purposes is not concerned with economic impact; rather, it looks only to the effect of this ordinance upon freedom of expression. This prompts essentially two inquiries: (i) Does the ordinance impose any content limitation on the creators of adult movies or their ability to make them available to whom they desire, and (ii) does it restrict in any significant way the viewing of these movies by those who desire to see them? On the record in this case, these inquiries must be answered in the negative. At most impact of the ordinance on these interests is incidental and minimal. Detroit has silenced no message, has invoked no censorship, and has imposed no limitation upon those who wish to view them. The ordinance is addressed only to the places at which this type of expression may be presented, a restriction that does not interfere with content. Nor is there any significant overall curtailment of adult movie presentations, or the opportunity for a message to reach an audience. On the basis of the District Court's finding, *ante*, at 71-72, n.35, 49 L. Ed. 2d 327, it appears that if a sufficient market exists to support them the number of adult movie theaters in Detroit will remain approximately the same, free to purvey the same message. To be sure some prospective patrons may be inconvenienced by this dispersal. But other patrons, depending upon where they live or work, may find it more convenient to view an adult movie when adult theaters are not concentrated in a particular section of the city.

In these circumstances, it is appropriate to analyze the permissibility of Detroit's action under the four-part test of United States v. O'Brien, 391 U.S.

367, 377, 20 L. Ed. 2d 672, 88 S. Ct. 1673 (1968). Under that test, a governmental regulation is sufficiently justified, despite its incidental impact upon First Amendment interests, "if it is within the constitutional power of the Government; if it furthers an important or substantial governmental interest; if the governmental interest is unrelated to the suppression of free expression; and if the incidental restriction on . . . First Amendment freedoms is no greater than is essential to the furtherance of that interest." Ibid. The factual distinctions between a prosecution for destruction of a Selective Service registration certificate, as in O'Brien, and this case are substantial, but the essential weighing and balancing of competing interests are the same. Cf. Procunier v. Martinez, 416 U.S., at 409-412, 40 L. Ed. 2d 224, 94 S. Ct. 1800, 71 Ohio Ops. 2d 139.

There is, as noted earlier, no question that the ordinance was within the power of the Detroit Common Council to enact. See Berman v. Parker, 348 U.S., at 32, 99 L. Ed. 27, 75 S. Ct. 98. Nor is there doubt that the interests furthered by this ordinance are both important and substantial. Without stable neighborhoods, both residential and commercial, large sections of a modern city quickly can deteriorate into an urban jungle with tragic consequences to social, environmental, and economic values. While I agree with respondents that no aspect of the police power enjoys immunity from searching constitutional scrutiny, it also is undeniable that zoning, when used to preserve the character of specific areas of a city, is perhaps "the most essential function performed by local government, for it is one of the primary means by which we protect that sometimes difficult to define concept of quality of life." Village of Belle Terre v. Boraas, 416 U.S., at 13, 39 L. Ed. 2d 797, 94 S. Ct. 1536 (Marshall, J., dissenting).

The third and fourth tests of O'Brien also are met on this record. It is clear both from the chronology and from the facts that Detroit has not embarked on an effort to suppress free expression. The ordinance was already in existence, and its purposes clearly set out, for a full decade before adult establishments were brought under it. When this occurred, it is clear—indeed it is not seriously challenged—that the governmental interest prompting the inclusion in the ordinance of adult establishments was wholly unrelated to any suppression of free expression. Nor is there reason to question that the degree of incidental encroachment upon such expression was the minimum necessary to further the purpose of the ordinance. The evidence presented to the Common Council indicated that the urban deterioration was threatened, not by the concentration of all movie theaters with other "regulated uses," but only by a concentration of those that elected to specialize in adult movies. The case would present a different situation had Detroit brought within the ordinance types of theaters that had not been shown to contribute to the deterioration of surrounding areas.

With which of these views, if any, do you concur?

2.   After the Supreme Court decision in Young v. American Mini Theatres, Inc., the city administration proposed an antipornography zoning ordinance that would sharply limit adult uses in New York City's midtown area. As Figure 7, on the next page, shows, fewer than thirty such uses would have survived in the entire midtown area, including only one adult-use establishment within 1000 feet of Times Square (where there are now dozens).

The plan never materialized, partly from doubts as to its validity, partly

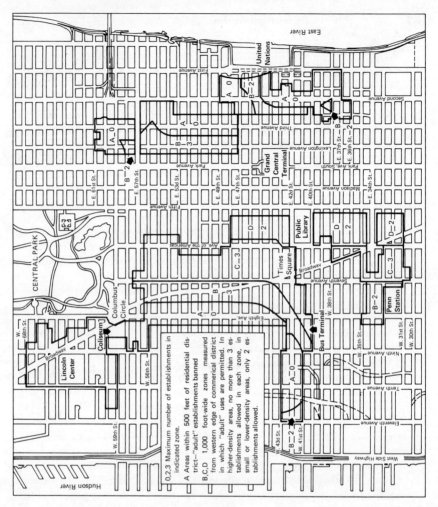

0,2,3 Maximum number of establishments in indicated zone.

A Areas within 500 feet of residential district—"adult" establishments banned

B,C,D 1,000 foot-wide zones measured from western edge of commercial district in which "adult" uses are permitted. In higher-density areas, no more than 3 establishments allowed in each zone, in small or lower-density areas, only 2 establishments allowed.

FIGURE 7

850

from concern that the plan would cause dispersal of adult uses into neighborhoods that had not previously experienced them.

3. The New York City proposal engendered the following exchange between the editorial writers of the New York Times and two of its readers.

More on the Zone Defense Against Smut

Two letters, below, object to a recent editorial that praised New York City for trying to deal with the blight of commercial sex through the zoning laws. We reassert that praise with the plea that the issues to be debated at least be clearly understood.

The story so far: Governments cannot, at least should not, censor films or books; most that have tried have failed; pornography and commercial sex have thus become big business, all the bigger where they have been able to concentrate visual and tactile services in dense clusters that overwhelm all other commercial and residential activity. Detroit, one of many cities struggling against this corrosion, amended its zoning ordinances against skid rows to limit the concentration but not to prohibit the offensive commerce. A divided Supreme Court upheld the effort, 5 to 4, inspiring an analogous move by New York.

We continue to believe that New York's effort is conscientious and progressive. As we said before, we also deem it "somewhat risky" because the new law ventures onto legal ground where the rights of free speech and the regulation of land use collide. We held the question could be well argued one way or the other and required a "Solomon-like justice" from the courts.

In other words, we think a good deal of the legal case that might be brought *against* the city in this matter; indeed, we think it can be a better case than that argued to us by the counsel of the New York Civil Liberties Union. What is more, we think it could be argued without resort to the fatuous charge that in worrying about the quality of New York neighborhoods The Times is looking after the value of its real estate.

We can recognize the legal tension in the new effort, even without benefit of counsel. The zoning law rests on the premise that the concentration of pornographic services and entertainments, including bookstores, movie houses, massage parlors, peepshows and topless bars, can destroy a neighborhood for other commercial or residential use. It holds, in effect, that what may be unthreatening in reasonable amounts becomes in volume a devastating blight and a magnet for noxious and dangerous traffic, including criminal traffic. These are the proper concerns of zoning. The new law seeks to avoid encroachment on First Amendment rights of free expression by providing rules under which "adult" business may operate, and in sufficient quantity to satisfy its market.

The zoning limits would apply to bookstores having a "predominant" portion of their stock in materials "distinguished or characterized by" an "emphasis" on specified sexual activity or portions of the human body, and to movie houses "used primarily" for films with the same emphasis.

So the essential constitutional problems turn on questions of intention and definition. The city must be able to demonstrate that it *intends* no inhibition on the production, sale or consumption of books or films, no matter how offensive they may be to some. It will have to prove that *concentrations* of the businesses in question, just like bars or junkyards or oil refineries, result in demonstrably undesirable side effects. If this argument holds, the city must further demonstrate that it can lawfully distinguish such offending businesses from other bookstores or movie houses, some of which also deal in sexual material.

In most cases, this distinction may be possible: bars that also sell soft drinks are not soda fountains; junkyards with some items of special value are not antique shops; "adult" bookstores are not just conventional booksellers that carry the Kinsey report. But what of a movie house that shows the fairly explicit "Last Tango in Paris" not for a month but for a year or two? Would it then be "used primarily" for films that give "emphasis" to sexual activity? Would there in fact be so many such difficult cases that we could not limit the location of so-called "adult" movie houses without limiting all movie houses?

The issues are well worth developing and arguing. When the stakes on both sides of a question are so great, the energies of the law are rightly consumed to see whether both can be served. Our correspondents believe that no law can safely draw these distinctions and that the squalor and crime which result from concentrations of commercial sex and which destroy other citizens' right of residence, commerce and entertainment, must be accepted as the price of free speech. Maybe so, but maybe not. If we can keep the debate at the proper level, the value of our real estate will take care of itself.

To the Editor:

Your Feb. 5 editorial discussing the city's proposals to zone "adult" bookstores and movie theaters, among other facilities, contains several statements that can only mislead the public on this important issue. They include:

The editorial repeatedly uses such phrases as "porn" and "filth" and "smut" to suggest that that's all the zoning plan applies to. However, the plan goes much further, applying to *all* books and movies dealing with sex, including, for example, such obviously non-obscene works as the Kinsey and the Masters and Johnson studies, several books on The Times' own best-seller lists and such popular and critically acclaimed movies as "Carnal Knowledge" and "Last Tango in Paris." Surely The Times does not consider such works "filth."

The editorial says that "a similar law in Detroit was recently upheld by the Supreme Court." However, the editorial fails to mention that there was no majority opinion for the Court on the crucial constitutional question raised, that Justice Powell's swing vote upholding the Detroit plan clearly signaled that he would disapprove such schemes as New York's and that the five Justices upholding the Detroit law repeatedly stressed that there would be no diminution of the availability of non-obscene "adult" materials in that city. In contrast, as the city now concedes, an express purpose of this proposal—a purpose apparently endorsed by The Times—is to reduce substantially the number and accessibility of facilities offering such materials so that, for example, not a single such facility could be opened in the entire borough of Brooklyn.

The editorial implies the New York proposals will somehow stop the "spread" of the "blight" of such facilities. However, as any number of community leaders have already observed, quite the opposite is the likely result of the plan, since plainly profitable outlets that are zoned out of one location will almost certainly relocate somewhere else, for example, in community shopping centers where they don't now exist—probably right next door to the local OTB parlor.

At first glance, it seems ironic that the same newspaper that went all the way to the Supreme Court in the Pentagon Papers case to vindicate what it viewed as a threat to the First Amendment in the guise of "national security" now talks of "balancing" free-speech rights against what it calls an "assault" on "sensibilities." But when one remembers how Times Square gets its name, and the fact that The Times' own sensibilities and real-estate values are at stake, the editorial becomes more understandable. It's too bad The Times itself wasn't included in the sweep of the new zoning plan—then perhaps it would have perceived the direct threat to the First Amendment that it entails.

Kenneth P. Norwick
Counsel, Legislative Department
New York Civil Liberties Union
New York, Feb. 7, 1977

To the Editor:

Your recent editorial on the city's proposed "adult uses" zoning plan took a regrettably shortsighted view of the serious First Amendment questions involved.

There is no doubt that the government may subject bookstores to a zoning ordinance, just as it may subject newspapers to a taxing ordinance. But to subject bookstores to differential zoning on the basis of the contents of the books they sell is no more permissible than to subject newspapers to differential taxation on the basis of the contents of the news stories they run.

The constitutional guarantee of a free press was instituted for the protection of unpopular messages, which need it, rather than popular ones, which do not.

If the material sold in these bookstores is of such slight social value that the public interest in morality outweighs any interest in the exposition of ideas, then the government is fully empowered under existing law to take appropriate action. The fact that it has been unable to do so—which is the genesis of the current attempt to end-run the First Amendment—clearly demonstrates the discriminatory nature of the zoning proposal.

The Times is properly proud of its opposition to the suppression of Communist viewpoints in the 1950's and antiwar viewpoints in the 1960's. But unless it is equally forthright in its opposition to the book burners of the 1970's, it may be too late to defeat the newspaper burners of the 1980's.

Eric M. Freedman
New York, Feb. 7, 1977

[New York Times, Feb. 15, 1977, at 30, col. 1, 3]

4. A student comment, which analyzed the decision in Young v. American Mini Theatres, Inc., *supra*, identified three criteria that an adult-use regulation must satisfy.

    (a) the regulation must be motivated not by distaste for the speech itself but by a desire to eliminate its adverse effects

    (b) the regulation must not sharply reduce the total number of "pornography outlets" and the number of potential customers who could conveniently patronize them

(c) the municipality must demonstrate an adequate factual basis for its conclusion that the ordinance will minify the evils at which it is aimed. Developments in the Law—Zoning, 91 Harv. L. Rev. 1427, 1557-59 (1978).

If concentration of adult uses tends to attract such harmful activities as prostitution and criminal assault and also tends to depress neighboring commercial and residential properties, shouldn't the community be able to curb this baleful influence even if the total number of adult-use outlets is greatly restricted?

5.   Is there a spectrum of constitutionally more and less protected adult uses? See, e.g., Kisley v. City of Falls Church, 212 Va. 693, 187 S.E.2d 168 (1972) (validated zoning amendment that barred cross-sexual massage parlors); Stansberry v. Holmes, 613 F.2d 1285 (5th Cir. 1980) (validated regulation of massage parlors, nude studios, modeling studios).

6.   After the Supreme Court decision in Young v. American Mini Theatres, Inc., courts have tended to evaluate adult-use regulations on the closeness of their modeling to that of the Detroit ordinance. Illustrations include:

(a) Bayside Enterprises, Inc. v. Carson, 450 F. Supp. 696 (M.D. Fla. 1978) (Jacksonville ordinance barred "adult businesses" from locating within 2500 feet of other such businesses, churches, or schools: ordinance invalid as effecting, for all practical purposes, a total ban on the establishment of new adult bookstores or movie houses).
(b) Purple Onion, Inc. v. Jackson, 511 F. Supp. 1207 (N.D. Ga. 1981) (Atlanta ordinance barred, inter alia, adult businesses from locating within 500 feet of "any property used for residential purposes"; Detroit ordinance spoke in terms of "any area zoned for residential use": because of this language change, and several others, Atlanta ordinance invalid).

7.   Might distressed neighbors sue the operator of an adult-use establishment on the grounds that it is a private nuisance? See Developments, Note 4 supra, 1564-68.

§16.4   Protection of the Environment

Rediscovery of the environment, with its attendant concern that humanity's very survival may rest upon its ability to preserve fragile, little-understood, natural balances, has led to a surge of protectionist legislation, which this course can only sample. Once again, government not only must define its goals but also must choose that mix of police power, eminent domain, taxing, and spending that can best satisfy the Constitution, the budget, and the political realities—and still achieve the environmental objectives.

Wetlands have been a prime target for control. Flood danger originally led to building restrictions in low-lying areas and to land-fill bans in marshes that form a natural detention basin for flood waters. More recently, growing alarm over water pollution, endangered wildlife, and a shaky ecological balance has spurred enactment of new wetlands controls, similar to the Maine law at issue in State v. Johnson.

STATE v. JOHNSON
265 A.2d 711 (Me. 1970)

MARDEN, J. On appeal from an injunction granted under the provisions of 12 M.R.S.A. §§4701-4709, inclusive, the Wetlands Act (Act),[1] originating in Chapter 348 P.L. 1967, which places restrictions upon the alteration and use of wetlands, as therein defined, without permission from the municipal officers concerned and the State Wetlands Control Board (Board). The Act is a conservation measure under the police power of the State to protect the ecology of areas bordering coastal waters. The 1967 Act has been amended in no way pertinent to the present issue except by Section 8 of Chapter 379 of the Public Laws of 1969, which authorized alternatively a mandatory injunction for the restoration of any wetlands previously altered in violation of the Act.

1. Pertinent portions are quoted.

> § *4701. Procedure; hearing*
>
> No person, agency or municipality shall remove, fill, dredge or drain sanitary sewage into, or otherwise alter any coastal wetland, as defined herein, without filing written notice of his intention to do so, including such plans as may be necessary to describe the proposed activity, with the municipal officers in the municipality affected and with the Wetlands Control Board. Such notice shall be sent to each body by registered mail at least 60 days before such alteration is proposed to commence. The municipal officers shall hold a public hearing on the proposal within 30 days of receipt of the notice and shall notify by mail the person proposing the alteration and the public by publication in a newspaper published in the county where the wetlands are located, the Wetlands Control Board and all abutting owners of the hearing.
>
> For purposes of this chapter, coastal wetland is defined as any swamp, marsh, bog, beach, flat or other contiguous lowland above extreme low water which is subject to tidal action or normal storm flowage at any time excepting periods of maximum storm activity. . . .
>
> § *4702. Permits*
>
> Permit to undertake the proposed alteration shall be issued by the municipal officers within 7 days of such hearing providing the Wetlands Control Board approves. Such permit may be conditioned upon the applicant amending his proposal to take whatever measures are deemed necessary by either the municipality or the Wetlands Control Board to protect the public interest. Approval may be withheld by either the municipal officers or the board when in the opinion of either body the proposal would threaten the public safety, health or welfare, would adversely affect the value or enjoyment of the property of abutting owners, or would be damaging to the conservation of public and private water supplies or of wildlife or freshwater, estuarine or marine fisheries. . . .

The appellants own a tract of land about 220 feet wide and 700 feet long extending across salt water marshes between Atlantic Avenue on the east and the Webhannet River on the west in the Town of Wells. Westerly of the lots fronting on Atlantic Avenue the strip has been subdivided into lots for sale. The easterly 260 feet approximately of the strip has been filled and bears seasonal dwellings. Westerly of this 260 foot development is marsh-land flooded at high tide and drained, upon receding tide, into the River by a network of what our Maine historical novelist Kenneth E. Roberts called "eel runs," but referred to in the record as creeks. Similar marsh-land, undeveloped, lies to the north and south of appellants' strip, and westerly of the River, all of which makes up a substantial acreage (the extent not given in testimony, but of which we take judicial notice) of marsh-land known as the Wells Marshes. Appellants' land, by raising the grade above high water by the addition of fill, is adaptable to development for building purposes.

Following the effective date of the Act, an application to the municipal officers, with notice to the Wetlands Control Board, for permission to fill a portion of this land was denied by the Board, an administrative appeal was taken and the case reported to this Court, which appears sub nom. Johnson v. Maine Wetlands Control Board, Me., 250 A.2d 825 (Case No. 1) and in which the constitutionality of the Act was challenged. We held, by decision filed March 11, 1969 that absent a record of evidence as to the nature of the land involved and the benefits or harm to be expected from the denial of the permit, the case would have to be remanded.

Subsequent to March 11, 1969 fill was deposited on the land in question, as the result of which the State sought an injunction, the granting of which brings this case before us on appeal (Case No. 2). It is stipulated that the evidence in this case should be accepted as the evidence lacking in (Case No. 1) and that the two cases be consolidated for final determination of both.

The record establishes that the land which the appellants proposed to build up by fill and build upon for sale, or to be offered for sale to be built upon, are coastal wetlands within the definition of the Act and that the refusal by the Board to permit the deposit of such fill prevents the development as proposed. The single Justice found that the property is a portion of a salt

---

§ 4704. *Appeal*

Appeal may be taken to the Superior Court within 30 days after the denial of a permit or the issuance of a conditional permit for the purpose of determining whether the action appealed from so restricts the use of the property as to deprive the owner of the reasonable use thereof, and is therefore an unreasonable exercise of police power, or which constitutes the equivalent of a taking without compensation. The court upon such a finding may set aside the action appealed from.

§ 4705. *Wetlands Control Board*

The Wetlands Control Board shall be composed of the Commissioners of Sea and Shore Fisheries and of Inland Fisheries and Game, the Chairman of the Water and Air Environmental Improvement Commission, the Chairman of the State Highway Commission, the Forest Commissioner and the Commissioner of Health and Welfare or their delegates.

§ 4709. *Violators are subject to fine or injunctive process.*

marsh area, a valuable natural resource of the State, that the highest and best use for the land, so filled, is for housing, and that unfilled it has no commercial value.

The issue is the same in both, namely, whether the denial of permit (Case No. 1) and the injunction (Case No. 2) so limit the use to plaintiffs of their land that such deprivation of use amounts to a taking of their property without constitutional due process and just compensation.[2]

DUE PROCESS

Due process of law has a dual aspect, procedural and substantive. 16 Am. Jur. 2d, Constitutional Law §548. . . .

It is this substantive due process which is challenged in the Act. In this connection it must be noted that §4704 (Footnote 1) by its terms equates a deprivation "of the reasonable use" of an owner's property with "an unreasonable exercise of police power."

The constitutional aspect of the current problem is to be determined by consideration of the extent to which appellants are deprived of their usual incidents of ownership,—for the conduct of the public authorities with relation to appellants' land is not a "taking" in the traditional sense. Our State has applied a strict construction of the constitutional provisions as to land. . . .

We find no constitutional definition of the word "deprive," Munn v. Illinois, 94 U.S. 113, 123, since the constitutionally protected right of property is not unlimited. It is subject to reasonable restraints and regulations in the public interest by means of the legitimate exercise of police power. 16 Am. Jur. 2d, Constitutional Law §363. The exercise of this police power may properly regulate the use of property and if the owner suffers injury "it is either damnum absque injuria, or, in the theory of the law, he is compensated for it by sharing in the general benefits which the regulations are intended . . . to secure." State v. Robb, 100 Me. 180, 186, 60 A. 874, 876. The determination of unconstitutional deprivation is difficult and judicial decisions are diverse. Broadly speaking, deprivation of property contrary to constitutional guaranty occurs "if it deprives an owner of one of its essential attributes, destroys its value, restricts or interrupts its common necessary, or profitable use, hampers the owner in the application of it to the purposes of trade, or imposes conditions upon the right to hold or use it and thereby seriously impairs its value." 16 Am. Jur. 2d Constitutional Law §367. See also State v. Union Oil Company, 151 Me. 438, 446, 120 A.2d 708.

Conditions so burdensome may be imposed that they are equivalent to an outright taking, although the title to the property and some vestiges of its uses remain in the owner. East Coast Lumber Terminal, Inc. v. Town of Babylon, 174 F.2d 106, [5-7] 110 (2 CCA, 1949).

2. Maine Constitution Article I §6. "He shall not be . . . deprived of his . . . property . . . but by . . . the law of the land."
"Section 21. Private property shall not be taken for public uses without just compensation. . . ."

A guiding principle appears in the frequently cited case of Pennsylvania Coal Company v. Mahon et al., 260 U.S. 393, 413 (1922) where Mr. Justice Holmes declared:

> Government hardly could go on if to some extent values incident to property could not be diminished without paying for every such change in the general law. As long recognized some values are enjoyed under an implied limitation and must yield to the police power. But obviously the implied limitation must have its limits or the contract and due process clauses are gone. One fact for consideration in determining such limits is the extent of the diminution. When it reaches a certain magnitude, in most if not in all cases there must be an exercise of eminent domain and compensation to sustain the act. So the question depends upon the particular facts.
>
> . . . We are in danger of forgetting that a strong public desire to improve the public condition is not enough to warrant achieving the desire by a shorter cut than the constitutional way of paying for the change. As we already have said this is a question of degree—and therefore cannot be disposed of by general propositions. (At page 416.)

See also Pumpelly v. Green Bay Company, 13 Wall. (U.S.) 166, 177-178 (1871).

Confrontation between public interests and private interests is common in the application of zoning laws, with which the Wetlands Act may be analogized, and the great majority of which, upon their facts, are held to be reasonable exercise of the police power. There are, however, zoning restrictions which have been recognized as equivalent to a taking of the property restricted . . .

The same result has been reached as to zoning laws which identify their purposes as ones of conservation. See Dooley v. Town Plan and Zoning Commission of Town of Fairfield, 151 Conn. 304, 197 A.2d 770, [5, 6] 773 (1964, flood control); and Morris County Land Improvement Company v. Township of Parsippany-Troy Hills et al., 40 N.J. 539, 193 A.2d 232, [6, 7] 241 (1963, swampland preservation), and the rationale expressed in Commissioner of Natural Resources et al. v. S. Volpe & Co., Inc., 349 Mass. 104, 206 N.E.2d 666 (1965, involving "dredge and fill" Act); and MacGibbon et al. v. Board of Appeals of Duxbury, 347 Mass. 690, 200 N.E.2d 254 (1964) and 255 N.E.2d 347 (Mass. 1970).

There has, as well, been restrictive conservation legislation which has been held not equivalent to taking. See Patterson v. Stanolind Oil & Gas Co., 182 Okl. 155, 77 P.2d 83, [1-3] 89 (1938, oil and gas "well spacing" Act); Iowa Natural Resources Council v. Van Zee, 158 N.W.2d 111, [10], [11] 117 (Iowa 1968, flood control Act), and Swisher v. Brown, 157 Colo. 378, 402 P.2d 62 (1965, marketing control Act). See also Greenleaf-Johnson Lumber Company v. Garrison, 237 U.S. 251, 260 (1914, directing removal of docks in navigable waters, with dissent), and Miami Beach Jockey Club, Inc. v. Dern,

66 App. D.C. 254, 86 F.2d 135 (1936, legislative prohibition of filling submerged land).

Of the above, the Massachusetts cases are of particular significance inasmuch as the "dredge and fill" Act discussed in *Volpe* is expressed in terms closely parallel to our Wetlands Act and the zoning ordinance in *MacGibbon* deals with facts closely akin to those before us.

Between the public interest in braking and eventually stopping the insidious despoliation of our natural resources which have for so long been taken for granted, on the one hand, and the protection of appellants' property rights on the other, the issue is cast.

Here the single Justice has found that the area of which appellants' land is a part "is a valuable natural resource of the State of Maine and plays an important role in the conservation and development of aquatic and marine life, game birds and waterfowl," which bespeaks the public interest involved and the protection of which is sought by Section 4702 of the Act. With relation to appellants' interest the single Justice found that appellants' land absent the addition of fill "has no commercial value whatever." These findings are supported by the evidence and are conclusive. [Citation omitted.]

As distinguished from conventional zoning for town protection, the area of Wetlands representing a "valuable natural resource of the State," of which appellants' holdings are but a minute part, is of state-wide concern. The benefits from its preservation extend beyond town limits and are state-wide. The cost of its preservation should be publicly borne. To leave appellants with commercially valueless land in upholding the restriction presently imposed, is to charge them with more than their just share of the cost of this state-wide conservation program, granting fully its commendable purpose. In the phrasing of *Robb, supra,* their compensation by sharing in the benefits which this restriction is intended to secure is so disproportionate to their deprivation of reasonable use that such exercise of the State's police power is unreasonable.

The application of the Wetlands restriction in the terms of the denial of appellants' proposal to fill, and enjoining them from so doing deprives them of the reasonable use of their property and within Section 4704 is both an unreasonable exercise of police power and equivalent to taking within constitutional considerations. . . .

Holding, as we do, that the prohibition against the filling of appellants' land, upon the facts peculiar to the case, is an unreasonable exercise of police power, it does not follow that the restriction as to draining sanitary sewage into coastal wetland is subject to the same infirmity. Additional considerations of health and pollution which are "separable from and independent of" the "fill" restriction may well support validity of the Act in those areas of concern. [Citations omitted.]

Within the provisions of Section 4704, the denial of the permit to fill (Case No. 1) and the injunction (Case No. 2) are "set aside."

Appeal sustained in both cases.

WEBBER, J., did not sit.

NOTES AND QUESTIONS

1. Just v. Marinette County, 56 Wis. 2d 7, 201 N.W.2d 761 (1972), offers contrast with State v. Johnson. Wisconsin passed the Water Quality Act of 1965, which directed counties to adopt shoreland zoning ordinances for approval by the State Department of Natural Resources. The act defined shorelands as lands within specified distances from various navigable waters. Pursuant to the act, Marinette County adopted a shoreland ordinance in 1967. Inter alia, the law established conservancy districts, within which certain landfill operations required a permit. Just owned swampland within a conservancy district. In 1968, without getting the necessary permit, Just hauled sand onto his property and filled in a sizeable parcel. Charged with a zoning violation, Just challenged the law as confiscatory (it should be assumed that the county would have denied the permit had it received an application).

Without dissent, the Wisconsin Supreme Court upheld the Marinette ordinance. The court did so fully aware of the Maine decision in State v. Johnson, *supra:*

> In State v. Johnson (1970), Me., 265 A.2d 711, the Wetlands Act restricted the alteration and use of certain wetlands without permission. The act was a conservation measure enacted under the police power to protect the ecology of areas bordering the coastal waters. The plaintiff owned a small tract of a salt-water marsh which was flooded at high tide. By filling, the land would be adapted for building purposes. The court held the restrictions against filling constituted a deprivation of a reasonable use of the owner's property and, thus, an unreasonable exercise of the police power. . . .
>
> It seems to us that filling a swamp not otherwise commercially usable is not in and of itself an existing use, which is prevented, but rather is the preparation for some future use which is not indigenous to a swamp. Too much stress is laid on the right of an owner to change commercially valueless land when that change does damage to the rights of the public. . . .
>
> The Justs argue their property has been severely depreciated in value. But this depreciation of value is not based on the use of the land in its natural state but on what the land would be worth if it could be filled and used for the location of a dwelling. While loss of value is to be considered in determining whether a restriction is a constructive taking, value based upon changing the character of the land at the expense of harm to public rights is not an essential factor or controlling. . . .
>
> We are not unmindful of the warning in Pennsylvania Coal Co. v. Mahon (1922), 260 U.S. 393: "We are in danger of forgetting that a strong public desire to improve the public condition is not enough to warrant achieving the desire by a shorter cut than the constitutional way of paying for the change." This observation refers to the improvement of the public condition, the securing of a benefit not presently enjoyed and to which the public is not entitled. The shoreland zoning ordinance preserves nature, the environment, and natural resources as they were created and to which the people have a present right.[6] The ordinance

---

6. On the letterhead of the Jackson County Zoning and Sanitation Department, the following appears: "The land belongs to the people . . . a little of it to those dead . . . some to those living . . . but most of it belongs to those yet to be born. . . ."

does not create or improve the public condition but only preserves nature from the despoilage and harm resulting from the unrestricted activities of humans.

Are you convinced by the Wisconsin court's treatment of State v. Johnson? Isn't landfill or grading often necessary before a tract is ready for development? What about timberland that first must be cleared? Is it meaningful to speak of the use of land "in its natural state"?

2. What is the source of the expectation, implicit in State v. Johnson, that every landowner has an unalienable privilege to build something on her soil?

3. The Maine court would require the state to pay Johnson for restricting his use of wetlands. If the state proceeded by eminent domain, what would it pay for? How would a court value the interests taken? To help you think about these questions, assume that Johnson owns 500 acres of swampland, for which he paid $10 per acre ten years ago. Valued as swampland today, it is still worth only $10 per acre. It is worth $100 per acre if zoned for one-family houses, one house to the acre; $200 per acre if zoned for one-family houses, three houses to the acre; $1000 per acre if zoned for "planned unit development," a mixture of one-family houses, apartments, and shopping.

What weight should be given to the following factors?

(a) The real estate tax assessment has remained at $10 per acre.
(b) Johnson has a contract to sell the acreage to a residential developer, contingent upon the right to build, for $100 per acre.
(c) $10 compounded at the rate of 12 percent annually would be worth $31 at the end of ten years.

4. The National Environmental Policy Act of 1969 (NEPA), 42 U.S.C. §§4321-4347 (1977), has been heralded as an "environmental bill of rights." Hanks and Hanks, An Environmental Bill of Rights: The Citizen Suit and the National Environmental Policy Act of 1969, 24 Rutgers L. Rev. 230 (1970). The act established an advisory Council of Environmental Qualities (CEQ), with a broad mandate to recommend national policies to improve the quality of the environment. NEPA also directs all federal agencies "to the fullest extent possible" to govern their activities in accordance with the policies of the act. More specifically, before undertaking any major federal action significantly affecting the quality of the environment, the responsible federal agency must prepare a detailed statement on

(a) the environmental impact of the proposed action,
(b) any adverse environmental effects which cannot be avoided should the proposal be implemented,
(c) alternatives to the proposed action,
(d) the relationship between local short-term uses of man's environment and the maintenance and enhancement of long-term productivity, and

(e) any irreversible and irretrievable commitment of resources which would be involved in the proposed action should it be implemented.

This environmental impact statement is expected to guide the agency decision. Moreover, it provides a basis for citizen challenge to any action having an adverse environmental impact.

Activities subject to the NEPA requirements include federally aided public housing, flood control, beach erosion, urban renewal, and power plant and highway construction. An early illustration of the statement's potential for decision making was a HUD judgment not to approve because of noise problems a public housing project that was to be located near the St. Louis Airport. F. Grad, Environmental Law 13-21 (1971). The courts' intent to enforce strict agency compliance with NEPA's *procedural* aspects became evident with the decision in Calvert Cliffs Coordinating Committee, Inc. v. U.S. Atomic Energy Commission, 449 F.2d 1109 (D.C. Cir. 1971) (court rejected AEC rules for reviewing environmental considerations; "the requirement of environmental considerations 'to the fullest extent possible' sets a high standard for the agencies . . . which must be rigorously enforced. . . .")

5.   Perhaps as important as NEPA's impact on federally aided activities has been its inspiration to state legislatures to enact similar laws governing state and local developmental programs. The California Environmental Quality Act of 1970, Cal. Pub. Res. Code §§21000-21151 (West), is typical. Section 21151 requires an environmental impact statement, similar to NEPA's, whenever a local governmental agency carries out a project having a "significant effect on the environment." The California Supreme Court has ruled that a privately developed mixed-use project, consisting of 184 condominium units, restaurant, and specialty shops on a 5.5-acre parcel, fell within the §21151 requirement, since a government permit was needed to build the project. Friends of Mammoth v. Board of Supervisors of Mono County, 8 Cal. 3d 247, 502 P.2d 1049, 104 Cal. Rptr. 761 (1972).

Suppose, as was claimed in *Friends of Mammoth*, that no development could proceed without impairing "one of the nation's most spectacularly beautiful and comparatively unspoiled treasures." Can the community constitutionally bar any development? If not, can the community permit only the "least impairing" development? What if it becomes prohibitively expensive for the developer to continue in the "least impairing" way?

California voters also approved "Proposition 20" at the 1972 general election. Known as the Coastal Conservation Act of 1972, this law required any development within 1000 yards of the shoreline to prove, before a permit would be issued, that no "substantial adverse environmental or ecological effect" would ensue. Where the topography involved estuaries or wetlands or a natural development area extending back to a mountain ridge, the protected zone could reach as much as five miles inland. In 1976, the legislature repealed this law, which all had regarded as an interim measure, and replaced it with the substantially similar, but expanded California Coastal Act. Cal. Pub. Res. Code §§30000 et seq. (West Supp. 1981).

In an editorial condemning Governor Edmund Brown, Jr. for "his performance in pushing the coastal zoning belt through the California legislature," the Wall Street Journal wrote: "This is naked class legislation which will serve to protect the enclaves of the prosperous already established on the coastline and block any further economic growth that might disturb the 'quality of life' of the affluent." Wall Street Journal, Sept. 14, 1976, at 26, col. 1.

The 1972 law has been upheld. Avco Community Development, Inc. v. South Coast Regional Commission, 17 Cal. 3d 785, 553 P.2d 546, 132 Cal. Rptr. 386 (1976).

6. The tiny town of Sanbornton, New Hampshire, has a year-round population of 1,000. Located in a major resort area, the town found itself under severe pressure from seasonal-home developers. In order to preserve the area's rural character, reduce water and air pollution, and protect smelt spawning in Black Brook, the town adopted a 6-acre minimum lot size requirement, which effectively stalled one developer's plans for a 510-acre parcel. Previous zoning would have permitted a lot area of 35,000 square feet (one acre = 44,000 square feet). Was there a taking? No, said the court in Steel Hill Development, Inc. v. Town of Sanbornton, 469 F.2d 956 (1st Cir. 1972):

We recognize, as within the general welfare, concerns relating to the construction and integration of hundreds of new homes which would have an irreversible effect on the area's ecological balance, destroy scenic values, decrease open space, significantly change the rural character of this small town, pose substantial financial burdens on the town for police, fire, sewer, and road service, and open the way for the tides of weekend "visitors" who would own second homes. If the federal government itself has thought these concerns to be within the general welfare, see, e.g., 42 U.S.C. §4321, et seq., (NEPA) we cannot say that Sanbornton cannot similarly consider such values and reflect them in its zoning ordinance. Though some courts may have rejected them within the suburban zoning context, as in [National Land and Investment Co. v. Kohn, 419 Pa. 504, 215 A.2d 597 (1965), page 891 *infra*], and its progeny or where permanent first homes are involved, [citations omitted] we think they are persuasive in the case before us. "Many environmental and social values are involved in a determination of how land would best be used in the public interest. The choice of the voters of [the city] is not lacking in support in this regard." Southern Alameda Spanish Organization v. City of Union City, 424 F.2d 291 (9th Cir. 1970).

Yet, though it may be proper for Sanbornton to consider the foregoing factors, we think the town has done so in a most crude manner. We are disturbed by the admission here that there was never any professional or scientific study made as to why six, rather than four or eight, acres was reasonable to protect the values cherished by the people of Sanbornton. On reviewing the record, we have serious worries whether the basic motivation of the town meeting was not simply to keep outsiders, provided they wished to come in quantity, out of the town. We cannot think that expansion of population, even a very substantial one, seasonal or permanent, is by itself a legitimate basis for permissible objection. Were we to adjudicate this as a restriction for all time, and were the evidence of pressure from land-deprived and land-seeking outsiders more real, we might well come to a different conclusion. Where there is natural population growth it has to go somewhere, unwelcome as it may be, and in that case we do not think it should be channelled by the happenstance of what town gets its veto in first. But, at this time of uncertainty as to the right balance between ecological and population pressures, we cannot help but feel that the town's ordinance, which severely restricts development, may properly stand for the present as a legitimate stopgap measure.

In effect, the town has bought time for its citizens not unlike the action taken in referendum by the City of Boulder, Colorado to restrict growth on an emergency basis until an adequate study can be made of future needs. 60 Georgetown L.J. 1363 (1972). See also Golden v. Planning Board of Town of Ramapo, 30 N.Y.2d 359, 334 N.Y.S.2d 138, 285 N.E.2d 291 (1972), *appeal dismissed,* 409 U.S. 1003 (1972). It was evident to the zoning board, and the district court, that haphazard and uncontrolled development of the town's hill areas would be inimical to present and future Sanbornton residents, see Candlestick Properties, Inc. v. San Francisco Bay Conservation & Development Comm., 11 Cal. App. 3d 557, 89 Cal. Rptr. 897 (1970), and that if the zoning laws do become "permanent barriers," then as the district court said, resort to the courts is always possible. *Steel Hill Development, supra,* 338 F. Supp. at 307. The zoning ordinance here in question has been in existence less than two years. Hopefully, Sanbornton has begun or soon will begin to plan with more precision for the future, taking advantage of numerous federal or state grants for which it might qualify. Additionally, the New Hampshire legislature, to the extent it expects small towns like Sanbornton to cope with environmental problems posed by private developments, might adopt legislation similar to the federal National Environmental Policy Act, 42 U.S.C. §4321 et seq., and thereby require developers to submit detailed environmental statements, if such power does not already reside within the town's arsenal of laws. Thus, while we affirm the district court's determination at the present time, we recognize that this is a very special case which cannot be read as evidencing a general approval of six-acre zoning, and that this requirement may well not indefinitely stand without more homework by the concerned parties.

Lastly, we find little merit to appellant's contentions that the zoning ordinance has resulted in a taking of appellant's property without just compensation or that it is discriminatory. As the district court found, appellant still has the land and buildings for which it paid $290,000. The estimated worth, had Steel Hill's original plans been approved, is irrelevant. Though the value of the tract has been decreased considerably, it is not worthless or useless so as to constitute a taking. Hadacheck v. Sebastian, 239 U.S. 394 (1915); Sibson v. State, N.H., 282 A.2d 664 (1971). Cf. State v. Johnson, 265 A.2d 711 (Me. 1970); Bartlett v. Zoning Comm. of Town of Old Lyme, 161 Conn. 24, 282 A.2d 907 (1971). As to appellant's claim of discrimination, we note that its land, like all other land zoned six acres, is essentially virgin forest. It is adjacent to, and its March 1971 re-zoning represented an extension of, the Forest Conservation District created in 1970. Thus the ordinance cannot be said to discriminate unreasonably against Steel Hill, be it the only developer in the town.

Affirmed.

As attorney for the town, or for the developer, how would you proceed for the next stage in the relentless struggle between builders and environmentalists? As the state representative from the town? As the legislative lobbyist for the real estate interests?

7. It is becoming increasingly clear that environmental impact means far more than a collision between developers and nature in remote outlying areas. See, e.g., City of Orange v. Valenti, 37 Cal. App. 3d 240, 249, 112 Cal. Rptr. 379, 386 (1974) ("the state may not put a traffic snarling, parking congesting activity, slam-bang in the middle of a quiet, single-family residential, area . . . without . . . an environmental impact report"); Jones v. District of Columbia Redevelopment Land Agency, 499 F.2d 502 (D.C. Cir. 1974) (NEPA applies to urban renewal planning); City of Rochester v. United States Postal Service, 541 F.2d 967 (2d Cir. 1976) (NEPA applied to new suburban postal facility where construction called for ultimate abandonment of an older city facility and for transfer of 1400 employees with consequent effect on commuter traffic); Trinity Episcopal School v. Romney, 523 F.2d 88 (2d Cir. 1975) (NEPA applies to public housing project on west side of Manhattan).

8. Another federal law affecting land development is the 1977 Air Pollution Prevention and Control Act, 42 U.S.C.A. §§7401 et seq. This act replaces earlier legislation, which included the 1955 Clean Air Act and the 1970 Clean Air Amendments Act. The law mandates the Environmental Protection Agency (EPA) to establish national ambient air quality standards, and directs each state to adopt a plan to achieve and maintain such standards. When applied to a proposed new parking facility at Boston's Logan Airport, the standards resulted in a ruling that the new facility could not increase by more than 10 percent the overall parking spaces at the terminal. Cf. Smith Terminal Corp. v. Environmental Protection Agency, 504 F.2d 646 (1st Cir. 1974). Clean air laws also have begun to hold up construction of large regional shopping centers, Wall St. J., Sept. 25, 1973, at 1, col. 6, and interstate highways such as New York City's Westway.

9. We have begun to see how foes of unwanted residential development are invoking environmental impact to prevent or stall the projects they do not like. See, e.g., Coalition for the Environment v. Volpe, 504 F.2d 156 (8th Cir. 1974) ("Earth City," a "balanced" new town of 12,000 residents eventually employing 29,000 persons). The delays and litigation costs may defeat even stouthearted and well-financed developers. The "Earth City" suit, to determine whether impact statements need be filed, began in 1971 and was still in the courts three years later. Cf. also Russian Hill Improvement Assn. v. Board of Permit Appeals, 44 Cal. App. 3d 158, 118 Cal. Rptr. 490 (1974) (permit issued Feb. 1972 for 343 units of luxury apartments; three years of litigation ensued, and more to come); Sierra Club v. Lynn, 502 F.2d 43 (5th Cir. 1974) (San Antonio Ranch New Town, planned for 88,000 residents, one-fourth having low or moderate income, obtained HUD financing guarantee in Feb. 1972; two and a half years of litigation ensued); Ackerman, Impact Statements and Low Cost Housing, 46 S. Cal. L. Rev. 754 (1973).

10. John Costonis, who earlier pioneered the concept of development

rights transfer as a means to compensate the owners of landmark properties, page 732, *supra,* proposed that the principle be extended to compensate the owners of ecologically sensitive lands who, under decisions like Just v. Marinette County, Note 1, *supra,* must otherwise absorb the full burden of regulation. Under the Costonis scheme, the regulated owner would receive development rights that he could then sell to landowners in "transfer zones" who wished to develop their parcels. The market value inherent in these transferable rights would provide the burdened owner with a reasonable investment return. Costonis, "Fair" Compensation and the Accommodation Power, 75 Colum. L. Rev. 1021 (1975).

The most extensive development rights transfer plan known to the author was authorized by the New Jersey legislature in 1979 and applied in 1981 to the Pine Barrens, a large expanse of fragile aquifer in the southern part of the state.

§16.5   Control of Development Pace and Sequence

We have learned sadly that uncontrolled growth has meant disregard not only for the American landscape and our historical heritage, but also for government finance, the sensibility of land-use relationships, and the amenity of day-to-day life. As we saw in the *Sanbornton* case, page 863 *supra,* high growth communities are at last becoming far more assertive in seeking to control and channel the developer's "own sweet will." Rather than assume that every acre of vacant land is instantly ripe for development whenever its owner is ready to proceed, some newer ordinances seek to establish a development rationale, which implies an orderly sequence and a timetable for population growth. The most celebrated of these ordinances, coming from the town of Ramapo in New York's Rockland County (on the fringes of New York City), is the subject of the case below.

GOLDEN v. PLANNING BOARD OF TOWN OF RAMAPO
30 N.Y.2d 359, 285 N.E.2d 291, 334 N.Y.S.2d 138, app. dismissed, 409 U.S. 1003 (1972)

SCILEPPI, J. Both cases arise out of the 1969 amendments to the Town of Ramapo's Zoning Ordinance. . . .

Experiencing the pressures of an increase in population and the ancillary problem of providing municipal facilities and services,[1] the Town of Ramapo,

_____

1. The Town's allegations that present facilities are inadequate to service increasing demands goes uncontested. We must assume, therefore, that the proposed improvements, both as to their nature and extent, reflect legitimate community needs and are not veiled efforts at exclusion (see National Land & Inv. Co. v. Easttown Twp. Bd. of Adj., 419 Pa. 504, 215 A.2d 597). In the

as early as 1964, made application for grant under section 801 of the Housing Act of 1964 (78 U.S. Stat. 769) to develop a master plan. The plan's preparation included a four-volume study of the existing land uses, public facilities, transportation, industry and commerce, housing needs and projected population trends. The proposals appearing in the studies were subsequently adopted pursuant to section 272-a of the Town Law, Consol. Laws, c. 62, in July, 1966 and implemented by way of a master plan. The master plan was followed by the adoption of a comprehensive zoning ordinance. Additional sewage district and drainage studies were undertaken which culminated in the adoption of a capital budget, providing for the development of the improvements specified in the master plan within the next six years. Pursuant to section 271 of the Town Law, authorizing comprehensive planning, and as a supplement to the capital budget, the Town Board adopted a capital program which provides for the location and sequence of additional capital improvements for the 12 years following the life of the capital budget. The two plans, covering a period of 18 years, detail the capital improvements projected for maximum development and conform to the specifications set forth in the master plan, the official map and drainage plan.

Based upon these criteria, the Town subsequently adopted the subject amendments for the alleged purpose of eliminating premature subdivision and urban sprawl. Residential development is to proceed according to the provision of adequate municipal facilities and services, with the assurance that any concomitant restraint upon property use is to be of a "temporary" nature and that other private uses, including the construction of individual housing, are authorized.

The amendments did not rezone or reclassify any land into different residential or use districts, but, for the purposes of implementing the proposals appearing in the comprehensive plan, consist, in the main, of additions to the definitional sections of the ordinance, section 46-3, and the adoption of a new class of "Special Permit Uses," designated "Residential Development Use." "Residential Development Use" is defined as "The erection or construction of dwellings on any vacant plots, lots or parcels of land" (§46-3, as amd.); and, any person who acts so as to come within that definition, "shall be deemed to

---

period 1940-1968 population in the unincorporated areas of the Town increased 285.9%. Between the years of 1950-1960 the increase, again in unincorporated areas, was 130.8%; from 1960-1966 some 78.5%; and from the years 1966-1969 20.4%. In terms of real numbers, population figures compare at 58,626 as of 1966 with the largest increment of growth since the decennial census occurring in the undeveloped areas. Projected figures, assuming current land use and zoning trends, approximate a total Town population of 120,000 by 1985. Growth is expected to be heaviest in the currently undeveloped western and northern tiers of the Town, predominantly in the form of subdivision development with some apartment construction. A growth rate of some 1,000 residential units per annum has been experienced in the unincorporated areas of the Town.

"All distances shall be computed from the proposed location of each separate lot or plot capable of being improved with a residential dwelling and not from the boundaries of the entire parcel. The Town Board shall issue the special permit specifying the number of dwelling units that meet the standards set forth herein." Ramapo Town Ordinances §46-13.1, quoted in 24 Zoning Digest 70 (1972).—Ed.

be engaged in residential development which shall be a separate use classification under this ordinance and subject to the requirement of obtaining a special permit from the Town Board" (§46-3, as amd.).

The standards for the issuance of special permits are framed in terms of availability to the proposed subdivision plat of five essential facilities or services: specifically (1) public sanitary sewers or approved substitutes; (2) drainage facilities; (3) improved public parks or recreation facilities, including public schools; (4) State, county or town roads—major, secondary or collector; and, (5) firehouses. No special permit shall issue unless the proposed residential development has accumulated 15 development points, to be computed on a sliding scale of values assigned to the specified improvements under the statute.[2] Subdivision is thus a function of immediate availability to the proposed plat of certain municipal improvements; the avowed purpose of the amendments being to phase residential development to the Town's ability to provide the above facilities or services.

Certain savings and remedial provisions are designed to relieve of potentially unreasonable restrictions. Thus, the board may issue special permits vesting a present right to proceed with residential development in such year as

---

2. D. *Standards for Issuance of Special Permit*
No special permit shall be issued by the Town Board unless the residential development has available fifteen (15) development points on the following scale of values:

(1) *Sewers*
    (a) Public sewers available in RR-50, R-40, R-35, R-25, R-15 and
        R-15S districts   5 points
    (b) Package Sewer Plants   3 points
    (c) County approved septic system in an RR-80 district   3 points
    (d) All others   0 points
(2) *Drainage*
    Percentage of Required Drainage Capacity Available
    (a) 100% or more   5 points
    (b) 90% to 99.9%   4 points
    (c) 80% to 89.9%   3 points
    (d) 65% to 79.9%   2 points
    (e) 50% to 64.9%   1 point
    (f) Less than 50%   0 points
(3) *Improved Public Park or Recreation Facility Including Public School Site*
    (a) Within ¼ mile   5 points
    (b) Within ½ mile   3 points
    (c) Within 1 mile   1 point
    (d) Further than 1 mile   0 points
(4) *State, County or Town Major, Secondary or Collector Road(s) Improved*
    with Curbs and Sidewalks
    (a) Direct Access   5 points
    (b) Within ½ mile   3 points
    (c) Within 1 mile   1 point
    (d) Further than 1 mile   0 points
(5) *Fire House*
    (a) Within 1 mile   3 points
    (b) Within 2 miles   1 point
    (c) Further than 2 miles   0 points

the development meets the required point minimum, but in no event later than the final year of the 18-year capital plan. The approved special use permit is fully assignable, and improvements scheduled for completion within one year from the date of an application are to be credited as though existing on the date of the application. A prospective developer may advance the date of subdivision approval by agreeing to provide those improvements which will bring the proposed plat within the number of development points required by the amendments. And applications are authorized to the "Development Easement Acquisition Commission" for a reduction of the assessed valuation. Finally, upon application to the Town Board, the development point requirements may be varied should the board determine that such a variance or modification is consistent with the on-going development plan.

The undisputed effect of these integrated efforts in land use planning and development is to provide an over-all program of orderly growth and adequate facilities through a sequential development policy commensurate with progressing availability and capacity of public facilities. While its goals are clear and its purposes undisputably laudatory, serious questions are raised as to the manner in which these ends are to be effected, not the least of which relates to their legal viability under present zoning enabling legislation, particularly sections 261 and 263 of the Town Law. The owners of the subject premises argue, and the Appellate Division has sustained the proposition, that the primary purpose of the amending ordinance is to control or regulate population growth within the Town and as such is not within the authorized objectives of the zoning enabling legislation. We disagree. . . .

[The court, while conceding that New York's enabling law does not explicitly authorize Ramapo's sequence and timing controls, finds that they come "within the perimeters of the devices authorized and purposes sanctioned" by the law.]

Undoubtedly, current zoning enabling legislation is burdened by the largely antiquated notion which deigns that the regulation of land use and development is uniquely a function of local government—that the public interest of the State is exhausted once its political subdivisions have been delegated the authority to zone (ALI, A Model Land Development Code [Tent. Draft No. 1], Intro. Mem., p. xxi). While such jurisdictional allocations may well have been consistent with formerly prevailing conditions and assumptions, questions of broader public interest have commonly been ignored (ALI, A Model Land Development Code [Tent. Draft No. 1], Intro. Mem., p. xxi; see, also, Roberts, Demise of Property Law, 57 Cornell L. Rev. 1, 19, 21; R. Babcock, The Zoning Game [1966] p. 19).

Experience, over the last quarter century, however, with greater technological integration and drastic shifts in population distribution has pointed up serious defects and community autonomy in land use controls has come under increasing attack by legal commentators, and students of urban problems alike, because of its pronounced insularism and its correlative role in producing distortions in metropolitan growth patterns, and perhaps more importantly, in crippling efforts toward regional and State-wide problem solving, be it pollution, decent housing, or public transportation (ALI, A Model Land Development Code [Tent. Draft No. 2, April 24, 1970], Intro. Mem., p. xv, citing Report of National Comm. on Urban Problems [Douglas Comm.], Building the American City [1969]; see, also, New York State Planning Law Revision Study, Study Doc. No. 4 [New York State Office of Planning Coordination, Feb., 1970]).

Recognition of communal and regional interdependence, in turn, has resulted in proposals for schemes of regional and State-wide planning, in the hope that decisions would then correspond roughly to their level of impact (see, e.g., Proposed Land Use and Development Planning Law, §§2-102, 4-101, 4-102; ALI, A Model Land Development Code, art. 7. Yet, as salutary as such proposals may be, the power to zone under current law is vested in local municipalities, and we are constrained to resolve the issues accordingly. What does become more apparent in treating with the problem, however, is that though the issues are framed in terms of the developer's due process rights, those rights cannot, realistically speaking, be viewed separately and apart from the rights of others " 'in search of a [more] comfortable place to live.' " (Concord Twp. Appeal, 439 Pa. 466, 474, n.6, 268 A.2d 765, 768, National Land & Inv. Co. v. Easttown Twp. Bd. of Adj., 419 Pa. 504, 527-528, 215 A.2d 597; see, generally, Sager, Tight Little Islands: Exclusionary Zoning, Equal Protection and the Indigent, 21 Stan. L. Rev. 767; Roberts, Demise of Property Law, 57 Cornell L. Rev. 1).

There is, then, something inherently suspect in a scheme which, apart from its professed purposes, effects a restriction upon the free mobility of a people until sometime in the future when projected facilities are available to meet increased demands. Although zoning must include schemes designed to allow municipalities to more effectively contend with the increased demands of evolving and growing communities, under its guise, townships have been wont to try their hand at an array of exclusionary devices in the hope of avoiding the very burden which growth must inevitably bring (see National Land & Inv. Co. v. Easttown Twp. Bd. of Adj., 419 Pa. 504, 532, 215 A.2d 597, *supra;* Girsh Appeal, 437 Pa. 237, 263 A.2d 395; Concord Twp. Appeal, 439 Pa. 466, 268 A.2d 765, *supra;* see, also, Roberts, Demise of Property Law, 57 Cornell L. Rev. 1, 5). Though the conflict engendered by such tactics is certainly real, and its implications vast, accumulated evidence, scientific and social, points circumspectly at the hazards of undirected growth and the naive, somewhat nostalgic imperative that egalitarianism is a function of growth. (See, generally, Lewis, Ecology and Politics: II, New York Times, March 6, 1972, p. 33, cols. 1, 2.)

Of course, these problems cannot be solved by Ramapo or any single municipality, but depend upon the accommodation of widely disparate interests for their ultimate resolution. To that end, State-wide or regional control of planning would insure that interests broader than that of the municipality underlie various land use policies. Nevertheless, that should not be the only

context in which growth devices such as these, aimed at population assimilation, not exclusion, will be sustained; especially where, as here, we would have
no alternative but to strike the provision down in the wistful hope that the
efforts of the State Office of Planning Coordination and the American Law
Institute will soon bear fruit.

   Hence, unless we are to ignore the plain meaning of the statutory delegation, this much is clear: phased growth is well within the ambit of existing
enabling legislation. And, of course, it is no answer to point to emergent problems to buttress the conclusion that such innovative schemes are beyond the
perimeters of statutory authorization. These considerations, admittedly real, to
the extent which they are relevant, bear solely upon the continued viability of
"localism" in land use regulation; obviously, they can neither add nor detract
from the initial grant of authority, obsolescent though it may be. The answer
which Ramapo has posed can by no means be termed definitive; it is, however, a first practical step toward controlled growth achieved without forsak-
ing broader social purposes.

   The evolution of more sophisticated efforts to contend with the increasing complexities of urban and suburban growth has been met by a corresponding reluctance upon the part of the judiciary to substitute its judgment as to
the plan's over-all effectiveness for the considered deliberations of its progeni-
tors [citation omitted]. Implicit in such a philosophy of judicial self-restraint is
the growing awareness that matters of land use and development are peculiarly within the expertise of students of city and suburban planning, and thus
well within the legislative prerogative, not lightly to be impeded [citations
omitted]. To this same end, we have afforded such regulations, the usual
presumption of validity attending the exercise of the police power, and have
cast the burden of proving their invalidity upon the party challenging their
enactment [citations omitted]. Deference in the matter of the regulations' overall effectiveness, however, is not to be viewed as an abdication of judicial
responsibility, and ours remains the function of defining the metes and bounds
beyond which local regulations may not venture, regardless of their profess-
edly beneficent purposes.

   The subject ordinance is said to advance legitimate zoning purposes as it
assures that each new home built in the township will have at least a minimum
of public services in the categories regulated by the ordinance. The Town
argues that various public facilities are presently being constructed but that for
want of time and money it has been unable to provide such services and
facilities at a pace commensurate with increased public need. It is urged that
although the zoning power includes reasonable restrictions upon the private
use of property, exacted in the hope of development according to well-laid
plans, calculated to advance the public welfare of the community in the future
[citations omitted], the subject regulations go further and seek to avoid the
increased responsibilities and economic burdens which time and growth must
ultimately bring [citations omitted].

   It is the nature of all land use and development regulations to circumscribe the course of growth within a particular town or district and to that extent such restrictions invariably impede the forces of natural growth [citations omitted]. Where those restrictions upon the beneficial use and enjoyment of land are necessary to promote the ultimate good of the community and are within the bounds of reason, they have been sustained. "Zoning [, however,] is a means by which a governmental body can plan for the future—it may not be used as a means to deny the future," National Land & Inv. Co. v. Easttown Twp. Bd. of Adj., 419 Pa. 504, 528, 215 A.2d 597, 610, *supra*. Its exercise assumes that development shall not stop at the community's threshold, but only that whatever growth there may be shall proceed along a predetermined course (Euclid v. Ambler Co., 272 U.S. 365, 387, *supra*). It is inextricably bound to the dynamics of community life and its function is to guide, not to isolate or facilitate efforts at avoiding the ordinary incidents of growth. What segregates permissible from impermissible restrictions, depends in the final analysis upon the purpose of the restrictions and their impact in terms of both the community and general public interest (see Euclid v. Ambler Co., 272 U.S. 365, 387, *supra*). The line of delineation between the two is not a constant, but will be found to vary with prevailing circumstances and conditions [citations omitted].

What we will not countenance, then, under any guise, is community efforts at immunization or exclusion. But, far from being exclusionary, the present amendments merely seek, by the implementation of sequential development and timed growth, to provide a balanced cohesive community dedicated to the efficient utilization of land. The restrictions conform to the community's considered land use policies as expressed in its comprehensive plan and represent a bona fide effort to maximize population density consistent with orderly growh. True other alternatives, such as requiring off-site improvements as a prerequisite to subdivision, may be available, but the choice as how best to proceed, in view of the difficulties attending such exactions (see Heyman & Gilhool, The Constitutionality of Imposing Increased Community Costs on New Suburban Residents through Subdivision Exactions, 73 Yale L.J. 1119; see, also, ALI, A Model Land Development Code, §3-104, subd. [6]), cannot be faulted.

Perhaps even more importantly, timed growth, unlike the minimum lot requirements recently struck down by the Pennsylvania Supreme Court as exclusionary, does not impose permanent restrictions upon land use (see National Land & Inv. Co. v. Easttown Twp. Bd. of Adj., 419 Pa. 504, 215 A.2d 597, *supra;* Concord Twp. Appeal, 439 Pa. 466, 268 A.2d 765, *supra*). Its obvious purpose is to prevent premature subdivision absent essential municipal facilities and to insure continuous development commensurate with the Town's obligation to provide such facilities. They seek, not to freeze population at present levels but to maximize growth by the efficient use of land, and in so doing testify to this community's continuing role in population assimilation. In sum, Ramapo asks not that it be left alone, but only that it be allowed to prevent the kind of deterioration that has transformed well-ordered and thriving residential communities into blighted ghettos with attendant hazards to health, security and social stability—a danger not without substantial basis in fact.

We only require that communities confront the challenge of population growth with open doors. Where in grappling with that problem, the community undertakes, by imposing temporary restrictions upon development, to provide required municipal services in a rational manner, courts are rightfully reluctant to strike down such schemes. The timing controls challenged here parallel recent proposals set forth by various study groups and have their genesis in certain of the pronouncements of this and the courts of sister States (see Proposed Land Use and Development Planning Law, §2-105, subds. 1, 2, par. [a], as proposed by Sen. No. 9028 of 1970 Legislature; ALI, A Model Land Development Code [Tent. Draft No. 2, April, 1970], §§2-101, 2-201, subd. [2], par. [c], §2-206; [Tent. Draft No. 1, April, 1968], §§3-101, 3-103, 3-104, 3-107, 3-108; see Westwood Forest Estates v. Village of South Nyack, 23 N.Y.2d 424, 427, 297 N.Y.S.2d 129, 132, 244 N.E.2d 700, 701; Concord Twp. Appeal, 439 Pa. 466, 475, 268 A.2d 765, *supra;* National Land & Inv. Co. v. Easttown Twp. Bd. of Adj., 419 Pa. 504, 532, 215 A.2d 597, *supra*). While these controls are typically proposed as an adjunct of regional planning (see Proposed Land Use and Development Planning Law, arts. 3, 4; ALI, A Model Land Development Code, art. 7), the preeminent protection against their abuse resides in the mandatory on-going planning and development requirement, present here, which attends their implementation and use (see, e.g., Proposed Land Use and Development Planning Law, §2-105).

We may assume, therefore, that the present amendments are the product of foresighted planning calculated to promote the welfare of the township. The Town has imposed temporary restrictions upon land use in residential areas while committing itself to a program of development. It has utilized its comprehensive plan to implement its timing controls and has coupled with these restrictions provisions for low and moderate income housing on a large scale. Considered as a whole, it represents both in its inception and implementation a reasonable attempt to provide for the sequential, orderly development of land in conjunction with the needs of the community, as well as individual parcels of land, while simultaneously obviating the blighted aftermath which the initial failure to provide needed facilities so often brings.

The proposed amendments have the effect of restricting development for onwards to 18 years in certain areas. Whether the subject parcels will be so restricted for the full term is not clear, for it is equally probable that the proposed facilities will be brought into these areas well before that time. Assuming, however, that the restrictions will remain outstanding for the life of the program, they still fall short of a confiscation within the meaning of the Constitution.

An ordinance which seeks to permanently restrict the use of property so that it may not be used for any reasonable purpose must be recognized as a taking: The only difference between the restriction and an outright taking in such a case "is that the restriction leaves the owner subject to the burden of payment of taxation, while outright confiscation would relieve him of that burden" (Arverne Bay Constr. Co. v. Thatcher, 278 N.Y. 222, 232, 15 N.E.2d 587, 592, *supra*). An appreciably different situation obtains where the restriction constitutes a *temporary* restriction, promising that the property may be put to a profitable use within a reasonable time. The hardship of holding unproductive property for some time might be compensated for by the ultimate benefit inuring to the individual owner in the form of a substantial increase in valuation; or, for that matter, the landowner, might be compelled to chafe under the temporary restriction, without the benefit of such compensation, when that burden serves to promote the public good (cf. Arverne Bay Constr. Co. v. Thatcher, 278 N.Y. 222, 232, 15 N.E.2d 587, 592, *supra*).

We are reminded, however, that these restrictions threaten to burden individual parcels for as long as a full generation and that such a restriction cannot, in any context, be viewed as a temporary expedient. The Town, on the other hand, contends that the landowner is not deprived of either the best use of his land or of numerous other appropriate uses, still permitted within various residential districts, including the construction of a single-family residence, and consequently, it cannot be deemed confiscatory. Although no proof has been submitted on reduction of value, the landowners point to obvious disparity between the value of the property, if limited in use by the subject amendments and its value for residential development purposes, and argue that the diminution is so considerable that for all intents and purposes the land cannot presently or in the near future be put to profitable or beneficial use, without violation of the restrictions.

Every restriction on the use of property entails hardships for some individual owners. Those difficulties are invariably the product of police regulation and the pecuniary profits of the individual must in the long run be subordinated to the needs of the community. [Citations omitted.] The fact that the ordinance limits the use of, and may depreciate the value of the property will not render it unconstitutional, however, unless it can be shown that the measure is either unreasonable in terms of necessity or the diminution in value is such as to be tantamount to a confiscation (see, e.g., Vernon Park Realty v. City of Mount Vernon, 307 N.Y. 493, 499, 121 N.E.2d 517, 520). Diminution, in turn, is a relative factor and though its magnitude is an indicia of a taking, it does not of itself establish a confiscation [citations omitted].

Without a doubt restrictions upon the property in the present case are substantial in nature and duration. They are not, however, absolute. The amendments contemplate a definite term, as the development points are designed to operate for a maximum period of 18 years and during that period, the Town is committed to the construction and installation of capital improvements. The net result of the ongoing development provision is that individual parcels may be committed to a residential development use prior to the expiration of the maximum period. Similarly, property owners under the terms of the amendments may elect to accelerate the date of development by installing,

at their own expense, the necessary public services to bring the parcel within
the required number of development points. While even the best of plans may
not always be realized, in the absence of proof to the contrary, we must assume
the Town will put its best effort forward in implementing the physical and
fiscal timetable outlined under the plan. Should subsequent events prove this
assumption unwarranted, or should the Town because of some unforeseen
event fail in its primary obligation to these landowners, there will be ample
opportunity to undo the restrictions upon default. For the present, at least, we
are constrained to proceed upon the assumption that the program will be fully
and timely implemented [citation omitted].

Thus, unlike the situation presented in Arverne Bay Constr. Co. v.
Thatcher, 278 N.Y. 222, 15 N.E.2d 587, *supra,* the present amendments propose restrictions of a certain duration and founded upon estimate determined
by fact. Prognostication on our part in upholding the ordinance proceeds upon
the presently permissible inference that within a reasonable time the subject
property will be put to the desired use at an appreciated value. In the interim
assessed valuations for real estate tax purposes reflect the impact of the proposed restrictions (cf. Arverne Bay Constr. Co. v. Thatcher, 278 N.Y. 222, 232,
15 N.E.2d 587, 592, *supra*). The proposed restraints, mitigated by the prospect
of appreciated value and interim reductions in assessed value, and measured
in terms of the nature and magnitude of the project undertaken, are within the
limits of necessity.

In sum, where it is clear that the existing physical and financial resources of the community are inadequate to furnish the essential services and
facilities which a substantial increase in population requires, there is a rational
basis for "phased growth" and hence, the challenged ordinance is not violative
of the Federal and State Constitutions. Accordingly, the order appealed from
should be reversed and the actions remitted to Special Term for entry of a
judgment declaring section 46-13.1 of the Town Ordinance constitutional.

BREITEL, J. (dissenting). . . . Holding zones, that is, areas reserved for
future development, if legislatively authorized and carefully circumscribed,
can validly and effectively implement land planning. Both the interests of
localities and the broader interests of the State and its large metropolitan areas
can be reconciled. Indeed it has been suggested by the National Commission
on Urban Problems that enabling legislation grant communities such power.
The devising and authorization of new powers, one of which is to create holding or delayed development zones, is a chief concern of the State Office of
Planning Coordination. Indeed, it plays a prominent role in its proposed legislation. Notably, in delayed development schemes limitations are invariably
suggested, limitations absent in the Ramapo ordinance (e.g., 3- to 5-year limits, regional and State agency review, provision for compensation). Such limitations may be essential if the delegation is to be valid constitutionally. Aside
from considerations of unlimited delegation, without the standards which universally circumscribe the conduct of administrative agencies, the limitations
reflect basic doctrine that even the State's zoning power is not unlimited. As

observed by the Pennsylvania Supreme Court, "Zoning is a means by which a governmental body can plan for the future—it may not be used as a means to deny the future" (National Land & Inv. Co. v. Easttown Twp. Bd. of Adj., 419 Pa. 504, 215 A.2d 597, *supra,* at p. 528, 215 A.2d at p. 610). Again, (in Concord Twp. Appeal, 439 Pa. 466, 268 A.2d 765, *supra*), it observed "Communities must deal with the problems of population growth. They may not refuse to confront the future by adopting zoning regulations that effectively restrict population to near present levels" (at p. 474, 268 A.2d at p. 768).

Either by legislation limited by decisional rule, or by decisional rule alone a limited amount of restraint in time has been held valid in controlling development, even without compensation. Thus, in the State of Washington it was suggested that the legislatively authorized right to impress "holding zones" on private property beyond the immediate reaches of present development, must be reasonably limited in its duration (State ex rel. Randall v. Snohomish County, 79 Wash. 2d 619, 488 P.2d 511; see, also, Westwood Forest Estates v. Village of South Nyack, 23 N.Y.2d 424, 428-429, 297 N.Y.S.2d 129, 132-133, 244 N.E.2d 700, 702-703). Significantly, the time limitations should be brief, or reasonably fixed, and justified by emergency or statutory authorization. . . .

Consequently, although the town had no power under the enabling act to adopt the ordinance in question, this does not mean that the town is not faced with a grave problem. It is. So are the many towns and villages in the State, and elsewhere in the country. But there is no doubt that the Ramapos, in isolation, cannot solve their problems alone, legally, under existing laws, or socially, politically, or economically. For the time being, the Ramapos must do what they can with district zoning and subdivision platting control. They may not declare moratoria on growth and development for as much as a generation. They may not separately or in concert impair the freedom of movement or residence of those outside their borders, even by ingenious schemes. Nor is it important whether their intention is to exclude, if that is the effect of their arrogated powers.

The exclusionary effect of local efforts to preserve the country's Edens has been largely noted. Professor Roberts, in an important essay, explores the conditions bedevilling places like Ramapo but also assesses the calamitous effects of ill-advised parochial devices (E. F. Roberts, The Demise of Property Law, 57 Cornell L. Rev. 1). The problems of development of the larger community run so deep, he suggests that:

> "Snob zoning," of course, may best be "solved" by the legislature. This really is the lesson contained in *Girsh* which seems, moderately enough, to suggest that a regional planning mechanism should be devised to create a pluralist suburbia in which each class could find its proper place. More interest, however, is being generated by the notion of statewide land-use planning which presumably would allow each class its niche outside center city. Whether this interest in formulating state planning derives from a concern for the lower orders or reflects instead an

irritation at the lack of order when a multitude of tiny hamlets makes any planning impossible, is difficult to tell. (at p. 37)

To leave vital decisions controlling the mix and timing of development to the unfettered discretion of the local community invites disaster. . . .

As said earlier, when the problem arose outside the State the judicial response has been the same, frustrating communities, intent on walling themselves from the mainstream of development, namely, that the effort was invalid under existing enabling acts or unconstitutional (National Land & Inv. Co. v. Easttown Twp. Bd. of Adj., 419 Pa. 504, 215 A.2d 597, *supra;* Girsh Appeal, 437 Pa. 237, 263 A.2d 395, *supra;* Bristow v. City of Woodhaven, 35 Mich. App. 205, 192 N.W.2d 322, *supra;* Lakeland Bluff v. County of Will, 114 Ill. App. 2d 267, 252 N.E.2d 765, *supra;* Concord Twp. Appeal, 439 Pa. 466, 268 A.2d 765, *supra;* Oakwood at Madison v. Township of Madison, 117 N.J. Super. 11, 283 A.2d 353, *supra*). The response may not be charged to judicial conservatism or self-restraint. In short, it has not been illiberal. It has indeed reflected the larger understanding that American society is at a critical crossroads in the accommodation of urbanization and suburban living, with effects that are no longer confined, bad as they are, to ethnic exclusion or "snob" zoning (see Roberts, op. cit., *supra,* at pp. 36-49). Ramapo would preserve its nature, delightful as that may be, but the supervening question is whether it alone may decide this or whether it must be decided by the larger community represented by the Legislature. Legally, politically, economically, and sociologically, the base for determination must be larger than that provided by the town fathers.

Accordingly, I dissent and vote to affirm the orders in both cases.

FULD, C.J., and BURKE, BERGAN, and GIBSON, JJ., concur with SCILEPPI, J.

BREITEL, J., dissents and votes to affirm in a separate opinion in which JASEN, J., concurs.

In each case: Order reversed, with costs and the case remitted to Special Term for further proceedings in accordance with the opinion herein.

NOTES AND QUESTIONS

1. Robert Freilich, Ramapo's attorney during the passage and successful defense of the ordinance, wrote afterwards:

What we have fought for and won was the right of a community to chart its own destiny within a framework of reasonable planning. Until we initiated the program in 1964 the pattern was for the developers and speculators to make the decisions as to where growth would take place. The only factor in their decision was the profit motive. It is not their concern as to how their development will affect demands for government service which will be reflected in higher taxes

and will have a tremendous impact on the lack of required secondary government investment. Nor are they especially concerned with the effects of their
development on the environment or in the social and economic composition of
the community. [Editor's Comments, Golden v. Town of Ramapo: Establishing
a New Dimension in American Planning Law, 4 Urban Lawyer ix, xii-xiii
(1972)]

A few years after the *Ramapo* decision, the town was issuing an average of
350 building permits annually, down from 620 before the new law. N.Y.
Times, Dec. 22, 1974, §4, at 3, col. 4.

2.   Fagin, Regulating the Timing of Urban Development, 20 Law and
Contemp. Prob. 298, 300-302 (1955), pioneered the argument for timing control:

But there are at least five well-considered motivations for regulating the
timing of urban development. These derive from the specific nature of modern
community-building activities and community requirements:

1.   *The need to economize on the costs of municipal facilities and services.* These
costs are strongly affected by the sequence in which the different areas of a
municipality are developed. This matter involves the efficient provision of police
and fire protection, schools, bus lines, streets and highways, utilities, and other
important facilities. The sequence of building operations determines, for example, whether linear facilities such as pipes and streets will have to be extended
inefficiently over long distances to serve scattered users or will be extended
gradually to serve areas built in careful phase with efficient facility growth.

The order in which the parts of a large community are built affects both
the initial expense of facilities and their costs of maintenance and operation.
Large-scale builders like the Levitts place great emphasis in their construction
operations on careful scheduling for the most economical possible sequence of
development, section by section. . . .

2.   *The need to retain municipal control over the eventual character of development.*
For example, the desired over-all future town pattern may require intensive
development served by public sewer and water lines in an extensive valley at
present remote from any utility lines. If there is no control over the timing of
building, however, the area in question may be the early subject of a substantial
amount of low-intensity construction served by individual wells and separate
sewage disposal fields. The existence of this type of development may later make
it impossible to convert the valley to the more intensive character required by
the evolving municipal pattern, even though important community-wide reasons
exist for doing so. In similar fashion, an important future industrial area may
become so cut-up by scattered small-scale factories as to preclude its eventual
development as a planned, coordinated industrial district when the time is ripe.

3.   *The need to maintain a desirable degree of balance among various uses of land.*
For example, it is essential to the economic stability of certain municipalities
which contain large areas of low-value homes that the service costs be offset by
tax income from commercial and industrial ratables. In such places it is essential
that new residential construction be timed in proper relation with business and
industrial expansion.

Another sort of balance involves the subtle relationship of areas of varied character. The village of Hastings-on-Hudson in New York has a policy exercised through the zoning ordinance which regulates the timing of apartment construction in relation to the rate of one-family home building in accordance with a 15 to 85 ratio. Thus, for instance, whenever 85 new one-family dwellings have been built, the village may issue permits enabling 15 dwelling-units in apartment buildings. This regulation is intended to maintain what is locally felt to be a desirable predominance of one-family dwellings in a commuter village, but at the same time to make possible a necessary though smaller supply of rental apartments. The device makes the timing of one element conditional on the timing of another related element.

4.   *The need to achieve greater detail and specificity in development regulation.* The growing awareness of this need is evidenced by the trends in zoning towards increased use of special permit devices subject to detailed requirements and conditions and by the popularity of "designed-district" provisions.

In Great Britain a desire for greater sensitivity of controls led to the present system of development permissions instituted after country-wide public acquisition of "development rights." Local authorities may grant or withhold permission to build, according to the needs of a development plan. At least in the negative sense—that is, being able to prevent development unless it accords with a municipally determined time schedule—the British regulations illustrate an application of control over timing to enable specific conformity with a detailed municipal plan. Under the British controls, for example, on a specific site in a developing area, permission for a store building may be denied on one day if the planning authority considers the construction premature, and at a later date permission may be granted.

There is, of course, a direct but generally unrecognized counterpart to this in the United States. Commonly, a municipality, petitioned to rezone a residential tract for a regional shopping center, refuses to do so when requested, but later decides the propitious moment has arrived and enacts the necessary amendment. . . .

5.   *The need to maintain a high quality of community services and facilities.* This requires during periods of rapid building expansion that adequate intervals of time be assured for the assimilation of residential, business or industrial additions to the community.

When newcomers are added faster than municipal facilities and services can be increased, the resulting overloads on existing capacities cause a decline in the quality of services. Uncontrolled, this deterioration can result in seriously substandard levels of water supply, sewage and waste disposal, public school education, and public recreation. Moreover, if the rate of sudden and unanticipated shopping or industrial expansion outstrips the pace of highway improvement, residential streets may be flooded by excessive traffic seeking to by-pass congestion. (It is possible that adequate time for the *social* integration of incoming families represents a sixth legitimate basis for regulating community growth.) . . .

3.   Examine §§1 and 3 of the Standard Zoning Enabling Act, pp. 762-763, *supra,* which correspond to the techniques and purposes sections of the New York law. Do you find language supporting the court's conclusion that Ramapo has not acted ultra vires?

4.   Several times before, New York courts had dealt with local ordinances that openly sought to slow down new development so as to bring public facilities into balance with population increase. Attempts to defeat the ordinances as ultra vires fared unevenly:

(a) A town board established annual quotas on residential building permits after school tax levies had spiraled upward 621 percent in fifteen years, tax rates had doubled, and bonded indebtedness had climbed 1000 percent. Albrecht Realty Co. v. Town of New Castle, 8 Misc. 2d 255, 167 N.Y.S.2d 843 (Sup. Ct. 1957) (ordinance invalid as ultra vires).

(b) A zoning law provided for minimum lot-size reduction from 40,000 to 22,500 square feet if the town board found that "existing [community] facilities or plans or reasonable possibilities for the expansion of such facilities [were] adequate to provide for the needs of future residents in the proposed development." Joseph sought a 22,500-square-foot special permit, which the town board denied because of the "inadequacy" of existing or planned school facilities. Joseph v. Town of Clarkstown, 24 Misc. 2d 366, 198 N.Y.S.2d 695 (Sup. Ct. 1960) (ordinance and its application valid).

In the *Albrecht Realty Co.* case, *supra,* the town had adopted no long-range plan for building new schools. Is this fact crucial on the issue of ultra vires? On the issue of substantive due process?

5.   You represent a landowner in the town of Ramapo whose acreage will qualify for development under the eighteen-year capital plan in 1985. It is 1976, the seventh year of the plan, and the town of Ramapo is currently three years behind schedule in carrying the plan out. Your client would like to develop his acreage without further delay. What advice do you give him?

6.   An attempt similar to New Castle's, Note 4(a) *supra,* to control population growth through a quota system eventually succeeded in the city of Petaluma, California, forty miles north of San Francisco. Construction Industry Assn. of Sonoma County v. City of Petaluma, 522 F.2d 897 (9th Cir. 1975), *cert. denied,* 424 U.S. 934 (1976). Between 1965 and 1972, the city's population rose from 20,000 to 30,000. In 1972, the city council passed a five-year Residential Development Program, which would allow only 2500 new dwelling units to be constructed during that period, at the annual rate of approximately 500 units. Eight to twelve percent of the allotment was reserved for low- and moderate-income housing. Elaborate criteria, including a point system similar to Ramapo's, were set forth to guide city officials in awarding building permits. On the eastern and northern edges of the city there was to be a greenbelt park, 200 feet in width. For ten to twenty years, no residential development could begin beyond the greenbelt. Eventually the city would acquire the greenbelt itself through subdivision exactions (see Note 9, *infra*).

Builders' associations and property owners joined in attacking the Petaluma ordinance. The plaintiffs' charges included: (a) the Petaluma law will invite similar, restrictive action by neighboring communities. Together, these population curbs will drastically alter migration trends, thereby interfering with constitutionally protected freedom of travel. Moreover, the forced curtailment of housing starts would impermissibly burden interstate commerce. (b) The greenbelt plan constitutes a taking of property by making this land unusable for up to twenty years.

The district court found the Petaluma plan invalid. 375 F. Supp. 574 (N.D. Cal. 1974). The court's findings included:

> [1] . . . The city created an "urban extension line" . . . to mark the outer limits of the city's expansion for twenty or more years. Within this perimeter, the city used . . . techniques to set a maximum population of . . . 55,000 as against the 1962 projection of 77,000 by 1985. [Id. at 576]
>
> [2] . . . The city has purposely limited . . . its public facilities . . . [so as] to serve a population lower than the market and growth rates would produce. [Id. at 577]
>
> [3] . . . When the "Petaluma Plan" was conceived in 1971, the city faced no immediate, serious or unusual difficulty in using or expanding the capacity of its public facilities to serve existing demographic and market growth rates in housing. [Ibid.]
>
> [4] . . . The San Francisco metropolitan region is generally self-contained and has a unitary housing market. Persons excluded from one suburb do not leave the region but seek housing elsewhere in the area. [Id. at 578-579]
>
> [5] . . . Limits on housing supply in the suburbs tend to keep people who would otherwise move to those suburbs in the center cities. [Id. at 579]
>
> [6] . . . If the "Petaluma Plan," limiting housing starting [sic] at approximately six percent of existing housing stock each year, were to proliferate throughout the San Francisco region, . . . for the decade of 1970 to 1980, the "shortfall" in needed housing would be approximately 105,000 [which] would occur primarily in "growth centers" [like Petaluma]. [Id. at 580]
>
> [7] . . . The specific housing most affected would be "threshold housing," that is, the least expensive housing available without government subsidy . . . loss of "threshold housing" means in turn, that persons of incomes of $8,000 to $14,000 per year would be deprived of housing to meet their needs. [Id. at 581]

The court in its conclusions of law held that the "Petaluma Plan" interfered with the freedom to travel, which was a fundamental right, and that the city might retain its plan only by showing a compelling state interest. The city failed to shoulder this burden, despite claims that uncontrolled population would overload sewage treatment and water supply facilities and destroy Petaluma's "small town character." The court believed the last concern unacceptable and the first two concerns factually unsupported.

For its own peroration, the court's opinion drew heavily from the plaintiffs' trial belief (id. at 588):

> As contended by plaintiffs on pages 7 and 8 of their Trial Brief, "This case is a study in anti-planning, the refusal of a city to come to grips with the fact that it has joined a metropolitan complex and is no longer the sleepy small town that

it once was. In a world in which nothing is as unchanging as change, Petaluma wants to stay the same. The means to that end is to draw up the bridge over the moat and turn people away. This is not the use of police power, but the abdication of that power. . . .

"In a large sense this case sets up the constitutional protections against a single small city's passing laws to keep people away, to maintain 'small town character' at the expense of depriving people of mobility, their right to travel, and of decent housing or perhaps any housing at all. . . .

"In a narrower sense, this case [holds] . . . that local police power may [not] be used to shift the burden of providing housing to other cities in a metropolitan region which have their own police power and their own problems. This issue . . . [questions] the jurisdiction of one town to visit its problems on another.

"The prospective resident turned away at Petaluma does not disappear into the hinterland, but presents himself in some other suburb of the same metroplex, perhaps in some town with as many problems or more than Petaluma. . . . By this means, Petaluma legislates its problems into problems for Napa, Vallejo or Walnut Creek. May Petaluma pass a law to bind the whole world? See, Bosselman, 'Can the Town of Ramapo Pass a Law to Bind the Rights of the Whole World?' 1 Fla. State L. Rev. 234 (1973). . . ."

In reversing the district court, the court of appeals avoided the landowner plaintiffs' right-to-travel claim, which had prevailed below. The appeals court held that plaintiffs lacked standing to assert the rights of the third persons (potential residents of Petaluma) whose travel, the complaint alleged, the Petaluma ordinance would impair.

Turning to the plaintiffs' substantive due process claim, the opinion states: "We conclude that . . . the concept of the public welfare is sufficiently broad to uphold Petaluma's desire to preserve its small town character, its open spaces and low density of population, and to grow at an orderly and deliberate pace." 522 F.2d at 908-09.

7. Boca Raton, Florida, a wealthy "Gold Coast" community, was a hamlet of 992 persons in 1950, a city of 28,000 in 1970. The citizenry voted in 1972 to cap the city's growth at 100,000 (40,000 dwelling units). When the cap was reached, no more building permits would be issued.

The Florida state court invalidated the Boca Raton ordinance as violating due process provisions of both the state and federal constitutions. It held that the cap did not bear a rational relationship to a permissible municipal purpose. City of Boca Raton v. Boca Villas Corp., 371 So. 2d 154 (Dist. Ct. App. 1979). The appeals court drew heavily from trial court findings that the city's utility systems were adequate, its water resources could abundantly withstand anticipated growth, its air quality and noise levels were normal, and that school congestion was a problem for the county, not city. Neither the trial nor appeals court was persuaded that Boca Raton could legitimately retain its "small-town" character purely for the sake of smallness.

Wholly apart from differences of opinion as to what, constitutionally, general welfare will and will not allow (and remember that state courts may read *their* constitutions more restrictively on this issue than would federal courts read the Fourteenth Amendment), why should not Boca Raton, or any other community, decide that it wants to cap its population? Is there any difference between planning a new town from scratch for a ceiling population of 100,000 and seeking to impose that curb upon an existing community? Is there any difference between an explicit population control (viz., 40,000 dwelling units and no more) and an unspoken, indirect one (viz., zoning density controls allowing 40,000 units)? Is there any difference between zoning for 70,000 units but allowing only the first 40,000 units to be built, and zoning initially only for 40,000 units?

8. "True other alternatives, such as requiring off-site improvements as a prerequisite to subdivision may be available. . . ." *Golden,* page 872 *supra.*

Judge Scileppi is referring to the widespread practice of requiring subdividers to bear some of the capital costs of servicing new residents. See page 915 *infra.* Improvements directly attributable to the development, such as the subdivision's own streets, sidewalks, or sewer mains, pose no serious legal issue when the developer must install and pay for them to gain subdivision approval. More likely to be objectionable are exactions that confer a significant benefit on persons living outside the subdivision or that pay for items that most communities still absorb themselves. See, e.g., Pioneer Trust & Savings Bank v. Village of Mount Prospect, 22 Ill. 2d 375, 176 N.E.2d 799 (1961). There, the court invalidated as a taking a local requirement that a residential subdivider donate 6.7 acres to the village for use as a public school.

Might it not be argued that the Ramapo "grace" provision, which allows developers to advance the date of subdivision approval by themselves providing the school site, firehouse, and collector roads that the town is not yet ready to pay for, is a veiled subdivision exaction that the courts would invalidate if it were required of all subdividers?

9. Local attempts to chill new development come in many guises. They include:

(a) Excessively large minimum lot size requirements. See, e.g., Steel Hill Development, Inc. v. Town of Sanbornton, 469 F.2d 956 (1st Cir. 1972), page 863 *supra;* Board of County Supervisors of Fairfax County v. Carper, 200 Va. 653, 107 S.E.2d 350 (1959) (2-acre restriction in western two-thirds of county in order to concentrate new development in the eastern one-third invalidated as arbitrary and bearing no relation to the general welfare); Santa Barbara, California, 1975 rezoning that placed most vacant land in one-acre zone, reduced potential new housing from 36,000 units to 8,300. Wall St. J., Feb. 8, 1978, at 1, col. 1.

(b) Refusal to expand services to accommodate new development. See, e.g., Wilson v. Hidden Valley Municipal Water District, 256 Cal. App. 2d 271, 63 Cal. Rptr. 889 (1967) (court will not interfere with water district refusal to enlarge its supply to service nonfarm activity); United Farmworkers of Florida Housing Project, Inc. v. City of Delray Beach, 493 F.2d 799 (5th Cir. 1974) (city's refusal to provide water and sewer services to federally aided housing project for low-income minority farmworkers held forbidden racial discrimination); Charles v. Diamond, 47 A.D.2d 426, 366 N.Y.S.2d 921 (4th Dept. 1975) (landowner entitled to damages where village had failed after nine years to modify its sewage system to accommodate new apartment development). See also Wall St. J., Feb. 8, 1978, at 1, col. 1, for article on water board of Goleta, California, which "simply refused" (1973 to 1978) to authorize new water hookups.

(c) Intolerable, illegal delay in handling applications for subdivision approval and building permits. Cf. generally Cutler, Legal and Illegal Methods for Controlling Community Growth on the Urban Fringe, 1961 Wis. L. Rev. 370.

(d) Two-year moratorium on rezoning of any land for residential purposes that is located in overcrowded school district, unless developer provides "satisfactory temporary alternative" to permanent school construction. See Builders Assn. of Santa Clara-Santa Cruz Counties v. Superior Court of Santa Clara County, 13 Cal. 3d 225, 529 P.2d 582, 118 Cal. Rptr. 158 (1974); no further residential permits to be issued until the city satisfactorily solves the problems of overcrowded classrooms, sewage pollution, and water rationing. Associated Home Bldrs. v. City of Livermore, 18 Cal. 3d 582, 557 P.2d 473, 135 Cal. Rptr. 41 (1976) (ordinance valid).

10. In an article describing California's "slow-growth" experience, the Wall Street Journal reported that growth control had contributed to skyrocketing prices of existing homes, the pricing of moderate-income and younger buyers out of the market, the scarcity of jobs that are growth-dependent (e.g., teachers, construction workers), and the loss of business and industry serviced by lower-income employees. Wall St. J., Feb. 8, 1978, at 1, col. 1.

The article concludes:

> Meanwhile, rancorous debate between pro- and anti-growth forces continues, both sides brandishing conflicting studies and projections. Anti-growthers are a mixed lot, including academics and students, the affluent and environmentalists. They are pitted against a coalition including labor, developers and business. Strong language is common: a pro-growth unionist calls environmentalist opponents "goofier than pet coons," and anti-growthers speak of their foes as if they were robber barons intent on raping the South Coast for personal profit.
>
> The more thoughtful anti-growthers concede that the policies adopted here have had some adverse social and economic impact, but they argue that too much growth would be worse. "What alternative do we have?" says Lawrence Schatz, an official at Westmont College in Montecito and a former Santa Barbara City councilman. He continues: "Anyone looking at cities of more than 100,000 sees increased crime, an expansion of government and taxes, more pov-

erty, more minorities, more social problems to deal with. That's what happens when cities grow. The limited capacity of a city to deal with this has to be faced eventually. We decided to face it earlier than most places."

11. In England, unlike America, landowners cannot argue a taking if they are refused permission to develop. The following extract appeared in a review (written by the editor) of a study of British development controls.

> The County of "E" is one of the Home Counties that ring London and, together with the central city, comprise the Greater London region. English population increases have been gentle during the 1950's; five percent compared with America's more robust percentage of 18.5. But echoing our experience, population pressures did not diffuse evenly about the island. There, too, the major urban areas, especially London and Birmingham, exerted a pulling force in the movement of people and jobs. But within the London region (or Birmingham) a counterthrust carried people away from the central core, as evidenced by a drop in the population of London proper during the 1950's. Its displacees (many the by-product of urban redevelopment or reduced crowding), and those attracted from beyond the region, sought housing in the surrounding Home Counties. Were "E" New York's Town of New Castle, the sum of many private decisions (builder, consumer, lender) would have settled the stock of new housing—in numbers and location—to accommodate this "over-spill." That "E" was unprepared for this new-resident onslaught, or that sites elsewhere were better suited for immediate housing development, would have made an interesting, but irrelevant, footnote.
>
> The British, however, do not accept for themselves the relatively free run with which we allow private decision to affect the land development process. Perhaps it is their greater tolerance for an overtly-planned society, fortified in this context by an earlier appreciation for the finite quality of land and wealth resources. Whatever the temperamental or cerebral underpinning, restraint upon the private developer is now a widely accepted axiom. Its credo is straightforward: the right to own land is constitutionally protected; but not so for the right to build a dwelling place or other structure upon it. This also applies even for one's own occupancy.
>
> To be sure, the American builder is hedged in customarily by assorted building codes, zoning ordinances, and subdivision regulations; but these all presuppose a right to develop once their "reasonable" demands are met. In England, on the other hand, the builder must await a critical preliminary evaluation, principally involving the question: does the community wish to allow development on the site proposed? Should the local planning authority decide not, and if review does not bring reversal, one skyline in particular will remain unchanged.
>
> Let us demonstrate by example the workings of British planning control. Squire Black owns a four-acre plot near the Village of Y in County "E." Several years before, the County development plan located Black's land within its green belt zone. After making some preliminary engineering and marketing surveys, Developer Jones has decided to erect ten cottages on the Black parcel, and has persuaded the Squire to part with legal title if development permission is available. A local bank is anxious to arrange the interim and permanent financing,

thereby rounding out the private decisions that are prelude to a building program.

The interested parties apply to the local planning committee for permission to erect the ten dwellings. The committee refers the application to its technical staff and a report including a recommendation follows which, in at least 95 percent of the cases, foreshadows the final disposition. Armed with the report, the planning committee meets in closed session, which not even the applicant attends, and there is no hearing. Deliberation is summary. Estimates of two minutes per agenda item recall the dispatch with which the United States Supreme Court presumably rushes through petitions for certiorari. A standardized form mailing notifies Squire Black of the committee action. If planning approval is denied, the usual conclusionary language buries the variables which might expose the process of decision: "Inside a Green Belt approval should not be given except in very special circumstances for the construction of new buildings or for the change of use of existing buildings, and it is considered undesirable that a [development of ten houses] should be introduced on this site."

Somewhat daunted, Squire Black may seek Ministry review. About one-quarter of the disappointed applicants do so. The appellate process is in four stages: the pleadings, wherein the local committee must detail more precisely its basis for rejection; the inquiry, a hearing before a Ministry inspector at which the developer, his real estate agents, the area planning officer and district engineer will probably testify; the inspector's on-site visit; and, finally, within the Ministry, the decision officer's evaluation of the appeal, relying heavily, it seems, upon the inspector's report. Here again, secrecy shrouds official action, since the report (which may include facts or attitudes not presented at the inquiry) is confidential, and the Minister's decision, when announced, resembles in its abstraction the initial refusal: "Decision: Dismissed. 'The appeal site is in a rural area which it is proposed shall form part of a Green Belt. [The Minister has] attached great importance to the Green Belt principle. . . . [T]he circumstances of this case are not such to justify its being treated exceptionally.' "

Have Squire Black and his developer vendee exhausted their remedies? With respect to this venture, yes, at least for the moment. Whereas the American judiciary hovers about a zoning and planning administrator like a jealous suitor, the British courts have been contrastingly stand-offish. Once the Minister establishes that the intended building is subject to permit (not even debatable in our example) and that compliance with statutory procedure has occurred, the "reasonableness" of his decision is beyond a court's concern. Some time later, Squire Black may reapply for a permit with the same or modified plans or he may seek to qualify for compensation upon a showing that his land has been stripped of development value. . . .

At first blush, this all seemes terribly high-handed for our tastes, as *in camera* decisions, shunning of precedent, lack of judicial review, even the inability of a disgruntled neighbor to appeal what he considers the unwise *issuance* of a permit are all foreign to the American approach. But the system is not especially footloose. Checks and balances do exist which leaven the risk of wholesale abuse, largely predicated upon the integrity and devotion of Britain's civil service, the continuity and central direction of the island's planning control, and Parliament's power, occasionally exercised, to challenge Ministry policy or action. Nevertheless, some procedural reform to make the checks more explicit is taking place and is likely to continue. [Berger, Review (Mandelker, Green Belts and Urban Growth) 61 Mich. L. Rev. 628, 630-631, 632-633 (1963)]

The ALI Model Land Development Code (1975) stands somewhere between Britain's "grace" and America's "inherent right" approach to development. The code would enable local communities to require development permits for a wide range of activities, as in England. Id. §1-202. The ordinance could distinguish between development for which permits would be granted "as of right" or only "after exercise of [administrative] discretion." Id. §2-102. A Land Development Agency (LDA) would administer the permit system. Id. §2-102. In issuing a discretionary permit ("special development permit"), the LDA could affix conditions "controlling the sequence of development, including when it must be commenced, and completed." Id. §2-103.

The Commentary to §2-103 indicates, however, that the ALI draftsmen may intend much less restrictive curbs on the tempo of new development than one finds in the Ramapo ordinance.

§16.6   Control over Population (Exclusionary Zoning)

What we will not countenance, then, under any guise, is community efforts at . . . exclusion. [Golden v. Planning Board of Town of Ramapo, page 872 *supra*]

Judge Scileppi's pointed warning was meant to quiet fears that, in the guise of regulating their rate of growth, suburban communities would keep out or sharply limit entry to unwanted groups, to wit: lower-income residents, of whom many are nonwhite. Such fears are not entirely groundless, since devices for slowing down growth, such as curbs on multibedroom apartments or excessive lot-size requirements, both restrict the supply and raise the cost of housing for less-privileged families. One critic of the Ramapo ordinance writes that "it will help the suburbs meet their development problems, but will do little to open up housing opportunities for middle- and lower-income families in suburban areas." May, Growth Controls, 24 Zoning Digest 67, 81 (1972).

Ramapo itself typifies the demography of most of the nation's fastest-growing suburbs. Ramapo Township in 1970 had 71,739 white and 4,563 black residents. Yet all but 416 of the black residents lived within the incorporated village of Spring Valley, an older community which had its own zoning laws. In those parts of the township where the Ramapo ordinance governed, the black percentage was less than 0.1! In the same area, the 1970 asking price for houses exceeded $50,000 in all but one census tract.

Since 1966, the town ordinance has not allowed multifamily housing. Sixty-five percent of the vacant residentially zoned land requires single-family houses on lots ranging from 25,000 to 80,000 square feet, and only one percent of the vacant land suitable for development allows houses on lots as small as

7,500 square feet. H. Franklin, Controlling Urban Growth—But for Whom? 11-15 (1973).

In this section we will examine specific zoning practices that separately and collectively have intensified the racial and economic polarity of our metropolitan areas. The conflict between outsiders seeking to open up the suburbs and entrenched local interests that, rightly or wrongly, want things to stay as they are grows sharper. As with many of the most difficult social issues of our time, courts have become a frequent arbiter.

a. Large-Lot Zoning

NATIONAL COMMN. ON URBAN PROBLEMS, BUILDING THE AMERICAN CITY

213-215 (1968)

The most widely discussed form of exclusion is large-lot zoning, by which a jurisdiction attempts to limit development in substantial portions of its territory to single-family residences on very large lots. The actual effects of this practice are not easy to isolate. Many factors determine the price which a particular lot will command in the market. In a weak market, large-lot zoning may make little difference, with a 4-acre tract selling for little more than a 2-acre tract, and both sizes providing sites for shacks. In a strong market, a change from a 4-acre minimum to a 2-acre minimum may not lower the price per lot since potential developers are concerned primarily with the number of units that can be built on a given tract and will bid up the price of the rezoned tract. Comparisons of different properties are difficult. A 2-acre lot may be more valuable than a 4-acre lot because of factors unrelated to size—location, topography, etc. Broad comparisons thus become extremely suspect. Nevertheless, it does appear that land prices per lot do diminish as minimum lot size is reduced, though usually not commensurately with the change in size. That is to say, a half-acre lot will cost less than a 1-acre lot, but will cost more than half the price. Table [15] gives figures for three suburban jurisdictions which serve to illustrate the point.

Even where prices per lot do not differ markedly from zone to zone, it does appear that large-lot zoning can have significant effects on the cost of housing. *First*, extensive large-lot zoning in a given area has the effect of substantially reducing the total amount of housing that can be accommodated. If demand for new housing is strong, this restriction of the supply of housing sites will increase residential land costs generally. Moreover, by limiting the amount of land for housing on smaller lots and multi-family units below that which the market demands, the prices for these sites may be increased.

Second, the increase in the total house-and-lot price may be greater than the increase in land price caused by large-lot zoning. Some builders will sim-

TABLE [15]

**Price of Vacant Lots by Residential Zoning Category in Greenwich, Conn.,
St. Louis County, Mo., and Montgomery County, Md.**

Zone	Minimum area per dwelling unit	Median sales price per lot
Greenwich, Conn.:[1]		
R-A-4	4 acres	$18,000
R-A-2	2 acres	19,700
R-A-1	1 acre	18,000
R-20	20,000 sq. ft.	12,500
R-12	12,000 sq. ft.	8,500
R-7	7,500 sq. ft.	8,000
R-6	7,500 sq. ft.	9,000
St. Louis County, Mo.:[2]		
R-1	1 acre	5,000
R-2	15,000 sq. ft.	2,000
R-3	10,000 sq. ft.	1,500
R-4	7,500 sq. ft.	1,111
R-5	6,000 sq. ft.	800
Montgomery County, Md.:[3]		
R-A	2 acres	18,000
R-E	40,000 sq. ft.	11,800
R-R	20,000 sq. ft.	7,650
R-15C	15,000 sq. ft.	5,400
R-90	9,000 sq. ft.	4,000
R-60	6,000 sq. ft.	3,600

1. Based on actual sales in 1966.
2. Based on interviews with local officials and developers.
3. Based on actual sales in 1967, available selling prices in Lusk's Real Estate Directory for Montgomery County, 1967 edition, and interviews with real estate developers and appraisers.
Source: Study prepared for the Commission by Department of Urban Affairs, Urban Research Center, Hunter College of the City University of New York.

ply not build the same house on a large lot that they will on a smaller lot, believing that a larger house is necessary. Furthermore, many builders observe a rule of thumb that the price of a lot should be some specified percentage of the total price of house and lot, e.g., 20 percent. If such a rule is strictly observed, a $1,000 increase in lot cost will result in a $5,000 increase in the price of the finished house and lot.

Third, large-lot zoning generally results in added costs for land improvements. Depending on specific requirements in the zoning ordinance regarding lot width, the effect can be to increase significantly the required linear feet of streets, sidewalks, gutters, sewers and water lines. Table [16] suggests the magnitude of such added costs.

In some instances the fiscal objectives behind large-lot zoning are quite clear. In St. Louis County, for example, the Parkway School District has

TABLE [16]

Land Improvement Costs per Lot by Residential Zoning Category in
St. Louis County, Mo., and Montgomery County, Md.

Zone	Minimum area per dwelling unit	Average frontage per lot (feet)	Improvement cost per lot[1]
St. Louis County, Mo.:			
R-1	1 acre	125	$4,375
R-2	15,000 sq. ft.	100	3,500
R-3	10,000 sq. ft.	80	2,800
R-4	7,500 sq. ft.	65	2,275
R-5	6,000 sq. ft.	55	1,925
Montgomery County, Md.:			
R-A	2 acres	150	5,250
R-E	40,000 sq. ft.	125	4,375
R-R	20,000 sq. ft.	100	3,500
R-150	15,000 sq. ft.	80	2,800
R-90	9,000 sq. ft.	75	2,625
R-60	6,000 sq. ft.	60	2,100

1. Estimated locally at $35 a foot of frontage.

Source: Study prepared for the Commission by Department of Urban Affairs Urban Research Center, Hunter College of the City University of New York.

calculated that any home costing less than $26,274 does not pay its own way in educational costs. On this basis, district officials oppose any change in zoning to permit lots of less than a quarter-acre, below which they believe housing costing less than this amount can be built. . . .

Large-lot zoning is a common and widespread practice in many major metropolitan areas. Data are scarce, however, since few metropolitan planning agencies or other regional groups have attempted to make consolidated area zoning maps or compile data on the total zoning maps or compile date on the total zoning pattern in the area. A Commission survey shows that 25 percent of metropolitan area municipalities of 5,000-plus permit *no* single-family houses on lots of less than one-half acre. Of these same governments 11 percent have some two-acre zoning; 20 percent have some one-to-two-acre zoning; 33 percent have some one-half-to-one-acre zoning; and more than 50 percent have some one-fourth-to-one-half-acre zoning. . . .

In Connecticut, more than half of the vacant land zoned for residential use in the entire State is for lots of 1 to 2 acres. In Greenwich, Conn., a community of about 65,000 within mass-transit commuting distance of New York City, more than four-fifths of the total undeveloped area is zoned for minimum lots of 1 acre or more—39 percent for 4 acres, 25 percent for 2 acres, and 17½ percent for 1 acre.

In Cuyahoga County, which contains the city of Cleveland, 85,200 acres of vacant land are zoned for single-family residential use. Of this amount, only 28,425 acres, or 33 percent, are zoned for one-half acre or less; 42,225 acres, or 50 percent, are zoned for one-half to 1.9 acres minimum lot sizes; and 14,550 acres, or 17 percent, are zoned for 2 acres or more. Thus, 67 percent of the vacant land zoned for single-family development in the core county of the Cleveland SMSA is zoned for minimum lots of one-half acre or more. In outlying Geauga County, for example, 85 percent of the residentially zoned area requires lots of 1 acre or more.

NATIONAL LAND & INVESTMENT CO. v. KOHN
419 Pa. 504, 215 A.2d 597 (1965)

ROBERTS, J. These appeals are taken from an order of the Court of Common Pleas of Chester County which held unconstitutional a provision of the Easttown Township zoning ordinance which required a minimum area of four acres per building lot in certain residential districts in the township. . . .

II.   VALIDITY OF FOUR ACRE ZONING

Easttown Township has an area of 8.2 square miles devoted almost exclusively to residential use. It is traversed in the north by the Main Line of the Pennsylvania Railroad as well as by U.S. Route 30, a heavily traveled highway which emanates in Philadelphia, 20 miles to the east, and heads west to Lancaster and eventually to the West Coast. It is along this strip that the township's sole commercial activity is conducted and where its two small industrial concerns are located.

The township finds itself in the path of a population expansion approaching from two directions. From the east, suburbs closer to the center of Philadelphia are reaching capacity and residential development is extending further west to Easttown. In addition, a market for residential sites is being generated by the fast growing industrial-commercial complex in the King of Prussia-Valley Forge area to the north of Easttown Township.

Easttown's vital statistics provide a good indication of its character. At present, about 60% of the township's population resides in an area of about 20% of the township. The remaining 40% of the population occupies the balance of about 80% of its area. Privately imposed restrictions limit lot areas to four, five and ten acre minimums on approximately 10% of the total area of the township, consisting of land located in the southern and western sections. Of the total 5157 acres in the township, some 898, or about 17%, have been restricted by the new zoning ordinance to minimum lots of two acres. Approximately 1565 acres composing about 30% of the township are restricted by the zoning ordinance to lots of four acres minimum area. About 5% of the population live in the areas zoned for two and four acre sites which together constitute about 47% of the township. Some 1835 acres, representing about 35% of the township, remain unaffected by the new zoning and continue, under the township's original zoning classification, to be zoned for building sites with a minimum area of one acre. . . .

U.S. Census figures show that Easttown's population grew from 2307 in 1920 to 6907 in 1960. As of April, 1963, the population estimate was 8400. Public school population through the sixth grade grew from 498 in the school year 1955-56 to 1052 in the school year 1963-64 and, as projected, will be about 1680 in 1969-70. New residential construction from 1951 through the first eight months of 1963, a twelve year period, consisted of 1149 units at an estimated cost of about $21,000,000, with an average of 100 building permits annually. At this rate of growth, allowing four persons per housing unit in Easttown, its population, related to new residences, would grow under the previous one acre minimum zoning at the rate of about 400 persons per annum. . . .

The task of considering the Easttown Township zoning ordinance and passing upon the constitutionality of its four acre minimum area requirement as applied to appellees' property is not an easy one. In the span of years since 1926 when zoning received its judicial blessing, the art and science of land planning has grown increasingly complex and sophisticated. The days are fast disappearing when the judiciary can look at a zoning ordinance and, with nearly as much confidence as a professional zoning expert, decide upon the merits of a zoning plan and its contribution to the health, safety, morals or general welfare of the community. This Court has become increasingly aware that it is neither a super board of adjustment nor a planning commission of last resort. See DiSanto v. Zoning Bd. of Adjustment, 410 Pa. 331, 189 A.2d 135 (1963); Joseph B. Simon & Co. v. Zoning Bd. of Adjustment, 403 Pa. 176, 168 A.2d 317 (1961). Instead, the Court acts as a judicial overseer, drawing the limits beyond which local regulation may not go, but loathing to interfere, within those limits, with the discretion of local governing bodies. Tidewater Oil Co. v. Poore, 395 Pa. 89, 49 A.2d 636 (1959). The zoning power is one of the tools of government which, in order to be effective, must not be subjected to judicial interference unless clearly necessary. For this reason, a presumption of validity attaches to a zoning ordinance which imposes the burden to prove its invalidity upon the one who challenges it. Cleaver v. Bd. of Adjustment, 414 Pa. 367, 200 A.2d 408 (1964); Bilbar Constr. Co. v. Easttown Twp. Bd. of Adjustment, 393 Pa. 62, 141 A.2d 851 (1958).

While recognizing this presumption, we must also appreciate the fact that zoning involves governmental restrictions upon a landowner's constitutionally guaranteed right to use his property, unfettered, except in very specific instances, by governmental restrictions. The time must never come when, because of frustration with concepts foreign to their legal training, courts abdicate their judicial responsibility to protect the constitutional rights of individual citizens. Thus, the burden of proof imposed upon one who challenges the validity of a zoning regulation must never be made so onerous as to foreclose,

for all practical purposes, a landowner's avenue of redress against the infringement of constitutionally protected rights.

The oft repeated, although ill defined, limitation upon the exercise of the
zoning power requires that zoning ordinances be enacted for the health, safety,
morals or general welfare of the community. See Cleaver v. Bd. of Adjustment,
414 Pa. 367, 200 A.2d 408 (1964). Such ordinances must bear a substantial
relationship to those police power purposes. Glorioso Appeal, 413 Pa. 194, 196
A.2d 668 (1964); Sylvester v. Pittsburgh Zoning Bd. of Adjustment, 398 Pa.
216, 157 A.2d 174 (1959). Regulations adopted pursuant to that power must
not be unreasonable, arbitrary or confiscatory. Eller v. Bd. of Adjustment, 414
Pa. 1, 198 A.2d 863 (1964). . . .

There is no doubt that in Pennsylvania, zoning for density is a legitimate
exercise of the police power. See Bilbar Constr. Co. v. Easttown Twp. Bd. of
Adjustment, 393 Pa. 62, 141 A.2d 851 (1958); Volpe Appeal, 384 Pa. 374, 121
A.2d 97 (1956). Every zoning case involves a different set of facts and circumstances in light of which the constitutionality of a zoning ordinance must be
tested. Therefore, it is impossible for us to say that any minimum acreage
requirement is unconstitutional per se. See Annot., 95 A.L.R.2d 716
(1964). . . .

We turn, then, to the question of the constitutionality of four acre minimum in the factual context of the instant case. Quite obviously, appellees will
be deprived of part of the value of their property if they are limited in the use
of it to four acre lots. When divided into one acre lots as originally planned,
the value of "Sweetbriar" (plaintiffs' parcel) for residential building was approximately $260,000. When the four acre restriction was imposed, the num-
ber of available building sites in "Sweetbriar" was reduced by 75% and the
value of the land, under the most optimistic appraisal, fell to $175,000. The
four acre minimum greatly restricts the marketability of this tract because,
with fewer potential lots, the cost of improvements such as curbing, streets and
other facilities is thus greater on each lot. In addition, each building lot being
larger, the cost per lot is automatically increased. The desire of many buyers
not to be burdened with the upkeep of a four acre lot also makes "Sweetbriar,"
so restricted, less desirable. Although there was some evidence in the record
that lots of four acres or more could eventually be sold, it is clear that there is
not a readily available market for such offerings.

Against this deprivation of value, the alleged public purposes cited as
justification for the imposition of a four acre minimum area requirement upon
appellees' land must be examined. . . .

[The court is unpersuaded by the argument that a four-acre zone is
needed to insure proper sewage disposal and to protect township water from
pollution.]

In addition to the alleged problem of sewage disposal as justifying the
four acre minimum, appellants cite the inadequacy of township roads and the
burden which continued one acre zoning for the entire township would impose
upon that road system. . . . Zoning is a tool in the hands of governmental

bodies which enables them to more effectively meet the demands of evolving and growing communities. It must not and can not be used by those officials as an instrument by which they may shirk their responsibilities. Zoning is a means by which a governmental body can plan for the future—it may not be used as a means to deny the future. The evidence on the record indicates that for the present and the immediate future the road system of Easttown Township is adequate to handle the traffic load. It is also quite convincing that the roads will become increasingly inadequate as time goes by and that improvements and additions will eventually have to be made. Zoning provisions may not be used, however, to avoid the increased responsibilities and economic burdens which time and natural growth invariably bring.

It is not difficult to envision the tremendous hardship, as well as the chaotic conditions, which would result if all the townships in this area decided to deny to a growing population sites for residential development within the means of at least a significant segment of the people.

The third justification for rezoning, and one urged upon us most assiduously, deals with the preservation of the "character" of this area. The photographic exhibits placed in the record by appellants attest to the fact that this is an area of great beauty containing old homes surrounded by beautiful pasture, farm and wood land. It is a very desirable and attractive place in which to live.

Involved in preserving Easttown's "character" are four aspects of concern which the township gives for desiring four acre minimum zoning. First, they cite the preservation of open space and the creation of a "greenbelt" which, as most present day commentators impress upon us, are worthy goals. While in full agreement with these goals, we are convinced that four acre minimum zoning does not achieve the creation of a greenbelt in its technical sense and, to the limited extent that open space is so preserved, such zoning as is here involved is not a permissible means to that end.

By suggesting that the creation of a greenbelt is a purpose behind this zoning, appellants betray their argument that there is a ready market for four acre plots. Only if there is no market for four acres lots will the land continue to be open and undeveloped and greenbelt created. This, however, would amount to confiscation of the property of Easttown landowners for which they must be compensated.

If the preservation of open spaces is the township objective, there are means by which this can be accomplished which include authorization for "cluster zoning" or condemnation of development rights with compensation paid for that which is taken. A four acre minimum acreage requirement is not a reasonable method by which the stated end can be achieved.

[The court then rejects as a "makeweight" the township's contention that four acre zoning will help create the proper setting for two historic sites, Old Swedes Church and the home of General Anthony Wayne.]

Closely related to the goal of protecting historic monuments is the expressed desire to protect the "setting" for a number of old homes in Easttown, some dating back to the early days of our Commonwealth. Appellants denominate this goal as falling within the ambit of promoting the "general welfare." Unfortunately, the concept of the general welfare defies meaningful capsule definition and constitutes an exceedingly difficult standard against which to test the validity of legislation. However, it must always be ascertained at the outset whether, in fact, it is the *public* welfare which is being benefited or whether, disguised as legislation for the public welfare, a zoning ordinance actually serves purely private interests.

There is no doubt that many of the residents of this area are highly desirous of keeping it the way it is, preferring, quite naturally, to look out upon land in its natural state rather than on other homes. These desires, however, do not rise to the level of public welfare. This is purely a matter of private desire which zoning regulations may not be employed to effectuate.

Appellants make some attempt to impose upon this area an aura of historic significance which deserves the protection of the township. Of course, the fact that these houses are old makes them architecturally and historically interesting. But it does not justify the creation of a special setting for them. They are all privately owned; most are already surrounded by substantial land holdings which, if their owners so desire, serve as protection against being "fenced in" by new residential development. In addition, there is nothing about south Easttown which differentiates it from any other area in the southeastern section of Pennsylvania. Surely, no one would seriously maintain that the entire southeast corner of the state should be declared immune from further development on areas of less than four acres simply because there are many old homes located there.

The fourth argument advanced by appellants, and one closely analogous to the preceding one, is that the rural character of the area must be preserved. If the township were developed on the basis of this zoning, however, it could not be seriously contended that the land would retain its rural character—it would simply be dotted with larger homes on larger lots.

Appellants point to the fact that the surrounding townships have similar low density zoning provisions. Although the zoning of the surrounding area is frequently a relevant consideration in assessing the validity of a zoning regulation, see Kubia Appeal, 396 Pa. 109, 151 A.2d 625 (1959); Act of May 1, 1933, P.L. 103, §2003, added by Act of July 10, 1947, P.L. 1481, §47, 53 P.S. §67003, it is not controlling on the issue presented. This is particularly so when we are dealing with a unique zoning classification such as is involved here. With most zoning classifications, there can be little question as to their suitability in any political subdivision; the only issue concerns their placement. With these classifications, the surrounding zoning is particularly relevant. As the classification itself becomes more questionable, however, similar classifications in surrounding districts become of less significance in supporting the validity of the restriction.

The briefs submitted by each appellant in this case are revealing in that they point up the two factors which appear to lie at the heart of their fight for four acre zoning.

The township's brief raises (but, unfortunately, does not attempt to answer) the interesting issue of the township's responsibility to those who do not yet live in the township but who are part, or may become part, of the population expansion of the suburbs. Four acre zoning represents Easttown's position that it does not desire to accommodate those who are pressing for admittance to the township unless such admittance will not create any additional burdens upon governmental functions and services. The question posed is whether the township can stand in the way of the natural forces which send our growing population into hitherto undeveloped areas in search of a comfortable place to live. We have concluded not. A zoning ordinance whose primary purpose is to prevent the entrance of newcomers in order to avoid future burdens, economic and otherwise, upon the administration of public services and facilities can not be held valid. Of course, we do not mean to imply that a governmental body may not utilize its zoning power in order to insure that the municipal services which the community requires are provided in an orderly and rational manner.

The brief of the appellant-intervenors creates less of a problem but points up the factors which sometime lurk behind the espoused motives for zoning. What basically appears to bother intervenors is that a small number of lovely old homes will have to start keeping company with a growing number of smaller, less expensive, more densely located houses. It is clear, however, that the general welfare is not fostered or promoted by a zoning ordinance designed to be exclusive and exclusionary. But this does not mean that individual action is foreclosed. "An owner of land may constitutionally make his property as large and as private or secluded or exclusive as he desires and his purse can afford. He may, for example, singly or with his neighbors, purchase sufficient neighboring land to protect and preserve by restrictions in deeds or by covenants inter se, the privacy, a minimum acreage, the quiet, peaceful atmosphere and the tone and character of the community which existed when he or they moved there."

In light of the foregoing, therefore, we are compelled to conclude that the board of adjustment committed an error of law in upholding the constitutionality of the Easttown Township four acre minimum requirement as applied to appellees' property. We therefore affirm the order of the Court of Common Pleas of Chester County.

Order affirmed.

JONES, J., dissents.

COHEN, J., files a dissenting opinion.

NOTES AND QUESTIONS

1. After this decision, plaintiffs and the township compromised their differences, and "Sweetbriar" was placed—to the plaintiffs' satisfaction—in a two-acre zone. Do any of the arguments, which Easttown had marshalled to

support four-acre zoning, serve the township any better to justify a two-acre requirement?

2. Appeal of Kit-Mar Builders, Inc., 439 Pa. 466, 268 A.2d 765 (1970), led to the rejection of another town's two- and three-acre zoning "under the test" set forth in the *National Land* case.

The township relied primarily upon a potential sewerage problem to support the ordinance. The court held that the township must rely upon alternative methods, not zoning, to treat the problem. The township's other arguments, viz., the inadequacy of roads and busses, and the protection of rural and historical surroundings, were called "so clearly makeweights as to barely require comment."

> . . . The two and three acre minimums imposed in this case are no more reasonable than the four acre requirements struck down in *National Land.* As we pointed out in *National Land,* there are obvious advantages to the residents of a community in having houses built on four- or three-acre lots. However, minimum lot sizes of the magnitude required by this ordinance are a great deal larger than what should be considered as a *necessary* size for the building of a house, and are therefore not the proper subjects of public regulation. As a matter of fact, a house can fit quite comfortably on a one acre lot without being the least bit cramped. (The Kaufmann's Department Store in Pittsburgh is built on approximately a one-acre lot, and clearly a house built on the same area would hardly want for elbow room.) Absent some extraordinary justification, a zoning ordinance with minimum lot sizes such as those in this case is completely unreasonable. [Id. at 470-471, 268 A.2d at 766-767]

3. "Any minimum lot requirement is, almost by its name, exclusive in some degree in purpose and effect. Indeed, if the minimum lot size in the present case had been one acre, and the appellee had planned to develop the tract in question in ³/₄ acre lots, or ¹/₂ acre lots, the reasoning of the majority opinion would appear to be equally applicable to permitting such use. Perhaps it is significant that the majority opinion in the case at bar does not cite *Bilbar* a single time." Id. at 495-496, 268 A.2d at 779 (dissent).

Justice Pomeroy, who wrote these dissenting words, believed that the township had justified its two- and three-acre zoning. He would not have demanded extraordinary justification.

Previously, the Pennsylvania court had upheld a township's one-acre zone. Bilbar Construction Co. v. Board of Adjustment, 393 Pa. 62, 141 A.2d 851 (1958). To a court that requires extraordinary justification for a two-acre minimum, how can a township defend a one-acre minimum?

4. Simon v. Town of Needham, 311 Mass. 560, 563-564, 42 N.E.2d 516, 518 (1942), offers a classic justification for the one-acre zone:

> The advantages enjoyed by those living in one family dwellings located upon an acre lot might be thought to exceed those possessed by persons living upon a lot

of ten thousand square feet. More freedom from noise and traffic might result. The danger from fire from outside sources might be reduced. A better opportunity for rest and relaxation might be afforded. Greater facilities for children to play on the premises and not in the streets would be available. There may perhaps be more inducement for one to attempt something in the way of the cultivation of flowers, shrubs and vegetables. There may be other advantages accruing to the occupants of the larger lots. The benefits derived by those living in such a neighborhood must be considered with the benefit that would accrue to the public generally who resided in Needham by the presence of such a neighborhood. In the four towns that adjoin Needham the minimum area restrictions for some residential lots have been fixed in one at twenty thousand square feet, in two others at forty thousand square feet, and in the fourth at an acre. Of eight other towns within a short distance from Needham, six have prescribed a minimum area of four [sic] thousand square feet for house lots, and two others have fixed the minimum area as an acre. Such evidence is not decisive that the imposition of a restriction of an area of an acre is reasonable and proper, but it is persuasive that many other communities when faced with an apparently similar problem have determined that the public interest was best served by the adoption of a restriction in some instances identical and in others nearly identical with that imposed by the respondent town.

Cf. also Senior v. Zoning Commission of Town of New Canaan, 146 Conn. 531, 153 A.2d 415 (1959) (four acres valid); Honeck v. County of Cook, 12 Ill. 2d 257, 146 N.E.2d 35 (1957) (five acres valid); Fischer v. Bedminster Township, 11 N.J. 194, 93 A.2d 378 (1952) (five acres valid); Dilliard v. Village of North Hills, 276 A.D. 969, 94 N.Y.S.2d 715 (2d Dept. 1950) (two acres valid).

5.   Isn't township-wide one-acre zoning even more pointedly exclusionary than four-acre zoning is? The latter often dries up virtually all development, whereas housing starts on one-acre lots will continue, but only for the well-to-do.

6.   Explicit in this controversy over minimum lot sizes is the presumption of legislative validity and whether courts must continue to respect the principle. The court in *National Land* and *Kit-Mar Builders*, over strenuous dissents, would, at some point, shift the burden of justification to the community. But why is any land use regulation presumptively invalid?

7.   Is there any way to reconcile the decision in *National Land* with that in *Town of Sanbornton*, page 863 *supra?* With that in *Town of Ramapo*, §16.5 *supra?* Was the township's mistake in *National Land* in cooking up the wrong rationale? In failing to produce an adequate long-range plan?

8.   Four-acre zoning seems to be neither an American nor a recent invention. King Henry VIII became worried about unchecked population increases beyond the walls of London and, beginning in 1480, directed a series of measures forbidding the building of any new houses in the "suburbs" with less than 4 acres of ground. The acts were not fully obeyed, but they did rechannel some of London's population growth back into the city proper. 1 Pevsner, The Buildings of England: London 51-52 (Cherry rev. 1973).

b.   Exclusion of Multiple Dwellings

NATIONAL COMMN. ON URBAN PROBLEMS, BUILDING
THE AMERICAN CITY

215 (1968)

Perhaps an even more important form of exclusionary zoning is the limitation of residential development to single-family houses. Again, motives are undoubtedly mixed. Apartments are viewed by many suburban dwellers as central city structures, having no place in the "pastoral" setting of suburbia. Apartment dwellers are sometimes stereotyped as transients who, not having the permanent ties to the community which home ownership provides, will not be sufficiently concerned about the community or their own residences. But fiscal motives are also present. There is a concern that apartments—especially those which have large units and thereby can accommodate large families—will not pay their way. Where low- or moderate-income units are involved, both fiscal and social concerns increase.

Multifamily housing units generally provide the best opportunities for housing persons of low and moderate incomes. The rental nature of such housing, and the savings produced by spreading land costs over a greater number of units, place such housing within the means of many who could not afford new single-family houses. Furthermore, many of the publicly assisted housing programs are multifamily programs and depend on the existence of zoning for multifamily structures.

Most jurisdictions have some zoning for multifamily structures, and it appears that more suburban zoning jurisdictions are permitting them than in the past. A Commission survey shows that 87 percent of municipalities and New England-type townships of 5,000-plus have at least one district in which multifamily housing can be built. But the figure fails to reveal the way in which such zoning comes about. In many suburban jurisdictions zoning for multifamily housing occurs only through a piecemeal rezoning process. There is at any one time little undeveloped land available for multifamily construction. The price of land zoned for such purposes is thus inflated because of the uncertainty about the total amount of land that may become available. Of the undeveloped land zoned for residential purposes in the New York metropolitan area, for example, 99.2 percent is restricted to single-family dwellings.

APPEAL OF GIRSH

437 Pa. 237, 263 A.2d 395 (1970)

ROBERTS, J. By agreement dated July 13, 1964, appellant contracted to purchase a 17½ acre tract of land, presently zoned R-1 Residential,[1] in

---

1. R-1 Residential zones require minimum lot sizes of 20,000 square feet. The most common of the permissible land uses under the R-1 Residential classification is a single-family detached dwelling.

Nether Providence Township, Delaware County. Appellant agreed to pay a minimum of $110,000 (later changed by agreement to $120,000) for the property. He further agreed to request the Township Board of Commissioners to change the R-1 Residential zoning classification so that a high-rise apartment could be built on the property and to pay $140,000 if this request were granted.

Nether Providence is a first-class township with a population of almost 13,000 persons and an area of 4.64 square miles. Approximately 75% of the Township is zoned either R-1 or R-2 Residential, which permit the construction of single-family dwelling units on areas not less than 20,000 and 14,000 square feet, respectively. Multi-unit apartment buildings, although not *explicitly* prohibited, are not provided for in the ordinance. The Township contains the customary commercial and industrial districts, as well as two areas where apartments have been permitted and constructed only after variances were secured.

After the Board refused to amend the zoning ordinance, appellant sought a building permit to construct two nine-story luxury apartments, each containing 280 units.[2] The permit was refused since the R-1 Residential classification does not permit multiple dwellings. Appellant appealed to the Zoning Board of Adjustment and announced that he would attack the constitutionality of the zoning ordinance in lieu of seeking a variance. The Zoning Board sustained the ordinance and denied relief. The Court of Common Pleas of Delaware County affirmed, and appellant took this appeal. We hold that the failure of appellee-township's zoning scheme to provide for apartments is unconstitutional and reverse the decree of the court below.

Initially, it is plain that appellee's zoning ordinance indeed makes no provision for apartment uses. Appellee argues that nonetheless apartments are not explicitly *prohibited* by the zoning ordinance. Appellee reasons that although only single-family residential uses are provided for, nowhere does the ordinance say that there shall be no apartments. In theory, an apartment use by variance is available, and appellee urges that this case thus is different from prior cases in which we severely questioned zoning schemes that did not allow given uses in an *entire* municipality. See Exton Quarries, Inc. v. Zoning Board of Adjustment, 425 Pa. 43, 228 A.2d 169 (1967); Ammon R. Smith Auto Co. Appeal, 423 Pa. 493, 223 A.2d 683 (1966); Norate Corp. v. Zoning Board of Adjustment, 417 Pa. 397, 207 A.2d 890 (1965).

Appellee's argument, although perhaps initially appealing, cannot withstand analysis. It is settled law that a variance is available *only* on narrow grounds, i.e., "where the property is subjected to an unnecessary hardship, unique or peculiar to itself, and where the grant thereof will not be contrary to the public interest. The reasons to justify the granting of a variance must be 'substantial, serious and compelling.' " Poster Advertising Company, Inc. v. Zoning Board of Adjustment, 408 Pa. 248, 251, 182 A.2d 521, 523 (1962). In

---

2. Appellant stated in court that he would reduce the number of units per building to 216.

light of this standard, appellee's land-use restriction in the case before us cannot be upheld against constitutional attack because of the *possibility* that an *occasional* property owner may carry the heavy burden of proving sufficient hardship to receive a variance. To be constitutionally sustained, appellee's land-use restriction must be reasonable. If the failure to make allowance in the Township's zoning plan for apartment uses is unreasonable, that restriction does not become any the more reasonable because once in a while, a developer may be able to show the hardship necessary to sustain a petition for a variance.[3] At least for the purposes of this case, the failure to provide for apartments anywhere within the Township must be viewed as the legal equivalent of an explicit total prohibition of apartment houses in the zoning ordinance.

Were we to accept appellee's argument, we would encourage the Township in effect to spot-zone a given use on variance-hardship grounds. This approach distorts the question before us, which is whether appellee must provide for apartment living as part of its *plan* of development. Cf. Eves v. Zoning Board of Adjustment, 401 Pa. 211, 164 A.2d 7 (1960).

By emphasizing the possibility that a given land owner *could* obtain a variance, the Township overlooks the broader question that is presented by this case. In refusing to allow apartment development as part of its zoning scheme, appellee has in effect decided to zone *out* the people who would be able to live in the Township if apartments were available. Cf. National Land and Investment Co. v. Easttown Twp. Board of Adjustment, 419 Pa. 504, 532, 215 A.2d 597, 612 (1965):

> The question posed is whether the township can stand in the way of the natural forces which send our growing population into hitherto undeveloped areas in search of a comfortable place to live. We have concluded not. A zoning ordinance whose primary purpose is to prevent the entrance of newcomers in order to avoid future burdens, economic and otherwise, upon the administration of public services and facilities can not be held valid.

We emphasize that we are not here faced with the question whether we can compel appellee to zone *all* of its land to permit apartment development, since this is a case where *nowhere* in the Township are apartments permitted. Instead, we are guided by the reasoning that controlled in *Exton Quarries, supra.* We there stated that "The constitutionality of zoning ordinances which totally prohibit legitimate business . . . from an entire community should be regarded

---

3. We must start with the basic proposition that absent more, an individual should be able to utilize his own land as he sees fit. U.S. Const. Amends. V, XIV. Although zoning is, in general, a proper exercise of police power which can permissibly limit an individual's property rights, Village of Euclid, Ohio v. Ambler Realty Co., 272 U.S. 365 (1926), it goes without saying that the use of the police power cannot be unreasonable. E.g., Eller v. Board of Adjustment, 414 Pa. 1, 198 A.2d 863 (1964). If the zoning ordinance is unreasonable, it is no saving that some people may show the requisite degree of hardship to obtain a variance. The hardship necessary to sustain an application for a variance borders on economic disaster, but this provides no protection for the individual who is disadvantaged to a substantial, but lesser, extent. This infringement on this latter individual's right to use his own property cannot be allowed unless it is reasonable.

with particular circumspection; for unlike the constitutionality of most restrictions on property rights imposed by other ordinances, the constitutionality of total prohibitions of legitimate businesses cannot be premised on the fundamental reasonableness of allocating to each type of activity a particular location in the community." 425 Pa. at 58, 228 A.2d at 179. In *Exton Quarries* we struck down an ordinance which did not allow quarrying anywhere in the municipality, just as in Ammon R. Smith Auto Co. Appeal, *supra*, we did not tolerate a total ban on flashing signs and in *Norate Corp., supra*, we struck down a prohibition on billboards everywhere in the municipality. Here we are faced with a similar case, but its implications are even more critical, for we are here dealing with the crucial problem of population, not with billboards or quarries. Just as we held in *Exton Quarries, Ammon R. Smith,* and *Norate* that the governing bodies must make some provision for the use in question, we today follow those cases and hold that appellee cannot have a zoning scheme that makes no reasonable provision for apartment uses.

Appellee argues that apartment uses would cause a significant population increase with a resulting strain on available municipal services and roads, and would clash with the existing residential neighborhood. But we *explicitly* rejected both these claims in *National Land, supra:* "Zoning is a tool in the hands of governmental bodies which enables them to more effectively meet the demands of evolving and growing communities. It must not and can not be used by those officials as an instrument by which they may shirk their responsibilities. Zoning is a means by which a governmental body can plan for the future—it may not be used as a means to deny the future. . . . Zoning provisions may not be used . . . to avoid the increased responsibilities and economic burdens which time and natural growth invariably bring." 419 Pa. at 527-528, 215 A.2d at 610. Cf. Delaware County Community College Appeal, 435 Pa. 264, 254 A.2d 641 (1969); O'Hara's Appeal, 389 Pa. 35, 131 A.2d 587 (1957). That reasoning applies equally here. Likewise we reaffirm our holding in *National Land* that protecting the character—really the aesthetic nature—of the municipality is not sufficient justification for an exclusionary zoning technique. 419 Pa. at 528-529, 215 A.2d at 610-611.

This case presents a situation where, no less than in *National Land,* the Township is trying to "stand in the way of the natural forces which send our growing population into hitherto undeveloped areas in search of a comfortable place to live." Appellee here has simply made a decision that it is content with things as they are, and that the expense or change in character that would result from people moving in to find "a comfortable place to live" are for someone else to worry about. That decision is unacceptable. Statistics indicate that people are attempting to move away from the urban core areas, relieving the grossly overcrowded conditions that exist in most of our major cities. Figures show that most jobs that are being created in urban areas, including the one here in question, are in the suburbs. New York Times, June 29, 1969, p. 39 (City Edition). Thus the suburbs, which at one time were merely "bedrooms" for those who worked in the urban core, are now becoming active business areas in their own right. It follows then that formerly "outlying", somewhat rural communities, are becoming logical areas for development and population growth—in a sense, suburbs to the suburbs. With improvements in regional transportation systems, these areas also are now more accessible to the central city.

In light of this, Nether Providence Township may not permissibly choose to only take as many people as can live in single-family housing, in effect freezing the population at near present levels. Obviously if every municipality took that view, population spread would be completely frustrated. Municipal services must be provided *somewhere,* and if Nether Providence is a logical place for development to take place, it should not be heard to say that it will not bear its rightful part of the burden.[4] Certainly it can protect its attractive character by requiring apartments to be built in accordance with (reasonable) set-back, open space, height, and other light-and-air requirements,[5] but it cannot refuse to make any provision for apartment living. The simple fact that someone is anxious to build apartments is strong indication that the location of this township is such that people are desirous of moving in, and we do not believe Nether Providence can close its doors to those people.

It is not true that the logical result of our holding today is that a municipality must provide for all types of land use. This case deals with the right of people to *live on land,* a very different problem than whether appellee must allow certain industrial uses within its borders.[6] Apartment living is a fact of life that communities like Nether Providence must learn to accept. If Nether Providence is located so that it is a place where apartment living is in demand, it must provide for apartments in its plan for future growth; it cannot be allowed to close its doors to others seeking a "comfortable place to live."

4. Perhaps in an ideal world, planning and zoning would be done on a *regional* basis, so that a given community would have apartments, while an adjoining community would not. But as long as we allow zoning to be done community by community, it is intolerable to allow one municipality (or many municipalities) to close its doors at the expense of surrounding communities and the central city.

5. As appellants indicate, the apartments here in question would cover only 2.7 acres of a 17.7 acre tract, would be located far back from the road and adjacent properties, and would be screened by existing high trees. Over half of the trees now on the tract would be saved.

It should be pointed out that much of the opposition to apartment uses in suburban communities is based on fictitious emotional appeals which insist on categorizing all apartments as being equivalent to the worst big-city tenements. See Babcock and Bosselman, Suburban Zoning and the Apartment Boom, 111 U. Pa. L. Rev. 1040, 1051-1072 (1963), wherein the authors also convincingly refute the arguments that apartments necessarily will: not "pay their own way"; cut off light and air; become slums; reduce property values; be destructive to the "character of the community"; and bring in "low-class" people.

6. Even in the latter case, if the Township instituted a total ban on a given use, that decision would be open to at least considerable question under our decision in *Exton Quarries, supra.*

In addition, at least hypothetically, appellee could show that apartments are not appropriate on the site where appellant wishes to build, but that question is not before us as long as the zoning ordinance in question is fatally defective on its face. Appellee could properly decide that apartments are more appropriate in one part of the Township than in another, but it cannot decide that apartments can fit in *no* part of the Township.

The order of the Court of Common Pleas of Delaware County is reversed.

BELL, C.J., files a concurring opinion.

JONES, J. (dissenting). Appellant attacks the constitutionality of the zoning ordinance in question on two levels. First, he maintains that it is unconstitutional for the Township to prohibit the construction of apartment buildings throughout the entire township. Second, he argues that the ordinance as applied to the Duer Tract in particular is unconstitutional because the property cannot reasonably be graded and developed for single-family residences. . . .

. . . [T]he natural expansion of the majority's conclusion is that Nether Providence must provide for all types of high-density, residential land use. This is an unsound result. It makes no more sense to require a rural township to provide for high-rise apartments than to provide for industrial zones; likewise, it would not make sense to require an industrial municipality to provide for agricultural uses. By concluding that the township must provide for high-rise apartments, the majority also impliedly holds that every possible use, having no greater detrimental effect, must also be allowed. In my opinion, this decision places us in the position of a "super board of adjustment" or "planning commission of last resort," a position which we have heretofore specifically rejected. National Land and Investment Co. v. Easttown Twp. Bd. of Adjustment, 419 Pa. 504, 521-22, 215 A.2d 597, 606-607 (1965).

Even if I were to accept appellant's logic, it must still be affirmatively demonstrated that high-rise apartment buildings are a *suitable* land use within the township. The court below held that appellant had failed to carry his burden of proof, and I find no fault in this decision. The evidence indicates that 90% of the township is presently already developed. A land planner and municipal consultant testified that he had studied the remaining undeveloped properties within the township and concluded that none of them was suitable for high-rise apartments. Furthermore, the township is residential in nature with a relatively sparse population. A high-rise apartment project would produce a significant increase in population which would tax the limited municipal services available in the township. Accordingly, I find it impossible to say on the face of this record that a township such as Nether Providence is constitutionally required to make provision for high-rise apartments in its zoning ordinances.[6]

I turn now to appellant's second contention, viz., that the zoning ordinance permitting only single-family dwellings is unconstitutional as applied to the Duer Tract in particular. Appellant's first argument under this heading is that the ordinance has no relation to the public health, safety and welfare. I cannot agree. The proposed apartment complex would be the largest of its

6. Decisions in other jurisdictions support this conclusion. See, e.g., Valley View Village, Inc. v. Proffett, 221 F.2d 412, 418 (6th Cir. 1955), (per Potter Stewart, J.); Fanale v. Borough of Hasbrouck Heights, 26 N.J. 320, 139 A.2d 749, 752 (1958) (per Weintraub, C.J.); Connor v. Township of Chanhassen, 249 Minn. 205, 81 N.W.2d 789, 794-795 (1957); Fox Meadow Estates, Inc. v. Culley, 233 App. Div. 250, 252 N.Y.S. 178 (1931), *aff'd per curiam*, 261 N.Y. 506, 185 N.E. 714 (1933); Guaclides v. Borough of Englewood Cliffs, 11 N.J. Super. 405, 78 A.2d 435 (1951) (per William Brennan, J.).

kind in Delaware County, housing an estimated 1,600 persons, and would increase the population of the township by 13%. We cannot refute the conclusion that such a large and rapid increase in population would place a strain on the township's limited municipal services and rural roads. Furthermore, except for the railroad tracks, the area surrounding the Duer Tract is composed exclusively of single-family dwellings. The proposed apartment towers would be incompatible with the existing residential neighborhood and would introduce a structure completely out of proportion to any other building in the township. Furthermore, the complex would present a density problem in this area of the township. The First Class Township Code specifically empowers local municipalities to zone for density; I conclude that the ordinance in question is a proper application of that power.

Appellant's second argument is that the ordinance is unreasonable, arbitrary and discriminatory as applied to the Duer Tract because of the prohibitive expense involved in grading and preparing the land for single-family residences. There is no question that the property contains some topographical features which are less than desirable for the construction of single-family homes. The record is replete with conflicting testimony, however, as to how much expense would be required to grade the tract and divert the creek which runs through the property. There is evidence in the record to support the court's conclusion that these preparatory expenses would not make the cost of the homes prohibitively expensive. The court pointed out that a development of single-family houses is now being constructed on a neighboring tract which is very similar topographically to the Duer Tract. Furthermore, appellant made a firm commitment to buy the property regardless of whether he was successful in having the zoning classification changed. Apparently when he purchased the property, therefore, appellant concluded that he could successfully build and sell single-family homes on the tract.

Therefore, I would hold that the Township is *not* constitutionally required to provide for multiple-unit apartment buildings in its zoning ordinance and that the ordinance in question is not unconstitutional as applied to the Duer Tract.

I dissent.

COHEN and POMEROY, JJ., join in this dissenting opinion.

NOTES AND QUESTIONS

1. Reread Justice Roberts's majority opinion. Which statement below better describes why the court invalidated the Nether Providence ordinance?

    (a) It was unreasonable in principle for the zoning law to bar all apartments from the township.

    (b) The township failed to give a sufficient reason for barring all apartments.

2. Reread Justice Roberts's majority opinion. Does the opinion identify whether the Nether Providence ordinance violates the federal constitution, the state constitution, or both? Might it make a difference?

3. The village of Belle Terre, New York, consists of 700 residents, and is seven miles from the State University of New York at Stony Brook. The village zoning ordinance allows only one-family dwellings. It defines "family" as "one or more persons related by blood, adoption or marriage, living and cooking together as a single housekeeping unit . . . or a number of [unrelated] persons but not exceeding two (2) living and cooking together as a single housekeeping unit."

Six students rented a six-bedroom house in the village, which they organized as a single housekeeping unit, dining together and sharing the chores. None of the occupants were related. They called this rental arrangement "pleasant, convenient, promotive of scholarly exchange, and within their pocket books." They preferred it to a college dormitory.

When the village sought to enforce the ordinance by serving an order to correct the violation within forty-eight hours or face criminal liability (disorderly conduct), three students and their landlord sued to invalidate the ordinance. The trial judge upheld the law. The Second Circuit Court of Appeals reversed, holding that the law denied equal protection to "voluntary" families (of unrelated individuals), since no rational basis supported the discrimination against them. 476 F.2d 806 (2d Cir. 1973).

The Supreme Court reinstated the ordinance in an opinion by Justice Douglas that surprised many:

> The present ordinance is challenged on several grounds: that it interferes with a person's right to travel; that it interferes with the right to migrate to and settle within a state; that it bars people who are uncongenial to the present residents; that the ordinance expresses the social preferences of the resident for groups that will be congenial to them; that social homogeneity is not a legitimate interest of government; that the restriction of those whom the neighbors do not like trenches on the newcomers' rights of privacy; that it is of no rightful concern to villagers whether the residents are married or unmarried; that the ordinance is antithetical to the Nation's experience, ideology and self-perception as an open, egalitarian, and integrated society.
>
> We find none of these reasons in the record before us. It is not aimed at transients. . . . It involves no "fundamental" right guaranteed by the Constitution. . . . We deal with economic and social legislation where legislatures have historically drawn lines which we respect against the charge of violation of the Equal Protection Clause if the law be "reasonable, not arbitrary . . . and bears a rational relationship to a [permissible] state objective."
>
> The regimes of boarding houses, fraternity houses, and the like present urban problems. More people occupy a given space; more cars rather continuously pass by; more cars are parked; noise travels with crowds.
>
> A quiet place where yards are wide, people few, and motor vehicles restricted are legitimate guidelines in a land use project addressed to family needs. . . . The police power is not confined to elimination of filth, stench, and un-

healthy places. It is ample to lay out zones where family values, youth values, and the blessings of quiet seclusion and clean air make the area a sanctuary for people. [Village of Belle Terre v. Boraas, 416 U.S. 1, 7-9 (1974)]

Does the decision in *Belle Terre* wash away holdings like *Girsh?* Is it significant that *Girsh* was a state case, while *Belle Terre* was a federal one? Compare Southern Burlington County NAACP v. Township of Mount Laurel, 67 N.J. 151, 336 A.2d 713 (1975), page 920 *infra*. Is it significant that Nether Providence had an area of 4.64 square miles and a population of 13,000, while Belle Terre had an area of less than one square mile and a population of 700? Is it significant that Nether Providence was a "logical place for development," while Belle Terre was a fairly settled community?

4. *Denial of Equal Protection.* Notice that equal protection underlies the constitutional discussion in *Belle Terre,* whereas due process has been the root of most of the zoning disputes we have seen before. The importance of *this* distinction should more properly be left to another course; yet a brief, highly oversimplified explanation might be helpful here. As you know, equal protection and due process are two branches of the Fourteenth Amendment. Both also appear, relatively unchanged, in most state constitutions. During the 1920s, when the Supreme Court decided *Euclid* and *Nectow,* and state courts began to examine local zoning laws, substantive due process was a far more powerful means than was equal protection for striking down objectionable state action. As a result, if landowners hoped to invalidate a zoning ordinance, they argued due process. Cf. Nectow v. City of Cambridge, page 789 *supra*. During the 1930s, the Supreme Court weakened the substantive muscle of due process. Federal courts were not to use this branch of the Fourteenth Amendment to reject state and local laws regulating business activity. This new learning little affected zoning laws, however: after the *Nectow* decision, zoning cases rarely reached the federal courts; moreover, state constitutional interpretations of due process may be more demanding than is the federal counterpart, and most due process attacks on local zoning laws charged both federal *and* state constitutional violations. In deciding these cases, state courts tended to ignore the curbs with which federal courts had surrounded the federal due process clause, implying that the state clauses did not suffer the same restraint.

It took the civil rights decisions, culminating in Brown v. Board of Education and its vast progeny, to vest the federal Equal Protection Clause with a striking-down power of the impact that due process had enjoyed a generation before.

While the rhetoric is different, the underlying judicial philosophy is quite similar. Federal courts currently assert a power to look hard at state and local laws that infringe on personal activities and, in some areas, to hold the laws to quite demanding substantive norms. The doctrine continues to evolve. Currently, one might voice it roughly as follows: where state action is directed against a suspect classification (e.g., race, religion, possibly gender) or impinges upon constitutionally protected (i.e., "fundamental") rights, the burden shifts to the state to establish that a "compelling state interest" justifies the measure. Cf. Shapiro v. Thompson, 394 U.S. 618 (1969). This is the "strict scrutiny" standard. In the absence of a suspect classification, or an impingement of a fundamental right, the measure need satisfy only the "minimal scrutiny" standard that there be some rational basis to explain the restriction against one group. Gunther, The Supreme Court, 1971 Term—Foreword: In Search of Evolving Doctrine on a Changing Court: A Model for a Newer Equal Protection, 86 Harv. L. Rev. 1, 8 (1972).

Activists have pressed the Supreme Court for a much longer list of fundamental rights. While the rights of association and privacy, to travel, to vote, and to prosecute a criminal appeal already appear on the list, the present Supreme Court seems reluctant to add others. Cf., e.g., Lindsey v. Normet, 405 U.S. 56 (1972) (housing not a fundamental right); Jefferson v. Hackney, 406 U.S. 535 (1972) (welfare payments not a fundamental right); San Antonio Independent School District v. Rodriguez, 411 U.S. 1 (1973) (education not a fundamental right).

5. In invalidating the Belle Terre ordinance, the Second Circuit itself fell short of adopting the strict scrutiny test. Instead, the court chose an intermediate test (between minimal and strict scrutiny) for weighing equal protection: Is the legislative classification *in fact* substantially related to the object of the statute? This means that a court need not accept on their face the village's reasons for the law. The village must also show a substantial relationship between the regulation and the goal. The following excerpt from Judge Mansfield's opinion illustrates this approach:

> We are further asked to speculate that "voluntary" families would pose greater parking, traffic and noise problems than would traditional families and that there would be a greater degree of transiency on the part of the former than the latter, thus weakening the stability of the community.
>
> If some or all of these hypothesized objectives were supportable, some form of such ordinance might conceivably be upheld as a valid exercise of state police power. Upon the record before us, however, we fail to find a vestige of any such support. To theorize that groups of unrelated members would have more occupants per house than would traditional family groups, or . . . would produce greater parking, noise or traffic problems, would be rank speculation, unsupported either by evidence or by facts that could be judicially noted. . . . [Boraas v. Village of Belle Terre, 476 F.2d 806, 816 (2d Cir. 1973)]

How did Justice Douglas dispose of the Mansfield formulation?

Compare Judge Mansfield's equal protection formulation with the reasoning of Justice White, writing for the plurality, in Schad v. Borough of Mount Ephraim, *supra,* page 834. Also compare Judge Mansfield's formulation with the state court opinion in National Land & Investment Co. v. Kohn, *supra,* page 891.

Why do we not require all legislation to meet a more exacting standard—such as that posed by Judge Mansfield—when laws are tested against the due process or equal protection clauses?

6.   An alternative theory for attacking exclusionary zoning has centered about the "suspect classification" leg of the strict scrutiny test. The argument goes that poverty is a suspect category, that any regulation tending to discriminate against the poor must promote a "compelling state interest," and that the protection of property values or the easing of financial burden is not "compelling." Some earlier support for the equation of "poor = suspect" appeared, cf. Douglas v. California, 372 U.S. 353, 361 (1963), but more recent cases have ended differently. See, e.g., James v. Valtierra, 402 U.S. 137 (1971); San Antonio Independent School District v. Rodriguez, 411 U.S. 1 (1973); Ybarra v. City of Town of Los Altos Hills, 503 F.2d 250 (9th Cir. 1974). In the *Rodriguez* case, the court said that the poor must show a complete inability to pay for some desired benefit and, thus, "an *absolute* deprivation of a meaningful opportunity to enjoy the benefit." 411 U.S. at 20. In the *Ybarra* case, where plaintiffs attacked a large-lot zoning ordinance as denying them the chance to live in Los Altos Hills, the court dismissed the action because plaintiffs, inter alia, failed to show that low-cost housing was unavailable elsewhere in the county, 503 F.2d at 253-254.

7.   Attempts to link racial discrimination to zoning actions that denied entry to the poor, in order to subject the actions to strict scrutiny, came nearly to a dead halt after Village of Arlington Heights v. Metropolitan Housing Development Corp., 429 U.S. 252 (1977). There, a nonprofit sponsor sought to build a federally subsidized, low-income project in a large, virtually all-white Chicago suburb. The village refused to amend its zoning to enable the project. The developer challenged the refusal and claimed, inter alia, that the village action had a racially discriminatory impact that only a compelling state interest, not shown here, could justify. To support the racial claim, plaintiffs alleged that in the Chicago area blacks represented 40 percent of the population able to qualify economically for the proposed 190-unit development. At the time only 170 of the 219,000 people who lived in Arlington Heights were black.

The trial court rejected the plaintiffs' challenge, finding that the village's decision was not racially motivated. 373 F. Supp. 208 (N.D. Ill. 1974). The Seventh Circuit reversed, holding that the refusal, when interpreted in light of its "historical context and ultimate effect" had a discriminatory impact and, thereby, was subject to strict scrutiny. 517 F.2d 409 (7th Cir. 1975). The Supreme Court reversed and reinstated the trial court judgment. In doing so, the Court held that plaintiffs' equal protection claim required a showing of an illicit purpose behind the challenged decision, which the trial court had not found. Although the zoning law's disproportionate impact upon blacks might be a circumstance from which a claim of illicit purpose could begin, impact alone was not sufficient to establish the constitutional violation.

Illicit purpose—even when it is strongly suspected—will usually be most difficult to prove if greater proof than the showing of disproportionate impact is required. For a discussion of the plaintiff's burden and some suggestions for carrying that burden, see Developments, 91 Harv. L. Rev. 1427, 1672-78 (1978).

8.   Plaintiffs seeking to establish an equal protection violation in the federal courts face a procedural barrier besides the substantive ones described above. In Warth v. Seldin, 422 U.S. 490 (1975), the Court dismissed a suit attacking as exclusionary the zoning ordinance of a Rochester, New York, suburb. Plaintiffs included present residents of the locality, a home-builders' association, and two public interest organizations concerned with low-income housing. The Court held that plaintiffs did not meet *prudential* standing requirements because they could not point to any specific projects that, but for the zoning, would have been built.

The project-specific standing requirement, which Warth v. Seldin seems to mandate, was satisfied in the *Arlington Heights* case, Note 7 *supra;* there plaintiffs included the project sponsor. His presence made possible the joinder, as a coplaintiff, the nonresident, minority, prospective occupant of the project who could then assert the equal protection claim. But how often will a developer, nonprofit or otherwise, be prepared to undergo the expense and delay incident to litigation to help vindicate the right of minority groups to obtain housing without racial discrimination?

9.   Although Warth v. Seldin and *Arlington Heights* have made federal courts an unpromising forum for parties seeking, in the case of local zoning, to establish racial discrimination under the Constitution, the Fair Housing Act of 1968, *supra,* pages 33-37, offers a statutory vehicle whose standing and substantive requirements plaintiffs continue to find less demanding. In *Arlington Heights,* for example, the Supreme Court, having dismissed the constitutional claim, remanded the case for a determination under the statute. In response, the Seventh Circuit held that the village's refusal to rezone could violate the statute despite the absence of proof of racial purpose sufficient to implicate the constitution. The court of appeals stopped short of ruling that every action producing a discriminatory effect would be illegal under the statute, but it listed several factors, including the degree of disproportionate impact, as responsive to the issue of whether a statutory violation has occurred. 558 F.2d 1283 (7th Cir. 1977), *cert. denied,* 434 U.S. 1025 (1978).

Similarly, the Supreme Court, relying upon congressional will, has defined standing in Fair Housing suits as coincident with that permitted under the Constitution, a more generous view than that expressed in Warth v. Seldin. Trafficante v. Metropolitan Life Insurance Co., 409 U.S. 205 (1972).

The *Arlington Heights* controversy finally came to an end in 1978 when the village board approved a tentative plan for the construction of 270 low-income housing units on two pieces of unincorporated land that the village would then annex. The district court approved a consent decree embodying the plan, despite the outcries of the neighboring village of Mount Prospect, whose officials feared that the project would increase congestion, the danger of flooding, the need for police protection, and would cause local property values to drop. 469 F. Supp. 836 (N.D. Ill. 1979), *aff'd,* 616 F.2d 1006 (7th Cir. 1980).

10. To return to the *Girsh* decision for a few further questions:

(a) The plaintiff sought to build 216 units of luxury apartments. After this decision, may a builder of subsidized units insist that land also be set aside for him? Cf. Willistown v. Chesterdale Farms, Inc., 7 Pa. Cmwlth. 453, 300 A.2d 107 (1973).

(b) Is Girsh absolutely entitled to build the apartments? Might Nether Providence respond to this decision by zoning someone else's land for apartments? Cf. Casey v. Zoning Hearing Board, 8 Pa. Cmwlth. 473, 303 A.2d 535 (1973) (town ordered to issue permit for Girsh site after town had rezoned land other than Girsh's for apartments), *reversed and remanded,* 549 Pa. 219, 328 A.2d 464 (1974) (landowner must first exhaust administrative remedies).

(c) After this decision, Nether Providence revises its ordinance to provide for a total of 500 apartment units. The units are built and rented. Thereupon a developer attacks the ordinance because there remains an unsatisfied demand for apartments in Nether Providence for which there is no zoning. How should the court respond, in light of *Girsh?*

c. Minimum House-Size Requirements

NATIONAL COMMN. ON URBAN PROBLEMS, BUILDING THE AMERICAN CITY

215 (1968)

The most blatant, though not most extensive, exclusionary practice takes the form of excluding housing which fails to contain a minimum floor area as set out in the zoning ordinance. Such requirements raise the lower limit of construction costs, and thus can be the most direct and effective exclusionary tool. An extreme application of the technique is found in Bloomington, Minn., an affluent suburb of the Twin Cities. Bloomington imposes a 1,700-square-foot minimum floor area. At a square foot construction cost of $15.82, the average for FHA Section 203 housing in the Minneapolis area in 1966, the smallest house permitted would require $26,894.00 in construction costs alone. . . .

NOTES AND QUESTIONS

1. Lionshead Lake, Inc. v. Township of Wayne, 10 N.J. 165, 89 A.2d 693 (1952), is a zoning classic. It approved a minimum house-size requirement

ranging from 768 square feet for a one-story house to 1200 square feet for a two-story dwelling. It also excited a literature of its own. See Haar, Zoning for Minimum Standards: The Wayne Township Case, 66 Harv. L. Rev. 1051 (1953) (criticism); Nolan and Horack, How Small a House?—Zoning for Minimum Space Requirements, 67 Harv. L. Rev. 967 (1954) (answer); Haar, Wayne Township: Zoning for Whom?—In Brief Reply, 67 Harv. L. Rev. 986 (1954) (reply).

The township defended its ordinance on the basis of a study showing the relation of minimum house-size to health. No one argues whether cramped quarters or overcrowding can endanger health. Housing codes routinely prescribe minimum room sizes or area per occupant. New York City, for example, requires not less than 80 square feet per person occupying a multiple dwelling, excluding the first child under four years of age in a family. New York City Charter and Code §D26-33.03 (1970). This means a minimum of 320 square feet of living space for a family of four which has no child under four. Compare that health standard with Wayne Township's standard of 768 to 1200 square feet. Is a minimum house-size requirement unrelated to the number of occupants a valid health measure? The New York City Code also fixes minimum room sizes: 150 square feet for a living room; 80 square feet for bedrooms. Id. §D26-33.01 (1970). This means a minimum of 310 square feet for a two-bedroom apartment, exclusive of kitchens and bathrooms. Once again compare that health standard with Wayne Township's. Is a minimum house-size requirement unrelated to the number of rooms a valid health measure?

While Wayne Township has set a higher standard than has New York City, are the differences, especially at the one-story level, of a degree of magnitude that warrants judicial interference with the local standard? Is it relevant even to compare the New York City requirement for apartments with the Wayne Township requirement for detached single-family homes? In establishing a health standard, does one consider the psychological expectation that a freestanding home has more roominess than does an apartment? In establishing a health standard, does one consider land and construction costs in the area?

2.   A two-story house containing 1200 square feet would occupy a 20′ × 30′ foundation, slightly smaller than the 24′ × 32′ foundation of a one-story house containing 768 square feet. However, a two-story house containing the 768 square feet required of a one-story house would be smaller than 20′ × 20′ at ground level; if freestanding, the house would *look* like a box. Apparently, Wayne Township's higher standard for a two-story dwelling may have had both health *and* appearance for its goals. If, independently, health and aesthetics are valid regulatory goals, do they lose or gain in combination?

3.   There comes a point, however, beyond which the health argument loses all persuasion. One is left with the argument that larger homes are more attractive than smaller homes. Is that reason enough to uphold the regulation? Cf. Senefsky v. Lawler, 307 Mich. 728, 12 N.W.2d 387 (1943) (1300-square-foot minimum for all residences held unreasonable).

d.   Exclusion of Mobile Homes

NATIONAL COMMN. ON URBAN PROBLEMS, BUILDING
THE AMERICAN CITY
216 (1968)

Exact figures are not available on the extent to which mobile homes are excluded from zoning jurisdictions, but it appears that a large number of governments exclude them entirely or limit them to industrial and commercial areas. A study in 1964 showed that in New York State, of 237 zoning ordinances reviewed, over half excluded mobile homes either explicitly or by imposing minimums relating to floor area, height, or other factors which mobile homes could not meet. Only 82 communities permitted mobile homes on individual lots, as distinguished from mobile home parks; and in all but 12 of these communities such lots had to be in areas zoned for industrial or commercial uses. Only 11 communities permitted mobile home parks to locate in residentially zoned areas.

The exclusion of mobile homes in large part reflects a stereotyping of their appearance and of their occupants. Many see mobile homes as unattractive and occupied by people who do not take care of their homes or neighborhood. Such images are often derived from viewing mobile homes in the midst of industrial districts, to which they are so often relegated. Moreover, there are sometimes fiscal reasons for exclusion in addition to those generally applicable to housing which might accommodate low- and moderate-income families. In many areas mobile homes are not taxable as real property. And in some States they are not subject to local personal property taxes because of special State levies, the imposition of which may exempt them from local taxes. In New York State, mobile homes are taxable as real property, and the fiscal motive for exclusion is accordingly reduced. The high exclusion rate in New York may thus indicate an even greater amount of exclusion in other States.

NOTES AND QUESTIONS

1.   Vickers v. Township Committee of Gloucester Township, 37 N.J. 232, 181 A.2d 129 (1962), upheld a total ban on trailer parks in a township twenty-three square miles in area and still largely rural. Ascribing a limited role for judicial review, the court noted also that "trailer camps . . . present a municipality with a list of problems [which] persist wherever such camps are located . . . [they] strike a discordance with, . . . [are] detrimental to property values, present and prospective, and retard the progress of the community."

Justice Hall's strongly worded dissent, which American City magazine called the zoning opinion of the year, disagreed both with the attitude of judicial laissez-faire and the pariah treatment of mobile homes:

Trailer living is a perfectly respectable, healthy and useful kind of housing, adopted by choice by several million people in this country today. Municipalities and courts can no longer refuse to recognize its proper and significant place in today's society and should stop acting on the basis of old wives' tales. A fair, modern appraisal is found in Note, "Toward an Equitable and Workable Program of Mobile Home Taxation," 71 Yale L.J. 702 (1962):

"Between 1951 and 1956 the mobile home population doubled; it currently totals over 3,000,000 persons. The number of mobile homes in use grew from 550,000 in 1953 to 1,200,000 in 1959. This figure has been augmented by mobile homes recently produced—produced at a rate which exceeds 10 percent of the private single family housing starts in this country.

"For many years communities viewed the house trailer as the source of at least three major problems: its presence was expected to blight surrounding areas, causing property values to fall; its occupants were often viewed as personally undesirable; and the municipal expense attributable to trailerites was expected to exceed the revenue which could be raised from them.

"Community fear of blight can be traced to the low quality of both the early trailers and their parking facilities. Economic conditions of the 'thirties, followed by wartime housing shortages and rapid relocations of the labor force, pressed many thousands of unattractive trailers into permanent use. Often these units were without running water or sanitary facilities. There were no construction standards to insure even minimum protection against fire or collapse. They were parked in areas which were usually crowded, poorly equipped, and generally unsuited to residential use. As a result, conditions in these parks seldom exceeded minimum health and sanitation standards. The specter of such parks teeming with tiny trailers made community apprehension understandable. But substantial improvements in the quality of both mobile homes and park facilities may have undermined the bases for this antipathy today. The mobile home currently produced is an attractive, completely furnished, efficiently spacious dwelling for which national construction standards have been adopted and enforced by the manufacturers' associations. Some of today's parks are landscaped, and feature ample lots imaginatively arranged around paved streets. Recreation facilities—such as swimming pools, boat docks and playgrounds—found in high quality parks could be the envy of conventional housing developments. *Although many parks have yet to match such progress, communities have ample power to require improvement of existing facilities and to set high standards for future park construction. They need only exercise it. . . .*" [Id. at 267, 181 A.2d at 148]

2. Mobile home proponents fared better in Degrindee Development Co. v. Charter Township of Warren, 359 Mich. 634, 103 N.W.2d 600 (1960) (exclusion of mobile home parks held unreasonable); Anderson v. Highland, 21 Mich. App. 64, 174 N.W.2d 909 (1969) (idem). See generally Comment, Validity and Application of Zoning Regulations Relating to Mobile Home or Trailer Parks, 42 A.L.R.3d 598 (1970); Williams and Norman, Exclusionary Land Use Controls: The Case of Northeastern New Jersey, 22 Syracuse L. Rev. 475, 500 (1971); Bartke and Sage, Mobile Homes: Zoning and Taxation, 55 Cornell L. Rev. 491 (1970).

3. Mobile homes typically are 14 feet wide and 30 feet long (420

square feet). Often two homes are coupled together to form a single unit. At 1973 prices, a new mobile home sold for $8 to $9 per square foot (exclusive of lot), compared with $18 to $19 per square foot for conventional housing. This price disparity helps explain why the 1972 production of mobile homes, 601,250, highest on record, accounted for more than 20 percent of all new housing and 75 percent of all single-family housing costing less than $20,000.

4. On the assumption that suburban communities may find courts acting more resistant to *total* exclusion, what kinds of mobile home regulation do you believe courts might accept? Why?

e. Excessive Subdivision Requirements

NATIONAL COMMN. ON URBAN PROBLEMS, BUILDING THE AMERICAN CITY

216 (1968)

Land improvement costs are becoming an increasingly important part of housing costs. Zoning, as discussed above, affects such costs by determining the number of linear feet of various improvements which are required to serve a given house. Subdivision regulations determine the precise specifications of such improvements, as well as the amount of land within a subdivision which can actually be devoted to housing. The more expensive these requirements are the greater the cost of housing.

Subdivision regulations differ widely from locality to locality. By demanding higher quality improvements, a jurisdiction can effectively increase the cost of housing and thereby exclude a greater number of potential home buyers from the market.

NOTES AND QUESTIONS

1. The regulation of land subdivision first began in the late 1800s with laws to enforce the uniformity and accuracy of surveying methods. More accurate title records was the avowed goal, in order to facilitate land transfer and to reduce friction between neighbors. Compliance was essential if one wished to record a subdivision plat, and although lots could still be sold legally without a recorded plat, the plat, once recorded, made unnecessary the tedious description (in deeds and mortgages) of each lot by metes and bounds. For many subdividers this was incentive enough to comply.

The land swindles of the 1920s, when many luckless buyers discovered they had paid for submerged lands and paper streets, gave new impetus to subdivision control. The prevention of consumer fraud was entrusted in several states to newly formed agencies—for example, the California Department of Real Estate—that would thereafter regulate all sales of subdivided lands.

Local fiscal considerations, today the most controversial basis for subdivision control, also are rooted in the experience of the 1920s. Prior to the Great Depression, cities regularly installed the streets, sewers, and water mains that would service a new neighborhood. However, the speculative overbuilding of residential tracts, and the premature extension of community facilities, left many cities financially prostrate—saddled by new debt as their revenues were falling. To prevent a recurrence communities were given power to shift this cost of new development from themselves to the subdivider, who now had to install or guarantee installation of roads, sewers, and water supply before a new plat could gain approval.

Despite the general prosperity of midcentury America, municipal finances often still remained straitened, largely because of an archaic tax structure that seemed resistant to significant change. In many suburban areas the insatiable demand of new residents for schools, parks, and recreational facilities further aggravated fiscal difficulties. Increasingly, communities raised the ante to the developer, requiring that he supply not only roads, sewers, and water, but also that he absorb part of the cost—through either a land dedication or a cash contribution—of schools and parks.

2.   Community control over the tract builder may occur at several stages of development: prior to the recordation of the plat; prior to the erection of the improvements; prior to the sale of the units; prior to the occupancy of the units. Map approval, building permits, sales permits, and certificates of occupancy are the authoritarian devices that, until granted, prevent the developer from moving ahead with his construction and marketing program.

3.   The Town of Islip, New York, required the installation of tract roads or, alternatively, the filing of a performance bond. In Brous v. Smith, 304 N.Y. 164, 106 N.E.2d 503 (1952), the court of appeals unanimously upheld the regulation. Replying to the builder's contention that the town should reimburse him for the roads since they would become public streets, the court wrote (id. at 170-171, 106 N.E.2d at 506-507):

> [N]o one may question that the town, were it desirous of constructing a road across petitioner's property, would have to condemn the necessary land and compensate petitioner. But the town has no such desire or design and does not seek to condemn land owned by petitioner. It is petitioner who wishes to construct dwellings on his property, and the town merely conditions its approval of such construction upon his compliance with reasonable conditions designed for the protection both of the ultimate purchasers of the homes and of the public. That the state may empower the town to do this is clear. . . .

4.   A 1952 survey of the New York City area, prepared by the Regional Plan Association, showed how the developer and local community shared the expense of various facilities; see Table [17].

5.   Subdivision exactions that go beyond the more traditional demands often invite court challenges. For example, Mount Prospect, Illinois, required as a condition to subdivision approval that the builder dedicate to the village

TABLE 17
Costs of Improvements Borne by Different Agencies*

(A = by developer; B = by municipality; C = by other means; None = no requirement.)

	A	B	C	None
Grading of streets	98%	0%	2%	0%
Surfacing	96	2	2	0
Curbs	87	0	2	11
Gutters	64	0	2	34
Sidewalks	72	0	6	22
Water mains	83	8	9	0
Sanitary sewers	70	0	2	28
Storm water drains	85	2	0	13
Fire hydrants	46	46	2	6
Street lights	15	57	6	22
Street signs	28	53	0	19
Street trees	49	25	2	24
Recreation areas	38	21	0	41

*Figures are percentages of the cities covered by the survey.
Source: Delafons, Land-Use Controls in the United States 62-63 (1962).

one acre of usable land for every sixty dwelling units shown on the plan. Such land was to be used for school and park purposes. The court upset the ordinance when the village could not show that the need for play and school facilities was uniquely attributable to the proposed subdivision. Pioneer Trust & Savings Bank v. Village of Mount Prospect, 22 Ill. 2d 375, 176 N.E.2d 799 (1961). By contrast, the New York court approved a village law requiring the builder either to set aside playland within his subdivision or to contribute $250 per lot to a fund that the village board could spend for park, playground, and recreational purposes where it chose within the community.

> Scarsdale and other communities, observing that their vacant lands were being cut up into subdivision lots, and being alert to their responsibilities, saw to it, before it was too late, that the subdivisions make allowance for open park spaces therein. This was merely a kind of zoning, like set-back and side-yard regulations, minimum size of lots, etc., and akin also to other reasonable requirements for necessary sewers, water mains, lights, sidewalks, etc. If the developers did not provide for parks and playgrounds in their own tracts, the municipality would have to do it since it would now be required for the benefit of all the inhabitants.
>
> But it was found, in some instances, that the separate subdivisions were too small to permit substantial park lands to be set off, yet the creation of such subdivisions, too, enlarged the demand for more recreational space in the community. In such cases it was just as reasonable to assess the subdividers an amount per lot to go into a fund for more park lands for the village or town. One

arrangement is no more of a "tax" or "illegal taking" than the other. [Jenad, Inc. v. Village of Scarsdale, 18 N.Y.2d 78, 84, 218 N.E.2d 673, 676 (1966)]

See also Jordan v. Menomonee Falls, 28 Wis. 2d 608, 137 N.W.2d 442 (1965) (land dedication or equalization fee requirement upheld).

6. Speaking for the Supreme Court of New Jersey, Chief Justice Vanderbilt wrote: "The philosophy of this ordinance is that the tax rate of the Borough should remain the same and the new people coming into the municipality should bear the burden of the increased costs of their presence. This is so totally contrary to tax philosophy as to require it to be stricken down." Daniels v. Borough of Point Pleasant, 23 N.J. 357, 362, 129 A.2d 265, 267 (1957). Any comment in the light of *Jenad* or *Jordan?*

7. Heyman and Gilhool, in The Constitutionality of Imposing Increased Community Costs on New Suburban Residents through Subdivision Exactions, 73 Yale L.J. 1119 (1964), offer a comprehensive discussion of the issues, including a cost-accounting model for allocating the cost of school facilities between new and old residents (at 1141-1146). See also Fagin, Financing Municipal Services in a Metropolitan Region, 19 J. Am. Inst. Planners 214 (1953).

8. Complaints about local autocracy are voiced regularly at builders' conventions. In an undated monograph, A Survey of Local Government Restrictions Affecting Home Building in New York State, prepared for the New York State Home Builders Association, Inc., examples of builder disaffection are many:

> In an upstate township, the community's Engineer arbitrarily increased the size of storm sewers from 30 to 42 inches. As a result of the increase in pipe sizes, the cost of storm sewers in one 350 lot subdivision was increased three times the original estimate.
>
> In Briarcliff Manor, Westchester County, a builder expressed strong criticism about a local demand for $75 per lot for recreational purposes and then Village insistence that the builder construct a roadway into undeveloped public land at a cost of approximately $14,000.
>
> In the metropolitan New York area, another builder criticized a conflict involving county and town officials "at odds" about the installation of septic tanks. The County people insisted on tile fields, while the Town approved seepage fields. The builder preferred the Town's proposal, although it resulted in additional cost for seven houses in an 82 lot subdivision. Eventually, the builder was permitted to install seepage fields but he was later accused by County officials of a "payoff" to Town representatives.
>
> A Yorktown Heights developer was required to give land to a Town for a proposed school site in order to obtain final approval on a subdivision plat. The builder turned over to the town property to widen two public roads in lieu of money for recreational purposes.

9. The ALI Model Land Development Code limits the power of local bodies to make subdivision exactions. Developers would still be required to

install or provide streets, other rights-of-way, utilities, parks, and other open space, or to make an in-lieu contribution, but the requirement "must be of a quality and quantity no more than reasonably necessary for the proposed development." Id. at §2-103 (1975).

f. Administrative Practices

NATIONAL COMMN. ON URBAN PROBLEMS, BUILDING
THE AMERICAN CITY
216-217 (1968)

Some of the most effective devices for exclusion are not discoverable from a reading of zoning and subdivision ordinances. Where rezoning is, in effect, necessary for many projects or where apartment development requires a special exception (as it does in some suburban communities), officials have an opportunity to determine the intentions of each developer with some precision. How many bedrooms will the units in his apartment house contain? What will be the rent levels? To whom does he plan to rent or sell? "Unfavorable" answers in terms of the fiscal and social objectives of such officials do not necessarily mean that permission will be denied outright. They may, however, mean long delays, attempts to impose requirements concerning dedications of land and provision of facilities over and above those which are properly required under the subdivision ordinance, and the like.

One witness heard by the Commission in Philadelphia stated the problem this way:

> Regulations are frequently written so that each apartment developer has to negotiate with the community in order to get in at all. He negotiates either to get a zoning amendment because there is no permitted area zoned for apartments in the community, or he negotiates in order to get a special exception because the zoning ordinance does not permit apartments outright. In both cases the negotiation process is one of trying to bid up the price or cost of the apartment structure in order to limit the number of people who can come in at lower cost. . . .
>
> A subdivision ordinance was used as a club in Abington against a veterans' cooperative which had intended to build about 250 free-standing houses which conformed with the zoning ordinance. This was in the late 1950's. I was a member. . . . It was an outright question of refusing to give the approval, and keeping the matter in the courts until the veterans' group broke up because they couldn't wait for housing. . . .

g. The Mount Laurel Decision

Southern Burlington County NAACP v. Township of Mount Laurel, 67 N.J. 151, 336 A.2d 713 (1975), offers the most sweeping repudiation yet of exclusionary zoning. Mount Laurel Township lies within ten miles of Philadelphia and seven miles of Camden, New Jersey. Its area is twenty-two square miles; its 1970 population exceeded 11,000, more than twice the 1960 population. Individual plaintiffs, Mount Laurel residents and former residents, were unable to acquire decent housing within the Township at prices they could afford. They blamed a congeries of zoning controls that, in the aggregate, made the construction of low-rent housing impossible. The controls included:

(a) minimum lot size requirements (9,375 square feet in one zone, 20,000 square feet in the other zone);

(b) residential areas zoned for only one type of housing, i.e., single-family detached dwellings; no area zoned for multifamily, row houses, or mobile home parks;

(c) minimum floor area of 1,100 square feet for one-story houses and 1,300 square feet for all other houses;

(d) planned unit developments allowing apartments by agreement only—units for the relatively affluent, and sharply limited as to numbers of bedrooms.

(e) 30 percent of township area set aside for industrial uses—far more than a 100-year supply.

SOUTHERN BURLINGTON COUNTY NAACP v. TOWNSHIP OF MOUNT LAUREL

67 N.J. 151, 336 A.2d 713 (1975)

HALL, J. This case attacks the system of land use regulation by defendant Township of Mount Laurel on the ground that low and moderate income families are thereby unlawfully excluded from the municipality. The trial court so found, 119 N.J. Super. 164 (Law Div. 1972), and declared the township zoning ordinance totally invalid. . . .

Plaintiffs represent the minority group poor (black and Hispanic)[3] seeking such quarters. But they are not the only category of persons barred from so many municipalities by reason of restrictive land use regulations. We have reference to young and elderly couples, single persons and large, growing families not in the poverty class, but who still cannot afford the only kinds of

---

3. Plaintiffs fall into four categories: (1) present residents of the township residing in dilapidated or substandard housing; (2) former residents who were forced to move elsewhere because of the absence of suitable housing; (3) nonresidents living in central city substandard housing in the region who desire to secure decent housing and accompanying advantages within their means elsewhere; (4) three organizations representing the housing and other interests of racial minorities. The township originally challenged plaintiffs' standing to bring this action. The trial court properly held (119 N.J. Super. at 166) that the resident plaintiffs had adequate standing to ground the entire action and found it unnecessary to pass on that of the other plaintiffs. The issue has not been raised on appeal. We merely add that both categories of nonresident individuals likewise have standing. N.J.S.A. 40:55-47.1; cf. Walker v. Borough of Stanhope, 23 N.J. 657 (1957). No opinion is expresssed as to the standing of the organizations.

housing realistically permitted in most places—relatively high-priced, single-family detached dwellings on sizeable lots and, in some municipalities, expensive apartments. We will, therefore, consider the case from the wider viewpoint that the effect of Mount Laurel's land use regulation has been to prevent various categories of persons from living in the township because of the limited extent of their income and resources. In this connection, we accept the representation of the municipality's counsel at oral argument that the regulatory scheme was not adopted with any desire or intent to exclude prospective residents on the obviously illegal bases of race, origin or believed social incompatibility.

As already intimated, the issue here is not confined to Mount Laruel. The same question arises with respect to any number of other municipalities of sizeable land area outside the central cities and older built-up suburbs of our North and South Jersey metropolitan areas (and surrounding some of the smaller cities outside those areas as well) which, like Mount Laurel, have substantially shed rural characteristics and have undergone great population increase since World War II, or are now in the process of doing so, but still are not completely developed and remain in the path of inevitable future residential, commercial and industrial demand and growth. Most such municipalities, with but relatively insignificant variation in details, present generally comparable physical situations, courses of municipal policies, practices, enactments and results and human, governmental and legal problems arising therefrom. It is in the context of communities now of this type or which become so in the future, rather than with central cities or older built-up suburbs or areas still rural and likely to continue to be for some time yet, that we deal with the question raised. . . .

I. THE FACTS

The record thoroughly substantiates the findings of the trial court that over the years Mount Laurel "has acted affirmatively to control development and to attract a selective type of growth" (119 N.J. Super. at 168) and that "through its zoning ordinances has exhibited economic discrimination in that the poor have been deprived of adequate housing and the opportunity to secure the construction of subsidized housing, and has used federal, state, county and local finances and resources[9] solely for the betterment of middle and upper-income persons." (119 N.J. Super. at 178.)

There cannot be the slightest doubt that the reason for this course of conduct has been to keep down local taxes on *property* (Mount Laurel is not a high tax municipality) and that the policy was carried out without regard for non-fiscal considerations with respect to *people,* either within or without its boundaries. . . .

---

9. Such "finances and resources" has reference to monies spent by various agencies on highways within the municipality, loans and grants for water and sewer systems and for planning, federal guarantees of mortgages on new home construction, and the like.

This pattern of land use regulation has been adopted for the same purpose in developing municipality after developing municipality. Almost every one acts solely in its own selfish and parochial interest and in effect builds a wall around itself to keep out those people or entities not adding favorably to the tax base, despite the location of the municipality or the demand for varied kinds of housing. There has been no effective intermunicipal or area planning or land use regulation. . . .

II. The Legal Issue

The legal question before us, as earlier indicated, is whether a developing municipality like Mount Laurel may validly, by a system of land use regulation, make it physically and economically impossible to provide low and moderate income housing in the municipality for the various categories of persons who need and want it and thereby, as Mount Laurel has, exclude such people from living within its confines because of the limited extent of their income and resources. Necessarily implicated are the broader questions of the right of such municipalities to limit the kinds of available housing and of any obligation to make possible a variety and choice of types of living accommodations.

We conclude that every such municipality must, by its land use regulations, presumptively make realistically possible an appropriate variety and choice of housing. More specifically, presumptively it cannot foreclose the opportunity of the classes of people mentioned for low and moderate income housing and in its regulations must affirmatively afford that opportunity, at least to the extent of the municipality's fair share of the present and prospective regional need therefor. These obligations must be met unless the particular municipality can sustain the heavy burden of demonstrating peculiar circumstances which dictate that it should not be required so to do. [10]

We reach this conclusion under state law and so do not find it necessary to consider federal constitutional grounds urged by plaintiffs. We begin with some fundamental principles as applied to the scene before us.

Land use regulation is encompassed within the state's police power. Our constitutions have expressly so provided since an amendment in 1927. That amendment, now Art. IV, sec. VI, par. 2 of the 1947 Constitution, authorized legislative delegation of the power to municipalities (other than counties), but reserved the legislative right to repeal or alter the delegation (which we take it means repeal or alteration in whole or in part). The legislative delegation of the zoning power followed in 1928, by adoption of the standard zoning enabling act, now found, with subsequent amendments, in N.J.S.A. 40:55-30 to 51.

---

10. While, as the trial court found, Mount Laurel's actions were deliberate, we are of the view that the identical conclusion follows even when municipal conduct is not shown to be intentional, but the effect is substantially the same as if it were.

It is elementary theory that all police power enactments, no matter at what level of government, must conform to the basic state constitutional requirements of substantive due process and equal protection of the laws. These are inherent in Art. I, par. 1 of our Constitution, [11] the requirements of which may be more demanding than those of the federal Constitution. Robinson v. Cahill, 62 N.J. 473, 482, 490-492 (1973); Washington National Insurance Co. v. Board of Review, 1 N.J. 545, 553-554 (1949). It is required that, affirmatively, a zoning regulation, like any police power enactment, must promote public health, safety, morals or the general welfare. (The last term seems broad enough to encompass the others.)

Frequently the decisions in this state . . . have spoken only in terms of the interest of the enacting municipality, so that it has been thought, at least in some quarters, that such was the only welfare requiring consideration. It is, of course, true that many cases have dealt only with regulations having little, if any, outside impact where the local decision is ordinarily entitled to prevail. However, it is fundamental and not to be forgotten that the zoning power is a police power of the state and the local authority is acting only as a delegate of that power and is restricted in the same manner as is the state. So, when regulation does have a substantial external impact, the welfare of the state's citizens beyond the borders of the particular municipality cannot be disregarded and must be recognized and served.

This essential was distinctly pointed out in *Euclid,* where Mr. Justice Sutherland specifically referred to " . . . the possibility of cases where the general public interest would so far outweigh the interest of the municipality that the municipality would not be allowed to stand in the way." (272 U.S. at 390, 71 L. Ed. at 311.) Chief Justice Vanderbilt said essentially the same thing, in a different factual context, in the early leading case of Duffcon Concrete Products, Inc. v. Borough of Cresskill, 1 N.J. 509 (1949), when he spoke of the necessity of regional considerations in zoning and added this:

> . . . The effective development of a region should not and cannot be made to depend upon the adventitious location of municipal boundaries, often prescribed decades or even centuries ago, and based in many instances on considerations of geography, of commerce, or of politics that are no longer significant with respect to zoning. The direction of growth of residential areas on the one hand and of industrial concentration on the other refuses to be governed by such artificial lines. Changes in methods of transportation as well as in living conditions have served only to accentuate the unreality in dealing with zoning problems on the basis of the territorial limits of a municipality. (1 N.J. at 513.)

See, to the same general effect, Borough of Cresskill v. Borough of Dumont, 15 N.J. 238, 247-249 (1954). . . .

11. The paragraph reads: "All persons are by nature free and independent, and have certain natural and unalienable rights, among which are those of enjoying and defending life and liberty, of acquiring, possessing, and protecting property, and of pursuing and obtaining safety and happiness."

This brings us to the relation of housing to the concept of general welfare just discussed and the result in terms of land use regulation which that relationship mandates. There cannot be the slightest doubt that shelter, along with food, are the most basic human needs. See Robinson v. Cahill, *supra* (62 N.J. at 483). "The question of whether a citizenry has adequate and sufficient housing is certainly one of the prime considerations in assessing the general health and welfare of that body." New Jersey Mortgage Finance Agency v. McCrane, 56 N.J. 414, 420 (1970). Cf. DeSimone v. Greater Englewood Housing Corp. No. 1, 56 N.J. 428, 442 (1970). The same thought is implicit in the legislative findings of an extreme, long-time need in this state for decent low and moderate income housing, set forth in the numerous statutes providing for various agencies and methods at both state and local levels designed to aid in alleviation of the need. [Citations omitted.]

It is plain beyond dispute that proper provision for adequate housing of all categories of people is certainly an absolute essential in promotion of the general welfare required in all local land use regulation. Further the universal and constant need for such housing is so important and of such broad public interest that the general welfare which developing municipalities like Mount Laurel must consider extends beyond their boundaries and cannot be parochially confined to the claimed good of the particular municipality. It has to follow that, broadly speaking, the presumptive obligation arises for each such municipality affirmatively to plan and provide, by its land use regulations, the reasonable opportunity for an appropriate variety and choice of housing, including, of course, low and moderate cost housing, to meet the needs, desires and resources of all categories of people who may desire to live within its boundaries. Negatively, it may not adopt regulations or policies which thwart or preclude that opportunity.

We have spoken of this obligation of such municipalities as "presumptive." The term has two aspects, procedural and substantive. Procedurally, we think the basic importance of appropriate housing for all dictates that, when it is shown that a developing municipality in its land use regulations has not made realistically possible a variety and choice of housing, including adequate provision to afford the opportunity for low and moderate income housing or has expressly prescribed requirements or restrictions which preclude or substantially hinder it, a facial showing of violation of substantive due process or equal protection under the state constitution has been made out and the burden, and it is a heavy one, shifts to the municipality to establish a valid basis for its action or non-action. Robinson v. Cahill, *supra*, 62 N.J. at 491-492, and cases cited therein. The substantive aspect of "presumptive" relates to the specifics, on the one hand, of what municipal land use regulation provisions, or the absence thereof, will evidence invalidity and shift the burden of proof and, on the other hand, of what bases and considerations will carry the municipality's burden and sustain what it has done or failed to do. Both kinds of specifics may well vary between municipalities according to peculiar circumstances. . . .

Without further elaboration at this point, our opinion is that Mount Laurel's zoning ordinance is presumptively contrary to the general welfare and outside the intended scope of the zoning power in the particulars mentioned. A facial showing of invalidity is thus established, shifting to the municipality the burden of establishing valid superseding reasons for its action and non-action.[19] We now examine the reasons it advances.

[The Court rejects as insufficient the chief reasons given by Mount Laurel for its zoning controls: the need for fiscal balance; the absence of sewer and water facilities.]

By way of summary, what we have said comes down to this. As a developing municipality, Mount Laurel must, by its land use regulations, make realistically possible the opportunity for an appropriate variety and choice of housing for all categories of people who may desire to live there, of course including those of low and moderate income. It must permit multi-family housing, without bedroom or similar restrictions, as well as small dwellings on very small lots, low cost housing of other types and, in general, high density zoning, without artificial and unjustifiable minimum requirements as to lot size, building size and the like, to meet the full panoply of these needs. Certainly when a municipality zones for industry and commerce for local tax benefit purposes, it without question must zone to permit adequate housing within the means of the employees involved in such uses. (If planned unit developments are authorized, one would assume that each must include a reasonable amount of low and moderate income housing in its residential "mix," unless opportunity for such housing has already been realistically provided for elsewhere in the municipality.) The amount of land removed from residential use by allocation to industrial and commercial purposes must be reasonably related to the present and future potential for such purposes. In other words, such municipalities must zone primarily for the living welfare of people and not for the benefit of the local tax rate.[20]

We have earlier stated that a developing municipality's obligation to afford the opportunity for decent and adequate low and moderate income housing extends at least to " . . . that municipality's fair share of the present and prospective regional need therefor." Some comment on that conclusion is in order at this point. Frequently it might be sounder to have more of such housing, like some specialized land uses, in one municipality in a region than

---

19. The township has not been deprived of the opportunity to present its defense on this thesis, since the case was very thoroughly tried out with voluminous evidence on all aspects of both sides.

20. This case does not properly present the question of whether a developing municipality may times its growth and, if so, how. See, e.g., Golden v. Planning Board of the Town of Ramapo, 30 N.Y.2d 359, 285 N.E.2d 291 (1972), *appeal dismissed,* 409 U.S. 1003, 93 S. Ct. 436, 440, 34 L. Ed. 2d 294 (1972); Construction Industry Association of Sonoma County v. City of Petaluma, 375 F. Supp. 574 (N.D. Cal. 1974), *appeal pending* (citation of these cases is not intended to indicate either agreement or disagreement with their conclusions). We now say only that, assuming some type of timed growth is permissible, it cannot be utilized as an exclusionary device or to stop all further development and must include early provision for low and moderate income housing.

in another, because of greater availability of suitable land, location of employment, accessibility of public transportation or some other significant reason. But, under present New Jersey legislation, zoning must be on an individual municipal basis, rather than regionally. So long as that situation persists under the present tax structure, or in the absence of some kind of binding agreement among all the municipalities of a region, we feel that every municipality therein must bear its fair share of the regional burden. (In this respect our holding is broader than that of the trial court, which was limited to Mount Laurel-related low and moderate income housing needs.)

The composition of the applicable "region" will necessarily vary from situation to situation and probably no hard and fast rule will serve to furnish the answer in every case. Confinement to or within a certain county appears not to be realistic, but restriction within the boundaries of the state seems practical and advisable. (This is not to say that a developing municipality can ignore a demand for housing within its boundaries on the part of people who commute to work in another state.) Here we have already defined the region at present as "those portions of Camden, Burlington and Gloucester Counties within a semicircle having a radius of 20 miles or so from the heart of Camden City." The concept of "fair share" is coming into more general use and, through the expertise of the municipal planning adviser, the county planning boards and the state planning agency, a reasonable figure for Mount Laurel can be determined, which can then be translated to the allocation of sufficient land therefor on the zoning map. See generally, New Jersey Trends, ch. 27, Listokin, Fair Share Housing Distribution: An Idea Whose Time Has Come? p. 353. [23] We may add that we think that, in arriving at such a determination, the type of information and estimates, which the trial judge (119 N.J. Super. at 178) directed the township to compile and furnish to him, concerning the housing needs of persons of low and moderate income now or formerly residing in the township in substandard dwellings and those presently employed or reasonably expected to be employed therein, will be pertinent.

There is no reason why developing municipalities like Mount Laurel, required by this opinion to afford the opportunity for all types of housing to meet the needs of various categories of people, may not become and remain attractive, viable communities providing good living and adequate services for all their residents in the kind of atmosphere which a democracy and free institutions demand. They can have industrial sections, commercial sections and sections for every kind of housing from low cost and multi-family to lots of more than an acre with very expensive homes. Proper planning and governmental cooperation can prevent over-intensive and too sudden development, insure against future suburban sprawl and slums and assure the preservation of open space and local beauty. We do not intend that developing municipalities shall be overwhelmed by voracious land speculators and developers if

---

23. The questions mentioned in this paragraph are more fully involved in Oakwood at Madison v. Township of Madison, *supra*, 128 N.J. Super. 438, *appeal pending*, unheard in this court.

they use the powers which they have intelligently and in the broad public interest. Under our holdings today, they can be better communities for all than they previously have been.

III. THE REMEDY

As outlined at the outset of this opinion, the trial court invalidated the zoning ordinance in toto and ordered the township to make certain studies and investigations and to present to the court a plan of affirmative public action designed "to enable and encourage the satisfaction of the indicated needs" for township related low and moderate income housing. Jurisdiction was retained for judicial consideration and approval of such a plan and for the entry of a final order requiring its implementation.

We are of the view that the trial court's judgment should be modified in certain respects. We see no reason why the entire zoning ordinance should be nullified. Therefore we declare it to be invalid only to the extent and in the particulars set forth in this opinion. The township is granted 90 days from the date hereof, or such additional time as the trial court may find it reasonable and necessary to allow, to adopt amendments to correct the deficiencies herein specified. It is the local function and responsibility, in the first instance at least, rather than the court's, to decide on the details of the same within the guidelines we have laid down. If plaintiffs desire to attack such amendments, they may do so by supplemental complaint filed in this cause within 30 days of the final adoption of the amendments.

We are not at all sure what the trial judge had in mind as ultimate action with reference to the approval of a plan for affirmative public action concerning the satisfaction of indicated housing needs and the entry of a final order requiring implementation thereof. Courts do not build housing nor do municipalities. That function is performed by private builders, various kinds of associations, or, for public housing, by special agencies created for that purpose at various levels of government. The municipal function is initially to provide the opportunity through appropriate land use regulations and we have spelled out what Mount Laurel must do in that regard. It is not appropriate at this time, particularly in view of the advanced view of zoning law as applied to housing laid down by this opinion, to deal with the matter of the further extent of judicial power in the field or to exercise any such power. See, however, Pascack Association v. Mayor and Council of the Township of Washington, 131 N.J. Super. 195 (Law Div. 1974), and cases therein cited, for a discussion of this question. The municipality should first have full opportunity to itself act without judicial supervision. We trust it will do so in the spirit we have suggested, both by appropriate zoning ordinance amendments and whatever additional action encouraging the fulfillment of its fair share of the regional need for low and moderate income housing may be indicated as necessary and advisable. (We have in mind that there is at least a moral obligation in a municipality to establish a local housing agency pursuant to state law to provide housing for its resident poor now living in dilapidated, unhealthy quarters.) The portion of the trial court's judgment ordering the preparation and submission of the aforesaid study, report and plan to it for further action is therefore vacated as at least premature. Should Mount Laurel not perform as we expect, further judicial action may be sought by supplemental pleading in this cause.

The judgment of the Law Division is modified as set forth herein. No costs.

[Justice Pashman wrote an extended concurring opinion urging that the court "go farther and faster" in implementing its principles. Justice Mountain wrote a brief concurring opinion resting his decision on a *statutory* reading of "general welfare" appearing in the zoning enabling law.]

NOTES AND QUESTIONS

1. The *Mount Laurel* decision brought a stream of favorable comment from civil rights advocates, but not much in the way of housing integration in the ensuing half-decade. Fifteen months after the decision, a survey of builders and state officials found agreement that immediate change had been negligible. The president of the state builders' association claimed: "Most towns are simply building new defenses. They didn't want it to begin with, and they still don't want it." New York Times, August 1, 1976, §8, at 1, col. 5. A follow-up survey in 1979 found that throughout New Jersey's developing towns "there was only a sprinkling of low-cost housing to serve as a monument to the controversial ruling." New York Times, Aug. 26, 1979, §8, at 1, col. 1.

One builder partially explained: "Zoning by itself isn't the answer. If a town allows an apartment project on a particular site, but refuses to provide municipal services like water and sewer lines, then it's just like zoning the Sahara Desert for skyscrapers." Jerome Rose, a professor of urban planning who has closely followed the *Mount Laurel* decision, further explained: "In spite of its noble objectives, the decision has had a minimal impact on the production of low-income and middle-income housing. Chief among the reasons for this is basic economics. The high cost of building materials, land and labor, and financing, together with the 'extra costs' caused by restrictive zoning and the long lead time required for production, make new housing expensive." Ibid.

Almost certainly the *Mount Laurel* decision has spawned greater profits for lawyers embroiled in litigation over the decision's scope than it has new housing for lower-income families. In Oakwood at Madison, Inc. v. Township of Madison, 72 N.J. 481, 371 A.2d 1192 (1977), the court invalidated the local ordinance, but refused to establish a judicial quota for the community's "fair share." Instead, the court said that it was "incumbent on the governing body to adjust its zoning regulations so as to render possible and feasible the 'least cost' housing, consistent with minimum standards of health and safety, which private industry will undertake, and in amounts sufficient to satisfy the deficit in the hypothesized fair share." 72 N.J. 512, 371 A.2d 1207. As to the size of that "fair share," although a trial court would not be required to specify the town's unit goal, the court would be expected to consider the testimony of the local planning advisor and of county and state planning bodies to ascertain whether the municipality would generally be meeting its "fair share" responsibilities.

Other lawsuits have involved communities that insisted they were not a "developing municipality" subject to the *Mount Laurel* obligation. See, e.g., Glenview Development Co. v. Franklin Township, 164 N.J. Super. 563, 397 A.2d 384 (1978) (defendant a rural, not a developing municipality); Pascack Ass'n, Ltd. v. Township of Washington, 74 N.J. 470, 379 A.2d 6 (1977) (defendant a developed, not a developing, municipality).

Mount Laurel itself returned to the courts when the NAACP challenged the zoning ordinance after it had been amended in response to *Mount Laurel I*. The revised ordinance involved only 20 acres out of the town's 22.4 *square miles:* 13 swampy acres zoned R-5 (townhouse garden apartments, minimum floor area 2000 square feet per bedroom, 10 units per acre); a small, low-lying, swampy parcel zoned R-6 (single-family district, minimum lot size 6,000 square feet); and an R-7 zone involving a continuing planned unit development whose housing restrictions would be relaxed. After an evidentiary hearing, the trial court agreed with the town that its revised ordinance satisfied the supreme court guidelines. Southern Burlington County NAACP v. Township of Mount Laurel, 161 N.J. Super. 317, 391 A.2d 935 (1978).

Finally, the New Jersey Supreme Court has again decided to illuminate its guidelines, using *Mount Laurel II* and several other cases as the vessel for deeper consideration. The court asked attorneys to discuss in their briefs and oral arguments more than twenty questions, which included the following.

(1) Is it economically feasible to provide housing opportunities for low- and moderate-income persons outside urban areas?

(2) Should the principles of *Mount Laurel* apply only to developing municipalities?

(3) What types of remedial devices should be available? For instance, is an order for site-specific rezoning a proper remedy? Can a court order a municipality to seek subsidies? Provide density bonuses? Institute rent-skewing?

2.   Another embattled suburban township is Brookhaven, New York. Located in Suffolk County, Long Island, the township's population had soared to 320,000 by 1975; nevertheless, more than 60,000 acres remained vacant and zoned for housing. During the township's era of rapid growth, the percentage of blacks dropped from 3.4 to 2.6; most blacks lived in four racial enclaves of deteriorating housing. The town zoning law barred apartments as of right, and where apartments were permitted as a special exception, builders were

discouraged from planning family-size units. Other provisions in the ordinance limited housing access for lower-income persons.

Four categories of individual and three of organizational plaintiffs challenged the ordinance as exclusionary. Individual plaintiffs included low-income residents of Brookhaven living in overcrowded rented quarters and a former resident forced to leave because she could not locate adequate housing for herself and two children. The organizational plaintiffs included the NAACP and the Brookhaven Housing Coalition, whose members were striving for a racially and economically integrated community.

In a preliminary procedural skirmish, the trial court denied the plaintiffs class-action certification (which under New York law would entitle the plaintiffs, if they later prevailed, to recover attorneys' fees). Suffolk Housing Services v. Town of Brookhaven, 69 A.D.2d 242, 418 N.Y.S.2d 452 (2d Dept. 1979).

Shortly after the suit began, a reporter for the New York Times interviewed a medley of town residents. Voicing a popular opinion, the town supervisor snorted: "If they can't afford it, they should go somewhere else." A young member of the town board replied: "Everybody wants to be the last person to settle in Brookhaven Town. There is a lot of fear about changes." The president of the Long Island Builders Institute stated: "The lawsuit is nebulous—it doesn't strike at the real issues. Even if I had a thousand acres zoned for low-cost housing, the cheapest I could produce is what is now in the marketplace. It's not the availability of land that's the problem—it's the price." But the town has stoutly refused to build public housing. Explaining that refusal, the supervisor said: "To build to suit somebody's needs—that's not for the town to do. That's up to private enterprise or the Federal Government." N.Y. Times, Dec. 13, 1975, at 29, col. 1.

Chapter 17

Toward Zoning Flexibility

§17.1 The Variance

One of zoning's key tenets has been district-wide, uniform classification: all parcels within a zoning district should suffer the same use and bulk restrictions. Yet zoners readily understood that universal classification might cause particular hardship to some landowners whose parcels, by reason of size, shape, location, or topography, were unsuited for the development prescribed for their district. To meet the hardship case, zoners adopted the variance procedure—an administrative appeal that allows a relaxing of the use or bulk restrictions if the landowner can satisfy statutory criteria. The materials in this section should give you some of the flavor of a typical variance appeal and its potential for abuse.

NEW YORK TOWN LAW
§267(5) (1965)

. . . Where there are practical difficulties or unnecessary hardships in the way of carrying out the strict letter of such ordinances, the board of appeals shall have the power in passing upon appeals, to vary or modify the application of any of the regulations or provisions of such ordinance relating to the use, construction or alteration of buildings or structures, or the use of land, so that the spirit of the ordinance shall be observed, public safety and welfare secured and substantial justice done.

TOWN OF HEMPSTEAD, BUILDING ZONE ORDINANCE
Art. 5 [1]

B RESIDENCE DISTRICTS

§B-1.0. In a B Residence District the following regulations shall apply:

A building may be erected, altered or used, and a lot or premises may be used for any of the following purposes and for no other:

B-1.1. Single family detached dwelling.

B-1.2. Club, Fraternity House or Lodge, when authorized as a special exception by the Board of Appeals.

B-1.3. A regularly organized institution of learning approved by the State Board of Regents; religious use; or philanthropic use when authorized as a special exception by the Board of Appeals.

B-1.4. Hospital, Sanitarium, Telephone Exchange or Golf Course when authorized as a special exception by the Board of Appeals.

B-1.5. Agriculture or Nursery, provided there is no display for commercial purposes or advertisement on the premises; Municipal Recreational Use; Railway Passenger Station.

B-1.6. Accessory use on the same lot with and customarily incidental to any of the above permitted uses, including a private garage. This shall be understood to include the professional office or studio of a doctor, dentist, masseur, teacher, artist, architect, engineer, musician, or lawyer, or rooms used for home occupations such as dressmaking, millinery or similar handicrafts; PROVIDED the office, studio or occupational room is located in the dwelling in which the practitioner resides and PROVIDED further, no goods are publicly displayed on the premises. Such accessory use, exclusive of a private garage, shall not include the erection or maintenance hereafter of any structures other than one erected on the ground and not exceeding two hundred fifty (250) cubic feet content unless *authorized as a special exception by the Board of Appeals.*

APPEAL TO THE BOARD OF ZONING APPEALS
In the Matter of Appeal of RICHARD W. BARNES
12 Bedell Avenue, P.O. Address Hempstead, N.Y.,
to the BOARD OF ZONING APPEALS TOWN OF HEMPSTEAD

The undersigned hereby appeals from the decision of the Building Inspector of the Town of Hempstead in denying application to construct private dwelling and funeral home.

"B" zone.

1. The following is adapted from the Record on Appeal, Matter of Clark v. Board of Zoning Appeals, 301 N.Y. 86, 92 N.E.2d 903 (1950), *infra.*

NW cor. Westminster Rd & Regent Pl, West Hempstead
GROUND OF APPEAL: Practical difficulties and unnecessary hardships.
Appeal made under Sec. 267 of the Town Law

RICHARD W. BARNES
(Owner-Agent-Lessee)
August 18, 1948

EXCERPTS FROM TRANSCRIPT OF HEARING BEFORE THE BOARD OF ZONING APPEALS

RICHARD W. BARNES, construct private dwelling & funeral home, N/W cor. Westminster Road (Rockaway Ave.) & Regent Place, West Hempstead. [See Figure 8, on the following page.]

Present in favor: NATHANIEL KAHN, attorney for the applicant
                     Various other witnesses.
Present opposed: ARTHUR W. RENANDER, attorney for the opposition
                     Various other witnesses. . . .

RICHARD W. BARNES, appearing in favor of this application, after being duly sworn, was questioned by Mr. Kahn and testified as follows:

Q. You are the applicant in this matter?
A. Yes.
Q. You are the owner of a parcel on the northwest corner of Westminster Road and Regent Place?
A. Yes.
Q. How long have you owned this piece of ground?
A. Three years.
Q. What is the frontage on Westminster Road?
A. 100 feet on Westminster Road.
Q. And the depth?
A. 110 feet.
Q. How much did you pay for the plot?
A. $5500.00.
Q. How is that property zoned at the present time?
A. "B" zone.
Q. What is immediately adjacent to it on the north?
A. A residence and doctor's office.
Q. That is Dr. McKenna's residence and office?
A. Yes.
Q. What is immediately adjacent to it on the south across Regent Place?
A. The same type, a residence and doctor's office.
Q. What is back of it, that is to the west?

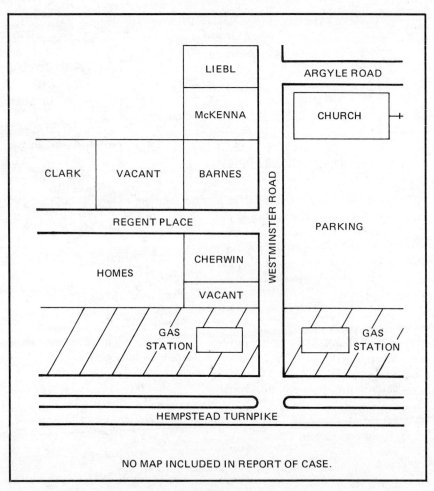

FIGURE 8
Editor's Conception of the Neighborhood

A. Vacant property.

Q. What is across Westminster Road on the east side of the road?

A. At the present time it is a parking space owned by St. Thomas, the Apostle.

Q. Adjacent to the parking space is the church and rectory?

A. That is right.

Q. Do you know whether there are any plans at the present time for the building of a Parochial School there?

A. Yes, there are plans for the building of a school.

Q. Do I understand that you propose to build if the variance is granted, a combined home for yourself and your family and a funeral home?

A. Yes.

Q. You are now in business and have a funeral home in a store around the corner on Hempstead Turnpike?

A. Yes. . . .

Q. I show you another photograph and ask you if this is a fair view looking north along Westminster Road showing where your parcel is located, and the gas station and doctor's office on the west side?

A. That is right. . . .

Q. Have you consulted with Mr. Mazzara, a builder, with respect to building the premises for you and the blue prints that have been submitted have been prepared by him or by an architect for him at your request?

A. That is right.

Q. Did you also have drawings made of the structure you propose to erect?

A. I did.

Q. And is this the drawing of the building you propose to erect?

A. Yes.

Mr. Renander: No objections.

    Drawing received in evidence and marked, "Applicant's Exhibit 5." . . .

REVEREND JOSEPH A. SMITH, 24 Westminster Road, was called by Mr. Kahn, and testified as follows:

Q. You are the Pastor, are you not, of the St. Thomas Apostle's Parish?

A. I am.

Q. Your church is located where?

A. Westminster Rd. at Argyle Rd. in West Hempstead.

Q. Adjacent to your Church and south of it is your Rectory?

A. Yes.

Q. What lies beyond that on the south?

A. At the present time a parking lot.

Q. Have any plans been made with respect to erecting a Parochial School on that property?

A. Plans have been completed but work, of course, hasn't started.

Q. That is the status of it, that plans have been completed and you are just waiting?

A. Waiting for money to build the school.

Q. Where is this proposed school with respect to Mr. Barnes' property?

A. Directly opposite Mr. Barnes' property is the proposed site of the school.

Q. You have known Mr. Barnes for how long?

A. Twenty-five years.

Q. Have you any objection to the granting of a variance here so that Mr. Barnes can build his residence and funeral home across from your property?

A. I have no objection whatever. . . .

Q. How long, Father, have you been in West Hempstead as a Pastor?

A. Seventeen years.

Q. And before that you were in Hempstead?

A. Some years ago I was in Hempstead, and in between I was in Brooklyn.

Q. During the seventeen years that you have been in West Hempstead, you have seen the community grow?

A. I have.

Q. You have taken an interest, I presume, in community affairs?

A. I have.

Q. Are you familiar with the type of structure that Mr. Barnes wishes to build?

A. Yes, Mr. Barnes has shown it to me and I have studied it very carefully.

Q. Do you believe that the granting of this variance to Mr. Barnes and the erection by him of the home which he seeks to build for himself, combined with a funeral home, will in any way hurt the community?

A. I don't think it will hurt the community in any sense, and even in the smallest way. . . .

Q. Now, Father, does Mr. Barnes conduct a good number of his funerals each year for people who are members of your parish?

A. I suppose about two-thirds of the number he has are in the parish.

Q. In those cases, two-thirds of his funerals, the funeral is conducted from your church?

A. That is right.

Q. So that such traffic conditions as may arise in connection with those funerals arise now with his funeral parlor around the corner on Hempstead Turnpike?

A. That is right. In coming to the church, the same conditions will be there.

Q. Would the granting of this variance and the building by Mr. Barnes of his funeral home and residence on Westminster Road in your opinion, in any way create any greater hazard to the children of the community than now exists?

A. I do not think so.

CROSS-EXAMINATION BY MR. RENANDER:

Mr. Renander: I do not wish to appear disrepectful and this questioning is not in that line. It is for laying the foundation for something which I wish to bring out later.

Q. You have testified as to the effect of this on the community, I ask you whether or not you believe a public dance hall conducted on the premises in question would be objectionable to the community?

A. I don't see any comparison.

Q. What about a shooting gallery?

A. I don't see any comparison and they are not relative at all.

Q. Or a theatre, a motion picture theatre?

A. I still say they are not relative, and I see no comparison between what you are trying to say and what we are trying to make our opinion.

Q. A freak show or a wax museum?

A. I still don't see any comparison, I think, on the other hand, it is disrespectful to speak of a funeral home in relation to such of those things you have mentioned.

Mr. Renander: I am glad you brought that up because in the City of New York and practically every large city in the country, a funeral home is placed in the same classification, and is prohibited in all retail districts.

Mr. Kahn: I object to any statement of counsel with respect to the provisions of any other district.

Mr. Renander: That is the experience of zoning experts. . . .

[Louis H. McMahan, a real estate and insurance broker, testifies that the Barnes parcel can not yield a reasonable return if used only for the purposes allowed under the Zoning Ordinance. His only explanation for this conclusion is that no one is "going to put up a beautiful home" which is one block north of the business zone and which faces a parking field and a church.]

Frank E. Wright, 7 Hempstead Turnpike, West Hempstead, after being duly sworn, was questioned by Mr. Kahn and testified as follows:

Q. What is your occupation or business?

A. Real Estate.

Q. How long have you been in the real estate business?

A. About twenty-nine years.

Q. Where is your place of business located?

A. 7 Hempstead Turnpike, West Hempstead.

Mr. Renander: I will concede his qualifications.

By Mr. Kahn:

Q. How long have you been in West Hempstead?

A. Since 1932.

Q. In your business in West Hempstead, have you had occasion to buy and sell or to assist in the purchase or sale of numerous homes in the Cathedral Gardens area?

A. I have.

Q. Are you familiar with the proposed application for a variance here?

A. Yes.

Q. Do you know Mr. Barnes?

A. Yes.

Q. You are familiar with the land on which he requests permission to build this combined home and funeral parlor?

A. I am.

Q. In your opinion would the granting of this variance in any way affect the community of Cathedral Gardens?

A. I do not think so.

Q. Why?

A. I think the type of building he is putting up and living in the house itself, and also the location that he is putting it up, I don't think it will hurt the community at all.

Q. You have been interested in Community welfare in that community for a number of years?

A. Quite a few.

CROSS-EXAMINATION BY MR. RENANDER:

Q. You testify that you have sold a number of homes in the Cathedral Gardens area?

A. I have.

Q. You testified that you do not believe that the granting of this variance for use of this premises as a funeral parlor has any derogatory effect as to the property in the area in general?

A. In general, that is right.

Q. Would you still testify that the location of the funeral parlor and the maintenance of the funeral parlor will affect any property in the area?

A. That is a big question. It would take me a little time to explain why.

Q. Will it affect the value? You know the Susan Clark property and you are familiar with the back porch, aren't you?

A. No, I am not.

Q. If I told you the porch was on the southeast corner, would you say no?

A. I have never taken notice of that. I don't know.

Q. If you were the owner of that property and were sitting on that porch having your tea in the afternoon, and you saw ambulances drive up to this site, discharging cadavas [*sic*]—

Mr. Kahn: I object.

Mr. Wright: Let me answer it.

Mr. Michaelis: Wait a minute. Do you press your objection?

Mr. Kahn: I do.

Mr. Renander: I withdraw my question.

Q. The property of Susan Clark, would it affect that, would it affect the value of her property?

A. In some ways it would if it was the location, at the location it is in, I don't believe it would harm the valuation very much and you have funeral services at the church now, and they can see it from the house, can't they? And they see them drive in Westminster Road and see them drive away. If they hold services across the street I can't see much difference. And also Mr. Barnes is making his home and the way this has been explained to me, they drive in and you don't see them any more. The hearses do not stand in the street. . . .

Mr. Renander: I have been a resident of Cathedral Gardens since 1930, one of the first members of the Civic Association, and I am still a resident there and I have been asked here because the attorney for the Civic Association is away on his vacation and to present this matter to the best of my ability, and I wish to offer in evidence the petitions, No. 1 through 13 inclusive, containing the verified objections of 240 residents in the area.

Mr. Kahn: I object to those petitions on two grounds, first because a great many of the signers live nowhere near the proposed building. Secondly because to my knowledge and perhaps I am equally, with counsel, aware of civic affairs in the West Hempstead community, to my knowledge these petitions were obtained under false and misleading circumstances, and unless counsel or somebody else who has obtained these petitions, comes in here and testifies, and I am given an opportunity to question them as to the contents pursued in obtaining these signatures, I must object to them. My information, and not only is it my information, but I know it as a fact, that these petitions were circulated together with other petitions in which the community was very vitally interested, and I represented this community, and that was in connection with the erection of an incinerator in West Hempstead.

Mr. Kane: You mean this is a tie-in?

Mr. Kahn: Yes, and they came back to me and I had some of these very petitions brought to me at the same time that they went around to get signatures to oppose an incinerator in West Hempstead. They tied this in and I certainly object to it.

Mr. Renander: I object. This is a public hearing.

By Mr. Michaelis [Member of the Board of Zoning Appeals]:

Q. Do the petitions indicate the addresses of the signers?

A. Yes.

Mr. Renander: I wish counsel would state after being sworn, and specifically state further the charges. I have six important witnesses here that I would like to bring up and prove that there has been no fraud.

Mr. Michaelis: Let me see the petitions.

Mr. Michaelis: We will take them for what they are worth. The objection is overruled.

Mr. Kahn: Exception.

Petitions received in evidence and marked, "Objector's Exhibit 'A'." . . .

Arthur W. Renander, after being duly sworn, testified as follows: I have been a resident in Cathedral Gardens at the same place where I now reside since 1930. I have been a member of the Cathedral Gardens Civic Association since that time. I am familiar with the premises which are the subject of this application. I am familiar with the properties immediately adjoining on the east, west, north and south. I am familiar with the nature of the improvement in all of the properties in the area generally. I know that there are approximately 238 private dwellings in the Cathedral Gardens area. The petitions which I have presented to this Board contain the names of 240 people, all of them property owners in this area of 238 homes. This does not represent all of the owners, because some of them were away on vacation and there are two signatures for some properties, because the properties sometimes are in a man and wife's name. The opposition represents, of the one family dwellings, approximately 90% of the owners. I was present at a meeting of the Cathedral Gardens Civic Association on October 16th, 1947, at which time the question of whether or not the Association would approve of the proposed variance which is before the Board today, was discussed, and thereafter, and a standing vote was taken with the result that 177 votes, all members of the Cathedral Gardens area were opposed to the granting of the variance and four were not. . . .

Mr. Renander: I wish to offer in evidence a copy of the minutes of that meeting.

Minutes of the meeting shown to Mr. Kahn.

Mr. Kahn: I object. I don't think you have to testify. I will concede that this probably took place, but I object to it being admitted in evidence as having any force in this application. The strange thing is that all of those 177 people, including the counsel, didn't even know that the property which is the subject of this application is in a different zone from theirs. I think the main thing they were concerned about was that this would affect zoning in their section of the community which is zoned "A," and I think if all of those people had been apprised of the true situation, they would not vote that way, and if all of the people who secured the petitions knew the true situation, they would not have signed the petitions.

Mr. Renander: Counsel, I am surprised. The man in the different zone is entitled to the benefits of the adjoining zone, you know that is the law. . . . [Query?—ED.]

NATHAN H. CHERWIN, 1 Westminster Road, West Hempstead, after being duly sworn, was questioned by Mr. Renander and testified as follows:

Q. You own the property on the southwest corner of Regent Place and Westminster Road?

A. Yes.

Q. Are you opposed to this application?

A. I am.

Q. Do you believe that the granting of this variance will have an adverse effect on the value of your property?

A. I do.

CROSS-EXAMINATION BY MR. KAHN:

Q. Don't you conduct your practice in your residence?

A. I do.

Q. You also live there?

A. I do.

Q. On the other side of Mr. Barnes' property does Dr. McKenna reside and conduct a practice?

A. Yes.

Q. Do you have office hours in your practice?

A. I do.

Q. What are the hours?

A. 1 to 2 and 7 to 8.

Q. Do patients come to your office during those hours?

A. Yes, and others.

Q. And they come by automobile?

A. Sometimes.

Q. Park their cars along Westminster Road?

A. No, they park on Regent Place, wherever they get a place to park. . . .

Q. Can you see the funerals coming from Mr. Barnes to the church?

A. I have never watched. I suppose I could see them.

Q. Are you esthetically affected by deaths?

A. I am accustomed to death.

Mr. Renander: I object to the line of questioning.

Mr. Michaelis: Objection overruled.

Dr. Cherwin: I have children in my house who are not in the same position that I am. A physician's children do not have to know the same things a physician knows, and I have female occupants of my house that are affected. . . .

EDWARD J. PHILLIPS, 2 Regent Place, West Hempstead, after being duly sworn, was questioned by Mr. Renander and testified as follows:

Q. How long have you lived on Regent Place?

A. 19½ years.

Q. And what number are you on Regent Place?

A. I am immediately adjoining Dr. Cherwin to the west.

Q. In other words, you would be the nearest house on the south side of Regent Place except for Dr. Cherwin, to the site which is the subject of this application?

A. Yes.

Q. Are you opposed to having a funeral parlor?

A. Yes.

Q. Will you give any additional reasons you may have to the Chairman of the Board?

A. When I purchased the house in the year 1929 we came there as a residential district. We bought the property knowing that the south, the abutting property to the rear would eventually become business but there was a zoning restriction that there was a certain amount of space that would have to come from my boundary line to the building on the Turnpike.

Mr. Michaelis: Counsel, out of burning curiosity all morning, what happened to the deed restrictions?

Mr. Renander: They all expired.

Mr. Phillips: That is my reason when I bought it, I bought it for a sum that if I wanted to buy in the business section, I could have bought on the Turnpike anywhere along from Franklin Square to Hempstead for the amount I paid for the house.

CROSS-EXAMINATION BY MR. KAHN:

Q. I suppose you are sorry that you did not buy a little property on the Turnpike in 1929?

A. I am not a speculator.

Q. From your rear porch or from your rear yard you can look out to Hempstead Turnpike?

A. Yes.

Q. And at the present time there are no stores there?

A. No.

Q. You can see Mr. Barnes' property very clearly?

A. Yes.

Q. If there were any cadavers brought into this property you could see them right now?

A. I could see them if my eyesight was a little better.

Q. If any box were brought in to Mr. Barnes' property on Westminster Road with the business entrance being on Westminster Road, you could not see them even if your eyesight were better?

A. I don't stand watching for boxes.

Q. Even if you watched, you could not see them?

A. I could, they would have to pass the corner of Regent Place.

Q. And all you would see would be a car driving past Regent Place?

A. Yes, that is all. . . .

Mr. Michaelis: Do you have any re-direct or do you go into argument?

Mr. Kahn: I have no re-direct and frankly, since this isn't a jury matter, I see no necessity for going into argument. If counsel wants to make some argument, I might feel called upon to answer what he says.

Mr. Renander: I wish to bring up two or three matters to explain some of the cross-examination.

Mr. Michaelis: Do you want to submit a written memorandum?

Mr. Renander: Not necessarily, it will only take me about two minutes.

Mr. Michaelis: We will allow each of you five minutes, and we will hear you first, Mr. Renander. Bear in mind that we sit here and we are a veteran of almost ten thousand variances. . . .

Mr. Renander: I contend that no hardship has been proved on the part of the applicant, because the applicant acquired the premises whle they were zoned for the present existing zoning, and there is no proof that the property can't be used for the purpose for which it is zoned. I call your general attention to the fact that irregardless of whether or not, and I am sure if Father Smith sponsors it, the type and personnel would be of the highest, but nevertheless, even when pork is worth a great deal, a pig may not be a nuisance unless you have him in your parlor, I say a funeral parlor in itself would not be objectionable in a proper place, but it would be objectionable in a very highly restricted residential area. I further contend that no proof of hardship being present, petitioner and this Board have no right to grant a nonconforming use which is wholly foreign to the spirit of the Ordinance. This Ordinance directly and explicitly says that it cannot be used for anything but a residential purpose and if this Board had the power, where there is no hardship to grant this variance, we would be giving to the Board the legislative power which it does not have and there is a long string of cases on that. I perhaps will be called to task with my questioning of Father Smith in relation to the things he would object to, but I wish to explain that. I also called attention to the decision in 244 N.Y. 280 which says explicitly that the power of the Board of Appeals is confined to variation in specific cases where there is some unusual emergency and some unusual hardship. I have had, perhaps, the privilege or the experience to practice before the various Boards of Appeals in Westchester and Nassau and New York City, the five Boroughs of New York City. I consider myself fairly familiar with the zoning laws and the reasons for them, and I also helped write the text some years ago on city improvements and city development, and in the course of my experience I have read a great number of treatises on zoning and what I wanted to press home here is the use of the building to be erected, the very use of the premises for undertaking establishment and funeral parlor, not only in the City of New York but in dozens of the major cities, is not permitted in either retail districts or in restricted retail districts and they class it with the kind of a nuisance that I have mentioned before. They say it is in the same classification, and there are twelve of them, of freak shows, or wax museums, theatre or motion picture, undertaking establishment, public dance hall, shooting gallery, skee ball or similar games. That is the experience of a great many other communities. It is not binding on your Board and I realize it when I bring it up, but I am bringing it out to show that this particular matter between denominations, as a matter of fact, I am here because the parishioners of St. Thomas have asked me to be here and it is their names on these petitions which is about 50-50 are non-parishioners, that has brought this thing on. Nobody has any axes to grind in this matter. Perhaps we are over vehement in our objection, perhaps not zealous enough but I want to leave this to your Board and respectfully ask that the application be denied, because this community has existed for twenty odd years without any nonconforming uses and it would like to continue to do so.

Mr. Kahn: Mr. Chairman, gentlemen, this is rather an unusual case in that if you were to take the position of the objectors seriously and by that I mean not only the witnesses and their experts, but also their counsel, this Board had better resign and disband itself because if you are going to have no nonconforming uses and you are going to have objection as we have here to every and any nonconforming use regardless of the merits, and that is what every one of the objectors testified, that they just don't want nonconforming uses in Cathedral Gardens regardless of the merits of the case. They concede that everything Father Smith sponsors will be good and run in a proper manner but they don't want nonconforming uses. If nobody wanted nonconforming uses and were all to take that seriously there would be no occasion for having a Board of Zoning Appeals. I believe that the Town Fathers, in providing for the ordinances for a Board of Zoning Appeals, were well aware that instances might arise, where although numbers of residents might not want a nonconforming use, there might be a particular hardship to one individual, and therefore this Board was created to handle that case and I am not going to belabor you by telling you what the law is. All of you men know it a lot better than I do, but it seems to me very simply that we have proven that we have a hardship where we have a piece of property which is unique in its general set up and surroundings and that hasn't been disputed in any way. The objectors can't show us another piece of property here in Cathedral Gardens which has the same situation as Mr. Barnes. He is suffering a hardship. It is testified to by Mr. McMahan who is certainly a qualified expert, his qualifications conceded by counsel. . . . They can look out into Westminster Road and bought their homes in back of the business property and it is not a hardship to Dr. McKenna because he is not here to oppose. It is not a hardship on the people who own the property immediately west of Mr. Barnes because they are not here to oppose it and Father Smith, who is directly across the street on the east, and [not] only is he not opposed, but he is highly in favor of it. . . . If I did not believe that this was a good thing for the community I would not be here and I know this and this Board well knows and counsel knows that if Father Smith, who has been the leading citizen of West Hempstead for seventeen years did not believe this was a good thing for the community he would not advocate it. I honestly and sincerely believe that the granting of this variance will bring an improvement, that what he hopes to build will be an improvement in the community, it will not hurt anybody in West Hempstead and it will give him an opportunity to utilize his property. I respectfully ask that the application be granted.

It was regularly moved, seconded and carried that the public hearing be closed. It was regularly moved, and seconded that the Board reserve decision. Motion carried, all voting "aye."

OBJECTORS' EXHIBIT A

TO THE BOARD OF ZONING APPEALS OF THE TOWN OF HEMPSTEAD:

WHEREAS, Richard W. Barnes petitioned the Board of Zoning Appeals of the Town of Hempstead for a variance to permit the erection of a funeral home on the northwest corner of Westminster Road and Regent Place, in West Hempstead, County of Nassau, State of New York; and

WHEREAS, the said property is presently zoned for residential purposes; and

WHEREAS, the immediate adjacent property and surrounding area is zoned for residential purposes and is fully developed, consisting of single one family homes;

NOW THEREFORE, we, the understanding property owners, hereby respectfully petition the Board to deny such application for a variance upon the following grounds:

1. To grant this application will adversely affect the value of real property in our community.

2. Our community is residential in nature and to permit a part of such area to be used for business purposes, and particularly for undertaking and embalming, would violate the spirit of the zoning ordinances, impair public safety and welfare, and would do substantial injustice not only to the owners of properties immediately adjacent to the proposed site, but to the owners in the entire neighborhood.

3. The vehicular traffic which is necessarily a part of a funeral parlor will add to the already heavy traffic on Westminster Road and create a hazard to pedestrians and particularly to our children who are obliged, in most instances, to cross Westminster Road going to and returning from school.

DECISION OF THE BOARD OF ZONING APPEALS

AFFIDAVIT OF WALTER G. MICHAELIS, MEMBER OF
THE BOARD OF ZONING APPEALS, ANNEXED TO ANSWER

SUPREME COURT, NASSAU COUNTY

STATE OF NEW YORK, ⎱ SS.:
COUNTY OF NASSAU. ⎰

WALTER G. MICHAELIS, being duly sworn, deposes and says that he is one of the respondents herein and a member of the Board of Zoning Appeals of the Town of Hempstead. That prior to the hearing upon the application of the petitioner herein a committee of the Board inspected the premises in this proceeding, as well as the surrounding neighborhood.

Hempstead Turnpike, running east and west and located approximately 250 feet south of the applicant's premises, is a six lane state highway. The property to the north of said state highway for 100 feet is zoned for business, and at either side of the intersection of Westminster Road and Hempstead Turnpike to the north of said state highway are located gasoline stations which are indicated in Applicant's Exhibits 1 and 3. Immediately west and across the street from the applicant's property there exists a Catholic church with a large public parking ground immediately adjacent to said church, which faces the applicant's property as described in Applicant's Exhibit 2. Adjoining the applicant's property to the north and south are the homes of two doctors who carry on their medical practice in their residences. There has been testimony to the effect that the erection of a school is contemplated on the unimproved site now occupied by the public parking field. The committee of the Board further considered the fact that the surrounding area was almost completely improved and its character fixed and not subject to change.

The committee of the Board, including your deponent, after viewing the premises of the applicant and the surrounding area, and considering the testimony adduced at the hearing, was of the opinion that the applicant's position, because of this exceptional environment, was unique and that his property did suffer hardship and that a variance would not damage nor depreciate the value of the existing surrounding property.

/s/   WALTER G. MICHAELIS.

(Sworn to by Walter G. Michaelis, Oct. 6, 1948.)

CLARK v. BOARD OF ZONING APPEALS
OF TOWN OF HEMPSTEAD

90 N.Y.S.2d 507 (Sup. Ct. 1948)

FROESSEL, J. This is a proceeding to review and annul the determination of the Board of Zoning Appeals of the Town of Hempstead, which granted a variance of the Building Zone Ordinance of said Town so as to permit the erection in a "B" Residence District of a two-story brick veneer building to be used as a private dwelling and funeral home. The premises in question are located on the northwest corner of Westminster Road and Regent Place, West Hempstead, Nassau County, and the respondent intervenor has been the owner thereof since 1945. . . .

The intervenor owner of the property in question, which is virtually on the edge of the residential area, claims that his land, situated as it is, and flanked by properties used as hereinbefore indicated, was unique, its uniqueness was not a general condition of the neighborhood, which is almost completely improved, that his said land cannot yield a reasonable return if restricted to a conforming use, that a case of hardship was presented, and that a variance would not damage or depreciate the value of existing surrounding property, nor alter the essential character of the locality.

A full and complete hearing was had and several of the six petitioners appeared and testified in opposition to the granting of the application. The petitioners were represented by experienced counsel. The members of the Board of Appeals, following the hearing, inspected the premises as well as the surrounding neighborhood, before the application was granted. I have read with care the record of the hearing, and am constrained to conclude that there is evidence to support the determination of the Board. It cannot be said upon the record before me that the Board's action was arbitrary, oppressive, capricious, nor an abuse of discretion.

Under all the circumstances, and notwithstanding the fact that a different result might well have been arrived at, this Court has no right to interfere, and to substitute its judgment for that of the administrative officers charged with the duty of making the determination [citations omitted]. The rule has been stated as follows in Matter of Foy Productions, Ltd. v. Graves (253 App. Div. 475, 478, *aff'd,* 278 N.Y. 498):

> And it has now become academic under our law that if there is evidence to constitute a reasonable basis for the determination of the Commissioner, if his determination is not arbitrary nor capricious, if the verdict of a jury reaching the same conclusion would not be set aside as against the weight of evidence, the court is not at liberty to disturb his finding. . . .

In the light of the foregoing, as well as the presumption that exists in favor of the determination by the Board (Werner v. Walsh, 212 App. Div. 635, 640, 209 N.Y.S. 454, *aff'd,* 240 N.Y. 689), I have no alternative but to deny that application to annul its determination.

Settle order.

ORDER OF AFFIRMANCE [2]

Order on Appeal from Final Order

At a Term of the Appellate Division of the Supreme Court of the State of New York held in and for the Second Judicial Department at the Borough of Brooklyn on the 6th day of June, 1949.

Present:—Hon. Gerald Nolan, *Presiding Justice.*

    Hon. John B. Johnston,

    Hon. Frank F. Adel,

    Hon. Charles W. U. Sneed,

    Hon. John MacCrate, *Justices.*

---

2. Record on Appeal at 134-135. Opinion reported at 275 A.D. 939, 89 N.Y.S.2d 916, leave to appeal and motion for reargument denied, 275 A.D. 1001, 91 N.Y.S.2d 838 (1949).

In the matter of the application of SUSAN H. CLARK, et al., Appellants,
To review a determination AGAINST
BOARD OF ZONING APPEALS OF THE TOWN OF HEMPSTEAD, et al., Respondents, and RICHARD W. BARNES, Intervenor-Respondent.

The above named Susan H. Clark, Nathan H. Cherwin, Walter E. Swansen, Ruth Swansen, Miriam R. Phillips, John E. Hahn, Dorothy Hahn, Michael Liebl and Mabel Liebl, the petitioners in this proceeding having appealed to the Appellate Division of the Supreme Court from a final order of the Supreme Court entered in the office of the Clerk of the County of Nassau on the 16th day of November, 1948, denying petitioners' application to annul a determination of the Board of Zoning Appeals of the Town of Hempstead in granting a variance of the building zone ordinance of said town so as to permit the erection of a funeral home in a residential zoned area; dismissing the petition and affirming the determination of said Board of Zoning Appeals, herein, and the said appeal having been argued by Mr. Irving H. Schafer of Counsel for appellants, and argued by Mr. George R. Brennan, Town Attorney, of Counsel for respondents, and argued by Mr. Nathaniel A. Kahn of Counsel for intervenor-respondent, and due deliberation having been had thereon; and upon the opinion and decision slip of the court herein, heretofore filed:

It is Ordered that the final order so appealed from be and the same hereby is unanimously affirmed, with one joint bill of $50, costs and disbursements to respondents and intervenor-respondent.

Enter:
JOHN J. CALLAHAN, Clerk.

MATTER OF CLARK v. BOARD OF ZONING APPEALS

301 N.Y. 86, 92 N.E.2d 903 (1950), motion for reargument denied, 301 N.Y. 681, 95 N.E.2d 44 (1950), cert. denied, 340 U.S. 933 (1951)

DESMOND, J. This proceeding was brought, under article 78 of the Civil Practice Act, to review a determination by respondent board of zoning appeals of the town of Hempstead, Nassau County, by which determination the board had granted to intervenor-respondent Barnes, a variance of the town zoning ordinance, so as to permit Barnes to erect, on a lot owned by him in a "B Residence District," a building to be used as a combined residence and funeral home. Petitioners-appellants are a few of the more than two hundred nearby residents who objected, before the board, to the application for this variance. Petitioners were defeated in the courts below, but we granted them leave to come here.

We hold that the board's action in authorizing this variance was without legal basis. The premises of intervener-respondent, as to which the variance was granted, is a vacant lot, 100 feet wide, on the west side of Westminster Road, in a section of the town of Hempstead known as Cathedral Gardens. When intervener-respondent bought that lot, in 1945, it was, and for some years had been, in a "B Residence District" under the town building zone ordinance. In such B residence zones, the permitted uses, under the ordinance, are: single residences, clubhouses, schools, churches, professional offices in dwellings, and some others. A funeral home, or undertaker's establishment, is not such a lawful use. Nevertheless, intervener Barnes purchased the lot, then applied for a variance. We could end this opinion at this point by saying that one who thus knowingly acquires land for a prohibited use, cannot thereafter have a variance on the ground of "special hardship" (Matter of Henry Steers, Inc., v. Rembaugh, 259 App. Div. 908, 909, *aff'd,* 284 N.Y. 621). But beyond that, we hold that the proof here made out, under applicable rules of law, no case for a variance.

At the hearing before the zoning board of appeals, intervener called witnesses to show that, about 260 feet south of his property, Westminster Road, on which his lot fronts, intersects the wide, much-traveled Hempstead Turnpike, that the lands along the turnpike are zoned for business, that on the corner lots at that Westminster-Hempstead intersection there are two gas stations, that the parcels nearest to intervener's, on the west side of Westminster Road, are both used for physicians' homes and offices, and that, just opposite to Barnes' lot on Westminster Road, the frontage, for 600 feet north from the gas stations, is owned by a church corporation, on it being a church, rectory, and (erected after the hearing) a parish school. All of these are, of course, specifically permitted uses, under the zoning ordinance, and there are no unauthorized uses anywhere in the vicinity. A real estate broker called by intervener testified, before the board, that intervener's parcel could not yield a reasonable profit if used only for purposes allowed under the ordinance. However, it is clear that the only basis for that conclusion was the witness' opinion that no one would be likely to buy that lot as the site for a fine residence, and it was not claimed that any effort had been made to sell the premises for any of the authorized uses. There was dispute, in the testimony heard by the board, as to whether the presence of a funeral parlor would depreciate values in the neighborhood. It was brought out, also, at the hearing, that intervener was then conducting his funeral establishment in a store around the corner on Hempstead Turnpike, but wished to move his business onto Westminster Road.

The proof just above summarized was insufficient for a variance. Section 267 of the Town Law empowers boards of appeals to vary the application of town zoning ordinances (subd. 5) "Where there are practical difficulties or unnecessary hardships in the way of carrying out the strict letter of such ordinances." But, as was recently held in Matter of Hickox v. Griffin (298 N.Y. 365, 370-371). "There must at least be proof that a particular property suffers a singular disadvantage through the operation of a zoning regulation before a variance thereof can be allowed on the ground of 'unnecessary hardship.' " Most frequently cited for that proposition is Matter of Otto v. Steinhilber (282 N.Y. 71, 76) where it is written that, before the board may vote a variance, there must be shown, among other things, "that the plight of the owner is due to unique circumstances and not to the general conditions in the neighborhood which may reflect the unreasonableness of the zoning ordinance itself." The board, being an administrative and not a legislative body, may not review or amend the legislatively enacted rules as to uses, or amend the ordinance under the guise of a variance (Dowsey v. Village of Kensington, 257 N.Y. 221, 227), or determine that the ordinance itself is arbitrary or unreasonable (Matter of Otto v. Steinhilber, *supra*). If there be a hardship, which, like the alleged hardship here, is common to the whole neighborhood, the remedy is to seek a change in the zoning ordinance itself (Arverne Bay Constr. Co. v. Thatcher, 278 N.Y. 222, 233; Matter of Levy v. Board of Standards & Appeals, 267 N.Y. 347). Nothing less than a showing of hardship special and peculiar to the applicant's property will empower the board to allow a variance [cases cited]. The substance of all these holdings is that no administrative body may destroy the general scheme of a zoning law by granting special exemption from hardships common to all.

The orders below should be reversed and the determination of the zoning board of appeals annulled, with costs in all courts.

DYE, J. (dissenting). I vote for affirmance. To reverse the action of the board of zoning appeals and annul its determination is to say that the granting of the variance was arbitrary and capricious and constituted an abuse of discretion. This we may not do on the record before us. It is axiomatic and no longer open to doubt that there is evidence to constitute a reasonable basis for the determination the court has no right to interfere and substitute its judgment for that of the administrative board charged with the duty of making a determination. . . .

LOUGHRAN, C. J., LEWIS and FULD JJ., concur with DESMOND, J.; DYE, J., dissents in opinion in which CONWAY, J., concurs; FROESSEL, J., taking no part.

Orders reversed, etc.

NOTES AND QUESTIONS

1. To keep the funeral parlor out of their neighborhood, the objectors were represented at the variance hearing and at the arguments before the state supreme court, the appellate division, and the court of appeals. In addition, unsuccessful motions for reargument were submitted to the appellate division and the court of appeals, and an unsuccessful petition for a writ of certiorari was filed with the United States Supreme Court. Estimate what the legal and printing expenses would run today for a dispute of this scale. The *Clark* outlays

were spread among scores of objectors, but you can see that one or two residential objectors may be no match for a business concern willing to spend almost anything to obtain a variance and to protect it on appeal. Small wonder that courts review only a tiny fraction of variance approvals.

2. The Philadelphia Zoning Board of Adjustment was the subject of a study published in 1955. At that time, the board was receiving yearly over 2,500 appeals from permit denials (including 600 to 800 requests for exceptions); the once-weekly docket of public hearings averaged 60 to 70 cases.

In the nine-week period covered by the study, the docket included 569 cases. Most numerous were those seeking bulk variances for multiple dwellings (198 cases); of these requests, 59.1 percent (104 of 176) were granted.

Next in number (160 cases) were those asking use variances to introduce a new use into a district, or to legalize an already existing use. This second group of cases was the subject of special scrutiny by the author, who counted, in all, 91 variances (56.8 percent) and only 45 refusals (another 24 cases were withdrawn before decision). The board was least pliable when the applicant could not show at least one similar use elsewhere on the block (denials in 34 of 46 cases). The cumulative impact of a nonconforming use can be inferred from the fact that variances were granted in 12 of the 15 cases where the only showing of "hardship" was the existence of a similar nonconforming use elsewhere in the block. The board tended also to continue the existing use of the parcel, seeming not to mind that such use might have been illegal. As one might suppose, the single most important variable was the presence (or absence) of aroused neighbors. In the 46 cases where protestants appeared at the hearing, only 11 variances were granted. See Note, Zoning Variances and Exceptions: The Philadelphia Experience, 103 U. Pa. L. Rev. 516 (1955).

3. The Lexington (Ky.)—Fayette County Zoning Board of Adjustment also was the subject of a study, published in 1962. Dukeminier and Stapleton, The Zoning Board of Adjustment: A Case Study in Misrule, 50 Ky. L.J. 273 (1962). The board's work for a seventeen-month period, ending in May 1961, was examined. In this period, the board had before it 167 cases, including not only variance applications, but also requests for special exceptions, *infra*, temporary permits for uses not conforming to the ordinance, home occupations (for example, beauty shops), and continuation or alteration of nonconforming uses. The statistical summary (id. at 321) appears in Table [18].

How the authors regarded these findings is self-evident from the title of their article. They wrote (id. at 322):

> Our general conclusion is that the Board has not operated in such a manner as to assure citizens equal protection of the law. It has not, during the seventeen months of our study, produced a pattern of consistent, sound, and articulate judgments. Nor have its operations assured the public that the comprehensive plan is not being thwarted through the variance device. We do not mean by this to imply any personal criticism of the individual members of the Board. To the best of our knowledge, they are all honest men and good citizens,

[TABLE 18]

Type of case	No. of petitions	Granted	Denied	Percentage granted	Percentage denied
Use variance	12[a]	3	7	30	70
Bulk variance					
Other than signs	51	44	7	86	14
Signs	41	29	12	71	29
Special exception[b]	17	15	2	88	12
Temporary use	6	5	1	83	17
Home occupation	28	24	4	86	14
Nonconforming use	4	3	1	75	25
Miscellaneous	8	8	0	100	—
TOTAL	167[a]	131	34	79	21
Planning staff					
recommendations	159[c]	69	90	43	57

a. This figure includes one petition that had not yet been finally disposed of and one petition that was granted as a use variance although the use was permitted as a special exception in the district. Neither of theses cases is reported as "granted" or "denied." Both are excluded in computing percentages.—ED.

b. Is it appropriate to combine data on variances and special exceptions? Cf. §17.2 *infra.*—ED.

c. The planning staff made no recommendation in eight cases.—ED.

serving without pay in a thankless job. Our criticism goes to the institution, which we find is functioning badly.

The authors then went on to explain why the institution was functioning badly (id. at 332-339):

    a.   The issues before the Board of Adjustment are not clearly focussed on by the petitioners (who are often not represented by counsel) or by the Board.

    b.   The Board frequently does not follow the law, but is moved instead by:

    (1)   Who the petitioner is ["Experienced builders and realtors seemed almost invariably to succeed."];

    (2)   A businessman's claim that without the variance, he would be at a competitive disadvantage;

    (3)   The presence of nonconforming uses in the neighborhood;

    (4)   The insubstantiality of the requested departure from the zoning ordinance;

    (5)   The presence of neighborhood opposition ["The Board granted 63% of the petitions where there were protestants, compared with 85% granted where there were no protestants."];

    (6)   The persistence of petitioner ["Where a petitioner, once denied, applied for a rehearing or applied a second time for a variance, his chance of success increased. The board heard fourteen such petitions and reversed itself in ten. The evidence in most of these reversals was substantially the same as was produced on first hearing"].

c. The Board's failure to find facts or state reasons inhibits the development of a system of administrative case law.

d. The Board members view themselves as "broker[s] for the individual citizen," not as impartial officials enforcing an impartial law. This is due in part to the members' business orientation, but it primarily reflects the difficulties inherent in a system of Euclidian zoning.

e. A high proportion of the variances granted seemed disruptive of the community plan.

4. Studies reaching similar findings based on the activity of zoning boards in all parts of the country appear with disturbing regularity. A representative sample would include Citizens Research Council of Michigan, Detroit Board of Zoning Appeals (1969) (variance approval rate more than 80 percent); Shapiro, The Zoning Variance Power, 29 Md. L. Rev. 1 (1969); Note, Syracuse Board of Zoning Appeals—An Appraisal, 16 Syracuse L. Rev. 632 (1965); Hagman, Wisconsin Zoning Practice 57 (1962); Comment, Zoning: Variance Administration in Alameda County, 50 Calif. L. Rev. 101 (1962); Am. Soc. of Planning Officials, Measures of Variance Activity (Info. Rep. 60, March 1954); Comment, 48 Nw. U.L. Rev. 470, 481 (1953); Administration of Zoning Variances in 20 Cities, 30 Pub. Management 70 (1940).

5. As Dukeminier and Stapleton (Note 3 *supra,* at 350) indicate, several writers have made proposals for reforming the zoning board of adjustment. These include:

(a) tightening up the procedures ("judicialization") of the board;
(b) abolition and replacement by a board of experts;
(c) abolition and replacement by a single local administrator with a right of appeal to
    (1) the local legislative body, or
    (2) a statewide board of appeal, or
    (3) a committee of the planning commission.

See Leary, A Model Procedure for the Administration of Zoning Regulations 72-92 (1958); Babcock, The Unhappy State of Zoning Administration in Illinois, 26 U. Chi. L. Rev. 509 (1959); Dallstream and Hunt, Variations, Exceptions and Special Uses, 1954 U. Ill. L.F. 213; Reps, Discretionary Powers of the Board of Zoning Appeals, 20 Law & Contemp. Prob. 280 (1955); Note, 74 Harv. L. Rev. 1396 (1961).

What advantages or disadvantages do you foresee for each proposal?

6. "Under an unfettered system of free enterprise, real estate in cities is simply one of several legitimate forms of private investment. Under that system, anyone courageous (or dumb) enough to invest his or her money in urban real estate (instead of, for example, in frozen pork-belly futures) has every right to use that real estate in every available way to improve his or her position. There are one or two laws that limit the use of real estate; for example, you are limited in the size of the building you may erect on your property,

because you shouldn't deprive your neighbors of all sunlight; and you are limited in the uses to which you may put your building, because you shouldn't deprive your neighbors of their lives by enveloping them in noxious fumes, or by exposing them to (let us say) nuclear radiation.

"But apart from such practical limitations, those who have shaped our economic system clearly believed and continue to believe in the sanctity of privately owned real estate. My guess is that this probably includes about 95 percent of the voters." Blake, Cityscape, New York Magazine, Dec. 23, 1974, at 57.

Widespread evasion of legal rules may also signal resentment against the rules themselves, as well as deficient procedures for enforcing them. Thus, rules which thwart human behavior that cannot or should not be curbed, such as laws against obscenity or prostitution, seldom work well, no matter how exertive their enforcement. Is it possible that Euclidian zoning falls into this category and that except for homeowners (and a few preservationists and environmentalists), land-use restrictions are so unpopular—so abhorrent to the development urge—that we should evince no surprise if variance boards freely ignore the rules?

7. The New York City Board of Standards and Appeals may now grant a variance based on practical difficulties or unnecessary hardship only if it finds:

(a) That there are unique physical conditions, including irregularity, narrowness or shallowness of a lot size or shape, or exceptional topographical or other physical conditions peculiar to and inherent in the particular zoning lot; and that, as a result of such unique physical conditions, practical difficulties or unnecessary hardship arise in complying strictly with the use or bulk provisions of the resolution; and that the alleged practical difficulties or unnecessary hardship are not due to circumstances created generally by the strict application of such provisions in the neighborhood or district in which the zoning lot is located.

(b) That because of such physical conditions, there is no reasonable possibility that the development of the zoning lot in strict conformity with the provisions of this resolution will bring a *reasonable return*, and that the grant of a variance is therefore necessary to enable the owner to realize a reasonable return from such zoning lot.

(c) That the variance, if granted, will not alter the essential character of the neighborhood or district in which the zoning lot is located; will not substantially impair the appropriate use or development of adjacent property; and will not be detrimental to the public welfare.

(d) That the practical difficulties or unnecessary hardship claimed as a ground for a variance have not been created by the owner or by a predecessor in title. Where all other required findings are made, the purchase of a zoning lot subject to the restrictions sought to be varied shall not itself constitute a self-created hardship.

(e) That within the intent and purposes of this resolution the variance, if granted, is the minimum variance necessary to afford relief; and to this end, the Board may permit a lesser variance than that applied for. [City of New York, Zoning Resolution §72-21 (1960)]

These stricter requirements seem to have done little to stanch the flow of variances. See Note, Zoning Variances in New York City, 3 Colum. J.L. & Soc. Prob. 120, 121 (1967).

8. Some courts hold applicants for a bulk variance to a less demanding standard of hardship than they require of applicants for a use variance. See, e.g., Hoffman v. Harris, 17 N.Y.2d 138, 144, 216 N.E.2d 326, 330, 269 N.Y.S. 2d 119, 123 (1966). Can you think of reasons why? Remember that bulk regulations govern lot area, setback, frontage, height, floor area, and density.

9. The ALI Model Land Development Code would create separate standards for granting bulk and use variances. To obtain a use variance, the landowner would be forced to show that development as permitted was not "reasonably capable of economic use." Id. §2-204. This would replace the present "unnecessary hardship" test and would require from the applicant dollars-and-cents evidence. Note to §2-204. By contrast, the code retains for bulk variances the "practical difficulties" test due to the parcel's unique physical characteristics. Id. §2-202.

10. "We could end this opinion at this point by saying that one who thus knowingly acquires land for a prohibited use, cannot thereafter have a variance on the ground of 'special hardship.' . . ." Matter of Clark v. Board of Zoning Appeals, page 946, *supra.*

The court did not, however, end the opinion at that point, which left unanswered whether purchase with knowledge, i.e., the self-inflicted hardship, disables the landowner from obtaining a use variance. Should it? Cf. In re McClure's Appeal, 415 Pa. 285, 203 A.2d 534 (1964) (bank seeking variance for branch office unable to claim unnecessary hardship when it bought land zoned residential); L. M. Pike & Son, Inc. v. Town of Waterford, 130 Vt. 432, 296 A.2d 262 (1972) (purchaser unable to claim unnecessary hardship despite his mistake in locating zoning boundaries).

Two appeals, decided on the same day by somewhat different panels of the New York Supreme Court, Appellate Division, Fourth Department, illustrate the illusiveness of the "self-inflicted hardship" rule. Each opinion cites Matter of Clark, but, otherwise, their similarity ends.

The facts in Paplow v. Minsker, 43 A.D.2d 122, 350 N.Y.S.2d 238 (4th Dept. 1973), were these: X purchased a two-family residence that had been converted from a one-family residence forty years before. The building, located in a one-family zone, had been vacant for twenty-one months before X's purchase. Since it was a nonconforming use discontinued for more than a year, the building could not legally be operated as a two-family residence. X applied for and received a variance to re-establish the nonconforming use.

In approving the grant of a variance, the court held that X was entitled to rely upon his belief—when he bought the property—that the property's use as a two-family house might continue, and that X had no duty to investigate further.

The facts in Kenyon v. Quinones, 43 A.D.2d 125, 350 N.Y.S.2d 242 (4th Dept. 1973), were these: Y purchased a commercial building, a nonconforming use in a two-family zone. Several years afterward, Y sought a variance to convert the structure into an apartment house containing eleven units. The area was then zoned for one-family residences.

In overturning the grant of a variance, the court held that Y bought the property with full knowledge of the use restriction and accordingly the hardship was of his own making.

The ALI Model Land Development Code would allow (but not require) denial of a use variance if the agency finds a self-created hardship. Id. at §2-204 and Note thereto.

11.   As a lawyer, do you see any ethical problem in advising your client to apply for a variance and helping him (as best you can) to proceed if you believe on the merits that the agency should turn him down but also believe, in the absence of heavy opposition, that the agency will not do so?

§17.2   The Special Exception

Although confused with the variance, the special exception serves zoning theory quite differently. Exceptions have nothing to do with individual hardship. Instead, they serve to shift from the legislature to an agency the authority to decide when various designated land uses can coexist with their surroundings. Notice, for example, the so-called Conditional Uses appearing in the summary of the San Francisco City Planning Code, pages 775-778 *supra*. In each case, the developer must apply to the city planning commission for approval to operate a nursery school in an R-1-D zone, or a hotel in an R-3 zone, etc. These are special exceptions. If there were no exception device, the zoning law must allow those uses as of right within the respective zones, or bar them entirely from the zones, or create many more zoning categories, or district the community with far greater detail. The exception, therefore, offers the community a sensible mean between rigid exclusion and carte blanche inclusion without forcing the ordinance into a priori decisions as to which parcels within the R-3 zone can best carry a new hotel. The special exception is also more attractive to the landowner than is rigid exclusion. If the hotel were barred entirely from an R-3 zone, the landowner must either seek a zoning change or pursue a (possibly illegal) variance.

Part of the confusion between the variance and special exception derives from their similarity in administration. In many communities the same agency, the zoning board of appeals, handles both procedures (although in other communities, the planning board—not the board of appeals—has charge of exceptions). Part of the confusion also stems from the common failure of ordinances to fix guidelines for reviewing the exception application, with agencies tending to apply (or misapply) variance criteria to the exception request.

SCHULTZ v. PRITTS
432 A.2d 1319 (Md. 1981)

DAVIDSON, J. This case presents [the question] whether the Board's denial of the conditional or special exception use[1] requested in this case was arbitrary, capricious, and illegal.

The respondents, Robert and Ann Pritts, are contract purchasers of a 2.74 acre tract of land located in Carroll County, zoned R-20,000 (single-family residential development—20,000 square feet minimum lot size). These contract purchasers filed an application with the Board requesting a special exception use to develop a funeral establishment and a variance for reduction of the minimum front yard requirements. The Board held a hearing at which the petitioners, Roger Schultz and others (protestants), appeared in opposition. After the hearing, the Board denied the requested special exception use and held that the request for the variance was moot.

The contract purchasers appealed to the Circuit Court for Carroll County which determined that there had been a denial of due process because the Board had considered evidence submitted after the close of the hearing. The Circuit Court reversed and remanded the matter to the Board for a new hearing. That Court specifically refused to consider the merits of the case and to decide whether a standard set forth in Gowl v. Atlantic Richfield Co., 27 Md. App. 410, 417-18, 341 A.2d 832, 836 (1975), was an appropriate standard to be applied on remand in determining whether the special exception use should be granted.

The protestants appealed to the Court of Special Appeals. The contract purchasers cross-appealed on the ground that the Circuit Court should have granted the special exception use. The Court of Special Appeals determined on its own motion that the Circuit Court's order remanding the case to the Board was not a final judgment and dismissed the appeal. That Court did not consider the merits of the case and did not decide whether the standard set forth in *Gowl* was an appropriate standard to be applied on remand in determining whether the special exception use should be granted.

The protestants filed a petition for a writ of certiorari, and the contract purchasers filed a cross petition. We granted both the petition and the cross petition. The case was argued on 3 June 1980. On 28 April 1981 a reargument was held limited to the following questions:

> (1) Was an appropriate standard established in *Gowl* . . . which held that it is arbitrary, capricious and illegal for a Board of Appeals to deny an application for a special exception when "the potential volume of traffic under the requested use would appear to be no greater than that which would arise from permitted uses"?

1. For the purposes of this opinion, the terms "special exception use" and "conditional use" are synonymous.

(2) Is the evidence sufficient when viewed in light of the standard deemed to be appropriate?

We have determined that the standard established in *Gowl* is inappropriate and that in the interest of justice we shall remand the case to the Board for further proceedings without affirmance or reversal. . . .

III. CROSS PETITION

The contract purchasers contend that the Board's decision denying the requested special exception use was arbitrary, capricious, and illegal. Initially, they assert that the Board did not apply the proper criteria in determining that the requested special exception use would result in dangerous traffic conditions. They claim that the Board failed to take into account the critical fact that the requested special exception use would generate less traffic than would be generated by permitted uses. In support of their position, they rely upon Gowl v. Atlantic Richfield Co., 27 Md. App. 410, 417-18, 341 A.2d 832, 836 (1975).

In *Gowl*, the Court of Special Appeals reversed a Board of Appeals decision denying a requested special exception use on the ground of traffic. There that Court stated that the proper standard by which to determine whether a requested special exception use should be denied on the ground of traffic is a comparison between the traffic problems that might arise under the requested special exception use and those that might arise under a permitted use. It held that when "the potential volume of traffic under the requested use would appear to be no greater than that which would arise from permitted uses," the requested special exception use must be granted. *Gowl*, 27 Md. App. at 417-18, 341 A.2d at 836. We do not agree.

This Court has frequently expressed the applicable standards for judicial review of the grant or denial of a special exception use. The special exception use is a part of the comprehensive zoning plan sharing the presumption that, as such, it is in the interest of the general welfare, and therefore, valid. The special exception use is a valid zoning mechanism that delegates to an administrative board a limited authority to allow enumerated uses which the legislature has determined to be permissible *absent any fact or circumstance negating the presumption.* The duties given the Board are to judge whether the *neighboring properties in the general neighborhood would be adversely affected* and whether the use in the particular case is in harmony with the general purpose and intent of the plan.

Whereas, the applicant has the burden of adducing testimony which will show that his use meets the prescribed standards and requirements, he does not have the burden of establishing affirmatively that his proposed use would be a benefit to the community. If he shows to the satisfaction of the Board that the proposed use would be conducted without real detriment to the neighborhood and would not actually adversely affect the public interest, he has met his burden. The extent of any harm or disturbance to the neighboring area and uses is, of course, material. If the evidence makes the question of harm or disturbance or the question of the disruption of the harmony of the comprehensive plan of zoning fairly debatable, the matter is one for the Board to decide. But if there is no probative evidence of harm or disturbance in light of the nature of the zone involved or of factors causing disharmony to the operation of the comprehensive plan, a denial of an application for a special exception use is arbitrary, capricious, and illegal. Turner v. Hammond, 270 Md. 41, 54-55, 310 A.2d 543, 550-51 (1973). [Other citations omitted.] These standards dictate that if a requested special exception use is properly determined to have an adverse effect upon neighboring properties in the general area, it must be denied.

The specific nature of the requisite adverse effect was defined in Deen v. Baltimore Gas & Electric Co., 240 Md. 317, 330-31, 214 A.2d 146, 153 (1965). There the Baltimore Gas and Electric Company requested a special exception use that would permit construction of high tension transmission lines above ground. At that time, the Baltimore County Zoning Regulations stated that a special exception use could not be granted if the requested use would "be detrimental to the health, safety, or general welfare of the locality involved." The Baltimore County Board of Appeals (Board) granted the requested special exception use for that portion of the proposed transmission lines that would traverse a rural area not then serviced by public sewer or water facilities. The trial court affirmed.

On appeal, this Court affirmed stating:

> Appellants assert that it was error for the Board to fail to consider the future effects which the high tension wires would have on the health, safety and general welfare of the locality "which could be reasonably anticipated in the normal course of its development." This factor was without relevance in this case, because *there was no evidence produced at the hearing which would show that the effect of high tension wires on the future health, safety and welfare of this area would be in any respect different than its effect on any other rural area. Section 502.1 implies that the effect on health, safety or general welfare must be in some sense unique or else a special exception could never be granted in such an area for the above ground location of high tension wires.* The only evidence as to future conditions was testimony revealing the possibility of future residential development of this land but such a possibility alone does not come close to showing a future deleterious effect upon the public health, safety or general welfare. *Deen,* 240 Md. at 330-31, 214 A.2d at 153 (emphasis added).

Subsequently, a similar analysis was employed in Anderson v. Sawyer, 23 Md. App. at 617-18, 329 A.2d at 720. There an owner requested a special exception use that would permit construction of a funeral home in a residential zone. Protestants presented evidence to show that the requested special exception use would tend to create congestion and unsafe conditions on neighboring roads and streets and would have a depressing psychological effect that would interfere with the enjoyment of the adjoining properties, make them less saleable, and prevent them from appreciating in value as much as other homes in the area. The Board found that the grant of the requested special exception use would create traffic problems and would, in fact, "be detrimental otherwise to the general welfare of the locality involved." It denied the requested special exception use. The Circuit Court for Baltimore County reversed.

The Court of Special Appeals affirmed the order of the Circuit Court requiring the grant of the requested special exception use. The Court of Special Appeals agreed with the trial court that there was no probative evidence to show any adverse effect. More particularly, with respect to the alleged depreciation of value and enjoyment of neighboring properties, it said:

> There can be no doubt that an undertaking business has an inherent depressing and disturbing psychological effect which may adversely affect persons residing in the immediate neighborhood in the enjoyment of their homes and which may lessen the values thereof. Indeed, it is precisely because of such inherent deleterious effects that the action of a local legislature in prohibiting such uses in a given zone or zones will be regarded as promoting the general welfare and as constitutionally sound. But in the instant case the legislature of Baltimore County has determined that as part of its comprehensive plan funeral homes are to be allowed in residential zones notwithstanding their inherent deleterious effects. By defining a funeral home as an appropriate use by way of special exception, the legislature of Baltimore County has, in essence, declared that such uses, if they satisfy the other specific requirements of the ordinance, do promote the heath, safety and general welfare of the community. As part of the comprehensive zoning plan this legislative declaration shares in a presumption of validity and correctness which the courts will honor.
>
> *The presumption that the general welfare is promoted by allowing funeral homes in a residential use district, notwithstanding their inherent depressing effects, cannot be overcome unless there are strong and substantial existing facts or circumstances showing that the particularized proposed use has detrimental effects above and beyond the inherent ones ordinarily associated with such uses.* Consequently, the bald allegation that a funeral home use is inherently psychologically depressing and adversely influences adjoining property values, as well as other evidence which confirms that generally accepted conclusion, is insufficient to overcome the presumption that such a use promotes the general welfare of a local community. *Because there were neither facts nor valid reasons to support the conclusion that the grant of the requested special exception would adversely affect adjoining and surrounding properties in any way other than would result from the location of any funeral home in any residential zone, the evidence presented by the protestants was, in effect, no evidence at all. Anderson,* 23 Md. App. at 624-25, 329 A.2d at 724 (emphasis added) (citations omitted).

These cases establish that a special exception use has an adverse effect and must be denied when it is determined from the facts and circumstances that the grant of the requested special exception use would result in an adverse effect upon adjoining and surrounding properties unique and different from the adverse effect that would otherwise result from the development of such a special exception use located anywhere within the zone. Thus, these cases establish that the appropriate standard to be used in determining whether a requested special exception use would have an adverse effect and, therefore, should be denied is whether there are facts and circumstances that show that the particular use proposed at the particular location proposed would have any adverse effects above and beyond those inherently associated with such a special exception use irrespective of its location within the zone.

In *Gowl*, the Atlantic Richfield Company requested a special exception use that would permit construction of above ground storage for more than 10 million gallons of fuel oil and gasoline to be located on approximately 19 acres of land zoned M-2 (Manufacturing-Heavy). At a hearing before the Board of Appeals for Howard County (Board), there was much evidence presented to show that the particular use proposed at the particular location proposed would have an adverse effect on neighboring properties in the general area. There was expert and lay testimony to show, among other things, that the access roads to the property were inadequate and dangerous and that the increased traffic could not be accommodated on the existing roads. The Board found, among other things, "that the proposed use would adversely affect the surrounding and vicinal properties by creating undue traffic congestion on a presently inadequate and hazardous road network. . . ." It denied the requested special exception use.

Atlantic Richfield filed an appeal in the Circuit Court for Howard County.

. . . [T]he trial court concluded that there was sufficient evidence to support the Board's finding that the particular use proposed at the particular location proposed would have an adverse effect on traffic above and beyond the adverse effect on traffic ordinarily associated with such uses. Notwithstanding the existence of this adverse effect, the trial court concluded that the Board's denial should be reversed and that the special exception use should be granted. In explanation, the trial court said:

> *The crux of the matter*, as pointed out by counsel for the appellant, *is that the proposed use in this instance* insofar as the evidence before the Board was concerned, *would not create any greater traffic congestion* on the presently inadequate and hazardous road network *than any number of uses permitted as a matter of right under the M-1 and M-2 zoning classifications.* For instance, among the uses permitted as a matter of right in the M-1 zoning district, such uses also being permitted as a matter of right in the M-2 zoning district, are truck terminals and warehouses, wholesale houses, merchandise distribution centers, and the manufacture of cement, cinder or slag products. In the M-2 zoning districts, among other uses permitted as a matter of right are: aircraft manufacture or assembly, automobile or truck assembly plants, food manufacturing, packing or processing plants and bituminous road material mixing plants. *Presumably any or all of these uses permitted as a matter of right in the area in question would create precisely the same, if not a greater, traffic hazard than the use in question here.* The fault, if any, lies not with the use proposed but with the zoning regulations and map in effect at this time. In other words, *an increase in traffic, including trailer trucks, or inadequate roads, is not a factor unique or peculiar to this proposed use.* (Emphasis added.)

. . . [T]he Court of Special Appeals agreed with the trial court that although the particular special exception use proposed at the particular location proposed had an adverse effect on traffic above and beyond that ordinarily associated with such uses, the requested special exception should be granted.

In reaching this conclusion, the trial court cited only *Deen,* 240 Md. at 330-31, 214 A.2d at 153, and the Court of Special Appeals cited no authority at all. Indeed, there is no persuasive authority that applies the *Gowl* standard or supports this conclusion.

An analysis of the rationale underlying the statutory scheme by which certain uses are delineated as either a permitted use or a conditional or special exception use leads to the conclusion that the *Gowl* standard is logically inconsistent and in conflict with the standards established in *Turner* as explicated by *Deen* and *Anderson.* . . .

Zoning provides a tool by which to establish general areas or districts devoted to selected uses. Ellicott v. Mayor of Baltimore, 180 Md. 176, 181, 23 A.2d 649, 651 (1942). Indeed, the very essence of zoning is the territorial division of land into use districts according to the character of the land and buildings, the suitability of land and buildings for particular uses, and uniformity of use. [Citations omitted.]

Generally, when a use district is established, the zoning regulations prescribe that certain uses are permitted as of right (permitted use), while other uses are permitted only under certain conditions (conditional or special exception use). [6] In determining which uses should be designated as permitted or conditional in a given use district, a legislative body considers the variety of possible uses available, examines the impact of the uses upon the various purposes of the zoning ordinance, determines which uses are compatible with each other and can share reciprocal benefits, and decides which uses will provide for coordinated, adjusted, and harmonious development of the district. P. Hagman, Urban Planning and Land Development Control Law 105 (1971). See Art. 66B, §4.03.

Because the legislative body, in reaching its determination, is engaged in a balancing process, certain uses may be designated as permitted although they may not foster all of the purposes of the zoning regulations and, indeed, may have an adverse effect with respect to some of these purposes. Thus, when the legislative body determines that the beneficial purposes that certain uses serve outweigh their possible adverse effect, such uses are designated as permitted uses and may be developed even though a particular permitted use at the particular location proposed would have an adverse effect above and beyond that ordinarily associated with such uses. For example, churches and

---

6. Art. 66B, §1.00 provides in pertinent part: " 'Special exception' [conditional use] means a grant of a specific use that would not be appropriate generally or without restriction and shall be based upon a finding that certain conditions governing special exceptions as detailed in the zoning ordinance exist, that the use conforms to the plan and is compatible with the existing neighborhood."

schools generally are designated as permitted uses. Such uses may be developed, although at the particular location proposed they may have an adverse effect on a factor such as traffic, because the moral and educational purposes served are deemed to outweigh this particular adverse effect.

When the legislative body determines that other uses are compatible with the permitted uses in a use district, but that the beneficial purposes such other uses serve do not outweigh their possible adverse effect, such uses are designated as conditional or special exception uses. [Citations omitted.] Such uses cannot be developed if at the particular location proposed they have an adverse effect above and beyond that ordinarily associated with such uses. For example, funeral establishments generally are designated as special exception uses. Such uses may not be developed if at the particular location proposed they have an adverse effect upon a factor such as traffic because the legislative body has determined that the beneficial purposes that such establishments serve do not necessarily outweigh their possible adverse effects.

More particularly, by definition, a permitted use may be developed even though it has an adverse effect upon traffic in the particular location proposed. By definition, a requested special exception use producing the same adverse effect at the same location must be denied. Thus, by definition, a church may be developed even if the volume of traffic that it generates causes congestion and unsafe conditions at the particular location proposed. By definition, however, a special exception use for a funeral establishment producing the same volume of traffic and, therefore, the same congestion and unsafe conditions at the particular location proposed must be denied. It is precisely because a permitted use may be developed even though it may have an adverse effect on traffic at the particular location proposed, whereas a special exception use may not, that to grant a requested special exception use on the ground that it generates traffic volume no greater than that generated by a permitted use is logically inconsistent and in conflict with previously established standards. Accordingly, the standard articulated in *Gowl* is inappropriate. We now hold that the appropriate standard to be used in determining whether a requested special exception use would have an adverse effect and, therefore, should be denied is whether there are facts and circumstances that show that the particular use proposed at the particular location proposed would have any adverse effects above and beyond those inherently associated with such a special exception use irrespective of its location within the zone. [Citations omitted.]

Here the purposes of the Carroll County Zoning Ordinance are "to promote the health, safety, morals, and the general welfare of the community, by regulating . . . the location and use of buildings . . . to provide for adequate light and air; to prevent congestion and undue crowding of the land; to secure safety from fire, panic, and other danger; and to conserve the value of property." Carroll County Zoning Ordinance §1.0. The local legislative body, the County Commissioners of Carroll County, after engaging in a balancing process, designated single-family dwellings, churches, schools, colleges, and community buildings such as libraries, cultural and civic centers as permitted uses in a R-20,000 Residence District. Carroll County Zoning Ordinance §7.1. As a result of this designation, such uses can be developed even if they have an adverse effect on traffic. The Commissioners also designated certain other uses of land, including funeral establishments, as special exception uses in a R-20,000 Residence District. Carroll County Zoning Ordinance §7.2. As a result of this designation, funeral establishments cannot be developed at a particular location if they have an adverse effect on traffic above and beyond that ordinarily associated with funeral establishments irrespective of location within the zone. Carroll County Zoning Ordinance §17.6.

Here the Board determined that the grant of the requested special exception use for the proposed funeral establishment would result in dangerous traffic conditions at the proposed location and, therefore, that the special exception should be denied. However, the record here shows that the evidence primarily relied upon by the Board was based on questionable assumptions. On appeal, the trial court did not decide whether a reasoning mind could reasonably have concluded, as did the Board, that the granting of the requested special exception use would result in dangerous traffic conditions. Rather, the trial court erroneously decided only that there had been a denial of due process and reversed and remanded the matter to the Board for a new hearing. The trial court specifically refused to determine whether, on remand, the *Gowl* standard was applicable.

The Court of Special Appeals did not decide whether the question of adverse effect on traffic was fairly debatable. Rather, it erroneously decided only that the trial court's order remanding the case to the Board was not a final judgment. It dismissed the appeal, without indicating whether the *Gowl* standard was applicable.

In our view, under all of these circumstances, the purposes of justice will be advanced by permitting further proceedings in this case through the introduction of additional evidence before the Board and the application of the appropriate standard set forth in this opinion. Accordingly, we shall remand the case to the Board without affirmance or reversal for further proceedings in accordance with this opinion. Md. Rule 871. . . .

SMITH, J., concurs in part and dissents in part.

SMITH, J. , concurring, and dissenting. I concur in the determination that the order of the Circuit Court for Carroll County was an appealable final order and that the applicant was not denied due process of law. I dissent, however, from Part III of the opinion dealing with the cross petition.

I

I do not think there was sufficient evidence before the Board of Zoning Appeals for Carroll County to warrant denial of the special exception here.

We all agree that the board of appeals may not arbitrarily and capriciously deny a request for a special exception. The problem is against what do we measure traffic in determining that it will have an adverse effect and produce a hazard warranting rejection of an application? Surely there must be some standard. It seems to me logically that since the legislative body has determined that in the district in question "[p]rincipal permitted uses" include "[c]hurches, schools and colleges," and "[b]uildings and properties of a cultural, civic, educational, social or community service-type such as libraries, ponds[,] . . . playgrounds [and] community centers," that it follows that in determining whether or not the board has been arbitrary one should measure the traffic to be generated by the proposed special exception against that generated by permitted uses. Why is it not arbitrary and capricious to deny permission for this funeral home on the basis of the traffic hazard when a church or certain others of the permitted uses may generate as much or more traffic?

Members of some religious denominations, e.g., the Protestant Episcopal Church, regularly have their funeral services from their church sanctuary. Thus, a church could be erected here which in the case of a funeral would generate exactly the same amount of traffic this funeral home would generate, but the church is a permitted use. Moreover, it is conceivable that after attendance at Sunday morning worship services, weddings, or other events on the church calendar the traffic which might pour out of its parking lot would be substantially in excess of that from the funeral home.

A playground is a permitted use. In my part of the State the traffic which would be generated by just an average Little League baseball game would dwarf that which is suggested as the average for a funeral in this instance. A hotly contested game between two bitter rivals obviously would produce even greater traffic.

A college is a permitted use. What amount of traffic might be expected to spew out of a parking lot adjacent to a college athletic field after a major football game?

To hold to the *Gowl* rule would not mean that every application for a special exception for a funeral home would have to be granted simply because the application is made. There can be a difference in funeral homes. All are not the same, by any means. Counsel for Pritts was asked at oral argument if he could articulate circumstances warranting denial by virtue of a demonstrable adverse effect upon surrounding property. In pointing out that all funeral homes are not the same he said:

> If a funeral home is one that does contract embalming work, for example, and has a lot of traffic in and out and has a laboratory facility, that is entirely different from the normal funeral home. If a funeral home is in the business of selling caskets to a lot of other funeral homes in the area, that is something larger than the normal funeral home. If a funeral home is in the business of selling grave markers or funeral paraphernalia, then I think in that circumstance you have something different than the normal funeral home.

I have known even in a town smaller than Westminister of a very busy funeral home that sometimes had as many as three funerals in one day. No such proposition was involved here.

When, as here, the special exception is denied on the basis that operation under the granted exception would create a traffic hazard and an identical or worse traffic hazard could arise from permitted uses, I must regard the action as arbitrary and capricious, such that should not be tolerated in a free land.

NOTES AND QUESTIONS

1. At issue in Schultz v. Pritts was whether, under the statute, the administrative agency had as much discretion to grant or deny the special exception as it sought to exercise. This problem arises when the zoning law seems to confer too great discretion on the agency. The Fremont (California) Municipal Code created an R-G garden apartment zone, in which agriculture was the principal permitted use, and dwellings were a conditional use, approval to be received from the city planning commission. The court, in striking down the ordinance, wrote:

> It can not be legitimately argued that a single-family dwelling, a duplex or a multiple dwelling present special use problems which cannot be resolved by restrictions of general application established legislatively.
>
> Other than some very general guide lines hereinafter mentioned, no attempt has been made to establish any criteria or standards for the guidance of the Planning Commission in deciding who in an R-G zone may build an apartment house, who may build a duplex, who may improve his land with only a single-family residence, or who must leave his land unimproved.
>
> To hold that the limitations imposed by the "purpose" section of the ordinance (F.M.C. 8-2700) or the other declared basic purposes of protecting "adjacent property" and promoting the "health, safety, peace, morals, comfort or general welfare" (F.M.C. 8-22502) are sufficient standards for the exercise of the discretionary power conferred on the Planning Commission to grant or reject conditional use permits, ignores the fact that the power to discriminate is nowhere curtailed. It also ignores the fact that these are the identical standards which governed the City Council in enacting the ordinance in the first instance. Thus, the power delegated to the Planning Commission is no less than that conferred on the City Council by the Government Code.
>
> The total effect of article 8 is—by the device of the conditional use permit—to delegate outright the entire legislative zoning function to the Planning Commission for it authorizes said Commission to rezone, parcel by parcel, the entire area embraced within any R-G zone until the character of the entire zone has been completely changed. The Planning Commission of a Government Code city possess no such independent legislative authority. (See Gov. Code, §§65460, 65654, 65656, 65800 and 65806.) (People v. Perez, 214 Cal. App. 2d 881, 885-886, 29 Cal. Rptr. 781, 783-784 (1963))

For further analysis of the delegation problem, and the courts' uneven response to it, see Mandelker, Delegation of Power and Function in Zoning Administration, 1963 Wash. U.L.Q. 60. Cf. also Flynn v. Zoning Board of Review of Pawtucket, 77 R.I. 118, 73 A.2d 808 (1950) (board authorized to approve any building use in harmony with character of neighborhood. Held: illegal delegation of legislative power).

2. The court in People v. Perez, *supra*, also warns against overutilization of the exception procedure. The opinion states the procedure "to be valid . . . should be limited to those uses only for which it is difficult to specify adequate conditions in advance, i.e., schools, hospitals, service stations, [social halls, nursing homes, public buildings, trailer parks]. 214 Cal. App. 2d 881, 885, 29 Cal. Rptr. 781, 783 (1963).

If the legislature has sufficiently articulated criteria to guide the administrative agency, do you see any policy objections to investing the agency with power to approve or disapprove a wide variety of uses, or mixtures of uses, including some not included on the court's list? In this regard, would it matter whether the planning commission or the board of appeals had charge?

3. Notice that architectural control and subdivision approval are procedures similar to the special exception. In each case, the landowner enjoys a presumption that he can proceed to development if he meets certain conditions, and in each case, an agency administers the procedure. Should approximately the same degree of specificity in all three cases govern the standards by which the developer gains approval?

4. Consider, for example, the frequent use of special exception procedures to screen apartment house development in suburban locales. What is the potential for abuse when a community can decide *which* projects will get built? Even if courts greatly limit an agency's discretion to reject outright a proposed project, might the agency still impose conditions upon the physical design or layout which—at the very least—would determine the project's cost and, ultimately, who lived there? Can you draft an exception procedure for apartments that will enable the agency to consider noise, traffic, and congestion, without also regulating bedroom distribution and recreational facilities?

5. In administering an exception procedure, should the agency have discretion to weigh the following variables?

(a) the business impact on existing merchants
(b) the number of school-age children that a project will generate
(c) the business reputation of the applicant
(d) the site's proximity to a high school; cf. Ward v. Village of Skokie, 26 Ill. 2d 415, 186 N.E.2d 529 (1962) (unreasonable for village to refuse to approve motel next to a high school, despite educators' testimony as to the effect on student morals)
(e) the applicant's readiness to accept restrictions as to the hours and days of a business operation; cf. Annot., 99 A.L.R.2d 227 (1965)

6. In §17.6 *infra,* you will encounter planned unit developments (PUDs) and floating zones. Be ready to discuss how they differ procedurally from the exception and whether these differences affect the legal issues.

§17.3 Conventional Rezoning

Your client owns a residentially zoned parcel on which she wishes to erect a small medical building with off-street parking. Such structures are not allowed in R zones, but are permitted in C-1 zones. Your client seeks approval for her plans, believes that local officials will be generally sympathetic, and hopes that neighborhood opposition will be relatively muted. One decision you must weigh is whether to apply for a variance.[3] If you decide not to, and if the ordinance is not constitutionally vulnerable, you will probably urge your client to seek rezoning.

Rezoning to meet your client's needs might take any of several forms:

(1) Rezoning of client's parcel from R to C-1.
(2) Rezoning of larger area including client's parcel from R to C-1.
(3) Redefining R zone to include medical buildings as either a permitted or special exception use.
(4) Creating a new M zone for medical buildings (or an R-M zone for residences *and* medical buildings) and placing your client's parcel (and several other parcels) within the new zone.

As you read the next group of materials, consider the practical and legal difficulties of each of these suggestions from two points of view: your client's and the local officials'.

BARTRAM v. ZONING COMMN. OF CITY OF BRIDGEPORT[4]

136 Conn. 89, 68 A.2d 308 (1949)

MALTBIE, C.J. This is an appeal by the defendants from a judgment sustaining an appeal from a decision of the zoning commission of the city of

---

3. Whether to seek a variance or apply for rezoning is both a practical and legal question. As the variance materials indicated, §17.1 *supra,* zoning boards far too often will ignore the legal standards and grant the variance even where the landowner appropriately should seek rezoning instead. Courts may have begun to take a harder look at this form of variance abuse. Cf. Topanga Ass'n for a Scenic Community v. County of Los Angeles, 11 Cal. 3d 506, 522 P.2d 12, 113 Cal. Rptr. 836 (1974).

4. Connecticut, perhaps alone among the states, has permitted its cities and towns to delegate broad zoning powers to a commission whose members may be appointed officials. Conn.

Bridgeport taken in accordance with the provisions of §845 of the General Statutes. The commission changed the classification of a Sylvan Avenue lot, with a frontage of 125 feet and a depth of 133 feet, from a residence zone to a business No. 3 zone.

With some corrections to which the defendants are entitled, the controlling facts found by the court are these: Zoning regulations became effective in Bridgeport on June 1, 1926. They provided for three classes of residence zones, two classes of business zones, and two classes of industrial zones. In 1937 the regulations were amended to establish business zones No. 3 and special regulations were adopted as to them. These regulations, as further amended, contain provisions as to the type of construction of buildings and require open yards about them, a setback of thirty feet from the street and parking facilities for cars on private property; the sale of liquors was originally restricted but this provision was amended to forbid sales of liquor under any permit for a tavern, restaurant or all-liquor package store. The territory surrounding the lot in question is contiguous to the northern boundary of the city and quite a distance from its shopping and business center. Previous to 1936, both sides of Sylvan Avenue to a depth of 100 feet had for a considerable distance been in a business No. 1 zone, but in that year the classification was changed to residence A; and since that date, as before, a considerable territory in the neighborhood of the premises in question has been in residential zones. When zoning was originally adopted, the area was sparsely built up and contained much farm land. Beginning before 1936, people desiring to get away from the noise and congestion of the center of the city began to build homes there; at present it is quite generally built up with residences, at least 40 percent of which have been constructed since 1936. Most of the houses in the immediate vicinity of the premises in question are comparatively new; they are neat, one-family homes, with well-kept lawns and attractive plantings; and they give every indication that a self-respecting community of people of moderate means have moved to this outlying section of the city. In the vicinity of the premises in question there exist as nonconforming uses four stores, three selling groceries or meat and one a liquor package store. One of the former is a small store in a building almost opposite the premises in question, the second floor of which is occupied as a residence. There is no drugstore in the vicinity. There is also, near the premises in question, a small church. Sylvan Avenue is a street sixty feet wide and it is a principal traffic artery to and from the section surrounding it.

The application for the change of zone was made by the defendant Rome. He presented to the commission at the hearing before it plans for a building he proposes to erect, which in all respects would comply with the regulations for a business No. 3 zone, which would contain provision for five places of business—a drug, a hardware and a grocery store, a bakeshop and a

---

Gen. Stat. Ann. §8-1 (Supp. 1981). Elsewhere, the counterpart to the zoning commission of this and the *Miss Porter's School* case (Note 5, page 1007 *infra*) would be the local legislative body.

beauty parlor—and which would provide for the parking of cars in the rear of the building, and between it and the street line. Aside from Rome, no one appeared to support his application, but ten residents and property owners in the neighborhood opposed it. They gave various reasons for the position they took, among them these: They desired to have the residential character of the section preserved from business development; in many instances they had purchased or developed their properties in reliance upon the residence zoning of the area and in the expectation that this zoning status would remain unchanged; they were fearful that the business zoning of any portion of the area would be destructive of the peace and quiet they desired to have preserved; they believed that the business zoning of any part of it, however small and wherever located, would have a tendency to break down the residence zoning of the area by making further business zoning in it more likely; and there was no present need for further and more adequate shopping facilities in the neighborhood. A remonstrance against granting the application signed by more than seventy residents in the neighborhood was also filed with the commission; but only some forty-six different addresses of the signers appear on it; in a number of instances the signers were husband and wife or two or more residing in the same house; and many of them lived at a considerable distance from the premises in question. Within a radius no longer than the distance to the addresses given by some of the signers are more than 200 residences.

The commission gave the following reasons for its decision: 1. The location is on Sylvan Avenue, a sixty-foot street, and there is no shopping center within a mile of it. To the north of this tract there is a very large development but only small nonconforming grocery stores to serve the people. 2. There is practically only one house, adjacent to this tract on the north, which will be directly affected by this change of zone. 3. Business No. 3 regulations, with their thirty-foot setback and liquor restrictions, were designed to meet conditions like this and help alleviate the great congestion in the centralized shopping districts. The court also found that a member of the commission testified that it was its policy to encourage decentralization of business in order to relieve traffic congestion and that, as part of that policy, it was considered desirable to permit neighborhood stores in outlying districts; and nowhere in the record is there any suggestion that this testimony is not true.

The trial court concluded that the change was an instance of "spot zoning." A limitation upon the powers of zoning authorities which has been in effect ever since zoning statutes were made applicable generally to municipalities in the state is that the regulations they adopt must be made "in accordance with a comprehensive plan." Public Acts, 1925, c. 242, §3 (Rev. 1949, §837). "A 'comprehensive plan' means 'a general plan to control and direct the use and development of property in a municipality or a large part of it by dividing it into districts according to the present and potential use of the properties.'" Bishop v. Board of Zoning Appeals, 133 Conn. 614, 618, 53 A.2d 659; State ex rel. Spiros v. Payne, 131 Conn. 647, 652, 41 A.2d 908. Action by a zoning authority which gives to a single lot or a small area privileges which are not extended to other land in the vicinity is in general against sound public policy and obnoxious to the law. It can be justified only when it is done in furtherance of a general plan property adopted for and designed to serve the best interests of the community as a whole. The vice of spot zoning lies in the fact that it singles out for special treatment a lot or a small area in a way that does not further such a plan. Where, however, in pursuance of it, a zoning commission takes such action, its decision can be assailed only on the ground that it abused the discretion vested in it by law. To permit business in a small area within a residence zone may fall within the scope of such a plan, and to do so, unless it amounts to unreasonable or arbitrary action, is not unlawful. Bishop v. Board of Zoning Appeals, *supra;* see Parsons v. Wethersfield, 135 Conn. 24, 29, 60 A.2d 771. The zoning regulations of Bridgeport were adopted under the provisions of the General Statutes which gave the commission power to divide the municipality into districts and in each district to regulate the construction and use of buildings and land, and to change the regulations from time to time. General Statutes, Rev. 1930, §§424, 425, as amended (Rev. 1949, §§837, 838); see De Palma v. Town Plan Commission of Greenwich, 123 Conn. 257, 265, 193 A. 868. The commission might be guilty of spot zoning either in the original regulations it made or in later amendments, but, if in one or the other it decides, on facts affording a sufficient basis and in the exercise of a proper discretion, that it would serve the best interests of the community as a whole to permit a use of a single lot or small area in a different way than was allowed in surrounding territory, it would not be guilty of spot zoning in any sense obnoxious to the law. That was the situation in this case, and we cannot sustain the conclusion of the trial court that the action of the commission was improper as an instance of spot zoning. . . .

How best the purposes of zoning can be accomplished in any municipality is primarily in the direction of its zoning authority; that discretion is a broad one; and unless it transcends the limitations set by law its decisions are subject to review in the courts only to the extent of determining whether or not it has acted in abuse of that discretion. First National Bank & Trust Co. v. Zoning Board of Appeals, 126 Conn. 228, 237, 10 A.2d 691. A court is without authority to substitute its own judgment for that vested by the statutes in a zoning authority. Piccolo v. West Haven, 120 Conn. 449, 455, 181 A. 615; Mrowka v. Board of Zoning Appeals, 134 Conn. 149, 155, 55 A.2d 909. In view of the facts present in this case, the trial court could not properly find that the policy which determined the decision of the commission would so clearly fail to serve the proper purposes of zoning in the city that the court might set aside that decision; nor do the facts show that it was unreasonable to apply that policy in the situation before us. This is illustrated by the fact that, had this lot been placed in a business No. 3 zone as an incident to the adoption of an original plan for zoning the city as a whole, that action could not on this record be held an unreasonable exercise by the commission of its power.

There is error, the judgment is set aside and the case is remanded with direction to enter judgment dismissing the appeal.

In this opinion BROWN and JENNINGS, JJ., concurred; ELLS and DICKENSON, JJ., dissented.

DICKENSON, J. (dissenting). This, as the trial court held, seems to be a clear instance of spot zoning. The trial court has found no comprehensive plan to permit single lots or small areas to be used for business purposes in residential zones. The only evidence of such a plan is the testimony of a member that it was the "policy" of the commission to encourage decentralization of business in order to relieve traffic congestion and permit stores in outlying residential areas. So radical a departure from the general purpose of zoning to separate business from residential districts should not be left to the whims of a zoning board. It should come within "a comprehensive plan for zoning the town." Parsons v. Wethersfield, 135 Conn. 24, 29, 60 A.2d 771.

I think there was no error.

NOTES AND QUESTIONS

1. Did the zoning commission win because the rezoning was "in accordance with a comprehensive plan," or was the rezoning "in accordance with a comprehensive plan "because the zoning commission won? Did the plaintiffs lose because they failed to establish "spot zoning," or was there no "spot zoning" because the plaintiffs lost? Are the terms "spot zoning" and "in accordance with a comprehensive plan" simply legal shorthand for a result, or do they also contain operative variables? What were the operative variables, if any, underlying the court's decision? the dissenting opinion? See generally, Haar, "In Accordance With a Comprehensive Plan," 68 Harv. L. Rev. 1154 (1955).

2. Contrast *Bartram* with Kuehne v. Town Council of East Hartford, 136 Conn. 452, 72 A.2d 474 (1950), decided one year later with Chief Justice Maltbie again writing the court's opinion. Langlois owned a 500-foot frontage in an R-A zone on East Hartford's Main Street. He applied for and received rezoning to Business-A, enabling him to erect a building on the site containing six to eight stores. Fifty-one nearby residents supported the change because the shopping center would benefit them. The owner of the parcel directly across Main Street opposed. The city council voted the change as in "the general welfare and [for] the good of the town in that section."

In upsetting the city's action as spot zoning and not in furtherance of a comprehensive plan, the court held:

> [I]t is obvious that the Council looked no further than the benefit which might accrue to Langlois and those who resided in the vicinity of his property, and that they gave no consideration to the larger question as to the effect the change would have upon the general plan of zoning in the community . . . [such as] the fact that only some 700 feet away was a tract of land already zoned for business which . . . was more easily accessible to most of the [51] signers of the petition than was the Langlois land.

Can you reconcile the two decisions? Is the court acting as a supraplanning agency when it decides two small shopping centers within 700 feet of each other would be one more than is needed? Can a court avoid the planning agency role when it must apply the "comprehensive plan" test to a rezoning decision?

3.   Compare the court opinion in *Bartram* with this quote from Levine v. Town of Oyster Bay, 46 Misc. 2d 106, 259 N.Y.S.2d 247 (Sup. Ct. 1964), where the court upset a rezoning from residential to industrial use:

> Thus in the Town's view, as expressed by its zoning expert, its "comprehensive zoning plan" is synonymous with "comprehensive plan." The plaintiffs planning expert and the Chief Planner for the Nassau County Planning Commission disagreed completely, maintaining that the zoning plan was merely a means or tool for effectuating the comprehensive plan. The Town's claim serves only to make the riddle of the "comprehensive plan" that much more puzzling. To say that the Town's "comprehensive zoning plan" is interchangeable with "comprehensive plan" is to say that zoning regulations . . . must be in "accordance" with themselves. This Court cannot believe that the Legislature intended or contemplated such a meaningless interpretation of these provisions.
>
> While a comprehensive plan need not be in writing [case cited], it should at least be amenable to statement when proper inquiry is made of those informed in such matters. If it is to be presented to exist in the mind of the Town Board, then of necessity the plan must bear the imprint of the varying ideas and peculiar experiences of the individual members. . . . It is doubtful that the Legislature intended that it should be that elusive.

Does this language help you to think about the *Bartram* dispute?

4.   Compare *Bartram* also with Udell v. Haas, 21 N.Y.2d 463, 235 N.E.2d 897 (1968). The village of Lake Success rezoned a narrow neck along Lakeville Road from business to residence. Plaintiff had owned his parcel some eight to nine years before the rezoning, which occurred shortly after plaintiff announced plans for a bowling alley and a supermarket. In the court's words, the "race to the statute books" took one month and was preceded by no planning activity showing the need for change; and while rightly concerned about traffic congestion, the village considered no other possible alternatives to residential rezoning.

Alluding to the state's "comprehensive plan" requirement, the court found that the village had such a plan in its zoning ordinance, first enacted in 1925, which since 1938 had set plaintiff's parcel in a business zone. In 1958, in the form of a zoning amendment, the village declared its "developmental policy" that, inter alia, continued the business classification for plaintiff's parcel and spoke of the need to strengthen the tax base of the community. The disputed rezoning occurred in 1960.

The court invalidated the change, holding that:

(a)   The comprehensive plan requirement is not a mere technicality, but the "essence of zoning."

(b)   The role of planning experts must be more than to rationalize actions already carried out. Planning input must *precede* the rezoning decision.

(c)   A zoning ordinance must not be lightly changed, because of the whims of either an articulate minority or even majority of the community. Moreover, any change must support a showing that it has not undermined the "community's basic scheme for land use."

(d)   The 1960 rezoning, which had no prior planning input, which did not deal explicitly with the goals set forth in the 1958 statement, and which did not weigh alternative measures for easing traffic congestion, failed to satisfy the comprehensive plan requirement.

Udell v. Haas is a noble statement by a fine judge (Keating). Yet even if the village had satisfied the court's procedures (and we can assume that the planning expertise would have been found), the court would have struck down the rezoning on the alternative ground that it discriminated against plaintiffs whose neighbors were already operating business premises.

This two-legged rationale illumines the tension between planning agencies and the courts, and our ambiguity about a suitable role for judicial review in the zoning area. On the one hand we have a strongly protective attitude and expect courts to intercede when private landowners are pushed around; some would add, when various nonlandowning groups are pushed around as well. On the other hand we (and the courts) believe in planning—the entire process that involves goals, alternatives, facts, professionals, and politicians; we insist that there be a comprehensive plan. Yet so elusive are goals, facts, alternatives, etc., and so flexible are pros and politicos, that one can have no assurance that the greater the planning input, the "better" the planning output. Moreover, there may still be a lot of the "pushing around" that leads to lawsuits. The court would then have before it a PLAN—which it could continue to set aside!

Does all this imply, therefore, that a comprehensive plan, whatever more that means than the *Bartram* court required, is a necessary, but not always sufficient basis for a zoning change—and that, conceivably, the planning input that precedes a zoning change should be marginally greater than whatever is required for the original ordinance?

One thing more: the court in Levine v. Town of Oyster Bay, Note 3 *supra,* calls it a fallacy to treat the comprehensive and zoning plans as equivalent. Yet Judge Keating in Udall v. Haas writes that the Lake Success comprehensive plan *was* its zoning ordinance. Are these statements reconcilable?

5.   Review the various rezoning choices listed in the text at page 968. Assume that the applicant and the municipality both do their planning homework. Are some of the choices more vulnerable to a charge of spot zoning?

6.   *Bartram* and *Kuehne* involved landowners who wanted their parcels rezoned; *Levine* and *Udall* involved landowners who wanted their parcels left alone. Levine and Udall claimed that they had been discriminated against (vis-á-vis unaffected neighbors). In the *Bartram* and *Kuehne* cases, might neighbors claim that the benefited landowners had been discriminated *for?* Does

that claim survive a showing that planning went into the zoning change? In the *Bartram* and *Kuehne* cases, might neighbors claim that they had been discriminated against because their parcels kept the original, more restricted classification? Does that claim survive a showing that planning went into the zoning change?

Are there any (other) ways it might matter whether a rezoning challenge came from a "Levine" or a "Bartram" neighbor?

7. Suppose that Bartram had failed to obtain rezoning: does he have judicial recourse? What does Bartram argue? What does the city argue? Is the legislature's refusal to rezone entitled to any greater presumption of validity than its decision to rezone? Suppose that Bartram had produced elaborate studies in support of the change, which the city had summarily dismissed without obtaining any news studies of its own. Is the city required to justify rezoning inaction?

8. Kahn, In Accordance with a Constitutional Plan: Procedural Due Process and Zoning Decisions, 6 Hastings Const. L.Q. 1011, 1027-30 (1979):

> A basic tenet of procedural due process is that it applies only to adjudicative decisions, and not to legislative acts. [Ordinarily] a legislative label will prevent a court from even reaching the question of how much process is due an individual. As many zoning decisions are made by municipal legislatures or by bodies that could be viewed as delegates of those legislatures, this has been a major hurdle to parties seeking to prove constitutional violations in zoning decisions. . . . Generally, enactments and amendments of zoning ordinances and comprehensive plans by elected bodies are regarded as legislative, while variances, permits and exceptions approval by boards of adjustment or appeal are deemed quasi-judicial. . . . Several recent decisions, however, have rejected making a distinction simply on the basis of whether the "rezoning" decision was made by a legislative or judicial body. [Cases cited from Colorado, Connecticut, Kentucky, Nevada, New Jersey, Oregon, Washington, and the District of Columbia.] According to these cases, although initial formulation of an entire zoning ordinance and major amendments to ordinances retain a legislative character, where a municipal legislature rezones a small parcel of land, affecting just a few owners, the action is quasi-judicial.

The author then indicates why this departure seems preferable.

(1) Municipal bodies are not the equivalent of state legislatures, because they are less subject to public scrutiny, and more susceptible to undue influence.

(2) Because rezoning often affects only a few landowners, citizens are almost powerless to remedy an adverse decision at the polls.

(3) Rezoning often does not involve questions of broad policy.

The Oregon courts, in treating rezoning as sometimes quasi judicial, have stated three factors that help draw the distinction: 1) the party initiating the change, i.e., whether a landowner or the municipality; 2) the size of the affected parcel; and 3) the number of affected owners and the diversity of their interests. Id. at 1030-33.

The author then argues for a more flexible, less dichotomous formula, which would require some hearing-type procedures (lesser procedures to smaller interests) for all rezoning legislation.

9.   California is one of many states that allow the initiative whereby legislation is proposed and acted upon by the electorate. Arnel Development Co. v. City of Costa Mesa, 28 Cal. 3d 511, 620 P.2d 565, 169 Cal. Rptr. 904 (1980), upheld a local initiative that rezoned a parcel from apartments to single-family use in order to thwart a proposed development. The unfortunate landowner had intended to build 539 apartment units on his 50-acre parcel. Objecting to the proposal, a neighborhood association circulated an initiative rezoning the Arnel parcel and two adjoining tracts to single-family residential use. Voters approved the initiative by a narrow margin.

The lower appellate court upset the initiative, holding that the rezoning of specific, relatively small parcels of private property was an adjudicatory act that could not be accomplished by initiative.

In rejecting that decision and reinstating the initative, the state supreme court refused to budge from the conventional view that rezoning is always legislative:

> . . . From the doctrine that zoning ordinances are legislative, but variances and similar administrative decisions are adjudicative,[11] derive a number of rules which facilitate the making of land use decisions and simplify litigation challenging those decisions. Among those rules are: (1) Zoning ordinances, but not administrative decisions, can be enacted by initiative (Associated Home Builders, etc. Inc. v. City of Livermore, 18 Cal. 3d 582, 135 Cal. Rptr. 41, 557 P.2d 473). (2) Zoning ordinances, but not administrative decisions, are subject to referendum (Dwyer v. City Council, 200 Cal. 505, 253 P. 320). (3) A zoning ordinance is reviewable by ordinary mandamus (Code Civ. Proc., §1084); an administrative decision, by administrative mandamus (Code Civ. Proc., §1094.5). (4) A zoning ordinance, unlike an administrative decision, does not require explicit findings (Ensign Bickford Realty Corp. v. City Council, 68 Cal. App. 3d 467, 473, 137 Cal. Rptr. 304). (5) A zoning ordinance is valid if it is reasonably related to the public welfare (see Miller v. Board of Public Works (1925) 195 Cal. 477, 488, 234 P. 381); administrative decisions must implement established standards and rest upon findings supported by substantial evidence. (Code Civ. Proc., §1094.5.) Under the views advanced by plaintiffs, however, the application of these rules is uncertain until a reviewing court finds whether the decision is legislative or an adjudicative act. Plaintiffs propose, however, no test to distinguish legislative and adjudicative actions with reasonable certainty.

---

11. A holding that rezoning of relatively small parcels is an adjudicative act would necessarily imply that decisions presently considered adjudicative, such as the grant of a use permit or the approval of a subdivision map, would henceforth be classified as legislative acts if they affected a relatively large parcel of property.

The factual setting of the present case illustrates the problems courts will face if we abandoned past precedent and attempted to devise a new test distinguishing legislative and adjudicative decisions. The Court of Appeal, for example, found here that the instant initiative was an adjudicative act because it rezoned a "relatively small" parcel of land. It is not, however, self-evident that 68 acres is a "relatively small" parcel; some cities have entire zoning classifications which comprise less than 68 acres. The size of the parcel, moreover, has very little relationship to the theoretical basis of the Court of Appeal holding— the distinction between the making of land-use policy, a legislative act, and the asserted adjudicatory act of applying established policy. The rezoning of a "relatively small" parcel, especially when done by initiative, may well signify a fundamental change in city land-use policy.

Plaintiffs alternatively urge that the present initiative is adjudicatory because it assertedly affects only three landowners. But this is a very myopic view of the matter; the proposed construction of housing for thousands of people affects the prospective tenants, the housing market, the residents living nearby, and the future character of the community. The number of landowners whose property is actually rezoned is as unsuitable a test as the size of the property rezoned. Yet without some test which distinguishes legislative from adjudicative acts with clarity and reasonable certainty, municipal governments and voters will lack adequate guidance in enacting and evaluating land-use decisions.

In summary, past California land-use cases have established generic classifications, viewing zoning ordinances as legislative and other decisions, such as variances and subdivision map approvals, as adjudicative. This method of classifying land-use decisions enjoys the obvious advantage of economy; the municipality, the proponents of a proposed measure, and the opponents of the measure can readily determine if notice, hearings, and findings are required, what form of judicial review is appropriate, and whether the measure can be enacted by initiative or overturned by referendum.

To depart from past precedent and embark upon a case by case determination, on the other hand, would incur substantial administrative cost. Such a rule would expose the municipality to the uncertainty of whether a proposed measure would be held to be legislative or adjudicative; it would entail cost to the litigants, and it would burden the courts with the resolution of these issues.

10.   City of Eastlake v. Forest City Enterprises, Inc., 426 U.S. 668, 96 S. Ct. 2358, 49 L. Ed. 2d 132 (1976), upheld a local law that would make rezoning ineffective unless the legislative action was also approved by 55 percent of persons voting in a referendum. The referendum procedure was added to the city charter shortly before the council approved a zoning amendment that would have allowed construction of high-rise apartments.

The Ohio Supreme Court had invalidated the referendum requirement. The state court reasoned that voters, lacking any standard to guide their decision, would be exercising the police power in an arbitrary and capricious manner. Such standardless delegation of legislative power was unlawful. 41 Ohio St. 2d 187, 324 N.E.2d 740 (1975).

In upholding the referendum requirement, Chief Justice Burger reasoned for the majority of his court that the people in establishing legislative bodies can reserve to themselves power to deal directly with matters that might otherwise be assigned to the legislature. Where such power is reserved, the doctrine requiring that legislative delegation to regulatory bodies be accompanied by discernible standards simply does not apply.

Justice Powell wrote a brief dissent:

> There can be no doubt as to the propriety and legality of submitting generally applicable legislative questions, including zoning provisions, to a popular referendum. But here the only issue concerned the status of a single small parcel owned by a single "person." This procedure, affording no realistic opportunity for the affected person to be heard, even by the electorate, is fundamentally unfair. The "spot" referendum technique appears to open disquieting opportunities for local government bodies to bypass normal protective procedures for resolving issues affecting individual rights. [426 U.S. at 680]

Justices Brennan and Stevens also dissented.

Are there no limits on popular referendum? Suppose that the proposal would strip the subject land of all value? prevent development of a church? bar federally subsidized housing project to be occupied principally by low-income minorities? not be in furtherance of a comprehensive plan? Cf. Blumstein, A Prolegomenon to Growth Management and Environmental Zoning Issues, 43 Law & Contemp. Prob. 74 (1979).

11. Professor Charles Haar directed a computer study of 79 rezoning cases decided between 1950 and 1975 by the Supreme Court of Connecticut. His objective was to learn whether one could build a computer model that would help litigants predict the eventual outcome of a rezoning dispute. Here are some of his observations:

> In our analysis several issues emerged which demand conscientious consideration by the court:
>
> 1. Before the court defers to the local zoning authority's judgment, there should be a standard against which the planning effort at the local level can be judged. As indicated by the computer analysis, the local zoning authority, in order to be in accordance with a comprehensive plan, need only avoid the following situations when it rezones a parcel: (a) creating a hazardous situation, (b) depriving the owner of all reasonable use of his property, (c) departing from large uniform blocks, (d) placing undue strain on the capacity of the streets, (e) causing an adverse economic impact on adjacent lots, and (f) locating the use in an area that is improving (see [Table 19, page 980]). This is not an adequate, functional interpretation of the statutory standard that requires overall coordination of policy. Is not additional meaningful reference to the quality of the planning effort at the local level necessary? Deference is given the zoning authority without determining the ability of that body to protect the public interest.
>
> 2. Though developers as defendants win cases in which they have the decision of the zoning authority on their side, in the cases decided during the 25 years considered in our study, they won only one of the cases where they had to

challenge the decision of the zoning authority. Is there a bias, perhaps an unconscious one, against developers and developments? When the court intervenes, are the judges reflecting the jaundiced view that developers are "bad guys" who warp the political process at the local level and must be curbed under any circumstances? Is unknown change more frightening than stagnation, as a matter of public policy? On the other hand, are the neighbors the "little guys" in need of protection by the court from unscrupulous developers? Or does the court cling to the naive view that planning and zoning decisions, since they are scientific and technical, are outside the political process—immune from improper exercise of discretion and arbitrary invocations of power?

3. Since the factors listed in [Table 19] are the key criteria for intervention, standards in each area should be clarified by the court. To be sure, some concepts, such as the likelihood of plan completion, have been well defined over a series of cases. But the concepts of large uniform blocks and relatively large area remain vague and unworkable. Each case seems to be evaluated separately. Statistical analysis of the court's use of size may provide a starting point, but it does not even purport to answer questions relating to the impact of the intensity of the use on the court's perception of relative size.

4. The political factors remain hardest to cope with. How is the court's definition of hazard affected by need for the use, or by the political climate in the town, or by the amount and source of opposition? Further computer analysis may yield insight into these issues, but the statistical tools are limited and quantification of such factors may not be possible. Therefore, it is the court that must look into the mirror, answer the tough questions for itself, and then clarify its views on those issues concerning the public interest.

5. Finally, the court must begin to look beyond the simple facts of the case before it to the broader policy issues in zoning litigation. Denial of one petition for a zone change does not constitute exclusionary zoning; there may be legitimate deficiencies in the location or nature of the proposed use. Rather, it is the pattern of decisions in a town which must be examined, and the plans on which such decisions are based are crucial. Are housing plans reasonably related to the rate of growth and the demands of the community? Are new industrial developments being designed without considering their accessibility to low-income residents? Are there plans for transportation to provide access to suburban jobs for central city residents?

If the plans are deficient in these respects, how can the community zoning decisions be "in accordance with a comprehensive plan"? The court's unwillingness to come to grips with the concept of comprehensiveness and its deference to the local zoning authority on the issue of need have allowed the development and perpetuation of housing patterns over the last 20 years which have increased racial and economic segregation.

Certainly the statutory mandate is vague, but it is not unworkable. The factors examined in this research would certainly be important considerations in the preparation of any comprehensive plan. A "good" comprehensive plan can be said to be one that prescribes evaluation of the recommended land use in terms of the substantive issues that planning professionals deem pertinent. Both the plan and the planning process, of which it is the outcome, can be evaluated in terms of the substantive and planning factors discussed in this research, and the weight given to the decision of the zoning authority can be determined by the quality of the process and the plan. . . .

Planners, Developers, and Zoning Authorities—Playing the Percentages

The lesson in this research for the zoning authorities is clear. At least in Connecticut, they have been given broad—if not unfettered—discretion to act as they wish as long as they avoid the specific problems highlighted in [Table 19]. Particularly where they follow the master plan or town plan of development, their judgment appears final.

In Connecticut, two crucial findings should provide guidelines for developers: (1) neighbors win cases, without the support of the zoning authority, and developers do not; and (2) the zoning authority's decision is pivotal. The developer will save time and money, as well as his nerves, if he cooperates with both the zoning authority and the neighbors in designing a workable, acceptable package. Cooperation, not litigation, is the road to success.

Given the strength of the zoning authority, the amount of negotiation over zoning amendments is bound to increase. If there is strong opposition, the zoning

TABLE [19]
Summary Table of Regression Analysis

	Value[b]
Constant[a]	.57

Variables:

Zoning authority denies zone change (Var. 012)	−.55
Court of common pleas approves zone change (Var. 011)	.16
Not a departure from large uniform blocks (from Scale 8)	.62
Streets inadequate (from Scale 7)	−.39
Adverse impact on value of adjacent lots (from Scale 6)	−.35
Physical hazard created (from Scale 7)	−.30
Area relatively large (from Scale 11)	.25
Completion of necessary improvements unlikely (from Scale 7)	−.24
Character of area improving (from Scale 6)	−.23
Character of area deteriorating (from Scale 10)	.13
Other municipal services adequate (from Scale 10)	.10
Retention of control (from Scale 4)	.07
Proposed use aesthetically compatible (from Scales 5 & 8)	.06[c]
Common zoning technique (from Scale 11)	.06
Specific, detailed limits in zoning ordinances (from Scale 4)	.05
More flexible land-use controls (from Scale 4)	.04
Adequate buffer (from Scale 4)	.02
Proposed use needed in neighborhood (from Scale 10)	.02
Existing zoning line a natural boundary (from Scale 8)	−.02

a. The constant term is the intercept a of the regression equation $y = a + b_1x_1 + b_2x_2 + \ldots b_nx_n$. For simplicity, the lawyer can consider it the initial probability of approval when no other information is known; all other variables change the probability from this starting point.

b. The sum of all relevant decision variables determines the prediction. A sum close to one predicts approval of the zone change by the court; a net value close to zero implies denial.

c. From this point in the Summary Table the variables add only marginally to the predictive capability of the model.

Source: Haar et al., Computer Power and Legal Reasoning: A Case Study of Judicial Decision Prediction in Zoning Amendment Cases, 1977 Am. B. Found. Research J. 651, 657, 747-50.

authority may also assume the role of arbitrator, helping the opposing factions reach an acceptable compromise. By knowing in the very specific terms presented in this research the importance of particular issues in determining the outcome of litigation before the supreme court, the parties will be encouraged to negotiate an acceptable development proposal.

The tremendous power of the zoning authority demands criteria for selecting members and staff adequate to protect the public interest. In Connecticut the court has stepped in to remedy cases where blatant conflict of interest was shown, but that is not sufficient to assure high quality, comprehensive planning. Since the court has chosen to avoid the responsibility of determining what constitutes adequate planning, the only current check on the abuse of this power lies in the process of appointing members to the planning and zoning agencies and in these members' conscientious performance of their tasks.

§17.4 Conditional Rezoning

Under conventional zoning theory, a landowner may develop his parcel for any use permitted within the district. If a San Francisco landowner were able to change his zoning classification from R-5 to C-1, for example, rezoning would permit him to develop the parcel not only for retail business, which might have been his original intention, but also for professional offices or parking lots, which, on rezoning, might prove more profitable. (See page 769 *supra*.) Unlike a variance or special exception—where the landowner seeks approval for a specified set of plans and where approval covers only those plans—rezoning creates an open-ended privilege to build whatever the new district enables.

Communities sometimes seek to modify conventional zoning theory by fixing conditions to any rezoning approval. Conditional rezoning, as you shall see, raises some difficult legal and policy issues, which the case below partly explores.

BAYLIS v. CITY OF BALTIMORE
219 Md. 164, 148 A.2d 429 (1959)

HENDERSON, J., delivered the opinion of the Court. This appeal is from a decree of the Circuit Court of Baltimore City dismissing a bill by residents and property owners to declare a rezoning ordinance invalid and to enjoin the owners of 5205 Frederick Avenue, in Baltimore City, from using their property as a funeral home or undertaking establishment. The Ordinance, as originally introduced, proposed a change of classification from a "Residential Use District" to a "First Commercial Use District." It was referred to the Board of

Municipal and Zoning Appeals, and also to the City Planning Commission, for reports and recommendations. The Board recommended approval, provided certain restrictions be included so that the property in question could be used only as a funeral home. The Planning Commission recommended disapproval on the grounds that no neighborhood need was shown, that the Ordinance would be "special privilege legislation," and that "legislation should not be based upon trades or conditions." After a hearing before the Council, certain amendments were made to the Ordinance to restrict the use of the property and reduce the area to be rezoned. In its final form, the Ordinance made the reclassification conditional upon the execution of an agreement, set out in the Ordinance, between the owners and the City, and the recording of such agreement among the Land Records of Baltimore City, so as to be binding upon the property owners, their successors, heirs and assigns.

The agreement provided that, in consideration of the rezoning, the owners would develop and maintain the property as a funeral home only, that the entrances and exits would be on Frederick Road, that adequate off-street parking facilities would be provided and maintained on the west side of the existing residence, and that all funerals would be formed on the property and not on the public streets. It was further provided that if said property should at any time not be used as a funeral home, the Ordinance would be "abrogated and repealed" and the zoning classification "automatically revert" to "Residential Use District"; if a new ordinance should be required to change the property back to "Residential Use District" (as the City Solicitor had advised), the property owners would not object to or oppose said Ordinance in any form.

The appellants contend that the Ordinance is invalid as "spot zoning" and that it is arbitrary and discriminatory, and has no substantial relation to the general welfare. They also contend that the special conditions contained in the Ordinance are ultra vires, and that the agreement is unenforceable.

"Spot zoning" is a term used in many of the zoning cases, but as a descriptive term rather than a word of art. As Judge Hammond, for the Court, said in Huff v. Bd. of Zoning Appeals, 214 Md. 48, 57, "Such zoning may be invalid or valid. If it is an arbitrary and unreasonable devotion of the small area to a use inconsistent with the uses to which the rest of the district is restricted and made for the sole benefit of the private interests of the owner, it is invalid. Cassel v. City of Baltimore, 195 Md. 348, 355. On the other hand, if the zoning of the small parcel is in accord and in harmony with the comprehensive zoning plan and is done for the public good—that is, to serve one or more of the purposes of the enabling statute, and so bears a substantial relationship to the public health, safety, morals, and general welfare, it is valid." [Citing cases.] The *Cassel* case involved a funeral home in a long established and built up residential district, and we found, on the facts, that there was no substantial basis for the reclassification. Cf. Jack Lewis, Inc. v. Baltimore, 164 Md. 146, 155, 159. It was noted in the *Cassel* case (p. 357), that the rezoning Ordinance contained a proviso that the premises should be used only as a funeral home, although the reclassification was from Residential to First Commercial, but the validity of the restriction was not raised or decided.

If we assume, without deciding, that there were distinguishing features in the instant case, on the facts, from those of the *Cassel* case, we think it is clear that the second contention of the appellants is well-founded. If it be true, as the City suggests, that the City has made a practice of imposing similar restrictions, it is all the more important that we pass on their power to do so under the statute and basic ordinance, when the point is squarely presented for the first time.

As the City concedes, Baltimore City derives its zoning powers from the State Enabling Act, Code (1957), Art. 66B, and not from its Charter. Cf. Scrivner v. Baltimore, 191 Md. 165. Sec. 3 provides that the regulation of uses by districts, authorized by Secs. 1 and 2, "shall be made in accordance with a comprehensive plan." The method of procedure for adopting such plan is set forth under Sec. 4. Sec. 5 provides that boundaries may be changed from time to time by the legislative body, after reports and recommendations by the Planning Commission and the Board of Zoning Appeals, and after study by those agencies of the proposed changes with respect to the master plan of zoning, and the need thereof. It is this section that applies in the instant case. It is clear that the City Council need not follow the recommendations. We are not here concerned with Sec. 7 of the Act or Sec. 35 of the Ordinance (1958 ed.), authorizing the appointment of a Board of Zoning Appeals, and delegating to it the power to make special exceptions or variances, for the simple reason that no such application was made to the Board, and there is no claim of practical difficulty or hardship. Cf. Marino v. City of Baltimore, 215 Md. 206, 215.

The City argues that because the Board, which recommended the conditions and restrictions, had the power to grant special exceptions, the City Council has the same power. But this does not follow. It seems clear that such power was not retained in the Council, but has been delegated to the Board for exercise in special types of cases. We find no express language in the Act or the Ordinance authorizing the Board itself to impose conditions or restrictions, even in cases where it may properly order a special exception or variance. Such authority is spelled out in the Baltimore County Regulations, Sec. 502.2. We are not referred to any similar provision in the City Ordinance, although Code (1957), Art. 66B, sec. 7(g)(4) provides that the Board shall have the power to approve "uses limited as to location under such rules and regulations as may be provided by ordinance of the local legislative body."

There is authority to the effect that reasonable conditions and restrictions may be imposed by a board in connection with a special exception or variance, at least where the power to do so is express, or may be fairly implied. Oursler v. Bd. of Zoning Appeals, 204 Md. 397, 406; Woodbury v. Zoning Board of Review, 82 A.2d 164 (R.I.); Selligman v. Western & Southern Life Ins. Co., 126 S.W.2d 419 (Ky.). See also 8 McQuillin, Municipal Corporations (3d ed. Rev.), §25.271, and 1 Yokley, Zoning (2d ed.), §144. This is so because the whole basis for the exception is the peculiar hardship to the applicant, and the Board is justified in limiting the exception in such a way as to mitigate the effect upon neighboring property and the community at large. But these considerations disappear when we deal with a reclassification involving a revision of the comprehensive plan and a change in the district or zone by the legislative body. We think it quite clear that the Council must consider factors not applicable in a special exception or variance. As pointed out in Baltimore County v. Missouri Realty Co., 219 Md. 155, in cases of reclassification the presumption of permanency must be overcome by proof of original mistake or change of conditions. Moreover, the Council, under the Enabling Act and Ordinance, has set up districts for Residential Uses, and First Commercial Uses. If it were permitted in special cases to allow inconsistent uses in such districts, it would destroy the uniformity required by Sec. 2 of the Enabling Act.

We said in Wakefield v. Kraft, 202 Md. 136, 149:

> If the decision of the County Commissioners was that the area called for the status of Commercial A, any of the nineteen uses permitted under that classification had a rank and force equal to any other. The County Commissioners are not a Planning Board, nor have they a right to exact conditions, or promises of a particular use in return for deciding that the public interest justifies that an area should be zoned commercial. . . . This is not to decide, and we do not, whether an administrative official or board may, as a prerequisite to the granting of a variance, attach reasonable conditions. Many Courts have held that, within limits, this can be done.

We find nothing to the contrary in Ellicott v. City of Baltimore, 180 Md. 176.

Courts in other states have reached the same conclusion as we did in the *Wakefield* case. [Citations omitted.] There seem to be three chief reasons for the rule stated in these cases: that rezoning based on offers or agreements with the owners disrupts the basic plan, and thus is subversive of the public policy reflected in the overall legislation, that the resulting "contract" is nugatory because a municipality is not able to make agreements which inhibit its police powers, and that restrictions in a particular zone should not be left to extrinsic evidence.

In terms of zoning, the primary objection is the effect of permitting additional districts which have little or nothing in common and are unlike the basic zones. While the uses permitted by variances, and to a much lesser extent special exceptions, may appear to give rise to comparable dissimilarity, the comparison is only superficial. The peculiar circumstances which must be shown to support a variance from the basic plan in those instances distinguish them from facts such as those in the instant case, where the action taken is based solely upon collateral promises. The former types of exception are, by their very nature, self-limiting; the latter has no inherent restriction.

For all of the reasons stated in this opinion, we must reverse the decree of the Chancellor and remand the case for the entry of a decree granting the relief prayed.

Decree reversed and case remanded; costs to be paid by appellees.

NOTES AND QUESTIONS

1. Would rezoning have survived the neighbors' attack if the Frederick Avenue property had been placed *unconditionally* in a First Commercial Use district? Would the neighbors even have brought suit except for their purists' view of correct legislative form?

2. Which of the following is the *Baylis* ratio decidendi?

(a) Only the board of zoning appeals may issue a special exception.
(b) The state enabling act does not authorize rezoning upon condition.
(c) The city ordinance does not authorize rezoning upon condition.
(d) Zoning regulations shall be uniform throughout a district.
(e) Legislative bodies shall not make deals.
(f) Any other.

3. The New York City Zoning Resolution (1960) authorizes the Board of Standards and Appeals to condition the grant of a variance "as it may deem necessary . . . to minimize the adverse effects of such variance upon other property in the neighborhood." Failure to comply with such conditions may result in a denial or revocation of a building permit or certificate of occupancy and the imposition of "all other applicable remedies." Id. §72-22.

Without passing on the issue directly, the *Baylis* opinion strongly implies that zoning boards may set conditions on variances *and* special exceptions. Are there different issues and policy considerations when conditions are imposed administratively rather than legislatively?

4. Other decisions disagree with *Baylis*. Chief among them is Collard v. Village of Flower Hill, 52 N.Y.2d 594, 421 N.E.2d 818, 439 N.Y.S.2d 326 (1981). Writing for an undivided court, Judge Jones reasoned:

> Probably the principal objection to conditional rezoning is that it constitutes illegal spot zoning, thus violating the legislative mandate requiring that there be a comprehensive plan for, and that all conditions be uniform within, a given zoning district. When courts have considered the issue (see, e.g., Baylis v. City of Baltimore, 219 Md. 164; Houston Petroleum Co. v. Automotive Prods. Credit Assn., 9 N.J. 122; Hausmann & Johnson v. Berea Bd. of Appeals, 40 Ohio App. 2d 432), the assumptions have been made that conditional zoning benefits particular landowners rather than the community as a whole and that it undermines the foundation upon which comprehensive zoning depends by destroying uniformity within use districts. Such unexamined assumptions are questionable. First, it is a downward change to a less restrictive zoning classification

that benefits the property rezoned and not the opposite imposition of greater restrictions on land use. Indeed, imposing limiting conditions, while benefiting surrounding properties, normally adversely affects the premises on which the conditions are imposed. Second, zoning is not invalid per se merely because only a single parcel is involved or benefited (Matter of Mahoney v. O'Shea Funeral Homes, 45 N.Y.2d 719); the real test for spot zoning is whether the change is other than part of a well-considered and comprehensive plan calculated to serve the general welfare of the community (Rogers v. Village of Tarrytown, 302 N.Y. 115). Such a determination, in turn, depends on the reasonableness of the rezoning in relation to neighboring uses—an inquiry required regardless of whether the change in zone is conditional in form. Third, if it is initially proper to change a zoning classification without the imposition of restrictive conditions notwithstanding that such change may depart from uniformity, then no reason exists why accomplishing that change subject to condition should automatically be classified as impermissible spot zoning.

Both conditional and unconditional rezoning involve essentially the same legislative act—an amendment of the zoning ordinance. The standards for judging the validity of conditional rezoning are no different from the standards used to judge whether unconditional rezoning is illegal. If modification to a less restrictive zoning classification is warranted, then a fortiori conditions imposed by a local legislature to minimize conflicts among districts should not in and of themselves violate any prohibition against spot zoning.

Another fault commonly voiced in disapproval of conditional zoning is that it constitutes an illegal bargaining away of a local government's police power (see, e.g., Hartnett v. Austin, 93 So. 2d 86 [Fla.], supra; Baylis v. City of Baltimore, 219 Md. 164, supra; Ziemer v. County of Peoria, 33 Ill. App. 3d 612, supra). Because no municipal government has the power to make contracts that control or limit it in the exercise of its legislative powers and duties, restrictive agreements made by a municipality in conjunction with a rezoning are sometimes said to violate public policy. While permitting citizens to be governed by the best bargain they can strike with a local legislature would not be consonant with notions of good government, absent proof of a contract purporting to bind the local legislature in advance to exercise its zoning authority in a bargained-for manner, a rule which would have the effect of forbidding a municipality from trying to protect landowners in the vicinity of a zoning change by imposing protective conditions based on the assertion that that body is bargaining away its discretion, would not be in the best interests of the public. The imposition of conditions on property sought to be rezoned may not be classified as a prospective commitment on the part of the municipality to zone as requested if the conditions are met; nor would the municipality necessarily be precluded on this account from later reversing or altering its decision (cf. Matter of Grimpel Assoc. v. Cohalan, 41 N.Y.2d 431).

Yet another criticism leveled at conditional zoning is that the State enabling legislation does not confer on local authorities authorization to enact conditional zoning amendments (see, e.g., Houston Petroleum Co. v. Automotive Prods. Credit Assn., 9 N.Y. 122, supra; Baylis v. City of Baltimore, 219 Md. 164, supra). On this view any such ordinance would be ultra vires. While it is accurate to say there exists no explicit authorization that a legislative body may attach conditions to zoning amendments (see, e.g., Village Law, §7-700 et seq.), neither is there any language which expressly forbids a local legislature to do so. Statutory silence is not necessarily a denial of the authority to engage in such a practice. Where in the face of nonaddress in the enabling legislation there exists independent justification for the practice as an appropriate exercise of municipal power, that power will be implied. Conditional rezoning is a means of achieving some degree of flexibility in land-use control by minimizing the potentially deleterious effect of a zoning change on neighboring properties; reasonably conceived conditions harmonize the landowner's need for rezoning with the public interest and certainly fall within the spirit of the enabling legislation (see Church v. Town of Islip, 8 N.Y.2d 254, *supra*).

One final concern of those reluctant to uphold the practice is that resort to conditional rezoning carries with it no inherent restrictions apart from the restrictive agreement itself. This fear, however, is justifiable only if conditional rezoning is considered a contractual relationship between municipality and private party, outside the scope of the zoning power—a view to which we do not subscribe. When conditions are incorporated in an amending ordinance, the result is as much a "zoning regulation" as an ordinance adopted without conditions. Just as the scope of all zoning regulation is limited by the police power, and thus local legislative bodies must act reasonably and in the best interests of public safety, welfare and convenience (Village of Euclid v. Ambler Realty Co., 272 U.S. 365, 387; Matter of New York Inst. of Technology v. Le Boutillier, 33 N.Y.2d 125, 130; Matter of Concordia Coll. Inst. v. Miller, 301 N.Y. 189, 196), the scope of permissible conditions must of necessity be similarly limited. If, upon proper proof, the conditions imposed are found unreasonable, the rezoning amendment as well as the required conditions would have to be nullified, with the affected property reverting to the preamendment zoning classification. [52 N.Y.2d at 599-603]

Cf. also Sylvania Electric Products, Inc. v. City of Newton, 344 Mass. 428, 183 N.E.2d 118 (1962); Scrutton v. County of Sacramento, 275 Cal. App. 2d 412, 79 Cal. Rptr. 872 (1969); Goffinet v. County of Christian, 30 Ill. App. 3d 1089, 333 N.E.2d 731 (1975), *aff'd,* 65 Ill. 2d 40, 357 N.E.2d 442 (1976).

5.   Cat-skinning may be done several ways. Suppose that the property owner (P) wants rezoning so he can run a service station, and the city (C) wants assurance that P will not use the property differently. Discuss from each party's vantage the strengths and weaknesses of the following arrangements:

(a) P for himself, his heirs, etc., covenants that the land will remain a service station for twenty-five years if C rezones the parcel to commercial use. P records the covenant. C rezones the parcel. (Unilateral contract).

(b) P for himself, his heirs, etc., covenants that the land will remain a service station for twenty-five years, and C promises to rezone the parcel to commercial use. The parties record the agreement. C rezones the parcel. (Bilateral contract.)

(c) P for himself, his heirs, etc. covenants that the land will remain a
service station for twenty-five years. P records the covenant. C rezones the parcel.

(d) C rezones the parcel on condition that P record a covenant restricting use to a service station for twenty-five years. P records the covenant.

Cf. Comment, Contract and Conditional Zoning: A Tool for Zoning
Flexibility, 23 Hastings L.J. 825 (1972).

6. In commenting on the *Baylis* case, one writer advised circumspection
if lawmakers wanted their actions to survive judicial review:

> If the legislative body of a municipality has permitted the rezoning on condition,
> the courts are disposed to allow it except in those cases where it is crudely
> handled. . . . It is difficult, of course, to overcome the objection of a contract
> where the express condition is set out in the ordinance in such manner that it
> looks like an offer and an acceptance. However, these appearances can be re-
> moved and the result still accomplished. Zoning is independent of deed restric-
> tions, and rezoning made unlikely because of neighborhood protest stands a good
> chance if the neighbors stay home from the hearing because petitioner has ex-
> ecuted a deed restriction running in their favor. The existence of the restrictive
> covenant could be mentioned by-the-by at the hearing. The objection might also
> be cured by the simple strategem of having the condition imposed by the plan
> commission before it will give approval. In any event, if the municipality gets
> what it wants, it seems unnecessary and risky to state the condition in the ordi-
> nance. [Hagman, Wisconsin Zoning Practice 11 (1962)]

7. "Many planning commission hearings have taken on the character
of an oriental bazaar where applicants wheel and deal with the commission on
conditions and restrictions to be imposed on zoning. Some hearings are more
like the ancient circuses in the coliseum of Rome in the days of Nero except
that the Christians then got a better deal from the lions than some applicants
do from the planning commission. Now instead of thumbs down or up the
planning commissioner asks for show of hands." Michalski, Zoning—The National Peril, paper presented at the 1963 ASPO National Planning Conference, Planning 1963, American Society of Planning Officials.

8. Ordinarily, a conditional rezoning ordinance will provide for its automatic repeal should the benefited landowner fail to carry out the conditions.
In at least one instance, however, a court has held that the ordinance of repeal
(after a purported violation) was a nullity since it did not comply with the
statutory requirements of notice, hearing and posting of the proposed zoning
change. Stiriz v. Stout, 210 N.Y.S.2d 325 (Sup. Ct. 1960).

Often the benefited landowner covenants not to oppose repeal should he
violate the conditions. Does the burden of his covenant run with the land? Cf.
Comment, Contract and Conditional Zoning: A Tool for Zoning Flexibility,
23 Hastings L.J. 825, 837 (1972).

Having imposed the conditions, may a local body subsequently waive them without enacting new legislation?

9.   For further reading: Shapiro, The Case for Conditional Zoning, 41 Temp. L.Q. 267 (1968); Comment, The Use and Abuse of Contract Zoning, 12 U.C.L.A.L. Rev. 896 (1965); Trager, Contract Zoning, 23 Md. L. Rev. 121 (1963); Note, Zoning Amendments and Variances Subject to Conditions, 12 Syracuse L. Rev. 230 (1960); R. Babcock, The Zoning Game (1966), chs. 1, 3.

§17.5   Cluster Zoning

CHRINKO v. SOUTH BRUNSWICK TWP. PLANNING BD.
77 N.J. Super. 594, 187 A.2d 221 (1963)

FURMAN, J.S.C. This prerogative writ action contests the validity of two ordinances of South Brunswick Township in Middlesex County permitting cluster or open space zoning. By their terms a subdivision developer may reduce minimum lot sizes by 20% or 30% and minimum frontages by 10% or 20% upon his concurrently deeding 20% or 30% of the subdivided tract for parks, school sites and other public purposes, with the approval of the planning board.

South Brunswick Township is in the western section of Middlesex County abutting Somerset and Mercer Counties. Its land area is over 41 square miles. The New Jersey Turnpike, three main arterial highways and the main line of the Pennsylvania Railroad bisect the township. Once predominantly agricultural, with settled communities at Kingston, Dayton, Monmouth Junction and Deans, South Brunswick has experienced an estimated doubling of its population in the three years between 1957 and 1960 and an onrush of new industry and commercial establishments, particularly along highways.

Downtown New York and downtown Philadelphia are within a radius of 35 miles, drawn from South Brunswick Township. The urban sprawl from the New York metropolitan area reaches within a few miles of the township on the north and east. Residential developments for the wage earners of Philadelphia, Trenton and vicinity are pushing towards South Brunswick from the south and west. Kendall Park, which was developed recently for one-family housing on lots approximately 13,500 square feet, now holds about 40% of the population of South Brunswick Township in an area slightly over one square mile along the northern boundary.

A similar project, Brunswick Acres, is proposed for a 235-acre tract in the Residential 20 Zone in the northeast corner of the township. This development is interwined with the legal and factual issues before the court. The plaintiffs contend that the cluster or open space ordinances were enacted for the special benefit of the owner, Yenom[5] Corporation. The defendants' position is that they responded with reasonable legislation, general in effect, to the problem of large subdivision developments without land areas available for schools, recreation areas and green spaces.

Facing multiple housing developments and a population upsurge, the South Brunswick Planning Board authorized a master plan from a firm of planning consultants in 1960. The master plan report, which recommended balanced growth, was submitted in late 1961. No master plan has been adopted. On the subject of cluster or open space zoning, the master plan report suggested an optional system parallel to that enacted in the zoning ordinances under attack here, but applicable only in zones with a minimum lot size of 45,000 square feet and allowing reductions of minimum lot sizes but not minimum frontages. The planning consultants label this recommended scheme "density zoning," stressing that no more homes can be built in a subdivision despite smaller size lots, because the land thus saved must be deeded to the municipality. . . .

Cluster or density zoning should meet judicial sanction as an implementation of the zoning and planning power to deal with a current and increasing problem, large subdivisions in previously rural communities. The Legislature has vested municipalities with legislative power in the field of zoning and planning pursuant to N.J. Const. Art. IV, §VI, par. 2. By specific delegation from the Legislature in N.J.S.A. 40:55-30 a municipality may: ". . . regulate and restrict the height, number of stories, and sizes of buildings, and other structures, the percentage of lot that may be occupied, the sizes of yards, courts, and other open spaces, the density of population, and the location and use and extent of use of buildings and structures and land for trade, industry, residence, or other purposes."

Although the state zoning law does not in so many words empower municipalities to provide an option to developers for cluster or density zoning, such an ordinance reasonably advances the legislative purposes of securing open spaces, preventing overcrowding and undue concentration of population, and promoting the general welfare. Nor is it an objection that uniformity of regulation is required within a zoning district, N.J.S.A. 40:55-31. Such a legislative technique accomplishes uniformity because the option is open to all developers within a zoning district, and escapes the vice that it is compulsory, Midtown Properties, Inc. v. Madison Tp., 68 N.J. Super. 197, 210, 172 A.2d 40 (Law. Div. 1961).

Zoning ordinances in rapidly growing municipalities may be founded on an outmoded concept that houses will be built one at a time for individual owners in accordance with zoning regulations, with latitude for variances in hardship or other exceptional cases, and that the municipality can take steps whenever warranted to acquire school, park and other public sites. Such a gradual and controlled development is not practicable in many municipalities

---

5. Yenom, backwards, spells. . . .—ED.

today. Confronted with a subdivision plan for several hundred homes in a tract meeting all water drainage, sanitation and other conditions, a municipality must anticipate school needs but without lands set aside for that purpose; it must anticipate a large population concentration without recreation areas, parks or green spaces, or lands for firehouses or other public purposes. Cluster or density zoning is an attempted solution, dependent, as set up in the South Brunswick zoning ordinance, upon the agreement of the large-scale developer whose specific monetary benefit may be only that he saves on street installation costs.

Other principles favoring cluster or density zoning are the presumption of validity attaching to zoning as well as other legislation, Ward v. Montgomery Tp., 28 N.J. 529, 539, 147 A.2d 248 (1959), and the liberal construction to be accorded to the powers of municipal corporations, including those granted by necessary or fair implication or incident to those expressly conferred, under the N.J. Const. Art. IV, §VII, par. 11.

In the pleadings and at the trial of this action the plaintiffs sought to establish that South Brunswick Township enacted the cluster or open space zoning ordinance for the special benefit of Yenom Corporation, not for one or more of the statutory zoning purposes, and without adequate consideration by the planning board.

The Brunswick Acres developer received preliminary approval of a subdivision of 526 lots with a minimum lot size of 13,500 square feet on December 9, 1959. The zoning ordinance at that time authorized minimum lot sizes of 13,500 square feet in the Residential 20 Zone, contingent upon an adequate water supply and sewage system. Otherwise the minimum lot size in the Residential 20 Zone was 20,000 square feet. By amendment in 1960 a minimum lot size of 20,000 square feet was fixed for all properties in the Residential 20 Zone.

Municipal officials were concerned with the prospect of 500 or so families moving into Brunswick Acres at the rate of 200 or 250 a year without adequate school or park sites, in accordance with the preliminary approval which extended for three years. N.J.S.A. 40:55-1.18. The experience stemming from the Kendall Park development had revealed how critical the problem was of rapid expansion in school population. Meetings were held between representatives of the township committee and planning board on one side and of Yenom Corporation on the other side in the late spring of 1962. A paramount object of these meetings was to work out terms for final approval of the Brunswick Acres subdivision, with an understanding that houses would be constructed at a rate acceptable to the municipality and that lands for public uses would be made available, in addition to the ten acres to be deeded as a school site under an agreement corollary to the preliminary approval.

Coordination of these objectives with the density control zoning concept of the master plan report was discussed and favored. Yenom Corporation submitted plans for the Brunswick Acres development embodying smaller lot sizes and extensive areas for public lands in July and August. The planning board informally rejected an initial proposal because the public lands were not suitable, apparently because of their location or drainage problems. On August 25, 1962, despite a petition with 500 signatures filed with the planning board by Joseph Rauch, one of the plaintiffs here, the planning board passed a resolution requesting the township committee to enact a zoning ordinance amendment to authorize plans such as the amended Brunswick Acres plan. At the same meeting the planning board specified 22 requirements to be fulfilled prior to final approval of Brunswick Acres, including, e.g., State Water Policy and Supply Division certification of the realignment, widening and deepening of Oakey's Brook, which meanders through the tract. Many of the 22 requirements are imposed under the Municipal Planning Act. L. 1953, c. 433, N.J.S.A. 40:55-1.1 et seq.

The South Brunswick Township Planning Board at its next meeting on September 11, 1962 adopted a second resolution endorsing specifically and recommending to the township committee enactment of a cluster or open space amendment to the zoning ordinance. Such an amendment was passed on first reading as ordinance No. 19-62 on September 18, 1962, with the accompanying ordinance No. 20-62. The planning board approved the two ordinances on September 26, 1962. Final passage by the township committee took place on October 2, 1962.

Yenom Corporation has submitted a new subdivision plan in accordance with the cluster or open space zoning amendment, with planning board action on final approval awaiting the outcome here. Any issue as to the specific terms of the amended subdivision plan or the right to build on 20% less than 13,500-square-foot lots is not within the framework of this prerogative writ action. Throughout the trial plaintiff conceded the applicability of ordinance No. 19-62 to 13,500-square-foot lot sizes on the Brunswick Acres tract, thus permitting construction of houses on 10,800-square-foot lots if the builder availed itself of the cluster or open space zoning option.

The broad charge that ordinances Nos. 19-62 and 20-62 were enacted to advance the special interest of Yenom Corporation is without support in the proof. Admittedly, the Brunswick Acres development was predominantly in the minds of Jack Stein, chairman of the planning board, and other municipal officials prior to the planning board resolutions and zoning ordinance amendments.

To avoid the consequences of a drastic expansion in population without green spaces or adequate school or other public sites, the municipality sought relief through legislation. The deadline of December 9, 1962 for final approval of the first Yenom Corporation plan was a significant consideration. Rebutting the contention that municipal officials acted in the interest of Yenom Corporation, not that of the municipality, are the statements of various officials on the witness stand that they voted for ordinances Nos. 19-62 and 20-62 because of projected growth, need for school sites, need for recreation sites and parklands and reduction of street maintenance costs.

The benefits to Yenom Corporation, other than a saving in street construction costs, are obscure. The same number of homes may be constructed, but on smaller lots. Lands aceptable to the planning board, including at least one five-acre parcel, must be deeded to the municipality. The paramount concern of the municipal officials, as one of them graphically described, was to avoid a "bad deal," the Brunswick Acres plan for 526 homes on 13,500-square-foot lots with only ten acres reserved for public use. Such an objective is valid, if enacted as ordinance No. 19-62 was enacted, as general, not special, legislation.

By overwhelming authority otherwise vald legislation is not nullified because it accomplishes an incidental benefit to one or a few private individuals. Kozesnik v. Montgomery Tp., 24 N.J. 154, 173, 131 A.2d 1 (1957); State v. Garden State Racing Ass'n, 136 N.J.L. 173, 54 A.2d 916 (E. & A. 1947), and 2 Sutherland, Statutory Construction, §2107, p. 27 (1943). The enactment of the cluster or open space zoning ordinance is concluded to have been in good faith, in accordance with legislative objectives in zoning and with only incidental benefit to Yenom Corporation as an individual developer.

The specific points raised by the plaintiffs, in support of the argument that the municipal officials favored Yenom Corporations, are that cluster or open space zoning deviates from the master plan report, that there are surface and subsurface drainage problems on the Brunswick Acres tract, that there are other lands available for public uses in the municipality, and that Yenom Corporation should have proceeded by application for a zoning variance.

Deviations from a master plan report are not fatal. Professional advice supports the good faith of a municipal governing body in promulgating a zoning ordinance or master plan, S & L Associates, Inc. v. Washington Twp., 61 N.J. Super. 312, 324, 160 A.2d 635 (App. Div. 1960), but it need not be followed to the letter. The legislative decision is the township's, not the planning consultant's. Testimony here amply supported the modifications of the master plan report. South Brunswick Township officials considered that cluster or density zoning was more advantageous in zoning districts permitting smaller lot sizes, with intensified school and parkland needs, and that reduction of minimum frontage as well as minimum lot size requirements, by smaller percentages, was a practical adjustment.

The master plan report advocated industrial-research zoning for the northeast corner of the township, including the proposed Brunswick Acres site, but this was in fact part of the Residential 20 Zone for which there was a pending and valid preliminary approval for a large subdivision for residential development.

Various engineers and soil specialists testified at the trial on the limitations of Brunswick Acres tract for dwelling sites because of flooding and drainage problems. The consensus was that these could be overcome, but no advantage facilitating building is discernible because of the cluster or open space amendments.

Public ownership of other lands in the 41 square miles of South Brunswick Township is of little relevance. One 74-acre tract, inaccessible by any road and spongy in soil texture, is in the Sand Hills area between Kendall Park and Brunswick Acres. While it may be of future value for public use in the municipality, the existence of this tract is not support for the claim that the cluster or open spacing zoning ordinance was enacted in the private interests of Yenom Corporation and not for valid legislative purposes.

Ordinance No. 19-62 is applicable in 60 to 65% of the land area in South Brunswick Township. Proper procedure was followed in amending the zoning ordinance to accomplish such a broad scale revision. Judicial decisions striking down zoning ordinances because they constitute spot zoning and by-pass the board of adjustment deal with single parcels or limited areas. Conlon v. Bd. of Public Works, Paterson, 11 N.J. 363, 94 A.2d 660 (1953); cf. Kozesnik v. Montgomery Tp., 24 N.J. 154, 131 A.2d 1 (1957). . . .

For all the foregoing reasons decision is in favor of the defendants. Will counsel submit an order.

NOTES AND QUESTIONS

1. Cluster development breaks with the pattern of each house to its own minimum-sized lot. Without adding to the area's overall housing density, the cluster subdivision usually contains many "undersized" lots; land spared from development may then retain its natural setting or become available for community facilities. See Figure 9. Apart from these advantages, the cluster concept invites considerable variety in both tract design and housing types, reduces street and utility installation costs, and, for the individual lot-owner, may even make grass-cutting and gardening a less onerous chore.

Radburn, New Jersey, begun in 1928, is a prototype cluster development. Its 149 acres contain 788 sites, 638 single-family detached, 50 duplex units, and 100 apartment units. There are also 23 acres of interior parks, which include two pools, three ballfields, and four tennis courts. All residents belong to the Radburn Association; members pay an annual assessment to maintain the common area. Urban Land Institute, The Homes Association Handbook 73-75 (Tech. Bull. 50, 1964).

Homebuilders, conservationists, and planners ardently inveigh against the rigidity of minimum lot-size zoning. See, e.g., Outdoor Recreation Resources Review Commission, Outdoor Recreation for America 150 (1962); W. Whyte, Cluster Development (1964).

Although cluster development has already gained wide acceptance, its proposed entry into a new area often means grim intransigence. What fears underlie such opposition?

2. The New York legislature has placed its imprimatur upon the clus-

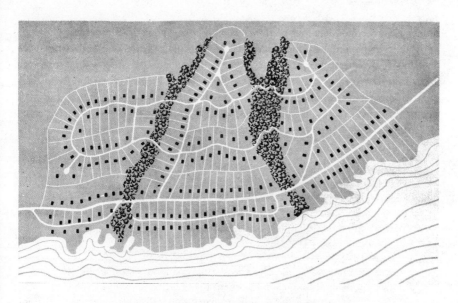

The same number of families can be accommodated in the cluster development below as in the conventional subdivision above.

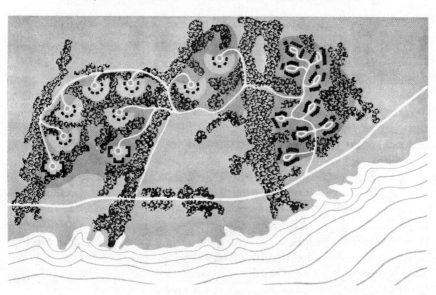

Source: Outdoor Recreation Resources Review Commission, Outdoor Recreation for America 151 (1962).

[FIGURE 9]

ter concept. The 1963 session amended Town Law §281 so that it now reads in part:

> The town board is hereby empowered by resolution to authorize the planning board, simultaneously with the approval of a plat or plats pursuant to this article, to modify applicable provisions of the zoning ordinance, subject to the conditions hereinafter set forth and such other reasonable conditions as the town board may in its discretion add thereto. . . . The purposes of such authorization shall be to enable and encourage flexibility of design and development of land in such a manner as to promote the most appropriate use of land to facilitate the adequate and economical provision of streets and utilities, and to preserve the natural and scenic qualities of open lands. The conditions hereinabove referred to are as follows:
>
> (a) If the owner makes written application for the use of this procedure, it may be followed at the discretion of the planning board if, in said board's judgment, its application would benefit the town.
>
> (b) This procedure shall be applicable only to lands zoned for residential purposes, and its application shall result in a permitted number of dwelling units which shall in no case exceed the number which could be permitted, in the planning board's judgment, if the land were subdivided into lots conforming to the minimum lot size and density requirements of the zoning ordinance applicable to the district or districts in which such land is situated and conforming to all other applicable requirements.
>
> (c) The dwelling units permitted may be, at the discretion of the planning board and subject to the conditions set forth by the town board, in detached, semi-detached, attached, or multi-story structures.
>
> (d) In the event that the application of this procedure results in a plat showing lands available for park, recreation, open space, or other municipal purposes directly related to the plat, then the planning board as a condition of plat approval may establish such conditions on the ownership, use and maintenance of such lands as it deems necessary to assure the preservation of such lands for their intended purposes. The town board may require that such conditions shall be approved by the town board before the plat may be approved for filing.

An earlier, less precise version of §281 was attacked as lacking sufficient standards for a lawful delegation of legislative power. A lower court rejected this contention, but ruled that the planning board had exceeded its authority by approving 49 homesites on a part of the parcel (33.1 acres) zoned for one-acre lots. In all, 100 acres were affected by the change. The developer intended to dedicate 37.4 acres for park purposes, and to build 79 homes on the remaining land. The plan seemed to satisfy the requirement that the total number of dwelling units not be increased, but the court excluded from its computation the land dedicated for park purposes. Matter of Hiscox v. Levine, 31 Misc. 2d 151, 216 N.Y.S.2d 801 (Sup. Ct. 1961). This decision prompted the more explicit language of revised §281.

3. Shouldn't you regard cluster zoning as a primitive scheme for the transfer of development rights? Cf. pages 732-733 and 865-866, *supra*.

§17.6   The "Floating Zone"—Planned Unit Development (PUDs)

In the more than half-century since *Euclid*, the scale of land development has grown enormously: huge subdivisions instead of the custom-built house; regional shopping centers instead of the commercial block; industrial parks instead of the factory building. Increased scale has also brought diversity within the development: a multiplicity of housing types; homes plus convenience shopping, parks, and schools; the entry of office buildings and motels into the shopping center. It is no surprise that a Euclidian straightjacket, which makes a priori judgments as to the use of every parcel, and which biases against many mixtures of land use because it cannot readily distinguish harmful mixtures from beneficial ones, does not serve present-day planning realities as well as zoning should. Subdivision control helps some, for it allows an administrative agency to make fairly fine decisions as to design and location, but it does not allow for use diversity, since the agency has no power to suspend the use restrictions of the underlying ordinances. Cluster zoning, §17.5 *supra,* suffers the same limitation.

The arrival of zoning for planned unit developments (PUDs) has helped significantly to loosen the Euclidian bind. PUDs may be residential, nonresidential, or mixtures thereof; invariably PUDs occupy relatively large plots (twenty acres or more); and, significantly, PUD districts often do not appear on the zoning map until after a landowner assembles acreage and applies to the governing body for permission to develop his parcel. It is this aspect of PUD that gives rise to the concept of "floating zone" and has caused legal problems not unrelated to those we have already discussed in connection with exceptions and conditional rezoning.

Eves v. Zoning Board of Adjustment of Lower Gwynedd Township, 401 Pa. 211, 164 A.2d 7 (1960), gave PUD theory an initial jolt. The influential Pennsylvania Supreme Court found a PUD ordinance doubly wanting: the state enabling law did not enable it; worse still, it violated the "comprehensive plan" requirement.

At issue in *Eves* was the "F-1" zone, a limited industrial district that the town board could map anywhere in Lower Gwyned, upon application of a landowner who satisfied various statutory criteria: a parcel 25 acres or larger; a "single architectural scheme"; a ceiling on lot coverage; prescribed building setbacks; satisfactory parking, landscaping, and buffering. In April 1958, the board authorized F-1 zoning (Ordinance 28). In September 1958, an industrial concern sought F-1 approval for its 103-acre tract within an A-residential zone. Despite 300 protesting residents at the public hearing, the board approved the zone change (Ordinance 34), whereupon Eves sued to invalidate the two ordinances.

On the "comprehensive plan" issue, the court's opinion reads:

> The adoption of a procedure whereby it is decided which areas of land will eventually be zoned "F-1" Limited Industrial Districts on a case by case basis

patently admits that at the point of enactment of Ordinance 28 there was no orderly plan of particular land use for the community. Final determination under such a scheme would expressly await solicitation by individual landowners, thus making the planned land use of the community dependent upon its development. In other words, the development itself would become the plan, which is manifestly the antithesis of zoning "in accordance with a comprehensive plan."

Several secondary evils of such a scheme are cogently advanced by counsel for the appellants. It would situations in which the personal predilections of the supervisors or the affluence or political power of the applicant would have a greater part in determining rezoning applications than the suitability of the land for a particular use from an overall community point of view. Further, while it may not be readily apparent with a minimum acreage requirement of 25 acres, "flexible selective zoning" carries evils akin to "spot zoning," for in theory it allows piecemeal placement of relatively small acreage areas in differently zoned districts. Finally, because of the absence of a simultaneous delineation of the boundaries of the new "F-1" district, no notice of the true nature of his vicinity or its limitations is afforded the property owner or the prospective property owner. While it is undoubtedly true that a property owner has no vested interest in an existing zoning map and, accordingly, is always subject to the possibility of a rezoning without notice, the zoning ordinance and its accompanying zoning maps should nevertheless at any given time reflect the current planned use of the community's land so as to afford as much notice as possible.

The *Eves* setback launched a torrent of academic criticism, led by Professor Krasnowiecki of the University of Pennsylvania School of Law.[6] Planners and builders were together on this one as well, and other communities, undaunted by *Eves*, ventured PUD zoning. In Donahue v. Zoning Bd. of Adjustment, 412 Pa. 332, 194 A.2d 610 (1963), the Pennsylvania Supreme Court seemed to retreat on the *Eves* front. Five years later, the court had still another chance to consider the PUD problem.

CHENEY v. VILLAGE 2 AT NEW HOPE, INC.

429 Pa. 626, 241 A.2d 81 (1968)

ROBERTS, J. Under traditional concepts of zoning the task of determining the type, density and placement of buildings which should exist within any given zoning district devolves upon the local legislative body. In order that this body might have to speak only infrequently on the issue of municipal planning and zoning, the local legislature usually enacts detailed requirements for the type, size and location of buildings within each given zoning district, and leaves the ministerial task of enforcing these regulations to an appointed

6. See, e.g., Krasnowiecki, Planned Unit Development: A Challenge to Established Theory and Practice of Land Use Control, 114 U. Pa. L. Rev. 47 (1965); Haar and Hering, The Lower Gwynedd Township Case: Too Flexible Zoning or an Inflexible Judiciary? 74 Harv. L. Rev. 1552 (1961); Reno, Non-Euclidian Zoning: The Uses of the Floating Zone, 23 Md. L. Rev. 105 (1963).

zoning administrator, with another administrative body, the zoning board of adjustment, passing on individual deviations from the strict district requirements, deviations known commonly as variances and special exceptions. At the same time, the overall rules governing the dimensions, placement, etc. of primarily public additions to ground, e.g., streets, sewers, playgrounds, are formulated by the local legislature through the passage of subdivision regulations. These regulations are enforced and applied to individual lots by an administrative body usually known as the planning commission.

This general approach to zoning fares reasonably well so long as development takes place on a lot-by-lot basis, and so long as no one cares that the overall appearance of the municipality resembles the design achieved by using a cookie cutter on a sheet of dough. However, with the increasing popularity of large scale residential developments, particularly in suburban areas, it has become apparent to many local municipalities that land can be more efficiently used, and developments more aesthetically pleasing, if zoning regulations focus on density requirements rather than on specific rules for each individual lot. Under density zoning, the legislature determines what percentage of a particular district must be devoted to open space, for example, and what percentage used for dwelling units. The task of filling in the particular district with real houses and real open spaces then falls upon the planning commission usually working in conjunction with an individual large scale developer. See Chrinko v. South Brunswick Twp. Planning Bd., 77 N.J. Super. 594, 187 A.2d 221 (1963). The ultimate goal of this so-called density or cluster concept of zoning is achieved when an entire self-contained little community is permitted to be built within a zoning district, with the rules of density controlling not only the relation of private dwellings to open space, but also the relation of homes to commercial establishments such as theaters, hotels, restaurants, and quasi-commercial uses such as schools and churches. The present controversy before this Court involves a frontal attack upon one of these zoning districts, known in the trade as a Planned Unit Development (hereinafter PUD).

Spurred by the desire of appellant developer to construct a Planned Unit Development in the Borough of New Hope, in December of 1964 Borough Council began considering the passage of a new zoning ordinance to establish a PUD district in New Hope. After extensive consultation with appellant, council referred the matter to the New Hope Planning Commission for further study. This body, approximately six months after the project idea was first proposed, formally recommended to council that a PUD district be created. Council consulted with members of the Bucks County Planning Commission on the text of the proposed ordinance, held public hearings, and finally on June 14, 1965 enacted ordinance 160 which created the PUD district, and ordinance 161 which amended the Borough zoning map, rezoning a large tract of land known as the Rauch farm from low density residential to PUD. Pursuant to the procedural requirements of ordinance 160, appellant presented plans for a Planned United Development on the Rauch tract to the

Borough Planning Commission. These plans were approved on November 8, 1965, and accordingly four days later two building permits, known as zoning permits 68 and 69, were issued to appellant. (Some question exists as to the current status of these permits, see text *infra*.) Subsequently, permit number 75 was issued. Appellees, all neighboring property owners opposing the issuance of these permits, appealed to the zoning board of adjustment. The board, after taking extensive testimony, upheld ordinances 160 and 161 and accordingly affirmed the issuance of the permits. Appellees then appealed to the Bucks County Court of Common Pleas. That tribunal took no additional testimony, but reversed the board, holding the ordinances invalid for failure to conform to a comprehensive plan and for vesting too much discretion in the New Hope Planning Commission. This Court granted certiorari under Supreme Court Rule 68½.

The procedural posture of this case is identical to that of National Land & Investment Co. v. Easttown Twp. Bd. of Adjustment, 419 Pa. 504, 523, 215 A.2d 597, 607 (1965). Our scope of review may thus be stated by reference to that decision: "The zoning enabling act being silent as to a right of appeal, we consider this case on broad certiorari, reviewing the testimony, the evidence, and the entire record. Keystone Raceway Corp. v. State Harness Racing Comm'n, 405 Pa. 1, 173 A.2d 97 (1961); Schmidt v. Philadelphia Zoning Bd. of Adjustment, 382 Pa. 521, 114 A.2d 902 (1955). Because the court below took no additional testimony, we will look at the decision of the board of adjustment to determine if, in upholding . . . [ordinances 160 and 161], the board committed an abuse of discretion or an error of law. Upper Providence Twp. Appeal, 414 Pa. 46, 198 A.2d 522 (1964)." Applying this standard, we hold that no error of law or abuse of discretion was committed by the New Hope Board of Adjustment, and that therefore the Court of Common Pleas of Bucks County must be reversed.

I

Approximately one year before the PUD seed was planted in New Hope, Borough Council had approved the New Hope Comprehensive Plan. This detailed land use projection clearly envisioned the Rauch tract as containing only single family dwellings of low density. The court below therefore concluded that the enactment of ordinance 160, and more specifically the placing of a PUD district on the Rauch tract by ordinance 161 was not "in accordance with a comprehensive plan," as required by the Act of February 1, 1966, P.L. (1965)—§3203, 53 P.S. §48203. See also Eves v. Zoning Bd. of Adjustment, 401 Pa. 211, 164 A.2d 7 (1960).

The fallacy in the court's reasoning lies in its mistaken belief that a comprehensive plan, once established, is forever binding on the municipality and can never be amended. Cases subsequent to *Eves* have made it clear, however, that these plans may be changed by the passage of new zoning ordinances, provided the local legislature passes the new ordinance with some demonstration of sensitivity to the community as a whole, and the impact that the new ordinance will have on this community. As Mr. Chief Justice Bell so artfully stated in Furniss v. Lower Merion Twp., 412 Pa. 404, 406, 194 A.2d 926, 927 (1963): "It is a matter of common sense and reality that a comprehensive plan is not like the law of the Medes and the Persians; it must be subject to reasonable change from time to time as conditions in an area or a township or a large neighborhood change." This salutary rule that comprehensive plans may be later amended by the passage of new zoning ordinances has been approved not only in *Furniss*, but also in Donahue v. Zoning Bd. of Adjustment, 412 Pa. 332, 194 A.2d 610 (1963) and Key Realty Co. Zoning Case, 408 Pa. 98, 182 A.2d 187 (1962).

Given this rule of law allowing post-plan zoning charges, and the presumption in favor of an ordinance's validity, see *National Land, supra*, 421 Pa. at 521-522, 215 A.2d at 607, we are not in a position, having reviewed the record in the present case, to say that the zoning board committed an abuse of discretion or an error of law when it concluded that ordinances 160 and 161 were properly passed. Presented as it was with evidence that the PUD district had been under consideration by council for over six months and had been specifically recommended by the borough planning commission, a body specially equipped to view proposed ordinances as they relate to the rest of the community, we hold that the board, within its sound discretion, could have concluded that council passed the ordinances with the proper overall considerations in mind. The PUD district established by ordinance 160 is not the type of use which by its very nature could have no place in the middle of a predominantly residential borough. It is not a steel mill, a fat rendering plant, or a desiccated egg factory. It is, in fact, nothing more than a miniature residential community.

Closely tied to the comprehensive plan issue is the argument raised by appellees that ordinances 160 and 161 constitute spot zoning outlawed by *Eves, supra*. Given the fact situation in *Eves*, however, as well as the post-*Eves* cases, we do not believe that there is any spot zoning here. In *Eves*, the municipality created a limited industrial district, F-1, which, by explicit legislature pronouncement, was not to be applied to any particular tract until the individual land owner requested that his own tract be so re-zoned. The obvious evil in this procedure did *not* lie in the fact that a limited industrial district might be placed in an area previously zoned, for example, residential. The evil was the *pre-ordained* uncertainty as to where the F-1 districts would crop up. The ordinance all but invited spot zoning hwere the legislature could respond to private entreaties from land owners and re-zone tracts F-1 without regard to the surrounding community. In *Eves*, it was almost impossible for the F-1 districts to conform to a comprehensive plan since tract would be re-zoned on a strictly ad hoc basis.

Quite to the contrary, no such "floating zone" exists in the present case. On the very day that the PUD district was created by ordinance 160, it was brought to earth by ordinance 161; and, as discussed *supra*, this *was* done "in

accordance with a comprehensive plan." Speaking of a similar procedure in
Donahue v. Zoning Bd. of Adjustment, 412 Pa. 332, 194 A.2d 610 (1963), this
Court faced squarely an attack based upon *Eves* and responded thusly:

> It was this case by case review [in *Eves*] which demonstrated the absence of
> a comprehensive plan and which sought to enable the Board of Supervisors [the
> local legislative body] to exercise powers they did not statutorily possess.
>
> In the instant case, the new classification was established and the zoning
> map amended within a very short period of time [in the case at bar, on the same
> day]. Under the rules of statutory construction which are likewise applicable to
> ordinances, see Cloverleaf Trailer Sales Co. v. Pleasant Hills Borough, 366 Pa.
> 116, 76 A.2d 872 (1950); Philadelphia to Use of Polselli v. Phillips, 179 Pa.
> Super. 87, 116 A.2d 243 (1955); these ordinances should be read together as one
> enactment. See Statutory Construction Act, May 28, 1937, P.L. 1019, §62, 46
> P.S. §562, 1952. So construed, Ordinances 151 [creating new zone] and 155
> [amending zoning map] do not create the "floating zone," anchored only upon
> case by case application by landowners, which we struck down in *Eves*. While it
> is true that the change here was made upon request of a particular landowner,
> this does not necessarily create the evils held invalid in *Eves* where the defects
> were specifically created by the very terms of the ordinances. It is not unusual for
> a zoning change to be made on request of a landowner, and such change is not
> invalid if made in accordance with a comprehensive plan (412 Pa. at 334-335,
> 194 A.2d at 611)

We think *Donahue* is completely controlling on the issue of alleged spot zoning
and compels the conclusion that ordinances 160 and 161 do not fall on that
ground. See also the excellent discussion of *Eves* and its progeny in Krasnowiecki, Legal Aspects of Planned Unit Development, Technical Bull. 52, Urban Land Institute, pp. 20-22 (1965).

II

The court below next concluded that even if the two ordinances were
properly *passed,* they must fall as vesting authority in the planning commission
greater than that permitted under Pennsylvania's zoning enabling legislation.
More specifically, it is now contended by appellees that complete project approval by the planning commission under ordinance 160 requires that commission to encroach upon legislative territory whenever it decides where,
within a particular PUD district, specific types of building should be placed.

In order to appreciate fully the arguments of counsel on both sides it is
necessary to explain in some detail exactly what is permitted within a PUD
district, and who decides whether a particular land owner has complied with
these requirements. Admittedly the range of permissible uses with the PUD
district is greater than that normally found in a traditional zoning district.
Within a New Hope PUD district there may be: single family attached or
detached dwellings; apartments; accessory private garages; public or private

parks and recreation areas including golf courses, swimming pools, ski slopes, etc. (so long as these facilities do not produce noise, glare, odor, air pollution, etc., detrimental to existing or prospective adjacent structures); a municipal building; a school; churches; art galleries; professional offices; certain types of signs; a theatre (but not a drive-in); motels and hotels; and a restaurant. The ordinance then sets certain overall density requirements. The PUD district may have a maximum of 80% of the land devoted to residential uses, a maximum of 20% for the permitted commercial uses and enclosed recreational facilities, and must have a minimum of 20% for open spaces. The residential density shall not exceed 10 units per acre, nor shall any such unit contain more than two bedrooms. All structures within the district must not exceed maximum height standards set out in the ordinance. Finally, although there are no traditional "set back" and "side yard" requirements, ordinance 160 does require that there be 24 feet between structures, and that no townhouse structure contain more than 12 dwelling units.

The procedure to be followed by the aspiring developer reduces itself to presenting a detailed plan for his planned unit development to the planning commission, obtaining that body's approval and then securing building permits. Of course, the planning commission may not approve any development that fails to meet the requirements set forth in the ordinance as outlined above.

We begin with the observation that there is nothing in the borough zoning enabling act which would prohibit council from creating a zoning district with this many permissible uses. The applicable section of the borough code is the Act of February 1, 1966, P.L. (1965)—§3201, 53 P.S. §48201. Under this section, council is given the power of regulate and restrict practically all aspects of buildings themselves, open spaces, population density, location of structures, etc., the only limitation on this power being that it be exercised so as to promote the "health, safety, morals or the general welfare" of the borough. Under the same act, section 1601, 53 P.S. §46601, empowers council to adopt ordinances to govern the use of public areas, such as streets, parks, etc., again with the only limitation being that such ordinances create "conditions favorable to the health, safety, morals and general welfare of the citizens." Thus, if council reasonably believed that a given district could contain *all* types of structures, without *any* density requirements whatsoever, so long as this did not adversely affect health, safety and morals, such a district could be created. In fact, it is common knowledge that in many industrial and commercial districts just such a wide range of uses is permitted. Given such broad power to zone, we cannot say that New Hope Borough Council abrogated its legislative function by creating a PUD district permitting the mixture of uses outlined *supra,* especially given the density requirements.

We must next examine the statutory power of the borough planning commission to determine whether such an administrative body may regulate the internal development of a PUD district. The Act of February 1, 1966, P.L. (1965)—§1155, 53 P.S. §46155 requires that all plans for land "laid out in building lots" be approved by the planning commission before they may be recorded. Thus, the traditional job of the commission has been to examine tract plans to determine whether they conform to the applicable borough ordinances. The ordinances most frequently interpreted and applied by the planning commission are those dealing with streets, sewers, water and gas mains, etc., i.e., the so-called public improvements. However, the statute contains no language which would prohibit the planning commission from approving plans with reference to ordinances dealing with permissible building uses as well. The primary reason that planning commissions have not traditionally interpreted this type of ordinance is that such regulations do not usually come into play until the landowner wishes to begin the actual construction of a particular building. By this time, the relevant subdivision plan has already been approved by the commission; thus the task of examining the plans for a particular structure to see whether it conforms to the regulations for the zoning district in which it will be erected devolves upon the local building inspector who issues the building permit.

However, in the case of PUD the entire development (including specific structures) is mapped out and submitted to the administrative agency at once. Accordingly, the requirements set forth in a PUD ordinance must relate not only to those areas traditionally administered by the planning commission, but also to areas traditionally administered by the building inspector. Therefore, quite logically, the job of approving a particular PUD should rest with a single municipal body. The question then is simply which one: Borough Council (a legislative body), the Planning Commission (an administrative body), or the Zoning Board of Adjustment (an administrative body)?

There is no doubt that it would be statutorily permissible for council itself to pass a PUD ordinance and simultaneous zoning map amendment so specific that no details would be left for any administrator. The ordinance could specify where each building should be placed, how large it should be, where the open spaces are located, etc. But what would be the practical effect of such an ordinance? One of the most attractive features of Planned Unit Development is its flexibility; the chance for the builder and the municipality to sit down together and tailor a development to meet the specific needs of the community and the requirements of the land on which it is to be built. But all this would be lost if the Legislature let the planning cement set before any developer could happen upon the scene to scratch his own initials in that cement. Professor Krasnowiecki has accurately summed up the effect on planned unit development of such planning. The picture, to be sure, is not a happy one:

> The traditional refuge of the courts, the requirement that all the standards be set forth in advance of application for development, does not offer a practical solution to the problem. The complexity of pre-established regulations that would automatically dispose of any proposal for planned unit development, when different housing types and perhaps accessory commercial areas are envisaged, would be quite considerable. Indeed as soon as various housing types are

premitted, the regulations that would govern their design and distribution on every possible kind of site, their relationship to each other and their relationship to surrounding properties must be complex unless the developer's choice in terms of site, site plan and design and distribution of housing is reduced close to zero. It is not likely . . . that local authorities would want to adopt such a set of regulations. (Krasnowiecki, Planned Unit Development: A Challenge to Established Theory and Practice of Land Use Control, 114 U. Pa. L. Rev. 47, 71 (1965))

Left with Professor Krasnowiecki's "Hobson's choice" of no developer leeway at all, or a staggering set of legislative regulations sufficient to cover every idea the developer might have, it is not likely that Planned Unit Development could thrive, or even maintain life, if the local legislature assumed totally the role of planner.

The remaining two municipal bodies which could oversee the shaping of specific Planned Unit Developments are both administrative agencies, the Zoning Board of Adjustment and the Planning Commission. As this Court views both reality and zoning enabling act, the Zoning Board of Adjustment is not the proper body. The Act of February 1, 1966, P.L. (1965)—§3207, 53 §48207(g) specifically sets forth the powers of a borough zoning board of adjustment. These powers are three in number, and only three. The board may (1) hear and decide appeals where there is an alleged error made by an administrator in the enforcement of the enabling act or any ordinance enacted pursuant thereto; (2) hear and decide special exceptions; and (3) authorize the grant of variances from the terms of existing ordinances. These powers in no way encompass the authority to review and approve the plan for an entire development when such plan is neither at variance with the existing ordinance nor is a special exception to it; nor does (1) above supply the necessary power since the board would not be reviewing an alleged administrative error.

Moreover, from a practical standpoint, a zoning board of adjustment is, of the three bodies here under discussion, the one least equipped to handle the problem of PUD approval. Zoning boards are accustomed to focusing on one lot at a time. They traditionally examine hardship cases and unique uses proposed by landowners. As Professor Krasnowiecki has noted: "To suggest that the board is intended, or competent, to handle large scale planning and design decisions is, I think, far fetched." Technical Bulletin 52, Urban Land Institute, p. 38 (1965). We agree.

Thus, the borough planning commission remains the only other body both qualified and statutorily permitted to approve PUD. Of course, we realize that a planning commission is not authorized to engage in actual re-zoning of land. But merely because the commission here has the power to approve more than one type of building for a particular lot within the PUD district does not mean that the commission is usurping the zoning function. Indeed, it is acting in strict *accordance* with the applicable zoning ordinance, for that ordinance, No. 160, *permits* more than one type of building for a particular lot.

To be sure, if the commission approved a plan for a PUD district where 30% of the land were being used commercially, *then* we would have an example of illegal re-zoning by an administrator. But no one argues in the present case that appellant's plan does not conform to the requirements of ordinance 160.

Nor is this Court sympathetic to appellees' argument that ordinance 160 permits the planning commission to grant variances and special exceptions. We fail to see how a development such as appellant's that meets every single requirement of the applicable zoning ordinance can be said to be the product of a variance or a special exception. The very essence of variances and special exceptions lies in their *departure* from ordinance requirements, not in their compliance with them. We therefore conclude that the New Hope Planning Commission has the power to approve development plans submitted to it under ordinance 160. . . .

NOTES AND QUESTIONS

1. The borough of New Hope enacted Ordinance 160 in June 1965. The state supreme court did not decide the appeal until April 1968. After the decision, other builders applied for and obtained PUD classification for their parcels. In view of the interval of nearly three years or more between adoption of Ordinance 160 and subsequent PUD approvals, does the court's decision in *Cheney* (relying upon language from *Donahue*) make all such later approvals vulnerable to upset? Note that the *Eves* interval between PUD enabling and the first attempt to gain PUD approval was only five months.

2. Do you believe that the *Cheney* decision handles successfully the comprehensive plan issue? If the validity of PUD zoning depends upon the simultaneous adoption of two ordinances, one creating the classification, one approving a PUD application, doesn't this contribute to the peddling of political influence—one of the dangers that worried the court in *Eves?* Moreover, if only the first PUD approval(s) (conceivably, several landowners might gain simultaneous approval) can satisfy the *Cheney* test, isn't there a fairness problem respecting later developers whose case for PUD approval may be no less compelling? And wholly apart from the issue of fairness, is *Cheney* responsive to the planning factors that lead to PUD zoning? If it makes good planning sense to introduce flexibility into the zoning ordinance, should not the community be able to consider PUD applications whenever they arise?

3. On the other hand, *Cheney* and *Eves* both responded to the image of a "floating zone" that might drop into anybody's back yard. Is this a concern that courts should properly respect? To what degree does a residential owner enjoy vestedness in the zoning of his surroundings, in the expectation that light industrial plants and apartment complexes will not enter a neighborhood that he believed would develop more compatibly? Should courts leave such owners to the political process, letting them rely upon their town board not to approve plans that defeat expectations? Do you agree or disagree with the following statements?

(a) The courts should protect the expectations of suburban homeowners that adjoining lands will contain expensive one-family homes.

(b) The courts should protect the desires of inner-city residents to move into subsidized apartments in the suburbs.

Can you reconcile your opinions?

Regardless of the merits of the vestedness issue, the *Cheney* formulation failed to protect residents who opposed Ordinances 160 and 161, since presumably they had no advance warning that a PUD would enter their low-density neighborhood. Indeed, one might even argue that as the interval lengthens between adoption of the enabling law and approval of PUD applications, the problem of vestedness fades, since all new landowners buy with notice of PUD zoning.

4. Are the legal and policy issues underlying the special exception procedure different from those affecting PUDs?

5. Whatever the theoretical controversy, PUDs have become a fait accompli. Spurred by the remarkable popularity of condominiums, many communities have created PUD zones, and one can expect that judicial dislike for the principle will diminish. See, e.g., Miss Porter's School, Inc. v. Town Plan and Zoning Commn. of Town of Farmington, 151 Conn. 425, 198 A.2d 707 (1964). One might still see, however, mild scrutiny of the statutory standards for PUD approval. Cf. Pacesetter Homes v. Village of Olympia Fields, 104 Ill. App. 2d 218, 244 N.E.2d 369 (1968); Model State Statute §3(f), Symposium on PUD, 114 U. Pa. L. Rev. 3, 170 (1965) ("all standards and criteria for any feature of a Planned Unit Development shall be set forth in such ordinance with sufficient certainty to provide reasonable criteria by which specific proposals can be evaluated. . . .")

§17.7   Farewell, Euclid

REPS, POMEROY MEMORIAL LECTURE: REQUIEM FOR ZONING [7]

. . . Zoning is seriously ill and its physicians—the planners—are mainly to blame. We have unnecessarily prolonged the existence of a land use control device conceived in another era when the true and frightening complexity of urban life was barely appreciated. We have, through heroic efforts and with massive doses of legislative remedies, managed to preserve what was once a lusty infant not only past the retirement age but well into senility. What is called for is legal euthanasia, a respectful requiem, and a search for a new legislative substitute sturdy enough to survive in the modern urban world. . . .

. . . What would be the broad outlines of that portion of a development

---

7. Paper presented at the 1964 ASPO National Planning Conference. Planning 1964, American Society of Planning Officials.—ED.

guidance system replacing our present system of zoning? How would we approach the control of bulk, use, intensity, location, and density?

First, I think it highly desirable to combine such zoning-type restrictions with other related public controls into a set of what might be called Development Regulations. From the standpoint of procedure we have already moved some distance in this direction. The use of floating zones, increased reliance on special exception or conditional use devices, and the requirements of site plan review as a condition of zoning permit approval, to name three among several methods that are currently employed, have all brought the procedure for securing permits under the zoning ordinance closer to that of subdivision control. I suggest that we pursue this approach much further and require most types of proposed development to be submitted to a local agency that would administer, through discretionary review, an ordinance combining at least zoning-type and subdivision regulations. This should simplify development control. Elimination of conflicting provisions and greater convenience for both administrative officials and land developers are but two of the advantages that would result.

Second, to guide administrative officials in reaching discretionary decisions, there should be a plan for community development and a comprehensive set of development objectives and standards. This plan should be made mandatory, it should be adopted by the legislative body, and review and readoption at fixed intervals should be required. Such plans should show generalized proposed future land uses, circulation systems, population density patterns, and community facilities.

Before the adoption of the plan by the legislative body, hearings would be required. After adoption, provisions of the plan would be subject to review by a state agency that would also be empowered to hear appeals submitted by those opposing details of the plan. The state review agency would have final authority to confirm or modify the plan. All discretionary review of development proposals would be guided by this plan. Appeals from local decisions could be taken to the state review agency. Further appeals to courts would be permitted only on matters of procedure or on the scope of statutory power, not on matters of substance.

I realize that in this era of "ad hocmanship," advocacy of a community plan to serve as a guide to public decision-making sounds faintly antiquarian. But the use of a plan as just described provides fresh meaning to the planning process and thrusts the general plan forward to a position of new importance.

Discretionary action limiting development in such a way as to cause severe deprivation of property rights would be accompanied by some form of compensation. This would, in Haar's words, add "the money lubricant . . . to the machinery of land use controls in order to achieve greater flexibility."[4]

Appeals to determine the amount of compensation, if an offer is de-

---

4. Haar, "The Social Control of Urban Space," Lowden Wingo, Jr. (ed.), Cities in Space: The Future Use of Urban Land (Baltimore: The Johns Hopkins Press, 1963), p. 216.

clined, would lie to the state review agency. In reaching such determinations the state agency would consider the degree of regulation that would be upheld under the most severe exercise of the police power and the value of the land burdened by such restrictions. Compensation would be payable only for the difference between that value and the value of the land if further restricted as specified by the local administrative body. After the payment of compensation, the restrictions imposed would be registered as part of the title. If, in future years, more intensive development were permitted, the amount of the compensation would be repayable by the owner.

Parenthetically, I should add that a system of betterment charges should also be devised to permit public recoupment of part of any increased land value conferred by public activities. Such a system might prove unnecessarily complex if applied to all land, but as a minimum a somewhat wider view of our present benefit assessment techniques should be investigated. David Levin, in a recent exploration of offsetting compensation with betterment charges in connection with highway access limitation, suggests that this approach "could be expanded substantially, giving a much wider recognition to benefits that in fact exist."[5]

Third, while I have referred to the discretionary administrative review body as local, I envisage this body ultimately as one with a geographical jurisdiction more extensive than the present city, town or borough boundaries. The new pessimists from the left bank of the Charles River have lately been stating that multipurpose metropolitan government is impossible to achieve and probably undesirable anyway. Perhaps they are correct, but as they point out, ad hoc metropolitan working agreements, authorities, special districts, and other single-purpose arrangements or agencies will be necessary as partial substitutes.

I suggest that sooner or later the general control of land use should be recognized as a responsibility to be located at the metropolitan level. In the absence of voluntary local action, the state agency previously mentioned should be empowered to establish broad guide plans in metropolitan areas and certain over-all land use control objectives and standards, against which local plans and land use objectives and standards would be reviewed. The next stage would be the creation of a metropolitan planning and discretionary control agency by action of the separate units of local government. Certain classes of development review might then well be left with smaller units of government, while other categories of development would be subject to metropolitan agency scrutiny. The alternative would be the direct exercise of land use controls by some agency of state government.

Fourth, the land use regulations themselves would need to differ substantially from those presently encompassed under zoning. Except as I will men-

5. David Levin, "Aspects of Eminent Domain Proceedings in the United States," Charles Haar (ed.), Law and Land: Anglo-American Planning Practice (Cambridge: Harvard University Press and the M.I.T. Press, 1964), p. 238.

tion later, no district boundaries—no zoning map—would exist. The comprehensive plan, expressed in graphic form and in statements of development objectives, would be one guide to the discretionary administrative body, which might be called the Office of Development Review. While ultimately the plan itself might be regarded as a sufficient standard or rule of conduct to guide discretionary action, probably we shall need in addition rather detailed standards enacted by legislative bodies. These would be similar to those we now find in the better ordinances which authorize floating zones, conditional uses, and site plan approval permits. I suggest that these standards need to do more than specify the public good as a rule of conduct. In other words, the standards should be fairly specific and should relate to defined categories of land use. Such requirements should take the form of performance standards, rather than rigid specifications. Permissible ranges of height and bulk, for example, should be expressed in such measures as floor area ratios and angles of light obstruction. Emphasis should be placed on such performance criteria as noise, traffic generation, smoke emission and air pollution, odor production, vibration, and the like. Even so, more specification standards would doubtless be needed.

Within this rather general framework of plans, goals and standards, the Office of Development Review would exercise broad discretionary power in granting or denying or modifying requests for development permission. Such permits would be for both tract development and single buildings on individual sites. As in most current floating zone procedures, approval would be for specific uses and building designs as shown on site plans, elevation drawings, and as described in supplementary text material. This procedure, then, would not be at all like present zoning, the effect of which is blanket permission for any of a wide range of uses permitted in the zoning district. The discretionary powers would be broad; the development permit would be narrow in the development rights that would be conferred.

Fifth, this type of discretionary review and control would be most appropriate at the urban fringe or applied to in-lying undeveloped areas. Some vestiges of the concept of districts might have utility. We would probably find it advantageous to establish a skeleton list of uses that would be permitted as a matter of right, along with a set of simplified district boundaries. One advantage of this approach would be to reduce the volume of detailed review that would otherwise be necessary if we relied on a wholly discretionary system. Another purpose would be to clothe the new system in some of the familiar garments of zoning to lend an air of respectability in gaining both public acceptance and judicial recognition.

In areas largely built-up, where most new construction would be on a discontinuous lot-by-lot basis, more of the present zoning techniques—district boundaries and use lists—could be retained, although modernized to incorporate many of the recent innovations in zoning.

For redevelopment areas, major reliance should be placed on deed restrictions as the chief control mechanism. Urban Renewal Commissioner William Slayton may have been only partially overstating the case when he recently asserted that zoning has no place at all in redevelopment. Since the redevelopment site passes through a period of public ownership there is an opportunity to condition the sale of such land with precise and detailed restrictions. Police power controls can safely be suspended in such areas, although held in readiness should some legal flaws develop in the system of covenants, or to be applied at the termination of the period specified in the deed restrictions.

This approach to land use controls put before you only in the broadest of outlines appears to me the most likely and desirable of several alternatives to the present system. Doubtless, many of you have recognized its similarity to the land control process operating in Britain since 1947. It thus has precedents in a country not wholly dissimilar to our own. Moreover, if I read the trends correctly, it seems to be a direction in which we are already heading. The land planning and zoning code prepared by Carl Feiss for Bratenahl, Ohio, is a first step along the lines I have suggested.[6]

Yet there are serious objections which can be raised and with which, in conclusion, I would like to deal. Seemingly this approach to land use control violates the cherished principles of certainty and predictability that are supposed to be the virtues of our present system of districts, use lists, and elaborate development standards. This theory, however, is deeply undercut by the multidude of zoning amendments, improper variances, special exception permits, floating zone approvals, and unenforced violations. What remains is the structure of certainty without the substance—a mere façade of respectable predictability masking the practice of unguided administrative and legislative discretion.

Would a system such as I have proposed, with discretionary judgments firmly based on an official plan serving as Haar's "impermanent constitution" and guided by stated development goals and standards, fundamentally reduce the degree of certainty that now prevails? I submit that it would not, and that it would be more honest to present the meat of reality rendered of its semantic fat.

Futher, I suggest we have little to fear from courts reviewing the legislative basis of such an approach to land development control. The little band of radicals in 1916 pushed the judicial clock further ahead in their time when they introduced comprehensive zoning than we would do in ours by pressing for additional dicretionary powers. Perhaps I betray a naive faith in judicial liberalism, but recent decisions in our higher courts seem to leave little to fear in this respect.

My reservations concerning the wisdom and practicality of adopting the system I have proposed lie in other directions. Are we planners, as those who would be charged with exercising such discretionary authority, ready to accept

6. Village of Bratenahl, Ohio, Land Planning and Zoning Code and Zone Map (July, 1962); Carl Feiss, Bratenahl Development Report (Washington, 1962).

the responsibility inherent in such an approach to development control? Are we confident that we possess the informed judgment to make intelligent decisions when granting or withholding development permission? Are we certain that we could withstand the inevitable political pressures that would be brought to bear on us? Does the present status of planning suggest that legislators would be willing to grant us such powers in the first place? Is there any clear evidence that the adoption of such a system would lead to development patterns significantly different or markedly better than we are currently achieving or which might be brought about by some less drastic modification in our traditional techniques?

Finally, could we produce personnel of the quality and in the quantity that would be demanded to provide careful review of development proposals in a period of rapid urban growth and change? The new breed of planners seemingly has less interest in and knowledge of the micro-physical environment than in the novelties of new analytical methods based on a computer culture, more applicable to macro-planning at the metropolitan scale. Can we safely trust site plan review to this new generation of urban scientists?

Although we may now answer these questions in the qualified negative, that does not mean we should reject the alternative control system I have described. The same question could have been posed in 1916. The answers then would surely have been equally discouraging. Who could have predicted, for example, the almost indecent haste with which state lawmakers clutched to their legislative bosoms the Standard State Zoning Enabling Act of 1922?

While I think it extremely doubtful that the episode of almost revolutionary legislative history will be repeated, we should not lose hope in evolutionary progress. If large increments of discretionary powers seem called for eventually, we should begin now to prepare the legislative and professional basis for the future.

Fortunately, there are grounds for optimism. The last ten years have witnessed the adoption and judicial approval of many techniques to ease the rigid Euclidian bonds of zoning districts, use lists, and precise standards. There are new signs of life in the corpse of state planning that was laid to rest in the 1930's. The experiment with statewide zoning in Hawaii promises to teach us some new lessons. A committee of the American Law Institute, aided by a substantial foundation grant, is now at work on a reassessment of American planning legislation. The proposals before Congress for broadening federal aid for such programs as open land acquisition, metropolitan planning, advance provision of neighborhood facilities sites, and the development of new towns will require new legislative responses at the state and local levels.

At this stage of our urban development we badly need imaginative experimentation in our fifty legislative laboratories. Where are the states that have placed metropolitan decision-making power at the metropolitan level, that require state or metropolitan approval of local plans, that provide for state or metropolitan review of local appeal decisions, that have reorganized the fiscal systems of municipalities so that land use decisions can be freed from the shackles of tax and revenue implications, that permit zoning-type regulations based on a community plan instead of a zoning map? And where have been the planners who should have been in the front ranks of those demanding reforms at the metropolitan and state level?

For half a century we have engaged in a kind of legislative Shintoism, worshipping at the shrine of the Standard State Zoning Enabling Act. Zoning served us well during a period when urban life was simpler and less dynamic. We should honor those who were responsible for its birth and early care—the Bassetts and the Bettmans and, later, the Pomeroys of our profession—all of whom demonstrated a fertility of intellect that we have failed to imitate. But we do these men, and ourselves as well, ultimate honor not by tending their legislative monuments at the end of the by now well-worn legal road they constructed but by carving new trails toward new frontiers to serve an emerging new urban America.

NOTES AND QUESTIONS

1. Three years later, Professor Reps wrote that "time has only strengthened my conviction that [my] assessment was correct." Reps, The Future of American Planning: Requiem or Renascence?, Planning 1967 (American Society of Planning Officials), at 47. His follow-up article strongly advocates the creation of COMSAT-like, mixed private-public agencies, or—alternatively—wholly public agencies to acquire raw land on the urban fringe, which they would prepare and make available for development in accordance with a comprehensive metropolitan growth plan. This scheme would further reduce the dependence upon Euclidian zoning, since the resale or lease of development sites would be subject to conditions similar to those imposed by urban renewal agencies.

2. The ALI Model Land Development Code echoes the Reps proposals in the following ways:

(a) It allows zoning and subdivision regulations to be combined into a single "development ordinance." §2-101(1).

(b) Any "development" activity would be subject to the development ordinance. This brings together a variety of activities often separately regulated, including demolition, mining, exterior alteration, outdoor advertising, etc. §1-202.

(c) Where communities adopt a local land development plan, it shall be a statement (in words, maps, illustrations, or other media of communication) setting forth its objectives, policies, and standards. §3-101. The code would not mandate local plans, but it would create strong incentives—in the nature of expanding the types of regulation permissible when plans exist—for the adoption of local plans.

(d) Although the code would retain local planning autonomy to a considerable degree, it would provide for modest state and regional planning and review activities. Articles 7 and 8.

(e) The code does not require the creation of use districts, with uniformity throughout, as does the Standard State Zoning Enabling Act.

Chapter 18

Eminent Domain

Eminent domain, the power to acquire privately held property "to answer the necessities of the State,"[1] is an inherent aspect of sovereignty. Indeed, it does not even appear among Congress's enumerated powers, so clear was it that this power went without saying.[2] What *needed* saying was that the power not be abused, a limitation appearing in the Fifth Amendment with these words: "Nor shall private property be taken for public use without just compensation."[3] State constitutions tend to repeat the federal pattern of implying the power by expressing the limitation. See, e.g., N.Y. Const. art. 1, §7. And one can even find an early state court decision where, in the absence of the limitation, private property was permitted to be taken without payment. Patrick v. Commissioners of Cross Roads, 4 McCord 541 (S.C. 1828). This would be impossible today, since the Fifth Amendment restraint also applies now to the states via incorporation into the Fourteenth Amendment. Fallbrook Irrigation District v. Bradley, 164 U.S. 112 (1896).

Through the nineteenth century, the power was used sparingly for several reasons: much of the nation's land was publicly held and could be devoted—or donated as in the case of the railways or land-grant universities—for essential purposes; the nature of the role of government was far more circumscribed than it is today; the automobile was not yet invented. Today, government at all levels spends many billions yearly in condemnation; the annual land acquisition cost of just one program, urban renewal, has run in the

---

1. Puffendorf, The Law of Nature and Nations, Book VIII, ch. 5, §7 (circa 1650). The term "dominium eminens" first appears in the writings of Grotius (circa 1625) and was roundly criticized by contemporary scholars who thought "imperium eminens" a more accurate phrase. Idem. "Dominium" is a civil-law property term that denotes proprietorship.

2. Cf. United States v. Jones, 109 U.S. 513 (1883). Strangely, Kohl v. United States, 91 U.S. 367 (1875), is the earliest Supreme Court decision to validate the power. One commentator notes that federal officials prior to the *Kohl* decision seemed uncertain if a federal condemnation power actually existed, so that they would ask state officials to condemn land for federal purposes. Stoebuck, A General Theory of Eminent Domain, 47 Wash. L. Rev. 553, 559 (1972).

3. One finds a more florid statement in the French Declaration of the Rights of Man, Aug. 26, 1789, art. 17: "The right to property being inviolable and sacred, no one shall be deprived of it, except in cases of evident public necessity, legally ascertained, and on condition of a previous just indemnity."

hundreds of millions, and the federal highway program is even more expensive. And, as we shall see, the power to condemn is not held by government alone.

In this chapter, you will examine the two major issues with which the law of eminent domain has been concerned. First, when (for what purposes) may the power be exercised? Second, what does the imperative "just compensation" require?

§18.1   What is "Public Purpose"?

TELL, DETROIT'S FRAY: PROGRESS v. PROPERTY
National L.J., June 1, 1981, at 1, cols. 1-3

Like an inmate on Death Row, Detroit's Poletown neighborhood is clinging to the last thread of hope that it can avert the final decree.

Poletown's remaining residents have mounted some last-ditch legal maneuvers as part of their strategy to stop the city's death sentence, which would clear the community for a new General Motors Corp. automotive assembly plant.

Legal battles between a community and the wrecker's ball are not new. Although Poletown's fate seems sealed by a long line of judicial precedents from around the country, the community's looming demise has been seized upon as a symbol by both ends of the political spectrum—conservatives who see it as a new threat to the sanctity of private property and those on the left who see it as a triumph of corporate and political power over a helpless neighborhood. Critics from both camps say Poletown could spark a renewed debate over similar protests across the nation.

The underlying issue in Michigan is survival, for Poletown and for Detroit. When GM threatened last year to move some important facilities out of the Detroit area, it gave the city a take-it-or-leave-it offer for the new plant on the 465-acre Poletown site.

The economically strapped city had no choice. It decided to take the GM offer—and to "take" by eminent domain more than 1,100 homes in one of the city's oldest, still-thriving ethnic neighborhoods, as well as the beautiful Church of the Immaculate Conception and the historic former Dodge "Main" assembly plant. . . .

With unemployment in Detroit at 18 percent and the city's economic mainstay, the auto industry, facing record losses, Mayor Coleman Young thinks that Detroit is getting a good deal from GM.

"I believe this program is beyond a doubt the most important single program that has been undertaken since I became mayor," he said at the first state court trial.

The project's supporters—who probably represent every powerful political, economic and social interest in the state—blast the Poletown residents and their lawyers as obstructionists who will bring the city to its knees. In their last-ditch effort to stop the project, they have "no hope of prevailing," says Mr. Christopher, the city's lawyer.

"They're not doing Detroit any good, they're not doing the neighborhood any good," he says.

Attorneys who are fighting the plant give different reasons for their persistence. Some say they object to the procedural short-cuts taken to push the project through at GM's behest. Others see it as a struggle between well-heeled corporate power and the individual citizen, outgunned by high-priced legal talent and GM's pressure tactics with the city.

But none deny that Detroit desperately needs the plant.

POLETOWN NEIGHBORHOOD COUNCIL v. CITY OF DETROIT

410 Mich. 616, 304 N.W.2d 455 (1981)

PER CURIAM. This case arises out of a plan by the Detroit Economic Development Corporation to acquire, by condemnation if necessary, a large tract of land to be conveyed to General Motors Corporation as a site for construction of an assembly plant. The plaintiffs, a neighborhood association and several individual residents of the affected area, brought suit in Wayne Circuit Court to challenge the project on a number of grounds, not all of which have been argued to this Court. Defendants' motions for summary judgment were denied pending trial on a single question of fact: whether, under 1980 PA 87; M.C.L. §213.51 et seq.; M.S.A. §8.265(1) et seq., the city abused its discretion in determining that condemnation of plaintiffs' property was necessary to complete the project.

The trial lasted 10 days and resulted in a judgment for defendants and an order on December 9, 1980, dismissing plaintiffs' complaint. The plaintiffs filed a claim of appeal with the Court of Appeals on December 12, 1980, and an application for bypass with this Court on December 15, 1980.

We granted a motion for immediate consideration and an application for leave to appeal prior to decision by the Court of Appeals to consider the following questions:

Does the use of eminent domain in this case constitute a taking of private property for private use and, therefore, contravene Const. 1963, Art. 10, §2?

Did the court below err in ruling that cultural, social and historical institutions were not protected by the Michigan Environmental Protection Act?

We conclude that these questions must be answered in the negative and affirm the trial court's decision.

This case raises a question of paramount importance to the future welfare of this state and its residents: Can a municipality use the power of eminent domain granted to it by the Economic Development Corporations Act, M.C.L. §125.1601 et seq.; M.S.A. §5.3520(1) et seq., to condemn property for transfer to a private corporation to build a plant to promote industry and commerce, thereby adding jobs and taxes to the economic base of the municipality and state?

Const. 1963, Art. 10, §2, states in pertinent part that "[p]rivate property shall not be taken for public use without just compensation therefor being first made or secured in a manner prescribed by law." Art. 10, §2 has been interpreted as requiring that the power of eminent domain not be invoked except to further a public use or purpose. Plaintiffs-appellants urge us to distinguish between the terms "use" and "purpose", asserting they are not synonymous and have been distinguished in the law of eminent domain. We are persuaded the terms have been used interchangeably in Michigan statutes and decisions in an effort to describe the protean concept of public benefit. The term "public use" has not received a narrow or inelastic definition by this Court in prior cases. Indeed, this Court has stated that " '[a] public use changes with changing conditions of society' " and that " '[t]he right of the public to receive and enjoy the benefit of the use determines whether the use is public or private' ".

The Economic Development Corporations Act is a part of the comprehensive legislation dealing with planning, housing and zoning whereby the State of Michigan is attempting to provide for the general health, safety, and welfare through alleviating unemployment, providing economic assistance to industry, assisting the rehabilitation of blighted areas, and fostering urban redevelopment.

Section 2 of the act provides:

> There exists in this state the continuing need for programs to alleviate and prevent conditions of unemployment, and that it is accordingly necessary to assist and retain local industries and commercial enterprises to strengthen and revitalize the economy of this state and its municipalities; that accordingly it is necessary to provide means and methods for the encouragement and assistance of industrial and commercial enterprises in locating, purchasing, constructing, reconstructing, modernizing, improving, maintaining, repairing, furnishing, equipping, and expanding in this state and in its municipalities; and that it is also necessary to encourage the location and expansion of commercial enterprises to more conveniently provide needed services and facilities of the commercial enterprises to municipalities and the residents thereof. *Therefore, the powers granted in this act constitute the performance of essential public purposes and functions for this state and its municipalities.* M.C.L. §125.1602; M.S.A. §5.3520(2). (Emphasis added.)

To further the objectives of this act, the legislature has authorized municipalities to acquire property by condemnation in order to provide industrial and commercial sites and the means of transfer from the municipality to private users. M.C.L. §125.1622; M.S.A. §5.3520(22).

Plaintiffs-appellants do not challenge the declaration of the legislature that programs to alleviate and prevent conditions of unemployment and to preserve and develop industry and commerce are essential public purposes. Nor do they challenge the proposition that legislation to accomplish this purpose falls within the Constitutional grant of general legislative power to the legislature in Const. 1963, Art. 4, §51, which reads as follows: "The public health and general welfare of the people of the state are hereby declared to be matters of primary public concern. The legislature shall pass suitable laws for the protection and promotion of the public health."

What plaintiffs-appellants do challenge is the constitutionality of using the power of eminent domain to condemn one person's property to convey it to another private person in order to bolster the economy. They argue that whatever incidental benefit may accrue to the public, assembling land to General Motors' specifications for conveyance to General Motors for its uncontrolled use in profit making is really a taking for private use and not a public use because General Motors is the primary beneficiary of the condemnation.

The defendants-appellees contend, on the other hand, that the controlling public purpose in taking this land is to create an industrial site which will be used to alleviate and prevent conditions of unemployment and fiscal distress. The fact that it will be conveyed to and ultimately used by a private manufacturer does not defeat this predominant public purpose.

There is no dispute about the law. All agree that condemnation for a public use or purpose is permitted. All agree that condemnation for a private use or purpose is forbidden. Similarly, condemnation for a private use cannot be authorized whatever its incidental public benefit and condemnation for a public purpose cannot be forbidden whatever the incidental private gain. The heart of this dispute is whether the proposed condemnation is for the primary benefit of the public or the private user.

The Legislature has determined that governmental action of the type contemplated here meets a public need and serves an essential public purpose. The Court's role after such a determination is made is limited.

> "The determination of what constitutes a public purpose is primarily a legislative function, subject to review by the courts when abused, and the determination of the legislative body of that matter should not be reversed except in instances where such determination is palpably and manifestly arbitrary and incorrect." Gregory Marina, Inc. v. Detroit, 378 Mich. 364, 396, 144 N.W.2d 503 (1966).

The United States Supreme Court has held that when a legislature speaks, the public interest has been declared in terms "well-nigh conclusive." Berman v. Parker, 348 U.S. 26, 32, 75 S. Ct. 98, 102, 99 L. Ed. 27 (1954).

The Legislature has delegated the authority to determine whether a particular project constitutes a public purpose to the governing body of the municipality involved. The plaintiffs concede that this project is the type contemplated by the Legislature and that the procedures set forth in the Economic Development Corporations Act have been followed. This further limits our review.

In the court below, the plaintiffs-appellants challenged the necessity for the taking of the land for the proposed project. In this regard the city presented substantial evidence of the severe economic conditions facing the residents of the city and state, the need for new industrial development to revitalize local industries, the economic boost the proposed project would provide, and the lack of other adequate available sites to implement the project.

As Justice Cooley stated over a hundred years ago, "the most important consideration in the case of eminent domain is the necessity of accomplishing some public good which is otherwise impracticable, and . . . the law does not so much regard the means as the need." People ex rel. Detroit & Howell R. Co. v. Salem Twp. Board, 20 Mich. 452, 480-481 (1870).

When there is such public need, "[t]he abstract right [of an individual] to make use of his own property in his own way is compelled to yield to the general comfort and protection of community, and to a proper regard to relative rights in others." Id. Eminent domain is an inherent power of the sovereign of the same nature as, albeit more severe than, the power to regulate the use of land through zoning or the prohibition of public nuisances.

In the instant case the benefit to be received by the municipality invoking the power of eminent domain is a clear and significant one and is sufficient to satisfy this Court that such a project was an intended and a legitimate object of the Legislature when it allowed municipalities to exercise condemnation powers even though a private party will also, ultimately, receive a benefit as an incident thereto.

The power of eminent domain is to be used in this instance primarily to accomplish the essential public purposes of alleviating unemployment and revitalizing the economic base of the community. The benefit to a private interest is merely incidental.

Our determination that this project falls within the public purpose, as stated by the Legislature, does not mean that every condemnation proposed by an economic development corporation will meet with similar acceptance simply because it may provide some jobs or add to the industrial or commercial base. If the public benefit was not so clear and significant, we would hesitate to sanction approval of such a project. The power of eminent domain is restricted to furthering public uses and purposes and is not to be exercised without substantial proof that the public is primarily to be benefited. Where, as here, the condemnation power is exercised in a way that benefits specific and identifiable private interests, a court inspects with heightened scrutiny the claim that the public interest is the predominant interest being advanced. Such public benefit cannot be speculative or marginal but must be clear and significant if it is to be within the legitimate purpose as stated by the Legislature. We hold this project is warranted on the basis that its significance for the people of Detroit and the state has been demonstrated.

Plaintiffs' complaint also alleged that the proposed project violates the Michigan Environmental Protection Act (MEPA), M.C.L. §691.1201 et seq.; M.S.A. §14.528(201) et seq., because it "will have a major adverse impact on the adjoining social and cultural environment which is referred to as Poletown". The trial court dismissed this claim, stating that " 'social and cultural environments' are matters not within the purview of the MEPA and outside its legislative intent". We agree.

M.C.L. §691.1202(1); M.S.A. §14.528(202)(1) permits maintenance of an action for declaratory and equitable relief against the state, its political subdivisions, or private entities, "for the protection of the *air, water and other natural resources* and the public trust therein from pollution, impairment or destruction." (Emphasis supplied.) The reference to "air, water and other natural resources" is also made in other sections of the act and in its title. Given its plain meaning, the term "natural resources" does not encompass a "social and cultural environment". Moreover, under the principle of ejusdem generis, where a statute contains a general term supplementing a more specific enumeration, the general term will not be construed to refer to objects not of like kind with those enumerated. 2A Sutherland, Statutory Construction (4th ed.), §§47.18-47.19, pp. 109-114.

The decision of the trial court is affirmed.

The clerk is directed to issue the Court's judgment order forthwith, in accordance with GCR 1963, 866.3(c).

No costs, a public question being involved.

COLEMAN, C.J., and MOODY, LEVIN, KAVANAGH and WILLIAMS, J.J., concur.

FITZGERALD, J. (dissenting). This Court today decides that the power of eminent domain permits the taking of private property with the object of transferring it to another private party for the purpose of constructing and operating a factory, on the ground that the employment and other economic benefits of this privately operated industrial facility are such as to satisfy the "public use" requirement for the exercise of eminent domain power. Because I believe the proposed condemnation clearly exceeds the government's authority to take private property through the power of eminent domain, I dissent.

In the spring of 1980, General Motors Corporation informed the City of Detroit that it would close its Cadillac and Fisher Body plants located within the city in 1983. General Motors offered to build an assembly complex in the city, if a suitable site could be found. General Motors set four criteria for the approval of a site: an area of between 450 and 500 acres; a rectangular shape (3/4 mile by 1 mile); access to a long-haul railroad line; and access to the freeway system. The city evaluated a number of potential sites and eventually made an in-depth study of nine sites. Eight of the sites were found not to be feasible,[1] and the ninth, with which we are concerned, was recommended. It occupies approximately 465 acres in the cities of Detroit and Hamtramck.[2] A plan was developed to acquire the site, labeled the Central Industrial Park,

---

1. Indeed, according to the Draft Environmental Impact Statement prepared by the city, none of the other eight sites studied met even the four basic criteria specified by General Motors.
2. Although approximately 145 of the 465 acres of the project lie within the City of Hamtramck, this case involves only the portion of the project located in Detroit.

under the Economic Development Corporations Act, 1974 PA 338. As authorized by the statute, the project plan contemplated the use of condemnation to acquire at least some of the property within the site. . . . I concur with the discussion of the environmental protection act issue, but disagree with the analysis of the eminent domain question.

The city attaches great importance to the explicit legislative findings in the Economic Development Corporations Act that unemployment is a serious problem and that it is necessary to encourage industry in order to revitalize the economy of this state, and to the legislative declaration that the use of eminent domain power pursuant to a project under the act, "shall be considered necessary for public purposes and for the benefit of the public". It is undeniable that such legislative pronouncements are entitled to great deference. However, determination whether a taking is for a public or a private use is ultimately a judicial question. E.g., Lakehead Pipe Line Co. v. Dehn, 340 Mich. 25, 39-40, 64 N.W.2d 903 (1954); Cleveland v. City of Detroit, 322 Mich. 172, 179, 33 N.W.2d 747 (1948). Through the years this Court has not hesitated to declare takings authorized by statute not to be for public use in appropriate cases. E.g., Shizas v. City of Detroit, 333 Mich. 44, 52 N.W.2d 589 (1952); Berrien Springs Water-Power Co. v. Berrien Circuit Judge, 133 Mich. 48, 94 N.W. 379 (1903). This is as it must be, since if a legislative declaration on the question of public use were conclusive, citizens could be subjected to the most outrageous confiscation of property for the benefit of other private interests without redress. Thus, while mindful of the expression of the legislative view of the appropriateness of using the eminent domain power in the circumstances of this case, this Court has the responsibility to determine whether the authorization is lawful.

Our role was well stated by Justice Cooley in "A Treatise on the Constitutional Limitations". Writing subsequent to the Court's decision in People ex rel. Detroit and Howell R. Co. v. Salem Township Board, 20 Mich. 452 (1870), he noted: "The question what is a public use is always one of law. Deference will be paid to the legislative judgment, as expressed in enactments providing for an appropriation of property, but it will not be conclusive." 2 Cooley, Constitutional Limitations (8th ed.), p. 1141.

Our approval of the use of eminent domain power in this case takes this state into a new realm of takings of private property; there is simply no precedent for this decision in previous Michigan cases. . . .

[I]n the present case the transfer of the property to General Motors after the condemnation cannot be considered incidental to the taking. It is only through the acquisition and use of the property by General Motors that the "public purpose" of promoting employment can be achieved. Thus, it is the economic benefits of the project that are incidental to the private use of the property.

The city also points to decisions that have found the objective of economic development to be a sufficient "public purpose" to support the expenditure of public funds in aid of industry. Advisory Opinion on

Constitutionality of 1975 PA 301, 400 Mich. 270, 254 N.W.2d 528 (1977); City of Gaylord v. Gaylord City Clerk, 378 Mich. 273, 144 N.W.2d 460 (1966). What constitutes a public purpose in a context of governmental taxing and spending power cannot be equated with the use of that term in connection with eminent domain powers. The potential risk of abuse in the use of eminent domain power is clear. Condemnation places the burden of aiding industry on the few, who are likely to have limited power to protect themselves from the excesses of legislative enthusiasm for the promotion of industry. The burden of taxation is distributed on the great majority of the population, leading to a more effective check on improvident use of public funds.

The majority relies on the principle that the concept of public use is an evolving one; however, I cannot believe that this evolution has eroded our historic protection against the taking of private property for private use to the degree sanctioned by this Court's decision today. The decision that the prospect of increased employment, tax revenue, and general economic stimulation makes a taking of private property for transfer to another private party sufficiently "public" to authorize the use of the power of eminent domain means that there is virtually no limit to the use of condemnation to aid private businesses. Any business enterprise produces benefits to society at large. Now that we have authorized local legislative bodies to decide that a different commercial or industrial use of property will produce greater public benefits than its present use, no homeowner's, merchant's or manufacturer's property, however productive or valuable to its owner, is immune from condemnation for the benefit of other private interests that will put it to a "higher" use. [15] As one prominent commentator has written:

> It often happens that the erection of a large factory will be of more benefit to the whole community in which it is planned to build it than any strictly public improvement which the inhabitants of the place could possibly undertake; but even if the plan was blocked by the refusal of the selfish owner of a small but necessary parcel of land to part with it at any price, the public mind would instinctively revolt at any attempt to take such land by eminent domain. 2A Nichols, Eminent Domain §7.61[1] (rev. 3d ed.).

The condemnation contemplated in the present action goes beyond the scope of the power of eminent domain in that it takes private property for private use. I would reverse the judgment of the circuit court.

RYAN, J., concurs.

RYAN, J. (dissenting). This is an extraordinary case. The reverberating clang of its economic, sociological, political, and jurisprudential impact is

_____

15. It would be easy to sustain the proposed project because of its large size and the extent of the claimed benefits to flow from it. The estimate is that approximately 6150 persons would be employed in the factory itself, with the generation of substantial other employment, business activity, and tax revenue as a result. However, it must be remembered that the dislocations and other costs of the project are also massive. The project plan indicates that a total of 3438 persons will be displaced by the project, that it will require the destruction of 1176 structures, and that the cost of the project to the public sector will be nearly $200,000,000.

likely to be heard and felt for generations. By its decision, the Court has altered the law of eminent domain in this state in a most significant way and, in my view, seriously jeopardized the security of all private property ownership. . . .

NOTES AND QUESTIONS

1. A little more background to the *Poletown* controversy. General Motors in 1980 had decided to build a modern, 3-million-square-foot assembly complex at a cost of $500 million to replace the aging Cadillac Assembly and Fisher Body Plants. These facilities employed more than 6000 workers. If suitable acreage could not be found in the Detroit area, General Motors talked of moving into a sunbelt state. At the time unemployment in the state of Michigan was at 14.2 percent, in the city of Detroit at 18 percent, and among black males at 30 percent.

2. Twenty years earlier, the New York courts had faced a similarly heated controversy involving the condemnation that led to erection of the World Trade Center, twin 1360-foot towers containing 10 million square feet of office space. The developer, a public authority, proposed to gather together as its tenants businesses relating to international trade, in order to strengthen the city's harbor activity. Opponents included merchants and landowners within the thirteen-block area whose parcels faced condemnation and private real estate investors whose office-building holdings faced competition. All legal attacks were finally beaten off. Courtesy Sandwich Shop v. Port of New York Authority, 12 N.Y.2d 379, 190 N.E.2d 402, 240 N.Y.S.2d 1 (1963), *app. dismissed*, 375 U.S. 78 (1963) (concept of World Trade Center fulfills public purpose); Port of New York Authority v. 62 Cortlandt St. Realty Co., 18 N.Y.2d 250, 219 N.E.2d 797, 273 N.Y.S. 337 (1966) (developer entitled to proceed with condemnation despite allegations that of 372 proposed tenants not over 103 would have real relation to World Trade functions).

3. In both the Poletown and World Trade Center situations, the project area was neither slum nor blighted. Would the controversy over the proposed reuse be without legal bearing if the legislature had declared (with appropriate factual findings) that the reuse area was physically substandard? Compare Yonkers Community Development Agency v. Morris, 37 N.Y.2d 478, — N.E.2d — (1975) ("substandard" land condemned to provide for expansion of Otis Elevator Company, one of the city's leading industrial employers; held: condemnation valid) and Miller v. City of Tacoma, 61 Wash. 2d 374, 378 P.2d 464 (1963) ("blighted area" condemned as part of comprehensive urban renewal plan; held: condemnation valid), with Hogue v. Port of Seattle, Note 4(a), *infra* (held: condemnation invalid).

4. Comment, The Public Use Limitation on Eminent Domain: An Advance Requiem, 58 Yale L.J. 599, 614 (1949):

Legal doctrines usually die quietly, if slowly. Their demise is generally accompanied by no more than soft sighs of relief at the courts' final acknowledgment of decay. But the theory of "public use" as a limitation on eminent domain—the notion that there are only certain limited "public purposes" for which private property may be expropriated—bulked so large in its prime and has taken so long in dying that, at the risk of disturbing the deathwatch, a few final words may be in order. . . . Doubtless the doctrine will continue to be evoked nostalgically in dicta and may even be employed authoritatively in rare, atypical situations. Kinder hands, however, would accord it the permanent interment in the digests that is so long overdue.

Consider, in the light of the following decisions, whether the words above are entirely prophetic.

(a) Civic leaders in the Seattle area had become concerned with the imbalance of industrial employment: one company, Boeing, engaged more than half the area's industrial work force. Believing that the lack of suitable plant sites was a major deterrent to a broadened industrial base, the leaders obtained a state law that enabled the Port of Seattle (a public body) to condemn so-called marginal land—fully developed agricultural and residential acreage—for resale as industrial sites.

The Supreme Court of Washington could not find a lawful public purpose. Hogue v. Port of Seattle, 54 Wash. 2d 799, 838-839, 341 P.2d 171, 193 (1959).

[T]he property owner is assured that, until our state constitution is amended, he may continue to own, possess, and use his property (for any lawful purpose) regardless of whether the state or any subdivision thereof may devise a plan for putting the property to a higher or better economic use than that to which the owner is currently devoting it. Unless the state or its subdivision can prove to the satisfaction of a court that it seeks to acquire the property for a "really public" use (and also pays just compensation for it), the owner may not be deprived of it without his consent.

But see Cannata v. City of New York, 11 N.Y.2d 210, 182 N.E.2d 395, 227 N.Y.S.2d 903 (1962) (95 acres of predominantly vacant residential tract condemned for industrial park; held: condemnation valid).

(b) The City of Charleston proposed a joint venture with a private concern whereby the city would condemn several parcels that would be leased to the concern for the construction and operation of a 500-car parking garage and convention center. On an adjoining two-acre parcel, which would be acquired privately, the concern would build a hotel, major department store, and restaurant. The convention center-hotel complex was intended to help revitalize downtown Charleston.

The South Carolina Supreme Court denied the city its power of eminent domain. The court concluded that the proposed undertaking failed constitutionally because it envisioned a taking of private property that would not be devoted to a public use. "However attractive the proposed complex, however desirable the project from a municipal planning viewpoint, the use of the power of eminent domain for such purposes runs squarely into the right of an individual to own property and use it as he pleases." Karesh v. City Council of City of Charleston, 271 S.C. 339, 247 S.E.2d 342 (1978).

(c) A bill pending in the Massachusetts legislature would have created a state agency to help finance mixed projects of "low" and "moderate" rental housing. The agency would make the mortgage loans to limited profit developers, but the precondition to a loan was an acceptable tenant selection plan. Tenants were to be selected so as "to avoid undue economic homogeneity." To help achieve this goal, the agency—through rent supplements—would additionally subsidize at least one quarter of the units in each project. The housing could be located anywhere, for the bill was not specifically directed to slum or blight removal.

The Supreme Judicial Court was asked to render an advisory opinion as to the legality of the proposed measure. At issue was whether the commonwealth's tax power, which, like eminent domain, must be used for a public purpose, could validly underwrite the program described above. Although the court implicitly endorsed the use of tax money to help clear slums or furnish low-rental housing, it boggled at a program that would encourage the building of "moderate" rental housing, for which no need had been asserted, in order to bring about mixtures of low- and middle-income families within a single project. Opinion of the Justices, 351 Mass. 316, 219 N.E.2d 18 (Mass. 1966).

But see People ex rel. City of Salem, 53 Ill. 2d 347, 291 N.E.2d 807 (1972) (state's Industrial Project Revenue Bond Act, which would stimulate private enterprise, held valid). Cf. also Pinsky, State Constitutional Limitations on Public Industrial Financing: An Historical and Economic Approach, 111 U. Pa. L. Rev. 265 (1963); Comment, State Constitutional Provisions Prohibiting the Loaning of Credit to Private Enterprise—A Suggested Analysis, 41 U. Colo. L. Rev. 135 (1969).

5. Do you believe there *should* be a "public purpose" limitation on how the legislature may spend its money for land acquisition via eminent domain, if the lawmakers have spoken and the city is ready to pay fair value? Consider this question in the light of the following situations:

(a) City A acquires a privately owned parcel for resale to a developer of luxury housing as part of a program to keep wealthy residents within the city.
(b) City B acquires a privately owned business building for resale to a minority owned bank as part of a program to stimulate minority enterprise.
(c) City C acquires some privately owned apartment houses for resale to an investment syndicate that will use the site for a professional sports arena and convention center.

(d) City D acquires some privately owned "holdout" properties for resale to an office developer who needs the sites to complete his land
assemblage. This is done to promote efficient and aesthetic office
development.

Would your views be any different if the cities instead were to give
various other subsidies to promote the several goals indicated?

In this connection, do you agree or disagree with the following?

> The conclusion is that there is no sufficient reason to limit the exercise of eminent
> domain any more than of other powers of government. All exercises, including
> regulations and taxations, are intrusions upon individual liberty, but they are
> necessary to prevent greater human losses in an interdependent society. Eminent
> domain poses no special threat to the individual that would require special
> limitations on the occasions of its exercise. It is not black magic, but merely one
> of the powers of government, to be used along with the other powers as long as
> some ordinary purpose of government is served. [Stoebuck, A General Theory of
> Eminent Domain, 47 Wash. L. Rev. 553, 597 (1972)]

6.   Do the "general welfare" limitation on police power and the "public
purpose" limitation on eminent domain mean the same thing? Professor Stoebuck argues above that eminent domain should not suffer any greater restraint
on the scope of its exercise than does the police power. Turn the statement
around. Should the police power suffer any greater restraint on the *scope* of its
exercise than does eminent domain?

7.   *Who may exercise the power of eminent domain?* In the United States a
long tradition exists of allowing certain regulated industries—e.g., railroads
and public utilities—to meet their land needs through eminent domain. More
recently, nonprofit institutions—for example, universities and hospitals—and
limited-profit companies formed to build below-market rental or sales housing, have been given the power to condemn. But when may the power be
validly delegated to private landowners who are not rendering a "public service"?

Consider the Utah statute before the Supreme Court in Clark v. Nash,
198 U.S. 361 (1905), which permitted persons to condemn privately held land
to obtain water for farming or mining. An individual, owning arid farmland,
sought to run an irrigation ditch across his neighbor's land that would connect
with the Fort Canyon Creek. Against the claim that the taking was for a
private use, the United States Supreme Court, through Justice Peckham,
wrote (at 367-368):

> In some States, probably in most of them, the proposition contended for
> by the plaintiffs in error would be sound. But whether a statute of a State
> permitting condemnation by an individual for the purpose of obtaining water for
> his land or for mining should be held to be a condemnation for a public use, and,
> therefore, a valid enactment, may depend upon a number of considerations

relating to the situation of a State and its possibilities for land cultivation. . . . It is not alone the fact that the land is arid and that it will bear crops if irrigated, or that the water is necessary for the purpose of working a mine, that is material; other facts might exist which are also material, such as the particular manner in which the irrigation is carried on or proposed, or how the mining is to be done in a particular place where water is needed for that purpose. The general situation and amount of the arid land, or of the mines themselves, might also be material, and what proportion of the water each owner should be entitled to; also the extent of the population living in the surrounding country, and whether each owner of land or mines could be, in fact, furnished with the necessary water in any other way than by condemnation in his own behalf, and not by a company, for his use and that of others.

Helped by findings that the condemnor had no alternative source of water supply, that his land would not produce without artificial irrigation, and that the condemnee's own water supply would not be impaired, the Court approved both the statute and its application.

The condemnee's damages, it should be noted, were only $40. Might the landowner have acquired the interest he sought, even against his unwilling neighbor, without benefit of eminent domain? Compare Berkeley Dev. Corp. v. Hutzler, page 552 *supra*. Might an inverted nuisance argument also be made? The refusal to permit a right-of-way essential for irrigation can be as damaging to the adjoining land as many of the forms of positive activity that courts would enjoin as a nuisance.

For further instances of the "private" exercise of eminent domain, see Strickley v. Highland Boy Gold Mining Co., 200 U.S. 527 (1906) (Court approved mining concern's use of the Utah statute to erect an aerial bucket line over privately owned lands to carry ore down to a railway station 1200 feet below the mines); Linggi v. Garovotti, 45 Cal. 2d 20, 286 P.2d 15 (1955) (landowner may be permitted to lay a private sewer line across an adjoining lot to connect with the public system); Estate of Waggoner v. Gleghorn, page 558 *supra*.

8.   Where the proposed re-use is one that is clearly "public"—a park or playground, for example—may a court look into the condemnor's motives to see if they are pure?

In several instances condemnation appears to have been used to thwart black or interracial housing from entering white neighborhoods. The most litigated attempt concerned the village of Deerfield, Illinois, a Chicago suburb. There, after approving two new subdivisions, the village learned of the builder's plan for an interracial development. Within days, the village park board voted to acquire the subdivision sites for park use, although the parcels had not previously been considered in discussions over park expansion. Condemnation was begun in the state court, which the developer then sought to block in the federal court. Both suits enjoyed a lively time of it as they stepped from trial to appellate stage and back again, but the outcome turned on the state court decision. There, in Deerfield Park District v. Progress Development Corp., 26 Ill. 2d 296, 186 N.E.2d 360 (1962), the Illinois Supreme Court refused to forestall the taking unless "its sole and exclusive purpose" was racially inspired. If the village could establish, as it ultimately did, both a need for parks and the suitability of the land in question, the condemnation was valid despite the accompanying motive. The United States Supreme Court denied certiorari, 372 U.S. 968 (1963). For a stirring account of the goings-on in Deerfield before the lawsuits began, see H. Rosen and D. Rosen, But Not Next Door (1962).

Similar occurrences have been reported around the country.

(a) Creve Coeur, Missouri—a black physician was unable to complete his house when his land (and that of two other families) was taken for a park and playground. Although conceding the questionability of improper motive, the court declared that "the motive which actuates and induces the legislative body to enact legislation is wholly the responsibility of that body, and courts have no jurisdiction to intervene in that area." City of Creve Coeur v. Weinstein, 329 S.W.2d 399 (Mo. Ct. App. 1959) (injunction denied).

(b) Western Springs, Illinois—after a black surgeon had purchased a homesite, the park district moved to condemn his lot.

(c) Rutledge, Pennsylvania—the borough selected the home of an NAACP official "for use as a site for a municipal building and other municipal purposes."

(d) Richland, Oregon—a water district voted to condemn the lot of a homebuilding black couple "to preserve sufficient land for future development and sanitation control."

In the last three instances injunctions to bar condemnation were reportedly issued.

Cf. also Blankner v. City of Chicago, 504 F.2d 1037, 1040-1041 (7th Cir. 1974), citing Green Street Assn. v. Daley, 373 F.2d 1, 6 (7th Cir. 1967), *cert. denied,* 387 U.S. 932 (1967) (if the area were in fact slum and blighted, the defendants' motives in designating it for renewal would be irrelevant).

9. *The necessity for the public use:*

(a) "The property of no person shall be taken for public use without just compensation." Conn. Const. art. 1, §11. This language, typical of that found in most state constitutions, was at issue in a 1965 statewide referendum. By a sharply divided vote, a constitutional convention had proposed an amendment to §11, reading: "No property shall be taken for public use unless the taking be necessary for such use, and then, only upon the payment of just compensation."

Consider the implications of this proposed change. Its chief drafter defended it by saying that "constitutional protection of property rights against greatly increased governmental agency land taking is of prime importance." The New Haven Register, Oct. 14, 1954. Opponents spoke of the added expense and delay. Some called the change "meaningless." Ibid.

After a bitter campaign, in which the Connecticut Urban Renewal Association spent large sums to fight the change, the electorate voted to leave the constitution as it was.

(b) "In all cases where land is required for public use, . . . it must be located in the manner which will be most compatible with the greatest public good and the least private injury. . . ." Mont. Code Ann. §70-30-110 (1975).

Without considering seriously whether it would be feasible to improve an existing right of way, the State Highway Commission decided to build a 14.2-mile parallel route that would cut across fertile farmland. On the "benefit" side, both the new and the old routes were of equal merit. Relying on the above statute, the court refused to allow condemnation if a detailed study, which the commission was directed to make, failed to show that the proposed route would cause "less private injury" than improvement of the existing route. State Highway Commn. v. Danielsen, 146 Mont. 539, 409 P.2d 443 (1965). Should every state have such a statute? How is "private injury" fixed? Is it simply computing what it will cost to acquire the right of way?

10. *Excess condemnation:* The state plans to widen an existing roadway from 60 feet to 100 feet. May it condemn a 190-foot strip—150 feet more than is now needed—to serve any of the following purposes?

(a) Should further widening become necessary, the state will have already acquired the needed frontage—at present-day prices.
(b) Since increased traffic is expected to cause a sharp rise in the value of abutting lands, the state can capture this value by selling off to private developers what it does not need; see, e.g., City of Cincinnati v. Vester, 33 F.2d 242 (6th Cir. 1929).
(c) The additional frontage will produce a less expensive source of land-fill than could be purchased commercially; cf. United States v. Certain Parcels of Land, 233 F. Supp. 544 (W.D. Mich. 1964).
(d) The additional frontage will help to protect the scenic view along the highway.
(e) The additional frontage, inter alia, will make it unlikely that the state will be forced to pay excess severance damages to abutting owners; cf. People ex rel. Dept. of Pub. Works v. Superior Court, 68 Cal. 2d 206, 436 P.2d 342, 65 Cal. Rptr. 342 (1968).

See generally 2A Nichols, Eminent Domain §7.5122 (rev. 3d ed. 1980); Matheson, Excess Condemnation in California; Proposals for Statutory and Constitutional Change, 42 S. Cal. L. Rev. 421 (1969).

11. *Extraterritorial condemnation:* When may community A accommodate its needs by acquiring land in community B? Must the state legislature first

give approval? If approval is given, will (should) the courts intervene to protect the "interests" of community B? Consider the following examples:

(a) A downstate city acquires an upstate watershed for water supply.
(b) A city acquires farmland in an unincorporated township (incorporated village) for a jetport.
(c) A city acquires woodland (a public golf course) in an unincorporated township (incorporated village) for a recreational center for city residents.
(d) A city housing authority acquires a 100-acre parcel in an unincorporated township (incorporated village) for a low-income housing project that will help to relocate the city's urban renewal site occupants.

See generally 1 Nichols, Eminent Domain §2.24 (rev. 3d ed. 1980).

§18.2 Problems of Just Compensation

a. Highest and Best Use

H. & R. CORP. v. DISTRICT OF COLUMBIA
351 F.2d 740 (D.C. Cir. 1965)

WASHINGTON, CIRCUIT JUDGE. This is a condemnation case. The District of Columbia took certain properties near Washington Circle, in the Northwest section of Washington, adjoining the central business area of the city, for use as a park and a police station. The owners demanded a jury trial as to the amount of compensation.

The measure of compensation is the fair market value of the condemned property just prior to the taking. United States v. Miller, 317 U.S. 369 (1943). In an effort to establish the market value of the property at that time, the owners asserted that there was a reasonable possibility that the property would be rezoned for a more profitable use—the construction of large apartment houses—than the existing zoning (for the construction of residences and small apartment houses) would allow.[1] Such rezoning, which they claimed would

1. Strictly speaking, the issue is not whether there is a reasonable possibility of rezoning at the time of taking; the issue is whether knowledgeable buyers thought that there was a reasonable possibility of rezoning at that time. Hence, a decision by the zoning commission that the property would or would not be rezoned, if such decision had not been made public at the time of taking, would not itself be relevant to this inquiry. Cf. Rapid Transit Co. v. United States, 295 F.2d 465, 466 (10th Cir. 1961); United States v. Meadow Brook Club, 259 F.2d 41, 45 (2d Cir.), *cert. denied,* 358 U.S. 921 (1958). These cases seem to focus on the question of the *actual* probability of a zoning change at the time of taking. While this approach is at odds with the fair market value standard, it would probably make no difference in most cases. Generally, a policy of the zoning commission would be well known and would have an impact on fair market value.

add about a third to the estimated fair market value of the land, had never in fact been requested, much less ordered. While the owners did not claim that they were entitled to this increased amount, they argued that the possibility of this increase in value should be taken into account in calculating market value at the time of taking. Two expert witnesses, testifying for the appellants, stated their belief that just prior to the time of taking, a knowledgeable buyer would have taken into account the reasonable probability that the land in question would be rezoned.

The trial judge apparently rejected this consideration as an element in fair market value. His charge, although it was somewhat confusing, reflected his opinion that the possibility of a zoning change should not be taken into account as affecting market value at the time of taking. He stated:

> You are instructed that all of the lots now under consideration in Square 37 were zoned R-5B on the dates of taking. There has been no testimony in this case from the Zoning Commission of the District of Columbia Government showing that on the dates of taking there was a reasonable probability that the zoning of any of the lots at issue would be rezoned to a higher density zoning.
>
> You are, therefore, instructed that you are not permitted to speculate as to what the Zoning Commission of the District of Columbia might have done with regard to rezoning this property, following the dates of taking.

It is true that the charge also contained a correct statement of the test that the jury was to apply:

> Fair market value is defined in the law as the price which a willing seller, who is not obliged to sell, would be willing to accept and the price which a willing buyer, who is not obliged to buy, would be willing to pay for the property. This definition of fair market value, of course, assumes that the buyer is knowledgeable and that the seller is knowledgeable. This means that both the buyer and the seller have full knowledge of all the present or potential elements of value involved in the transaction into which they are willing to enter. . . .
>
> . . . Fair market value is the criterion and this fair market value is based upon the probabilities as they appear to the willing buyer and the willing seller.

However, the charge is at best ambiguous. And the specific language instructing the jury not to speculate on a zoning change would probably override the general instruction to look to "the probabilities as they appear to the willing buyer and the willing seller." We think that the net result of the charge was to give the jury the mistaken impression that they could not consider the possibility of rezoning.

The judge has a responsibility to prevent the jury from indulging in baseless speculation about future changes in zoning. In our view the judge's responsibility is to determine whether a jury would be justified in concluding on the evidence that a willing buyer at the time of taking would have taken into account the possibility of rezoning in deciding the fair market value of the condemned property. If it would, the judge should instruct the jury to take into account the possibility of a zoning change. Only if the trial judge is satisfied that a jury could not reasonably conclude that the possibility of a zoning change would affect the fair market value should he instruct the jury to disregard that element of value. In deciding whether there is sufficient evidence for the jury, the trial court should not resolve questions of credibility. But a jury question is not presented by a witness' bare assertion that zoning change was probable. His opinion must have some foundation in fact. "It is axiomatic that a witness must explain the 'observational basis' of his testimony . . . in order to meet even the test of admissibility. 2 Wigmore, Evidence §562." Rollerson v. United States, 119 U.S. App. D.C. 400, 406, 334 F.2d 269, 275 (1964). In this case there was a clash of credible testimony, based on a reasonable foundation, regarding the probability of a change in zoning. Under such circumstances, the judge should have submitted the matter to the jury for its decision under proper instructions. Contrary to the trial judge's charges, Zoning Commission testimony need not be adduced in order to put the issue before the jury. [2]

Appellants also protest the trial judge's decision on the admissibility of evidence. He ruled that a report of the Zoning Advisory Council, rendered to the Zoning Commission, concerning land somewhat similarly situated, was inadmissible in evidence because it was irrelevant. [3] The text of the proferred report is as follows:

> The Council invites attention to our report in Case No. 1 heard on December 5, which is incorporated therein by reference. For convenience, the application [sic] portion of this report is quoted: "By memorandum of April 12, 1962, all Commission members were reminded by the staff that expansion of the R-5-D district [zoned for high rise apartment houses] is essential. This is a conclusion based on the assumption that Commission policy endorsing high rise apartment development peripheral to the Central Business District is sound and that the rate of construction reached during 1960-61 ought to be maintained. This building pace should not be slowed as a result of two few available sites and inflated land costs, a combination which results in high rents and undue investment risk. (R-5-D areas total only three-tenths of one percent of the City's zoned area.)
>
> "We think here, and in a similar case opposite on the south side of L Street, which is to be heard on December 10th, that the only pertinent issues are minor and solely those of adjustment of boundary lines of that well-established portion of the R-5-D district known as the New Hampshire coridore [sic]. All issues and policies should be considered, however, and we believe the Commission should not loose [sic] sight of basic objectives."

2. One Government witness testified: "I don't think the Zoning Commission, to the best of my knowledge, ever adopts any official position except with respect to specific properties."

3. The Zoning Advisory Council is a statutory body, established to advise the Zoning Commission concerning proposed amendments to the Commission's regulations and maps. See D.C. Code §5-417 (1961).

As to two of the appellants the report was properly excluded. The declarations of taking of the property of appellants Norair Realty Company and Olga Ruppert May, et al., were filed on October 18, 1962. Appellant H. & R. Corporation had two pieces of property taken, one on October 18, 1962, and one on January 16, 1963. The report of the Zoning Advisory Council was submitted to the Zoning Commission on December 10, 1962. It seems clear that the report had not been written on October 18, 1962, so that it cannot go to establish the value of the land taken on that date. [4] As to H. & R.'s property taken in January, 1963, assuming that the report had been made public before the day of taking, the admissibility of the report depends on a balance of the probative value of the report and the delay and confusion that its admission would cause. It is true that this report related to different property than that here at issue: that the Advisory Council is not the ultimate policy-making body; that the staff of the Zoning Commission may not have been correctly quoted; and that the jury might have to be instructed to use the report for some purposes and not for others. On the other hand, knowledge of the contents of this report would probably have increased the amount that an informed buyer would have paid for this property. In deciding whether or not to admit the report, the trial judge should make some inquiry into the significance attached to such reports by the Zoning Commission and the real estate community.

The decision of the District Court is

Reversed and the cases remanded for further proceedings not inconsistent with this opinion.

DANAHER, CIRCUIT JUDGE (dissenting): My colleagues conclude that the District Court erred in its exclusion of a December 10, 1962 report of the Zoning Advisory Council, the text of which they have quoted. The proffer rested upon the ground that the report contained a statement of policy by the Zoning Commission. Apparently the Zoning Commission had never acted on the report submitted by the Council. There was no showing that any of the property owners in the affected area had ever applied for a change in zoning. There was no evidence that the Zoning Commission had adopted or even contemplated a change in policy. The District's appraisers had submitted their opinions as to the highest and best use of the land without regard to any possibility, either reasonably or remote, that in the future some higher value might be attributed to the property because of a zoning change. Thus the "report" was not rebuttal.

The Supreme Court has told us that "The highest and most profitable use for which the property is adaptable and needed or likely to be needed in the reasonably near future is to be considered, not necessarily as the measure

---

4. The Advisory Council report of December 10, 1962, contains statements purporting to characterize Commission policy and a previous staff report. While we think that these statements are inadmissible, except to show what the Advisory Council considered the Commission's policy to be, it is open to the appellants to try to prove Commission policy by the introduction of competent evidence in a new trial.

of value, but to the full extent that the prospect of demand for such use affects the market value while the property is privately held." Olson v. United States, 292 U.S. 246, 255 (1934). . . .

In the *Olson* case, a unanimous Court added [id. at 257]:

> The determination is to be made in the light of all facts affecting the market value *that are shown by the evidence* taken in connection with those of such general notoriety as not to require proof. Elements affecting value that depend upon events or combinations of occurrences which, while within the realm of possibility, are not fairly shown to be *reasonably probable,* should be excluded from consideration for that would be to allow mere speculation and conjecture to become a guide for the ascertainment of value—a thing to be condemned in business transactions as well as in judicial ascertainment of truth. (Emphasis supplied.)

The trial judge excluded the proferred report and in my view, his ruling was quite within the guidelines thus spelled out. He could readily discern the absence of foundation for its admissibility. He could see the infirmities noted by my colleagues—as they were bound to do on this record: "It is true that this report related to different property than that here at issue; that the Advisory Council is not the ultimate policy-making body; that the staff of the Zoning Commission may not have been correctly quoted. . . ."

There was no showing on this record that the Council's "report" had even been announced prior to the time of the second H. & R. Corporation taking on January 16, 1963, yet my colleagues indulge in another "assumption" in ruling with reference to it.

I fail to understand how any such "report" subject to the various infirmities I have mentioned, can be deemed to constitute relevant evidence to establish a substantial possibility, much less a "reasonable probability," that rezoning would be based upon it and that higher valuations might thereupon follow.

I believe that the ruling of the trial judge was not erroneous and that his charge, taken as a whole, was adapted to the issues and fairly instructed the jury as to the proper basis for ascertainment of its awards. I would affirm the judgments.

LEVIN v. STATE OF NEW YORK

17 A.D.2d 335, 234 N.Y.S.2d 481 (1962), aff'd, 13 N.Y.2d 87, 192 N.E.2d 155, 242 N.Y.S.2d 193 (1963)

COON, J. The Court of Claims has awarded $557,365 to claimants as compensation for land taken and for consequential damages to land not taken. The claimants contend they are entitled to $1,056,695. The State asserts claimants are entitled to approximately $257,615. This great differential is not only due to the difference of value opinion between expert appraisers, but is largely dependent upon the consideration of the effect of a profitable lease which was existent at the time of the taking. In general, the State claims that it should pay for only unimproved land on an acreage basis, while claimants contend that they are entitled to compensation for the loss of a highly profitable executed lease of most of the land which was taken.

Claimants, through their corporate agent, Rebrug Corp., had been trying for about a year to find a suitable and adequate site for the operations needed by Reeves Instrument Corp., an electronics manufacturer. The requirements were difficult to find in the area, including: (1) proximity to a labor source; (2) elevation to "sight" instruments on distant objects; (3) adequate parking for employees who would be largely dependent upon private car transportation. Finally claimants' agent, Rebrug Corp., found a desirable site and, after many consultations with Reeves, purchased three contiguous parcels of land totaling 49 acres, locally zoned as residential. The cost of the unimproved land on all three parcels, zoned as residential, was $3500 per acre. On October 6, 1954, claimants' agent, Rebrug Corp., contracted to buy the 49 acres at that price. On October 26, 28.2 acres were rezoned to light industrial use, which opened the door for the Reeves plant. On December 1, 1954, Rebrug took title, and on December 4 Rebrug conveyed the title to claimants, and on the same day the lease from the claimants to Reeves was executed. This lease provided for the construction of buildings, with specifications attached, and for the payment of rental for the improved land of $380,900 per year for 23 years. On December 31, 1954, the State appropriated 34.1 acres, 21.1 of which was from the parcel rezoned industrial, and thereby rendered the performance of the lease impossible.

Aside from fringe differences as to the consequential damage to the remaining industrially zoned property and two zoned classes of residential property, the fundamental difference between the parties is whether any consideration should be given to the value of the existing lease. Claimants contend that the loss of clearly expected future earnings constitutes a damage, while the State contends that inasmuch as the buildings had not been actually constructed, it need pay only the value of the unimproved "raw" land.

At this point it should be noted that the good faith of claimants is conceded. But, beyond the concession, it appears in the record that prior to acquiring title and the execution of the lease to Reeves, claimants and their agent had reason to believe (upon proposed maps and information from State engineers) that only an inconsequential (if any) part of the subject property would be taken. The State thereafter changed the plans and appropriated the major part of the property which had the highest potential value.

It is also conceded that Reeves was a "prime" tenant, meaning that its financial responsibility to perform its obligations under the lease was unquestioned.

An expert witness for claimants has capitalized the agreed rental less the estimated cost of the improvements, and has considered that factor, among other things, in arriving at claimants' damage. The Court of Claims has found, with evidence to support the findings, that the cost of improvements could be ascertained with reasonable certainty. This evaluation of reasonably expected earnings has been approved in Mattydale Shopping Center v. State of New York (303 N.Y. 974, *revg.* 279 App. Div. 704) and explained in St. Agnes Cemetary v. State of New York (3 N.Y.2d 37, 45). The State's expert refused to consider the executed lease at all in evaluating claimants' damage except for limitation purposes, mentioned later herein. The Court of Claims was not bound to accept his rejection of any value to the lease. The fact that claimants stood to make a handsome profit from their favorable acquisition of the subject property and subsequent favorable lease to Reeves should not deprive claimants of the rewards of a successful business enterprise, which was lost because of the appropriation.

Claimants not only had the executed lease with a prime tenant, they had obtained a favorable rezoning, spent substantial sums for plans and engineering work, obligated themselves to completion of agreed improvements by a certain date under penalty, and had actually progressed substantially in clearing and grading the land. To say that claimants' successful business venture, of which they were deprived, is worth nothing more than the present value of the barren land originally acquired, is ignoring the realities of commercial transactions.

The single factor of the lease which the State's expert did consider was a provision giving Reeves the option to purchase the land at $7500 per acre, plus the cost to date of the improvements, if the improvements were not completed by an agreed date. This agreement between the parties, dependent upon a contingency not likely to happen, should not benefit the State. Its purpose was collateral to true evaluation and it was designed to encourage prompt construction of the improvements. It was in no sense a valuation of the property in a free market with a willing buyer and a willing seller.

There is evidence in the record of comparable sales which demonstrate the fantastic value of land space in the area of the subject property. The State claims that they are not comparable because a few miles distant and closer to New York City. These sales are of evidentiary value and the trial court undoubtedly weighed their nature and location in relation to the subject property.

We think the trial court properly considered the reasonably expected income fixed by firm contract and not dependent upon speculative profits from a nonexistent business, as in Levitin v. State of New York (12 A.D.2d 6). The buildings are nonexistent here, but the cost of them in accordance with agreed specifications and plans presents a factual question for the trial court. The Court of Claims has obviously not accepted either the evidence of claimants or that of the State at face value, but has fixed a market value and consequential damage which is well within the range of the testimony. Upon all of the evidence relevant to market value of the property at the time of taking, the Judge of the Court of Claims who heard the witnesses and viewed the property, has fixed a value upon the land taken and the consequential damage to the remainder. Upon this record we see no compelling reason to either lower or raise that evaluation.

The judgment should be affirmed, without costs.

BERGAN, P.J. (dissenting). On October 6, 1954 claimants through their agent contracted to buy 49 acres of unimproved land for a little over $171,000 at $3500 an acre, title passing to claimants on December 1, 1954. Within a month the State appropriated 34.1 acres of this unimproved land.

An award of $557,365 has been made. This amount, which is over 300% more for 34.1 acres than claimants paid within a few weeks for 49 acres is in our judgment grossly excessive. The award reaches these huge proportions because claimants intended to erect improvements on the land; had obtained a zoning change; and had entered into contractual arrangements with a third party for the ultimate rental of the projected improvements.

But there were no improvements on this land when the State appropriated it. To treat a plan to put up a building as a building that has been put up; and then to capitalize the rent reserved in the lease as though the building had been put up and occupied and the lease had successfully run its full course to the end, seems an unrealistic approach to a proper award in condemnation.

Indeed, it charges to the public authority condemning land an obligation to carry out a projected commercial enterprise on the land to a successful termination with no risk, no effort, and no investment by the claimants. A party is entitled to "just compensation" but this is for the land taken and its improvements. Just compensation requires a consideration of the value of land as it may be affected by potential growth under favorable circumstances; but it ought not to include as completed improvements the mere intention and purpose of the owners to improve the land.

An improvement is a physical entity and not a contract; and in these circumstances a "lease" to use land in the future after it has been actually improved does not spell out an "improvement." All this is still merely the intention of private parties to do something with land in the future which they had not done in the present.

No case in New York has gone as far as this. The decision in Mattydale Shopping Center v. State of New York (303 N.Y. 974, *revg.* 270 App. Div. 704) was essentially a fact evaluation by the Court of Appeals in one of the rare situations when on successive reversals a question of fact comes to that court. The court held, merely, that the Appellate Division decision was not in accordance with the weight of evidence. It cannot be read to sanction as a matter of law the right of owners of unimproved land in all cases to recover as "improvements" in the full value of what they expect to put on the land in the future.

Moreover, the theory by which the capitalization of this projected improvement was treated by the Court of Claims as though it had been actually carried out and the use of this as a measure of damage was disapproved in the opinion in St. Agnes Cemetery v. State of New York (3 N.Y.2d 37, 45).

The judgment should be modified to allow claimants $257,615.

GIBSON and HERLIHY, JJ., concur with COON, J.; BERGAN, P.J., dissents and votes to modify the judgment in an opinion in which REYNOLDS, J., concurs.

Judgment affirmed, without costs.

NOTES AND QUESTIONS

1. Both H. & R. Corp. and Levin assume that the condemnor must pay top dollar for the land that it takes, reflecting the most favorable set of valuation circumstances. Why is that?

2. Suppose that the H. & R. Corp. parcel had already been zoned for large apartment houses when condemnation occurred. Might the condemnor offer evidence that the zoning commission had been considering a zoning change that would *decrease* the parcel's value?

3. Suppose that the H. & R. Corp. parcel had been zoned for large apartment houses, but three months prior to condemnation the city had rezoned the parcel to permit only small apartment houses. Might the landowners successfully set aside the rezoning by arguing that the city acted in order to reduce the condemnation award? May courts explore legislative motive in this situation?

4. Suppose that Rebrug (Levin) had been denied rezoning on grounds that condemnation was likely, as evident from proposed maps. Might Rebrug successfully overturn this denial by arguing that the town acted in order to reduce the condemnation award? What if the town replied that Rebrug sought rezoning in order to inflate the condemnation award? Also, is it relevant that the state and not the town had condemned the property?

5. When does zoning become vested for purpose of valuation in eminent domain: is it at the same time that vesting would assure an owner the right to continue and complete his development? Putting the question in context, if *Levin* had been an attack on the town's decision to rescind a shopping center classification (and not a condemnation case), would Rebrug have a sufficiently vested interest to prevent the rezoning?

b.　Loss of Goodwill and Business Advantage

COMMUNITY DEVELOPMENT AGENCY v. ABRAMS

15 Cal. 3d. 813, 126 Cal. Rptr. 473, 543 P.2d 905 (1975)

Supra, page 4.

NOTES AND QUESTIONS

1. During World War I, the federal government acquired a large tract of land in Maryland for the Aberdeen Proving Ground. One parcel, consisting

of 440 acres, was used by plaintiffs in the business of growing and canning whole-grain shoe-peg corn, a special grade for which their lands were especially adapted. In the condemnation proceeding, plaintiffs were paid for their land and buildings, but denied compensation for the loss of business that could not be re-established elsewhere. The Supreme Court upheld the judgment for the defendant. Mitchell v. United States, 267 U.S. 371, 45 S. Ct. 293, 69 L. Ed. 644 (1925).

Justice Brandeis wrote the opinion.

> The special value of land due to its adaptability for use in a particular business is an element which the owner of land is entitled, under the Fifth Amendment, to have considered in determining the amount to be paid as the just compensation upon a taking by eminent domain. . . . Doubtless such special value of the plaintiffs' land was duly considered by the President in fixing the amount to be paid therefor. The settled rules of law, however, precluded his considering in that determination consequential damages for losses to their business, or for its destruction. . . . No recovery therefor can be had now as for a taking of the business. There is no finding as a fact that the Government took the business, or that what it did was intended as a taking. There can be no recovery . . . if the intention to take is lacking. [267 U.S. at 344-45]

2.   "There is no finding as a fact that the Government took the business, or that what it did was intended as a taking. . . ." (Mitchell opinion.)

When does a "taking" of a business occur? Consider, by contrast, Kimball Laundry v. United States, 338 U.S. 1 (1949). Here, the War Department condemned claimant's laundry plant for successive one-year terms from 1942 to 1946, and used the plant facilities for army personnel. Having no other means of servicing its own customers, the laundry suspended business. With four justices dissenting, the Court fixed the measure of damage to include the value of claimant's trade routes during the period of army occupancy. Justice Frankfurter, who wrote for the Court, spoke approvingly of *Mitchell* but was able to distinguish it. Can you see how? Justice Douglas's dissent read in part (id. at 23-24):

> The truth of the matter is that the United States is being forced to pay not for what it gets but for what the owner loses. The value of trade-routes represents the patronage of the customers of the laundry. Petitioner, I assume, lost some of them as a result of the government's temporary taking of the laundry. But the government did not take them. There was indeed no possible way in which it could have used them. Hence the doctrine that makes the United States pay for them is new and startling. It promises swollen awards which Congress in its generosity might permit but which it has never been assumed the Constitution compels.

Which is the more valid measure of compensation—value to the condemner or loss to the condemnee?

If government acquires (nationalizes?) a going business and continues its operation, it must pay for the "going-concern" value of the business. See, e.g., Omaha v. Omaha Water Co., 218 U.S. 180 (1910); In re Fifth Ave. Coach Lines, Inc., 18 N.Y.2d 212, 219 N.E.2d 410, 273 N.Y.S.2d 52 (1966).

3.   One author distinguishes two forms of good will: the increment attributable to trade advantage that may derive from a strategic location (quasi monopoly), and the increment attributable to the personality or business acumen of the proprietor (a laundry route, for example). One indication of the second is that a prospective buyer would demand either a management contract with the seller or his promise not to compete for a specified time.

Those who would not compensate for good-will damages argue that the businessman is a risk-taker, and that the prospect of an uncompensated taking is simply another risk he should shoulder along with those of increased competition, technological change, population movement, etc. In reply, one might ask whether businessmen do, in fact, account for this risk; if so, might they not overcompensate and become chary of new investment; finally, is not the risk often borne by the small operator who is already insecurely financed?

Also opposed to compensation is the argument that the loss of a quasi monopoly should not entitle one to be made whole. Yet, competitors (if there are any) will benefit from the removal—and they are *not* assessed; the cost of public improvement is partly concealed and, more important, unevenly distributed. See generally Note, 53 Colum. L. Rev. 660 (1953).

4.   Most American state courts subscribe to the federal rule and refuse to compensate for loss of good will. See Banner Milling Co. v. State of New York, 240 N.Y. 533, 148 N.E. 668 (1925); 4 Nichols, Eminent Domain §13.3 (1980). But a few courts, even while stating the rule, seem to have fudged. See, for example, Housing Authority of Bridgeport v. Lustig, 139 Conn. 73, 90 A.2d 169 (1952) (poultry slaughterer awarded $16,500 for loss of building valued at $6,500 *qua* building; higher award based on building's location and "suitability" for business); State v. Williams, 65 N.J. Super. 518, 168 A.2d 233 (1961) (gas station owner awarded $60,000 after testifying to business losses as evidence of the suitability of the site for a gas station).

Can it be argued that the value of land necessarily includes the "quasi monopoly" advantage of the site that should be capitalized—based on business income—in the same way that a site bearing an office building or apartment house is valued?

The courts of Britain and Canada have long required compensation for loss of good will. See, e.g., White v. Commissioners, 22 L.T.R. (n.s.) 591 (Ex. 1870); Re McCauley and City of Toronto, 18 Ont. 416 (ch. 1889).

5.   Also, occasional American statutes such as the newly enacted California law in the *Abrams* case, *supra*, require compensation for loss of good will. See also Fla. Stat. Ann. §73.071(3)(1979) (business of more than five years' standing); 19 Vt. Stat. Ann. §221(2)(1968); New York City Admn. Code §§K51-44.0 (acquisitions in upstate New York for expansion of New York City water supply). The latter statute, which dates from 1906, was imposed upon

the city by a none-too-friendly state legislature. Under its terms, a business-man may also recover for the loss of customers forced to leave their homes even though his site has not been condemned. Matter of Huie, 18 A.D.2d 270, 239 N.Y.S.2d 178 (3d Dept. 1963).

Might a New York City condemnee, for whom the loss of good will is usually noncompensable, claim a denial of equal protection in view of the statute cited above?

6.   Other noncompensable expenses, in the absence of statute, may in-clude the removal cost of business equipment and inventory, moving expenses, and "starting-up" expenses at a new location. See generally 4A Nichols, Emi-nent Domain §14.2471 (1980). For a statutory attempt to mitigate these losses in urban renewal and other federally aided acquisitions, see 42 U.S.C.A. §§4601 et seq. (1973).

c.   **Consequential Damages**

DENNISON v. STATE
22 N.Y.2d 409, 239 N.E.2d 708, 293 N.Y.S.2d 68 (1968)

KEATING, J. Like most programs undertaken in the name of Twentieth Century progress, the massive public highway construction launched in recent years has produced its share of problems and inconveniences. Of particular concern has been the damage done to the quiet beauty of many once remote and inaccessible areas, as well as the intrusion of the seemingly endless line of asphalt and concrete into the enclaves which many people have sought as surcease from the hustle and bustle of modern day life.

The home of Ira and Dorothy Dennison located in a remote wooded area in Lake George, New York, was unfortunately in the path of one such highway, the Luzerne Road-Lake George Interchange. The area in which the Dennisons' colonial frame house was located, as described in the opinion of the Court of Claims, consisted of generally high and beautifully wooded and land-scaped land. The west area of the property sloped downward sharply to the south and west and was covered with a natural stand of trees. The entire eastern section of the property was surrounded by many tall pine, maple, birch, oak and fruit trees. There were no telephone or electric poles as all services were underground. A stream which ran into Lake George formed one border of the property. The landscaping included exotic shrubs and trees. Large shade trees bordered on the lawns. A pine grove at the south end of the property protected the residence from the elements. A raspberry and aspara-gus garden and dwarf apple trees were part of the landscaped area. In sum, as the Court of Claims Judge concluded, the property "was entirely secluded, quiet and peaceful". (48 Misc. 2d 778, 780.)

The aftermath of the condemnation of a portion of the property and the construction of the highway is vividly described in the opinion of the Court of Claims:

As a result of the appropriation, a new highway has been constructed which crosses Old Mill Brook at a point westerly of claimants' residence and continues across the westerly part of the claimants' premises at a distance of about 200 ± feet from said residence. In place of the beautiful view of forest and mountain, which claimants could see from their westerly windows and living areas on the west side of their residence, has been substituted the new highway supported by an embankment approximately 27 feet above grade level at its crossing of Old Mill Brook and averaging approximately 20 feet in elevation above the westerly lawns of claimants' property. All of the sylvan beauty afforded by the forest pre-existing the highway and the privacy and quiet it provided are gone, for the State necessarily removed the trees in the course of constructing the new highway. The complete privacy and quiet the claimants enjoyed has been taken from them because the new highway presents a stream of automobile traffic with its attendant noise, lights and odors (*supra,* pp. 782-783).

In awarding damages for the partial taking of the Dennisons' property, the Court of Claims took into consideration "the loss of privacy and seclusion, the loss of view, the traffic noise, lights and odors all as factors causing consequential damage to the remaining property". The Appellate Division (Third Department) unanimously affirmed. We granted leave to appeal.

The State argues that the courts below were in error in considering noise as a factor in making an award for consequential damages and urges that the order be reversed and the case remanded to the Court of Claims for a new trial at which the court should make an award without considering the injury to the value of the claimants' property caused by the noise of passing traffic.

The State concedes that it is well settled in this State that, where there is a partial taking, consequential damages which ensue upon the taking are to be considered in determining the award and that, among other things, damages which arise from the use of the parcel taken are entitled to consideration (see, e.g., South Buffalo Ry. Co. v. Kirkover, 176 N.Y. 301).

The State argues, however, that not all elements of consequential damages resulting from the use to be made of the condemned property are to be considered. To be excluded from consideration are elements of damage which are not peculiar to the owner of the remaining property but are suffered by the public generally. Thus, the State points to the fact that, where there has been no partial taking of property, an owner whose property adjoins a public highway would not be entitled to damages resulting from the depreciation of his property due to the noise of cars and trucks passing on the highway. (See, e.g., Mathewson v. New York State Thruway Auth., 11 A.D.2d 782 [2 Dept.], *affd.* 9 N.Y.2d 788; Bennett v. Long Is. R.R. Co., 181 N.Y. 431; Nunnally v. United States, 239 F.2d 521 [4th Cir.].) Therefore, a property owner should not be entitled to compensation for such damages merely because of the fortuitous circumstance that a portion of his property was needed to construct the highway.

While this argument is not without some merit, we believe that it overlooks the method by which the courts below awarded damages and the practical difficulties involved in adopting the rule it suggests.

The courts below did not make a separate award for damages due to noise but rather merely considered it as one factor in determining the decrease in value to the remaining property. As we view the case, it would have been practically impossible for the court to separate the noise element from the other elements which, it is conceded, were properly considered—the loss of privacy, seclusion and view. Any reduction which would be made on remand would be purely arbitrary and at best speculative. How could it be determined which portion of the diminution in value was due to loss of privacy and view and which portion was due to noise? The State does not suggest an answer but argues steadfastly that such a determination must be made.

This does not answer the question and is clearly contrary to cases in this and other jurisdictions which have recognized that, where there has been a partial taking of property of the kind present here, the noise element may be considered as one of several factors in determining consequential damages (South Buffalo Ry. Co. v. Kirkover, *supra;* Shano v. Fifth Ave. & H St. Bridge Co., 189 Pa. 245; Crawford v. Central Nebraska Public Power & Irrigation Dist., 154 Neb. 832).

In conclusion, we would note that we are not unmindful of the State's argument that there are certain inconveniences which property owners must endure without monetary compensation if we are to have the advantages of modern means of transportation (see, e.g., Bopp v. State of New York, 19 N.Y.2d 368, 373). In the instant case and cases of like kind, however, we believe that the practical difficulties attendant upon accepting the State's theory of evaluating damages outweighs any benefit likely to be derived from applying it.

The order of the Appellate Division should be affirmed, with costs.

CHIEF JUDGE FULD (concurring). I agree with Judge Keating and would simply add that we are not, contrary to intimations in the dissenting opinion, "accept[ing] future traffic noise as an element of consequential damage" (p. 414) in "quite unrestricted form" (p. 415).

The essential factor which distinguishes the case before us from the general run of cases—and, perhaps, relates it to those involving hospitals and cemeteries (see, e.g., Mount Hope Cemetery Assn. v. State of New York, 11 A.D.2d 303, 313, *affd.* 10 N.Y.2d 752)—is the quietude, the tranquility and the privacy of the property, qualities which the claimant prized and desired and which undoubtedly are items that would be taken into account by an owner and a prospective purchaser in fixing the property's market value.

BERGAN, J. (dissenting). It is, unfortunately, not made altogether clear in the majority opinion whether the reason that leads the court to accept future traffic noises as an element of consequential damage is the difficulty in segregating this element from other well-established items; or whether, as a matter of policy, future traffic noise should be the subject of consequential damages, even if it stood alone. The two questions are rather different.

At one point the opinion observes that it would have been "practically impossible for the court to separate the noise element from the other elements" and concludes that any reduction on remand "would be purely arbitrary and at best speculative".

Although the opinion regards the State's answer (or nonanswer) to this question of segregation unacceptable, it also treats the State's answer as being contrary to South Buffalo Ry. Co. v. Kirkover (176 N.Y. 301) and to two cases in other States. In its final paragraph the opinion again reverts to the "practical difficulties" in accepting the State's theory as outweighing any benefit likely to be derived from accepting it.

Thus the stress in the *rationale* of the majority seems to fall on the difficulty in segregating damages. But the burden is on a claimant to show that the consequential damage asserted by him flows from the taking; and it is strange doctrine, indeed, to say that a man is entitled to an item of damage not recoverable if it stood alone because he is unable to segregate that item from other items of damage properly recoverable.

Nor is segregation necessarily practically impossible in this case. No attempt was made by the claimants to separate damage from future traffic noise from other items; and the impossibility of the segregation is thus one which has merely been assumed on appeal. Moreover, expert witnesses and trial courts are accustomed to separating elements of damage that are proper from those elements not proper. This covers a wide range of subjects and it does not seem unreasonable to require a claimant having the burden of proof to make the segregation, or if not made to fail in his claim for undifferentiated damage.

This leads to the broader implication of the present decision, beyond the impossibility of segregation which was decisive at the Appellate Division (28 A.D.2d 28, 29) and which seems largely controlling in this court. That other and broader question beyond segregation is whether future traffic noise is a legitimate part of consequential damage at all.

Traffic noise on highways and streets is a universal condition of modern life. The nearer one gets to the beneficial public conveniences of rapidly moving transportation, the more pervasive the noise.

Millions of residents of New York are exposed to it along the Long Island Expressway, the East River Drive, the West Side Highway, the Route 17 Quickway and the Thruway, to suggest some notable examples. Its effects are not limited to people whose property adjoins the highway. It can be heard with more or less intensity for remarkable distances. That it has, indeed, a consequence on market value wherever it is heard is undoubtedly true. But there are some unpleasant consequences of modern life which are not the proper subject of damages in a law court.

The very universality of traffic noise presents a quite different problem from the items customarily allowed as consequential damages in condemnation. If a tree which shades a man's home is cut down or his access to a highway is destroyed or his view from his property affected detrimentally, these are things directly and specially tied into the land.

But traffic noise is heard by everyone within the range of sound; and since it is a consequence that one takes by choosing to live in a country which builds modern highways, with resulting economic and transportation advantages to everyone, damage ought not, as a matter of policy, be allowed in general and unlimited scale for this kind of consequence.

The court seems by implication to sanction future noise damage in quite unrestricted form. If it does this, it ought to reconsider the cases such as Bennett v. Long Is. R.R. Co. (181 N.Y. 431) and Mathewson v. New York State Thruway Auth. (11 A.D.2d 782, *affd.* 9 N.Y.2d 788) which it cites with approval and in which damage for noise was disallowed in the absence of a taking.

It is not easy to support the justice of a distinction between a man from whom a small slice of land is taken for a road who may get damages for future traffic noise and a man who is just as near the road and suffers every bit as much damage but from whom no land is taken. . . .

Care must be taken, too, in accepting uncritically some of the out-of-State decisions. The Pennsylvania decisions, for example, rest upon a grouping of damage elements which are left generally to a jury under the rules peculiar to that State (see, e.g., Shano v. Fifth Ave. & H St. Bridge Co., 189 Pa. 245).

And in some other States, the rule which this court ought to adopt as at least a minimal limitation on its decision is that, where noise is an element of damage, it must be shown that its effect on the claimants is not common to other owners (see, e.g., Mississippi State Highway Comm. v. Colonial Inn, 246 Miss. 422; People v. Symons, 54 Cal. 2d 855).

The order should be reversed and the claim remitted to the Court of Claims to require claimants to establish their consequential damages independently of the element of future traffic noise.

JUDGES BURKE and JASEN concur with JUDGE KEATING; CHIEF JUDGE FULD concurs in a separate opinion; JUDGE BERGAN dissents and votes to reverse in an opinion in which JUDGES SCILEPPI and BREITEL concur.

Order affirmed.

NOTES AND QUESTIONS

1. "The term 'consequential damage' is ambiguous in character . . . In the proper sense of the term, all damages must of necessity be consequential, since all damage is the consequence of an injurious act." 4A Nichols, Eminent Domain §14.1 (rev. 3d ed. 1980). The treatise then describes several different ways in which courts have used the term, often indiscriminately:

    (a) Damage so remote as not to be actionable.
    (b) Damage to property no part of which is physically appropriated.
    (c) Damage to property remaining when part of a tract is physically appropriated.

Which usage describes the situation in the *Mitchell* case, *supra*, p. 1040? In the *Dennison* case?

2. The universal rule entitles the landowner whose tract is partially taken to recover not only for the direct taking but also for depreciation in the value of the remainder area. Courts often use the term "severance damages" to describe the remainder's loss of value. Two widely used methods exist for computing just compensation in the case of a partial taking:

(a) just compensation = value of parcel taken + (value of remainder area before taking − value of remainder area after taking).
(b) just compensation = value of entire parcel before taking − value of remainder area after taking (the "before and after" rule). 4A Nichols, Eminent Domain §14.23 (rev. 3d ed. 1980).

The annotation to Nichols indicates that in many states the courts use both formulations. Compare City of Amarillo v. Nelson, 428 S.W.2d 141 (Tex. Civ. App. 1968), with County of Nueces v. Salley, 348 S.W.2d 397 (Tex. Civ. App. 1961)

Can you devise a factual situation in which it might matter which method is used? Where difference results, should the claimant receive the higher award?

3. Sometimes a partial taking will add to the value of the remainder area. Can you explain how? What should courts do about this? Cf. Annot., 13 A.L.R. 3d 1149 (1967); Cal. Code Civ. Proc. §1248(3) (West 1972).

4. If no part of the Dennisons' parcel had been lost to eminent domain, they could not have recovered for their loss of privacy, seclusion, and view or for their discomfort resulting from noise pollution. Why does the right to compensation hinge on a concurrent physical taking? Is it only because the Constitution so defines the right? Cf. Michelman, Property, Utility, and Fairness: Comments on the Ethical Foundations of "Just Compensation" Law, 80 Harv. L. Rev. 1165, 1225-1229 (1967).

5. Which of these makes good policy: noise discomfort (loss of privacy) should yield compensation even in the absence of a concurrent physical taking? only in the presence of a concurrent physical taking? Noise discomfort (loss of privacy) should not yield compensation even in the presence of a concurrent physical taking?

6. Compare Metropolitan Atlanta Rapid Transit Authority v. Trussell, 247 Ga. 148, 273 S.E.2d 859 (Ga. 1981). Marta operated subway trains underneath plaintiffs' condominium apartments. Sympathetic vibrations caused the buildings to vibrate, shaking china, pictures, and furniture within the buildings. When negotiations with the plaintiffs concerning remedies collapsed, Marta sought to condemn "a noise and vibration easement" that would allow it to operate trains at a maximum vibration of 94 decibels (well above current levels). Plaintiffs in turn sued to enjoin the condemnation and

the running of trains underneath their apartments at speeds beyond eighteen miles per hour. The trial court granted the injunction and the state supreme court affirmed (three judges dissented).

The Georgia Constitution of 1976 provides that "private property shall not be taken, *or damaged,* for public purposes, without just and adequate compensation being first paid . . ." [emphasis added]. The court read this language as imposing liability upon the state for any consequential damages, and as barring the state from causing property damage without a taking. The court then reasoned that although the state in this situation had both the power and the duty to acquire a fee simple or any lesser interest through eminent domain, this meant "the taking of an actual property interest and [not] the right merely to buy a right to damage."

> We do not find that the people, in adopting the constitution . . . intended to allow a public body to condemn the right to damage property without also taking a property interest. A condemning authority may not purchase the right to shake the very walls and ceilings down upon the heads of those dwelling within. [273 S.E.2d at 861].

Recall Boomer v. Atlantic Cement Co., *supra,* page 685. Defendants were allowed to buy an entitlement to pollute. Is that a property interest? If so, isn't an entitlement to cause vibrations similarly a property interest?

d. Loss of Benefit of Deed Restrictions

BOARD OF PUBLIC INSTRUCTION v. TOWN OF BAY HARBOR ISLANDS

81 So. 2d 637 (Fla. 1955)

DREW, J. This is an appeal from a final decree of the Circuit Court of Dade County requiring the Board of Public Instruction of Dade County, Florida, hereafter called the Board, forthwith to perform the terms and conditions of a contract of sale of certain lands located within the corporate limits of the appellee Town of Bay Harbor Islands, hereafter called the Town, from William G. Mechanic and his wife and, at the same time, permanently enjoining and restraining the Board from locating, erecting or operating a public school building or any building for school purposes on such property. . . .

Two questions are involved in this appeal. The first is whether the restrictions, *infra,* which were placed upon the subject lands at the time and which formed a part of a general plan of subdivision of lands composing the municipality, are broad enough to prohibit the use of said lands for school purposes and, if so, whether they may be enforced against the Board. The second is whether such restrictions constitute property in those in whose favor such restrictions exist for which compensation must be made in the event said lands are acquired for public purposes. A negative answer to the second question would obviate the necessity of answering the first question; hence we proceed to a discussion of the latter proposition.

The restrictions are:

> Except for Lots 1 and 2 in Block 1; Lots 36 and 37 in Block 4; all of Blocks 11, 12, 20 and 21; and Tracts A, B, C, D, E and F of the East Island, no building shall be erected or constructed or maintained on any lot in the East Island other than residences, duplexes, apartments, apartment hotels, hotels or club hotels; no business building may be erected on said lands or any part of said lands, and no business may be conducted thereon except such business as is directly concerned with and incidental to each individual apartment house, apartment hotel, hotel or club hotel, as the case may be. If any such incidental business is conducted in any building on said land, then no shop or store or concession for any such business shall have any outside entrance or outside store-front or outside signs or displays, lighting or advertising; access thereto being exclusively limited to and through the inside of the building.

At the threshold we emphasize that the restrictions quoted above and with which we are concerned in this case do not fall within the category of true easements, such as the right of passage, use, or rights of light, air and view. See 18 Am. Jur., Eminent Domain, p. 786, Sections 156-158, especially Section 158. Easements such as these fall into a separate category from easements such as those we are dealing with in this case. These latter easements have been defined, and we think correctly, as negative easements [*sic*] or equitable servitudes. Such so-called easements are basically not easements in the strict sense of the word but are more properly classified as rights arising out of contract. It may well be that the failure of some of the courts to recognize this real difference has led to the confusion and the "irreconcilable conflict" in the decisions.

The courts are not in agreement as to whether such easements or restrictions are binding upon the acquiring authority when such lands are acquired for a public use. The author states in Note, 1939, 122 A.L.R. 1464, that "in determining whether the right thus created is one of property for which compensation must be made when land subject to such rights is taken by eminent domain or is voluntarily deeded to be used for public purposes, the courts remain in irreconcilable conflict." In 18 Am. Jur. 788, Section 157, it is said that "building restrictions are a property right, and where, through the exercise of the power of eminent domain, there is a taking or damage of such property rights, then owners of property for whose benefit the restrictions are imposed are entitled to compensation for the loss of the easements created by such restrictions, *although there are a few cases to the contrary.*" (Emphasis supplied.)

The whole subject is discussed at length in Nichols on Eminent Domain (3rd ed. 1950), Volume 2, Section 5.73, as follows:

5.73   Restrictive covenants

A rather perplexing situation arises out of the existence of what are commonly called "building restrictions." A large tract of land is often cut up into lots and sold for residential purposes, and each lot is sold subject to restrictions against use for various purposes, the restriction upon each lot being for the benefit of all the others. So far as such restrictions are reasonable in their character, they are enforced by courts of equity in favor of the original owner, so long as he continues to own any part of the tract for the benefit of which the restrictions were created, as well as in favor of the owner of any one of the lots into which the tract was divided, and against the owner of any of the lots who attempts to disregard the restrictions.

A conflict of opinion has arisen in the disposition of the question whether a person in whose favor such a restriction exists has a compensable interest in a condemnation proceeding which prevents compliance with such restriction.

[1] Majority view.

The majority view holds that such a restriction, often characterized as an equitable servitude, constitutes property in the constitutional sense and must be compensated for if taken. Such restrictions constitute equitable easements in the land restricted, and when such land is taken for a public use and will violate the restrictions, there is a taking of the property of the owners of the land for the benefit of which the restrictions were imposed. The owners of such property cannot maintain proceedings for damages against the original owner or enforce the restrictions against the condemnor, but they are entitled to an award of compensation for the destruction of their easements.

If the existence of the easement diminished the value of the land subject thereto, as is ordinarily the case when the easement is of such a character as a right of way, the compensation of the holder of the easement might well be deducted from the sum awarded to the owner of the servient tenement. In the case of mutual building restrictions, however, the existence of the restrictions often enhances rather than decreases the value of the land, and the owner of the land taken might consequently well object to receiving in any event less than the fair market value of his property as a piece of real estate.

[2] Minority view.

On the other hand, objection has been raised to paying more than such value for all the interests in the property taken and by reason thereof negative easements belonging to other owners have been taken without payment of compensation.

It has been argued that such restrictions were not intended to apply as against public improvements;—that, since all property is held subject to the power of eminent domain, the rights of the condemnor are impliedly excepted from the operation of the restrictive covenant.

It has further been held that such restrictions could not possibly inhibit the action of the sovereign because any such attempt would be void as against public policy since they constitute an attempt to prohibit the exercise of the sovereign power of eminent domain. Since the state has the power to condemn the fee prior to the imposition of a restrictive covenant, the placing of the additional burden upon the land does not create a new compensable interest.

Denial of compensation has also been justified upon the ground that such restrictions do not constitute property at all, but are merely contract rights which need not be compensated for in eminent domain. Such contract rights, it has been reasoned, are enforceable as against individuals but not as against the state.

The final argument in support of a denial of compensation in a specific case is predicated upon a construction of the particular restrictive covenant in such manner that the prospective use does not constitute a violation thereof.

Our study of the problem leaves considerable doubt in our minds that, at this time, the view stated in American Jurisprudence and Nichols on Eminent Domain, *supra,* to be the majority view is actually that. The recent trend, and we think the better view, if it is not actually the majority view, is that so ably presented and adopted by the Georgia Supreme Court in 1939 in the case of Anderson v. Lynch, 188 Ga. 154, 3 S.E.2d 85, 122 A.L.R. 1456, a case of first impression in that court. There it was concluded, after a review of the cases on the subject, and in full recognition of the substantial authority to the contrary, that restrictions of the kind we are concerned with here, and which were being dealt with in that case, convey no interest in the land, are not true easements, and at best may be relied upon and enforced between the parties thereto and their successors with notice. That Court concluded, and we think correctly, that such restrictions do not vest in the owners of other lands in the subdivision a property right for which compensation must be made in the event said lands are taken for and devoted to a public use even though such use is inconsistent with the use to which said lands are restricted by private agreement.

It is a well recognized rule that damages may not be recovered because of the depreciation in value of nearby property which may result by the construction of a public building in the vicinity. . . .

We think the conclusion reached by us is not only supported by what we believe to be the best considered cases but also by logic and reason. Were we to recognize a right of compensation in such instances, it would place upon the public an intolerable burden wholly out of proportion to any conceivable benefits to those who might be entitled to compensation. In the event of the construction of a public building in a large subdivision containing many separate ownerships, a determination of the varying degrees of damage, if any, which might be claimed by the individual lot owners would present obstacles of an unwarranted nature in the exercise of the sovereign power. It would afford little, if any, actual benefit to the landowner.

Moreover, were we to adopt the rule contended for by appellee and hold that restrictions of the nature which we have been discussing constitute property for which compensation must be made, it would be necessary in all instances where streets or highways were extended or enlarged through subdivisions having restrictions of such nature that the consent of every property owner in such subdivision be obtained or his interest acquired by eminent domain before such improvement could lawfully be made. It would be just as much a violation of a restriction limiting the use of specific property to residential purposes to construct a road or a sidewalk over it as a school or fire house or town hall. While these considerations are not controlling, where there is respectable authority both ways, they would be compelling and forceful factors in the determination of which way the scales of reason and justice incline. In such cases the courts should consider practical matters and problems as well as theories.

Having reached the conclusion we have, it becomes unnecessary for us to pursue the first question further except to observe that the answer we have given to the second question necessarily determines that the restrictions may not be enforced against the Board.

The portion of the final decree requiring the Board to consummate the purchase of the subject land from the appellee Mechanic and his wife be and the same is hereby affirmed but that portion of the decree which enjoins the Board from using said lands for school purposes is hereby reversed with directions to the lower court, if found to be essential to the orderly and proper disposition of this litigation, to enter a revised decree in accordance with the views herein expressed.

Reversed in part and affirmed in part.

MATHEWS, C.J., and THOMAS and BUFORD, JJ., concur.

NOTES AND QUESTIONS

1. In a 1964 opinion (which denied recovery), the states of Connecticut, Massachusetts, Michigan, Missouri, New Jersey, New York, North Carolina, Tennessee, Virginia, and Wisconsin all were said to treat the "destruction" of a restrictive covenant as a compensable event. The states of California, Colorado, Florida, Georgia, Louisiana, Ohio, Texas, West Virginia, and the District of Columbia were said to hold otherwise. Arkansas State Highway Commn. v. McNeill, 238 Ark. 244, 381 S.W.2d 425 (1964). Cf. also Annot., 4 A.L.R.3d 1137 (1965).

2. When compensation is allowed, what is the date of taking—when the servient estate is condemned, or when the infringing improvements are built?

3. United States v. Certain Lands, 112 F. 622 (C.C.R.I. 1899), *aff'd sub nom.* Wharton v. United States, 153 F. 876 (1st Cir. 1907), still remains a leading statement against compensation. There, a colony of summer homes had become the site for coastal fortifications. In refusing to compensate the homeowners whose lands had not been taken, the trial judge reasoned (112 F. at 678): "Suppose a deed to contain the condition that the grantee's property should never be used by the United States for a fort, or by the state for a state capital, armory, or school house; would not such a condition on its face be void, as against public policy? . . . Can it be possible that these owners, by mutual agreements or covenants that they or their successors in title will not do things which may be necessary for national defense, and by agreeing that these things are noxious and offensive to them, compel the United States to

pay them for the right to do, upon lands taken, what is necessary for the protection of the nation?" How might you reply to this argument?

4. A forthright stand for compensation, upon an unusual set of facts, appears in Adaman Mutual Water Co. v. United States, 278 F.2d 842 (9th Cir. 1960). The corporate claimant supplied water for a reclamation project in Maricopa County, Arizona. Each consumer owned a proportionate interest in the corporation based on the acreage being served; this interest entitled him to water and subjected him to operating assessments. A transfer of land within the project automatically included the corporate interest—much like the sale of a proprietary lease in a stock cooperative.

The United States condemned one twelfth of the project acreage and settled out of court for the direct taking. But the water company, acting in behalf of the remaining landowners, sought an award for the "diminution of the assessment base upon which the operating costs were shared." Treating the duty to pay assessments as an equitable servitude in which all remaining landowners held a beneficial interest, the court upheld the claim (278 F.2d at 848): "Why should a party receive compensation for an easement right which enhances the value of his property and yet be denied compensation for a right obtained by a restrictive covenant which similarly adds to the value of his holdings?"

How would you establish the amount of damages for loss of assessment base? If the company had issued revenue bonds, might the bondholders—on the analogy to waste—also have a claim against the condemnor on the theory that their security had been impaired?

e. Condemnation Blight

CITY OF BUFFALO v. CLEMENT
28 N.Y.2d 241, 269 N.E.2d 895, 321 N.Y.S.2d 345 (1971)

SCILEPPI, J. This is a case of first impression which requires that we consider in detail the somewhat amorphous and apparently perplexing concept of de facto appropriation in the hope of clearly defining and firmly establishing its perimeters. Specifically, we have before us the question of whether there can be a de facto taking absent a physical invasion or the imposition of some direct legal restraint. Needless to say, the dictates of precedent, practicality and public policy guide us in seeking a just result.

On or about December 10, 1954, J. W. Clement Company received notice of a hearing to be held in the office of the Buffalo City Clerk on December 21, concerning what has since come to be known as the Buffalo Redevelopment Project. This in turn prompted a request of Clement, directed to the local Chamber of Commerce, that the matter be further investigated. Pursuant to that request, a meeting of the chamber was held at which several city officials, including members of the City Planning Commission and the

Commissioner of the Redevelopment Board, spoke, describing the project and advising what properties were to be taken. The record shows that from that time there were frequent meetings, official and otherwise, news releases and advice to owners in the project area indicating when the properties would be appropriated. In August, 1957 the executive secretary of the planning board advised Clement that the taking would be started between 1960 and 1962; and in December, 1957 an Urban Renewal Clinic sponsored by the Buffalo Redevelopment Foundation was held, at which time it was restated that Clement's property would be taken.

The record further discloses that Clement's business was and continues to be the printing of national magazines, including Time and Life, as well as paperback books, the latter approximating some one hundred million per annum. Significantly, its printing machines are enormous, requiring, therefore, an appreciable amount of time to prepare for operation and production. Considering both the nature of production and demands of publication, it is readily apparent that, as the Appellate Division found, Clement felt a sense of urgency in ascertaining its status with respect to the project. Apparently, total exclusion was initially sought; and only when those efforts proved futile did Clement undertake a relocation project.

In June 1960, the secretary of the City Planning Commission informed the company's president that the premises would have to be vacated within three or possibly four years. By September of that year, the estimate was reduced to within two or three years. Finally, in February, 1961 the Commissioner of the Redevelopment Board advised that all industry would have to vacate within the next 18 to 24 months. Relying on these "official" representations, Clement embarked on its relocation project; and having successfully applied for a building permit in Depew, New York, bought a site for the projected plant. A new press which it had purchased for installation in the subject plant was deferred and redirected for placement in the new plant. On July 18, 1962 the Mayor of Buffalo and the Commissioner of Urban Renewal advised Clement's president that negotiations for the subject property were scheduled for the following spring.

With appropriation imminent, Clement continued to redirect machinery to the Depew site, then in the final stages of construction. Early in 1963 Clement was advised via letter that acquisition was scheduled for May, 1963. The substance of this correspondence was orally confirmed soon thereafter. Removal was completed by April of that year.

The record, of course, is replete with instances of widespread publicity, including various newspaper reports and the minutes of concerned public agencies, all of which demonstrate what loosely may be termed a pattern of continuous agitation. Additionally, the City Assessor testified that as early as 1959 the city had begun lowering property assessments in the redevelopment area; and the Department of Buildings had been directed to deny all applications for building permits in the area, issuing perhaps one temporary permit after 1962.

Additional evidence was furnished to show that vacancies were common and that the subject area fell into general disrepair. Indeed, the city's principal appraisal witness acknowledged that by reason of the threat of condemnation property values were drastically reduced. Defendant Clement's property was characterized as both unsalable and unrentable after 1963, and all efforts to procure even a short-term tenant proved unsuccessful. Clement, however, as owner in fee, continued to pay taxes and insurance and to maintain the property at its own expense while urging the city to complete the condemnation. . . .

[In January 1967,] the city commenced a proceeding in accordance with its charter provision (art. 21) to condemn Clement's waterfront property for redevelopment purposes under its urban renewal plan, denominated Waterfront Development Project No. U.R.N.Y. R-35, and funded in large part by Federal and State grants. After trial, judgment was entered awarding Clement $2,030,306.96. . . .

The trial court found that the acts of the city, including its protracted delay, had "destroyed the value of the property to the defendant and made the property no longer fit to be used as the defendant had been using it and had planned to use it in the future." In addition, it found that the city, by its threat of condemnation, had forced the Clement Company to move its business operation and that in view of the nature of its business Clement "waited to do this until the last possible moment that a prudent businessman could wait." On the basis of these findings, the trial court held that there was a de facto taking of Clement's property as of April 1, 1963 and that its value should be determined as of the year 1962. This holding was affirmed by the Appellate Division, reasoning that there was "a de facto taking . . . inasmuch as the city's acts forced Clement to move from its property . . . rendering the property not only unsalable but unrentable and yielding no income whatever." (34 A.D.2d 31-32.)

Preliminarily, it is well to note that our consideration of the problem posed by the present appeal is, of course, guided by constitutional guarantees. Both the Federal and State Constitutions provide in sum, that private property shall not be taken for public use without just compensation. This, of course, marks only the beginning of the inquiry, as the nicer questions relating to precisely what constitutes a taking, as well as just compensation in the constitutional sense remain to be determined.

Although the condemning authority is generally not liable to a condemnee until title to the property is officially taken (Condemnation Law, §4; Court of Claims Act, §10; 17 Carmody-Wait 2d New York Practice, §108.19; 19 N.Y. Jur., Eminent Domain, §§78-79), it has long been recognized by the courts of this State that the constitutional provision against the taking of property without just compensation may be violated without a physical taking. Indeed, injuries which in effect deprive individuals of full or unimpaired use of their property may constitute a taking in the constitutional sense (29A C.J.S., Eminent Domain, §110; see, also, Leeds v. State of New York, 20 N.Y.2d 701;

Matter of Keystone Assoc. v. Moerdler, 19 N.Y.2d 78; Oswego & Syracuse R.R. Co. v. State of New York, 226 N.Y. 351; Forster v. Scott, 136 N.Y. 577; Lambert v. State of New York, 30 A.D.2d 582; American Woolen Co. v. State of New York, 195 App. Div. 698, 704). Thus, we held in Forster v. Scott (136 N.Y. 577, *supra*) that whenever a *law* deprives the owner of the beneficial use and free enjoyment of his property, or imposes restraints upon such use and enjoyment that materially affect its value, it deprives him of his property within the meaning of the Constitution. And it is not necessary, in order to render a statute obnoxious to the restraints of the Constitution, that it must in terms or in effect authorize an actual physical taking of the property, so long as it affects its free use and enjoyment or the power of disposition at will of the owner. These words are pervasive and would at first blush require affirmance herein. However, the concept of de facto taking has traditionally been limited to situations involving a direct invasion of the condemnee's property or a direct legal restraint on its use (Leeds v. State of New York, 20 N.Y.2d 701, *supra;* Matter of Keystone Assoc. v. Moerdler, 19 N.Y.2d 78, *supra;* Oswego & Syracuse R.R. Co. v. State of New York, 226 N.Y. 351, *supra;* Forster v. Scott, 136 N.Y. 577, *supra*), and to hold that there can be a de facto appropriation absent a physical invasion or direct legal restraint would, needless to say, be to do violence to a workable rule of law. It is our view that only the most obvious injustice compels such a result. The Appellate Division, discerning so substantial an interference with the use of the subject property, found the essential elements of ownership to have been destroyed and held that the city's action constituted a de facto taking. We firmly disagree with that determination.

There is in fact a marked distinction between those cases which by reason of the cloud of condemnation, resulting in so-called condemnation blight, permit the claimant to establish his true value at the time of the taking but as if it had not been subjected to the debilitating effect of the threat of condemnation (Niagara Frontier Bldg. Corp. v. State of New York, 33 A.D.2d 130, *affd.* 28 N.Y.2d 755, decided herewith), and those cases which go even further and declare that the acts of the condemnor constitute a de facto taking long before the filing of appropriation maps (Matter of Keystone Assoc. v. Moerdler, 19 N.Y.2d 78, *supra;* Forster v. Scott, 136 N.Y. 577, *supra*). One is the product of acts which result, realistically speaking, if no less than an out and out appropriation of property, requiring in turn that the owner be fully compensated, while the other relates more properly to certain affirmative value-depressing acts on the part of the condemning authority, requiring only that evidence be received of value prior to such acts in an effort to arrive at just compensation. Both concepts owe their existence to the law's efforts to secure full compensation; they differ only insofar as one involves essentially the rules of appropriation while the other relates to the rules of evidence.

Nor, as the present appeal clearly suggests, is the distinction merely academic. Clearly, both the award itself and the award as increased by the interest allowance are directly proportionate to the time of the taking and to hold that the taking was complete at an earlier date would, of necessity, require that interest run from that date; surely, no incidental matter, as it presently involves some $459,603.86. The distinction has, however, at times been ignored and lower courts have been wont to confuse the concepts, often speaking of one in terms of the other (see, e.g., City of Buffalo v. Irish Paper Co., 31 A.D.2d 470, 475-476).

Despite this obvious confusion, it is clear that a de facto taking requires a physical entry by the condemnor, a physical ouster of the owner, a legal interference with the physical use, possession or enjoyment of the property or a legal interference with the owner's power of disposition of property. On the other hand, "condemnation blight" relates to the impact of certain acts upon the value of the subject property. It in no way imports a *taking* in the constitutional sense, but merely permits of a more realistic valuation of the condemned property in the subsequent de jure proceeding. In such a case, compensation shall be based on the value of the property at the time of the taking, as if it had not been subjected to the debilitating effect of a threatened condemnation.

The facts herein fail to disclose any act upon the part of the condemning authority which could possibly be construed as an assertion of dominion and control. Indeed, it cannot be said that the city, by its actions, either directly or indirectly deprived Clement of its possession, enjoyment or use of the subject property. We simply have a manifestation of an intent to condemn and such, even considering the protracted delay attending final appropriation, cannot cast the municipality in liability upon the theory of a "taking" for there was no appropriation of the property in its accepted legal sense. As the Supreme Court has held: "A reduction or increase in the value of property may occur by reason of legislation for or the beginning or completion of a project. Such changes in value are incidents of ownership. They cannot be considered as a 'taking' in the constitutional sense" (Danforth v. United States, 308 U.S. 271, 285). This reasoning, it may be added, has been applied time and time again to deny compensation based upon the asserted theory that the threat of condemnation constitutes an actual taking (see, e.g., Matter of City of New York [Boston-Secor Houses—Rusciano], 28 A.D.2d 658; Housing Auth. of City of Decatur v. Schroeder, 222 Ga. 417; Town of Swampscott v. Remis, 350 Mass. 523; St. Louis Housing Auth. v. Barnes, 375 S.W.2d 144, 146-148, [Mo.]; City of Houston v. Biggers, 380 S.W.2d 700, 704-705, [Tex.]; Bakken v. State Highway Commn., 142 Mont. 166; Chicago Housing Auth. v. Lamar, 21 Ill. 2d 362; Sorbino v. City of New Brunswick, 43 N.J. Super. 554; A. Gettelman Brewing Co. v. City of Milwaukee, 245 Wis. 9; State ex rel. City of St. Louis v. Beck, 333 Mo. 1118), and the rule has evolved in this State denying direct recovery for the manifestation of an intent to take (Waller v. State of New York, 144 N.Y. 579, 599) or threat to condemn (2 Nichols, Eminent Domain [3d ed.], §6.1, subd. [1]).

Moreover, strong public policy considerations prohibit a finding of a de facto taking in the instant case. To hold the date of the *announcement* of the impending condemnation, whether directly to the condemnee or by the news media, constitutes a de facto taking at that time, would be to impose an "oppressive" and "unwarranted" burden upon the condemning authority. At the very least, it would serve to penalize the condemnor for providing appropriate advance notice to a property owner. And to so impede the actions of the municipality in preparing and publicizing plans for the good of the community, would be to encourage a converse policy of secrecy which "would but raise [greater] havoc with an owner's rights" (City of Buffalo v. Clement Co., 34 A.D.2d 24, 39 [dissenting opn.]).

Again, although we have not yet arrived at a point where an expression of an intent to appropriate, absent some act on the part of the condemning authority toward executing the appropriation (for example, taking possession or exercising some form of control over the use or enjoyment of the property) [sic], that is not to say that interferences short of physical invasion of the condemnee's property may not be sufficient to constitute a taking, as it has long been settled that a de facto taking does occur where the property has been the subject of some direct legal restraint on its use (supra). As noted above, direct legal restraint has traditionally embraced only laws which by their own force and effect, deprive owners of property or materially affect its beneficial use and free enjoyment (see, e.g., Matter of Keystone Assoc. v. Moerdler, 19 N.Y.2d 78, supra; Forster v. Scott, 136 N.Y. 577, supra). While there is authority supportive of the proposition that in the absence of such a law de facto taking does not occur without either actual physical invasion or ouster of possession (Cicci v. State of New York, 31 A.D.2d 733), the idea that there can be a de facto taking in the absence of a physical invasion or direct legal restraint is not without current support and finds some viability in the decisions of sister States and the broader pronouncements of other courts (see, e.g., City of Detroit v. Cassese, 376 Mich. 311; Foster v. City of Detroit, 254 F. Supp. 655, affd. on other grounds, 405 F.2d 138, 147).

Despite these divergent lines of authority, the policy of this State has been to deny recovery in the absence of a substantial impairment of the claimant's right to use or enjoy the property at any time prior to the date of final appropriation. Accordingly, the mere announcement of impending condemnations, coupled as it may well be with substantial delay and damage, does not, in the absence of other acts which may be translated into an exercise of dominion and control by the condemning authority, constitute a taking so as to warrant awarding compensation.

Nor can we agree with the Appellate Division's emphasis upon the fact that there were a number of meetings with city officials regarding the impending condemnation. It is important to note that the city never, by its statements or actions, directly or indirectly, interfered or sought to exercise any control over the property, thus inferentially depriving the claimant of its possession, enjoyment or use. Neither can we agree with the majority below that the acts of the city, "so interfered with the use of the subject property that essential elements of ownership have been destroyed" (34 A.D.2d 32). There is nothing in the record that indicates any element of ownership was destroyed by an act of the city on April 1, 1963.

In sum, therefore, there was no appropriation which would permit an award of damages prior to the de jure taking. This, however, is not to say that the aggrieved property owner is without remedy. Indeed, the aggrieved property owner has a remedy where it would suffer severely diminished compensation because of acts by the condemning authority decreasing the value of the property (Niagara Frontier Bldg. Corp. v. State of New York, 33 A.D.2d 130, *affd.* 28 N.Y.2d 755, decided herewith). In such cases where true condemnation blight is present, the claimant may introduce evidence of value prior to the onslaught of the "affirmative value-depressing acts" (City of Buffalo v. Irish Paper Co., 31 A.D.2d 470, 476) of the authority and compensation shall be based on the value of the property as it would have been at the time of the de jure taking, but for the debilitating threat of condemnation (see, also, City of Detroit v. Cassese, 376 Mich. 311, 317-318, *supra;* City of Cleveland v. Carcione, 118 Ohio App. 525; 4 Nichols, Eminent Domain [3d ed.], §12.3151; Owen, Recovery for Enhancement and Blight in California, 20 Hastings L.J. [Univ. of Cal.] 622, 643-649 [Jan., 1969]. This, in turn, requires only that there be present some proof of affirmative acts causing a decrease in value and difficulty in arriving at a value using traditional methods (City of Buffalo v. Irish Paper Co., 31 A.D.2d 470, *affd.* 26 N.Y.2d 869, *supra*).

Thus, when damages are assessed on the claim for the de jure appropriation, the claimant's property should be evaluated not on its diminished worth caused by the condemnor's action, but on its value except for such "affirmative value-depressing acts" of the appropriating sovereign. This, it appears, would provide adequate and just compensation. As the defendant offered no evidence of value in 1968 based upon market data nor did the city offer any valid appraisal evidence, we lack competent evidence upon which an award could be fashioned. Accordingly, a new trial is required, at which evidence of proper valuation could be taken. . . .

NOTES AND QUESTIONS

1. "Both concepts owe their existence to the law's efforts to secure full compensation; they differ only insofar as one involves . . . the rules of appropriation while the other relates to the rules of evidence." *City of Buffalo* opinion, page 1056 *supra.*

The claimant failed to establish a de facto taking (rules of appropriation) but succeeded in having valuation fixed to reflect condemnation blight (rules of evidence). The immediate issue was when to accrue interest on any award, since the city had no duty to pay damages, or interest thereon, until a taking. But in seeking to dispel the "obvious confusion" between the two concepts, has the court created a culture that will breed difficulties untold? Consider, for example, how New York courts, "guided" by the *City of Buffalo* case, might resolve the following hypothetical disputes:

(a) The Clement Co. vacates its plant in 1963. The condemnation threat continues until 1967. Then the city of Buffalo abandons the urban renewal project without formally taking title to the Clement Co. property. Is the company entitled to compensation? Cf. Danforth v. United States, 308 U.S. 271, 284-285 (1939), where the Supreme Court stated: "Until taking, the condemnor may discontinue or abandon his effort. . . . A reduction or increase in the value of property may occur by reason of legislation for or the beginning or completion of a project. Such changes in value are incidents of ownership. They cannot be considered as a 'taking' in the constitutional sense." (But cf. Klopping v. City of Whittier, 8 Cal. 3d 39, 104 Cal. Rptr. 1, 500 P.2d 1345 (1972)).

Is there an analogy between the *Danforth* rule as to abandonment, and the rule of consequential damages, pp. 1053-1059 *supra*, which grounds a recovery for noise pollution or loss of privacy upon nothing less than a partial taking? Is it possible to formulate a workable rule that will fully protect the property owner no matter what the cause of condemnation blight?

(b) The Clement Co., not believing the condemnation threat serious, sought a building permit in 1959 to expand its capacity 50 percent. Under orders from the commissioner of urban renewal, the department of buildings refused to issue the permit. The company did not appeal the denial. It claims, however, that a taking occurred in 1959.

(c) The owner of an office building claims that he suffered rental losses beginning in 1954, when the city held its first hearings on the redevelopment project, and that by 1963, all major tenants had left the building, which then stood virtually empty. How is compensation fixed? Cf. Niagara Frontier Building Corp. v. State of New York, 28 N.Y.2d 755, 269 N.E.2d 912 (1971).

2. Was it only unwillingness to "backdate" interest that led the court to reject the argument of "de facto" taking?

3. The New York Court of Appeals, while recognizing that courts should consider condemnation blight in fixing damages, remanded the *City of Buffalo* case for a new trial on valuation evidence. What is the difference between the trial court's theory, which found value as of 1962, and the court of appeals' theory, which would set value as of 1968 except for such "affirmative value-depressing acts of the appropriating sovereign"? Do the two theories translate into dollars-and-cents differences in the basic award exclusive of interest? The court of appeals denied a motion to clarify its opinion. 29 N.Y.2d 640, 273 N.E.2d 315 (1971).

4. As the opinion indicates, many states will not let the condemnee show how official statements depressed market value prior to the taking. Courts speak of this injury as "necessarily incident to the ownership of property . . . for which the law does not . . . afford relief." Eckhoff v. Forest Preserve Dist., 377 Ill. 208, 212, 36 N.E.2d 245, 247 (1941); accord, Sorbino v. City of New Brunswick, 43 N.J. Super. 554, 129 A.2d 473 (Law Div. 1957).

5. The obverse of condemnation blight is the rise in value—often speculative—that follows a public announcement. Ordinarily the courts will

not allow recovery for such enhancement if the parcel was "probably within" the project area when announcement was made. See, e.g., United States v. Miller, 317 U.S. 369 (1943). Suppose, however, that after a project site is first announced its boundaries are later enlarged, or that after one project is completed a second project—in an adjoining neighborhood—is begun. Should a landowner be compensated for whatever provable value has been added to his site because of government-initiated improvement nearby?

6. English experience is pertinent. The Town and Country Planning Acts of 1925 and 1932 provided that if a planning scheme diminished the value of one's property ("injurious affection"), compensation was to be given; if, however, a planning scheme enhanced value, the local authority might recoup a percentage of the betterment that accrued. 15 Geo. 5, c. 16; 22 & 23 Geo. 5, c. 48. Recoupment was not a success, but its precept was carried into post-World War II legislation, the Town and Country Planning Act of 1947, 10 & 11 Geo. 6, c. 51. Development rights were "nationalized." Thereafter, any landowner who gained permission to improve his parcel was required to pay a "development charge" equal to the land's enhancement—above 1947 values—for the requested development. Reacting to public dissatisfaction, a government newly elected in 1953 abolished the development charge. Once again, in the Town and Country Planning Act of 1959, Britain dealt with the issue of betterment; this time, it adopted a characteristically American solution. For a landowner to benefit from government planning was beside the point unless his parcel was taken by eminent domain ("compulsory acquisition"). In that event, he was entitled to market value less any increment due to the development scheme that gave rise to the government's acquisition—in essence, the *Miller* rule. 7 & 8 Eliz. 2, c. 53.

f. Valuation of Divided Interests

ALAMO LAND & CATTLE CO. v. ARIZONA
424 U.S. 295, 47 L. Ed. 2d 1, 96 S. Ct. 910 (1976)

MR. JUSTICE BLACKMUN delivered the opinion of the Court. This case presents an issue of federal condemnation law—as it relates to an outstanding lease of trust lands—that, we are told, affects substantial acreage in our Southwestern and Western States.

Under §24 of the New Mexico-Arizona Enabling Act, 36 Stat. 572 (1910), specified sections of every township in the then proposed State were granted to Arizona "for the support of common schools." By §28 of the same Act, 36 Stat. 574, as amended by the Act of June 5, 1936, c. 517, 49 Stat. 1477, and by the Act of June 2, 1951, 65 Stat. 51, the lands transferred "shall be by the said State held in trust, to be disposed of in whole or in part only in manner as herein provided and for the several objects specified . . . and . . . the

. . . proceeds of any of said lands shall be subject to the same trusts as the lands producing the same." Arizona, by its Constitution, Art. 10, §1, accepted the lands so granted and its trusteeship over them.

Among the lands constituting the grant to Arizona were two parcels herein referred to as Tract 304 and Tract 305, respectively. On February 8, 1962, Arizona, as lessor, and petitioner Alamo Land and Cattle Company, Inc. (Alamo), as lessee, executed a grazing lease of these tracts for the 10-year period ending February 7, 1972. App. 6-14. By Arizona statute, Ariz. Rev. Stat. Ann. 37-281D (1974), incorporated by general reference into the lease, App. 7, Alamo may not use the lands for any purpose other than grazing.

On May 31, 1966, while the two tracts where subject to the grazing lease and were utilized as part of Alamo's larger operating cattle ranch, the United States filed a complaint in condemnation in the United States District Court for the District of Arizona in connection with the establishment of a flood control dam and reservoir at a site on the Bill Williams River. The tracts in their entirety were among the properties that were the subject of the complaint in condemnation. The District Court duly entered the customary order for delivery of possession.

Thereafter, the United States and Arizona and, separately, the United States and Alamo, stipulated that "the full just compensation" payable by the United States "for the taking of said property, together with all improvements thereon and appurtenances thereunto belonging" was $48,220 for Tract 304 and $70,400 for Tract 305, and thus a total of $118,620 for the two. 1 Rec. 156,162.

At a distribution hearing held to determine the proper allocation of the compensation amounts, the only parties claiming an interest in the awards for the two tracts were respondent Arizona, asserting title through the federal grants to it, and petitioner Alamo, asserting a compensable leasehold interest in the lands and a compensable interest in the improvements thereon. The State conceded that Alamo was entitled to receive the value of the improvements, but contested Alamo's right, as lessee, to participate in the portion of the award allocated to land value. The District Court, with an unreported opinion, App. 1-5, awarded Arizona $57,970 for its fee interest, and awarded Alamo $3,600 for the improvements and $57,050 for "its leasehold interest at the time of taking, and its reasonable prospective leasehold interest." 1 Rec. pp. 227-228. On appeal, the United States Court of Appeals for the Ninth Circuit, while recognizing that Alamo was entitled to compensation for the improvements, held that under the Enabling Act Arizona "had no power to grant a compensable property right to Alamo," and that "Alamo therefore never acquired a property right for which it is entitled to compensation." United States v. 2562.92 Acres of Land, 495 F.2d 12, 14 (1974). The Court of Appeals thus reversed the judgment of the District Court insofar as it concerned the leasehold interests. It remanded the cause for the entry of a new judgment in accordance with its opinion. Id., at 15. . . .

It has long been established that the holder of an unexpired leasehold interest in land is entitled, under the Fifth Amendment, to just compensation for the value of that interest when it is taken upon condemnation by the United States. United States v. Petty Motor Co., 327 U.S. 372, 90 L. Ed. 729, 66 S. Ct. 596 (1946); A.W. Duckett & Co. v. United States, 266 U.S. 149, 69 L. Ed. 216, 45 S. Ct. 38 (1924). See United States v. General Motors Corp., 323 U.S. 373, 89 L. Ed. 311, 65 S. Ct. 357, 156 A.L.R. 390 (1945); Almota Farmers Elevator & Warehouse Co. v. United States, 409 U.S. 470, 35 L. Ed. 2d 1, 93 S. Ct. 791 (1973); 2 P. Nichols, Eminent Domain §5.23 (Rev. 3d ed. 1975); 4 id. §12.42 [1]. It would therefore seem to follow that when a lease of trust land is made, the trust must receive from the lessee the then fair rental value of the possessory interest transferred by the lease, and that upon a subsequent condemnation by the United States, the trust must receive the then full value of the reversionary interest that is subject to the outstanding lease, plus, of course, the value of the rental rights under the lease. The trust should not be entitled, in addition to all this, to receive the compensable value, if any, of the leasehold interest. That, if it exists and if the lease is valid, is the lessee's. See State ex rel. La Prade v. Carrow, 57 Ariz. 429, 433-434, 114 P.2d 891, 893 (1941).

Ordinarily, a leasehold interest has a compensable value whenever the capitalized then fair rental value for the remaining term of the lease, plus the value of any renewal right, exceeds the capitalized value of the rental the lease specifies. The Court has expressed it this way:

> The measure of damages is the value of the use and occupancy of the leasehold for the remainder of the tenant's term, plus the value of the right to renew . . . , less the agreed rent which the tenant would pay for such use and occupancy. United States v. Petty Motor Co. 327 U.S., at 381, 90 L. Ed. 729, 66 S. Ct. 596.

See Almota Farmers Elevator & Warehouse Co. v. United States, *supra*. A number of factors, of course, could operate to eliminate the existence of compensable value in the leasehold interest. Presumably, this would be so if the Enabling Act provided, as the New Mexico-Arizona Act does not, that any lease of trust land was revocable at will by the State, or if it provided that, upon sale or condemnation of the land, no compensation was payable to the lessee. The State, of course, may require that a provision of this kind be included in the lease. See United States v. Petty Motor Co., 327 U.S., at 375-376, and n.4, 90 L. Ed. 729, 66 S. Ct. 596; see also 4 Nichols, *supra*, §12.42[1], pp. 12-488 and 12-489.

A difference between the rental specified in the lease and the fair rental value plus the renewal right could arise either because the lease rentals were set initially at less than fair rental value, or because during the term of the lease the value of the land, and consequently its fair rental value, increased. The New Mexico-Arizona Enabling Act has a protective provision against the initial setting of lease rentals at less than fair rental value. This is specifically prohibited by §28. The prohibition is given bite by the further very drastic provision that a lease not made in substantial conformity with the Act "shall be null and void." Thus, if the lease of trust lands calls for a rental of substantially less than the land's then fair rental value, it is null and void and the holder of the claimed leasehold interest could not be entitled to compensation upon condemnation.

On the other hand, the fair rental value of the land may increase during the term of the lease.[9] If this takes place, the increase in fair rental value operates to create a compensable value in the leasehold interest. It is at this point, we feel, that the Court of Appeals erred when it held that the Act by its terms, and apart from the extent to which it incorporated Arizona law by reference, barred Arizona from leasing trust land in any manner that might result in the lessee's becoming constitutionally entitled to just compensation for the value of its unexpired leasehold interest at the time of the federal condemnation. Instead, the Act is completely silent in this respect.

Arizona, however, suggests that this usually acceptable analysis may not be applied under the New Mexico-Arizona Enabling Act. It argues, as the Court of Appeals held, 495 F.2d, at 14, that under the Act the State, as trustee, has no power to grant a compensable property interest to Alamo, as lessee. It bases this thesis on the Enabling Act's provision in §28 that no "mortgage or other encumbrance" of trust land shall be valid, and it claims that a lease is an encumbrance, citing, among other cases, Hecketsweiler v. Parrett, 185 Or. 46, 52, 200 P.2d 971, 974 (1948) (agreement to sell real estate free and clear of encumbrances), and Hartman v. Drake, 166 Neb. 87, 91, 87 N.W.2d 895, 898 (1958) (partition). One seemingly apparent and complete answer to this argument is that §28 goes on to authorize specifically a lease of trust land for grazing purposes for a term of 10 years or less, and further provides that a leasehold, before being offered, shall be appraised at "true value." See n.2, *supra*. These provisions thus plainly contemplate the possibility of a lease of trust land and, in so doing, intimate that such a lease is not a prohibited "mortgage or other encumbrance." Furthermore, Arizona statutes in other contexts specifically protect the lessee's interest. Ariz. Rev. Stat. Ann. §§41-511.06, 37-291 (1974). See Ehle v. Tenney Trading Co., 56 Ariz. 241, 107 P.2d 210 (1940). To this the State responds that, while a lease is possible, it falls short of being a compensable interest when the property is sold because the Act prohibits the sale unless the trust receives the full appraised value of the land. The argument assumes that such compensation is to be measured by the entire land value despite the presence of the outstanding lease. That approach overlooks the actuality of a two-step disposition of interests in the land, the first at the time of the granting of the lease, and the second at the time of the condemnation. Full appraised value is to be determined and measured at

---

9. The Arizona statutes governing grazing leases of trust lands recognize this possibility and provide for adjustment of rent at specified times to account for fluctuations in fair rental value. Ariz. Rev. Stat. Ann. §§37-283, 37-285 (1974). Indeed, under §28 of the Enabling Act, at the termination of a lease, a re-evaluation would appear to be required before release or renewal.

the times of disposition of the respective interests, and if the State receives those values at those respective times, the demands of the Enabling Act are met. The State's argument would serve to convert and downgrade a 10-year grazing lease, fully recognized and permitted by the Act, into a lease terminable at will or into one automatically terminated whenever the State sells the property or it is condemned. The lessee is entitled to better treatment than this if neither the Enabling Act nor the lease contains any such provision. We have noted above that the Act or the lease, or both, could provide for that result. The Act, however, does not specifically so provide. Whether either the Act or the lease does so through incorporation of state law is an issue not addressed by the Court of Appeals, and it is to be considered on remand. We merely note that the fact that it is within Arizona's power to insert a condemnation clause in a lease it makes of trust land does not mean that the State may claim the same result when its lease contains no such clause. . . .

The judgment of the Court of Appeals is reversed, and the case is remanded for further proceedings consistent with this opinion.

It is so ordered.

Mr. Justice Stevens took no part in the consideration or decision of this case.

Mr. Justice White with whom Mr. Justice Brennan joins, dissenting.

NOTES AND QUESTIONS

1.　L owns rental property that has just become vacant when condemnation occurs. All experts agree that the property's annual rental value is $100,000. What amount should L receive as just compensation? Assume that the market expects a 10 percent return on property similar to L's. An 8 percent return? A 15 percent return?

Suppose that L and T enter into a ten-year lease of this property commencing January 1, 1980. The annual reserved rental is $100,000. On January 1, 1983, the *entire* parcel is condemned. The annual rental value has held steady at $100,000. What is the award? How is the award divided between L and T? (Assume that the market expects a 10 percent return.)

Suppose that the rental market drops between 1980 and 1983. The annual rental value for the premises T occupies falls to $90,000. Should L get $1 million, or more or less than $1 million? What does T get?

Suppose, instead, that the rental market rises between 1980 and 1983. The annual rental value for the premises T occupies climbs to $120,000. Should L get $1 million, or more or less than $1 million? What does T get?

2.　Most leases contain a so-called condemnation clause terminating the lease in the event of condemnation or a negotiated purchase in lieu of condemnation. See, e.g., Model Apartment Lease ¶8, p. 240 *supra*. Despite their frequent unfairness to the tenant, such clauses are enforceable. See United States

v. Petty Motor Co., 327 U.S. 372, 376 (1946). Wherever possible, though, a court will make use of any ambiguity, either in the clause or in the landlord's conduct, to find that the clause does not apply. See, e.g., City of Columbus v. Huntington Nat'l Bank, 143 N.E.2d 874 (Ohio Ct. App. 1956) (lease to be terminated if premises "rendered untenantable by public authority"; held: clause did not refer to condemnation); United States v. 40,438 Square Feet of Land in Boston, 66 F. Supp. 659 (D. Mass. 1946) (lease to be terminated at landlord's "election"; held: landlord failed to prove election); 2 Powell, Real Property ¶247[2] (Rohan ed. 1974). Should not the courts sometimes regard such clauses as unenforceable on the analogy to a contract of adhesion?

3. Premises are conveyed to church "so long as premises are used for church purposes." While the church is in possession, the premises are condemned. How should the award be distributed? See Restatement of Property §53, Comment b (1936); Note, 60 Colum. L. Rev. 408 (1960).

4. X holds an unexercised option to purchase land for $100,000. Before the option expires, the parcel is condemned and an award of $120,000 is made. Is X entitled to share in the award? In what amount? Cf. County of San Diego v. Miller, 13 C. 3d 684, 532 P.2d 139, 119 Cal. Rptr. 491 (1975).

5. What problems might arise if in a "lateral" condominium—for example, a group of townhouses—only part of the project were taken in eminent domain? See generally Rohan and Reskin, Condominium Law and Practice §12.04 (1981).

§18.3 Inverse Condemnation

We have seen many kinds of official action impinging heavily upon a landowner's use and enjoyment. When regulation is present, the landowner may seek to invalidate the control by arguing that a taking has occurred without compensation. If the landowner wants to complete his plans, however, it is primarily relief from the control that he prefers, not compensation. Indeed, whether he is even entitled to compensation, as we shall shortly see, remains a lively issue. But as to some other forms of official action, relief from the action may not be possible, no matter how burdensome to the individual owner. Courts rarely enjoin the building of dams, cf. United States v. Willow River Power Co., §18.4 *infra*, or the widening of roads, or the operation of airports, for example. The term "inverse condemnation" has come to describe suits against government where the property owner complains of official action so interfering with his use and enjoyment that compensation is due him, as if there had been a formal taking. Today, this issue arises frequently in suits by airport neighbors seeking to recoup their damages from aircraft noise, fumes, and vibration.

BATTEN v. UNITED STATES
306 F.2d 580 (10th Cir. 1962), cert. denied, 371 U.S. 955 (1963)

BREITENSTEIN, CIRCUIT JUDGE. This case presents the novel question whether a taking of property, compensable under the Fifth Amendment, occurs when there is no physical invasion of the affected property but the operation and maintenance of military jet aircraft on an Air Force Base of the United States produce noise, vibration, and smoke which interfere with the use and enjoyment of the property. The appellants-plaintiffs, owners of 10 homes at Pauline, Kansas, sued the United States under the Tucker Act and base their claims on the use of jet aircraft at Forbes Air Force Base which adjoins the subdivision in which they live. They acquired their homes prior to the enlargement of the Base to accommodate jets. Recovery was denied on the ground that there was no taking of property in violation of the Fifth Amendment for which the United States was liable under the Tucker Act.

The facts are not disputed. Forbes Air Force Base, originally known as Topeka Army Air Field, was a temporary World War II base used for training in the operation of propeller-driven aircraft. It was deactivated at an undisclosed date prior to 1948. In that year a tract, the southeastern corner of which adjoined the northwestern corner of the Base, was platted as a residential subdivision. The homes of the plaintiffs were built and acquired in the period 1949-1955. After the Korean War started the United States obtained land adjacent to the subdivision on the east to enlarge the Base for the accommodation of jet aircraft. Use of a lengthened runway, known as 13-31, began in September, 1955, and a ramp parking area, and warm-up pad for jet planes were put into operation in the spring of 1956.

Since the enlargement of the Base, about 100 RB-47 and B-47 six-engine jet aircraft and about 40 KC-97 six-engine propeller-driven aircraft have been located there. Aircraft movements average about 4000 monthly or about 130 daily and of these 70% are attributable to jets. This activity occurs usually between dawn and dusk, Monday through Friday, but occasionally on the week ends and at night.

The plaintiffs do not rely on flights over their properties to sustain their claims. The trial court found: "The Pauline Subdivision is outside the flying pattern of all aircraft operating from Forbes Air Force Base, and the Government does not claim or exercise any right to fly any planes over plaintiffs' property. However, on a few occasions, RB-47 and B-47 jet aircraft did fly directly over the plaintiffs' homes in Pauline, Kansas, Subdivision at low altitudes."

The jets use the 13-31 runway almost exclusively. The operating procedure is for the engines to be started on the parking ramp about 30 minutes before take-off. The ramp is 900 feet wide and at its nearest point is 650 feet from any property of the plaintiffs. After about 10 minutes the plane is taxied to the warm-up pad, located 2000 feet from the nearest property of the plaintiffs, where final pre-flight checks are performed. During this period all 6 engines are running at idling speed. The plane is then moved to the take-off point. About one-half of the flights begin at the end of the 13-31 runway near Pauline and at a point 2280 feet from the nearest property of the plaintiffs. About 30 seconds before take-off the engine power is advanced to maximum output. The planes are airborne some 50 seconds after start.

From April through October a water-alcohol injection system is used to increase the maximum power by 23%. The RB-47 and B-47 jets leave a characteristic trail of black smoke which is increased by the use of the water-alcohol injection system and which is quite heavy for about 70 seconds after the brakes have been released for take-off but which is exhausted within a mile from the end of the runway.

Maintenance work on the planes was done on the ramp 3420 feet from the nearest property of the plaintiffs until May, 1960, when it was moved to a location about 1 1/2 miles therefrom. In the maintenance operations jet engines are run at power settings of from 50% to 100%. During a typical month the engines were operated for 84 hours in the 100% RPM range and for 211 hours in less than that range for maintenance purposes.

Ground power generators are used on the parking ramp to provide auxiliary power to start the jet engines and to recharge the batteries of the planes. From 4 to 10 of these generators may operate at the same time and on occasion they run from 8 to 10 hours at any time during the day and sometimes at night.

The mentioned activities produce sound and shock waves which cross the plaintiffs' properties and limit the use and enjoyment thereof. Strong vibrations cause windows and dishes to rattle. Loud noises frequently make conversation and the use of the telephone, radio, and television facilities impossible and also interrupt sleep. During engine operation in the 100% range the sound pressure level measured in decibels varies from 90 to 117 decibels on the plaintiffs' properties. Ear plugs are recommended for Air Force personnel when the sound pressure level reaches 85 decibels and are required at or above 95 decibels.

In the summer months when there is an easterly wind, the black smoke developed during jet take-offs occasionally blows across the plaintiffs' properties leaving an oily black deposit on the houses and laundry of the plaintiffs.

The court found that: " . . . plaintiffs have suffered a substantial interference of the use and enjoyment of their properties, which interference did not exist prior to the construction and activation of the new runway in September, 1955, and the new ramp in March or April, 1956."

The court further found that such interference "is of the same character as that noticed in varying degrees in the general area surrounding the Base" with greater adverse effect on the plaintiffs because of the proximity of their property to the Base.

Diminution in value of the 10 homes was found in amounts which varied from $4700 to $8800.[3] The trial court deemed United States v. Causby, 328 U.S. 256 . . . to be a controlling precedent and held that there was no taking of an interest in the plaintiffs' properties for which compensation had to be paid.

The case at bar is one of first impression in the federal appellate courts and presents an issue of widespread current interest. The jet airplane is a great boon to the traveler but a veritable plague to the homeowners near an airfield. The noise, vibration, and smoke incidental to the operation and maintenance of jet planes disturb the peace and quiet in every residential area located near an airport used by the jets. This disturbance is felt not only by those whose property is crossed by the planes on take-offs or landings but also by those who live outside of the established flight patterns. The Supreme Court has allowed recovery under the Tucker Act to a landowner whose property was crossed by low-elevation flights of military planes on take-offs and landings.[4] The novelty in the instant case is that liability is asserted not because of disturbance in conjunction with any over-flights but because of the noise, vibration, and smoke alone which harass the occupants of nearby properties. The amount of harassment varies with the proximity of the property to the scene of jet operations.

No amount of sympathy for the vexed landowners can change the legal principles applicable to their claims. We do not have either a tort or a nuisance case. The plaintiffs sue under the Tucker Act and whether the applicability of that Act depends on a taking without compensation in violation of the Fifth Amendment or on an implied promise to pay for property taken, the claims are founded on the prohibition of the Fifth Amendment, "nor shall private property be taken for public use, without just compensation."

In construing and applying this constitutional provision the federal courts have long and consistently recognized the distinction between a taking and consequential damages. In Transportation Company v. Chicago, 99 U.S. 635, 642, the Supreme Court held that governmental activities which do not directly encroach on private property are not a taking within the meaning of the Fifth Amendment even though the consequences of such acts may impair the use of the property. The principle was repeated in United States v. Willow River Power Co., 324 U.S. 499, 510, the Court saying that "damage alone gives courts no power to require compensation." We have recognized the rule in this circuit by our holding in Harris v. United States, 10 Cir., 205 F.2d 765, 767, that under the federal constitution "damages to property not taken are compensable only as a consequence of or incidental to an actual taking."

Because of this rule which denies the recovery of consequential damages in the absence of any taking, many state constitutions provide in substance that private property shall not be taken or damaged for public use without

---

3. Stated in terms of percentages the diminution in value ranged from 55.3% to 40.8%.
4. United States v. Causby, *supra*. See also Griggs v. Allegheny County, 369 U.S. 84. . . .

compensation. However, the federal obligation has not been so enlarged either by statute or by constitutional amendment.

In *Causby* the Supreme Court held that the continuous invasions of the airspace superadjacent to the property of the landowner by military planes taking off and landing at a nearby base was "in the same category as invasions of the surface" and that the damages were not "merely consequential" but "the product of direct invasion of respondent's domain." The plaintiffs argue that the actual damage in *Causby* resulted from noise and vibrations and that if recovery is permitted for sound and shock waves traveling vertically, it should also be allowed for such waves traveling laterally. The unacceptability of this theory was demonstrated in Nunnally v. United States, 4 Cir., 239 F.2d 521, where recovery was denied because of diminution in value of a recreational cottage by practice bombing on an adjoining federal proving ground. The Fourth Circuit pointed out that there was no physical invasion of the plaintiff's property and that there was at the most a "sharing in the common burden of incidental damages" because the annoyance was the same as that to which everyone living in the vicinity was subject to varying degrees. The court said that to permit recovery would be to obliterate the carefully preserved distinction between "damage" and "taking."

We are cited to no decisions holding that the United States is liable for noise, vibration, or smoke without a physical invasion. In *Causby, Griggs,* and a number of lower court decisions such as Highland Park, Inc. v. United States, 161 F. Supp. 597, 142 Ct. Cl. 269; Herring v. United States, 162 F. Supp. 769, 142 Ct. Cl. 695, and Matson v. United States, 171 F. Supp. 283, 145 Ct. Cl. 225, there were regular flights over the property. Absent such physical invasion recovery has been uniformly denied.

Plaintiffs cite no cases with either facts or issues analogous to those with which we are concerned. Richards v. Washington Terminal Company, *supra,* allowed recovery because smoke and fumes were driven out of a tunnel by an exhaust fan in such manner that they were directed across plaintiff's property, but in so doing expressly recognized the invasion principle. United States v. Cress, 243 U.S. 316, and United States v. Kansas City Life Insurance Co., 339 U.S. 799, cases of flooding and underflooding respectively, applied the same principle. Swetland v. Curtiss Airports Corporation, 6 Cir., 55 F.2d 201, was an action to enjoin a private nuisance and the decision rests on theory of balance of conveniences.

In Armstrong v. United States, 364 U.S. 40, 48, the Court held that the total destruction of a lien was a compensable taking. Baltimore & Potomac Railroad Company v. Fifth Baptist Church, 108 U.S. 317, 332, sustained a recovery by a church for a nuisance created by a railroad operating in the District of Columbia under congressional authorization and the Court expressed doubt that such authorization would justify total deprivation of use without compensation. In discussing the meaning of the word "taken," the Court said in United States v. General Motors Corp., 323 U.S. 373, 378, that governmental action short of occupancy was a taking "if its effects are so complete as to deprive the owner of all or most of his interest in the subject matter."

In the instant case there is no total destruction and no deprivation of "all or most" of the plaintiffs' interests. The plaintiffs do not suggest that any home has been made uninhabitable or that any plaintiff has moved because of the activities at the Base. The record shows nothing more than an interference with use and enjoyment.

Congress has placed the navigable airspace in the public domain and has authorized administrative regulation of minimum altitudes of flight. [10] The regulations so far as pertinent fix the minimum altitudes at 1000 feet over congested areas and 500 over sparsely populated areas. [11] The airspace below such minimums is within the dominion of the landowner. The over-flights considered in *Causby* invaded that dominion. In the situation confronting us the warm-ups occur 2000 feet, the take-offs 2280 feet, and the maintenance 1 1/2 miles from the nearest property of the plaintiffs. *Causby* contains nothing indicating that recovery could be had for noise, vibration, or smoke coming from the same vertical distances.

Each of these disturbing conditions is brought to the plaintiffs' properties through the air and they do not effect an actual displacement of a landowner from space within which he is entitled to exercise dominion consistent with recognized concepts of real property rights. Such displacement is a fact when occasioned by repeated airplane flights. Sound waves, shock waves, and smoke pervade property neighboring that on which they have their source but the disturbance caused thereby is only a neighborhood inconvenience unless they are intentionally directed to some particular property as was the case in Richards v. Washington Terminal Co., *supra,* or unless they force the abdication of the use of space within the landowner's dominion. The activities of which the plaintiffs complain are not directed against them or their property and do not arrogate to the government any of the plaintiffs' dominion over their properties. The situation is common to that found on all the property surrounding the Base.

The vibrations which cause the windows and dishes to rattle, the smoke which blows into the homes during the summer months when the wind is from the east, and the noise which interrupts ordinary home activities do interfere with the use and enjoyment by the plaintiffs of their properties. Such interference is not a taking. The damages are no more than a consequence of the operations of the Base and as said in United States v. Willow River Power Co., *supra,* they "may be compensated by legislative authority, not by force of the Constitution alone." As we see the case at bar, the distinctions which the Supreme Court has consistently made between "damages" and "taking" control and compel denial of recovery.

Affirmed.

10. 49 U.S.C. §§1301(24) and 1348(a).
11. 14 C.F.R. §60.17.

MURRAH, C.J. (dissenting). It is agreed that subsequent to the establishment of the homes of these plaintiffs, the Government constructed these run-
ways and warm-up pads nearby, for Jet Engine operation, and that, as a
direct result of this operation, the "plaintiffs have suffered a substantial interference of the use and enjoyment of their properties . . .," with consequent
substantial diminution of the values of such properties. It seems also agreed
that the right asserted, i.e., the peaceful enjoyment of their homes, is a constitutionally protected property right, and that the admitted injury to such right
is peculiar to these plaintiffs, who are similarly situated. In any event, "the
constitutional provision is addressed to every sort of interest the citizen may
possess" (see United States v. General Motors, 323 U.S. 373), and certainly
includes the right to the peaceful possession of residential property. The economic interest asserted here, is no different from that "taken" in *Causby* and
Griggs.

Both the trial Court and this Court have denied compensation, upon the
premise that an actual physical invasion of the property damaged is a sine qua
non to a constitutional taking, and the injury is, therefore, merely consequential; hence, not constitutionally compensable. It is my thesis that a constitutional taking does not necessarily depend on whether the Government
physically invaded the property damaged.

It is true that, in the very nature of things, most constitutional takings
are accompanied by actual physical invasion. . . . But, the Government may
surely accomplish by indirect interference, the equivalent of an outright physical invasion. "If regulation goes too far it will be recognized as a taking."
Pennsylvania Coal Co. v. Mahon, *supra*, 260 U.S. [393, at] 415. Thus, a
"taking" was effected in Armstrong v. United States, 364 U.S. 40, by the
destruction of the liens on property through governmental acquisition of title.
The closing of a gold mine, by force of a wartime governmental regulation,
without physical invasion was held not to be a constitutional taking in United
States v. Central Eureka Mining Co., 357 U.S. 155, but not without recognizing that "action in the form of regulation can so diminish the value of property
as to constitute a taking." There was forceful argument in dissent to the effect
that to make the property owner's right to compensation turn on the physical
act of taking, was to "permit technicalities of form to dictate consequences of
substance." (See Mr. Justice Harlan's dissent, p. 181.) It is admitted that the
compensable damage in Richards v. Washington Terminal, 233 U.S. 546, was
not accompanied by an actual invasion, though the case is said to have been
decided on the invasion theory. The facts and reasoning there are analogous to
our situation, and serve to prove the recognition of a constitutional taking by
indirect interference. The principle is analogous to trespass and nuisance. See
cases collected in Harvard Law Review, June 1961, p. 1581.

As I view the precedents, especially in the context of their contrariety,
the decisional process involves an analysis and evaluation of competing interests, i.e., the public versus private, within the framework of our social order—
a jurisprudence of interest, if you please, in which the State imposes its will,

subject only to the constitutional covenant that it will pay "just compensation" for "private property" which is "taken." The critical and definitive words are, to be sure, constitutional language which, as we know, are subject to formulations, depending upon a point of view. We start with the agreed proposition that not every governmental interference, which adversely affects a private economic interest, amounts to a constitutional taking. See United States v. Willow River Power Co., 324 U.S. 499; Armstrong v. United States, *supra;* and Nunnally v. United States, *supra.* "Frustration and appropriation are essentially different things." Omnia Company v. United States, 261 U.S. 502. As I reason, the constitutional test in each case is first, whether the asserted interest is one which the law will protect; if so whether the interference is sufficiently direct, sufficiently peculiar, and of sufficient magnitude to cause us to conclude that fairness and justice, as between the State and the citizen, requires the burden imposed to be borne by the public and not by the individual alone.

Indeed, my brothers impliedly embrace this theory when they indicate that if the governmental interference in this case had rendered the plaintiffs' homes totally uninhabitable, the damages would have been compensable, as for a constitutional taking. But, they then say, that since there is "nothing more than an interference with use and enjoyment" of the property, the admitted damages are merely "consequential." This leaves me in doubt as to whether compensation is denied because the interest asserted is not one which the law will protect, as in United States v. Willow River Power Co., *supra,* or whether the interference with a protectable property right was not sufficiently direct, peculiar and grave to justify a conclusion of "taking." If the decision is based on the latter premise, I must inquire at what point the interference rises to the dignity of a "taking"? Is it when the window glass rattles, or when it falls out; when the smoke suffocates the inhabitants, or merely makes them cough; when the noise makes family conversation difficult, or when it stifles it entirely? In other words, does the "taking" occur when the property interest is totally destroyed, or when it is substantially diminished?

My point of view leads me to conclude, contrary to my brothers, that the interference shown here was sufficiently substantial, direct and peculiar to impose a servitude on the plaintiffs' homes, quite as effectively as the overflights in *Causby* and *Griggs,* and the smoke and gases in *Richards.* I would, therefore, hold the damages constitutionally compensable.

NOTES AND QUESTIONS

1. Most state courts faced with the *Batten* issue have granted recovery to the landowners. See, e.g., Aaron v. City of Los Angeles, 40 Cal. App. 3d 471, 115 Cal. Rptr. 162 (1974), where 581 property owners recovered from $400 to $6000 each for the jet noise emanating from the nearby Los Angeles International Airport; Parker v. City of Los Angeles, 44 Cal. App. 3d 556, 118

Cal. Rptr. 687 (1975) (idem, 9 plaintiffs, $224,000); Thornburg v. Port of Portland, 233 Or. 178, 376 P.2d 100 (1962), second appeal 244 Or. 69, 415 P.2d 750 (1966); Martin v. Port of Seattle, 64 Wash. 2d 309, 391 P.2d 540 (1964), *cert. denied,* 379 U.S. 989 (1965); City of Jacksonville v. Schumann, 167 So. 2d 95 (Fla. App. 1964), second appeal 199 So. 2d 727 (Fla. App. 1967), *cert. denied,* 390 U.S. 981 (1968); Johnson v. City of Greeneville, 222 Tenn. 260, 435 S.W.2d 476 (1968).

2. Many state constitutions, including those of California and Washington, provide that property may neither be "taken" nor "damaged" without compensation. See, e.g., Calif. Const. art. 1, §14; Wash. Const. art. 1, §16, amend. 9. On the *Batten* facts, should the government lose wherever the "damage" clause appears in a constitution and win wherever it does not?

3. The *Batten* opinion refers to the public domain of airspace over 1,000 feet above congested areas and 500 feet above sparsely populated areas. Does the dissenting judge answer the public domain argument? Does a good answer exist?

4. Clearance zone regulations of the Federal Aviation Administration set a ceiling on the height of structures near airports. Cf. Federal Aviation Act of 1958, 49 U.S.C. §1348. These regulations require a 50:1 approach-to-departure clearance surface (for every 50 feet traveled horizontally, ascend one foot). Thus, one-quarter mile from the runway, the height restriction is 26.4 feet; the FAA must approve any construction higher than the limit. Surprisingly, however, if the landowner fails to obtain approval, he may still proceed, since Congress apparently intended to shift to local authorities the responsibility and the cost of hazard-free approaches. Cf. Kupster Realty v. State of New York, 93 Misc. 2d 843, 404 N.Y.S.2d 225 (Ct. Cl. 1978). Thus, when an airport builds a new runway or lengthens an old one, the airport operator, when necessary, must acquire a *navigation* easement. Where such takings occur, the measure of compensation becomes quite complex. Cf., e.g., Kupster Realty v. State of New York, *supra;* 3775 Genesee Street v. State, 99 Misc. 2d 59, 385 N.Y.S.2d 587 (Ct. Cl. 1979).

5. How should courts decide the following analogous situations?

(a) A neighboring landowner complains of freeway noise, fumes, and dust. Cf. People ex rel. Dept. Pub. Wks. v. Volunteers of America, 21 Cal. App. 3d 111, 98 Cal. Rptr. 423 (1971); Dennison v. State, page 1042 *supra.*

(b) The operator of a gasoline station complains of a three-month business shutdown when repairs force a shutdown of the highway on which he fronts. Cf. Farrell v. Rose, 253 N.Y. 73, 170 N.E. 458 (1930).

6. Suppose that the *Batten* airfield had been privately owned and operated: might the plaintiffs have sued and recovered in nuisance? Cf. Boomer v.

Atlantic Cement Co., page 685 *supra*. If so, why did plaintiffs not couple nuisance to their suit in inverse condemnation against the United States? Do nuisance and inverse condemnation suits based upon airport noise present identical issues? Cf. Stoebuck, Condemnation by Nuisance: The Airport Cases in Retrospect and Prospect, 71 Dick. L. Rev. 207 (1967).

State courts quite consistently have refused to award damages in inverse condemnation as a remedial alternative to declaring invalid a zoning (or other) regulation that was deemed a "taking." See, e.g., Fred F. French Investing Co. v. City of New York, 39 N.Y.2d 587, 350 N.E.2d 381, 385 N.Y.S.22 587 (1976), *cert. denied*, 429 U.S. 990 (1976). But the issue is far from settled. The United States Supreme Court has recently become involved, and although the Court has yet to find a satisfactory vehicle for installing a general rule, the opportunity may be close at hand.

In 1980, the Court heard argument in Agins v. City of Tiburon, 447 U.S. 255, 100 S. Ct. 2138, 63 L. Ed. 2d 106 (1980). The Aginses had paid $50,000 for five acres of unimproved land having a splendid view of San Francisco Bay. When they purchased their parcel, the zoning law permitted one house per acre. Several years later, Tiburon adopted an "open space" ordinance placing the Aginses' parcel in a more restricted zone; density would be determined when property owners applied for a building permit, and density under this ordinance might be as low as 0.2 houses per acre. The Aginses filed a $2 million damages claim against the city, contending that the new zoning had destroyed the value of their property. The city rejected the claim, and a complaint for damages in inverse condemnation followed. In their complaint, plaintiffs alleged that the regulation had taken their property without just compensation.

The California Supreme Court held for the defendant, 24 Cal. 3d 266, 598 P.2d 25, 157 Cal. Rptr. 372 (1979). It ruled that the regulation did not deprive the landowner of substantially all reasonable use of the property. But even if the regulation had been invalid, the court continued, declaratory relief, not compensable damages, was the appropriate remedy.

When the Supreme Court noted probable jurisdiction in the *Agins* case, "there was a somewhat breathless expectation in planning and zoning circles that the court was about to hand down a modern day Village of Euclid v. Ambler Realty decision that would serve as the new touchstone for determining the constitutionality of land use regulations." Smith, Nat'l L.J., Aug. 4, 1980, at 52, cols. 3-4. The suspended breath went for naught, however; all that the Court produced was a brief unanimous opinion holding that the zoning ordinance on its face did not take the Aginses' property without just compensation, and that the record did not concretely present an "as applied" issue because the Aginses had not submitted a development plan for their parcel. As to whether inverse condemnation might be an available remedy, the court was unwilling to consider that issue until a taking had occurred.

Expectations were created again during the following term when the

Court considered the case that follows. Once again, the Court did not like the vehicle it chose, but Justice Brennan's dissent, in which *five* justices expressed some agreement, deserves close attention.

SAN DIEGO GAS & ELECTRIC CO. v. CITY OF SAN DIEGO
450 U.S. 621, 101 S. Ct. 1287, 67 L. Ed. 2d 551 (1981)

JUSTICE BLACKMUN delivered the opinion of the court. Appellant San Diego Gas & Electric Company, a California corporation, asks this Court to rule that a State must provide a monetary remedy to a landowner whose property allegedly has been "taken" by a regulatory ordinance claimed to violate the Just Compensation Clause of the Fifth Amendment. This question was left open last Term in Agins v. City of Tiburon, 447 U.S. 255, 263 (1980). Because we conclude that we lack jurisdiction in this case, we again must leave the issue undecided.

I

Appellant owns a 412-acre parcel of land in Sorrento Valley, an area in the northwest part of the city of San Diego, Cal. It assembled and acquired the acreage in 1966, at a cost of about $1,770,000, as a possible site for a nuclear power plant to be constructed in the 1980's. Approximately 214 acres of the parcel lie within or near an estuary known as the Los Penasquitos Lagoon.[2] These acres are low-lying land which serves as a drainage basis for three river systems. About a third of the land is subject to tidal action from the nearby Pacific Ocean. The 214 acres are unimproved, except for sewer and utility lines.[3]

When appellant acquired the 214 acres, most of the land was zoned either for industrial use or in an agricultural "holding" category.[4] The city's master plan, adopted in 1967, designated nearly all the area for industrial use.

Several events that occurred in 1973 gave rise to this litigation. First, the San Diego City Council rezoned parts of the property. It changed 39 acres

---

2. Appellant claims that only the 214 acres have been taken by the city of San Diego. Throughout this opinion, "the property" and any similar phrase refers to this smaller portion of the 412 acres owned by appellant.

3. Apparently other portions of the 412-acre parcel have been developed to some extent, and some parts sold.

4. The city had classified 116 acres as M-1A (industrial) and 112 acres as A-1 (agricultural). The latter classification was reserved for "undeveloped areas not yet ready for urbanization and awaiting development, those areas where agricultural usage may be reasonably expected to persist or areas designated as open space in the general plan." San Diego Ordinance No. 8706 (New Series) §101.0404, reproduced in Brief for Appellee C-1. A small amount of the land was zoned for residential development. (These figures total more than 214 acres. When the California courts described the zoning of the property, they did not distinguish between the 214 acres that allegedly were taken and 15 other acres that the trial court found had been damaged by the severance.)

from industrial to agricultural, and increased the minimum lot size in some of the agricultural areas from 1 acre to 10 acres. The Council recommended, however, that 50 acres of the agricultural land be considered for industrial development upon the submission of specific development plans.

Second, the city, pursuant to Cal. Govt. Code Ann. §65563 (West) (Supp. 1979), established an open-space plan. This statute required each California city and county to adopt a plan "for the comprehensive and long-range preservation and conservation of open-space land within its jurisdiction." The plan adopted by the city of San Diego placed appellant's property among the city's open-space areas, which it defined as "any urban land or water surface that is essentially open or natural in character, and which has appreciable utility for park and recreation purposes, conservation of land, water or other natural resources or historic or scenic purposes." App. 159. The plan acknowledged appellant's intention to construct a nuclear power plant on the property, stating that such a plant would not necessarily be incompatible with the open-space designation. The plan proposed, however, that the city acquire the property to preserve it as parkland.

Third, the City Council proposed a bond issue in order to obtain funds to acquire open-space lands. The Council identified appellant's land as among those properties to be acquired with the proceeds of the bond issue. The proposition, however, failed to win the voters' approval. The open-space plan has remained in effect, but the city has made no attempt to acquire appellant's property.

On August 15, 1974, appellant instituted this action in the Superior Court for the County of San Diego against the city and a number of its officials. It alleged that the city had taken its property without just compensation, in violation of the Constitutions of the United States and California. Appellant's theory was that the city had deprived it of the entire beneficial use of the property through the rezoning and the adoption of the open-space plan. It alleged that the city followed a policy of refusing to approve any development that was inconsistent with the plan, and that the only beneficial use of the property was as an industrial park, a use that would be inconsistent with the open-space designation.[6] The city disputed this allegation, arguing that appellant had never asked its approval for any development plan for the property. It also contended that, as a charter city, it was not bound by the open-space plan, even if appellant's proposed development would be inconsistent with the plan, citing Cal. Govt. Code Ann., §§65700, 65803 (West) (1966 and Supp. 1979).

Appellant sought damages of $6,150,000 in inverse condemnation, as well as mandamus and declaratory relief. Prior to trial, the court dismissed the mandamus claim, holding that "mandamus is not the proper remedy to chal-

---

6. Appellant abandoned its plan to construct a nuclear power plant after the discovery of an off-shore fault that rendered the project unfeasible. Tr. 73. Its witnesses acknowledged that only about 150 acres were usable as an industrial park, and that 1.25 million cubic yards of fill would be needed to undertake such a development. Id., at 711, 905.

lenge the validity of a legislative act." Clerk's Tr. 42. After a nonjury trial on
the issue of liability, the court granted judgment for appellant, finding that:

> 29.   [Due to the] continuing course of conduct of the defendant City
> culminating in June of 1973, and, in particular, the designation of substantially
> all of the subject property as open space . . . , plaintiff has been deprived of all
> practical, beneficial or economic use of the property designated as open space,
> and has further suffered severance damage with respect to the balance of the
> subject property.
>
> 30.   No development could proceed on the property designated as open
> space unless it was consistent with open space. In light of the particular charac-
> teristics of the said property, there exists no practical, beneficial or economic use
> of the said property designated as open space which is consistent with open
> space.
>
> 31.   Since June 19, 1973, the property designated as open space has been
> devoted to use by the public as open space.
>
> 32.   Following the actions of the defendant City in June of 1973, it would
> have been totally impractical and futile for plaintiff to have applied to defendant
> City for the approval of any development of the property designated as open
> space or the remainder of the subject property.
>
> 33.   Since the actions of the defendant City of June of 1973 the property
> designated as open space and the remainder of the larger parcel is unmarketable
> in that no other person would be willing to purchase the property, and the
> property has at most a nominal fair market value. App. 41-42.

The court concluded that these findings established that the city had
taken the property and that just compensation was required by the Constitutions of both the United States and California. A subsequent jury trial on the
question of damages resulted in a judgment for appellant for over $3 million.

On appeal, the California Court of Appeal, Fourth District, affirmed.

The Supreme Court of California, however, on July 13, 1978, granted
the city's petition for a hearing. This action automatically vacated the Court
of Appeal's decision, depriving it of all effect. Knouse v. Nimocks, 8 Cal. 2d
482, 483-484, 66 P.2d 438 (1937). See also Cal. Rules of Court 976(d) and
977. Before the hearing, the Supreme Court in June 1979 retransferred the
case to the Court of Appeal for reconsideration in light of the intervening
decision in Agins v. City of Tiburon, 24 Cal. 3d 366, 598 P.2d 25 (1979), aff'd,
447 U.S. 255 (1980). The California court in *Agins* held that an owner who is
deprived of substantially all beneficial use of his land by a zoning regulation is
not entitled to an award of damages in an inverse condemnation proceeding.
Rather, his exclusive remedy is invalidation of the regulation in an action for
mandamus or declaratory relief.

When the present case was retransferred, the Court of Appeal, in an
unpublished opinion, reversed the judgment of the Superior Court. App. 63. It
relied upon the California decision in *Agins* and held that appellant could not
recover compensation through inverse condemnation. It, however, did not

invalidate either the zoning ordinance or the open-space plan. Instead, it held that factual disputes precluded such relief on the present state of the record:

> [Appellant] complains it has been denied all use of its land which is zoned for agriculture and manufacturing but lies within the open space area of the general plan. It has not made application to use or improve the property nor has it asked [the] City what development might be permitted. Even assuming no use is acceptable to the City, [appellant's] complaint deals with the alleged overzealous use of the police power by [the] City. Its remedy is mandamus or declaratory relief, not inverse condemnation. [Appellant] did in its complaint seek these remedies asserting that [the] City had arbitrarily exercised its police power by enacting an unconstitutional zoning law and general plan element or by applying the zoning and general plan unconstitutionally. However, on the present record these are disputed fact issues not covered by the trial court in its findings and conclusions. They can be dealt with anew should [appellant] elect to retry the case. App. 66.

The Supreme Court of California denied further review. App. to Juris. Statement I-1. Appellant appealed to this Court, arguing that the Fifth and Fourteenth Amendments require that compensation be paid whenever private property is taken for public use. Appellant takes issue with the California Supreme Court's holding in *Agins* that its remedy is limited to invalidation of the ordinance in a proceeding for mandamus or declaratory relief. We postponed consideration of our jurisdiction until the hearing on the merits.— U.S.—(1980). We now conclude that the appeal must be dismissed because of the absence of a final judgment. [10]

II

In *Agins,* the California Supreme Court held that mandamus or declaratory relief is available whenever a zoning regulation is claimed to effect an uncompensated taking in violation of the Fifth and Fourteenth Amendments. The Court of Appeal's failure, therefore, to award such relief in this case clearly indicates its conclusion that the record does not support appellant's claim that an uncompensated taking has occurred. Because the court found that the record presented "disputed fact issues not covered by the trial court in its findings and conclusions," App. 66, it held that mandamus and declaratory relief would be available "should [appellant] elect to retry the case." Ibid. While this phrase appears to us to be somewhat ambiguous, we read it as meaning that appellant is to have an opportunity on remand to convince the trial court to resolve the disputed issues in its favor. We do not believe that the Court of Appeals was holding that judgment *must* be entered for the city. It

---

10. Title 28 U.S.C. §1257 grants jurisdiction to this Court to review only "[f]inal judgments or decrees rendered by the highest court of a State in which a decision could be had."

certainly did not so direct. This indicates that appellant is free to pursue its quest for relief in the Superior Court. The logical course of action for an appellate court that finds unresolved factual disputes in the record is to remand the case for the resolution of those disputes. We therefore conclude that the Court of Appeal's decision contemplates further proceedings in the trial court.

Because §1257 permits us to review only "[f]inal judgments or decrees" of a state court, the appeal must be, and is, dismissed.

It is so ordered.

JUSTICE REHNQUIST, concurring. If I were satisfied that this appeal was from a "final judgment or decree" of the California Court of Appeal, as that term is used in 28 U.S.C. §1257, I would have little difficulty in agreeing with much of what is said in the dissenting opinion of Justice Brennan. . . .

JUSTICE BRENNAN, with whom JUSTICE STEWART, JUSTICE MARSHALL, and JUSTICE POWELL join, dissenting. Title 28 U.S.C. §1257 limits this Court's jurisdiction to review judgments of state courts to "[f]inal judgments or decrees rendered by the highest court of a State in which a decision could be had." The Court today dismisses this appeal on the ground that the Court of Appeal of California, Fourth District, failed to decide the federal question whether a "taking" of appellant's property had occurred, and therefore had not entered a final judgment or decree on that question appealable under §1257. Because the Court's conclusion fundamentally mischaracterizes the holding and judgment of the Court of Appeal, I respectfully dissent from the Court's dismissal and reach the merits of appellant's claim.

Since the Court of Appeal held that no Fifth Amendment "taking" had occurred, no just compensation was required. This is a classic final judgment. See North Dakota State Board of Pharmacy v. Snyder's Drug Stores, Inc., 414 U.S. 156, 163 (1973); Grays Harbor Logging Co. v. Coats-Fordney Logging Co. 243 U.S. 251, 256 (1917). I therefore dissent from the dismissal of this appeal, and address the merits of the question presented. . . .

III

The Just Compensation Clause of the Fifth Amendment, made applicable to the States through the Fourteenth Amendment, Webb's Fabulous Pharmacies, Inc. v. Beckwith,—U.S.—, —(1980); see Chicago, B. & Q. R. Co. v. Chicago, 166 U.S. 226, 239, 241 (1897), states in clear and unequivocal terms: "[N]or shall private property be taken for public use, without just compensation." The question presented on the merits in this case is whether a government entity must pay just compensation when a police power regulation has effected a "taking" of "private property" for "public use" within the meaning of that constitutional provision. Implicit in this question is the corollary issue whether a government entity's exercise of its regulatory police power can ever effect a "taking" within the meaning of the Just Compensation Clause.

In Penn Central Transportation Co. v. New York City, 438 U.S. 104 (1978), the Court analyzed "whether the restrictions imposed by New York City's [Landmark Preservation] law upon appellants' exploitation of the [Grand Central] Terminal site effect a 'taking' of appellants' property within the meaning of the Fifth Amendment." Id., at 122. Canvassing the appropriate inquiries necessary to determine whether a particular restriction effected a "taking," the Court identified the "economic impact of the regulation on the claimant" and the "character of the governmental action" as particularly relevant considerations. Id., at 124; see, id., at 130-131. Although the Court ultimately concluded that application of New York's Landmark law did not effect a "taking" of the railroad property, it did so only after deciding that "[t]he restrictions imposed are substantially related to the promotion of the general welfare and not only permit reasonable beneficial use of the landmark site but also afford appellants opportunities further to enhance not only the Terminal site property but also other properties." Id., at 138 (footnote omitted).

The constitutionality of a local ordinance regulating dredging and pit excavating on a property was addressed in Goldblatt v. Town of Hempstead, 369 U.S. 590 (1962). After observing that an otherwise valid zoning ordinance that deprives the owner of the most beneficial use of his property would not be unconstitutional, id., at 592, the Court cautioned: "That is not to say, however, that governmental action in the form of regulation cannot be so onerous as to constitute a taking which constitutionally requires compensation," id., at 594. On many other occasions, the Court has recognized in passing the vitality of the general principle that a regulation can effect a Fifth Amendment "taking." See, e.g., Pruneyard Shopping Center v. Robins,—U.S.—, —(1980); Kaiser Aetna v. United States, 444 U.S. 164, 174 (1979); Andrus v. Allard, 444 U.S. 51, 65-66 (1979); United States v. Central Eureka Mining Co., 357 U.S. 155, 168 (1958).

The principle applied in all these cases has its source in Justice Holmes' opinion for the Court in Pennsylvania Coal Co. v. Mahon, 260 U.S. 393, 415 (1922), in which he stated: "The general rule at least is, that while property may be regulated to a certain extent, if regulation goes too far it will be recognized as a taking." The determination of a "taking" is "a question of degree—and therefore cannot be disposed of by general propositions." Id., at 416. While acknowledging that "[g]overnment hardly could go on if to some extent values incident to property could not be diminished withtout paying for every such change in the general law," id., at 413, the Court rejected the proposition that police power restrictions could never be recognized as a Fifth Amendment "taking." Indeed, the Court concluded that the Pennsylvania statute forbidding the mining of coal that would cause the subsidence of any house effected a "taking." Id., at 414-416.

Not only does the holding of the California Court of Appeal contradict precedents of this Court, but it also fails to recognize the essential similarity of regulatory "takings" and other "takings." The typical "taking" occurs when a government entity formally condemns a landowner's property and obtains the fee simple pursuant to its sovereign power of eminent domain. See, e.g., Berman v. Parker, 348 U.S. 26, 33 (1954). However, a "taking" may also occur without a formal condemnation proceeding or transfer of fee simple. This Court long ago recognized that

> [i]t would be a very curious and unsatisfactory result, if in construing [the Just Compensation Clause] . . . it shall be held that if the government refrains from the absolute conversion of real property to the uses of the public it can destroy its value entirely, can inflict irreparable and permanent injury to any extent, can, in effect, subject it to total destruction without making any compensation, because, in the narrowest sense of that word, it is not *taken* for the public use. Pumpelly v. Green Bay Co., 80 U.S. (13 Wall.) 166, 177-178 (1872) (emphasis in original).

See Chicago, R. I. & P. R. Co. v. United States, 284 U.S. 80, 96 (1931).

In service of this principle, the Court frequently has found "takings" outside the context of formal condemnation proceedings or transfer of fee simple, in cases where government action benefiting the public resulted in destruction of the use and enjoyment of private property. E.g., Kaiser Aetna v. United States, *supra*, 444 U.S., at 178-180 (navigational servitude allowing public right of access); United States v. Dickinson, 331 U.S. 745, 750-751 (1947) (property flooded because of government dam project); United States v. Causby, 328 U.S. 256, 261-262 (1946) (frequent low altitude flights of Army and Navy aircraft over property); Pennsylvania Coal Co. v. Mahon, *supra*, 260 U.S., at 414-416 (state regulation forbidding mining of coal).

Police power regulations such as zoning ordinances and other land-use restrictions can destroy the use and enjoyment of property in order to promote the public good just as effectively as formal condemnation or physical invasion of property. From the property owner's point of view, it may matter little whether his land is condemned or flooded, or whether it is restricted by regulation to use in its natural state, if the effect in both cases is to deprive him of all beneficial use of it. From the government's point of view, the benefits flowing to the public from preservation of open space through regulation may be equally great as from creating a wildlife refuge through formal condemnation or increasing electricity production through a dam project that floods private property. Appellee implicitly posits the distinction that the government *intends* to take property through condemnation or physical invasion whereas it does not through police power regulations. See Brief for Appellee, at 43. But "the Constitution measures a taking of property not by what a State says, or by what it intends, but by what it *does*." Hughes v. Washington, 389 U.S. 290, 298 (1967) (Stewart, J., concurring) (emphasis in original); see Davis v. Newton Coal Co., 267 U.S. 292, 301 (1925). It is only logical, then, that government action other than acquisition of title, occupancy, or physical invasion can be a "taking," and therefore a de facto exercise of the power of eminent domain, where the effects completely deprive the owner of all or most of his interest in the property. United States v. Dickinson, *supra*, 331 U.S., at 748; United States v. General Motors Corp., 323 U.S. 373, 378 (1945).

IV

Having determined that property may be "taken for public use" by police power regulation within the meaning of the Just Compensation Clause of the Fifth Amendment, the question remains whether a government entity may constitutionally deny payment of just compensation to the property owner and limit his remedy to mere invalidation of the regulation instead. Appellant argues that it is entitled to the full fair market value of the property. Appellee argues that invalidation of the regulation is sufficient without payment of monetary compensation. In my view, once a court establishes that there was a regulatory "taking," the Constitution demands that the government entity pay just compensation for the period commencing on the date the regulation first effected the "taking," and ending on the date the government entity chooses to rescind or otherwise amend the regulation. This interpretation, I believe, is supported by the express words and purpose of the Just Compensation Clause, as well as by cases of this Court construing it.

The language of the Fifth Amendment prohibits the "tak[ing]" of private property for "public use" without payment of "just compensation." As soon as private property has been taken, whether through formal condemnation proceedings, occupancy, physical invasion, or regulation, the landowner has *already* suffered a constitutional violation, and " 'the self-executing character of the constitutional provision with respect to compensation,' " United States v. Clarke, 445 U.S. 253, 257 (1980), quoting 6 P. Nichols, Eminent Domain §25.41 (3d rev. ed. 1972), is triggered. This Court has consistently recognized that the just compensation requirement in the Fifth Amendment is not precatory: once there is a "taking," compensation *must* be awarded. In Jacobs v. United States, 290 U.S. 13 (1933), for example, a government dam project creating intermittent overflows into petitioners' property resulted in the "taking" of a servitude. Petitioners brought suit against the government to recover just compensation for the partial "taking." Commenting on the nature of the landowners' action, the Court observed:

> The suits were based on the right to recover just compensation for property taken by the United States for public use in the exercise of its power of eminent domain. That right was guaranteed by the Constitution. The fact that condemnation proceedings were not instituted and that the right was asserted in suits by the owners did not change the essential nature of the claim. The form of the remedy did not qualify the right. It rested upon the Fifth Amendment. Statutory recognition was not necessary. A promise to pay was not necessary. Such a promise was implied because of the duty to pay imposed by the Amendment. Id., at 16.

See also Griggs v. Allegheny County, 369 U.S. 84, 84-85, 88-90 (1962); United States v. Causby, *supra,* 328 U.S., at 268. Invalidation unaccompanied by payment of damages would hardly compensate the landowner for any economic loss suffered during the time his property was taken.

Moreover, mere invalidation would fall far short of fulfilling the fundamental purpose of the Just Compensation Clause. That guarantee was designed to bar the government from forcing some individuals to bear burdens which, in all fairness, should be borne by the public as a whole. Armstrong v. United States, 364 U.S. 40, 49 (1960). See Agins v. City of Tiburon, *supra,*— U.S., at—; Andrus v. Allard, *supra,* 444 U.S., at 65. When one person is asked to assume more than a fair share of the public burden, the payment of just compensation operates to redistribute that economic cost from the individual to the public at large. See United States v. Willow River Power Co., 324 U.S. 499, 502 (1945); Monongahela Navigation Co. v. United States, 148 U.S. 312, 325 (1893). Because police power regulations must be substantially related to the advancement of the public health, safety, morals, or general welfare, see Village of Euclid v. Ambler Realty Co., 272 U.S. 365, 395 (1926), it is axiomatic that the public receives a benefit while the offending regulation is in effect. If the regulation denies the private property owner the use and enjoyment of his land and is found to effect a "taking," it is only fair that the public bear the cost of benefits received during the interim period between application of the regulation and the government entity's rescission of it. The payment of just compensation serves to place the landowner in the same position monetarily as he would have occupied if his property had not been taken. Almota Farmers Elevator & Warehouse Co. v. United States, 409 U.S. 470, 473-474 (1973); United States v. Reynolds, 397 U.S. 14, 16 (1970).

The fact that a regulatory "taking" may be temporary, by virtue of the government's power to rescind or amend the regulation, does not make it any less of a constitutional "taking." Nothing in the Just Compensation Clause suggests that "takings" must be permanent and irrevocable. Nor does the temporary reversible quality of a regulatory "taking" render compensation for the time of the "taking" any less obligatory. This Court more than once has recognized that temporary reversible "takings" should be analyzed according to the same constitutional framework applied to permanent irreversible "takings." For example, in United States v. Causby, *supra,* 328 U.S., at 258-259, the United States had executed a lease to use an airport for a one-year term "ending June 30, 1942, with a provision for renewals through June 30, 1967, or six months after the end of the national emergency, whichever [was] the earlier." The Court held that the frequent low-level flights of Army and Navy airplanes over respondent's chicken farm, located near the airport, effected a "taking" of an easement on respondent's property. Id., at 266, 267. However, because the flights could be discontinued by the government at any time, the Court remanded the case to the Court of Claims: "Since on this record *it is not clear whether the easement taken is a permanent or a temporary one,* it would be premature for us to consider whether the amount of the award made by the Court of Claims was proper." Id., at 268 (emphasis added). In other cases where the government has taken only temporary use of a building, land, or equipment, the Court has not hesitated to determine the appropriate measure of just compensation. See Kimball Laundry Co. v. United States, 338 U.S. 1, 6 (1949); United States v. Petty Motor Co., 327 U.S. 372, 374-375 (1946); United States v. General Motors Corp., *supra*, 323 U.S., at 374-375.

But contrary to appellant's claim that San Diego must formally condemn its property and pay full fair market value, nothing in the Just Compensation Clause empowers a court to order a government entity to condemn the property and pay its full fair market value, where the "taking" already effected is temporary and reversible and the government wants to halt the "taking." Just as the government may cancel condemnation proceedings before passage of title, see P. Nichols, 6 Eminent Domain §24.113, at 24-21 (3d rev. ed. 1980), or abandon property it has temporarily occupied or invaded, see United States v. Dow, 357 U.S. 17, 26 (1958), it must have the same power to rescind a regulatory "taking." As the Court has noted, "an abandonment does not prejudice the property owner. It merely results in an alteration of the property interest taken—from full ownership to one of temporary use and occupation. . . . In such cases compensation would be measured by the principles normally governing the taking of a right to use property temporarily." Id.; see Danforth v. United States, 308 U.S. 271, 284 (1939).

The constitutional rule I propose requires that, once a court finds that a police power regulation has effected a "taking," the government entity must pay just compensation for the period commencing on the date the regulation first effected the "taking," and ending on the date the government entity chooses to rescind or otherwise amend the regulation. Ordinary principles determining the proper measure of just compensation, regularly applied in cases of permanent and temporary "takings" involving formal condemnation proceedings, occupations, and physical invasions, should provide guidance to the courts in the award of compensation for a regulatory "taking." As a starting point, the value of the property taken may be ascertained as of the date of the "taking." United States v. Clarke, *supra*, 445 U.S., at 258; Almota Farmers Elevators & Warehouse Co. v. United States, *supra*, 409 U.S., at 474; United States v. Miller, 317 U.S. 369, 374 (1943); Olson v. United States; 292 U.S. 246, 255 (1934). The government must inform the court of its intentions vis-à-vis the regulation with sufficient clarity to guarantee a correct assessment of the just compensation award. Should the government decide immediately to revoke or otherwise amend the regulation, it would be liable for payment of compensation only for the interim during which the regulation effected a "taking." Rules of valuation already developed for temporary "takings" may be particularly useful to the courts in their quest for assessing the proper measure of monetary relief in cases of revocation or amendment, see generally Kimball Laundry Co. v. United States, *supra;* United States v. Petty Motor Co., *supra;* United Sates v. General Motors Corp., *supra,* although additional rules may need to be developed, see Kimball Laundry Co. v. United States, *supra,* 338 U.S., at 21-22 (Rutledge, J., concurring); United States v. Miller, *supra,* 317 U.S., at 373-374. Alternatively the government may choose formally to condemn the property, or otherwise to continue the offending regulation: in either case the action must be sustained by proper measures of just compensation. See generally United States v. Fuller, 409 U.S. 488, 490-492, (1973); United States ex rel. Tennessee Valley Authority v. Powelson, 319 U.S. 266, 281-285 (1942).

It should be noted that the Constitution does not embody any specific procedure or form of remedy that the States must adopt: "[t]he Fifth Amendment expresses a principle of fairness and not a technical rule of procedure enshrining old or new niceties regarding 'causes of action'—when they are born, whether they proliferate, and when they die." United States v. Dickinson, *supra*, 331 U.S., at 748. Cf. United States v. Memphis Cotton Oil Co., 288 U.S. 62, 67-69 (1933). The States should be free to experiment in the implementation of this rule, provided that their chosen procedures and remedies comport with the fundamental constitutional command. See generally Hill, The Bill of Rights and the Supervisory Power, 69 Colum. L. Rev. 181, 191-193 (1969). The only constitutional requirement is that the landowner must be able meaningfully to challenge a regulation that allegedly effects a "taking," and recover just compensation if it does so. He may not be forced to resort to piecemeal litigation or otherwise unfair procedures in order to receive his due. See United States v. Dickinson, *supra*, 331 U.S., at 749.

V

In Agins v. City of Tiburon, *supra*, 24 Cal. 3d, at 275, 598 P.2d, at 29, the California Supreme Court was "persuaded by various policy considerations to the view that inverse condemnation is an inappropriate and undesirable remedy in cases in which unconstitutional regulation is alleged." In particular, the Court cited "the need for preserving a degree of freedom in land-use planning function, and the inhibiting financial force which inheres in the inverse condemnation remedy," in reaching its conclusion. Id., at 276, 598 P.2d, at 31. But the applicability of express constitutional guarantees is not a matter to be determined on the basis of policy judgments made by the legislative, executive, or judicial branches. Nor can the vindication of those rights depend on the expense in doing so. See Watson v. City of Memphis, 373 U.S. 526; 537-538 (1963).

Because I believe that the Just Compensation Clause requires the constitutional rule outlined, *supra*, I would vacate the judgment of the California Court of Appeal, Fourth District, and remand for further proceedings not inconsistent with this opinion.

NOTES AND QUESTIONS

1. Read Justice Brennan's dissent carefully. Does the opinion provide any standard for testing whether the regulation *is* a taking?

2. Assume that Justice Brennan's views eventually prevail. How should a court measure just compensation during the interval when the regulation remains on the books? Consider that issue in the *San Diego* case. The utility company had assembled a 412-acre parcel in 1966 at a cost of $1,770,000. Of the 214 acres in question, 116 acres were zoned industrial and the remainder were "agricultural" (. . . areas where agricultural usage may be reasonably expected to persist or areas designated as open space in the general plan). In 1973, rezoning placed all but 39 acres in the agricultural zone, and much of the company's tract was included in the open-space plan. About this time, the company abandoned its plans for a nuclear plant and began to consider an industrial park development.

For starters, what value should be placed on the disputed parcel: the 1966 purchase price "properly" allocated or the 1973 "value"? If the latter, should the value reflect the 1966 zoning (which was already quite restricted) or some less restrictive zoning—e.g., the industrial usage that the company preferred? What consideration should one give to the fact that the property tax assessment reflected the parcel's agricultural zoning, or that an industrial park takes years to develop—during which time farming may well be the land's only productive use? And how does one establish an investment rate of return during the "taking" interval? Should it be the same as the statutory interest rate that the state pays on condemnation awards (measured from the date of taking), or should it reflect the investment yield on "comparable" investments? And, if the latter, what is the yield on raw land?

3. Municipalities have long believed that a "temporary" moratorium on new development would be constitutionally acceptable when the community wanted reasonable time either to devise a new comprehensive plan or to install needed infrastructure—e.g., water and sewer lines. Cf., e.g., Golden v. Town of Ramapo, *supra*, page 866. Is Justice Brennan now saying that a temporary moratorium would require the payment of just compensation?

4. Smith, Natl. L.J., Aug. 4, 1980, at 52, col. 3; at 54; col. 1:

> Compensation as a remedy for constitutionally invalid regulation has a superficial attractiveness, particularly to landowners who believe that establishing the principle that municipal caprice can be costly will make local councils more amenable to development proposals. The concept is not without its drawbacks, however. Unless the courts can be persuaded to award compensation in inverse condemnation for mere diminution in the value of land, which seems very unlikely, condemnation will remain a remedy for those comparatively rare cases in which the landowner can plausibly argue that when the city zoned the land, it also bought it and the only question remaining is the amount to be paid for the conveyance. The zeal of the average landowner to pursue an inverse condemnation remedy may be considerably dampened by the explanation that if he wins he does not get to keep the property.
>
> The difficulty with the compensation remedy is that it does not come to grips with the central problem in most land use litigation, which is that invalidation of constitutionally impermissible regulation does not ordinarily free the

landowner or developer to use his property without regard to the invalidated regulation. A municipality that finds that its land use ordinance has been declared invalid, either facially or as applied, need only revise its regulations in a manner that still forbids the proposed development and then invite the plaintiff to bring suit to invalidate the new restrictions.

Do Justice Brennan's views meet any of the problems described above?

§18.4. The Navigation Servitude

UNITED STATES v. WILLOW RIVER POWER CO.
324 U.S. 499, 65 S. Ct. 761, 89 L. Ed. 1101 (1945)

Certiorari, 323 U.S. 694, to review a judgment for the plaintiff in a suit against the United States to recover a compensation for an alleged taking of property. . . .

MR. JUSTICE JACKSON delivered the opinion of the Court. The Willow River Power Company has been awarded $25,000 by the Court of Claims as just compensation for impaired efficiency of its hydroelectric plant caused by the action of the United States in raising the water level of the St. Croix River. Reality of damage and reasonableness of the award are not in issue. Our question is whether the damage is the result of a "taking" of private property, for which just compensation is required by the Fifth Amendment.

Willow River in its natural state was a non-navigable stream,[4] which flowed to within a few rods of the St. Croix River, turned and roughly paralleled it for something less than a mile, and then emptied into the St. Croix. Many years ago an earth dam was thrown across the Willow about a half-mile above its natural mouth. A new mouth was cut across the narrow neck which separated the two rivers and a dam was built across the artificial channel close to or upon the banks of the St. Croix. Here also was built a mill, which operated under the head produced in the pool by the two dams, which obstructed both the natural and the artificial channel of the Willow River. [See Figure 10.]

4. The Willow wasn't much of a river. The Court of Claims judge wrote of it:

We are clearly of the opinion that the Willow River is not a navigable stream in the sense that the United States may regulate commerce thereon. There is no commerce thereon to be regulated and there never has been. The only transportation the river has ever afforded is to float down logs in times of spring freshets. Except at these times logs cannot be floated down the river. The river is but 40 miles long in a straight line and 70 miles long following its meanders. In some places it is so narrow that the branches of trees on one bank are interlocked with the branches of trees on the other bank. The depth of the water varies from 2 inches to 12 or 14 inches. Fencing extends across the stream in agricultural areas. . . . [101 Ct. Cl. 222, 227-228 (1944).—ED.]

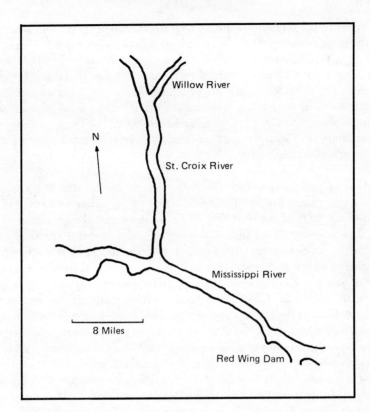

FIGURE 10

These lands and appurtenant rights were acquired by the Willow River Power Company, a public utility corporation of the State of Wisconsin, and were devoted to hydroelectric generation for supply of the neighborhood. The plant was the lowest of four on Willow River operated by the Company as an integrated system. The powerhouse was located on land owned by the Company above ordinary high water of the St. Croix. Mechanical energy for generation of electrical energy was developed by water in falling from the artificial level of non-navigable Willow River to the natural level of navigable St. Croix River. The elevation of the head water when at the crest of the gates was 689 feet above mean sea level. The operating head varied because elevation of the tail water was governed by the fluctuating level of the St. Croix. When that river was low, the maximum head was developed, and was 22.5 feet; when the river was at flood stage, the operating head diminished to as little as eight feet. The ordinary high-water mark is found to have been 672 feet, and the head available above that was seventeen feet.

The Government, in pursuance of a Congressional plan to improve navigation, in August of 1938 had completed what is known as the Red Wing

Dam in the upper Mississippi, into which the St. Croix flows. This dam was some thirty miles downstream, but it created a pool which extended upstream on the St. Croix beyond respondent's plant at an ordinary elevation of 675 feet. Thus the water level maintained by the Government in the St. Croix was approximately three feet above its ordinary high-water level at claimant's property. By thus raising the level at which tail waters must flow off from claimant's plant, the Government reduced the operating head by three feet, using ordinary high water as the standard, and diminished the plant's capacity to produce electric energy. The Company was obliged to supplement its production by purchase from other sources.

Loss of power was made the only basis of the award. The Court of Claims found as a fact that "The value of the loss in power as a result of the raising of the level of the St. Croix River by three feet above ordinary high water was $25,000[5] at the time and place of taking," and it rendered judgment for that amount. There is no finding that any fast lands were flooded or that other injury was done to property or that claimant otherwise was deprived of any use of its property. It is true that the water level was above high-water mark on the St. Croix River banks and on claimant's structures, but damage to land as land or to structures as such is not shown to be more than nominal and accounts for no part of the award. The court held that the Government "had a right to raise the level of the river to ordinary high-water mark with impunity, but it is liable for the taking or deprivation of such property rights as may have resulted from raising the level beyond that point." Turning, then, to ascertain what property right had been "taken," the Court referred to United States v. Cress, 243 U.S. 316, 329, 330, which it said was identical in facts, and held it had no option but to follow it and that "It results that plaintiff is entitled to recover the value of the decrease in the head of its dam."

The Fifth Amendment, which requires just compensation where private property is taken for public use, undertakes to redistribute certain economic losses inflicted by public improvements so that they will fall upon the public rather than wholly upon those who happen to lie in the path of the project. It does not undertake, however, to socialize all losses, but those only which result from a taking of property. If damages from any other cause are to be absorbed by the public, they must be assumed by act of Congress[6] and may not be awarded by the courts merely by implication from the constitutional provision. The court below thought that decrease of head under the circumstances was a "taking" of such a "property right," and that is the contention of the claimant here.

5. The amount of just compensation was that sum which, invested at a specified yield, would produce yearly the revenue that the respondent lost by reason of the power reduction. Id. at 230. Property valuation is an art that many lawyers must make their own.—Ed.

6. Congress reacted to this suggestion and, in February 1950, directed the Secretary of the Treasury to pay $25,000, together with interest, to the trustees of the Willow River Power Company. Priv. L. No. 378, c. 32, 64 Stat. A13 (1950).—Ed.

It is clear, of course, that a head of water has value and that the Company has an economic interest in keeping the St. Croix at the lower level. But not all economic interests are "property rights"; only those economic advantages are "rights" which have the law back of them, and only when they are so recognized may courts compel others to forbear from interfering with them or to compensate for their invasion. The law long has recognized that the right of ownership in land may carry with it a legal right to enjoy some benefits from adjacent waters. But that a closed catalogue of abstract and absolute "property rights" in water hovers over a given piece of shore land, good against all the world, is not in this day a permissible assumption. We cannot start the process of decision by calling such a claim as we have here a "property right"; whether it is a property right is really the question to be answered. Such economic uses are rights only when they are legally protected interests. Whether they are such interests may depend on the claimant's rights in the land to which he claims the water rights to be appurtenant or incidental; on the navigable or non-navigable nature of the waters from which he advantages; on the substance of the enjoyment thereof for which he claims legal protection; on the legal relations of the adversary claimed to be under a duty to observe or compensate his interests; and on whether the conflict is with another private riparian interest or with a public interest in navigation. The claimant's assertion that its interest in a power head amounts to a "property right" is made under circumstances not present in any case before considered by this Court. . . .

The property right asserted to be appurtenant to claimant's land is that described in United States v. Cress, 243 U.S. 316, 330, as "the right to have the water flow away from the mill dam unobstructed, except as in the course of nature" and held in that case to be an "inseparable part" of the land. The argument here is put that the waters of the St. Croix were backed up into claimant's tailrace, causing damage. But if a dike kept the waters of the St. Croix out of the tailrace entirely it would not help. The water falling from the Willow must go somewhere, and the head may be preserved only by having the St. Croix channel serve as a run-off for the tail waters. The run-off of claimant's water may be said to be obstructed by the presence of an increased level of Government-impounded water at the end of claimant's discharge pipes. The resulting damage may be passed on to the Government only if the riparian owner's interest in "having the water flow away" unobstructed above the high-water line is a legally protected one. . . .

Cress owned riparian lands and the bed as well as a non-navigable creek in Kentucky. He built a dam which pooled the water and diverted it to his headrace; after it turned the wheel of his mill, it was returned to the stream by his tailrace. The Government built a dam in the navigable Kentucky River which backed up the water in this non-navigable tributary to a point one foot below the crest of the mill dam, leaving an unworkable head. The Court concluded that Cress was entitled to compensation as for a taking. It found that Cress had the right as a riparian owner to the natural flow-off of the water in this non-navigable stream. The *Cress* case is significant in that it measured the rights of a riparian owner against the Government in improving navigation by the standard which had been evolved to measure the rights of riparian owners against each other. The rights of the Government at that location were held to be no greater than those of a riparian owner, and therefore, of course, not paramount to the rights of Cress.

We are of opinion that the *Cress* case does not govern this one and that there is no warrant for applying it, as the claimant asks, or for overruling it, as the Government intimates would be desirable. The Government there was charged with the consequences of changing the level of a non-navigable stream; here it is sought to be charged with the same consequences from changing the level in a navigable one. In the former case the navigation interest was held not to be a dominant one at the property damaged; here dominance of the navigation interest at the St. Croix is clear. And the claimant in this case cannot stand in the *Cress* shoes unless it can establish the same right to have the navigable St. Croix flow tail waters away at natural levels that Cress had to have the non-navigable stream run off his tail waters at natural levels. This could only be done by an extension of the doctrine of the *Cress* case. As we have already said, it "must be confined to the facts there disclosed." United States v. Chicago, M., St. P. & P.R. Co., 312 U.S. 592, 597.

On navigable streams a different right intervenes. While riparian owners on navigable streams usually were held to have the same rights to be free from interferences of other riparian owners as on non-navigable streams, it was recognized from the beginning that all riparian interests were subject to a dominant public interest in navigation. . . .

It is conceded that the riparian owner has no right as against improvements of navigation to maintenance of a level below high-water mark, but it is claimed that there is a riparian right to use the stream for run-off of water at this level. Highwater mark bounds the bed of the river. Lands above it are fast lands and to flood them is a taking for which compensation must be paid. But the award here does not purport to compensate a flooding of fast lands or impairment of their value. Lands below that level are subject always to a dominant servitude in the interests of navigation and its exercise calls for no compensation.[7] United States v. Chicago, M., St. P. & P.R. Co., 312 U.S. 592; Willink v. United States, 240 U.S. 572. The damage here is that the water claimant continues to bring onto its land through an artificial canal from the Willow River has to leave its lands at an elevation of 675 instead of an elevation of 672 feet. No case is cited and we find none which holds a riparian owner on navigable waters to have such a legal right. The *Cress* case which the Court of Claims relied upon does not so hold and does not govern here.

Rights, property or otherwise, which are absolute against all the world

---

7. For a full discussion of the navigation servitude, see Morreale, Federal Power in Western Waters and the Rule of No Compensation, 3 Nat. Resources J. 1 (1963).—ED.

are certainly rare, and water rights are not among them. Whatever rights may be as between equals such as riparian owners, they are not the measure of riparian rights on a navigable stream relative to the function of the Government in improving navigation. Where these interests conflict they are not to be reconciled as between equals, but the private interest must give way to a superior right, or perhaps it would be more accurate to say that as against the Government such private interest is not a right at all.

Operations of the Government in aid of navigation ofttimes inflict serious damage or inconvenience or interfere with advantages formerly enjoyed by riparian owners, but damage alone gives courts no power to require compensation where there is not an actual taking of property. . . . Such losses may be compensated by legislative authority, not by force of the Constitution alone.

The uncompensated damages sustained by this riparian owner on a public waterway are not different from those often suffered without indemnification by owners abutting on public highways by land. It has been held in nearly every state in the Union that "there can be no recovery for damages to abutting property resulting from a mere change of grade in the street in front of it, there being no physical injury to the property itself, and the change being authorized by law." This appears to be the law of Wisconsin. . . . It would be strange if the State of Wisconsin is free to raise an adjacent land highway without compensation but the United States may not exercise an analogous power to raise a highway by water without making compensation where neither takes claimant's lands, but each cuts off access to and use of a natural level.

We hold that claimant's interest or advantage in the high-water level of the St. Croix River as a run-off for tail waters to maintain its power head is not a right protected by law and that the award below based exclusively on the loss in value thereof must be reversed.

MR. JUSTICE REED concurs in the result on the ground that the United States has not taken property of the respondent.

MR. JUSTICE ROBERTS. I think the judgment of the Court of Claims should be affirmed.

. . . The respondent owned the land on either side of the Willow River at and above the point where its dam was constructed. Under the law of Wisconsin the respondent owned the bed of Willow River, and both by common and statute law of Wisconsin it had the right to erect and use the dam. That right was property; and such a right recognized as private property by the law of a state is one which under the Constitution the federal government is bound to recognize. Monongahela Navigation Co. v. United States, 148 U.S. 312 [citations omitted].

Unless United States v. Cress, 243 U.S. 316, is to be disregarded or overruled, the respondent is entitled to recover for the property taken by the reduction of the efficiency of its dam due to the raising of the high-water mark. If the respondent's power dam had been in Willow River at a distance of one hundred yards or more above the confluence of the two streams, there can be no question that the decision in the *Cress* case would require payment for the injury done to its water power. Since under local law the owner of the land and the dam was entitled to have the water of the non-navigable stream flow below his dam at the natural level of the Willow River, which is affected by the natural level of the St. Croix, the raising of that level by navigation works in the St. Croix invaded the respondent's rights. This is the basis of decision in the *Cress* case. The fact that the respondent's dam is close to the high-water mark of the St. Croix River can not call for a different result.

The court concludes that the *Cress* case is inapplicable by ignoring the finding of the trial court that the increase in level of the St. Croix above high-water mark has diminished the head of respondent's dam by three feet. But to reach its conclusion the court must also disregard the natural law of hydraulics that water seeks its own level. At the confluence of the two rivers at normal high water of the St. Croix, both the St. Croix and the Willow are at the same level. Any increase in the level of the St. Croix above high-water mark must result in raising the natural level of the Willow to some extent. The court below has found that the increase in the level of the St. Croix operates to diminish the head at respondent's dam by the specified amount. The facts thus established are in all relevant respects precisely those on the basis of which this court sustained the recovery of damages in the *Cress* case.

If the fact is that respondent discharges the water from its power plant through a tailrace extending below high-water mark of the St. Croix, that fact is irrelevant to the problem presented. Respondent claims, and the court below has sustained, only the right to have the flow of the Willow maintained at its natural level. That level has been increased by raising the level of the St. Croix above its high-water mark. The increase in the level of the St. Croix above high-water mark has operated to raise the level below the respondent's dam to an extent which has damaged respondent by diminishing the power head. To that extent respondent has suffered damage and is entitled to recover on principles announced in the *Cress* case.

United States v. Cress has stood for twenty-eight years as a declaration of the law applicable in circumstances precisely similar to those here disclosed. I think it is a right decision if the United States, under the Constitution, must pay for the destruction of a property right arising out of the lawful use of waters not regulable by the federal government because they are not navigable.

The CHIEF JUSTICE concurs in this opinion.

KAISER AETNA v. UNITED STATES

444 U.S. 164, 100 S. Ct. 383, 62 L. Ed. 2d 332 (1979)

MR. JUSTICE REHNQUIST delivered the opinion of the Court. The Hawaii Kai Marina was developed by the dredging and filling of Kuapa Pond, which was a shallow lagoon separated from Maunalua Bay and the Pacific Ocean by a barrier beach. Although under Hawaii law Kuapa Pond was private property, the Court of Appeals for the Ninth Circuit held that when petitioners converted the pond into a marina and thereby connected it to the bay, it became subject to the "navigational servitude" of the Federal Government. Thus, the public acquired a right of access to what was once petitioners' private pond. We granted certiorari because of the importance of the issue and a conflict concerning the scope and nature of the servitude.

I

Kuapa Pond was apparently created in the late Pleistocene Period, near the end of the ice age, when the rising sea level caused the shoreline to retreat, and partial erosion of the headlands adjacent to the bay formed sediment that accreted to form a barrier beach at the mouth of the pond, creating a lagoon. It covered 523 acres on the island of Oahu, Hawaii, and extended approximately two miles inland from Maunalua Bay and the Pacific Ocean. The pond was contiguous to the bay, which is a navigable waterway of the United States, but was separated from it by the barrier beach.

Early Hawaiians used the lagoon as a fishpond and reinforced the natural sandbar with stone walls. Prior to the annexation of Hawaii, there were two openings from the pond to Maunalua Bay. The fishpond's managers placed removable sluice gates in the stone walls across these openings. Water from the bay and ocean entered the pond through the gates during high tide, and during low tide the current flow reversed toward the ocean. The Hawaiians used the tidal action to raise and catch fish such as mullet.

Kuapa Pond, and other Hawaiian fishponds, have always been considered to be private property by landowners and by the Hawaiian government. Such ponds were once an integral part of the Hawaiian feudal system. And in 1848 they were allotted as parts of large land units, known as "ahupuaas," by King Kamehameha III during the Great Mahele or royal land division. Titles to the fishponds were recognized to the same extent and in the same manner as rights in more orthodox fast land. Kuapa Pond was part of an ahupuaa that eventually vested in Bernice Pauahi Bishop and on her death formed a part of the trust corpus of petitioner Bishop Estate, the present owner.

In 1961, Bishop Estate leased a 6,000-acre area, which included Kuapa Pond, to petitioner Kaiser Aetna for subdivision development. The development is now known as "Hawaii Kai." Kaiser Aetna dredged and filled parts of Kuapa Pond, erected retaining walls, and built bridges within the development to create the Hawaii Kai Marina. Kaiser Aetna increased the average depth of the channel from two to six feet. It also created accommodations for pleasure boats and eliminated the sluice gates.

When petitioners notified the Corps of Engineers of their plans in 1961, the Corps advised them they were not required to obtain permits for the development of and operations in Kuapa Pond. Kaiser Aetna subsequently informed the Corps that it planned to dredge an 8-foot-deep channel connecting Kuapa Pond to Maunalua Bay and the Pacific Ocean, and to increase the clearance of a bridge of the Kalanianaole Highway—which had been constructed during the early 1900's along the barrier beach separating Kuapa Pond from the bay and ocean—to a maximum of 13.5 feet over the mean sea level. These improvements were made in order to allow boats from the marina to enter into and return from the bay, as well as to provide better waters. The Corps acquiesced in the proposals, its chief of construction commenting only that the "deepening of the channel may cause erosion of the beach."

At the time of trial, a marina-style community of approximately 22,000 persons surrounded Kuapa Pond. It included approximately 1,500 marina waterfront lot lessees. The waterfront lot lessees, along with at least 86 nonmarina lot lessees from Hawaii Kai and 56 boatowners who are not residents of Hawaii Kai, pay fees for maintenance of the pond and for patrol boats that remove floating debris, enforce boating regulations, and maintain the privacy and security of the pond. Kaiser Aetna controls access to and use of the marina. It has generally not permitted commercial use, except for a small vessel, the Marina Queen, which could carry 25 passengers and was used for about five years to promote sales of marina lots and for a brief period by marina shopping center merchants to attract people to their shopping facilities.

In 1972, a dispute arose between petitioners and the Corps concerning whether (1) petitioners were required to obtain authorization from the Corps, in accordance with §10 of the Rivers and Harbors Appropriation Act of 1899, 33 U.S.C. §403 [33 U.S.C.S. §403], for future construction, excavation, or filling in the marina, and (2) petitioners were precluded from denying the public access to the pond because, as a result of the improvements, it had become a navigable water of the United States. The dispute foreseeably ripened into a lawsuit by the United States Government against petitioners in the United States District Court for the District of Hawaii. In examining the scope of Congress' regulatory authority under the Commerce Clause, the District Court held that the pond was "navigable water of the United States" and thus subject to regulation by the Corps under §10 of the Rivers and Harbors Appropriation Act. 408 F. Supp. 42, 53 (1976). It further held, however, that the Government lacked the authority to open the now dredged pond to the public without payment of compensation to the owner. Id., at 54. In reaching this holding, the District Court reasoned that although the pond was navigable for the purpose of delimiting Congress' regulatory power, it was not navigable for the purpose of defining the scope of the federal "navigational servitude" imposed by the Commerce Clause. Ibid. Thus, the District Court denied the Corps' request for an injunction to require petitioners to allow public access and to notify the public of the fact of the pond's accessibility.

The Court of Appeals agreed with the District Court's conclusion that the pond fell within the scope of Congress' regulatory authority, but reversed the District Court's holding that the navigational servitude did not require petitioners to grant the public access to the pond. 584 F.2d 378 (1978). The Court of Appeals reasoned that the "federal regulatory authority over navigable waters . . . and the right of public use cannot consistently be separated. It is the public right of navigational use that renders regulatory control necessary in the public interest." Id., at 383. The question before us is whether the Court of Appeals erred in holding that petitioners' improvements to Kuapa Pond caused its original character to be so altered that it became subject to an overriding federal navigational servitude, thus converting into a public aquatic park that which petitioners had invested millions of dollars in improving on the assumption that it was a privately owned pond leased to them.[3]

II

The Government contends that petitioners may not exclude members of the public from the Hawaii Kai Marina because "[t]he public enjoys a federally protected right of navigation over the navigable waters of the United States." Brief for United States, 13. It claims the issue in dispute is whether Kuapa Pond is presently a "navigable water of the United States." Ibid. When petitioners dredged and improved Kuapa Pond, the Government continues, the pond—although it may once have qualified as fast land—became navigable water of the United States. The public thereby acquired a right to use Kuapa Pond as a continuous highway for navigation, and the Corps of Engineers may consequently obtain an injunction to prevent petitioners from attempting to reserve the waterway to themselves.

The position advanced by the Government, and adopted by the Court of Appeals below, presumes that the concept of "navigable waters of the United States" has a fixed meaning that remains unchanged in whatever context it is being applied. While we do not fully agree with the reasoning of the District Court, we do agree with its conclusion that all of this Court's cases dealing with the authority of Congress to regulate navigation and the so-called "navigational servitude" cannot simply be lumped into one basket. 408 F. Supp., at 48-49. As the District Court aptly stated, "any reliance upon judicial precedent must be predicated upon careful appraisal of the purpose for which the concept of 'navigability' was invoked in a particular case." Id., at 49.

It is true that Kuapa Pond may fit within definitions of "navigability" articulated in past decisions of this Court. But it must be recognized that the concept of navigability in these decisions was used for purposes other than to delimit the boundaries of the navigational servitude: for example, to define the scope of Congress' regulatory authority under the Interstate Commerce Clause, see, e.g., United States v. Appalachian Power Co., 311 U.S. 377, 85 L. Ed. 243, 61 S. Ct. 291 (1940); South Carolina v. Georgia, 93 U.S. 4, 23 L. Ed. 782 (1876); The Montello, 20 Wall 430, 22 L. Ed. 391 (1874); The Daniel Ball, 10 Wall 557, 19 L. Ed. 999 (1871), to determine the extent of the author-

---

3. Petitioners do not challenge the Court of Appeals' holding that the Hawaii Kai Marina is within the scope of Congress' regulatory power and subject to regulation by the Army Corps of Engineers pursuant to its authority under §10 of the Rivers and Harbors Appropriation Act, 33 U.S.C. §403.

ity of the Corps of Engineers under the Rivers and Harbors Appropriation Act of 1899, and to establish the limits of the jurisdiction of federal courts conferred by Art. III, §2, of the United States Constitution over admiralty and maritime cases. Although the Government is clearly correct in maintaining that the now dredged Kuapa Pond falls within the definition of "navigable waters" as this Court has used that term in delimiting the boundaries of Congress' regulatory authority under the Commerce Clause, see, e.g., The Daniel Ball, *supra*, at 563, 19 L. Ed. 999; The Montello, *supra*, at 441-442, 22 L. Ed. 391; United States v. Appalachian Power Co., *supra*, at 407-408, 85 L. Ed. 243, 61 S. Ct. 291, this Court has never held that the navigational servitude creates a blanket exception to the Takings Clause whenever Congress exercises its Commerce Clause authority to promote navigation. Thus, while Kuapa Pond may be subject to regulation by the Corps of Engineers, acting under the authority delegated it by Congress in the Rivers and Harbors Appropriation Act, it does not follow that the pond is also subject to a public right of access.

In light of its expansive authority under the Commerce Clause, there is no question but that Congress could assure the public a free right of access to the Hawaii Kai Marina if it so chose. Whether a statute or regulation that went so far amounted to a "taking," however, is an entirely separate question. Pennsylvania Coal Co. v. Mahon, 260 U.S. 393, 415, 67 L. Ed. 322, 43 S. Ct. 158, 28 A.L.R. 1321 (1922). As was recently pointed out in Penn Central Transportation Co. v. New York City, 438 U.S. 104, 57 L. Ed. 2d 631, 98 S. Ct. 2646 (1978), this Court has generally "been unable to develop any 'set formula' for determining when 'justice and fairness' require that economic injuries caused by public action be compensated by the government, rather than remain disproportionately concentrated on a few persons." Id., at 124, 57 L. Ed. 2d 631, 98 S. Ct. 2646. Rather, it has examined the "taking" question by engaging in essentially ad hoc, factual inquiries that have identified several factors—such as the economic impact of the regulation, its interference with reasonable investment backed expectations, and the character of the governmental action—that have particular significance. Ibid. When the "taking" question has involved the exercise of the public right of navigation over interstate waters that constitute highways for commerce, however, this Court has held in many cases that compensation may not be required as a result of the federal navigational servitude. See, e.g., United States v. Chandler-Dunbar Co., 229 U.S. 53, 57 L. Ed. 1063, 33 S. Ct. 667 (1913).

The navigational servitude is an expression of the notion that the determination whether a taking has occurred must take into consideration the important public interest in the flow of interstate waters that in their natural condition are in fact capable of supporting public navigation. . . .

For over a century, a long line of cases decided by this Court involving Government condemnation of "fast lands" delineated the elements of compensable damages that the Government was required to pay because the lands were riparian to navigable streams. The Court was often deeply divided, and the results frequently turned on what could fairly be described as quite narrow distinctions. But this is not a case in which the Government recognizes any obligation whatever to condemn "fast lands" and pay just compensation under the Eminent Domain Clause of the Fifth Amendment to the United States Constitution. It is instead a case in which the owner of what was once a private pond, separated from concededly navigable water by a barrier beach and used for aquatic agriculture, has invested substantial amounts of money in making improvements. The Government contends that as a result of one of these improvements, the pond's connection to the navigable water in a manner approved by the Corps of Engineers, the owner has somehow lost one of the most essential sticks in the bundle of rights that are commonly characterized as property—the right to exclude others.

Because the factual situation in this case is so different from typical ones involved in riparian condemnation cases, we see little point in tracing the historical development of that doctrine here. . . .

. . . The nature of the navigational servitude when invoked by the Government in condemnation cases is summarized as well as anywhere in United States v. Willow River Co., 324 U.S. 499, 502, 89 L. Ed. 1101, 65 S. Ct. 761 (1945):

> It is clear, of course, that a head of water has value and that the Company has an economic interest in keeping the St. Croix at the lower level. But not all economic interests are "property rights"; only those economic advantages are "rights" which have the law back of them, and only when they are so recognized may courts compel others to forbear from interfering with them or to compensate for their invasion.

We think, however, that when the Government makes the naked assertion it does here, that assertion collides with not merely an "economic advantage" but an "economic advantage" that has the law back of it to such an extent that courts may "compel others to forbear from interfering with [it] or to compensate for [its] invasion." United States v. Willow River Co., *supra*, at 502, 89 L. Ed. 1101, 65 S. Ct. 761.

Here, the Government's attempt to create a public right of access to the improved pond goes so far beyond ordinary regulation or improvement for navigation as to amount to a taking under the logic of Pennsylvania Coal Co. v. Mahon, 260 U.S. 393, 67 L. Ed. 322, 48 S. Ct. 158, 28 A.L.R. 1321 (1922). More than one factor contributes to this result. It is clear that prior to its improvement, Kuapa Pond was incapable of being used as a continuous highway for the purpose of navigation in interstate commerce. Its maximum depth at high tide was a mere two feet, it was separated from the adjacent bay and ocean by a natural barrier beach, and its principal commercial value was limited to fishing. It consequently is not the sort of "great navigable stream" that this Court has previously recognized as being "incapable of private ownership." We have not the slightest doubt that the Government could have refused to allow such dredging on the ground that it would have impaired navigation in the bay, or could have conditioned its approval of the dredging on petitioners' agreement to comply with various measures that it deemed appropriate for the promotion of navigation. But what petitioners now have is a body of water that was private property under Hawaiian law, linked to navigable water by a channel dredged by them with the consent of the Government. While the consent of individual officials representing the United States cannot "estop" the United States, see Montana v. Kennedy, 366 U.S. 308, 314-315, 6 L. Ed. 2d 313, 81 S. Ct. 1336 (1961); INS v. Hibi, 414 U.S. 5, 38 L. Ed. 2d 7, 94 S. Ct. 19 (1973), it can lead to the fruition of a number of expectancies embodied in the concept of "property"—expectancies that, if sufficiently important, the Government must condemn and pay for before it takes over the management of the land-owner's property. In this case, we hold that the "right to exclude," so universally held to be a fundamental element of the property right, falls within this category of interests that the Government cannot take without compensation. This is not a case in which the Government is exercising its regulatory power in a manner that will cause an insubstantial devaluation of petitioners' private property; rather, the imposition of the navigational servitude in this context will result in an actual physical invasion of the privately owned marina. Compare Andrus v. Allard, *ante*, at 65-66, 62 L. Ed. 2d 210, 100 S. Ct. 318, with the traditional taking of fee interests in United States ex. rel. TVA v. Powelson, 319 U.S. 266, 87 L. Ed. 1390, 63 S. Ct. 1047 (1943), and in United States v. Miller, 317 U.S. 369, 87 L. Ed. 336, 63 S. Ct. 276, 147 A.L.R. 55 (1943). And even if the Government physically invades only an easement in property, it must nonetheless pay just compensation. See United States v. Causby, 328 U.S. 256, 265, 90 L. Ed. 1206, 66 S. Ct. 1062 (1946); Portsmouth Co. v. United States, 260 U.S. 327, 67 L. Ed. 287, 43 S. Ct. 135 (1922). Thus, if the Government wishes to make what was formerly Kuapa Pond into a public aquatic park after petitioners have proceeded as far as they have here, it may not, without invoking its eminent domain power and paying just compensation, require them to allow free access to the dredged pond while petitioners' agreement with their customers calls for an annual $72 regular fee.

Accordingly the judgment of the Court of Appeals is reversed.

MR. JUSTICE BLACKMUN, with whom MR. JUSTICE BRENNAN and MR. JUSTICE MARSHALL join, dissenting. The Court holds today that, absent compensation, the public may be denied a right of access to "navigable waters of the United States" that have been created or enhanced by private means. I find that conclusion neither supported in precedent nor wise in judicial policy, and I dissent. . . .

The conclusion that the navigational servitude extends to privately created or enhanced waters does not entirely dispose of this case. There remains the question whether the Government's resort to the servitude requires compensation for private investment instrumental in effecting or improving navigability. The Court, of course, concludes that there is no navigational servitude and, accordingly, that assertion of public access constitutes a compensable taking. Because I do not agree with the premise, I cannot conclude that the right to compensation for opening the pond to the public is a necessary result. Nevertheless, I think this question requires a balancing of private and public interests.

Ordinarily, "[w]hen the Government exercises [the navigational] servitude, it is exercising its paramount power in the interest of navigation, rather than taking the private property of anyone." United States v. Kansas City Ins. Co., 339 U.S. 799, 808 94 L. Ed. 1277, 70 S. Ct. 885 (1950). See also United States v. Willow River Co., 324 U.S. 499, 509-510, 89 L. Ed. 1101, 65 S. Ct. 761 (1945); Lewis Blue Point Oyster Co. v. Briggs, 229 U.S. 82, 87-88, 57 L. Ed. 1083, 33 S. Ct. 679 (1913); Gibson v. United States, 166 U.S. 269, 276, 41 L. Ed. 996, 17 S. Ct. 578 (1897). The Court's prior cases usually have involved riparian owners along navigable rivers who claim losses resulting from the raising or lowering of water levels in the navigable stream, or from the construction of artificial aids to navigation, such as dams or locks. In these cases the Court has held that no compensation is required for loss in water power due to impairment of the navigable water's flow, e.g., United States v. Twin City Power Co., 350 U.S., at 226-227, 100 L. Ed. 240, 76 S. Ct. 259; United States v. Chandler-Dunbar Co., 229 U.S., at 65-66, 57 L. Ed. 1063, 33 S. Ct. 667; for loss in "head" resulting from raising the stream, United States v. Willow River Co., 324 U.S., at 507-511, 89 L. Ed. 1101, 65 S. Ct. 761; for damage to structures erected between low- and high-water marks, United States v. Chicago, M., St. P. & P. R. Co., 312 U.S. 592, 595-597, 85 L. Ed. 1064, 61 S. Ct. 772 (1941); for loss of access to navigable water caused by necessary improvements, United States v. Commodore Park, Inc., 324 U.S. 386, 390-391, 89 L. Ed. 1017, 65 S. Ct. 803 (1945); Scranton v. Wheeler, 179 U.S. at 163, 45 L. Ed. 126, 21 S. Ct. 48; or for loss of value to adjoining land based on potential use in navigational commerce, United States v. Rands, 389 U.S. 121, 124-125, 19 L. Ed. 2d 329, 88 S. Ct. 265 (1967). The Court also has held that no compensation is required when "obstructions," such as bridges or wharves, are removed or altered to improve navigation, despite their obvious commercial value to those who erected them, and despite the Federal Government's original willingness to have them built. See, e.g., Greenleaf Lumber Co. v. Garrison, 237 U.S. 251, 256, 258-264, 59 L. Ed. 939, 35 S. Ct. 551 (1915); Union Bridge Co. v. United States 204 U.S. 364, 400, 51 L. Ed. 523, 27 S. Ct. 367 (1907).

These cases establish a key principle that points the way for decision in the present context. In most of them, the noncompensable loss was related, either directly or indirectly, to the riparian owner's "access to, and use of, navigable waters." United States v. Rands, 389 U.S., at 124-125, 19 L. Ed. 2d 329, 88 S. Ct. 265. However that access or use may have been turned to account for personal gain, and no matter how much the riparian owner had invested to enhance the value, the Court held that these rights were shared with the public at large. Actions taken to improve their value for the many caused no reimbursable damage to the few who, by the accident of owning contiguous "fast land," previously enjoyed the blessings of the common right in greater measure. See, e.g., United States v. Commodore Park, Inc. 324 U.S., at 390-391, 89 L. Ed. 1017, 65 S. Ct. 803. The Court recognized that encroachment on rights inhering separately in the adjoining "fast land," United States v. Virginia Electric Co., 365 U.S. 624, 628, 5 L. Ed. 2d 838, 81 S. Ct. 784 (1961), or resulting from access to *nonnavigable* tributaries, see United States v. Cress, 243 U.S. 316, 61 L. Ed. 746, 37 S. Ct. 380 (1917), might form the basis for a valid compensation claim. But the principal distinction was that these compensable values had nothing to do with use of the navigable water.

Application of this principle to the present case should lead to the conclusion that the developers of Kuapa Pond have acted at their own risk and are not entitled to compensation for the public access the Government now asserts. See Union Bridge Co. v. United States, 204 U.S., at 400, 51 L. Ed. 523, 27 S. Ct. 367. The chief value of the pond in its present state obviously is a value of access to navigable water. Development was undertaken to improve and enhance this value, not to improve the value of the pond as some aquatic species of "fast land." Petitioners do not question the Federal Government's plenary control over the waters of the Bay, and they have no vested right in access to its open water. Since the value of the pond and the motive for improving it lie in access to a highway of commerce, I am drawn to the conclusion that the petitioners' interest in the improved waters of the pond is not subject to compensation. Whatever expectancy petitioners may have had in control over the pond for use as a fishery was surrendered in exchange for the advantages of access when they cut a channel into the Bay.

In contrast, the Government's interest in vindicating a public right of access to the pond is substantial. It is the very interest in maintaining "common highways, . . . forever free." After today's decision, it is open to any developer to claim that private improvements to a waterway navigable in interstate commerce have transformed "navigable water of the United States" into private property, at least to the extent that he may charge for access to the portion improved. Such appropriation of navigable waters for private use directly injures the freedom of commerce that the navigational servitude is intended to safeguard. In future cases, of course, the Army Corps of Engineers may alleviate this danger by conditioning permission for connection with other waterways on a right of free public access. But it seems to me that the inevitable result of today's decision is the introduction of new legal uncertainty in a field where I had thought the "battles long ago," *ante,* at 177, had achieved some settled doctrine. . . .

PART VII

REAL ESTATE TRANSACTIONS

Chapter 19

Introducing the Real Estate Transaction

Few areas of legal practice retain their parochial ways as persistently as real estate. The lawyer from Illinois would find much about Indiana practice unfamiliar; indeed, if he practiced in Chicago, he might even be unfamiliar with the usages in many of the state's rural counties. This variation from one state to another—and, in large, heavily populated states, from one locale to another—makes it difficult to generalize about the basic elements of the real estate transaction: the documents; the forms of title protection; the role of brokers, lawyers, insurers. Even the recent surge of interstate real estate activity, led by lenders investing in out-of-state mortgages, title companies operating from coast to coast, and home buyers purchasing across state lines, has not carried standardization very far. Suffice it to say that the real estate lawyer must learn the folkways of any community in which he decides to practice.

Yet the sale of most real property (and in this chapter we shall deal exclusively with sales) follows a sequence that, viewed by the purchaser, consists of:

(a) the formation of the contract,
(b) the executory interval,
(c) the closing,
(d) the post-closing period.

This is the sequence that we shall follow also, as we open the gateway to a field whose tax and financing complexity will require much beyond this course.

§19.1   The Formation of the Contract

On a Sunday afternoon, in response to a full-page newspaper ad, the Smiths visit a tract development where they immediately fall for a three-bedroom

Georgian Colonial, which the broker assures them is a steal at $60,000. If the broker is typically earnest, he is likely to urge the Smiths to leave a deposit check and sign a binder before they depart. If the Smiths are typically inexperienced, they will do as they are asked. On the spur of the moment, without a lawyer at their side, the Smiths may legally commit themselves to the largest financial undertaking they will ever make, outside of marriage itself.

The first step in a real estate transaction is the formation of a binding contract of sale between seller and buyer. Even a relatively short, simple document, four or five provisions long, may be enough in many places to cement the parties to the transaction. The "binder" that the Smiths signed may contain no more than the parties' names, the property address, the sales price, mortgage terms, and the closing of title date; yet it might suffice to create a right of action in either the seller or buyers should the other party later change his or their mind.

The legal "minimum" for a binding contract of sale is an issue often before the courts (M. Friedman, Contracts and Conveyances of Real Property §1.3, Binders, Memoranda and Incomplete Contracts (1963)). Courts handle these cases in terms familiar from contracts courses: "preliminary negotiations, indefiniteness, significance of formal contract to follow," etc. Rather than re-work familiar, if unsettled, ground, it seems more useful for you to examine a "finished" contract of sale form. We can assume that the Smiths either signed a "binder" of this completeness or, several days after their visit to the tract, signed a second document—the "formal" contract of sale.

The form we have selected is a standard form—i.e., mostly boiler plate. It typifies those used in the Chicago area. Usually, the selling broker will complete the blanks, a practice unsuccessfully challenged by the Chicago Bar Association as an unauthorized practice of law. Chicago Bar Assn. v. Quinlan & Tyson, Inc., 34 Ill. 2d 116, 214 N.E.2d 771 (1966). Cf. Florida Bar v. Irizarry, 268 So. 2d 377, 379 (Fla. 1972) ("where the broker has no interest in the transaction except as broker, he may not complete standard conveyancing forms such as deeds, mortgages, notes, assignments and satisfactions" [but broker may prepare the contract of sale]).

As you study the Chicago form, try to think through the significance of its many provisions.

CONTRACT OF SALE
Chicago Title & Trust Co. (rev. 1968)

1. Sale. _____ (Purchaser) agrees to purchase at a price of $_____ on the terms set forth herein, the following described real estate in _____ County, Illinois: [_If legal description is not included herein at time of execution,_ _____ _is authorized to insert it thereafter._] commonly known as _____, and with approximate lot dimensions of _____ × _____, together with the following personal property presently located thereon: (strike items not applicable)

(a) storm and screen doors and windows; (b) awnings; (c) outdoor television antenna; (d) wall-to-wall, hallway and stair carpeting; (e) window shades and draperies and supporting fixtures; (f) venetian blinds; (g) electric, plumbing and other attached fixtures as installed; (h) water softener; (i) refrigerator(s); (j) _____ stove(s); and also _____.

    2. Encumbrances. _____ (Seller) agrees
(Insert names of all owners and their respective spouses)
to sell the real estate and the personal property described above at the price and terms set forth herein, and to convey or cause to be conveyed to Purchaser or nominee a good title thereto (in joint tenancy) by a recordable _____ deed, with release of dower and homestead rights, and a proper bill of sale, subject only to: (a) covenants, conditions and restrictions of record; (b) private, public and utility easements and roads and highways, if any; (c) party wall rights and agreements, if any; (d) existing leases and tenancies; (e) special taxes or assessments for improvements not yet completed; (f) installments not due at the date hereof of any special tax or assessment for improvements heretofore completed; (g) mortgage or trust deed specified below, if any; (h) general taxes for the year _____ and subsequent years; and to _____.

    3. Payments. Purchaser has paid $_____ (and will pay within _____ days the additional sum of $_____) as earnest money to be applied on the purchase price, and agrees to pay or satisfy the balance of the purchase price, plus or minus prorations, at the time of closing as follows: (*strike subparagraph not applicable*)

    (a)   The payment of $_____

    (b)   The acceptance of the title to the real estate by Purchaser subject to a mortgage (trust deed) of record securing a principal indebtedness (which the Purchaser [does] [does not] agree to assume) aggregating $_____ bearing interest at the rate of _____% a year, and the payments of a sum which represents the difference between the amount due on the indebtedness at the time of closing and the balance of the purchase price.

    4. Loan Commitment. This contract is subject to the condition that Purchaser be able to procure within _____ days a firm commitment for a loan to be secured by a mortgage or trust deed on the real estate in the amount of $_____, or such lesser sum as Purchaser accepts, with interest not to exceed _____% a year to be amortized over _____ years, the service charges for such loan not to exceed _____%. If, after making very reasonable effort, Purchaser is unable to procure such commitment within the time specified herein and so notifies Seller thereof within that time, and if Seller within a like period of time following the Purchaser's notice does not procure for Purchaser such a commitment or notify Purchaser that Seller will accept a purchase money mortgage upon the same terms, this contract shall become null and void and all earnest money shall be refunded to Purchaser. [strike paragraph if inapplicable]

    5. Closing. The time of closing shall be on _____, or 20 days after notice that financing has been procured if paragraph 4 is operative (whichever date is later), unless subsequently mutually agreed otherwise, at the office of _____ or of the mortgage lender, if any, provided title is shown to be good or is accepted by Purchaser.

6. **Possession.** Seller shall deliver possession to Purchaser on or before _____ days after the sale has been closed. Seller agrees to pay Purchaser the sum of $_____ for each day Seller remains in possession between the time of closing and the time possession is delivered.

7. **Broker's Commission.** Seller agrees to pay a broker's commission to _____ in the amount recommended in the present schedule of commissions of the _____ Real Estate Board applicable to this sale.

8. **Depositary.** The earnest money shall be held by _____ for the mutual benefit of the parties.

9. **Representation.** If the building or structure located on the real estate is subject to the provisions of "An Act relating to contracts to sell multiple dwelling units", passed by the General Assembly of the State of Illinois and approved August 11, 1967, Seller warrants that no notice from any city, village or other governmental authority of a dwelling code violation which existed prior to the execution of this contract has been issued and received by Seller or his agent.

10. **Delivery of Contract.** A duplicate original of this contract, duly executed by the Seller and his spouse, if any, shall be delivered to the Purchaser within _____ days from the date hereof, otherwise, at the Purchaser's option, this contract shall become null and void and the earnest money refunded to the Purchaser.

This contract is subject to the Conditions set forth on the back page hereof, which Conditions are made a part of this contract.

Dated _____
Purchaser _____   (Address) _____
Purchaser _____   (Address) _____
Seller _____   (Address) _____
Seller _____   (Address) _____

CONDITIONS

1. **Title Insurance Policy.** Seller shall deliver or cause to be delivered to Purchaser or Purchaser's agent, not less than 5 days prior to the time of closing, a title commitment for an owner's title insurance policy issued by the Chicago Title and Trust Company in the amount of the purchase price, covering title to the real estate on or after the date hereof, showing title in the intended grantor subject only to (a) the general exceptions contained in the policy, (b) the title exceptions set forth above, and (c) title exceptions which may be removed by the payment of money at the time of closing and which the Seller may so remove at that time by using the funds to be paid upon the

delivery of the deed. The title commitment shall be conclusive evidence of good title as therein shown, subject only to the exceptions as therein stated. Seller also shall furnish Purchaser an affidavit of title covering the time of closing, subject only to the title exceptions permitted by this contract.

2. **Defects in Title.** If the title commitment discloses exceptions relating to title other than those referred to in the preceding paragraph, Seller shall have 30 days from the date of the delivery thereof to have these exceptions removed from the commitment. If Seller fails to have these exceptions removed within this time, Purchaser may terminate this contract or may elect, upon notice to Seller within 10 days after the expiration of the 30-day period, to take title as it then is with the right to deduct from the purchase price liens or encumbrances of a definite or ascertainable amount. If Purchaser does not so elect, this contract shall become null and void without further action of the parties.

3. **Adjustments at Closing.** Rents, premiums under assignable insurance policies, water and other utility charges, fuels, prepaid service contracts, general taxes, accrued interest on mortgage indebtedness, if any, and other similar items shall be adjusted ratably as of the time of closing. If the amount of the current general taxes is not then ascertainable, the adjustment thereof shall be on the basis of the amount of the most recent ascertainable taxes. Existing leases and assignable insurance policies, if any, shall then be assigned to Purchaser. Seller shall pay the amount of any stamp tax imposed by law on the transfer of the title, and shall furnish a completed Real Estate Transfer Declaration signed by the Seller or the Seller's agent in the form required pursuant to the Real Estate Transfer Tax Act of the State of Illinois.

4. **Destruction of Improvements.** If prior to closing, the improvements on said real estate shall be destroyed or materially damaged by fire or other casualty, this contract, at the option of the Purchaser, shall become null and void and the earnest money shall be returned to the Purchaser.

5. **Application of Earnest Money on Termination.** If this contract is terminated without Purchaser's fault, the earnest money shall be returned to the Purchaser, but if the termination is caused by the Purchaser's fault, then at the option of the Seller and upon notice to the Purchaser, the earnest money shall be forfeited to the Seller and applied first to the payment of Seller's expenses and then to payment of broker's commission; the balance, if any, to be retained by the Seller as liquidated damages.

6. **Option for Escrow.** At the election of Seller or Purchaser upon notice to the other party not less than 5 days prior to the time of closing, this sale shall be closed through an escrow with Chicago Title and Trust Company, in accordance with the general provisions of the usual form of Deed and Money Escrow Agreement then in use by Chicago Title and Trust Company, with such special provisions inserted in the escrow agreement as may be required to conform with this contract. Upon the creation of such an escrow, anything herein to the contrary notwithstanding, payment of purchase price and delivery of deed shall be made through the escrow and this contract and

the earnest money shall be deposited in the escrow. The cost of the escrow shall be divided equally between seller and purchaser. (*strike paragraph if inapplicable*)

7. Time of the Essence. Time is of the essence of this contract.

8. Notices. All notices herein required shall be in writing and shall be served on the parties at the addresses following their signatures. The mailing of a notice by registered or certified mail, return receipt requested, shall be sufficient service.

NOTES AND QUESTIONS

1. Try to locate a standard contract-of-sale form used in the vicinity of your law school. Compare it with the Chicago form. What are their similarities? Differences?

2. *Legal description:* The property's post office address is rarely the same as its legal description, which usually identifies the parcel either in metes-and-bounds terms, or as a lot number in a recorded subdivision plot, or by government survey.[1] Below are samples of each:

> Beginning at the SW corner of Main Street and Elm Street, in the City of Beacon, County of Salem, State of New Hampshire, thence southerly along the west line of Elm Street for a distance of 100'; then westerly at right angles for a distance of 50'; thence northerly at right angles for a distance of 100' to the southerly line of Main Street; thence easterly along the southerly line of Main Street to the point of beginning.

> In the County of Queen, State of Washington, lot 1 in the J. B. Priestly Subdivision, according to plot thereof recorded in volume 7 of plots, page 35, records of said county.

> The N.W. ¼ of the N.W. ¼ of section 3, Township 3 North, Range 2 West of the Third Principal Meridian, containing 40 acres.[2]

Occasionally someone will get the legal description wrong, either in the contract of sale or in a deed, mortgage, etc. Disputes between the seller and buyer as to what exactly is being sold set misdescription issues in one context. Disputes between neighbors, or between a mortgagor and mortgagee as to what exactly a deed or mortgage has conveyed, present another facet of the

---

1. Sometimes a legal description will combine two or even all three methods.

2. By a succession of statutes starting before 1800, the Congress directed the division of public lands into *sections*, one mile on a side, containing 640 acres. A grid system, consisting of townships 6 miles square, each divided into 36 sections, took its reference from degrees of longitude and latitude. The Third Principal Meridian is in central Illinois; it is shorthand for lat. 38° 28' 27" N, long. 89° 08' 54" W. Cf. Axelrod, Berger, and Johnstone, Land Transfer and Finance 435 (2d ed. 1978).

misdescription problem. Full discussion of the issues appears in Axelrod, Berger, and Johnstone, Land Transfer and Finance 431-465 (2d ed. 1978).

3.   Re-examine paragraph 2, Encumbrances, in the Chicago form. What perils might await the buyer who signs the contract with this paragraph unchanged? Cf., e.g., Lundberg v. Gage, 22 Ill. 2d 249, 174 N.E.2d 845 (1961).

4.   Re-examine paragraph 6, Possession. Describe the legal relationship between seller and buyer if the seller stays in possession after the closing.

5.   Does this contract envision any role for a seller's lawyer? For a buyer's lawyer? In this connection, what is intended by paragraph 6 (Option for Escrow) of the Conditions?

§19.2   The Executory Interval

Very rarely does someone agree to buy and also to take title to real property at one time. Ordinarily some weeks elapse between the two events. During this interval both parties to the transaction are busy. The buyer must arrange his financing, satisfy himself that the seller's title meets the contract standard, and prepare to take possession. For his part, the seller must prepare the title documents and the closing adjustments, arrange for evidence of title, and prepare to give possession. Buildings under construction must be completed. Sometimes problems will arise with the state of seller's title, the condition of the premises, or the quality or pace of construction, and the parties must try to iron out their differences. Sometimes deals disintegrate between the contract signing and the formal closing.

We call this period of some weeks the *executory interval*. *Legal* title to the real estate remains in the seller; it will not pass to the buyer until the formal closing. But the contract gives buyer some interest in the real estate; and under a doctrine known as equitable conversion, courts have said that the buyer holds *equitable* title to the premises. By dint of equitable conversion, the buyer is able to seek and obtain specific performance of the sales contract if the seller does not perform. Cf. Stone, Equitable Conversion by Contract, 13 Colum. L. Rev. 369, 386 (1913).

a.   Damages to the Premises During the Executory Interval

The doctrine of equitable conversion generates a series of knotty legal problems that the sales contract may fail to address. One quite vexing problem has been the risk of loss if the premises are damaged or destroyed before the formal closing. Suppose, for example, that a house burns down and insurance does not cover the entire value: must buyer perform the contract anyway? If so, must buyer pay the full contract price, or may he get an abatement to reflect the uninsured loss? Who gets the insurance proceeds? Does it matter whether buyer is at fault for the damage or not?

Consider how the following case handles these questions.

SKELLY OIL CO. v. ASHMORE
365 S.W.2d 582 (Mo. Sup. Ct. en banc, 1963)

HYDE, J. [In March 1958, defendant-sellers were the owners of improved business premises. The premises were subject to a $7,200 mortgage and were leased to a tenant through 1961 at a rental of $150 per month.

Defendants, that same March, agreed to sell the premises, subject to the lease but free of the mortgage, to Skelly Oil Company for $20,000. Skelly, owning premises adjacent to those in the suit, planned at some later date to combine the tracts for a gas station. The closing was set for April 16, 1958. On April 7, 1958, the building on the lot was destroyed by fire without fault of either party. Seller had a $10,000 insurance policy, and, according to its terms, the insurance company paid off the $7,200 mortgage and gave the $2,800 balance to defendants. Plaintiffs sued for a decree compelling defendants specifically to perform but seeking an abatement in the purchase price of $10,000 as the amount of the insurance policy proceeds. The trial court decreed plaintiffs' requested relief; defendants appealed. The opinion states the facts, dismisses defendants' contention that there was no enforceable contract, and continues:]

The contract of sale here involved contained no provision as to who assumed the risk of loss occasioned by a destruction of the building, or for protecting the building by insurance or for allocating any insurance proceeds received therefor. When the parties met to close the sale on April 16, the purchaser's counsel informed vendors and their attorneys he was relying on Standard Oil Co. v. Dye, 223 Mo. App. 926, 20 S.W.2d 946, for purchaser's claim to the $10,000 insurance proceeds on the building. . . . It is stated in 3 American Law of Property, §11.30, p. 90, that in the circumstances here presented at least five different views have been advanced for allocating the burden of fortuitous loss between vendor and purchaser of real estate. We summarize those mentioned: (1) The view first enunciated in Paine v. Meller (Ch. 1801, 6 Ves. Jr. 349, 31 Eng. Reprint 1088, 1089) is said to be the most widely accepted; holding that from the time of the contract of sale of real estate the burden of fortuitous loss was on the purchaser even though the vendor retained possession. (2) The loss is on the vendor until legal title is conveyed, although the purchaser is in possession, stated to be a strong minority. (3) The burden of loss should be on the vendor until the time agreed upon for conveying the legal title, and thereafter on the purchaser unless the vendor be in such default as to preclude specific performance, not recognized in the decisions. (4) The burden of the loss should be on the party in possession, whether vendor or purchaser, so considered by some courts. (5) The burden of loss should be on vendor unless there is something in the contract or in the relation of the parties from which the court can infer a different intention, stating "this rather vague test" has not received any avowed judicial acceptance, although it is not inconsistent with jurisdictions holding the loss is on the vendor until conveyance or jurisdictions adopting the possession test. As to the weight of the authority, see also 27 A.L.R.2d 448; Tiffany, Real Property, 3rd ed., §309.

We do not agree that we should adopt the arbitrary rule of Paine v. Meller, *supra,* and Standard Oil Co. v. Dye, *supra,* that there is equitable conversion from the time of making a contract for sale and purchase of land and that the risk of loss from destruction of buildings or other substantial part of the property is from that moment on the purchaser. Criticisms of this rule by eminent authorities have been set out in the dissenting opinion of Storckman, J., herein and will not be repeated here.

We take the view stated in an article on Equitable Conversion by Contract, 13 Columbia Law Review 369, 386, Dean Harlan F. Stone, later Chief Justice Stone, in which he points out that the only reason why a contract for the sale of land by the owner to another operates to effect conversion is that a court of equity will compel him specifically to perform his contract. He further states:

> A preliminary to the determination of the question whether there is equitable ownership of land must therefore necessarily be the determination of the question whether there is a contract which can be and ought to be specifically performed *at the very time when the court is called upon to perform it.* This process of reasoning is, however, reversed in those jurisdictions where the "burden of loss" is cast upon the vendee. The question is whether there shall be a specific performance of the contract, thus casting the burden on the vendee, by compelling him to pay the full purchase price for the subject matter of the contract, a substantial part of which has been destroyed. The question is answered somewhat in this wise: equitable ownership of the vendee in the subject matter of the contract can exist only where the contract is one which equity will specifically perform. The vendee of land is equitably entitled to land, therefore the vendee may be compelled to perform, although the vendor is unable to give in return the performance stipulated for by this contract. The non sequitur involved in the proposition that performance may be had because of the equitable ownership of the land by the vendee, which in turn depends upon the right of performance, is evident. The doctrine of equitable conversion, so far as it is exemplified by the authorities hitherto considered, cannot lead to the result of casting the burden of loss on the vendee, since the *conversion depends upon the question whether the contract should in equity be performed.* In all other cases where the vendee is treated as the equitable owner of the land, it is only because the contract is one which equity first determines should be specifically performed.
>
> Whether a plaintiff, in breach of his contract by a default which goes to the essence, as in the case of the destruction of a substantial part of the subject matter of the contract, should be entitled to specific performance, is a question

which is answered in the negative in every case except that of destruction of the subject matter of the contract. To give a plaintiff specific performance of the contract when he is unable to perform the contract on his own part, violates the fundamental rule of equity that . . . *equity will not compel a defendant to perform when it is unable to so frame its decree as to compel the plaintiff to give in return substantially what he has undertaken to give* or to do for the defendant.

The rule of casting the "burden of loss" on the vendee by specific performance if justifiable at all can only be explained and justified upon one of two theories: first, that since equity has for most purposes treated the vendee as the equitable owner, it should do so for all purposes, although *this ignores the fact that in all other cases the vendee is so treated only because the contract is either being performed or in equity ought to be performed;* or, second, which is substantially the same proposition in a different form, the specific performance which casts the burden on the vendee is an incident to and a consequence of an equitable conversion, whereas in all other equity relations growing out of the contract, the equitable conversion, if it exists, is an incident to and consequence of, a specific performance. Certainly nothing could be more illogical than this process of reasoning. (Emphasis ours.)

For these reasons, we do not agree with the rule that arbitrarily places the risk of loss on the vendee from the time the contract is made. Instead we believe the Massachusetts rule is the proper rule. It is thus stated in Libman v. Levenson, 236 Mass. 221, 128 N.E. 13, 22 A.L.R. 560: When

the conveyance is to be made of the whole estate, including both land and buildings, for an entire price, and the value of the buildings constitutes a large part of the total value of the estate, and the terms of the agreement show that they constituted an important part of the subject matter of the contract . . . the contract is to be construed as subject to the implied condition that it no longer shall be binding if, before the time for the conveyance to be made, the buildings are destroyed by fire. The loss by the fire falls upon the vendor, the owner; and if he has not protected himself by insurance, he can have no reimbursement of this loss; but the contract is no longer binding upon either party. If the purchaser has advanced any part of the price, he can recover it back. Thompson v. Gould [*supra*] 29 Pick. [37 Mass.] 134, 138. If the change in the value of the estate is not so great, or if it appears that the buildings did not constitute so material a part of the estate to be conveyed as to result in an annulling of the contract, specific performance may be decreed, *with compensation for any breach of agreement,* or relief may be given in damages. (Emphasis ours.)

. . . An extreme case, showing the unfairness of the arbitrary rule placing all loss on the vendee, is Amundson v. Severson, 41 S.D. 377, 170 N.W. 633, where three-fourths of the land sold was washed away by the Missouri River (the part left being of little value) and the vendor brought suit for specific performance. Fortunately for the vendee, he was relieved by the fact that the vendor did not have good title at the time of the loss, although the vendor had procured it as a basis for his suit. However, if the vendor had then held good title even though he did not have the land, the vendee would have been required to pay the full contract price under the loss on the purchaser rule. (Would the vendee have been any better off if the vendor had good title from the start but did not have the land left to convey?) The reason for the Massachusetts rule is that specific performance is based on what is equitable; and it is not equitable to make a vendee pay the vendor for something the vendor cannot give him.

However, the issue in this case is not whether the vendee can be compelled to take the property without the building but whether the vendee is entitled to enforce the contract of sale, with the insurance proceeds substituted for the destroyed building. We see no inequity to defendants in such enforcement since they will receive the full amount ($20,000.00) for which they contracted to sell the property. Their contract not only described the land but also specifically stated they sold it "together with the buildings, driveways and all construction thereon." While the words "Service Station Site" appeared in the caption of the option contract and that no doubt was the ultimate use plaintiff intended to make of the land, the final agreement made by the parties was that plaintiff would take it subject to a lease of the building which would have brought plaintiff about $6,150.00 in rent during the term of the lease. Moreover, defendants' own evidence showed the building was valued in the insurance adjustment at $16,716.00 from which $4,179.00 was deducted for depreciation, making the loss $12,537.00. Therefore, defendants are not in a very good position to say the building was of no value to plaintiff. Furthermore, plaintiff having contracted for the land with the building on it, the decision concerning use or removal of the building, or even for resale of the entire property, was for the plaintiff to make. Statements were in evidence about the use of the building and its value to plaintiff made by its employee who negotiated the purchase but he was not one of plaintiff's chief executive officers nor possessed of authority to bind its board of directors. The short of the matter is that defendants will get all they bargained for; but without the building or its value plaintiff will not.

We therefore affirm the judgment and decree of the trial court.

EAGER, LEEDY and HOLLINGSWORTH, JJ., concur.

STORCKMAN, J., dissents in separate opinion filed.

WESTHUES, C.J., and DALTON, J., dissent and concur in separate dissenting opinion of STORCKMAN, J.

STORCKMAN, J. (dissenting). . . . I cannot assent to the holding that the plaintiff is entitled to specific performance on any terms other than those of the purchase contract without reduction in the contract price. . . .

The evidence is convincing that Skelly Oil Company was buying the lot as a site for a service station and that in so using it they not only wanted the Joneses' lease terminated but intended to tear down and remove the building in question. The contract documents support this conclusion. Both the option and the letter of acceptance refer to the property as a "service station site" and contain escape clauses permitting Skelly to avoid the purchase agreement if proper permits could not be obtained or if zoning laws prohibited such use.

From the time the option was first granted on July 31, 1957, through its various extensions, until the letter of March 4, 1958, Mr. Busby, Skelly's real estate representative, was cooperating with and urging Mr. Ashmore and his attorney to secure a termination of the Joneses' lease (which was on the entire property) even to the extent of filing an ejectment suit against the lessee. Then after the fire Skelly's legal department prepared as one of the closing documents an agreement to be executed by the Ashmores and the Joneses for mutual cancellation of the lease. The purchase contract calls for an assignment of the Joneses' lease by the Ashmores to Skelly and its honoring the lease; but, at the request of Mr. Busby, the Ashmores on April 17, 1958, with the approval of their attorney, executed and delivered to Mr. Busby the mutual cancellation agreement. This conduct is consistent with its prior activities, but is inconsistent with plaintiff's present contention that the building and its rental under the lease represented a substantial part of the consideration for the purchase of the real estate.

Count 1 of the petition is for specific performance in accordance with the terms of the purchase contract; Count 2 seeks a declaration that the defendants hold the $10,000 insurance proceeds in trust for the benefit of the plaintiff and that the defendants be required to pay the proceeds to the plaintiff or that the amount thereof be applied in reduction of the purchase price of the property. Count 2 alleges that the concrete block, single-story building which was used as a grocery store was totally destroyed by fire, that the defendants collected the insurance thereon, and that "said building was a valuable appurtenance on said real estate worth more than $10,000.00 and that its destruction reduced the value of said real estate more than the sum of $10,000.00."

In spite of the issue made by Count 2 as to the effect of the destruction of the building upon the value of the real estate, the trial court refused to permit cross-examination of plaintiff's witness to establish that the purpose and intent of Skelly was to remove the building from the premises when the lease was terminated, and the court rejected defendants' offer of proof to the same effect. In this equity action the testimony should have been received. It did not tend to vary or contradict the written contract but dealt with an issue made by plaintiff's petition based on a partial destruction of the subject matter subsequent to the acceptance of the option. Nevertheless, there was other evidence from which it could be reasonably inferred that the use of the real estate as a filling station site necessitated the removal of the building. Mr. Ashmore testified that he originally asked $27,000 for the property but reduced his price on Mr. Busby's representation that the improvements had no value to Skelly and that Skelly would be glad to have Mr. Ashmore remove them.

The plaintiff introduced no evidence of the market value of the property before or after the fire in support of the allegations in Count 2. The amount paid by the insurance company is of little or no benefit as evidence of the actual value of the building because of the valued policy law of Missouri which provides that in case of the total destruction of a building by fire, insurance companies shall not be permitted to deny that the property insured was worth at the time of issuing the policy or policies the full amount for which the property was insured. Sections 379.140 and 379.145, R.S. Mo. 1959, V.A.M.S.[3] Defendants' evidence tended to prove that the real estate was worth more as a site for a service station after the fire than before and that the value of the real estate after the fire was in excess of $20,000.

The claim of neither party is particularly compelling insofar as specific performance in this case is concerned. The destruction of the building by fire, its insurance, and the disposition of the insurance proceeds were matters not contemplated by the parties and not provided for in the purchase contract documents. Skelly's representative did not know that Mr. Ashmore carried insurance on the building until after the fire, and he then told Mr. Ashmore that despite the fire the deal would be closed on the agreed date. Skelly's present claims are an afterthought inconsistent with its conduct throughout the negotiations and prior to the closing date.

In short, as to both Skelly and the Ashmores, the destruction of the insured building was a fortuitous circumstance supplying the opportunity to rid the property of a vexatious lease, to dispose of the building, and at the same time resulting in a windfall of $10,000. And the problem, in fact the only seriously contested issue between the parties, is which of them is to have the advantage of this piece of good fortune. Skelly contracted to pay $20,000 for the property. If it is awarded the $10,000 windfall, it will receive a $20,000 lot for $10,000. If the Ashmores retain the $10,000, they will in fact have realized $30,000 for a piece of property they have agreed to sell for $20,000.

In claiming the proceeds of the Ashmores' fire insurance policy, Skelly did not contend that the value of the real estate as a service station site had decreased. After learning of the fire and the existence of the insurance policy, Skelly's counsel did some research and, as he announced when the parties met in Joplin to close the deal, Skelly was relying on a case he had found, Standard Oil Company v. Dye, 223 Mo. App. 926, 20 S.W.2d 946. And in its basic facts the case admittedly is quite similar to this one although there were no attendant circumstances such as we have in the present case. As authority for its decision, the court in that case relied almost wholly on William Skinner & Sons' Shipbuilding & Dry-Dock Co. v. Houghton, 92 Md. 68, 48 A. 85. The doctrine of these two cases laboriously evolved from Paine v. Meller, (1801) 6 Ves. Jr. 349, 31 Eng. Reprint 1088, is "that a contract to sell real property vests the equitable ownership of the property in the purchaser, with the corollary that any loss by destruction of the property through casualty during the pendency of the contract must be borne by the purchaser." Annotation 27 A.L.R.2d 444, 446. The twofold rationale of this doctrine is a maxim that "equity regards as done that which should have been done," from which it is said the "vendor becomes a mere trustee, holding the legal title for the benefit

---

3. About half the states have valued policy statutes. These change the usual fire insurance rule under which the liability of the insurer is confined to the lower of the value of the destroyed subject matter and the coverage of the policy. Fraud is a possible defense to overvaluation under a valued policy statute. See Vance on Insurance §157 (3d ed. 1951).—Ed.

of the purchaser or as security for the price." 27 A.L.R.2d 444, 448, 449. All of the experts and scholars seem to agree that this doctrine and its rationale is misplaced if not unsound. To illustrate see only 4 Williston, Contracts §§928-943B, pp. 2605-2639. As to the maxim, Williston said, "Only the hoary age and frequent repetition of the maxim prevents a general recognition of its absurdity." 4 Williston, Contracts, §929, p. 2607. As to the corollary, Williston points out that while the purchaser may have an interest in the property, it is equally clear that the vendor likewise has an interest, and as for the vendor's being a trustee for the purchaser observes, "However often the words may be repeated, it cannot be true that the vendor is trustee for the purchaser." 4 Williston, Contracts, §936, p. 2622. See also Pound "The Progress of The Law—Equity", 33 Har. L.R. 813, 830.

Nevertheless, adapting this doctrine and following a majority opinion in another English case, Rayner v. Preston, (1881) L.R. 18 Ch. Div. 1 (CA), the rule as stated in the *Dye* case has evolved: "Where the purchaser as equitable owner will bear the loss occasioned by a destruction of the property pending completion of the sale, and the contract is silent as to insurance, the rule quite generally followed is that the proceeds of the vendor's insurance policies, even though the purchaser did not contribute to their maintenance, constitute a trust fund for the benefit of the purchaser to be credited on the purchase price of the destroyed property, the theory being that the vendor is a trustee of the property for the purchaser." Annotation 64 A.L.R.2d 1402, 1406. Many jurisdictions have modified or do not follow this doctrine, some take the view that the vendor's insurance policy is personal to him, and Parliament has enacted a statute which entirely changes the English rule. 4 Mo. L.R. 290, 296. The rule is not as general as the annotator indicated, and as with the rule upon which it is founded, all the experts agree that it is unsound, their only point of disagreement is as to what the rule should be. See 4 Williston, Contracts, §§928-943; Vance Insurance, §131, p. 777, and 34 Yale L.J. 87; Vanneman, "Risk of Loss, Between Vendor and Purchaser", 8 Minn. L.R. 127; Pound, "The Progress of The Law", 33 Har. L.R. 813, and the excellent student note to Standard Oil Co. v. Dye in 4 Mo. L.R. 290. . . .

Professor Williston was of the view that the risk of loss [pending transfer of legal title] should follow possession (4 Williston, Contracts, §§940, 942), and that view has been written into the Uniform Vendor and Purchaser Risk Act, 9C U.L.A., p. 314 and 1960 Supp., p. 82. Eight states have adopted that act and four of those, California, New York, South Dakota, and Oregon, are listed among the fifteen jurisdictions said by the A.L.R. annotator (64 A.L.R. 1406) to follow the *Dye* case. . . .

Vance is of the opinion that a rule of "business usage" should be adopted, but he ruefully adds, "Here we have another instance in which business usage substitutes the insurance money for the insured property, despite the general rule that the two are not legally connected; and, as usual, the courts are sluggishly following business." Vance on Insurance, §131, p. 781. Dean Pound assails Vance's contention that the insurance money is any part of the thing bargained for and he also vigorously attacks the theory that the vendor is a trustee for the vendee. 33 Har. L.R., 1. c. 829, 830; 4 Mo. L.R. 1. c. 296. . . .

Automatic application of the doctrine that "equity regards that as done which ought to be done", in the circumstances of this case, begs the question of *what ought to be done*. Because the insurance proceeds may be a windfall to those legally entitled does not necessarily mean that justice will be accomplished by transferring them elsewhere. The substance of the purchase contract and the use to which the property is to be put must be considered. A resort to equity should involve a consideration of other equitable principles or maxims such as the equally important maxims that "equity follows the law" and "between equal equities the law will prevail".

A valid legal excuse is a sufficient reason for refusal of specific performance. . . . Destruction of a particular thing upon which the contract depends is generally regarded as a legal excuse for nonperformance according to 12 Am. Jur., Contracts, §372, pp. 944-945, wherein it is stated:

> In the absence of a contrary provision, if the act to be performed is necessarily dependent on the continued existence of a specific thing, the perishing thereof before the time for performance, without the fault of the promisor, will excuse nonperformance of the contract. This is especially true where, from the nature of the contract, it appears that the parties must, from the beginning have known that it could not be fulfilled unless when the time for the fulfillment of the contract arrived, some particular specified thing continued to exist. The contract is not, in the absence of any express or implied warranty that the thing shall exist, to be construed as a positive contract, but as subject to an implied condition that the parties shall be excused in case, before breach, performance becomes impossible from the perishing of the thing without default of the contractor. . . .

The plaintiff's petition alleges that the building destroyed by fire "was a valuable appurtenance on said real estate worth more than $10,000.00 and that its destruction reduced the value of said real estate more than the sum of $10,000.00." So far as Skelly's use of the property as a service station site is concerned, this allegation cannot be true if Skelly's intent was to tear down and remove the building. On the other hand, if the plaintiff retained the property or sold to an investor who proposed to rent the building for a store or a similar business purpose, then the loss would be substantial and the insurance proceeds would be necessary to restore a suitable building. The petition asserts that "as a matter of law" the defendant held "said $10,000.00 insurance proceeds in trust for the benefit of plaintiff as the vendee of the defendants." I know of no equitable or legal principle that justifies the award of the insurance proceeds automatically to the purchaser in the circumstances of this case.

If plaintiff's contention is that there has been a substantial failure or impairment of the consideration of the contract by reason of the destruction of the building, then I do not think that the Ashmores should be entitled to specific performance, and because of the theory of mutuality it would seem that Skelly would not be entitled to specific performance unless it was willing to perform its legal obligations under the purchase contract as drawn. We would not be justified in making a new contract for the parties to cover the building insurance, and a court of equity will not decree specific performance of a contract that is incomplete, indefinite or uncertain. . . . Nor can the courts supply an important element that has been omitted from the contract. . . .

If the subject matter of the purchase contract was not as well or better suited to Skelly's purpose after the fire than it was before, then it appears from the authorities above discussed that Skelly could avoid the contract entirely or that it could clearly establish the amount and manner in which it was damaged. What would the situation be if the building had not been insured or for only a small amount? The fact that the building was insured and the amount thereof are hardly determinative of Skelly's alleged injury.

But Skelly did not after the fire or in this action elect to abandon the contract although the Ashmores gave it the opportunity to do so rather than to sell at the reduced price. It is quite evident that Skelly had received one windfall as the result of the fire in that the lease is terminated and the site can be cleared at less cost. It has not shown itself to be entitled to another, the one now legally vested in the Ashmores. Ideally the purchase contract should be set aside so that the parties could negotiate a new one based on the property in its present condition. But the plaintiff by its election to take title has foreclosed this possibility.

The foregoing part of this dissenting opinion was directed primarily at the Division 2 opinion by Bohling, C., and the first opinion by Hyde, J., en banc. I respectfully suggest that the second opinion written en banc by Hyde, J., still falls short of establishing and applying dependable standards for a case of this kind. This opinion, which will be referred to as the majority opinion, employs conflicting rules or theories. It purports to adopt one but applies another. It professes to repudiate the equitable conversion theory and to adopt unequivocally the Massachusetts rule, stating: "Instead we believe the Massachusetts rule is the proper rule." This rule as shown by the opinion's quotation from Libman v. Levenson, 236 Mass. 221, 128 N.E. 13, 22 A.L.R. 560, is that the sales contract will no longer be binding if the buildings are destroyed by fire and "the value of the buildings constitutes a large part of the total value of the estate, and the terms of the agreement show that they constituted an important part of the subject matter of the contract". In the same quotation from the *Libman* case, the circumstances and terms under which specific performance is granted are stated as follows: "If the change in the value of the estate is not so great, or if it appears that the buildings did not constitute so material a part of the estate to be conveyed as to result in an annulling of the contract, specific performance may be decreed, *with compensation for any breach of agreement, or relief may be given in damages.*" Emphasis added.

Obviously the majority opinion did not find the value of the building constituted "a large part of the total value of the estate" or "an important part of the subject matter of the contract", else it would have declared the sales contract no longer binding under the Massachusetts rule. What it had to find was that the value of the building was not so great or such a material part of the estate to be conveyed as to interfere with the decree of specific performance.

But at this point the majority opinion abandons any pretense of following the Massachusetts rule and switches back to the equitable conversion theory and awards the insurance proceeds as such to the vendee without a determination of compensation for breach or relief to be given in damages. The value of the building for insurance purposes or as a structure to house a retail store is not necessarily the proper measure of the compensation or damages to which the plaintiff is entitled. It might be considerably less than such a figure if Skelly intended to remove the building as soon as it had the legal right to do so. Obviously the Massachusetts rule is not tied in with insurance at all and that is as it should be. Logically the majority opinion should have remanded the case for a determination of the amount of actual damages suffered by Skelly or the compensation to which it is entitled if it still wants specific performance. This is undoubtedly what the Massachusetts rule contemplates. I would find no fault with such a procedure.

Such evidence would also have a bearing on whether specific performance should be decreed at all, which was the first matter to be determined. Actually without such evidence the court does not have any basis for its finding as to the value of the building to the vendee and whether it was "an important part of the subject matter of the contract". Such a determination is a necessary prerequisite to granting or denying specific performance under the Massachusetts rule before the assessment of damage is reached. As the opinion stands, the adoption of the Massachusetts rule is more imaginary than real. The equitable conversion theory is *applied,* not the Massachusetts rule.

The opinion simply awards the *proceeds* of the fire insurance policy. It does not, and could not on the evidence in the present record, ascertain the compensation or damages, if any, to which Skelly is entitled by reason of the destruction of the building. Evidence of this sort was excluded by the trial court. Count 2 of the plaintiff's petition claims the insurance proceeds on the theory of a trust fund as a matter of law and that seems to be the basis of the majority opinion's award of the insurance fund to the purchaser. This is the antithesis of the Massachusetts rule which contemplates the ascertainment of the amount of compensation or damages that will assure the vendee receiving the value for which it contracted, and no more. . . .

Although the entire court now seems to be in agreement that the theory of equitable conversion should not be adopted and that the equitable rules which should govern are those that require an allowance of compensation or damages to fit the particular case, nevertheless a majority of the court have concurred in an opinion which makes the amount of insurance proceeds the yardstick. This is the rejected doctrine of equitable conversion regardless of the name given to it.

On the present record the plaintiff has failed to show a superior equity in the insurance proceeds under the Massachusetts rule or otherwise, and on well-established equitable principles I would leave the legal title to that fund where it is. I would find against the plaintiff on Count 2 of its petition, but award it specific performance under Count 1 on the condition that it pay to the defendants the agreed purchase price of $20,000 less the amount of compensation or damages, if any, that it could establish against the defendants (not the insurance funds) at a plenary hearing of that issue in the trial court.

NOTES AND QUESTIONS

1. Some states have now adopted the Uniform Vendor and Purchaser Risk Act, which readjusts the common-law rights and duties, except where the contract expressly provides otherwise. The act's key points are as follows:

  (a) If the seller retains possession, and damage occurs without fault of the buyer, the seller may not enforce the contract, and the buyer may recover his deposit.
  (b) If the buyer is in possession, and damage occurs without fault of the seller, the buyer is not relieved of his duty to complete the contract.
  (c) The above rules also apply if all or part of the premises is taken by eminent domain.

New York has embellished the uniform act where the seller has kept possession and only an *immaterial* part of the premises is damaged by fire or taken by eminent domain. Here the seller may continue to enforce the contract provided he accepts appropriate abatement of the purchase price. N.Y. Gen. Oblig. Law §5-1311 (McKinney 1964).

In *Skelly Oil*, seller's tenant was in possession at the time of the fire; buyer bought subject to that tenant's rights. How would the uniform act apply?

2. Re-examine the Chicago contract of sale form. What are the parties' rights and duties in the event of condemnation of the entire premises? Of an immaterial fire damage? Of vandalism? Cf. House of Realty, Inc. v. Ziff, 9 Ill. App. 3d 419, 292 N.E.2d 71 (1973). Assume that Illinois has (has not) adopted the uniform act.[4]

Is there an arguable distinction between the fire and condemnation cases? Might it turn on the quality of the seller's title? Cf., e.g., Friedman, Contracts and Conveyances of Real Property §4.11 (3d ed. 1975).

3. Your client has just agreed to buy a $30,000 house. She wishes to know whether she should obtain fire insurance during the executory interval, and, if so, how much. How do you advise her? Cf. Raplee v. Piper, 3 N.Y.2d 179, 143 N.E.2d 919, 164 N.Y.S.2d 732 (1957). Suppose that your client has just agreed to sell a $30,000 house and asks whether she should retain coverage during the executory interval: how do you advise her?

---

4. Illinois has adopted the uniform act. 29 Ill. Ann. Stat. §§8.1 et seq. (1969).

4.   The doctrine of equitable conversion may surface in various non-damage contexts as well.

   (a) During the executory interval, does the seller's creditor levy on the seller's interest in the land or garnishee the buyer? Cf. Mueller v. Novelty Dye Works, 273 Wis. 501, 78 N.W.2d 881 (1956).
   (b) Seller dies during the executory interval. Pursuant to his will, real property goes to X, personal property goes to Y. Who is entitled to the sales proceeds? Cf. In re Estate of McDonough, 113 Ill. App. 2d 437, 251 N.E.2d 405 (1969).
   (c) The Internal Revenue Code treats beneficially long-term capital gains, where the taxpayer has held property for more than one year. Int. Rev. Code of 1954, §§1222, 1223, 1202. When does the holding period begin—with the signing of the contract or the formal closing? When does the holding period end—with the signing of the contract or the formal closing? Cf. Merrill v. Commissioner, 40 T.C. 66 (1963), aff'd, 336 F.2d 771 (9th Cir. 1964); Edwards Industries, Inc. v. Commissioner, 33 T.C.M. 569, Dec. 32, 581(m) T.C. Memo 1974-120; Rev. Rul. 54-607, 1954-2 C.B. 177. Does it really matter, provided that all sellers and buyers are treated alike?

b.   Financing the Acquisition

   Buyers of improved real estate seldom pay the entire purchase price in cash. Partly this is because few persons can raise the large sums that even a modest transaction requires. Partly this is because most buyers—even when they have the cash in hand—prefer to put their cash in more liquid outlets than real estate. Partly, as to income-producing property, an investor can lever his investment return into a higher yield by reducing his cash or equity position.[5]

---

5. "To explain how leverage works, let us start with an investor who buys a $1 million apartment house that throws off $150,000 after expenses. On an all cash purchase, he will earn a 15 percent cash yield on his investment. Suppose instead that he borrows to make the purchase: first $500,000, then $900,000. If the mortgages bear 9 percent interest, and if the annual debt service (that is, the combined amount of interest and principal reduction) is sufficient to pay off the mortgages in 25 years, the cash flow and cash yield appear below:

(a)	$500,000 mortgage, ($500,000 cash down-payment)	
	Cash flow before debt service	$150,000
	Less debt service	50,500
	Cash flow after debt service	$ 99,500
	Cash yield on $500,000 down-payment	19.99%
(b)	$900,000 mortgage, ($100,000 cash down-payment)	
	Cash flow before debt service	$150,000
	Less debt service	90,900
	Cash flow after debt service	$ 59,100
	Cash yield on $100,000 down payment	59.1%

In the sales contract, therefore, the parties must agree not only on the purchase price but also on the buyer's plan for paying the purchase price. To give us some numbers for discussing this situation, suppose that the buyer has agreed to pay $60,000 for a house, toward which he can make a $15,000 down payment.

In at least two cases, our buyer would not have to search for a $45,000 loan to complete the purchase. There may already be a $45,000 mortgage on the property, which buyer can take over at the formal closing. Alternatively, the seller may agree to finance the purchase price himself by accepting $15,000 in cash and taking back a $45,000 mortgage. Either situation would relieve buyer from finding a bank or other third-party lender ready to invest $45,000 in the buyer's credit and the property's value as security.

Since a trip to a lender often awaits the buyer of real property, you should know who the lenders are that your client is likely to deal with. Table 20 summarizes the major sources of real estate finance.

When your client borrows anew (whether from seller or a third-party lender) or takes over an existing mortgage, he will want to know not only the

TABLE 20
Mortgage Debt Outstanding by Class by Property—1981*
(in billions of dollars)

	One- to four-family houses	Multi-family	Commer-cial	Farm
Commercial banks	166.8	12.8	85.8	9.2
Mutual savings banks	65.2	17.3	17.1	—
Savings and loan assns.	429.2	39.0	46.3	—
Life insurance cos.	18.1	20.0	83.9	13.1
Govt. Natl. Mortgage Assn. (GNMA)	0.7	4.3	—	—
Fed. Natl. Mortgage Assn. (FNMA)	52.2	5.5	—	—
Federal land banks	2.4	—	—	40.3
Federal Home Loan Mortgage Corp. (FHLMC)	4.0	1.2	—	—
GNMA pools	98.1	2.5	—	—
FHLMC pools	14.1	3.6	—	—
Farmers Home Administration pools	17.0	3.1	5.6	8.4
Individuals and others**	120.8	27.0	27.5	37.5

*Data derived from Federal Reserve Bulletin, Sept. 1981.
**Other holders include mortgage companies, real estate investment trusts, state and local credit agencies, state and local retirement funds, credit unions, and pension funds.

"If we were to continue to project cash yield based on ever-shrinking down payments, the investment return would approach infinity. And by placing elsewhere the cash that mortgaging replaces, the investor can expand and diversify his holdings." Axelrod, Berger, and Johnstone, Land Transfer and Finance 103 (2d ed. 1978).

size of the loan but also the loan's repayment terms. Some years ago Professor Charles Haar coined the phrase "credit trio" to describe the variables of a mortgage loan, to which we would like to add a fourth member. Our credit "quartet" consists of loan-to-value ratio, length of loan, rate of interest, and rate of amortization. Let us discuss each.

(1) Loan-to-Value Ratio

The loan-to-value ratio states, in a percentage, the relationship between the amount of money borrowed and the real estate's (appraised) value; for example, $45,000 borrowed on a $60,000 property results in a 75 percent loan. All lending institutions must keep their loan-to-value ratios within the ceiling set by the applicable state or federal laws. Ceilings vary from state to state, and, also, within any one state may be set differently for commercial banks and savings banks, for owner-occupied one-family houses and apartment houses, etc. Moreover, federally insured or guaranteed mortgages carry their own loan-to-value ratios, which either Congress or an agency sets.

Value, the ratio's denominator, need not be identical to the property's cost, although much of the time the two will coincide. Statutes use different adjectives to qualify value—for example, "appraised value," "reasonable value," "estimated replacement cost"—and the phrasing choices may conceal significant social policy decisions, where they actually affect the potential size of the minimum down payment. Moreover, lenders may themselves appraise "generously" or "conservatively" to reflect their eagerness to make a loan; the inexactitude of the appraisal art readily allows this. Nor are lenders required to give a maximum loan; as a matter of policy, either to discourage borrowing or to strengthen their security, lenders may insist upon larger down payments than the law requires.

(2) Length of Mortgage

Back in the 1930s, in an effort to stimulate a depressed housing market, Congress provided for 90 percent loans on federally insured home purchases. For the buyer of a $15,000 house, this meant only a $1,500 down payment, an unparalleled opportunity at the time. But two factors affect one's ability to purchase real estate: the size of the down payment *and* the cost of carrying the property. If one must borrow $13,500 to finance his purchase, he has more debt to repay and potentially higher carrying costs than if he need borrow only $10,000.

Since Congress did not want to undo the good effects of increased loan-to-value ceilings, it met the carrying cost problem by stretching out the life of the loan. As Table 21 shows, a $32,000 loan repayable at 12 percent interest in equal monthly installments over 25 years cost the borrower little more monthly than does a $20,000 loan all due and payable in 10 years. The principle of stretch-out, which was a fairly revolutionary reform fifty years

TABLE 21
Monthly Debt Service Related to Length of Mortgage and Loan-to-Value Ratio
(in dollars) ($40,000 value)
(12 percent interest)

Loan-to-Value Ratio	Loan	10 years	25 years	40 years
50 percent	$20,000	286.94	210.64	201.70
80 percent	32,000	459.10	337.03	322.72
90 percent	36,000	516.50	379.16	363.06

ago, now enjoys wide acceptance, so that mortgages of 30, 40, and even 50 years often appear. Again, state or federal laws govern the maximum duration of most real estate loans.

An extended maturity is not all to the borrower's advantage. The longer he repays the loan, the larger will be his total interest charges. A $32,000 25-year loan, at 12 percent, costs $69,109 in interest; the interest on a 40-year loan costs $122,905. And since the loan balance drops more slowly as the mortgage is stretched out, this increases the peril for borrower and lender alike that the value of the property may not cover the unpaid debt if a default happens somewhere down the line.

(3) Rate of Interest

Because interest payments are the largest item of housing expense for most homeowners and landlords, interest rate levels have much to do with the ability of consumers to afford decent shelter and with the willingness of both consumers and suppliers to engage in new shelter investment. Abnormally high interest rate levels invariably signal a sharp decline in the volume of housing starts, and the volume seldom revives until the next downturn in rates. A family earning $23,000 yearly would exhaust its entire housing budget on interest costs alone if its shelter (whether owned or rented) were financed by a $40,000, 14.0 percent, 30-year mortgage—not a fanciful illustration at all, since in many areas even modest apartments can no longer be built for less than $50,000. During the early 1970s, the primary federal housing subsidy programs for lower-income families, the FHA sections 235 and 236 programs, were pegged to an interest reduction payment that lowered effective interest rates to as little as one percent.

(a) Variable-rate mortgages

Since the early 1950s, interest rates on home mortgages have tripled. Inflation, unparalleled credit demands, and restrictive monetary policy have all brought about this steep rise, not only for mortgage rates but also for the rates on comparable long-term government and corporate securities. Because real estate loans compete with many other forms of long-term debt for a place in the lender's portfolio, and because real estate borrowers compete with each other for available mortgage funds, the past decade has seen, in addition to interest rates that would have shocked the conscience (and violated most laws against usury) not so long ago, periodic shortages of mortgage credit, especially for potential home-owners.

Disintermediation occurs when depositors withdraw their deposits from thrift institutions—the mutual savings banks and savings and loan associations that recycle deposits primarily into home mortgages—and place the withdrawn funds into money market and other higher-yield outlets. Heavy disintermediation intensifies the mortgage crunch. To curb withdrawal, lending institutions now offer depositors a choice of higher-yield savings accounts—6- to 30-month certificates that pay considerably more than regular passbook deposits earn. But in seeking to solve one problem, mortgage lenders have aggravated a second, which results from the spread between current interest yields and the (much) lower interest rates on older, unmatured loans. At any one time, a lender's mortgage portfolio will have an average age of five to ten years; this *is* inevitable because of the relatively long-term maturities of mortgage debt. Having "borrowed" short and loaned long (at *fixed* rates), the lender is fairly helpless, either to staunch a heavy outflow of funds, if he fails to adjust upward his rates on current deposits, or to suffer a heavy spilling of red ink, if he seeks to compete for current deposits. For thrift institutions, especially, the choice has been Hobsonian.

A fairly recent innovation, the variable-rate mortgage (VRM), seeks to improve the balance between portfolio yield and current borrowing costs. The VRM theory is remarkably simple: as current interest levels rise, the lender may lift interest rates on unmatured mortgages. Conversely, should current interest levels drop, the mortgage borrower would (usually) see a lowering of his interest rate. But VRM practice has led to a confusing array of "floating-rate" schemes. Consider, for example, the following possibilities.

Suppose that R borrows $50,000 on a VRM, which calls for an initial interest rate of 10.0 percent, a 25-year maturity, and annual debt service (based on quarterly payments) of $5465. Five years later, interest rates have risen to 11.0 percent and a VRM adjustment is required. What is the VRM adjustment? Under present theory, it might take one of three forms:

(1) *Maturity remains constant; debt service rises to reflect increased interest rate.* At the end of five years, R will have reduced the mortgage balance from $50,000 to $47,047. The interest rate having risen to 11.0 percent, the debt service must be adjusted upward so as to pay off the unpaid balance, at the higher rate, in the remaining 20 years. The revised annual debt-service increase: $378.

(2) *Debt service remains constant; maturity extended.* This formula would seek to avoid entirely the risk of default that might follow higher debt-service payments. In order to maintain the level of debt service, while adjusting for higher interest rates, the mortgage term must be

extended. After five years, when R's mortgage balance is $47,047, the annual debt service of $5465—adjusted for an 11.0 percent interest rate—will require nearly 27 more years in which to amortize that balance. Thus, the VRM maturity must be extended nearly seven years. Consider, however, what the effect would be if interest rates had risen from 10.0 to 12.0 percent during that five-year interval.

(3) *Combination of debt service increase and maturity extension.* This formula would seek to reduce the risk of default that might follow higher debt-service payments while avoiding extreme extensions of the mortgage term. The parties might agree, for example, that any maturity extension would not exceed a fixed duration, viz., 25 years; and that the borrower would pay higher debt service to complete the adjustment. In the illustration above, R would be obliged after five years to pay an adjusted annual debt service of $5547, to reflect an extended maturity from 20 to 25 years. The annual debt service increase: only $82.

One important variable is the index to which interest rates are geared. Because the Consumer Price Index measures *current* inflation, whereas interest rates reflect *anticipated* inflation, the CPI does not seem entirely suitable. Some banks have tied their indexes to the cycle of rates paid on three-month U.S. Treasury bills or other short-term paper. An alternative, more widely used index is the cost-of-funds index, which reflects the rates that lenders must pay currently to attract deposits. One might also conceive of a VRM index that would measure the yields on corporate industrial bonds and intermediate or long-term government securities.

Outside the United States, the VRM has wide usage in such developed countries as Britain, France, Germany, Italy, Sweden, Australia, and the Union of South Africa. In this country, not everyone loves the VRM. Consumer advocates argue that the entire risk of inflation shifts from the lender to the borrower and that VRM will make borrowing more difficult for lower-income and fixed-income persons, because lenders will regard them as poor risks to pay debt-service increases as they become due. At one time, some states even banned the VRM, although the present mood is to enable, but closely regulate, VRM usage. California, where the VRM has become commonplace, has a typical, elaborate regulatory scheme. Cal. Civ. Code §1916.5 (West Supp. 1981). This requires, inter alia, that:

1. the prescribed standard for interest rate changes shall apply identically to movements in either direction;
2. no interest rate change shall occur for the first semi-annual period;
3. no interest rate change shall occur more often than once during any semi-annual period, nor more often than once every six months;
4. no interest rate change shall be greater than one-quarter of one percent during any semi-annual period;
5. the maximum interest rate increase shall be limited to 2.5 percent;

6. the borrower shall have the right of prepayment without charge within 90 days after notification of any interest rate increase.

In the federal system, the Federal Land Banks, a network of twelve cooperative agricultural banks supervised by the Farm Credit Administration, have been making variable-rate rural home mortgages since mid-1972. Borrower acceptance has been described as "good," even though the mortgage rate is unindexed and can be varied at any time at the discretion of the FLB Board of Directors (with the approval of the Farm Credit Administration). On a much broader front, the Federal Home Loan Bank Board in 1973 began seeking to allow federally chartered savings and loan associations to issue VRMs. Early in 1975, the FHLBB issued regulations that would have authorized VRMs on terms fairly similar to those permitted in California, *supra*, but Congress, responding to the cries of consumer groups, refused to allow the plan, and the proposed regulations were withdrawn. The FHLBB tried again in 1978. This time, the regulations called for four new mortgage types, including VRMs, where they were "required to preserve competitive balance" (from state-chartered thrift organizations). In the wake of the successful VRM experience both of the Federal Land Banks and of state-chartered lenders, Congressional opposition softened, and the new regulations became effective on January 1, 1979. Not surprisingly, California became the first state in which a competitive disadvantage was deemed to exist.

(b) Limitations on the Rate of Return

In setting their interest rate, lenders have had to consider—in addition to profitability, risk, and market demand—one other constraint: the legal ceiling, set either by state law or, in the case of federally insured loans, by Congress. A loan exceeding the legal ceiling is usurious, and where a borrower can show usury, sanctions ranging from a loss of the excess interest to a loss of the entire interest and principal may await the lender. The earliest usury laws, which appear in the Bible, forbade the taking of any interest (cf. Leviticus 25:36 and Deuteronomy 23:20). Centuries later, Aristotle argued that money, as an inorganic object, cannot breed new coins; therefore he who demands payment for the lending of money causes money to beget money and thus defies the laws of nature. During the Middle Ages, the church treated the exaction of any interest as a mortal sin punishable by excommunication. But as the Western world turned to capitalism, and as credit became a precondition to economic growth, laws fixing interest ceilings replaced the absolute bar against interest. One might still ask, however, why interest—of all charges made for goods and services—continues to be one of the most consistently regulated.

State usury statutes vary widely, as to rates, penalties, covered transactions, defenses, exemptions, statutes of limitations, etc. In addition, the courts have added an enormous body of usury doctrine in sorting out the illegal from legal loan.

Thus, purchase-money mortgages—those mortgages that the seller "takes back" from the buyer to help finance the purchase price—are generally not subject to usury limits. See, e.g., Mandelino v. Fribourg, 23 N.Y.2d 145, 242 N.E.2d 823, 295 N.Y.S.2d 654 (1968). At least thirty states have enacted a corporate borrower exception, which would remove any ceiling from loans made to a corporation. See, e.g., N.J. Stat. Ann. §31:1-16 (1963). In some of these states, however, the exception does not apply to a corporation whose principal asset is a one- or two-family dwelling if the corporation was formed so recently as to suggest evasion. See, e.g., N.Y. Gen. Oblig. Law §5-521(2) (McKinney 1977).

State usury controls, however, may have become far less important in the wake of recent federal legislation. Section 501 of the Depository Institutions Deregulation and Monetary Control Act of 1980 gives the Federal Home Loan Bank Board power to adopt regulations pre-empting state usury laws with respect to federally related first mortgages made after March 31, 1980. Federally related mortgages embrace virtually all residential loans issued by institutional lenders. Accepting its powers, the FHLBB immediately issued regulations, which remain in force. The statute gives all states a three-year period in which to override the regulation, but few states, if any, have yet taken that option. Note, however, that Congress did not empower the FHLBB to substitute a federal rate ceiling for the pre-empted state limits. Thus, except for certain federally originated or insured loans, e.g., FHA insured mortgages regulated by the Department of Housing and Urban Development, and for secondary mortgages, residential lending has become virtually interest-unregulated.

(4) Method of Amortization

Debt service payments have two components, interest and principal reduction, which are usually called amortization. Most real estate mortgages are *self-amortizing*, that is, each installment contains enough amortization to reduce the loan balance to zero when the borrower pays his final installment. Mortgages that are not self-amortizing, that is, not self-liquidating by regular debt service installments, are said to have a *balloon*. One finds balloon mortgages on investment properties, and sometimes as second mortgages on homes. While a balloon mortgage could be written to require interest payments only, more often the rate of amortization simply falls below that needed to achieve self-liquidation. For the property owner, the balloon arrangement has the key advantage of improving his cash flow during the loan period (because debt service is reduced); but he must be ready, when the mortgage matures, either to find cash to discharge the balloon or to obtain a new or extended mortgage.

Self-amortizing loans come in two forms: *level payment* and *constant amortization*. The former signifies that each installment of debt service remains constant throughout the mortgage term. Table 22 will enable you to determine the monthly debt service needed to self-amortize various amounts of debt at varying interest rates and maturities.

TABLE 22

Monthly Level Payments to Amortize $1000. Various Amortization Periods and Interest Rates

(in dollars)

Interest Rate (percent)	Term in Years						
	10	15	20	25	30	35	40
9.0	12.67	10.14	9.00	8.39	8.05	7.84	7.71
10.0	13.21	10.75	9.65	9.09	8.78	8.60	8.49
11.0	13.77	11.37	10.32	9.80	9.52	9.37	9.28
12.0	14.35	12.00	11.01	10.53	10.29	10.16	10.08
13.0	14.93	12.65	11.72	11.28	11.06	10.95	10.90

Problem: Compute the level payments required monthly to amortize a $40,000, 15-year mortgage at 12.0 percent interest; a $50,000, 20-year mortgage at 9.0 percent.

A major characteristic of the level payment mortgage is the fact of ever-changing components of interest and principal; with each successive installment the interest component gets smaller while the amortization grows. Let us take a $40,000, 11 percent, 25-year mortgage, carrying a monthly debt service of $392. Normally each installment of debt service is applied first to the payment of interest on the unpaid balance; whatever sum remains is then applied to principal reduction. Allocation of interest and principal for the first three months appears in Table 23.

In contrast to level-payment debt service, constant amortization mortgages provide the same amount of principal reduction in each installment. Again using the example of a $40,000, 11 percent, 25-year mortgage, the schedule of debt service that results appears in Table 24.

Over the 25 years, if the hypothetical mortgages go to term, the level-payment loan will be far the more costly—over $22,000 in extra interest. Yet the greatly reduced cost of the level-payment mortgage in the loan's early years makes it a far more popular borrowing device in financing the sale of housing. Note, for example, that a family able to afford the $500.00 initial debt service of a 25-year constant amortization mortgage could handle a

TABLE 23

Month	Installment	Interest	Principal	Principal Balance After Monthly Payment
1	$392.00	$366.67	$25.33	$39,974.67
2	392.00	366.43	25.57	39,949.10
3	392.00	366.20	25.80	39,923.30
. . .	. . .	. . .	. . .	. . .
300	392.00	3.56	388.44	0

TABLE 24

Month	Installment	Interest	Principal	Principal Balance After Monthly Payment
1	$500.00	$366.67	$133.33	$39,866.67
2	498.77	365.44	133.33	39,733.34
3	497.55	364.22	133.33	39,600.00
. . .	. . .	. . .	. . .	. . .
300	134.55	1.22	133.33	0

15-year level payment loan, whose monthly payments would come to only $454.80.

Since the income of many homebuying households tends to rise during the mortgage term, both in real and inflated dollars, this might argue for a mortgage whose debt service starts quite low and later steps up. (One close analogy is the life insurance policy calling for premium increases after three to five years to anticipate the policy holder's greater income.) To test the practice, the Federal Home Loan Bank Board issued regulations in 1978 that would allow Federal savings and loan associations to issue *graduated payment* mortgages in states where state-chartered thrift institutions were permitted to do so. The board proposed a range of mortgages whereby payments could increase for up to five years by as much as 7.5 percent a year, and could fall for up to ten years to 3.0 percent. Then the payment would stay level for the remainder of the term. Because of negative amortization in the early years of the loan, borrowers seeking the maximum loan-to-value ratio would be required to make a somewhat larger down payment, since the regulations require compliance with regular loan-to-value limits throughout the term of the loan.

Congress also moved in 1974 to give the FHA the power experimentally to insure graduated payment mortgages. To date, HUD has not implemented this authority.

c.   Forms of Security Devices

(1)   The Mortgage
AXELROD, BERGER, AND JOHNSTONE, LAND TRANSFER AND FINANCE

156-158 (2d ed. 1978)

We have already used the word "mortgage" repeatedly and have done so as a layman would—to describe a loan on real property. The lawyer knows better. A mortgage is not the loan itself, but is a security interest in property given to an obligee (usually a lender) to secure the loan or, occasionally, some other obligation. Such other obligation might be the promise of the obligor to act as surety for the debts of a third person; in that instance the mortgage would be called a collateral security mortgage. The party who holds a mortgage is called the *mortgagee;* the party whose property is subject to a mortgage is called the *mortgagor.* Very often neither the mortgagee nor the mortgagor will be the original mortgaging parties, since the mortgage will have been sold or assigned or the mortgaged property will have been transferred. The mortgages dealt with in this text are mostly mortgages on real estate, not mortgages on personalty, which are called chattel mortgages. . . .

Where a mortgage is given to secure a loan, the loan usually is evidenced by the obligor's note or bond which accompanies the mortgage. Although the terms often are used interchangeably, technically a bond is a sealed instrument and a note is an unsealed instrument; until the 1966 repeal of the federal excise tax on corporate bonds mooted the difference, a corporate mortgagor could avoid the tax by issuing a note instead of a bond. For an instance in which the archaic difference may still matter, see N.J.S.A. 2A:50-3 (1952); 79-83 Thirteenth Ave., Ltd. v. De Marco, 44 N.J. 525, 210 A.2d 401 (1965).

What does the mortgagee get when it receives a mortgage? The answer to that question has varied greatly over the course of centuries, but today, for most practical purposes, the mortgagee receives a lien[23] against the mortgagor's property as of the time that the mortgage is recorded. (Between the mortgaging parties, the lien is effective when the mortgage is executed and delivered, but since most disputes over priority involve third parties, the critical date is that of recordation.) In an earlier era, the mortgagee obtained title to the mortgagor's property subject to divestment if the debt were paid on the due or law day. Often this arrangement meant hardship for the mortgagor, for a late tender of payment, late even by so little as one day, would not bring a return of title unless the mortgagee volunteered to give it. In time, chancery intervened in behalf of defaulting mortgagors by letting them "redeem" the property from the mortgagee if they tendered payment within a reasonable period after the law day. This equitable right of redemption[24] grew into an implied term of every mortgage bargain.

---

23. Even in states where conveyancing practice still uses language in the mortgage instrument that signifies the transfer of legal title to the mortgagee, all that he gets is a lien interest. At an earlier time, American courts differentiated between the interest of a mortgagee holding title and the interest of a mortgagee having a lien only; today, most of the differences have disappeared. There remains, however, one. In a few states, known as title states, the mortgagee has the continuing right to possession, as he does in England. In one or two other states, known as "hybrid" or "intermediate" theory states, the mortgagee is entitled automatically to possession immediately upon default. Everywhere else, the mortgagee must petition the court for the right to take possession—via a court-appointed receiver—to protect the security from waste or dissipation of the rents; usually the petition is received and granted as part of a foreclosure proceeding.

24. Be sure not to confuse the equitable right of redemption, which the mortgagor holds until the default hardens into foreclosure, with the statutory right to redeem. The latter operates only after the equity of redemption is extinguished and entitles the mortgagor, in states where the right exists, to buy back the real estate from the purchaser at the foreclosure sale.

Now the mortgagee faced hardship—the hardship of uncertainty—for he could not be sure, after default, when his title would indefeasibly vest. A late tendering mortgagor might yet persuade chancery that the tender was not unreasonably delayed. Taking the initiative, mortgagees began to petition the courts to cut off, or foreclose, the mortgagor's equity of redemption. In this way, the procedural remedy of foreclosure was born. The decree of foreclosure, which was issued some months after the law date and upon notice to the defaulting mortgagor, vested the mortgagee's title to the real estate security; prior to the decree redemption was possible, but after the decree, it was not.

If, when foreclosure occurred, the real estate was worth more than the mortgage debt, still another source of hardship remained for the mortgagor. Since foreclosure vested title in the mortgagee, he stood to benefit, while the mortgagor stood to lose, from any surplus in property value. No restitution was necessary. By the early 1800s, state legislatures began to respond to the evident harshness of this situation; mortgagees who applied for a foreclosure decree were ordered to sell the property at a public sale and to pay over to the mortgagor (and to any junior lienors) the surplus moneys from the sale, i.e., the moneys not needed to satisfy the claims of the foreclosing mortgagee. (Sometimes, of course, the sales price fails to satisfy the debt, and this may give rise to further claim for a deficiency judgment.) In a substantial majority of states, *foreclosure by judicial sale* has become the exclusive or generally used process, and it is available everywhere. The process it supplanted, which for obvious reasons became known as *strict foreclosure,* survives in only a few states as a permitted remedy.[25]

One other form of foreclosure deserves mention, for it does not depend upon judicial decree. Where the mortgage instrument gives the mortgagee the power, and state law does not prevent its exercise, a sale arranged for by the mortgagee may be held to transfer the interest of the defaulted mortgagor. A *mortgage with power of sale* grew out of the efforts of English lawyers to avoid Chancery; by the mid-1800s, statutes confirmed the practice, and today, in England, the practice prevails. The 1951 volume of Osborne on Mortgages indicates the widespread use of the power of sale in eighteen American states. In England the sale may be held privately, the mortgagor being deemed protected sufficiently by the requirement that the sale must be "bona fide to a stranger and at a reasonable price." In the United States the sale is invariably

---

25. Strict foreclosure, while not permitted in the original foreclosure proceeding, may sometimes be used to correct an error in the original proceeding. Take this example: X, who holds a first mortgage, obtains a foreclosure decree and bids in (i.e., purchases) the property at the public sale. Then X discovers that service on Y, who held a second mortgage or a subordinate judgment lien against the property, was omitted in the foreclosure action, so that his lien survives the decree. Rather than reinstitute the sale, X may be able to apply for a decree of strict foreclosure—upon notice to Y, of course—that would cut off Y's interest in the real estate and relegate Y to a claim against the mortgage proceeds. Whether the decree is granted or not would probably depend on the showing of the relationship between the value of the property and the sales price and on the circumstances of Y's nonservice.

public and statutes carefully regulate the conduct of the sale and the method of giving notice.

The purchaser in theory obtains the same rights in the property he would enjoy had he purchased at a judicial sale, since the mortgagee is selling the title as it existed when the mortgage containing the power of sale was given. Nevertheless, the costlier, slower, and more cumbersome judicial sale is frequently preferred because it creates a permanent court record of the events leading to the transfer of the mortgagor's interest, while the purchaser at a nonjudicial sale may have only the recitals in his deed to establish the regularity of his title.

State law varies as to whether a mortgagee may bid at any sale that he conducts pursuant to the power of sale. Generally he will be permitted to do so if the mortgage gives him the privilege or if the sale is actually conducted by a public officer. What arguments do you see for and against letting the mortgagee participate in the bidding?

If the sale results in surplus moneys, the foreclosing mortgagee will usually bring a bill of interpleader joining the mortgagor and junior lienors so that their rights to the surplus may be decided judicially.

MORTGAGE NOTE
(FAMILY HOME)

US $_____   _____, New Jersey
                                                                City

_____, 19 ____

FOR VALUE RECEIVED, the undersigned ("Borrower") promise(s) to pay _____ _____, or order, the principal sum of _____ _____ _____ Dollars, with interest on the unpaid principal balance from the date of this Note, until paid, at the rate of _____ _____ percent per annum. Principal and interest shall be payable at _____ _____, or such other place as the Note holder may designate, in consecutive monthly installments of _____ _____ Dollars (US $ _____), on the first day of each month beginning _____, 19_____. Such monthly installments shall continue until the entire indebtedness evidenced by this Note is fully paid, except that any remaining indebtedness, if not sooner paid, shall be due and payable on _____.

If any monthly installment under this Note is not paid when due and remains unpaid after a date specified by a notice to Borrower, the entire principal amount outstanding and accrued interest thereon shall at once become due and payable at the option of the Note holder. The date specified shall not be less than thirty days from the date such notice is mailed. The Note holder may exercise this option to accelerate during any default by Borrower regardless of any prior forbearance. If suit is brought to collect this Note, the Note holder shall be entitled to collect all reasonable costs and expenses of suit, including, but not limited to, reasonable attorney's fees.

Borrower shall pay to the Note holder a late charge of four (4%) percent of any monthly installment not received by the Note holder within fifteen (15) days after the installment is due.

Borrower may repay the principal amount outstanding in whole or in part. Any partial prepayment shall be applied against the principal amount outstanding and shall not postpone the due date of any subsequent monthly installments or change the amount of such installments, unless the Note holder shall otherwise agree in writing.

Presentment, notice of dishonor, and protest are hereby waived by all makers, sureties, guarantors and endorsers hereof. This Note shall be the joint and several obligation of all makers, sureties, guarantors and endorsers, and shall be binding upon them and their successors and assigns.

Any notice to Borrower provided for in this Note shall be given by mailing such notice by certified mail addressed to Borrower at the Property Address stated below, or to such other address as Borrower may designate by notice to the Note holder. Any notice to the Note holder shall be given by mailing such notice by certified mail, return receipt requested, to the Note holder at the address stated in the first paragraph of this Note, or at such other address as may have been designated by notice to Borrower.

The indebtedness evidenced by this Note is secured by a Mortgage, dated even date herewith.

_____(Seal)

_____   _____(Seal)

_____   _____(Seal)

      Property Address   *(Execute Original Only)*

MORTGAGE (FAMILY HOME)

THIS MORTGAGE is made this _____ day of _____, 19_____, between the Mortgagor,

_____ (herein "Borrower"), and the Mortgagee _____

_____, a corporation organized and existing under the laws of _____, whose mailing address is _____

_____ (herein "Lender").

WHEREAS, Borrower is indebted to Lender in the principal sum of ____ _____ Dollars, which indebtedness is evidenced by Borrower's note dated _____ (herein "Note"), providing for monthly installments of principal and interest with the balance of the indebtedness, if not sooner paid, due and payable on _____;

To SECURE to Lender (a) the repayment of the indebtedness evidenced by the Note, with interest thereon, the payment of all other sums, with interest thereon, advanced in accordance herewith to protect the security of this Mortgage, and the performance of the covenants and agreements of Borrower herein contained, and (b) the repayment of any further advances, with interest thereon, made to Borrower by Lender pursuant to paragraph 21 hereof (herein "Future Advances"), Borrower does hereby mortgage, grant and convey to Lender the following described property located in the _____ _____, State of New Jersey:

which has the address of _____, _____
                                  [Street]   *[City]*
_____ (herein "Property Address");
       [State and Zip Code]

TOGETHER with all the improvements now or hereafter erected on the property, and all easements, rights, appurtenances, rents, royalties, mineral, oil and gas rights and profits, water, water rights, and water stock, and all fixtures now or hereafter attached to the property, all of which, including replacements and additions thereto, shall be deemed to be and remain a part of the property covered by this Mortgage; and all of the foregoing, together with said property (or the leasehold estate if this Mortgage is on a leasehold) are herein referred to as the "Property".

Borrower covenants that Borrower is lawfully seised of the estate hereby conveyed and has the right to mortgage, grant and convey the Property, that the Property is unencumbered, and that Borrower will warrant and defend generally the title to the Property against all claims and demands, subject to any declarations, easements or restrictions listed in a schedule of exceptions to coverage in any title insurance policy insuring Lender's interest in the Property.

UNIFORM COVENANTS. Borrower and Lender covenant and agree as follows:

1. Payment of Principal and Interest. Borrower shall promptly pay when due the principal of and interest on the indebtedness evidenced by the Note, prepayment and late charges as provided in the Note, and the principal of and interest on any Future Advances secured by this Mortgage.

2. Funds for Taxes and Insurance. Subject to applicable law or to a written waiver by Lender, Borrower shall pay to Lender on the day monthly installments of principal and interest are payable under the Note, until the Note is paid in full, a sum (herein "Funds") equal to one-twelfth of the yearly taxes and assessments which may attain priority over this Mortgage, and ground rents on the Property, if any, plus one-twelfth of yearly premium installments for hazard insurance, plus one-twelfth of yearly premium install-ments for mortgage insurance, if any, all as reasonably estimated initially and from time to time by Lender on the basis of assessments and bills and reason-able estimates thereof.

The Funds shall be held in an institution the deposits or accounts of which are insured or guaranteed by a Federal or state agency (including Lender if Lender is such an institution). Lender shall apply the Funds to pay said taxes, assessments, insurance premiums and ground rents. Lender may not charge for so holding and applying the Funds, analyzing said account, or verifying and compiling said assessments and bills, unless Lender pays Bor-rower interest on the Funds and applicable law permits Lender to make such a charge. Borrower and Lender may agree in writing at the time of execution of this Mortgage that interest on the Funds shall be paid to Borrower, and unless such agreement is made or applicable law requires such interest to be paid, Lender shall not be required to pay Borrower any interest or earnings on the Funds. Lender shall give to Borrower, without charge, an annual account-ing of the Funds showing credits and debits to the Funds and the purpose for which each debit to the Funds was made. The Funds are pledged as additional security for the sums secured by this Mortgage.

If the amount of the Funds held by Lender, together with the future monthly installments of Funds payable prior to the due dates of taxes, assess-ments, insurance premiums and ground rents, shall exceed the amount re-quired to pay said taxes, assessments, insurance premiums and ground rents as they fall due, such excess shall be, at Borrower's option, either promptly re-paid to Borrower or credited to Borrower on monthly installments of Funds. If the amount of the Funds held by Lender shall not be sufficient to pay taxes, assessments, insurance premiums and ground rents as they fall due, Borrower shall pay to Lender any amount necessary to make up the deficiency within 30 days from the date notice is mailed by Lender to Borrower requesting pay-ment thereof.

Upon payment in full of all sums secured by this Mortgage, Lender shall promptly refund to Borrower any Funds held by Lender. If under paragraph 18 hereof the Property is sold or the Property is otherwise acquired by Lender, Lender shall apply, no later than immediately prior to the sale of the Property or its acquisition by Lender, any Funds held by Lender at the time of applica-tion as a credit against the sums secured by this Mortgage.

3. **Application of Payments.** Unless applicable law provides otherwise, all payments received by Lender under the Note and paragraphs 1 and 2 hereof shall be applied by Lender first in payment of amounts payable to Lender by Borrower under paragraph 2 hereof, then to interest payable on the Note, then to the principal of the Note, and then to interest and principal on any Future Advances.

4. **Charges; Liens.** Borrower shall pay all taxes, assessments and other charges, fines and impositions attributable to the Property which may attain a priority over this Mortgage, and leasehold payments or ground rents, if any, in the manner provided under paragraph 2 hereof or, if not paid in such manner, by Borrower making payment, when due, directly to the payee thereof. Borrower shall promptly furnish to Lender all notices of amounts due under this paragraph, and in the event Borrower shall make payment directly, Borrower shall promptly furnish to Lender receipts evidencing such payments. Borrower shall promptly discharge any lien which has priority over this Mortgage; provided, that Borrower shall not be required to discharge any such lien so long as Borrower shall agree in writing to the payment of the obligation secured by such lien in a manner acceptable to Lender, or shall in good faith contest such lien by, or defend enforcement of such lien in, legal proceedings which operate to prevent the enforcement of the lien or forfeiture of the Property or any part thereof.

5. **Hazard Insurance.** Borrower shall keep the improvements now existing or hereafter erected on the Property insured against loss by fire, hazards included within the term "extended coverage", and such other hazards as Lender may require and in such amounts and for such periods as Lender may require; provided, that Lender shall not require that the amount of such coverage exceed that amount of coverage required to pay the sums secured by this Mortgage.

The insurance carrier providing the insurance shall be chosen by Borrower subject to approval by Lender; provided, that such approval shall not be unreasonably withheld. All premiums on insurance policies shall be paid in the manner provided under paragraph 2 hereof or, if not paid in such manner, by Borrower making payment, when due, directly to the insurance carrier.

All insurance policies and renewals thereof shall be in form acceptable to Lender and shall include a standard mortgage clause in favor of and in form acceptable to Lender. Lender shall have the right to hold the policies and renewals thereof, and Borrower shall promptly furnish to Lender all renewal notices and all receipts of paid premiums. In the event of loss, Borrower shall give prompt notice to the insurance carrier and Lender. Lender may make proof of loss if not made promptly by Borrower.

Unless Lender and Borrower otherwise agree in writing, insurance proceeds shall be applied to restoration or repair of the Property damaged, provided such restoration or repair is economically feasible and the security of this Mortgage is not thereby impaired. If such restoration or repair is not economically feasible or if the security of this Mortgage would be impaired, the insurance proceeds shall be applied to the sums secured by this Mortgage, with the excess, if any, paid to Borrower. If the Property is abandoned by Borrower, or if Borrower fails to respond to Lender within 30 days from the date notice is mailed by Lender to Borrower that the insurance carrier offers to settle a claim for insurance benefits, Lender is authorized to collect and apply the insurance proceeds at Lender's option either to restoration or repair of the Property or to the sums secured by this Mortgage.

Unless Lender and Borrower otherwise agree in writing, any such application of proceeds to principal shall not extend or postpone the due date of the monthly installments referred to in paragraphs 1 and 2 hereof or change the amount of such installments. If under paragraph 18 hereof the Property is acquired by Lender, all right, title and interest of Borrower in and to any insurance policies and in and to the proceeds thereof resulting from damage to the Property prior to the sale or acquisition shall pass to Lender to the extent of the sums secured by this Mortgage immediately prior to such sale or acquisition.

6.   Preservation and Maintenance of Property; Leaseholds; Condominiums; Planned Unit Developments.   Borrower shall keep the Property in good repair and shall not commit waste or permit impairment or deterioration of the Property and shall comply with the provisions of any lease if this Mortgage is on a leasehold. If this Mortgage is on a unit in a condominium or a planned unit development, Borrower shall perform all of Borrower's obligations under the declaration or covenents creating or governing the condominium or planned unit development, the by-laws and regulations of the condominium or planned unit development, and constituent documents. If a condominium or planned unit development rider is executed by Borrower and recorded together with this Mortgage, the covenants and agreements of such rider shall be incorporated into and shall amend and supplement the covenants and agreements of this Mortgage as if the rider were a part hereof.

7.   Protection of Lender's Security.   If Borrower fails to perform the covenants and agreements contained in this Mortgage, or if any action or proceeding is commenced which materially affects Lender's interest in the Property, including, but not limited to, eminent domain, insolvency, code enforcement, or arrangements or proceedings involving a bankrupt or decedent, then Lender at Lender's option, upon notice to Borrower, may make such appearances, disburse such sums and take such action as is necessary to protect Lender's interest, including, but not limited to, disbursement of reasonable attorney's fees and entry upon the Property to make repairs. If Lender required mortgage insurance as a condition of making the loan secured by this Mortgage, Borrower shall pay the premiums required to maintain such insurance in effect until such time as the requirement for such insurance terminates in accordance with Borrower's and Lender's written agreement or applicable law. Borrower shall pay the amount of all mortgage insurance premiums in the manner provided under paragraph 2 hereof.

Any amounts disbursed by Lender pursuant to this paragraph 7, with interest thereon, shall become additional indebtedness of Borrower secured by this Mortgage. Unless Borrower and Lender agree to other terms of payment, such amounts shall be payable upon notice from Lender to Borrower requesting payment thereof, and shall bear interest from the date of disbursement at the rate payable from time to time on outstanding principal under the Note unless payment of interest at such rate would be contrary to applicable law, in which event such amounts shall bear interest at the highest rate permissible under applicable law. Nothing contained in this paragraph 7 shall require Lender to incur any expense or take any action hereunder.

8. Inspection. Lender may make or cause to be made reasonable entries upon and inspections of the Property, provided that Lender shall give Borrower notice prior to any such inspection specifying reasonable cause therefor related to Lender's interest in the Property.

9. Condemnation. The proceeds of any award or claim for damages, direct or consequential, in connection with any condemnation or other taking of the Property, or part thereof, or for conveyance in lieu of condemnation, are hereby assigned and shall be paid to Lender.

In the event of a total taking of the Property, the proceeds shall be applied to the sums secured by this Mortgage, with the excess, if any, paid to Borrower. In the event of a partial taking of the Property, unless Borrower and Lender otherwise agree in writing, there shall be applied to the sums secured by this Mortgage such proportion of the proceeds as is equal to that proportion which the amount of the sums secured by this Mortgage immediately prior to the date of taking bears to the fair market value of the Property immediately prior to the date of taking, with the balance of the proceeds paid to Borrower.

If the Property is abandoned by Borrower, or if, after notice by Lender to Borrower that the condemnor offers to make an award or settle a claim for damages, Borrower fails to respond to Lender within 30 days after the date such notice is mailed, Lender is authorized to collect and apply the proceeds, at Lender's option, either to restoration or repair of the Property or to the sums secured by this Mortgage.

Unless Lender and Borrower otherwise agree in writing, any such application of proceeds to principal shall not extend or postpone the due date of the monthly installments referred to in paragraphs 1 and 2 hereof or change the amount of such installments.

10. Borrower Not Released. Extension of the time for payment or modification of amortization of the sums secured by this Mortgage granted by Lender to any successor in interest of Borrower shall not operate to release, in any manner, the liability of the original Borrower and Borrower's successors in interest. Lender shall not be required to commence proceedings against such successor or refuse to extend time for payment or otherwise modify amortization of the sums secured by this Mortgage by reason of any demand made by the original Borrower and Borrower's successors in interest.

11. Forbearance by Lender Not a Waiver. Any forbearance by Lender in exercising any right or remedy hereunder, or otherwise afforded by applicable law, shall not be a waiver of or preclude the exercise of any such right or remedy. The procurement of insurance or the payment of taxes or other liens or charges by Lender shall not be a waiver of Lender's right to accelerate the maturity of the indebtedness secured by this Mortgage.

12. **Remedies Cumulative.** All remedies provided in this Mortgage are distinct and cumulative to any other right or remedy under this Mortgage or afforded by law or equity, and may be exercised concurrently, independently or successively.

13. **Successors and Assigns Bound; Joint and Several Liability; Captions.** The covenants and agreements herein contained shall bind, and the rights hereunder shall inure to, the respective successors and assigns of Lender and Borrower, subject to the provisions of paragraph 17 hereof. All covenants and agreements of Borrower shall be joint and several. The captions and headings of the paragraphs of this Mortgage are for convenience only and are not to be used to interpret or define the provisions hereof.

14. **Notice.** Except for any notice required under applicable law to be given in another manner, (a) any notice to Borrower provided for in this Mortgage shall be given by mailing such notice by certified mail addressed to Borrower at the Property Address or at such other address as Borrower may designate by notice to Lender as provided herein, and (b) any notice to Lender shall be given by certified mail, return receipt requested, to Lender's address stated herein or to such other address as Lender may designate by notice to Borrower as provided herein. Any notice provided for in this Mortgage shall be deemed to have been given to Borrower or Lender when given in the manner designated herein.

15. **Uniform Mortgage; Governing Law; Severability.** This form of mortgage combines uniform covenants for national use and non-uniform covenants with limited variations by jurisdiction to constitute a uniform security instrument covering real property. This Mortgage shall be governed by the law of the jurisdiction in which the Property is located. In the event that any provision or clause of this Mortgage or the Note conflicts with applicable law, such conflict shall not affect other provisions of this Mortgage or the Note which can be given effect without the conflicting provision, and to this end the provisions of the Mortgage and the Note are declared to be severable.

16. **Borrower's Copy.** Borrower shall be furnished a conformed copy of the Note and of this Mortgage at the time of execution or after recordation hereof.

17. **Transfer of the Property; Assumption.** If all or any part of the Property or any interest therein is sold or transferred by Borrower without Lender's prior written consent, excluding (a) the creation of a lien or encumbrance subordinate to this Mortgage, (b) the creation of a purchase money security interest for household appliances, (c) a transfer by devise, descent or by operation of law upon the death of a joint tenant or (d) the grant of any leasehold interest of three years or less not containing an option to purchase, Lender may, at Lender's option, declare all the sums secured by this Mortgage

to be immediately due and payable. Lender shall have waived such option to accelerate if, prior to the sale or transfer, Lender and the person to whom the Property is to be sold or transferred reach agreement in writing that the credit of such person is satisfactory to Lender and that the interest payable on the sums secured by this Mortgage shall be at such rate as Lender shall request. If Lender has waived the option to accelerate provided in this paragraph 17, and if Borrower's successor in interest has executed a written assumption agreement accepted in writing by Lender, Lender shall release Borrower from all obligations under this Mortgage and the Note.

If Lender exercises such option to accelerate, Lender shall mail Borrower notice of acceleration in accordance with paragraph 14 hereof. Such notice shall provide a period of not less than 30 days from the date the notice is mailed within which Borrower may pay the sums declared due. If Borrower fails to pay such sums prior to the expiration of such period, Lender may, without further notice or demand on Borrower, invoke any remedies permitted by paragraph 18 hereof.

NON-UNIFORM COVENANTS. Borrower and Lender further covenant and agree as follows:

18. Acceleration; Remedies. Except as provided in paragraph 17 hereof, upon Borrower's breach of any covenant or agreement of Borrower in this Mortgage, including the covenants to pay when due any sums secured by this Mortgage, Lender prior to acceleration shall mail notice to Borrower as provided in paragraph 14 hereof specifying: (1) the breach; (2) the action required to cure such breach; (3) a date, not less than 30 days from the date the notice is mailed to Borrower, by which such breach must be cured; and (4) that failure to cure such breach on or before the date specified in the notice may result in acceleration of the sums secured by this Mortgage, foreclosure by judicial proceeding and sale of the Property. The notice shall further inform Borrower of the right to reinstate after acceleration and the right to assert in the foreclosure proceeding the non-existence of a default or any other defense of Borrower to acceleration and foreclosure. If the breach is not cured on or before the date specified in the notice, Lender at Lender's option may declare all of the sums secured by this Mortgage to be immediately due and payable without further demand and may foreclose this Mortgage by judicial proceeding. Lender shall be entitled to collect in such proceeding all expenses of foreclosure, including, but not limited to, attorney's fees permitted by Rules of Court, and costs of abstracts, title reports and documentary evidence.

19. Borrower's Right to Reinstate. Notwithstanding Lender's acceleration of the sums secured by this Mortgage, Borrower shall have the right to have any proceedings begun by Lender to enforce this Mortgage discontinued at any time prior to entry of a judgment enforcing this Mortgage if: (a) Borrower pays Lender all sums which would be then due under this Mortgage, the Note and notes securing Future Advances, if any, had no acceleration occurred; (b) Borrower cures all breaches of any other covenants or agreements of Borrower contained in this Mortgage; (c) Borrower pays all reasonable expenses incurred by Lender in enforcing the covenants and agreements of Borrower contained in this Mortgage and in enforcing Lender's remedies as provided in paragraph 18 hereof, including, but not limited to, reasonable attorney's fees; and (d) Borrower takes such action as Lender may reasonably require to assure that the lien of this Mortgage, Lender's interest in the Property and Borrower's obligation to pay the sums secured by this Mortgage shall continue unimpaired. Upon such payment and cure by Borrower, this Mortgage and the obligations secured hereby shall remain in full force and effect as if no acceleration had occurred.

20.   Assignment of Rents; Appointment of Receiver; Lender in Possession.   As additional security hereunder, Borrower hereby assigns to Lender the rents of the Property, provided that Borrower shall, prior to acceleration under paragraph 18 hereof or abandonment of the Property, have the right to collect and retain such rents as they become due and payable.

Upon acceleration under paragraph 18 hereof or abandonment of the Property, Lender, in person, by agent or by judicially appointed receiver, shall be entitled to enter upon, take possession of and manage the Property and to collect the rents of the Property including those past due. All rents collected by Lender or the receiver shall be applied first to payment of the costs of management of the Property and collection of rents, including, but not limited to, receiver's fees, premiums on receiver's bonds and reasonable attorney's fees, and then to the sums secured by this Mortgage. Lender and the receiver shall be liable to account only for those rents actually received.

21.   Future Advances.   Upon request of Borrower, Lender, at Lender's option prior to release of this Mortgage, may make Future Advances to Borrower. Such Future Advances, with interest thereon, shall be secured by this Mortgage when evidenced by promissory notes stating that said notes are secured hereby. At no time shall Future Advances secured by this Mortgage, not including sums advanced in accordance herewith to protect the security of this Mortgage, exceed US$3,500, nor shall such Future Advances plus the unpaid principal balance of the Note exceed the original principal amount of the Note.

22.   Release.   Upon payment of all sums secured by this Mortgage, Lender shall cancel this Mortgage without charge to Borrower. Borrower shall pay all costs of recordation, if any.

23.   No Claim of Credit for Taxes.   Borrower will not make or claim credit on or deduction from the principal or interest on the sums secured by this Mortgage by reason of any municipal or governmental taxes, assessments or charges assessed upon the Property, nor claim any deduction from the taxable value of the Property by reason of this Mortgage.

IN WITNESS WHEREOF, Borrower has executed this Mortgage.
Signed, Sealed and Delivered
in the Presence of:

_____   _____ (Seal)
                                         —*Borrower*
_____   _____ (Seal)
                                         —*Borrower*

STATE OF NEW JERSEY, _____County ss:

On this _____ day of _____, 19_____, before me, the
subscriber, personally appeared _____
_____ who, I am satisfied, _____
the person(s) named in and who executed the within instrument, and thereupon _____ acknowledged that _____ signed, sealed
and delivered the same as _____
act and deed, for the purposes therein expressed.

_____
                                    Notary Public

This instrument was prepared by:

Receipt of a true copy of this instrument, provided without charge, is hereby
acknowledged.
Witness:

_____   _____ (Seal)
                                         —*Borrower*
_____   _____ (Seal)
                                         —*Borrower*

——— (Space Below This Line Reserved For Lender and Recorder) ———

(2)   *The Trust Deed Mortgage (Deed of Trust)*

AXELROD, BERGER, AND JOHNSTONE, LAND TRANSFER AND FINANCE

159 (2d ed. 1978)

Many states, both in lien and title, recognize a device called a trust deed
mortgage [deed of trust],[25a] which creates a three-party mortgage transaction.
When the mortgage is made, the borrower transfers the real estate security to
a trustee, usually an institution specializing in that role. The trust provides
that if the obligation is performed, title will be reconveyed to the mortgagor,

---

25a. Deed of trust should not be confused with the *land trust,* a device for concealing real
estate ownership that is especially popular in the Chicago area. See Garrett, Land Trusts, 1955 Ill.
L. Forum 655. Under the usual "Illinois" land trust, record title is held by a corporate trustee (a
bank or title insurance company), but the trustee's powers are restricted by an unrecorded trust
agreement whereby the beneficiary (and "real" owner) retains full powers of management and
control. Advantages asserted for the land trust, in addition to privacy of ownership, are avoidance
of probate, facilitation of multi-ownership, and insulation of the real estate form the claims of
judgment creditors.

but if a default occurs, the trustee must arrange a public sale of the mortgagor's interest—very much like a mortgage with power of sale. The mortgagee may be likened to the cestui que trust until performance takes place, after which the trustee's primary duties run to the mortgagor. Assignment of the mortgagee's interest does not result in a change of trustee; instead, only the note or other evidence of debt is transferred and the new mortgagee gains a beneficial interest in the trust.

While the differences between the straight mortgage and the trust deed mortgage may have been significant at one time, that no longer is the case. Courts and legislatures recognize the functional connection between the two mortgage forms, and, in a lien state, for example, the rights and powers of the settlor-mortgagor are not curtailed because he parts with legal title. Thus, the mortgagor retains the right to possession until the trustee realizes on the security by sale or until a receiver is named; the mortgagor may sell, lease, or further mortgage the real estate, subject, of course, to the trust. The particular mortgage form most widely used by any state today is mainly a matter of custom.

NOTES AND QUESTIONS

1. Examine the mortgage note form. Does it call for level payment or constant amortization debt service? Does it call for self-amortization?

2. Examine the prepayment paragraph in the mortgage note form. If the paragraph were removed, would the obligor be privileged to pay off in advance any part of the debt? Cf. Peter Fuller Enterprises, Inc. v. Manchester Savings Bank, 102 N.H. 117, 152 A.2d 179 (1959).

3. What is the function of covenant paragraph 2, Funds for Taxes and Insurance, in the mortgage form?

Some states now require the lender to place escrow funds—as these tax and insurance deposits are called—into interest-bearing accounts for the mortgagor's benefit. Cf., e.g., N.Y. Gen. Oblig. Law §5-601 (McKinney Supp. 1980).

4. Examine covenant paragraph 7, Protection of Lender's Security, in the mortgage form; similarly, covenant paragraph 18, Acceleration. As a consumer spokesman, what reasonable changes might you suggest to strengthen the rights of borrowers without needlessly impairing the lender's security?

5. Examine covenant paragraph 10, Borrower Not Released, in the mortgage form. What is its function? Cf., e.g., Alropa Corp. v. Snyder, 182 Ga. 305, 185 S.E. 352 (1936).

d. Examining the Seller's Title

In the absence of contrary language in the sales contract, the seller of real property implicitly covenants to deliver a "marketable title" on the day of closing. The meaning of "marketable title" occupies a 300-page annotation in American Law Reports (57 A.L.R. 1253 (1928)) and 129 pages in the earliest commercial land transactions casebook: M. Handler, Cases on Vendor and Purchaser (1933). Very generally, a marketable title consists of a fee simple absolute in the subject premises, free of encumbrances such as leases, liens (mortgage, tax, etc.), marital rights, easements, private use restrictions, or encroachments. In point of fact, few parcels *are* any longer marketable, and as your study of the Chicago sales contract showed, the parties invariably restate the basic obligation (paragraph 2, Encumbrances, page 1107 *supra*). Accordingly, we might more accurately speak of the seller's duty to furnish the buyer with a "contract title."

Under the doctrine of merger, the seller's promise of contract title expires with the formal closing. If the buyer wants seller to covenant title beyond the closing, he must get new assurances in the deed itself (page 1154 *infra*). Often, the seller will refuse to give these assurances. In any case, most buyers will want to learn, before they pay over the purchase price, whether they are getting the very title they have bargained for. Therefore, two key events during the executory interval are the seller's proof of title and the buyer's examination thereof.

(1) Methods of Title Examination

AXELROD, BERGER, AND JOHNSTONE, LAND TRANSFER AND FINANCE

537-538 (2d ed. 1978)

In the United States there are three major forms of title search and examination, each dominated by a different skill group or combination of skill groups. In the first, lawyers in private practice make both searches and examinations and provide their clients with title opinions, usually in writing. These opinions ordinarily state who has title, indicate whether or not title is marketable, and describe any defects.

Under the second form of search and examination, lawyers in private practice do the examining and provide their clients with opinions but do not search the public records. Searching is done by professional abstracters who prepare written summaries of the titles to individual land parcels as disclosed by the public records. These summaries, or abstracts as they are called, are histories of the titles to particular parcels. An abstract has a series of entries, normally arranged chronologically, each entry being a synopsis of or excerpt from a recorded document or other public record relevant to the land title in question. To the extent that the abstract is an accurate and complete reflection of the public records, it will have an entry for every step in the public record history of the title: every deed, mortgage, will, judicial decree, or other instrument or event bearing on the title and appearing in the public records will be referred to in a separate abstract entry. By carefully examining these entries a competent lawyer can determine the nature of the record title, including its current marketability. The companies that prepare abstracts are staffed by specialists in title searching, although few abstracters are lawyers. Many title insurance companies originally started as abstract companies, and some of the insurers still prepare and sell abstracts.

The third major form of title search and examination is one in which both search and examination functions are performed by a title insurance company as preliminary steps to issuance of title insurance policies. When a policy is ordered, company employees assemble and evaluate data requisite to insurability. Those employees who search rarely are lawyers; those who examine often are.

In counties where there is not enough title work to justify search and examination staffs, some companies, on request, will issue policies based on opinions of expert title lawyers in private practice. Thus title insurance is fairly frequent even under lawyer or lawyer-abstracter forms of title search and examination. In New England and most rural and small-town communities in the United States, title searches and examinations generally are still monopolized by lawyers or lawyers and abstracters. The Far West is an exception to this, for there and in most of the larger urban areas demand for title insurance is so great that insurers do a high percentage of all searches and examinations. Where title insurance companies have moved into title searching and examination, private practitioners of law have often been displaced in performing one or both of these functions. In some communities, especially most major metropolitan centers, this displacement is almost complete, and the title work of lawyers in private practice is restricted to clearing defective titles and negotiating with title insurers to limit the scope of coverage exceptions. The shift away from title work has had important implications for the private practice of law, as at one time such work was a major source of income to lawyers in all parts of the United States. This loss of title searching and examination illustrates the vulnerability of lawyers in private practice to competition from specialized, high volume businesses and professions. Other occupations that have been particularly effective in cutting in on the work of private law firms include collection agencies, banks in their probate and trust work, and accountants dealing with tax matters.

(2) Recording Acts

AXELROD, BERGER, AND JOHNSTONE, LAND TRANSFER AND FINANCE

531-534 (2d ed. 1978)

Fundamental to title protection in the United States are the recording acts, statutes in effect in every state.[1] The term "recording acts" has a variety

---

1. On recording acts generally, in addition to the standard real property texts, see the following: B. Webb, The Law of Record of Title (2d ed. 1891); Cross, Weaknesses of the Present Recording System, 47 Iowa L. Rev. 245 (1962); and Philbrick, Limits of Record Search and Therefore of Notice, 93 U. Pa. L. Rev. 125, 259, 391 (1944-1945).

of meanings, but here it is used in a narrow sense common to discussions of real property law. It means only those statutes that provide for land conveyancing records to be maintained by recorders of deeds (or equivalent public officials) and that establish priorities among successive purchasers of land interests. Under some circumstances these acts reverse the common law rule that priority among successive purchasers of land interests from the same grantor is dependent on priority in time of execution. Although they differ in detail, all the recording acts provide for (1) centralized filing of documents creating or transferring land interests, (2) maintenance of systems of public records, consisting primarily of copies of the filed documents, and (3) priorities for those interests appearing in the public records as against those that do not.

Public land records provided for by the recording acts are generally maintained in the office of a designated public official of the county where the lands are located. In many states this official bears the title of county recorder of deeds. Most of the records he keeps are open for public inspection and are the principal source of land title data sought by professional searchers. But records kept pursuant to the recording acts are not the only sources of information about land titles; and, on theories of notice or priority irrespective of notice, interests not apparent from an examination of these records may be outstanding and superior to any others. Such interests may be ascertainable from other public records, including court and tax records, and from an examination of the premises. Title examinations frequently involve inspection of these other sources, but some outstanding land interests still may not be uncovered, nor may any reasonable kind of search prove successful. The existence of such interests is an off-record risk that usually cannot be eliminated, although through title insurance or other means the risk may be passed on to someone else.

American recording acts were highly developed by the close of the colonial period.[2] In their early evolution they were probably influenced by English legislation, by the statute of enrollments and registry acts for the counties of Middlesex and York, and by English judicial decisions that purchasers with notice of unregistered conveyances were not protected by the registration statutes. But a general system of recording never developed in England as it did in the United States, and original title instruments kept in private hands have been the main sources relied on in title examinations of English lands. Registration similar to that provided for by the American Torrens system is, however, gradually replacing this so-called title deeds system in England.

It is conventional to classify American recording acts into three main groups, emphasizing the varied significance of notice and the act of recording. The three types are often referred to as race, notice, and race-notice statutes. Under the race type statute, a purchaser who records has priority over any interest then unrecorded, whether or not the purchaser had notice of the unrecorded interest when he took title. In other words, the race to the recorder's

2. On the history of the recording acts, see 4 American Law of Property §§17.4 and 17.5 (Casner ed. 1952); and 6A Powell, The Law of Real Property ¶912 (Rohan ed. 1980).

office determines who prevails. Under a notice type statute, a purchaser takes priority over all prior unrecorded interests of which he had no notice when he took. Once such a purchaser takes title, it is advisable for him to record in order to protect himself from subsequent purchasers, but he need not record to be protected against prior but unrecorded interests of which he had no notice. Race-notice type statutes are similar to notice statutes, except that for a purchaser under a race-notice statute to prevail over a prior unrecorded interest of which he had no notice when he took, he must record before the prior unrecorded interest holder does. Thus, under a race-notice statute, the subsequent uninformed purchaser is not accorded automatic protection against a prior unrecorded but recordable interest, as is the case under the notice statute. The term race-notice is applied to statutes so designated because under them both the race and the notice are material to determination of priority.

Only two states, Louisiana and North Carolina, have race statutes applicable to conveyances generally; several other states have them for mortgages. Of the remaining states, about half have notice statutes and half have race-notice statutes.[3] Florida, Illinois and Massachusetts are among the notice states; and California, Michigan and New York among the race-notice ones.

Filing for record under the recording acts is not essential to validity of an unrecorded but recordable instrument. Such an instrument is valid between the parties and is effective as against subsequent takers not protected by the recording acts. When recording act priorities do not apply, then priority among successive conflicting interests in the same land parcel normally is determined by the common law preference for the interest senior in time of execution.

Public records kept pursuant to the recording acts have evidentiary value in judicial proceedings. In many states the recorded copies of instruments are primary evidence, with no requirement that the original be produced or accounted for. In other states contents of an instrument may be proven from the recorded copy, but only after accounting for the original.

The recording acts, with their stress on readily accessible public land records and priorities for interests appearing in these records, have been largely responsible for creating enough certainty in American land titles to meet the needs of a highly developed industrial society extensively based on private property rights. But there are serious weaknesses in the recording acts that have resulted in more title uncertainty than is necessary and high costs of title protection to minimize the risks inherent in the system. Weaknesses in the recording acts include: the extensive and complex searches that must be made, both on and off record, to determine the apparent state of a title; inefficiently maintained and indexed public records; the risk of outstanding title interests that cannot be ascertained from any reasonable search; and limited effectiveness of recording due to possible errors by recorders and chain of title restric-

---

3. For a listing of states by types of recording statutes, see 4 American Law of Property §17.5 n.63 (Casner ed. 1952).

tions on search obligations. What was no doubt a very good system in earlier days when title histories were short and searches comparatively easy is now a cumbersome and expensive procedure, particularly in highly urbanized communities. Following are representative recording acts, including examples of race, notice, and race-notice statutes.

WASHINGTON REVISED CODE ANNOTATED (1966)

[*Race-Notice:*] §65.08.070. *Real property conveyances to be recorded.* A conveyance of real property, when acknowledged by the person executing the same (the acknowledgment being certified as required by law), may be recorded in the office of the recording officer of the county where the property is situated. Every such conveyance not so recorded is void as against any subsequent purchaser or mortgagee in good faith and for a valuable consideration from the same vendor, his heirs or devisees, of the same real property or any portion thereof whose conveyance is first duly recorded. An instrument is deemed recorded the minute it is filed for record.

TEXAS REVISED CIVIL STATUTES (1969)

[*Notice:*] Art. 6627. *When sales, etc., to be void unless registered.* All bargains, sales and other conveyances whatever, of any land, tenements and hereditaments, whether they may be made for passing any estate of freehold of inheritance or for a term of years; and deeds of settlement upon marriage, whether land, money or other personal thing; and all deeds of trust and mortgages shall be void as to all creditors and subsequent purchasers for a valuable consideration without notice, unless they shall be acknowledged or proved and filed with the clerk, to be recorded as required by law; but the same as between the parties and their heirs, and as to all subsequent purchasers, with notice thereof or without valuable consideration, shall be valid and binding.

ARKANSAS STATUTES ANNOTATED (1947, 1971 REPLACEMENT)

[*Race:*] §51-1002. *Lien attaches when recorded.* Every mortgage of real estate shall be a lien on the mortgaged property from the time the same is filed in the recorder's office for record, and not before; which filing shall be notice to all persons of existence of such mortgage.

NOTES AND QUESTIONS

1. To test your understanding of how race, race-notice, and notice systems differ from one another, work through the following priority disputes under each form of statute:

(a) X, the fee owner, to A, a mortgagee. A does not record.
    X to B, B having no notice of the X-A mortgage. B records his deed.
    A records his mortgage.
(b) X, the fee owner, to A, a mortgagee. A does not record.
    X to B, B having notice of the X-A mortgage. B records his deed.
    A records his mortgage.
(c) X, the fee owner, to A, a mortgagee. A does not record.
    X to B, B having no notice of the X-A mortgage. B does not record
    his deed.
    A records his mortgage.
    B records his deed.

2.   The concept of notice is critical to all but race systems. The relevant
date for notice is when the party seeking recording act protection (i.e., the
grantee, mortgagee, etc.) obtains delivery of his title instrument (i.e., the deed,
mortgage, etc.). Notice of an earlier transaction, received prior to the delivery
date, disables the party from claiming a superior interest. Notice received after
that date is nondisabling even when—under a race-notice setup—the party
has not yet recorded his title instrument.
3.   We have already met the doctrine of notice in this course, fleetingly,
when we discussed implied easements and the burden of covenants and easements on successor owners of the servient estate (pages 538 and 586-587,
supra). *Actual* notice means that a party has direct information about the earlier transaction. This may come from an examination of the records, or from
off-record sources brought directly to the party's attention. *Constructive* notice
leads us to impute notice to a party who has means of knowledge that he is
duty-bound to use but fails to. *Record* notice is a form of constructive notice;
this is the notice that a party would gain of outstanding interests were he to
make a proper examination of the records. A second form of constructive
notice might be called *inspection* notice. Parties who acquire an interest in real
property are expected to inspect the premises carefully before they close. Facts
that such an inspection would disclose—whether inspection is actually made
or not—will be imputed to a party seeking recording act priority over an
earlier interest-holder. For example, if X acquires a lease from O but fails to
record it,[6] O's subsequent mortgagee Y still takes subject to X's lease if X has
occupied the premises. X's possession places Y on constructive notice.
    This discussion of notice, especially constructive notice, might be greatly
expanded. What constitutes a "proper" examination of the records depends on
the chain of title that an examiner must trace and retrace. Courts disagree as
to what this chain should consist of. Similar disagreement underlies the inspection of the premises requirement. Moreover, the doctrine of constructive notice
requires a questioning attitude in the party making the examination or inspec-

6. In many jurisdictions, short-term leases cannot even be recorded. See, e.g., N.Y. Real
Prop. Law §290 (McKinney 1980) (lease not exceeding 3 years).

tion. If a well-worn path leads from the road front to the pond behind the lot, there need not also be a billboard warning "This is an easement" to serve notice of a possible outstanding interest. In this connection, recall the (extreme) facts that led to constructive notice in Van Sandt v. Royster, page 538 *supra* (implied easement).

§19.3   The Closing

If the buyer obtains financing, if the seller tenders contract title, if the premises have not burned down, and if nothing else has gone amiss, the parties will close title—and legal ownership will pass from seller to buyer. Title closings lack the ceremony of earlier centuries, when the parties, with their witnesses, went together on or within sight of the land, and the grantor (called the "feoffor") delivered to the grantee (called the "feoffee") a twig, clod, key, or other symbol in the name of the whole. Oral, rather than written, words of conveyance usually attended the transfer: the feoffor spoke the Latin for "I give to him and his heirs," to transfer a fee simple absolute, or appropriate other words to transfer other freehold estates. While the parties could also use a writing, and sometimes did when fairly complex interests were involved, the requirement of a written instrument to convey freehold estates awaited the English Statute of Frauds in 1677. Even then, this ceremony, *livery of seisin*, theoretically remained essential to transfer freehold estates until its abolition by the Real Property Act of 1845.

In fact, a competing system for the transfer of title grew up in chancery. It depended exclusively on the use of written documents. Codified by the Statute of Uses in 1535, this system relied upon so-called bargain and sale contracts, or "contracts to stand seized"—contracts made for consideration that chancery would execute. (To this day, the phrase "bargain and sale" marks certain deed forms.) In addition, common-law conveyances, with the same ingenuity that led to fine and common recovery, page 149 *supra*, invented the system of "lease and release," which also avoided livery of seisin. Since only transfers of present freehold estates required the ceremony, the owner would execute two instruments outside the ritual: first, a lease (usually in the form of a bargain-and-sale deed of an estate for one year); second, a release to the lessee of the owner's reversionary interest. This fiction also gave way by the mid-nineteenth century.

The modern American closing is mostly a humdrum paper-shuffle, with occasional breaks for a signature, explanation, and writing of checks. The venue may be the recorder's office, or the offices of a lawyer, escrow agent, or title company. A handshake wishing the buyers good luck as they assume the burdens of ownership will usually seal the event.

a. The Deed

Modern statutes of frauds require a written instrument, signed by the grantor or his duly authorized agent, for the transfer of a freehold interest in land. This instrument, the deed, still retains much of the litany that seventeenth-century conveyancers would have found familiar; but stripped of its legalese veneer, the deed's essential parts are:

(1) grantor's name,
(2) grantee's name,
(3) description of the property,
(4) indication of the legal interest (e.g., fee simple absolute),
(5) words denoting intent to transfer an interest, and
(6) grantor's signature.

Any scrap of writing that contains these vitals would satisfy the Statute of Frauds. But as you examine the form below, you will notice, besides the mumbo-jumbo, other elements as well.

WARRANTY DEED

This indenture, made the _____ day of _____, nineteen hundred and _____, between _____, party of the first part, and _____, party of the second part,

Witnesseth, that the party of the first part, in consideration of Ten Dollars and other valuable consideration paid by the party of the second part, does hereby grant and release unto the party of the second part, the heirs or successors and assigns of the party of the second part forever.

All that certain plot, piece or parcel of land, with the buildings and improvements thereon erected, situate, lying and being in the _____.

Together with all right, title and interest, if any, of the party of the first part of, in and to any streets and roads abutting the above-described premises to the center lines thereof; Together with the appurtenances and all the estate and rights of the party of the first part in and to said premises; To Have and To Hold the premises herein granted unto the party of the second part, the heirs or successors and assigns of the party of the second part forever.

And the party of the first part, in compliance with Section 13 of the Lien Law, covenants that the party of the first part will receive the consideration for this conveyance and will hold the right to receive such consideration as a trust fund to be applied first for the purpose of paying the costs of the improvement and will apply the same first to the payment of the cost of the improvement before using any part of the total of the same for any other purpose.

And the party of the first part covenants as follows: that said party of the first part is seized of the said premises in fee simple, and has good right to convey the same; that the party of the second part shall quietly enjoy the said premises; that the said premises are free from incumbrances, except as aforesaid; that the party of the first part will execute or procure any further necessary assurance of the title to said premises; and that said party of the first part will forever warrant the title to said premises.

The word "party" shall be construed as if it read "parties" whenever the sense of this indenture so requires.

In witness whereof, the party of the first part has duly executed this deed the day and year first above written.

In presence of: _____

State of New York }
County of _____ } ss.

On the _____ day of _____, 19____, before me personally came _____, to be known to be the individual __ described in and who executed the foregoing instrument, and acknowledged that _____ executed the same.

State of New York }
County of _____ } ss.

On the _____ day of _____, 19____, before me personally came _____, to me known, who, being by me duly sworn, did depose and say that __he resides at No. _____; that __he is the _____ of _____, the corporation described in and which executed the foregoing instrument; that __he knows the seal of said corporation; that the seal affixed to said instrument is such corporate seal; that it was so affixed by order of the board of directors of said corportion, and that __he signed h__ name thereto by like order.

State of New York }
County of _____ } ss.

On the _____ day of _____, 19____, before me personally came _____, the subscribing witness to the foregoing instrument, with whom I am personally acquainted, who, being by me duly sworn, did depose and say that __he resides at No. _____; that __he knows _____ to be the individual described in and who executed the foregoing instrument; that __he, said subscribing witness, was present and saw _____ execute the same; and that __he, said witness, at the same time subscribed h__ name as witness thereto.

NOTES AND QUESTIONS

1. *Recital of consideration.* Deed forms rarely lack a paragraph denoting consideration. As between the parties, however, consideration is not needed for a valid legal transfer. Consider, for example, that one may make a gift of real property. The recital avoids the implication that the grantor intended to cre-

ate a resulting trust, under which the grantee holds property as trustee for the benefit of the grantor. The recital is also a vestige of the chancery practice that we described above, page 1153.

2. *Acknowledgment clause.* The party signing the deed acknowledges the authenticity of his signature before a notary public, or other person having the authority to take acknowledgments. Generally, the transfer is good even without the acknowledgment, but recording acts require either acknowledgment or some equivalent (for example, attestation by witnesses) before the instrument may be accepted for recordation. Why this requirement?

3. *Types of deed: quitclaim and warranty.*

It oversimplifies to classify instruments into two categories, *warranty deeds* in which seller-grantor has responsibility for after-discovered title flaws and *quitclaims* in which he does not. Each term is used to describe a number of different sorts of instruments, and the classification into quitclaim or warranty deed has significance for legal issues other than title liability. Thus a warranty deed serves to pass title from grantor to grantee where grantor acquires that title *after* the delivery of the deed, while a mere quitclaim supposedly does not. Yet courts, in the after-acquired property situation, have strained to thrust particular instruments into the former category, so that an instrument entitled *quitclaim deed* (as against mere *quitclaim*) has been held to carry after-acquired property. 18 Baylor L. Rev. 618 (1966). . . .

A warranty deed is one which contains one or more of six "covenants for title." These covenants split into two triads, the first of which consists of the covenants of *seisin, right to convey,* and *against encumbrances.* The first two generally guarantee that grantor owns what he purports to grant, and the last that the estate is free of liens, mortgages, easements, etc. except as otherwise noted in the deed. The first two are generally regarded as indistinguishable (but see the detailed discussion of all the covenants for title in Aigler, Smith, and Tefft, Cases on Property 737-749 (1960)), and in the cases they blur into the last.

This first group represents guarantees against title flaws extant at the date of the conveyance and thus differ in form from the second triad in which grantor promises in the future to defend and hold grantee harmless against hostile claimants or encumbrancers. Of this latter triad, the covenants of *quiet enjoyment* and *warranty* are again indistinguishable, and the last, that of *further assurances,* is little used in the United States.

You will notice that the first triad is phrased in present tense and the second is phrased in future tense. This has resulted in controversy over whether the first group can run with the land so as to benefit subsequent grantees. Since these covenants are broken, if at all, upon delivery of the deed, they become mere choses in action, which do not run. However, some courts have found that the chose in action passed to a subgrantee by implicit assignment when the subgrantee received his deed. The future-phrased covenants do run with the land. (Query: How can a covenant for title run with the land to a subgrantee when the original grantor didn't own the land for the covenant to run with?) . . .

The protection afforded by the warranties is not generous; the warrantor's liability generally is limited to the consideration he received for the land. Mc-Cormick, Damages §185 (1932). You can see how negligible a recovery this would produce for an evicted buyer of California land who sues against a remote grantor-warrantor. Convenantee may also recover his expenses in reasonable though unsuccessful defense of the title. [Axelrod, Berger, and Johnstone, Land Transfer and Finance 505, 506 (2d ed. 1978)]

4. *Grantee's signature.* Ordinarily the grantee does not sign the deed. However, if the grantee is taking over an existing mortgage and intends to assume it—i.e., to become personally liable for the underlying debt—statutes generally require that the assumption be in writing. See, e.g., Cal. Civ. Code §1624(7) (West 1973); N.Y. Gen. Oblig. Law §5-705 (McKinney 1977).

5. The operative event for the transfer of legal title—i.e., the instant when grantee becomes the new owner—comes not when grantor signs the deed, or when he acknowledges his signature, but when grantor *delivers* the deed to grantee or his agent and grantee accepts the conveyance. We usually infer acceptance from the grantee's parting with the purchase price, his taking the deed without comment, his recording of the deed, or his entry into the premises and bestowing ownership upon them; but sometimes in the donative situation we may have to look harder to see whether the grantee-donee has acceded to the gift. (Be aware that ownership of real property may carry more burdens than benefits.) The subject of delivery, especially of gifts, creates more troublesome problems. The sampling below will introduce you to problem areas:

(a) X signed a deed conveying property to his nephew, N. X and N lived together on the property, where the deed was kept. Both had access to the deed. X told others that he had deeded the property to N, but X continued to operate the property and to enjoy its benefits as he had before. Has there been a valid conveyance? Cf. Berigan v. Berrigan, 413 Ill. 204, 108 N.E.2d 438 (1952). Compare Noble v. Fickes, 230 Ill. 594, 82 N.E. 950 (1907).

(b) Y was indebted to his mother. He signed a deed conveying land to her and gave the instrument to his brother with oral instructions: "Give this to Mother if I predecease her." Y died fifteen years later, predeceasing his mother. Y's widow claims that delivery was conditioned upon Y's predecease of his mother, that this made the transfer testamentary, and that, as a testamentary transfer, the deed failed to satisfy the formal requirements of the statute of wills. Y's mother argues that Y made a present gift of a future interest, and that delivery occurred when Y placed the deed in third-party hands. Inter vivos gift or testamentary transfer? Cf. Atchison v. Atchison, 198 Okla. 98, 175 P.2d 309 (1946).

(c) S and B enter into a contract of sale. The contract names an escrow agent to whom S will give the deed with the understanding that the agent will record the deed when B pays him the purchase price. The agent absconds with the purchase price after recording the deed.

Does B have title? See generally Annot., 15 A.L.R.2d 870 (1951); cf. also Doherty v. Elskamp, 58 Misc. 2d 653, 296 N.Y.S.2d 127 (Civ. Ct. 1968), *aff'd,* 58 Misc. 2d 654, 298 N.Y.S.2d 743 (App. T. 1969).

In some areas escrow agents commonly handle the details of a real estate transaction:

> Brown, in The Lawyer's Prescription, 30 Unauth. Prac. News 1, 7 n.3 (1964), estimates that over 90 percent of home sales in southern California take place without a lawyer directly representing either buyer or seller. Closings there are handled by independent escrow agents.
>
> Escrows are possible as closing devices since buyer and seller each satisfy their contract obligations by providing appropriate pieces of paper for the other: in the seller's case, principally a deed and some sort of title assurance; in the buyer's, a certified check for the price (and where appropriate a mortgage to the bank which lends him the money to buy the property). Under escrow arrangements, after the contract of sale is executed, the parties enter an escrow agreement, which provides that the parties are to deposit the required pieces of paper with the escrow agent. If all the paper comes in within a specified time, the escrow is closed; the escrow agent then files for record the appropriate documents and gives each party the instruments to which he is entitled. If the transaction is not timely closed, papers are returned to the depositors who can then decide who sues whom for what.
>
> Escrow provides a convenient device for handling the procurement and deposit of the parties' papers at times convenient to them individually, as well as an efficient institution for handling other closing mechanics. For example, escrow agents may request a title search; obtain reports; draft deeds or other documents; obtain rent statements; pay off authorized demands; adjust taxes, rents and insurance between the parties; compute interest on loans; and acquire insurance for title, fire or other liability. California Real Estate Transactions 507 (State Bar of California 1967).
>
> There is a rule of law which gives escrow a further advantage over the ordinary transaction of contract of sale followed by lawyer's office closing three weeks hence. In such a transaction if seller dies during the interim, buyer, to enforce his rights, has to get entangled with the administration of decedent seller's estate, whereas if a deed is deposited in escrow, even if the seller dies before the escrow is closed, the escrow can proceed to normal closing. (However, hypercautious local practice may require buyer's attorney to clear the transaction with the court of probate.)
>
> Past litigation involving escrow agents raises such questions as which party bears the loss for various sorts of escrow agent default; whether a written escrow agreement satisfies the statute of frauds so as to make binding a contract of sale not otherwise evidenced; and whether to define the parties' obligations according to the contract of sale, when the escrow agreement calls for party actions different from those specified in the contract. See Aran, Escrows in California Real Estate Transactions 503 (State Bar of California 1967). [Axelrod, Berger, and Johnstone, Land Transfer and Finance 66-67 (2d ed. 1978)]

b. The Closing Adjustments

Re-examine paragraph 3 of the conditions of the Chicago contract of sale form, page 1109 *supra*. To test your ability to calculate the adjustments to the purchase price that fairly must be made at the closing, consider in the following problem: first, whether seller or buyer should receive a credit; and second, what the size of the credit should be. In doing so, keep as your guiding principle that the benefits and burdens of ownership should inure to the party having legal title, unless the parties have agreed differently.

Problem: S and B have entered into a contract of sale. The contract price is $60,000. B has agreed to pay $20,000 in cash. For the balance, B will take over an existing mortgage of $40,000. The mortgage bears interest at 12 percent per annum payable monthly in advance. S made the payment due April 1. The property has one tenant, who pays his monthly rental of $600 in advance. He has paid his April rental. The real estate taxes are payable quarterly in advance. Taxes of $900 for the April-June quarter are unpaid. There is a full tank of oil in the basement for which S has paid $500. The closing occurs on April 10. Compute the mortgage interest, rent, real estate taxes, and fuel adjustments. (The convention is to treat B's ownership as beginning on April 11.)

c. Title Insurance

AXELROD, BERGER, AND JOHNSTONE, LAND TRANSFER
AND FINANCE

666-667, 674-675 (2d ed. 1978)

In many parts of the United States, including nearly all metropolitan areas, title insurance is the prevailing form of title protection. It is an American innovation and little such insurance is written outside the United States. The first American title insurance company was formed in 1876, and by World War II some title insurance was being written on lands in most all parts of the United States, with well-established companies in nearly all big cities. But the great expansion of this kind of coverage has come mostly since the mid-1940s, a period marked by extensive real estate activity, a tremendous volume of new subdivisions and a vast number of new conveyances and mortgages. Title insurance has grown in both absolute and relative terms, for it has gradually cut in on other forms of title protection, particularly title search and examination by lawyers in private practice. In a number of big cities private practitioners of law have been eliminated from both title search and examination; and in some areas, notably in the Far West, this has happened in many middle and small-sized cities as well. In these communities the title work of the private bar is reduced largely to occasional efforts at curing title defects that title companies will not insure or negotiating with title insurers to waive minor defects. But in all of New England and in much of the Midwest and South outside large metropolitan centers, private law firms still do a great deal of title examination work, and in some communities they do title searching as well.

There are two major types of title insurance operations. In one the title company merely insures in reliance on the title opinion of a lawyer in private practice, the lawyer making a title examination and he or an abstracter making the search. In the other the title company performs all functions itself, commonly maintaining a title plant to facilitate searching. A title plant consists principally of duplicate copies of public records pertaining to all land parcels in a particular county, arranged and indexed to enable accurate and speedy searching of titles for individual parcels. Most highly developed plants are in counties with large populations.

The phenomenal growth of title insurance is attributable to a series of factors. For one thing, the big national lenders, especially the life insurance companies, like the relatively standardized coverage given by mortgagees' policies wherever written. This makes it easier for these large volume operators to determine the acceptability of mortgages originated for them or that they purchase in the secondary market. They also like the risk insurance feature. Demand for title insurance by national lenders is probably the single most significant reason for expansion in this type of title protection since World War II. Another reason for title insurance growth is that in large metropolitan areas public records pertaining to land have become so voluminous and difficult to search that only specialists with a large volume of title work can operate efficiently. And only the mass volume operator can afford a title plant, an essential to maximum efficiency in many big counties. Still another reason why title insurance has expanded so is that, being businesses, title companies can and do vigorously solicit work, whereas their lawyer and Torrens competitors are inhibited from doing so, lawyers by their canons of ethics and Torrens registrars by the usual reluctance of government agencies to spend money advertising their services.

Title insurance differs from most other kinds of insurance in that it does not insure against future risks but only against those existing at the time coverage is obtained. Further, it is issued only after a careful title search and examination and excludes any risks of substance disclosed by this process. As a result, loss ratios are low, with principal risks being negligence in search and examination and relatively rare defects not apparent from customary public record searches. Only one premium is paid for title insurance, and this includes a charge for search and examination if made by the title company. It is common, at the time land is sold, for a title company to issue two separate policies of insurance for which separate premiums are paid: one policy to the mortgagee and the other to the purchasing owner. Owners' policies do not cover grantees from the insured; if a buyer wishes coverage he must order and pay for a new policy, even though his grantor was covered. Mortgagees' policies usually cover assignees. In addition to fee owners and mortgagees, long-term lessees and holders of valuable oil and gas rights frequently obtain title insurance coverage. . . .

Title insurance protects insured from loss as the result of title deficiencies not excepted by the policy. Most policies contain a number of exceptions: any material defects uncovered by the insurer in its search of the particular title, and certain risks that in standard printed clauses the insurer excludes in all coverage of the kind in question. For an added premium, there are companies that will provide extended coverage by eliminating some of their standard exceptions. State insurance regulations in some states control the kinds of extended coverage permitted.

Most title policies insure the title against both record and off-record claims, subject, of course, to stated exceptions. Coverage of off-record risks is desired by many knowledgeable insureds because of the difficulty, often the impossibility, of ascertaining that such risks exist. However, one type of policy, sometimes referred to as a title guarantee, insures only the record title. The policy states, in essence, that the insured has good record title, subject to any listed exceptions, and then obligates the company to pay any losses incurred by the insured should the record title be otherwise. [It not only protects] against negligence in search and examination of the public records, but [also] guarantees that the record title is as represented, thus protecting against non-negligent search and examination errors. This limited form of policy was extensively written at an earlier stage in the evolution of title insurance.

In addition to protecting against title deficiencies, title insurance policies commonly provide certain benefits in case of litigation. These benefits usually include a commitment by the insurer, at its cost, to defend the insured in litigation over the title based on any claim not excepted by the policy. Failure of the insurer to defend can result in it being obligated to pay defense counsel retained by the insured.

As is true of other kinds of insurance, the scope of title insurance coverage is determined in large part by standard provisions in the insurers' policies. All companies use printed policy forms and their terms are often borrowed from state or national trade association approved documents. Of special importance have been the title policy forms developed and approved by the American Land Title Association, a national association of commercial title insurance companies, abstracters and title lawyers, including counsel for large lending institutions.

CHICAGO TITLE INSURANCE COMPANY

SUBJECT TO THE EXCLUSIONS FROM COVERAGE, THE EXCEPTIONS CONTAINED IN SCHEDULE B AND THE PROVISIONS OF THE CONDITIONS AND STIPULATIONS HEREOF, CHICAGO TITLE INSURANCE COMPANY, a Missouri corporation, herein called the Company, insures, as of Date of Policy shown in Schedule A, against loss or damage, not exceeding the amount of insurance stated in Schedule A, and costs, attorneys' fees and expenses which the Company may become obligated to pay hereunder, sustained or incurred by the insured by reason of:

1. Title to the estate or interest described in Schedule A being vested otherwise than as stated therein;

2. Any defect in or lien or encumbrance on such title;

3. Lack of a right of access to and from the land; or

4. Unmarketability of such title.

In Witness Whereof, **CHICAGO TITLE INSURANCE COMPANY** has caused this policy to be signed and sealed as of the date of policy shown in Schedule A, the policy to become valid when countersigned by an authorized signatory.

SPECIMEN POLICY

CHICAGO TITLE INSURANCE COMPANY

By

President.

ATTEST:

Secretary.

IMPORTANT

This policy necessarily relates solely to the title as of the date of the policy. In order that a purchaser of the real estate described herein may be insured against defects, liens or encumbrances, this policy should be reissued in the name of such purchaser.

EXCLUSIONS FROM COVERAGE

The following matters are expressly excluded from the coverage of this policy:

1. Any law, ordinance or governmental regulation (including but not limited to building and zoning ordinances) restricting or regulating or prohibiting the occupancy, use or enjoyment of the land, or regulating the character, dimensions or location of any improvement now or hereafter erected on the land, or prohibiting a separation in ownership or a reduction in the dimensions or area of the land, or the effect of any violation of any such law, ordinance or governmental regulation.

2. Rights of eminent domain or governmental rights of police power unless notice of the exercise of such rights appears in the public records at Date of Policy.

3. Defects, liens, encumbrances, adverse claims, or other matters (a) created, suffered, assumed or agreed to by the insured claimant; (b) not known to the Company and not shown by the public records but known to the insured claimant either at Date of Policy or at the date such claimant acquired an estate or interest insured by this policy and not disclosed in writing by the insured claimant to the Company prior to the date such insured claimant became an insured hereunder; (c) resulting in no loss or damage to the insured claimant; (d) attaching or created subsequent to Date of Policy; or (e) resulting in loss or damage which would not have been sustained if the insured claimant had paid value for the estate or interest insured by this policy.

CONDITIONS AND STIPULATIONS

1. DEFINITION OF TERMS

The following terms when used in this policy mean:

(a) "insured": the insured named in Schedule A, and, subject to any rights or defenses the Company may have had against the named insured, those who succeed to the interest of such insured by operation of law as distinguished from purchase including, but not limited to, heirs, distributees, devisees, survivors, personal representatives, next of kin, or corporate or fiduciary successors.

(b) "insured claimant": an insured claiming loss or damage hereunder.

(c) "knowledge": actual knowledge, not constructive knowledge or notice which may be imputed to an insured by reason of any public records.

(d) "land": the land described, specifically or by reference in Schedule A, and improvements affixed thereto which by law constitute real property; provided, however, the term "land" does not include any property beyond the lines of the area specifically described or referred to in Schedule A, nor any right, title, interest, estate or easement in abutting streets, roads, avenues, alleys, lanes, ways or waterways, but nothing herein shall modify or limit the extent to which a right of access to and from the land is insured by this policy.

(e) "mortgage": mortgage, deed of trust, trust deed, or other security instrument.

(f) "public records": those records which by law impart constructive notice of matters relating to said land.

2. CONTINUATION OF INSURANCE AFTER CONVEYANCE OF TITLE

The coverage of this policy shall continue in force as of Date of Policy in favor of an insured so long as such insured retains an estate or interest in the land, or holds an indebtedness secured by a purchase money mortgage given by a purchaser from such insured, or so long as such insured shall have liability by reason of covenants of warranty made by such insured in any transfer or conveyance of such estate or interest; provided, however, this policy shall not continue in force in favor of any purchaser from such insured of either said estate or interest or the indebtedness secured by a purchase money mortgage given to such insured.

3. DEFENSE AND PROSECUTION OF ACTIONS—NOTICE OF CLAIM TO BE GIVEN BY AN INSURED CLAIMANT

(a) The Company, at its own cost and without undue delay, shall provide for the defense of an insured in all litigation consisting of actions or proceedings commenced against such insured, or a defense interposed against an insured in an action to enforce a contract for a sale of the estate or interest in said land, to the extent that such litigation is founded upon an alleged defect, lien, encumbrance, or other matter insured against by this policy.

(b) The insured shall notify the Company promptly in writing (i) in case any action or proceeding is begun or defense is interposed as set forth in (a) above, (ii) in case knowledge shall come to an insured hereunder of any claim of title or interest which is adverse to the title to the estate or interest, as insured, and which might cause loss or damage for which the Company may be liable by virtue of this policy, or (iii) if title to the estate or interest, as insured, is rejected as unmarketable. If such prompt notice shall not be given to the Company, then as to such insured all liability of the Company shall cease and terminate in regard to the matter or matters for which such prompt notice is required; provided, however, that failure to notify shall in no case prejudice the rights of any such insured under this policy unless the Company shall be prejudiced by such failure and then only to the extent of such prejudice.

(c) The Company shall have the right at its own cost to institute and without undue delay prosecute any action or proceeding or to do any other act which in its opinion may be necessary or desirable to establish the title to the estate or interest as insured, and the Company may take any appropriate action under the terms of this policy, whether or not it shall be liable thereunder, and shall not thereby concede liability or waive any provision of this policy.

(d)   Whenever the Company shall have brought any action or interposed a defense as required or permitted by the provisions of this policy, the Company may pursue any such litigation to final determination by a court of competent jurisdiction and expressly reserves the right, in its sole discretion, to appeal from any adverse judgment or order.

(e)   In all cases where this policy permits or requires the Company to prosecute or provide for the defense of any action or proceeding, the insured hereunder shall secure to the Company the right to so prosecute or provide defense in such action or proceeding, and all appeals therein, and permit the Company to use, at its option, the name of such insured for such purpose. Whenever requested by the Company, such insured shall give the Company all reasonable aid in any such action or proceeding, in effecting settlement, securing evidence, obtaining witnesses, or prosecuting or defending such action or proceeding, and the Company shall reimburse such insured for any expense so incurred.

4.   NOTICE OF LOSS—LIMITATION OF ACTION

In addition to the notices required under paragraph 3(b) of these Conditions and Stipulations, a statement in writing of any loss or damage for which it is claimed the Company is liable under this policy shall be furnished to the Company within 90 days after such loss or damage shall have been determined and no right of action shall accrue to an insured claimant until 30 days after such statement shall have been furnished. Failure to furnish such statement of loss or damage shall terminate any liability of the Company under this policy as to such loss or damage.

5.   OPTIONS TO PAY OR OTHERWISE SETTLE CLAIMS

The Company shall have the option to pay or otherwise settle for or in the name of an insured claimant any claim insured against or to terminate all liability and obligations of the Company hereunder by paying or tendering payment of the amount of insurance under this policy together with any costs, attorneys' fees and expenses incurred up to the time of such payment or tender of payment, by the insured claimant and authorized by the Company.

6.   DETERMINATION AND PAYMENT OF LOSS

(a)   The liability of the Company under this policy shall in no case exceed the least of:

(i)   the actual loss of the insured claimant; or

(ii)   the amount of insurance stated in Schedule A.

(b)   The Company will pay, in addition to any loss incurred against by this policy, all costs imposed upon an insured in litigation carried on by the Company for such insured, and all costs, attorneys' fees and expenses in litigation carried on by such insured with the written authorization of the Company.

(c) When liability has been definitely fixed in accordance with the conditions of this policy, the loss or damage shall be payable within 30 days thereafter.

7. LIMITATION OF LIABILITY

No claim shall arise or be maintainable under this policy (a) if the Company, after having received notice of an alleged defect, lien or encumbrance insured against hereunder, by litigation or otherwise, removes such defect, lien or encumbrance or establishes the title, as insured, within a reasonable time after receipt of such notice; (b) in the event of litigation until there has been a final determination by a court of competent jurisdiction, and disposition of all appeals therefrom, adverse to the title, as insured, as provided in paragraph 3 hereof; or (c) for liability voluntarily assumed by an insured in settling any claim or suit without prior written consent of the Company.

8. REDUCTION OF LIABILITY

All payments under this policy, except payments made for costs, attorneys' fees and expenses, shall reduce the amount of the insurance pro tanto. No payment shall be made without producing this policy for endorsement of such payment unless the policy be lost or destroyed, in which case proof of such loss or destruction shall be furnished to the satisfaction of the Company.

9. LIABILITY NONCUMULATIVE

It is expressly understood that the amount of insurance under this policy shall be reduced by any amount the Company may pay under any policy insuring either (a) a mortgage shown or referred to in Schedule B hereof which is a lien on the estate or interest covered by this policy, or (b) a mortgage hereafter executed by an insured which is a charge or lien on the estate or interest described or referred to in Schedule A, and the amount so paid shall be deemed a payment under this policy. The Company shall have the option to apply to the payment of any such mortgages any amount that otherwise would be payable hereunder to the insured owner of the estate or interest covered by this policy and the amount so paid shall be deemed a payment under this policy to said insured owner.

10. APPORTIONMENT

If the land described in Schedule A consists of two or more parcels which are not used as a single site, and a loss is established affecting one or more of said parcels but not all, the loss shall be computed and settled on a pro rata basis as if the amount of insurance under this policy was divided pro rata as to the value on Date of Policy of each separate parcel to the whole, exclusive of any improvements made subsequent to Date of Policy, unless a liability or value had otherwise been agreed upon as to each such parcel by the Company and the insured at the time of the issuance of this policy and shown by an express statement herein or by an endorsement attached hereto.

11.   SUBROGATION UPON PAYMENT OR SETTLEMENT

Whenever the company shall have settled a claim under this policy, all right of subrogation shall vest in the Company unaffected by any act of the insured claimant. The Company shall be subrogated to and be entitled to all rights and remedies which such insured claimant would have had against any person or property in respect to such claim had this policy not been issued, and if requested by the Company, such insured claimant shall transfer to the Company all rights and remedies against any person or property necessary in order to perfect such right of subrogation and shall permit the Company to use the name of such insured claimant in any transaction or litigation involving such rights or remedies. If the payment does not cover the loss of such insured claimant, the Company shall be subrogated to such rights and remedies in the proportion which said payment bears to the amount of said loss. If loss should result from any act of such insured claimant, such act shall not void this policy, but the Company, in that event, shall be required to pay only that part of any losses insured against hereunder which shall exceed the amount, if any, lost to the Company by reason of the impairment of the right of subrogation.

12.   LIABILITY LIMITED TO THIS POLICY

This instrument together with all endorsements and other instruments, if any, attached hereto by the Company is the entire policy and contract between the insured and the Company.

Any claim of loss or damage, whether or not based on negligence, and which arises out of the status of the title to the estate or interest covered hereby or any action asserting such claim, shall be restricted to the provisions and conditions and stipulations of this policy.

No amendment of or endorsement to this policy can be made except by writing endorsed hereon or attached hereto signed by either the President, a Vice President, the Secretary, an Assistant Secretary, or validating officer or authorized signatory of the Company.

13.   NOTICES, WHERE SENT

All notices required to be given the Company and any statement in writing required to be furnished the Company shall be addressed to its principal office at 111 West Washington Street, Chicago, Illinois 60602, or at any branch office of the Company.

Form 1523
R-6-70

SCHEDULE A

Number	Date of Policy	Amount of Insurance

1. Name of Insured.

SPECIMEN POLICY

2. The estate or interest in the land described herein and which is covered by this policy is:

    Fee Simple

3. The estate or interest referred to herein is at Date of Policy vested in the Insured.

4. The land herein described is encumbered by the following mortgage or trust deed, and assignments:

    and the mortgages or trust deeds, if any, shown in Schedule B hereof.

5. The land referred to in this policy is described as follows:

Form 1823
R-8-70

SCHEDULE B

This policy does not insure against loss or damage by reason of the following exceptions:

General Exceptions:

(1) Rights or claims of parties in possession not shown by the public records.

(2) Encroachments, overlaps, boundary line disputes, and any matters which would be disclosed by an accurate survey and inspection of the premises.

(3) Easements, or claims of easements, not shown by the public records.

(4) Any lien, or right to a lien, for services, labor, or material heretofore or hereafter furnished, imposed by law and not shown by the public records.

(5) Taxes or special assessments which are not shown as existing liens by the public records.

Special Exceptions: The mortgage, if any, referred to in Schedule A.

SPECIMEN POLICY

Countersigned

_____

Authorized Signatory

Schedule B of this Policy consists of   pages

NOTES AND QUESTIONS

These questions will test your reading of the policy and suggest potential problems for the buyer's lawyer.

1.   X has purchased a 50-acre parcel, intending to develop it for a shopping center. After he acquires title, which is insured under the standard policy form, X discovers that tract restrictions bar the sale of alcoholic beverages. How would you determine whether X has a claim against the insurer? Suppose, instead, that X learns that only 40 acres are zoned for commercial development: any recourse against the insurer? Suppose, instead, that X orders a survey that shows that the parcel contains only 48.5 acres: any recourse under this policy?

2.   Y acquires an apartment house for $1 million. Her title is insured for the purchase price. Two years later, Y signs a contract to sell the property for $1.2 million, but her buyer rejects Y's title as partly defective. The records contain a forged deed of an undivided one-half interest in the property, reducing Y's valid interest by 50 percent. What recourse, if any, does Y have under this policy? Suppose that Y had signed to resell the property for $900,000?

3.   Z buys a lakeside cottage, which the seller's daughter and her family have used for several summers. During this period, Z has rented the cottage next door. Z obtains a title policy at the closing. A few months later, Z learns that the seller's daughter holds an unrecorded lease for the cottage, good for three summers more. The lease bears the fair market rental. What recourse, if any, does Z have against his insurer? The policy does not mention the lease.

§19.4   After the Closing

a.   The Condition of the Premises

Under the doctrine of merger, any promises that the parties make in the sales contract expire at the closing, unless the deed incorporates the promises or the contract contains survival clauses. Thus, the seller's duties respecting title, as we have seen, do not obligate him beyond the closing unless he executes new title assurances in the deed (page 1154 *supra*). Seller may continue—even after the closing—to be independently liable in fraud where, for example, he has sold the same property twice; but this is another, and not very common, matter.

Somewhat related to title is the seller's continuing duty, if any, respecting the condition of the premises. Take, for example, a fairly common misfortune—the flooded basement in the new home, or similarly, the leaky roof in the older home. Must buyer lick his own wounds (or dry his own body)? It was not long ago that courts still echoed the seventeenth-century view: "Note, that by the civil law, every man is bound to warrant the thing that he selleth or conveyeth, albeit there be no express warranty, either in deed or in law; but the common law bindeth him not, for caveat emptor. . . ." 2 Coke, Littleton, c. 7, §145 (1633). Or to put the matter more colorfully: "When you buy a $10,000 house, you just can't expect gold doorknobs." [7]

Caveat emptor, in this age of consumerism, is losing its grip in realty sales, paralleling the changes in real estate leases, and the more advanced doctrine in personalty sales. The case below now has its counterpart in many jurisdictions.

YEPSEN v. BURGESS
269 Or. 635, 525 P.2d 1019 (1974)

O'CONNELL, C.J. Plaintiffs, purchasers of a new house built and sold to them by defendants, bring this action to recover damages allegedly incurred as the result of defendants' breach of an implied warranty that the structure had been built in a proper and reasonably workmanlike manner and was fit for habitation. The trial court sustained defendants' demurrer to the complaint and plaintiffs appeal.

According to plaintiffs' complaint, defendant Sylvester Burgess is a "builder engaged in the occupation of building new homes." It is alleged that on or about May 8, 1972, defendants sold to plaintiffs certain land and a new home, which had been built by defendant Sylvester Burgess on the land described. It is further alleged that two of the septic tank drain field lines were defectively located and installed so that when the owner of the adjoining lot graded an area for a driveway he severed one of the lines, causing sewage from plaintiffs' septic tank to flow onto and collect on the adjoining lot as a result of which plaintiffs were required to acquire an easement in the adjoining lot and to construct a new drain field.

On appeal plaintiffs concede that in order for them to prevail this court must overrule Steiber v. Palumbo, 219 Or. 479, 347 P.2d 978, 78 A.L.R.2d 440 (1959), in which it was held that no implied warranties exist in sales of real property. This decisions was based on dual grounds: (1) that ORS 93.140, providing that "No covenant shall be implied in any conveyance of real estate, whether it contains special covenants or not," constituted a legislative proscription against implying a covenant of fitness for inhabitability, and (2) that even in the absence of statute, the prevailing case law in other jurisdictions denied recovery on the theory of implied warranty of fitness in the sale of new houses, including those sold by the builder.

With respect to the first ground recited above, we are of the opinion that the court misinterpreted ORS 93.850 in *Steiber*. It is to be noted that the statute refers to "covenants," a term which when used in connection with the

---

7. A Memphis, Tenn. builder, quoted in Bearman, Caveat Emptor in Realty Sales, 14 Vand. L. Rev. 541, 573 (1961).

conveyance of land ordinarily refers to the quality of title, such as the modern covenants of warranty, quiet enjoyment, seisin and against encumbrances, or the ancient covenants of right to convey and for further assurance. At the time ORS 93.140 and comparable statutes in other states were adopted, the extent to which various covenants of title could be implied in the transfer of land was a matter of some confusion. It is reasonable to regard these statutes as a legislative effort to clarify the law in this respect.

Other jurisdictions having statutes similar to ORS 93.140 have reached the same result, although on somewhat different reasoning. Thus in Weeks v. Slavick Builders, Inc., 24 Mich. App. 621, 180 N.W.2d 503, 507, aff'd, 384 Mich. 257, 181 N.W.2d 271 (1970), the court said:

> Our extension of an implied warranty of fitness for purpose intended to new residential dwelling houses is in no way affected by M.C.L.A. §565.5 (Stat. Ann. 1970 Rev. §26.524) upon which appellant relies, since appellees have not alleged that the implied warranty arises from the conveyance of real estate, but from the sales agreement entered into between the appellees and appellant. Such executory contracts are specifically excluded from the definition of "conveyance" by M.C.L.A. §565.35 (Stat. Ann. 1970 Rev. §26.552), thereby rendering the import of M.C.L.A. §565.5 (Stat. Ann. 1970 Rev. §26.524) inapplicable to the particular facts of this case.

Finding no statutory impediment to the recognition of implied covenants other than covenants of title, we turn to a re-examination of the cases refusing to recognize an implied covenant of fitness for habitation upon the sale of a dwelling house.

Steiber v. Palumbo, 219 Or. 479, 347 P.2d 978, 78 A.L.R.2d 440 (1959), and the cases upon which it relied, denied recovery to the purchaser on the ground that the principle of caveat emptor applied in the sale of real property, including structures regarded as a part of the land. Since the date of decision in the *Steiber* case at least 14 states have cast aside the principle of caveat emptor in the sale of new houses by the builder-vendor and have recognized an implied warranty of workmanlike construction and habitability.[3] These

---

3. Cochran v. Keeton, 287 Ala. 439, 252 So. 2d 313 (1971); Wawak v. Stewart, 247 Ark. 1093, 449 S.W.2d 922 (1970); Pollard v. Saxe & Yolles Development Co., 32 Cal. App. 3d 390, 108 Cal. Rptr. 174 (1973); Carpenter v. Donohoe, 154 Colo. 78, 388 P.2d 399 (1964); Vernali v. Centrella, 28 Conn. Supp. 476, 266 A.2d 200 (1970); Gable v. Silver, 258 So. 2d 11, 50 A.L.R.3d 1062 (Fla. App. 1972); Bethlahmy v. Bechtel, 91 Idaho 55, 415 P.2d 698 (1966); Hanavan v. Dye, 4 Ill. App. 3d 576, 281 N.E.2d 398 (1972); Theis v. Heuer, 280 N.E.2d 300 (Ind. 1972); Weeks v. Slavick Builders, Inc., 24 Mich. App. 621, 180 N.W.2d 503, aff'd, 384 Mich. 257, 181 N.W.2d 271 (1970); Smith v. Old Warson Development Co., 479 S.W.2d 795 (Mo. 1972); Schipper v. Levitt & Sons, Inc., 44 N.J. 70, 207 A.2d 314 (1965); Padula v. J.J. Deb-Cin Homes, Inc., 298 A.2d 529 (R.I. 1973); Rutledge v. Dodenhoff, 254 S.C. 407, 175 S.E.2d 792 (1970); Waggoner v. Midwestern Development, Inc., 83 S.D. 57, 154 N.W.2d 803 (1967); Humber v. Morton, 426 S.W.2d 554, 25 A.L.R.3d 372 (Tex. 1968); Rothberg v. Olenik, 128 Vt. 295, 262 A.2d 461 (1970); House v. Thornton, 76 Wash. 2d 428, 457 P.2d 199 (1969).

For an indication of the extent of change which has occurred in the past decade and a half, compare Annot.: Implied Warranty by Seller, in Absence of Fraud or Misrepresentation, as to Fitness, Condition, or Quality of New Dwelling, 78 A.L.R.2d 446 (1961) with Annot.: Liability of

cases, reflecting a change in the morals of the market place, more specifically rest their holdings on the ground that the underlying theory of caveat emptor, predicating an arm's length transaction between seller and buyer of comparable skill and experience, is unrealistic as applied to the sale of new houses. The courts of this persuasion recognize that the essence of the transaction is an implicit engagement upon the part of the seller to transfer a house suitable for habitation. It is also recognized that the purchaser is not in an equal bargaining position with the builder-seller of a new house and is forced to rely upon the latter's skill and knowledge with respect to the ingredients of an adequately constructed dwelling house. It is further explained that, although a house becomes a part of the realty according to the technical law of accession, the purchaser sees the transaction primarily as the purchase of a house with the land only as an incident thereto. Looked at in this light, there is no substantial difference between the sale of a house and the sale of goods and it follows, therefore, that the implied warranties of fitness for use attendant upon a sale of personal property should attach to a sale of a house.

The foregoing reasoning, which we regard as sound, compels us to overrule Steiber v. Palumbo, *supra,* and to join the ranks of those courts recognizing an implied warranty of fitness in the sale of new dwelling houses. Our holding limits the implication of such a warranty to those cases where the seller is a builder-vendor, i.e., one who builds new houses upon land for the purpose of sale to the general public.[4] This rule is applicable only to the sale of new houses. The sale under such circumstances is deemed to carry with it a warranty that the house is constructed in a reasonably workmanlike manner and is fit for habitation. A more precise definition of the scope of this warranty must await delineation on a case by case basis.[5] Similarly, resolution of problems concerning the commencement of the running of the statute of limitations,[6] and the possible extension of the doctrine to include industrial as well as residential structures,[7] or non-privity as well as first party purchasers must be postponed until we have the benefit of briefs and argument on these issues.

In the present case the complaint alleges the sale of a new house by a builder-vendor. It further alleges that the house "was not erected in a proper

---

Builder-Vendor or Other Vendor of New Dwelling for Loss, Injury or Damage Occasioned by Defective Condition Thereof, §6, 25 A.L.R.3d 383, 413-415 (1969). Supp. 1973, 9-10.

In addition, some courts have adopted the so-called English rule that an implied warranty of reasonable workmanship arises when the sales transaction occurs during the course of construction. See Annot.: 25 A.L.R.3d, *supra,* §6[b], 415-419 (1969).

4. Cf., Elderkin v. Gaster, 447 Pa. 118, 123; 288 A.2d 771, 774, fn. 10 (1972).

5. Mulhern v. Hederich, 163 Colo. 275, 430 P.2d 469 (1967); Elderkin v. Gaster, *supra* 288 A.2d at 776, fn. 13. See Note, 47 Temple L.Q. 172 (1973).

6. Note, Contracts-Sales-Houses—An implied warranty of fitness extends to the purchase of new residential housing. Rule of caveat emptor no longer applies, 49 J. Urban Law 195, 199 (1971); Comment, Real Property-Implied Warranties-Sale of House by Builder-Vendor Creates an Implied Warranty of Fitness and Habitability. 24 Ala. L. Rev. 332, 338-339 (1972).

7. Cf., Robertson Lumber Co. v. Stephen Farmers Co-op Elev. Co., 274 Minn. 17, 143 N.W.2d 622 (1966). Note, Products Liability-Implied Warranty in the Sale of a New House, 38 Mo. L. Rev. 315, 319-320 (1973); 24 Ala. L. Rev., *supra* note 6, 338-339.

and reasonably workmanlike manner as impliedly represented and warranted by defendants." The defects are more specifically described as the improper construction of the septic tank and drain field system. Although these defects do not constitute inadequate workmanship in the construction of the dwelling structure itself, they are the product of the builder's work upon the land in conjunction with the construction and sale of the structure. Moreover, the septic tank and drainage system are so essential to the use of the house that for warranty purposes their proper installation may be deemed a part of the structure sold. The use of the house is so dependent upon the proper disposition of waste through a properly operating septic tank and drain field system that the house would not be habitable without them.

The judgment of the trial court is reversed and the cause is remanded for further proceedings.

NOTES AND QUESTIONS

1. Where seller gives an express warranty "made in lieu of any and all implied warranties," what are the arguments for and against strict interpretation of this disclaimer? Cf. Tennessee Carolina Transp. Inc. v. Strick Corp., 283 N.C. 423, 196 S.E.2d 711 (1973); N.Y.U.C.C. §2-316 Official Comment (McKinney 1981).

2. The buyer of a tract house scalds himself badly when he cannot reduce the temperature of the hot water below 190° F. He learns that the builder chose not to install a mixing valve which would have prevented this mishap. The installed valve would have cost $18. The buyer sues seller on two theories: (a) negligence—in view of the likelihood and gravity of the danger and the ease with which it could have been avoided, builder failed to exercise reasonable care in the design and installation; (b) breach of implied warranty of habitability where a dangerous condition resulting from defective construction has caused injury. What outcome? Cf. Schipper v. Levitt & Sons, Inc., 44 N.J. 70, 207 A.2d 314 (1965). Should it matter under either theory whether plaintiff is the original or a subsequent owner of the premises? Recalling your contracts and torts, discuss the significant differences between the two theories.

3. A lender fails to inspect the progress of tract homes whose construction it is financing. The builder negligently erects the homes without regard to soil conditions at the site. Two years later, the foundations badly crack. Builder by then is broke. Does the bank have any obligation to the homeowners for failing to weathereye the construction? Compare Connor v. Great Western Savings and Loan Ass'n, 69 Cal. 2d 850, 447 P.2d 609, 73 Cal. Rptr. 369 (1968) (liability), with Jemison v. Montgomery Real Estate & Co., 47 Mich. App. 73, 210 N.W.2d 10 (1973) (no liability). Compare Note, Liability of the Institutional Lender for Structural Defects in New Housing, 35 U. Chi. L. Rev. 739, 758 (1968); Cal. Civ. Code §3434 (West Supp. 1981) (*Connor* overruled). If contingent liability does exist, may lender avoid exposure by obtain-

ing exculpatory clauses in its loan agreements and providing that such clauses run with the land?

Might the owner of a house negligently or defectively built recover from the mortgage insurer (FHA), on the theory that the FHA—like the construction lender—has a duty to see that the house is prudently built and that it conforms to plans and specifications? Cf. United States v. Thompson, 293 F. Supp. 1307 (E.D. Ark., W.D. 1967), *aff'd*, 408 F.2d 1075 (8th Cir. 1969).

4.   What are the arguments for and against extending the implied warranty of habitability to the sale of "used" houses?

b.   Mortgage Default

(1)   Foreclosure

PRATHER, FORECLOSURE OF THE SECURITY INTEREST
1957 U. Ill. L.F. 420, 427-430

METHODS OF FORECLOSURE

After a default by the borrower, the lender or his successor in interest must seek to realize upon the real property security by selling or acquiring ownership of the land, at the same time extinguishing any equitable rights belonging to the borrower. The process is called foreclosure, which in its dictionary definition means "to shut out; exclude or bar."

In the early days of English mortgage law there was no necessity for foreclosure. The courts enforced the mortgage in accordance with its written terms, and a failure of the borrower to pay his debt when due simply extinguished all of his rights in the land. Because of the gradual development of a borrower's equitable right to redeem the land at a later date, however, foreclosure became necessary to extinguish the right.

Methods of foreclosure vary greatly from state to state. In some states foreclosure is quick and cheap; in others it is a long and expensive process.

Foreclosure procedures available for use must be sought under the laws of the state where the property is situated. While the diversity of state foreclosure laws is formidable, the most prevalent methods in use are foreclosure by sale in judicial proceedings, and foreclosure by exercise of a power of sale contained in the mortgage. . . . Although in some states one method is exclusive, in many states the mortgagee may elect which method he will pursue, including an election to proceed on the note alone, on the mortgage, or on both concurrently.

STRICT FORECLOSURE

In jurisdictions which permit its use, strict foreclosure usually is one of several remedies, although ordinarily it is confined to cases where (1) the mortgagor is insolvent, (2) the mortgaged premises are not of sufficient value to pay the debt, and (3) there are no outside creditors or encumbrancers. The process begins with a complaint or a petition to foreclose. The complaint is brought against not only the owner but all persons who may have the right to redeem, including a spouse, tenants, and junior lien holders, if any. After summons either by personal delivery, or by publication and mailing of notice where personal summons is not possible, the defendants are given the opportunity to introduce defenses such as invalidity of the mortgage, prior payment, or failure of consideration.

After hearing any defenses, the court will determine if there has been a default and if the mortgagee has the right to foreclose. A degree or judgment is then entered, setting out the amount due to the lender, and specifying a period, ordinarily from two to six months, in which the borrower may redeem by payment of the amount due. The decree provides also that if the property shall not have been redeemed within the period specified, the borrower and all persons claiming under him shall be forever barred and foreclosed. As of the time the specified period expires, the mortgagee becomes the sole owner of the property. No sale of the premises is involved.

Some courts have called strict foreclosure a harsh remedy since it transfers the property to the mortgagee without a sale, the value appearing not to be taken into account.

FORECLOSURE BY SALE IN JUDICIAL PROCEEDINGS

Under this method, the procedure is identical with that of strict foreclosure until the point that judgment or decree is about to be entered. At this time, the procedure becomes different, due to the widespread belief that if the land is sold at a public sale it might bring more than the mortgage debt, leaving something for the borrower. Although judicial sale predominates in most parts of the country, it later will be shown that in practical operation the theory seldom works out in accordance with the original purpose.

At the time of entering the decree, the court determines the amount due to the mortgagee. The decree provides that a specified period of notice shall be given to the public that the property is to be sold at public auction. The notice, usually by newspaper publication, must include a description of the property, the time, place, and terms of the sale, and the officer designated to conduct the sale. The officer usually is a master in chancery, a sheriff, or other officer appointed or authorized by the court.

The mortgagee customarily is permitted to bid at the auction, and in practice, the mortgagee almost invariably is the only or the highest bidder. If such bids are confined to the unpaid amount of the mortgage, the mortgagee may avoid parting with any cash. The bid price is merely applied to the mortgage debt.

Upon receiving a report of the auction, the court will determine the equity and propriety of the sale, and if it approves, the officer is ordered to execute either a deed to the purchaser or, as in Illinois, a certificate of sale. If the state law does not provide statutorily for a further period in which the borrower may redeem, the purchaser at this point becomes the sole and absolute owner of the land.

FORECLOSURE BY EXERCISE OF POWER OF SALE

In a great many states, a mortgage may be foreclosed without recourse to the courts, and the usual method is that of foreclosure by exercise of a power of sale contained in the security instrument. Power of sale mortgages are used primarily because they afford a less expensive as well as a more convenient and expeditious mode of foreclosure, and the mortgagor is not required to pay the greater expenses of a regular foreclosure action.

Foreclosure by power of sale specifically must be authorized in the mortgage instrument. Such clauses spell out what shall be considered a default, and, in the event of such default, confer power on the mortgagee (or trustee in the case of a trust deed) to sell the property after public notice at public auction.

Ordinarily personal notice of the proposed sale to the borrower is necessary, but certain states permit notice by advertisement. In order to be able to bid in at his own sale, the mortgagee or trustee must have expressly provided such authorization in the mortgage instrument, otherwise he is barred from the bidding. A deed is issued by the mortgagee as conductor of the sale to the highest bidder. Almost invariably this is the mortgagee himself. Again, while the equity of redemption is cut off by the process, statutory redemption may or may not be allowed, depending upon state statutory provisions. While the purchaser at the sale obtains immediate possession in states having no period of redemption, in states allowing a redemption period the majority allow the mortgagor to remain in possession, although the statute or the mortgage may contain different stipulations as to rents. To exercise the power of sale there is no need for the mortgagee to make entry. . . .

Problem: On April 1, 1972, R mortgaged Blackacre to E. At the time, L held a 20-year lease to Blackacre due to expire in 1990. L later assigned the lease to L-1. On April 1, 1973, R mortgaged Blackacre to F. On April 1, 1974, R sold Blackacre to S, who assumed both mortgages. On April 1, 1975, S sold Blackacre to T, who took subject to both mortgages. On April 1, 1976, C obtained and docketed a judgment against T. On April 1, 1977, T granted an easement of right of way across Blackacre to A. On April 1, 1978, E assigned a half interest in his mortgage to X; E agreed that he would continue to service the mortgage. On April 1, 1980, with the first mortgage in default, E brought an action to foreclose. Whom should E name as parties defendant? As parties plaintiff? Why? See Osborne on Mortgages 923-926, 931-935 (1951).

(2)   Recovery of Deficiency Judgment

NEW YORK REAL PROPERTY ACTIONS AND PROCEEDINGS LAW

§1371 (McKinney 1963)

1.   If a person who is liable to the plaintiff for the payment of the debt secured by the mortgage is made a defendant in the action, and has appeared or has been personally served with the summons, the final judgment may award payment by him of the whole residue, or so much thereof as the court may determine to be just and equitable, of the debt remaining unsatisfied, after a sale of the mortgaged property and the application of the proceeds, pursuant to the directions contained in such judgment, the amount thereof to be determined by the court as herein provided.

2.   Simultaneously with the making of a motion for an order confirming the sale, provided such motion is made within ninety days after the date of the consummation of the sale by the delivery of the proper deed of conveyance to the purchaser, the party to whom such residue shall be owing may make a motion in the action for leave to enter a deficiency judgment upon notice to the party against whom such judgment is sought or the attorney who shall have appeared for such party in such action. Such notice shall be served personally or in such other manner as the court may direct. Upon such motion the court, whether or not the respondent appears, shall determine, upon affidavit or otherwise as it shall direct, the fair and reasonable market value of the mortgaged premises as of the date such premises were bid in at auction or such nearest earlier date as there shall have been any market value thereof and shall make an order directing the entry of a deficiency judgment. Such deficiency judgment shall be for an amount equal to the sum of the amount owing by the party liable as determined by the judgment with interest, plus the amount owing on all prior liens and encumbrances with interest, plus costs and disbursements of the action including the referee's fee and disbursements, less the market value as determined by the court or the sale price of the property whichever shall be the higher.

3.   If no motion for a deficiency judgment shall be made as herein prescribed the proceeds of the sale regardless of amount shall be deemed to be in full satisfaction of the mortgage debt and no right to recover any deficiency in any action or proceeding shall exist. . . .

NOTES AND QUESTIONS

1.   The New York statute both confirms the mortgagee's right to a deficiency and limits the deficiency to the difference between the amount of claim and the "fair and reasonable market value," not to the difference between the amount of claim and the foreclosure sale price. In practically every

state the mortgagee may obtain a judgment for a deficiency—usually without benefit of statute. Through the years, however, courts and legislatures have devised methods to protect the debtor from being victimized by superficial bidding at the sale. There are, of course, provisions for the giving of notice, the time, place, manner and terms of conducting the sale. A court of equity may refuse to confirm a sale or may set it aside upon evidence of chilled bidding or upon a showing of inadequacy so gross as to "shock the conscience or raise a presumption of fraud or unfairness." See Ballentyne v. Smith, 205 U.S. 285 (1907). Where foreclosure is by power of sale, the mortgagee is not permitted to buy unless the mortgagor has given his consent or, under some statutes, a public officer conducts the sale. Nearly half the states allow the mortgagor (and junior lienors) to redeem from the foreclosure sale upon payment of the sale price plus specified interest; these *statutory rights to redeem*, dating back to the panic of 1837, were intended to dissuade a perfunctory bid on the theory that too low a price would invite redemption. (Since the redemption period may run six months or longer, redemption may cause the very lackluster interest on the part of potential bidders it was expected to prevent.)

The depression of the 1930s gave new impetus to the effort to protect mortgage debtors, for even in normal times the result of a forced sale does not usually reflect the "reasonable" market value of the property. Some states, like New York, abandoned the sale price as the presumptive measure of fair value and forced the mortgagee who was seeking the deficiency judgment to prove "fair and reasonable market value." This was fine in theory, except during the 1930s no market existed. Wrestling with this conundrum, some lower courts went back to predepression values, until the New York Court of Appeals held that the statute was intended to set up a new "equitable standard" in lieu of market value, in which market transactions, if any, were only one item. See Heiman v. Bishop, 272 N.Y. 83, 4 N.E.2d 944 (1936). The values found on the new test were said to approximate tax assessments. See Friedman, Personal Liability on Mortgage Debts in New York, 51 Yale L.J. 382, 396 (1942).

The United States Supreme Court has approved the New York statute both as an emergency measure—Honeyman v. Jacobs, 306 U.S. 539 (1939)—and as a permanent provision applying to existing and future mortgages—Gelfert v. National City Bank, 313 U.S. 221 (1941). In both cases, however, the purchaser was also the mortgagee. Should the result be different if the purchaser is a third party?

Some states went even further and barred deficiency judgments altogether, or barred them as to some mortgagees. See, for example, Cal. Civ. Proc. Code §580b (West 1970): "No deficiency judgment shall lie in any event after any sale of real property for failure of the purchaser to complete his contract of sale, or under a deed of trust, or mortgage, given to secure payment of the balance of the purchase price of real property." This language kept California lawyers guessing for years as to who was disabled (e.g., a bank that lends the balance of the purchase price) and as to who was insulated (e.g., a guarantor of a purchase money mortgage). These issues seem now to be settled. The bank is not disabled: Cf. Roseleaf Corp. v. Chierighino, 59 Cal. 2d 35, 378 P.2d 97, 27 Cal. Rptr. 873 (1963). The guarantor is not insulated: See Heckes v. Sapp, 229 Cal. App. 2d 549, 40 Cal. Rptr. 485 (1964). For further analysis of the California statute, see Hetland, Deficiency Judgment Limitations in California—A New Judicial Approach, 51 Calif. L. Rev. 1 (1963).

California also bars deficiency judgments where the security is sold pursuant to a power of sale in either a mortgage or a deed of trust. Cal. Civ. Proc. Code §580(d) (West 1970). Thus, the holder of a deed of trust wishing to obtain a deficiency judgment—and not otherwise ineligible—must foreclose by judicial action. If he does so, however, the debtor may then invoke his statutory right to redeem, a right that is denied him when the creditor proceeds by power of sale. Cal. Civ. Proc. Code §§700a, 701, 725a (West 1970). Do you see the connection between statutory redemption and deficiency limitation?

2.   Military personnel are entitled to the benefits of The Soldiers' and Sailors' Civil Relief Act of 1940, 50 U.S.C.A. §§501-590 (1969). This law tolls the statute of limitations during military service, permits the mortgagor to reopen foreclosure after his release from duty on proof of a meritorious defense, and authorizes a court to stay foreclosure or execution on a money judgment. The serviceman must be able to show, however, that military service has "materially affected" his ability to meet his debts or to defend an action. See Comment, 37 N.Y.U.L. Rev. 1128 (1962).

PHILLIPS, FROM THE CRASH TO THE BLITZ 1929-1939
2-3 (1969)

It was bitterly cold in the little town of Lemars, Iowa, on the morning of January 4, 1933. On the snow-packed ground before the entrance to the Plymouth County Courthouse, eight hundred roughly dressed farmers and townsmen were packed shoulder to shoulder. They had begun assembling before daybreak. They were restless and in an ugly mood, the breath from their mutterings and occasional catcalls congealing in gray wisps of fog above their heads. The farm of one of their neighbors, John A. Johnson, was posted to be auctioned from the courthouse steps at ten o'clock. The sale was to satisfy a $33,000 mortgage held by a New York insurance company. After two summers of searing drought and with the price of corn dropping to 10 cents a bushel (the actual cost of raising it had been about 80 cents), Johnson had fallen hopelessly behind in his payments. The court had granted the company's petition to foreclose, as it had on a score of other debt-ridden farms in the county in the preceding months.

The people gathered at Lemars did not intend to prevent the sale of John Johnson's farm (mobs in other communities had tried to prevent such sales). But they were going to see to it that the property was bid at the full face of the mortgage, so that the Johnson livestock and family possessions would not have to be sacrificed to make up the deficiency. So, when Sheriff Ripley stood up on the portico, read off the court order, and asked, "What am I bid," the only response came from an obvious "city fellow" standing at his elbow, Herbert S. Martin, an attorney representing the insurance company.

"Thirty thousand," Martin said in a nervous, scarcely audible voice.

"No! No!," the crowd yelled. Individual voices cried out: "Full value!" "Thirty-three thousand or nothing!" "Stop the sale!"

The sheriff held up his hands to restore quiet. "Mr. Martin says that is as high as the mortgage holder has authorized him to go," he shouted. "Unless I hear another offer I'll be forced to knock it down to him. Do I hear another bid?"

Again the crowd broke out into a bedlam of shouts. "No! No! Full value or no sale! Let's show 'em we mean business. Get Martin! Get Ripley!"

As the mob surged forward up the steps, the sheriff and the lawyer made a dash for the courthouse door, but not in time. The two men were roughly seized and pushed out into the center of the seething, pummeling mob. A heavy rope with a hangman's noose was slipped over the distraught lawyer's head. "We'll hang him from the highest tree in town," someone yelled, and the crowd took up the chant.

Frantically, Martin implored for time to telegraph his principals asking permission to raise his bid. His wire ended with this desperate plea: "Rush answer. My neck at risk." Two hours later his bid of $33,000 for the Johnson farm was accepted with the grudging consent of the mob, and the crisis of law and order at Lemars, Iowa, was ended.

TABLE OF CASES

1183

INDEX